PUBLIC PAPERS OF THE PRESIDENTS
OF THE UNITED STATES

PUBLIC PAPERS OF THE PRESIDENTS

OF THE UNITED STATES

Jimmy Carter

1980-81

(IN THREE BOOKS)

BOOK III—SEPTEMBER 29, 1980 TO JANUARY 20, 1981

UNITED STATES GOVERNMENT PRINTING OFFICE

WASHINGTON : 1982

Published by the
Office of the Federal Register
National Archives and Records Service
General Services Administration

For sale by the Superintendent of Documents, U.S. Government Printing Office
Washington, D.C. 20402

Foreword

This is the ninth and final volume in this series of the Public Papers of my Presidency, but it does not complete my relationship with the publisher, the National Archives and Records Service. That, in fact, is only beginning.

While President, I sought to make my administration the most open in history. Secrecy is necessary at times, but this should not be assumed to protect officials from public scrutiny. I maintain my conviction that in our government of the people, for the people, and by the people, the people have the right and the need to know what their government is about.

It is now my goal to open to historians, as soon as possible, the massive collection of the records of my administration. I am myself currently engaged in research and writing about my Presidency and am moving ahead with plans for a Presidential library to be managed by the National Archives. I will continue to advocate and encourage openness.

My farewell address, which is included in this volume, gives my sentiments upon leaving office. I need not repeat them here, except to say thank you to those who served me in my administration and thank you to the American people who gave me the opportunity to serve them.

Jimmy Carter

Preface

This book contains the papers and speeches of the 39th President of the United States which were issued by the White House Press Office during the period September 29, 1980–January 20, 1981. The material has been compiled and published by the Office of the Federal Register, National Archives and Records Service, General Services Administration.

The material is presented in chronological order within each week, and the dates shown in the headings are the dates of the documents or events. In instances when the release date differs from the date of the document itself, that fact is shown in the textnote. Every effort has been made to ensure accuracy. Tape recordings are used to protect against errors in transcription of Presidential remarks, and signed documents are checked against the original to verify the correct printing. Textnotes, footnotes, and cross references have been provided by the editors for purposes of identification or clarity. Speeches were delivered in Washington, D.C., and other documents released there, unless indicated. All times noted are local times.

The index covers Books I, II, and III of the 1980–81 volume. In addition to the usual subject-matter entries in the index, the material has been classified in categories reflecting the type of Presidential activity or document. For example, a reader interested in the President's speeches will find them listed in the index under "Addresses and Remarks."

The Public Papers series was begun in 1957 in response to a recommendation of the National Historical Publications Commission. An extensive compilation of messages and papers of the Presidents covering the period 1789 to 1897 was assembled by James D. Richardson and published under congressional authority between 1896 and 1899. Since then, various private compilations have been issued, but there was no uniform publication comparable to the Congressional Record or the United States Supreme Court Reports. Many Presidential papers could be found only in the form of mimeographed White House releases or as reported in the press. The Commission therefore recommended the establishment of an official series in which Presidential writings, addresses, and remarks of a public nature could be made available.

The Commission's recommendation was incorporated in regulations of the Administrative Committee of the Federal Register, issued under section 6 of the Federal Register Act (44 U.S.C. 1506), which may be found in Title 1, Part 10, of the Code of Federal Regulations.

Preface

A companion publication to the Public Papers series, the Weekly Compilation of Presidential Documents, was begun in 1965 to provide a broader range of Presidential materials on a more timely basis to meet the needs of the contemporary reader. Beginning with the administration of Jimmy Carter, the Public Papers series expanded its coverage to include all material as printed in the Weekly Compilation. That coverage provides a listing of the President's daily schedule and meetings, when announced, and other items of general interest issued by the White House Press Office. Also included are lists of the President's nominations submitted to the Senate, materials released by the Press Office which are not printed full-text in the book, and acts approved by the President. This information is compiled on a weekly basis and appears at the end of each week's coverage.

Volumes covering the administrations of Presidents Hoover, Truman, Eisenhower, Kennedy, Johnson, Nixon, and Ford are also available.

This series is under the direction of John E. Byrne, Director, Office of the Federal Register, and is produced by the Presidential Documents and Legislative Division, Robert E. Lewis, Director. Editors of this book were Katherine A. Mellody, Brenda A. Robeson, Kenneth R. Payne, and Wilma P. Greene. The index was prepared by Walter W. Rice.

The frontispiece and photographs used in the portfolio were supplied by the White House Photo Office.

The typography and design of the volume were developed by the United States Government Printing Office under the direction of Danford L. Sawyer, Jr., Public Printer.

Robert M. Warner
Archivist of the United States

Gerald P. Carmen
Administrator of General Services
August 1982

Contents

Administration of Jimmy Carter

1980-81

New York, New York

Remarks at the International Ladies Garment Workers Union 37th Tri-Annual Convention. September 29, 1980

President Chick Chaikin, Governor Carey, Lieutenant Governor Cuomo, Congresswoman and next United States Senator Liz Holtzman:

Sometimes I have a hard time deciding which I like best, "Hail to the Chief" or "Look for the Union Label." [*Laughter*] But with your endorsement, I'd like to make a prediction right now that when November the 4th comes we're going to be singing both of them as a duet, and they're going to go very well together.

To President Chaikin and Secretary-Treasurer Shelley Appleton, your secret weapon in Washington, Evie Dubrow, ILG'ers, friends:

Chick, I want to thank you for that wonderful introduction and the words you said before I came in here. I was listening very carefully. That may have been one of the two best speeches I've heard you make all year. [*Laughter*] The other one, of course, was when you nominated me at the Democratic National Convention. Chick has the makings of a great orator, if he just wasn't so timid and would go ahead and speak up and say what he has to say. [*Laughter*] All of you need to help me help Chick overcome his bashfulness. [*Laughter*]

Before I came here to speak to you, he asked me a very serious question, one that I've been asked about many times. And I would like to respond here in this public

place and in a very sober way. It's a matter of great concern to us, and that is Israel and its relationship with the United Nations General Assembly.

The United States has opposed and we will continue firmly to oppose any attempt to deprive the State of Israel of its legitimate rights as a respected member of the international community.

I noted with great pleasure the UNESCO Conference which met in Belgrade last week and which rejected an effort to question Israel's credentials. We will strongly oppose any effort to exclude Israel from the United Nations General Assembly.

There is absolutely no doubt that Israel is a bona fide member of the United Nations, and Israel has the right to participate fully in that organization and all of its specialized agencies. The illegal expulsion of a member of the family of nations from the General Assembly would be a challenge to the basic principles of the United Nations. It would raise the gravest questions about the future of the General Assembly and further participation of the United States and other nations in the deliberations of that body. We will not permit it.

I am proud to be President of a great nation that stands up for human rights, not only in our own country but around the world, just as this union was standing up for human rights long before most of us were born.

I'm proud to have Chick Chaikin as my friend and ally in that struggle because he is one of the most forceful spokesmen for the rights of free trade unions in the entire world, and your support makes it possible for him to be that valuable spokesman everywhere.

And I'm also proud to stand before you as the standard-bearer of the one political party that represents the historic concerns of America's working people, and that is your and my Democratic Party of the United States.

I lead this party as its nominee in the crucial election of 1980 because of your help. And I am proud to share that leadership with a great friend of labor and the best Vice President that any President ever had, Fritz Mondale.

There are a lot of things that bind us closely together. I'm very proud to run with the support of a union that believes that our society has a moral obligation to do the most for those who have the least. That's what compassionate, democratic government is all about. That is what this campaign is all about. That is why you and I are fighting side by side, and that is why you and I are going to win November the 4th.

I feel confident about that prediction because this union has been fighting and winning for 80 years. You have fought for better wages, better working conditions for your own members, but you've done something more than that. For 80 years, you've fought to make our country live up to its own ideals. You've never cared what color someone might be or what nationality or what language they might speak or what sex they are or what religion they practice, because this union is serious about equality and social justice and democracy.

Five weeks from tomorrow the American people will make a choice that will affect every gain that you have fought so hard to achieve for the last 80 years. All of those gains, all of that progress is at stake, from the minimum wage to human rights. Never in my lifetime has our country faced such a stark choice—between two parties, yes, between two candidates, yes, between two totally different philosophies, yes; also, between two futures, for you, for your families, for those you love, and for our country.

I came here to talk to you briefly about that choice and what it means to working people and, especially today, about working women. It should be an easy choice, because all you have to do is follow the same good advice the ILG has been giving for years. When you pick a candidate and when you pick a party, just look for the union label.

Before a candidate tells you what he's going to do, first find out what he's already done. I think that's a pretty good standard. Before someone says he's a friend of the working people, take a look at his record. Look at which candidate stands up for the needs of America's working people, which party looks out for the people who have to work day in and day out, which candidate has fought with you, alongside of you, when the working people's interests were at stake.

Let me tell you briefly where I stand, what I've been fighting for with your help since the first day I was inaugurated President.

I believe, as you do, that people have a right to a decent living, and that's why we fought together for the largest and most certain continual increase ever in history in the minimum wage. We won that fight over tremendous opposition, and now 4 million Americans are living better lives today and all Americans, because of that, really live better lives.

I believe, as you do, that in the nation with the richest agriculture in the history of the entire world there can be no excuse for allowing anyone to go hungry. And that's why you and I fought to eliminate the cash requirement for purchasing food stamps. And we won that fight, and a lot of people today are not hungry because we fought together.

And I believe, as you do, that every worker has a right to be employed in a place that's safe and healthy. And that's why we've worked to improve OSHA and successfully defended it against attempts to destroy it. These attempts might still be launched in the future, but with you and I working together they will not succeed, and Americans will be protected where they work.

And I believe, as you do, that the best way to put young people to work is not to guarantee them lower wages, but to give them the training and the work experience they need to fit into the job market. I want to make sure there's a job for every young person to fill. As a matter of fact, I want to be sure that in America, there is a job for every person who's able to work to fill.

Full employment is my goal, and full employment is your goal. And that's why I'm working with the ILG to protect jobs from unfair import competition. And that's why you and I've worked together to increase American textile exports. In the last 2 years, we've had some success. Textile imports in the last 2 years are down, and in the last 2 years, American exports of textiles are up $2 billion. That trend is in the right direction, and we're going to keep it moving that way. This is your characteristic, because for 80 years you have fought to eliminate the sweatshop. And we must not let the sweatshop win, from abroad, the battle that you won against the sweatshop here at home.

And for many reasons that I will not go into today, I believe that Government has the responsibility to deal with the challenge of foreign oil dependence. Recent news broadcasts make this vividly clear.

I do not believe that the answer to that challenge is to do away with the windfall profits tax and to turn our energy future over to the oil companies. And if I should lose this election, that's what'll happen. Therefore, we will not lose.

And I also do not believe that the answer to our Nation's complex economic problems is a monstrous, ill-conceived tax giveaway to the very rich—Reagan-Kemp-Roth, a plan that would give the most to those who already have the most, a plan that may be the most ill-advised and inflationary proposal ever put before the Congress. I believe that the real answer is for you and me to work together not only to defeat Reagan-Kemp-Roth but also to defeat those who support it.

And more general in nature but equally important, I believe that the real answer is a good partnership between labor, business, and the public, to revitalize and to modernize American industry, to help American workers become even more productive and where necessary, better trained. With your help we will build that partnership and achieve those goals. Every one of these positions and many more that I could name carries the ILG union label, and so does this one: All Americans, women and men alike, should have the same fundamental rights. And those rights should be enshrined where the rights of Americans are supposed to be enshrined, in the Constitution of the United States of America.

We simply cannot afford top public officials who ignore the real problems of American working women, who would deny women the constitutional protection of their equal rights, who seem to believe that women, like children, should be seen and not heard. I totally reject that view. I support ERA. Not only do I support ERA, but my six predecessors in the White House also supported it, Democratic and

Republican Presidents. Even the Republican Party supported ERA for 40 years, until this year. The new Republican leaders have turned their backs on American women. Some of them say they are not opposed to women's rights; they just want to let the States do it. That's what the enemies of women's suffrage said 70 years ago, "Leave it to the States." That's what the enemies of civil rights said 20 years ago, "Leave it to the State."

Throughout the United States there are hundreds and hundreds of laws that discriminate against women. Fragment this series of laws among 50 different States, and you get some idea of what leaving it to the States really means. Make no mistake, this is not just a theoretical question. Equal rights for women is a bread and butter issue. For every dollar that men are paid, women are only paid 59 cents for the same amount of work. That is wrong. In many parts of our country women cannot work or borrow or dispose of their property on equal terms. That, too, is wrong. Equal pay for equal work!

Equal pay for equal work is a standard that ILG set a long time ago. It's the time now that the rest of the country caught up with you. Women make up 43 percent of the work force; a fourth of American households are headed by women—more and more American families depend on the wages that women bring home. When we help women to achieve greater economic rights, we are helping the American family. That's why we must put muscle behind our anti-discrimination laws, why we've toughened the Equal Employment Opportunity Commission, why I personally have appointed more women to top Federal positions and more women judges to the Federal bench than all previous Presidents in the 200-year history of our Nation combined. And that's why we have

boosted women employees in the Federal Government by 66,000, at a time when overall Federal employment was going down because of increased efficiency. And that's why we've strengthened the support of day care, why we've pioneered pacesetting innovations like flexitime and compressed time to help women meet both job and family responsibilities.

I'm the father of a little girl, and I'm also the grandfather of a little girl, and I want them to have the same kind of opportunities that my sons and my grandsons have.

I'd like to remind you again that ERA is not just a question of laws; it's a clarion call to end an historic injustice. It's a signal that we are really one Nation, with liberty and justice for all—all men and, at long last, all women. You understand the special problems of working women, because more ILG'ers are working women, women who work to support themselves and their families, women whose paychecks are not a luxury but a necessity.

You've not had an easy historic road. The men and women of the ILG have worked to send your sons and daughters to college, to law school, to medical school, sometimes based on the lowest possible wage. One of my own assistants in the White House, in fact the one who helped me write this speech, is the grandson of two members of the old local 38. His grandmother was a sweatshop seamstress at a time when the great shirtwaist strike of 1909, when 20,000 people, most of them women, rose up to demand the right to be treated with simple human decency. That strike holds a lesson for today's battle for ERA. On the ILG picket lines, immigrant girls of 14 and 15 years of age were joined by wealthy women from the suffragist movement; the women of 5th Avenue and the women of the Lower East Side joined together in solidarity because both believed in the dignity of women as human beings and also because both groups of women believed in the promise of America.

All of us who are fighting for ERA today are part of that same battle which began so many years ago. We must persevere until the battle is won and the equal rights amendment is inscribed in the Constitution of the United States.

But let me say, in closing, that the rights of women, the rights of minorities, the rights of those who are afflicted and oppressed, the rights of free speech and free expression, the rights of working people to organize and bargain collectively—these are fundamental human rights. They are the rights that our Nation represents. These are the rights that are worth fighting for, and these are the rights of our Nation which I will defend as long as I am President.

Let me dip just once more into ILG history before I close. Many of you will remember the old Italian Dressmakers Local 89 radio program on WEVD. The program always began with a song. The title of the song was "Bread and Roses." That same phrase—"Bread and Roses"—was one of the most famous rallying cries of the early American labor movement. It meant, of course, that labor was not struggling only for material benefits, but for the value and the ideals that give life its meaning and its beauty.

That old rallying cry is as good a description as any of what our country means to our own people and also to people all over the world. I want to continue that struggle side by side with you over the next 4 years. So let us go forward together to win an election and to build a future that gives us bread—and roses, too.

Thank you very much, and God bless you.

NOTE: The President spoke at 12:39 p.m. in the Imperial Ballroom at the Sheraton Centre Hotel.

Following his arrival in New York earlier in the day, the President went to Metzger's Garment Factory and toured the fourth floor factory area.

New York, New York

Remarks to the New York Business/Labor Committee for Carter/Mondale.
September 29, 1980

As I listened to the emotionalism and the objectivity and the cold economic analysis and the political judgment of the speakers that came before me, I couldn't help reminding myself that all the members of the union who look to Victor Gottbaum and Chick Chaikin are my constituents. And all the New Yorkers who were there with Abe Beame and now with Ed Koch are my constituents. And all those who live in the State of New York and are constituents of Hugh Carey are also mine. And all the customers of the business men and women assembled here are my constituents. I consider New York City to be my responsibility.

It's not as though there's an alien President who lives in the White House and who works in the Oval Office who deals from afar with leaders who are responsible for the future of this great city—I'm part of it. It's my city, and I'm determined that it will not suffer. I'm determined that it will be economically viable. And to summarize these feelings in four words—I love New York.

I came here first to campaign when the city was filled with discouragement and despair, when there was a sense of alienation between New York City and the White House, when Congress was responsive to a President who did not believe that this true partnership should exist, and I've seen that change in the eyes and in the hearts and minds of people on the streets. I've been here for two momentous occasions in my own life—when the Democratic National Committee and Convention nominated me for President. I've been here, probably, 15 times to ride down the street with Ed Koch as mayor and with Hugh Carey as Governor and with other leaders and looked in the faces of people alongside who gave me a friendly greeting, because I believe they honestly knew that I had their best interests at heart.

I know how much has been accomplished, but I also realize what great things we still have to do. Every New Yorker can take pride in what we have done, but every New Yorker must share the responsibility for the future—economic development, public transit, the allotment of funds for human services to meet the legitimate needs of people who are hungry, who are unemployed, who want a better chance in life, who are interested in equality of opportunity, who want a better education.

I'm very proud that in this city we have added in the last 3½ years, up through August, including the recession time, 248,000 jobs, and I remember that when I was inaugurated President the unemployment rate throughout New York State was 11 percent. It has decreased, as of last month, by 30 percent. Good progress, yes; not yet enough. But this was because we did the most necessary things as a top priority. We acted when we had to act, and we worked together. I don't think there's ever been an absence of the fullest kind of communication and cooperation and a sense of partnership although, as

almost everyone has said, we haven't always agreed on everything.

The $1.6 billion loan guarantee program is now the cornerstone of New York City's recovery program, and it's important that it be assessed constantly and kept alive. We won that monumental fight, but there's going to be more to fight for in the future. Right now, as you know, in the Senate an attack is being mounted which seriously threatens the $300 million in additional loan guarantees for which the city has recently applied. I'm determined, you and I together, to defeat that measure and to protect our hard-won gains.

Last night between 9 o'clock and 11 o'clock from my own study in the White House, I was calling members of the House and Senate Appropriations Committees, including the Senate Majority Leader, to ask them that when that conference committee comes out with the continuing resolution that there is congressional expression in the conference report that it's the sense of Congress that the Federal Government shall honor its obligation to continue the guarantee of loans for New York City. And I can tell you that as soon as that legislation is passed, protected as I've described, the Treasury will issue your guarantees without delay.

All the work's been done. There is no obstacle except that particular item, and I hope that all of you will help me with the members of the conference committee to protect what we've done.

Soon my opponent will be coming to New York, and we can predict that he'll try to make us forget what has been done in the past, his record, that he's the candidate with aspirations for the Presidency in the time of New York's greatest need who said, and I quote, "I have included in my morning and evening prayers every day the prayer that the Federal Government will not bail out New York City." Fortunately, it seems that the Lord does not always hear such prayers. [*Laughter*]

And I don't think that the people of New York or the other major cities of this country are going to pay much attention to candidates who make positive statements just during the few weeks immediately before a campaign is concluded. I hope that when my opponent comes to New York that you could do me a favor. I have been hoping that in a man-to-man debate, I could ask him some questions. Since he refuses to debate with me, there's one question that perhaps you can put to him, and I'll have to depend on the people of New York to ask it.

He proposes that we put the entire cost of the welfare program on State and local governments. The question is, how much would this proposal cost the taxpayers of New York? How much would State and local taxes have to be raised to pay for this one proposal? That's the question that he needs to answer in every city and town across this country, and I think tomorrow in New York is a good place for him to start.

We are going to continue our fight not only for a better city and a better State of New York but for a better nation; for a country that's strong and at peace; for a country that stands for the rights of Israel and our other allies to be secure and to live at peace; for energy security without the threat of blackmail from those who could bring us to our knees by the deprivation or overcharge for oil; for the military security of this country; for a vigorous economy and productive jobs, particularly in our cities; for social justice and quality of education; for equal rights for women and human rights around the world; for peace on Earth. And through all of this, of course, no matter how dif-

ficult the trials might be, my support for New York City will never wane.

The truth is that the Nation needs a strong and a healthy New York, not only for the obvious reasons of its commercial and cultural and international preeminence but for the example of what it offers to the Nation, of what people and politics can accomplish when we work together. By working hard and without falling victim to simple slogans and implausible promises, we'll keep on making steady, day-by-day progress. By working together without falling victim to divisions between black and white or Jews and Christians or North and South or urban and rural areas, we'll reach our goal of renewed greatness for this city and also for our country.

It's equally true that New York needs the support and the understanding of the rest of this Nation. As you know very well, particularly those of you who have spent time on Capitol Hill and in Washington, keeping the slender support of Congress is not easy. The President doesn't always have a lot of adequate influence in the Congress. But on closely divided issues, when public support around the Nation is absolutely crucial, the President's voice can make a difference in the Congress between success and failure. That's why when the Republicans were in the White House, New York could not succeed, and that's why when Fritz Mondale and I took over the leadership of this country, we were narrowly able to succeed.

Well, it's important to have your support. The full breadth of it could make the difference. It's almost theoretically impossible—practically, I'm sure, it's impossible—to figure out how I can win reelection without New York State. You can make the difference, not only with your financial contributions but with your voice, because you are the leaders to whom others listen, not only about the past, what has occurred, and the present problems that must be resolved together, but about the future that will extend even beyond the next 4 years.

A few people can make all the difference in the world. In 1960, if just 28,000 Texans had voted differently and just a few thousand in Illinois, John Kennedy would never have been President. And as all of you know, to your great regret and to mine, in 1968 just a few people working a little bit harder would have put Hubert Humphrey in the White House instead of Richard Nixon.

This year we face another crucial test of that same kind—not just a contest between two candidates or two parties, but between two futures for our country. The choice could not be more stark nor more critical. Will America have a secure future with abundant energy from sources that are as old as the Sun and as new as synthetic fuels, or will it face a precarious future, excessively dependent on OPEC and also the oil companies? Will America unite in fighting hard to fight inflation and compete abroad by rebuilding our industrial muscle, which needs a reinvestment to give American workers the tools and factories to keep their productivity high, or will it yield to transient political appeal of a massive inflationary election year Federal tax cut scheme known as Reagan-Kemp-Roth?

There's a question about whether America will care for its women and its children and its unemployed men or turn its back on traditions of compassion. Will America stand with those who struggle for equal rights and better lives for minorities and for the poor and for women, or will others hide behind codewords and evasions? Will America continue to build military power and strong alliances in a steady and responsible way, or will we throw away our wealth and our security and perhaps world respect and perhaps our peace on a doomed nuclear arms race? Will America keep laboring to strengthen the fragile bonds of peace among nations, or will we threaten them and our own safety with ill-considered, unnecessary interventions around the world as have been advocated repeatedly in the past few months? Will America continue to stand up for human rights at home and abroad?

My friends, there is no choice. We are proud that America once again stands for principle. We need not be ashamed of what our country is. We remember our founding commitments and ideals, and that sort of message is sent through every nation on Earth.

Above all, we must keep America standing firm with those—every President since Harry Truman has advocated—who have sought to control nuclear weapons and to lift their clouds of terror from the future of mankind. This could change, and we could be embroiled in a nuclear arms race that would endanger the existence of the world. Right now, in this crucial year of choice, the actions that you take will affect the lives and the futures of human beings everywhere.

You and I know how hard we have fought to put this country on the right road to the right future. I was with you then, and now I'm with you now. I'll be with you when the time comes to fight again.

I do not promise we can have everything immediately or exactly as you might wish. I do not promise that everything will be better all at once. If we accept the lessons of our past and face the facts of our life and welcome the challenges of the future, then I can promise you that our Nation will continue to prosper. I can promise you that our Nation will continue to grow stronger. I can promise you that our Nation will continue to use its beneficial impact on people throughout the world. I can promise you that our highest objective will be a secure nation at peace. I can promise you that human suffering will not be ignored, and I can promise you hope.

Together, I have no doubt that you and I will win this election, and together we'll keep the greatest nation on Earth firmly on course toward a future of security, of justice, of prosperity, of hope, and of peace. That's my promise to you. If you stay my partners and do your share on November the 4th, we will not lose.

Thank you very much.

NOTE: The President spoke at 2:10 p.m. in the Georgian Ballroom "A" at the Sheraton Centre Hotel.

Scientific and Technological Cooperation With Egypt and Israel

Message to the Congress Transmitting a Report.   September 29, 1980

To the Congress of the United States:

Pursuant to Section 8 of Public Law 96–35, I am pleased to transmit the report outlining plans for United States' participation and support of scientific and technological activities involving Egypt and Israel.

It is clear that science and technology have played an important role in strengthening U.S. bilateral cooperation with these countries. Recognizing this, my Administration fully supports the view that encouraging trilateral cooperation on activities of a scientific and technological nature can contribute much to building a permanent structure of peace in the Middle East. We will continue to support the

development and strengthening of scientific and technological activities that enhance relations between the peoples of Egypt, Israel and the United States.

JIMMY CARTER

The White House,
    September 29, 1980.

NOTE: The 49-page report is entitled "Planning for Trilateral Scientific and Technological Cooperation by Egypt, Israel, and the United States."

United States Sinai Support Mission

Message to the Congress Transmitting a Report.   September 29, 1980

To the Congress of the United States:

I am pleased to transmit herewith the Tenth Report of the United States Sinai Support Mission. It covers the Mission's activities during the six-month period ending October 1, 1980. This report is provided to the Congress in conformity with Section 4 of Public Law 94–110 of October 13, 1975.

The Peace Treaty of Egypt and Israel signed in Washington on March 26, 1979, called for the United States to continue its monitoring responsibilities in the Sinai until January 25, 1980, when Israel's armed forces withdrew from areas east of the Giddi and Mitla Passes. This mission was completed on schedule and to the satisfaction of all parties.

Trilateral talks in Washington in September of 1979 resulted in agreement that the United States would use the Sinai Field Mission to perform certain functions, among those specified in Annex I of the Treaty, relating to the verification of military constraints applicable to limited forces zones located in the western two-thirds of the Sinai. The Egyptian and Israeli Governments subsequently confirmed orally their acceptance of three articles on the operations of the Sinai Field Mission from an agreement still under negotiation which deals with arrangements in the Sinai up to the time of final Israeli withdrawal in April 1982. Administration officials have conveyed the text of these three articles to appropriate Congressional committees and have briefed them on the other aspects of the proposed agreement. They will continue to keep the Congress fully informed of progress in the negotiations on the remainder of the proposed agreement.

This year's funding of the Sinai Support Mission is authorized under Chapter 6, Part II of the Foreign Assistance Act, "Peacekeeping Operations." At my request, Congress restored 6 million dollars and approved an additional FY–1980 funding of 3.9 million dollars so that the Sinai Support Mission could perform verification functions entrusted to it.

The American peacekeeping effort in the Sinai has been a highly successful one. I know the Congress will continue its support of this mission as part of the larger U.S. effort to achieve our goal of permanent peace in the Middle East.

JIMMY CARTER

The White House,
September 29, 1980.

NOTE: The report is entitled "Report to the Congress—SSM: United States Sinai Support Mission" (13 pages plus appendices).

Accidents at Nuclear Power Facilities

Executive Order 12241.   September 29, 1980

NATIONAL CONTINGENCY PLAN

By the authority vested in me as President of the United States of America un-

der Section 304 of Public Law 96–295 (94 Stat. 790) and Section 301 of Title 3 of the United States Code, and in order to provide for the publication of a plan to protect the public health and safety in case of accidents at nuclear power facilities, it is hereby ordered as follows:

1–101. The functions vested in the President by Section 304 of Public Law 96–295 (94 Stat. 790) are delegated to the Director, Federal Emergency Management Agency.

1–102. A copy of the National Contingency Plan shall, from time to time, be published in the FEDERAL REGISTER.

JIMMY CARTER

The White House,
September 29, 1980.

[Filed with the Office of the Federal Register, 11:21 a.m., September 30, 1980]

NOTE: The Executive order was released on September 30.

Fish and Wildlife Conservation Act of 1980

*Statement on Signing H.R. 3292 Into Law.
September 30, 1980*

I have signed H.R. 3292, the Fish and Wildlife Conservation Act of 1980.

For over 50 years, in what has been one of the most successful and harmonious relationships in our Federal system, Federal and State agencies have labored together to conserve the fish and wildlife resources of our Nation. However, as I stated in my 1977 environmental message to Congress, almost always our activities have been focused on species that are harvested by hunters and fishermen. Usually, it is only when a species is threatened with extinction that we take note of the nongame species of wildlife—and then it is often too late.

This legislation will benefit the vast

majority of species which have too often been neglected, and, quite wisely, the legislation establishes a system within the existing framework of Federal-State relations. H.R. 3292 sets up a Federal-State planning process to inventory nongame wildlife species, identify their habitats, determine problems affecting their survival, and develop priorities for protecting them, if necessary. The Federal Government will assist them financially and technically to achieve this objective. This program will not diminish the support we give to game species, but it will encourage the comprehensive planning we need to conserve the full spectrum of our Nation's wildlife.

I wish to congratulate the Members of Congress, the conservation organizations, and the State fish and game agencies, who have worked for the passage of this bill. I salute their determination, and I am proud to be able to sign this bill into law.

NOTE: As enacted, H.R. 3292 is Public Law 96–366, approved September 29.

American Steel Industry

Remarks Announcing the Revitalization Program.   September 30, 1980

This is an important event in my own life as President, I think, in the life of our country, not only what it means to our Nation but also a demonstration of how government and industry, labor, public citizens groups, environmentalists can work together to deal with a very complicated and very challenging problem. A healthy and modern steel industry is vital to our Nation's economy and also to our Nation's security. Working together we now have a good opportunity to revitalize this basic industry.

Economically our Nation is living in a constantly changing world, a new world. We must meet foreign competition. We

must reverse our declining productivity— still, by the way, the highest in the world. We must protect our environment. And we must create jobs for a constantly growing work force. These are serious challenges, and all of them are closely interrelated. They require thoughtful, long-range analysis and attacks on many fronts at the same time. In today's real world a quick fix of one particular problem easily means quick trouble with another or others.

A few weeks ago I presented to the Nation a thorough plan for rebuilding the industrial base of America. Its carefully targeted public and private investment programs would put people back to work, attacking the two long-range problems of declining productivity and energy dependence that brought us both higher inflation and unemployment in the first place. We will modernize our industrial capacity, advance our technology, create new jobs and skills, rebuild our transportation system, reduce our energy dependence, and regain our competitive edge all at the same time. The entire program which I outlined is noninflationary in nature, a very important aspect at this time in our economic growth.

These goals can only be met by creating a new spirit of determined cooperation, and this meeting today is a milestone along that path of progress. The comprehensive steel agreement that we've reached is proof that the proper role of government is to be a partner in economic change, not an impediment and also not an uninterested or indifferent spectator.

The American steel industry is our third largest, exceeded only by petroleum and automobiles. Not only is the revitalization of these basic industries important to our economic health, it's necessary to preserve our national security, our ability to defend ourselves in case of a crisis. No nation can be a world power, with the ability to defend itself and to deter aggression, no nation can adequately defend itself without a strong industrial base to provide the necessary implements of national defense. Obviously, steel is perhaps the most crucial of all these industries.

Resolving conflicts among business, labor, and government in the steel industry has not been a simple matter of getting off each other's backs. It's required us to work together and to hammer out ways to keep America producing and working. The Steel Tripartite Advisory Committee has worked hundreds of hours over the last 2 years, reviewing every possible approach to our industry's future. This industry, we all recognized from the very beginning, is vital, and it also has inherent strengths that has constantly give us hope.

The hard work of the members of this Committee has shown that this industry can indeed modernize, that it can do so in a way that protects our environment, and that it has the will to regain its competitiveness and also its health. The Committee has now given me their conclusions on how the Federal Government can help the steel industry in its own efforts. They've recommended to me policies that will help workers, their families, and steelmaking communities overcome the challenges of a restructured steel industry, assist in capital formation, and increase investment, to discover and develop new technologies, to maintain free and fair trade, to guarantee that the industry can and will meet our environmental requirements.

I'm pleased to be able to accept the thrust of these recommendations, and I propose ways to achieve them in a detailed statement which we are releasing today, which will be described in just a few minutes. Secretary Klutznick, the Secretary of Commerce, Secretary Marshall, the Secretary of Labor, Doug Costle, Ambassador Askew, our Special Trade Representative, and Stu Eizenstat from my staff will now present the elements of that program.

On behalf of the workers and managers and the communities who give life to one of America's vital industries and who derive life from it, I want to thank the Secretaries of Commerce and Labor and all the members of this Committee for their efforts. They've proven that the proper role of government in our economy is in helping our industry and our workers to help America, and that's the path of the better future, which I am determined that our Nation will follow. And with your help, I have no doubt that we will be successful.

Again, my thanks to all of you, particularly those men and women who have served so well in evolving this plan. I believe that you will be pleased with it. I'm determined to carry it out, and I'm also equally determined that it will be successful.

Thank you very much.

NOTE: The President spoke at 10:03 a.m. in Room 450 of the Old Executive Office Building.

American Steel Industry

Statement on the Revitalization Program. September 30, 1980

Almost 2 years ago, I formed a Steel Tripartite Advisory Committee, to advise me and my administration on problems within the U.S. steel industry. Since that time, the Committee has served as the forum for constructive talks among government, management, and labor. Last week, the Committee completed a review of industry conditions and recommended to me a series of measures by which the government can assist the American steel industry in its efforts to modernize and regain competitive strength.

I have already acted, in my Economic Revitalization Program, to introduce measures that will help steel, as well as other industries, to accelerate the technological innovation and capital investment that are necessary to our economic growth, in ways that do not rekindle inflation.

Based on the proposals in my Economic Revitalization Program, the recommendations of the Steel Tripartite Advisory Committee, and recent developments in the trade area, I have initiated a new steel industry program consisting of:

• Measures to assist the steel industry in making the investments necessary to modernize its plants and equipment.

• Initiatives to encourage research and development of new steelmaking technologies.

• Reinstatement of an improved trigger price mechanism (TPM) that will provide expeditious investigation of unfair trade practices. The United States Steel Corporation has indicated its intention to withdraw its anti-dumping complaints. These decisions will help ensure a fair environment for trade in steel products during the transition period that both domestic and foreign steelmakers have begun.

• A program for industry compliance with environmental requirements that will, at last, ensure that the steel industry can and will attain our goals of a cleaner environment and a healthier workplace.

• Programs to help workers, their families and communities heavily affected by changes in the industry.

• A renewed commitment to address the problems of the steel industry through the tripartite process.

The challenge of revitalizing this essential industry must be met primarily by the industry itself. The government will de-velop policies that provide the climate for accelerated modernization, enhanced productivity, lasting and stable employment, and the protection of the environment. If the goals that all share for this industry are to be realized, however, the industry—management, stockholders and labor—must look beyond short-term interests. Attractive short-term investment or diversifying activities should not be permitted to delay or interfere with investment for modernization, a task that will require the full financial resources of the industry. Wage demands must be moderate and consistent with productivity gains, to ensure improved longer-term employment prospects. Once the industry, both labor and management, and government have demonstrated to the financial community and the public their commitment to each of these efforts and to continued cooperations, the industry will be able to meet its capital requirements.

My steel program will help improve the condition of the steel industry. The immediate effects will be a pickup in production, improved job opportunities for steelworkers, increased revenues for steel producers, and a new sense of certainty and stability for international trade in steel products. Over the longer term the program will lead to substantial increases in investment and the introduction of advanced technologies into the steel industry. Those steps will improve productivity, hold down costs and make the industry more competitive at home and in the international marketplace. The end result will be more secure jobs and more prosperous communities.

PRINCIPLES AND OBJECTIVES

In announcing this steel program, I agree with the general conclusions of the Steel Tripartite Advisory Committee. The program is guided by the following principles and objectives, which set both its goals and its limits.

Steelmaking is a basic industry within our economy. With annual sales reaching $57 billion in 1979, the steel industry is larger than any other U.S. industry except for petroleum and autos. Steel remains an essential ingredient in a vast array of the goods that we require. Its size, and the major role it plays in our industrial base, makes an efficient steel industry a prerequisite for a revitalized domestic economy.

The size of the industry will ultimately be determined by market forces, by the demand for steel products and by competition in the U.S. market and in international trade. American consumers and steelworkers will benefit from the efficient, modern steelmaking that will result.

But *trade in steel must be conducted according to the established rules of fairness.* Unfairly priced imports disrupt our home market for steel products, making it difficult for domestic producers to plan and invest for the future. The American steel industry must be prepared to meet fair international competition, but it is the government's responsibility to take action when injury is the result of competition violating established rules of fairness. Prompt and effective enforcement of our trade laws will help establish conditions in which industry modernization can go forward rapidly.

The industry has exceptional capital needs. Modernization of the American steel industry will call for high levels of investment in new plant and equipment for a number of years. Compliance with environmental laws will require the industry to invest even more. Combined, these expenditures will be very large, much larger than the investment requirements for many other American industries. While estimates differ substantially, almost all studies agree that the industry faces a substantial capital shortfall.

In the past the industry has not been sufficiently profitable to finance its capital requirements. Under current and anticipated business conditions, without changes in Federal policies, it is questionable whether over the next few years the industry would be able to do so.

The government does have a responsibility, working with the private sector, to ease the burden of adjustment for workers and communities that are heavily affected by economic change. Where jobs and communities are adversely affected, new jobs must be created, workers retrained, and economic development encouraged.

Prompt and full industry compliance with our pollution laws is critical to meet our environmental goals. Although the steel industry has spent substantial sums and made considerable progress in the past few years on pollution control, it continues to lag far behind other industries in achieving compliance with air and water pollution control requirements. Since steelmaking is an inherently dirty process, further progress in compliance will contribute substantially to overall attainment of our national environmental goals. Modernization and the use of new, cleaner technologies will result in a more competitive *and* cleaner steel industry in the years ahead.

For all these reasons, *the situation of the steel industry is unique.* The magnitude of the effort necessary to modernize and regain competitiveness will require the full cooperation of the industry and government. Modernizing the steel industry will also take time. A coordinated and integrated set of initiatives, maintained for a substantial period, will be necessary to set the industry on a new path. Our aim must be to have a steel industry that is as productive and efficient as possible, one that is completely competitive by world standards.

Working together, we will do so.

THE PRESIDENT'S PROGRAM

MODERNIZATION AND INVESTMENT

Modernization of the domestic steel industry will require sustained investment at high levels, as well as research, development and use of advanced steelmaking technologies. The proposals contained in my economic revitalization program will help the industry in this effort.

My proposals to liberalize and simplify the current depreciation system will help the steel industry finance its long-term modernization program. Under the new system of constant rate depreciation, the rate of depreciation for equipment (which accounts for 85–90 percent of the steel industry's fixed capital) would be about 40 percent greater than is permitted under current law.

In addition, the full 10 percent regular investment tax credit (ITC) will be made available for all new equipment with a useful life of more than one year. (Current law provides for a reduced credit in the case of short-lived assets.) Furthermore, an extra 10 percent credit will be allowed for up to $10 billion of capital investments which provide job opportunities and contribute to the economic base in distressed regions; this credit should be of particular benefit to steelmakers, in light of the location of many of their existing facilities.

Another important measure for the steel industry is my proposal to make the regular investment tax credit partially refundable and the special credit fully refundable. This proposal, which represents a major innovation in Federal tax policy, will extend the benefits of the ITC to firms that have no current tax liability. It provides the bulk of immediate tax relief for steel industry modernization.

These proposals will improve the outlook for investment in steel in several ways. In addition to their substantial direct benefits to steel companies, the new capital recovery provisions will yield important indirect benefits in the near term as a result of new investment and increased steel demand in other industries. In addition, diversified steel firms may realize direct short-term benefits by reducing tax liabilities in profitable non-steel areas.

DEVELOPMENT AND USE OF NEW TECHNOLOGY

Increased use of new technology is essential to make the United States steel industry more efficient, productive and competitive. Some U.S. firms are world leaders in the development and use of advanced steelmaking technologies. Others, however, have lagged considerably. For the most part, firms will modernize if the industry's ability to generate the funds for investment in new technology improves; my tax proposals will help in this regard. However, programs to develop and test important technical advances, under actual steelmaking conditions, will also be required.

Many promising technical opportunities have been identified. After extensive review, the Steel Tripartite Advisory Committee concluded that both existing and prospective steel technology is moving toward continuous, closed operations, which offer significant progress in manufacturing productivity, energy utilization, environmental protection, and worker health and safety. The Committee also concluded there were promising opportunities in broader application of continuous steel casting, formed-coke technology, dynamic control systems for steelmaking, recycling and recovery technologies, and a range of advanced process technologies.

Examples of additional possible areas of cooperation to be explored include coal-based direct reduction of iron ore and basic research on high performance steel alloys, plasma technology, and the physical chemistry of steel and steelmaking.

As announced in my recent Economic Revitalization Program, I am committed to providing an additional $600 million over the fiscal years 1981 and 1982 for the support of basic research and other scientific programs to improve the performance of the U.S. economy. These funds will be used to maintain a real annual growth rate of 3% in Federal funding of basic research and also to support increased collaborative research among government, industry, and universities. The steel industry, among others, will benefit from these steps.

I believe industry and government should cooperate to ensure full consideration of the opportunities that can put domestic producers back at the forefront of steelmaking technology. I have therefore instructed the Director of the White House Office of Science and Technology Policy, the Secretary of Commerce, and other senior officials to review carefully the technical proposals outlined by the Steel Tripartite Advisory Committee and others. I am further directing these officials to explore promptly, in collaboration with industry, the feasibility of establishing a cooperative basic and applied research program.

EFFECTIVE ENFORCEMENT OF TRADE LAWS

Under the United States trade laws, the Federal government is responsible for ensuring that domestic producers are subject to fair competition in the international marketplace. Our trade laws are fully consistent with the obligations we have accepted under the Multilateral Trade Agreements. My Administration has often stated our insistence on vigorous and prompt enforcement of these laws.

My Administration has continued to work towards an environment in which international trade in steel products is free of government obstruction, is determined by competitive conditions, and is conducted without injurious dumping or subsidization. The steps announced today advance these goals.

Today, the Commerce Department is announcing that the trigger price mechanism (TPM), which was suspended in March 1980, will be reinstated. The TPM, which has been improved in several respects, will help achieve prompt and effective enforcement of the trade laws during the transition period in which the industry—both here and abroad—will modernize and restructure, for a period of not more than five years.

At the same time, the United States Steel Corporation is announcing immediate withdrawal of its anti-dumping complaints against steel producers in seven European countries.

Administration of the TPM, particularly monitoring efforts, is being improved. In addition, a change will be introduced in the method of calculating trigger prices in order to reduce the distortions from short-term exchange rate fluctuations. Furthermore, a procedure is being established to review import surges which may be the result of dumping or subsidies. (Details are being announced today by the Commerce Department.) As before, the TPM will impose no quantitative restrictions, will guarantee no market share, and will not impede fair international trade.

Reinstatement of the TPM will help ensure that unfair import competition does not disrupt the steel industry's modernization program. Indeed, the reinstatement of the TPM is premised on the industry's readiness to undertake such a program. The new TPM system will be reviewed after three years; continued operation of the TPM beyond three years is specifically conditioned on the industry's undertaking the investments necessary to ensure its long-term competitiveness.

The new TPM is thus designed to cover only a transitional period for domestic and foreign steel producers. The United States Government has received assurances from European Community authorities that they will press forward with their efforts to restructure the European steel industry during the period when the TPM is in operation.

In no longer than 5 years, the TPM will be terminated, and there will be no special administrative procedures for steel imports. Should trade complaints arise, they will be handled through the normal enforcement of our antidumping or countervailing duty laws.

As the Committee suggested, I am directing the United States Trade Representative and the Secretary of Commerce to review the other trade issues identified in the Committee's report. Also, the Secretary of Commerce will follow closely the situation in specialty steel trade, and advise me if inclusion of specialty steels is necessary and feasible.

ENSURING COMPLIANCE WITH ENVIRONMENTAL LAWS

I believe that prompt compliance with the Clean Air and Water Acts is absolutely essential for the health and quality of life of the American people. The steel industry is, by the nature of its operations, one of the country's largest sources of air and water pollution. It is particularly important, therefore, that the steel industry comply with the environmental laws. This package is intended to get that job done.

The problems of environmental compliance are unique to steelmaking. Because steel production is an inherently dirty process, the clean-up costs are very great. Although the industry has spent substantial sums, during a period of declining profits, and made considerable progress in the past few years on pollution control, it continues to lag far behind other industries. Full compliance will require large additional expenditures at the very time that the industry must also make major investments for modernization.

Modernization of the industry is critically important to the well-being of the steel workers, their families, steelmaking communities, and the economy generally. But modernization is equally important to environmental objectives, since modern facilities are inherently much cleaner, and all parties (including the industry) have agreed they will use the most modern technology available.

For these reasons, I agree with the Committee report that, for this industry *uniquely,* flexibility is needed to assure that the goals of modernization and environmental protection will both be met.

The program announced today is designed to make sure that the steel industry *can* and *will*, at last, comply with the environmental statutes. It will encourage and enable the industry to raise the capital necessary for compliance by fostering modernization and technological development and providing tax incentives. It will allow companies the time necessary to secure capital for achieving compliance by providing flexibility on deadlines in those individual cases where it is necessary. And it will ensure that there *will be* environmental compliance by requiring strict schedules spelled out in compliance orders and enforced by the courts.

I am firmly committed to the reauthorization of a strong Clean Air Act next year. I do not intend to endorse an across-the-board relaxation of deadlines for this industry or others. I recognize, however, that the unique conditions of the steel industry identified in the Tripartite report may require some modification of compliance deadlines for a limited number of steel facilities. So that these special needs can be addressed without distorting the general debate on the Clean Air Act, I will recommend legislation to deal separately with the unique situation of the steel industry immediately after the Congress convenes in January. I will not recommend an automatic deferral of compliance deadlines—there are steel facilities that can comply without further delays—but rather, a discretionary, case-by-case stretchout of required action.

In preparing the amendment, the Administration will consult with the Congress, the Committee (which will be expanded to include public members with respect to its work on environmental matters), with representatives of environmental organizations, and with the National Commission on Air Quality. The amendment would allow the EPA Administrator to grant an individual steel source an extension for up to three years of the deadline for compliance with the requirements of the Clean Air Act. The Ad-

ministrator could grant the extension only where the following conditions are met:

1. The extension is no longer than necessary to allow the company to make modernization expenditures on iron and steel facilities; and

2. Funds which would have been spent to comply with the deadline will be expended in the same time period for modernization and in existing steelmaking communities; and

3. The company will have sufficient capital to meet all air pollution control requirements in a timely manner; and

4. The company is under a company-wide judicial order which

—establishes a schedule for each violating source to comply with as expeditiously as practical, consistent with any extensions granted; and

—provides means to assure no degradation of air quality during the deferral period.

Existing consent decrees will remain in force until, in particular cases the Administrator is granted by legislation, and uses, this extension authority.

In the Committee report, all parties—including the industry—agreed that effective implementation of their recommendations would resolve the major health-related environmental regulatory issues concerning the steel industry. It will make an important contribution to the modernization of the industry. I am accepting this and the Committee's other proposals because doing so will remove the need for further amendments to the Clean Air Act as it affects the steel industry during reauthorization by the next Congress. My decision is also premised on my understanding that the steel industry has committed to comply with the Clean Air Act. The conditions for obtaining extensions of deadlines will be strict, and I have been assured by the industry that when a source obtains a deadline deferral, efforts to improve air quality will continue. The amendment would only allow a stretch-out—not a postponement—of investments on controls.

The amendment recommended by the Tripartite Committee would allow the Administrator to extend the deadline for a facility to permit investment in modernization of other steel facilities owned by the company. I believe it is appropriate to require that the investments made possible by the deadline extension should be for facilities located in existing steel communities.

The Committee also recommended that "to the extent substantial additional expenditures will be required" by forthcoming EPA regulations to meet water pollution control requirements, the Clean Water Act should be amended in the same manner. The regulations will be proposed in December and the level of expenditures required by new regulations is not now known. My Administration will then take appropriate action in light of the Committee's recommendation, taking into account whether substantial additional expenditures will be required by the forthcoming regulations and whether the overall capital requirements of the industry are as high as projected. Before my Administration forwards any amendment, we will consult with all interested parties.

EPA has already begun work to effect the Committee's recommendations that it explore ways to increase the availability of the "bubble concept" to the industry, and that discharge permits under the water act not be modified until EPA's revised regulations take effect next year. I accept both recommendations as important to the modernization of the steel industry.

WORKER AND COMMUNITY ASSISTANCE

The modernizing and restructuring of the steel industry will result in the competitive industry that is necessary to ensure the stability of steelworkers' jobs. As the modernization process takes hold over a period of years, productivity will improve. Nonetheless, job losses can be reduced or avoided, especially since the modernization will take place in steel-making communities. However, some dislocation must be anticipated. Both government and industry can and will take steps to help relieve the anguish and uncertainty that accompany these changes, but change cannot be avoided entirely. Failure to modernize the steel industry would lead to still greater economic and personal distress, with permanent shutdowns of major plants.

Trade Adjustment and Other Current Efforts

The Federal Government has in recent years provided substantial financial assistance through trade adjustment programs for workers and communities harmed by temporary layoffs or permanent plant closings. From 1975 to the present, for example, over 100,000 steelworkers have received nearly $200 million in trade adjustment assistance (TAA) benefits to supplement unemployment payments from other sources. Similarly, over $30 million had been disbursed since 1977 in adjustment assistance to communities affected by steel plant closings. Earlier this year I requested and Congress approved an additional $1.5 billion for trade adjustment benefits in fiscal 1980 and 1981, part of which will go to steelworkers. My Administration has also supported legislation that would extend TAA benefits to workers in supplier industries.

Over the past year, guided by the deliberations of the Steel Tripartite Advisory Committee, the government has begun a number of important steps to channel Federal aid to workers and communities more effectively. In 1979, my Administration, in cooperation with the companies and the United Steelworkers of America, established a task force to respond to the problems posed by steel shutdowns on an individual plant basis. This task force has served as a useful vehicle for improving the flow of unemployment benefits and employability service information to the site of plant closings, for speeding up the application and payment of TAA benefits to unemployed workers, and for developing action plans specifically geared to the needs of individual groups of workers and communities. A joint Commerce-Labor Adjustment Action Committee has worked in eleven of the communities most severely hurt by steel layoffs and shutdowns, helping to organize and expedite financial, training and job finding help for workers and, in six communities, helping secure Economic Development Administration funds. The Committee also recommended that Federal officials be assigned to work fulltime with local governments, labor and managements to ensure that available Federal assistance programs be delivered as quickly as possible; this program, too, has begun.

New Initiatives

My proposals for worker and community adjustment assistance, as announced in my Economic Revitalization Program, draw upon the adjustment experience gained from the steel industry and indicate my commitment to expand these efforts. The proposals include the following:

Supplemental Unemployment Benefits: As a temporary measure my proposal to authorize 13 additional weeks of unemployment compensation will provide immediate and direct financial assistance to steelworkers and workers in related industries who have lost their jobs.

Job Training/Assistance: I have proposed a $300 million expansion of current job training programs under CETA, some of which will help retrain skilled workers. In addition, the Department of Labor will establish in 1981 about a dozen pilot programs to test innovative new ways to assist in retraining and relocation of workers affected by industrial change. I have instructed the Department of Labor to conduct some of these pilot programs in steelmaking communities. If the demonstrations prove successful, I will propose a full-scale program offering dislocated workers throughout the Nation similar training and assistance.

Targeted Investment Tax Credit: My proposed targeted investment tax credit will be of special benefit to steel communities. Many steel communities are older cities and towns suffering not only from temporary or permanent shutdowns of steel plants but also from general declines in economic activity. Many would qualify as eligible sites for the targeted investment tax credit. For these communities the modernization of the steel industry, in combination with the targeted investment tax credit, should be an important step towards revitalizing their economic bases.

Programs Assisting Communities: The Federal government, through agencies such as the Economic Development Administration (EDA) of the Department of Commerce and the Department of Housing and Urban Development (HUD), provides a wide variety of programs aiding the development of businesses in steelmaking communities, including loan guarantees, development grants, direct loans, and interest subsidies.

My proposal for increased program levels for economic development of $1 billion in 1981 and $2 billion in 1982 will allow a significant expansion of these programs benefiting steel communities.

CONTINUING PARTNERSHIP

In large part, my Administration's program is a result of the continued discussion and collaboration within the Steel Tripartite Advisory Committee. The Committee's deliberations have shown the value to Government decisionmaking of close cooperation and discourse with business and labor. In recognition of this contribution, I decided to create an Economic Revitalization Board to advise on matters of economic policy affecting all industry.

To obtain additional guidance, and help in monitoring the progress of the program being announced today, I have directed Secretaries Marshall and Klutznick to renew the Committee's charter, which expires next January. I have also directed them to modify the Committee's charter to include representatives of the public with respect to its work on environmental matters.

National Railroad Passenger Corporation

Nomination of Charles Luna To Be a Member of the Board of Directors. September 30, 1980

The President today announced that he will nominate Charles Luna, of Dallas, Tex., for reappointment as a member of the Board of Directors of the National Railroad Passenger Corporation (Amtrak) for a term expiring in 1984.

Luna, 73, has been a member of this Board since 1970. He was previously president and chairman of the board of the United Transportation Union and was elected president emeritus of that union on his retirement in 1972.

He began work as a switchman in the Dallas area in 1928 when he joined the Brotherhood of Railroad Trainmen. He served as president of that union from 1962 until 1969, when it merged with three other unions into the United Transportation Union, of which he was the first president.

American Education Week, 1980

Proclamation 4797.   September 30, 1980

By the President of the United States of America

A Proclamation

Nothing is of greater importance to the future of America than education. The survival of our free institutions, the health of our economy, the power of our ideals depend on the vitality of our educational system.

The theme of this year's American Education Week—an event we have celebrated for more than sixty years—is "Education in the 80's: Preparation for the Future." Our future will be determined by how well we pass along our knowledge and our values to our children.

American Education Week affords all of us time to think about the needs, the importance, and the hopes for education. And it gives us a time to acknowledge the accomplishments of an education system that serves more than 58 million young people and adults.

We have much to be proud of—our schools, our teachers, and the administrators who make the system work. But there is more progress to be made and more work ahead of us.

I invite all Americans to join me in reaffirming our commitment to the excellence and equality of the educational opportunity offered to every individual in our Nation. Education is everyone's concern.

Now, THEREFORE, I, JIMMY CARTER, President of the United States of America, do hereby designate the period of November 16 through 22, 1980, as American Education Week.

IN WITNESS WHEREOF, I have hereunto set my hand this thirtieth day of September in the year of our Lord nineteen hundred and eighty, and of the Independence of the United States of America the two hundred and fifth.

JIMMY CARTER

[Filed with the Office of the Federal Register, 3 p.m., September 30, 1980]

Synthetic Fuels

Executive Order 12242. September 30, 1980

By the authority vested in me as President by Sections 305 and 703(a) of the Defense Production Act of 1950, as amended (50 U.S.C. App. 2095, and 2153(a)), and Section 301 of Title 3 of the United States Code, and in order to achieve production of synthetic fuel to meet national defense needs and to provide for an orderly transition of synthetic fuel responsibilities to the United States Synthetic Fuels Corporation, it is hereby ordered as follows:

1-101. The functions vested in the President by Sections 305(f)(1) and 305(f)(2) of the Defense Production Act of 1950, as amended (50 U.S.C. App. 2095

(f)(1) and (2)), are delegated to the Secretary of Defense.

1-102. The Secretary of Defense shall, after consulting with the Secretary of Energy, determine the quantity and quality of synthetic fuel which is needed to meet national defense needs from time to time. This determination shall be made in accord with Section 305(f)(1) of the Defense Production Act of 1950, as amended, and shall promptly be furnished to the Secretary of Energy.

1-103. In accord with Section 305(f)(1) of the Defense Production Act of 1950, as amended, the Secretary of Defense shall ensure that his determination of the national defense needs for synthetic fuel does not include any synthetic fuel which the Secretary anticipates will be resold by the Government.

1-104. The functions vested in the President by subsections (b)(1)(A)(i) and (ii), (c)(1)(B), (c)(3), (d)(2), (d)(3), (d)(5), (d)(6), (e), and (g)(2)(C) of Section 305 of the Defense Production Act of 1950, as amended (50 U.S.C. App. 2095), are delegated to the Secretary of Energy.

1-105. The Secretary of Energy, to the extent practicable, shall apply laws regarding the procurement of goods and services by the Government to the terms and conditions contained in purchase contracts awarded under subsection (b)(1)(A)(i) of Section 305 of the Defense Production Act of 1950, as amended. The terms and conditions of these contracts shall be subject to the concurrence of the Secretary of Defense.

1-106. The Secretary of Energy shall, after consulting with the Secretary of Defense, exercise the functions delegated to him under Section 305 of the Defense Production Act of 1950, as amended, in order to meet the national defense needs for synthetic fuel as determined by the Secretary of Defense.

1–107. The Secretary of Energy shall exercise the functions delegated to him under Section 305 of the Defense Production Act of 1950, as amended, in a manner consistent with an orderly transition to the separate authorities established pursuant to the United States Synthetic Fuels Corporation Act of 1980, as provided by Section 305(a)(1)(B)(iii) of the Defense Production Act of 1950, as amended.

1–108. The Secretary of Energy, after consulting with the Secretary of Defense, shall prepare for the President's transmittal to the Congress the report required by Section 106 of the Energy Security Act (Public Law 96–294). The proposed report shall be submitted to the President for his consideration no later than thirty days prior to the date on which it is to be transmitted to the Congress.

1–109. No new awards for purchases or commitments for financial assistance shall be made under the provisions of this Order after the date on which the President determines that the United States Synthetic Fuels Corporation is established and fully operational. That determination is to be made in accord with Section 305 (k) of the Defense Production Act of 1950, as amended (50 U.S.C. App. 2095 (k)), and in accord with the appropriations to the Departments of Energy and the Treasury pursuant to the Supplemental Appropriations and Rescission Act, 1980 (P.L. 96–304; 94 Stat. 857, 880–882).

1–110. No award for a purchase or commitment for financial assistance shall be made which would preclude projects or actions initiated by the Secretary of Energy under the provisions of this Order from being transferrable to the United States Synthetic Fuels Corporation.

1–111. Prior to issuing any loan guarantee under the provisions of this Order, the Secretary of Energy shall obtain the concurrence of the Secretary of the Treasury with respect to the timing, interest rate, and substantial terms and conditions of such loan guarantee. In establishing an interest rate, the current average yield on outstanding marketable obligations of the United States with comparable remaining periods of maturity shall be considered. To the extent practicable, the timing, interest rate, and substantial terms and conditions of such guarantees shall have the minimum possible impact on the capital markets of the United States, taking into account other Federal direct and indirect securities activities.

JIMMY CARTER

The White House,
    September 30, 1980.

[Filed with the Office of the Federal Register, 3:01 p.m., September 30, 1980]

Synthetic Fuels

Statement on Signing Executive Order 12242. September 30, 1980

The rapid development of a viable synthetic fuels industry is an essential part of my overall program to reduce our dependence on imported oil. This program must include both increasing domestic energy supplies and reducing demand through conservation. Great strides have been made in the past year in both of these areas, but much remains to be done. Our program to increase the supply of domestic energy includes:

—Increased reliance on our vast coal deposits;

—Use of renewable resources;

—Greater exploration, development,

and production of domestic oil and gas;

—Development of alternate fuels.

The United States Synthetic Fuels Corporation (SFC) was created by the Energy Security Act. It will be the principal Federal instrument to ensure that the synthetic fuels industry becomes a reality. That same legislation recognized that it would take time for the SFC to become operational and therefore provided interim authority under the Defense Production Act for a "fast-start" program for the development of synthetic fuels to meet the needs of national defense.

I am pleased today to sign an Executive order which formally assigns responsibilities to the Departments of Energy and Defense to carry out this interim program until the SFC becomes fully operational. This effort is well underway in both departments. The Department of Defense has identified its short-term synthetic fuel needs and is testing the compatibility of fuel derived from oil shale with existing equipment. The tests to date have been highly successful. The Department of Energy has issued a draft solicitation to industry requesting proposals for financial assistance for synthetic fuels projects to meet the national defense needs.

The synthetic fuels program is a matter of the highest national priority. The use of this "fast-start" interim authority will permit immediate financial aid to the synthetic fuels industry and provide a smooth transition to the SFC. I will take all appropriate steps to assure that the SFC is able to begin full-scale operation at the earliest practical time.

Under the Energy Security Act, I must declare when the SFC is fully operational for the purposes of termination of the Defense Production Act. In exercising this authority, I shall, of course, be aware that this declaration will terminate the interim authority. I am confident that it will be possible both to utilize the interim authority and to provide a smooth transition to the SFC. The Departments of Defense and Energy are both committed to this goal, and I intend to declare the Corporation fully operational at a time that will avoid adverse impact on the activities underway at the Department of Energy. Projects awarded under this interim program shall be transferrable to the Corporation or shall remain with the Department of Energy under the interim program and will be transferred to the Corporation for its consideration.

World Bank Group and International Monetary Fund

Remarks at the Annual Meetings of the Boards of Governors. September 30, 1980

Thank you very much, Secretary Miller, Chairman Jamal, Mr. de Larosière, Mr. McNamara, Governors of the Fund and the Bank, distinguished delegates and guests:

It's a special pleasure for me as President of our country to welcome you again for this meeting, which is so important to the entire world. This is the 35th annual meeting of its two great institutions. And it's also a special pleasure for me to welcome the new members.

Your presence here symbolizes a commitment of more than 140 countries to a dynamic system of international economic cooperation and to its central institutions, as you well know, the International Monetary Fund and the World Bank. Your commitment strengthens the prospects for a lasting peace, because peace cannot be assured if hundreds of millions of people are offered no hope of escape from hunger or poverty or economic instability or deprivation. The Bank and the Fund provide that hope.

Both institutions are rapidly adapting to new circumstances and new changes and also new challenges. We support this process of adapting to change. The response of a changing world can best be charted within these institutions, acting in your own fields of competence and experience. Your work should not be diverted by extraneous political disputes. And as you mold and adapt, you must be assured that your decisions will not be determined or renegotiated in some other meeting. Your record of success justifies this vote of confidence. Any political pressure or unwarranted influence from any international forum which might undermine your integrity would be neither necessary nor desirable.

The Fund is the world's principal official source of balance-of-payments financing. So far this year, Fund programs of more than $5½ billion have been arranged; even more is needed. An action is underway to expand these resources. The IMF is also adopting important changes in policy, making it more responsive to changing needs and the concerns of its members.

During the last 12 months, the World Bank Group has lent more than $12 billion to developing member countries. Nearly $4 billion of that was provided on concessional terms to the poorest nations.

The Bank is mounting initiatives to enable developing countries to find and produce more energy, while also carrying out other important bank functions. An enlarged World Bank program for energy exploration and development would benefit all of us. The World Bank has also launched a program of lending and advisory services to help developing nations and to help them make the structural adjustments required by higher energy prices.

It's not possible for me to discuss the role of the World Bank without paying personal and professional tribute to the leadership and the dedication of Robert McNamara over the last 12 years. Under Bob McNamara's outstanding leadership, the Bank has become the focus of world cooperation to improve the human condition and a fine example of how such cooperation can be effective. Bob, you will leave to your successor a high standard and a firm foundation for the future, based on an open heart, sensitivity about people's human needs, and the sound economic judgment that has maintained the integrity of the World Bank.

U.S. support of the Fund and the Bank reflects both our fundamental humanitarian principles and also our own economic interests. Legislation enabling our participation in the IMF quota increase passed the House of Representatives last week. I'm now pressing for a passage of this legislation in the Senate, and I will sign it as soon as it reaches my desk. Moreover, I will urge the Congress of our country to give high priority to the sixth IDA replenishment later this year. Next year we will submit legislation for our subscription to the general capital increase of the World Bank. Both the Fund and the World Bank Group must have all the resources they need for their crucial work.

Let me also mention several other steps the United States has taken that will help to stabilize the world economy. We've adopted a strong anti-inflation program of fiscal and monetary restraint. We've begun a nationwide program to revitalize our own industrial base and to accelerate productivity growth. This new program would increase the portion of our own gross national product devoted to investment in new industry and in new jobs and in new production. The program will reduce inflation. It will restore innovation and vigor to our economy. And we've also put into place a comprehensive program to rebuild my country's energy base.

This new program is already paying rich dividends; it's already bearing fruit.

In the last 3 years, for instance, we've reduced oil imports by 24 percent. This year we are drilling more oil and gas wells than any other year in history. And this year we are producing more coal in my country than in any previous year in history. We are acting to ensure that the United States can meet much of the world's need for coal. We've started a massive investment program to increase production of synthetic fuels. We're spending $4 billion per year on energy research and development and additional billions of dollars on incentives to use energy more efficient in our homes, in our industries, our commerce, and our transportation.

Because of sustained oil production and because of worldwide conservation measures, the world's oil stocks are now at an alltime high, and these reserves will help to offset the effect of temporary reductions in supply, such as that which has been caused by the present conflict between Iran and Iraq. However, we are keenly aware that some nations are seriously threatened by even a temporary interruption in normal oil supplies. Thus we are working with your countries in the United Nations and through other public, international fora to end this conflict as quickly as possible.

Our energy program is part of a far-reaching effort to which we pledged ourselves at the recent Venice economic summit conference. Our common goal there, as expressed by the seven nations involved, is to conserve more oil and to produce the equivalent in alternative fuels of 15 to 20 million barrels of oil per day by the end of this decade. This will ease pressure on world oil markets. It will alleviate balance-of-payments problems and will let developing countries obtain a larger share of the world oil supply now and in the future.

The common purpose of all countries, in both our domestic and international energy actions, should be to strengthen the world economy and to assure fair treatment for all nations. Our common goal should be to minimize the threat of abrupt changes in the price of oil, to assure a reasonable, predictable level of supply of energy, to avoid compounding inflationary pressure that rob us all. The oil-importing countries and the oil-exporting countries as well can all contribute to this effort. We all have a stake in its outcome.

This meeting comes at a crucial time for us all. The world has come to place enormous confidence in your judgment, in the judgment and the services of the World Bank and the International Monetary Fund. That confidence, down through the years, has never been misplaced, and I'm certain that it will be even more justified by your actions and your services in the future.

On behalf of the United States of America, I assure you that we intend to remain active in the decisions made within these two institutions and supportive of the work which lies ahead of us all. Congratulations on what you've accomplished. My full support and best wishes now and in the future.

Thank you very much.

NOTE: The President spoke at 11:17 a.m. in the Plenary Hall at the Sheraton Washington Hotel to representatives of the International Monetary Fund, the International Bank for Reconstruction and Development (World Bank), the International Development Association, and the International Finance Corporation.

In his opening remarks, the President referred to Secretary of the Treasury G. William Miller, Amir H. Jamal, Minister for Finance of Tanzania and chairman of the 35th annual meetings, Jacques de Larosière, Managing Director and Chairman of the Board of Executive Directors of the International Monetary Fund, and Robert S. McNamara, President of the World Bank.

Environmental Protection Agency

Nomination of Jeffrey G. Miller To Be an
Assistant Administrator. September 30, 1980

The President today announced that he will nominate Jeffrey G. Miller, of Chevy Chase, Md., to be an Assistant Administrator of the Environmental Protection Agency (EPA). He would replace Marvin Durning, resigned. Miller has been with EPA since 1971 and has been Associate Assistant Administrator for Enforcement since earlier this year.

He was born August 15, 1941, in Muncie, Ind. He received an A.B. from Princeton University in 1963 and an LL.B. from Harvard University Law School in 1967.

From 1968 to 1971, Miller was an associate with the Boston firm of Bingham, Dana & Gould. He helped develop a consumer rights program with the Boston Legal Assistance Projects.

Miller was Chief of the Enforcement Branch of EPA for Region I from 1971 to 1973 and Director of the Enforcement Division for Region I from 1973 to 1975. From 1975 to 1980, he was Deputy Assistant Administrator of EPA for Water Enforcement.

National Transportation Safety Board

Nomination of Elwood T. Driver To Be a
Member. September 30, 1980

The President today announced that he will nominate Elwood T. Driver, of Reston, Va., for reappointment as a member of the National Transportation Safety Board. On confirmation by the Senate, he will be redesignated as Vice Chairman of the Board.

Driver, 49, has been Vice Chairman of this Board since 1978. He was previously Acting Director of the Office of Crashworthiness, Motor Vehicle Programs, at the National Highway Traffic Administration.

United States International Trade Commission

Nomination of Gardner Patterson To Be a
Member. September 30, 1980

The President today announced that he will nominate Gardner Patterson, of Washington, D.C., to be a member of the U.S. International Trade Commission for a term expiring in 1981. Patterson has been a senior adviser to the General Agreement on Tariffs and Trade (GATT) and a consultant to the World Bank since earlier this year. He was Assistant Director General, then Deputy Director General, of GATT from 1966 to 1980.

He was born May 13, 1916, in Burt, Iowa. He received a B.A. (1938) and M.A. (1939) from the University of Michigan and a Ph. D. in economics from Harvard University in 1942.

From 1942 to 1946, Patterson served in economic intelligence with the U.S. Treasury Department and U.S. Navy. From 1946 to 1948, he was a member of the International Currency Committee in Athens, Greece. In 1948–49 he was a professor of economics at the University of Michigan.

From 1949 to 1969, Patterson was a professor of economics at Princeton University. In 1955 and 1956 he also served as economic adviser to the State Department in Ankara, Turkey. He served as head of the economic mission at the State Department in 1961 and as an economic adviser to the State Department in Tel Aviv, Israel, in 1963.

NOTE: On the same day, the President announced that he will withdraw the nomination of Robert Baldwin to be a member of the U.S. International Trade Commission, at Mr. Baldwin's request. Mr. Baldwin was nominated for this position on November 30, 1979.

Billy Carter's Activities With the Libyan Government

White House Statement on a Draft Report by a Subcommittee of the Senate Judiciary Committee. September 30, 1980

On September 24, 1980, the subcommittee of the Senate Committee on the Judiciary requested by September 29 information relating to the President's knowledge as to certain issues the subcommittee believed to be unresolved in the record of the Billy Carter hearings. The President's Counsel submitted this information to the subcommittee on September 29 as requested.

Unfortunately, before this information could be reviewed and reflected in the subcommittee's report, a draft report previously prepared by the subcommittee's staff has been leaked and reported in the press. The White House has not seen a copy of this draft report and is not in a position to comment on it. We would expect that the final report will reflect the information provided to the subcommittee on September 29 at its request. Because the draft report has already been leaked, we have informed the subcommittee we are now releasing the information it requested.

The news articles which we have seen describing the draft report indicate that the subcommittee staff has found no significant impropriety but has raised certain issues involving questions of judgment.

As is to be expected, after-the-fact opinions may differ on judgmental issues.

We look forward to a final report which will present in an impartial and balanced manner the facts learned by the subcommittee and the conclusions it has reached.

NOTE: On the same day, the White House also released a letter, dated September 29, from Alfred H. Moses, Special Counsel to the President, to Philip W. Tone, Special Counsel of the Senate subcommittee; a list of contacts between Zbigniew Brzezinski, Assistant to the President for National Security Affairs, and Secretary of State Cyrus R. Vance; and a portion of Dr. Brzezinski's testimony in executive session before the Senate subcommittee on September 19.

Mental Health Systems Legislation

Statement on Congressional Approval of the Conference Report. September 30, 1980

I am delighted that the House of Representatives today joined the Senate in accepting the conference report on the mental health systems act. This bill, which had its origins in the hard work of the President's Commission on Mental Health and which owes its success to the talent and dedication of Senator Edward M. Kennedy, Congressman Henry A. Waxman and Tim Lee Carter, and their staffs, is a landmark piece of legislation.

The mental health systems act will encourage the provision of services for the chronically mentally ill, severely disturbed children, the elderly, minorities, and other priority population groups. It will also, for the first time, make grants available for the prevention of mental illness and the promotion of mental health. In addition, it will refine and enhance the partnership between Federal, State, and local levels of government.

It is a fine bill, and I look forward to signing it into law.

1980 Democratic Victory Dinner

*Remarks at the Democratic National
Committee Fundraiser. September 30, 1980*

It's always wonderful to listen to an absolutely unbiased and objective introduction. *[Laughter]* I know a lot of Presidents of this great Nation have been blessed with many assets and with many degrees of support during the crises that we have faced in past years and generations together, always successfully. There has never been a President in the history of this Nation blessed with so close and so fine a Vice President as the one I have.

If you notice any degree of nervousness among those of us who are on the public payroll tonight, we are a little bit like Cinderella. Unless the continuing resolution passes this evening, the Government comes to a screeching halt and all salaries stop. This afternoon I got a call from Tip O'Neill and Bob Byrd and they said, "Mr. President, you know the continuing resolution has not yet passed. We've got a choice to make, whether to come to the Democratic National Committee dinner and help raise money for the party or stay here and get the continuing resolution passed." I thought about it—*[laughter]*—not very long. And I said, "Stay. Stay on the Hill and do your duty. Our financial security—I mean our national security comes first. *[Laughter]* We've got to have that bill!"

It's always good to be with friends, Democratic friends. Although Tip and Bob can't be here and some of those who are with them, at least we've got Bob Strauss. Bob is to politics what Ethel Merman is to music. *[Laughter]* When those two are finished performing you don't know exactly what they said or what they meant, but you are sure that you have heard it and heard it loud and clear. Bob, I'm glad to have you tonight. And I'm particularly glad with the way Bob can inspire a group of prospective contributors. He says, "The President has to pitch in and do his part; the voters have to pitch in and do their part; and you have to pitch in and do your part, or," as Bob says, "come November we won't have a part to pitch in." *[Laughter]*

Well, Bob Strauss—I hope the fidelity is good—Bob Strauss is a man of many parts—most of them still working. *[Laughter]* And as you know, he just came back from Texas with a secret assignment to write that endorsement that's been mentioned a couple of times already by Leon Jaworski. And I'm very grateful that Leon made his endorsement; otherwise, our speechwriters would have had a dearth of material for this evening. *[Laughter]*

Leon is kind of old; he's getting confused. They asked him who was the last Democrat he voted for, and he said he thought it was Calvin Coolidge—*[laughter]*—but he wasn't quite sure.

Among those of us in this room tonight, I must admit that there have been some disputes and some disagreements and some arguments—that's all part of being Democrats. But there's one thing I know that we all agree on, and that it that we're going to whip the Republicans on November the 4th as bad as they have ever been whipped in this country.

On a few occasions I've been given a little advice. They say, "Mr. President, just lay back and let the Republicans defeat themselves." But I say, "Why should we let them have all the fun?" *[Laughter]* I want to get in there and help them defeat themselves. Right? *[Applause]*

The Republicans in their attitude to the people are exemplified by the Reagan-Kemp-Roth tax bill. It's a Godsend to the property tax collectors of this country. You know it gives gigantic tax breaks to the rich, while looking down their nose at everyone else.

Their theory is to forget about inflation. We can have a 30-percent tax cut, plus an all-out arms race, plus essential programs, plus a balanced budget. It's an interesting theory, but I think the Republican candidate is blithely singing a solo version of "The Impossible Dream." And unfortunately, his running mate is serenading him with a kind of note of discord from a famous Cole Porter lyric, "Do do that voodoo that you do so well." [*Laughter*] It's bad to have two running mates on the same ticket who are still debating each other.

We have in this party a tremendous opportunity for the future. And I want to talk a little about the future. But before I do, I want to discuss a few more serious issues along the lines of those I've already mentioned.

I'd like to address myself to an area of gross misunderstanding. Some members of the press have accused me of running a mean campaign. That accusation is patently false. I will say here and now that I believe all Republican candidates to be people of genuine principle. I'm sure you've all heard of the "Peter Principle." [*Laughter*] The fact is that if I did want to run a mean campaign, I could use such rhetoric as this: The Republican candidate has refused to debate me one-on-one, but I won't say it; I don't want to cut too deep. [*Laughter*] I have observed, however, that the muzzle is back in place and he is, once again, being led around the country by a group of senior advisers. I must say they're all doing a good job, though. When he speaks, you can hardly see their lips move. [*Laughter*]

Now, that kind of remark has no place in this campaign. [*Laughter*] But I have to admit that in order to point out the differences between what I'm doing and what a mean campaign really is, it might be necessary now and then, between this

and November, to give you many examples of this kind of out-of-bounds rhetoric, purely, of course, for illustration and clarity. We simply must keep the political debate on a very, very high plane. But, as a matter of fact, even the subject of debates has become a very controversial one.

Offered the opportunity to meet me in a head-on-head debate, my Republican opponent has taken his own version of the Rose Garden approach. There's just one item that he failed to overlook—he doesn't have a Rose Garden. [*Laughter*] And we're going to see to it that he never gets one.

Some of my advisers have finally come up with a good solution to this debate question. First, I debate Governor Reagan, and then Fritz debates Pat and George, and then Rosalynn debates Nancy and Kiki. [*Laughter*] And after that, Amy debates Maureen and John, Junior, and then whichever two groups come out on top then meet in a special winner-take-all version of "Family Feud." [*Laughter*]

Well, you know, speaking of Hollywood and television—well, I'll be more serious than that. I know you've all heard me speak of my vision for the future. I also have a recurring nightmare—[*laughter*]—and that is the Hollywood-izing of Washington. In it I see every bill signing ceremony on the South Lawn taking place at night with huge spotlights, and I see Pennsylvania Avenue turning into the Avenue of the Stars, and I see visiting foreign dignitaries putting their boot prints into cement on the South Lawn—[*laughter*]—and I see the most important news personality in America is Rona Barrett. [*Laughter*] And then I wake up and I realize immediately that it's only a bad dream. And the reason I know it's a bad dream is because of where I wake up. And thanks to you and millions of other concerned Americans, that's where I'm going to be waking up for the next 4 years.

This campaign has already had some lighthearted moments. It's had some frivolous moments. It's had some times when the major issues were obscured by tangential debates. Sometimes the obscurity was deliberate, but it's important for us as Democrats and as leaders, as supporters of this party and as lovers of this Nation, not to forget the deep and penetrating issues that are involved in this election of 1980. It could not possibly be more sharply drawn in the vision that we have for the future between myself and my opponent, between the Democratic Party of history and of today—which is the same—and of the radically different Republican Party which was pictured so clearly in the recent convention and the platform that was evolved from it.

We're talking about the future of this Nation. We're talking about the life and the quality of that life and the fruitfulness of that life and the prosperity of that life of every human being who lives now and who will live in this country in the years ahead.

We're talking about a difference in basic philosophy: what our government is; how precious is a human ambition; how damaging is a human frustration or alienation; what it means to be deprived of equality of opportunity; what it means to be despised if you're different; what it means to have hopes for continued progress where children lead a better life than their parents led; whether consumers will have a voice in Washington on the Hill and in the Oval Office; whether the quality of our land and our air and our water will be maintained or even improved; whether working people will feel that they're part of societal structure, now and in the future, on the inside of those delib-

erations when the future is planned, or whether they'll be outside, excluded, searching for some peripheral way just to let their voice be heard; whether there'll be an alienation of black from white or Christian from Jew or North from South or rural from urban, or whether the Nation will be unified with a common purpose, a search for peace, sound judgment, consultations, a clear vision of where our Nation's going to be—continued prosperity, better education, better homes, an end to discrimination, a healing of past wounds inflicted on this Nation before Fritz Mondale and I took over the responsibilities for the Government, harmony between the Congress and the White House being continued, major threats to our Nation met before they become crises. Those kinds of questions penetrate the existence of this Nation and the existence of every person who lives here, and it's my responsibility as the standard bearer of our party, as the incumbent President of the greatest nation on Earth, and as the nominee of yours for reelection to lead you and to work with you in defining those issues in the clearest terms for the American people to understand.

I have no doubt that if our voice can be heard and if we can describe those issues clearly that the American people will make the right judgment. But it's not easy to get that message across clearly, because of the circumstances I described to you just a few minutes ago—the confusion, the withdrawing, the muzzling, the lack of an adequate debate forum between the nominees of our two parties. It's a travesty to know that that has not been possible to arrange, when the American people need it and it ought to be offered to them. I'll do the best I can the next few weeks, and the weeks are not very long and not very many before the American people make a judgment about what kind of future this Nation will have.

You have helped time after time after time, some of you for decades, to keep this party together through thick and thin. Our party's strong now. Our party is solvent. Our party is united, more than I ever remember it, certainly in my time in the political arena. We've got a wonderful opportunity to let our philosophy be known, to let our standard be raised, to let millions of Americans join us and to face the future with confidence—not only in our government but in one another.

There are some ideals that we espouse that would be a dreadful loss to the world if they were abandoned. And we cannot permit our Nation to abandon them. Every one of you here tonight is a leader, with varying degrees of influence, perhaps measured by the number of people who will listen to your voice. But there is no one here who couldn't reach a thousand, and there are many of you who could reach millions of ears between now and November the 4th.

I'm going to do the best I can; there's no doubt in my mind that Fritz Mondale will continue to do so. But I need for you to leave here tonight not just having been self-congratulated or thanked by me or John White for your financial contribution, which is crucial to us, but determined to be an equal partner with me and Fritz Mondale in giving our views to the Nation in a clear, unvarnished, absolutely truthful way about the choice that will be made on election day in November.

I don't believe that you will ever have a more important responsibility. It's much more important than which college your child might attend. It's much more important than whether your income might be $100 thousand a year or $50 thousand a year or $20 thousand a year, because we're talking about the character of the future of our Nation, and we're talking about the character of the opportunity or absence of opportunity that your children, whom you love, might have.

If you'll help me in a dedicated, even a sacrificial way, above and beyond what you had dreamed of doing when you came here tonight, there is no doubt that we will win, because you're here from Florida, a close State; Texas, a close State; New York, a close State; Pennsylvania, close; Michigan; Illinois; Ohio; Connecticut; Virginia, close; California, close. You know what happened in 1968 when many of you, and I, had we done what I'm asking you to do now, would have put Hubert Humphrey in the White House instead of Richard Nixon. You know it.

And I don't appeal to you out of a lack of confidence, because if I have one common criticism from the press or observers, it's not that I lack confidence. I won in 1976 over overwhelming odds because many of you helped me and we had a fervor and a spirit and kind of a crusade that permeated our campaign, particularly in the primary days. And I see no reason why we couldn't have that same crusade now, because much more is at stake. I tell you, in 1980 much more is at stake than it was in 1976. You know that what I say is true, and you know why I'm saying it, and I don't say it in derogation of any particular person, but because the issues are greater than two people.

Well, I'm confident. I do not intend to lose this election and, with your help, when November the 4th comes that bright future and not that relatively dismal future or doubtful future will be in store for the people of the greatest nation on Earth, which you and I love.

Will you help me? [*Applause*] Okay. Thank you.

NOTE: The President spoke at 10:21 p.m. in the International Ballroom at the Washington Hilton Hotel.

Continuing Appropriations for Fiscal Year 1981

Statement Concerning Congressional Action on the Resolution. October 1, 1980

The failure of Congress to approve a continuing resolution for fiscal year 1981, which begins today, will cause an interruption of services if not rectified promptly.

Since the Attorney General has ruled that Federal workers should report to work, any serious disruption can be avoided if the Congress acts today. In the strongest possible terms, I urge them to do so. Once they have acted, the resolution will be forwarded to me and signed immediately.

NOTE: Later on the same day, the Congress approved the continuing resolution. The President's statement on signing the resolution is printed on page 2015.

National Commission for Employment Policy

Appointment of Three Members and Designation of Chairman. October 1, 1980

The President today announced the appointment of three persons as members of the National Commission for Employment Policy for terms expiring in 1983. They are:

PEDRO GARZA, of Austin, Tex., national director of SER-Jobs for Progress, one of the Nation's largest employment and training agencies.

ELI GINZBERG, of New York City, Hepburn professor emeritus of economics and special lecturer at Columbia University. He has been director of the Conservation of Human Resources Project at Columbia since its establishment in 1950 and has been Chairman of this Commission and its predecessor agencies since 1962. He has been redesignated Chairman.

LEON HOWARD SULLIVAN, pastor of Zion Baptist Church in Philadelphia and founder of the Opportunities Industrialization Centers, a program sponsoring job training and retraining, which operates in more than 135 cities and has trained more than 600,000 persons since its establishment in 1964.

Pennsylvania Avenue Development Corporation

Appointment of Julia M. Walsh as a Member of the Board of Directors. October 1, 1980

The President today announced the appointment of Julia M. Walsh, of Washington, D.C., as a member of the Board of Directors of the Pennsylvania Avenue Development Corporation for a term expiring in 1984. She would replace Elwood Quesada, whose term has expired.

Walsh is chairman of the board of Julia M. Walsh and Sons, Inc., a securities and investment management firm.

Budget Deferrals

Message to the Congress. October 1, 1980

To the Congress of the United States:

In accordance with the Impoundment Control Act of 1974, I herewith report 22 deferrals of fiscal year 1981 funds totalling $619.1 million. The deferrals are primarily routine in nature and do not, in most cases, affect program levels.

The details of each deferral are contained in the attached reports.

JIMMY CARTER

The White House,
October 1, 1980.

NOTE: The attachments detailing the deferrals are printed in the FEDERAL REGISTER of October 6, 1980.

Official Dealings Between Federal Employees and the President's Family

Memorandum From the President.
October 1, 1980

Memorandum for the Heads of Executive Departments and Agencies

Subject: Guidelines Concerning Official Dealings with Members of the President's Family

The purpose of these guidelines is to caution government employees against dealing with members of the President's family in ways that create either the reality or the appearance of impropriety.

The primary responsibility to avoid impropriety of course rests on the President and the members of his family. The President has cautioned members of his family not only to observe these guidelines, but also not to place government employees in a position where the appearance of impropriety can occur.

There are three situations which need to be distinguished:

First are the cases where a member of the President's family is performing the duties or exercising the rights of any other citizen. The payment of taxes, military service, and entitlements to Social Security, agricultural, or educational benefits are typical examples. In all such cases, members of the President's family are to be treated the same way as anyone else. They are to seek no special favor, nor are they to be granted any.

Second are the cases where the President calls on a member of his family to act as his official representative at a ceremony, function or meeting in the United States or abroad. In such cases, government employees should afford the designated members of the President's family the courtesies and amenities appropriate to his or her official status and to the occasion—no more, no less.

When members of the President's family take personal trips or where the government has information that their personal security may be threatened, they should be accorded the same treatment and protection as any other public figure.

Third are the cases in which a member of the President's family is seeking to do business with the government on his or her own behalf or to act as an agent for another person, firm or government seeking to do business with our government. Examples are the discretionary award of government contracts and the discretionary granting of valuable licenses.

In this third class of cases, there is a strong presumption against such dealings with a family member. Even though the family member's proposal or request may be entirely meritorious, and the government employee's response is the same as it would be regardless of the family relationship, many will believe, without any other evidence, that the government's response was influenced by the family member's status as such. While it could be argued that members of the President's family have the same right as any other citizen to have the government engage in discretionary dealings with them, this is a right that is best relinquished during the President's incumbency. The President has therefore cautioned family members from making such proposals or requests, and urges all government employees not only to reject all such proposals and requests, but to report their occurrence to the head of the department or agency, who should advise the Counsel for the President. In extraordinary cases where the responsible employee believes the proposal or request should be approved—for example when the family member's business relationship with the government predates the President's incumbency and the relationship has not been exploited during his incumbency—the approval of the department or agency head shall first be obtained.

Government employees should also apply a strong presumption against the discretionary disclosure to family members of information of potential economic value about existing or planned government policies or actions that is not generally available to the public.

These guidelines apply only to family members. They do not apply to any business entity with which a family member may be associated, so long as the family member does not participate in any way, and the family member's association is not otherwise exploited, in the entity's dealings with the government.

For purposes of these guidelines, the President's family consists of the President's parents, brothers, sisters and children, and the spouses of his brothers, sisters and children.

JIMMY CARTER

[Filed with the Office of the Federal Register, 12:07 p.m., October 1, 1980]

Energy and Water Development Appropriation Act, 1981

Statement on Signing H.R. 7590 Into Law. October 1, 1980

Today I have signed the Energy and Water Development Appropriation Act, 1981. It is the first appropriations bill to be enacted this year, and the amounts appropriated are very close to those recommended in my 1981 budget.

Included in this bill are appropriations for a variety of energy and water development programs in the Department of Energy, the U.S. Army Corps of Engineers, the Tennessee Valley Authority, and re-

lated agencies. Most of these programs have been supported by my administration, and on balance, it is a bill that represents a constructive compromise among contending interests. However, there remain elements in this bill that depart significantly from my water resource development policy. In signing H.R. 7590, I want to note my continued interest in working with the Congress to press for reforms in water resources policy.

As an important part of that effort, this bill provides for continuation of the Water Resources Council and therefore gives us an opportunity to work with Congress next year to establish in that agency the independent review that is necessary to ensure that projects are planned and designed as both economically feasible and environmentally acceptable. It contains a relatively small number of unbudgeted new projects, compared to past congressional practice, thus preserving our opportunity to complete economic and environmental studies on the remaining current candidates for new construction starts. It has also not provided funding for many of the projects I have opposed in the still pending omnibus water resources project authorization bill.

My administration has worked diligently to restore credibility to the Federal water resources development program, and with the support of many in the Congress, we have made significant progress. I am especially pleased with our record in the following respects:

1. We have established economic and environmental guidelines for planning water projects, to be consistently applied by all water resource program agencies.

2. Water conservation practices have been applied by Federal agencies in the administration of their water related programs.

3. An expanded grant program has been implemented to strengthen the

ability of States to control planning for water resources within their jurisdictions.

4. We are working cooperatively with States in resolving longstanding problems related to Federal reserved water rights, in-stream flow maintenance, and groundwater management, in ways that do not infringe on State authorities.

5. We have provided for environmental mitigation funding concurrently with water resource development project funding.

My administration will continue to consult with the Congress and the public on ways to further implement the unfinished proposals still pending, and we will work vigorously for the reform measures that will allow us to better plan for the water resource needs of this Nation.

NOTE: As enacted, H.R. 7590 is Public Law 96–367, approved October 1.

Wayne, Michigan

Remarks to Employees of the Ford Automobile Assembly Plant. October 1, 1980

Thank you very much, Phil and Doug, John, for the good tour through this wonderful plant.

Congressman Brodhead, Congressman Ford, and my fellow automobile workers:

I'm very glad to be with you. As a matter of fact, I'm a member of local 900, not the Atlanta local—dues paid up for a lifetime. [*Laughter*] And also I've got my coat to prove that I'm one of the chief inspectors of this wonderful plant.

As you know, there is a new spirit here, because this area is an area of winners, all the way from this new Ford plant at Wayne to the Detroit Lions. And when this new model year is over, I know you'll be able to point to the foreign competition, no matter where it might come from,

and say, "Another one bites the dust." And after the football season's over, I'm going to get Billy Simms to help me with the automobile industry everywhere and to keep the world at peace and to do other important things that I know he can help handle.

Well, this is an exciting day for me. It's exciting because my heart is filled with gratitude for what I've seen. I wish that every single citizen of the United States of America could have gone with me through this plant. I've just seen some of the best designed, best built, most up-to-date automobiles in the world rolling off this assembly line at full capacity. This is American ingenuity and it's American teamwork at its best, and I'm very proud of every one of you and grateful for what you're doing here.

The new model introductions each fall have always been exciting. I remember, as a boy in Georgia living on a farm, studying the magazine ads as the new models for each year were revealed, and then as soon as I could get a chance to go to the county seat over in Americus, Georgia, I would go there and look with wide-open eyes at the new American cars in the local automobile dealerships.

This visit here, though, is doubly exciting, not just because of the new models I've seen but because this will be the year that we begin to turn around the American economy, and especially in our automobile industry. We have been hit by severe shocks. The origin of them is the multiplication of the price of OPEC oil.

American consumers attitudes have changed, and you have responded to meet that challenge. And I can tell you, with the greatest sense of being absolutely right, that there's a new spirit of cooperation and partnership and friendship and consultation and shared responsibility between the Government, the management of our automobile manufacturers, the automobile workers, to face the future with success. There is no other automobile industry on Earth that could have accomplished more quickly or more completely this fundamental shift that's taking place in our country in automobile production.

Since 1974 alone, the fuel economy performance of American-built cars has improved by nearly 50 percent—and the rate of improvement now is much greater than it has been even in the earlier years—while the mileage of foreign competitors since 1974 has stayed the same. In just 1 year, fuel efficiency in this country has increased by 20 percent in some models. No other competing country even comes close.

No other country builds safer cars that offer more protection in a collision. No other country makes cars that are more durable. I know that you put your best in building them and the workers are more directly involved now than before in quality control, because your stamp of workmanship and pride is on every automobile that rolls off this assembly line. I know that you're proud of them, and I believe that all Americans are proud of the dramatic progress that you've made.

Today, as President, I urge American consumers to go into the showrooms around this country and test drive these new American cars. There's not a better built, safer, more durable, or more efficient car today than these new American models, and the American buyers ought to remember that because it's important to us all.

And I urge other countries who want to sell their cars in the United States to do as some foreign manufacturers have already done—locate more of their plants in this country and employ American workers. Perhaps when Americans go new-car shopping, they'll ask their dealers,

was this car built in the United States. That's a good question. American automobile workers deserve the chance to compete, and as President, I urge American buyers to give you that chance.

In the next few months we'll be buying thousands of new cars and trucks with American taxpayers' money, and I'm going to make certain that they'll be American-made automobiles and trucks, because they are first rate and they're world class, but they're only the beginning. In the next 5 years—this is almost hard to believe—our automobile industry will invest almost $80 billion to produce even more fuel-efficient, high-quality advanced cars that the American public will be eager to buy. This is twice the cost of the Apollo program that went to the Moon, in just half the time.

And I pledge to you that as President I'll use the full resources of my own office to ensure that the American automobile industry has access to the capital it needs to retool, to compete, and to maintain its rightful share of the American automobile market. That's been my commitment in the past, it's my commitment now, and it will be my commitment in the future. And Phil Caldwell has pointed out to you, which I need not repeat, some of the steps that we've already taken.

My administration—President, Vice President, Secretary of Transportation, and everyone else—will stay right in the trenches with the UAW and the American automobile industry until we restore this industry to its full productive health. I will not rest until the working men and women in the auto industry are back on the job with full-time, steady work.

As President I've made it absolutely clear to our foreign competitors that the United States will not abandon any portion of our share of the domestic automobile market. We've asked the ITC to give us an early ruling on the claims that have been made by the UAW about unfair foreign competition. And as you know, I have also authorized the imposition of a 25-percent duty on trucks that were previously assembled by subterfuge in this country. I expect our foreign competition to practice restraint during this time of transition, as I've counseled them to do.

I also want you to know that you're part of something larger than the automobile industry. Something special is happening in this country—the rebuilding of our entire economic base. To do the job right, we need to include labor, business and Government in a solid partnership, something that we've already begun in the automobile industry. Yesterday I announced a similar move which will revitalize the steel industry in our country.

The economic revitalization program that labor helped to develop will create an additional 1 million new jobs in the next 2 years, jobs in growing and competitive industries. We'll modernize our basic industries, such as steel and automobiles. We'll encourage high-technology industries. We'll expand research and development to keep us in the forefront, on the cutting edge of progress. We'll rebuild our transportation system, so important to you. And we'll expand exports. We'll aid communities and workers that are hit hard by inevitable change. And when we are finished, the American economy will be a full-employment economy, and the American worker will continue to outwork, outproduce, and outcompete the workers of any other country on Earth. And you can depend on that, if we work together.

The reason I'm so confident is because the auto industry is again taking the lead. I remember that during the depression, Franklin D. Roosevelt asked autoworkers and makers to move up the new model year introductions to help our staggering economy. The industry responded and helped to stimulate the economy at its lowest point. During World War II, the President again turned to the auto industry, and you helped to make America the arsenal of democracy. I see that same spirit exactly here today, and I'll leave here much more encouraged than I have been before.

Let me make just one final point. Just 5 weeks from now, as Doug pointed out, the American people will make an important decision. I'm not going to mention politics, but I'll just say that I intend to be your President when a constant stream of ships full of American-built cars are unloading in Tokyo and Yokohama, and I want your help to make that come true.

Thank you very much.

NOTE: The President spoke at 12 noon outside the plant. In his opening remarks, he referred to Philip Caldwell, chairman of the board of directors, Ford Motor Co., and Douglas Fraser, president of the Automobile Workers of America.

Prior to his remarks, the President met separately with Ford Motor Co. executives and UAW officials and then was given a tour of the plant.

Flint, Michigan

Remarks and a Question-and-Answer Session at a Townhall Meeting.   October 1, 1980

THE PRESIDENT. It is really great for me to be here on my birthday in Viking country. Everybody has told me that Flint Northern High is a school of champions. Is that right? [*Cheers*] That's what I heard. And that's in athletics, academically, and otherwise. And I'm very proud to be able to come here on this special day for me.

AMERICAN AUTOMOBILE INDUSTRY

I wish everyone could have been with me this morning when I had a chance to see a display of America's brand new 1981 automobiles at the airport in Detroit and then to visit one of our modern production lines in Wayne County, where some of the best designed, best built, safest, most up-to-date, most efficient automobiles in the world are being made in the United States.

It's really a thrill for a President of our great country to see this demonstration of American ingenuity and American team-work helping us to overcome one of the most difficult transition periods that the world has ever seen, with the enormous increase in the price of OPEC oil, with the change in buying habits, which has afflicted our Nation as nothing ever has before in the history of the automobile industry, or to see the fine working men and women, with tremendous investments now and in the future, modernizing our automobile industry faster than any other nation on Earth could possibly even attempt. And to see the pride in the workmanship and quality is indeed a thrill for me.

And I do not hesitate to repeat my call, which I made early this morning in the Detroit area, that American buyers all over this country should cast their eyes first at automobiles that are built in the United States of America. There may have been times in the past when buyer preferences changed and foreign cars met needs that couldn't be met by American automobiles. If that is the case, when the American consumers now get ready to spend American dollars on a new car, my advice is for them to look first and fore-most at the fine, new American cars that can meet any competition and come out safer and better all around.

I will not rest as President until our automobile industry is completely competitive and has its tax laws written and economic assistance provided and invest-ment capital ready and the protection of American workers that's necessary for us to make our entire American automobile industry competitive in every sense of the word. We've seen this serious threat, brought about by OPEC, in changing buying preferences very vividly.

This morning I rode from Washington to Detroit, from Detroit up to Flint with Doug Fraser and other leaders in the UAW, and we discussed in great depth the new partnership that has been forged between the Government and manage-ment in automobile industry and Amer-ican automobile workers to face the future with confidence and with commitment and with success.

You can all think back 3 or 4 years ago, where there was an adversary relation-ship, a competitive relationship between Government and the automobile industry and between management and labor. About the only time we faced each other across the table was to bargain and to argue and to debate about Government regulations and about wage settlements. That time has passed, in that we now sit regularly around the negotiating table thinking how we all can work on the same team to overcome these threats to our Nation's basic industry. And what is happening in automobiles is now begin-ning to happen in steel.

And with the new energy policy now intact, we can move to the future and completely rebuild the American eco-nomic system, to modernize basic indus-tries, such as steel and autos, to encourage high-technology industry that keeps us in the forefront of production, research and development, to keep us on the cutting edge of new changes so that America, as it always has been in the past, will be the first ones to get bright ideas to be competitive on an international basis. We're going to rebuild our transportation system—it's sadly in need of overhaul—expand our exports, and aid communities and workers which happen to be hit hard by those inevitable changes that we have faced so far. When we're through, the American economy will be a full-employment economy with stable prices, and the American workers will continue to outwork, outproduce, and outcompete the workers of any other nation on Earth.

Before I take the first question, I want to make just one other point. We've faced challenges together before. In the Depression years when our economy was strangled and everyone was doubtful about the next month, President Franklin D. Roosevelt called on the automobile industry and the workers and said, "Move the time for introduction of your new models up." And the automobile industry responded, and workers turned out those cars earlier, and hundreds and thousands of people went back to work in the depth of the Depression. And later on, in World War II, the same President Roosevelt called on the industry and said, "Our country is in danger. I need for you to help turn America into the arsenal of democracy." And the same spirit prevailed then, and the automobile industry kept our Nation free. And now we find the same spirit prevailing as we face this economic threat, not quite so severe, as a matter of fact, as we faced on those other two occasions. And I don't have any doubt that we will be successful.

And finally, let me repeat a point that I made earlier today. Just 5 weeks from now, the American people will make an important decision. I won't mention politics, but I'd like to say this: I intend to be the President when a constant stream of American ships filled with American-built automobiles are unload-

ing every week and every month in Tokyo and Yokohama, and I want you to help make that pledge come true.

QUESTIONS

CUBAN REFUGEES

Q. *De parte de los estudiantes de la escuela norte que deseamos darle las felicitaciónes. Feliz cumpleaños, querido Señor Presidente.* [On behalf of the students of Northern High, we'd like to offer you congratulations. Happy birthday, dear President Carter.]

THE PRESIDENT. *Muchas gracias, señora. Es us placer para mí estar aquí y las felicidades son muy buenas. Gracias.* [Thank you, ma'am. It's a pleasure for me to be here and your greetings are very good. Thank you.]

Q. *De nada.* [You're welcome.] You'll get an A in my class.

THE PRESIDENT. I'd get an A in her class. [*Laughter*] I'd hate to ask her what her class is. [*Laughter*]

Q. Spanish.

What is your long-range solution to the Cuban refugee problem?

THE PRESIDENT. I think the Cuban refugee problem has been one of the most difficult human problems I've had since I've been in the White House.

As you know, throughout the world 3 or 4 million people are refugees from their own country because of pressure on them from totalitarian, primarily Communist, governments that deprive them of freedom. I would guess that unless there are some native Indians here, that almost everyone came here, other than the blacks from Africa who came as slaves originally, to seek freedom and to find a better life in this country.

The Cubans came here in a flood in the

first few weeks when Castro finally gave them the right to go to freedom. We received about 3,000 Cuban refugees per day—a very difficult problem. Now, we cut that down to about 150 per day by using the Navy and the Coast Guard to stop the flood of small boats coming from Mariel Harbor in Cuba to the United States.

My responsibility is to administer the laws of the United States and the constitutional provisions, and I'm sworn to do that. So, I tried to stop the illegal flow of Cubans and others into this country. Now the Cuban officials have announced that no more will the boats be encouraged to come to Mariel Harbor and no more will they be permitted to bring Cubans back to the southern part of the country, primarily Florida.

With that stopping of the Cuban refugee flow, we'll now be able to handle the matter, I think, well. We will put a few Cuban refugees, that have been in excess and haven't yet been placed, in Puerto Rico. I talked to the Governor of Puerto Rico, after I took off from Washington this morning on Air Force One, to explain to him what was going to happen. We will continue to place those refugees in places where the unemployment rate is lowest and where they have family members that can help them get assimilated into our society. We're trying to handle them humanely. We have stopped the flow. I will not let that flow recommence. And we will abide by the laws of the United States, using the Coast Guard, the Navy, and the full resources that I have to enforce the laws.

Good morning.

FLINT, MICHIGAN

Q. Mr. President, Flint is an important automotive industrial city in the Nation, but I feel that Flint doesn't get enough recognition for what it does. Flint is the cradle of GM, and in 1937 there was a sit-down strike, which created all labor unions. And GM is where Flint started and not Detroit. Flint may not be a very big city population-wise, but it's just as important.

THE PRESIDENT. I agree with you. When I asked Doug Fraser and the UAW officials about the origin of General Motors and the UAW, they don't make any bones about it; they say Flint, Michigan.

And it's not an accident that I've come here. There are tens of thousands of places in the United States, as you know, that I could have chosen to come for this townhall meeting, and I think I would have been welcomed in almost all of them, but I chose to come to Flint. I might say, too, that there was one place, at the end of a long 1976 campaign for President— when I hadn't really had a chance to be on the same platform with my running mate, Vice President Walter Mondale— that I chose to be the night before the election. Do you remember where that was? Flint, Michigan, right?

This is my fifth visit to Flint, Michigan, and I always enjoy coming here. And I particularly wanted to come here this morning—and in a way I hate to say this, but I'm going to be frank with you— because of all the cities that have been hurt by the changes that have taken place in the automobile industry, with excessive imports and too slow a change to new models, Flint has been hurt the most. As President, my heart goes out to those who suffer, and I know that the people in Flint, Michigan, have been suffering. And I came here to let you know that I, as President, Vice President Mondale, Secretary Goldschmidt of Transportation, my whole administration is working with the leaders of UAW and all the manufacturing leaders in the automobile industry to put Flint, Michigan, back on its feet economically and to provide jobs for you workers. That's why I came.

And I have to admit there is another reason. I'll just make this remark off the record. George Bush said that I didn't have the guts to come here. It doesn't take any guts to come here, with friends who share with me a hope for the future. And also, I was invited to meet here to have a man-to-man debate with Governor Reagan. I'm here. And anytime he's willing to meet me back here on a two-man debate proposition, I'll make my sixth visit to Flint, Michigan.

SENIOR CITIZENS

Q. Happy birthday, Mr. President.

THE PRESIDENT. Thank you, ma'am.

Q. I have a birthday this month, too. [*Laughter*]

THE PRESIDENT. I won't ask you how old you are if you won't tell anybody how old I am.

Q. I don't care, really. I'm going to be a senior citizen, that's for sure, and that's what my question is about. I want to know what the future is for us senior citizens of a better life to live?

THE PRESIDENT. I'll be glad to tell you.

Q. Some of us have a pretty rough time.

THE PRESIDENT. I know that. I'll be glad to tell you. A lot of the future life for senior citizens will depend on the decisions that will be made in the ballot boxes of voting places on November the 4th.

We have a need to protect the social security system, to keep it sound, to make sure that social security payments are never taxed, to make sure they're never reduced, to make sure that when inflationary pressures impose themselves on

retired people, that social security payments are increased to accommodate the changes of inflation. We need to make sure that we protect the Medicare program, also Medicaid. We need a nationwide comprehensive health program for our people.

And we also need to recognize that senior citizens—and if I am reelected President I'll be 60 years old 4 years from now—we need to recognize that people who've reached retirement age still have a lot to contribute in ways that are beneficial to our country. And I want to make sure that in the future, as we have since I've been in the White House, that we give senior citizens a chance to work, part-time if they choose or enjoy themselves without working as they choose. But there's a full life to be lived even during retirement years.

So, to protect retirement benefits, to protect our health programs and improve them, to make sure that we index payments so that inflation doesn't rob those who are retired, and to make sure we don't tax income—those are some of the things that you can count on if I'm in the White House. And I believe that the Congress will back me up on all those items.

Thank you, ma'am.

Q. Happy birthday, Mr. President.

THE PRESIDENT. Thank you very much.

JAPANESE AUTOMOBILE IMPORTS

Q. My name is Ted Gallimat; I'm a resident of Flint Township. I have supported you since September 10th, 1975. I wish you well for the next 4 years as President.

THE PRESIDENT. Thank you very much. So far, I like your question very much. [*Laughter*]

Q. I could say I'll vote for you if you vote for me, but I won't.

Is there any possibility in the future of generating equal trade with our friends in Japan by their removing the tariff or by the U.S.A. imposing them in regard to the automobile?

THE PRESIDENT. That's an excellent question. I don't believe I can answer it about what will happen years in the future, but let me tell you what we are doing and the prospects as I see them.

First of all, when Japan abuses privileges, as they did with the recent assembly loophole on small trucks, I am determined to act forcefully. I have imposed, as you know, a 25-percent duty on the small trucks that have come into our country almost assembled and then just a little bit of assembly went into them, and I believe that's very important. And I just got word that the Japanese manufacturers of those small trucks will increase their price 25 percent beginning in the near future, which will make the American small and efficient trucks competitive. So, meeting competition in that respect and preventing dumping and unfair competition is very important to me.

Secondly, we're trying to encourage the Japanese to restrict their shipment of automobiles to this country this year during this transitional phase. Recently, a top Japanese official announced that their shipments of cars to this country would not be increased further, that their total shipments would not exceed those of 1979, and that the last 6 months of this year the anticipated rate of Japanese automobile shipments would be down 200,000 below what we had thought it would be. That helps.

In addition, we are encouraging Japanese who are going to sell their cars in this country to put their manufacturing plants or assembly plants in the United States, to employ American workers to make Japanese cars. When I got into the airport this morning in Detroit, there was a Volkswagen there, manufactured in this country. And the man who represented Volkswagen-America told me that 70 percent of all the Volkswagens sold in this country are manufactured in the United States with American workers. The only two things they import from Germany now is the transmission and the motor itself.

In addition, we are trying to get the Japanese to buy spare parts and parts for assembly of their own automobiles in the United States. And we're trying to force them to lower tariff barriers—that's important—but also distribution techniques that in the past have almost completely excluded American cars from the market in Japan. All those items put together will help.

I've also asked the ITC, the International Trade Commission, to make a quick ruling on whether or not unfair competition has been exerted against American workers by the Japanese automobile imports. They will have hearings in about a week and make a determination then about whether we can restrain excessive and improper shipments of Japanese and other cars into this country. If and when the ITC rules, my intention is as quickly as possible to consult with the Japanese leaders and provide some means to communicate with them, either through Reubin Askew, our Special Trade Representative, or, perhaps later on after the election, with the Japanese leaders themselves with me.

So, in all those areas we're trying to make sure that we impress upon the Japanese, one, they've got to be fairly and properly competitive and secondly, that the American automobile industry does not intend to relinquish to the Japanese or anyone else any part of the automobile production scheme in this Nation.

Q. Thank you.

THE PRESIDENT. Thank you.

AMERICAN HOSTAGES IN IRAN

Q. Mr. President, I was going to ask you how it felt to be 21-plus, but you already told us. So, I'll ask my other question now—Happy birthday to you anyway.

THE PRESIDENT. Thank you.

Q. Do you think that the war between Iran and Iraq is a threat to our hostages, and what do you think we should do about it or what is going to be done about it?

THE PRESIDENT. I don't believe that the present war between Iran and Iraq has changed the status of the hostages as far as their safety is concerned. I don't believe it's threatened their lives further, and I don't believe it's changed, as far as I can determine, the prospect for their return to their homes and to freedom.

Yesterday, the Majles, or the parliament or congress, of Iran was debating the hostage question, ignoring, at least for those few hours, the threat to their nation's existence from Iraq. The problem with Iran is that we have not had any government with which we could deal. And they have now finally got a President, a Prime Minister, a parliament elected, a speaker of the parliament, and they're getting a cabinet put together now. Once that's done, I think we'll have a good prospect of improving the chances to get those hostages home.

We have been very cautious since the very beginning to do two things: First of all is to protect the honor and the integrity and the interest of our Nation—that's my responsibility; and secondly, not to do anything from the White House or from my own public statements that would endanger the lives or safety of the hostages and their chance to come back home to freedom. I've never seen any incompatibility between doing both those things at the same time.

And I'm being very cautious in this trying time for Iran, to let them know that we're staying neutral, that we'll do nothing to try to punish Iran, that we want our hostages back. We want Iran to be a secure nation. We want their own people to choose their own government and in the future, when it's mutually advantageous, to restore normal relationships between our two countries. But I need to get every American to understand that our priorities are twofold: to protect our Nation's interests and to protect those hostages and to keep our country at peace. These are the things that are important to us.

The last thing I'd like to say is this: It's always difficult for a powerful nation to be patient and not to capitalize in a political way over a tragedy like the capturing of our innocent hostages. But the American people have shown that patience; we've acted in a very mature way. And I believe we'll continue that process and that attitude.

My constant prayers are that the hostages will be released safely and will come back home. And I don't believe that war, as serious as it is—and we're trying to end it—has further endangered those precious 52 Americans about whom we're so concerned.

Q. Thank you, Mr. President.

ECONOMIC ASSISTANCE FOR MICHIGAN RESIDENTS

Q. Yes. Mr. President, I'd like to ask what you plan to do to help Flint, Michigan's, economic problem.

THE PRESIDENT. All right, I'll try to answer that.

I've been very conscious of the need to

have extended unemployment benefits for those who have been made unemployed by the change that's taken place in the automobile industry. Secondly, we've asked the Congress now for a 13-week extension, above and beyond the 52 weeks that's authorized under the present law, for unemployment compensation.

The special training assistance that goes to provide help economically and training for workers who have to change jobs is also available there for most workers. And we're trying to get it extended to some other workers, 50 percent of whose jobs are related to an industry that's impacted by imports from overseas, as has been the automobile industry in our own country.

In the last 3½ years, just for the State of Michigan, we've put in here about $3 billion of economic development assistance, CETA programs which provide jobs for citizens, plus the youth employment jobs. That's above and beyond the new programs that we've put into effect all over the Nation for education, for better transportation, and so forth. Three billion dollars is a lot of money. It's not my money; it's the taxpayers' contribution. And Michigan and the Flint area deserve it.

So, we're trying to make sure that as this industry works out of its transition phase, back into full production with the new style automobiles and with the elimination of unfair competition from overseas, that we can keep intact the economic security of people who live here in Flint.

The last point is—I'll repeat myself briefly—we've formed a new and very close partnership, that never has existed before, between the Federal Government and the executives who make the decisions with the automobile industry and the executives who represent the automobile workers. We've only done that in one

other industry in our Nation—and I announced it yesterday—and that was the steel industry. So, that's the kind of forward-looking partnership that will pay rich dividends in the future.

Those are some of the things that we're doing that will help to alleviate the concerns that I share with you about the people who live here in Flint.

Q. Thank you.

THE PRESIDENT. It's a good question, and I thank you for it.

CAMPAIGN ISSUES

Q. My name is Marlene Laro, and this is my sister Rachel. My daddy is a Republican, and my mom is undecided. What is the difference between a Republican and you, so I can tell my parents how to vote? [*Laughter*]

THE PRESIDENT. Very good. Is your first name Marlene—and Rachel, right?

Q. Right.

THE PRESIDENT. That's an excellent question, Marlene. I thank you for it.

There are several very important differences. One is a basic difference between the two parties, the Democratic and Republican Party. The Democratic Party has always been the one that cared most about human beings, about humans who have not had a good opportunity that exists for those who are rich or powerful or well educated or socially prominent or who have had every advantage in life. The Democrats believe that those who do suffer, like retired people, or those who are out of a job or those who might be black or those who speak a different language are given a chance to stand on their own feet and to compete and have equality of opportunity. The Democrats have always been on the forefront of that.

We've also always seen that there were special needs at certain times in history. For instance, during the Great Depression, which I remember, but of course you don't, back in the thirties and forties, there was no security for people who got to be 60 years old or 65 years old and couldn't work full time. Social security was put forward. The Democrats were for it; the Republicans were against it.

I lived on a farm in Georgia, and the Democrats felt that we ought to have rural free delivery of mail, that a farmer ought to get mail just like a city person. Democrats were for it; Republicans were against it.

There was a time when American workers were cheated, when people worked all day, sometimes 18 hours a day, and didn't get much pay. And there was no law that said you had to pay a person a certain amount of money to work. If somebody was out of work, a person that owned a factory could say, "I'll give you 10 cents an hour or 15 cents an hour to work in my factory," and if that person didn't have any bread to eat, they had to say, "Okay." So, a proposal was put in the Congress to have a minimum wage, and the minimum wage proposed was 25 cents an hour. The Democrats were for it; the Republicans were against it.

This was a concern about working people. When the time came for giving black people a guaranteed right to vote and to have equality of opportunity in getting jobs and going to public buildings and going to the same schools, the Democrats under President Kennedy and President Johnson were in the forefront of saying, "Let's treat all Americans fairly." This is another very important difference.

So, between the two parties there's a great deal of difference all the way down through history.

I was for Medicaid and Medicare. My opponent was against Medicaid and Medicare. Many times my own opponent who's running in this election said that he thought that social security should be a voluntary program, which in effect would spell the end to social security. When New York got on its knees and was about to go bankrupt, my opponent said, "I pray the first prayer every morning, I pray the last prayer every night that the Government won't bail out New York." When Chrysler Motor Company was just about to go under and hundreds of thousands of jobs were at stake all over the country, I and the Congress were working to guarantee loans—not to give away a nickel, but just to give Chrysler a right to borrow money. And my opponent, who is a Republican, said, "I don't see anything wrong with bankruptcy." This is the kind of difference that exists now.

Another very important difference is this: I believe that we ought to control nuclear weapons and have an agreement worked out between us and the Soviet Union, the other major power, to have equal and constantly lowered arsenals of atomic weapons that could destroy the Earth. We spent years under President Nixon, President Ford, and myself, developing a SALT agreement, so-called, to limit those atomic weapons. Every President since Harry Truman, including all the Republican Presidents, like Eisenhower, all the Democratic Presidents, have believed in this process. My opponent is against the SALT treaty that we're trying to get ratified now, and he believes we ought to have a nuclear arms race to convince the Soviet Union that we are the most powerful nation on Earth. With a nuclear arms race there would be no way for the Soviet Union to agree to balanced reductions in atomic weapons.

Those are some of the differences that are very important to me. I felt it was important for us to have a Department of Energy and a Department of Education to deal with crises in these areas.

Q. Thank you.

THE PRESIDENT. Marlene, one other point. Just yesterday my opponent said that if he was elected President that he was going to eliminate the Department of Energy and abolish the Department of Education.

So, there's a lot of difference historically between the two parties, but there's even more difference now between myself and the Republican nominee this year. So, I hope you'll ask your parents to vote for me and give them some good reasons.

Q. Thank you.

THE PRESIDENT. Thank you.

UNITED STATES STRENGTH

Q. Happy birthday, Mr. President.

THE PRESIDENT. Thank you.

Q. As a young man about to enter the future, I'm very concerned about the possibility of a draft. And are we militarily ready should there be an emergency with another country?

THE PRESIDENT. What was the last part of your question? I heard the part about the draft.

Q. Okay. Are we militarily ready if there should be an emergency to this country?

THE PRESIDENT. Yes. There's no doubt about that. Our country is the strongest nation on Earth, militarily, economically, politically, and I think morally and ethically as well. We have strong allies. And we are bound together with our allies, because we have mutual interests and it's a matter of voluntary cooperation and teamwork. We also have the most advanced technology, research and development, new concepts.

We've got a well-balanced geographical advantage in that we've got broad areas of our Nation with access to both oceans. We have friendly nations to the south in Mexico, to the north in Canada, quite different from what the Soviet Union has with a major border with a sworn enemy in the People's Republic of China. Our country is almost invulnerable to any sort of land attack or sea attack.

We also have, I believe, a very balanced strategic advantage. Right now oil seems to be the strategic weapon that could be used, not by the Soviet Union but by some of the Arab countries. All the Arab OPEC nations combined have about 6 percent of the world's energy reserve. Our country alone has 24 percent of all the energy reserves, and ours are different in nature, with oil and gas and shale and with tar sands and geothermal supplies. We've got a broad range of energy reserves.

Our country's a peace-loving nation, and a lot of nations around the world are trying to build governments based on freedom, based on democracy, based on the value of a human being, like ours, using us as a pattern. I don't know of a single other nation on Earth that's trying to structure their own government patterned after the Soviet Union.

Our country is also at peace, and we are opening up new friendships as rapidly as we can with other countries. Not much more than a year ago we formed diplomatic relations and opened up trade opportunities and other friendships with the People's Republic of China, a billion people, almost a fourth of all the human beings on Earth. So, that adds an additional dimension to our strength.

Our country espouses human rights, which is a hunger that exists among people in every nation, no matter where they might live.

Militarily, our country's constantly growing stronger. We've got Trident submarines, cruise missiles, the new MX missile that's coming along, that'll make us very competitive still with any nation on Earth. And I might add that the SALT II treaty requires the Soviet Union to eliminate about 10 percent of all their missiles if it's put into effect. We don't have to eliminate any of ours.

The last point is that our people are unified. We are comprised of citizens from almost every nation and ethnic group on Earth. But once we become Americans, we become part of a team that's confident and innovative. The free enterprise system, our freedom of religion gives us a motivation to protect ourselves and the will to stand up over any difficulty that's been exhibited many times in the last few hundred years.

So, I think in every aspect of life, our country is strong, is able, and is willing and eager to defend itself. And I might say, there's not going to be any draft. The registration is to prevent the need for a draft and to keep our country free.

Thank you very much.

SUBMARINE COMMUNICATIONS SYSTEMS

Q. Mr. President, it's an honor to be here, to speak to you and represent the veterans of Flint and Michigan.

THE PRESIDENT. Very good.

Q. My name is William Palo, Flushing Township in Michigan. I'm the chairman of the ELF Committee, District 10, Veterans of Foreign Wars and member of the Chevrolet Motor Post in Flint. I'm also, I was in twice—two wars. I couldn't get it across; I'm sorry, sir.

Mr. President, my question is: The American Legion, the Disabled American Veterans, the Submarine Veterans of World War II, and the Veterans of Foreign Wars in Michigan and nationally have passed resolutions in support of the Navy's proposed extremely low frequency submarine communication system. We believe that you, as an ex-submarine officer and from your various statements to the press, that you believe we need it, but you haven't been able to make a decision because of political pressure. You also know that the VFW has endorsed Governor Reagan for President partly because of the indecisiveness on your part. The veterans here in Michigan and across the country might vote for you if you showed the courage to make the decision now.

This coil is a sample of what we would like—130 miles—for you to make a decision where to deploy this. The coil would be put in the ground with a transmitter to communicate with our Trident nuclear submarine. At present it must come to the surface for a message, and our potential adversaries can see them. They are not based at the present time. Ten million dollars or more for a submarine, and this would be far less cost compared to the loss in manpower and the deterrent from war. Please comment, Mr. President.

THE PRESIDENT. I'll be glad to. I was in the Navy for 11 years, as a submarine officer for the last 5 years. I understand very clearly, as Commander in Chief of all our military forces, the need to have a strong defense and especially to communicate adequately with our submarines under water. We have several different means to communicate adequately with those submarines.

In 1976 I stated to the people in Michigan and other citizens in this part of the country that we would not move forward with the then ELF system, which was 2,400 miles of underground transmitter cables, without coming into the communities and ascertaining accurately the attitude of the people involved and to give them the arguments before I made a decision. We've worked on this question, and we'll make a decision when it's necessary to do so.

There has been no delay in the decision because of pressure, because I've not had any delegations come into the White House to see me, I've not had any appreciable pressure through the mail or otherwise on me. The decision will be made by me, by the Secretary of Defense, by the Joint Chiefs of Staff when the time comes. It'll obviously have to be made with the Congress as well.

Since I've been in office, we have reduced the impact—whatever the impact might be—environmentally more than tenfold below what it was when the original system, as you know, was to be considered. We've assessed the possibility of the placement of the underground transmitter cables in other parts of the Nation. That assessment is still ongoing. As soon as I get a recommendation from the Secretary of Defense and the Joint Chiefs of Staff, no matter when it might come, I will not hesitate to make a decision without delay.

At the present time, I can tell you that our communications capability with our submarines is adequate to defend ourselves. It's obvious that in the future we might need additional capabilities to defend ourselves and communicate with the submarines. When that time comes, I will have no hesitation about making a decision publicly and instantly. But if I make a decision to come into this area, then I will meet the commitment that I made in '76 to explore it, to have public hearings myself with the leaders involved before I make a public decision on the subject.

Q. Mr. President, public hearings have been held in the Upper Peninsula, and at the present time Wisconsin is also applying for this system.

THE PRESIDENT. Yes, I know.

Q. The Chief of Naval Operations has issued you a letter, plus the Defense Secretary has, also. I have copies myself where he has asked you to go ahead on it.

THE PRESIDENT. You're mistaken. Mr. Palo, there is no difference between me and the Secretary of Defense. And when I get a recommendation from the Secretary of Defense either to go ahead with the system or not to go ahead with it and the location that they advocate, I will not hesitate. I have not gotten such a recommendation. When I get one I'll make the decision.

KU KLUX KLAN

Q. Mr. President?

THE PRESIDENT. Yes?

Q. Mr. President, my name is Angela Sawyer, and I'm a senior here at Northern. And I would like to welcome you to Viking country.

THE PRESIDENT. Thank you, Angela.

Q. I would like to know what can be done about the Ku Klux Klan and their secret training camps in the South, if anything can be done?

THE PRESIDENT. The secret training camps are minimal. The Ku Klux Klan is looked on by southerners, black and white, as a despicable and obnoxious blight on the free society of America. In my judgment they are a group of cowards who have disgraced our country. And their strength and influence is much lower now than at any time I remember during my lifetime. In the past they have been a major influence in States like Indiana and others and down through the South, but I think that time is gone permanently.

I have had the Klan demonstrate against me, both when I was Governor, and even recently I had Klansmen, a few, in northern Mississippi [Alabama] [1] when I opened my campaign on Labor Day. But I can assure you that the FBI is cooperat-

---

[1] White House correction.

ing fully with local and State officials to make sure that there is no illegal act performed by the Klansmen or anyone else of their ilk who try to deprive American citizens of their rights, and who are filled with hatred based on a person's color or religious preference. I'll do everything I can to make sure that what I say is true now—and it is—continues to be true in the future.

EMPLOYMENT AND TRAINING PROGRAMS

Q. President Carter, my name is Karen West. And I'm very concerned about jobs in Flint, because I deal with unemployment every day. Therefore, I'm very concerned about the talk in Congress of cutting CETA money for the next fiscal year, also the talk that has been going around of completely wiping out title VI money that deals with cyclical unemployment, which is rampant here in Flint at this time. Therefore, I would like to know what the administration can do to ensure that Flint, which has had the highest unemployment rate in the nation for several months, which is no honor—how can you ensure that we get those CETA dollars and other jobs programs directly to us?

THE PRESIDENT. In addition to the CETA jobs and the others that I outlined as an answer to an earlier question, we're also trying to get an extra billion dollars in countercyclical aid, which means—the word countercyclical means that the money is focused on those communities in our Nation where the need is greatest. In other words, the higher the unemployment rate is, the more money is focused on job programs.

In addition, we have before the Congress now an act, which I believe will pass—it's already through the House and

is almost through the Senate—called the Youth Act of 1980, which will add $2 billion to programs to train and to employ young people. This is above and beyond all the existing young persons employment programs and above and beyond all existing CETA programs that are there now. I believe that Congress will pass this bill.

We now have $4 billion in special programs for youth employment, and this will increase by 50 percent to $6 billion. What it does, in a nutshell, is: A young person who's at the, roughly, the junior and senior year in high school or older who does have a need for a job is placed in a private employer's job, and for the first few months the Government pays part of that salary of the young person as they become qualified to work full time and do productive labor. In addition, it's tied in with the Department of Education so that if that young person needs a special skill, say, mathematics or something of that kind, to hold that permanent job, they're given extra work at the high school itself.

This is the first time we have ever had a major program where Education and Labor, those two departments, work hand in hand to address a problem together. In the past we've had too many graduates of high school, too many graduates of vocational schools, too many graduates of junior colleges, and otherwise, who went out into the community where they lived and found their skills didn't match the jobs that were available. The Labor Department is responsible for filling jobs, the Education Department has been turning out graduates. So, I think this will be a major quantum step forward in providing that opportunity.

So, to protect the jobs that we have

now, to add a billion dollars in counter-cyclical aid focused on the special cities, to have an expanded EDA program, or economic development program, again focused on the crippled cities where unemployment is high, and to add the brand new youth job program, which has excellent chance of being put into effect this year—those are some of the things that we're doing that will have a direct benefit to the people of Flint.

Q. Thank you.

TRADE READJUSTMENT ASSISTANCE FOR TEAMSTERS

Q. I would like to say happy birthday, Mr. President.

THE PRESIDENT. Thank you, sir.

Q. My name is Clarence Murphy, and I'm a driver for local 332. The company that I work for hauls brand new trucks out of General Motors and Chevrolet plants. And what I'd like to talk to you about is, there's been some rumors that the Secretary of Labor has said that car haulers can haul most anything, and, you know, I'm here to let you know that we can't. If we could put some wire around those trailers there, we'd haul peanuts or whatever we could. [*Laughter*] I don't think the freight haulers would like that. But——

THE PRESIDENT. No, they wouldn't.

Q. ——but there's been some saying that we are not affected by the Japanese imports, and because of that House rule 1543 has not been passed and it's waiting in the Senate to be signed there.

I believe that you are a very fair man, as fair as you were when you first were elected. And I see no need for a person to lose their home and their family if it can be helped.

Now, it was denied us. We're in the Teamsters. And UAW has received this TRA, as it's called, and we are not qualified. They are saying that we're not qualified because we don't have anything to do with the making of the product. But the product is not finished until it reaches the dealership. And we have quite a few drivers that they're losing their homes, and quite a few of us have lost our homes. And we're depending on you. We're definitely depending on you. I don't think it's fair for them to—I mean before we can take care of anything else, we've got to take care of our own, and we're not being taken care of.

THE PRESIDENT. Clarence, let me say this. You've made your case very well. I don't think anyone could have made it better or clearer.

There has to be a line drawn somewhere on the TRA between jobs that are directly affected by imports and those that are not. That's the way the law is written. The position that we have taken, the way I understand it, is that if 50 percent of your kind of work is related to the industry, like automobiles, then we favor the coverage of TRA for that group.

If you would give one of my aides your name and telephone number, let me go back and talk to the Secretary of Labor and give you a call. The reason I want to call you back personally is that I've told you all I know about this subject, and I'd rather find out a little bit more. But I will call you when I get back in Washington, okay?

EMPLOYMENT AND TRAINING PROGRAMS

I'm sorry, I don't have enough time for another question. Tell me what your name is.

Q. Kevin McKenzie.

To the honorable President of the United States, Mr. Carter, I would like to say happy birthday and welcome to Flint. I am a young high school student at Flint Northern High School. I would like to know what can you do to help provide jobs for us young people? For example, here in Flint there's only the car industrials, and when they are down, everything is down. The CETA program is not for all. What other alternatives can you assure us with as far as jobs are concerned?

THE PRESIDENT. Let me ask you this: Did you hear my answer to the question that I just gave the lady in the back?

Q. Yes.

THE PRESIDENT. Well, this summer—and also, I can assure you, next summer—we had a million jobs for young people during the summer months. And this new youth program, that I believe will pass before the Congress adjourns this year, would add another massive program, $2 billion, which will be a 50-percent increase in the program, to give young people a chance to work. So, if I did have time to answer your question that's what I would have told you. Okay?

Thank you.

Let me close by saying——

Q. Mr. President?

THE PRESIDENT. I've got to—yes, ma'am?

Q. The President of the United States of America?

THE PRESIDENT. Yes, but I——

Q. I was elected to say something to you.

THE PRESIDENT. All right. Let me say one other thing before you say something, okay?

Q. Yes.

THE PRESIDENT. No, you go ahead. Ladies first. [*Laughter*]

Q. To the President of the United States of America, my name is Ophelia Bonner of—[*cheers*]—wait a minute—of

Christ Fellowship Missionary Baptist Church, Reverend Erobbs, pastor, of the United States of America to you today. We are so glad to have you here. In your travels now in the different cities and different congregations, do you have the faith and confidence to believe that you'll be reelected President of the United States in '81?

THE PRESIDENT. If you all will help me, I have that faith, yes.

Let me say one other thing, please. I'm going to have to go, but let me say one other thing.

Q. Mr. President, I'm Andrew Jackson—[*inaudible*]—a former Congressman from this district.

THE PRESIDENT. Oh, great. Well, Congressman, it's an honor. You go right head.

Q. All right. Now, my question is this: I believe in this campaign the overriding issue is the atomic bomb and the control of it, and I think you've answered this somewhat.

THE PRESIDENT. I agree with that.

Q. But I think I would—I know it's better for you to have the panic button than "Ronald Ray-gun."

THE PRESIDENT. Thank you, sir. Thank you, Congressman.

Let me close, in just about one minute summarizing something that hasn't been said. I've come here to Flint because we face difficult problems.

When I became President, the most serious problem we had was the threat of energy and our dependence on too much overseas oil and our possible loss of our Nation's security and our independence, because if people control you or control the product you've got to have, then it takes away part of our freedom. In the last 3½ years we've made good strides on energy, and today we are importing 2 million barrels of oil less every day than we were the first year I was in office. And it's made good progress because of you.

Now we are faced with a very serious problem of change in the automobile industry and challenge to the steel industry. Again we are making very good progress, because we've spelled out for ourselves a road to the future that we can follow successfully.

The point is, our Nation has faced much more serious challenges and much more serious problems in years gone by than any that I have seen since I have been in the White House—the Great Depression, the First World War, the Second World War, Watergate, the Vietnam war. Those kinds of things have shocked this country and endangered our very existence and our Nation's security.

We've got problems now. I don't want to underestimate them. There are no easy answers. But our country, when we were united and when we understood the problem or the challenge or the obstacle, has never failed. And I don't have any doubt in my mind, as President of this country, that the United States of America, a united people, as we face the future together we will not fail. And you can depend on that.

Thank you very much. God bless you.

NOTE: The President spoke at 2 p.m. in the Flint Northern Community High School gymnasium.

Niagara Falls, New York

Remarks on Signing the West Valley Demonstration Project Act and the Love Canal Agreement.   October 1, 1980

THE PRESIDENT. This is a good day for me.

AUDIENCE MEMBER. Happy birthday.

THE PRESIDENT. Well, that's part of it.

[*At this point, the audience sang "Happy Birthday."*]

Well, it has been a very good birthday for me. I've had a chance to go to Detroit and to Flint to look at an exciting development in the automobile industry of our Nation, which affects you here as well. And I think this occasion, the signing of these two extremely important documents, will be another historic event not only for this particular locality and the entire State of New York but for our Nation. I'm grateful that Senator Moynihan and Senator Javits are here, Governor Hugh Carey, Congressman Lundine, Congressman LaFalce; also, of course, our candidate for United States Senator, Liz Holtzman. When I say "our," I'm talking about we Democrats. And also Mayor O'Laughlin and Mayor Griffin is here. This is a very fine day for us all.

I'm honored to be in Niagara Falls—back in Niagara Falls, I've been here several times before—to sign these two documents. Both of them represent a significant step forward. Each of them in its own way addresses a problem that Americans are only beginning to recognize, one recognized because of a potential tragedy, the other one recognized because it's becoming a worldwide threat. But the people of this area understand too well what the problems of dangerous waste can be.

The first document that I will sign is an act of Congress, the West Valley Demonstration Project Act, which is Senate act number 2443, and the second one that we will sign, myself and Governor Carey, an agreement between the United States Government and the government of the State of New York that will permit the State to purchase the homes of residents of the Love Canal area.

The West Valley Demonstration Project Act, which has kind of a complicated name, but a very simple meaning, was sponsored by Congressman Lundine and Senator Moynihan and supported by Congressman Nowak and others here on this stage with me. Governor Carey was a constant proponent of the passage of this important legislation. It's an example of the forward-looking responses that we are now developing to the question of nuclear waste disposal.

I was in the nuclear program early in the 1950's, living in New York, as a matter of fact, in Schenectady. And at that time we studied the future of nuclear power production and also thought at that time that the problems of waste disposal would be handled in a routine manner because of established, understood, routine government policies. That hope and expectation did not materialize. I supported this bill enthusiastically, as a former nuclear engineer and as President and as the Governor of a State on whose borders is the Savannah River Project. It's a vital part of the nuclear waste management policy so important to us all.

We've been pursuing modern techniques of dealing with the large backlog of high-level nuclear waste all around the country. These techniques involved locking the liquid waste, highly radioactive, into virtually indestructible solid masses to cool the waste, solidify them into these masses which can almost withstand any destructive force.

This new act provides a production-scale demonstration of high-level waste solidification technology. In addition, it provides for environmental and safety reviews and creates a mechanism for independent assessment and monitoring by the Nuclear Regulatory Commission of how the Department of Energy plans to carry out the project.

On the way out here, Governor Hugh Carey and I were discussing how close a cooperative relationship existed between the State of New York, the communities involved, and the Department of Energy. Our hope is that this project will help to resolve the problem of high-level waste disposal in a way that protects the environment and safeguards the health and the safety of the public.

I want to remind everyone that this West Valley legislation would never have been enacted without the strong and unwavering support of Congressman Lundine and Senator Moynihan, Senator Javits, and the others on the stage with me. These men and women are responsible and determined legislators. They deserve great credit for their dedication to what has often been written off as a controversial and politically thankless cause. They believe, as I do, that the safe disposal of nuclear waste is both a national problem and also a State problem. Governor Carey agrees, and he's worked in close cooperation with us in developing the formula for Federal-State costsharing on the West Valley Project.

The second document that I will sign, following the West Valley project act, involves another kind of hazardous waste. Maybe some of you in Niagara Falls area have heard about it, the toxic chemicals that have caused so much suffering and so much anxiety to families in the area of the Love Canal. This agreement which Governor Carey and I will sign provides a Federal loans and grant program that will permit the State of New York to purchase the homes of Love Canal residents.

There have been arguments and a lot of confusion over scientific studies of the Love Canal area, but there can be no argument about the human reality of the problem. People have suffered and are suffering still. The financial and physical suffering has been bad enough, but perhaps worst of all has been the mental anguish and the terrible uncertainty to which those families have been subjected. There's really no way to make adequate restitution for that kind of suffering, but this agreement will at least give the families of the area, some 750 of them, the financial freedom to pack up and leave if they choose to do so.

I want to recognize four people in particular who have championed the cause of the Love Canal residents. First, Congressman John LaFalce, who has been at the forefront of this battle from the very beginning. Second, Mayor Michael O'Laughlin of Niagara Falls, who's made many trips to Washington to argue the case of the people of this city. Third, Governor Hugh Carey, who I don't believe has ever overlooked an opportunity to remind me about the problem in Love Canal. [*Laughter*] And fourth and most important, the grassroots leader of the Love Canal residents, Lois Gibbs. Without her empassioned advocacy and dedication there might have never been a Love Canal emergency declaration, and this agreement might never have come to pass.

The whole question of the disposal of hazardous waste, especially toxic chemicals, is going to be one of the great environmental challenges of the 1980's. As a nation we must look ahead, just as we are doing in dealing with nuclear wastes. As a nation we must make this resolution for our own sake and, more importantly, for the entire Nation: There must never be in our country another Love Canal.

Thank you very much.

Just to recapitulate briefly, this bill that I will sign now will provide a joint Federal-State partnership which will be innovative in nature, set a standard for the rest of the country in the disposal of nuclear waste materials.

[*At this point, the President signed the bill.*]

And the second document which will now be signed, both by myself and Governor Carey, will provide the loan guarantees and the grants for the people of the Love Canal area, about 750 families, to provide for their opportunity to move from the area which has been contaminated if they so choose and to have some financial guarantee that they won't lose the equity in their own homes.

[*At this point, the President and the Governor signed the agreement.*]

NOTE: The President spoke at 6:10 p.m. at the ceremony in Rooms 3 and 4 of the Niagara Falls International Center.

As enacted, S. 2443 is Public Law 96–368, approved October 1.

Niagara Falls, New York

Remarks at the Annual Convention of the Civil Service Employees Association. October 1, 1980

President Bill McGowan and Governor Hugh Carey, Senator Moynihan, distinguished Members of the Congress, Speaker Fink, and others who are so important in my life and in your life:

I'm glad to be here. If I can't be at home with Rosalynn and Amy, I can't think of any place I'd rather be than here with you and the CSEA.

I've been several places today: in Washington, on Air Force One, I've been in Detroit, I've been in Flint, Michigan. I just had a chance to sign two very important documents that will affect the lives of people in New York. And I have to confess to you that that's not the first time I have heard "Happy Birthday" sung, but I can tell you without fear of contradiction that was the most beautiful rendition I have heard today. Beautiful.

One of the important things that a

President must do is to look for qualified people to work with me on important elements of human life in the United States, people whose reputation and whose influence might be in a local community or a State community. The most difficult kinds of positions to fill are not those that relate to academics or science, but those that relate to human problems, because there you have to have a person with the qualifications of sound judgment, influence, experience, idealism, and a heart filled with love.

My wife and I have made a professional lifetime of commitment to those who have mental problems, the mentally retarded children of all ages of our Nation. And yesterday I chose a person to serve on the President's Commission on Mental Retardation that fills all those requirements in a very fine way, and that's your president, Bill McGowan. Later on this month, in a few days, I will be signing into law a landmark piece of legislation called the mental health bill of 1980, and Bill McGowan will be helping me on a nationwide basis to make sure that law is implemented in the fullest degree for the benefit of our people.

That's not why I came up here. I came up here because of my respect for you and what you mean, but I came up here in particular because of my deep respect and friendship and my admiration for Jerry Wurf, because Jerry Wurf not only champions the cause of all of you but also the working families and the poor and the elderly and the afflicted and the deprived people of this entire Nation and indeed to a fairly unlimited way the people of the world. He is a man of great ideals and great influence, and I think that he has the makings of a great labor leader. The only thing is, I believe his career would be enhanced if he would just speak up

more often. He's a little bit too timid. [*Laughter*] So, Jerry, just don't be so bashful. If you've got something to say, speak up, speak up. [*Laughter*]

And I want to thank you for inviting me. It's a good way for me to spend the latter part of a special day in my life, and I'm especially grateful for your endorsement. Your president told me that this is the first endorsement of anyone for President in 70 years, and it's honored me and I hope I can honor you. Thank you for it.

I'd like to say just a few things to you, and I will try to be brief. But on November the 4th the people of this Nation will make a choice that will affect the quality of all your lives, the quality of the lives of people in your own family, of others that you love, and those who look to you for leadership. It's a choice as to whether we'll have a continuation of five decades of social and economic progress and whether or not our Nation will stand behind its commitments to justice and to equality and to freedom.

During the last 3½ years you and I together and the State and public officials at the local levels have formed a very fine new partnership. Our urban program, our rural program has now been substantially implemented. When I was campaigning throughout this State and others in 1976, one of the common concerns expressed to me everywhere I went was our local communities have been severely damaged, our prospects for the future are dismal, the central city areas are deteriorating, we cannot let our voice be heard in Washington, we need a new partnership to be established. We've done that, and I believe in addition to that we've addressed some of the crucial issues of this Nation outside the government arena that are important to all of you.

Our Nation was becoming dependent upon foreign oil with a steady upward increase in imports, making us not only rob ourselves and import oil and inflation and unemployment but also put our Nation potentially under the control or influence of foreign powers who don't share the commitments and ideals that we hold so dear.

I've only been in office 3½ years, but we've made good progress. With the help of Pat Moynihan and the Congressmen who are here with me we've now forged a national energy policy. It's only been a brief time since those laws were on the books. But the American people have rallied, and we have actually cut the importing of foreign oil by 24 percent. And we've also measured it so that each day now, in 1980, we import 2 million barrels of oil less than we did the same day in 1977. At the same time, we've put into the consciousness of America the knowledge that we must conserve energy and produce more energy of our own.

I just came this morning from Detroit, from Flint, and saw a remarkable demonstration of the production of high-quality, safe, durable, efficient automobiles that made me proud as President, as an American, and I hope will make you just as proud, and I hope that in the future, when you get ready to trade your automobiles, that you'll go to the showrooms where American cars are sold and look at those new products. Compare and I don't think you'll find the American product wanting in any respect. I was really proud of what I saw this morning.

This year we'll produce more coal than any year in history. We're drilling more oil wells, more natural gas wells, than any year in history. And we have proven again to the rest of the world that when this country is faced with a serious challenge or a problem or an obstacle or a question, when we understand and unite together that this country has never

failed. And I don't believe that we will ever fail.

So, now we've got a good basis in energy to move forward to address some other problems; some are economic. We need to rebuild the industrial structure of our country. I saw a little part of it this morning. Yesterday we unveiled a program that will revitalize our entire steel industry. We've got a lot of progress already under our belt, but we need to make sure that our Nation is committed to full employment, modern tools, modern factories, competitive exports, so that in the future every person in this country who wants a job can get a good job and hold it. That's what our goal is.

That's one of the measures of the quality of life. But another measure of the quality of life is the quality of the community within which one lives—jobs, yes, in the industrial sector. Most of our jobs are private jobs, five out of six. Others are public service jobs, and those one out of six in the broad range of our great country are what determines how people in America live—a safe nation, a secure nation, happy nation, a well educated nation, a nation where the responsibilities of a community are held together, where the poor and the weak and the elderly have adequate services, where the police, the firemen, streets, the homes, the services, that pull a community together and inspire Americans to be even better than we have been in the past, to give our children a better life than even we've enjoyed. That's the role that's played by you; that's the role that's played by the President of the United States.

There's a partnership that exists—those of us who give our lives or a major portion of our lives to serving others. Sometimes it's a sacrificial commitment, because many in this room could make more money and perhaps even to be more socially prominent and more influential if you worked in the private sector of our economy. That's the way it's always been. But to those of you who feel the gratification of taking what talent God gives you and letting that talent be used in the most extraordinary and productive way, not only for yourself but for others, I congratulate you and thank you for what you mean to me as President and to our country.

I just want to mention a few other things that we've still got to do. We need to reform our welfare system so that we can channel more benefits to our people and more fiscal relief to local and State communities, particularly those in New York, where you bear such a heavy burden. We need to make an emphasis on the work opportunities to make it always attractive; we need to provide more support from the Federal Government for the State and local governments. We need to work toward the $1 billion counter-cyclical aid program that's now being considered by the Congress, social security rebates of $680 million, and continuation of the shared responsibility for dealing with these and problems in the future that we might not even be able to foresee at this time.

The important thing is to have a continuum, day after day, week after week, month after month, year after year, where there need be no fear of one another and a recognition that we're not aliens or antagonists or enemies, but that we're on the same team, because every one of your constituents, every person that you serve is my constituent, and I feel that very deeply. We've got unmet needs in civil rights, in human rights. And one of the most important things that's impressed on my mind today: I'm the father of a beautiful little girl; I'm the grandfather of a beautiful little girl, and I want to be sure

that when my daughter and granddaughter face the future, they have the same equal rights as men guaranteed in the Constitution of the United States.

I have to admit to you that I cannot understand people who deliberately distort this ERA amendment. What it says is—and listen to this—what it says is not anything about homosexuality; it's not anything about men and women using the same bathroom; it's not anything about women being drafted. That's a bunch of baloney. What the amendment says is that neither the Federal Government nor any State government can pass a law which discriminates against women. It's all it says. Got that? That's what it says.

That's the kind of future that can only be spelled out through the political process. It's not just a matter of theoretical rights. It's a matter of guaranteeing working women, whose children depend on them, that when they do a full day's work equal to the man next to them, they get the same pay. Now a woman on the average in this country for the same level of work gets only 59 cents for every dollar received by men. There are hundreds of different laws all over this Nation, from one State to another, that deprive women of a right under certain circumstances to own an automobile or to get property if their husband dies, or to know how she can be continued in a productive and safe financial life. That's a serious blight on our country.

I don't want to mislead you, because you've endorsed me and because this is a happy day for me to be here. There will be times when I as President, even in spite of what I've said about partnership, will not always agree with you. That's obvious. I can't agree with every proposal you make and also agree with every proposal that other groups in this country make, as President. I cannot promise you that there'll be unlimited Federal resources to meet every demand that's presented to my desk in the Oval Office. I can't promise that every new program will be passed through the Congress without delay, even if you and I agree that it ought to be done. I can't promise you that there will not be difficult challenges in the future and tough decisions to be made. But I do tell you that we share the same goals and the same ideals and the same hopes in the future.

And as this election approaches, you need to remember what the consequences might be if the wrong decision is made, because I face a Republican candidate formidable in his political strength and in the finances accruing to his campaign, who offers us an uncertain kind of future based on improbable promises and ill-considered proposals that affect us at home and also affect us abroad.

He's spoken about the problems of working families and of the poor, yet he proposes the same formulas that long ago broke faith with the majority of Americans. He's praised publicly the newborn free trade unions of Poland, but he's failed to provide the same support for the free trade unions of the United States.

He's against full rights for American workers. He opposes the minimum wage. It's hard for me to believe that working people would vote for a President who has said, not a long time ago, but this year, and I quote: "The minimum wage has caused more misery and unemployment than anything since the Great Depression." He also said this about the Humphrey-Hawkins bill: "The Humphrey-Hawkins bill was a design for fascism." And he also said, "Fascism was really the basis for the New Deal."

Only a year and a half ago he backed the elimination of the Occupational Safety and Health Act, and he still talks about drastically weakening OSHA. He once called unemployment compensation little more than paid vacations for free-loaders. He opposed Medicaid and was a nationwide leader in the campaign against Medicare.

He was against aid to New York City and against aid to Chrysler. As a matter of fact, when Chrysler was on the verge of bankruptcy, he said, "What's wrong with bankruptcy?" And his attitude toward New York City was identical when he said, "Every morning my first prayer and every night my last prayer of the day is that the Federal Government will not bail out New York City." Now, a few weeks before the election, he said he's changed his mind. But when hundreds of thousands of jobs were at stake and the integrity of our greatest city was at stake, his voice was loud and clear.

Despite his record, he's campaigning as a friend of the working people and the man with all the simple answers. He says solving the energy problem is simple: No windfall profits tax—just turn it over to the oil companies; they'll make the decisions for us.

And solving our economic problems is just as simple: Pass a massive election-year tax cut, Reagan-Kemp-Roth. It would be a windfall for the rich and an inflationary disaster for the working people. And when he got a chorus of criticism from economists of almost every persuasion, he revised his economic program about a month ago. But his numbers don't add up. Instead of budget surpluses or even a balanced budget, it would bring on massive new budget deficits and unpredictable levels of inflation, over $100 billion deficit in 1985 alone. And between now and 1987, the tax cuts that he proposes from the Federal Government amount to a thousand billion dollars.

This tax cut would pump those billions

of dollars, consumer dollars, into an already inflationary economy and bid up the price of every consumer item that you would have to buy, without investing first, at all, in the productive capacity of the Nation, that we need. Only one dollar out of ten of his tax cut would go for job-producing investments, and what's more, there's nothing in his simplistic answer for rebuilding the economy of our older cities, of the Northeast or the Midwest. There's nothing for ports, nothing for railroads, nothing for retraining workers, nothing for research. The result would be an inflationary whirlwind that would steal back in higher prices the few dollars an average family would get in tax cuts.

Because of its inflationary impact even Business Week and former President Ford oppose this Reagan-Kemp-Roth tax cut, and George Bush earlier called it, accurately, "voodoo economics."

My opponent has another simple solution for Government spending. Two weeks ago he repeated his promise to place the burden of massive Federal programs on State and local governments. As you know, he had a similar proposal 4 years ago to turn back $90 billion in Federal programs. He said recently he wanted to put those Federal programs back, but of course, the price had gone up because of inflation.

This year he left out the details. What are all these programs he wants to turn back to be financed by local and State government? How will the local taxpayers pay for them? How much will property taxes have to rise, for instance, on your local and State governments if you have to pay the full cost of welfare? Think about the property tax burden that will fall on you. He owes the American people some of these answers, but so far we've not had any of those answers.

We don't need that one-dimensional kind of thinking that government is the source of all problems and that the solutions are so simple and so easy. The plain fact is that our problems require everyone to work together, a partnership of government and labor and management and business and the American public. We need to draw the best out of everyone to deal with problems that are genuinely difficult and complicated. We need to draw on our strength as we have when our Nation's been threatened in the past, with the First World War, the Second World War, the Great Depression, the Vietnam war, the social problems that were brought about by the end of racial discrimination. Those are the kinds of challenges that our Nation has met successfully if and when we worked together. They weren't resolved by simply lashing out at scapegoats like the Government or providing simplistic answers that wouldn't work.

Those are some of the reasons why I'm so happy to have your endorsement, because I know that this country has the best and most productive public employees—Federal, State, and local—of any nation on Earth. I've worked at every level of government for the past quarter-century. I know from personal experience the dedication that you bring to your careers, public service. Most people know that public employees keep our Nation safe, our roads in good condition, our schools open, our water and air clean, our work places healthy and safe, our elderly and our sick cared for, our laws enforced, and perform countless other necessary services day and night. And I'm glad to give thanks where it's due. I thank you for the hard work and the professional skills that you bring to your jobs, and I thank you for your support.

I don't want you to forget the importance of a decision to be made 5 weeks from now. I'll do all I can; so will Fritz Mondale, your friend; so will my wife and others in my Cabinet and those on the stage. But the decision will be made by you and people like you. And I hope that this next 5 weeks that you will add some of the sacrifice that you have devoted to your own jobs to this campaign, because the result of what happens November 4th could have more of an impact on your life and on the future of your family and the future of this Nation than perhaps any other decision that you will make in a long time.

So, I hope you'll join me not only as partners in administering government but partners in this campaign. Your endorsement is wonderful, but your personal voice and your influence among your friends and those who listen to you and respect you, this next 5 weeks, will be crucial. New York State can make the difference in the entire election outcome for the Nation, and what happens in this region here and what happens in your own communities all over this State can spell out the difference for the future of our country.

I want to join together with you in sweeping New York State on November 4th. One more word: If you do your share, I'll do mine, and on November 4th we will whip the Republicans together. Right? [*Applause*]

NOTE: The President spoke at 6:54 p.m. in the Niagara Falls International Convention Center ballroom.

Flint, Michigan

Interview With Joe Stroud and Remer Tyson of the Detroit Free Press. October 1, 1980

UNEMPLOYMENT IN AUTOMOBILE INDUSTRY

Q. Well, let's start off with the unemployment, which a lot of people are talking about in Michigan—in view of the

hardship that some people in Flint, as you pointed out, have endured and so forth, explain to us how you can ask somebody who's unemployed to vote for you again. Why should he?

THE PRESIDENT. Well, first of all, you have to analyze the source of the unemployment and the reasons for it. I believe we've done everything we could to add jobs in this Nation, at an increase of 8½ million in the last 3½ years. The unemployment rate has been fairly stable now in spite of the tremendous adverse impact of oil prices doubling. And we've had a chance to assess the problems, specifically in the automobile industry, which is crucial to this particular area.

The fact that OPEC prices went up 120 percent in 1 year—and the cumulative effect of that and the previous increases have made Americans shift their buying habits for cars—has created I think what's a transient problem in the automobile industry of this Nation. The manufacturers have announced collectively that they will invest about $80 billion in modernization over the next 5 years—an unprecedented investment, I might say, in any industry in our country. And I think that the new desire of American people to both produce cars and to buy the kind that we are making now is a healthy thing for the future.

We've extended unemployment compensation. The TRA program has helped to provide a transient opportunity for workers to shift and to accommodate unfair import impact. We've had a chance to increase the commitment of funds for CETA and are trying to expand the youth program. We are opening up additional opportunities for the export of American goods. We've tried and successfully tried, to keep the dollar stable. I believe that what we've done in the economic area so far has minimized the damage caused by uncontrollable and unpredictable change in American buying habits and its impact on the automobile industry.

The other thing that we've done for this industry is to form a working partnership between government and the automobile industry and, I think, we've helped to form a working partnership between management and labor in the automobile industry to deal with this crisis, but which will have a permanently beneficial impact.

I think you know that we've provided loan guarantees for Chrysler, when my opponent said, you know—what did he say exactly?

Q. "What's wrong with bankruptcy?"

THE PRESIDENT. Yes, "what's wrong with bankruptcy?" He's also characterized unemployment compensation as "prepaid insurance for loafers." He's been against the minimum wage. He's been against many of the programs that we've advocated that would be helpful in this respect.

So, I think when you compare what we've done, what we have in mind for the future, the new partnership that we have which has enthusiastically been endorsed by all the elements involved, and in comparison between me and Reagan, the arguments for voting for me are very formidable.

Q. But what you're saying is, as tough as the problems are and how the difficulty overcome, the voter would be a lot better off with you than if he was with Reagan?

THE PRESIDENT. Yes. I think there's no doubt about that. And the primary measure of an objective analysis would be the United Automobile Workers, and I think they've analyzed it probably as deeply and as personally and as intensely as any group could possibly do. And I believe that the message that they are sending out is to confirm what I just described to you.

POLITICAL ROLE OF RELIGIOUS GROUPS

Q. One of the questions that came up in the Baltimore debate and has had a good bit of attention has been the question of the proper role of organized religion in politics. There's been discussion of it both in terms of the right-wing evangelicals and the Catholic bishops. As a born-again Christian, what do you think is the proper role of religion on such questions as abortion and prayer in the schools and equal rights, other issues?

THE PRESIDENT. Well, I think anyone has a right to voice a personal opinion, whether it be a believer in a particular religious faith or a minister or pastor or rabbi who is a leader of a congregation or a flock. I see nothing wrong with that, and I believe it's vital in our society to let those views be expressed.

When there is an organized attempt, highly financed, to shape the outcome of an election by a religious group, using tax-exempt status or using the right to the public airwaves, it brings into the scope of the question an additional concern. Also, the attempt to equate a belief, on whether or not we have a Department of Education or whether or not there's a treaty between us and Panama, with a particular definition of whether that person is a Christian I think that exceeds the boundary of what has been the case in the past with acceptable religious groups.

I have never found any incompatibility between my own religious faith and my duties as President. I believe in the separation of church and state. I don't believe that these "radical" groups are going to have a profound effect on the political system of our country, because I trust the sound judgment of the American people. And although there might be some transient effect because of the newness of it and the fact that Americans haven't yet assessed the long-range impact, I believe that there won't be any permanent adverse consequences from it.

U.S. MILITARY STRENGTH

Q. Ronald Reagan says your vacillation and our military weakness has led to an imbalance of power in the Middle East, and that's led to the war there. And also, today you mentioned over at Flint High School that he said he'd withdraw the SALT II treaty because "the one card that's been missing in these negotiations has meant the possibility of an arms race, Now the Soviets have been racing, but with no competition." Have we been letting military power get away from us?

THE PRESIDENT. The Republicans ran the White House for 8 years before I got there. Seven of those years we had a real decrease in expenditures for defense in dollars, discounting inflation. I'm a professional military officer—that's my training—and I'm also from the South, where strong defense is a major commitment of almost any person who runs for public office. And when I became President, I believed that we needed to strengthen our defense commitment instead of letting it deteriorate further as the Republicans had done.

We've had a steady, sustained, predictable, well-organized increase each year in real dollars, above and beyond inflation, in our defense establishment. We had to change some of the ill-advised Republican proposals like, for instance, the B–1 bomber and shift toward more efficient means of protecting our so-called triad in the strategic weapon field by the air-launched cruise missiles. The Trident submarine program was at a stalemate when I took over. We're now progressing on schedule with the Trident submarines and the associated missiles with it. And, of course, the MX missile needs to be deployed, and we've worked out a mobile system for deployment that will make it relatively invulnerable to Soviet attack.

I'm deeply concerned about what Governor Reagan said concerning abandoning the SALT II treaty and injecting, for the first time since Harry Truman was President, the concept of an arms race, nuclear arms race, as a factor in the control of those weapons that could destroy the world. This is a radical departure from what other Presidents have done. And as you know, the SALT II treaty was the culmination of negotiations that were originated under President Nixon, carried out by President Ford, and concluded by me.

I have a reluctance to comment specifically on this matter, because it is so profoundly important a matter, until I can study what Reagan actually said and assess the consequences of what he would propose on our relationship with the Soviet Union, prospects for future control of nuclear weaponry, the impact on our allies, who are deeply concerned about successful implementation of SALT treaties. I think until I have a chance to consider more carefully the far-reaching effect of his proposal or the implementation of it for our country, I'd rather limit my response to what I've already said.

PRESIDENT'S CAMPAIGN STYLE

Q. Mr. President, there's been some talk lately—and the Reagan camp has made a good bit of it—about what's sort of called the "meanness issue," that there's somehow a mean side of Jimmy Carter that shows up in such issues as the Atlanta speech and the painting of Reagan as warmonger. Would you talk a little about that? I saw an editorial just a few days ago that speculated at some length about that.

THE PRESIDENT. In your paper?

Q. No. [*Laughter*]

THE PRESIDENT. There've been a couple of editorials in your paper that I've read. I have always tried to be very moderate in my campaign. I very seldom mention my opponents' names. And I try to spell out issues so the audience can understand them. And when I have, in an extemporaneous forum, as a candidate for State senator or Governor or President in '76 or President now, made some comment that was misinterpreted or which because of brevity didn't adequately describe my real feelings, I've always tried immediately to correct any misimpressions.

After the Atlanta speech, I had a national press conference, as you remember. I think I had four questions on the subject. In each case I said I did not intend to imply and did not imply in my mind that Reagan was a racist. I do not think he is and have never thought he was. I did deplore the injection into the campaign from any source of the Ku Klux Klan or racism.

Also, following the statement in Los Angeles, I was going down a litany of differences that might exist between success or failure, prosperity and so forth, and war and peace as a result of the outcome of the election. I didn't intend to imply and did not imply that any President, including Reagan if he should become President, wanted a war. But immediately I had a television interview, which was distributed—a transcript—to all of the press—and then Jody pointed out that on many occasions in the last few years, eight or ten occasions, Governor Reagan has indeed advocated the injection of American military forces into an area of the world that was troubled, where the solution to the trouble was obviously diplomatic in scope. This involved Peru, Cyprus, Lebanon, Angola, and other places around the world, Korea, Cuba.

I don't know what Reagan would do if he were President, if a crisis like that should arise—whether his inclination to put military forces into a troubled area would be terminated if he should become President, or if that would be part of his attitude towards the crisis.

I do know this—that the Presidency is a lonely job. You have to make a decision on your own. You can't turn over the Presidency to advisers or to a Vice President. On almost every crucial issue, advisers are divided in their counsel to you, and the more vivid an issue is, the more important it is, and the more profoundly significant it might be, the more likely the advisers are to be 50–50 or divided almost equally. The best thing for a President to do if faced with a potential crisis is to handle it so it does not become a crisis, so that it doesn't affect hundreds of lives or hundreds of millions of lives.

I think that that judgment and that management of a crisis, that general inclination towards peace or a peaceful settlement of a dispute or the attempt to settle a dispute by weapons is a legitimate issue in the campaign. And I say that being cautious about my words, but also reemphasizing that I'm not accusing Reagan of wanting a war. But I do know that in a troubled world, on the closest possible margins of decision, there is the option of either the use of weapons or the commitment to try to resolve a dispute peacefully, and that's a judgment that the American people will have to make.

AMERICAN HOSTAGES IN IRAN

Q. There's another thing that Reagan has said, and as a matter of fact, I think he said it today. I heard on a newscast that you were accused of using the hostage issue in the primaries for your political gain. And he would expect an October surprise, and he wouldn't be surprised if the hostages came home before election. If you're trailing Reagan in the polls in the last week in October, are the hostages coming home before election day?

THE PRESIDENT. I would pray that the hostages would come home at the earliest possible moment regardless of the date of the election. I have never failed, any morning when I woke up, to pray that God would let those hostages come home safe at the earliest possible moment. I've never used the hostage issue for political purposes and never will.

The allegation that I would play with the lives of innocent hostages for political purposes or delay their coming home to have some good news just before an election is ridiculous, and his further statement that I somehow or another caused the war between the Iranians and the Iraqis is, you know, is ridiculous.

Q. Talk just a minute about——

THE PRESIDENT. —— try to avoid saying things, you know, about that.

Q. I didn't mean to interrupt you.

THE PRESIDENT. It's all right.

Q. But there was an awfully early press conference just before the Wisconsin primary—not a press conference, but appearance—and you talked about the hostages, and a lot of people said, "There's Jimmy Carter now trying to get onto the 'Today' show so he can stop Teddy Kennedy in Wisconsin to win." And I'd just like for you to respond to that.

THE PRESIDENT. One time since last November we have had every element in Iran committed to let those hostages go, and that was that particular morning. It happened to be the morning of some primaries. We had an average, I think, of six primaries a week during that whole

period. I mean it was almost impossible to find a time that wasn't before or after or during a primary.

We got up at 4 o'clock that morning, waiting for the final culminating public statement from the President of Iran that would confirm that the negotiations that we had formed with them were successful. The militant students had agreed to let the hostages go, the President of Iran had agreed to let the hostages go, the Revolutionary Council had agreed to let the hostages go, and the Foreign Minister had agreed to let the hostages go. The only thing we had to do was to wait until, I believe, 11 o'clock or 12 o'clock noon in Iran, when the President of that nation was going to make a public statement confirming that the agreement was legitimate.

He made that statement publicly. We monitored it very quickly. It was transmitted to me in the White House. The Secretary of State was there; the Secretary of Defense was there; the national security adviser was there; the Vice President was there; Jody [Powell] was there. We'd been there since 4 o'clock in the morning. And when that message got to me confirming that point, I went before the American people and said we believe we have finally arrived at the point where the hostages will be coming home.

Because of timidity on the part of some of the Iranian officials and some argument about things like how will the hostages be actually carried physically out of the compound to the airport, there was a delay. And subsequent to that, instead of having the Revolutionary Council prevail, with only two dissenting votes—I think there are 15 or 20 on the Revolutionary Council—Bani-Sadr, the President, said, "We've got to have a unanimous vote in the Revolutionary Council." And the agreement that we had evolved, using intermediaries and the most detailed negotiating techniques, did not come to pass. It was a great surprise to us, a disappointment, a profound disappointment.

That's the only time during this whole period when we thought we had a final agreement involving all of the people involved in Iran.

Q. But the Wisconsin primary wasn't on your mind during that time?

THE PRESIDENT. Well, I knew the Wisconsin primary was there, but the Wisconsin primary was not any more important to me than the Minnesota primary or the Michigan primary or the Illinois primary or the New York primary or the Florida primary. We had primaries and caucuses, and I was in all of them.

What we did was wait until the public statement was made in Iran. We analyzed—we had it translated into English from Farsi. We read the statement to make sure that the agreement was confirmed publicly, and then I went to the American people. It was a very logical time schedule. This is the first time I've ever explained that, by the way.

VIEWS ON THE PRESIDENCY

Q. This is a question that probably we wouldn't have asked before seeing the Roger Mudd interview of Ted Kennedy last fall. But what is it that would drive you through all this long process? What is it you hope to do with a second term? Why is it that you want to be President for a second term? What do you hope to do for the country?

THE PRESIDENT. Well, I think there's a normal human trait that arouses legitimate ambition, to analyze your own talent or ability or opportunity and to make the most of one's life, whether it's in the field of journalism or education or science or medicine or politics. Also there is a con-

fluence of events or circumstances sometimes that makes it possible for a southerner—a person from Georgia, a southerner—to have a chance to be elected, to heal the Nation's wounds following the civil rights transition, a Democrat to be coming into the White House following the embarrassment of Watergate and the trauma of Vietnam, the CIA revelations— that was what let it be possible for me to serve as President.

We've got ongoing programs now that I think are very important. I want to keep the country at peace. We've been at peace under difficult circumstances for the last $3\frac{1}{2}$ years. I believe I can do that. I've got an understanding and a degree of experience on the knowledge of other nations and their leaders, of the complexities of regional and worldwide interrelationships—that I believe I could use for the benefit of our Nation in maintaining peace.

I've got clear in my own mind the route toward adequately strengthening our Nation's defenses in an orderly way, a predictable way, with harmony existing between me and the Joint Chiefs of Staff and the Congress, and I think an understanding of the American people. I see the need to control nuclear weapons. And I believe that having gone through this torturous process of negotiating the SALT II treaty that I'm almost uniquely qualified to take this Nation towards success in a further reduction, leading towards the ultimate goal, many years in the future, of complete elimination of the threat of nuclear weaponry from the world.

We've got a remarkably united Democratic Party now and programs concerning better health for our Nation, better education for our people, more security for the aged, better job opportunities for all Americans and particularly for young people; the correlation of different agencies, Labor plus Education, to match training with job opportunities, the enhancement of civil or human rights that are now still in a transient stage. We're approaching the culmination of securing, once and for all, equality of opportunity for all our people, including not just minority groups but women. This is important to me.

The economic shock that has hit the world, primarily resulting from OPEC oil price explosions, has to be assimilated in the steel industry, the coal industry, the entire energy concept, automobiles. I think we're well on the way toward bringing it together—government, labor, management—in those key basic industries to our country.

Reagan would dismantle the Energy Department. He would eliminate the windfall profits tax. He would denigrate the commitment that we've made to conservation. I think this would be a shock to our country and to the rest of the world, if we abandoned the leadership role that we have carefully forged in this first term.

So, the culmination of what I've already implemented and the realization of those kinds of hopes and dreams for our country, I think, can only be carried out effectively, in my perhaps biased judgment, by someone who has been there, who's experienced, and who knows all the very complicated factors involved.

RONALD REAGAN

Q. What kind of President do you think Reagan would make?

THE PRESIDENT. I don't think he would be a good President. I think his election would not be good for this country.

Q. Why do you say that?

THE PRESIDENT. Well, I think that the answer to that question is so complicated.

It involves, I would say, almost everything that we've discussed in this interview.

Q. Thank you very much.

THE PRESIDENT. Thank you very much.

NOTE: The interview began at approximately 3:30 p.m. at Bishop Airport.

The transcript of the interview was released on October 2.

Continuing Appropriations for Fiscal Year 1981

Statement on Signing H.J. Res. 610 Into Law. October 2, 1980

I am pleased that the Congress acted on the continuing resolution for 1981 in time to avoid disruption in Government activities at the start of this fiscal year. I urge the Congress to pass the remaining regular appropriations bills promptly upon its return next month.

While I signed the continuing resolution yesterday, I think it is important to make clear my concerns about several of its provisions:

1. The funding levels in the resolution do not in all cases represent the levels I will be supporting in the regular appropriation bills.

2. A provision in the resolution prevents the Secretary of Education from adopting or enforcing required guidelines under title VI of the Civil Rights Act of 1964 for services to students of limited English-language proficiency before June 1981. I believe it is inappropriate for the Congress to interpose itself between the courts and a Cabinet officer on this matter.

3. The resolution prohibits programs that would prevent voluntary prayer and meditation in public schools. No such programs exist, nor are any planned. This issue has been dealt with adequately by the Supreme Court. Raising this issue in

the appropriation process is therefore unnecessary and misleading.

NOTE: As enacted, H.J. Res. 610 is Public Law 96–369, approved October 1.

Solar Energy and Energy Conservation Bank

Nomination of Joseph S. Bracewell To Be President.   October 2, 1980

The President today announced his intention to nominate Joseph S. Bracewell, of Houston, Tex., to be President of the Solar Energy and Energy Conservation Bank. This is a new position created by Public Law 96–294.

Bracewell was born February 12, 1947, in Houston, Tex. He attended Harvard University from 1965 to 1969 and received an M.B.A. from Stanford University in 1971.

Since 1972, Bracewell has been president of The Brianco Corp. From 1972 to 1975, he was executive vice president and director of the Metropolitan National Bank. Bracewell has been chairman of the board, president and chief executive of First National Bank of West University Place since 1975.

Billy Carter's Activities With the Libyan Government

White House Statement on the Final Report of a Subcommittee of the Senate Judiciary Committee.   October 2, 1980

The Senate subcommittee today released its report on Billy Carter. It confirms the statements in the President's report of August 4 that there was no interference by the White House in the Department of Justice's investigation of Billy Carter under the Foreign Agents Registration Act and that Billy Carter had no influence or effect on any U.S. Government policy or actions concerning Libya. These conclusions were reached after an investigation extending over 2 months, in which several thousand documents were voluntarily produced by the White House and executive branch agencies, and testimony was taken from more than thirty witnesses. No wrongdoing was found by the subcommittee.

In its conclusions, the subcommittee differs from the President's views and those of his staff on certain questions of judgment, such as the use of Billy Carter in seeking Libyan help in urging Iranian authorities to release the American hostages in November 1979. This decision was made shortly after the seizure of our Embassy and at a time when our Government was employing all available channels to persuade Muslim nations to urge the release of the hostages.

The subcommittee's report questions the decision by the President's National Security Adviser to caution Billy Carter not to take any action that could embarrass our Government or the President in connection with Billy Carter's efforts to obtain an increased allocation of Libyan oil for an American oil company. The President has previously stated that when Dr. Brzezinski told him about his conversation with Billy Carter and the intelligence report on which it was based, he approved of the action taken. The report also questions whether the President should have made further statements disassociating himself from Billy Carter in light of Billy Carter's decision to make a second trip to Libya. The President and his Press Secretary made it clear on a number of occasions well before Billy Carter's second trip to Libya that Billy Carter was acting as a private citizen and was acting without prior consultation with the White House in his associations with Libya.

Finally, the report questions whether in the spring of 1980 the intelligence agencies and the Attorney General should have brought certain sensitive intelligence information to the President's attention and to the attention of the Justice Department trial attorneys. This decision, like the others questioned by the subcommittee, involved a weighing of comparative risks and benefits, including the risk, if the President or the trial attorneys had sought to utilize the information, of compromising valuable intelligence sources and methods.

As the subcommittee recognizes in its conclusions after "full and careful reflection," there may be differing views on such judgmental matters. Even in the light of hindsight, the President respectfully differs with the subcommittee's views and believes that each of these decisions was correct.

The subcommittee's views on the future handling of intelligence information and, in particular, whether there is need for improved procedures for coordinating interagency dissemination and use of this information, will be carefully reviewed by the President and his advisers.

Metropolitan Opera Labor Dispute

Telegram to the Principal Parties Negotiating New Labor Contracts.   October 2, 1980

I have been informed by the Director of the Federal Mediation and Conciliation Service that intensive negotiations for new contracts between the Metropolitan Opera Association and the seventeen unions representing workers at the Metropolitan have thus far been unsuccessful.

I am personally concerned that the Metropolitan Opera has therefore announced the cancellation of the 1980–81 season.

Several thousand employees will be without work and thousands of others will be adversely affected in many ways if the Metropolitan Opera does not perform this season. More importantly, the Metropolitan is an institution that is beloved all around the world. Both its regular season in New York and its traveling season—which includes performances at the Kennedy Center in Washington and in many other communities across the country—are supported by full houses at every performance.

I know that with the assistance of the Mediation Service, both parties have tried earnestly to resolve their differences and that the decision taken by the Board of the Metropolitan Opera Association to cancel the season was made with great reluctance and sorrow. I know also that the cancellation is more than an economic burden on the performers, all of whom have a strong sense of loyalty and affection for the Metropolitan Opera.

For all these reasons, I ask the parties to these negotiations to reassess their positions, and I am directing Wayne Horvitz, Director of the Federal Mediation and Conciliation Service, to ask both management and the unions to resume negotiations in another effort to open the 1980–1981 season.

JIMMY CARTER

Dayton, Ohio

Remarks and a Question-and-Answer Session at a Townhall Meeting.   October 2, 1980

THE PRESIDENT. *Senator Metzenbaum, Mayor Jim McGee, Congressman Tony Hall, Paula MacIlwaine, Treasurer Joe Shump:*

It's really an honor for me to be here with you in Miami Valley, Montgomery County, Dayton. I've only been here a few minutes, but I think I can already agree with your city's motto, and it's right on the mark. It's "Great in Dayton." There's no question about that.

Yours is a great city, a dynamic city. It's vibrant and alive with new construction and new ideas and new vigor and a new zest and confidence in the future. It's typical of the life and the attitude of more than 220 million Americans, who are blessed by God with one of the greatest opportunities for freedom and the preservation of life and to guarantee to our children that they'll have even a better life than we've had. Your downtown restoration effort shows that you can be proud not only of what you've done already but what you expect to accomplish in the months and the years ahead.

It's a privilege for me to come here as President to answer your questions and to share your views about our Nation's future. I have no idea at all what the questions will be. But when this session is over about an hour from now, I will have learned a lot about you and your community, and I hope you will have learned a lot about me and the rest of the Nation.

This is a good place for a President to come. You are builders; you are workers; you're people who know how to get a job done. And I'm glad to come to the birthplace of aviation, because it proves down through history that you've known what innovation and technical progress and also courage means—you see a problem, you're not afraid to tackle it headon, and our country needs that kind of spirit.

CAMPAIGN ISSUES

As you know, we face some historic tests right now. We discussed this in the car on the way here from Air Force One with some of your officials, Mayor McGee and others, about how our Nation has been able and willing to face difficult questions down through the ages, questions and problems much more serious than the ones we face now—a Great Depression, social shock that swept through this Nation when we eliminated racial discrimination, the First World War, the Second World War, Vietnam, Watergate. We've had those tests of our Nation, much more serious than any problem we face today, and when our people were united and understood what the problem was, we've never failed to solve any problem.

And we've kept high the principles and ideals on which our Nation was founded and on which it still rests. We've never abandoned those ideals. And the other thing is that we've come here from all over the world. Our people came here as immigrants, found freedom—for some it took a long time, but never abandoned hope—to worship as we please. And we, in that process, honor each individual person as a precious son or daughter of God.

We've made a lot of progress even against the tremendous test or challenge of the energy crisis. Last year the price of oil went up 120 percent. It rose more in price in 1 year than the price of oil had increased since it was first discovered back in the 1800's. But our country has weathered that shock. And this year we'll produce more American coal than any other year in the history of our Nation. We'll be producing more and using more of the coal from Ohio, even the high-sulphur coal, to develop clean fuels. It'll be used in the years ahead. And I'm determined to see OPEC oil in the future replaced as a major energy source by Ohio coal.

And finally, before I take the first question, let me say that having come through this first 3½ years of my administration, working with Congress to forge a good, sound energy policy, we've laid the groundwork or the foundation or the base for an exciting new technological revolution in this country, when the American working people, men and women, already the most productive workers on Earth, will now have new investments, new tools, new factories, to keep them at the forefront in the years ahead. What our Nation does will provide an example for the rest of the world. And I want to be sure that 10 years from now, 20 years from now, the end of this century, that American workers will be the most productive, the best paid, the most united, the most free, and the most idealistic workers on Earth. That's my goal. With your help, we'll reach that goal together.

And now we have 54 minutes left for questions. I'll take the first one.

QUESTIONS

TAX CREDIT FOR COLLEGE EDUCATION

Q. Hi, Mr. President, welcome to Dayton.

THE PRESIDENT. I feel welcome. Thank you.

Q. My name is Lou Ann Clingman. And I'm a senior at Fernwell High School, and I'm an advanced high school student at Miami University. And my first question for you this afternoon is: I'm entering college full-time next year, and I was wondering if you're going to give the families of college students a tax credit next year?

THE PRESIDENT. I'll be glad to answer. No. [*Laughter*] But let me explain. Since I've been in office just 3½ years, there have been very few goals that I have accomplished absolutely. One of them is that I wanted to make sure that every young person in our Nation who was mentally able to do college work could get a full college education no matter how poor the family might be. And I can guarantee you, that when you get ready to go to college, no matter what the financial condition of your family might be, you will be financially able to go to college, through grants or loans or work-study programs. There's no reason anymore in this country after the great work that the Congress has done in the last 3½ years for any young person to be deprived of a college education because of economic circumstances.

So, we've done that, it's a great achievement and I think that we'll build on it.

Q. Good afternoon, Mr. President, and happy birthday to you.

THE PRESIDENT. Thank you very much. It was yesterday, but thank you. I heard "Happy Birthday" sung so many times yesterday, I almost turned against it. But then I got home and Amy had practiced on her violin all week, and she surprised me last night by playing "Happy Birthday" on the violin. It sounded beautiful once again. So, thank you very much.

MINORITY EMPLOYMENT PROGRAMS

Q. My name is Howard T. Smith, and I'm a resident of the city of Dayton, Ohio. Before I ask my question, I'd like to say, Mr. President, I attended your Inauguration in January of 1977, and I intend to be present at your Inauguration ceremony in January of 1981.

THE PRESIDENT. Thank you. So far, that's my favorite question. [*Laughter*]

Q. I've read recently that one of five black families receives public assistance. In addition, black youth are traditionally hardest hit in periods of recession. Mr. President, what new programs are you proposing to help blacks find jobs?

THE PRESIDENT. I might say that four times as many white families receive public assistance as do black families, but you're absolutely right in your basic question that the minority citizens of our country still suffer most from any sort of economic problems that we have—and by minority citizens I'm going to stretch the definition a little bit by including women, because women are still cheated in this country as are the black people as well. For equal work women only get paid 59 cents out of every dollar that men get, and that's black women and white women as well.

But to answer your specific question, we've been able in the last 3½ years, in spite of all these economic shocks that I've described, to make good progress on employment. We've had a net increase of 8½ million jobs. About 400,000 more people are at work in Ohio today than there were in January when you attended that first Inauguration. As a matter of fact, about 1.3 million more black people are at work today than there were in January of 1977. That's not enough, because we still have a lot of people unemployed.

In the last 4 months or so the unemployment rate has not increased. It's been about 7.7, 7.8 percent. We're doing the best we can to get it down. We've tried to channel opportunities for minorities in

this country to places outside of government jobs, that the taxpayers have to finance, into permanent jobs in the private free enterprise system. For instance, I've been very eager to see black ownership of some radio and television stations, because in the past, because of discrimination, they've been excluded from that. We've tripled the number of black-owned or -controlled stations in the last 2 years.

I've also been very eager to see that when the Government has local development funds spent for public works or when the Government buys things like file cabinets or uniforms or stationery and so forth, that a certain portion of those expenditures—and you help pay the taxes—go to minority-owned businesses. That's been a very fruitful pursuit, and we've more than tripled the purchases from black-owned companies. And we've had about 15 percent of our total public works channeled into minority-owned businesses, that's helped. Another thing that we're doing now is trying to increase the so-called countercyclical aid to communities where the unemployment rate is high. We have a billion dollar program that I believe the Congress will pass before it adjourns this year.

And the last point I want to make is this. No, I want to make two more points quickly. One is that we've tried to protect as best we could the downtown urban areas which were deteriorating so rapidly 3 or 4 years ago. It's good for the suburbs to build up, that's inevitable, but while they do that, I don't want to see downtown Dayton or downtown Atlanta or downtown Washington, D.C., go down and become a ghetto area. So, we in all of our programs, housing, transportation, we've tried to defend them.

And the last thing is that we have before the Congress now, that I believe will be passed, a $2 billion program for youth employment. This program will tie together for the first time the Labor Department and the Education Department to make sure that when a young person gets out of high school or out of a junior college or out of vocational technical school, that his or her talents are matched with the particular jobs available in that community. We've never done this before. This will be a 50-percent increase in youth employment programs, keeping intact what we've already got. A lot of these jobs will be channeled to minority youth, of course, and this will be a very helpful, additional boon to what we've done already.

So, those are some of the programs very hurriedly that we're working on, many of them already established and very helpful; the record already very good; the future looks much brighter.

Q. Thank you very much.

THE PRESIDENT. Thank you, Howard Smith.

CHEMICAL WARFARE

Q. Mr. President, I'm Harlan Hullinger, and I'd like to know what your current position and future policy is on chemical warfare and whether you intend to make it a part of your defense policy or if you had some intention of stopping funding of the current facility proposal before Congress?

THE PRESIDENT. What we've done, as you know, ever since the First World War, is taken the leadership as a nation in trying to eliminate the threat of chemical warfare from the arsenals or policies of the nations of the world. We have ongoing negotiations with the Soviet Union even now to outlaw chemical warfare. We have indications that they've used chemical warfare against the Afghan people and also that the Vietnamese have used Soviet

chemicals against the poor people of Cambodia. We have reserve supplies of some chemicals on hand, because we've got to keep those in order to induce the Soviets to join with us in the elimination of this threat.

The present proposal, which I think is ill-advised by the Congress, is to move immediately toward the production of so-called binary chemicals that can be used against human beings. The binary approach is a good one, in that you have two different chemicals that are not mixed until they're actually used, so that if you were to spill them at some storage place, say, an Air Force base in our country, nobody would be injured. Only it's when you mix them would they be used. And eventually we'll replace our existing limited stockpiles of old-fashioned, already mixed, and very dangerous chemicals with the binary chemicals that are not dangerous until the time of war comes.

So, that's the combination that we'll use to move to a modern small supply of chemicals of a binary nature that are not dangerous in storage, but to continue to work with the Soviet Union and all nations to eliminate the threat of chemical warfare altogether.

Q. Thank you.

THE PRESIDENT. Thank you very much, Harlan.

You can see the breadth of the questions that we get in a townhall meeting. I had no idea I was going to get that question. I'm glad I was familiar with the answer. [*Laughter*] I've been studying it lately.

FEDERAL ASSISTANCE TO STATES

Q. Good afternoon, President Carter. My name is Gene Hawk, and I live and work here in Dayton, Ohio. For the past 3 years, the State of Ohio has received approximately 75 cents back from the

Federal Government for every dollar it pays in Federal taxes. This ratio is about the same for most of Midwestern industrial States, while in the South, the situation is just the opposite. They receive more aid than they pay in. My question is: Why are the tax dollars from Ohio and other industrial States allowed to drain into the South when we have been hit the hardest by the recession?

THE PRESIDENT. That's a good question. I'm afraid your question is going to get more applause than my answer. But let me try to explain it. It's not something new, as you know.

Ever since 1913 when a constitutional amendment was passed authorizing income tax, the policy of our Nation—all Presidents, Democratic and Republican; all Congresses, Democratic and Republican majorities—has been to collect for the Federal revenues money depending upon the wealth or income of an American citizen no matter where that citizen might live.

Rich people pay more taxes than poor people to the Federal Government. In State and local governments that's not necessarily the case, because local governments are primarily financed, in many States, by sales tax, and the poor people pay just as much sales tax on a loaf of bread as a rich person. It's a lot higher percentage of their income, of course.

And then the Congress, through its laws, that have to be signed by a President, send those moneys that are collected from the income tax to communities and to services as they are needed, to defend our Nation through the military—and a lot of the military bases are located in the South; you have an outstanding military base here in Dayton—to build highway systems; to help with education, primarily designed for the more deprived children and the poorer children, just to

supplement what the local and State governments can do; to rebuild cities by matching funds, as we are doing with your urban development program; and of course, to pay unemployment compensation when people are temporarily out of work, as is the case with many people here in Dayton. I was in Flint, Michigan, yesterday.

So, the programs that Congress passes to spend money is designed primarily to defend our country; to provide uniform transportation services, say, with the Interstate Highway System; and to meet pockets of need that vary from one community to another, whether they're in the North or South, East or West; and also to meet transient needs until the State and local governments can catch up with a general trend, like controlling pollution or building up an energy program.

I would guess that in the future this policy will continue. If Ohio had a very low income level, then you would pay much less money to the Federal Government than you got back. If you had a lot of poverty and a lot of deprivation in Ohio, you would get a lot more money back than you paid in, because you wouldn't have much income tax, right? And the poor people would get more welfare payments, more unemployment compensation. So, what has happened in the past is a measurement of the progress and wealth, or income, of the States involved.

I'm from the South, as you know. Georgia's a very progressive State, making a lot of progress, not nearly up to the income level of Ohio yet. But it's equalizing, the trend. And eventually I believe that Ohio will get back about what it pays in.

I might say that just since I've been in office, the average income of a family in Ohio has gone up 36 percent in less than 4 years. You're still making a lot of progress, and your employment in Ohio has gone up 10 percent, in this entire State—as I said earlier, more than 400,000 jobs.

So, to answer your question, I don't think it's going to change, that policy. I don't think it ought to change. But the reason for it is that on the average, Ohio families have a higher level of income, and they pay income tax based on how much they have coming in and the moneys that the Federal Government pays out for social programs go to those that have very low incomes. So far, you have more low-income families on the average in the South, but I believe it's equalizing.

Did I explain it so you could understand it?

Q. Yes, you did.

THE PRESIDENT. You may not like the answer, but that's accurate, I believe.

Thank you very much.

TAX POLICIES

Q. Hi. My name is Amy Bechtel, and I'm a senior at Centerville High School. And I've been studying economics and government a lot, and Ronald Reagan has proposed to cause more tax cuts with particular emphasis on big business. This is, I think, in order to stimulate growth of business and consequently increase employment and put money back into the economy. My question is: Do you feel that this is a productive way to check inflation and help the U.S. economy?

THE PRESIDENT. No, that's one of the worst proposals that I have ever heard of and one of the most inflationary things that's ever been suggested for presentation to the Congress. Let me explain why.

The so-called Reagan-Kemp-Roth proposal is what you're referring to. Only 10 percent of the benefits of that proposal would go to stimulate new investments in

business and new tools and the modernization of American production plants. Ninety percent would go to personal income tax reductions, primarily for the rich people. For instance, a family that makes $200,000 a year under Reagan's proposal would get 35 times more tax benefits than a family that makes $20,000 a year. You'd have a heavy channeling of benefits or tax moneys into the pockets of the rich families and very little going to business that would help them invest in new plants and provide more jobs for the American workers.

Business Week, which is a very conservative magazine, has disavowed any support of Reagan's proposal. Former President Ford, a Republican who supports Reagan for President, has said he could not support Reagan's proposal. Those are not exactly biased analysts. I think one of the closest political observers to Reagan is his own Vice-Presidential running mate, George Bush. George Bush said that the Reagan-Kemp-Roth proposal would create inflation rates in this country of over 30 percent, and George Bush said the best way he could think of to describe it was "voodoo economics."

So, it's not just me as a Democrat who thinks this is a ridiculous proposal. It would be extremely damaging to the working families of this country, would deprive them of an opportunity for jobs, and would saddle them with enormous inflationary pressures, and the rich families would benefit tremendously.

We have proposed, on the other hand, that we not have any tax cuts during an election year. I think it's the wrong time for the Congress to consider it, because there's too much politics involved. But our proposal would be very cautious in nature and designed, with 50 percent of the total benefits going to stimulate jobs and to create new investments in the steel industry, the automobile industry, and associated ones like the ones that produce tires, and at this same time we would add some personal reductions, but very few. The only two that amount to anything much is to have an income tax credit beginning next year that would just offset the increase in social security payments to keep the social security system sound. That ought to be done. And the other thing that we are proposing is that we should eliminate the so-called marriage penalty. Now if a husband and wife live together and both work, they have to pay a lot higher income taxes than if a man and woman are living together not being married when they both work, and I don't think that's right to preserving the sanctity of marriage. So, we want to eliminate that marriage penalty. That's one other point.

And I think that's the best brief description I could make of the so-called Reagan-Kemp-Roth proposal.

This same foolish idea was put forward in 1978 in the election when Members of Congress were running for reelection, and before the election time was over almost all the Republican candidates who had earlier endorsed it said, "It's like a millstone around our neck, because once people look at it and see what it does, it's not a politically attractive proposal." Other than that it's okay. [*Laughter*]

THE MIDDLE EAST

Q. Good afternoon, Mr. President.

THE PRESIDENT. Good afternoon.

Q. My name is Tony Mann, and I'm from Dayton, Ohio. My question is, with the conflict and terrorism continuing in the Middle East, what new measures are the United States now taking or planning to take to bring stability and lasting peace to that area of the world?

THE PRESIDENT. Our security is directly related to stability in the Middle East and particularly to the preservation of the existence and the freedom and, hopefully, the peace of Israel.

One of the most exciting times of my administration so far has been when President Sadat, Prime Minister Begin, and I forged the Camp David accords, followed up by a treaty between Egypt, that's by far the most powerful and influential Arab nation, and her neighbor, Israel. And now, of course, they have normal commerce, the borders are open, the tourists go to and from Israel and Egypt, they have ambassadors in both countries. Instead of confronting each other across barbed wire with machine gun bullets and tanks, they confront each other now with negotiating. This is a very fine development and, I think, helps to stabilize the western part of the Mideast area, that is, the part that borders on the Mediterranean.

The other part of the so-called Mideast—I think you might want to extend it to the Persian Gulf; I won't try to make geographical definitions here—is still a very troubling part of the world. The revolution in Iran has not yet been replaced with a stable, coherent government. The Iranians have had a very difficult time in putting together their own government. They have finally got a parliament elected—they call it a Majles—they've got a speaker of the parliament, they've got a Prime Minister, and a President now, they're putting together a cabinet. And we believe that when they get a government intact that the country might be more stable. But that process has been interrupted, as you know, by the attack on Iran by Iraq.

So far, we have been instrumental in confining that conflict to just those two nations and trying to discourage [encourage] [1] both those countries to sit down and negotiate their differences. We can get along without oil from Iran and Iraq, but we cannot get along without oil, ourselves or the rest of the world, from the rest of the Persian Gulf region. The United Arab Emirates, Kuwait, and Saudi Arabia ship about 12 million barrels of oil every day out of the Straits of Hormuz, and we will use whatever means is required to keep the Straits of Hormuz open.

In the meantime, we want to prevent any further disturbance that might precipitate a Soviet involvement in Iran or Iraq. We use our alliances with France and Australia and Great Britain and other western countries, plus our friendship with Saudi Arabia, with Pakistan, and other Moslem countries, to dampen down any conflict there. In the future we'll continue these policies.

One of the things that we will do after the election is to go ahead with another summit meeting between myself and President Sadat and Prime Minister Begin, to followup on further progress toward a comprehensive Mideast peace.

In the meantime we are working with the King of Jordan, trying to stabilize the situation in Lebanon, hoping that later the Syrians will come into a peaceful relationship with Israel, and a resolution of the Palestinian question, which all three of us want to see done. That's a quick summary of the circumstances in the Mideast Persian Gulf region and what we have in mind for the future.

THE FEDERAL BUDGET

Q. Good afternoon, Mr. President. My name is Steve Schier, and I teach politics at Wittenberg University in Springfield, Ohio. I was surprised to learn this

---

[1] White House correction.

week that you and I have the same birthday. So, I wish you a happy birthday.

THE PRESIDENT. Same to you.

Q. My question is this: The congressional budget process in recent days has gone off the rails. Taxing and spending limits have been deferred for final resolution until after the election. The problem of controlling annual budget spending is compounded by the fact that an estimated 75–80 percent of annual spending is uncontrollable—entitlements, multi-year contracts. Can you promise to discipline Congress to eventually balance the budget, and at what cost to Government programs should the budget be balanced? Finally, could you compare yours and Ronald Reagan's proposals for eventually bringing the budget into balance?

THE PRESIDENT. Yes. I'll be glad to.

You're right in the analysis of what the Congress has done the last few days. But one of the greatest steps forward that I know the Congress has taken in my lifetime has been the development of the budget process—the formation of the Budget Committees and the self-imposed discipline on the Congress that formerly just did not exist. Now the Budget Committees set overall limits of spending, as you know, in different areas of American life, and then the Appropriations Committees, that formerly had unlimited authority, have to comply with those limits. So, it's a very good improvement in responsibility and predictability about the Government process.

The Congress has done a yeoman's job this year, in my judgment, in trying to bring about a balanced budget. It's easy to use "if's"—but if we had 6-percent unemployment in 1982 fiscal year, in this year that started yesterday, 1981 fiscal year, then we would have a balanced budget. What has caused the budget to be unbalanced is the increased unemployment compensations that are being made to workers who are out of jobs, particularly in areas relating to automobiles and a few other industries, but that's the main one. We cannot abandon those workers, and I have asked the Congress to extend unemployment compensation another 13 weeks when their present authorization expires. We have, I think, a good prospect to continue this discipline on spending in the future.

There are two things that will make it hard to carry out the goal that you described, no matter who the President might be: One is my commitment that during the next 5 years, counting the year that just started, we will have a continual, predictable, adequate increase in real-dollar expenditures for defense capability. For the 8 years before I became President, out of 7 of those years we had a decrease in spending for defense under the Republican administration. We've had a steady predictable increase built in that'll continue. And the other thing is that we have a very serious problem with the meeting of needs of the constituent groups because of inflation. Social security, for instance, must be kept sound.

When I was campaigning in 1976, there was an imminent prospect of a failure or bankruptcy of the social security system. We've put it back on its feet, and it will be kept sound. One of the provisions for social security, though, is as the inflation rate goes up for retired people, their social security payments go up enough to compensate for inflation, because those payments are low enough so they're already very restraining. So, with those built-in guarantees of certain groups of people, like social security recipients, that they can have a stable and predictably good life in the future, and the need for a strong defense, it's not going to be easy to have a balanced budget. That's still

my goal, and I believe the Congress shares that goal.

Last March we had a balanced budget committed. We did not anticipate the downturn in the economic situation of the entire world brought about by OPEC price increases and the increase in welfare payments and unemployment compensation payments that go along with it. And of course, when you get more people unemployed and those unemployment compensation payments go up, you also get less income tax being paid by those same people who have formerly paid interest into the Federal revenue chest.

I made the answer awhile ago to Ann Bechtel over here about the Reagan-Kemp-Roth proposal. My total economic proposal, that I outlined so briefly, is anti-inflationary in nature. The replacement of social security payments by tax credits has an anti-inflationary impact. Reagan's proposal is highly inflationary in nature, and if his proposal is put into effect, I see no possible way that the deficits could be less than $100 billion a year by 1985. But I think my proposal is much better designed to meet the needs of our people to have equity in the income tax system, to have discipline on the Congress, and work toward a balanced budget.

FEDERAL SUPPORT FOR EDUCATION

Q. Mr. President, my name is Terence Walton, and I'm a 10th-grade DE student at Patterson Co-op. And I'd first like to bring you greetings from the distributive education department and everyone at Patterson. Now, first of all, if Ronald Reagan were here I'd ask him why he isn't striking like all the rest of the actors, but I'd like to ask you: Do you have any plans for allocating additional funds for vocational education or education in general in the coming years?

THE PRESIDENT. Yes. Just since I've

been in office we have done two things basically—three things for education that are very notable. One is, we have created the new Department of Education, because formerly education was buried under health and welfare, and there was no way for a local school board, a teacher or a parent or a Governor who is interested in better education in a community or State to find who in Washington was directly responsible for education. So, now we've got a new Department of Education, a new Secretary of Education, a highly qualified woman, and that's one step in the right direction.

Another one is what I described earlier about the guarantee that any young person who finishes high school without regard to economics can go to college and find a way to finance it. All they've got to do is qualify to do college work.

And the third thing is that we've increased substantially our commitment in Federal money for education. In just this brief first 3 years we've increased Federal money going to education by 73 percent, an enormous increase. At the same time I've been very careful to leave control of the school system at the local level. I don't think the Federal Government ought to get involved in the curriculum or the hiring of teachers or how to handle education as it relates to the student teacher. But we do provide assistance in general for those who live in very poor areas or near a military base, where the taxes are not paid and the students are there, or problems of that kind—on vocational education of all kinds, distributive education would be included. We have had substantial increases, and we will continue that trend upward in the commitment of Federal funds for that need.

One very important connective part is the youth act that I described earlier in answer to one of the questions about minority employment. This $2 billion that

we'll put into youth employment will be a 50-percent increase in the next 2 years. It'll provide literally hundreds of thousands of jobs for young people like you at the junior and senior high school level or perhaps a little bit older, who in the past have not been able to get a job.

The good thing about this for taxpayers is that these jobs will not be in government jobs. They'll be in private employment, where a young person can go to work there and for the first few weeks the government will help pay part of the salary until that young person goes through a training program and then can handle the full job himself or herself. And if they need a special remedial course in high school, say, like in mathematics, then they'll get that remedial course at night while they hold a full-time job in a local business opportunity.

So, that will be a tremendous, $2 billion increase above and beyond what we've already done, specifically designed for youth education and employment that would tie directly to the program that you're in.

MILITARY PERSONNEL AND ENLISTMENT

Q. Good afternoon, sir. I'm Major Paul Davis from Wright-Patterson Air Force Base, and I'm a firm believer in a strong and smart military as a deterrent to conflict. In your recent signing of the military pay increases you offered some inducement for the all-volunteer force, and while it is a step, it certainly doesn't go all the way to help us recruit and retain the topnotch people that we need in tomorrow's military. What additional inducements are you going to offer in your next administration to help us?

THE PRESIDENT. We've had several appropriations bills that I have signed since I've been in office, amounting to more than $2 billion in increased pay and benefits for military people. The last one, the so-called Nunn-Warner bill, was just signed recently, and that's the one to which you refer. It primarily increases pay in general. It also provides more housing allowance and also helps with transportation allowance, and, I believe, in addition will help encourage people to reenlist, particularly at the mid-skill level among petty officers who in the past have not done so.

I'm committed to the volunteer military force. The registration for the draft which I supported strongly does not lead to a draft. It's just the registration of young people 18 and 19 years old so that we'll know where they are, and if we do have to mobilize our forces it can be done expeditiously. It'll save us 90 to 100 days. One of the things that we've done in that registration in which about 95 percent of the young people signed up on time, was to have a block on the form that they fill out if they want to get more information about a career in the military forces. Fifteen percent of all those who signed up said they would like to get information about a career in the military forces. That will help us with recruitment. That's part of the answer to your question.

Another thing is that we are trying to explore ways now to extend the time that military personnel are assigned to one particular location, to minimize how much time they have to spend going to and from training courses, of schools, and going to a new assignment. I think a more stable assignment of military people will help to let their lives be better and to tie them more closely with the civilian community around them.

I was in the Navy for 11 years, 7 years after I finished at Annapolis, and spent the last part of my life in submarines. A lot of that time was at sea. We have had some very long, extended cruises for some of our ships in the Indian Ocean, as you know, since the hostages were captured by Iran, but in general we're trying also to explore ways where the families of military people, men or women, can be both closer to them, assigned to the same place where the military persons are assigned, and to let that rotation from unpopular or unpleasant foreign stations be more rapid.

That's the combination of a few things that we'll do in the future, and I think there's a general trend upward in the number of women who are volunteering for the military forces. We see a great opportunity there for good careers for women and, of course, only the actual combat roles are excluded for women's service now. And I think this will open up opportunities for Americans that didn't have it before, and this is a very fine chance for me to put in a plug for that.

Thank you very much, Major. I'm glad to talk to you.

Q. Thank you, sir.

REGISTRATION AND THE DRAFT

Q. Good afternoon, Mr. President. My name is Mary Turner, and my home is here in Dayton, Ohio. My question is about the young men 18 and over that are now registered for the draft and are attending college.

THE PRESIDENT. Yes.

Q. I would like to know, if and when the time should come that they would be called to duty to defend this country, how long would they have to attend college, would they be able to finish the year, and when they come back, would they be able to attend college under some kind of education program like the last bill of rights for GI's?

THE PRESIDENT. Mary, let me answer. That's a good question and it's probably on a lot of people's minds.

First of all, there is not going to be any draft imposed anytime in the future. I hope we will never see the reimposition of the draft. The only circumstances under which we could have draft of young people would be if our national security was in danger, that we had to defend ourselves, and even then the Congress would have to pass a new law setting up authorization for young people to be drafted. That's one part of the question. So, you need not worry about some unforeseen threat to our Nation that we're going to have any draft at all. We're going to continue with the volunteer military forces.

Secondly, if we ever do have another draft, I am not in favor of excluding college students. I want them to be drafted along with everybody else, because in the past, quite often the children of the poorer families were the ones that were drafted, and anybody that could scrape up enough money to put their young men in college avoided the draft. I think if we do have another threat to our national security serious enough to have the draft, we will not have a college exclusion, as far as I'm concerned.

And the third thing is that we will continue the GI bill benefits, certainly, if that should ever come to pass. It's not going to come to pass. We won't give college students special privileges. If it should come to pass, then we will certainly have GI privileges and other benefits for veterans as we have had in the past.

INFLATION

Q. Good afternoon, Mr. President. My name is Johnnie Pope, and welcome to Dayton.

THE PRESIDENT. Thank you, Johnnie.

Q. My first question is: Does Federal deficits contribute to inflation? Also, if reelected, what's your long-range plan to combat inflation?

THE PRESIDENT. Fine. Yes, Federal deficits do contribute to inflation. I don't think there's any doubt about it. The Federal deficit size is one of the major factors in the attitude of people. The financial community, the business community, the average family, all of their attitudes are influenced by how big the Federal deficit is.

When I was running for President in 1976, the Federal deficit was 4½ percent of our gross national product; that is, it was 4½ percent of everything this Nation produced. Now, we've cut that deficit down to about a third as much of our gross national product, and we're still making progress to bring it down.

Other things are much more inflationary in nature than just the Federal deficit. How much money is available in the community—by the community I mean the whole Nation—is a very serious cause of inflation. If you have a lot of money available floating around for a given amount of bread and clothes and automobiles and refrigerators, then people tend, in effect, to bid against each other and force the price of those products up. One cause of a lot of money floating around is people don't save the money. And Americans need to save more of their money in order to reduce the amount of inflationary pressure there.

Another factor, of course, is the price of goods over which we have no control. The biggest cause of inflation right now has been—the biggest single cause has been the explosion in the price of OPEC oil, where they, as I said earlier, more than doubled the price of oil in 1 year. So, that kind of price forced on us is a very important cause of inflation.

What we've done there and what we'll continue to do in the future is to hold down the Federal deficits, try to encourage people to invest in new plants and new tools, and also to save their money so that it can be loaned to people to buy new houses and so forth, and to cut down our dependence on imported oil.

We've passed now legislation to set up a very good national energy policy—the first time we've ever had one in our history—and we're saving energy and not wasting it anymore and producing more American energy, not only producing more coal than any year in history, but we also have more oil wells and natural gas wells being drilled this year than any year in history. So, as we cut down on the amount of oil we bring into this country, we control inflation. We'll continue that in the future. This day and every day in 1980 we're buying 2 million barrels of oil less than we were the first year I was in office. We're making good progress there.

So, those are the kind of things that we're doing now and in the future to hold down inflation.

Q. Thank you, sir.

THE PRESIDENT. Thank you. Good question.

NATIONAL SECURITY

Q. Good afternoon, Mr. President. I'm Dave Ponitz, and I live in Centerville. Being 13 and being aware of this summer's registration for the draft and its direct effect on me, I wonder if you intend to reinstate the draft or anything similar in the foreseeable future?

THE PRESIDENT. Okay. David, by the time you get to be 18 or 19, I believe that we will still have a nation militarily strong enough and with a philosophy of commitment to peace that will prevent the need for draft. Our country is the strongest on Earth. Militarily, economically, politically, we're the strongest nation on Earth. Our influence is greater than that of any other nation. Our moral and ethical standards, I believe, are unequaled anywhere on Earth. The Ameri-

can people are committed to peace, and I believe that that will continue.

This election will help to shape those attitudes for the future. One of the elements of maintaining peace, in my judgment, is the control of nuclear weapons. Ever since Harry Truman was President back in 1948–1952, every President, Democrats or Republicans—Eisenhower, Nixon, Ford, Johnson, Kennedy—have favored negotiating with the Soviet Union an agreement to have equal nuclear weapon arsenals to limit how many weapons we can both have and, over a period of time, to lower those levels.

We have concluded the SALT II treaty. Ford and Nixon began the negotiations. I concluded them. Yesterday I read an article where Governor Reagan said that we should abandon the SALT II treaty and use a nuclear arms race as a new card to play against the Soviet Union to try to induce them to lower their commitment to nuclear weapons. This is the kind of thought or proposal that is very serious in its consequences. If the American people get the idea, which is mistaken, that a nuclear arms race on our side is going to cause the Soviets to quit building nuclear weapons on their side, they are silly, because we would not let the Soviets build theirs up to a high level and then have us hide in a closet and say, "Okay, go ahead and take over." And there's no way that we or the Soviet Union would negotiate for future arms control, nuclear weapons, if both sides were madly building as many nuclear weapons as the nation could support.

Also, this kind of talk or proposal directly violates the commitments that our Nation has made in the past to our allies around the world and to countries that don't have nuclear weapons. And it's a very serious matter to depart from a national commitment to peace and the control of weapons and propose a departure from that policy.

I believe the American people have sound judgment. And I believe the American people want to see nuclear arms controlled, and I don't believe the American people want to see a nuclear arms race begun by this country that might aggravate an already dangerous situation. And I believe that the American people are going to make the right judgment in 5 weeks that will continue us on the path to nuclear arms control and therefore to peace, and I believe that's what's going to happen. So, I don't think you have to worry.

Q. Mr. President, my name is Harlan Louis, and I go to school at Northmont Junior High.

THE PRESIDENT. What's your first name?

Q. Harlan.

THE PRESIDENT. Harlan. Thank you.

Q. Again, I'd like to wish you a very happy birthday.

THE PRESIDENT. Thank you.

PRESIDENTIAL CANDIDATES

Q. I would like to know—just suppose that you could not or you wouldn't run for President. Who would you rather become President, John Anderson or Ronald Reagan? [*Laughter*]

THE PRESIDENT. Well, during every townhall meeting I try to pick out one question that I don't answer. [*Laughter*] I believe the country would prefer a Democratic President, and if I could not run and could not be elected, at this moment my choice would be Fritz Mondale.

You'd make a good news reporter. [*Laughter*]

Q. Thank you.

THE PRESIDENT. What are you going to do when you finish school?

Q. I'm planning on being an attorney.

THE PRESIDENT. Oh, you'd be a good lawyer. I hope if I ever get into a lawsuit you're not on the other side. [*Laughter*]

Thank you, Harlan, very much.

VIEWS ON THE PRESIDENCY

Q. My name is Ken Day, and I'm a resident of Dayton, Ohio, and I'm a senior at Northridge High School. My question is: There have been predictions that every 20 years or election years ending in zero, the President dies in office. Are you concerned about this?

THE PRESIDENT. I've seen those predictions. I'm willing to take the chance. I don't say that in a silly way but even if I knew I would die in office if I were a President, I would still run for the office, because I think it's the most exciting and challenging and important position in the free world.

It's the highest elective office in the world; it's the office that's revered by the American people. For anybody in politics, you know, it's the ultimate achievement. The American people have given me an honor that I never dreamed of when I was your age, and I think it would be worth it even if I knew that it would end in some kind of tragedy.

The Presidency is a special job; it's a lonely job. You know, when you're elected President you're the only one that has authority to represent everyone in this Nation. The decisions that come to my desk are the most difficult and complicated that anybody gets. The ones that come to the Oval Office are the ones that can't be solved in your own family or in the city hall or country courthouse or in the Governor's office or State legislature; if they can't solve the questions there they come to me. It's a very serious challenge, but also a very exciting opportunity. Also you have good advisers; I've got an outstanding Cabinet. The Congress and I have had remarkably good cooperation in this first 3½ or so years.

We've been able to keep our Nation at peace. We've been able to keeping it move forward. And I'd like to continue those policies that we've established. It's been a long time since this country had a President who served two full terms. Eisenhower, who was elected in 1952—28 years ago—was the last President who served two terms. And I think it would be beneficial to our Nation to have a President who was experienced, who knew the job, who was dealing with a nation's problems in a period of transition and trial, when the rest of the world was looking to us for leadership, to continue to keep stability and progress moving as we've already established.

So for all those reasons, I'm not afraid. If I knew it was going to happen, I would go ahead and be President and do the best I could till the last day I could.

Q. Thank you.

THE PRESIDENT. One more question.

WHITE-COLLAR UNEMPLOYMENT

Q. Good afternoon, Mr. President. My name is Jeff Pace, and I am a public information officer for DAVEST, the Dayton Volunteer Employment Service Team. The Carter administration has made strides into the reemployment of unemployed Americans who wish to be reemployed. However, the bulk of the administration's energies has seemingly been toward the labor market. My question to you is: What programs are you initiating to reemploy the unemployed white-collar professional?

THE PRESIDENT. It is hard to provide special programs for the white-collar professional because of the lack of concentration of that particular group of employees in a certain location; also, because of the fact that the white-collar profession, most of them, has a fairly high educational level, and is comparatively mobile in that, if a certain class of jobs, say an insurance auditor or a certified public accountant job, should be lost in a certain community, they can find ready employment in a different community.

I don't have any plans to provide a resettlement or a retraining program for those who have lost their jobs specifically in the white-collar, executive, professional level. But in the military there's a very fine opportunity. We're not employing people in the Government service right now; we're trying to cut down on the total number of employees. But I think that there is an opportunity for college training with Federal assistance for those who need to be retrained for a different kind of career. And that college training with loans and grants, work-study programs are available to adults beyond the normal college age if they should require retraining for a different kind of profession.

I haven't answered your question well. It's a difficult question. I've really not thought it through as I should have; I haven't gotten his question before. But I think in our Nation with the employment force growing rapidly that someone who's qualified to do the kind of work you described will not have a permanent disability on a job.

You might be interested in knowing, for instance, that last month alone, even though we've had some problems with unemployment, we added about a half a million jobs—I think 470,000 jobs—in this country, and even in the automobile industry, each week for the last 6 weeks, we've added back about 4,000 automobile workers. So, I think the recession has bottomed out, and although I haven't answered your question adequately for you, with that narrow definition of employee, the prospects in my judgment to minimize the damage from the recession is much less [better] [2] than it was a few weeks ago.

Thank you very much.

Let me add another point. I don't have time for another question, I'm sorry.

I'm really sorry. Let me say this in closing. It's very helpful for me to come here to meet with you in an exciting community where you obviously have been in the forefront of American progress, and you've always been both eager and qualified to meet changing times. In a modern technological world there's no way to avoid change. We wouldn't want to stop change if we could. And every time we've had a shocking change, in most cases we've benefited from it. Our space program has added enormously to the breadth of benefits of American life in medicine, in science, and so forth.

When we changed many years ago from oil [wood] [3] to coal and later from coal to oil, American life was benefited with electricity for even rural homes and so forth. Now we are faced with the time of changing away from dependence on imported oil to a dependence on American energy and American ingenuity and American ability to conserve energy of all kinds that can give us an exciting life in the future. The OPEC Arab nations all put together only have about 6 percent of the world's energy reserves—6 percent. The United States by itself has 24 percent of all the energy reserves on Earth,

and ours are not just oil and gas—we've got a lot of that—but ours are geothermal supplies and shale oil and coal and tar sands, almost every kind of energy you can imagine.

I see in the future an exciting opportunity for Americans to have a better life, a life with families stronger, a life of more leisure and enjoyable time, a life with a higher quality of air and water and land, a life with greater freedom, a life with more equality of opportunity among Americans who are different from one another, a life where discrimination is eliminated, a life of more trust of government in itself, and a closer relationship between the average citizen and the people who are our elected officials. I see an America even stronger in the future than we've been in the past, with more friends around the world like the 1 billion new friends that we've just added recently in the People's Republic of China. And I see America using that strength for the maintenance of peace and the enhancement of human rights among all people on Earth.

This is the kind of future that we face. We don't face a future of which we need to be afraid or which we need to dread; it'll be an enjoyable, exciting, dynamic future. It's typical of what Americans have always demanded, always expected, and always had. And I would believe that my little daughter, Amy, who will be 13 this month and my granddaughter, Sarah, who is almost 2, will have a much better life in the future than I've experienced in my own. And we've already got, just the folks sitting here, the best life in the greatest nation of Earth.

Thank you very much.

NOTE: The President spoke at 12:02 p.m. in the Dayton Convention and Exhibition Center ballroom.

---

[2] White House correction.
[3] White Hourse correction.

Lansdowne, Pennsylvania

Remarks and a Question-and-Answer Session With Local Residents.   October 2, 1980

THE PRESIDENT. First of all, let me say to Joe and Bertha and their small family how delighted I am to be here. They've just about got the Nation covered with college students, and I've been very pleased to meet them.

Before I start I'd like to ask all of you in your own way, later on, to say a prayer for my mother. She's in the operating room right at this moment. She fell this morning and broke her hip, and she's very strong and very vigorous and in good spirits. I don't know whether she was riding a skateboard or surfing, but she's very active, as you know—82 years old, and I hope that she'll be all right.

I would like to say that this is a delightful experience for me to be in a neighborhood that's obviously well groomed. It's a little noisy; I don't see how you ever get any sleep with this crowd on the street. But I've really enjoyed having a chance to get ready to come out here.

Before I answer questions, I want to take just a couple minutes to remind all of you how God has blessed us in a nation of strength and freedom and diversity and concern about one another. Our Nation has been through a lot of trial and testing, through periods of difficulty when our existence was threatened and when the harmony of our people was really put to the severest possible challenge: in World War I, World War II, the Korean war, the Vietnam war, the Great Depression, the social changes that shocked our country when we removed the last vestiges of legal discrimination against black people, the threat to the integrity of the White House by the Watergate embarrassments. These kinds of things have afflicted our

country from time to time, but we've always pulled ourselves together. We've never lost our faith in God or in each other, and when our Nation was unified and when we could see clearly the question or the challenge or the problem or the obstacle, we've never failed to overcome it or to answer the questions.

Nowadays we've got some problems. The whole world has problems; almost every nation has much more serious problems than do we. And what you see in the news and hear on the radio is the argument and the debates and the differences and the temporary inconveniences and the changes that are taking place in our lives that we can't stop and don't want to stop that cause us to be concerned about the future. But what we need to remember is the underlying basic strength of the American people and our government.

This is a time of reassessment to think about our past and present and also to make plans for the future, and I'm very delighted to be with you to share for a few minutes your thoughts and your concerns and your questions. I hope to learn about your own community and about you in the few minutes we have together and also hope that you can learn something about me and about our country from the perspective of the Oval Office when I respond to your questions. So, I'll be glad to answer questions. I don't know who's going to decide——

Q. [*Inaudible*]

THE PRESIDENT. Thank you very much. I'm sorry—thank you very much.

Q. [*Inaudible*]

FEDERAL EMPLOYEES

THE PRESIDENT. Right on. Yes, sir— with the attractive white moustache.

Q. My question is, Mr. Carter, why you have not cut down the size of the Federal bureaucracy as you said you would?

THE PRESIDENT. As a matter of fact, we have. I've been in office 2½ years. We've had an inevitable growth with a 75-percent increase in Federal funding for education, with a steady upward growth in our military, with the new Energy Department, with a lot of things that our people need to have, better transportation systems. But on top of all that we've had several tens of thousands fewer Federal employees now than when I took office, and by now we've probably reduced the Federal rolls about 45,000. We've cut down on waste, and we've increased efficiency. We've still got a ways to go. But my hope and my commitment is to continue this downward trend in total number of Federal employees at the same time we have to meet the needs of an increasing population. And, of course, lately we've had an increase in the problems that have been brought on us by the unexpected increase, almost doubled and doubling the price of OPEC oil.

So, we've cut down on the total number of employees, We've cut down on the number of agencies and departments and at the same time increased services— still have a long way to go to improve it further.

Yes, ma'am?

HEALTH CARE PROGRAMS

Q. I'd like you to know that we certainly do pray for you and your wife. You're under a lot of pressure with things the way they are. We're concerned—I'm concerned in this part of the world that Federal funding is not available for mental health and child care.

Some of our agencies have had to close down. Do you see in the future help for that, for Federal funding?

THE PRESIDENT. Yes, ma'am. We have just gotten through the Congress—I have not yet signed into law—a landmark Mental Health Systems Act of 1980. It will strengthen mental health programs of all kinds. This is a result of a study that was done the first 2 years I was in office. My wife was the chairman of the group. She had hearings, I think, in 22 different cities around the Nation to let people who were experts in mental health care and who know the problems at the local and State level give her and then, through her and a commission, to me advice on what could be done.

I would guess next week I will go to one of the mental hospitals in the Washington or Virginia, Maryland area and sign this legislation, which would be the basis in the future for the entire mental health program.

On child health we've made substantial progress already. We put forward a so-called CHAPS legislation, which hasn't yet passed. But as far as programs like immunization and the prevention of disease is concerned, we've got that fairly well under control, with tremendous improvement in the percentage of young people who are immunized against preventable disease.

We need to have a nationwide comprehensive health insurance program, and the first implementation of that will be compatible with what we want to do to save money and to minimize Federal intrusion into the lives of our people. I'm in favor, for instance, of keeping the relationship between the private person and the choice of one's own physician. I'm in favor of continuing to use the private insurers as much as possible to provide the insurance coverage. And I'm in favor of having a maximum emphasis on prevention of disease rather than treatment of extended disease that could have been prevented. I'm in favor of having an emphasis on out-patient care rather than the incarceration of a patient permanently in the hospital or for an extended period in the hospital when it can be avoided. We also are going to emphasize the first phase step toward increased care for women and children—women during the prenatal period of childbearing and children with each year the age increasing until they're covered up to maybe 14 years old, but starting with the infants and then the small children.

This is the kind of program combined with a catastrophic health insurance for all families in the Nation. It will be the first step toward a more comprehensive program. But those are the principles involved. The emphasis has been and will be on the care for children under the general health, and I believe that you'll be pleased with the new bill that has been passed on mental health.

Thank you.

EQUAL RIGHTS AMENDMENT

Q. Mr. President, as a classroom teacher I'd like to first thank you for the strong support and commitment that you have given to improving public education in this country. I'd like to also, if you could, share with us your views as to why you think it is important that the ERA be passed soon and what significance do you attach to the fact that the Republicans have seen fit to exclude it from their goals for America?

THE PRESIDENT. Every Republican President in modern history has favored the equal rights amendment, and the Republican Party platform has strongly supported the equal rights amendment for 40 years. This is the first departure by the Republican Party from a commitment to the ERA. As a matter of fact, the Republican Party actually endorsed in its national platform the equal rights amendment before the Democrats did. It's hard for me to understand why the Republicans now have withdrawn their support for the ERA.

There's a lot of reasons to pass it, and I need not go into all of them, but it's important to women to have their rights protected. A lot of distortions have been put forward about ERA that have been absolutely misleading. The thought that it would eliminate American families, would encourage homosexuality, would require men and women to go to the same bathrooms, would mean that young girls would be drafted into the military forces—all those lies have been put forward in, so far, a very effective, highly publicized campaign to defeat ERA. What ERA says is this and this is the amendment: That [neither] [1] the Federal Government and no State governments can pass a law discriminating against women. That's it. And that is the amendment that's being opposed by people in such a fervent way. That's the amendment that's being opposed by Governor Reagan. I do not understand why.

There are hundreds and hundreds of laws all over this Nation in different States that deprive women of a right to own property if their husbands should die; that require a husband's signature before they can get title to an automobile, or in some places even a driver's license; the guarantee that at this time in the enlightened Nation that we love, a woman

---

[1] White House correction.

doing the same work for the same length of time requiring the same skills only gets 59 cents as much as a man gets a dollar for doing the same work. The fact is that women are the heads of a lot of households. Women have a normal lifespan greater than men, and there are a lot of widows, for instance.

I remember in Plains once there were 32 widows at one time and only 1 widower, and that's the total town and the widower was my wife's grandfather. But the point is that women have rights that have not yet been guaranteed in the Constitution, and it's the last remaining major need in our Nation, to realize the hopes and ambitions of our original founders that people would have an equal opportunity in this country.

So, I'm strongly in favor of it. We've got three States to go. I'll do all I can to get it passed.

PRESIDENT'S CAMPAIGN STYLE

Q. Mr. President, in the early days of your campaign the tone of your political commercials was very upbeat and positive as to your leadership qualities and to the loneliness of the job, et cetera. However, in the last week or so, the negative aspects of your campaign strategy have been evident in some unclear rhetoric in political television commercials attacking your opponents, et cetera—for instance, the Jesus Christ amendment and Mr. Anderson. Please comment on your use of religious institutions as a forum and if you approve of these TV commercials and the use of a little mudslinging maybe?

THE PRESIDENT. I've never heard of the TV spot that you referred to about Anderson and the Jesus Christ amendment. And, in fact, I've very carefully avoided any reference to Congressman

Anderson as well for political, tactical reasons, as well as others.

It is my responsibility as a candidate in the give-and-take political world that's part of a democracy not only to point out what I have done in the last 4 years, and not only to point out what I intend to do the next 4 years, but to point out in a legitimate and accurate way the differences between me and my major opponents.

For instance, the question about the equal rights amendment, it is a legitimate issue for me. It's not just enough for me to say, "I'm for it." I think it's legitimate for me to say that Ronald Reagan is against it and then let the people decide. There are many people who are against ERA, and when I make that point, that means they can decide if they wish that that's the only issue to vote for Mr. Reagan.

On the question of peace—which is another item that has come up recently in the news—I don't claim and have never thought that any President if they got in the Oval Office and were faced with crises in that lonely job would want war. But, it's legitimate for me to point out that in the last 8 or 10 years, whenever there's been a dispute around the world in a certain troubled region, Governor Reagan has repeatedly called for the sending of American military forces there. Off the coast of Equador, for instance, he advocated sending in the American Navy. Off the coast of Angola, in Cyprus, in Lebanon, in North Korea, in the Mideast—Mr. Reagan, I think 8 or 10 times, has called for the sending in of military forces when the obvious judgment made by me, since I've been President, and by Nixon and Ford and Johnson and Kennedy and Eisenhower and Truman, has been to avoid conflicts and to try to resolve those issues in a very troubled, tense part of the world in a diplomatic way. What Governor Reagan would do if he was in the Oval Office, I don't know. But that fact that he's called for military forces to be used repeatedly, time after time after time, is troubling to me.

There's another crucial issue that's come up in the last 2 days, and that is the control of nuclear weapons. Every President since Truman has tried to spell out the goal of SALT negotiations, the control of strategic arms or nuclear weapons. Nixon and Ford before me worked to get a SALT II treaty. I finally concluded the SALT II treaty with President Brezhnev. It puts limits on both the Soviets and us at roughly equivalent levels and would require the Soviets to go, incidentally, to dismantle about 10 percent of their total missiles.

Governor Reagan said the day before yesterday that he was going to do away with SALT II if he were elected, start a nuclear arms race, and use it as a card to be played against the Soviet Union. That is an extremely serious proposal, and I think his inability to understand the consequences of it and the attitude of American people who have, in the past, Democrats and Republicans, been in favor of limiting arms. And now for a potential President to advocate a nuclear arms race is a shocking thing to many people and of concern to me, just the atmosphere in our own country. Also, our allies in Europe and around the world are intensely interested in the United States being committed to controlling nuclear weapons. And the Soviet Union is also committed to the control of nuclear weapons. And for Mr. Reagan to think that if we start a massive nuclear arms race, which he proposes, and that the Soviet Union is going to all of a sudden abandon their construction of nuclear weapons, he's mistaken. We wouldn't do

that on the other side. And that's the kind of threat, I think, that the stability of the peaceful inclination of the world that I feel obligated to point out.

I'm not insinuating that Mr. Reagan wants war. I'm not insinuating that he's a warmonger. The thing that I'm insinuating or stating clearly is that all the previous Republican Presidents have advocated the most fervent continual negotiations to limit, have equal, and then reduce nuclear weapons. Mr. Reagan's proposal is a radical departure from what they've advocated in the past.

So, this is the kind of thing that might have the tone of being negative, but is really a legitimate part of the political debate that has always taken place in this country during a Presidential election. And I think I would be doing myself a disservice and the Nation a disservice if I only pointed out how great and how good I am, or the accomplishments we've had for the last 4 years, all the hopes that I have for the next 4 years, and not draw vividly in the minds of the American people the real differences between me and Governor Reagan.

TRADE POLICIES

Q. Mr. President, in the past several years we have seen our garment industry, our auto industry, and our steelmill production go down; a lot of them have closed up because of foreign imports. In your next 4 years in office, do you have plans to have some of these foreign countries do more business in the United States to put our people back to work and limit some of the imports that we're taking in from their country?

THE PRESIDENT. Yes. We've had good luck already with the so-called Multilateral Trade Negotiation settlements on textiles.

Not too long ago I was down in Spartanburg, South Carolina, and their whole economy is built around textiles. And I noted then that in the last 2 years alone, since we had this new phased bill passed, that we have increased our textile exports by $2 billion and by several hundred million square yards; we have reduced the total amount of textile imports coming into our country. So, this is a very new achievement that was unlikely 3 years ago, with imports going down and American textile exports going up.

Secondly, on steel—yesterday, day before yesterday now, as a result of 2 years of hard work with me and the Steel Workers Union member leaders and the executives of the steel industry we worked out an approach to put the steel industry back on its feet. Actually imports from overseas of steel have gone down with the trigger price mechanism that we put into effect after I became President. We are now seeing a steady increase of American steel production along with it and a high utilization of the steel facilities than we had before. We've advocated for passage next year, not now, a special tax program that would make investment tax credits refundable and also to give accelerated depreciation allowances for steel companies that could invest and modernize our plants.

Not long ago I was in Perth Amboy, New Jersey, to visit a small steelplant that's modern just to show what America can do. It's the most modern steelplant in the world. The average worker in that Perth Amboy steelplant produces more steel per year than in any other plant in the world. I asked them what they were doing with the steel. They make steelrods about as big as my little finger and in big bales a ton at a time, and 50 percent of all their steel is going halfway around the world to China. An American steel company with modern techniques, and we're better than anybody in doing the modern things, can make steel and ship it that far and sell it to China cheaper than the Japanese can produce it and ship it just a few hundred miles across the China Sea to China. That's the steel industry. I think that's the one in good shape.

Yesterday I was in Detroit and Flint, Michigan, visited the Ford plant in Wayne County, Detroit. They are now producing American automobiles that are safer, more durable, and just as energy efficient as any you can buy in the world. I don't know how many of you all have foreign automobiles, but I hope the next time you go to trade that you'll go into the American showrooms and look over the American products. now and compare it with what you can buy from overseas. You can think about American jobs if you want to, but make your own judgment about what's best for your family and what's best for our country. Make your own judgment, but I can tell you that every one of those new automobiles rolling off the assembly line, there's somebody waiting to buy it.

One of the cars that I had waiting for me at the airport when I arrived in Detroit was a Volkswagen, and then I had American Motors and Chrysler and Ford and Chevrolet cars there too, just to show me what the new products look like. I asked the Volkswagen-America manager what portion of all the Volkswagens that are sold in our country are now made in our country. Seventy percent of the Volkswagens sold in the United States are now built in the United States, and we're getting the Japanese to move more and more into our country, not only to buy our parts for their cars but also to build the Japanese-made cars in the United States. So, we're putting as much legitimate influence or pressure on those foreign countries to treat our workers right as we possibly can.

So, in those industries that you mentioned—textiles, steel, and automobiles—making good progress.

Coal, of interest to some Pennsylvanians—you might be surprised to know that this year the United States will produce more coal than any year in the history of our Nation. And we could produce more if we had the port facilities to load it and ship it overseas. But we've had such an explosion in production and foreign sale of American coal that we really literally don't have a way to load it fast enough on ships and send it to the customers overseas. That's coming very rapidly, and the coal industry is going to really be healthy in the future. And my hope is that eventually as a major energy source we can replace OPEC oil with Pennsylvania coal. That's what I want to see happen.

One other point is this: You've got anthracite coal, and I just came from Ohio where they have very high-sulfur coal. With our new windfall profits tax fund we'll be producing now from coal synthetic fuels, clean-burning gas, clean-burning liquids, from those kinds of coal that in the past have not been popular. And this will give us a new opportunity to increase further coal to be used in our own Nation. And we've got a proposal in the Congress now that will require electric powerplants to shift away from burning oil and natural gas to burning American coal. So, in every way we're moving forward on the energy front. And I think now that we've got an energy policy in place, that Bob Edgar and the other Members of the Congress helped me get done, we've got a foundation to revitalize the entire American economic system and to give us an exciting future.

It was a shock to this country when we changed from wood to coal, but the result was we had millions of new jobs and a better life for people. It was a shock to this State and other States when we shifted from coal to oil, but it gave us a new possibility for a better life. And I predict to you that shifting away from foreign oil to more conservation and more American energy will give us a new chance in the 1980's to have an even more exciting life than we've had in the past, and using American high technology and research and development and our superb education system and our free enterprise system that encourages innovation, we'll be on the cutting edge of progress and change and benefit not only our country but other countries as well.

So I look forward to the future with confidence, not with fear.

FEDERAL RESERVE SYSTEM

Q. Mr. President, about a year ago the Fed changed its way of dealing with monetary policy.

THE PRESIDENT. Yes, I know.

Q. As you know. Since that time do you think that the experience has been that this new method has shown us that the monetary supply can be, in fact, controlled by the Government, that it is a better way to deal with the problems of inflation? And finally, how would you evaluate Mr. Volcker's performance in dealing with the new policy?

THE PRESIDENT. Let me predicate my reply by saying that under the American law, the Fed is independent of the President. It's just like the judicial system. I don't have any influence on it, but that doesn't mean I have to sit mute. My own judgment is that the strictly monetary approach to the Fed's decision on the discount rate and other banking policies is ill-advised. I think the Federal Reserve Bank Board ought to look at other factors and balance them along with the supply of money.

Now, in my judgment, too much of their decision is made just by measuring the amount of money available in our system, both the M–1, M–2 supplies of money. I think that the Fed ought to look at the adverse consequences of increased interest rates on the general economy as a major factor in making their own judgments.

I might add that the Congress and I together would have the ultimate authority to override some of the consequences of a Fed decision. But that's a very complicated process and creates unwise conflict and controversy within the economic system. I think Paul Volcker is an outstanding Chairman, a highly qualified, very brilliant man, and he has to look, as do I also, at the value of the dollar overseas, the international stability that must be maintained in the monetary system of the entire world. He has to look at our trade balance, and he has to look at the economy and how it grows and the impact on our gross national product. All those things are some minor factors, but I think they put too much of their eggs in the money supply basket and are not adequately assessing the other factors that I've outlined.

I've got to answer one more question. Yes, right here.

VIEWS ON THE PRESIDENCY

Q. Mr. President, there are so many demands on you. Please tell me what you'd like us to do to make your job easier during the next 4 years.

THE PRESIDENT. Okay. I wouldn't say you would make my job easier the next 4

years depending on what you do in the next 5 weeks. [*Laughter*]

Well, let me close. I think it might be good and interesting to you, to close, just to outline my own feelings about the Presidency itself.

For anyone involved in politics, I think the ultimate goal would be to occupy the Oval Office as the President of this great country, because it's the highest elective office, certainly, in the free world. It's also an office that is respected and revered by the American people, because I'm the only elected officer with authority to represent all the American people.

It's a lonely job. And there are a lot of crises that come to my desk in the Oval Office. If I handle those crises well, then the likelihood is that you never know about it. If I handle the crises poorly, it could have an adverse effect on every life in the United States and perhaps the entire world. I have good advisers; I have a superb Cabinet. They're politically sensitive as well as being highly qualified. They work with me on issues that are important to our country, but there's a limit to what a Cabinet can do.

The questions that I get as President are the most difficult ones of all. They are the questions that can't be answered in your own family or in a city hall or county courthouse or they can't be answered in a Governor's office or a State legislature. If they can be answered in those places, then I don't ever hear about them. But if they cannot be answered there, they come to me and I have to make an ultimate judgment. I consult with my counselors.

My experience has been though that if the question is extremely serious and important and very difficult to answer, that my advisers are most likely to be split fifty-fifty, with half of them saying no and half of them saying yes, because you have a natural difference, for instance, between the Secretary of Treasury on the one hand, and the Secretary of Labor on the other, because the Secretary of Labor and those Secretaries responsible for health and for human services and for education are naturally inclined to want to spend more money to alleviate the need of their constituency group. The Secretary of Commerce, the Secretary of Treasury, and others are much more inclined to want fiscal stability and a restraint on spending and lower deficit and more rigid attention to the bureaucracy of government. So, when an issue is extremely important the responsibility comes down to the President. I don't deplore it, but I just point out to you the importance of the office and the gratitude that I have to be able to hold it.

I've learned a lot in the last 3½ years. I was in local government, I was in the State senate for two terms, I was Governor of Georgia, I campaigned for President for a long time. But I was not prepared in any of those ways for what I found when I got to the White House, and no one else could be who hasn't actually served there, because it's a unique job. A Congressman or U.S. Senator cannot prepare himself or herself to be President through past experience. I've been in there for 3½ years; I've learned a lot. I've learned about our own country; I've learned about our people, the conflicting demands that are made on government; I've learned about the organizational structure of our Government; I've learned about foreign countries; I've learned about the leaders of foreign countries; I've learned about the troubled places in the world and what can we do to avoid war and to perpetuate peace. I've negotiated with people who see things differently.

I've tried to be a peacemaker when I could. I've tried to exert the beneficial influence of our Nation in human rights and in other areas for the benefit of the other people of the world. So, I think the experience that I've had will pay rich dividends in the next 4 years.

I can do a better job, I think, the next 4 years. I've made some mistakes. I'm sure I've done many things with which all of you disagree. But I have to balance all of the conflicting interests that come before the Government and essentially work in harmony with the Congress.

The reassuring thing about all this political job of being President in this country is that I have a lot of partners. I've got 230 million partners who feel that you're a part of me and part of our country, part of its problems, part of its glory, part of its weaknesses, when there are weaknesses, part of its strength, part of its failures, part of its achievement. And I don't feel lonely because of that, and what I need most of all is to stay as close as possible to the American people. To the extent that you know the issues and you understand the reasons why I make decisions, my voice is stronger and I'm less likely to make a serious mistake.

When we have made serious mistakes in recent years—Watergate, maybe Vietnam, the CIA revelations—when we were embarrassed, it's been because things were done in secret and the American people were misled, not told the truth, or weren't involved in making the decisions. So, the best insurance that I have is for you to understand my job, and that's why I'm so grateful to Joe and to Bertha for letting me meet with you in their backyard this afternoon. I've learned a lot, and I think I'll be a better President because of it.

Bob, I'm glad to see you. I'm glad you came.

Representative Edgar. Mr. President,

I jogged from Lansdowne Avenue over to visit with you. I came in from Washington on the last plane possible, and I just wanted to say on behalf of all of the people who are here and on behalf of the people of Delaware County, we not only thank you for coming to Delaware County today to participate in this public forum, but we thank you for the *Saratoga*, the Defense Contracting Agency, the compromise on the Blue Route, the Reynolds plant, and a lot of other things that you've done.

Thank you.

THE PRESIDENT. If I've got one final thing to thank you for, it's for sending a Congressman like Bob Edgar to Washington to help me.

NOTE: The President spoke at 4:42 p.m. outside the home of Mr. and Mrs. Joseph Phillips.

Philadelphia, Pennsylvania

Remarks at a Democratic National Committee Fundraising Reception.
October 2, 1980

My good friend, Mayor Bill Green, wonderful ally and strong supporter of mine and friend of yours and mine, Bill Batoff, fine city comptroller, Tom Leonard, other fellow Democrats, some of whom I've already met and shaken hands with, others whom I will meet in a few minutes:

That introduction was beautiful, and I appreciate it. It's kind of put me back in the best spirits. When I drove up in front of the hotel, a lot of people were very disappointed at my modest means of transportation this evening. I arrived by automobile. The Vice President arrived by aircraft carrier. [*Laughter*] And it just shows where I stand in the Carter/Mondale partnership. I do want to thank and congratulate Fritz. He arrived with an adequate degree of flair.

As a matter of fact, before he descended in the helicopter and came in, he even wanted to borrow my old Navy uniform which I had to lend him. Also, he came to Philadelphia Navy Yard for the first time as Vice President, and as some of you may know, I came to the Philadelphia Navy Yard for the first time as an ensign in the U.S. Navy in 1946, very shortly after Rosalynn and I were married. He made the front page and when I came there for the first time, I don't recall it being on the front page.

I think the arrival of the *Saratoga* here was a very important, tangible achievement, and it was not easy as many of you know. It was a very important symbolic achievement as well, because what we are going to accomplish with the *Saratoga* is exactly what Bill Green referred to in our desire and our commitment to accomplish for the entire Nation's economic system—refitting it, overhauling it, revitalizing it, modernizing it, providing jobs in the process, and showing the rest of the world that we can produce more, use it more efficiently, and make ours a better nation.

It also symbolizes our determination to keep this America secure, to keep it strong through a carefully considered and efficient program, to modernize and strengthen our national defense. I'm a professional military officer; I served in the Navy for 11 years. I'm a graduate of Annapolis. I was a submarine officer. I came here to go to radar school as a young ensign.

When I became President and went into the White House for the first time, I realized that in the 8 years preceding my inauguration, 7 of those years we had a decrease in the commitment of American dollars to strengthen American defenses.

We were going steadily downhill. Since then, every year since I've been in office, and the commitment for this fiscal year that just began yesterday and for the next 4 years, we'll have a steady increase in our commitment to our Nation's defense in real dollars above and beyond inflation.

It's been more than 50 years since a President could stand before a group like this and say, "Since I've been in the White House, I've not had to send an American soldier into combat." And I pray to God that when I go out of office, I will have a sustained record of peace. The peace must come from American strength. The best weapon is one that's never fired in combat, and the best soldier is one that never has to shed his blood on the field of battle. Our Nation's strength gives us peace. It also gives us the influence and the flexibility and the commitment and the idealism and the desire and the goal of the American people to extend that beneficial peaceful influence to others. That's one of the choices that is going to be made on November the 4th.

A crucial element of peace is the dealing with crises in the Oval Office. They arrive there often, a steady stream of them. And if they are handled properly, quite often you never know about them; they never become a headline in the news. But if a potential crisis is handled improperly, it can affect the life of every person in this Nation, perhaps every person in the entire world.

This is not a partisan commitment, to handle crises and to keep our Nation on the road toward sustained peace, with the consciousness of every American exemplifying that desire. Every President since Harry Truman, Republican and Democrat, has been committed to the proposition that our Nation has as its major goal the protection of our security and, along with it, the control of nuclear weapons. President Ford, President Nixon before him, and I worked to forge the SALT II treaty with the Soviet Union to provide for balanced, limited, and then reducing the level of nuclear armaments.

Yesterday I read the report where my opponent said that he's going to abandon the SALT II treaty and substitute for it an American nuclear arms race as a card to be played against the Soviet Union. That concerns me very deeply as President. And I believe that the lack of understanding of Governor Reagan about its impact on the consciousness of America and about the attitudes of our allies and the attitudes of nations all over the world who don't have nuclear weapons and the attitude of our potential adversaries, including the Soviet Union, can be quite profound.

There is no way for our Nation to embark on a nuclear arms race to try to force the Soviet Union into abandoning their commitment to escalated nuclear armaments. It would spell the end, in my opinion, of any possibility of this sustained effort that all Presidents have maintained.

There are other sharp differences. Everywhere I go, I get questions about the equal rights amendment. Our Nation has made steady progress since it was founded in concept here in your city to constantly broaden the commitment of our country to equality of opportunity, to give voting rights to people to elect their own senators, to give young people, black people, women the right to vote.

Every Republican President in modern days, the Republican Party platform for 40 years has committed itself to the equal rights amendment until this year. This is abandonment of the right of women to be treated equally. All this amendment says is that neither the Federal Government nor any State government can pass a law which discriminates against women. That's all it says—a simple, but very important commitment of the American people. And for one who hopes to be President of this country to abandon that commitment, to me, is a profound change, not only in this country's policies but in the policies of the Republican Party. I think we have got to guarantee women's rights in the Constitution of the United States of America.

There's another choice that will be made on November the 4th that affects every one of you, and that's the economic future of this Nation. We've been shocked the last few years, since 1973, with pressure from suppliers of oil, foreign countries, OPEC, Arab nations. We had a constant escalation in the percentage of oil we imported prior to the time that I became President.

We began working on an energy policy, which the Congress, with Bob Edgar's help, has now put into effect. The American people have been convinced by me as President and by others, including some of you, that we've got to conserve energy and produce more American energy. We've already had beneficial results. This year every day we are importing 2 million barrels of foreign oil less than we did the first year I was in the White House—a sustained protection of our Nation's economy and also our Nation's security, because anyone who thinks will know that we are not free to exercise our foreign policy if we should become subject to blackmail from foreign oil suppliers. And to achieve our energy security is an important commitment of this Nation. It's one that I've exemplified. It's one that the Nation has responded with effectiveness.

My opponent wants to abolish the windfall profits tax. He said the day be-fore yesterday he wants to abolish the Department of Energy. He wants to eliminate conservation measures, including the 55-mile-per-hour speed limit. He wants to let the oil companies decide the energy policy of our country. This is a sharp departure from what America has decided and, in my judgment, would have severe consequences for our country.

The base that we've built now with an energy policy will permit us to go forward toward a vitalized, exciting, dynamic, successful new economic system. American workers are already the most productive on Earth. We need to keep them that way by giving them new tools and new factories. Coal production, the highest this year of any year in the history of our Nation. Oil and gas wells, the highest number being drilled this year of any year in history.

The day before yesterday—yesterday, rather, I was in Detroit, in Flint, Michigan, seeing brand new American automobiles coming off the assembly line, safer, more durable, and just as fuel efficient as any produced on Earth; workers excited about the quality of their product, asking American buyers, now that the products are here, to go into their American dealers' showroom and look at those products and then make a judgment about what's best for your family and our country in your decision for a new automobile.

The steel industry, which has been on its knees, is now prepared, through refundable tax credits and a commitment that I have for next year to give accelerated depreciation and to reestablish the trigger price mechanism to protect our industry from excessive foreign imports and dumping. This has revitalized the possibility of this basic industry to restore itself.

We've got so many advantages economically that if we can take advantage of our free enterprise system, the entrepreneurial attitude of Americans, the freedom and worth of the individual human being, our superb research and development capabilities and education institutions, there is no doubt in my mind that we can move forward and be the cutting edge of progress and set an example not only for Americans but for the rest of the world. But it's going to require a firm hand at the tiller of the ship of state and a policy that will be progressive in nature.

The Reagan-Kemp-Roth tax proposal, which could be implemented in the future, would be a devastating blow to the economy of our country. Instead of investing in new investments, it has 90 percent of it going for personal tax breaks primarily to the wealthy Americans, perhaps to many of you. But it's highly inflationary in nature, and it's not fair to the American people. This kind of an approach also would put a tremendous additional burden on the property taxpayers of this Nation if major Federal programs are shuffled away from the Federal Government responsibility onto State and local government.

The last thing I'd like to say to you, as Democrats and as my friends, is that Philadelphia and Pennsylvania will play an important role in the outcome of this election and in the future of our Nation. It's happened in the past, as you know. You played a major role for me in 1976, and you played a major role back in 1960 when the Democratic organization, led by Bill Green's father, Congressman William Green, decided the outcome of the race in Philadelphia, Pennsylvania, and nationwide. And as all of you remember, in 1968 if just a few of us had had a deeper commitment to support a wonderful Democrat, Hubert Humphrey, the course of history would have been different, and he would have been President instead of Richard Nixon.

These last few weeks will make the difference on November the 4th, and that will make the difference, not just in the next 4 years but I believe for the rest of this century, to set a course for our Nation to follow.

I'm grateful for Bill Green. I know what he can do. It's really good for us now to be on the same side, and this time he and I both are going to win.

And I think I'd like to close my remarks by referring to another person on the stage with me, Bill Batoff, a man who made this reception possible, who's been my staunch friend and supporter through thick and thin, who's helped me politically and personally and financially. He stands with the Democratic Party as a staunch leader. He's a man who loves this country dearly. He's a man who supports the great principles on which it was founded. He's a man who believes in peace for us and peace in the Middle East.

My most vivid impression or memory of Bill Batoff is when he and I sat at the same table at the White House with President Anwar Sadat of Egypt, as we honored the historic treaty between Israel and its most powerful Arab neighbor. I remember Bill because he and Sadat were the only two smoking pipes that evening. And I know that he shares my commitment to a lasting peace; that's a very important thing.

A secure Israel at peace with its neighbors is a direct investment in security and peace for our country. It's not a gift or a handout or an act of benevolence. It's an investment that I have, as a President, in the security and peace of my own country. And I'm committed to that proposition—that if I live and if I stay in office, we're going to have a comprehensive peace for Israel and the entire Middle East.

Shortly after the election, I expect to be having another summit meeting with

President Anwar Sadat and Prime Minister Begin. We'll be pursuing then the obstacles that still remain. It's just one of a vast array of items still on the agenda, including those I've already mentioned to you where we've made good progress.

We have a great deal of which we can be proud, but our work has not yet been completed. I need a lot of partners, and some of the partners I have are here tonight. And I am very grateful to you as my partners as you work together to make the greatest nation on Earth even greater in the future.

And now I would like to shake the hands of everyone here and thank you personally for your commitment and your support and our confidence in our country.

Thank you very much.

NOTE: The President spoke at 6:18 p.m. in the North Cameo Room at the Fairmont Hotel.

Philadelphia, Pennsylvania

Interview With Correspondents of WCAU–TV. October 2, 1980

Q. We are live in the Ambassador Suite of the Fairmont Hotel in Philadelphia with the President of the United States, Jimmy Carter. Welcome to Philadelphia, Mr. President.

THE PRESIDENT. I'm glad to be here.

ADMINISTRATION ACCOMPLISHMENTS

Q. Some of the questions that we're including in this program were solicited from our viewers last night. They phoned it in at 6 and 11 o'clock last night. And I'd like to begin with a question from Nicholas Schiller, of Windmore. He says, "Mr. President, you asked to be elected in 1976 because you said you could restore confidence. Confidence is nowhere to be seen. Why should you be reelected now?"

THE PRESIDENT. I think we've got a lot more confidence now than we had in '76. At that time we were coming out of the time of great shock to our Nation, with the Vietnam war, the Watergate scandals, the CIA revelations. The unemployment rate was extremely high. Farm income was at an abysmal low.

Since then we've had, I think, notable success. Our country's been at peace for 3½ years. We created 8½ million jobs. We've made good progress in resolving the biggest single threat to our domestic and economic prosperity, and that was the energy crisis brought about by excessive dependence on foreign oil. And now with that energy base intact, we're ready to revitalize the American industrial complex. We've also begun to weather the threat that existed to the steel industry. I think the new steel program will put it back on its feet.

This year, for instance, we will produce more coal than any year in the history of our Nation. We'll drill more oil and gas wells than any year in our history. And we've got a good prospect in the future to have OPEC oil as a major worldwide energy source replaced with Pennsylvania coal. So, there's plenty of reason to be confident now about the future.

NEW JERSEY ELECTION RESULTS

Q. Mr. President, in the past few hours you've talked to voters, both here in Philadelphia and its suburbs, and now by being with us here on TV tonight you're also talking to the voters of New Jersey, which is the State I cover and which is a State that you must win. You didn't carry New Jersey 4 years ago. Given your track record there, coupled with the Anderson factor on the ballot this year, how do you expect to win New Jersey's 17 electoral votes?

THE PRESIDENT. Well, it's hard to depend on a State, but a lot can happen between now and November the 4th. The Anderson factor is significant because, in my judgment, a vote for Congressman Anderson is the same as a vote for Reagan. Lately there's been some indication that that factor is not as important as it was a few weeks ago.

I think we've got a good record for New Jersey people. They're interested also in the energy crisis. They're interested also in the revitalization of the steel industry. They're interested in the production of new jobs for Americans and in the modernization of tools and factories. I think they've seen that our Nation has stayed at peace, that our defense structure is much stronger than it was 4 years ago. So, I believe the same factors that are important in Pennsylvania and New York will also permeate the consciousness of the people in New Jersey.

I remember a couple years before, Brendan Byrne ran for reelection. I went to New Jersey to campaign with him, and his prospects were virtually almost nonexistent. And he came through with a roaring victory for the best interests of the people of New Jersey. So, I can't predict flatly that I'll win, but we've got a much better chance to carry New Jersey than we had in 1976.

Q. Is it a key State for you?

THE PRESIDENT. Yes, it is; certainly is.

AUTOMOBILE INDUSTRY

Q. Mr. President, as a consumer reporter I was very interested in your statement yesterday that America makes the most efficient and safest cars in the world. So, I have a related question. What has your administration done and what does it plan on doing about the widespread failure of the American car manufacturers to promptly and fairly act on complaints about defects of workmanship? In the tristate area, all the consumer protection agencies that I've talked to say the efforts of the American manufacturers range from inadequate to disgraceful.

THE PRESIDENT. We're going through a phase now of unbelievable change in the automobile manufacturing industry of our country, brought about primarily by the explosion in OPEC oil prices last year. The price of oil increased more in 1 year than it had since oil was first discovered. And the American automobile industry is retooling.

I was in a plant in Wayne County around Detroit yesterday and then went later to Flint. I went through the plant and drove off the assembly line one of the new Ford models and examined at the airport the new Ford, Chevrolet, American Motors, Chrysler, and Volkswagen American cars. In my judgment, those cars now in workmanship and those cars in durability and those cars in safety are as good or better than any in the world, and on efficiency they're very competitive.

We've learned a lesson in this country on automobile production. We were taking it for granted. There's a new interrelationship, too, between the automobile workers and the industrial management leaders and the Government. Three years ago we were all adversaries—the Government versus the industry, labor versus management. Now we're working as a team with the interests of the American automobile buyer as a first interest and the most important factor. And I believe that in the future, now and in the future, when Americans go to shop for an automobile, they'll see that this is a highly competitive car in workmanship and quality with any in the world, highly efficient, and that the automobile industry of our country deserves a fair chance with American buyers.

There have been defects in the past in the absence of efficiency and different buying styles for the country, but I don't have any doubt that in the future that quality will be there.

Q. What I was getting at was, what has the administration done to require the automobile industry to pay attention to the problems and complaints of the consumer? In other words, they're not taking care of them. Someone suggested, for example, that in return for all of the loans and loan guarantees, that the Government require some kind of arbitration program, because people are simply left out in the cold. They have no remedy today. They can't afford to take a lawsuit ordinarily. And the American manufacturers, in effect, are turning their back on the American people as far as settling complaints.

THE PRESIDENT. Well, I think both the Federal Trade Commission and the Department of Transportation have the authority to require an automobile manufacturer, either a domestic or a foreign manufacturer, to take back from a consumer an unsafe automobile or one that has an inherent defect in it and to repair that defect at no cost to the consumer. And the high publicity that is promulgated through all the news media of our country when there is a serious defect, in a tire or some component part of the automobile, is additional protection. As I say, we've not lowered but we've raised our standards for both the quality of American workmanship in automobiles and also the meeting of the efficiency standards that we've never had to meet before.

PRESIDENT'S CAMPAIGN STYLE

Q. As President, both John Anderson and Ronald Reagan have criticized you for "abusive remarks" and "scare tactics." Do you think that you're really taking the high road of this 1980 campaign?

THE PRESIDENT. Yes, I do. It's part of the American political system for candidates to do three things: one, to point out the previous record; secondly, to point out their visions or commitment for the future; and third, to point out the differences that exist between myself and my major opponents. That's been a part of democracy. And other than presenting those three views, the voters would have, I think, an inadequate basis on which to make a choice on November 4th. There are some honest differences between us.

I have never felt that Ronald Reagan was going to lead this Nation deliberately into war. But it is a legitimate issue to point out, for instance, that on numerous occasions the last 8 or 10 years, or even quite recently, he has advocated in trouble spots in the world the sending of American forces, American combat forces there to resolve differences—with Ecuador, with Cuba, with North Korea, Cyprus, Lebanon, many other places—when the incumbent President, myself or even my Republican predecessors, were trying to solve those same problems not with gunboat diplomacy or with American military forces but by diplomatic means.

Another very important thing on the so-called war and peace issue is the handling of nuclear weapons. Every President since Harry Truman, Democrat and Republican, including, of course, Eisenhower, Ford, Nixon—all the Presidents have been committed to a SALT agreement that would limit, balance, and then reduce nuclear weapons. Presidents Ford and Nixon, before me, and I culminated a SALT II agreement.

Day before yesterday Governor Reagan announced that he was going to abandon the SALT II agreement and replace it with an American nuclear arms race, to use his words, "to play as a card against the Soviet Union." This indicates to me that he has misunderstood the tremendous importance of that radical change from previous postures of Presidents since the nuclear weaponry came into being, beacuse the change in the psychology or attitude of American people, influenced by a President, away from controlling nuclear weapons and the impact on our allies and friends and the impact on nations that don't have nuclear weapons and the impact on the Soviet Union to know that it's no longer fruitful for them to join in with us in limiting nuclear weapons is a very, very important issue. And I feel the responsibility as a candidate to make clear that extreme difference between me and him on that important issue.

Q. But isn't it kind of harsh to suggest in a Presidential campaign that a vote for Ronald Reagan could be a vote for war? Isn't that kind of strong?

THE PRESIDENT. That would be too harsh, yes; that certainly would be.

Q. Haven't you sort of insinuated that?

THE PRESIDENT. No, I don't think so. You know, when you make a long speech, quite often extemporaneously, or when you answer questions that you don't know will come, quite often because of brevity you use fewer words than you would if you have time to explain in detail all the nuances that I've just tried to do for you. And I have always made very clear that I'm not criticizing my opponents personally.

But the American people will have to go to the polls on November the 4th and decide—because of my past record of maintaining this Nation at peace, my past record of trying to control nuclear weapons, my past record of working in harmony with our allies and friends for the peaceful commitment around the world, here, in the Middle East, and other places, compared with the statements and policies that Governor Reagan has put forward as a candidate, day before yesterday and over a period of years consistently—which candidate is most likely to keep our Nation strong militarily on the one hand and deeply committed to peace. I think that's legitimate.

VIEWS ON CAMPAIGNING

Q. Mr. President, 4 years ago it seemed that you had a lot of fun during your campaign for President. I recall specifically the Peanut Brigade. You say it's better this time, but many of my colleagues seem to think that the joy has gone out of your campaign this time. What's the difference between now and then? Does incumbency change things?

THE PRESIDENT. Not as far as the candidate is concerned. I think as far as the news media is concerned, it changes things. There's a more sober analysis of an incumbent President and what I say and what I do than it was in 1976, when at first I was a lonely candidate with no friends and no chance to win and then later grew up to be a candidate who had the nomination of my party.

For instance, this morning in Dayton, Ohio, in a townhall meeting, I think there were, in a 1-hour exchange with the audience, there were probably 10 or 15 times when laughter swept the convention hall. And everybody felt in a very good and an enjoyable mood. And recently in a suburban backyard, near Philadelphia here, again the atmosphere was one of give and take and friendship and enjoyment.

I really like the political life and enjoy every day that I'm President, in spite of the crises and the sometimes loneliness of the job and the difficulties of the White House. But I think there is a more sober careful judgment of the actions of a President than there is of a candidate who's running against the President.

HOUSEHOLD PRODUCT WARNING LABELS

Q. Mr. President, for the last 4 years we at Channel 10 have been trying to get out thousands of mislabeled household products off the market that, according to virtually all medical experts, are likely to kill little children, because products, which are poison, carry first-aid instructions that are erroneous and that if followed will kill the victim.

Despite continued appeals to Federal agencies and a personal visit to the White House to see your special adviser on consumer affairs, no action has been taken. And only yesterday the EPA told me it will probably take another 10 years to get this mess straightened out. Mr. President, isn't that a little slow and a little ridiculous, even by the standards of Federal regulatory agencies?

THE PRESIDENT. Yes, it is. I would be glad to have you present the material directly to me, and I will guarantee you that it'll get immediately, that day, to the Federal Trade Commission or the EPA or whatever agency is directly involved in that product.

One thing that happened last week—I think it may have been covered by your network—was that we signed the infant formula bill, where manufacturers of baby formula—and it's made out of soybean

oil base—had a defect in the formula. And babies were becoming ill; they couldn't eat; they were losing weight and even having convulsions. A doctor in Tennessee finally believed that it was the formula. And we investigated it as rapidly as we could and found that it was, indeed, an absence of chloride. And the Congress passed a bill, I signed it into law, and gave us the authority under the Health and Human Services Department now to monitor baby formulas, when formerly we didn't have that right under law.

But if you'll give to me personally the information that you have about these dangerous products, I will see to it that same day that I get the product information, that it goes to the appropriate agency, and we'll also give you a report back on what action is taken.

Q. I'll send it to you immediately. But I guess I should ask why can't these Federal agencies move more quickly than that? I know that you can get the job done in 15 minutes, but why should a Federal agency take 14 years to take household labels off the market that all the experts say are going to kill little children? There's no argument over it. Everybody admits that this is wrong, and they're just not doing it.

THE PRESIDENT. That's a question I can't answer. But I've given you my answer. I haven't heard about it before. But now, having heard about it from you, there will be no delay in its being investigated and managed.

Q. Thank you very much.

FINANCIAL ASSISTANCE FOR PRIVATE SCHOOLS

Q. Paul Walkr, a viewer from northeast Philadelphia, wants to know your stand—and this is a very important local issue——

THE PRESIDENT. Yes.

Q. ——on tax credits to parents of children who attend Catholic and other nonpublic schools.

THE PRESIDENT. I'm not in favor of tax credits to be given to parents, but I am in favor of greatly improving the Federal programs that go to ease the financial burden on parents who send their children to private schools.

Q. Why do you oppose the tax credits, Mr. President?

THE PRESIDENT. Well, the Attorney General believes and his predecessors in the Attorney General's office believed that there are constitutional prohibitions against the Federal Government paying directly for religious instruction in the schools and the buying of books that relate to religious instruction.

But in order to avoid that constitutional prohibition we have done other things. We have expanded the title I programs for disadvantaged children to include private schools for the first time. We've added substantially to the amount of money that goes to the private schools for the school lunch program. The amount of aid that goes for college students going to private colleges has now made it possible for any young person in this Nation to go to a college if they're academically qualified to do the work, regardless of the financial status of that family. There just are different ways to approach the same problem. We also have established now a Department of Education and, for the first time, have within it a special agency to enhance the quality of private education without having the Federal Government interfere in the free exercise of management over those private schools.

So, within constitutional boundaries, as defined by my top legal adviser, the nation's top legal adviser, the Attorney General, we are moving to give Federal assistance to the private schools, including the religious schools, for instance, with the Catholic Church.

NATIONAL ECONOMY

Q. Mr. President, the prime rate went up again today to 14 percent at one of the major banks. In our area the construction and the housing industries are suffering very badly and so are the people who would like to borrow money to buy new homes. When will things ever get better for them?

THE PRESIDENT. It depends on where you draw the comparison line. Compared to last March, things are much better. We've had a sustained housing construction industry in this Nation—the first 3 years I was in office, almost 2 million homes per year on the average. Recently, the interest rates have begun to go up again. It's something that I deplore very seriously. It would be obviously much better for me as a candidate for election if the interest rates were going down.

The Federal Reserve Bank, the Board that manages it, is an absolutely independent agency. Under law, the President has no influence over the decisions made by the Federal Reserve Board. They have a formula that they have developed that if the supply of money in the economy gets too great, there's too much money for any given level of products, then this would cause inflation to escalate, and they use that formula to raise the interest rates by the Government, and the banks sometimes follow suit.

We are trying to work as best we can to keep inflation rates, and the interest rate down and to provide a source of funding so that the homebuilding industry can continue to be strong. The last reports I got were that the homebuilding industry was still improving each month in the number of homes constructed and the new housing starts that were authorized by permits. I think the last figures I got were over 1.4 million homes per year rate, which is fairly good.

I don't know what will happen with the new interest rate increases. My hope is that they will turn downward soon and help me politically and obviously help our Nation economically.

Q. Do you see a prime rate of 10 percent again in the foreseeable future?

THE PRESIDENT. I can only say I hope so, yes. I owe a good bit of money myself in my warehouse business down in Plains and I have to pay interest at the prime rate plus 1 or 2 percent. So, it hurts me personally when these interest rates go up.

We have tried to minimize the adverse consequences in the construction industry and throughout the economy that have been brought about by the interest rates tied directly to the inflation rate, primarily foisted on this country by the more than doubled price of OPEC oil, a decision made by foreign oil producers.

One of the best things that can be done to hold down interest rates and inflation rates in the future is to continue to save energy and produce more American energy of all kinds. The new energy program is doing that. For instance, every year [day] [1] in 1980, we are buying from foreign countries 2 million barrels of oil less every day. And this will hold down the flood of foreign oil, which also brings with it inflation and unemployment. So, to become more energy-secure and move toward energy independence is a major commitment of our Nation. That will be a major factor in the future in helping to control interest rates and inflation.

---

[1] White House correction.

Q. Just one followup question: What good are those new homes if people can't get the mortgage money to move into them? They might be sitting empty next year or the year after.

THE PRESIDENT. Well, the data that I gave you are predicated on existing interest rates, and there has been a fairly good recovery since last March. It's hard to predict the future of the homebuilding industry, but I think, in general, the homes are still being built. There's still a pretty heavy demand for them.

And one of the things that I've done, in spite of a very tight and restrained budget, is to increase substantially the number of federally assisted homes, where the rental rates and the interest rates charged on loans have been helped by the Federal Government, so that the people can go ahead and buy a home. For instance, since I've been in office, the Farmers Home Administration has loaned more money than it has in its 45 previous years of existence. And we have increased greatly the number of homes that will be built in this current fiscal year, that began yesterday, so that the Federal Government can have a beneficial effect on the homebuilding industry throughout the country.

TOXIC WASTE DISPOSAL

Q. Mr. President, we've been doing a story on toxic chemicals in this area.

THE PRESIDENT. Yes.

Q. One theme emerges. The people of Collegeville, Pennsylvania, for example, whose wells have been poisoned by the chemical TCE, say Federal officials are not helpful and have to be badgered and pressured and beaten into taking action. Why can't your agencies, such as the EPA and others, convince these people that the Federal Government is able and willing to help?

THE PRESIDENT. My own belief is that the EPA is a very dedicated and able agency that's made tremendous strides forward in controlling the toxic material that you've mentioned.

Yesterday, in Niagara Falls, New York, I signed two documents. One was a new bill that permits us for the first time to solidify nuclear waste into an almost impregnable solid so that it can be stored safely. The other bill I signed was an agreement with the Governor of New York to help those who had been hurt with the Love Canal contamination to move to a safe neighborhood without suffering financial damage.

We've gotten through the Congress to the House now the so-called superfund bill, which addresses for the first time in the history of this Nation an insurance fund that will correct toxic dump sites in the future, which will be paid for out of a small fee charged the chemical companies as they produce potentially toxic products to sell to the American public and also will help to clean up the more than 2,000 dangerous dump sites that exist in this country.

These are problems on nuclear waste disposal and toxic materials disposal that have never been addressed before. It takes a long time to convince the Congress, sometimes with the concerted opposition of chemical companies and the nuclear companies, that we must move. It took me 3 years to get through the Congress energy legislation. We've been working on toxic materials now for about a year, and the bill I signed last night in Niagara Falls is the first legislation ever signed in the history of this country to deal with the disposal of nuclear waste.

So, we are making progress. I can't tell you that it's fast enough, but it's as fast as I can move in setting up laws that give us the authority to do as you want.

Q. Of course, Mr. President, though, I'm not talking about legislation or regulation or authority. I'm talking about the heart and soul of the agencies. These people simply feel that these agencies are not their friends. They should be. Government is supposed to protect these people. And why do they view them as just a bunch of bureaucrats who don't act and won't act? Isn't that a problem?

THE PRESIDENT. You ask a question with an underlying premise with which I disagree. I know Doug Costle, who heads up the Environmental Protection Agency. He is as dedicated a human being as I know to do the job that's his under the laws of this country, to protect the health and the safety of American people. He works day and night at it, just as hard as you do being a consumer advocate through the television media. There is no doubt in my mind that his people who work under him are doing the best they can within the constraints of the law to protect the health of the American people against toxic materials.

The point is that quite often these toxic dump sites and nuclear waste sites have never been under the protection of the Federal Government before. And you have to get a law passed, through a very reluctant Congress at times, over unbelievable opposition from interest groups, to give the Federal Government the authority to act quickly, without delay, to protect the lives and the safety of our people.

LILLIAN CARTER

Q. Mr. President, before we conclude tonight, of course your mother, Miss Lillian, broke her hip today in a fall in Plains, Georgia. How's she doing?

THE PRESIDENT. Yes. I just got a report, when I was walking into this room, from the White House physician, who's talked to Mama's physician. She just came out of surgery a few minutes ago. She was in there for an hour and a half. They had to operate on her hip. The upper femur, the large leg bone, was fractured and displaced substantially. They implanted a steel pin in the marrow of the bone and put a plate on her hip. She's in good physical shape. Her heart is strong. She's 82 years old, which makes it more serious. But the reports that I have is that although she's still under the effect of the anesthesia, the doctor says the operation was successful.

I thank you for asking about it.

Q. Okay. President Carter, thanks for joining us tonight. We've been talking live in the Ambassador Room, the Ambassador Suite at the Fairmont Hotel with President Jimmy Carter. Right now, for Lorrie Yapczenski and Herb Denenberg, I'm Larry Kane. Good night.

NOTE: The interview began at 7 p.m. and was broadcast live from the Ambassador Suite at the Fairmont Hotel.

The National Economy

White House Statement on Recent Economic Data.   October 3, 1980

It's gratifying to have two pieces of good economic news.

The President is pleased that two rates have fallen—the producer price index and unemployment.

The producer price index declined in September for both food and other items. End-of-the-model-year rebates on autos and trucks—collected for the first time by the Bureau of Labor Statistics in its efforts to improve the index—were an important factor. But even if we were to exclude this new factor, the rise in wholesale prices would be quite small.

While the inflation rate does tend to fluctuate from month to month, the trend in recent months has clearly been downward.

The unemployment rate, meanwhile, has fallen for the second straight month. The rise in total hours worked, especially noticeable in construction and manufacturing, indicates a basic improvement in the economic situation.

The fight against inflation is far from over, and the economic recovery is still in its early stages. But the President believes that today's economic data, and those of the last several months, indicate that his economic policies are working and provide the basis for a healthy and noninflationary recovery.

Meeting With President Mohammad Zia-ul-Haq of Pakistan

Remarks to Reporters Following the Meeting.   October 3, 1980

PRESIDENT CARTER. First of all, I'd like to express to the people of our country and Pakistan the deep honor that I consider having been paid to us and to our country by the visit of President Zia. I've told him privately and would like to express publicly that the people of the United States have the greatest admiration for the courage of the people and the leaders of the great nation of Pakistan.

They live in a troubled region. Their security has been threatened as has the security of other nations in the region. And the tenacity with which they've adhered to their own deep commitments for peace and for sharing their responsibility for the maintenance of peace has indeed aroused the renewed admiration of the entire world. In addition, the humanitarian attitude of the people of Pakistan in receiving hundreds of thousands of refugees from Afghanistan is a matter that causes great admiration for the people of President Zia's country.

In my State of the Union message this year, I pointed out that the independence and the freedom and security of Pakistan was very important to our country. On a mutual basis we understand that the relationship between our countries is of the utmost importance. Our commitment to consult very closely with Pakistan was expressed in an agreement signed in 1959; if Pakistan should be in danger, that commitment stands today as it did in 1959 and at the time of the State of the Union message that I delivered this January.

In addition, our countries share with almost every other nation on Earth the belief that the Soviet invasion of Afghanistan is contrary to the laws of peace-loving nations, contrary to the peace and stability of the entire world, and that the Soviets should withdraw their occupying forces immediately. This was expressed by more than a hundred countries through the United Nations earlier this year. Our commitment to this United Nations action still stands even though time has passed.

In addition, we are deeply grateful for President Zia's role as a spokesman for the Islamic Conference. His recent visit to Tehran and then to Baghdad to try to limit the combat, the loss of blood, and also to bring to an early conclusion the war between Iran and Iraq is of great importance to us all.

And finally let me say that we are honored personally by his visit. He's a military man who received part of his train-ing in our country. He's familiar with our Nation. His knowledge of the sensitivities and ideals of America make him particularly dear to us. And his role now as the President of that great country has shown by all of his actions the political leadership and its worth not only to the people of Pakistan but to that entire troubled region and to our country as well.

President Zia, we are deeply grateful to you and your associates for coming here on a mission of great importance to the United Nations and now to Washington. We wish you well and express again the great value of the friendship that exists between our two people. Thank you again, and welcome.

PRESIDENT ZIA. Ladies and gentlemen of the press, through the President of the United States, President Carter, I wish to thank you for giving me this opportunity.

I am very grateful to President Carter himself for giving me this opportunity, particularly at the time when he's so busy with a very crucial campaign at home. We wish him all the best.

I'm also very grateful to him for giving me this opportunity of establishing personal contact. Being an army man, I've learned one thing—that it is different talking to a man to a man rather than communicating from 12,000 miles away. I have found it equally true today in my meeting with President Carter, whom I found exactly a little more than my expectations were—a man of deep understanding, a humane personality, and who has at the bottom of his heart love of humanity, the rights of men to live as men, as free men. As President of the United States, I found him a competent personality to bear the beacon of light that the free world expects of him to bear.

I think this meeting has been very purposeful. And if the relationship between Pakistan and the United States continues to be meaningful and purposeful, as we wish, and if Pakistan, a developing country, is smothered and helped in more than the economic field and if the burden, on humanitarian grounds, that we are bearing of over a million refugees from the neighboring country of Afghanistan is shared, as is being done by the United States of America, I think we'll have something to offer to humanity.

I once again thank President Carter for all his kindnesses, his hospitality, his generosity to receive me at this time when he's so busy, and my colleagues and my delegation. On my own behalf, on behalf of the people of Pakistan, through you, ladies and gentlemen of the press, I want to thank him and thank the people of the United States of America for the very practical understanding of the problems of Pakistan and people of Pakistan.

I thank you, sir.

PRESIDENT CARTER. Thank you, Mr. President, very much.

NOTE: The President spoke at 12:15 p.m. on the South Lawn of the White House.

National Association of Women Judges

Remarks at a White House Reception.
October 3, 1980

I just had the exciting experience of meeting personally some of the judges that I've been able to appoint since I've been in the White House. These are names all very famous to me because the selection process, before it's made public, is a very long and detailed one. And to meet you personally is indeed an honor and a pleasure.

I met Judge Joan Dempsey Klein and Judge Vaino Spencer a good many months ago, I think about 2 years ago, in

Los Angeles. They were on the platform when I addressed the Bar Association. Several people in the audience demanded equal time after I got through with my speech. [*Laughter*] But I've reread the speech, and I meant every word of it and wouldn't change it if I had to make it now.

This is an opportunity for me to come and see you. And I'm also grateful to see how many of you there are—many representing others in one of the finest and most gratifying developments in which I've been a part since I've been President. It's a special pleasure to have you here at the White House, because you are a special part of a significant breakthrough in our country.

Susan B. Anthony said in 1897, and I quote from her: "There never will be complete equality until women themselves help to make laws and elect lawmakers." Radical as that statement was back in that time, it does not go far enough, as I'm sure all of you would agree. She left out a very crucial point, and that is the interpretation and the administration of the law.

My own political career began in Georgia at a time of great change in this country, especially in my region. The judiciary, and especially the Federal judiciary, played a vital role in that change, not only in matters of racial discrimination, which were sensitive and difficult to accommodate, but also in matters of political discrimination based on where people lived.

The courts had outlawed the white primary in the 1940's. In the 1950's and the 1960's they insisted that the dual school systems must go, that all votes must be counted alike, and that discrimination of all kinds under the law must end. No longer would it take hundreds of votes in Atlanta to equal one vote in some of the small counties of my State under the unit rule, nor could the legislature decide whether or not it wanted to reapportion congressional and legislative districts. The courts were in the forefront of those changes that freed us from the twin fetters of undemocratic government and enforced legal racial discrimination.

Many of the judges involved had to be men of great courage and sound legal scholarship. But the phrase that became the rallying cry of the political equality was, "One man, one vote." And when I say the men who were judges it kind of grates on me now—[laughter]—because I don't use that kind of phrase any more, and to say, "One man, one vote," is indeed at this time an anachronism. Behind us we are reminded that there were no women on those courts, although about half the people of Georgia were women. There were no blacks on the district and circuit courts that made those decisions in my State or anywhere in the South, although one-third of the people in my State were black.

I learned, too, the vast authority and influence and power that local judges could have, particularly in the human kinds of interrelationships involving criminal cases. I went into the law office of a young black legislator in Savannah, Georgia, when I was running for Governor in 1970, and he had a photograph on his wall that told the story in vivid terms. It was a photograph of a white person standing in the criminal docket as the accused, and the judge was black and all 12 jurors were black and the sheriff was black and the baliff was black—[laughter]—and all those in audience in the court were black. I think that impressed me more than any photograph or even public demonstration that I've ever seen.

My own election to the State senate finally rested on a court decision involving voting irregularities. I learned the first time I ran for public office the importance of justice. There were only 330 ballots that had been officially cast in one precinct where the election hung in balance; 330 people had voted. There were 433 ballots in the box—[laughter]—and the last 126 had voted in alphabetical order. [Laughter] And when the officials went there to recount the ballots and unfolded the ballots, sometime there would be eight ballots inside of one folded document. Many of the people on the list were dead or in prison or had moved away a long time ago. Reform in that county that was proposed afterwards, that was that no one could vote who had been dead more than 3 years. [Laughter] Well, those kinds of travesties of justice not only afflicted black citizens and those who don't speak Spanish [English] well and women, but they also afflicted others without political or social or financial influence.

So, you hold tremendous power, whether you are a Federal, State, or local judge, whether the cases that you consider are capital cases or child custody cases or disputes over contracts or over political matters or over an interpretation of what our Constitution says. You have the power to make our system work and to administer the laws in a sensitive and humane way, to stop those who would misuse power against their less powerful fellow citizens, to hold us all to the very high standards set forth in our Constitution, the power to see that justice includes mercy.

In my judgment, our system of justice still has a long way to go. The innovation for the removal of injustice ought to originate among lawyers and among those who are professionally trained, but in the past that has not been the case. Because I knew the power and importance of judges, I was determined when I became

President to get the very best people possible to serve on the Federal bench. I was also determined to see that women and minorities, whose destinies have so often depended upon the kind of justice that our courts can provide, should be included in those judgeships. The highest possible quality and women and minorities—I have found no conflict in those two aims.

When I became President, only 10 women had ever been appointed to the Federal bench in more than 200 years. I've appointed 40 more. And if the process was not so complicated, involving the United States Senators who represent a particular State—[*laughter*]—there would have been more still. [*Laughter*] And some of the delay in making the appointments of those represented here today had been because of long and extended arguments, almost always done in private, to induce progressive, sometimes even liberal, Members of the United States Senate to change their previous practices and consider women and blacks and those who speak Spanish.

And I have to confess to you that I also took one excellent Federal judge away— Shirley Hufstedler. But education has always been one of my prime interests, and when I was ready to fill the new office of Secretary of Education, I wanted the very best. And I've not been disappointed. Shirley Hufstedler is one of only six women in the history of our Nation who have ever held a Cabinet post, and I appointed three of them. Patricia Harris, who was speaking to your group, is another one who's served superbly in two Cabinet posts.

As you know, Federal judges are not only powerful but they're also more or less permanent. [*Laughter*] And I was amazed a few minutes ago, when I looked at that group, how young women judges are. [*Laughter*] Few things that a President

does will have as much long-term effect as the judges that are appointed. When I leave this office in January of 1985, I hope—[*laughter*]—my successor can turn out my Cabinet, as you know, and other officials in the executive branch of Government. They can reverse or dismantle the executive decisions that I've made. They can change the programs that have been initiated. They could even convince the Congress to repeal laws that I've proposed or supported. But the judges that I've appointed will remain.

I'm concerned, as are many of you, that some groups around this country are attempting to set up ideological eligibility tests for judges. It's never been done before. It's a radical departure from what all previous Presidents, Democratic or Republican, have done. And as long as I'm President, potential judges will not be subjected to tests of religion or gender or race or personal beliefs on someone's list of so-called "right" attitudes.

I know that your association is on record favoring the appointment of a woman Supreme Court justice, and some of you are hoping that I will promise today that, should the need arise for me to fill a vacancy on the Supreme Court, that my next appointment will be a woman. I would be honored to be the first President to appoint a woman to the Supreme Court, but I cannot make such a promise. I can promise, based on my record so far, that women and members of minority groups will be fully considered, but I will not rule out anyone—male or female—on the basis of sex or race or religion or national origin. To do that, to me, to promise ahead of time that I would comply with your wish would violate the principles for which you and I have both fought so hard and would violate the trust that's been placed in me as President. I know that you, whose lives are full of critical decisions and who have experienced personal discrimination because you're female and arbitrary exclusion because you are women, understand that better than most people.

I'm proud of what I've been able to do this past 3½ years, but I'm not through yet. We still have a full agenda before us, including the passage of the equal rights amendment, which has been so grossly distorted and about which so many lies have been told. The amendment simply says that neither the Federal Government nor any State can pass a law which would discriminate against women—a simple, obviously badly needed amendment. And I want to see that embedded in the Constitution of the United States so that every judge, male or female, will have a clear constitutional standard to follow in the years ahead.

We share a lot together—you as exciting new public servants in the system of administering justice in our Nation and myself as the President of the same Nation. I'm honored by that shared partnership, and I'm deeply grateful for what you have already and will contribute to make our wonderful Nation even greater in the future.

Thank you very much.

NOTE: The President spoke at 1:08 p.m. in the East Room at the White House.

Sterling, Virginia

*Remarks on Signing the Education
Amendments of 1980 Into Law.
October 3, 1980*

THE PRESIDENT. *President Ernst and distinguished members of the faculty and student representatives of this fine college, Secretary Hufstedler, Senator Pell, Senator Jennings Randolph, Congressman* *Ford, Congressman Biaggi, Congressman Fisher, Congressman Buchanan, Congressman Petrie, representatives of the American Federation of Teachers:*

It's really a pleasure for me to be here. I had a wonderful welcome outside and almost decided not to come in. [*Laughter*] But because of the historic nature of this event I'm very grateful to all of you for letting me perform this act here in one of our fine centers of education of which we are all so proud.

We've come to this splendid new campus to celebrate the enactment of the Education Amendments of 1980, truly an historic piece of legislation for education. It's appropriate that we've come to a community college to sign this bill. This campus is a symbol of extraordinary enterprise that is American education. The task of that enterprise is one of the most audacious ever undertaken by any nation in history—nothing less than the education of an entire people.

One of Virginia's greatest sons, about whom I think frequently, living in the White House, Thomas Jefferson, set forth the dream of a system of general education which shall reach every description of our citizens from the richest to the poorest. Making Jefferson's dream live and come true has been the business of our Nation under Presidents and Congresses of both parties. President Lincoln signed the Morrill Act, which opened up the great land grant universities of this Nation. President Truman signed the GI bill, which has enabled thousands and thousands of veterans to benefit from higher education which they would not otherwise have gotten.

President Eisenhower signed the National Defense Education Act, which for the first time made Federal loans available to undergraduate students. President Johnson signed the Elementary and Secondary Education Act of 1965, the land-mark Civil Rights Act of 1964, and the Higher Education Act of 1965. And as President I've also been busy. I've sought to breathe new life into this national tradition of devotion and commitment to education.

My first public job was as a member of the Sumter County Library Board, and later during the crucial years of racial integration in the South, I was on a local county school board. I ran for the Georgia State Senate, because I was concerned about education. When I got to Atlanta my only request was to be put on that committee. I was chairman of the higher education committee of the Georgia Senate and later served as Governor with a major portion of my time and commitment devoted to improving the education system in our State.

We have now expanded, with this legislation, the Elementary and Secondary Act, and we've also been able to increase, in spite of severe fiscal constraint, the budget increases for education by 75 percent, for education in general and for Head Start and other programs for deprived children in particular.

We've doubled funds for student aid and for educating handicapped children. We've tripled funds for basic skills education and provided new funds for the disadvantaged students in our urban centers. Through the Middle Income Student Assistance Act we've brought college within the reach of every single student in this Nation who's qualified for higher education. The idea that lack of money should be no barrier to a college education is no longer a dream, it's a reality.

We've put more Federal resources behind the historically black colleges, which award nearly half the degrees received by black students in our country. And by creating the new Department of Educa-

tion we've given education its proper place in the highest councils of government.

When Congress reconvenes on November 12 I hope that we will soon be able to add the Youth Act of 1980 to that list. It will provide jobs and basic education skills to millions of impoverished young men and women, and will ultimately prepare large numbers of students to take advantage of community college educations.

This legislation will, for the first time, bind in an official way the Department of Labor and the Department of Education so that in the future the products of high schools, community colleges, vocational and technical schools, and senior colleges will be more accurately oriented toward career opportunities in the communities where the graduates will live.

The legislation I'm signing today reflects the diversity and adds to the strength of American higher education. It helps parents and students pay college costs. It strengthens our research universities. It strengthens our black colleges. It strengthens our Hispanic colleges. It supports teacher training, language and areas studies, and graduate studies as well. It provides support to students in all kinds of institutions, public and private universities, communities and junior colleges, and private technical institutions as well, to the National Institute of Education and the Fund for the Improvement of Post-Secondary Education. It supports research that helps us to explore the nature of teaching and the nature of learning. And through a new urban grant university program it helps to bring the resources of the university into our cities and our neighborhoods.

Let me say something about why this bill and the activities it supports are so important. Alexis de Tocqueville wrote some 150 years ago, and I will quote from him, "America is a land of wonders . . .

No natural boundary seems to be set to the efforts of man; and in his eyes what is not yet done is only what he has not yet attempted to do." That was prophecy.

Over the generations American creativity has erased natural boundaries. American ingenuity has pushed back the frontiers of technology. American imagination has given us a more rich and a more bountiful life. But most important of all, American liberty has brought meaning to the material achievements of our rich society. American education is both a source and a beneficiary of these values. No matter how rich we are, without freedom our wealth would not be of value.

Literature, mathematics, science, history, language, the arts, specialized education are all part of a truly national effort to expand, as de Tocqueville said, the natural boundary of human effort. To millions education means opportunity. It's a door through which we walk to attain happier lives, better jobs, and if we are lucky, a measure of wisdom. It's the mechanism by which the American dream, the dream of taking our talents and our abilities as far as we can, is realized in this Nation of refugees and immigrants. It's a vehicle for understanding the diversity that is America, and it's a unifier of our ideals and values among people that are different one from another.

The act I'm signing today emphasizes to us how vital our educational system is, because it reminds us of how enduring our national ideals have become. It also asks of all of us a major question. What will be our legacy to those who will follow us? When generations to come cast their minds back to our times, will they write and will they teach that we began to close the door to knowledge, that we slammed shut opportunities for some of our people, that we succumbed to a narrow, exclusionary vision of our land? Or will our legacy be one of building our national diversity—opening wide the flow of ideas, casting broadly our net of respect and tolerance? I have no doubt of the answer.

We Americans do not fear competition in the marketplace of ideas. We do not repress those who have a different ideology from us. We do not stifle competing thoughts. Instead we followed Jefferson's advice, "Enlighten the people generally," he said, "and tyranny and oppressions of body and mind will vanish like evil spirits in the dawn of a new day."

We often hear the argument that education deserves our support because it contributes to the economic strength of our Nation. That's certainly true. But the real meaning of education goes far beyond that, much deeper. In its broadest sense, education, the question of understanding and knowledge of ourselves, our fellow human beings and God's universe, is not a means to some end, but rather an end in itself.

Education and liberty are part of the same search for truth, and education and liberty are unthinkable without each other. Let me quote Jefferson once more. "The education of the people," he wrote, "can alone make them the safe, as they are the sole repository of our political and religious freedom." So, political and religious freedom depend upon education.

Today we strengthen American education, and by doing so, we enlarge a precious possession—American liberty. In the process, we strengthen and enlarge both our inner lives as individuals and also our common life as a democratic society. That's why I'm honored to be here with you. And that explains in brief and perhaps fumbling words the historic significance of this event.

And now I would like to introduce to you our Nation's first Secretary of Education, Shirley Hufstedler.

SECRETARY HUFSTEDLER. Mr. President, it gives me very great pleasure to be here this afternoon as you sign into law the Education Amendments of 1980. This is the first major piece of education legislation that has been signed since the new Department of Education was created, formally inaugurated 5 months ago. I am confident that the second piece of legislation will be the Youth Act of 1980. That critically important bill represents your major domestic initiative, and it will be the first and most dramatic original education legislation in the last decade. That takes nothing away at all from the historic moment of the education legislation you are signing today.

The Education Amendments of 1980 have traveled a long and very intricate route through Congress. I want not only to recognize all the persons in the House and in the Senate who worked so hard on this bill who are not here; I want to, however, especially acknowledge the indispensible help of two persons on this platform without whose ardent, selfless work we would not be here today, Senator Claiborne Pell and Congressman Bill Ford.

The result of all the work of the great leaders who are represented here today in favor of education has resulted in a bill of which you can be very justly proud. The legislation furthers some of the most important objectives of American education. It reaffirms our determination that postsecondary education will remain accessible to every single person in this country whose inclinations and aptitudes lead them to education beyond high school.

It permits a sharing of burdens and responsibilities for the cost of that education while making sure that no one will have the door on higher education closed by reason of financial want. The amendments protect the very diversity and pluralism that is at the heart and strength of

American society, and particularly, the American educational systems. They will continue to provide assistance directly to students who will remain therefore free to make choices about which institutions can best meet the students' needs, and they will offer new support in a number of areas where colleges have compelling needs for help.

Some of the major accomplishments of the new law include a restructuring of the National Direct Student Loan program to allow more flexibility and an extended payment for borrowers who have financial hardships. It enacts a new loan program for parents which allows parents to spread their contributions to their children's education over a much longer period of time. It adopts a standard needs analysis system and a single application form. For all of those of you who have had to fill out so many of them, you can now feel very grateful. We are cutting down the paperwork in this bill. And you will see when we implement the bill, by regulations that we are going to work out in the closest cooperation with Congress, that you ought to—[*laughter*]—we hope the Hill is going to be as happy as you are with the results.

We are consolidating and broadening Federal support for international education activities, a subject of such tremendous importance to the United States. You know, not many months ago I wouldn't be surprised if most persons in the United States thought that Kabul was some kind of comfy slipper. The amount of ignorance—by which I mean not "stupidity," I mean "unknowing"—about international affairs, has been a cause of very serious concern in the United States. Accordingly, President Carter has doubled for this fiscal year, commitment to international education. And we are going to continue the upward path to making international education available in a much more meaningful way to all interested students.

And finally, we don't want to forget that, although it's a higher education bill, it is going to provide very significant and essential support for the research efforts of the National Institute of Education—and perhaps touching everybody in the country, it provides very significant help for libraries.

The Education Amendments of 1980 are evidence of a continuing momentum of the Congress and, I must say, under Democratic leadership and on the ongoing commitment of this administration to expand and improve the opportunities for education of all citizens in America.

I could not possibly speak to this audience in this setting without referring to the motto of the Department of Education, because it has very great meaning here. The motto of the Department of Education is "Learning never ends," and I say that is of such importance here, because this set of community colleges has done such an outstanding job in adult education. It is not alone enough to educate our children; we must all keep educating ourselves all our lives if we are to reach the full potential for our country and for ourselves.

As the President has said, education is an end in itself even though it leads to all kinds of things that enhance the quality of life in America. Universities and colleges have to have some hardware within which to do our work, but we must always remember the hardware is not an end, it is a means to the enhancement of the human spirit, of the quality of intellectual life, and to the sustaining joy of knowledge which we all hope will ultimately lead us to wisdom.

Thank you.

THE PRESIDENT. Shirley has already bragged on him, but I would like to take the opportunity to introduce to you the key worker and a visionary man who can put his thoughts into practical benefits for the people of our country, Senator Claiborne Pell.

SENATOR PELL. Thank you, Mr. President.

Machines, means of production, construction, transportation, communication, even of destruction, do not really determine the strength—the true strength—of a nation. The true strength of a nation is the sum total of the education and the character of its people, and this is what we're here today to celebrate. And this is the bill that President Carter has just signed, because it brings to reality the dream that some of us have had that any American who desires a college education and can cut the mustard in achieving it can secure it, and this bill really does ensure that that happens.

So, I say thank you, President Carter; thank you, colleagues in the Congress; thank you, particularly staff, with whom we depend in the Senate very much indeed; thank you, lobbyists, for keeping us on our toes; and thank you, everybody.

THE PRESIDENT. Now I'd like to introduce as the final speaker a man who's a driving force in the House of Representatives, who knows from practical experience in his own district the need for better education for the working people of our Nation, and whose staunch support and courage in hammering out this detailed but very significant legislation has been very important to me as President, to all those that take pride in our country. Congressman William Ford.

REPRESENTATIVE FORD. Thank you, Mr. President, Madam Secretary, and my colleagues from the Congress.

I'm sure that those of you here fully realize how proud we are to be here for the reason that we are here, and, Mr.

President, it needs to be said that the two pieces of higher education legislation that you will have signed now within the space of 2 years probably goes further to keep promises that Harry Truman made to the people than we have been able to move in our party ever since the time of Truman at any one time. Even the great days of the Johnson administration pale by comparison in dollar amounts to the initiatives that you've put in place.

With the signing of the Middle Income Student Assistance Act you gave to higher education the largest single increase in commitment that's occurred at any time since the adoption of the GI bill in World War II. With the signing of this bill today the President is committing us to authorizing $10 billion a year for each of the next 5 years, taking us well into the decade of the eighties. And when people ask the frequent question—"What is education going to be in the eighties?"—you can be optimistic because, as the President has already indicated, under his leadership our commitment at the Federal level has increased by over 70 percent, a little bit more in higher education than in other areas, but over 70 percent above the commitment of the Federal Government measured in dollars when he became President.

Mr. President, you are, indeed, entitled to a place in the history books of this country as an education President, and we're very proud to be a part of your team and to be here with you for this momentous occasion.

THE PRESIDENT. And now comes a difficult decision in the life of a President. I've had good advice from these people on the stage, but I have to decide now whether to sign this bill or veto it. [*Laughter*]

I'd like to ask all those of you who think I should sign the bill to please raise your hand. [*Laughter*] It seems to be unanimous. Thank you very much. That's genuine participatory democracy. [*Laughter*]

NOTE: The President spoke at 2:05 p.m. at the Loudon Campus of the Northern Virginia Community College. Following his remarks, the President signed the bill.

As enacted, H.R. 5192 is Public Law 96–374, approved October 3.

Variable Housing Allowance
Executive Order 12243.   October 3, 1980

By the authority vested in me as President of the United States of America under Section 403 of Title 37 of the United States Code and under Section 4 of the Military Personnel and Compensation Amendments of 1980, and in order to provide for the implementation of a variable housing allowance, Section 403 of Executive Order No. 11157, as amended, is hereby further amended by adding thereto the following new subsections (c) and (d):

"(c) For purposes of Section 403 of Title 37 of the United States Code, a member shall be deemed to be living in a "high housing cost area" whenever the average monthly cost of housing, including utilities, for housing appropriate for the member's grade, exceeds 115 percent of the amount of the basic allowance for quarters of that member."

"(d) During fiscal year 1981, members may be paid a variable housing allowance as permitted by Section 4(c) of the Military Personnel and Compensation Amendments of 1980 (94 Stat. 1125; Public Law 96–343; 37 U.S.C. 403 note); a member shall be deemed to be living in a "high housing cost area" whenever the estimated average monthly cost of housing, including utilities, appropriate for the member's grade, exceeds 115 percent of the amount of the basic allowance for quarters of that member.".

JIMMY CARTER

The White House,
    October 3, 1980.

[Filed with the Office of the Federal Register,
    3:34 p.m., October 3, 1980]

National Port Week, 1980

Proclamation 4798.   October 3, 1980

*By the President of the United States
of America*

A Proclamation

Our Nation's seaports and river ports, operated by local and State authorities, are indispensable to our national prosperity and international commerce.

Historically, waterborne commerce has been a key element in the development and growth of most of the Nation's major population and commercial centers. Today public and privately owned marine terminals, valued at about $54 billion, are expected to handle almost two billion short tons of foreign and domestic ocean-borne cargo in 1980.

In addition to the economic benefits provided by our ports, they play a leading role in logistical support of our military forces. Our port system has been and will continue to be vital in maintaining our national security.

The Congress has by House Joint Resolution 551 requested the President to designate the seven calendar days beginning October 5, 1980, as National Port Week.

Now, THEREFORE, I, JIMMY CARTER, President of the United States of America, in order to remind Americans of the importance of the port industry of the United States to our national life, do hereby designate the seven calendar days beginning October 5, 1980, as National Port Week. I invite the Governors of the several States, the chief officials of local governments, and the people of the United States to observe such week with appropriate ceremonies and activities.

IN WITNESS WHEREOF, I have hereunto set my hand this third day of October in the year of our Lord nineteen hundred and eighty, and of the Independence of the United States of America the two hundred and fifth.

JIMMY CARTER

[Filed with the Office of the Federal Register,
    4:21 p.m., October 3, 1980]

The 96th Congress

*Letter to the Speaker of the House and the
Majority Leader of the Senate.
October 3, 1980*

I am writing to congratulate you on the productive session that the 96th Congress has had to date. Through your strong and effective leadership and our cooperation, we have addressed the critical energy, economic, national security and social issues that had been too long ignored by previous Administrations and Congresses. I am proud of our cooperative relationship and our achievements to date, and I know you agree that a great deal more must be accomplished in the post-election session.

Through our cooperative efforts, we have enacted legislation that will be the building blocks of our Nation's energy policy for decades to come. The Synthetic Fuels Corporation Act, the Crude Oil Windfall Profits Tax Act, the Low-Income Energy Assistance Act, the Emergency Energy Conservation Act, the

Stand-by Gasoline Rationing Plan, the Conservation and Solar Bank Act, a major new gasohol program, and the Wind Energy Systems Act will make major contributions to strengthening our country and reducing our Nation's dependence on foreign oil. Already the initiatives we have taken in the last four years have helped to reduce oil imports by 2 million barrels per day below 1977 levels.

With your leadership, we have enacted legislation to deregulate the railroad, trucking and banking industries, and passed the Regulatory Flexibility Act to reduce the burden of regulations on small business. These bills are a major step forward in our efforts to reduce the unneeded intrusion of Federal regulation into our free market system. They represent the most profound change in relations between government and the private sector since the New Deal.

We have created a new Department of Education, reorganized the government's programs to assist developing nations, and approved a plan reorganizing our international trade activities. These actions will streamline our government and make it more effective and responsive to the needs of our citizens.

Together, we have worked to reduce the growth in Federal spending and to strengthen our Nation's economy. Our efforts this year in the budget, appropriations, and reconciliation processes will achieve efficiencies amounting to tens of billions of dollars in the coming years. I am particularly proud that you and the Congressional Democrats beat back Republican attempts to enact a hastily developed, ill-conceived, inflationary, election-year tax cut.

While we have tightened the budget, we also have expanded programs that specifically meet the needs of our Nation's unemployed and disadvantaged citizens.

We have extended the time period for ratification of the Equal Rights Amendment; expanded funding and eligibility for veterans programs, particularly for Vietnam-era veterans; passed an expanded authorization for higher education programs; enacted new authorizations for our community development, urban development, and housing programs; enacted new authorizations for our agriculture and farm credit programs; provided full voting rights to the District of Columbia; and enacted reforms in the food stamp, social services, child welfare, and disability insurance programs.

With your cooperation, we have strengthened our Nation's commitment to a strong national defense and improved our relations with our Allies and the Third World. We have enacted a Defense Authorization bill and military pay legislation that will strengthen our armed services and ensure that our defense capability is second to none. We have enacted legislation that will enhance our relations with the People's Republic of China; approved legislation to improve oversight of our intelligence activities; and enacted the legislation required to implement the Middle East peace treaty.

While the record of the 96th Congress is one of which we can all be proud, substantial work remains to be done in the post-election session to complete action on the Budget Resolution, appropriations bills, and a number of essential pieces of legislation. Substantial progress already has been made on these bills, but final action is essential. It is unfortunate that the partisan tactics of some Republican Members have prevented final action on many of these proposals until the post-election session.

I am pleased with the work of the 96th Congress thus far and I look forward to continuing our strong working relationship.

Sincerely,

JIMMY CARTER

NOTE: This is the text of identical letters addressed to Thomas P. O'Neill, Jr., Speaker of the House of Representatives, and Robert C. Byrd, Majority Leader of the Senate.

Americus, Georgia

Informal Exchange With Reporters Following a Visit With Lillian Carter.
October 3, 1980

THE PRESIDENT. I've had a chance to visit with my mother and also talk to the doctors who performed the operation on her yesterday, and I've also looked at the X-rays and talked about the future.

Mother's feeling much better. I asked her if she had any message for the outside world, and she said to thank everyone who's sent telegrams and letters and flowers and please not to send any more flowers, that she has to have room to breath in the room. And everybody's been so nice to her that she's got enough flowers, but she really appreciates them.

Also, the doctors say that she had the operation very successfully. They put a stainless steel plate and pin in the upper part of her legbone near the hip, and it was a very successful operation, took about 2 hours. She's likely to be sitting up in a wheelchair tomorrow or the next day. She'll have to stay between the wheelchair and the bed for about 3 months, but her heart is strong, she's very vigorous, in good spirits, and feels much better today than she did yesterday.

Q. How long will she be in the hospital, Mr. President?

THE PRESIDENT. I would guess 2 or 3 weeks, until the doctors make sure that the bone is healing back well.

Q. How does she feel about not being able to campaign for you for the rest of the campaign?

THE PRESIDENT. Well, she might be campaigning by telephone.

Q. Have you heard of the latest Reagan charges on the Stealth?

THE PRESIDENT. Yes, I've heard it, but I don't want to comment on that today.

Q. How about Zia? Did he give you any report on the Persian Gulf war?

THE PRESIDENT. Not lately.

Q. Mr. President?

THE PRESIDENT. Yes?

Q. Mr. Reagan accused you of covering up the Stealth leak.

THE PRESIDENT. I've already made a statement on that before, and I stand by what I said.

Thank you very much.

REPORTER. Thank you, Mr. President.

NOTE: The President spoke at 5:32 p.m. outside the Sumter County Memorial Hospital. Following the President's visit, he returned to the White House.

Cuban and Haitian Refugees

Executive Order 12244.   October 3, 1980

EXEMPTION FOR FORT ALLEN

By the authority vested in me as President by the Constitution and statutes of the United States of America, including Section 313 of the Federal Water Pollution Control Act, as amended (33 U.S.C. 1323), Section 118 of the Clean Air Act, as amended (42 U.S.C. 7418), Section 4 of the Noise Control Act of 1972 (42 U.S.C. 4903), and Section 6001 of the Solid Waste Disposal Act, as amended (42 U.S.C. 6961), and in order to provide for the immediate relocation and temporary housing of Haitian and Cuban nationals, who are located in the State of Florida and presently in the custody of the United States, at a Federal facility known as Fort Allen, located in the Commonwealth of Puerto Rico, and having determined it to be in the paramount interest of the United States to exempt Fort Allen from all the requirements otherwise imposed on it by the said statutes, it is hereby ordered as follows:

1-101. Consistent with the provisions of subsection (a) of Section 313 of the Federal Water Pollution Control Act, as amended (33 U.S.C. 1323(a)), each and every effluent source located at Fort Allen is exempted from compliance with the provisions of that Act; except that no exemption is hereby granted from Sections 306 and 307 of that Act (33 U.S.C. 1316 and 1317).

1-102. Consistent with the provisions of subsection (b) of Section 118 of the Clean Air Act, as amended (42 U.S.C. 7418(b)), each and every particular emission source located at Fort Allen is exempted from compliance with the provisions of that Act; except that no exemption is hereby granted from Sections 111 and 112 of that Act (42 U.S.C. 7411 and 7412).

1-103. Consistent with the provisions of subsection 4(b) of the Noise Control Act of 1972, as amended (42 U.S.C. 4903(b)), each and every single activity or facility, including noise emission sources or classes thereof, located at Fort Allen, are exempted from compliance with the provisions of that Act; except that no exemption is hereby granted from Sections 6, 17 and 18 of that Act (42 U.S.C. 4906, 4916, 4917).

1-104. Consistent with the provisions of Section 6001 of the Solid Waste Disposal Act, as amended (42 U.S.C. 6961), each and every solid waste management facility located at Fort Allen is exempted from compliance with the provisions of that Act.

1-105. The exemptions granted by this Order shall be for the one-year period beginning October 2, 1980, and ending October 1, 1981.

JIMMY CARTER

The White House,
October 3, 1980.

[Filed with the Office of the Federal Register, 10:44 a.m., October 6, 1980]

Digest of Other White House Announcements

The following listing includes the President's public schedule and other items of general interest announced by the White House Press Office and not included elsewhere in this issue.

September 28

The President returned to the White House from Camp David, Md.

September 29

The President met at the White House with Zbigniew Brzezinski, Assistant to the President for National Security Affairs.

September 30

The President met at the White House with:

—Dr. Brzezinski;
—Representative Parren J. Mitchell of Maryland;
—Governor Bob Graham of Florida;
—Representative James C. Corman of California and artist Peter Max, who donated a lithograph of the Statue of Liberty to the Democratic Campaign Committee to raise money for Democratic candidates.

The President announced the recess appointments of three persons as Representatives and four persons as Alternate Representatives to the 35th Session of the General Assembly of the United Nations. These persons were nominated on September 22, but were not confirmed by the Senate before it adjourned. They are:

Representatives

DONALD F. McHENRY, U.S. Representative to the United Nations;

WILLIAM J. VANDEN HEUVEL, Deputy U.S. Representative to the United Nations;

HANNAH D. ATKINS, Oklahoma State representative.

Alternate Representatives

NATHAN LANDOW, president, Landow and Co., Bethesda, Md.;

BARBARA NEWSOM, trustee and secretary, the L. S. B. Leakey Foundation, Pasadena, Calif.;

RICHARD W. PETREE, Deputy U.S. Representative to the Security Council of the United Nations;

H. CARL McCALL, U.S. Alternate Representative for Special Political Affairs in the United Nations.

The President announced that he will nominate Brig. Gen. Hugh Granville Robinson, of the U.S. Army Corps of Engineers, to be a member of the Mississippi River Commission. He would replace Maj. Gen. Richard Harris, who is retiring. Robinson, 48, is division engineer of the Army Engineer Division, Southwestern.

October 1

The President met at the White House with Dr. Brzezinski.

October 2

The President met at the White House with Dr. Brzezinski.

The White House announced that the President declared a major disaster for the State of California as a result of flooding, beginning on September 26, which caused extensive property damage.

October 3

The President met at the White House with:

—Dr. Brzezinski;

—Secretary of Defense Harold Brown, Secretary of State Edmund S. Muskie, Deputy Secretary of State Warren M. Christopher, Lloyd N. Cutler, Counsel to the President, Jody Powell, Press Secretary to the President, and Dr. Brzezinski;

—Frank B. Moore, Assistant to the President for Congressional Liaison.

NOMINATIONS SUBMITTED TO THE SENATE

The following list does not include promotions of members of the Uniformed Services, nominations to the Service Academies, or nominations of Foreign Service officers.

Submitted September 30, 1980

CHARLES LUNA, of Texas, to be a member of the Board of Directors of the National Railroad Passenger Corporation for a term expiring July 18, 1984 (reappointment).

BRIG. GEN. HUGH GRANVILLE ROBINSON, 577–44–1975, United States Army, to be a member of the Mississippi River Commission, under the provisions of section 2 of an act of Congress, approved 28 June 1879 (21 Stat. 37) (33 U.S.C. 642).

ELWOOD THOMAS DRIVER, of Virginia, to be a member of the National Transportation Safety Board for the term expiring December 31, 1985 (reappointment).

JEFFREY G. MILLER, of Maryland, to be an Assistant Administrator of the Environmental Protection Agency vice Marvin B. Durning, resigned.

GARDNER PATTERSON, of the District of Columbia, to be a member of the United States International Trade Commission for the remainder of the term expiring June 16, 1981, vice Italo H. Ablondi, resigned.

NOMINATIONS—Continued

Withdrawn September 30, 1980

ROBERT E. BALDWIN, of Wisconsin, to be a member of the United States International Trade Commission for the remainder of the term expiring June 16, 1981, vice Italo H. Ablondi, resigned, which was sent to the Senate on November 30, 1979.

FRANK T. CARY, of Connecticut, to be a member of the Board of Directors of the United States Synthetic Fuels Corporation for a term of 6 years, which was sent to the Senate on September 19, 1980.

CHECKLIST OF WHITE HOUSE PRESS RELEASES

The following listing contains releases of the White House Press Office which are not included in this issue.

Released September 29, 1980

Advance text: remarks at the 37th Tri-Annual Convention of the International Ladies Garment Workers Union in New York, N.Y.

Advance text: remarks to the New York Business/Labor Committee for Carter/Mondale in New York, N.Y.

Released September 30, 1980

Fact sheet: revitalization program for the American steel industry

News conference: on the revitalization program for the American steel industry—by Philip M. Klutznick, Secretary, and Robert E. Herzstein, Under Secretary for International Trade, Department of Commerce; Senator Jennings Randolph of West Virginia, Stuart E. Eizenstat, Assistant to the President for Domestic Affairs and Policy; Ambassador Reubin O'D. Askew, United States Trade Representative; Douglas M. Costle, Administrator, Environmental Protection Agency; Lloyd McBride, president, United Steelworkers of America; and William DeLancey, president, Republic Steel

Advance text: remarks at the annual meetings of the World Bank Group and International Monetary Fund

Released October 1, 1980

Advance text: remarks to employees of the Ford Automobile Assembly Plant in Wayne, Mich.

CHECKLIST—Continued

Released October 1—Continued

Advance text: opening remarks at the townhall meeting in Flint, Mich.

Advance text: remarks on signing S. 2443 into law at a ceremony in Niagara Falls, N.Y.

Advance text: remarks at the annual convention of the Civil Service Employees Association in Niagara Falls, N.Y.

Released October 2, 1980

Advance text: opening remarks at the townhall meeting in Dayton, Ohio

Released October 3, 1980

Advance text: remarks at a White House reception for the National Association of Women Judges

Fact sheet: H.R. 5192, Education Amendments of 1980

News conference: on the administration's legislative accomplishments and the status of pending legislation—by Frank B. Moore, Assistant to the President for Congressional Liaison; James T. McIntyre, Jr., Director, Office of Management and Budget; William H. Cable, Deputy Assistant for Congressional Liaison (House); and Mr. Eizenstat

---

ACTS APPROVED BY THE PRESIDENT

Approved September 29, 1980

H.R. 3292_____ Public Law 96–366
Fish and Wildlife Conservation Act of 1980.

Approved October 1, 1980

H.R. 7590_____ Public Law 96–367
Energy and Water Development Appropriation Act, 1981.

S. 2443_____ Public Law 96–368
West Valley Demonstration Project Act.

H.J. Res. 610_____ Public Law 96–369
A joint resolution making continuing appropriations for the fiscal year 1981, and for other purposes.

Approved October 3, 1980

H.R. 7825_____ Public Law 96–370
An act to establish the Ice Age National Scenic Trail, and for other purposes.

ACTS APPROVED—Continued

Approved October 3—Continued

H.J. Res. 551_____ Public Law 96–371
A joint resolution authorizing and requesting the President of the United States to issue a proclamation designating the seven calendar days beginning October 5, 1980, as "National Port Week", and for other purposes.

S.J. Res. 209_____ Public Law 96–372
A joint resolution providing for temporary extension of certain Federal Housing Administration authorities and for rural housing authorities.

H.R. 6395_____ Public Law 96–373
An act to amend the Consumer Product Safety Act to modify certain postemployment restrictions applicable to officers and employees of the Consumer Product Safety Commission.

H.R. 5192_____ Public Law 95–374
Education Amendments of 1980.

ACTS APPROVED—Continued

Approved October 3—Continued

H.R. 5278_____ Public Law 96–375
An act to authorize the Secretary of the Interior to engage in feasibility investigations of certain water resource developments, and for other purposes.

S. 2489_____ Public Law 96–376
An act to authorize appropriations for the Coast Guard for fiscal year 1981, to authorize supplemental appropriations for fiscal year 1980, and for other purposes.

H.R. 7478_____ Public Law 96–377
An act to facilitate the management of the public debt by permitting an increase in the investment yield on United States savings bonds above the existing 7 per centum ceiling, and by increasing the amount of the bonds paying interest in excess of 4¼ per centum which may be outstanding.

Ambassador at Large and Special Representative of the President for the Law of the Sea Conference

Exchange of Letters on the Resignation of Elliot L. Richardson.   October 3, 1980

To Ambassador Elliot Richardson

Thank you for your letter. I accept with reluctance your resignation as Ambassador at Large and Special Representative of the President of the United States of America for the Law of the Sea Conference and Chief of Delegation, effective on a date to be determined.

I deeply appreciate your contributions to the conduct of our foreign policy. You have ably represented the interests of the United States. Your contributions to the Law of the Sea Conference and the delicate negotiations encompassing it have been especially meaningful. I greatly appreciate your valuable insights and tireless efforts.

With best wishes,
Sincerely,

JIMMY CARTER

[The Honorable Elliot L. Richardson, Ambassador at Large and Special Representative for the Law of the Sea Conference, Department of State, Washington, D.C.]

———

September 26, 1980

Dear Mr. President:

I respectfully request that you accept my resignation as your Special Represent-ative to the Law of the Sea Conference as of October 3, 1980.

The goal of a mutually acceptable Convention on the Law of the Sea is now close to fulfillment. Although several important issues remain to be settled at the Tenth Session of the Conference, there is now every likelihood that the Convention can be completed and opened for signature before the end of next year. Knowing that the remaining tasks will be in the hands of an extremely competent and experienced delegation, I feel able in good conscience to let personal considerations bring about my long-deferred return to private life.

It has been a great privilege to have had a part during the past nearly four years in an undertaking that can have so much importance for the prevention of conflict and the extension of the rule of law. The effort has been difficult, demanding, and sometimes frustrating, but never boring. I leave it reluctantly and with sincere appreciation for your confidence and support.

I hope, in any case, to continue to be useful in furthering the objectives of the Conference and would be happy to be called upon in a private capacity to assist in any appropriate way to bring the negotiations to a final and fruitful conclusion.

Respectfully,

ELLIOT L. RICHARDSON

[The President, The White House.]

NOTE: The text of the letters were made available on October 4, when the White House announced that the President had accepted Ambassador Richardson's resignation.

2073

Synthetic Fuels Corporation

*Statement on the Recess Appointments of
Five Members of the Board of Directors.
October 5, 1980*

Although we continue to make progress in reducing America's dependence on foreign sources of oil, the current conflict in the Persian Gulf region serves as a reminder of our need to achieve energy independence without delay. Therefore, I am today announcing the recess appointments of five members of the Board of Directors of the Synthetic Fuels Corporation. I am taking this action because the United States Senate failed to confirm these nominees before it adjourned last week. A number of congressional leaders, including Senator Robert Byrd and Senator Henry Jackson, have encouraged me to proceed with recess appointments.

The Synthetic Fuels Corporation can now begin immediately its work to design, build, and operate plants which will convert coal, shale, tar sands, and other American natural resources into synthetic fuels. This corporation for energy security is the cornerstone of our national energy policy.

I urge the Senate to move quickly to confirm each of these recess appointments when it reconvenes in November.

NOTE: On the same day, the President announced the recess appointments of John C. Sawhill, Lane Kirkland, Frank Savage, Catherine B. Cleary, and John D. DeButts as members of the Board of Directors of the Synthetic Fuels Corporation. For the announcements of their nominations, see pages 1700 and 1717 of this series.

Peace Corps Advisory Council

Executive Order 12245.   October 6, 1980

By the authority vested in me as President of the United States of America, and in accordance with the Federal Advisory Committee Act, as amended (5 U.S.C. App. I), and in order to provide for Co-Chairpersons on the Peace Corps Advisory Council, Section 1–202 of Executive Order No. 12137 of May 16, 1979, is hereby amended to read as follows:

"1–202. The President shall appoint not more than 30 individuals to serve on the Council and shall designate two members to serve as Co-Chairpersons. Members shall serve at the pleasure of the President.".

JIMMY CARTER

The White House,
   October 6, 1980.

[Filed with the Office of the Federal Register, 10:52 a.m., October 7, 1980]

Peace Corps Advisory Council

*Appointment of 29 Members and
Designation of Cochairpersons.
October 6, 1980*

The President today announced the appointment of 29 persons as members of the Peace Corps Advisory Council. They are:

MUHAMMAD ALI, former World Boxing Council heavyweight champion of the world;

THOMAS JOSEPH BARRETT, of St. Paul, Minn., managing attorney for Migrant Legal Services of Minnesota and North Dakota, a former Peace Corps volunteer;

CAROL BELLAMY, president of the New York City Council and a former Peace Corps volunteer (also designated Cochairperson);

ALVA T. BONDA, of Bratenahl, Ohio, chairman of the board of Penril Corp., an electronics firm, and a member of the board of trustees of Brandeis University;

HARLAN CLEVELAND, of Princeton, N.J., director of the Aspen Institute program in international affairs, a former U.S. Ambassador to NATO;

ANTHONY J. ESTEVEZ, of Miami, Fla., an architect and planner who is president of a building and development firm and owner of several residential and commercial properties and a heavy equipment company;

GREGORY MICHAEL FLAKUS, of Omaha, Nebr., a graduate assistant in the department of communications at the University of Nebraska, a former Peace Corps volunteer, and president of the National Council of Retired Peace Corps Volunteers;

ZOLTAN GOMBOS, of Cleveland, Ohio, editor of several Hungarian-language newspapers and president of the Liberty Publishing Co.;

LESTER GROSS, of Columbia, S.C., president of Harbison Development Corp., a member of the Urban Land Institute and of the board of trustees of the United States League of New Community Developers;

SAMUEL HALPERIN, director of the Institute for Educational Leadership at George Washington University, former Deputy Assistant Secretary of Health, Education, and Welfare;

TERRY HERNDON, of Bethesda, Md., executive director of the National Education Association and a director of the United Nations Association and the Council on Hemispheric Affairs (also designated Cochairperson);

YOLANDA KING, of Atlanta, Ga., an actress and director, member of the board of directors of the Martin Luther King, Jr., Center for Social Change and the Commission for the Advancement of Policy Affecting Youth, the Disadvantaged, and the Poor;

MAXINE HONG KINGSTON, of Honolulu, Hawaii, a professor at the University of Hawaii and author of "The Woman Lawyer";

LORETTA LYNN, of Hurricane Mills, Tenn., award-winning country singer and author of the autobiography "Coal Miner's Daughter";

GRACE D. McCULLAH, of Mesa, Ariz., executive director of the Navajo Ford Product Industry, personnel director of the Navajo Tribe, and executive director of the Indian Development District of Arizona;

MARY TYLER MOORE, actress and entertainer;

HENRY MORGENTHAU, of Cambridge, Mass., special assistant to the president of the University of Massachusetts for audiovisual communications and a former executive producer for WGBH-Television in Boston;

ANTONIA PANTOJA, president and founder of the Graduate School for Urban Resources and Social Policy in San Diego, Calif., founder and the first executive director of ASPIRA, and founder of the Puerto Rican Association for Community Affairs;

RUBY B. PERNELL, professor of social work at Case Western Reserve University and former social welfare attaché at the U.S. Embassy in New Delhi, India;

EVELYN PERRY, of Cary, N.C., coordinator of volunteer services for the city of Raleigh, a former Peace Corps volunteer, who also served as Peace Corps special projects assistant and Peace Corps program officer for radio and television;

DONALD E. POST, of Austin, Tex., professor of anthropology and sociology and director of Third World studies at St. Edward's University;

YOLANDA SANCHEZ, of the Bronx, N.Y., executive director of the East Harlem Council for Human Services and project director for the East Harlem Neighborhood Health Center, a founding member and board member of the New York chapter of the National Conference of Puerto Rican Women;

SIDNEY SUHER, of Rochester, N.Y., an attorney specializing in family law;

GENE TACKETT, of Bakersfield, Calif., president of the Central California Health Planning Organization and member of the Kern County Board of Supervisors, a former Peace Corps volunteer and Peace Corps recruiter;

FAYE WATTLETON, of New Rochelle, N.Y., president of the Planned Parenthood Federation of America, a former assistant director of public health nursing services for the city of Dayton, Ohio;

DAVID WINFIELD, captain and outfielder with the San Diego Padres baseball team, founder of the David Winfield Foundation for Underprivileged Children;

JOAN T. WINN, of Dallas, Tex., a judge of the 191st Judicial District Court of Texas and a former Peace Corps volunteer;

FRANCE YANAI WONG, of Los Angeles, Calif., an elementary school teacher with the Los Angeles Unified School District, former chairperson of the cultural and student exchange program of the Los Angeles-Nagoya, Japan Sister Cities program;

ANDREW J. YOUNG, president of Young Ideas, former U.S. Ambassador to the United Nations.

The President also announced that Mrs. Lillian Carter will serve as honorary Chair of this Council.

West Allis, Wisconsin

Remarks at the West Campus of the
Milwaukee Area Technical College.
October 6, 1980

Well, first of all let me say that I'm delighted to be here.

As President it's always helpful to bask in the glory of two very fine and popular political leaders—Gaylord Nelson, who is looked upon throughout this Nation as the protector of the small business enterprises of our Nation, the protector of the free enterprise system, and one of the most dedicated men I've ever known to helping provide a better life and better jobs for all the people of America. You are indeed fortunate to have him specifically concentrating not only on nationwide problems but on the opportunities in this great State of Wisconsin.

And Clem Zablocki, chairman of the Foreign Affairs Committee of the House, is one of those men that I have to work with on a daily basis in trying to keep our Nation strong, first of all, and keep our Nation and the world at peace. It's always good to have a man like him, who's completely versed in the very complicated international affairs, but still who keeps his roots very close to the people of this Nation. And he understands the particular makeup of our great country, a country of refugees, a country of immigrants, a country of people who've come here from almost every other nation on Earth and who've invested our lives in better opportunities for our children and also more freedom for ourselves.

So, I'm indeed honored to be with these two fine men.

I had a chance to ride with Mayor Maier and his wife from Washington, and I was welcomed outside by Mayor Barlich.

I'm very proud to have both of them here. And the officials of the school, the instructors, the students have already made my visit a successful one, even in the brief time that I've had to spend.

This school, which is the largest one of its kind in the entire world, serves during a year's period of time about 70,000 Americans, those who already have a good life that want to have a better life. And this school, in my judgment, represents what our Nation is all about. We Americans believe in carrying our own weight. We believe in independence for ourselves and also for our beloved country. And this school offers the skills and the knowledge that all of us need, particularly the graduates of this school, to be productive citizens. It helps you to help yourselves, and it helps our Nation in the process.

You all have your own personal goals, you in this room and all those listening to my voice. You want to become even stronger breadwinners for your families. You want to become independent and respected members of a cohesive community. You want to plan for the future. You, like I, want to give your children an even better life than the one we've enjoyed, and we want to be secure in our retirement years.

Today we do face tough economic problems in this country. They're complicated; there's nothing simple or easy about them. Those challenges, if not met successfully, can stand in our way to the fulfillment of the life that we want so much. They can obstruct our economic goals, they can prevent our children having a better life than we have, and they can also prevent our Nation from being secure, prosperous, and at peace. As President, I am determined to meet those economic challenges and to resolve the economic problems for the best interests of all Americans. I've worked very closely with the working families of this country and the leaders who represent them, in and out of the labor union movement itself.

We've got to face, also, specific challenges like the overdependence on foreign oil, which was becoming a debilitating circumstance for our Nation. Over the few years before I became President, every year we were importing more and more of our oil and had reached the point where about half of the total oil consumed in this Nation came from overseas.

As we import a shipload of oil, we also import inflation and unemployment. So, the Congress and I have worked closely together, hammering out for ourselves an energy policy for our Nation. It's been remarkably successful already, although it's only been on the books a short time. We've cut down our imports of foreign oil by about 24 percent, and each day this year we import about 2 million barrels of oil less than we did the same day the first year I was in office—a remarkable achievement by the people of this country, who see this threat to our economic future. I'm determined that we'll continue this progress to make sure that our Nation is independent on energy and that we control inflation and unemployment resulting from this high dependence on imported oil.

We're also facing the problem of declining productivity growth. American workers are still the most productive on Earth. We produce more per hour worked, per year worked in this country than any other people on Earth. But our rate of increase of production per hour or per year has not been going up well; in fact, it's been declining a little bit lately. And that's because we've not had enough money invested in giving our workers the new tools and new factories that would

let them continue to be more productive as time goes along and to compete with foreign suppliers of goods. But I think now we've turned the corner on that.

We've got to do it by revitalizing American industry—here again, a very complicated process, because you've got to do it with tax provisions that will let people invest in those new factories and new tools, and you've got to do it with the maximum dependence on the freedom of our free enterprise system. We've tried to get the Government's nose out of the private affairs of the free enterprise system and have had remarkable success recently with the deregulation of the airline industry, the trucking industry, the rail industry, the financial institutions industry. Cut down on paperwork and let competition give industry a better chance to survive on its own, in freedom, and at the same time give consumers better prices for high-quality products.

America's strength doesn't come from giant corporations; it doesn't come from the Federal Government; it doesn't come from the State or local governments, either. It comes from the work and the ingenuity and the dedication and the skills of American workers. I'm determined to see our country make the most of this great strength, and I want to make sure that all those who graduate from this school and other schools like it around the Nation have the greatest possible opportunities to provide for yourselves and for your own families. This also, in the same process, provides for the best future of our country.

To improve worker productivity, we need to build the new plants and modernize those that presently exist. There's no way to stop change; circumstances economically in our own country, in a given community, and around the world are going to change. But Americans have never been afraid of change. We've always been on the cutting edge of change. Ready with the freedom that we have, with the good education systems that we have, with the research and development that we know, we've been the ones that carve out the benefits from new ideas and to make our competition with other nations in the world more and more successful. But I have to tell you that world competition is becoming more challenging, more difficult every year. And we need to win that competition. But you don't win a war with obsolete weapons; you don't win a competition, economic war with obsolete tools.

I'd like to point out, since this is a political year, the stark difference between myself and my opponent for President in how to deal with these questions I've just described to you. Governor Reagan proposes a tax program called Reagan-Kemp-Roth. This proposal would provide massive inflationary tax cuts across the board, amounting between now and 1987 to a Federal income tax reduction of a thousand billion dollars, a trillion dollars. These tax cuts would add billions and billions of dollars to the Federal deficit and would mean the printing of more and more Federal money, dollars that would become more and more worthless, and inflation would rob every family.

This Reagan-Kemp-Roth proposal is like quicksilver; it glitters. It promises quick results, easy answers, but it ends up being worthless except for the very rich, who would benefit greatly at the expense of the working families of this country. It's been condemned even by Business Week as inflationary. George Bush, who is Governor Reagan's running mate as Vice President, said it would create inflation in excess of 30 percent, and he called

it "voodoo economics." Even President Ford, who supports Governor Reagan, says it's too inflationary for him to support.

We can't deal with our problems offering something for nothing just in the last few weeks or a month of a political campaign. We have to face the facts, and sometimes these facts are very difficult; sometimes, almost always, they are very complicated. And the facts are that you can't give giant tax cuts, giant increases in spending for a nuclear arms race, balance the budget, stop inflation, all at the same time. I have great confidence in the sound judgment of the American people, and I have no doubt that they'll reject this Republican economic program of implausible promises, improbable assumptions, and ill-considered proposals. This creates in the people's minds increasingly, day by day, uncertainty and doubt about the future.

There's another Republican proposal that I'd like to mention to you now that concerns me very deeply and ought to concern every person that lives in our country, and especially those who live in Wisconsin, who pay State taxes and who pay local property taxes. Governor Reagan has proposed that the programs for education and welfare be shifted to the shoulders of the local and State governments. This for Wisconsin means a shift of about a billion dollars a year to pay for the welfare programs that he would put as your responsibility.

There are only two ways he could do it. He's called for some sort of change in tax sources. This would either require that property tax and other taxes in Wisconsin would have to go up a billion dollars, which would cost the average family in this State $870 a year in increased property taxes; or else he would have to transfer literally billions and billions of dollars from the Federal Government to local governments in some sort of a massive, undefined, revenue-sharing program that he's never spelled out to the American people. If he did that, it would further aggravate the tremendous cost in inflation and Federal deficits of the Reagan-Kemp-Roth tax proposal.

This kind of confusion creates doubt and uncertainty about the future. As you know, Governor Reagan has refused to debate with me. What I think we ought to have and what I know we ought to have, for the benefit of the American people, is a man-to-man debate between me and Governor Reagan, so that I can say to him, "I've got a question I want to ask. As you put the burden of welfare and education on the shoulders of local property tax payers, how is it going to be paid for by those already overburdened Americans? Or if you're going to transfer some sort of tax source to them to finance this program, how is the Federal Government going to handle the enormous deficits and the enormous inflationary results of that transfer?"

The point is that in an election year it's extremely important for candidates to be responsible, to be sound, to be clear, to be honest, not to mislead the American people by offering simplistic answers to complicated questions, and if questioned on an issue so important as the one I've just described to you, to explain very clearly to the American people what the answers are.

There's a very clear difference between me and my opponent. There's a very clear difference between the Democratic Party and what it stands for and the Republican Party. That difference is much more vivid in 1980 than it's been before. We're talking about a difference in two futures for America. I know that all of you are search-

ing now, during the last few weeks of this election year, for the answers to this basic question: What is the future of our Nation going to be? Will my family be stable? Will my taxes be moderate? Is my future predictable? Are we going to control nuclear weapons? Are we going to avoid war and keep peace for our Nation? Will education and welfare and other programs be handled in a responsible way? Will job opportunities be provided? Will tax programs be fair?

These are the kinds of questions that must be determined in the mind of every single individual American who goes to the polls to vote on November the 4th. The responsibility is yours. And that's why I came here to this fine school to talk to you and to listen to you and to talk to your students and the faculty of this school and to learn how you feel our Nation's future will be shaped.

I started out my remarks by saying that this school stands for what America is all about, and I believe it's also what our economic programs are all about. There are no easy answers. The American people want frankness. The American people do not believe in living on handouts. The American people believe that an able-bodied person should have a job and if it's offered to them, that that person ought to take the job. The American people want to carry their own weight. And I want to make it easier for those aspirations and those commitments and those principles that have guided our Nation for so long to be carried out.

As I said before, we Americans come from a lot of different countries, and we've all come with the same common dream— a dream of freedom, a dream of opportunity, a dream of a better future for our families. And I'm determined to make this dream of America a living and a breathing reality. With your help, we will not fail. The future of our great country will be even brighter than the present and the past that we free Americans have known.

Thank you very much. God bless you all.

NOTE: The President spoke at 12:12 p.m. to faculty, students, and community leaders in Room A105–111 of the Main Building.

Prior to his remarks, the President took a walking tour of the college facilities.

Milwaukee, Wisconsin

Excerpt From an Interview With John McCullough of WTMJ–TV.
October 6, 1980

MR. McCULLOUGH. Have you talked, Mr. President, to President Brezhnev about the Middle East?

THE PRESIDENT. We've exchanged letters about it, and Secretary Muskie recently has met personally and had extended conversations, several hours, with Foreign Minister Gromyko, representing the Soviet Union. And at that time, Foreign Minister Gromyko delivered me another personal letter from President Brezhnev. So, we have means of communicating back and forth on a fairly regular basis.

MR. McCULLOUGH. Are they as anxious as you to keep it confined?

THE PRESIDENT. I hope so. My belief is that the Soviets don't want war to break out in a general way throughout the Persian Gulf.

The biggest threat to our security would be if the Soviets should be tempted to move into Iran or to move into an area where they can control the Persian Gulf itself or the access to it. This would be a direct threat not only to our own security but the security of other Western nations who depend on oil supplies from that region for economic well-being.

We've developed now an energy policy since I've been in office that is reducing very rapidly our dependence on foreign oil. That's the best way for our economic security to be maintained. It's the best way for us to have an independent foreign policy free of unwarranted control or influence by the OPEC nations, who might try to use the oil weapon as blackmail as they did in '73 and '74.

MR. McCULLOUGH. You mentioned Senator Muskie. There was a report that perhaps he might not be a part of your second administration, if that would come to be. Is there anything you could say about that?

THE PRESIDENT. That's a false report. I talked to Secretary Muskie last night. I won't use the exact language, but he said it was absolutely false. He enjoys his job. He and I have a very fine relationship. The good relationship exists with the national security adviser, as well. And I think if you were to ask Secretary Muskie the same question, he would give you the same answer. He likes his job; he's pleased with what he's doing. And my hope is that he'll continue there.

NOTE: The interview began at approximately 1:25 p.m. at General Mitchell Field.

Addison, Illinois

Remarks and a Question-and-Answer Session with Du Page County Residents.
October 6, 1980

THE PRESIDENT. Can you all hear me okay? Very good.

Well, first of all I want to thank Bud and Margaret Loftus for letting me come and be with them at their home and to meet with you. In 1976 Bud had a choice between having me in his backyard or Senator Lloyd Bentsen—[*laughter*]—and he decided to choose Lloyd Bentsen, right? [*Laughter*] So, this is kind of to equal the score.

I would like to say that Bud not only takes care of the present but also the future—I just met nine children, I think, in the house. [*Laughter*] And I'm also interested in the future.

CAMPAIGN ISSUES

This afternoon I'd like to spend just a few minutes talking to you briefly about some of the things that are important to all of us, and then answer your questions for a half an hour or so.

Our Nation is the strongest country on Earth. Militarily, politically, economically, we're the strongest nation on Earth. But we faced and are facing some very serious questions and problems brought about primarily by the troubled areas in the world, in the Mideast, in Africa, in Asia, and also brought about by the increase in oil prices imposed on the rest of the world by the OPEC countries.

Last year the price of oil increased more in one year than it had the entire time since oil was first discovered in the 1800's. And this economic fact has swept across our Nation, and it's hurt us severely. But this impact has not been too strong for our country to assimilate, because, as you all know, every time in the past our Nation has been challenged and our country was unified, we've been able to meet that challenge or answer that question or resolve that problem as a united country.

We're a country of great diversity, people here from all over the world, almost every country on Earth, represented here, trying to keep our heritage and our religious convictions and our family structures close, to remember our history, but still at the same time to be Americans first of all and to keep our country strong because we are diverse in nature.

This election is one that involves the future, perhaps as much as any election I ever remember, and the election is a contest between the sharpest differences between me and Governor Reagan, between the Democratic Party and what it stands for and what the Republican Party now stands for and between the two futures that we face.

We have a problem of controlling nuclear weapons. Every President since Harry Truman, including all the Republicans and the Democrats, have worked to carve out with the Soviet Union an agreement whereby we could limit and balance and then reduce the dependence on atomic weapons. Governor Reagan has thrown that out, saying that he would withdraw the SALT II treaty from the Senate, that he would start a nuclear arms race as a card to be played against the Soviet Union. This is a very dangerous proposal, and it shows Governor Reagan's lack of understanding of how important it is, and also the adverse impact on the attitude and consciousness of our own country, and also what it means to our allies and friends, the countries around the world that don't have nuclear weapons, and also the attitude of our relationship between us and the Soviet Union.

We've got to have a balance in military strength on the one hand, and arms control on the other. It takes two wings for an airplane to fly, and you can't just fly with military strength alone, a nuclear arms race, and not work toward maintaining peace and maintaining arms control. The same thing with economics.

Energy is the greatest threat right now. You've got to have a combination of conservation on the one hand and increased energy production on the other. A plane's got to have two wings to fly. We've had a very balanced approach to the energy question. We've cut down on our consumption; we have insulated homes; we've had a very restrained attitude on the part of the American people to eliminate waste. At the same time we've increased production of energy in our country.

This year for instance, we'll produce more coal than any other year in history. We'll drill more oil and gas wells this year than any year in history. And my hope is to continue that progress and eventually to replace as an energy basis for the rest of the world OPEC oil and substitute Illinois coal. I think it would be a very good development.

Also it's important to realize that here again the differences are very sharp. Governor Reagan wants to eliminate the Department of Energy. He wants to repeal or drastically change the windfall profits tax. He doesn't believe in conservation, and he wants to do away with the 55-mile-per-hour speed limit, for instance, and put our country back into a position that might be excessively dependent on the OPEC nations for oil. We've cut back 2 million barrels a day on how much oil we buy from overseas since I've been in office. And the program has just now been put into effect.

And the last point I want to make before I answer your questions is on taxation. It's very important for us to have a balanced and fair tax program with a proper delineation of responsibility between the Federal Government on the one hand, and local and State government on the other. We've done a lot to get the Gov-

ernment's nose out of the private affairs of Americans and the private enterprise system and let competition work. We've deregulated the trucking industry, the airline industry, the rail industry, the financial institutions industry of this country, working on communications, trying to get the Government to let competition work.

Governor Reagan, on the other hand, wants to put the burden of welfare and education programs off the Federal Government onto the shoulders of people in your community and communities all over Illinois and the rest of this country. In Illinois the amount of money that the Federal Government contributes to the welfare and education programs is more than $2 billion, and if that was put on you, away from the Federal Government income tax system, it would mean that your property taxes and other taxes would have to go up an average of about $750 per family or either the Federal Government would have to give up that much more revenue and make the Reagan-Kemp-Roth tax bill be even more costly and even more inflationary and even more unbalanced.

So far, these kinds of issues have not been debated adequately between me and my Republican opponent, because he won't debate me on a two-man debate. And if that's not possible, because he refused in the future, then you need to make your judgment by November 4 based on what is best for you. The control of nuclear weapons, or not; an energy policy that's controlled by the people, or one that's turned back over to the oil companies; or the kind of tax program and education programs, welfare programs that are balanced between the Federal Government, local and State government, or put back on the shoulders of the local people. Those are the kinds of issues, just hurriedly, that illustrate the sharp differences between us, and I hope that you'll keep that in mind as you go to the polls on November 4.

And now, I'd like to answer your questions. I've talked enough, and I'll be glad to start over here on the right.

QUESTIONS

DU PAGE COUNTY WATER PROJECT

Q. The question I have, Mr. President, we in Du Page County, one of our personal pressing needs is the availability of water. We have Lake Michigan 20-some miles to the east of us; we have a plan; we have the engineering done; we have the association of all the communities of Du Page County who can avail themselves of Lake Michigan water. If we get Lake Michigan water, we reduce the dependence on the deep water aquifers, which are being depleted. We need the help of the Federal Government on the basis of a low-interest loan to finance the construction of the tunnel, the deep tunnel from the city of Chicago to Du Page County, and I'd like to know what your thoughts are on this. You have a report now from the Urban Water Supply Task Force, and you have not addressed that as yet.

THE PRESIDENT. I'm not familiar with that issue, but I'll find out and let you know. We have, as you know, a very strong program in the Environmental Protection Agency to provide freshwater supplies and also sewage systems for governments that have been increased substantially. But that particular project to supply fresh water to Du Page, I'm not familiar with it.

Q. Yes, you've addressed the western part of the country, but there has been no policy on the urban water system, which we are part of.

THE PRESIDENT. Well, we do have a policy on urban water systems, but I'm just not familiar with that particular issue. But if you'll give one of my staff members your name and address, I'll find out the answer and call you back or let them do it, one or the other.

Q. Thank you.

THE AMERICAN FAMILY

Q. Mr. President, I have a two-part question. First, do you agree that the strength of a nation comes from the unity of the family? And second, if you agree, do you have any proposals for promoting the unity of the American family?

THE PRESIDENT. Karen asked about the importance of the unity of the American family—what it means to our country and how we could promote it. The answer is obviously, yes. Our country is so diverse in nature, with people coming here from like 120 nations on Earth, that the structure that holds our country as a unified entity is the families being cohesive and the communities being self-reliant and sharing responsibilities for the future.

It's very important that we don't overlook the principles and ideals and religious faith that preserves the sanctity of the marriage vows and also let the family be stable in its relationship to one another. Having good schools, good transportation systems, and good jobs, and not having a disruptive society also helps substantially. We have, for instance, in our proposal for tax reductions, one element that would help people to keep the families together all over the country, and that is to eliminate the so-called marriage penalty. Now if a husband and wife live together, both of them working, they pay more taxes, more income taxes than a man and woman living together, both working, who are not married. And we will propose to the Congress for passage next year the elimination of that marriage penalty.

We've also had very good programs put into effect to let there be a good day-care center for wives who work. And of course, I think it's crucial that we pass the equal rights amendment, in my judgment, which would strengthen the American family structure. Too many women, now, a lot of women have to work, and they are in effect the breadwinners of the family. And if they only receive for the same hours and the same quality of work 59 percent as much as a man—if a man gets a dollar for doing a certain amount of work, the women on the average only get 59 cents— this tends to hurt the structure and the self-respect of the American family.

We've had an increase, for instance, in allocation of funds for education, almost 75 percent since I've been in office in just 3½ years. In addition to that, we've had a commitment that I've shared that any young person in this Nation who finishes high school can go to college now if they're qualified academically to do the work without regard to the economic income or wealth of the family itself.

There's hardly a single element of American life that's not directly related to the family, whether you're trying to maintain peace, whether you're trying to keep the unemployment rate down and employment up, whether you're trying to have a good education system, good water supply, equal rights for women and others, that doesn't affect the family. And the basic protection of Americans' rights to equal opportunity and the strengthening of religious and other ethical and moral standards, I think, are also important.

So, yes, the family's the basis for our economic and our social structure. Everything that the government can do ought to be done to preserve the family structure.

INFLATION

Q. Mr. President, as individuals, what can we do to help the administration and our country to fight the inflation that is going on?

THE PRESIDENT. Very good. One of the most important contributions to inflation is the rapid increase in oil prices and our dependence on foreign oil for our energy supply. Every person in our country can help to save energy. This is a program that we've addressed in the last 3½ years that's bigger than the Interstate Highway System, the total space program, and the Marshall plan that rebuilt Europe, all put together. And it's the kind of thing, unlike the Moon shots, where every person, even Amy, who's 12 years old, and my little Sarah, who's a year and a half old, can contribute a little bit to it, and every family in their home, on the job, and going to and from work can help to save energy. That's the most important single thing to control inflation.

Another thing that you can do is to help me revitalize the American industrial society. We've now got a base of energy that will let us look to the future with confidence. American workers are the most productive on Earth, but we haven't been increasing American productivity as much as some other countries like Germany and Japan. So, to rebuild the American industrial system to give American workers modern tools and modern factories is a very exciting prospect where all Americans can participate.

Businesses that have profits can invest them back into modernizing their own plants, and Americans can save money and let that money be used in stocks and in loans by banks and otherwise to revitalize the American industrial system. That will let each worker produce more and make us competitive and hold down inflation.

Another thing you can do is to help reduce the Federal deficit. The Federal deficit does contribute some to inflation, and it sets kind of a tone or attitude in the Nation that makes it very difficult for people to believe that we're serious about controlling inflation.

So, those kinds of things—to save energy, to save your own earnings, to invest in a better productivity for American workers, and to help hold down the budget deficit by going along with efficiency in Government, not making too many demands on Government—all those things can help a great deal to control inflation.

And of course, the other thing is to buy wisely. When you get ready to shop, I think it's very important how you make a decision on major expenditures in the family budget. Lately, for instance, I visited some of the new and modern American automobile plants. The new cars coming off the assembly lines, in our own country, are more durable, they're safer, and they're just as fuel-efficient as any foreign car you can buy. And I hope that the next time you go to trade automobiles, you'll go in the showrooms that have American cars and give the American cars a chance to compete with those foreign cars, because there again, you're making an investment in our country, you're creating more jobs for Americans, and if you don't find the car you want, of course you can buy otherwise. But I hope you'll give the American cars a chance. So, just common sense will help a lot.

POLLUTION STANDARDS AND THE STEEL INDUSTRY

Q. Considering your outstanding records on environmental issues, how would you account for your recent proposal to Congress that would lift restrictions on the steel industry, enabling them to inject more pollutants into the environment? I realize that our steel industry must be modernized, but should it be at the expense of the environment?

THE PRESIDENT. No. One of the things that we've had to do is to deal with a few basic industries that have been severely damaged by, primarily, oil price increases—coal is one. I've told you already that we are producing more coal this year than any other year in history. Automobiles is another, and the American buying habits have changed on cars so that now people want the smaller, more efficient cars, and the industry is planning to spend $80 billion in the next 5 years to revitalize the automobile industry. And the other one is steel.

We have worked out with the steel industry and with other industries a good tax program to encourage new investments and to let them take credit quicker for building new machines and new factories. Another part of our proposal for the steel industry has been worked out very carefully with them and with the environmental community, Chris. So far as I know, every environmental group in the Nation has endorsed me for reelection as President. And one of the reasons is that we've been very careful before we made a decision to make sure that it was compatible with clean air and clean water and good quality and clean land.

The steel industry will have longer period of time to bring up their plants to meet air and water pollution standards provided they agree on a planned program approved by the Environmental Protection Agency to remodel and to revise those plants to bring them in compliance with the law. In the past, they've been able to delay year after year after year, and not ever correct their air and water pollution problems. Now, if they go ahead and invest in a new plant with pollution control devices, we'll give them a couple years longer to complete their work if they sign an agreement ahead of time not to pollute the air and water anymore in the future.

Q. I was wondering—do you know who shot J. R.?

THE PRESIDENT. No. If I did, I'd raise enough money to pay for my campaign. [*Laughter*]

SYNTHETIC FUELS

Q. Mr. President, how do you see synthetic fuels and synthetic lubricants as affecting our reliance on the foreign oil that we're talking about here today.

THE PRESIDENT. Well, there are two parts to dealing with the foreign oil import question. There's one, to save energy; the other one's to produce American energy. The OPEC Arab nations, all put together, have about 6 percent of the world's energy reserves. We've got 24 percent in this country, and it's oil and natural gas; it's geothermal supplies; it's tar sands and shale oil and coal—all kinds of energy that we've got here.

One of the important new developments will be the development of synthetic fuels, that is, clean-burning oil and clean-burning gas that's gotten out of oil shale and coal. Some of the Illinois coal, for instance, has high sulfur, but you can take that same coal that now has to have very expensive scrubbers and put it through a chemical process, as you probably know, and out of it you can get the cleanest burning gas and oil. So, we will have, in the next 10 years, about $80 billion available to put into the production

of synthetic fuels in this country, which means that our almost unlimited supply of coal of all kinds, both high sulfur and low sulfur, bituminous and anthracite coals, that have in the past not been used for various reasons, can now be used to produce synthetic fuels. And this will give us a chance to be self-reliant and also open up tremendous numbers of hundreds of thousands of new jobs to produce the synthetic fuel.

So, synthetic fuel in the future will play a major role in making us more energy secure or energy independent, along with solar power, conservation, and of course, the production of oil and gas in this country.

SCIENCE AND TECHNOLOGY

THE PRESIDENT. Maybe in the back row. Yes, ma'am?

Q. Mr. President?

THE PRESIDENT. Yes. Go ahead, I can hear you.

Q. You can hear me? My name is Olga Sudless. I'm sure you know you are within a very short distance of two great national laboratories. I feel we live in a technological and scientific civilization. And I feel that the scientific research is very inadequately supported. If the Government, through the people, does not support the research, who's your supporters, and are they indeed aware of what is lacking and where it will bring us, for the future indeed lies within research.

THE PRESIDENT. Well, since I've been in office for the last 3½ years, every year in the Federal budget we've increased substantially the percentage of our budget alloted for basic research, for research and development. This has not only been in the educational institutions, like universities, but also in the Department of Energy, the Department of Defense, the Department of Education, the Department of Health. And I will continue this process of improving the percentage of the total expenditure in our country in the budget for research and development.

One of the things that we've agreed to do, for instance, on the steel industry is to allot several hundreds of millions of dollars over the next 5 years to research on more efficient ways to produce steel. In addition to that, we've made the same commitment to the automobile industry to help share with them not applied research, but basic research. And when I met in Tokyo not too long ago, last year, with the leaders of Japan and Germany, France and Italy, Great Britain and Canada, we agreed among the heads of nations that we would share basic research findings on transportation—like the reduction of friction formed between an automobile tire and the road, and a more efficient production of engines, and so forth.

The other thing that we've commited ourselves to do in the new economic stimulation program or revitalization program is to increase the amount of Federal money being granted to the universities and other research centers around the country. The space program is obviously still an ongoing program—several billions of dollars every year. I think the last part is on cancer research, and in all kinds of research concerning health, we've also increased it.

I have a scientific background of my own. I'm an engineer by education, but I did research work in science as well, in physics, and I'm very deeply committed to that. Frank Press, who's my science and technology adviser, has also been going to different countries around the world. He was recently in China; he's been in Russia

before; he's been to several countries in Africa to try to get international cooperation on basic research that might help people have a better life—in food production and health matters and things of that kind.

So, I agree with you completely. I think our record's very good. And if you are more interested in details, if you'd write Dr. Frank Press, P-r-e-s-s, he can give you kind of a summary of other things that we've done that I don't have time to outline.

Q. What was the address?

THE PRESIDENT. Frank Press, The White House.

VIEWS ON THE PRESIDENCY

Q. Mr. President?

THE PRESIDENT. One more question? Can I get one more? Okay.

Q. Mr. President, I'm a registered Republican who plans to vote for you in November.

THE PRESIDENT. I love you. [*Laughter*]

Q. Some Americans believe that Russia will gamble on war in the eighties. What are your plans to increase both the numbers and the level of preparation for the military personnel in this country?

THE PRESIDENT. The question was, some people think that the Soviets might gamble on war in the 1980's. What are my plans to make sure our defense is strong, particularly relating to personnel?

My number one responsibility above everything else is to keep our Nation secure and at peace. The question illustrates, I think, perhaps better than any other question we've had the crucial nature of the Presidency itself and the decisions that are made in the Oval Office. It's not a place for simplistic answers. It's not a place for shooting from the hip. It's not a place for snap judgments that might have very serious consequences. I have a lot of potential crises that come to my desk on which I need to make a decision. If I make the right judgment, then you never know about it. But if I should make an error in judgment, then my error would cause a crisis that would affect every life here or perhaps every life in the whole world.

One of those constant series of judgments that I have to make is how to protect our Nation's interest—our security, our economy, and the influence that we have around the world—and still maintain the peace. I thank God that I have never had to order a soldier into combat since I've been in the White House. We've had peace. No President can say that for the last 50 years, and my prayer is that I'll go out of office, hopefully at the end of 8 years, with that record intact, with the Nation at peace. Strong, yes, because our ability to keep our Nation at peace depends on our strength, our known strength. We've not only got to be strong, but the American people have got to know we're strong, our allies have to know we're strong, and our potential adversaries have to know we're strong.

My belief is the Soviets also want peace. As long as they know we are strong enough to defend our interests, to protect our own country, to help protect Western Europe, to provide economic stability for the world, then we will stay at peace. But an important element of keeping our country at peace is what I described to you with the first airplane that only had one wing. If you've got just a strong military and you're jingoistic in spirit—that is, you want to push everybody around and just show the macho of the United States— that is an excellent way to lead our country toward war. You've got to have

strength militarily. You've got to also have arms control. And you've got to have a stable, sound policy that's well understood, that our Nation is strong, we'll protect our interests, but we want to live at peace. That's what we've done so far.

To abandon nuclear arms control, in my judgment, is probably the most serious mistake that this country could make in keeping our relationships with the Soviet Union sound. My background is as a military officer. I was in the Navy 7 years after I finished at the Naval Academy. I was a submarine officer. When I got to the White House, the 8 years before me had been Republican administrations. The amount of money spent on our national defense for 7 of those years had gone down, in real dollars, above inflation.

Since I've been in office, we've had a steady growth in our commitment to our national defense in dollars above and beyond the cost of inflation. It's careful, considered, steady, predictable improvement in the quality of our defenses. I think that's the best investment we can make. We spend about 5 percent of our gross national product in the strength of our Nation, in military strength.

The last thing I'd like to remind you of is that the best weapon is one that's never fired in combat, and the best soldier is one that never dies or sheds his blood on the field of battle. So, we do need the weapons; we do need the soldiers. But they're designed to deter war, to prevent war, not to push people around.

If you look at Mr. Reagan's record the last 8 or 10 years, including recently, many times when there was a troublespot in the world, when diplomacy was obviously the best approach, and my predecessors in office, Democrats and Republicans, resolved those issues peacefully, Governor Reagan has advocated the sending in of American military forces. In countries in this hemisphere like Ecuador, or Cuba, Angola, Cyprus, Lebanon, North Korea, and other places, he has advocated sending in American military forces. That's as a Governor or as a candidate for President. What he would do in the Oval Office I don't know.

But it's a serious question about the attitude of a President, who's a lonely man in many ways while he's in the Oval Office. You have very serious judgments to make. But how to keep our Nation strong and at peace, how to have a strong military and arms control, how to have tax reductions, but an improvement in the quality of American life and better jobs for our people, how to have energy conservation and the increased production of American energy—those kind of balances are very important and very difficult. And I've found that when the questions are most serious, that's when my advisers, who are very fine men and women, are most likely to be split fifty-fifty, and that question has to be answered by me as President. And those questions that come to my desk are perhaps the most difficult of all, because if a question's easy to answer, you'll answer it yourself or you'll do it in your home or you'll do it in a county courthouse or city hall or maybe a State legislature or the Governor's office. But if none of those places can find the answer to a question, then it finally gets to me, and I share it with the Congress.

So, the crucial nature of who's in the White House and what kind of judgment a President has can affect the quality of life of every person here and every person in this country, perhaps the whole world. That's why it's so important.

It's not a bad job. I like it. And the reason I do it is that in a democracy I have you to help me, and to the extent that you're involved in the political process,

like backyard meetings like this and town-hall meetings and exchanges on television, radio, and so forth, to that extent I feel that I have your support and your partnership. It's good to have partners like you.

Thank you very much, and I've enjoyed it.

NOTE: The President spoke at 3:45 p.m. outside the home of Mr. and Mrs. Hubert Loftus.

Chicago, Illinois

Remarks at a Voter Registration Rally.
October 6, 1980

Mayor Jane Byrne, George Dunn, John Touhy, distinguished State and local officials, Members of the Congress, my fellow Democrats:

What a wonderful and exciting welcome; what a great introduction from your fine mayor. Tony Bennett may have left his heart in San Francisco, but I left my heart right here in Chicago. I'm particularly glad to be in this plaza, named after one of the greatest mayors that this Nation has ever known—your own beloved Mayor Daley, who's been so great to me when I was running for President in 1976.

This is the greatest Democratic city in America. Chicago Democrats put Illinois in the Democratic column in 1960 and elected John Fitzgerald Kennedy President, and I look for Chicago Democrats and Cook County Democrats to do exactly the same thing for me in 1980. I want you all to remember what Adlai Stevenson said: "You have to vote like a Democrat if you want to live like a Republican." Right? And by the way, I'd like to remind you that in 1952 and in 1956, my

State, Georgia, voted for Adlai Stevenson, not Dwight Eisenhower, for President. So, we know how to select them in Georgia, too.

Tomorrow I want you to turn out all the unregistered voters in Chicago and Cook County, get them registered to vote, and then turn them out on November the 4th so they can vote Democratic. Tomorrow is the last day for registration, and I want you to work this next 24 hours as though the entire election depended on every voter that you get elected [registered] tomorrow, as if every vote counts this year, because there's no doubt that it does.

This is a crucial election. It's not just an election between two candidates. It's not just an election between two parties—and you know the difference between the Republican and the Democratic Party. This is an election between two futures that will affect the life of every person here. It will affect the life of everyone in your family. It will affect the life of everyone you love or care for. Your choice will have an impact on whether this country continues to strive for justice and compassion, whether we build or not for peace in the future, and whether or not we have a solid economy that provides a job for every person who wants to work in this country. That's what the Democrats stand for.

I have confidence that you and the people of this Nation will make the right judgment and the right choice on November the 4th, because I know the people of this country, like the people of Chicago, are builders. The same spirit that built the magnificent skyline of this city is building a new future for our Nation.

We have already built a new energy base for America. From coast to coast, we're moving forward on this very disturbing new element of American life, and that is OPEC oil, and they're charging us

for it at more than twice as much today as they did less than 12 months ago. Our new program is now producing more coal than any year in history, and I'm looking forward to seeing the energy supplies of the world be not OPEC oil but Illinois coal.

And based on that energy policy, we're now getting ready to build a new industry society for America. We have the most productive workers on Earth. You and others must have new tools and new factories to remain more productive than any other workers in any nation on Earth.

I've seen in recent days new energy facilities, high-technology facilities in so-called Silicone Valley, the most modern textile mills and steel mills in the world, and last week I saw 1981 cars rolling off the American assembly lines—more safe, more durable, just as efficient as any cars on Earth. That shows what American workers can do if given a chance. And in every one of those places I saw the spirit of building something new and something good for this country. I saw the hope for our cities and the working families of America. I could see the future of this country, and it's a good, strong future.

This country believes in hard work. We believe in opportunity. We believe in strong families. We believe in strong neighborhoods. And we believe in laying a foundation for an even stronger America. That's what we Democrats believe in. I hope you will not let anyone tell you different. Don't let anyone tell you that this is not the strongest nation on Earth—the strongest militarily, the strongest politically, the strongest politically and economically, the strongest morally, and the strongest ethically. This country can meet every challenge put before us. We can make this Nation even greater in the future.

There are some people who've given up, who say our Nation is weak, who say our people cannot meet any challenge. And they'll tell you not what they're for, they'll tell you what they're against, or they'll tell you that our hope is a trillion dollar tax reduction for rich people, to put the burdens of inflation on the working families of this country.

We've got to know among ourselves that this country is going to job security, health care, care for the elderly, a clean environment, and the last 50 years, under Democratic leadership, has given us a nation that's the strongest on Earth. And it's going to stay that way.

And if we forget all that, the Republicans want us to believe that the solutions to our problems are all simple, that major Federal programs that cost billions of dollars should be loaded on the back of local property tax payers, that the Department of Education should be abolished, the Department of Energy should be dismantled, the windfall profits tax should be repealed, and the oil companies unleashed to handle the energy problem. The American people are not simple minded.

I meet with average Americans every day, not in the big banks and the country clubs, but on the streets, in the schools, Americans who work on farms and in the factories, and I can tell you and I can tell the Republican Party that Americans are ready to build, not tear down. We're ready to face facts and get on the job of rebuilding our economy from the ground up. They're ready to provide jobs for all able-bodied Americans, ready to protect social security and to help the poor and the weak and the elderly have a life of security and self-respect. That's where the future of this country is. The future is in the commonsense and the good judgment and the building spirit and the compassion and the concern of the American people, and that's exactly the spirit of the Democratic Party.

And finally I want to tell you that what happens on November the 4th is going to depend on what you do—what you do the next 24 hours in getting your neighbors and people who will listen to your voice to register to vote and, in the next 4 weeks, think about the future. Think about your family. Think about your jobs. Think about tax being equal. Think about our Nation staying at peace. Think about nuclear arms control. Think about the equality that must exist among all Americans.

Remember, 1980 is the year of a great Democratic victory. I want you to remember that we win elections from the precinct up. We defeat Republican candidates, despite all their money, up and down the ticket. But most of all, I want you to be able to tell your children and your grandchildren that you had confidence in yourself, confidence in the Democratic Party, confidence in this Nation, and in 1980 we began to rebuild America. I'll do my part, and what I'd like to ask is this: Will you do your part? [*Cheers*] We'll win together. We'll whip the Republicans from top to bottom on November the 4th.

Thank you very much. God bless you all.

NOTE: The President spoke at 5:30 p.m. at the Daley Plaza. In his opening remarks, he referred to George Dunn, Cook County Democratic chairman, and John Touhy, Illinois State Democratic chairman.

Chicago, Illinois

Remarks at a Democratic National Committee Fundraising Reception. October 6, 1980

THE PRESIDENT. Thank you very much, Chairman Jack Touhy, Mayor Jane Byrne.

It's wonderful to be here in Chicago, one of the great industrial centers of the Nation. I'm particularly proud of the one thing that you produce best, and that's good Democrats. And now at least you and I know what I really mean when I say we want to increase productivity, right, throughout the country? [*Laughter*]

This next 4 weeks is important. It's also impressive to be with a group like you and to see what creative and imaginative people Democrats are. Nobody else could find such an infinite number of things to disagree on as Democrats do. But I know there's one thing that every person in this room agrees with tonight, and that is on November the 4th we're going to whip the Republicans from top to bottom.

A lot of people have said I've been running a mean campaign.

AUDIENCE MEMBER. Right on. [*Laughter*]

THE PRESIDENT. No matter how much you might approve, that's not exactly the case, because I think there's definitely a place in our political society for Republican candidates, and that's second place. Right? Second place. And this year we're going to use all the Democratic power we can exert to keep them in second place.

Well, I've been very eager since the first of the campaign to have a man-to-man, one-on-one debate with my opponent, Governor Reagan, because he and I represent our two parties. He and I are the product of months and months of primary and caucus competition. He and I are the choices of the two great conventions of the parties of our Nation, and the choices between us are extremely important. There has never been in my lifetime a more sharp, stark, important decision for the American people than the differences that exist this year, not just between me and him, not just between the

Democratic Party and its platform compared to the Republican Party and its relatively radical platform, compared to previous years, but between the two futures that'll be spelled out for our people. And I'm very eager to see these issues debated during the next 4 weeks.

We have important work to do among us. My responsibility is the same as yours. You and I are partners in every sense of the word. Ours is a party of history, a party of Jefferson and Jackson, of Franklin Roosevelt and Harry Truman, a party of Lyndon Johnson and John Kennedy. And those memories that come back to Democrats' minds, whether old or young, just from the listing of those names are warm memories. They are memories of progress. They are memories of commitment to peace. They're commitment to the equality that ought to exist among Americans of all backgrounds and all faiths and all interests and all national origin. They're the party that's closest to the lives of average Americans, of working families.

We are the party that believes in nuclear arms control. We're the party that believes in jobs for all Americans. We're the party that believes in fair and equitable tax systems. We're the party that believes that the energy crisis is being resolved through courage, and the new energy policy will be the foundation for a revitalization of the American industrial complex. We're the party that believes in a better life for minorities and the poor and working families and for the elderly and those that might not have a powerful voice because they're not rich or influential, but who have a powerful voice because they are represented by a party both of compassion and of competence.

We're talking tonight about the future of our Nation. We're talking tonight about the future of our own lives and about the future of the lives of people that we love.

Ours is a nation that believes in strength, and we believe in using that strength to maintain peace. In the last 8 years before I became President, when Republicans were in the White House, 7 of those years we had a decrease in the allotment of budget funds to keep our Nation strong. In the last 3 or 4 years, since I've been in office, we've had a steady, planned, meticulous, deeply committed, orderly, and effective increase in our allotment for defense. And as long as I'm President, we're going to have a strong nation, because only through strength can our Nation stay at peace. And in the last 3½ years, and I pray God for the next 5½ [4½] years, I've not had to send a single soldier of the American Government or the American people to combat, to die in war.

I just want to say a couple of other things to you. This month, the month of October and 3 or 4 days in November, will be crucial moments of choice. The actions that you take will literally decide the lives of millions of people in our country and indeed throughout the world.

You'll have to determine whether consumers have a voice on Capitol Hill and in the White House, whether the quality of our land and our water and our air will be maintained and improved. And you'll also determine whether there'll be jobs for all Americans, whether working people will be on the inside counsels, around the table, when decisions are made about the future of our Nation or excluded on the outside, alienated, driven from the counsels of government and therefore frustrated. You'll determine whether or not this America will be unified or, if I lose the election, whether Americans might be separated, black from white, Jew from Christian, North from South, rural from

urban; whether this Nation will be guided by a sense of long-range commitment to peace, sound judgment, and broad consultations; whether we'll have a close feeling of community and consultation with our allies; whether our adversaries will be tempted to end the peace for which we all pray.

These kinds of questions and many others ought to be on your minds and hearts as we go through this next 24 hours of registering people to vote and go through the next 4 weeks of making the best basic decision. Although you are my partners, I, as the President of this country, as the nominee of our party, as the standard bearer, nominated at the convention, will be the leader, along with Fritz Mondale, one of the best Vice Presidents, perhaps the best that this Nation has ever seen.

And finally we need to think about the candidate who's been chosen by the Republican Party. I don't believe this country needs a President who believes that the best way to control nuclear weapons is to start a nuclear arms race and play a trump card against the Soviet Union. I don't believe we need a candidate for President who believes that the proliferation of nuclear weapons, and I quote, "is none of our business." I don't believe that Americans want a President who thinks that Americans who draw unemployment compensation are just on a prepaid vacation for freeloaders. I don't believe we want a President—those of us who grew up during the Depression as I did—who says that the New Deal was based on facism or that those tonight who believe and love Hubert Humphrey believe, as Governor Reagan does, that the Humphrey-Hawkins bill is a design for facism.

It's difficult to get the message across to the American people in the hurlyburley of a campaign, when the Republicans have unlimited finances, to explain those deep and penetrating differences that exist in the lives of people of this country in the future depending on the choice that will be made on November the 4th. I'll do the best I can during these last 4 weeks.

This is my last campaign, the last political race that I will ever run. I do not intend for it to end by turning the Government of the United States over to people whose political philosophy and views about this country are directly contary to everything in which I believe with all my heart and soul. But I must remind you again that 29 days is not a very long time.

Many of you have helped the Democratic Party and helped candidates like Hubert Humphrey and John Kennedy and Lyndon Johnson and Franklin Roosevelt, Harry Truman, perhaps through your entire adult life. You've helped to keep this party together through thick and thin. Our party is strong now. Our party is united now. Senator Ted Kennedy and I are campaigning together in many ways, in many places. And I appreciate what you've done in the past, what you've done tonight, and what you've pledged to do during the next few days. I congratulate you on your service in the past. I thank you for your service now.

But we must get our voice through to the American voters, in a clear, undistorted, truthful, and unvarnished way, about the choice to be made on election day in November. You've given this party your contribution; you've given this party your hearts. But you cannot walk out of here tonight satisfied that you have fulfilled your obligation even though you've given a major contribution in funds tonight and in dedicated work and service in the past.

The job is not yet done. We still must have your leadership, your voice, your dedication, your energy, and your spirit. I need it all, working together. And if we have it, with everyone here a leader—no one in this room who cannot reach at least a hundred people—many of you can reach thousands of people between now and November the 4th. If you do that and realize the important responsibility on all of us, then there is no doubt in my mind that Illinois will be a key to the victory that we will celebrate in the evening of November the 4th for the Democratic Party and for our Nation.

In 1960 if just 28,000 people in Texas had voted differently and just a few people here in Illinois had voted differently, John Kennedy would never have served in the White House. In 1968 if all of you and I had done just a little more during that crucial election, Hubert Humphrey would have been our President and Richard Nixon would **never** have served in the White House. Those ifs are very important, but they show in a vivid way the crucial nature of a Presidential election, the impact of an election on the well-being and attitude and stature of our country and the catastrophe that can result if the outcome of those elections go the wrong way.

I tell you that there is much more at stake in 1980 with me versus Governor Reagan than there was in 1976 in the election between me and Gerald Ford— much more at stake. The Republican Party is different. The consequences of the election are much more profound. To lead this country through a threshold to a bright and secure future, we must work together, because the alternative is too doubtful, too bleak to contemplate.

I do not intend to lose this election, and I want to know: Will you help me? [*Applause*] Right on. We're ready together, and we will not lose. Right? [*Applause*] Right on.

NOTE: The President spoke at 7:31 p.m. in the Grand Ballroom at the Palmer House.

Visit of President Alhaji Shehu Shagari of Nigeria

Remarks at the Welcoming Ceremony.
October 7, 1980

PRESIDENT CARTER. It is a distinct honor for me this morning to be able to welcome to our country President Shagari of the great nation of Nigeria. Mr. President, we are delighted to have you here. We appreciate your patience in opening the automobile door. [*Laughter*] We hope that this delay in getting out of the car will be matched by your delay in leaving our country.

We are very pleased, particularly at the distinguished nature of the delegation traveling with you. President Shagari has brought to our country experts on trade, agriculture, foreign affairs, science, technology, development, and our consultations during this day and subsequently will be extremely useful to both countries.

President Shagari is the first freely elected leader of one of the greatest democracies on Earth, a nation which celebrated its independence 20 years ago on the 1st of October, and this is the first anniversary, on the 1st of October, of the inauguration of this great new President.

We share a great deal with Nigeria. We have enormous trade relationships with that great country. The political co-operation that exists, the sharing of concepts of freedom, the concepts of equality of opportunity, the concepts of the elimination of racial discrimination in our own nations and throughout the world, the basic concepts of human rights have been exemplified by the orderly development during this last 20 years of this great nation.

President Shagari exemplifies the finest aspects of his own country. He's a teacher, a poet, an historian, statesman, and I'm also glad to say, a farmer. He comes from one of the great ground-nut producing areas of the world, known in south Georgia as peanuts—[*laughter*]—but we also share that in common.

When I became President it was my resolve that we should open up a new and ambitious diplomatic and trade effort in the continent of Africa, an area too long neglected by my predecessors in this office. We recognize that among the 150 nations of the world that there is a great diversity and also a need for each nation to be treated as an individual people, even though the diverse nature of its own people might be quite exemplary. We have made visits now to the continent of Africa and to its nations, myself and the Vice President. As a matter of fact, in 1978 I made the first official visit by an American President to that great continent. And of course, I was honored to visit the people of Nigeria on that occasion.

This is President Shagari's first official visit outside the continent of Africa, and we are extremely honored that he chose Washington and our great country for the place of his first visit. The relationships between our two nations are growing. Our trade increases every year enormously. Our commitment to democracy is now being studied very carefully by other nations in Africa, and the recent development of freely elected democratic governments in Zimbabwe, Niger, Chad, the Upper Volta, has also been of great benefit to us all. This example which has been established is an exemplification of what our two nations espouse as concepts and practice in practical politics, government, and statesmanship.

We were particularly gratified to cooperate with Nigeria in helping to see established the new democracy in Zimbabwe. This must be followed by a sustained commitment to see the same development of a government based on majority rule and an end to racial discrimination in Namibia. We are cooperating not only with this great country but also through the United Nations, and we hope to see the consummation of our efforts in the early future. The elimination of apartheid, the elimination of racial discrimination, is a goal that we share with deep commitment and with fervent effort.

And finally, I'd like to say that the meetings today will indeed be beneficial to both countries. We are honored to share these concepts and ultimate goals with the great nation of Nigeria. And in my meetings this morning with President Shagari and his distinguished delegation, followed by other meetings between the delegation members and the members of my Cabinet, there is no doubt in my mind that both nations will continue the benefits derived from the close friendship and common concepts about the present and the future.

Mr. President, welcome to our Nation. You have honored us with this visit.

PRESIDENT SHAGARI. *President Carter and Mrs. Carter, Secretary of State Muskie, distinguished ladies and gentlemen:*

I thank you on behalf of my delegation, in the name of the people of Nigeria, and on my own behalf for the wonderful reception and warm welcome which you and your Government has accorded us since we arrived on the soil of this great country. I'm highly honored to have been invited to visit your beautiful capital at the conclusion of my participation at this year's session of the General Assembly of the United Nations.

Mr. President, your invitation, extended to me, even at this very busy time for you, when the affairs of state are pressing and indeed demanding, is a confirmation of the high esteem and honor in which you and your Government hold me and my country. It mirrors the friendship and generosity of your people towards Nigeria.

One visible evidence of this bond of friendship is the presence among us here today of a number of Nigerians resident in your country. The traditional American hospitality continues to be enjoyed by these Nigerians who, in their scores of thousands, come to your schools, colleges, and universities to acquire skills and knowledge most urgently needed in our task of nation-building and of development. I thank you and the American people for making our people welcome among you.

This friendship between our two countries, which is born out of shared values of democratic principles, of our common respect for peace and freedom and for basic human rights and dignity everywhere, has been demonstrated with the increasing cordiality many times within the life of your administration.

We also recall with pleasure the warm hospitality which you and your friendly people accorded my predecessor, General Olusegun Obasanjo, the then Nigerian

Chief of State in the autumn of 1977, when he visited you here at your invitation.

Your own state visit to our country in the spring of 1978, the first by any President of the United States, remains for us in Nigeria an historic landmark in our bilateral relations. And for Africa it demonstrated the beginning of a welcome change in American policy towards our continent. More recently, only last July, we were very happy to receive your dynamic Vice President and Mrs. Mondale in Lagos during those successful economic talks between our two Governments.

This close friendship has been beneficial beyond the ideas of our bilateral relations. It has permitted very close cooperation between our two Governments on the international scene. We have been able, when necessary, to share our concern and anxiety, and at other times when our views and interests have been close, we have moved forward on issues of vital international importance. For example, I'm sure that your Government and mine derived tremendous satisfaction and a sense of relief from the final liberation of Zimbabwe and the installation of a government representative of true aspirations of the people of that country.

We both had worked very hard toward such an outcome. And I hope that we will dedicate our best efforts towards the achievement of similar solutions in Namibia and elsewhere in the area of the African Continent. I hope also that we can cooperate and bring about peace and stability wherever they are needed in other parts of our one world.

Mr. President, we have taken the occasion of our presence in New York these past few days to familiarize ourselves with various groups in your society with whom we Nigerians share common interest—

cultural, ethnic, and economic. I'm encouraged by their general enthusiasm with a bold experiment in democratic government upon which Nigeria has embarked and most modest success which we have achieved since my administration peacefully succeeded a military regime a year ago. We are confident in the knowledge that the atmosphere of real and lasting stability which we're endeavoring to create in our country seems to them a conducive one in which to cooperate with us in our national development to the mutual advantage of our two countries.

Mr. President, in the next few hours, we will be holding discussions with your good self and your officials, seeking ways of further consolidating and enhancing the very friendly relations which so happily exist between our two Governments and peoples. We will explore new possibilities and, I hope, set ourselves new goals in order that we may achieve that ultimate objective of happiness: peace with justice and dignity for all mankind.

Thank you, Mr. President.

NOTE: President Carter spoke at 10:41 a.m. on the South Lawn of the White House.

Veterans' Disability Compensation and Housing Benefits Amendments of 1980

Statement on Signing H.R. 7511 Into Law. October 7, 1980

Today I am very pleased to sign into law H.R. 7511, the Veterans' Disability Compensation and Housing Benefits Amendments of 1980. Consistent with the administration's recommendation, the bill provides significant cost-of-living increases in rates of compensation for over 2¼ million service-disabled veterans and over 375,000 of their survivors, effective October 1, 1980.

These benefits are an expression of our gratitude to the men and women who were injured or died as a result of service to their country. I am proud that annual increases in these benefits have been enacted during each year of my administration.

The bill will also benefit veterans by increasing maximum loan guaranties for the purchase of condominiums, conventional and mobile homes, and will permit veterans who have previously used their loan guaranty entitlements to take advantage of reduced lending rates. It also provides special housing grants for certain veterans who are blind or have lost the use of their hands as a result of service injuries.

I am pleased that H.R. 7511 does so much for the many Americans who have sacrificed for their country.

NOTE: As enacted, H.R. 7511 is Public Law 96–385, approved October 7.

Mental Health Systems Act

Remarks on Signing S. 1177 Into Law.
October 7, 1980

THE PRESIDENT. *Senator Kennedy and Congressman Waxman, Congressman Harris, Congressman Fisher, Secretary Harris, and all of you who are so interested in this particular aspect of American life:*

This is indeed a thrilling occasion for me and for my wife, Rosalynn, and I know for all of you. It's also an historic occasion, and I was particularly glad to come here to the Woodburn Center to have this cere-

mony to commemorate where people are served a new opportunity for service by us all.

Woodburn Center has served citizens for more than 30 years, and I'm particularly delighted to have with me today two Members of the Congress who serve this particular area, Congressman Joe Fisher and Congressman Herb Harris. We're grateful that you've come to be with us.

I've been looking forward to this day for a long time. And those of the audience and those on the stage with me who've worked on this legislation so persistently know what I mean by saying that. As you know, my wife, Rosalynn, has been very instrumental in helping to develop this legislation, and while mental health is of importance to all of us, it has a special significance to me, above many issues with which I have to deal, because of my wife's intense involvement. Today I want to make clear the depth of my personal commitment to assuring that our Nation, so full of opportunity for so many of us, offers greater opportunity for decent care to those with mental and emotional difficulties.

Rosalynn and I became interested in mental health as a public service in Georgia. We observed lives wasted because of needs which were long unmet. When I was Governor we worked to increase and to improve those services and to bring into the awareness of Georgia people the special faults and failures that existed then in the care or lack of care for those suffering with mental problems.

When I came to Washington we also recognized a new opportunity to assess the standard of care and prevention of mental illness from the perspective of the White House. And less than a month after I took office I issued an Executive order creating the President's Commission on Mental Health. I asked Rosalynn to serve as Honorary Chairman, which she did, and under the leadership of Dr. Tom Bryant the Commission studied the mental health needs of the Nation for more than a year. In April of 1978 they presented their recommendations, which have served as a blueprint for this act which will be signed today.

The legislation was submitted to the Congress in May of 1979 and was further developed through the dedicated efforts of Senator Kennedy and Senator Schweiker, Congressman Waxman, and Congressman Dr. Carter. Without their persistent efforts to shepherd it through the Congress we would not be here today.

The Mental Health Systems Act I'm signing this afternoon is designed to provide vital services to the most underserved group in this Nation, a group that has not been served well even by those who've dedicated their lives, as you have, to their care. The States, which have long borne the major burden of care for chronic mental illness, will be able now to provide better services to all.

This is the most important piece of Federal mental health legislation since President John Kennedy signed the Community Mental Health and Mental Retardation Facilities Act 17 years ago. I'm proud that my family and his family, personified by Ted Kennedy, my good friend, and also by other members of his family—Mrs. Shriver, who's here—have been able to work harmoniously and in a partnership on this far-reaching legislation.

I would particularly like to express my thanks to the Kennedy family. Outside of government, with the Special Olympics effort and many other things to which they've devoted their lives, they have in-

deed been an inspiration to the world, and I'm greatly indebted to them as President, representing the 220 million Americans who admire and appreciate what they've done.

I'd like to ask Mrs. Shriver to stand up. Eunice, would you stand?

As a matter of fact, the first time that the Kennedy family and we became well acquainted was while I was Governor, when Eunice and Mrs. Robert Kennedy and others came down on the Special Olympics program, took my wife away from me for literally weeks at a time, and formed that close partnership then.

Despite advances in research, increases in the number of mental health personnel, and the dramatic shift from inpatient to community-based care, many of our citizens still do not have access to high-quality mental health care at a reasonable cost. This act is specifically aimed at addressing the problems of underserved groups—minorities, people who live in rural areas, the poor—and it targets new funds for services to severely disturbed children, to adolescents, and to the elderly.

Special emphasis is placed on the care and treatment of chronic mental illness to ensure that mental health support and aftercare services are available at the community level. The act also provides Federal grants for the first time for projects to prevent mental illness and to promote mental health care. It also includes grants to initiate advocacy programs to protect the rights, the legal and other rights, of the mentally ill.

In the past a lack of flexibility in Federal funding of community-based services has prevented some communities from providing any services at all and has limited programs for underserved populations and others. This act creates significant new opportunities for communities to address the most pressing needs first and forges a more flexible partnership between the Federal and State governments so that they can chart a new course that is comprehensive and responsive to the needs of all our people.

One of the great benefits of this act must be and will be the improved care of emotionally disturbed within families, especially when handicapped persons such as mentally retarded individuals are involved. We've come a long way since the days when handicapped and disturbed people, especially children and the elderly, were routinely separated from their families and shut away from society. We know how important the love and support of the family can be to those who are most vulnerable among us. But too often families have not had readily at hand the help and the services they need. I'm convinced this act will reduce the suffering of millions of Americans who are robbed of satisfying lives by mental illness.

This act expands our national commitment to mental health with the ultimate aim that all who need mental health services receive prompt care by qualified people, whatever their need, wherever they may live, however they might come into the system.

So, to summarize briefly, this provides help for those who are most in need, who've been most underserved in the past. It gives the States a greater role for assuming their administrative responsibilities with a minimum of interference from the Federal Government. It provides much more flexibility than the past laws have permitted. It emphasizes prevention of mental illness and it protects patients' rights. Those goals have been met very well in this legislation.

And now I'd like to introduce to you the Chairman of the President's Commission on Mental Health, Rosalynn Carter.

MRS. CARTER. Thank you. The Honorary Chairperson of the President's Commission on Mental Health Health. They wouldn't let me be Chairman.

I've looked forward to this day for a long time too. And I'm very grateful, and there are so many people I want to thank—first, Jimmy, because he encouraged me from the very beginning; Senator Kennedy and Congressman Waxman, who never wavered in their support and their efforts to guide the legislation through Congress. I want to thank Senator Schweiker and Dr. Tim Lee Carter also, because they demonstrated that mental health is not a partisan issue, that it is a bipartisan issue.

I want to thank Dr. Tom Bryant and all the members of the President's Commission on Mental Health and the members of the task panels and so many people who worked on the report. I see so many of you here today who worked very hard, and there were literally hundreds of people who worked to develop the report of the President's Commission on Mental Health and then to develop the legislation.

The past 3½ years have been extraordinary and fulfilling. There were some frustrating moments but now the Mental Health Systems Act is law, or will be as soon as Jimmy's signature is on that bill. And it's an exciting day for me and for all of us, but especially for those people who need help and who need care. It represents a great victory for the vulnerable people in our society, those who are struggling with mental and emotional difficulties, and also it represents a victory for those people all over our country, dedicated professionals and private citizens who work every day to try to provide comprehensive, humane care for those who are vulnerable in our society.

So, I'm very proud today, and this is landmark legislation. Someone told me the other day that there are going to be reports written about it for years. I'm very proud of it, and I want to again thank all who made it possible.

Thank you very much.

THE PRESIDENT. I've already said a few words about the next speaker, who represents a great family—the Kennedy family. But he also represents the quality of leadership in the United States Senate that's indeed inspirational to those who observe him in his leadership role. He's a man of compassion and sensitivity, whose heart has always been filled with love for those who need help most in our community. He's never forgotten them, and they never forget him. And it's with a great deal of friendship, admiration, and appreciation that I introduce to you now for a few words about legislation which he helped to evolve and bring to consummation, Senator Edward Kennedy.

SENATOR KENNEDY. Thank you very much.

Mr. President and Mrs. Carter and Secretary Harris, my colleagues in the Congress:

Last January Mrs. Carter was asked about her New Year's resolutions. And she listed four New Year's resolutions. She said that first of all that she wanted the Mental Health Systems Act passed into law. Secondly, she wanted the equal rights amendment achieved. Third, she wanted her husband renominated and reelected as President of the United States. And fourth, she wanted to keep her diary up. [*Laughter*] And now it is just the question

of keeping her diary up—[*laughter*]—I'm for all four of those.

Well, this is a proud day for her and for all of us, and it's an important day for the cause of mental health. This bill is the most significant step forward in this area since 1963, and at that time, as President Carter mentioned, President Kennedy, in sending a special message to the Congress on mental illness and mental retardation pointed to the national neglect of the mentally ill and mentally retarded. And President Kennedy said of that neglect, "It has been tolerated too long, it has troubled our national conscience, but only as a problem unpleasant to mention, easy to postpone and despairing of solution." And today millions of Americans, the very young and the very old, the urban poor and the migrant farmworker, the mentally retarded and the chronically mentally ill, black and Hispanic Americans still lack essential mental health services. For them the system of mental health care remains a nonsystem and a job yet to be done. This legislation represents new and important progress towards making such care a right for all those who need it.

This bill emphasizes the programs for those of all ages suffering from chronic mental illness, the severely disturbed children and adolescents, the elderly, for the minority who are not white and the majority who are women. This bill emphasizes prevention, and it continues our commitment to a national network of community health centers and will create a landmark advocacy program for the mentally ill. My sister Eunice, who has been a leader in the national fight to improve the quality of life for the mentally retarded, many of whose needs are effectively addressed by this legislation, joins me in offering the special note of thanks to the First Lady.

This Mental Health Systems Act emerged from the recommendations of the President's Commission on Mental Health. In a large measure the effectiveness of that Commission, indeed its very existence, are due to the energy and skill, the dedication and compassion of its Honorary Chairperson, Mrs. Carter.

As the first lady of Georgia, she volunteered 1 day a week to work with patients and families at the State Mental Health Hospital. She participated in the International Special Olympic Games for the mentally retarded; an active member of the Georgia Mental Health Association, she helped Governor Carter develop and implement the State health programs.

Now, as the First Lady of the United States, she's been instrumental in helping President Carter focus the national attention on the plight of the mentally ill. Her commitment is deeply felt and personal. The legislation President Carter signs today is a living monument to her commitment and to her concern, and I'm proud that all of us—Jimmy Carter, Henry Waxman, Dick Schweiker, Tim Lee Carter, and I—helped you, Mrs. Carter, to pass this bill.

Thank you.

THE PRESIDENT. It's difficult enough in the Senate with a hundred Members to get a complicated and controversial bill like this passed, but the House has 435 Members, and there it takes an extraordinary degree of tenacity and leadership in order to have the success that has been achieved by Chairman Henry Waxman. He did create in the House a bipartisan approach recruiting Republicans to help him in this noble endeavor. He's a very fine and cooperative Congressman with ideas of his own, yes. But he's the kind of person that all those with disparate views can go to for the consolidation of those views into achievable legislation. And I'm grateful to him for the contribution that he has made in making this day possible.

Now Congressman Henry Waxman from California.

REPRESENTATIVE WAXMAN. Thank you very much, Mr. President, for those kind words of introduction. It's been an honor for me to have worked with your administration in seeing this legislation come to this point where it's about to be signed into law. I want to join in paying tribute to, I think, the one person to whom this legislation stands as a monument, and that is the First Lady, Rosalynn Carter.

She may have been the Honorary Chairman of this Commission, but she took her duties very seriously. And every step of the way in the legislative process it was clear to me—it was clear to everyone involved—that her compassion, her concern, her dedication was all focused on this legislation. She wanted this to become law. She wanted the recommendations of the President's Commission to be followed through, particularly when she saw, as she had us see, the gaps in our mental health system which allow the chronically mentally ill to be dumped from State hospitals without having available to them community services so that they can live and function in the community, to see that the elderly who could so benefit from the outpatient services of the community health center didn't have available to them such a center, and the disturbed children and adolescents who are looking for some guidance, for some help, also had nowhere else to turn despite the fact that we had a law, a pledge for a program for community mental health centers around the country.

What she proposed and the Commission recommended was that we set up a way of focusing in on those priority populations, a way of working a relationship between the Federal Government and the State and local governments to work together to fill in those gaps, to see that all people who were in need of mental health services had them available to them, not just in expensive institutions, but in the community level, where people live, are able to function, are able to be with their loved ones and their neighbors if they have that extra help that a community mental health centers program could give them.

So, I'm just delighted to be here personally and very proud to have worked with the President and his administration, particularly the First Lady and Senator Kennedy in fashioning the bill that is now before us and will, with the stroke of a pen in a minute, become law.

Thank you very much.

THE PRESIDENT. And now I'd like to introduce the person who has to carry this tremendous responsibility and opportunity on her shoulders in the months and years ahead.

Pat Harris is a superb administrator. When I became President, the Department of Housing and Urban Development had a very bad, I think, well-deserved reputation. It was not a Department of which the Nation could be proud. She made it a source of pride to me and of outstanding service to this country and cemented the relationships between the Federal Government and local officials that had been sadly lacking. When a vacancy occurred in the Department of Health, Education, and Welfare I didn't have to think very long before I came to the conclusion that Pat Harris would be

the best Secretary there. She was reluctant to take on the job. But I asked her to, and she decided to do so.

Now Education is separate and Health and Human Services is her responsibility. She administers the third largest budget in the world. It's less only than the entire Federal Government of the United States, the Government of the Soviet Union budget, and that's all. She does it with competence, with strict enforcement of efficiency in that for a given level of personnel staffing and a given level of money available, the services are highest quality. That's the best definition of efficiency.

She will now be charged with the responsibility of administering the Mental Health Act of 1980, and I'm very grateful that she is here to assume that responsibility. I have no doubt that those with mental problems will now be served by the Mental Health Systems Act through the utmost degree commensurate with the opportunities that we offer her.

Ladies and gentlemen, Secretary of Health and Human Services Patricia Harris.

SECRETARY HARRIS. *Mr. President and Mrs. Carter, Senator Kennedy, Congressman Waxman, Congressman Harris, and Congressman Fisher:*

This day has been a long time in coming. It has taken a long time for the Mental Health Systems Act to travel from proposal into law, but it has taken even longer to bring the subject of mental health out of the shadows and into the sunshine.

Throughout most of our history, the mentally ill have been bound up in dark suspicion, victims of fear and ignorance, confined to institutions and trapped by popular stereotypes. The mentally ill have been isolated, demeaned, ignored, and misunderstood. Dorothea Dix, crusader for prison and asylum reform, was once told that the mentally ill don't need any heat, because they don't have any feeling. And too often our society has behaved as if the mentally ill do not have feelings, as if they do not have rights or talents or hopes for the future. The Mental Health Systems Act will not change these attitudes or those conditions overnight, but it is an essential beginning.

This far-reaching act will give us greater flexibility in helping States and communities meet the mental health needs of our citizens. It will emphasize health for children, adolescents, and the elderly. It will strengthen services for the poor in rural areas and in inner-city neighborhoods. This act has been a labor of love for many people, but it is appropriate today to single out the steadfast support Mrs. Carter has given this cause for more than a decade.

Her advocacy and leadership in the area of mental health has been instrumental in making this day possible, and I know her commitment will result in further progress in years ahead. And one of the first conferences I had after I became Secretary of Health, Education, and Welfare, was with Mrs. Carter on the Mental Health Systems Act.

Mr. President, this is a proud beginning. I join you in expressing determination that the Mental Health Systems Act be quickly implemented and that we build on its foundation a new, more just and humane mental health policy in the years to come. The Department of Health and Human Services is ready.

[At this point, the President signed the bill.]

THE PRESIDENT. You might be interested in knowing that all during the spring campaign, when Senator Kennedy and I were communicating through the media—*[laughter]*—quite often I would

come in and find Rosalynn and him communicating very intimately about the Mental Health Systems Act. So, it kind of bridged the gap during the political campaign, and I'm very grateful that all of us have been able to share in this delightful and exhilarating and gratifying experience.

Thank you all for being part of a historic occasion.

NOTE: The President spoke at 2:35 p.m. in the Woodburn Center for Community Mental Health in Annandale, Va.

As enacted, S. 1177 is Public Law 96–398, approved October 7.

Visit of President Shagari of Nigeria

White House Statement.   October 7, 1980

President Carter and President Alhaji Shehu Shagari of the Federal Republic of Nigeria met this morning at the White House for a comprehensive and cordial discussion of bilateral and international issues of mutual concern. They were accompanied by senior foreign affairs advisers, including on the U.S. side, Secretary of State Edmund S. Muskie, Assistant to the President for National Security Affairs Zbigniew Brzezinski, Assistant Secretary of State for African Affairs Richard M. Moose, and U.S. Ambassador to Nigeria Stephen Low. Minister of External Affairs Ishaya Audu and Ambassador to the United States Olujimi Jolaoso were among those who accompanied President Shagari.

In reviewing bilateral relations, the Presidents discussed the U.S.-Nigerian Joint Agricultural Consultative Committee, which was established as a result of the fifth bilateral economic talks in Lagos in July 1980. President Shagari will meet tomorrow, October 8, with the American members of this Committee, which was created to encourage joint investment in Nigerian agriculture. Both Presidents expressed satisfaction with the progress in this field and reaffirmed their commitment to promote further extensive agricultural cooperation. In addition, they explored other means of diversifying and strengthening bilateral relations in trade, investment, science, and technology.

President Carter and President Shagari also discussed priority items in African and international affairs, with particular attention to the hostilities in the Sahara and the continuing effort to bring about a peaceful transfer of power to majority rule in Namibia and South Africa, as well as the impact of events in the Middle East.

sions in the international monetary system. Many Americans do not realize that of the entire membership of the IMF, the United States is itself the second largest user of IMF resources. For example, we drew $3 billion in German marks and Japanese yen from the IMF in November 1978—a critical part of our highly successful program to combat speculative attacks against the dollar and restore its strength and stability, which have remained ever since.

The appropriation for the quota increase passed the House by a large margin on September 25. The Senate was unable to complete action before it recessed last week. It is extremely important to our Nation and the world that the Senate take this up as a priority item and complete legislative action when it reconvenes in November.

NOTE: As enacted, S. 2271 is Public Law 96–389, approved October 7.

International Monetary Fund Quota Increase

Statement on Signing S. 2271 Into Law.
October 7, 1980

This act authorizes United States participation in a 50-percent increase in quotas in the International Monetary Fund. The quota increase is essential to enable the IMF to support a stable international monetary system and the open world economy so important to our own economy and the strength of the dollar.

Our participation is important not only because we have a deep self-interest in the health of the world economy but also because our quota gives us important financial rights and influence over deci-

Magnetic Fusion Energy Engineering Act of 1980

Statement on Signing H.R. 6308 Into Law.
October 7, 1980

I have today signed H.R. 6308, the Magnetic Fusion Energy Engineering Act of 1980, a bill authorizing a magnetic fusion research, development, and demonstration program within the Department of Energy. The bill establishes as a national goal the successful operation of a magnetic fusion demonstration plant in the United States by the year 2000. The scientific results of magnetic fusion experiments have been highly encouraging so far, and there is considerable confidence that controlled fusion reaction can be achieved. Congressman McCormack and Senators Church, Tsongas, Baker, and Domenici are to be commended for their foresight in obtaining the enactment of H.R. 6308.

Fusion power offers the potential for a limitless energy source with manageable environmental effects, and H.R. 6308 represents a bipartisan effort to develop fusion as a viable energy option for the United States. Our Nation is the undisputed leader in developing this advanced technology, and H.R. 6308 will help us keep it that way. This bill represents a reasonable approach to the broad advancement of fusion research and technology. I sign it into law with pleasure.

NOTE: As enacted, H.R. 6308 is Public Law 96–386, approved October 7.

United States Holocaust Memorial Commission

Statement on Signing H.R. 8081 Into Law. October 7, 1980

I am pleased and honored to sign into law H.R. 8081, an act that authorizes the continuation of the United States Holocaust Memorial Council, which was established by Executive Order 12169, October 26, 1979, and supplemented by Executive Order 12213, May 2, 1980.

The principal responsibility of the Council, under the leadership of the distinguished author and survivor, Elie Wiesel, is to create a permanent national memorial museum to commemorate the systematic, state-sponsored extermination of 6 million Jews and the murder of millions of other victims of the Nazi Holocaust. In addition to planning, overseeing

construction of, and operating the memorial museum, the Council shall create and administer an educational and research foundation; establish a committee on conscience to warn of threats of genocide anywhere in the world; and encourage and sponsor appropriate annual observation of Days of Remembrance throughout the United States as a national commemoration of the Holocaust.

It is my hope and expectation that the memorial museum and other related programs assigned to the Council by this legislation should symbolize our national commitment to human rights and make us resolve that such a crime against decency, civility, and humanity never again be allowed to occur. This memorial should serve to remind us for all time that when any fellow human being is stripped of humanity, tortured, or defiled, or is victimized by terrorism, prejudice, or racism, that all human beings are degraded.

At this moment my thoughts return to May 1978, when a reception was held at the White House to celebrate the 30th anniversary of the State of Israel. On that occasion, I announced my intention to establish a commission to erect an appropriate national memorial to those who perished in the Nazi Holocaust, a memorial that would renew and refresh our commitment to human rights and human dignity everywhere. It is with this expectation in mind that I sign H.R. 8081.

I congratulate the congressional leadership, the congressional members of the Council, and the officers and members of the Council who made this legislation possible, and I look forward to the dedication of the national Holocaust memorial museum in the near future.

NOTE: As enacted, H.R. 8081 is Public Law 96–388, approved October 7.

National Highway Safety Advisory Committee

Appointment of 10 Members.
October 7, 1980

The President today announced the appointment of 10 persons as members of the National Highway Safety Advisory Committee for terms expiring in 1983. They are:

PHILIP T. ABRAHAM, of Portland, Oreg., presiding judge of the Oregon District Court for Multnomah County and chairman of the special courts committee of the Oregon Judicial Conference charged with revising the Oregon Motor Vehicle Code.

HARPER BREWER, JR., of Memphis, Tenn., a four-term member of the Tennessee State house of representatives and speaker pro tempore for two terms.

JANE CEASE, of Portland, Oreg., an Oregon State representative and member of the house transportation committee.

SANFORD CLOUD, JR., of Hartford, Conn., a Connecticut State senator and counsel in the Law Department of Aetna Life & Casualty.

DAVID WAYNE ELIZANDRO, of Arlington, Tex., an assistant professor in the department of industrial engineering at the University of Texas at Arlington, former coordinator of public safety for the State of Arkansas.

JACK O. HICKS, mayor of LaRue, Ohio, former national commander of the Disabled American Veterans, a member of the executive board of the Marion County Area Drivers Reeducational Committee, and an adviser to the county government on architectural and transportation barriers to handicapped persons.

ROBERT W. LANDON, of Olympia, Wash., chief of the Washington State Patrol.

LAURENCE P. OURSO, of Baton Rouge, La., supervisor of the motorcycle operator training program of the Louisiana State Department of Education, who has won several awards for his contributions to improving motorcycle safety.

SANDRA JOAN THOMSON, of Brookline, Mass., an associate in orthopedic surgery at Children's Hospital Medical Center in Boston and an instructor in orthopedic surgery at Harvard Medical School.

PATRICIA F. WALLER, of Chatham County, N.C., a staff associate with the University of North Carolina Highway Safety Research Center, where she conducts research on highway safety and works with State personnel to develop new programs (reappointment).

Federal Mine Safety and Health Review Commission

Designation of Richard V. Backley as Chairman. October 7, 1980

The President today announced that he has designated Richard V. Backley, of Fairfax, Va., as Chairman of the Federal Mine Safety and Health Review Commission. He replaces Jerome R. Waldie, who has resigned. Backley has been a member of this Commission since 1978.

He was born July 21, 1927, in Chicago, Ill. He received an LL.B. from De Paul University in 1955.

Backley practiced law in Chicago from 1955 to 1957 and was a trial counsel for Montgomery Ward from 1957 to 1960. From 1960 to 1967, he was district attorney for the Trust Territory of the Pacific Islands.

From 1967 to 1970, Backley was attorney-adviser to the Interior Department's Federal Water Pollution Control Administration (now the Environmental Protection Agency). In 1970 he became a senior trial attorney with the newly formed Division of Mine Health and Safety at Interior.

From 1974 to 1975, Backley was assistant solicitor of the Division of Mine Health and Safety. He was an administrative law judge at the Department of Health, Education, and Welfare in 1975, and at the Civil Aeronautics Board from 1975 to 1978.

Visit of President Shagari of Nigeria

Toasts at the State Dinner. October 7, 1980

PRESIDENT CARTER. I can already tell that this is going to be a delightful evening, because there's kind of a spirit of friendship and excitement in the guests that we've had here at the White House. The reason for that is that we've got a great new leader of a wonderful new democracy who's come here representing one of the largest and most influential democracies in the entire world.

I've been trying to find something where I was better than he was to make me feel better tonight. He's younger than I am. I thought he was born in 1924, he's born in 1925. I've got four children, he's got nine children. [*Laughter*] And he's got 3 more years to serve in this term, I've only got a few more months to serve in this term. [*Laughter*] I grow peanuts; he told me he grows ground-nuts on his farm, which is a much more all-pervasive worldwide name for the same genus. And I'm very delighted that we've already had a chance to get acquainted and to become, I believe, at least embryonic personal friends.

We have as a guest tonight a man who represents a great nation, 80 million freedom-loving people committed to free elections and democracy, the end of racial discrimination throughout the continent of Africa, a nation committed to peace, a nation like ours blessed by God with great natural resources, the nation of Nigeria, committed to preserving those resources for the benefit in perpetuity of the people who look to him for leadership, a nation which has had an unbelievable transformation from a military regime, under General Obasanjo and his Cabinet, whom

I know very well, in the most generous and constructive change that I have ever known in politics, where they all voluntarily committed themselves not to seek further office, but let the people of the nation choose through free and unrestrained elections a civilian government. And none of those former leaders who did such a superb job for Nigeria were willing or able through their own self-imposed constraints to serve in the new government. It's an exciting thing to see the spread of democracy and the spread of influence of this great, new nation throughout the continent of Africa and indeed the entire world.

Obviously, there is a need for exchange of ideas. The first official visit that an American President ever made to a nation in Africa was made when I visited Liberia and Nigeria in April of 1978. I visited Nigeria first, and it was not an accident that I chose Nigeria in all the 50 or more nations in the continent of Africa to express our country's new commitment to the interests and the importance of the continent of Africa, which had been neglected too long by my predecessors who've lived in this house.

Later, indeed this year, Vice President Mondale made a return visit to Lagos. He was received with hospitality and warmth. And then following that we had a very constructive economic mission who went to Lagos to explore new ways that we could share in a partnership fashion the economic development and the innovations that can benefit all of our people by this close cooperation in trade and commerce. And only 2 weeks ago my science and technology adviser, Dr. Frank Press, went back to Nigeria to explore ways where new ideas can be used to benefit the lives of both our peoples.

We have literally thousands of young Nigerian students who come to our universities. This is a further tie that binds the people of these two great nations together. I think, perhaps, more important of all though is the spirit that permeates the consciousness of the people, a spirit dedicated to freedom, a spirit dedicated to democracy, a spirit dedicated to deep religious convictions and the right of each person to choose his or her own religion, a spirit that permeates the consciousness that a human being is a precious thing in the eyes of God, and that government has a responsibility and a duty to enhance the worth of that individual and to let whatever talents that person might have be expanded.

The President of Nigeria, who's our honored guest tonight, along with one of the most distinguished delegations that has ever come to our country, is a man of great experience in government. He's also a farmer who loves the earth and sees in his country the tremendous potential for the future of greater production of food and fiber and things that are good for people in a peaceful way. And he's also a teacher, he's also an author, and he's also a poet. A man of ideas and a man of action. So, in many ways, this is an exciting evening which is important to us all.

Nigeria is now using its tremendous economic and political influence throughout the continent of Africa to promote stability and to honor international boundaries, but to let the aspirations which are legitimate among people who have been too long suffering from suppression and discrimination be realized. And to promote majority rule and to promote the end of apartheid and the end of racial discrimination is a deep commitment of the people of Nigeria which we share.

There's never been any equivocation in my own administration about a common approach to these concepts of the enhancement of freedom and the enhancement of the worth of individual human beings.

And finally, I'd like to say that we have worked together very closely. It wasn't very many months before I became President in the previous administration here that the borders of Nigeria were closed to the Secretary of State of our country. But we've opened those borders and those arms of friendship in a mutually beneficial way across the ocean, and we have worked together to promote majority rule and democracy and independence of Zimbabwe. And we're now working to realize the same aspirations in Namibia cooperating closely. And throughout South Africa we're working to end apartheid and to see this same concept that's been exemplified in Zimbabwe under Prime Minister Mugabe extended to all people who live there.

And finally, let me say that as a leader in the Organization of African Unity, President Shagari and the people of Nigeria have a great reason to be proud. One top official in the OAU said that Nigeria acts as an umbrella over the continent of Africa to realize the finest aspirations of all people who live there. And I'm very glad to raise my glass in a toast tonight to the man who holds that umbrella and who exemplifies to the utmost degree the qualities and aspirations of the people who he leads.

I'd like to ask you all to rise and join me in a toast: to President Shagari, to the great and free and independent and democratic nation of Nigeria, and to the people who join with us in friendship and in peace to the promotion in the finest way of human rights for all. Mr. President.

PRESIDENT SHAGARI. *President Carter and Mrs. Carter, Vice President Mondale and Mrs. Mondale, Your Excellencies, distinguished guests, ladies and gentlemen:*

It is 1 year since I was in an electioneering campaign, and you are, Mr. President, now in a period of election, which from my own experience, I know, is a period which is a very busy period. And the fact that you can spare the time to meet us and entertain us, I, more than anybody else, know that it is a great sacrifice, and it is done in your love to Africa and to Nigeria, which we greatly appreciate.

I feel highly honored to be your special guest, and I want to take this opportunity to thank you, Mr. President, your Government, and the people of the United States for the wonderful hospitality accorded to me and my entourage since our arrival in your great country. The toast which you have proposed to me and to my country is an expression of the deep and true friendship that has always existed between our two countries.

We in Nigeria, indeed, I daresay in all Africa, welcome and value this friendship with your country, a friendship which we have consistently enjoyed since the beginning of your administration. Before your time Africa and African affairs did not receive adequate and positive American attention as a matter of official policy. While it is true to say that African leaders have always been welcomed to the White House, it is also a fact that you, Mr. President, are the first American President to make an unprecedented visit to Nigeria, in the spring of 1978. Your state visit, which was in return for the visit of my predecessor, General Obasanjo, whom you received in this same gracious setting, is a landmark in the friendly relations between our two peoples.

These and other activities between our two countries reflect your commitment not only to seek to understand us better but also to build a very strong bond of friendship and cooperation between our two countries. In that way Nigeria and the United States have come to treat each other with the deserving respect and now cooperate in the material advantage of our two peoples.

Our relationship is one which is based on interdependence. The friendship which characterizes it has made it possible for us to maximize those advantages that are derivable from it. We have, for example, set up the machinery of bilateral economic cooperation between our two Governments to provide the framework within which contacts at various levels in the public and private sectors of the economy will be facilitated. Our population of some 80 million people needs to be fed, housed, educated, and provided with good medical services to enable us to engage unhindered in the task of nation-building. Also, we know that your country is the biggest and most advanced producer of food in the world. We will, therefore, need expertise and investment by your people in our green revolution, to which my administration attaches the greatest importance and has devoted substantial proportion of our resources.

In addition, we take this opportunity to invite your planners, architects, and engineers to collaborate with their Nigerian counterparts to plan, design, and construct low-cost housing for our people. We will welcome, in short, American participation and partnership in the national development, as we have welcomed other countries. The combination of American technology and our own resources and manpower will enable us to contribute our output to the challenge of providing the material needs of our people. Massive American investment in the relevant areas of our development programs, apart from having many other advantages for our own two countries, will be yet another method to reverse the payment deficit which the U.S. now runs in its trade with Nigeria. I know that this is a matter of considerable importance to you, Mr. President, and all Americans.

Mr. President, the voluntary return of the Nigerian armed forces to their military function and the assumption of power by democratically elected government both guarantee an atmosphere of stable government security and security for those who may wish to come to our country. Our laws in this regard are fair and the most likely to assure mutual satisfaction and political stability.

Mr. President, we in Nigeria realize clearly that in order to achieve our goal of national development we need an atmosphere of international peace and security. The United States is one of the superpowers of this world whose actions help to determine the future of mankind. It is for this reason that we have watched with great interest and concern the fortunes of your talks with other superpowers in respect of nuclear disarmament and the control of strategic arms. Indeed, we applauded your efforts in the conclusion of the SALT II treaty last year, because we believe that mankind deserves to live without the fear of nuclear annihilation and that the treaty was one positive step towards freedom from nuclear holocaust. We are your friends and we trust that you will not relent in your efforts to save us this anxiety.

The fear of nuclear catastrophe, dreadful as it may be to contemplate, is not only our main concern. The yawning gap between the North and the South cannot fail to demand our prime attention, because in spite of our oil resources we belong to the Third World.

My friends, this is not the time to bother you with data on economic control of the wealth of the world by developed nations, data of deprivation of essentials of life in the South, data on the staggering rise in death through famine and starvation, data on the soaring number of refugees in Africa and other parts of the world, and endless data of procrastinations and refusals on the part of developed countries to respond to calls from the poor South to come to meaningful agreements. However, I feel this is an opportune moment for me to call on America, an influential voice in the North, for a rethink on the matter which poses a real threat to the stability of the world if not arrested.

For those of us gathered here tonight we must realize that failure to act meaningfully to correct this economic imbalance between the two worlds may mean the loss of democracy and human rights as we know them in this part of the world. I believe America has the will and the capacity to lead the rest of the North in coming to an understanding of the developing countries. It is in your best interest to lead the way be opening up to the demands of the developing countries. On the other hand, the message should also go out to our friends in Eastern Europe that they need to ensure this world stability by extending substantial development aids to the developing countries. To argue, as they have done in the past, that they were never colonial powers and therefore unable to enter meaningful dialog is nothing but an escapist posture.

Another equally pressing problem is that of racism, which you have mentioned, Mr. President. The problems of colonialism and apartheid in southern Africa from the beginning—I have to say that I am particularly pleased with the fact that the efforts of our two countries contributed immensely to the final liberation of Zimbabwe. However, we in Nigeria do not regard our independence as complete so long as there remains a parcel of land in Africa, on the African Continent, which is still under foreign domination, nor shall we rest in our struggle so long as racism and racial discrimination as a philosophy of government is practiced in our continent.

Your Vice President restated very clearly your Government's policy in this regard when he was in Lagos a few months ago, and we were very pleased to hear it anew. But may I ask, Mr. President, to let us work more closely and more diligently together to eradicate this evil which the whole international community has declared abominable. It is our hope that your administration and the entire American people, who have purged racism from your own society by law, will collaborate with us in doing the same by our votes in the United Nations in the case of our continent. It is better for South Africa to heed the voice of these nations now and work for peaceful change than to wait to be engulfed in a violent upheaval.

In closing, Mr. President, let me entertain the pleasant wish that these happy relations between the friendly peoples of the United States of America and the peoples of the Federal Republic of Nigeria, which we celebrate here tonight, will endure and that they will serve to make this world a better habitat for all mankind.

Your Excellencies, distinguished guests, may I, in the fond hope, invite you to raise your glass and drink with me a toast: to the personal well-being of the President and Mrs. Carter, to the happiness of the American people.

PRESIDENT CARTER. Thank you, Mr. President.

NOTE: President Carter spoke at 8:15 p.m. in the State Dining Room at the White House.

Housing and Community Development Act of 1980

Remarks on Signing S. 2719 Into Law. October 8, 1980

THE PRESIDENT. *Senator Pete Williams and Senator Paul Sarbanes, Congressman Moorhead, Secretary Landrieu, other distinguished members of my administration, and citizens from around the country:*

I'm very grateful to be participating this morning in a ceremony that has far-reaching impact on the future of our Nation, on individual communities which have been hard-pressed and have benefited from the UDAG and the community block grants.

We have also a great benefit, I think, for people who want to rent and to own reasonably priced homes and to alleviate an unconscionable burden on some of the condominium owners, particularly in the Miami and south Florida area, a project on which I have worked for 3 solid years and where we've finally made some progress.

I'm very happy to be here today to sign this bill. It's a major step forward for housing and for community and urban development programs. I want to give special recognition to the men behind me, particularly to Representative Moorhead and to Representatives Ashley and Reuss, who are not here, Senator Pete Williams and Senator Proxmire for their leadership, and Representative Stanton and Senator Garn who exemplify the bipartisan nature of what has been done with this legislation. Senator Sarbanes provided a special insight into the needs of this kind of change in the laws of our country.

This is the second such reauthorization bill that's been signed during my own administration. The first, in 1977, I believe had historic connotations and benefits because it highlighted our UDAG program, which has been one of the most effective programs that I have ever seen in government, a program that has expanded tremendously, through a multiplication factor, the small investment of Federal funds and efforts and the enormous concentration and cooperation between local and State funds and particularly private investments, a minimum of paperwork, a minimum of delay, a maximum of local participation and control. This has been an outstanding success in attracting private investment to the disturbed or deteriorating areas in our cities, and today with this bill we are building on that good foundation.

First, this bill authorizes funding for up to 290,000 section 8 and public housing units. This is a 30-percent increase in this current fiscal year, which began on October the 1st, a 30-percent increase over 1980 fiscal year. The section 8 program will soon pass the milestone of 1 million families served. To put this into perspective, it took the public housing program 30 years to reach 1 million units.

Secondly, under this bill, we can now respond rapidly to a decline in the housing industry. This bill gives us the powers to avoid a serious housing downturn. We are monitoring conditions very carefully in case this authority needs to be used.

Third, Congress has finally provided the remedy for condominium and cooperative owners burdened by unconscionable long-term leases. Many owners, especially the elderly in Florida, have had their savings consumed by recreation leases. When I campaigned for President in 1976, this was the most burning issue that was brought to me by many distressed homeowners. And we've worked on this issue, as I've said, for 3 solid years. I'm deeply gratified that they'll finally have the chance to seek judicial relief for unfair leases signed by them when they thought they were purchasing a good bargain in a home.

Fourth, this bill reauthorizes for 3 years the community development bloc grant program and provides $675 million for the very successful UDAG program, major tools for neighborhood and for urban revitalization. For example, the first $1½ billion of UDAG funds generated $8½ billion of investment and created over 400,000 jobs—all targeted in our most distressed cities.

Fifth, the Congress has adopted my recommendation that the Home Mortgage Disclosure Act be extended and strengthened. This is a clear reaffirmation of our determination to stem redlining and to secure the lifeline of credit for all neighborhoods.

And finally, I'm pleased with two initiatives. The bill creates a program to modernize 1.2 million units of public housing, to provide energy-efficient homes there, and to revitalize seriously troubled projects. Also, the bill includes my proposal to permit HUD to make payments if a homeowner cannot make the payments because of unemployment or illness.

This bill is an important achievement, but we also must look candidly at our Nation's remaining housing requirements. High home prices and interest rates have made it increasingly hard for American families to buy homes, and we also need to produce more rental housing. I'm committed to American home ownership. This bill increases the FHA mortgage limits from $67½ thousand to $90 thousand, allowing many more American families to buy their own homes.

Lately, there's been a lot of controversy about high interest rates, the interrelationship among my administration, the Congress, the Federal Reserve Board, and also, of course, the individual banks in this country. Right now, increases in mortgage interest and construction financing costs threaten the housing recovery that began in June. I'm deeply concerned about the recent upsurge in interest rates. They reflect in part an overreaction by financial institutions, which are not justified by the state of the economy.

I remain committed to disciplined tax and spending policies to reduce inflationary pressures and to encourage productivity gains. These policies are designed to achieve an objective which is critical to housing and economic growth, and that is lower interest rates.

To deal with our long-term problems, I'm forming an administrative task force on housing to work very intimately with all the elements of my own administration. It will determine what actions are necessary, to assure a steady and affordable flow of mortgage credit and to provide adequate levels of multi-family housing construction. I'm also appointing an advisory committee of distinguished representatives of all segments of the housing industry and its related interests. I'm pleased to announce that this committee will be chaired by Robert Weaver, our first Secretary of Housing and Urban Development.

It is with great pleasure that I sign this important legislation. Thank you very much for being here.

[*At this point, the President signed the bill.*]

Now I'd like to ask three gentlemen to comment who have been so instrumental in the passage of this legislation, each one representing a large number of others who have also worked very hard for this accomplishment. First, Senator Pete Williams, representing the Senate.

SENATOR WILLIAMS. Thank you very much, Mr. President. Just a moment to say that I think everybody here appreciates— we have a comprehensive response to both our housing needs and our community development needs in this legislation, and your constancy has been of such great importance to us in the Congress to come to this point where we had this program together and signed into law.

It's been rather a long journey, difficult at times, but we know this administration has stayed with the basics of a very fine response to our needs. You mentioned them all, Mr. President. For one, I'm particularly proud to report that the urban development action grants, UDAG, certainly have brought a new spirit, a new hope, a new opportunity for our cities and, indeed, our towns to develop their potential. And we hope that with your task force and other developments that we can even improve and grow on our foundations in housing that's so desperately needed in today's market for housing.

Thank you, Mr. President, very much.

THE PRESIDENT. And now, representing the House, I'd like to ask Congressman Bill Moorhead to make a few remarks. Bill?

REPRESENTATIVE MOORHEAD. Thank you, Mr. President, my colleagues from the Senate. I want to join with Senator Williams, Mr. President, in mentioning the UDAG, urban development action grants. They were the major innovation in housing in your administration. We in the Congress were able to fight back against drastic cuts, because your administration administered those grants so effectively.

Thank you, Mr. President.

THE PRESIDENT. And now, representing my administration is Moon Landrieu, who's done such a superb job in carrying out the laws that exist now and who can do a much better job with the new legislation that I've just signed. Moon Landrieu.

SECRETARY LANDRIEU. Thank you. Mr. President, on behalf of the some 16,000 representatives of HUD and the constituent groups across the country, I want to express our appreciation to you for the leadership which you have consistently demonstrated in enacting this legislation. Some 16 years or 15 years, really, since HUD was formed—and it's a great pleasure to have Bob Weaver, our first Secretary, the man who set the pattern for the operation of so many programs that are effectively working today. And it's a great pleasure, Mr. Secretary, that you would accept the chairmanship of this housing task force to assist your Government, once again, in attacking what is a very serious problem for us but one which we know is well within our reach of solution, and that is the housing costs that we're facing today.

Mr. President, I'm happy to report to you that after 3 years of this administration, that while there are still difficulties in America's cities and towns, that enormous progress has been made. One can hardly go into a city or town today without seeing a rebirth of those places—some downtown development, some neighborhood development. And wherever we go, we find people living in housing that was not available to them before, whether that be families or the elderly.

And so I think the Senate, Members of the Congress, members of the administration, particularly you, can take great pride in the progress that's been made in America's cities in both community development and housing. Thank you very much for signing today.

THE PRESIDENT. Since those comments were so pertinent and so brief, I have time to call on an additional speaker. I'd like to ask Dick Hatcher, mayor of one of our great cities, to comment from a recipient's and the partnership point of view. Mayor Dick Hatcher.

MAYOR HATCHER. Thank you, Mr. President. I would like to say on behalf of the U.S. Conference of Mayors and all the mayors and city officials, that the signing of this bill this morning represents one more step towards the rebuilding and the rebirth of America's cities.

When you took office, Mr. President, the cities of this country were mired in almost despair, and what has happened in the 3 years or so that you have been in office is nothing short of miraculous. We believe that the cities of America have been turned around as a result of the efforts and the actions of your administration. And we want to express our appreciation for it and to say that this morning's bill and the programs that it represents—particularly UDAG has been referred to already—with the assistance, tremendous assistance of the Congress of the United States, reaffirms once more a statement that you made at the time you first took office, and that is that you would be the best friend that the cities of America have ever had. You've done that, Mr. President. Thank you.

THE PRESIDENT. I'm glad I called on Dick Hatcher to say a few words. [*Laughter*]

I think if there has been one bipartisan or nonpartisan achievement in this last 3½ years that has been both exhilarating and also unanimously acclaimed, it is the revitalization of our cities. The urban policy was evolved, based upon consultation and advice and a full partnership with the local and State officials. It didn't add enormous new programs. It provided some incisive elimination of redtape and delay, bureaucratic confusion. It gave a few dollars to stimulate enormous investments from the private sector in rebuilding the downtown areas, and this has been a very gratifying experience.

I'm grateful again that Secretary Weaver will head up our housing task force to give me constant advice on how we can improve this important element in the future. I'm very grateful that we are all harnessing our efforts to hold down unwarranted increase in interest rates. And I would also like to say, with Congressman Bob Garcia here, that there is an additional approach to improving the quality of life—particularly in our urban areas—that's important, and that is the strengthening of our communities.

I've just issued a memorandum to all the agencies and departments in the Federal Government asking them to review every Federal program which affects neighborhoods and community-based organizations to make sure that the cooperation is at a maximum level and to make sure that any impediments to the close working relationship or partnership between the Federal Government and all its agencies and neighborhood-based organizations are absolutely removed. We must have this cooperation. It's a very fine thing.

I've also established a liaison for this purpose, to neighborhoods and community-based organizations, within the White House itself. I'm glad Congressman Garcia's here, because this has been one of his major interests.

Again, let me express my thanks to all of you for participating in this historic event. I think we have a better prospect in the future for stronger cities, better neighborhoods—rural and urban—effective housing programs, a move toward lower interest rates, an end to the unwarranted abuse of those who've signed long-term leases, better efficiency in our existing homes, and a stronger housing program for the entire country.

Thank you again. It's been an honor for me to be with you.

NOTE: The President spoke at 9:07 a.m. in the Rose Garden at the White House.

As enacted, S. 2719 is Public Law 96–399, approved October 8.

Neighborhood and Community Programs

Memorandum From the President.
October 8, 1980

Memorandum for the Heads of Executive Departments and Agencies

Throughout my Administration I have stressed that neighborhoods are the soul of every community. Each opportunity to include neighborhood organizations in the partnership to rebuild America's cities and towns should be taken. All Federal programs should be administered in a manner which complements neighborhood efforts.

Over three years ago I appointed, with Congressional approval, the National Commission on Neighborhoods to conduct a study of the important issues affecting the residents of America's neighborhoods. The Commission membership represented a broad spectrum of American concerns and included members of Congress, local elected officials, leaders of neighborhood organizations, and private citizens from many walks of life.

Following an exhaustive study, the Commission presented over two hundred recommendations to the Administration for consideration. The Secretary of Housing and Urban Development and the Assistant Secretary of HUD for Neighborhoods, Voluntary Associations and Consumer Protection coordinated a review of the Commission's recommendations, most of which were agreed to by the agencies.

To ensure that the Administration continues to make progress in working with the nation's neighborhoods, it is essential that the findings and recommendations made by the Commission and accepted by each agency be carried out as expeditiously as possible.

It is important that Federal officials be sensitive to the needs of neighborhoods and include neighborhood representatives in the planning and implementation of Federal programs whenever neighborhood interests are affected.

A review of Federal programs affecting community and neighborhood based organizations to assess and improve the effectiveness of current efforts is an appropriate step in this process.

A liaison to neighborhoods is being established in the White House Office of Intergovernmental Affairs to work with your Departments and Agencies and with neighborhood organizations, mayors, county representatives and Governors to accomplish these goals.

Gene Eidenberg, or his designee, will soon be contacting you regarding these important matters.

JIMMY CARTER

Advisory Committee for Trade Negotiations

Appointment of Eight Members.
October 8, 1980

The President today announced the appointment of eight persons as members of the Advisory Committee for Trade Negotiations for 2-year terms. They are:

ALVIN J. BOUTTE, president of the Independent Bank of Chicago, the Nation's largest black commercial bank.

PHILIP CALDWELL, chairman and chief executive officer of Ford Motor Co.

JANE REIS-BRIAN ENGELHARD, of Far Hills, N.J., chairman of the board of Engelhard Hanovia, Inc., and a director of Engelhard Minerals and Chemicals Corp.

MILTON N. FISHER, of Miami, Fla., president of Panelfab International Corp. and Dicoa Corp., both exporting firms, and chairman of the Florida District Export Council.

PEDRO A. GRANA, of Houston, Tex., president and chairman of the board of Lone Star Shipping, Inc., and a director of numerous other shipping and terminal services of the Port of Houston.

THOMAS L. HOLTON, chairman and chief executive of Peat, Marwick, Mitchell & Co.

EDWARD H. JONES, of New York City, president of International Commercial Resources, Ltd., an export firm doing business in West Africa and the Caribbean.

ROBERT E. RUBIN, of New York City, a general partner in the firm of Goldman, Sachs & Co., and a member of the board of directors of the New York Futures Exchange.

Tri-City Municipal Airport, Tennessee

*Remarks at a Carter/Mondale Rally.
October 9, 1980*

I am glad to be home in the South.

Thank you, Jim Sasser—a great Senator, right? [*Applause*] Thank you very much.

Senator Jim Sasser, Congressman Gore, Congressman Ford, Congressman Jones, Congressman Bouquard, Congressman Boner, Speaker Ned Mc-Wherter, Lieutenant Governor John Wilder, Mayor John Love, Mayor Easley, Mayor Pyree, and all my good friends in Tennessee:

You've got more people than I thought you had in the Tri-City area. Four years ago Tennesseans helped to get me a good job in the city and to keep me in the White House for this last 4 years. You came in second to Georgia in the strength of the vote that I got here in the general election, and I'd like to know if you think you might even beat Georgia in 1980. How about that? [*Applause*] I'd like to have that job in the city just 4 more years and then come back south to home, because it's hard to know until you've been away a while how strong our feelings are for the South and what it stands for.

For generations my people have lived here in the South near Tennessee, in Georgia. We share the same basic commitments to what a great nation means. We have a conviction that a better life must depend on hard work, on a belief in God, on strong families, on farming the land, on giving people the chance for a job, on taking care of those who can't care for themselves. We believe in a strong nation, a nation whose military strength is second to none on Earth. And that's the way we are keeping and will keep the United States of America.

We also believe in peace, and we know that our country, as powerful as it is, the most powerful nation on Earth militarily, the most powerful nation on Earth economically, the most powerful and influential nation on Earth politically—can stay that way and keep the peace if the people of this Nation are united in common commitment. The South has never forgotten those very important and enduring values.

This year, as you all know, is a very important election year. This year the people will make a judgment, not just between two candidates, not just between two parties, the Democratic and Republican Party, but between two futures. And I would like to ask you in this next 4 weeks to think about what this election will mean to you, to your family, to the people that you love, and to the status of the Nation which we love.

A campaign is a good opportunity in a democracy to spell out the specific issues so that our people can make the right judgment on election day, Tuesday after the first Monday in November. It's incumbent on a candidate, each candidate to stick to the issues, to analyze one's own record, what has been said, what has been done, what has been accomplished in the past; also, and secondly, to spell out one's vision for the future, what we have in mind for the months and the years and the generations ahead; and third, to compare one's record and one's plans for the future with the record and the plans for the future of one's opponent. This is not only the right of a candidate, it's the duty of a candidate.

We have had to address in the last 4 years many very difficult issues which have no easy answers and which are profoundly important to the people of this Nation. On energy, this has been our most serious domestic threat. Last year alone, the OPEC nations increased the price of oil more in one year than the oil prices had increased since oil was first discovered back in the 1800's. Our Nation has addressed this question courageously, and with the help of the Tennessee delegation, we're making good progress now. This year our country is importing from foreign countries, every day, 2 million barrels of oil less than we did in 1977. That's a great credit to you, to the Congress, and to this administration.

This year the United States will have more oil and gas wells drilled than any year in history, and this year—and this may be a surprise to you—our country will produce more coal than any year in the history of our Nation. My hope is that in years ahead on the energy market we will replace OPEC oil with Tennessee coal. It'll be good for the whole world.

I might point out to you that the future is bright if we manage our affairs soundly. The OPEC Arab nations all put together only have 6 percent of the world's energy resources. The United States alone has 24 percent of the world's energy reserves. We've made good progress now in this first 3½ years in laying a basis for future progress. But it's important for you to realize that my opponent against whom I'm running on November 4 would change all this. He would reverse the progress that we have made.

He says that his energy policy, and I quote, is to repeal the energy legislation that has been passed, to abolish the Department of Energy, and to turn the oil companies loose to manage the energy affairs of this country in the future. That would be a very serious judgment for you to make and for your neighbors to make on November 4.

The economy of our country is also very important. We've had shocks, yes, in the last 3½ years with this unwarranted increase in the price of oil. But our country has made steady progress. In this last 3½ years we have had a net increase of 8½ million jobs in the United States. Today, in Tennessee alone, compared to 1977, when I was sworn in as President, 144,000 more people have full-time jobs. Our cities have been put back on their feet. Farmers will have the highest gross income, the highest net income, of any administration in the history of this Nation, and we are increasing agricultural exports far beyond what anyone dreamed would be possible just 4 years ago.

We've set world records on agricultural exports in 1977, 1978, 1979, and 1980. This year we'll have the biggest increase in history, $8 billion more in agricultural exports this year than last year, $40 billion in all. The American farmers, in spite of droughts, have a great prospect ahead. This cannot be undone. As a farmer I am determined that American agriculture will continue to be the world's greatest resource for peace and Americas' greatest resource for economic progress, and you can depend on that.

I might add about the economy very briefly that now that we have an energy policy in place, it can serve as a foundation for the entire revitalization of the American industrial economy. This is important, because American workers now are the most productive on Earth. But we've not been increasing our productivity enough in recent years. This must be continued.

The South suffered many generations from wages that were too low to finance the affairs and the needs of a family. I remember the first proposal for the minimum wage was for 25 cents an hour. The Democrats supported that minimum wage; the Republicans were against it. My first job as a high school senior was for the minimum wage of 40 cents an hour. The Democrats supported that minimum wage; the Republicans were against it. Now we have a sound minimum wage program in our country, and my Republican opponent says that there's been more hardship and suffering brought about by minimum wage than we got from the Great Depression. He also says that unemployment compensation, so vital to a nation when temporary unemployment comes, my opponent said that unemployment compensation is just a free paid vacation for freeloaders. This is the kind of attitude toward working people that's contrary to the basic concepts of the South and contrary to the basic concepts of our Nation. And that's the kind of choice that will be made on November 4 by this Nation.

The last point I want to make this morning is about our Nation's defense and about peace. Eight years before I was President, we had Republicans serving in the White House. Seven of those years American Government budget for defense went down—7 out of 8 years, down. Since I've been in office we've had a steady, predictable, deeply committed, orderly, and fruitful increase every year in our Nation's commitment to defense in real dollars above and beyond inflation.

We must have a strong defense in order to keep our Nation at peace. We also know that it takes two wings on an airplane for that airplane to fly. You can't just have massive armaments, which we do have, and depend on that to keep our Nation at peace. You've got to have arms control, you've got to have sound relationships with our allies, and you've got to have a steady course and a willingness to settle major differences around the world, which are inevitable, with diplomatic means, and not by American soldiers and sailors and airmen in a time of crisis.

This is what we've done. We have worked hard for peace, and we've kept our Nation at peace. I have not ordered a single American soldier into combat in the last 3½ years, and I pray to God that when I go out of office at the end of 4 more years we'll still have a record of peace intact.

Every President since Harry Truman has known the extreme importance of controlling nuclear weapons, to negotiate SALT treaties with the Soviet Union so that we could have a balanced, controlled, predictable, known, and reducing level of atomic weapons. It would be a mistake for us to forget the horrible worldwide destruction that could come from abandoning nuclear arms control. Every President has worked on this. I concluded SALT II treaty terms with the Soviet Union following the work that had been done by President Ford and President Nixon. That's crucial to every family, every life in this Nation, and to everyone in the entire world.

Just recently my opponent said that he would withdraw SALT II, not ask the Senate to ratify it, that he would launch a nuclear arms race, and play a trump card against the Soviet Union. This would be the end to any fruitful effort to negotiate control of nuclear arms and would be a destabilizing factor in the entire world that would shake the foundations of our alliances and create unwarranted tensions among nations that either have or do not have atomic weapons.

In the last few years myself and my predecessors have had to deal with a constant stream of potential crises. If they are handled properly you may not ever know about them. But if a President makes a serious misjudgment, a small crisis can become a major one and can affect every life represented here. Time after time after time my opponent in the last few years has called for the injection of American military forces into diplomatic troubled regions of the world—in Korea, Ecuador, Cuba, the Middle East, Pakistan, Angola. Time after time after time when there was a problem my opponent has said, "Let's send American military forces there to settle the dispute." Fortunately, Democratic and Republican Presidents have not done that. We've tried to ease those tensions and resolve those differences in a peaceful way, letting the influence of our Nation be strengthened by strong military forces. That is the kind of judgment that American voters will make on November 4.

I'd like to close by saying this: America's defense will be kept strong, but the best weapon is the weapon that's never fired in combat, and the best soldier is the soldier that never lays down his life or sheds his blood on the field of battle.

That's what sound judgment and proper leadership can do.

Let me close by saying we've got less than 4 weeks to go. This is a very close election. Major issues are at stake. I've only outlined two or three of them, but the sharp differences that exist between me and my opponent are perhaps unequaled in the recent political history of this country. Think very seriously about the consequences of your vote and the decision that America will make on November 4.

I want a nation strong and at peace. I want a nation where people have a chance for a better life. I want a chance to see Americans at work with a good education. I want to see the Nation united, North and South united, black and white united, rural and urban united. I want to make sure that our Nation moves forward with progress, predictable progress, steady, based on the great resources, human and natural resources that God's given us. That's the vision that I have for our country—a nation strong, confident, hopeful, at peace, filled with respect one for another, using our beneficial impact around the world to enhance human rights.

If you'll help me on November 4, we'll have a tremendous victory, we'll whip the Republicans again and keep this Nation on the proper road.

Thank you very much. God bless you.

This is a beautiful crowd, a wonderful welcome to Tennessee and the South, I thank you from the bottom of my heart. God bless all of you.

Go to work now for me, right? [*Applause*]

NOTE: The President spoke at 9:36 a.m. at the airport terminal building.

Blountville, Tennessee

Remarks at a Democratic National Committee Fundraising Reception.
October 9, 1980

My friend, Jim Sasser, and my equally good friend Mrs. Cauldwell, and all my east Tennessee friends who've come here this morning to be with me:

First of all, I want to thank Mrs. Cauldwell for making it possible for me to visit her beautiful home and to sign the door as Jimmy Carter, President of the United States. You don't know how nice it is to sign something that I don't have to get through Congress first. [*Laughter*]

I notice in more ancient history there are few Republican names on some of those doors. I can tell they sign them in a hurry, because you know Republicans— once they get in, don't stay in very long. [*Laughter*] And I hope from now on all those doors will be covered with Democratic names. But, Mrs. Cauldwell, it is a delight and a pleasure and an honor to come here and to participate in part of the history of our Nation and the history of the South, the history of Tennessee, that makes all of us so proud.

You've come here because of your confidence in our party, because of your respect for Jim Sasser, Ned McWherter, other Democrats who are here with me this morning, and also because of your respect for the Presidency itself and for your belief in the future of our country. I've never seen a more thrilling and excited and supportive audience than I had at the Tri-Cities Airport a few minutes ago. It was a delight for me and a reassuring thing for me to see the expectation and confidence in their faces.

We face a very important election on November 4. I'm not going to repeat the issues that I discussed at the airport, but I would like to say just in the quiet setting of this beautiful yard a few words about the Presidency itself.

This is an office, as you know, with Andrew Johnson and with Andrew Jackson and with other great Presidents of the past, that is revered by the American people, the office itself, because there is a realization that in a very strange but tangible and heartfelt way the President represents what this Nation is. He represents the fears and concerns and troubles and problems and challenges that confront the American people and has to deal with them, and he also represents the hopes and the dreams and aspirations and confidence and a unity of our Nation as we look to the future.

It's a good job. It's one that is gratifying for anyone interested in politics or government. It's the greatest elective office in the free world, certainly, perhaps the entire world. It's an office that is not easy, sometimes a lonely job. In the confines of the Oval Office, in the privacy of the White House, major decisions have to be made concerning questions of unbelievable complexity and difficulty. The problems that come to my desk or the questions that come to my desk in the Oval Office can't be solved in your own life or in your family or in a city hall or a county courthouse or a State legislature or the Governor's office. And if they are that difficult, eventually they wind up on the desk of the President, and then the President consults very closely and works very closely with the Congress. And we've had extraordinary good relationships with the Congress the last 3½ years.

Many crises or potential crises come to that desk and to that one sometimes lonely man. If the issue is dealt with effectively, with common sense and sound judgment, with the reminder of what this

Nation is and the principles that have always guided leadership in the White House, then those potential crises are never known by you. They simply pass into the history books, maybe the private memoirs of a President or his adviser. If a President makes a wrong judgment or a snap judgment or an ill-advised judgment or is unsure of the strength of our country or must test his bravery by making a rash statement or a rash action, then that potential crisis becomes a real crisis, and it can affect adversely the life of every person in this country or perhaps every person in the entire world.

I'm not complaining about the job, because there's a reassuring part of it too, in that although it's a lonely job, the President is not alone. You have the realization of the strength of the ties that exist all the way from the grassroots precincts into the Oval Office itself, a kind of a structure or a stable organization, a relationship or friendship or partnership that ties the people of this country together. And the thing that I recall most vividly now that I'm in the White House is that our Nation has faced much more difficult problems than we face today.

We complain sometimes about interest rates—and they concern me deeply—or the level of unemployment—it concerns me deeply—or the threats to our peace and security in the Persian Gulf—obviously that's a constant concern to me. But if you go back and analyze where we stand today, with the material blessings that God has given us, with a nation at peace, a nation that's strong, a nation unified, a nation that's not embarrassed anymore by Watergate and CIA revelations or divided by the Vietnam war, if you go back and compare the present circumstances with the Great Depression, when I grew up, or the First World War, where my daddy went, or the Second World War or the Korean war or the

Vietnam war or the embarrassments that I've outlined previously, if you compare all those extreme difficulties with what we have today, indeed we are a blessed nation.

The Revolutionary War, referred to earlier, the Civil War, that tore our Nation apart, those were tests of the American people. And the point to remember in closing is that when we've been presented by those tests—in war, in depression, in the potentially divisive issue of the relationship in the South between black and white citizens—our Nation has never failed, never failed to meet every challenge, to solve every problem, to answer every question, to overcome every obstacle. And that inner strength, that's easy to inventory when you think back through history, is still here.

We're a nation of diversity. We're a nation of immigrants. We're a nation of refugees who've come here looking for a better life, keeping intact as best we could our religious convictions, our heritage, our family patterns, our attitudes, our friendship and blood ties with European and Asian and Latin American and African countries. But once we get here we know that the paramount consideration is the unity and strength of our country, because that's where lies the chance for our families to be closer, for our children to have a better life than we've got even, for our Nation to perpetuate peace, to strengthen human rights, to strengthen democracy all over the world. And we extend a hand of friendship, not war, to those who are different from us.

As our Nation stays at peace and strong we can help the Mideast be stable and at peace. We can see new nations formed, like Zimbabwe, where a large number of people who've always been deprived of even a chance to vote, now running their own affairs very well. In the past we've never had, for many years, friendship or any relationships at all with the 1 billion people that live in China—now new friends, new opportunities for trade and for stability, strategic interrelationships, not based on war or threats to anyone else, but just based on a sharing of common principles that do bind us together in many ways.

So, the point I want to make is this: The issues that I outlined at the airport are crucial. We need confidence in our Nation. We need to emphasize the unity that binds us together, and we particularly need to review in our own minds the importance of that partnership that I described, from the White House to your house.

You are my partners in every sense of the word, whether you're a United States Senator or the speaker of the house in Tennessee or a State senator or Member of the Congress or Mrs. Cauldwell, who has many visitors come to see her, or a farmer, maybe even unemployed. But we're partners, and I have no doubt that this election will see the right judgment made, the principles of our Nation and our party preserved, and our Nation perpetuated as a strong nation at peace, a great nation to be even greater in the future. That's my prayer, and I believe you'll help that prayer come true.

Thank you very much.

NOTE: The President spoke at 10:38 a.m. outside the Old Deery Inn.

Nashville, Tennessee

Remarks and a Question-and-Answer Session at a Townhall Meeting.   October 9, 1980

THE PRESIDENT. It is really good to be back down home. You probably think I came down here to campaign for President, but I really came down here to hear Bill Monroe and his band.

Not long ago Bill Monroe and his wonderful band were at the White House, on the South Lawn, playing some of the best music the White House has ever heard in 200 years. And it brought back memories to me then, because, as you know, I grew up listening to that music and other like it coming from Nashville when I was a small boy on the farm.

We didn't have electricity, but we had a battery radio. And I had two ambitions then. My daddy said, "Forget it." One was to be President of the United States and the other one was to stand on the stage at the Grand Ole Opry. I have to admit I never dreamed at the time that I'd have to be President in order to stand on the stage—[*laughter*]—at the Grand Ole Opry, but I'm really glad to be here with you.

Unlike Georgia, as you know, Tennessee has been the home of great Presidents, not only Andrew Jackson, one of the fathers of the Democratic Party and a man who planted the big magnolia trees that are just outside the entrance of the White House, where Bill Monroe played, but Andrew Johnson, who had a lot of trouble with those radical Republicans in Washington, and also, of course, James K. Polk, was a Tennessean. In 1976 the only thing the press knew about James K. Polk or could remember, apparently, was that he was the last southerner to be elected President of the United States, and that was in 1844.

So, the chances of a southern boy becoming President of this country at that time were very remote. And I have to say that I would not be in the White House had it not been for people like you who had confidence in me then. As a matter of fact, second only to Georgia, Tennessee gave me the biggest victory of any State in the Nation, and I want to thank you for it.

We're going to spend an hour together. I'm going to spend almost all our time answering your questions, but before I do, there's one particular issue that I would like to discuss with you that concerns me very much. It's kind of a serious issue, but it's been my custom to describe one before the question period at all my townhall meetings.

CAMPAIGN ISSUES

First of all, we have lived under the threat of war ever since World War II—under the terrible new threat of nuclear war, atomic weapons that could wipe out an entire city and destroy hundreds of millions of people in our country in just a few hours if that kind of combat took place. We've said these words now and reminded ourselves of it for a full generation. Yet, we've not yet learned how to deal with the real meaning of that serious threat. But we have learned one thing in the last 20 or 30 years, and that is that peace is no accident.

I said those words on the front lawn of the White House not much more than a year ago when we signed the treaty between Israel and Egypt, that peace and the maintenance of peace is not an accident. War with all its horror can be an accident, a terrible misunderstanding, a critical miscalculation of intentions or will or capability or a misguided concept of what honor really is. But peace is no accident. It has to be won every day, against all the forces willing to sacrifice others for their causes, against all who would gamble the fate of nations and the world. People everywhere long for peace. But the peace of all nations is in danger.

We live in a troubled world and, as you know, in Iran, Iraq, other places, they don't know peace today. The first responsibility of every President—Johnson, Jackson, Polk, other Presidents—is for the security of our Nation. It's a responsibility that's on my shoulder every moment.

I was trained as a naval officer, later in the nuclear submarine force, trained for nuclear warfare, and I know what it can do. I chose a military career not because I loved war, but because I knew that a strong, well-trained, dedicated, and prepared military was the surest way to keep the peace. I've watched the awesome power of nuclear weapons grow all my adult life, and I'm not about to do anything that would risk letting that kind of devastation threaten to rain death on any American city.

I'm not saying that we don't face serious challenges and that we don't have serious problems, but the strength of the United States and of our allies is unequaled, unsurpassed, and our strength is growing. That's good for us.

During the 8 years before I became President, in 7 of those years we had a decrease in budget commitment for adequate defense. Our expenditures on defense during the 8 years before I became President went down 35 percent. Since I've been President, we've had a steady, predictable, assured, effective increase every year in commitments for defense, in strategic weapons, nuclear weapons. Before I became President, the commitment had gone down steadily, 20 percent. Now, we've had a steady, predictable, wise increase.

We're overcoming the problems that I faced when I became President. The Trident submarine and its missiles were stalemated. We weren't building any.

Now the first one's getting its sea trial, the second one is ready for launching. There was no long-range cruise missile program; now we've got one, a good one. We had no main battle tanks to fight conventional war on the ground. We didn't have any modern infantry fighting vehicle in production; now we do.

I want to say that there is no solution to the problem without commitment. We didn't have any way to solve the threat of vulnerability of our intercontinental ballistic missiles; now there is a mobile MX missile program. There was a growing gap in the long-range missiles between NATO Europe and Eastern Europe and the Soviet Union; now we're closing that gap. There was no comprehensive plan for improving our military forces in Europe. Now we've got a good, solid 15-year plan to build, steadily and predictably, strength for peace. All of us, all of our allies, are joining in the same program.

This is an election year, and I have to say that the state of our defenses is a legitimate subject for political debate. But political candidates make a mistake when they run down America's strength. When they say falsely that America is weak, it causes Americans ourselves to be concerned. It causes our allies to lose confidence in us. It gives our potential adversaries false hope that they might prevail against us in a showdown.

In every campaign when a candidate charged that the Russians were ahead of us, after the campaign those charges were proven to be false. A perfect example is my Republican opponent's recent suggestion that United States weakness is what caused us to stay neutral in the war between Iran and Iraq. It's a sign of weakness if you have to get involved militarily in a combat. It's a sign of strength if you can protect our Nation's interests peacefully. He also said that somehow or another, our Nation being weak, which it's not, helped even to cause the war between Iran and Iraq. That kind of statement doesn't help.

We've got two carrier battle groups and almost 150 aircraft in that region of the Persian Gulf. We have clear naval superiority; we've got clear air superiority in that whole region. These aircraft include F–14's, which are capable of tracking six enemy aircraft at the same time and shooting them down. If candidates want to contribute to American security, the most important thing they can do is to talk accurately about our military strength in a more balanced and a more responsible manner. It's a subject that's too important to be discussed any other way. It's a point I wanted to make to you, one of many important issues that face our country.

Ours is such a strong country. It's such a good country. It's such a united country. And I just don't like anybody to be saying that we're weak or that somebody else can push us around, because it's not true.

Now, the first question.

QUESTIONS

PRESIDENT'S FUTURE PLANS

Q. My name is Linda Turner. I'm thrilled and honored to be here. Before I ask my question I would like to tell you that I am a Democrat all the way. You have done a good job for the past 4 years, and you will continue to do the same good job in the next 4 years.

THE PRESIDENT. That's enough already if you want to stop right there. [*Laughter*] Go ahead.

Q. Mr. President, you will be reelected in November, but what I would like to know, in case you are not reelected, what are your plans for the future? [*Laughter*]

THE PRESIDENT. That's one of the most hypothetical questions I ever heard. [*Laughter*]

I am a southerner, a Georgian, and after I finish my service in the White House in January of 1985—[*laughter*]—I intend to go back and live in Plains, Georgia. My family's been there for a long time. My own Carter ancestors, who were born in the 1790's, are buried right there near Plains. My wife's ancestors, who were born in 1787, are buried right there in Plains. They're the first people who lived on the farm we still own, after the Indians moved out back in 1828.

So, my roots are deep in the South, and I look forward to coming back to the South after I get through being President.

EDUCATION IN RURAL AREAS

Q. Mr. President, before I ask my question I'd also like to say that I'm very definitely a Jimmy Carter supporter.

THE PRESIDENT. Thank you.

Q. Judging from the answer to your last question, I'll take it for granted that you are from a rural background and that your roots do lie in rural communities, and, being from a rural background, this question is twofold, Mr. President. How do you feel about small country schools, and the learning that takes place in these schools? And secondly, isn't the present trend to consolidate these schools, to tear down the small country schools and build the large multimillion dollar building programs, isn't this very inflationary and isn't this bad for us at the present time?

THE PRESIDENT. That's a good question. It's one that's had to be faced every-

where. I think I know what answer you would prefer.

I might say that in my own graduating class I had 23 classmates, and I went on to become Governor of Georgia and then become President of our country. Nowadays, of course, the breadth of technological instruction, the need to study foreign languages, the enormous pressures on a person to compete in a world where a career or training is important, I think, are more significant than when I was a boy.

As President my commitment has been to keep the Federal Government's nose out of the affairs of the local school boards and the local schools. I think that's extremely important. But let me say one more thing.

If the local country school cannot provide the curriculum and the background and the educational program that the children need, obviously sometimes they have to be consolidated to make the classrooms adequate to provide a good staff and a good curriculum and a good offering. But that's just a judgment that has to be made locally.

I'm not trying to avoid the answer to your question, but I wouldn't want to comment, because you're probably referring to a local situation where you live, and I don't want to say that it ought to be consolidated or not consolidated. I'll take the typical politician's attitude. I've played it both ways.

I was on the school board in Sumter County, and on occasion we had to consolidate some schools. I might give you the reason why, and I'll be very brief. This is a southern audience, and you'll understand what I'm saying.

I came out of the Navy in '53, and my first political job was the local school board. It was when we were going through the years of school integration—difficult issue, difficult times for the South. I was a typical white, prosperous member of the community. It took me a long time on the school board before I realized that the white kids were riding buses to school and the black kids were walking. It took me a long time—and I was a member of the school board—to realize that the only schoolbooks the black kids had were the ones that were too dilapidated and worn out for the white kids to use anymore. And so, when it finally dawned on me after several months, I asked the school board members, the other four, to join me and go around and look at some of the schools in the county.

The white kids were in pretty nice schools, some old; the black children were going to school in the back kitchen of houses and on the porches and in the basements of old dilapidated churches and so forth. We had 26 black grammar schools in that county, and the total population was about 30,000 total people. So, there was a case where we were cheating the black children without realizing it, and so we made changes and had to do some consolidation.

And later the people in the South were very courageous in changing a way of life to give black children an equal chance. It's one of the best things that ever happened to the South. And I would not be President if it hadn't happened.

So, I'll let the local school boards decide about consolidation, but that's a couple of experiences that I've had. I came from a tiny school and did okay in politics. But on occasion, consolidation is necessary.

INTEREST RATES

Q. How are you doing, Mr. President?
THE PRESIDENT. Fine.

Q. My name is Jamie Lucas, and my question is on interest rates and on housing. And I'd like to know what you and the Federal Government would do to lower these interest rates so the people like myself could afford to buy a home and the people in the construction industry and real estate can earn more money?

THE PRESIDENT. Thank you, Jamie.

For the last 3 months we've had a steady increase in the number of houses being built or begun in this country. We're up now almost to 1½ million homes per year as a rate. As you know, back in March—first of March and before that—the interest rates were up around 18 or 19 percent. Now they're down around 13 percent, which is still too high.

We've taken several steps during that time to bring those interest rates down, and they went down, as you remember, about 1 percent per week for several weeks. We put some restraint on credit in order to encourage American people to save more money. We've got the lowest level of savings of perhaps any developed nation on Earth. We spend about 96 or 97 percent of all we earn, and we save about 3 or 4 percent. In the other countries, like, say, Japan or Germany, they save 15 or 20 percent and spend 80 or 85 percent. So, how much people save and invest in savings and loan institutions and maybe put in savings accounts in banks and so forth determines how much money is available to be loaned. And also it takes money out of circulation in the country so that the price of products is not bid up with inflation. That's one point.

Another one is the policies set by the Federal Reserve Board. It's a completely independent agency. I don't have a thing in the world to do with how they function or what decisions they make. I have said that I think the narrow formula that they use—just measuring money supply and nothing else, almost nothing else—is not an adequate basis on which to make a decision about their policies that drive up interest rates on occasion. And I think recently, the Citibank in New York and a few others have raised their prime rate too much, more than the economic circumstances in our country warrant.

The other thing that we can do is to hold down unnecessary Government spending and make sure that our deficits are constantly reduced. We've had tremendously good luck since I've been in the White House in cutting out unnecessary expenditures and holding down the deficits. We've not yet reached a balanced budget, but that's one of my goals. We've got 44,000 fewer Federal employees right now than we had the day I took office, and we're giving better services, I think, to the American people.

And the other thing is to provide federally assisted homes, where the Federal Government supplements interest rates and monthly payments and also encourages under section 8 and other programs, the construction of homes available to people, keep the GI bill strong, and keep homes for the elderly being built. I just signed a bill day before yesterday that will provide about a 30-percent increase in this fiscal year, that started the 1st of October, compared to last fiscal year on federally assisted housing.

Those are some of the things that can be done by the public, in saving more money; by the Federal Reserve Board and the banks, in holding down interest rates; by myself as President and the Congress, in determining expenditures from the Federal budget; and in the housing industry itself, helping people to buy homes.

We've also raised the value on homes that can be subject to Federal assistance.

And another thing that we've done is on homes that are federally assisted when the husband or wife making the payments is temporarily ill or unemployed, then the Housing and Urban Development Department in the Federal Government now, HUD, can make those payments for the family for a few months until the husband or wife is well or back on the job so the family doesn't lose a home where they've already bought a lot of equity in it.

Briefly, those are a few things that can be done. The interest rates are too high now. I believe that you'll see them coming down in the future.

INFLATION

Q. Mr. President, I'm Suzanne Lowenstein. Everyone makes mistakes. What do you think has been the greatest mistake you have made since you took office close to 4 years ago?

THE PRESIDENT. Thank you a lot. That's a great question.

You're right. Everyone makes mistakes, even Presidents. It's hard to know how to address that question, because looking back on history, if I had known 3 years ago what I know now and was a fortune teller, I could have made different judgments.

I would say the most important one was the lack of adequate preparation for the enormous increase in oil prices last year. We were concentrating on putting American people back to work, because when I took office we had a very high unemployment rate, and the inflation rate was fairly low, because OPEC had not raised their oil prices all during 1976. It was a kind of a stable economy. So, we emphasized the first year I was in office jobs. In this first 3½ years we have added 8½ million net new jobs in America—never done before in the history of our country in wartime or peace. But in the process we didn't adequately restrain inflation.

Last year, in '79, OPEC increased the price of oil more in 1 year than oil prices had increased since oil was first discovered back in the 1800's, and this enormous buildup in oil prices has driven inflation high and interest rates high all over the world. Had I known ahead of time that that would happen, I would have put much more emphasis the first couple of years on controlling inflation than I did. In retrospect it's obvious, but no one, I believe, could have anticipated that enormous increase in OPEC oil prices. So, that's the kind of thing that you can look back on and say, "I wish I had done it differently." At the time we consulted and, I think, made good decisions.

And I might point out too that we've come through it fairly well. You know, we still have very high employment. The unemployment rate is reasonably low. The housing industry is fairly stable. And we've made enormous progress now in cutting down our dependence on foreign oil. So, in the future, if OPEC should jack up its prices too high, we're not importing nearly as much as we were. We've cut oil imports 24 percent since I've been in office. This day and every day in 1980 we are importing 2 million barrels a day less each day from overseas than we did the first year I was in office.

We're making progress, but if I had it to do over again, I'd put more emphasis on inflation.

PRIVATE EDUCATION

Q. Mr. President, my name is Jerry Jarrett, and I'm a junior at Brentwood Academy, and that's a private high school outside of Nashville. And with the situation that public education is in today, a lot of people feel that they might not have any choice other than to send their children to private schools. But there's been a lot of talk lately about the proposal by the IRS to take the tax-exempt status off of our schools, and I was wondering what your feelings are on this proposal and your feelings on private education in general?

THE PRESIDENT. What's your first name?

Q. Jerry.

THE PRESIDENT. Jerry. Thank you.

I think there's a real important place in our Nation for both private and public schools at all levels, from kindergarten all the way up through graduate schools. This is important for our Nation to understand, that ever since the early 1600's we've had both private and public education on this continent.

I'm not in favor of the IRS taking away the tax-exempt status for private schools. But—I've got to have a "but"—but if the private school is organized and designed and functions just to exclude children who are a certain race or have a certain religious belief, that's a violation of the United States Constitution as interpreted by the court. And under that circumstance, I think that the tax-exempt status should be withheld, but I also believe that the burden of proof that that is the case ought to be on the Government. So, if— with that one exception, I believe that the tax-exempt status ought to be retained, and if there is an allegation or a charge that the school is discriminating against the person because of their race or beliefs, then I think the Federal Government, IRS, ought to have to prove that the school is guilty before the tax exempt status is withheld.

THE MIDDLE EAST

Q. Mr. President, I'm Christie Newkirk from Nashville, and I'd like to say I think you've done a tremendous job under very difficult situations.

THE PRESIDENT. Thank you.

Q. I do have a question for you. In view of the inflammable situation in the Middle East, especially the prolonged Iran-Iraq conflict and the willingness of some Arab leaders to supply arms and other war materials to these nations and the ever-present potentials for increased Soviet influence in the situation, what specific role do you foresee for the United States to play in promoting peace in the area, ending the American hostage crisis, and checking Soviet influence and/or aggression in the Persian Gulf area?

THE PRESIDENT. Good question. That's a very important and a very thoughtful question, Christie, and I thank you for it.

In my opening comments, I tried to make clear that our Nation can only stay at peace if we are strong. That's an important concept. But in order to fly an airplane has to have two wings. You can't just have a strong military in order to keep a nation at peace. You've got to also have a commitment of the American people to work for arms control and not to use our military forces around the world every time some troubled area develops.

I've not been in office yet a single day when there wasn't an intense focusing of trouble or problems somewhere in the world. And the best way I know how to deal with this is to keep our people aware, our allies knowledgeable, and also our potential adversaries knowing that we are there and that we are strong and we're going to protect American interests peacefully—peacefully.

I had a chance, as you know, in the Afghanistan situation, when the Soviets invaded Afghanistan, to either take military action or economic and political action. We decided to take economic and political action. It's been very effective. Now in the Iran-Iraq war our country is staying neutral. We're not going to inject ourselves into that combat, and we're not staying neutral because we are weak.

We do have, however, vital interests in the Persian Gulf region. From the Persian Gulf the rest of the world gets about 15 million barrels of oil per day—from Iran, Iraq, Kuwait, United Arab Emirates, and, primarily, from Saudi Arabia. If that Persian Gulf was closed and tankers couldn't go in and out to load and bring their oil to us and to other nations, it would be a devastating blow to the rest of the world. Oil prices would skyrocket, nations would have to shut down their industrial plants, and we would be threatened. Our security would be threatened. So, I have announced that we will take action, if necessary, to keep the Strait of Hormuz open and to make sure that that Persian Gulf region is accessible to the rest of the world.

I can't spell out to you this morning in public what I would do or will do. But we will take necessary action to make sure that goal is realized. We've also consulted very closely with our allies and friends to say, "What would you do to help us if the Strait of Hormuz is threatened to be closed and if the rest of the world is threatened with this deprivation of oil?"

We're working for peace between Israel and her neighbors. The peace treaty that was signed between Israel and Egypt is a major step forward in preserving a democracy there, an ally of ours, a strong and staunch defender of freedom, and a stabilizing force. We're going to do what we can. We'll do whatever is necessary to keep Israel secure and to keep Israel at peace. It's a tiny nation, about 3 million people, surrounded by hundreds of thousands of Arabs. And we work very closely with some of her Arab neighbors as well.

The biggest and strongest Arab nation, of course, in the world, is Egypt. And I'm very pleased that now, because of our influence to some degree, instead of facing each other through barbed wire and with guns and ships and planes killing each other, they now face each other across a bargaining table, a peace table. So, we try to use our influence there, just to calm things down.

One of the things that concerns me about Governor Reagan is that over the last few years in many instances when myself or President Nixon or President Ford or President Johnson were faced with one of these troubled times or places—we've tried to use diplomatic means to resolve the problems peacefully; but Governor Reagan on those occasions has called repeatedly for the use or injection of American military forces there. I don't know what he would do in the Oval Office, but I know what he's said as a candidate or a potential candidate for President. He has said, send American military forces to Ecuador, to Cuba, to the Middle East, to North Korea, to Pakistan, to Angola, and other places around the world when those areas were troubled. That's not the way to deal through strength to keep peace.

And the last thing is the Soviet Union. We have let the Soviet Union know very clearly that any encroachment on the Persian Gulf region by them would be a threat to our own security. I said this in my State of the Union speech last January, and the message went very clearly to them. I communicate on occasion with President Brezhnev. He writes me letters; I write him letters. We exchange ideas also through normal diplomatic channels. And so, the Soviets know very clearly that we would look upon this as a threat to our Nation's security, if the Soviet Union should move into that Persian Gulf region with their military forces.

So, just letting other nations, friends or potential adversaries, know clearly what we will do is a good way to restrain them from further threatening the peace. We'll also do all we can to end the Iran-Iraq war as quickly as possible, and if we can't end it soon, to keep it confined just to those two countries.

PRESIDENT'S JOGGING HABITS

Q. Mr. President, welcome to Tennessee and Nashville.

THE PRESIDENT. Thank you.

Q. As a jogger I'd like to ask you something about your jogging. [*Laughter*]

THE PRESIDENT. Okay.

Q. How long, how much, and are you going to run in New York? [*Laughter*]

THE PRESIDENT. I'm going to run in the election in New York November 4. [*Laughter*]

Last year I ran 6 or 7 miles a week—I mean, a day. Excuse me. I ran about 30, 35 miles a week. This year I've cut that about half because of the extra duties that I have to perform during an election year, but I get exercise every day, and my wife runs a couple of miles, and I generally run 3 or 4 miles. I'm not very fast. I generally, if I want to really try, I can do 3 miles in about 20 minutes. That's the best I can do. I'm 56 years old—not getting any younger—and stay in good physical shape.

My favorite pastime, though, is fishing. Whenever I get a chance I go fishing. I've been doing that ever since I was a little boy. But I would like to say that I think one of the best things that's happened to our country in recent years has been the new interest in personal physical fitness, and around the streets in Washington and New York and San Francisco, I'm sure Nashville, you can see a lot of people running or jogging and in the parks playing softball. I think that's a very fine thing for us to continue to do.

I stay in good shape, and jogging's something that I do daily.

EMPLOYMENT PROGRAMS

Q. Mr. President, I'm Norma Walker from Gladeville, Tennessee, and my question is: For several years our Government has had programs providing public jobs. I'd like to know why these programs can't be coordinated through State and local welfare offices and then those deserving people be given a job instead of a check?

THE PRESIDENT. Thank you. We have a welfare reform bill before the Congress that I think has a good chance of passing next year, that will—I can't say force, but will strongly encourage every able-bodied person to get off welfare and take a job. Under the present confused laws it sometimes means that that person loses income if they take a full-time job. But with the combination of tax credits, the low-income tax credits, and the income that would come from a job under my new proposal, which is before the Congress now, it would always be attractive for that person to get a job.

I don't believe that it would be advisable for the welfare department to handle, though, the public job business. I think the Labor Department is better able to do that. We're also now moving toward a new youth bill—which has already passed the House of Representatives, has a good chance to pass the Senate this year—that would tie together for the first time, much more closely, the Labor Department, that knows in an area where the jobs are available, and the Education Department, with all of its breadth of graduates from high school, vocational technical schools, and so forth, that want jobs.

This would provide about $2 billion in training for young people from the junior high school, senior high school level, and on up, to get jobs not in the government, but in private industry. And during the first few weeks when that new jobholder is learning how to do simple arithmetic work and how to get there on time, how to punch a timeclock and so forth, the Government would help pay part of the salary. But the Government role would be phased out very rapidly, and then that person could stand on his or her own and hold that job.

So, we are moving strongly, and as rapidly as the Congress will, to encourage people who are able to work to work, and at the same time, we are trying to tie together an opportunity for everybody to have a job through cooperation between the Labor Department, the welfare department, and also, of course, the Education Department.

AMY CARTER

Q. Mr. President, my name is Amy Jo Kee, and I am in the fifth grade at Walton Ferry School in Hendersonville, Tennessee. Does Amy ever have any of her friends in Georgia to come and visit her at the White House? [*Laughter*]

THE PRESIDENT. Your name is Amy Jo?

Q. Yes.

THE PRESIDENT. Beautiful name. [*Laughter*]

Yes, Amy's a very active young girl. She's 12 years old, as you know—soon be 13. She has a lot of her classmates and friends come from—she goes to the public school in Washington, D.C.—to come to the White House often. And whenever possible, when anybody from Plains or that we've known in Georgia, comes to Atlanta [Washington],[1] they come by to see Amy; sometimes they spend the night with her. Amy is a fairly good student, and she's taking violin lessons, and she has a lot of outside activities.

Would you like to come and visit Amy?

Q. Yes.

THE PRESIDENT. Are your parents here, Amy Jo? Where are they?

Q. Over there.

THE PRESIDENT. If Amy invited Amy Jo to come and visit her, would you see that she gets there? [*Laughter*] I'll let one of my staff members get Amy Jo's address and phone number, and Amy will give you a call before long. And you can come up and see us, Amy Jo. Okay?

TENNESSEE VALLEY AUTHORITY

Q. Mr. President, my name is June Landers, and I'm delighted to see you in Nashville, Tennessee, today. My question is this: How do you feel about the decision of the TVA Board of Directors to finance construction of expensive nuclear powerplants beyond its projected energy needs of the Tennessee Valley?

THE PRESIDENT. I don't think the TVA ought to build plants above and beyond their needs. I think the hard question

_____
[1] White House correction.

that they have to answer, June, is what will be the needs 6 years from now, 8 years from now, 10 years from now, when this entire region that depends on TVA continues to grow, with new industry and new jobs and a larger population and more need for electricity. That balance is a very difficult one to reach, because you have to guess what's going to happen in the economy in the future.

I've been quite disturbed lately and have talked to the Chairman of the TVA and also have talked to some of your congressional leaders that are here today with us about the recent rapid increase in TVA rates. And I've asked the TVA Board, over whom, as you know, I have no control, to make sure that they implement the maximum amount of efficiency of operation to cut out waste; secondly, that they encourage the maximum amount of conservation in individual homes so electricity is not used and wasted, and also in factories and plants in the Southeast, where they serve to lower the amount of electricity capacity that will be needed in years to come; and, third, that they minimize construction for future years and don't build excessive capacity as you've described. I think that the TVA Board is now very much aware of my concern and your concern and that they will do all three of those things, and that in the future they'll be cautious like electric power companies all over the Nation in not building capacity that will not in the future be needed.

It's time for a reassessment, because Americans have much more commitment now to buying efficient automobiles and to keeping their homes insulated, cutting out lights when they're not needed, and reducing the cost of their electricity each month because the price has gone so high.

I might add, though, just in fairness to TVA, that even with their projected rate increases you will still pay in the TVA region 30 percent less for electric power than the national average, so TVA has done a good job in holding down rates in years gone by. They're going to be much more cautious in months ahead not to put additional plants in that are not needed, and my hope, and I'm sure your hope, is that any increase in the future in rates will be minimized.

FOREIGN POLICY

Q. Mr. President, I'm Jim Hobson. And in the last year it's become increasingly clear that foreign policy is playing a very big role in the United States. My question is, there seems to be a constant rivalry between Dr. Brzezinski and your Secretary of State, Edmund Muskie. Is this playing a very devastating role in our foreign policy, and how is it affecting our foreign policy?

THE PRESIDENT. Jim, first of all that report is false. It's an error. The President is the one who makes foreign policy. I make the foreign policy. There have been Presidents in the past, maybe not too distant past, that let—[laughter]— their Secretaries of State make foreign policy. I don't. I make my own decisions on foreign policy, and when there is a mistake made, now or in the future, as long as I'm in the White House, it would be wise and accurate for you to say, "The President made a mistake," not "Ed Muskie made a mistake," or "Dr. Brzezinski made a mistake." It's the President. Hopefully, if we have some successes in the future you can say, "The President made a good decision," and not the others.

Now, let me point out the need to have some diversity in advice. I meet frequently—not every single day, but almost every day—with the Secretary of Defense, Secretary of State, and my national security adviser, and the Vice President's there, and a couple of other people, a very small group. We go through the broad range of foreign policy questions that I have to address. It's extremely complicated—150 or more nations on Earth. Each one of them has different desires and different neighbors and different problems and different kinds of people, different kinds of leaders, and I have to understand them. It takes a lot of homework and a lot of study, of a lot of reading, a lot of prayer.

I can't just let the State Department give me advice on what to do in a time of trouble, because quite often the origin of the State Department opinion is a particular desk officer who has the responsibility just for one nation or for one small part of the world. He concentrates on that nation or that little group of nations, and his prime interest is to have extra good relationships between our country and that particular nation of his, although he's loyal to our country. But there'll be 150 other nations involved and our allies and friends and the Soviet Union and troubled areas in the Persian Gulf. So, I have to make sure that I get a breadth of understanding and advice.

I have to admit to you that sometimes there is a sharp division of opinion between, say, the Vice President and the Secretary of State, or between the Secretary of State and the Secretary of Defense, or between Dr. Brzezinski and Harold Brown, the Secretary of Defense. I admit that. And they present their conflicting views to me, and I make a decision.

When I got ready, for instance, to go to Camp David with Prime Minister Begin and President Sadat, I believe it's accurate to say that none of my advisers thought I ought to go, because the prospects for success were so remote and the embarrassment to me of a failure was potentially so great, they thought I ought to be more cautious. I decided to go, and it worked out well. Other times I've used my own initiative and it hasn't worked out nearly so well as that.

But I can guarantee you, there's no need for me to mislead anyone—I'm a man of honor and a man of truthfulness—I can tell you that there are no problems or differences between Brzezinski and Muskie that need cause you any concern or need be of any concern to the American people. On 95 percent of the cases they agree completely, and when they do have a difference of agreement, they both present their case to me. I make the judgment, and I stand by it. I take responsibility for it. That's the way it is.

DEPARTMENT OF EDUCATION

Q. Hello, Mr. President, my name is Carol Boehms, and I'm a fourth grade public schoolteacher in Cheatham County. And I thought you'd like to know we held a Presidential election in our room, and you won. [*Laughter*]

THE PRESIDENT. Very good.

Q. You beat out Reagan and Anderson and your brother too. [*Laughter*] My children really want an autograph from you if I can get one. I am a nervous wreck.

THE PRESIDENT. You'll get it.

Q. My question is if you can tell me how the newly formed Department of Education will help the public schoolteachers as well as the students?

THE PRESIDENT. All right. For too long in this country we've had education buried under health and welfare. I've said this many times, but when I was Governor, I probably spent at least 25 percent of my time on education, trying to get a better system, private and public schools, in Georgia.

When I got to be President, I was kind of taken aback by the fact that the only time I got involved in education was at a Cabinet meeting when there was some argument about a lawsuit or civil rights or how many players on a girls basketball team or something like that, and I feel that the Federal Government has a very important role to play in education. As I said earlier, in answer to Jerry's question about—I think it was Jerry's question—I think that the decision of our curriculum, the location of schools, consolidation of schools, the hiring of teachers, ought to be left completely to the local and State people. The Federal Government ought not to get involved in that. But we should provide some aid in money to help, particularly the poorer districts and particularly the poorer children who would not otherwise have an adequate education. And when our country has a special need, like after the Soviets put up Sputnik, the Federal Government provided under President Eisenhower, a Republican President, some additional help for science and mathematics. So, these kinds of things the Federal Government ought to do.

There's no doubt in my mind that the new Department of Education, under Shirley Hufstedler, will now be able to concentrate its effort on better cooperation between the Federal, State, and local governments and the private sector if they choose. They'll be able to concentrate their efforts on experimentation, new ideas for teaching, new use of communications. Also they'll be able to resolve the differences that arise before they get into the Federal courts. In the past if a school board member or a Governor had a problem with the Federal Government about education in Tennessee, there was nowhere to go. I mean if you went to the Secretary of HEW that Secretary was bogged down with health and welfare and all the thousands of things that they had to do.

Now everybody in education knows you go to Shirley Hufstedler, the Secretary of Education. When we have a Cabinet meeting she's there. She understands what all the other departments do, and I believe that through this process we'll have a much better chance for a problem that arises that involves the quality of life for teachers and how well you do your job, then we can resolve that problem through negotiation and understanding and communication. She can come to Tennessee and meet with the Governor. She can meet with the local school board if necessary and keep these lawsuits from ever taking place and keeping the Federal Government's nose out of local affairs and keeping us out of the Federal courts.

So, I think in every aspect of education protecting the local and State rights to run the schools the Federal Government can do a better job now and make the teachers' job more effective and avoid conflict that in the past has quite often debilitated the partnership that ought to exist in giving kids a better chance in life.

PRESIDENT'S CAMPAIGN STYLE

Q. Hello, President Carter. My name is David Mangum, and I'm in an American Government class at David Lipscomb High School. I have to say that Mr. Reagan and you have made my class much more interesting.

THE PRESIDENT. Very fine.

Q. It would just be great to see you at a day at the office.

I have read a lot of literature and watched many news shows. I believe that all Democrats agree that you are the most qualified for the 1980 Presidential election. Sir, why is it that if you are the right man for the job that you and your staff have to lower yourselves to the extent of slinging mud and making slanderous statements with your rival, Ronald Reagan? I've been brought up by being taught to respect other peoples' ideas and beliefs, and if I disagree with them I should not cut down their program, but I should show the good of my own.

THE PRESIDENT. Thank you, David. Good question.

I think in the last few weeks, the campaign has gotten sidetracked on too many personal references between me and Governor Reagan and between Governor Reagan and me. I was interviewed yesterday by Barbara Walters on ABC, and I explained to her that in my judgment, it was much better for the Nation to devote its time to the proper conduct of a campaign that was suitable for candidates for the highest office in the world, certainly in this land.

I have never intended to criticize Governor Reagan personally. Some issues affect me very deeply, and there have been occasions when the press has not covered the issue at all, that I consider to be extremely important. I'll just give you one quick example, because we've run out of time.

Not too long ago, last week, Governor Reagan said, for instance, that the SALT II treaty, which has been negotiated by President Nixon and Ford and me, ought to be withdrawn from the Senate and not considered. And he expressed a belief that an arms race might be commenced as a trump card or card to be played against the Soviet Union. That may sound on the surface to be a reasonable approach, but when I read it, knowing the importance of this issue and how the American people have got to be committed to nuclear arms control, and how our allies are depending on us to be the leaders in the world to prevent a nuclear war, and how a proper peaceful relationship between ourselves and the Soviet Union has got to be maintained, and how disturbing this would be to future negotiations on arms control, I felt motivated to speak out. And I got maybe overly enthusiastic about it.

Every President since Truman, Eisenhower, all the way through Johnson, Kennedy, Ford, and Nixon, have worked for arms control, and to abandon that concept now would be a radical change from what we've had in the past. I felt that the press should have covered that issue. Do you agree? [*Applause*]

That night I watched the evening news networks. ABC did not mention it. CBS did not mention it. NBC did not mention it. They covered the technique of the campaign and who was going to debate whom and all that kind of stuff—didn't even give one word to this, perhaps the most important issue that a President has to face. You know, when I decided to run for President, I had to make a decision: If I get in the Oval Office and if I have to, could I use nuclear weapons? That's the kind of issue about which candidates need to discuss.

The last point I'd like to make is this: There are three things in a campaign that not only are a privilege, but a duty of a campaigner, a candidate. One is to discuss my record, what I've done about education and about health and about peace and about war and about weapons and about defense and about jobs; second, to spell out what I'll do in the future, next 4 years; and third, is to point out the differences that exist between me and my opponents. That's a legitimate role to play.

I have accepted five or six invitations to debate Governor Reagan. He's refused to debate me without other people on the platform. He wants to debate with Anderson there, with others. I think that he and I, as the nominees of our two parties, ought to get on a platform like this, be questioned and question each other, to let the American people know these sharp differences between us. And if I have misinterpreted what he says——

Q. It's important that we get back to the basics.

THE PRESIDENT. It is important.

Q. If we can do that, maybe we can solve our problems easier.

THE PRESIDENT. I'm determined this last 26 or 27 days, whatever it is, to be sharp in my accurate description of the differences between us and to spell out those issues. Yesterday, a television station in Tampa, Florida, invited me and Governor Reagan to a joint televised appearance tomorrow. The reason is, coincidentally, that both of us will be in Tampa, same day. They invited us to be cross-examined by reporters, maybe even in separate rooms—I don't know the exact details. I accepted immediately, just like I accepted the League of Women Voters invitation to debate Governor Reagan and then later to debate him and Anderson both. I understand that he's turning it down.

I hope that Governor Reagan will accept the invitation of that Tampa TV station to debate me tomorrow. I will be very eager to do it. It's unfortunate that he has decided not to debate. You have probably noticed lately that he is very cautious. He doesn't have townhall meetings like this. He doesn't have press conferences anymore. He's very cautious about what he says. So, I'll have to reserve the right, even though I'm going to be very careful to be both accurate and not attack him as a person, to spell out the sharp differences between me and him, and I'll try to do it in such a way that'll make you proud of me, yes.

Q. Thank you. I want to be.

THE PRESIDENT. Thank you all very much. Let me say one other thing, a brief 1-minute statement. We've gone a little bit over time.

Our country's got problems. Our country faces critical choices. One of the most critical will be on November 4. I'm not going to make a campaign request here, but let me point this out: The situation in our Nation now is much better than we generally are willing to acknowledge. God has blessed this country with material wealth, with strength, with unity, and with peace.

Think back on the time when James K. Polk was running for President or Andrew Johnson was running for President, Andrew Jackson was running for President. The Revolutionary War, the Civil War, World War I, World War II, the divisive Vietnam war, the civil rights revolution, you might call it, the embarrassments of Watergate, the Great Depression—a lot of you experienced some of those things. They were troublous times, much worse than the times we live in today. But in every one of those times when the country was challenged the United States of America never failed. We have never failed to resolve a difficult problem. We have never failed to answer

the toughest questions. We've never failed to overcome the most insurmountable obstacle. We have never failed to lead the world toward a better life.

And that's the message that I want to leave with you. We've got a great country.

NOTE: The President spoke at 12:04 p.m. in the Grand Ole Opry.

Nashville, Tennessee

Remarks at a Carter/Mondale Fundraising Reception.   October 9, 1980

First of all, I want to thank Tom T. and Dixie for being so nice to me as to host this reception, and all of the performers behind me have really thrilled my heart. I've been a fan of theirs ever since they've been performing and I've been old enough to listen to the radio. Don't you think you got your money's worth just for them? [*Applause*]

As you know, I'm part of the Carter family. [*Laughter*] I'm the politician in the family; they are the musicians. If I could just politick as well as they can sing, I wouldn't have any problems at all— [*laughter*]—this year.

Since I've been in the White House, I've had a chance to let the world know about my love for country music and about the value of country music to our Nation and to the world. There is no other form of music, in my opinion, that has such a heartfelt expression of the real, few, intense human yearnings and expressions of love and disappointment, ambition and hope, sense of the family, of history, as is expressed through country music. It's as modern as the daily newspaper, it's as true to the past as a history book, and I think it looks to the future with a great deal of anticipation and confidence and enjoyment.

I'm not going to make a political speech, because I want to spend my time here shaking hands personally with every one of you who've come to express your confidence in me and also come to express your confidence in our Nation. I just had a very exciting townhall meeting with 4,400 people in the Grand Ole Opry. And to me, this relationship with you as partners in the future development of our country and the exchange of ideas and questions with that many people in Nashville is part of what makes our country great.

I'm determined, if I am reelected in November, to continue to make the greatest nation on Earth even greater, and I'm determined also to be elected in November. With your help, we won't fail.

Thank you very much.

NOTE: The President spoke at 1:22 p.m. in the Knoxville Room at the Opryland Hotel. In his opening remarks, he referred to Mr. and Mrs. Tom T. Hall.

Winston-Salem, North Carolina

Remarks to Residents of Forsyth County and the Surrounding Area. October 9, 1980

THE PRESIDENT. Jim, I particularly thank you for that wonderful introduction. It's a real pleasure for me to be here. There is no way that I could search the United States of America and find a better Democratic ticket to run with than here in North Carolina, the one you've put together, and I thank you for it.

My background, as you know, is the South. And my present is the South, and my future is the South as well, because I've never found any difference between what was best for this region compared to what is best for the entire United States.

But in the long time prior to 1976, the South was not given the opportunity to have one of our sons seek the highest office of this land successfully. When I began to campaign in 1976, many of my southern friends said, "Jimmy, it won't be possible because the last President who was a southerner who was elected was James K. Polk in 1844." But I came to North Carolina and asked you for your help; you gave it to me, and now I'm in the White House. I'm going to stay there 4 more years.

And I might have a few weaknesses, you know, but——

AUDIENCE. [*Shouting*] No!

THE PRESIDENT. Some people say I have. I agree with you, I think. [*Laughter*] But one of the things that gives me both enthusiasm and also confidence in North Carolina is to be on this same unity campaign with one of the finest, strongest, most distinguished Governors in the United States, Jim Hunt.

And I'd like to say just one special word on behalf of a man of great courage. I am the President, sometimes lonely, making in the Oval Office decisions that are not easy, because the questions that come to me can't be solved by you personally or within your own home or in a city hall or a county courthouse or a State legislature or the Governor's office. They're the most difficult questions of all. And for a President, eager for a strong nation, eager for a nation that uses its strength to stay at peace, I'm grateful to you that you let Jim [Bob] Morgan represent you and me and this Nation in the United States Senate—Bob Morgan. Bob Morgan is a great man.

Bob is a man who has been under attack, as you know, on your televisions, from outside forces spending hundreds and hundreds of thousands of dollars against a great North Carolinian. And I hope that you here in North Carolina will show those outside, rich, political, misguided Americans what you think of Bob Morgan.

In 1974—I was Governor—I came here to Winston-Salem at the request of a young man running for Congress. A lot of people said he didn't have a chance. I had confidence in him. He has assumed a major leadership role in the House of Representatives. He's grown every year politically in wisdom and judgment and in influence. He truly represents your best interests in our National Capital, and I'm very glad to come back here as President and express to you my pride in Steve Neal, who I hope you will keep there for a long, long time.

Well, I'm proud of all of them, but I'm going to be even prouder of the people of North Carolina on November the 4th when you vote the Democratic ticket back in office, from the White House all the way to the courthouse.

I think a lot of you know that North Carolina is my second home. My people came from Bertie County, North Carolina, and moved to Georgia. They moved down there about 10 years before the Revolution. They were tobacco farmers, and I think they surely grew some goobers as well. [*Laughter*] But my ties of kinship and friendship with you are very strong. And for generations I've shared also with you and other southerners certain convictions that are important to working people—a pride, almost a reverence, for hard work; a deep personal belief in God; a commitment to maintain strong families; a belief that we are stewards of a wonderful gift of the land; a belief that these principles are the bedrock of our society.

And I pray to God that the people of the South and the people of this Nation will never lose their commitment to these enduring values.

I've come back home to the South to ask you to join with me in one of the most crucial campaigns in recent times. This is not just a contest between two men. It's not just a contest between Republicans and Democrats. It's a contest that will spell out for you, for your families, for those you love and for this Nation two different futures. The choice will affect how we respond and how we search for justice and compassion, how we meet the challenge of keeping America strong and using that strength to maintain peace, whether or not we'll have a strong economy, a growing economy, confidence in the future, whether we hold down inflation, whether we have fair taxes, whether we provide jobs for every American able to work and make sure that all those that are able to work will take a job if it's offered to them.

I know that America and the people, within 4 weeks from now, on November the 4th, will make the right choice. And I know the people of this country, like the people of North Carolina, are builders. I'd like to say just a word about that—builders.

I've seen the South suffer economically. I remember the days when the Congress was passing a minimum wage bill— 25 cents an hour was what we wanted to have. The Democrats were supporting that legislation, the Republicans almost down the line were against it. And later, before I finished high school, the minimum wage was raised to 40 cents an hour. That's where I got my first job—40 cents. Democrats were for it; Republicans said that working people weren't worth 40 cents an hour.

I remember in the Depression years when Franklin Roosevelt said we need social security to give the elderly people a chance for self-respect and decency and security. Republicans were against it. And I remember in history— I lived on a farm—rural free delivery of mail. The Democrats were for it; the Republicans against it. And I remember the rural electrification program. I think the brightest day of my life, the best day of my life was when electricity got to our house. I was 13 or 14 years old, and the REA came in under Franklin Roosevelt. The Democrats were for it; Republicans were against it.

The man I run against represents the Republican Party, and he's said that the minimum wage has caused more suffering and hardship than the Great Depression. And I have a heartfelt concern about people that are temporarily out of work, and my opponent, Governor Reagan, says that unemployment compensation is just a paid vacation for freeloaders. This is a man that four times has said, "Let's let social security be voluntary," which would mean the end of that program. He's campaigned across this Nation against Medicare. It provides a little bit of health care for older people. These are the kinds of issues that are at stake in less than 4 weeks, and the decisions about those economic issues will affect your life.

We've now got a good energy base in this country, for the first time an energy policy that's making progress. We're saving energy now, having good conservation in our homes, automobiles, at work. We're producing more American energy. This year we'll dig more American oil and gas wells than any year in history. This year we'll produce more American coal than any year in history. And this day and every day in 1980, we are import-ing from foreign countries 2 million barrels of oil less than we did the first year I was in office. That's progress, thanks to you.

My opponent says, "Let's eliminate the windfall profits tax; let's abolish the Department of Energy; and let's let the oil companies be unleashed to run the energy program for us." That's the kind of issue that will be decided on November the 4th.

With that energy base in place, we now have a chance to revitalize the American industrial program. We've got the greatest country on Earth economically. The American producers, the workers are the most productive on Earth. We've not been making as good progress in recent years as we ought to to increase production. We've got to have new tools and new factories to do it.

In recent days, I've been in some places that show what America can do now that we have an energy program in place. I was in a steelmill in Perth Amboy, New Jersey, a modern steelmill where the workers in that factory produce more steel per year per worker than in any factory on Earth. They're exporting their steel, about half of it, to the People's Republic of China. They can make steel, United States, using scrap metal, ship it halfway around the world, and sell it to China, cheaper than the Japanese can make it and just send it a few hundred miles over to their neighbors in China.

Not long ago, I was in the Atlanta airport, a vision of the future, a dynamic demonstration of what the South is now and will be in years to come. Not long ago, I was in a modern textile mill in Spartanburg, South Carolina—typical of what we've got throughout the South.

Jim Hunt pointed out that we've increased exports of American textiles to foreign countries for a change—$2 billion in the last 2 years—and at the same time, we have cut imports from foreign countries in textiles to our country. That's the kind of progress I'm talking about now and in the future.

One other example: Last week I was in Detroit, Michigan, and Flint, Michigan, and I saw rolling off those assembly lines the best built, best designed, safest, most durable automobiles in the world. And the next time you trade cars, I want you to go to an American dealer, take a look at them, give them a chance, because none can beat the cars we're making in this country now.

I've just come from East Tennessee. I'll save time by moving very quickly to Winston-Salem, North Carolina. No one who's come to this State and to this region can doubt that the economic and industrial progress that I've just outlined to you is taking here as well. I know that R. J. Reynolds has just announced a $1 billion plan to expand capacity and to improve productivity.

In every one of these places, your community and mine, east and west coast, I see the spirit of building something new and something good for the country that we love. I see the hope for better communities, the hope for working families to live a better life, for young people to enjoy their talents and the use of them even more than we have had a benefit to do in our own generation. I see the future of this country strong and secure and good. Don't let anyone tell you different. Don't let anyone tell you that this country is weak or washed up, that we don't have it in us to make this great country of ours even greater.

There are people, and you hear from them every night on television, who've given up on this country. They'll tell you that we have to change our priorities on job safety to let workers be endangered, on health care to abandon our elderly, on aid for schools, on a clean environment. They tell you that our military is second rate. This is one of the worst things you could say about a nation, because it creates in our own people the false sense of concern, and it expresses doubts which lessen the commitment to our alliances by those who depend on us in Europe, and it raises a false expectation among potential adversaries that our Nation might be vulnerable to a possible attack. Our Nation, militarily, is the strongest nation on Earth, and we'll never be second to any other country in military strength.

I don't want you to forget the important issues at stake. We don't want to do away with Medicare. We don't want to change and weaken social security. And also, my opponent, to get to agriculture, said that farm price supports, and I quote from him, "subsidize the inefficient." The Republican candidate has repeatedly suggested that programs such as welfare, education, mass transit, be turned over to the States and the local governments to pay for. He hasn't explained it, but if those suggestions were implemented, the impact would be much higher property taxes, State income taxes, State sales taxes, State business taxes in every part of the country.

North Carolina now receives, from your income tax dollars paid to Washington, $910 million a year in Federal aid for those programs. You'd have to raise State and local taxes by 99 percent, almost exactly twice, or $644 for every family of four. That's not my idea of how to help the people of North Carolina.

If that's not enough, he also wants a massive election year tax cut for the rich.

Under the Reagan-Kemp-Roth proposal, a family making $200,000 a year would get 35 times as much benefits as a family making $20,000 a year. Only 10 percent of this ridiculous tax cut would go for job-producing investment. The rest of it would set off an inflationary whirlwind so severe that even President Ford, who supports Governor Reagan, says he could never support this tax program, and the Republican candidate for Vice President, George Bush, said it sounds like voodoo economics to him and would increase inflation rate over 30 percent.

Well, I don't want to make another longer list, but the point I'm trying to make to you is that in national security, economics, human affairs, local and State property taxes, respect for one another—these kinds of things are at stake.

The American people are not simple-minded; they've not given up on this country nor its values. I meet average Americans every day, and I can tell you that Americans throughout this country are ready to build again, not tear down. We're ready to continue the program to improve our armed services with the finest, best trained fighting men and women on Earth, remembering that the best weapon is one that's never fired in combat, and the best soldier is the one that never has to give his life or shed his blood on the field of battle.

And finally, let me say this: We're also ready to sustain our farm programs. The American farm family wants nothing more than stable agricultural programs with stable prices and orderly marketing. I'm committed to that, including, and especially including, a sound loan support program for tobacco.

I know that tobacco farmers are seriously concerned about the treatment of imported tobacco by the Customs Service.

I share that concern, particularly over the report that leaf tobacco is being shredded overseas expressly for the purpose of circumventing our United States laws. I intend to see that the loophole that permits this practice is closed once and for all.

I'm directing the Department of Agriculture to determine what the quality of this imported tobacco is. And if it's determined, as a result of this information, that the necessary relief cannot be provided promptly under existing law and authority, I will propose to the Congress as soon as they reconvene that they promptly enact legislation granting me that authority. And I want to be sure that Bob Morgan and Steve Neal and the other Congressmen from North Carolina are up there to help me correct this deficiency in our law.

Two million farm families in this country, a lot of them in Georgia, depend on the tobacco industry, and I won't ever forget that.

Finally, let me say to you that we recognize that to rebuild our economy is important, it's going to take a while, but the Americans have never failed to do what we set to do as a goal. Think back in history. Some of you are even older than I am. You remember the days of the Great Depression. Our Nation was tested. Some of you remember even the First World War. Our Nation, democracy itself, was tested. Many of you remember the Second World War, the Korean war, the divisive Vietnam war that separated one from another among Americans. You remember the disgrace and embarrassment of Watergate. You remember the time when the South was struggling to overcome discrimination and separation of black from white and how we had to go through those tortuous years to change our way of life—one of the best things that ever happened to us. But this is an example of a few things that this country has faced in the past—in the *past*.

Nothing that we face now equals the difficulty or the trial or the tribulation or worry of those experiences. I won't even mention the War Between the States or the Revolutionary War, other times when our Nation's been tested. But you remember this: Whenever our Nation has been tested, with the American people unified we have never failed. We have **never failed** to answer any question, no matter how difficult. We've never failed to solve any problem, no matter how much effort it took. We've never failed to scale any obstacle, no matter how great. And we have never failed to set an example for the rest of the world. Our country has always been on the cutting edge of progress. We raise high the banner of human rights, freedom, a belief in the average human being, a belief in God, a commitment that our children will have a better life even than the one we have. Those are the kinds of concepts that have made this Nation great, and with your help and with the help of God in the years ahead, we'll make the greatest nation on Earth even greater.

Thank you very much. Work hard this next 4 weeks. God bless you.

I want the entire Nation to remember farmers and agriculture. And the Congress has passed a proclamation setting aside a special time for this country to pause, to thank God, and to remember what agriculture, what our land, what our stewardship means to this country, now and in the future. And I'm going to sit down at this table on my left now, surrounded by your fine North Carolina leaders, and sign this proclamation into law. And I want to make sure that we

never forget we've got a tremendous responsibility to make the Earth clean and productive, to make sure that neighbors respect one another, to make sure we never lose our confidence and our faith and never forget to thank God who gave us all our blessings.

Thank you very much.

NOTE: The President spoke at 5:19 p.m. at the grandstand area of the Dixie Classic Fairgrounds. Following his remarks, the President signed the joint resolution.

As enacted, H.J. Res. 560, a bill requesting the President to proclaim March 9, 1981, as National Agriculture Day, is Public Law 96–416, approved October 9.

Clemmons, North Carolina

Remarks at a Carter/Mondale Fundraising Reception.   October 9, 1980

Thank you very much, my good friend, Jim Hunt. Jim Hunt calls me often enough to tell me what North Carolina needs—*[laughter]*—and in between times, Bob Morgan is right there at my elbow to make sure that I never forget. He says, "I want you to be as good a President for North Carolina as Jim Hunt would be if he was in the Oval Office." And that's a pretty high standard to meet, but I try to meet it. [*Laughter*]

This is a beautiful place—isn't it?— and a beautiful nation, with people who have confidence in the future, people who have never failed to meet any challenge presented to us, people who are confident in one another, who believe in God, who love the land, who want strong families and communities that are making progress; a nation that's strong militarily and economically, whose political influence is felt beneficially all over the world; a nation committed to peace, peace not through weakness, but peace through strength; a nation whose government is admired and emulated in many parts of the world; a nation that's unselfish, that sometimes tries to help others maybe a little too much; a nation which has always kept intact the commitment to high principles and moral standards that never change; a nation that faces tribulation and answers questions and overcomes obstacles and solves problems without fail; a nation that's on the cutting edge of progress, that looks to the future not with doubt and fear and trepidation, but with anticipation and hope. That's the kind of nation we have.

God's really blessed us, and I'm very glad to be here today to share that blessing with you.

This is an election year. We're running a hard, difficult campaign. It's not easy. We face enormous bankrolls with all kinds of groups, financed with unlimited resources that don't even count, as you know, in the campaign for United States Senator here, when Bob Morgan is attacked every day with thousands and thousands of dollars from outside the State—a man who's courageous and who's committed to those principles that I've outlined to you. I'm glad to be on a ticket with him and with Steve Neal and with Jim Hunt.

The Democratic Party is one that's not perfect. We've made mistakes perhaps in the past, but those mistakes were always open. They were not mistakes of the devious kind. They were made after consultation with people. We couldn't always anticipate what OPEC was going to do. We couldn't always anticipate the difference between the emphasis on jobs and the control of inflation. That's not possible for anyone to do. But the Democratic Party is a party of competence and commitment and compassion. I'm proud to be a part of it.

I'm also proud to be a southerner. As I told the people at the fairgrounds, my people came from North Carolina way back. My cousin, Willard Slappey, Dr. Willard Slappey, is back here with his wife. Our people moved down from North Carolina to Georgia 10 years before the Revolutionary War, but our ties have always been close ones. And I think the concepts that I've just outlined to you have epitomized the concepts of the South.

I'm the first President elected from the South since James Polk was elected in 1844. It was not possible prior to the change in civil rights laws for a southerner to be considered seriously for President. That change was not easy. I look out on this crowd and see black and white people, friends, neighbors, sharing the present, sharing the future. It's an exhilarating, almost emotional thing for me. But that concept has stood us in good stead.

And we in this country have to remember that we are a nation of refugees, we're a nation of immigrants, each one of us different, family blood ties to almost every nation on Earth, which gives us a great advantage, because we have a special sense of the preservation of the past, which is part of the southern consciousness too, and a knowledge of the diversity of human beings which makes us respect every single person, no matter how great, no matter how small. And that's part of our strength. That doesn't fragment us one from another. It just let us put together our varied kind of interests and talents and abilities and concepts and commitments in a beautiful mosaic that makes up America.

We've opened up the rest of the world for new friendship. Africa was never part of the political consciousness of this country before I became President. This week we had the president of Nigeria, the greatest black nation on Earth. When Henry Kissinger was Secretary of State not long ago, he tried to go to Nigeria; they wouldn't let him come in. We've seen Zimbabwe, a new nation formed recently, democratic nation, free elections, majority rule, equality—great step forward. We helped do that. Lately we've opened up the People's Republic of China, a billion people, one out of every four people on Earth, with whom we haven't had any diplomatic relationships in decades. And now they're our friends. In the process we've expanded trade with Taiwan. This gives us a new opportunity to let the benefits of America be expressed all over the world.

Finally, let me say that this election in less than 4 weeks is crucial. It'll determine the future of our country. It'll determine whether that progress continues, whether we can work as the Democratic Party for the things that I've outlined to you as guiding lights in our life. And I say that with a proper degree of humility and also a proper understanding of the difficulties we face, but with confidence, because I believe that with partners like you— President, in one of the most difficult jobs on Earth, a sometimes lonely job, dealing with crises that you never know about unless the President makes a mistake, and then a crisis becomes something that might devastate your life or change the life of every person on Earth.

The job that I have is a good one. It's the highest office certainly in the free world. It's one revered by American people. It's one where difficult problems and questions arise, because if you can't solve a problem in your own life or in your home, county courthouse, city hall, State legislature, Governor's office, it comes to me, and I work with the Congress and try to deal with it.

Well, it could be lonely and unpleasant, but it's not because I don't feel alone. I feel that every one of you, in a tangible way, is my partner, and that's why I've come here to North Carolina again to let you know that in this next 4 weeks I need you. I need you to do more than just contribute $500—that's a lot—I need for you to set as your goal an all-out commitment to success for the Democratic ticket on November the 4th, because the decision made that day could be one of the most important decisions in your lifetime. It could be more important than the level of your income next year. It could be more important than what kind of college your child might attend in the future. It could be more important than the quality of automobile you buy or exactly where you live in a neighborhood.

And I hope that you will set aside a substantial portion of your time and contact directly the people that look to you for leadership and who trust your judgment. There's no one in this group that can't reach 100 people, most of you can reach 1,000, maybe 10,000 people, to say, "I've got confidence in Bob Morgan and Jim Hunt, Steve Neal, Jimmy Carter, and I hope you'll help them continue to lead our State and our Nation."

That's why I've come here, to thank you, first of all, and let you know you're my partners. And I believe with that partnership we'll make the greatest nation on Earth even greater in the years ahead.

Thank you very much. And now, I'll go around and shake hands with all I can reach.

Thank you very much.

NOTE: The President spoke at 6:30 p.m. outside the Tanglewood Park Clubhouse.

Tallahassee, Florida

*Remarks at a Fundraising Fish Fry for State
Democratic House Nominees.
October 9, 1980*

*Governor Bob Graham, Speaker Ralph
Havens, my friends and neighbors:*

I've got two or three things to say to
you to start with. First of all, I am really
glad to be home in the South. That is a
great feeling. I remember your commissioner of agriculture said when I ran for
Governor in 1970 that I did so well in
south Georgia that I swept Georgia and
carried four counties in Florida.
[*Laughter*] It's always been hard for me
to tell where the line was. [*Laughter*]
You know, to me it's just one people who
love each other.

Secondly, I'm here because I came to
remind you that we've got 26 days to get
ready to whip the Republicans, from the
courthouse to the White House, on November the 4th. I'll never forget what
Florida did for me in 1976. My wife spent
113 days campaigning in Florida before
that most significant primary election, and
you gave me those expressions of support.
In the general election the Florida electors voted for me. This spring, as you
know, it was a very tough campaign. You
gave me another strong expression of support. You've established a wonderful
tradition—[*laughter*]—which I know
you're going to continue to carry out in
4 weeks. Right? [*Applause*]

And I might say that since I've been in
the White House, a very special place,
holding the highest elective office, in the
free world at least, perhaps in the entire
world, an office respected and revered by
the American people, I have called on
Florida leaders to help me.

One of the greatest troublespots that
we have is our next door neighbors in the
Caribbean. And when I got ready to put
together a nationwide organization of
leaders from education, from local and
State government, from business, and from
labor, I cast about in my own mind for
the best person in this entire Nation, a
leader with integrity, sensitivity, courage,
who could head this commission to recement relations with this crucial part of
the world. And I settled on the best man
I could find, and that's Bob Graham,
your Governor.

Our country has a lot of domestic challenges, opportunities, but internationally
our country is growing by leaps and
bounds. In the last 3½ years, we have
opened up, for United States beneficial
influence, the entire continent of Africa,
about 50 nations, a vast area of the world,
with hundreds of millions of people that
had never been touched really by American diplomacy or American trade. We've
formed now a friendship with a billion
new people in the People's Republic of
China, one-fourth of the total population
on Earth, and we've kept intact and have
increased the trade with the people on
Taiwan at the same time. This hand of
friendship opens up opportunities for us
that will touch the life of every person
here and every person who looks to you
for leadership.

We're increasing our agricultural products sales to those countries. We've put
some restraints on sales this year to the
Soviet Union, but in spite of that, we've
had the largest increase in agricultural
exports in the history of the world. We
have increased exports to $40 billion this
year, $8 billion more than 1979. 1979 set
a world record, 1978 set a world record,
1977 set a world record on agricultural
exports. One of the reasons for that is
that we've come down here to Florida
to get two men, one to be our Special

Trade Representative to open up opportunities in textiles, automobiles, steel, agriculture—and you trained him well—Reubin Askew, your former Governor. And I thank you for him.

And I've got one special love, I have to admit. My folks have lived in the South for a long time, since before this country was formed. We've all been farmers. My father nor his father nor anyone back ever finished high school until I came along. Our roots are in the earth. We believe in the same thing you do—strong families, strong communities, God, the stewardship of the land, integrity, neighborliness, patriotism. Those characteristics are very important.

And to me, agriculture is the greatest single resource that God has given us in this country. And I needed someone to represent the South, who understood thoroughly agriculture, to put in at a top position in the Department of Agriculture. And you trained Jim Williams for that job. And he's done a superb job with it.

And you gave me Fred Schultz for the Federal Reserve Board and Jay Janis to help get the home loan industry back on its feet. We're making good progress with that. Every month for the last few months, 4 or 5 months in a row, we've had an increase in new home starts.

And I'm just grateful to you and wanted to point out very quickly some of the reasons why my ties to Florida are permanent.

There are a lot of things I could talk about tonight. I'm just going to talk about one, because as you go around the country as Democrats, running for the State legislature, it's important for you to carry a message—a message of sharp comparison between the principles of our party, represented by Franklin Roosevelt, Lyndon Johnson, Jack Kennedy, Harry Truman, who've seen clearly the same things we see.

Those of us who grew up in the Great Depression remember the elderly living in poor folks' homes, with no sense of self-decency or respect and no security. And Franklin Roosevelt proposed social security; Republicans were against it, but it passed.

We believe that a man who works or a woman who works ought to be paid a decent wage. This has not always been the case. I remember the first minimum wage bill proposed, when I was a very young man—25 cents an hour. Democrats supported it, finally got it passed, Republicans against it. My first job as a high school senior—at the minimum wage of 40 cents. That enormous increase from 25 to 40 cents Democrats supported, Republicans opposed. The working families have always been important to us.

My Republican opponent has said that the minimum wage has caused more suffering and hardship than the Great Depression, and he's said that fascism is the basis for the New Deal that gave us social security, gave us REA, gave us the minimum wage. He said that unemployment compensation for husbands and and wives who are temporarily out of a job is a prepaid vacation for freeloaders. When Medicare was proposed, to give some modicum of health care for old people, he traveled this Nation back and forth, working to defeat it.

The sensitivity to human beings is important, and those things affect you and those who look to you to lead them in the Florida legislature in the future.

But the point I want to make to you tonight is as a President, responsible for our Nation's defense, because this is an issue that has been distorted too much in this campaign. It is a crucial issue. It affects the life of every person who lives in this country, perhaps the entire world.

Republicans were in the White House 8 years before I got there. My background is in the military. I'm a Naval Academy graduate, a submarine officer. For 7 of those years, our Nation's expenditure for defense went down. In 8 years our defense commitment decreased by 35 percent. Since I've been in the White House, every single year we've had a steady, predictable, orderly, constructive increase in the commitment that our Nation has made for defense. This is important, but I'd like to remind you that the reason for a nation to have a strong defense is not to kill or be killed; it's to keep peace. We've kept the Nation at peace.

And it doesn't help our country for false statements to be made that our Nation is militarily weak, because of two or three reasons. One, it creates a sense of uneasiness or concern in the minds of American people when they hear statements like this that are not true. It also weakens the ties that bind our country to our Western European allies and to other allies around the country [world] like Australia, New Zealand, South Korea, Japan, and others. The worst thing it does, when these false statements are made that the United States is somehow militarily weak and vulnerable, is it might lead a potential adversary to misjudge us and to challenge us, in a way that would be suicidal, based on a distorted picture of what our Nation is. Our Nation militarily is the strongest nation on Earth, and we will never be second to any nation on Earth.

Just two more quick points. One is that a plane with only one wing wouldn't fly, and a nation with just a strong defense establishment cannot preserve the peace. Along with that strong defense capability must go the realization that the best weapon is one that's never used in combat and, secondly, the best soldier is one that never lays his life down on the field of battle or sheds his blood in war. That's important to remember.

So, along with a strong defense you've got to have two other things. One is arms control, particularly nuclear arms control. Ever since Truman was in the White House, every President—Republican and Democrat, Eisenhower, Ford, Nixon, all the Democrats who've preceded me in the White House—have worked to negotiate with the Soviet Union, an agreement to limit nuclear weapons, to have rough equivalency or balance, strict limits, and a way to prove compliance with the SALT treaties, and then the goal of lowering those limits to eliminate nuclear weapons.

Recently Governor Reagan announced that SALT II treaty would be withdrawn from consideration if he should become President, and he advocated the end to this treaty, which has been negotiated by me, Nixon, and Ford, and somehow advocated a nuclear arms race or a playing of a card with the threat of a nuclear arms race against the Soviet Union. This is a profoundly important and radical departure in the attitude of our Nation. It hurts our people, because Americans ought to be eager to remove the threat of nuclear destruction from the world in a balanced way. Our allies and friends, those who have nuclear weapons and who don't have nuclear weapons, would be deeply disturbed with this new departure. And of course, we want to be at peace and negotiate with the Soviet Union for this ultimate goal. That's one thing that bothers me in this campaign, a very serious development.

And the other thing is that no matter who's in the White House, you have crises that come up. I've not been there one day since I was inaugurated that there wasn't a trouble spot in the world somewhere that directly impinged on my decisions. I and all my predecessors, Republican and Democratic, when those trouble spots arose, have tried to deal with them in a diplomatic way, without the use of American military forces, to negotiate or to work them out not through weakness but through strength.

Repeatedly, for the last 8 or 10 years, my opponent has time after time after time called for the injection of American military forces into those sensitive trouble areas, in our own hemisphere, in Ecuador, in Cuba, in Korea, in the Middle East, Cyprus, Angola, Pakistan. Eight or 10 times, either as a candidate for President or potential candidate for President, he has called for the use of American military forces in those troubled areas. I don't have any idea what he would do if he was in the Oval Office, but that pattern concerns me deeply.

The point I want to make to you in closing is that a lot is at stake in this election, and your responsibility as supporters of the Florida Democratic legislative candidates and as future members of the legislature, as well, are the same responsibilities as mine. We represent the same party, the same concept, the same principles, the same ideals, the same heritage, the same commitments. There's no way to separate you from me.

The Presidency is a lonely job, because I deal with problems that are important to you. If I deal with them properly, with sound judgment, in accordance with that heritage that I've just outlined to you, you may never know about them. But if I make a mistake or a misjudg-ment, that potential crisis can affect your life or the life of everyone on Earth. It is a lonely job, but I don't feel neglected or secluded or isolated, because of the partnership I've just described to you, because I've got people like Reubin Askew and Bob Graham and others to work with me to represent you. And many of you in this room feel that you're part of my administration.

And as a Democratic President, the nominee of our party, the titular head of the Democratic Party itself, I'm part of your organization. And as you take your message in this next 4 weeks to the people of Florida, to be reelected or elected to the State legislature, hope you'll remember those principles that do not change, the things that bind us together.

We've got the greatest nation on Earth. We have never had, when this country was unified, a question that we could not answer or a problem that we could not solve or an obstacle that we could not overcome. We've got some problems now, yes. But don't let anybody fool you about this Nation being weak or about us being debilitated or our problems being insoluble, because we've faced much more problems, much more serious ones than the ones we face now. The First and Second World Wars, the Korean war, the Vietnam war that divided us, the Great Depression, the social changes between blacks and whites in the South, the Watergate scandals—all those things were much more serious than what we face now.

And I'd just like to remind you that we've got a great country, a unified people, a strong party, a platform on which we can run with pride, a future that holds promise and confidence, not despair and fear and trepidation. We've always been on the cutting edge of progress. Our party, our Nation are the greatest on Earth. And if we are victorious on November the 4th, with common commitments and hard work—and there's no shortcut that I know in politics—we'll make the greatest nation on Earth even greater in the years ahead. That's my goal. You help me to do it.

NOTE: The President spoke at 9:36 p.m. at the North Florida Fairgrounds.

Following his appearance at the fish fry, the President went to the Governor's Mansion in Tallahassee, where he stayed overnight.

Tallahassee, Florida

Remarks on Signing the Refugee Education Assistance Act of 1980 Into Law.
October 10, 1980

Mr. Speaker, Governor Graham, Senator Chiles, Senator Pepper, Bill Gunter, my other good friends who are here in this beautiful new building typical of the present progress of Florida and the future dreams of an even greater State, members of the State cabinet who've come this morning and honored me, members of the State legislature:

I think of all the human problems that I've had since I've been in the White House, this has been the most severe for me personally, as well. Hardly a day has gone by in the last few months that I haven't had direct communication, either with your Governor or other officials in the State of Florida or with the congressional delegation in Washington, representing your views and your ideas and your problems and concerns.

It would have been easy to demagogue this issue, perhaps some were tempted to

do so, but the thing that always impressed itself on my mind was that ours is a nation of immigrants. My parents and grandparents were immigrants, and I would guess that unless some of you are Native Americans, that all of your ancestors were immigrants. It's been difficult for those who came here in generations gone by to be assimilated into a new society. Almost all of us, with the possible exception, of course, of the slaves who came here earlier, came actively seeking freedom, a better life, a chance to worship as we chose, a chance to escape from oppressive regimes, a chance to be assimilated into a heterogeneous society that's America, a chance to worship freely. There was a lot of prejudice against some of those immigrants who came here from Ireland, who came here from Italy, Poland, Indonesia, China, Japan, because they didn't speak our language well and their societal structure and their family structure were different from ours. And that prejudice was real and tangible and was felt very strongly against immigrants ever since our Nation was founded.

Those who'd come here a little earlier said, "We've got our freedom. We've been assimilated into this great country, now let's don't let others come and disturb our privileged way of life." That could have been the attitude expressed by Floridians in this last few troubled months, but it was not, and I'm proud of what you've done.

I want to congratulate Senator Dick Stone for the good work he did on this bill, and Dante Fascell who worked day and night, Ed Stack who was in the forefront of making sure that the problems absorbed by Florida were shared by the Federal Government in financial terms, and the men and women on this stage with me, a couple of whom will speak after I do.

This bill signing is important, not only to you but to this country, because this is not just a Florida problem, it's a Federal problem, it's a national problem. And I want to let you know this morning—as I have felt from the very beginning, constrained as I was by the law and by appropriations and by restraints of a bureaucracy that's not quick to move—that I assume the responsibility, as President, for the problem generated recently by the unexpected immigration from Cuba and particularly from Haiti as well.

I'm glad this morning to sign the Refugee Education Assistance Act, and there's no better place to sign it than here in the beautiful Florida Capitol. This legislation means that $100 million will immediately be available to the communities of Florida and a few other States to help reimburse them for expenses involved in the recent influx of people from Cuba and from Haiti.

The amount of the Federal share of this cost is flexible; it's up to me. The judgment that I have made is that the Federal Government should assume 100 percent of the cost. The items for which the Federal Government's responsibility will lie will be a matter of agreement between our agencies and those of Florida and Dade County and others involved. We also have funds in this continuing resolution to help in the resettlement problem.

This has been a difficult period for you, especially. It's required a massive emergency effort to accommodate this large number who are seeking freedom and a new life in this country. It could not have happened under more difficult circumstances. As many as three or four thousand people per day were pouring into the southern part of Florida in one particular time period. We've processed them

at centers in Florida, as you know, and Arkansas where the problems were very difficult, in Wisconsin where the cooperation was hard to find, in Pennsylvania, other places in this country. And we're presently preparing a center to be used, if necessary, in Puerto Rico.

Now we're carrying out the equally difficult task of helping these newcomers enter the mainstream as productive members of our society. The most immediately important features of the bill I'm signing is title 5, the Fascell-Stone amendment. Congress has already appropriated $100 million in reimbursements for cash and medical assistance and social services provided to these newcomers; this amendment makes that money available. Also, I pledge to seek from Congress additional funds, as necessary, to meet the Federal Government's responsibility in these programs.

Another significant feature of this act will help Florida communities. It's a 3-year program of grants to States to help local education agencies meet the needs of Cuban and Haitian adults and children. The bill also authorizes aid to school districts greatly affected by the influx of children from Indochina.

Many of you here worked conscientiously, tirelessly, to help meet the urgent needs created overnight by these extraordinary circumstances. This has not been easy for you; it's not been easy for the other people of Florida; it's not been easy for the President or for other people in this country.

The behavior of the Cuban officials during this exodus period violated international law and standards of common decency. The only recent precedent was the flight of the boat people from Vietnam. As you know, in recent months, some who fled from Cuba died on the voyage, and more would have died had not our Coast Guard and Navy carried out more than 1,000 rescue missions so effectively. I have deployed a whole flotilla of ships between the Florida Keys and Mariel Harbor to try to make sure that we could restrain the flow of boats down to Cuba, but once they were loaded with human beings and coming back to this country that those human beings' lives were not endangered. In my judgment, that was compatible with the principles and ideals of a great humanitarian and freedom-loving country.

Also, we're continuing to identify those Cuban entrants with criminal histories and mental illnesses and are placing them in appropriate institutions. And while we've emphasized our difficulties, I believe history will write that we did well. About 90 percent of those who entered have already been resettled satisfactorily in the United States. The Federal Government worked closely and effectively with State and local leaders, with volunteer agencies, and with individual families.

This act is a good example of that kind of partnership. Finally we've shown that once again, the American people accepted and gave new hope to yet another group of people accepting and yearning for and finally acquiring freedom. This is one of our Nation's oldest and most humane traditions. You were indeed a part of history.

History has never been easy. When people are tested and stand the test, then the history of our country has been good. And America has seldom failed to meet humanitarian needs and to marshal our resources in a proper fashion when we have been tested under stress. The people of Florida have indeed made me proud.

It's with a great deal of pleasure that I now sign this act, following which I would like to ask Senator Lawton Chiles and then Senator Claude Pepper to respond.

[At this point, the President signed the bill into law. Following the remarks of the other officials, the President resumed speaking as follows:]

That would be a good finale for this— *[laughter]*—session, but I would like to add one additional word. Our problems are not completely over, as you know. This will undoubtedly be a responsibility that we'll share for months in the future. I've decided to move all of the remaining refugees who've not yet been settled into Arkansas, and Bill Clinton and the Arkansas Legislature are cooperating very well with this necessary move.

We have still a desire, commitment to let those Cubans who have come here and have changed their mind be returned to Cuba. We also have a commitment that those who've come here as so-called undesirables who have serious criminal records be returned to Cuba, as they should be, and we won't stop in our effort to settle this entire problem in a way compatible with our own ideals and with the American law. In the use of emergency funds that I've alloted to Florida in recent months, I have to admit that I may have stretched the law just a little bit, but it was necessary, and I think the Congress and the courts would understand the special circumstances involved.

As Lawton Chiles pointed out, our American laws just have not contemplated large numbers of refugees, several hundred or several thousand per day, arriving here not having been screened and assessed and with no preliminary plans having been made. But I will continue to work closely with you. And as the weeks go by, if the circumstances should change, we have formed a kind of a sense of partnership that, in my judgment will stand us in good stead with any unanticipated developments in the days to come.

Again, I'd like to repeat the deepest feelings of my heart by saying again how proud I am of the people of Florida.

NOTE: The President spoke at 8:03 a.m. before a joint session of the Florida State Legislature in the House of Representatives Chamber of the State Capitol.

As enacted, H.R. 7859 is Public Law 96–422, approved October 10.

Tallahassee, Florida

Interview With a Correspondent From the Florida News Network.   October 10, 1980

REPORTER. It's nice to have you in Florida, sir.

THE PRESIDENT. I'm glad to be back.

CUBAN-HAITIAN REFUGEE SITUATION

THE PRESIDENT'S ROLE

Q. I'd like to ask you a couple of questions, first of all, about the refugee problems as many south Floridians see the problem now.

THE PRESIDENT. All right.

Q. Some observers feel the $100 million refugee appropriation is nothing more than a token gesture by the Government; more importantly, that the Government failed to act responsibly and decisively in handling the refugees. In looking back, how would you have handled it differently?

THE PRESIDENT. There's no way I could have handled it differently. The law under which I was operating was de-

signed to handle refugees who had been screened in an orderly fashion ahead of time, before they ever arrived on our shores. The law did not contemplate and did not give me the authority to act in a way where several hundred or several thousand each day were arriving here directly from their former home, of Cuba primarily. As a matter of fact, I probably stretched the law a little bit in allotting emergency funds, over which I did have some control, to alleviate the problem financially in Dade County and other affected areas.

We proposed to the Congress months ago legislation which would permit me to have money available to pick up the burden from Florida, and this $100 million is designed to alleviate the financial problem. We also have flexibility on how much of this cost to absorb by the Federal Government under the present law, and I've decided that it ought to be 100 percent.

Florida has responded well, in the tradition of our Nation, to people seeking freedom. And I want to make sure that everyone understands this is a national problem for which I personally, as President, assume responsibility. We'll still have some problems in the future, but I think the partnership that's been formed and the close relationship that we've developed, with almost daily consultations between myself and the Governor, local officials in south Florida, particularly, and the Florida congressional delegation, will stand us in good stead in the future.

We've tried to handle this in a way, understanding the humanitarian aspects involved. We've not made a political football out of it. We've been very careful not to demagogue this issue. And in my judgment, the Florida officials and I have worked very closely and harmoniously under the most difficult circumstances, not covered at all by the previous American laws.

THE CONGRESSIONAL ROLE

Q. You say yourself as President have——

THE PRESIDENT. Yes.

Q. ——assumed the full responsibility. How about the Congress? They have to play a role in this, perhaps more directly than yourself, even.

THE PRESIDENT. Well, the Congress has now passed authorization and appropriation laws, working very closely with me, that permits this financial burden to be assumed by the Federal Government, and that will be done.

Q. People in south Florida are concerned that—what happens now in terms of the continued education for the refugees and possibly future resettlement of refugees, in terms of more appropriations should it be needed?

THE PRESIDENT. Yes, we'll get more appropriations if necessary to continue this process that I've already initiated, and I think the Congress has learned a lesson, too. It won't take so long in the future to pass the necessary laws. This legislation would have been passed earlier, but it was attached to the foreign aid bill as a vehicle in the legislative process. That bill is still in conference committee. We have not yet got it passed. So we had to attach this legislation to an education bill just to get it through the Congress in a hurry before the Congress recessed.

Also, I've decided to move all the remaining refugees who've not yet been processed and settled into one location. It happens to be in Arkansas. And we're working now very well with the Governor of Arkansas and with the officials of that State to make sure that the entire process is handled in an orderly fashion.

POLITICAL ATTACKS ON THE HANDLING OF THE SITUATION

Q. Governor Reagan, of course, most recently—and then I believe last week John Anderson, again attacking your administration, you as the President, for not taking a position sooner on the refugees. How do you respond to that at this point?

THE PRESIDENT. That's a ridiculous attitude on the part of Governor Reagan. He's tried to have it both ways, depending on what audience he was addressing. Back in May when the crisis was at its peak, and I was trying to enforce the American laws and restrict the flow of aliens into this country with a flotilla of Coast Guard ships and Navy ships, Governor Reagan criticized me for that obstacle that I was placing in the ocean to enforce the American law. He also called for an air flotilla to be sent to Cuba to pick up anyone who wanted to come here and was very critical of the effort that I was making with the Florida officials to handle these refugees in an orderly and legal way.

Now that the process is over, he completely reverses himself and tries to take political advantage of this difficult humanitarian problem by taking a completely different position on the whole issue.

But throughout this process, I think the Florida people have seen that it was not something to be used for political advantage, that there were very serious legal and humanitarian problems involved. And regardless of what Governor Reagan has tried to do for his own political advantage, the Florida officials, the Dade County officials, and the congressional delegation from Florida have all worked very well with me on it.

OUTCOME OF PRESIDENTIAL ELECTION IN FLORIDA

PRESIDENT'S CONFIDENCE IN WINNING

Q. Mr. President, are you confident of countering the Reagan surge in this State, even though his percentage preference at this point in the popular polls at this point is slightly more than yours?

THE PRESIDENT. I think so. I have a close kinship with the people of Florida, both as a neighbor and also politically. We'll be mounting a major campaign in the next 3 or 4 weeks, as we have for a long time past. I recall the strong support that I got here in Florida in the 1976 primary. It was perhaps the most crucial election of the whole year when I defeated Governor Wallace in Florida and other candidates as well.

Florida gave me the electoral vote margin in 1980 and helped put me over the top. And again this spring in the campaign for the Democratic primary contest, Florida again responded very well to me. My judgment is that there's a great compatibility between my basic philosophy and my attitudes on major issues and the people of Florida. As a farmer, as a southerner, as a former Governor who worked well with Reubin Askew and now with Bob Graham, as one who's been a champion of the rights of the elderly, who works very closely with Senator Pepper and others on matters that relate to retired people directly, I think we've got a good base for strong support in Florida. So, I feel reasonably confident but recognize that we have a lot of hard work to do.

SENATOR STONE'S PRIMARY DEFEAT

Q. There is speculation already that Senator Dick Stone's defeat in Florida's primary run-off this week may perhaps cause some degree of erosion in terms of your support in Florida heading into the November election. Do you agree with that assessment?

THE PRESIDENT. It's hard for me to know about that. That's a judgment for the Florida people to make. I've had a very good working relationship with Dick Stone. He's been, I think, an outstanding Member of the United States Senate, and I hope that Senator Stone in future months and years will continue to play a major role in international affairs, as he has done so well in the Senate itself. That's a judgment for him to make.

But Bill Gunter is also a good man, and if he's elected to the Senate I feel that he'll represent Florida well and work closely with me. So I don't believe that that will have a direct impact on the outcome of the election for President.

Q. Okay. Mr. President, thank you very much.

THE PRESIDENT. Thanks, Joe. I've enjoyed it.

NOTE: The interview began at approximately 8:30 a.m. at the Florida State Capitol.

St. Petersburg, Florida

Remarks and a Question-and-Answer Session at a Town Meeting With Senior Citizens. October 10, 1980

THE PRESIDENT. *Senator Chiles, Governor Bob Graham, Senator Claude Pepper, distinguished friends of mine representing the tens of thousands of retired Americans who live in this great State of Florida:*

I think you all realize that today is Senior Citizens Day throughout the Nation. Vice President Mondale is at a senior citizens event in New York. My son Chip is doing a similar event in Los Angeles. My wife is with senior citizens groups every day of the year. And of course, my mother, if her hip wasn't recently broken, would be out with a senior citizens group somewhere, also. So, our family, including Claude Pepper and Lawton Chiles, are part of your group almost every day of the year, and we're glad to be with you.

CAMPAIGN ISSUES

Four years ago, I pledged as I traveled through Florida that one of the top priorities of my own administration would be the preservation of the integrity of the social security system, because then, everywhere I went, the senior citizens knew that the biggest threat to your lives and to your security was the impending or threatened bankruptcy of the social security system. I can tell you today, as President, that with the help of these two fine chairmen of the committees in the House and Senate, we have kept the social security system sound. And it's going to stay sound and solvent as long as we have got a Democrat in the White House, and you can depend on it.

I'd like to point out to you that America is growing older. The average age is increasing, because of better health care, because of better security, and because we have become so deeply aware of the value of the lives of Americans who are sometimes called "retired." The precious life of those who have reached an age, 65 or 70 or 75 or 80—my mother is 82—has got to be recognized by all those in public office and all the other citizens of our country, because the value of contribution that can be of benefit to our country with that deep involvement in improving America is something we should never overlook. I want you to have vital, fruitful, active lives, as well as secure lives, with good medical care and attention and the proper respect which your great contribution deserves.

When I got to the White House, there was a broad agenda of things that Claude Pepper and Lawton Chiles and others presented to me and which my mother kept ever vivid in my mind, and my wife and others. As you know, there was a mandatory retirement age in this country, sometimes 60, sometimes 65. For most people the mandatory retirement age has been completely eliminated, and for some still in the private sector it's been raised to 70.

We've provided extra help for housing for the elderly. In the brief 3½ years that I've been in office, we have doubled Federal contributions for housing. We have doubled Federal contributions for nutrition programs for the elderly, particularly the Meals on Wheels. We've seen a Comprehensive Older Americans Act of 1978, landmark legislation putting together greatly improved services in social, housing, employment, nutrition for the elderly.

Most important of all, we have protected senior citizens from the ravages of inflation. Recently I fought for—shoulder to shoulder with Senator Chiles, Congressman Pepper, and others—a 14.2 percent increase in social security payments so that inflationary burdens would not fall on your shoulders. And we're going to keep that social security system improved every time inflation goes up so that your buying dollar will stay sound, just like the system itself is going to stay sound.

Another problem that was presented to me was that for many people the outside earnings were too low, and with the help of this fine delegation here, we've raised that, as you know, from $3,200 to $5,000. That helps you, and it also helps America.

The last thing I'd like to say is that this election, which will come up now in less than 4 weeks, could be the most important decision that you ever make in your lives in politics.

I grew up as a young man during the Depression years. I remember a Democratic administration under Franklin D. Roosevelt that said, "We have got to have security for the older people of our Nation," and he put forward the concept of social security. Democrats worked hard for it; the Republicans were against it. Later, a Democratic President said, "We need Medicare to help the senior citizens of our Nation stay in good health. The Republicans opposed it.

My opponent, who's running for President now, Governor Ronald Reagan, took a nationwide tour as the leader against Medicare. On four different occasions, at least, he has advocated that the social security system be made voluntary. That means that anyone who wants to withdraw from social security can do so. As all of you know, that would cripple and destroy the social security system. These attitudes, expressed publicly and repeatedly by the man running against me as a Republican, are of great importance to every one of you.

Democrats have always been concerned about those who had to work for a living. I remember as a young man the proposal, which Claude Pepper and I were discussing on the way here from the airport, to set up a 25-cent minimum wage, 25 cents an hour. The Democrats were for it; the Republicans against it. I got my first job as a high school graduate at 40 cents an hour, which was the minimum wage then. The Democrats were for that increase in minimum wage; the Republicans were against it. That has not changed. My opponent seeking the Presidency this year has said that the minimum wage has caused more suffering than anything since the Great Depression. To pay working people a fair wage for what they do is an important aspect of American life.

A lot is at stake. And I ask you, as we go through this question period this morning, to keep in the back of your mind, in fact in the forefront of your mind and in the bottom of your heart the deep concerns that can be imposed on this Nation depending upon the outcome of the election on November the 4th.

There are many other things that I could mention to you that we have accomplished in the last 3½ years. We've got a lot to do in the next 4 years. But I want to be sure that you and I are partners, working with Claude Pepper, working with Lawton Chiles, working with Bob Graham, working with the broad range of senior citizens organizations. The leaders of almost every one have endorsed me for reelection, to make sure that this country has a brighter future for all Americans and particularly those of you who've already contributed so much to this country and have so much to give in the years ahead.

And now I'd be glad to answer your questions. God bless all of you.

QUESTIONS

VETERANS BENEFITS

Q. Mr. President, my name is George Hernandez, from St. Petersburg, and I'd like to ask you, what have you done for veterans?

THE PRESIDENT. All right, sir.

What we've done since I've been in office is that for the first time in the history of our Nation, we have had an increase every year in veterans payments to make sure that you, as a veteran, are compensated for the increase in the cost of things that you have to buy with your pension funds.

We've also had a substantial increase in the quality of medical care for veterans since I have been in office. We've opened up centers around the Nation, under the leadership of Max Cleland, a veteran of the Vietnam war, to make sure that those younger veterans who have mental problems derived from war and combat had a chance to be rehabilitated.

And we've had enormous numbers, hundreds of thousands of new jobs made available for those who are veterans. We've tried to eliminate discrimination against veterans and to revitalize the veterans programs, not only in education, employment, and housing and medical care but in the status of veterans in our society.

This has never been done before, to have an annual increase every year to make sure that veterans did not suffer from the additional burdens of inflation. My intention is to continue doing this as long as I'm in the White House.

Thank you, sir.

MEDICAL COSTS AND NATIONAL HEALTH
INSURANCE

Q. Mr. President?

THE PRESIDENT. Yes, sir.

Q. I'm very pleased to have you here.

THE PRESIDENT. Thank you.

Q. [*Inaudible*]

THE PRESIDENT. I want to hear about it.

Q. That's what I'm here for. My name is Joseph P. Carroll. I'm from Connecticut, and I live here. But what I want to say is this. Recently we had a 14.3 increase, and then later on, right away, you turned around and increased what I have to pay for Medicare. I don't think that's right. I think something should be done about that, because a lot of people cannot afford it—[*inaudible*]—a couple of hundred dollars or—[*inaudible*]. Is there something that could be done, sir?

THE PRESIDENT. Yes, sir, I believe so. I used to live in Connecticut myself. My youngest son was born there, and we have a lot in common there.

One thing that I'd like to point out is that, as your congressional delegation well knows, one of the continued attempts that I have put to the Congress has been to initiate hospital cost containment legislation, to prevent the hospital costs from going up much more rapidly than the general inflation rate. We've been just on the verge of getting that bill passed. We have not yet got it through. We've also encouraged States individually to impose hospital cost containment within each State boundary. Some States have done an outstanding job in holding down those unwarranted, unnecessary, excessive increases in the cost of medical care.

My commitment to you and to this whole group and to the Nation is to pass national health insurance for a comprehensive program for the future to make sure that all citizens can have better health care at a reasonable price.

I might point out, since this is an election year, that Governor Reagan is strongly and consistently against any national health insurance program. This is a sharp difference that ought to be kept in the minds of voters who go to the polls on November the 4th.

So, the best way to hold down the cost of Medicare and other services that are important to senior citizens is to make sure that we have hospital cost containment passed and a national health insurance coverage that would be comprehensive in nature, emphasizing prevention of illness, caring for those quickly who need it, emphasizing outpatient care when the patient is able to stay out of a permanent incarceration in the hospital.

And also, one other aspect is to increase the competitive nature of the charges by doctors themselves. We have passed legislation, as you know, that has resulted in the lowered cost of eyeglasses, 20 to 40 percent, and we've also passed legislation that now lets doctors advertise as to whether or not they will treat Medicare patients.

So, those things put together, I believe, particularly national health insurance, will alleviate your problem in the future.

Thank you, sir, very much.

Q. I lost 20 years.

HANDICAPPED PERSONS

Q. My name is Ann Kuzak, of Clearwater, Florida. What can you do to help speed up the compliance with section 504 of the vocational rehab act of 1973? And at this time, Federal offices like social security and Medicare do not provide all of the required services for the handicapped, in particular interpreters for the deaf.

THE PRESIDENT. Lawton, do you want to——

SENATOR CHILES. [*Inaudible*]

THE PRESIDENT. Ann, I'm very glad to have your question.

The section 504—I wasn't familiar with the number of the bill—but under both Joe Califano, who was a Secretary of HEW, and more recently under Patricia Harris, Secretary of Health and Human Services, we've made tremendous strides forward in having adequate programs for the handicapped. The legislation has been passed, as you know, and this was a major step forward. The problem now, as Lawton Chiles has just pointed out, is getting Congress adequately to fund these programs. And the fact that you have a good interpreter in front of you and we have another good interpreter up here in front of this crowd shows that the new attention given to the problems of the deaf and dumb and other handicapped are being addressed.

Another program that I have pursued personally as President is to make sure that the network television coverage has the subtitles available for the deaf so that you can understand at least key programs that are important for you to keep informed and also to be entertained.

I believe there's a new awareness in our Nation now of the problems of the handicapped. We're making good progress, and with adequate funding in future years by Congress, we'll meet those needs that you have outlined so well this morning.

Thank you, and may God be with you. Yes, sir.

NATIONAL HEALTH INSURANCE

Q. Mr. President, I have the honor to have the same name as yours; mine is Ted Carter, from Tampa, Florida. I also have a brother, Jimmy Carter, who is 20 minutes away from you.

THE PRESIDENT. Oh, really? I'm always glad to meet my cousins. It's a pleasure to be with you. [*Laughter*]

Q. I wanted to ask you whether or not any legislation is pending or if so, would you favor it, which could defer medical payments for the elderly?

THE PRESIDENT. Defer?

Q. Right. Because when they reach that age, and all of a sudden their assets are gone, all their savings are gone and they're faced with additional medical payments which they have no way of earning the money, if it could be deferred say, until insurance payments were due, or something like that, upon death?

THE PRESIDENT. Yes, sir. The national health insurance program that we advocate and I hope that the Congress will pass will indeed take care of that need that you've described. It'll be phased in year by year, and this is the best way, I believe, to get Senator Long and Senator Kennedy, on both extremes of the issue together moving forward. Senator Ribicoff has also been a strong proponent of this kind of insurance program.

We'll start out with hospital cost containment and catastrophic insurance to make sure that if a health bill, hospitals or doctors, is too high for a particular family's income that the Federal Government would take care of that bill in the very early stages of the national health insurance program being implemented nationwide.

The additional emphasis would be on the prevention of illness for people for all ages. The third thing would be to emphasize outpatient care, rather than inpatient care in the hospitals, to hold down the total cost of the program and also the total bills given to those who might be sick. And the other thing that I'd like to mention is a special emphasis on mothers and tiny children, even the mother before the child is born, and then year by year the coverage for children who are a little bit older would be expanded. But the first and earliest part of it would be to take care of those catastrophic illness bills that are above and beyond the family's ability to pay.

I think we have a good chance to pass this legislation if I'm reelected.

Q. Thank you, sir.

THE PRESIDENT. Yes, sir.

CONDOMINIUM RECREATION LEASES

Q. Good morning, Mr. President.

THE PRESIDENT. Good morning.

Q. We're glad to have you here today. I am George—[*inaudible*]—from—[*inaudible*]—Florida. We have had bad leases on our 274 condominium building units. We have to pay land and recreation leases, also property taxes on both, plus escalation on both places, and upkeep on the recreation building and the pool area. [*Inaudible*] On account of this, I had to sell—[*inaudible*]. What can you do to get rid of this burden?

THE PRESIDENT. I am glad you asked that question.

When I campaigned through Florida in 1975 and 1976, everywhere I went in the condominium areas, people told me that these unconscionable so-called recreation leases were robbing them by increasing the cost every year above and beyond what they ever anticipated when they bought or began payments on the condominium.

Just this past week, I finally signed into law a bill that will give you relief. It lets any condominium leaseholder who's subject to that abuse concerning recreation now go to the Federal courts and get relief that was not available before. Lawton Chiles, Bob Graham, Claude Pepper, every Member of the Florida delegation was in there fighting alongside me to get this bill passed through the Congress. There was a lot of opposition to it, because the real estate lobby and other people in the Nation don't feel the need for this, of course, as much as the people in Florida.

But now you do have relief, and I think a few test cases by leaseholders, like you perhaps, in the Federal courts will set landmark decisions that will relieve the the leaseholders now of being abused in the future. So, finally, after 3 years, we got your legislation through the Congress, and you do have relief now under the law. The next steps will be much easier.

If you hadn't asked me that question, I was going to point that out before I left here, because it's very important.

Q. Thank you.

THE PRESIDENT. Yes, ma'am.

SENATOR EDWARD KENNEDY

Q. Mr. President, we welcome you to St. Petersburg, and I'm so happy to see you. We admire you, and we think you've been a marvelous President in the last 4 years.

THE PRESIDENT. That's a beautiful question. Thank you very much.

Q. I'm Mrs. Fred Peters; we're from St. Petersburg. My question is: Have you received any support from Senator Kennedy throughout your campaign, and if not, do you expect any in the next few weeks?

THE PRESIDENT. Yes. Senator Kennedy is working almost full time for me and my campaign. I'll be with him in New York shortly. He and I had a joint fundraising effort in Los Angeles earlier this month. He's campaigning for me in the New England States today, as a mat-

ter of fact. We'll have a joint fundraising effort in Washington, D.C., on the 19th of October, a major fundraising effort together in New York City again on the 20th of October. He will be campaigning for me in southern Texas and in California, hopefully perhaps in Florida to let people know that I have his unequivocal support.

He and I and my wife, Rosalynn, were together, as a matter of fact, earlier this week in, I think, Annandale, Virginia, where he and I signed—or I signed, he was there—the Mental Health Systems Act of 1980 on which he and I have worked harmoniously.

I might add that it's very good for me to have Senator Kennedy on my side, working with me for victory in November, because he recognizes, as I do, that the few differences that we did emphasize during the spring period of the primaries are insignificant compared to the major differences that separate me and him on one side, from Ronald Reagan and his supporters on the other.

So, Kennedy is a strong supporter. He would tell you the same thing I've just told you then.

Q. Thank you.

HOMEOWNERSHIP FOR SENIOR CITIZENS

Q. Mr. President, I'm Lillian Rauh, from Mandalay Shores, one of the senior citizens of the nonprofit co-op. We are the hardest hit by inflation and fixed income. Our members are too elderly to be forced into condominiums, and we would like to have ownership. And we need you to help us for a nonprofit co-op for our homes, of the HUD project. What can you do now, *now* to help us—*now*? [*Laughter*]

THE PRESIDENT. All right. When? When?

Q. Now, now, now! [*Laughter*]

THE PRESIDENT. Sometimes the Federal Government moves too slowly; I can't deny that.

It was only this week that many of the Florida delegation and I think about 20 senior citizens came up to be with me in the Rose Garden as I signed the housing and urban development act, the housing act of 1980. This act will provide the kind of assistance that you described, assistance by the Federal Government for senior citizens and others in making sure that you'll be able to buy homes, with subsidies for interest payments as those interest rates go up and down.

We also have increased enormously, by about 40 percent this year, the number of federally assisted housing units, both individual homes, condominiums, and rental units, that will be available in the future.

As Lawton knows, the holdup was in the Senate for a long time. The bill has now been passed, and you'll see the results of the bill in the very near future. As a matter of fact, you can see the results of the bill now.

Q. We have waited 14 months, though.

THE PRESIDENT. Thank you very much.

I might say that, as the congressional leaders know, this has been a difficult year. I guess a Presidential election year always shows a much sharper partisan delay in legislation being passed than would ordinarily be the case. And my belief is that after this election is over, many of the things that are obviously of benefit to the Nation that have been held up by Republican leaders in the House and the Senate because of the contest that goes on, which is very good, will be passed either in the lameduck session after November 4th or early next year.

I think we've got a good chance now to move on some of these major programs, so important to all of you, that have been delayed for the last few months.

Thank you very much. One more question, I think.

INFLATION AND THE ECONOMY

Q. Mr. President, my name is Orman Compton, and I am from—born in Tennessee, lived in Michigan all my life, retired to Florida 8 years ago. And we love it, we appreciate you coming here to Florida. I'll tell you, my question is this, but wait just a second. I want to thank you very kindly, because I happened to work in one of those big corporations in Detroit. You yourself okayed a certain loan. I'm 63 years old. If you hadn't okayed the loan, I'd be out here looking for a job. Your opponent, Mr. Reagan, in Detroit, in one of the factories, made a statement that he didn't see nothing wrong with a big company going bankrupt and if he was President, he would never have voted for this loan. So, praise the Lord for you, brother Carter.

THE PRESIDENT. Thank you, sir.

Q. And God bless you.

THE PRESIDENT. Thank you.

Q. My question is—I retired 8 years ago, and I'm on a fixed income. Now, what has happened, I'm on the same retirement—I retired—a little bit less—in '72, and this is '80. And the only thing about it, every year the prices keep agoin', and it's pretty hard for me to keep up with those prices. What are you going to do about inflation? I would like to know, please.

THE PRESIDENT. I'll try.

I might say that I appreciate your pointing out Governor Reagan's position on the Chrysler bankruptcy bill. He said at the time that bankruptcy might be advisable and that he would not bail out the Chrysler company. You've made a point that many people have forgotten. Not only would several hundred thousand workers have been out of jobs in our country, not only would the American automobile industry have been hit a major blow, but tens of thousands of retirees like you would have lost your income altogether.

And this is a case of a good investment, where the American Government said, "We're not going to give the taxpayers' money away, but we're going to back up the loan that Chrysler can get from banks, from insurance companies, and others." My guess is that we will not lose anything from the Federal Government Treasury. But we have Chrysler on its feet, kept American workers employed, and kept retirees like you from suffering the hardships of poverty and deprivation.

The biggest source of inflation in this country this year has been the enormous and unpredicted increase in the price of OPEC oil imposed on all the world last year. In 1 year alone, 1979, the price of oil increased more than the price had increased ever since oil was first discovered in the 1800's. Our country has tried to accommodate, along with nations all over the world, this enormous and serious blow to stability in the economic markets. We've done fairly well.

As you know, the inflation rate did go up, up until March, to 18 or 19 percent. We imposed some restraints on budgeting, on credit, and encouraged Americans to save more money out of what is earned, invest it back in our economic system. And also, we moved to stabilize interest rates. Every week after that, interest rates dropped about 1 percent per week, and the inflation rate went down so that in July we had a zero infla-

tion rate, at least for that 1 month, the first time in 13 years. There is no doubt that the inflation rate is still too high.

But what we are doing now, along with other nations in the world, is to try to reduce our excessive dependence on imported oil. You have a major responsibility for the success that we have enjoyed. Today and every day in 1980, we are importing from overseas 2 million barrels less of oil than we did the first year I was in office. This is because we're conserving more oil and other energy, we're not wasting it as much, and we're increasing the production of energy of all kinds in our country.

There's no reason for us to be afraid about the future. All the OPEC Arab countries put together have about 6 percent of the energy reserves in the world. The United States by itself has 24 percent of all the energy reserves, and those reserves are in oil, natural gas, geothermal, coal, shale, tar sands. We've got rushing streams for hydroelectric power. We've got beautiful sunshine, as you know, for solar power.

And so, as we cut down on the buying of oil overseas, we also cut down on the importing of inflation and also the importing of unemployment.

The windfall profits tax, which we have imposed on the unearned income of the oil companies, is the key to the future stability of the energy program in our Nation. Part of that windfall profits tax, as you know, goes to make low-income payments to those of you who need to have help in paying your energy bills.

I might point out, since this is a political year, that Governor Reagan has advocated eliminating the Department of Energy, doing away with the legislation we've passed to set up this energy program. He'd like to do away with the windfall profits tax and, as he says, "unleash or let loose the oil companies and let them solve the energy problem for us." There's another example of how the elderly would be directly affected depending upon the outcome of the election this year.

It's very important that we take this Federal assistance for low-income families to help pay your energy bills and not do away with it by repealing the windfall profits tax, but let it be increased year by year as energy costs inevitably go up. I don't want to mislead you, Orman, because there's no way that I can see, in the future, that energy prices are going to go down. Oil will become more scarce, and I think the prices are going to go up. But what we'll have to do is continue on the program that we've finally got in place.

You might be interested in knowing, as proud and patriotic Americans, that this year we will have more oil and gas wells dug in the United States than any year in the history of our Nation, and you might be surprised to know that this year we'll produce more American coal than any year in history. And my hope is that soon, not too distant future, we will replace a major part of OPEC oil in the international energy trade with American coal. That's the kind of things that we can do to get that inflation rate down and hold it down.

And the last point is this: Now that we've got this energy legislation passed, it's time for us to revitalize American industry. One major factor in the inflation rate is how productive American workers are. The more American workers produce for the salaries they receive, the lower the inflation rate is. Right now the American workers are the most productive in the whole world. But what we need is new investments to make sure that American

workers have modern tools and modern factories that they can use to be even more productive in the future.

So, high productivity, cutting down on imported oil, restraining the waste of energy, keeping the windfall tax on the books, helping you to have lower medical costs with a nationwide comprehensive national health insurance program, protecting Medicare, keeping social security sound, helping you with housing programs, protecting you from abuse of any kind, letting you work and have productive lives as long as you live, for the benefit of this Nation—those are the kinds of things that I'm committed to. If you help me, we'll do them together.

Thank you very much, and God bless you all.

NOTE: The President spoke at 11:04 a.m. in the Grand Ballroom at the Princess Martha Hotel.

St. Petersburg, Florida

Interview With Hugh Smith of WTVT-TV.   October 10, 1980

MR. SMITH. Thank you, Leslie. We are here live at the Princess Martha Hotel with President Carter. Mr. President, welcome to the Tampa Bay area.

THE PRESIDENT. Well, I'm glad to be back. This is one of my favorite places in the world.

MR. SMITH. We're very pleased to have you here.

THE PRESIDENT. Thank you.

SOCIAL SECURITY

MR. SMITH. Mr. President, as you know, both you and your opponent, Governor Reagan, have been giving a good deal of attention to the issue of social security. At his Tampa appearance this morning, Governor Reagan said, and this is pretty much a quote, the elderly are the prisoners of your inadequate leadership. The Governor said, "I will preserve and strengthen social security," but that you want to tax social security benefits. How would you respond to that?

THE PRESIDENT. That's completely false. As long as I'm in the White House, social security benefits will not be taxed. No one in my administration has advocated that they be taxed, as Mr. Reagan well knows. As a matter of fact, on four different occasions in the past, Governor Reagan has called for making social security participation voluntary, which would bring social security to its knees. I understand this morning—I haven't seen the exact quote—that he's even advocated now paying social security benefits to millionaires, which would really rob the average American retired person of a chance to keep the social security system sound.

One thing that I heard everywhere I went in Florida when I was campaigning here in '75 and '76 was that the social security system was on the verge of bankruptcy, which it was under the Republican administration. Now we've made social security sound. It will not go into bankruptcy, and it will be kept sound as long as we have a Democrat in the White House.

PENSION FUNDS

MR. SMITH. Mr. President, Governor Reagan has also said while he has been in Florida that you are playing what he calls "retirement roulette" with people's pension plans, through your proposal that pensions would be invested in companies having financial problems.

THE PRESIDENT. It's difficult to respond to ridiculous things like this repetitively, but I think it's necessary for me to do it since you've asked the question.

What has been proposed is that American workers' pension funds, which are enormous, billions and billions of dollars, be used in the future to invest in increased productivity of American industry to provide jobs for America. Lane Kirkland, who's the president of the AFL-CIO, came to me and made this proposal personally. He will respond to Governor Reagan's silly statement later on today, but what President Kirkland said was that the workers' funds now in retirement areas are being invested in foreign countries in different ways through the large banks, without contributing to the increased stability in our own country and job opportunities for Americans.

One point that Governor Reagan deliberately overlooked is that these funds would be guaranteed by the Federal Government. There would be no chance for workers' pension funds to be lost. You know, this is a kind of a typical response by a Republican to proposals that would help the average Americans who come from working families or who might be on insecure grounds.

I remember that when Medicare was proposed as a program that Governor Reagan led the fight against it. He went all over the Nation making speeches against Medicare, calling it socialized medicine, saying that the doctors would be, in effect, servants of the Federal Government. I just happened to read a quote from him. As part of his effort to kill Medicare Governor Reagan said, "It's very easy to disguise a medical program as a humanitarian project." He said, "It would be just a short step before the Government was telling the doctors where they could practice and who they could treat." Mr. Reagan predicted that soon this would be expanded to all Americans until, and I quote, "Pretty soon your son won't decide when he's in school where he will go or what he will do for a living. He will wait for the Government to tell him where he will go to work and what he will do." This is what Mr. Reagan predicted would happen if Medicare passed.

You know, it's obviously without foundation and obviously an exaggeration, and it was a rightwing kind of Republican response to a Medicare program, which they opposed just as they opposed, by the way, social security when Franklin Roosevelt and the Democratic Congress passed it.

1980 ELECTION RESULTS

MR. SMITH. Mr. President, the race at this point is said to be very, very close——

THE PRESIDENT. Yes.

MR. SMITH. Not only here in Florida but in other parts of the country. How do you assess it at this point? Let me ask you, sir, if the election were held today, who would win?

THE PRESIDENT. It's hard to say. I think it is close. In my judgment the next 3 or 4 weeks will be a time when Americans are brought to the realization that the outcome of the election on November 4 will indeed affect the future of their country. It will affect the future of every single person, every family, everyone who's loved in this Nation.

I don't recall any election in my lifetime when the differences between myself and my opponent or the Republican and Democratic platforms have been so stark and sharp as they are in 1980. The only possible exception is when Barry Goldwater ran against Lyndon Johnson in 1964. But with that one exception I've never known any differences to be so sharp. And as the American people begin to see how deeply the issues are divided between me and Governor Reagan, I think they'll come to the conclusion that November 4 can be a turning point in their life.

I'm determined that we'll continue the progress that has been made under myself and previous Democrats who served in the White House in meeting the legitimate needs of the American people.

"OCTOBER SURPRISE"

MR. SMITH. The Reagan people have said more than once, Mr. President, that you are planning some kind of October surprise which would benefit your candidacy. If in fact you are, is that a domestic kind of surprise or something having to do with foreign policy?

THE PRESIDENT. It'll be a surprise to me too.

I don't know of anything planned. Every day a President has to deal with very important issues that are important to everybody in the country, indeed, the entire world. As I sit in the Oval Office and make those decisions on potential crises, if I make the right decision the American people never know what I've done. If I should make a misjudgment or make the wrong decision, that potential crisis could affect adversely the life of every American or every person in the whole world. So, each day in the life of a President you have that enormous responsibility of trying to answer questions that couldn't be answered anywhere else and dealing with problems that can't be dealt with anywhere else.

The difficulty of the job is that if a question can be answered easily it's answered in the life of an average citizen or within the home or in a county courthouse or a city hall or perhaps a State legislature or Governor's office. But if the question's so complex and so difficult that it can't be addressed in any of those places, then it comes to the Oval Office, to the President's desk.

And there's no way to contrive some sort of a false surprise to be sprung on the American people just before an election. Obviously every day I try to do the best I can for this country and for the people that elected me to serve them.

AMERICAN HOSTAGES IN IRAN

MR. SMITH. In talking about the so-called October surprise the Reagan people have mentioned the American hostages. Are there any signs of a breakthrough on that at all? And do you think, Mr. President, that the fact that these people had been held captive almost a year now is an indication of this country's inability to deal with the situation, or has it became a symbol of that?

THE PRESIDENT. Never a day goes by, never an hour goes by that I don't think about those hostages, and I pray for them every day. It's been one of my most serious problems as President, and I hope they'll be returned as soon as possible. There's no way I can predict when.

I've done two things from the very beginning, and I've never changed our policy as a Nation or myself as a President. One is I've protected the interests and the integrity and honor of my country, and at the same time I've done everything I could to avoid making a statement or an action that might endanger the lives or the safety of those hostages or put an obstacle in the way of their return-

ing home to freedom. I'll continue to do that in a very cautious way.

It's a serious mistake for any candidate, Governor Reagan or myself or anyone else, to inject the question of the American hostages into the political campaign. I think it's not good for the hostages themselves, it's not good for our relationships with Iran, and it might create an impediment to a successful resolution of this problem and the return of the hostages to our homes.

MR. SMITH. Can you tell us, Mr. President, whether there might be a breakthrough very soon on this matter of the hostage issue?

THE PRESIDENT. I have no idea. I have hoped from the very beginning of their incarceration in Iran that each week would bring some progress. We've been persistently and repeatedly disappointed.

The problem has been that there is no government in Iran with the authority to speak. We had negotiated their release, as you may remember, I think in the month of May, with their President, their Foreign Minister, the revolutionary council, even with the militants who were holding the hostages. It was announced by their President they would be released. But they reversed themselves and have not done so. Now there is a parliament, called a Majles, in Iran. They have a speaker elected, they have a Prime Minister now and a President. They don't at this time have a Foreign Minister, but most of the cabinet's intact.

We have hope—that's all—but no expectation of any release at a certain time.

MR. SMITH. Since the one military attempt failed, would you rule out any future military attempts to get them?

THE PRESIDENT. I don't anticipate the use of any rescue operation at this time or in the future.

IRAN-IRAQ WAR

MR. SMITH. Another problem you have to deal with, of course, is the war between Iran and Iraq, which seems to be getting more serious with every growing day. And today, according to the Libyan News Agency, Libya has declared its support for Iran. Some 10 planes per day, we are given to understand, are flying from Libya, passing over the Soviet Union to Iran. Does this concern you?

THE PRESIDENT. From Libya over the Soviet Union?

MR. SMITH. Well, at any rate Libyan support is being given, and I wonder if that's a matter of concern to you?

THE PRESIDENT. I see. Yes, it is. It's a concern to me, because we want to see that combat over. And if it should be stalemated or continued over a period of time we want to see it confined just to those two nations, Iran and Iraq. We've used all the influence that we can to discourage other nations from becoming militarily involved.

We have major naval and air forces in the Persian Gulf region, in the northern part of the Indian Ocean, that can protect our own interests, if necessary, by keeping the Strait of Hormuz open.

Libya, as you know, is a radical terrorist regime under Colonel Qaddafi, and they are unpredictable. I think they exemplify the threat of terrorism throughout the world. This is a blight on the entire universe of civilized nations, even absent a war between Iran and Iraq.

Recently we've seen, for instance, in France terrorism against people because they're Jews, attacks on synagogues. This is abhorrent to me and to the American people and to the entire civilized world. I think one of the things that we can do to hold down this terrorism in the future

is when I have another summit conference with the leaders of other developed democratic nations, is to have us jointly address the question of terrorism.

Obviously terrorism in the Mideast, the Persian Gulf region, is a contributory factor to the combat that presently exists between Iran and Iraq. But stamping out terrorism all over the world, and particularly based on racism, or religious beliefs, is something that addresses me, the American people, and all civilized people.

MR. SMITH. Mr. President, you recently ordered four special surveillance planes to Saudi Arabia, and Jordan is being supplied with a number of tanks because of the war between Iran and Iraq. Do you see any parallel between this kind of American involvement and the situation which got us into Vietnam a number of years ago in which our participation in that began in a very small way and then escalated?

THE PRESIDENT. No, we're not involved in any nation where combat is being conducted. Obviously, it's important to us to stabilize the Middle East based on the treaty between Israel and Egypt, which we hope to extend to Jordan and to Syria and to Lebanon in the future.

The Saudi Arabians on the Persian Gulf, far removed from Israel, obviously is a nation that we want to see protected and kept at peace. The four airplanes that you described, we call them AWACS planes, it's an aircraft early warning plane. It goes up into the air with very elaborate and effective radar coverage of a large area, stays way back from the combat area, and just provides information for those who want to defend themselves in case there is an aerial attack.

So, I think that this is a peaceful contribution to prevent an unwarranted attack on a peaceful nation, Saudi Arabia.

It's not an injection under any circumstances of American military forces into a combat area.

FOREIGN POLICY

MR. SMITH. Mr. President, should you be reelected, I want to ask this question. There have been some reports out of Washington which hint at some friction between two members of the staff very close to you, your Secretary of State, Mr. Muskie, and your national security adviser, Mr. Brzezinski. Should you be reelected, do you intend to retain both of those gentlemen, or what other changes might you be making in your administration, should you be reelected?

THE PRESIDENT. Well, it's too early for me to say about what's going to happen for the next 4 or 4½ years. My present intention is to keep them on, yes.

The reports about conflict between Brzezinski and Muskie, both of whom happen to be Polish Americans, are false and in any instance, highly exaggerated. I meet, almost daily, several times a week with Secretary of State Muskie, with my national security adviser, with Secretary Brown, Secretary of Defense, and also with the Vice President. We discuss the important issues around the world, 150 nations, troublespots in different parts of the world, and what our Nation should do to address it. We sometimes have differences of opinion among us.

I'd say 95 percent of the time the national security adviser, the Secretary of State agree in making a recommendation to me. On those times when they do disagree, honest disagreements, I make the judgment. But if our foreign policy is successful, the responsibility is mine. If our foreign policy is unsuccessful, the responsibility is mine. And when we are able to bring peace to Israel, when we're able to open up a billion new friends for the United States in the People's Republic of China, when we are able to see military dictatorships replaced with democratic governments, when we are able to see some of the new emerging countries in Africa who've never known us now become our staunch friends and allies who are able to stabilize international trade, those are things that are the result of a common approach. But I don't remember any of my advisers, for instance, telling me they thought that I ought to go to Camp David to meet with President Sadat and Prime Minister Begin, but I decided to go.

And I can tell you that I will always have strong advisers around me. Sometimes they are inevitably going to give me conflicting advice, but I'll be the one to make a judgment on what should be the foreign policy of our country and let it be known to the American people, consult with the Congress as appropriate, and I believe in that way, prevent the kind of serious mistakes that were made in the past when things were done secret, in a closet, like Watergate, the CIA violating American laws, and the extended and unnecessary aspect of the war in Vietnam.

MR. SMITH. Well, would both gentlemen be a part of your administration if you are reelected, sir?

THE PRESIDENT. Well, that's my present plan. Secretary Muskie has said that he's never had anything better happen to him in his life than my choice of him as the Secretary of State. My plan would certainly be that if he's willing to stay on that I would keep him on. And I have no present plans to change the members of my White House staff.

RONALD REAGAN

MR. SMITH. We have less than a minute, Mr. President.

There's been a good deal of talk about the calming down of rhetoric lately between you and Governor Reagan and the campaign.

THE PRESIDENT. Yes.

MR. SMITH. Give me your assessment of Governor Reagan as President if he should be elected.

THE PRESIDENT. I think it'd be a bad thing for our country if Governor Reagan should be elected. I think a lot of his advisers are very concerned about what he would say in an open and free exchange of ideas with the American people in a townhall meeting, like I just concluded, or in an interview like this or an open debate. Your station invited me and Reagan, Governor Reagan, to meet on this station since we both happened to be in Tampa, and have a debate, as you know. I accepted immediately, as I've accepted the League of Women Voters invitation to debate and three or four other invitations for us to have a two-person debate. He's refused all those opportunities for a debate.

And I don't know what he would do in the White House, but his opposition to the SALT II treaty, his opposition to Medicare, his opposition to many of the programs that are important like the minimum wage or unemployment compensation, his call for the injection of American military forces into place after place after place around the world when diplomatic means ought to solve those problems indicate to me that he would not be a good President, a good man to trust with the affairs of this Nation in the future.

MR. SMITH. We have used up all of our time. I appreciate very much the time you have given us. Thank you, Mr. President.

THE PRESIDENT. It's good to have this one-sided part of the debate.

MR. SMITH. Thank you, Mr. President. Now back to Leslie Spencer.

NOTE: The interview began at 12 noon at the Princess Martha Hotel.

Martin Luther King, Junior, and Boston African American National Historic Sites

Remarks on Signing H.R. 7218 and H.R. 7434 Into Law.   October 10, 1980

THE PRESIDENT. To Coretta King and Representative McLin, to Byron Rushing, to Cecil Andrus, Secretary of Interior, to other men and women of our Nation, and also to young people as well who believe that quite often government, which moves slowly, can correct a long overdue omission in the social and educational development of our country, this is a very good occasion. The two bills that I will sign today represent a three-pronged effort to preserve a vital, but long neglected part of American heritage: the history and culture of Americans of African ancestry and their role in the history of our Nation.

First, I will sign a bill that designates and establishes the Martin Luther King, Junior, National Historic Site and Preservation District in Atlanta to preserve the area where Dr. Martin Luther King, Jr., lived and worked and worshiped and where he's buried, as a living memorial to the civil rights movement which he came to symbolize.

The second bill establishes a Boston African American National Historical Site, including the African-American

Meeting House, which was the center of the 19th century free African American community on Beacon Hill. That bill also provides for the establishment of a national center for the study of Afro-American history and culture with headquarters in Wilberforce, Ohio.

Wilberforce University was founded in 1856 for the education of runaway slaves and free black people and has a proud history of service and distinguished faculty and also, obviously, distinguished alumni. It was named for the British abolitionist, William Wilberforce, who secured passage of the act ending the British slave trade and who worked for the worldwide abolition of slavery. These two historic sites will preserve for all Americans some of the physical surroundings of two important periods in the history of black Americans.

From the early days of our country, free black Americans had helped to gain freedom for the slaves by their writing, their speeches, and direct action. They were an important force in arousing the conscience of our Nation to the evil of slavery that ate at the heart of our most fundamental principles.

The contributions of black Americans in all fields of human endeavor were largely forgotten or overlooked until just recent years to the detriment of all Americans. In this century, the writings, speeches, and direct action of black Americans culminating in the civil rights movement again aroused the conscience of all Americans to the evils of lingering discrimination that threaten to deny black people freedom, justice, and opportunity.

The creation of a national center for the study of Afro-American history and culture will give new impetus to the effort of many scholars and organizations to extend our knowledge and understanding of black experience in America and to make this heritage known to all our people. We must put the pain and prejudice of the past behind us, but in so doing, we must not deny ourselves the valuable lessons that can teach us or let the truth be lost to future generations.

If the truth is to set us free, we must study and to understand our own past and how it affects the present and the future. It is for this purpose that this national center is to be established. I hope the preservation of these sites and the creation of this center will provide all Americans with a new source of knowledge and inspiration at the same time they give black Americans new insights into their own roots.

Preserving some of these sites that were a part of these two great historic movements to free the slaves and the American civil rights movement in this century will help present and future generations appreciate not only the events of the past but the principles and dreams that gave these movements power and allowed them to overcome almost insurmountable obstacles. The Historic Preservation District in Atlanta will include the Martin Luther King, Jr. Center for Social Change, which is dedicated to continuing the nonviolent struggle for justice and equal opportunity in this country and for human rights around the world.

It houses historic tapes and photographs that contain much of the record of the tragedy and the triumph of the civil rights movement, but it also speaks to what Dr. King called the "fierce urgency of now." He longed for the day when all people would be judged, and to quote him, "not by the color of their skin, but by the content of their character." The character of future generations will be shaped by the understanding of the past and their ability to build on it a world where all people will be able, as in his dream, to join hands and to sing together "Free at Last."

And now I'd like to sign these two historic documents establishing centers and preserving sites where the black Americans were finally given freedom from slavery and, finally in our recent lifetime, to the courage and commitment of Dr. Martin Luther King, Jr., reminded us what peace meant and let us remove the threat and the oppression of legal discrimination from our land.

The first act is designed to establish the Martin Luther King, Junior, National Historic Site in the State of Georgia and for other purposes.

[*At this point, the President signed H.R. 7218.*]

I forgot to ask Coretta if I should sign it or veto it. [*Laughter*]

Mrs. King. You did the right thing.

The President. Well, I think that's a fine bill. Thank you very much.

I think before I sign the other act it might be good to let Coretta respond, if you don't mind.

Mrs. King. Thank you, Mr. President.

This is indeed an historic occasion for those of us who represent the family of Martin King. My son, Marty King—Martin III—is with me, members of the board of directors and trustees of Martin King Center—John Cox, Jeri Allen, Al Nellum, and Pastor Joe Roberts of the Ebenezer Baptist Church—and all of the friends and supporters, representatives from the city of Atlanta, from the State of Georgia—Liz Lyons, former Commissioner Gibson, two council persons, I believe, Rob Pitts and Arthur Langford, here——

The President. Daddy King's here in spirit today.

Mrs. King. Daddy King is here in spirit——

The President. He was going to be here, but he just couldn't make it.

Mrs. King. He couldn't make it. He had a little accident, but I think he's going to be all right.

We have members of the Park Service Committee, National Park Service, Mr. Brown, Dr. Janet Wolf, others. And Bill Whelan, former Director of the Park Service—I am especially pleased to see him, Mr. President, because he started early on with us, and Mr. Whelan went about this with great dedication, and we're just deeply appreciative.

Other members of the Park Service have been so helpful to us. Certainly Mr. Andrus, Secretary Andrus, and Assistant Secretary Deputy, Deputy Secretary Hutchinson——

The President. Director.

Mrs. King. Director. [*Laughter*] I'm making you Secretary. I'm getting in trouble. [*Laughter*] Congressman Bereuter came down and saw the site and was extremely helpful to us, and we're just grateful that he could be here today and for all of the other friends and supporters of the Martin Luther King Center and those who are working to make the dream a reality.

I can assure you that this act, Mr. President, which you have signed today will be a tremendous inspiration and encouragement, but it also will help us to continue to develop the site, to develop the area where Martin grew up and to revitalize that total community, because we're concerned not only about the physical revitalization but the spiritual revitalization as well, creating the beloved community. Again, Martin King was concerned about a community, a city, a State, a nation, and a world where people could live together with feelings of security, equal opportunity, justice and peace. And I feel that this site is not only a symbolic representation of all that Martin stood for and the representation of his dream, but it is in fact a beginning where we can demonstrate what can happen in a small way. This will become a model community, I believe, Mr. President. We want to thank you.

THE PRESIDENT. Thank you very much. And, of course, the other bill is for the establishment of the Boston African American National Historic Site in the Commonwealth of Massachusetts, and of course, the Wilberforce Center, the National Center for the Study of Afro-American History and Culture. It's a great pleasure for me to do this. I know that in our lifetime we've seen the need for Americans to remember the exciting but sometimes torturous path that our country has played toward achieving equality of opportunity and realizing the dream that existed in the hearts and minds of those who founded this country. And I'm very glad to be present on this historic occasion.

[At this point, the President signed H.R. 7434.]

We've got two new laws now. I think Representative McLin might want to comment on the Wilberforce——

REPRESENTATIVE McLIN. Well, Mr. President, especially those of us in Ohio who have worked long and hard to try to get the National Museum Centers established, we appreciate it. I think this will be a lasting compository and repository for Afro-American history and culture; long we have needed such a place that we can have a center that we can place those historical items in. And on behalf of the Afro-American and Dr. Taylor and Dr. Newsom of both Central State and

Wilberforce University, we want to thank you very much and Congress for carrying this law past.

Thank you very much.

THE PRESIDENT. Thank you very much, Representative McLin.

And now I'd like to ask Byron Rushing, the president of the Museum of Afro-American History in Boston, to say a word.

MR. RUSHING. In 1790, when the first census was taken in this country, Massachusetts was the only State in the Union that had no slaves, and so this community that we are preserving in this act is truly the oldest free black community in the United States. And the center part of the 16 sites that will be preserved by this act is the African Meeting House, which is now the oldest black church building still standing in the United States. For various reasons we are very proud that all of that happened in Boston, Massachusetts.

We're also very proud that our Congressman Joe Moakley and our Senator Paul Tsongas understood the importance of this legislation and moved very effectively to have it passed. We want to especially thank at this time, not only our own, of course, in-house supporters, our board members and all those people who love us dearly, but especially the staff of the National Park Service. And I think of two names that come out immediately, and that's Ira Hutchinson and Bob Nunn, who I don't think is here today, who just did a tremendous job in helping us in this legislation. And I want to thank you very much, Mr. President, for signing this.

THE PRESIDENT. Thank you very much.

Well, I was going to call on Cecil Andrus to say a final word representing the administration, but as usual, he's quite modest. He does the work, shepherds the legislation through the Congress, works very closely with his subordinates in the Interior Department, also cooperates completely with private and public officials in the local and State government and with those who are interested in the improvement of our country. And I want to express my deep thanks to him, my confidence that in his Department, the true intent of the Congress and the highest ideals to these two bills will be carried out to the fullest. Cecil, thank you again along with those others assembled here.

Thank you very much, everybody. Have a good day.

NOTE: The President spoke at 3:35 p.m. in the Cabinet Room at the White House.

As enacted, H.R. 7218 is Public Law 96–428, and H.R. 7434 is Public Law 96–430, both approved October 10.

Maine Indian Claims Settlement Act of 1980

Remarks at the Bill Signing Ceremony. October 10, 1980

THE PRESIDENT. *Governor Brennan and Secretary Muskie, Senator Mitchell, representatives of the Passamaquoddy and the Penobscot and Maliseet Tribes:*

This is indeed a culmination of a great deal of effort on behalf of everyone in this room—and a lot of those who are not assembled here today because the room is not large enough to hold those who have worked on this important legislation. This is also a great day for all the people of Maine, for the Indian tribes involved, for Maine's landowners, and also a good day for the Congress of the United States, because they are all satisfied with the settlement act. Because we have a settlement act, rather than lengthy and extremely costly litigation, a mutual consent agreement, rather than acrimonious debate and further division among the people of Maine, it's a good day for me as President as well.

When I first came to office in 1977, I was determined to help resolve the uncertainty surrounding the land ownership question in Maine. It was an intolerable situation. On the one hand, the Federal Government had failed to live up to its responsibility to the Maine Indians. On the other hand, the citizens of Maine were subjected to fear and uncertainty about the title to land they considered to be their own. The Federal Government owes a special responsibility to all the people of Maine, of course, Indian and non-Indian, to settle this claim.

In 1977 I appointed a very distinguished former Georgia Supreme Court Justice, William Gunter, to evaluate the claims and advise me on an appropriate course for the Federal Government to follow. At his suggestion, we appointed a working group which undertook extensive negotiations with the tribes and with the representatives of various landowners in the State of Maine. These negotiations have paved the way for a satisfactory out-of-court settlement of what might otherwise have been a lengthy and costly and bitter lawsuit.

The settlement authorizes a permanent land base and trust fund for the tribes and also resolves once and for all the title to the land for all the people who reside in Maine. The settlement act does something else as well. It's a reaffirmation that our system of government works.

A hundred and ninety years after the Passamaquoddy and Penobscot Indians and Maine settlers fought side by side to protect Maine's borders and help defend all Thirteen Colonies in the Revolutionary War, the people of Maine have again shown themselves to be an example of us all, by working together, by acting with patience and fairness and understanding. This should be a proud day for everyone who was involved in this effort, many of whom are here today—the tribes, who placed their trust in the system that has not always treated them fairly, the leaders of the State of Maine who came openly to the bargaining table, the landowners who helped make the settlement a reality by offering land for sale that they might not otherwise have wanted to sell, the Members of Congress who realize the necessity of acting, and all the citizens of Maine who have worked together to resolve this problem of land title.

And now it's with a great deal of pleasure that I, as President of our country, sign into law this bill, which settles once and for all in a fair and equitable manner a dispute that has concerned all of us over many years.

[At this point, the President signed the bill.]

I think I'll let a few of the people comment if you all have just a brief period of time. Governor, would you say a word first?

GOVERNOR BRENNAN. Mr. President, I wish to thank you and commend you and your administration for a superb response to solving the most difficult problem that has faced Maine in its history. By virtue of the efforts of your administration in the signing of this bill, an economic cloud has been removed from Maine, and the opening of a new relationship between Indians and non-Indians will begin.

Thank you very, very much.

THE PRESIDENT. Senator?

SENATOR MITCHELL. Well, I'd just like to add my thanks to those of the Gov-

ernor, Mr. President. This is but one example of your responsiveness to the problems of the people of Maine that has existed since you took office. With Loring Air Force Base, the Bath Iron Works, this settlement, your prompt response to the Governor's request last week for disaster recognition for the Maine coast demonstrated a concern and responsibility in dealing with the problems of the citizens of Maine. And I know everybody in Maine is deeply appreciative of that and very thankful to you.

Thank you.

THE PRESIDENT. Ed, would you like to say a word?

SECRETARY MUSKIE. Mr. President, as I contemplate the history of this complicated problem, I can only think of one appropriate word to say. Amen. *[Laughter]*

THE PRESIDENT. Well, I'll let you choose someone to represent the Indian tribes, if you don't mind. Tom?

MR. TUREEN. I don't know why I get chosen.

THE PRESIDENT. You're chosen.

MR. TUREEN. Mr. President, we thank you. It's a problem not just for these tribes but for our whole system. If it hadn't been for your courage, who knows what would have happened in these cases. There's a temptation to turn your back on what was right, and you resisted that, and we'll all be appreciative.

Thank you very much.

THE PRESIDENT. I might say as a personal note that this is one of the most difficult issues I've ever gotten involved in. I've aroused the animosity and the criticism of almost everyone—*[laughter]*—at least for transient periods of time. But I felt it was my responsibility, as President representing all the people of this country, to stay with it, and I imported a very fine and distinguished jurist from Georgia to help me with it. And I think that his basic recommendation and the courage of all those here to face a difficult issue head-on has resulted in a settlement that's gratifying to everyone involved.

Again, I want to thank all of you for coming here. I think the people of Maine have responded well to a very difficult and potentially permanently divisive issue in your State. And I think that the final resolution has been a credit to our system of government.

SECRETARY MUSKIE. Mr. President, if I may mention one other person who is not to be forgotten, who can't be with us, and that's Governor Jim Longley——

THE PRESIDENT. Absolutely.

SECRETARY MUSKIE.——who really fought for Maine's best interests, who persisted with you. And I think his involvement and contribution ought to be recognized.

MR. PRESIDENT. Thank you, Ed, very much.

NOTE: The President spoke at 3:56 p.m. in the Cabinet Room at the White House.

As enacted, H.R. 7919 is Public Law 96–420, approved October 10.

Ronald Reagan

Informal Exchange With a Reporter on Departure for Camp David.
October 10, 1980

Q. Mr. President, did you mean to suggest that Reagan is untrustworthy in your interview?

THE PRESIDENT. Very trustworthy.

NOTE: The President was asked the question as he departed from the South Portico of the White House at 4:55 p.m.

Digest of Other White House Announcements

The following listing includes the President's public schedule and other items of general interest announced by the White House Press Office and not included elsewhere in this issue.

October 4

The President left the White House for a weekend stay at Camp David, Md.

October 5

The President returned to the White House from Camp David.

October 6

The President met at the White House with:

—Zbigniew Brzezinski, Assistant to the President for National Security Affairs;

—Representative Joseph L. Fisher of Virginia.

October 7

The President met at the White House with:

—Dr. Brzezinski;

—Frank B. Moore, Assistant to the President for Congressional Liaison.

October 8

The President met at the White House with:

—Dr. Brzezinski;

—Mr. Moore;

—a group of ethnic leaders.

The White House announced that the President has directed the Department of Justice to make an expedited appeal to the First Circuit Court of Appeals of a district court decision handed down in Puerto Rico that enjoins the Federal Government from continuing to set up a processing center for Cuban and Haitian refugees at Fort Allen, Puerto Rico.

October 9

The President met at the White House with Zbigniew Brzezinski, Assistant to the President for National Security Affairs.

October 10

The President left the White House for a weekend stay at Camp David, Md.

NOMINATIONS SUBMITTED TO THE SENATE

NOTE: The Congress being in recess, no nominations were submitted to the Senate during the period covered by this issue.

CHECKLIST OF WHITE HOUSE PRESS RELEASES

The following listing contains releases of the White House Press Office which are not included in this issue.

Released October 5, 1980

Announcement: recess appointments of five members of the Board of Directors of the Synthetic Fuels Corporation

Released October 6, 1980

Advance text: remarks at the Milwaukee Area Technical College in West Allis, Wis.

Released October 7, 1980

Fact sheet: S. 1177, Mental Health Systems Act

Released October 8, 1980

Fact sheet: S. 2719, Housing and Community Development Act of 1980

Fact sheet: President's Task Force on Housing for the Eighties and white paper on housing

Released October 9, 1980

Announcement: Federal assistance for the development of small hydroelectric projects

Released October 10, 1980

Fact sheet: Refugee Education Assistance Act of 1980

Fact sheet: Martin Luther King, Junior, and Boston African American National Historic Sites

Fact sheet: Maine Indian Claims Settlement Act of 1980

ACTS APPROVED BY THE PRESIDENT

Approved October 6, 1980

H.R. 5164_____ Public Law 96–378
An act to amend certain inspection and manning laws applicable to small vessels carrying passengers or freight for hire, and for other purposes.

S. 1895_____ Public Law 96–379
An act to change the name of the Los Esteros Dam (New Mexico) to the Santa Rosa Dam and Lake, and to designate Clark Hill Dam and Lake on the Savannah River, Georgia and South Carolina, as "Clarks Hill Dam and Lake".

H.R. 6242_____ Public Law 96–380
An act to establish a Towing Safety Advisory Committee in the Department of Transportation.

S. 1123_____ Public Law 96–381
An act to amend section 204 of the Marine Protection, Research, and Sanctuaries Act of 1972 to authorize appropriations for title II of such act for fiscal year 1980.

H.R. 3748_____ Public Law 96–382
An act to provide for a uniform national three-year statute of limitations in actions to recover damages for personal injury or death, arising out of a maritime tort, and for other purposes.

H.R. 8018_____ Public Law 96–383
An act to rename a reservoir and dam in the Little Miami River Basin, Ohio, as the "William H. Harsha Lake" and the "William H. Harsha Dam".

H.R. 8024_____ Public Law 96–384
An act to change the name of Aubrey Lake, Texas, to Ray Roberts Lake.

Approved October 7, 1980

H.R. 7511_____Public Law 96–385
Veterans' Disability Compensation and Housing Benefits Amendments of 1980.

H.R. 6308_____Public Law 96–386
Magnetic Fusion Energy Engineering Act of 1980.

S. 1442_____Public Law 96–387
An act to authorize the documentation of certain vessels as vessels of the United States, and for other purposes.

H.R. 8081_____Public Law 96–388
An act to establish the United States Holocaust Memorial Council.

ACTS APPROVED—Continued

Approved October 7—Continued

S. 2271_____Public Law 96–389
An act to amend the Bretton Woods Agreements Act to authorize consent to an increase in the United States quota in the International Monetary Fund, and for other purposes.

H.R. 4792_____ Public Law 96–390
An act to name a certain Federal building in Houston, Texas, the Bob Casey Federal Building—U.S. Courthouse.

H.R. 5410_____ Public Law 96–391
An act to amend title 5, United States Code, to require any Federal employee who elects at the time of retirement not to provide survivorship benefits for the employee's spouse to notify (or take all reasonable steps to notify) the spouse of that election.

H.R. 5732_____ Public Law 96–392
An act to designate the Federal Building located at 33 West Twohig, San Angelo, Texas, as the "O. C. Fisher Federal Building".

H.R. 6531_____ Public Law 96–393
An act to name a certain Federal building in Indianapolis, Indiana, the Minton-Capehart Federal Building.

H.R. 7414_____Public Law 96–394
An act to designate the building known as the Federal Building and United States Courthouse in Amarillo, Texas, as the "J. Marvin Jones Federal Building".

H.R. 7450_____Public Law 96–395
An act to designate the United States Post Office Federal Building in Waterbury, Connecticut, as the "John S. Monagan Federal Building".

H.R. 7782_____Public Law 96–396
An act to amend the District of Columbia Police and Firemen's Salary Act of 1958 to provide for the same adjustments in the basic compensation of officers and members of the United States Secret Service Uniformed Division as are given to Federal employees under the General Schedule.

H.R. 8202_____Public Law 96–397
An act to continue in effect any authority provided under the Department of Justice Appropriation Authorization Act, Fiscal Year 1980, for a certain period.

S. 1177_____Public Law 96–398
Mental Health Systems Act.

ACTS APPROVED—Continued

Approved October 8, 1980

S. 2719_____Public Law 96–399
Housing and Community Development Act of 1980.

Approved October 9, 1980

H.R. 7831_____ Public Law 96–400
Department of Transportation and Related Agencies Appropriation Act, 1981.

S. 2126_____ Public Law 96–401
An act relating to certain leases involving the Secretary of the Interior and the Northern Cheyenne Indian Reservation.

S. 91_____ Public Law 96–402
Uniformed Services Survivor Benefits Amendments of 1980.

H.R. 7670_____ Public Law 96–403
An act to amend title II of the Social Security Act to make necessary adjustments in the allocation of social security tax receipts between the Federal Old-Age and Survivors Insurance Trust Fund and the Federal Disability Insurance Trust Fund.

S. 341_____ Public Law 96–404
An act to authorize the Three Affiliated Tribes of the Fort Berthold Reservation to file in the Court of Claims any claims against the United States for damages for delay in payment for lands claimed to be taken in violation of the United States Constitution, and for other purposes.

S. 1795_____ Public Law 96–405
An act to authorize the Blackfeet and Gros Ventre Tribes to file in the Court of Claims any claims against the United States for damages for delay in payment for lands claimed to be taken in violation of the United States Constitution, and for other purposes.

S. 2398_____ Public Law 96–406
An act to extend the provisions of the General Exchange Act, as amended, to certain lands in order that they may become parts of the Umatilla and Wallowa National Forests, and for other purposes.

H.R. 3956_____ Public Law 96–407
An act granting the consent of the Congress to Hewson A. Ryan to accept the office and title of Honorary Consul of Honduras.

H.R. 7130_____ Public Law 96–408
An act to designate the building known as United States Court House and Federal Building in Syracuse, New York, as the "James M. Hanley Federal Building".

ACTS APPROVED—Continued

Approved October 9—Continued

H.R. 7309_____ Public Law 96–409
An act to designate the Federal building in Portland, Oregon the "Edith Green Federal Building".

H.R. 7544_____ Public Law 96–410
An act to designate the United States Federal Building in New Haven, Connecticut, as the "Robert N. Giaimo Federal Building".

H.R. 7588_____ Public Law 96–411
An act to redesignate the United States Post Office and Courthouse Building in Concord, New Hampshire, as the "James C. Cleveland Federal Building".

H.R. 7770_____ Public Law 96–412
An act to name the Environmental Research Center in Cincinnati, Ohio, the "Andrew W. Breidenbach Environmental Research Center".

H.R. 8161_____ Public Law 96–413
An act to designate the United States Federal Building in Pittsburgh, Pennsylvania, as the "William S. Moorhead Federal Building".

H.J. Res. 472_____ Public Law 96–414
A joint resolution designating October 19, 1981, as a "Day of National Observance of the Two Hundredth Anniversary of the Surrender of Lord Cornwallis to General George Washington at Yorktown, Virginia."

S. 2801_____ Public Law 96–415
An act to designate the Indian Health Facility in Ada, Oklahoma, the "Carl Albert Indian Health Facility".

H.J. Res. 560_____ Public Law 96–416
A joint resolution to proclaim March 19, 1981, as "National Agriculture Day".

H.R. 6538_____ Private Law 96–61
An act to authorize and direct the Secretary of the Interior to reinvest oil and gas lease New Mexico 33955.

Approved October 10, 1980

S. 1654_____ Public Law 96–417
Customs Courts Act of 1980.

H.R. 7301_____ Public Law 96–418
Military Construction Authorization Act, 1981.

S.J. Res. 201_____ Public Law 96–419
A joint resolution to provide for the designation of a week as "National Lupus Week".

H.R. 7919_____ Public Law 96–420
Maine Indian Claims Settlement Act of 1980.

ACTS APPROVED—Continued

Approved October 10—Continued

S.J. Res. 82_____ Public Law 96–421
A joint resolution to designate the week commencing with the third Monday in February of 1981 as "National Patriotism Week".

H.R. 7859_____ Public Law 96–422
Refugee Education Assistance Act of 1980.

S. 2730_____ Public Law 96–423
Federal Railroad Safety Authorization Act of 1980.

S. 3180_____ Public Law 96–424
An act to repeal a provision of the Refugee Education Assistance Act of 1980.

S. 2475_____ Public Law 96–425
Automobile Fuel Efficiency Act of 1980.

S. 3148_____ Public Law 96–426
An act to name the Federal Building located at 444 Southeast Quincy, Topeka, Kansas, the "Frank Carlson Federal Building".

H.R. 7666_____ Public Law 96–427
Federal Employees' Group Life Insurance Act of 1980.

H.R. 7218_____ Public Law 96–428
An act to establish the Martin Luther King, Junior, National Historic Site in the State of Georgia, and for other purposes.

S. 3044_____ Public Law 96–429
An act to designate the United States Federal Building in Hartford, Connecticut, as the "Abraham A. Ribicoff Federal Building".

H.R. 7434_____ Public Law 96–430
An act to provide for the establishment of the Boston African American National Historic Site in the Commonwealth of Massachusetts, and for other purposes.

H.R. 6065_____ Public Law 96–431
An act to amend title 5, United States Code, to provide that military leave be made available for Federal employees on a fiscal year rather than a calendar year basis, to allow certain unused leave to accumulate for subsequent use, and for other purposes.

H.R. 6331_____ Public Law 96–432
An act to amend the Act of July 31, 1946, as amended, relating to the United States Capitol Grounds, and for other purposes.

H.R. 7939_____ Public Law 96–433
An act to amend the Securities Investor Protection Act to increase the amount of protection available under such Act to customers of brokers and dealers, and to provide for the applicability of the Right to Financial Privacy Act of 1978 to the Securities and Exchange Commission.

ACTS APPROVED—Continued

Approved October 10—Continued

S. 1796_____ Public Law 96–434
An act to authorize the Assiniboine Tribe to file in the Court of Claims any claims against the United States for damages for delay in payment for lands claimed to be taken in violation of the United States Constitution, and for other purposes.

ACTS APPROVED—Continued

Approved October 10—Continued

H.R. 7411_____ Public Law 96–435
An act authorizing the Secretary of the Interior to accept the conveyance of the United First Parish Church in Quincy, Massachusetts, and authorizing the Secretary to administer the United First Parish Church as a national historic site, and for other purposes.

Cuban and Haitian Entrants

Executive Order 12246. October 10, 1980

By the authority vested in me as President of the United States of America by Section 501 of the Refugee Education Assistance Act of 1980 and Section 301 of Title 3 of the United States Code, and in order to provide for assistance to be made available relating to Cuban and Haitian entrants, it is hereby ordered as follows:

1–101. All the functions vested in the President by Section 501(c) of the Refugee Education Assistance Act of 1980, are hereby delegated to the Secretary of State.

1–102. In carrying out the functions delegated to him by this Order, the Secretary of State shall ensure that among the actions he takes or directs from time to time, he shall promptly take action which provides assistance for those Cuban and Haitian entrants located or to be located at Fort Indiantown Gap, Fort McCoy, Fort Chaffee, Fort Allen, existing processing and reception sites in Florida, and such other sites as he may designate.

JIMMY CARTER

The White House,
October 10, 1980.

[Filed with the Office of the Federal Register, 11:16 a.m., October 14, 1980]

NOTE: The Executive order was released on October 11.

National Lupus Week, 1980

Proclamation 4799. October 10, 1980

By the President of the United States of America

A Proclamation

Systemic lupus erythematosus (also known as lupus, or SLE) is a serious connective tissue disorder, affecting an estimated 500,000 Americans. Almost 90 percent of its victims are young women.

In the systemic form, lupus can affect almost any part of the body, often producing abnormalities in the kidney, heart, skin, joints, and other internal organs.

The outlook for victims of lupus has vastly improved in recent years. In 1955, the survival rate for lupus victims was only 50 percent four years after diagnosis. Now, more than 80 percent of lupus patients are alive 10 years after their disease has been identified. This increased survival is due to a greater awareness of the disease, better diagnostic methods, and development of more effective drug therapies. Nevertheless, an estimated 50,000 new cases are diagnosed each year, and much additional research is needed to pinpoint the underlying cause of this disease and to discover methods for preventing or halting its progression.

In the last few years, progress has been made toward better understanding of lupus. Public and privately-supported medical research and education mean that

2183

each year thousands of patients can look forward to improved treatment, and the opportunity to live happier and more productive lives. However, new research findings and new approaches for improved treatment and diagnosis are needed if we are ever to eliminate lupus as a cause of human suffering and to improve the quality of life in our society for its victims.

The Congress has, by Senate Joint Resolution 201, authorized and requested the President to designate the week of October 19 through October 25, 1980, as National Lupus Week.

Now, THEREFORE, I, JIMMY CARTER, President of the United States of America, do hereby proclaim the week of October 19 through October 25, 1980, as National Lupus Week. I invite the Governors of the States, the Commonwealth of Puerto Rico, and officials of other areas subject to the jurisdiction of the United States to issue similar proclamations.

I urge the people of the United States and educational, philanthropic, scientific, medical, and health care organizations and professions to provide the necessary assistance and resources to discover the cause and cure of systemic lupus erythematosus and the other rheumatic diseases and to alleviate the suffering of all persons struck by these disorders.

IN WITNESS WHEREOF, I have hereunto set my hand this tenth day of October, in the year of our Lord nineteen hundred and eighty, and of the Independence of the United States of America the two hundred and fifth.

JIMMY CARTER

[Filed with the Office of the Federal Register, 11:17 a.m., October 14, 1980]

NOTE: The proclamation was released on October 11.

Martin Luther King, Junior, National Historic Site

Statement on Signing H.R. 7218 Into Law. October 11, 1980

It is an honor for me to sign into law H.R. 7218, a bill to establish the Martin Luther King, Junior, National Historic Site and Preservation District in Atlanta, Georgia.

Dr. King's tragic death deprived our Nation of one of its greatest leaders. He had become a symbol for all the world of the power of the nonviolent struggle for human rights. The establishment of this unique National Historic Site will protect the places where Dr. King lived, worked, and worshiped and where he is buried, for the benefit, inspiration, and education of present and future generations. The Preservation District will also include the Martin Luther King, Jr. Center for Social Change, which is committed to carrying out the ideals and mission for which Dr. King lived.

Martin Luther King had a dream that all people would be free and equal under the law. His life was sacrificed for this cause, but his dream is still not a reality. It is my hope that, by preserving the physical environment in which Dr. King developed his concept of social justice, our people will come to understand more fully what we have accomplished and what remains to be done. May it be a perpetual reminder of Dr. King's great work and inspire people everywhere to strive for the realization of his dream of equal rights and equal opportunity for all.

NOTE: As enacted, H.R. 7218 is Public Law 96–428, approved October 10.

Maine Indian Claims Settlement Act of 1980

Statement on Signing H.R. 7919 Into Law.
October 11, 1980

I am pleased to sign into law H.R. 7919, the Maine Indian Claims Settlement Act of 1980.

In March of 1977, I appointed retired Georgia Supreme Court Justice William Gunter to review the land claims of the Indian tribes of Maine. Those claims, which were based on alleged violations of Federal law, had clouded the title of some two-thirds of the State of Maine, an area in which some 350,000 people reside. Justice Gunter recommended that a settlement of the claims be negotiated rather than litigated because of the length of time litigation would require and the hardship that an extended period of clouded land titles would impose on the people of Maine.

In line with Justice Gunter's recommendation, I directed that officials of my administration work with representatives of the tribes, the State of Maine, and the major landowners involved to negotiate a settlement of the claims. I am pleased that a reasonable compromise has been reached which reflects the unique circumstances involved and avoids an extensive and damaging period of litigation.

NOTE: As enacted, H.R. 7919 is Public Law 96–420, approved October 10.

Customs Court Act of 1980

Statement on Signing S. 1654 Into Law.
October 11, 1980

I have signed into law, S. 1654, the Customs Court Act of 1980.

This legislation, which contains many of the provisions proposed by the administration, creates a comprehensive system for judicial review of civil actions arising out of import transactions and Federal statutes affecting international trade. The bill enhances the importance and effectiveness of the new Court of International Trade, formerly the Customs Court. I am pleased to have signed this major judicial reform bill into law.

Unfortunately the bill retains a political affiliation requirement which stipulates that no more than five of the nine members of the Court of International Trade can be from the same political party. This provision is inappropriate as applied to the present Customs Court. The appointment of judges to a court created under Article III of the Constitution should be on the basis of merit, not political affiliation.

I urge that the 97th Congress pass legislation deleting this unfortunate requirement.

NOTE: As enacted, S. 1654 is Public Law 96–417, approved October 10.

Military Construction Authorization Act, 1981

Statement on Signing H.R. 7301 Into Law.
October 11, 1980

I am signing into law H.R. 7301, the Military Construction Authorization Act for 1981.

This act is important to increasing our Nation's security at home and abroad. It provides $5.5 billion for highly necessary facilities in 49 States, the District of

Columbia, Puerto Rico, and in 16 foreign countries, which support not only the military services and their reserve components but the defense agencies and the Military Family Housing program as well. These facilities will help us continue to achieve higher degrees of military readiness and mobilization capability. They will also improve the quality of life for many of our military personnel and their families.

The bill also provides support for three other essential elements of our national defense. One is our contribution to the NATO Infrastructure Program for continued upgrading of overall readiness in Europe. Another is the enhancement of our military position in Indian Ocean and Persian Gulf areas where critical United States interests may be threatened. The third is consideration for high priority national programs such as energy conservation and pollution abatement.

While the bill's primary purpose is to meet urgent military requirements, a side benefit to the economy of our country and to the American construction industry will be the creating of an estimated 100,000 to 150,000 direct jobs and, perhaps, an equal number of indirect jobs.

I also want to take this opportunity to express my gratitude to Chairmen Price and Stennis and Subcommittee Chairmen Hart and Nedzi for their dedicated work in securing the passage of this bill. And I want to particularly pay tribute to Mr. Nedzi, whose long and faithful service will be dearly missed when he retires from Congress following the completion of his current term.

NOTE: As enacted, H.R. 7301 is Public Law 96–418, approved October 10.

Automobile Fuel Efficiency Act of 1980

Statement on Signing S. 2475 Into Law. October 11, 1980

I have signed S. 2475, the Automobile Fuel Efficiency Act of 1980. This bill is another step in my administration's efforts to make Federal regulations more responsive to the needs of our Nation's automobile industry.

S. 2475 includes several necessary modifications to the corporate average fuel economy (CAFE) standards, all of which were requested by the administration. First, the bill allows low-volume automobile producers, those producing less than 10,000 cars annually, to request alternative CAFE standards for 2 years or more and exempts these producers from burdensome reporting requirements. This provision should ease the regulatory burden on small auto manufacturers, without having any consequential effect on our Nation's efforts to conserve energy.

Second, the bill provides additional flexibility in the CAFE standards for foreign manufacturers to encourage them to produce and assemble cars in this country. This provision is part of my effort to encourage foreign automobile companies to increase their investments in the United States.

Finally, the bill provides all manufacturers greater flexibility in achieving the fuel economy standards in any particular year. This provision will permit the automobile companies to meet the standards more easily without reducing our commitment to energy conservation.

The revitalization of our Nation's domestic automobile industry is essential to the health of our economy. In the past several months we have made progress toward this goal. My administration has modified existing regulations to save the auto industry more than $600 million in the years to come. As part of my economic renewal program, I have proposed a 40-percent increase in depreciation allowances to give the industry the tax incentives that it needs to retool. I also have proposed a refundable investment tax credit to help the domestic companies, which currently are not profitable, to invest in the future.

To help the communities and workers that currently are suffering from the downturn in the auto industry, I have proposed substantial financial help to the States, cities, and counties that are experiencing the highest unemployment. I also have proposed substantial additional benefits for workers in the automobile and related industries, by extending unemployment benefits for 13 additional weeks and extending trade adjustment assistance to workers in many supplier industries.

I have expressed concern to the Japanese about the level of Japanese imports, and I have stated quite clearly that the United States does not intend to abandon any portion of our share of the domestic auto market. I have also encouraged Japanese car companies to increase their investments in the United States and urged Japan to reduce the barriers to the sale of U.S. cars and parts in Japan. This bill will contribute to that effort.

In addition, the Administrator of the General Services Administration recently announced the fulfillment of a commitment I had made some time ago to accelerate the Federal Government's purchase of automobiles and trucks. The General Services Administrator also announced that for the first time we will be purchasing American-made light duty trucks that meet our fuel economy standards.

Finally, to ensure that government, business, and labor continue to work together to address the problems of this vital industry, I have established a tripartite Presidential Auto Industry Committee.

The steps that we have taken over the last 6 months lay the foundation for recovery in the automobile industry. There is no question that more remains to be done. I look forward to working with the Congress, business, and labor in the upcoming months to ensure swift enactment of the legislation that we need to ensure that the recovery in autos is strong and lasting.

NOTE: As enacted, S. 2475 is Public Law 96–425, approved October 10.

Federal Employees' Group Life Insurance Act of 1980

Statement on Signing H.R. 7666 Into Law. October 11, 1980

I am happy to sign into law H.R. 7666, the Federal Employees' Group Life Insurance Act of 1980. This legislation, which was proposed by the administration, will make some greatly needed improvements in the group life insurance program for Federal civilian employees.

The life insurance program for Federal employees has gone largely unchanged in the quarter century it has existed and in recent years has become less and less comparable to the insurance plans of other large employers. This has led many new employees to waive participation in the program, largely because younger employees can obtain better coverage per premium dollar elsewhere.

H.R. 7666, will make a number of changes to solve these problems. First, effective October 1, 1981, it will increase the amount of regular life insurance offered to employees under age 45, with no increase in the premium they pay. To offset this new expense, employees who retire after 1989 will be required to pay premiums until age 65 for the insurance which is currently provided at no cost to retirees. The bill will also permit retiring employees to puchase improved post-age-65 regular insurance coverage at their own expense. Finally, the bill will offer new optional insurance plans allowing employees to purchase additional life insurance at very reasonable group rates and also to purchase insurance to cover members of their families.

These program improvements have been carefully designed to provide greater protection for employees at a minimum cost to the Government. I commend the Congress, and Congresswoman Gladys Spellman in particular, for enacting this legislation, which is both fiscally responsible and responsive to the needs of Federal employees.

NOTE: As enacted, H.R. 7666 is Public Law 96–427, approved October 10.

honor the brilliant and determined individuals who won for the American press the freedom it enjoys in reporting and interpreting current events. We also rededicate ourselves to perpetuating, in a way that would make them proud, the great tradition they have passed on to us. And we applaud those members of our press who have consistently displayed the sensitivity, integrity, wisdom and accuracy which their profession demands.

As a nation we recognize the extent of our dependence on our fellow citizens who gather and report the news. And we are in awe of the grave responsibility they bear as they cover events that affect the lives of millions of Americans and the future of our country.

We believe as they do that the freedom they possess can protect the freedoms we cherish. And we look to them to exercise their freedom wisely, responsibly and with a daily awareness of the tremendous power they wield.

Rosalynn and I are proud to join with all Americans at this time in tribute to our nation's newspapers and to the dedicated men and women behind them.

JIMMY CARTER

National Newspaper Week, October 12–18, 1980

Message of the President.   October 11, 1980

A free and unmanaged press is one of the proudest symbols of our democratic government and one of its boldest champions. And, conversely, an open government is one of the staunchest protectors of the free press and of the people whose trust it holds.

During National Newspaper Week, we

Newspaper Carrier Day, October 18, 1980

Message of the President.   October 11, 1980

I urge all Americans to join me in this traditional salute to those who deliver newspapers in cities and towns across our country.

The carrier's job builds qualities of responsibility, integrity and good citizenship. It is a wonderful preparation for any future employment, and it often provides a useful base for later success in a chosen career.

I admire the dedication and energy of our nation's newspaper carriers, and I hope that their paper routes will continue to bring them rewarding experiences that will enrich their lives in years to come.

JIMMY CARTER

Mille Lacs Band of the Minnesota Chippewa Indians

Message to the Senate Returning S. 1464 Without Approval.   October 11, 1980

To the Senate of the United States:

I am returning without my approval S. 1464 "To direct the Secretary of the Interior to acquire certain lands for the benefits of the Mille Lacs Band of the Minnesota Chippewa Indians."

S. 1464 would require the Secretary of the Interior to acquire approximately 105 acres of land, in Mille Lacs County, Minnesota from a commercial land developer and subsequently hold such land in trust for the Mille Lacs Band. Under the terms mandated by S. 1464, the cost to the Federal government of acquiring this land could not be less than $670,000, and could be $910,000 or more.

I am disapproving S. 1464 because the Secretary of the Interior already possesses the authority to purchase an amount of land he determines appropriate for the benefit of the Mille Lacs Band, and because he and the tribe agree that the bill would require purchase of the land at a price the Secretary has heretofore determined excessive.

In order to obtain a swift resolution of the issues which prompted Congressional action on S. 1464, I am, however, instructing the Secretary of the Interior to con-

duct as expeditiously as possible a new appraisal of the 25 acres of land in question and to make a fair and reasonable offer based on that appraisal for purchase of those 25 acres.

JIMMY CARTER

The White House,
    October 11, 1980.

NOTE: The text of the message was released on October 12.

The Nation's Economy

Radio Address to the Nation.
October 12, 1980

This is President Jimmy Carter, speaking to you from the Oval Office in Washington. I want to talk to you today about our country's future, about the goals I've set for the decade of the 1980's, and how we can achieve these goals together.

Too often in political campaigns the focus is on the contest itself, debates about the debates, charges and countercharges among candidates, the endless speculation about who is ahead. Too often the meaning of the election, the real decision facing our country, is lost or forgotten. During the next 3 weeks, candidates owe the American people a clear vision of what we see for our country's future.

The choice before this country on November 4th is not just between me and Governor Reagan, it's not just between the Democratic Party and the Republican Party; it's a choice between two vastly different sets of beliefs. The meaning of that choice is not just in what we say, but in the consequences of our words, the consequences of what we believe, the consequences of what we will do. They will be more enduring than any campaign rhetoric. Those consequences will shape the whole philosophy of our society, our country's approach to social responsibility, to economic opportunity, to the quality of our environment, to protection of consumers, to older Americans, to the well-being of working men, to the well-being and the opportunities of working women. The choice will affect our security both at home and abroad.

So, today and on the next two Sundays I want to describe the consequences of the coming election. Next week I'll discuss the Nation's military security, America's role in the world, and our vital quest for peace. Today I will describe my vision, my hopes, and my plans for our country's economic future. And later this week I will present a more detailed and extensive economic statement.

As you know, we and other nations around the world have recently been shocked by OPEC oil prices, which more than doubled in just 12 months. But our country has been strong enough to withstand this blow. The economic outlook after this period of real difficulty has now brightened. We see the beginnings of recovery along with a reduction in inflation. The number of jobs is increasing. Unemployment is declining. Our policies are working. But to stay on the road to full recovery, we need to keep on attacking the roots of our problems—inflation, foreign oil dependence, slow productivity growth.

I'm especially concerned about the human impact of these problems—temporary unemployment, the uncertainty of rapid technological change, interest rates too high. I know that some people have questions about earning a good living, providing for a family. I know from personal experience how it felt when my three sons were small. Will I be able to care for my family, to give my children what they need, to provide for their future? These human questions are always on my mind. My heart goes out to families who are threatened or who suffer.

Some of our Nation's economic problems are deep-rooted, interrelated, and complex. Solving them cannot be simple. We must face the facts. If we try to stimulate the economy too fast, we may speed up inflation. High inflation triggers high interest rates, which choke off recovery. And we end up back where we started. That's why creating jobs and controlling inflation must go together. That's why I've fought so hard to prevent a massive tax cut this year in the heat of an election campaign, and why I support a targeted tax cut to be enacted next year, focused on the most urgent needs.

Inflation is caused by many forces, therefore we are attacking it on many fronts.

One is the Federal budget. By slowing the growth of Government spending and by avoiding imprudent tax cuts, we've reduced one source of inflationary pressure. We'll continue this budgetary restraint.

Deregulation is another front. We've now acted to free from unnecessary regulation some of our biggest industries—airlines, trucking, energy, banking, railroads—so that the American free enterprise system, with maximum competition, can give us better services with less inflation.

But most important of all, we have met head on our country's number one economic challenge, the primary cause of inflation as well as unemployment—excessive dependence on foreign oil. The dimensions of this challenge are staggering. Foreign oil costs our Nation $85 billion a year—$85 billion that could be spent on American industry, American products, American jobs.

No country, no matter how strong, can afford to send this kind of money abroad year after year without paying an enormous economic cost. The problem was neglected for too long. Now we have acted. From the very first days of my Presidency, I sought to alert the American people and the Congress to this problem. At first there was doubt and even ridicule, but I kept at it and you responded. We've rallied to meet the energy challenge, as we've met other serious problems in the past.

Until recently, most of us never even thought about where our gasoline came from—just from the local service station. We don't think that way any more. We've all come to realize that the service station is at one end of a very precarious supply line. The line is 12,000 miles long, and at the other end is one of the most unstable regions of the world—the Persian Gulf.

We've cut our foreign oil consumption by 20 percent in the last year alone, some 1½ million barrels a day. No other country has matched that record. That is extremely important to every American. The war between Iraq and Iran puts this achievement in perspective. Today the United States alone is saving almost half the amount of oil exported before the war by both those countries combined. We've made ourselves and our allies that much less vulnerable to international blackmail or to a break in the world's oil lifeline.

We're also building up our own ability to produce energy. This year in the United States, we will drill more oil and gas wells than ever before. We've won approval of the most sweeping program in history to develop solar power, synthetic fuels, to conserve energy, and to create other new energy sources.

That program is being financed in large part by a most important and equitable revenue program—the windfall profits tax on the oil companies. This windfall profits tax finally passed this year, after a long and difficult political struggle. It will permit us to take some of the billions of dollars we spend on oil and invest them in creating new American energy sources and new American jobs.

Also, we are making rapid strides in coal production. This year we will produce more coal than ever before in history. With better transportation and seaport facilities, we can triple this production. As the major world energy source, I want to see OPEC oil replaced with American coal.

We have come a long way in a very short time—in conservation, in production, and in public understanding. Our attack on energy can now serve as a historic first step in a drive to strengthen the other economic foundations of our country.

American workers are still the most productive in the world, because we've had the best machinery and equipment, the best plants and factories. But now in some industries that equipment is growing older, and countries that have newer factories are outproducing us. We cannot ask our workers to compete with out-of-date equipment, any more than we would ask our soldiers to fight with obsolete weapons. America will need to spend billions of dollars building new plants and refurbishing old ones.

Recently I outlined a broad-ranging program to renew our economic momentum. This program will have some immediate benefits. It will add a half-million additional new jobs during the coming year and a million new jobs by the end of 1982. It will also meet our long-term challenges by encouraging greater investment, higher productivity, and reduced inflation. Half of the tax reductions under this program will go for encouraging investment and creating new jobs rather than for encouraging consumption and more inflation. What I'm proposing is the next major step in building a brighter economic future.

Our efforts to meet the energy challenge, our program to modernize American industry can set the stage for an American economic renaissance to propel us past our current economic obstacles and build the new foundations for economic greatness. Let me describe that future.

It will be a time of enhanced productivity, with modern plants and equipment to keep American industry at the cutting edge of international progress.

I see us turning American coal and shale and American farm products into American fuel for American cars and trucks, and the light of the Sun into heat and electricity for American homes. And I see those buildings and vehicles that will house us and move us in comfort, using a lot less energy.

I see modern railbeds and ports making American coal into a powerful rival of OPEC oil, and new industries that bring the convenience of modern communications and futuristic computer technology into millions of American homes and offices and factories.

I see an America of full employment, of people working to modernize existing American industry and to create whole new American industries.

It will be a time of purer air, cleaner water, and freedom from the threat of toxic wastes.

This is not just a dream. It's a practical vision that we can bring to life by taking the right actions today, by investing in our future. This is part of the American character. Our families invest in homes, in education. We parents invest not just in our own future but in the future of our children.

I see this kind of progress already in the exciting revitalization of our Nation's urban centers. I've seen it in our ability to produce 8½ million new jobs in just 3 years, a record never before achieved in any President's term, in times of either war or peace.

I've seen it in Michigan, where modern, safe, durable, and fuel-efficient cars roll off American production lines, cars that can now compete with any in the world. I've seen it in American steel production, that's beginning to use the most advanced level of technology on Earth. I've seen this progress in our agricultural heartland, with outstanding production setting world export records every year that I've served in this office.

There can now be an exciting era of increased prosperity and fruitfulness of our land, built upon the new conservation ethic and technological developments using biomass from growing crops to help meet our energy needs. And I've seen the beginnings of progress in our synthetic fuels production and in our new commitment to basic research and to scientific and technological progress in a broad range of American industries.

I'm asking our entire country to drive these programs forward. If we are to succeed, it cannot be because of government alone or business alone or labor alone. It must be because government, business, labor, and the public work together to make this future a certainty for our country. We've seen this partnership at work already in our efforts to assist the automobile industry and the steel industry. It will be further strengthened by the new Economic Revitalization Board.

This kind of partnership is at the very heart of America. Almost 40 years ago, in the midst of World War II, President Franklin D. Roosevelt put it this way: "The most significant fact in American history is the ability of the American people to face a tough situation and to take orderly and united action in their own behalf—and in behalf of the things in which they believe." That was true in 1942. It's true today. And I'm determined that it will be true in the future.

And I also know that we will achieve this future only if we make the conscious decision to invest in it and plan for it *now*. A good life in the 1980's and in the 21st century can only be built on American ingenuity, American dedication, American values.

The economic challenges which we and the world must face are difficult and complex, extraordinarily complex. But if the proud history of this country teaches us anything, it's this: We can solve even the most difficult and complex problems if we recognize them for what they are and put our minds and our hearts to work on the solutions. History tells us something else, something that illustrates the most basic and important choice before us in 1980: When nations fail to address their challenges realistically and look for simplistic solutions to their problems, then they run into trouble.

This is a choice that affects our economy, but it is also a choice that goes to the very heart of our national spirit:

Are we mature enough and strong enough to accept the realities of the 1980's and to take the difficult but rewarding steps that are needed, or will we close our eyes and dream of earlier times, simpler problems, and painless solutions?

I have faith in America. I have faith in Americans. We will face up to these challenges. We will work together. We will build for the future, a future of greatness for the country that we love.

Thank you very much.

NOTE: The President spoke at 12:10 p.m. from the Oval Office at the White House. The address was broadcast live on the Mutual Broadcasting System.

New York, New York

Remarks at a Meeting With Civic and Community Leaders.   October 13, 1980

THE PRESIDENT. *Rabbi Bokser—[shouts from audience]—Rabbi Bokser, Senator Jackson, Senator Moynihan—[shouts from audience]*——

AUDIENCE [*chanting*]. We want Jimmy!

THE PRESIDENT. Fine. Thank you.

As I was saying, Rabbi Bokser, Senator Jackson—[shouts from audience]— Senator Moynihan, President Don Manes— [shouts from audience]——

SPEAKER. It's never unanimous, Mr. President.

THE PRESIDENT. I know.

Would you like to hear what I've got to say?

AUDIENCE. Yes!

THE PRESIDENT. Good. We don't expect you to be unanimous.

——*members of the Forest Hills Jewish Community Center which marks this year your 50th year of service to the Borough of Queens and the people who look to you for leadership throughout this Nation:*

I'm proud to have the support and the counsel of Senator Scoop Jackson. He is a tremendously effective fighter for a strong defense, for American energy security, for help to New York City and to other great cities, for the cause of Soviet Jewry, and for a strong and secure Israel. And I might say that I share with some of you the belief that Scoop Jackson would be or would have been a great President.

You might want to know that at the Democratic Convention in Miami in 1972 the person who nominated Senator Scoop Jackson for President of the United States was Governor Jimmy Carter.

I want to express my thanks, too, for the members of the New York congressional delegation who are here this morning, Ben Rosenthal, Congressman Addabbo, Congressman Ferraro, who's helping me all over the country, Congressman Biaggi, and Chairman Baranello, who's come here representing the Democrats of this entire State.

This is a session which I consider to be very important. It's crucial to our Nation; it's crucial for the leaders of the rest of the world to know where a President of the United States stands on current and major issues. I want the people of Forest Hills and of Queens to know exactly where I stand on these crucial issues. There has been misunderstanding, which is legitimate. There has also been misrepresentation, which is not legitimate.

For instance, I saw a political advertisement in one of the community papers. It was placed by an independent committee supporting my Republican opponent and completely misrepresented the policy—past, present, and future—of the United States of America and my administration toward the PLO. Let there be no doubt where I stand. The United States opposes and I oppose any PLO state.

The United States of America will never recognize nor negotiate with the PLO as long as it refuses to recognize Israel's right to exist and refuses to accept U.N. Resolution 242. The United States does not deal with organizations which attempt to accomplish their objectives by means of terrorism. Terrorism is a crime against decency and humanity, whether it occurs on the streets of Paris or on the streets of Jerusalem, whether those responsible in Paris are neo-Nazis or in Jerusalem members of the PLO.

The recent acts of violence in Paris and other French cities remind us that after so many centuries, in so many countries, anti-Semitism has still not been eradicated. At the next summit meeting of the industrial democracies, among our major allies, we will discuss collectively what can be done to counter such terrorist acts wherever they might occur throughout the world.

The world must never forget the lessons of the Holocaust. That is exactly the reason which after all these years I established the Holocaust Commission to plan a memorial in our country, both to look at and to listen to as a constant memory for the victims of Nazi terror. That's also why after 40 years of Government inaction I set up a special unit in the Department of Justice to root out Nazi war criminals who may be in hiding in the United States. The Congress has appropriated $2.8 million especially for this task.

Senator Moynihan, Scoop Jackson, and I also share a deep concern about the freedom of Soviet Jews to emigrate. The year before I became President, Jewish emigration from the Soviet Union was about 14,000. Last year it was up to 50,000, the highest level in more than 10 years. This year's lower rate in the wake of the Soviet invasion of Afghanistan is of great concern. We will not rest until every Soviet Jew is free to emigrate. This will be an important item on the agenda of the Madrid conference. The Soviets have an obligation to honor their Helsinki commitment.

Let's be absolutely frank with each other, without mincing words. I want to answer directly and personally a question that I know has been raised by some in our country who deeply care about Israel: "What about after the election? The record so far is very good," they say, "but isn't there a danger that President Carter might reverse United States policy and turn his back on Israel sometime in the future?" My answer is: Never.

I want each of you, even including the demonstrators, to go back to the people in your communities and neighborhoods and tell them this: The President will never turn his back on Israel. I never have and I never will. This President will never do as the previous administration has done, and I quote, "reassess America's relationship with Israel." This President never has and I never will. And this President will never use economic and military aid to Israel as a lever against Israel, not in the last 4 years, not now, and not in the next 4 years.

AUDIENCE [*chanting*]. We want Jimmy!

THE PRESIDENT. You've got me. Thank you, you've got me.

My own belief is that even in a nation where freedom of speech is important, it's also important for interested citizens like you to be able to hear from the President of the United States the policy of our Government towards Israel.

These policies have been demonstrated during the last 4 years. These policies are firmly embedded in the consciousness and commitment of myself as a human being, of myself as a President, and in the consciousness of the people of America. And these policies will not change—and you can depend on that.

Scoop Jackson knows that. That's why he came here on his own volition all the way from Seattle, Washington, to be with us this morning. Immediately after this meeting, he has to fly back to his own home State of Washington. He knows and I know that the United States has a moral commitment to Israel, and also a strategic commitment to Israel.

General David Jones, Chairman of the Joint Chiefs of Staff of our country, and Robert Komer, Under Secretary of Defense for Planning, recently went to Israel to improve our strategic relationship with Israel's defense planners and top leaders.

I sent them there to continue laying the foundations for our mutual defense requirements for the next decade. As a strong democracy in a troubled part of the world, Israel is a major strategic asset. A strong secure Israel is not just in Israel's interest; it's in the interest of the United States and in the interest of the entire free world.

On Jerusalem, let me repeat the policy of the United States. We believe in an undivided Jerusalem. We believe in a Jerusalem with free access for all faiths to the holy places. We believe that the future of Jerusalem can only be decided through negotiations with the concurrence and with the agreement of Israel—[*shouts from audience*]——

AUDIENCE [*chanting*]. We want Jimmy!

THE PRESIDENT. Thank you very much. That's fine.

I think it might be important for this group to hear the fact that the future of Israel and the future of Jerusalem can only be decided with the strong support of the United States for the principles and the ideals and commitments which we share and that any future of Jerusalem can only be decided through negotiations with the concurrence and the agreement of Israel.

As I told the International Ladies Garment Workers Union 2 weeks ago, we will oppose any effort to reject Israel's credentials at the United Nations General Assembly. If it did so, that would raise the gravest doubts about the future of the General Assembly itself and further participation of the United States and other nations in the deliberations of that body. If the matter should ever come to the Security Council, of course, we would veto it—[*shouts from audience*].

AUDIENCE [*chanting*]. We want Jimmy!

THE PRESIDENT. That's good. You've got me. Thank you very much.

At his cabinet meeting last week Prime Minister Begin praised the United States for protecting Israeli membership and legal status in such international forums as the General Assembly, UNESCO, General Convention at Belgrade, and the International Tourist Organization. And, as you know, we have worked hard to prevent the injection of PLO politics into the International Monetary Fund. Israel can count on that kind of backing from us now and always.

Obviously, our Government and the Government of Israel are not always going to agree on everything. We do not agree on everything with any of our friends and allies. But in the next 4 years our country is going to continue to support Israel and to work with Israel not just as a mediator but as a partner.

AUDIENCE [*chanting*]. Four more years!

THE PRESIDENT. Thank you very much.

We are going—this is very important— we are going to persevere in the Camp David process, which has already brought the peace treaty between Israel and Egypt, the first peace ever between Israel and one of her neighbors. This is a treaty between Israel and her most powerful Arab nation [neighbor].[1] There are now open borders between the two countries. They have now exchanged ambassadors, as you well know, full diplomatic relationships, regular airline flights between the major cities of Egypt and the major cities of Israel. Tourists regularly visit each other in those neighboring countries, and negotiations are now continuing to perpetuate permanent peace and secure borders by Israel and between her and her neighbors.

Tomorrow, Sol Linowitz, the American Ambassador and negotiator, will resume negotiations with the top officials of Israel

---

[1] White House correction.

and Egypt to build a broader peace. These negotiations will commence in Washington.

The choice in this election is not a matter of personalities or intentions, it's a matter of consequences—the consequences for the future of policies our Government will follow for the next 4 years. The choice could not be more critical nor more clear.

On one side is a Republican candidate who said a few months ago, and I quote, "Urban aid programs are one of the biggest phonies that we have in this system." On the other side is a Democratic administration that has pushed through the first comprehensive national urban policy in our history.

On one side is a Republican candidate who wants to put an end to Federal aid for mass transit. That proposal would mean higher local taxes, more pollution, higher transit fares, and more dependence on foreign oil, for New York, to Los Angeles, from Portland to Atlanta. On the other side is a Democratic candidate who is committed to decreasing the burden on local taxpayers, to continuing full support for public transportation, decreasing our dependence on foreign oil, and making our cities a better place in which to live.

AUDIENCE [*chanting*]. Four more years!

THE PRESIDENT. Thank you very much.

On one side is a Republican candidate who prayed morning and night, according to his own words, that the Federal Government would never come to the aid of New York City. On the other side is a Democratic administration that worked with the people of this, the greatest city in the world, to see to it that New York was saved. And we still have a lot more to do together for this city and its people. Now, I'm not saying that the Lord does not listen to the prayers of people who pray against New York. [*Laughter*] I

just think the people of New York out-
prayed him, and all of us outworked him.

On one side of the choice is a Republican candidate who last week proposed
that we play the nuclear arms race card.
On the other side there's a Democratic administration that is committed to mutual
and balanced controls and future substantive reductions in the terrible weapons of
nuclear annihilation.

On one side is a Republican candidate
who, at a time of growing concern about
the possibility that such nations as Iraq
might develop nuclear weapons, says that
nuclear proliferation is, and I quote him,
"None of our business." On the other side
is a Democratic administration that believes that halting the spread of nuclear
weapons is the business not only of the
United States Government but of every
government and every human being.

On one side is the Republican candidate who summed up his energy program
this way: "What needs to be done is for
the Government to repeal the energy legislation and then turn the industry loose."
On the other side is a Democratic administration that fought successfully for the
windfall profits tax and for a massive new
energy program that has already helped
to reduce our oil imports by one-third
compared to this time last year. Every
drop of oil that we do not have to buy
from OPEC increases our security and
that of our friends, including Israel. We
must not allow our progress on energy to
be reversed, and we must not let this country become subservient to nor excessively
dependent upon nor vulnerable to blackmail from those who might want to use
oil as a weapon against us if we don't build
up our energy security.

On one side is a Republican candidate
who launched his political career as a
spokesman for the anti-Medicare lobby,
and who now says, and I quote, "I am

firmly opposed to national health insurance." On the other side is a Democratic
administration that's committed not only
to a national health plan but also to the
integrity of great programs of social betterment this country has adopted under
Democratic Presidents ever since Franklin D. Roosevelt.

On one side is a candidate whose party
platform promises ideological loyalty tests
for prospective judges, including members of the United States Supreme Court.
On the other side is a Democratic administration pledged to the kind of independent, qualified judiciary the founders of
our Nation envisioned.

On one side is a Republican candidate
who has turned his back on 40 years of his
own party's support for the equal rights
amendment. On the other side is a Democratic President who has pledged to fight
until the rights of women, like the rights
of men, are inscribed in the Constitution
of the United States of America.

On issue after issue—and I could go
on—the choice is clear, and the stakes for
our country are very high. This is a tough
race. The polls say we may be behind.
The Republicans are outspending us by
tens of millions of dollars. Fritz Mondale
and I are going to need the help of every
person in this room and a lot more besides. New York City and the Borough
of Queens are very important in this effort. Your influence can go throughout
the United States. For the sake of this
city, and for the sake of everything we've
done together in the past, for the sake of
everything we will do together in the future, let's let our message get across to
every New Yorker and to every American.

Just one more comment and one serious
reminder. We have just a short time to
go, 3 weeks and 1 day. So, let's every one
of us buckle down together and get to

work for the future of our own Nation, for the future of Israel, for the peace of our country, for the peace and security of Israel, for the stability of the entire world, for the control of the spread of nuclear weapons, and for a bright future of peace and brotherhood and sisterhood together.

Let's win a victory for the whole Democratic ticket in New York. And most important of all, for the beliefs and convictions and ideals we all share, on November 4 let's have a tremendous victory for the entire Democratic ticket in New York and around the country.

Thank you.

NOTE: The President spoke at 10:45 a.m. in the Forest Hills Jewish Community Center ballroom.

New York, New York

Remarks on Proclaiming Italian-American Heritage Week.   October 13, 1980

Distinguished Members of the United States Congress, Mr. Mayor, leaders of New York State and New York City and the surrounding areas, all of the great Americans of Italian descent and all of the rest of us who join you today:

If there's one thing I love, it's a good parade, and I believe this will be one of the greatest and best ones ever seen in our country. And I might say there's another parade that I like very much, a very favorite of mine. It comes ever 4 years in January. And I'm planning on leading that one, even though Luciano Pavarotti leads this one.

Four hundred and eighty-eight years after Columbus came, you and I, all of us are still discovering America, the greatness of this country, and the potential that we have to make it even greater.

Four hundred and eighty-eight years after the first Italian landed on the shores of America, Italian Americans are continuing that great tradition—the tradition of Enrico Caruso, Mother Cabrini, Enrico Fermi, Fiorello LaGuardia, and Luciano Pavarotti, who will lead the parade today. It is a tradition, as you know, which means a lot to all Americans, a tradition strong on family, a tradition strong on patriotism, a tradition strong on the dignity of work and the importance of education and religion and the power of love.

Our Nation's character is drawn from the diversity of our people, joined together in our separate identities in the greatest miracle of government ever known, in this magnificent amalgam called America.

Just as an Italian was the first to discover the new world, an Italian was the first to give it its name. And while this day is meant to honor Columbus, it's also meant to honor all the generations of Italians who have followed him to this great land, and to show our gratitude for all that you and they have done. As President of our great country, on behalf of more than 220 million Americans, I want to tell you how proud we are of Italian Americans, what you've meant to our Nation.

Happy Columbus Day, a greater future for us all.

Thank you very much.

And now I would like to sign a proclamation, in accordance with the law passed by the United States Congress.

[*At this point, the President read the text of and signed the proclamation.*]

Thank you very much.

NOTE: The President spoke at 11:55 a.m. on the steps of the New York Public Library. Following the ceremony, the President joined other officials in leading the Columbus Day parade up Fifth Avenue.

As enacted, H.J. Res. 568 is Public Law 96–443, approved October 13.

Italian-American Heritage Week, 1980

Proclamation 4800.   October 13, 1980

By the President of the United States of America

A Proclamation

Columbus Day is a symbol of the debt our Nation owes to Italian-Americans.

During the past four hundred years, millions of Italians have become Italian-Americans. Many of them arrived in this country without money or property or friends. They had only the hope of opportunity and the strength of their character. They took advantage of opportunities which America offered and the result has been an extraordinary contribution to every facet of American life.

In recognition of the many contributions of Italian-Americans to our country, the Congress, by House Joint Resolution 568, has requested the President to designate the week of October 12 through October 19, 1980, as Italian-American Heritage Week.

Now, THEREFORE, I, JIMMY CARTER, President of the United States of America, do hereby designate the week of October 12 through October 19, 1980, as Italian-American Heritage Week. I call upon the people of the United States, State and local agencies, and interested organizations to observe that week with appropriate ceremonies, activities, and programs.

IN WITNESS WHEREOF, I have hereunto set my hand this thirteenth day of October, in the year of our Lord nineteen hundred and eighty, and of the Independence of the United States of America the two hundred and fifth.

JIMMY CARTER

[Filed with the Office of the Federal Register, 11:18 a.m., October 14, 1980]

West Frankfort, Illinois

Remarks to Miners and Employees of Old Ben Coal Mine No. 25.   October 13, 1980

President Evans, Congressman Paul Simon, President Sam Church, also distinguished members of mine who are friends who've helped me understand better the opportunities and the challenges of the coal industry:

I'm particularly glad to have with us today Congressman Ken Gray, who, working with the UMW, is trying to establish the National Coal Mining Museum.

I just came through West Frankfort, stopped to shake hands with several hundred people along the streets, and remembered the Christmas of 1951, when the whole world was shocked to hear about the death of 120 brave coal miners. That is a tragedy which, I believe, is the worst of any mining disaster in the United States. And it reminds me, as President of our great country, of the great contribution that you make in providing not only for your needs and your families' needs but also the responsibilities of the operators and the Government to make sure that your working conditions are safe and healthy.

My voice today will go not just to this group but, through television, radio, and through the news media, throughout our country and throughout the world, and I particularly want the world to know what I have seen here this afternoon in the brief time that I've had a chance to visit with you.

The last time there was a crisis in the Persian Gulf, during the Iranian revolution, the world oil supplies were cut by about 4 million barrels per day. We had long gas lines and fears of worse, as you know. Today, as the war between Iran and Iraq continues, again oil supplies throughout the world have been cut roughly 4 million barrels per day, about the same.

2199

But this time our country has been ready. We are ahead of that crisis. And you've not seen any lines, and you've not seen the world brought to its knees by a temporary shortage of oil.

For the first time in a century, in history, America now has a national energy policy. It's working, and we're improving our energy security every day. We are showing that this country can produce more and discover more and conserve more energy and that we can use American resources, American knowledge, and American jobs to do it. Nothing illustrates this better than your industry—coal. America indeed is the Saudi Arabia of coal, and my goal as President of the United States is to see on the world energy markets Arab oil replaced with Illinois coal.

When I was Governor of Georgia a number of years ago, we made a basic decision, then and before, that our electric power would stick with coal as a major energy resource and not shift to oil and to natural gas. As you know, these two mines connected here where we're standing were originated in their concept basically because of orders from Georgia Power Company. So, I have a special deal with you—right?—as a Georgian, good customer, and also as President.

I'm proud that we've been able in my administration, with the help of people like Paul Simon, to do more for the coal industry than any other in the history of our country.

Domestic coal production will hit a record high this year. We will produce more coal in 1980 than has ever before been produced in the United States of America, exceeding 800 million tons for the first time. Before this year, you might be interested in knowing, we had never before been able to produce 17 million tons of American coal in any one week. This year we've had 15 weeks in which

we've gone over 17 million tons per week. This is the first year in our history in which more than 50 percent of all our Nation's electricity has been produced from coal. Our exports of coal have hit an alltime high.

And we're just now ready to take a giant step, which we've not yet taken, that will be another tremendous boost for the coal industry, and that is our Synthetic Fuels Corporation. It will create a massive program for producing liquid and gaseous fuels from coal. We will provide, out of the windfall profits tax on the excess profits of oil companies, $88 billion in the next 10 years. About 75 percent of that will go as loans, loan guarantees, price and market guarantees to the private sector to build synthetic fuel plants using coal to get oil and gas from your coal, which will stimulate the demand for as much as 300 million tons of coal by the end of this century and 150 to 200 million tons of coal during the 1980's.

Over the past several weeks, we've signed historic agreements to finance and to guarantee the construction of synthetic facilities, including the SRC–1 in Kentucky, the SRC–2 in West Virginia, and the Great Plains Gasification plant in North Dakota. This year alone, getting ready to do much more in the future, we'll have over $1 billion spent on research and development on better ways to use coal. These demonstration plants, soon to be joined, as you well know, by others, will be among the largest and the best advanced facilities of their type in the entire world and will increase demand for coal by several million tons annually in just a few short years.

We're also mining and using coal more safely. We're finding solutions to environmental problems. We cannot afford to waste our natural resources. The American people have to accept coal as both a clean fuel and a safe fuel if we are ever to achieve our goals for energy security and for vastly greater coal use.

I'd like to give you a warning while I stand here, one very important. Do not let anyone convince you that the best way to produce and use more American coal is to eliminate air quality standards and water quality standards. That's the best way to turn the American people and the rest of the world against the use of coal.

What Sam and I have done together, as your president in both cases, is to try to make sure that all these projected increases in the use of coal are built on a quality environment, because if the American people ever are believing that the use of coal will destroy the quality of air and water, then they will turn against the use of coal. This is not necessary to do that, because we can have pure air, we can have clean water, and meet all these goals that I've just described to you for the rapid increase in the use of coal. With improved railroads, improved highways, improved loading facilities at our ports on the east and west coast and the Gulf area, there's no doubt in my mind that we can triple the production of American coal in the next 15 years.

I know that you're concerned sometimes because you hear false and misleading statements about the economic impact of the Clean Air Act. So, I have directed Doug Costle, who heads up EPA, to include a careful analysis of job impact with each proposal for any amendments that might come up when that Clean Air Act is renegotiated and repassed by the Congress next year. I will not propose any amendment to the Clean Air Act without full consideration of its effect on American jobs.

The Department of Interior has shown that the coal leasing program can proceed without compromising valuable public lands. The Office of Surface Mining has shown that sound management and reclamation practices can coexist with record production levels. The important goals of a growing and productive economy with jobs for all Americans and a healthy environment for all Americans can be served by careful study, full understanding of the complexities, and close consultation. Those who would dismiss lightly or deny the validity of either concern are simply wrong.

I might add here that since I've been in office, the last 2 years, with the help of Sam Church and the producers of coal, we've got a new era of harmony and understanding and consultation and cooperation between the operators and the coal miners. In the past about the only time when there was any conversation between the miners and the owners was when a contract was being renegotiated. Now there's a new spirit of protecting your interests on health, safety, working conditions, and waste levels, but at the same time a recognition that a steady supply of coal, dependable supply of coal is the way we build up customers in this country and overseas.

Just as we can no longer afford to waste energy, we can no longer afford to add untreated wastes to the environment. Just as we must conserve energy for ourselves and for our children and grandchildren, so we must conserve the environment. And we can do both, we will do both, at the same time.

A balance has also been struck, as I've said earlier, between coal management and labor. I believe that with my own commission, which I established to give me advice on what to do about coal, working with the Members of Congress from coal mining areas, with representatives of the UMW, and also with representatives of those who own and operate coal miles, we've reached a new level of cooperation unparalleled in recent history.

I believe that you recognize that coal production is not only good for you and your families, with a sustained income and a healthy life, but also to the economic and the national security of the United States. I've been working to increase coal production for 4 years, and I do not intend to quit until it's at a maximum, until your mines are all producing and America's miners are all working. And I'd appreciate it if you'd help me keep my job for 4 more years, too.

Thank you very much. God bless you all.

I might add one other thing that I forgot to say because it wasn't on my notes, and that is that later on this month we will have a conference at the White House, between the people that run the railroads, the people that operate the coal loading facilities in our port cities like Norfolk and Philadelphia and Baltimore and others, plus foreign buyers from France and Belgium, from Japan, plus UMW officials, of course, including Sam Church, and owners of the coal mines, to make sure that we plan for the long-range contracts for the delivery of American coal overseas. We are expanding that export opportunity as rapidly as possible, and I believe this bodes well for you and for the best interests of our country.

Thank you again for letting me add that postscript. God bless you.

NOTE: The President spoke at 4:36 p.m. outside the mine company's headquarters. Prior to his remarks, he was given a tour of Old Ben Coal Mine No. 25.

Marion, Illinois

*Remarks to Carter/Mondale Supporters.
October 13, 1980*

THE PRESIDENT. *Congressman Simon, Congressman Evans, others leaders of one of the finest political parties in the world:*

I want to ask you one question before we start. How many of you believe that in 3 weeks and 1 day we're going to whip the Republicans from top to—[*cheers*].

I may be mistaken, but I don't think I am. Throughout this country in the last few days, I've seen a renewed interest in the political campaign for President, the reelection of Democratic Congressmen and State officials throughout this country. It's extremely important what happens on November the 4th. I'll do all I can. Fritz Mondale, Rosalynn, my Cabinet, the Democratic candidates for Congress, for United States Senate, Governor, will do all we can. But as you know, the results of the election has always depended on people like you.

How many of you were delegates for me? Would you raise your hand? I'd just like to thank you personally. Stand up, if you don't mind. Thank you. Now, that's a good looking bunch of folks, don't you think? [*Laughter*]

I want to say just a couple of things, then I'd like to spend as much time as I can shaking hands, because I want to thank you personally.

I've just come from one of the newest and finest and most productive coal mines in this Nation and in the world. I discovered, when I began to study about what I would see, that both the new mines that I've just visited were designed primarily to provide coal for the Georgia Power Company. So, I feel a close relationship already to the folks of this area. [*Laughter*] And I've already made a speech out at the coal mine to the workers, who've come up from the bottom, from the shaft, to talk to me and to meet with me.

But in this brief time together, I'd like to point out to you that not only does Illinois have the greatest reserve of coal of any State in this Nation but you also, as you know, are number one in the production of corn, number one in the production of soybeans, number two in the production of swine, number one in agricultural exports. My background is a farmer. All of my people have lived in this country for the last two or three hundred years, my family, have been farmers. And when I fly over your beautiful land and see what's happening here in Illinois, I'm doubly proud of what you have to contribute to the well-being of your own families in this country but also to the security of our Nation.

A lot of people are concerned because the OPEC oil companies, the Arab oil nations have 6 percent of the world's energy reserves. This country alone has 24 percent, and ours are in a breadth of different kinds of energy resources. But the most valuable resource we have of all is the land that God gave us.

We've got a good sound agricultural program. And during my own administration, so far, we've had the highest gross income for farmers; the highest net income for farmers; the highest level of exports in 1977, set world records; 1978, we set new records; 1979, we set additional new world records; and this year we'll export $8 billion more American agricultural products than we did even last year.

We interrupted some of the sales of grain to the Soviet Union, but we made sure that we didn't do what the Republicans did when they imposed agricultural embargoes to force down the prices. We imposed grain sale restrictions to protect the security of our Nation and the peace

of the world. In the process, we committed ourselves not only to find alternative customers for American grain but to hold up the prices. And if you compare agricultural prices now with what they were in the early part of January, you'll see that we've done very well—sometimes a little slow getting started, I admit that.

But in the process, we have now opened up tremendous new permanent buyers for American grain and American agricultural products. This year we will sell to Mexico 10 million tons of American grain. Exports to Mexico in total this year will be three times as great as they were just 4 years ago. And we're now negotiating what we hope will be an eight- or a nine-million-ton-per-year grain sale to the People's Republic of China. This is a tremendous opportunity for us, to have permanent customers, high quality customers for American grain.

I'm very proud of what we have done, but I'm especially proud of the people of Illinois. It means a lot to me to have your support on November the 4th. And if we work together, we Democrats, we'll take the treasures that God's given this Nation, we'll stay good stewards of it, we won't waste the quality of our land, we won't waste the natural resources with which God's blessed us. We'll have a better life for ourselves. We'll rebuild the industrial complex of America to keep American workers the most productive on Earth, which they are now, with new tools, new factories, based upon a new energy policy, a new agricultural policy that'll be stable, predictable, and also profitable for us all.

As we have a better life for ourselves, taking advantage of the blessings we've been given, we'll also prepare for a nation with greater security, because we've been living now at the end of a 12,000-mile pipeline half-way around the world to one of the most troubled areas on Earth. With the new energy policy, we have already cut back oil imports from overseas by over 20 percent just compared to this time last year—over 1½ million barrels of oil a day less that we buy from overseas. That's something you've done; that's something you've done.

And I want to see Saudi Arabian oil replaced as a treasure—it already has been, people don't know it—with American soil, and I want to make sure that in the future, as a source for energy for the rest of the world, that we replace OPEC oil with Illinois coal. That's my goal. We'll do it together.

Thank you very much.

Are you all going to help me?

AUDIENCE. Yes!

THE PRESIDENT. Right on.

Well, let me say one other thing in closing, and I want to go down and shake hands.

AUDIENCE [*chanting*]. Four more years!

THE PRESIDENT. I don't need to say it. You say it.

Thank you very much. God bless you.

AUDIENCE [*chanting*]. Four more years!

THE PRESIDENT. You do your share; I'll do mine. We'll have a great victory on November the 4th.

Thank you.

NOTE: The President spoke at 5:32 p.m. in the Ban Dor Motor Inn ballroom.

St. Louis, Missouri

Remarks and a Question-and-Answer Session at a Townhall Meeting.
October 13, 1980

THE PRESIDENT. *Senator Tom Eagleton, Governor Teasdale, Congressman Bob Young, Congressman Harold Volkmer, Chancellor Arhold Grobman, Mayor James Conway, ladies and gentlemen:*

It's a great pleasure to be with you in this beautiful city, so dynamic and so friendly. I'm always glad to come and feel and experience the hospitality of the St. Louis area, but I particularly wanted to visit the home of that outstanding soccer team, the Rivermen, and also, of course, the Riverwomen, who do such a good job in this modern day of full equality. So, here I am, and I've come here to talk with you about our choices in one of the most crucial elections in recent times.

CAMPAIGN ISSUES

Three weeks from tomorrow the American people will choose not just between two Presidential candidates, not just between two major political parties, but between two futures, two very different and significant futures that will affect the life of everyone in this audience and those you love and throughout this country.

I feel confident that the American people will make the right choice. I know that they, like the people of Missouri, are builders. The same spirit that built the strong industries and communities of this area is building a new future now for America. We are already building a new energy base for this country. We've conserved energy dramatically. Every day this year, in 1980, we are importing 2 million barrels of oil less from foreign countries than we did the first year I was in office. Thanks to you, because you've seen the challenge and, as has been the character of America through thick and thin, through difficult times, through challenges, through troubled times, you've never failed to respond; we've also not only conserved energy, but coast to coast we're developing new energy resources as never before in our history. This year, in the United States, we'll drill more oil and gas wells than any year in history, and this year in the United States we'll produce more coal, American coal, than any year in history.

What we've done on energy under the most difficult possible circumstances where OPEC oil prices more than doubled in one year, 1979, is now giving us a base on which we can build a new industrial program for the entire country. This program which I've already unleashed and which will be put into effect next year, will create a million additional new jobs in the next 2 years in growing and competitive industries.

The American worker is still the most productive on Earth, producing more goods and services in a year than workers in any country on Earth. But a lot of our industries have become old. They need remodeling. We need to stay on the forefront, on the cutting edge of progress. And you can't ask workers to continue to be the most productive on Earth unless they've got new tools and new factories with which to do it.

In recent weeks, as President, I've had a chance to go around this country and visit sites to see what revitalization is already going on. I visited workers in a modern textile mill in South Carolina, and almost unbelievably in the last 2 years, America has increased textile exports by over $2 billion. And we, at the same time, have cut down imports, because now we can be competitive, even with well-paid workers, in that very important element of American life.

I've been to a new steelmill in Perth Amboy, New Jersey, the most modern steelmill in the world. There the workers produce more steel per year than in any steelmill on Earth. Half of their total production, made from scrap metal that used to go overseas, is being sold to the People's Republic of China. The workers

in that factory can now produce steel and ship it halfway around the world and sell it cheaper to the people of China than the same steel can be produced in Japan and shipped a few hundred miles.

And I've seen a major grain elevator on the west coast of our country—growing by leaps and bounds in exports to the Far East, because now we've got a billion new friends that we never had before in the People's Republic of China. And at the same time we've kept our friendship and our trade with the people on Taiwan.

It's extremely important for an American farmer to be productive, to have storage on his farm or her farm so that you can market grain and other products when prices are good, so prices don't fluctuate wildly and rob the housewife, the homeowners each time the markets change.

We now have set records since I've been in office: the highest gross income in history for American farmers, the highest net income in history for American farmers. In 1977 we set a world's record on agricultural exports. In 1978 we broke that record. In 1979 we broke it again. In 1980 we increased American exports of farm products $8 billion, and this year $40 billion worth of American farm products are going overseas and bringing those good dollars back home where they belong. That's what we're doing.

And just a few hours ago I was in the southern part of Illinois, near Marion, in a mine 600 feet deep, one of the most modern coal mines on Earth. This year, as I said, we're producing more coal than we've ever produced before, and we can export as much coal as we can mine, ship to seaports, and load on ships. My goal is in the near future as a major energy source on Earth to replace OPEC oil with American coal. That's what we can do.

And finally, let me point out to you that I've also been in some excellent automobile assembly plants in Michigan, where the most modern, most durable, most safe, and fuel-efficient cars on Earth are now being built. American cars can match any built anywhere, and I just ask you, as Americans, the next time you get ready to change cars and buy a new model, give those new American cars and those new American automobile workers a chance.

The future of this country is extremely bright, but the brightest part of all is that ours is a nation not only of economic but military strength. We're a nation whose military strength is second to none, and that means that it's possible for us to stay at peace. I thank God that for the last 3½ years this Nation has stayed at peace, and I pray God that when I finally go out of the Oval Office, we'll still be at peace.

And now I'd like to spend the next 51 minutes answering your questions about anything on your mind. I'll do the best I can. Don't know all the answers, but I'll try.

I think the first one's over here.

QUESTIONS

THE NATION'S STRENGTHS

Q. I'm Thelma Jean Coutt, and I live in University City, Missouri. Mr. President, why are you telling us you can cure the Nation's woes in the next 4 years when it has gone down so far in the first 4 years of your administration?

THE PRESIDENT. I don't claim to have all the magic answers, and I don't think there are any simple or easy answers to the complex economic problems that we face. What we have to remember is that this country has been blessed by God with tremendous human and natural resources. All the OPEC Arab countries put to-

gether, for instance, have 6 percent of the world's energy reserves—6 percent. We've got 24 percent. We've just now put into effect a new energy policy, and we've made tremendous progress in cutting down the vulnerability that I inherited when I went in the Oval Office.

You probably remember, Thelma Jean, a couple of years ago or more when we lost, the whole world lost, about 4 million barrels of oil per day with the Iranian revolution. You remember there were gas lines and a lot of despair and skyrocketing prices. Recently the Iran-Iraq war erupted and we again lost about 4 million barrels of oil per day. No gas lines. No despair. Stable prices. The reason is that our Nation was prepared. When I came into office we had a very despairing outlook on farm income, agriculture, exports—in the pits. We did have very low net and gross income. I've already given you the statistics. I won't repeat it. But we've made good progress now.

In addition, we were very high in unemployment. In the last 3½ years we have added a net increase of 8½ million new jobs in America, never before done in any President's term, in war or peace. We've got a long way to go.

I could stand here and give you all the statistics about great things that have been done, but let me point this out: We face very serious challenges. The point is that we have now taken steps, sometimes with tremendous political difficulty, to put into effect a new energy policy and to prepare America for the future by saving energy in this country and producing more American energy. I think in the future it's going to be a lot better.

But I don't want to mislead you. America has got to be ready to face unforeseen challenges, tests of our strength, trade competition, and we have got to be prepared to sacrifice on occasion.

We've never had it easy in this country; we've never asked for the easy way out. But one final thing I'd like to say is this: We've got it better now than many people realize.

I'm old enough to have gone through the Second World War, the Great Depression. I grew up then. I've seen the divisiveness of the Vietnam war and the embarrassment of Watergate and some here might be old enough to have gone through the First World War. Our country has faced those challenges, much more serious than anything we face now, successfully. We have never failed in this country, no matter how complicated the question, to find the right answer.

We have never failed, no matter how difficult the problem, to find a solution. We have never failed, no matter how high the obstacle, to find a way over it, if this country was united and confident. And that's why I believe that with the full support of the American people, a united nation, blessed by God with great resources, we'll find a better future even than we have. We've got a darn good present in this country.

DEPARTMENT OF HEALTH AND HUMAN SERVICES

Q. Mr. President, my name is Lawrence Connor from St. Louis City. I read recently where one Department, Health and Human Services, has more people in it than the United States military, and its budget exceeds that of many foreign countries, and this bothers me very much. Could you please tell me what specific actions, if any, you would take during the next administration to reduce the growing influence of the Federal bureaucracy and to help get some government off our backs?

THE PRESIDENT. I'll try to answer that. You're right. Health and Human Services has the third largest budget in the world, second only to the U.S. Government and to the Soviet Union. The reason for that is, primarily, the enormous amount of money handled by social security, where people pay in social security taxes all their lives and when they are at the retirement age, HHS, or Health and Human Services Department, handles that money in a very efficient and humane and proper way and channels it back to people that have paid it in for security when they retire.

I believe this Department now is as efficient as its ever been. We had a very confused Department up until about a year or so ago with health and welfare and education in the same Department. We've taken education out now, and the reason we've done that is so that education can stand on its own so that local people, State officials, school board members, parents, when they have a problem with the schools that might wind up in the courts will now know one Cabinet officer to go to to get an answer to a question or try to resolve a problem before the Federal courts stick their nose in local peoples' business.

In the entire Federal Government, outside of the military, we've had substantial growth in the population of our country and in people served, with cancer research, better health services, immunization programs for little children, and the social security, SSI, Meals on Wheels for the elderly, that sort of program. We have 44,000 fewer Federal employees on a fulltime basis now than we had the day I came in office, in spite of the increase in services provided because of a growing population and growing demands and so forth. I think this trend can continue. I'm determined to make sure we get the Government's nose out of peoples' affairs and also hold down the bureaucracy and give better efficiency, that is, better services.

One other point I'd like to make, not relating to HHS specifically: My philosophy is probably the same as yours. I think the less government you have involved in peoples' lives in the free enterprise system the better off we are. We've tried to do some unprecedented things and had good success. We have deregulated—first time—the airline industry. We have deregulated for the first time the railroad industry. We have deregulated for the first time the trucking industry. We have deregulated for the first time financial institutions, banks, and so forth, and we are now working on a deregulation of the communications industry. We have also deregulated over a phased period of time the energy industry to make sure that we have more American energy produced to cut down our dependence on foreign oil.

So, we are withdrawing the Government from involvement in the free enterprise system and also the private lives of American citizens, let the free enterprise system work the way it ought to be with maximum competition, maximum services, and a minimum of inflation and intrusion into the private lives of Americans. We're going to keep the rate of Federal employment going down steadily as we can, continue to increase the efficiency of government as we have this first 3½ years.

INTERNATIONAL TRADE

Q. Mr. President, I would like to know, when you go in a store you find imported goods and you don't find American-made goods.

THE PRESIDENT. And you want to know why?

Q. Yes.

THE PRESIDENT. What's your name?

Q. Erin O'Neill.

THE PRESIDENT. What's your first name?

Q. Erin.

THE PRESIDENT. Erin?

Q. Yes.

The PRESIDENT. Beautiful name.

Q. Thank you.

THE PRESIDENT. Erin, it's very important for us not to build a wall around our country and isolate ourselves from the rest of the world, because we have to buy things from foreign countries and also produce things in this country with American workers and have other people in foreign nations buy things from us. If we say to a foreign nation, we won't buy any of your goods—we won't buy any of your bauxite to make aluminum, we won't buy any of your chromium to help make better steel, we won't buy any of your raw materials with which we can use to make our own products—then they would say in return, we won't buy any American goods, and we'll put your workers out of work.

It's much better also for us to have friends in those foreign countries. Some of those countries are struggling just to stay alive, economically. They are poor countries. Quite often they only have one product that they can export—one raw material like the ones I just mentioned, chromium or molybdenum. Sometimes they have sugar, sometimes they might have coconuts, sometimes they might have coffee, and if we don't buy anything from them, then their children go hungry, their parents can't find jobs. The products that they grow on their farms can't find a market.

So, the best way you can have competition and at the same time have low prices and at the same time have a broad range of goods to buy, it's better for us to sell our products overseas and for those overseas countries to sell products to us.

Now, if you or your parents don't want to buy foreign goods, you don't have to.

You know, you can just say, "I don't want to buy anything but goods that are made in America," and that's your privilege. And our country could get along and maybe the other countries could survive as well. That's the good thing about a democracy. We've got such a broad range of products made in our Nation that you can buy American goods, if you want to—like automobiles.

I just mentioned a while ago, it would suit me fine if Americans would decide now and in the future to buy more American cars. But a year ago, foreign cars—like those made in Japan and Germany and Sweden and other places, because their gasoline has always been so high priced—were smaller, and they got more miles per gallon, and Americans were still manufacturing large cars that use a lot of gasoline, because our gas had always been so cheap. Now, however, American manufacturers see that American buyers want the small and efficient cars, right? So, they're making the kind of cars that Americans want.

So, international trade lets us sell our products and, at the same time, gives us competition. But if you don't want to buy foreign goods, you don't have to.

This State of yours, Missouri, is a tremendous agricultural producing State. We sell $40 billion worth of American agricultural products overseas. If we didn't buy some goods from overseas, the people wouldn't buy our grain and a lot of Missouri farmers couldn't produce corn and soybeans and rice and other things that they export, because nobody would buy them.

So, it's better to trade back and forth. Use your own judgment though about whether you want to buy foreign goods or American goods. If I had a choice, I'd buy American goods, all things being equal.

ENERGY

Q. Good evening, Mr. President. Welcome to St. Louis. My name is Louise Whittenburg, and I'm from Florissant, Missouri. By the way, you're not only in the home of good soccer country, you're 10 miles away from the school district of our National Teacher of the Year, Beverly Bimes.

Could you please create what we in education call a behavioral objective, that is, one: State a specific economic problem that you wanted to address yourself to 4 years ago. Two: List the steps you took to remediate that problem. And three: Tell what changes you have observed which you think indicate you have been successful.

THE PRESIDENT. Okay. Louise, I think the most important one that I faced when I was elected President was energy. And since I've already covered it fairly well, I'll be extremely brief.

We did not have any energy policy in this country. We had had an enormous increase in the amount of oil we imported from foreign countries before I became President. It had been growing by leaps and bounds each year. I decided that we would face that problem head-on.

So, I made a speech, a fireside chat to all the American people in April of 1977. That same night I made a speech to the Congress of the United States and spelled out an energy program for our country. It was not popular then. I pointed out in my radio-TV talk that my public opinion polls would go down 15 percent because of this issue. It went down a lot more than that, I might say.

But the Congress began to address it, and as the Congress Members here know,

Tom Eagleton and the other Members of the House, it took us 3 solid years to overcome the tremendous influence of the oil companies on Capitol Hill in Washington, because prior to that time, the consumers had not had a voice in energy that could equal the tremendous influence of the American oil companies. But we've built up that interest and that commitment over a period of months until finally, by a thread—one vote in the House, one vote in the Senate—we built a program to conserve energy and to produce more American energy.

We've finally this year passed the windfall profits tax on the oil companies, on the unearned income of the oil companies. That money can be used now to produce synthetic fuels, to insulate homes, to encourage research and development, to produce solar power, to conserve energy, all these things can be done in the future plus improving our rapid transit systems and helping the poor families, particularly elderly, to pay their higher fuel bills as the price of OPEC oil goes up.

All that has now resulted in a tremendous reduction, for the first time, in how much oil we import, because when we imported oil we were importing inflation and also unemployment. It was a very difficult battle, perhaps the most complicated issue which the Congress has ever faced in the history of our country.

Not only have we reduced imports, but we've done it by improving the production of American energy, and, as I said earlier, this year, strangely enough, will be the highest production of coal and also the highest number of oil and gas wells drilled. And in the next 15 years it will be completely conceivable to triple the amount of coal that we produce in this country.

I think Americans are living a better life by having their homes better insulated, by having automobiles more efficient, by having the factories produce more goods with less consumption of energy. So, that's the kind of complicated goal that I set for myself and this Nation. It was actually ridiculed at first. You remember I said it was the moral equivalent of war, and there were a lot of cartoons drawn and fun made of the seriousness of it. That is the domestic side.

One other sentence: We've also restored a major part of our Nation's strategic security, because in the past when we were overly dependent on Persian Gulf oil, by squeezing down on the supply to us they could almost bring us to our knees economically. Now they can't do it. Now we are much more secure, because we've taken these steps. That's a typical example that you asked for.

CUBAN IMMIGRANTS

Q. My name is Sharon Daniels, and I'm from St. Louis. Okay. Mr. President, since the Cubans entering the U.S. will undoubtedly be minorities in our society, what will be your economic plan to keep these minorities from adding to the already large number of people on welfare and in the unemployment lines?

THE PRESIDENT. Did you say the Cuban refugees?

Q. Yes.

THE PRESIDENT. What's your first name?

Q. Sharon.

THE PRESIDENT. Sharon?

Q. Yes.

THE PRESIDENT. Thank you. Sharon, this has probably been my most serious human problem since I've been President. As you know, throughout the world now literally millions and millions of people are trying to escape totalitarian governments and find freedom. This is going on in Cambodia, where the Vietnamese have invaded. It's going on in Afghanistan, where the Soviet Union has invaded. It's going on in Ethiopia, where people are trying to seek a life of freedom, and in other countries around the world. Some people are escaping extreme poverty, like is the case in Haiti, and of course, in Cuba the Castro regime has imposed on its people a loss of freedom and also poverty at the same time.

We've got laws on the books that the Congress has passed to deal with refugees in an orderly fashion. The presumption has been that a refugee, before they come to our country, would be screened somewhere else to see if they were qualified to come to our Nation and brought in in a very orderly and predictable way.

All of a sudden early this spring Fidel Castro opened up Mariel Harbor on the northern coast of Cuba and said that people that want to leave could leave. A lot of Cuban families who live in our Nation paid boats to go down and haul those people to our country. Along with their relatives Castro also sent some—not many, but some—criminals and some people who had mental problems. We were getting about 3,000 a day and trying to handle them as best we could. The people of Florida were angry. I had to put some of those refugees in camps in Arkansas, Pennsylvania, Wisconsin. Those people were angry.

But at the same time I remembered—and you're not going to like this, some of you—I remembered that they are human beings. They were trying to escape communism. They were looking for freedom, to live a life as they chose. They wanted to worship God and escape from a Communist, atheistic nation.

I also remembered that my parents came to this country looking for a better life, looking for the freedom to worship. And every time a wave of immigrants has come to our country—whether they are from southern Europe—Italians, Greeks, and so forth—or whether they are Jews from the Soviet Union or whether they were people from Ireland, who came here during the potato famine—no matter when they came, the people that were already here had a tendency to say, "We've got it made now in this great country. Let's don't let any more of those immigrants come in."

Our country has been a nation of immigrants, a nation of refugees. We have been strengthened by it, not weakened by it. And every time people have come here with a different color skin or a different kind of language or religious habits, there's been a general tendency to say, well, they're going to create a real problem. But every time our country has gotten stronger and better.

Now we've got 125,000 Cubans that have come in here. There are none coming in now. We cut off the flow. I put Coast Guard boats and Navy boats down there, because I'm sworn on my oath to uphold the laws of the country and to let people come in here in accordance with the quota system after they've been screened. So, we stopped the flow. But the ones that are already here, we're trying to deal with them as human beings that we care about. We are placing them in communities that want them and where jobs are available, where the unemployment rate is relatively low. And we're placing them with families, quite often who are their own relatives.

We've already put into communities about 90 to 95 percent of them; we've got a few left. All of them now are in Arkansas, and eventually by the end of this year, they'll all be placed. That's 125,000 out of 230 million. They're not going to hurt our country. But we're giving them a new life, and I predict to you, that although this has not been an easy thing for me politically or for the people of Florida to accommodate, now I am very proud that our country has once again proven that we've not lost the ideals and the human beliefs and the religious beliefs and the generosity that has made this country great.

Our country's not going to be hurt. It's going to be helped.

Q. Mr. President——

THE PRESIDENT. I might add one point. I'm going to do everything I can to enforce the American immigration laws. But don't be disturbed, because, as I said in closing when you were applauding, our country has not been hurt by this episode; I think it's been helped. Not only here, but people around the world know that America has not changed. It still has every element of greatness.

PROGRAMS FOR THE ELDERLY AND HANDICAPPED

Q. Mr. President, my name is Reverend Quinton Ross, and I live in Florissant, Missouri. My question is: There are many elderly and handicapped in our Nation, and I need to know, are there any programs that will address the issue of the handicapped and elderly that have no one to look after them or have no other means of support than fixed incomes?

THE PRESIDENT. All right. Yes, we have greatly improved the programs for the handicapped and the elderly. In the Department that I discussed earlier, Health and Human Services, both those respon-sibilities rest there. For an elderly person who's poor, of course social security or SSI, Meals on Wheels, health care is available, and for the handicapped the same thing applies.

If you have a particular family in mind that might need help and doesn't know how to get help for themselves, if you'd—is that the case?

Q. The case is something of that nature, but widespread.

THE PRESIDENT. Good. I would like for you either to see me or one of my staff members and give me the name of the family or either your name, and we'll contact you privately to make sure that that family or that elderly person or that handicapped person gets the help they need and deserve.

Q. Thank you.

THE PRESIDENT. Will you get the name and address? Fine.

NATIONAL DEFENSE

Q. I'm Jack Hughes from Bellefontaine Neighbors, Missouri. First of all, Mr. President, I'd like to welcome you to the beautiful and friendly city of St. Louis.

THE PRESIDENT. Right on.

Q. Mr. President, many Americans are concerned about our military strength. I'm wondering if you have any plans to raise the salaries of our Armed Forces up to an adequate level in order to retain trained and skilled personnel for a strong defense?

THE PRESIDENT. Fine. As Tom and Harold and Bob know, just a few weeks ago I signed the so-called Nunn-Warner act, which gave another raise to the people in the military to help pay for housing, transportation, higher reenlistment bonuses, and also an increase in salary.

One of the very serious problems that I inherited when I went into the White House was a constant decline in the allotment of funds for defense purposes all put together. My profession is a military officer. I went to Annapolis. I was a submarine officer and resigned from the Navy after serving 11 years. The 8 years before I was inaugurated was a period of steady decline. Seven of those years we actually had a decrease compared to the previous year in Federal budgeted funds for defense.

Since that time of my inauguration, every year we've had a steady, predictable, substantial increase in commitments in our budget for defense, above and beyond inflation. We'll continue this for the next 5 years. I've already allotted to the Congress my version of what ought to be done for the next 5 years. The Senate and the House have basically said this is a good plan.

In addition to that we now have a 15-year plan worked out with our NATO Allies, so they have agreed to join with us in a steady, progressive buildup in military strength in the European theater, which is the most likely to see the outbreak of some sort of combat with the Soviet Union or the Warsaw Pact in the future. I hope it won't.

We've also addressed specific programs. I won't go into detail about them, but just very quickly the nuclear deterrent: It was vulnerable. We now have in all three legs of our nuclear deterrent—air, the new air-launched cruise missiles are small, relatively inexpensive, penetrating missiles, high accuracy, that can go into the Soviet Union, no matter what they do with their civil aerial defense. Secondly, the Trident submarine. The program was almost dead. It was stalemated before I became President. We now have completed sea trials

on the first Trident submarine with new missiles. The next one is ready to be launched shortly. So, the sea leg is also intact. And the MX missile, mobile in deployment, makes it relatively invulnerable to any sort of preemptive strike by an ICBM from the Soviet Union. So, in all three of those areas, plus the Rapid Deployment Force, naval force buildup in the Persian Gulf region, and so forth, we've made good progress.

The last point I want to make is this: All I've told you comprises about 5 percent of our gross national product, a very reasonable expenditure for a nation which is determined never to be equaled by any other country in military strength.[1] I believe that the reason we've kept our Nation at peace and been able to extend peace to Israel and to Egypt and other countries around the world is because of our military strength.

I have no apology to make for the high budget levels on defense expenditures. I think it's a good investment. It's not wasted. The best weapon is one that's never fired in combat, and the best soldier is one that never has to shed his blood on the field of battle.

The last point is this, because we're in a college community and I want to make this point clear: I strongly favored the registration for the draft. The young men of this country responded to an extraordinary degree, much better than we anticipated. We don't anticipate any time in the future having to implement the draft, unless our Nation's security is directly threatened. But we'll be prepared for that if we have to do it.

Fifteen percent of all the young men who signed up for registration indicated

---

[1] The President's point is that we will not be outdone in military strength by any other country. [White House correction.]

that they were interested in having more information about a career in the military forces. As a person who's now become President and who had a military career, I found that it did not interfere at all in my political development or my economic status in life nor my ability to operate a farm or a successful small business. And I would hope that many of our young men and women would take advantage of a chance to get a good career, to serve our Nation, to contribute to peace, to contribute to the strength of American ideals. And in the process, we'll continue to increase and improve the pay, the status, the esteem, the self-respect, the excitement, and the quality of service in the military forces.

As Commander in Chief, that's one of my major responsibilities, and I will not shirk it.

RONALD REAGAN

Q. Hello, hello. My name is Pam Huggins, and I live in St. Louis County. I think my questions have been adequately, satisfactorily addressed. So, instead, I ask you to speculate about which part of the world Mr. Reagan would prioritize for military action?

THE PRESIDENT. Okay. I've got a very strict policy of being careful about what I say—[*laughter*]—and I'm going to bend over backwards to be accurate and fair. [*Laughter*]

My belief is that every President would like to keep this Nation strong and at peace. Secondly, I don't believe that our Nation is likely to be brought into a war just because of a change in administration. However, there are some trends put forward by my opponent that concern me.

Every President since Harry Truman, Republican and Democratic, have worked to control nuclear weapons, have tried to have a balance between ourselves and the Soviet Union, equality, with a steady reduction or control over one another, and a guaranteed means to assure that the agreement that we signed, either SALT agreements or the test ban agreements, were carried out.

Governor Reagan has departed from that. He has advocated not a balance, but nuclear superiority. It sounds not too bad, but the Soviets would not accept our having nuclear superiority anymore than we would accept the Soviets saying, "We demand nuclear superiority, and then we'll negotiate with you on equal and balanced nuclear controls." That is a very serious issue.

Mr. Reagan has referred to the fact that an arms race might be advisable, and he has also said, as you know, that he was going to play a card of an arms race to force the Soviets to do this or that. A nuclear war would be the worst thing. It would make energy and economics and education and caring for the elderly and trade insignificant as an issue. That is a very serious matter.

In the past Governor Reagan has advocated the use of American military forces in many instances when other Presidents, myself and Republican Presidents, have settled troubled times diplomatically. He's advocated, for instance, using American military forces in North Korea, Ecuador, Cuba, the Mideast, Cyprus, Pakistan, Angola, Rhodesia. Those are a few places——

Q. Right. Very good.

THE PRESIDENT.——that I know he has advocated the use of American military forces.

I want to make it clear I'm not insinuating that he would do that as President, because there is a much more serious responsibility on a person once they are in the Oval Office.

Let me add one other human thing, because we've got time. That job is a special job. Nobody can prepare for it ahead of time adequately. It's a lonely job. It's difficult, because the questions that come to my desk in the Oval Office are ones that cannot be solved in a person's private life or in a family's home or in a local city hall or a courthouse or in a State legislature or in a Governor's office. If they can be solved then, I don't ever hear about them. But the ones that come to me are the most difficult ones, and I share them with Tom Eagleton and other Members of the Congress, and we try to work out solutions, sometimes very close calls.

I have good advisers. My Cabinet is as good as any Cabinet that ever served, and they give me good advice. But when that issue is so important and so difficult my experience is that the advice is often fifty-fifty. Half the people say yes; half the people say, "Mr. President, no." I have to make a decision. That's all right.

A lot of crises come to my desk. We've had troubled times every day since I've been in office, domestically and internationally. I deal with those crises. If I deal with them properly, you never hear about them, Pam. But if I make a mistake in dealing with a crisis, then it might affect your life and the life of everyone in this country or even the entire world. So, soundness of judgment and temperament and compatibility with the peaceful ideals of America is a very important element of any President, Democratic or Republican, and I think experience in the office means something as well.

My belief is that any President who serves in that office, Democrats or Republicans, in the past or the future, will do the best they can. And it's not a lonely job, because the President has partnership with you, with people in this auditorium, and people like you all over the country, and the more we are open with our mistakes, with the arguments pro and con, with the difficulties and with the opportunities, the more we guarantee that we don't make a serious mistake like Watergate. That's the kind of thing that a President has to do.

So, I think we'll have a good administration in the future. I think we'll have a better one if the people make the right decision November 4.

VICE PRESIDENT MONDALE

Q. Mr. President, my name is Joe Beckerle, and I'm from the Cranolet area of the city of St. Louis. I would like to preface my question by saying that I'm a very ardent admirer of Fritz Mondale. Now, my question is: If you and Mondale are reelected to another 4-year term, will you give him more of an input and let him put more of an input into both foreign and domestic affairs?

THE PRESIDENT. Thank you, Joe. I share your admiration for Fritz Mondale.

It would be almost impossible to give him more responsibility than he already has. Any observer of the White House operation will tell you that there has never been a closer relationship between a President and a Vice President that exists today between me and Fritz Mondale. Since I've been in office, he has never been excluded from any private session that I have had—with a foreign leader, a domestic leader, or anyone else. He has responsibilities now for the military that no Vice President has ever before had. I trust him with every element of the responsibilities which I share. He has an office right down the hall from me. In the past, the Vice President was across the street in a different building. He and I share staff members. We consult with each other constantly.

So, I don't know that I could give Fritz any more responsibility than I presently give him, but if I think of any way—[*laughter*]—to put additional responsibility on his shoulders, I guarantee you I'll take your advice and let him have it, because he can handle it.

FEDERAL BUDGET DEFICITS

Q. Good evening, Mr. President. My name is Jack Schreiber, and I'm from Normandy, Missouri. It's also the home of this university. During your 1976 campaign, you pledged that if elected the Federal budget would be balanced by 1980. Since that time, the level of Government spending has increased significantly to the point where we are now faced with the prospect of a budget deficit in 1980 of $60 billion. Estimates for 1981 already indicate a budget deficit in the excess of $30 billion. During this same period, we've experienced the highest level of inflation in recent history, much of which has been attributed to the dramatic increase in the price of oil.

My question: Have not Government deficits and the Federal Reserve Bank's willingness to finance these deficits been a major cause for inflation, and if so, and if reelected, what hope can you give us that we will ever see a reduction in the growth of Government spending, a balanced budget, and some relief for the American taxpayer? Thank you.

THE PRESIDENT. It was my hope and my expectation that the present budget the Congress is dealing with for this current fiscal year would be balanced. In March of this year, I presented to the Congress a balanced budget. Unfortu-

nately, after then we went into a recession which we had not anticipated, brought about, fairly well on a worldwide basis, by the fact that oil prices increased more in a 12-month period than they had since oil was first discovered in the 1800's.

That meant two things, Jack. One was that more people were unemployed or partially employed. Unemployment compensation payments went up. Welfare payments also went up. Trade Recovery Act payments—like in the automobile industry, to retrain workers—also went up. And while those payments were going up to people who were unemployed temporarily, they obviously stopped paying income tax, and so the Federal revenues went down. That is where the budget became unbalanced.

It was something that we did not anticipate. It was something that I wish had never happened. Nothing would please me more than to stand here before you and say, "We have finally balanced the Federal budget." When I ran for President in 1976, our budget deficit was about $60 billion, which at that time was about 4½ percent of the gross national product. Now the budget deficit is not as high as you say. We think it'll be about $40 billion, which is less than 2 percent of the gross national product. If we continue to have good recovery and people continue to go back to work, then we have an excellent chance to balance the budget.

Those budget deficits are much lower, as a percentage of gross national product, than they are, for instance, in other major trading countries like Germany, very prosperous, or Japan or Great Britain. We are bringing those deficits down. But sometimes when you try to get them exactly balanced and you have an unexpected downturn in the economy, then there's no way you can control a small deficit.

I might add this: Since March we have seen the situation improve. July, as you know, showed a zero inflation rate—first time in 13 years. It was an aberration, and we will have a continued inflation rate, maybe 8, 9 percent for a while. We have proposed for next year an economic program that will be anti-inflationary in nature and will also provide at least 50 percent of tax reductions for investment in more modern tools and more modern factories, which I believe will stimulate the economy, put more people back to work— about a million new jobs by the end of the following year—bring in more revenue, because people pay more income taxes, and modernize so that we can be more competitive and more productive.

As you know, the thing that causes inflation is the deficit plus the fact that people don't save very much in our country lately, plus the fact that American workers are not as productive as they should be. So, we're trying to deal with those root causes of inflation. The most important one is the one you mentioned— the excessive dependence on imported oil. We're making excellent progress on that. I think the progress will continue.

Finally, let me say I wish we could have the balanced budget immediately. That's still my goal. I can't guarantee you exactly when it'll happen. But it's at the top of my priority list in dealing with the Federal budget to meet the needs of our Nation, first of all, adequately, to keep an efficient government, to deregulate the private industry, let it function in a competitive way, and continue as we have already, very successfully, to drive that deficit steadily lower.

I wish I had a better report for you. I don't want to mislead you. That's as accurate a statement as I can make.

I don't think I have time for another one. They tell me my time's up. I'm sorry. Let me make one other point, and I pretty well covered the issues on a broad basis here, all the way from energy to deficits to the people who are unemployed or the elderly or the afflicted.

Finally, let me say this: I don't claim that we've never made mistakes. We've learned in the process. I don't claim that our country doesn't have problems. We have some. Most of those problems are challenges that we can adequately meet. A President must bear the responsibility for successes or failures. The President serves today, but the decisions he makes affect our Nation in the future. That's why this campaign that will take place in almost exactly 3 weeks is so important to you. The differences between myself and my opponent are sharp, stark differences. I've not tried to dwell on them tonight, as you know—the only time I have is when I got a specific question about defense.

But my hope and my judgment is that the American people will consider the blessings that we have, the problems that we face, the fact of our greatness, the blessings God has given us, a chance to participate as you've done tonight, and give me the support that I need as President, hopefully as the next President, to make the greatest nation on Earth even greater in the future. That's my prayer. I hope you'll join me.

Thank you very much.

NOTE: The President spoke at 7:30 p.m. in the gymnasium of the University of Missouri at St. Louis.

Privacy Protection Act of 1980

Statement on Signing S. 1790 Into Law.
October 14, 1980

I am pleased to sign the Privacy Protection Act of 1980, a bill which provides vital safeguards for our free press.

The Supreme Court's 1978 decision in *Zurcher* v. *Stamford Daily* raised the concern that law enforcement authorities could conduct unannounced searches of reporters' notes and files to seek evidence. Such a practice could have a chilling effect on the ability of reporters to develop sources and pursue stories. Ever since the Court's decision, my administration has been working with Congress to prevent this result by enacting legislation.

This bill requires Federal, State, and local authorities either to request voluntary compliance or to use subpoenas—with advance notice and the opportunity for a court hearing—instead of search warrants when they seek reporters' materials as evidence. The bill also covers others engaged in first amendment activities such as authors and scholars. Searches are allowed only in very limited situations.

The bill also directs the Attorney General to issue guidelines for Federal law enforcement officers to minimize intrusion when documentary evidence of a crime is sought from innocent third parties who are not members of the press. Those guidelines are already being written and the Attorney General expects to issue them in the near future. I am pleased that the Federal Government is taking the lead in providing these privacy protections. I urge the States to follow suit.

This bill provides important civil liberties protections without hampering legitimate law enforcement investigations. I congratulate Senators Birch Bayh, Edward Kennedy, and Strom Thurmond, and Congressmen Robert Drinan, Robert Kastenmeier, Tom Railsback, and Peter Rodino, who played crucial roles in passing this legislation.

The Privacy Protection Act is an integral part of my administration's strong, ongoing commitment to a national privacy policy. In this wide-ranging program, we have reversed the historic growth in collection of personal data by the Government. We have reduced the size of these Government files by more than 10 percent. Congress has nearly completed action on legislation I submitted last year to protect medical records. I expect that bill to pass in the November session, and I look forward to working with the next Congress to enact credit, banking, and insurance privacy legislation. Finally, I am pleased that the first international guidelines on transfer of personal data across borders have just been adopted by the member countries of the Organization for Economic Cooperation and Development, including the United States.

I also wish to note the progress we are making on other aspects of civil liberties. The Justice Department is today announcing final guidelines requiring Federal lawyers to oppose closing trials and other legal proceedings except in very limited circumstances. The principle that justice should be done in public is a basic part of our legal tradition.

This legislation and these other actions have helped preserve our country's basic freedoms.

NOTE: As enacted, S. 1790 is Public Law 96–440, approved October 13.

The Nation's Economy

Remarks and a Question-and-Answer Session at the National Press Club.
October 14, 1980

THE PRESIDENT. It was indeed a good omen when, back in 1974, I came here and made a speech and then later became President of the United States. I hope the same thing doesn't happen to Jerry Falwell. [*Laughter*] He has a place in the pulpit is the reason—separation of church and state. [*Laughter*]

I consider this to be a very important message, because 3 weeks from now the American people face a critical choice, a choice with historic consequences for America and indeed the entire world. I want the American people to focus hard on those consequences of the election between now and election day. I want every voter to get answers to the important questions about each candidate—three important questions: How does he intend to build a stronger economy; how does he intend to ensure a more peaceful world; and how does he intend to create a more just society here at home?

I'm taking up these questions in a series of nationwide radio broadcasts. I offered a broad answer to the first question on Sunday. I described the kind of economic future our country must build, and this afternoon I want to give a more extensive report, a more thoughtful report perhaps, on the same subject.

First, I want to describe what is happening to our economy right now.

As you know, we and other nations around the world have recently been shocked by OPEC oil prices, which more than doubled in just 12 months. This has been a very difficult and painful period of high inflation and unemployment, particularly painful to some Americans who have, in their own families, suffered most.

Fortunately, our Nation has been able to withstand this blow. The economic outlook has now brightened. We see the beginnings of recovery. We see a reduction in inflation, an increase in the number of jobs, a decline in the unemployment rate. I'm confident about our future, not simply because the immediate outlook is improving but because, at long last, our country is coming to grips with some of its chronic, underlying economic challenges.

America's great economic strength is founded on economic freedom. Every day millions of economic decisions are made in factories, in automobile showrooms, in banks, and in brokerage houses, on farms and around kitchen tables, where family budgets are prepared. These millions of choices are not made by official command, but according to private needs and private, individual judgments.

Nevertheless, the economic impact of government is profound. Government collects taxes; it enacts laws; it issues regulations; it borrows and lends money. Government policies can limit economic opportunities or expand them. If we choose the right policies for the future, we can encourage abundance, opportunity, and stable prices. If we choose the wrong policies for the future, we can accelerate inflation, jeopardize savings and jobs, and discourage investments in the future. No President and no Congress has never intentionally chosen to be wrong in shaping economic policies for our country, but there have been occasions when the effect of their policies was to worsen the already negative trends that existed in our economy.

In the past 15 years we've had several major inflationary episodes. Each ended in a recession. Each time we were left with a higher underying level of inflation than we had before.

The first of these episodes occurred during the military buildup for the war in Vietnam. We needed to raise adequate revenues during that period when Government expenditures both for defense and for new social programs were rising. But this failure to do so left a persisting inflationary hangover. Our underlying inflation rate rose from 1 percent in the first half of the 1960's to over 4 percent at the beginning of the 1970's.

Several years later, in 1972, there was a worldwide grain shortage. Food prices went up sharply. Once again fiscal excesses added to the inflationary pressures. In 1973 came the Arab oil embargo and a tremendous increase in OPEC petroleum prices. Soon afterwards, our economy suffered the worst recession in 40 years. Once again the underlying inflation rate failed to drop. Once again it was ratcheted upward, now to 7 percent.

Again, in 1979, the OPEC countries imposed another huge increase in oil prices on the world economy. Again the underlying inflation rate was ratcheted upwards, this time to about 9 percent.

We've learned by hard experience the strength of the inflationary forces in our economy and how firmly we must resist the temptation to overstimulate the economy. That is why it is so important to resist the massive, across-the-board tax cuts of the Reagan-Kemp-Roth proposal; why we need targeted tax cuts that encourage economic growth, but at the same time hold down inflation. Creating jobs and controlling inflation must go together. Right now, just as we are beginning to bring inflation down, is exactly the wrong time for election-year proposals that would drive prices up again.

We have therefore learned what has caused our current inflation: the failure to raise adequate revenues at a time of greatly increased public spending, like in the Vietnam war; natural events, such as grain shortages in the early 1970's; overstimulation of the economy, sometimes for political purposes; the staggering increases in imported oil prices; and the long decline in our productivity growth in the United States. To overcome inflation, we need to attack its causes directly and at their roots.

First, we need to pursue prudent overall fiscal policies. We've made substantial progress in controlling the budget. The rate of real growth in Government spending is half what it was when I took office, and the budget deficit has been reduced by more than half as a percentage of the gross national product.

We can exercise real fiscal restraint and still maintain a compassionate and a progressive society. We need to eliminate waste. We need to target Government programs to areas and citizens who are most in need. We cannot assume that all boats rise with the tide. We need to attract and encourage private investment to join with government in achieving our various economic and social goals.

This brings me to one of the central issues of the campaign: Do we want policies that encourage growth without driving up inflation, through needed investments in new plant and new equipment, or do we want to place our emphasis on immediate consumption, through a quick, regressive, across-the-board tax cut?

On August the 28th I proposed a major program to revitalize America's industry. The major part of my proposed tax reductions will go to encourage investment and to create new jobs—an investment in our country's economic future.

In contrast, this is what Governor Reagan has proposed: first, a large, across-the-board tax cut plus a liberalization of business depreciation allowance that by 1983 would cost some $110 billion; second, a removal of the so-called work-test under the social security program, costing another 6 or 7 billion dollars annually; third, a sharp increase in Government subsidies for the merchant marine; fourth, a system of tuition tax credits for those attending private schools, which at even a modest level would add 3 to 5 billion dollars to the budget; next, an increase in military spending beyond the substantial increases that we've already planned, which would cost more than $20 billion extra a year; and also, a substantial repeal of the windfall profits tax that would give at least $10 billion in lost Federal revenues back to the oil companies in 1983.

These, Governor Reagan's tax and spending proposals, would add $130 billion at least to the 1983 budget deficit. In recent weeks Governor Reagan has been saying that he can avoid the highly inflationary consequences of these tax and spending programs by cutting other parts of the budget sufficiently to prevent a deficit. By cutting this, by doing what he proposes, he's promised to protect social security and other entitlement programs. But all the rest of the Federal Government—and listen to this—out of which the $130 billion in cuts would have to come, will amount to only $150 billion in 1983. He has not specified, of course, which programs would be cut. I call upon him to do so, for it's clear that the only way he could balance the budget under his program is to eliminate almost all of the Federal Government except for defense and entitlement programs.

On the other hand, it may be that Governor Reagan thought he had the answer to this difficult budgetary problem early this year when he said, and I quote: "We could use the increased resources the Federal Government would get from this tax decrease to rebuild our defense capabilities." I'd like to repeat that. "We could use the increased resources from the Federal Government which it would get from this tax decrease to rebuild our defense capabilities."

As I said earlier, I'll leave the assessment of the Reagan-Kemp-Roth proposal to the good sense and judgment of the American people.

I propose that we reject quick, inflationary tax cuts that pile up Federal deficits and erode the value of the money of our country. I propose instead that we rely on the same values and the same common sense that built our country in the first place. I propose that we encourage capital investment in new plant and equipment, the investments we need to increase worker productivity. If living standards are to rise, productivity must grow. There's no way around this. It's an economic fact of life.

During the 1950's and 1960's, productivity grew at an average of about 3 percent per year. During the 1970's, productivity growth began to slow down, and today it is hardly growing at all. There are many theories for this decline in productivity growth, but there is one sure prescription for it: providing American workers with a growing stock of modern plant and equipment.

Our workers can continue to be the most productive in the world if given the proper tools. To do that, government must encourage investment. We must make sure that American research and development does not lag behind. We must provide the kind of tax incentives that will help to modernize the Nation's industries.

I've listed two elements in the administration's economic program: fiscal prudence and encouraging productivity. A third, the most important of all, concerns energy.

During the 1970's, the price of oil rose by more than 10-fold. We will pay about $85 billion to import oil this year, 30 times what we paid just 10 years ago. Only in the last 2 years have we really launched the right kind of energy programs, with new legislation passed by Congress, to stimulate new production of oil, coal, and natural gas, to encourage conservation in homes and in businesses, to develop synthetic fuels from our coal and oil shale resources, to make nuclear energy production safer and more reliable, and to tap the power of the Sun.

As a result of these and other energy measures, we've cut our foreign oil consumption by 2 million barrels per day, almost 25 percent, since I took office. No other country can match that record. We have loosened but not yet broken the grip of foreign oil dependency. Those who ignore this challenge, those who discount conservation, those who believe we can leave the energy challenge to the oil companies alone have failed to grasp what may well be the central challenge of our time.

The fourth element of our economic policy is aimed at putting people back to work and creating jobs for the millions of men and women who will be entering the work force in the 1980's. To accomplish our goal of full employment, we need to do several things.

We need to insist, first of all, on fair rules of trade with other nations in every product. Our program to help the American steel industry will help to achieve this kind of fairness. We're awaiting a decision from the International Trade Commission to determine if action should be taken with regard to Japanese automobiles. We must not embark on the kind of trade war that wrecked the world economy of the 1930's.

The way to full employment does not lie in escalating an already persistent inflation. It lies in the right kind of tax incentives. It lies in measures that bring about investment in modern plant and equipment. It lies in controlling inflation, so that industry can plan for the future with confidence and so that interest rates can be brought down within the reach of homebuyers and consumers. It lies in stimulating competition, deregulating the airlines, the railroads, the financial institutions, energy, the truck lines, and communication industries, just as we have done.

Creating jobs is what my economic revitalization program is all about. I have proposed that in areas suffering high unemployment and a declining industrial base, an additional tax credit be allowed for qualifying investments; also, that depreciation schedules be simplified and depreciation rates accelerated; and that investment tax credits be made partially refundable, which will help new companies and those hit by cyclical downturns whose profits are not high enough to pay high rates of taxation.

I've also recognized that economic change sometimes requires difficult adjustment. I have proposed tax incentives and the establishment of an industrial development authority to channel public and private resources to help industries and communities adjust to inevitable economic change.

All these proposals have one thing in common: They put people to work in real jobs without triggering higher prices. Inflation is beginning to decline. We need to maintain that trend. To make further progress, we will consult with business, labor, and other groups about how to improve our voluntary wage and price policies. We also need to work together to design future tax reductions that help to moderate the wage and price spiral.

Government can help to build an exciting and healthy economic future for our country, but if we are to succeed, it cannot be because of government alone or business alone or labor alone. It must be because government, business, labor, and the public work together.

Our programs to meet the energy challenge and to modernize American industry can set the stage for American economic renaissance. If we follow through with these steps, we can have a future of modern plants, a future where American coal and shale and farm products fuel American cars and trucks, a future where modern railbeds and ports make American coal a powerful rival of OPEC oil, a future of full employment of American men and women, working to modernize American industry and to create whole new American industries.

I believe that if the American people understand the nature of their choice in this absolutely crucial campaign issue and the consequences of the choice they will make, they will choose the right course for the economic future of this country. Americans proved that by facing up to the reality of our energy problem and reversing several decades of increasing dependence on foreign oil. That achievement gives us a foundation now on which to realize the hopes and dreams and expectations which I've just outlined to you.

If we fight for economic progress as hard as we've been fighting for America's energy security, then I am confident that we can build a future of full employment, stable prices, rising exports, a more modern, competitive industry, and a stronger, more prosperous, and a more productive America. That is my goal. It's a goal that I intend to achieve.

Thank you very much.

QUESTIONS

INTEREST RATES

Mr. Von Bergen. Thank you. We'll have a few questions.

The first question: You have complained that interest rates are too high. Do you think the Federal Reserve should intervene in the market and drive down interest rates?

The President. No, I don't. I think we have a proper balance now between the private sector—the financial community and the economic and commercial community—on the one hand; the Federal Reserve Board, which is independent, on the second hand; the Congress, independently from me; and I, as Executive of our country.

I make proposals, make decisions on regulations, change priorities in the budget, emphasize certain aspects of American life to the public through my statements and actions. The Congress makes decisions on budget levels and passes legislation concerning tax programs. The Federal Reserve observes all these matters and makes their decisions. The financial community reacts. I think it's a good, sound system.

I do, however, believe that recently the financial institutions, the banks have overreacted, and I believe that at this time the interest rates are too high compared with the economic circumstances that prevail. It's my own judgment; I believe it's sound. And I hope that the sound of my voice in the financial institutions will prevail, and the interest rates will come down where they ought to be. But I don't want to intercede artificially, as a President or through an administration, to directly affect interest rates.

AGRICULTURAL POLICIES

MR. VON BERGEN. Mr. President, along economic lines, a lot of people think grocery prices are too high, but farmers feel their returns for their products are too low. What do you think, and what does Mrs. Carter think? [*Laughter*]

THE PRESIDENT. My wife's enough of a politician to realize that there are two sides to this very important issue. [*Laughter*]

I inherited, when I came into office, a time of economic deprivation and uncertainty among farmers, with an excessive intrusion of the Federal Government into their affairs and a rapid, changing cycle of supply and demand and therefore wild rises, quite often, in farm or agricultural prices after the grain or other products had left the farmer.

We approached this in several ways, the most important aspect of which was to build up substantial storage of farm products on the farms. We encouraged farmers to keep their products under their own control. We arranged Government programs to assist them and put literally hundreds of millions of dollars on loans, which the farmers are repaying on a timely basis, to build storage for them to hold their grain.

This means that there's a much more stable supply of grain now. If we have an excess harvest, above the average or expected level, then that grain goes into the farmer-held reserve. If we have a shortage in our country or worldwide basis, then the farmers can take grain out of their reserve, at a carefully prescribed price, in advance and market it to keep our country sound and the world supply sound. I think this has done a good job in stabilizing prices.

We have had reasonable gross income for farmers and reasonable net income for farmers. At the same time, since I've been in office, both gross and net income for farmers has increased more than in any administration in history. One of the reasons for this has not been an excesive burden on the American consumer, who still get food at a lower level, compared to their other income and compared to other people, than anybody on Earth, but because we have escalated so greatly the exporting of American agricultural products.

We set a world's record on exports of our agricultural products in 1977. We broke that record in '78. We broke it again in '79. And this year, in spite of the interruption of some of our sales to the Soviet Union, we've had the greatest increase in history, increasing exports by $8 billion this year alone, up to a level of $40 billion for American-exported agricultural products. You might be interested in knowing that this year we'll sell Mexico 10 million tons of American grain.

I tried the best I could to stabilize American farm prices, in spite of the interruption of sale of some grain to the Soviet Union, and at the same time to open up in the rest of the world more permanent customers for American agricultural products. In the long historic perspective, our biggest single strategic asset of a peaceful nature is the productivity of our land. It's much more important on a historical scale than OPEC oil, for instance.

And so, I believe we've got a very sound farm economy now, stable prices compared to what they were, good bargains for American consumers. And I would guess that in the future these prices would increase only at very moderate rates, compatible with market pressures that are much less fluctuating than they were before.

RONALD REAGAN

MR. VON BERGEN. Mr. President, in criticizing Governor Reagan you have used outdated statements he has since repudiated, like his 1966 comments about making social security voluntary. Is this fair campaigning, since just in the past 4 years you have changed your position on a number of major issues, like your 1976 campaign pledge to cut defense spending, your former opposition to decontrol of oil prices, and your one-time opposition to any form of national health insurance?

THE PRESIDENT. When we quote Governor Reagan on these matters of interest to the American people, we always make a point to give to the news media the time and the place of the statement which he has made.

Recently, in the last few days, I understand, he has said that he has not changed his positions, that his positions are consistent with what they've been for the last 20 years. Sometimes they are in conflict, but I think the basic underlying philosophy is there.

When he says, for instance, that the minimum wage has caused more damage than anything since the Great Depression, that's an expression of a philosophy about working people that's still pervasive, I think, in his own mind and also in the platform of his party. When he says that unemployment compensation is a prepaid vacation for freeloaders, to me that's a statement that still prevails, although he may have said it a while ago.

When he took on his role as the nationwide opponent or spokesman against Medicare and traveled this country speaking against Medicare, he said that this would lead to the Government's intrusion into private affairs, so that Government would later tell a young man or woman where they could go to work or where a family could live. Recently he repeated a similar statement, even this year.

And his most disturbing statement was one recently made about withdrawing SALT II treaty from the Senate, speculating on the advisability of a so-called nuclear arms race to induce the Soviets to be more forthcoming in SALT negotiations, and saying that he was, in effect, playing a card against the Soviet Union. This kind of talk, to me—made quite recently, within the last couple of weeks—is extremely dangerous.

And the repeated nature of some of his statements when he was either a candidate for President or had the hopes of being a President—the pattern is still there.

For instance, all of us who serve in the Oval Office recognize the sensitivity of the decisions we make, the dealing with potential crises which might, if mishandled, become real crises and affect the life of everyone in this Nation and perhaps the world. My predecessors in office, Republican and Democrat, and I deal constantly with a series of trouble spots in the world, and we try to manage those potential problems in a diplomatic way, without the use of military force.

Repeatedly, there's a pattern of Governor Reagan's calling for the injection of military forces by the United States into those trouble spots in the world—in Ecuador, Cuba, in Cyprus, Pakistan, North Korea, the Middle East, Angola, Rhodesia, just to name a few. This kind of inclination, to me, although some of those statements were made recently, some of them longer ago—the pattern is what causes me concern.

So, we are trying to be extremely accurate in quoting Governor Reagan precisely and also putting the right tone and not misinterpreting what he says and giving the dates without misleading the American people about the timeliness of them.

MR. VON BERGEN. Thank you. Mr. President, before asking you one final question, I would like to present you with a National Press Club certificate of appreciation for being here and also a Press Club jacket, which we hope you will wear. [*Laughter*]

THE PRESIDENT. Very good.

"OCTOBER SURPRISE"

MR. VON BERGEN. The final question: Mr. President, your opponents expect from you an October surprise, a political trick-or-treat. To put their minds to rest, will you tell us what the surprise is, or do we have to wait? [*Laughter*]

THE PRESIDENT. First of all, let me say that I'll treasure this certificate the rest of my life. [*Laughter*] Thank you very much.

It's not possible for a President to contrive a significant surprise. We deal in the Oval Office with questions of profound importance and difficulty. We try without delay to solve any problems that arise. I think every President who's served there has tried to do the best he could to meet the needs of our country.

It would be very pleasant for me if we could come up with a zero inflation rate or a zero unemployment rate or a boon to our economy that was significant or if the Japanese would say they would never ship any more cars to our country unless they were given away free, or something like that—[*laughter*]—but you know, that's the kind of hopes that always exist.

I think it would be a bad thing if I tried to delay good news or to conceal bad news to create some sort of surprise just to orient the election. So, you need not expect any such surprise between now and November. If it's a surprise to you, I guarantee you it will also be a surprise to the President. [*Laughter*]

Thank you. I've enjoyed being with you.

NOTE: The President spoke at 1:05 p.m. in the National Press Club ballroom.

Drew Von Bergen of United Press International, president of the National Press Club, read the questions submitted earlier by members of the press.

Staggers Rail Act of 1980

Remarks on Signing S. 1946 Into Law. October 14, 1980

THE PRESIDENT. There are a lot of smiles on the faces of the men and women behind me, who've worked so hard on this legislation.

I'd like to begin by acknowledging the leadership of Senator Howard Cannon, who has been so important this last 2 years in our deregulation effort. This bill is the result of a strong bipartisan support, both in the House and the Senate. Senator Russell Long, Senator Bob Packwood made outstanding efforts to help passage in the Senate. In the House, of course, the leadership of Chairman Jim Florio, Congressman Matsui, Congressman Edward Madigan, Nick Joe Rahall, who's also here, James Broyhill, were all critical to our success.

It's especially fitting that the Congress has decided to name this act after Congressman Harley Staggers, a great chairman who has capped his illustrious career with this key effort to pass this major reform bill.

The Staggers Rail Act of 1980 is the capstone of my own efforts to get rid of needless and burdensome Federal regulations which benefit nobody and which harm all of us. This effort is crucial to promote more competition, to improve productivity, and to hold down inflation. We deregulated the airlines, we deregulated the trucking industry, we deregulated financial institutions, we decontrolled oil and natural gas prices, and we negotiated lower trade barriers throughout the world for our exports.

Where we needed continued regulation, we required agencies to analyze carefully the costs of their new proposals. We now have a sunset review program for major new regulations. We have cut, with the help of the Congress, Federal paperwork by 15 percent. I established a Regulatory Council to weed out inconsistencies and to encourage innovation, saving hundreds of millions of dollars while still meeting our most vital regulatory goals. Most recently I signed the Regulatory Fexibility Act to remove unnecessary burdens on small businesses.

All of us here heard for years the campaign rhetoric of regulatory reform. We heard so much rhetoric and saw so few results in that time that many of us could have given up, but we didn't. And together in these 3½ years, we've carried out the most fundamental restructuring of our economy, the relationship between government and the private enterprise system, since Franklin D. Roosevelt's time

and the initiation of the New Deal. It will be a major boost for the revitalization of the American economy, a revitalization that I intend will restore America's competitive edge and make possible full employment and, at the same time, stable prices.

The railroad deregulation act strips away needless and costly regulations in favor of market forces, competitive market forces, whenever possible. It will help to restore the financial health to the railroad industry. It will help shippers by allowing the railroads to improve equipment and to tailor services to shippers' needs, and it will help American consumers with better and more efficient service. It will allow railroads to adjust rates to at least cover out-of-pocket costs and to earn a reasonable return without red-tape.

For the first time, railroads and shippers can contract for terms of service, as is the case in other industries. The act will curtail collective rate-setting practices among railroads in favor of individual price competition. It will simplify and shorten ICC rate and railroad restructuring procedures. This act also will allow Conrail to provide more effective services. At the same time, it will help protect captive shippers and utilities using coal. It will facilitate the reorganization of the Rock Island Railroad lines so vital to the Midwest, and it will expand and revise the existing financial program which helps our Nation's railroads.

The importance of this act is clearly reflected in the outstanding and diverse group of people who are assembled here today for this ceremony—representatives from railroad management, from labor, from such shippers as automobiles and steel and coal, retail stores, farm organizations, and also from environmental organizations.

Let me also commend the ICC. The ICC has made substantial progress toward reducing regulatory burdens. The Staggers act builds on and reinforces these crucial reforms, and I look to the Commission for aggressive implementation of the act's objectives.

I now take great pleasure in signing the Staggers Rail Act of 1980.

[At this point, the President signed the bill.]

I also want to welcome former Congressman Fred Rooney back. It's a pleasure to have you here.

REPRESENTATIVE ROONEY. Nice to be with you.

THE PRESIDENT. Thank you very much.

I'd like to ask Jim Florio to say a word if he will and then Congressman Staggers.

REPRESENTATIVE FLORIO. Thank you very much, Mr. President.

You've obviously summarized the bill very well. There's not much more that has to be said except this was a really good example of how the legislative process is supposed to work, attempting to harmonize all the divergent interests, and it was a good tribute to the way that the legislature is supposed to enact legislation. You have representatives, as you said, of the community, the shipping community, rail management, rail labor, public and private sectors.

So, I'm pleased to be associated with it; certainly think it's appropriate, as you've mentioned, that this be named after Mr. Staggers, who has devoted so much of his time and energies over the great number of years that he's been in the Congress to working to ensure the fact that we have a healthy railroad system. We hope this legislation will get us back to that point.

So, thank you very much.

THE PRESIDENT. Thank you very much. Well, Mr. Staggers, will you say a word for us, please?

REPRESENTATIVE STAGGERS. Mr. President, and all those present, I congratulate you on your leadership in sending to the House and to the Senate legislation which would do what has taken place today, because it was under your leadership that the legislation has been enacted.

I would like to congratulate, on our side, very much Jim Florio—He has worked so hard—and Mr. Madigan of Illinois, because there were so many obstacles they had to overcome, factors they had to stop, consideration of the bill one time and then came back.

THE PRESIDENT. Just once? *[Laughter]*

REPRESENTATIVE STAGGERS. More than that, in fact. *[Laughter]*

THE PRESIDENT. More than once.

REPRESENTATIVE STAGGERS. But there were so many who had a part in it—Nick Rahall and Matsui and many others that I could mention who were on our committee. But actually Jim Florio and Mr. Madigan were the two leaders.

THE PRESIDENT. Yes.

REPRESENTATIVE STAGGERS. And they maneuvered, manipulated the bill on the floor—*[laughter]*—and worked it out, so that it could really be worked into legislation.

But I would like to also congratulate the shippers and the railroad management and railroad labor and all the rest who have entered into this agreement to try an experiment that might, and we think will, help the future of the railroad industry, help to build it and make this a better transportation system in the land and make it a better nation in which to live.

So, we congratulate everyone who had a part in working on it. And thank you so very much, Mr. President.

THE PRESIDENT. Thank you.

I think the word "maneuver" is good. [*Laughter*] The word to "guide" or to "steer" it through the very tortuous legislative process is significant and appropriate.

This is legislation of far-reaching significance that touches on the lives of almost every American. And of course, the people who use the railroads and who are very interested in seeing rates as low as possible and service as good as possible, representing those who ship grain and cotton and other agricultural products, the retail merchants who want their goods to arrive in a timely fashion and with minimum freight rates added, the major basic industries like automobiles and steel, worked very closely with Mr. Florio and his equals, equivalents in the Senate, with the railroad management, that want to see a sound railroad industry, with laborers, who see the inevitability of economic and social and transportation change, wanting to have their own lives protected.

The complexity here was very profound. It's similar to the complexities that we did face, I think even exceeds the complexities that we faced in either airline deregulation or even trucking deregulation, and perhaps even more so than even the financial institutions regulation.

But to move the governments out of the free enterprise system when regulations are onerous or costly and at the same time have additional protection for consumers, to stimulate an industry that has been ailing in some way, and to let the free enterprise system actually work with intense competition is an achievement that brings credit to all those assembled here.

And I want to express my thanks to all of you for being willing to help with this very fine legislation that moves our Nation one step forward, one major step forward toward the revitalization that is necessary in giving our economy a new stimulus, keeping our people at work, with improved services for the American people, and at the same time reducing inflation and enhancing the quality of our environment. This has accomplished all these goals, and all of you deserve a great deal of credit. I'm proud to be part of this group and this achievement.

Thank you very much.

NOTE: The President spoke at 2:47 p.m. in the Cabinet Room at the White House.

As enacted, S. 1946 is Public Law 96–448, approved October 14.

Staggers Rail Act of 1980

Statement on Signing S. 1946 Into Law.
October 14, 1980

Today I take great pleasure in signing the Staggers Rail Act of 1980. This legislation builds on the railroad deregulation proposal I sent to Congress in March 1979. It is vital to the railroad industry and to all Americans who depend upon rail services.

By stripping away needless and costly regulation in favor of marketplace forces wherever possible, this act will help assure a strong and healthy future for our Nation's railroads and the men and women who work for them. It will benefit shippers throughout the country by encouraging railroads to improve their equipment and better tailor their service to shipper needs. America's consumers will benefit, for rather than face the propsect of continuing deterioration of rail freight service, consumers can be assured of improved railroads delivering their goods with dispatch.

The importance of this act is demonstrated by the wide array of individuals and groups who support it, including railroad management and labor, major shippers such as automobile, steel, and coal companies, retail stores, farm organizations, and environmental and other public interest representatives. This act would not have been possible without the outstanding leadership of Senators Howard Cannon, Robert Packwood, and Russell Long, and Congressmen Jim Florio, Edward Madigan, and James Broyhill.

It is especially appropriate that this legislation is named after Harley O. Staggers, who is retiring from Congress this year and who has done so much to achieve passage of this bill as well as other major legislation throughout his illustrious congressional career.

This act is the capstone of my efforts over the past 4 years to get the Federal Government off the backs of private industry by removing needless, burdensome regulation which benefits no one and harms us all. We have deregulated the airlines, a step that restored competitive forces to the airline industry and allowed new, innovative services. We have freed the trucking industry from archaic and inflationary regulations, an action that will allow the startup of new companies, encourage price competition, and improve service. We have deregulated financial institutions, permitting banks to pay interest on checking accounts and higher interest to small savers and eliminating many restrictions on savings institutions loans.

Where regulations cannot be eliminated, we have established a program to reform the way they are produced and reviewed. By Executive order, we have mandated regulators to carefully and publicly analyze the costs of major proposals. We have required that interested members of the public be given more opportunity to participate in the regulatory process. We have established a sunset review program for major new regulations and cut Federal paperwork by 15 percent. We created a Regulatory Council, which is eliminating inconsistent regulations and encouraging innovative regulatory techniques saving hundreds of millions of dollars while still meeting important statutory goals. And Congress recently passed the Regulatory Flexibility Act, which converts into law my administrative program requiring Federal agencies to work to eliminate unnecessary regulatory burdens on small business. I am hopeful for congressional action on my broad regulatory reform proposal now pending, to help complete congressional action on my regulatory reform proposals.

Today these efforts continue with deregulation of the railroad industry and mark the past 4 years as a time in which the Congress and the executive branch stepped forward together in the most significant and successful deregulation program in our Nation's history. We have secured the most fundamental restructuring of the relationship between industry and government since the time of the New Deal.

In recent decades the problems of the railroad industry have become severe. Its 1979 rate of return on net investment was 2.7 percent, as compared to over 10 percent for comparable industries. We have seen a number of major railroad bankruptcies and the continuing expenditure of billions of Federal dollars to keep railroads running. Service and equipment have deteriorated. A key reason for this state of affairs has been overregulation by the Federal Government. At the heart of this legislation is freeing the railroad industry and its customers from such excessive control.

The Interstate Commerce Commission (ICC), under the able leadership of Chairman Gaskins, has made substantial progress toward reducing regulatory burdens, and I commend the Commission for the progress it has made. The bill I am signing today builds upon and reinforces these crucial reforms, and I look to the Commission for prompt and effective implementation to achieve its deregulatory objectives.

The Staggers act places a gradually increasing jurisdictional threshold on ICC review of rate decisions, thereby providing railroads with much-needed freedom to set rates while also affording shippers appropriate protection. It encourages a realignment of the joint rate system that now results in some carriers losing money on many hauls, and for the first time explicitly authorizes railroads and shippers to contract for rates and services like other private industries. Competition is increased by significantly curtailing the collective rate-setting practices of the railroad industry, and remaining ICC rate and railroad restructuring procedures are simplified and shortened.

The act also reforms the existing system of labor protection for Conrail employees and will allow Conrail to provide more effective service to those who depend on it. In addition, the legislation amends the Rock Island Railroad Transition and Employee Assistance Act to help assure that displaced former Rock Island employees will receive financial assistance necessary to make the transition to other employment. As a result, the reorganization of Rock Island lines, so vital to Midwest shippers, should be facilitated.

Finally, the act authorizes expansion and revision of the existing financing program which provides funds to help our Nation's railroads. It is my expectation that these Federal funds be directed to the maximum extent possible at rail restructuring projects, and the Secretary of Transportation has assured me that he will give the highest priority to using the funds provided in that manner.

All Americans will benefit from the Staggers Rail Act of 1980.

NOTE: As enacted, S. 1946 is Public Law 96–448, approved October 14.

Hostage Relief Act of 1980
Statement on Signing H.R. 7085 Into Law. October 14, 1980

The tragic circumstances which make the Hostage Relief Act of 1980 so necessary have occurred all too often in recent years. In particular, the holding of 52 Americans in Tehran has made this legislation urgent.

I am pleased that speedy and thoughtful action on the part of both Houses of Congress has brought to my desk a bill which will go a long way toward alleviating some of the burdens faced by the families of those held hostage and will ensure that adequate medical treatment will be provided to hostages and to their loved ones when they return.

All those held captive in Iran and others in similar situations since November 4, 1979, irrespective of whether they are in the Armed Forces or are civilian

Government employees, will receive the education and health benefits provided for in this bill. Additionally, all of the hostages will be excused from Federal taxes for the period of time spent in captivity.

With the enactment of this legislation, we take a small but extremely important step toward providing a measure of compensation for the severe hardships hostages and their families endure. I am extremely pleased to sign this bill into law.

NOTE: As enacted, H.R. 7085 is Public Law 96–449, approved October 14.

Intelligence Authorization Act for Fiscal Year 1981

Statement on Signing S. 2597 Into Law. October 14, 1980

It is with pleasure that I sign into law the Intelligence Authorization Act for Fiscal Year 1981. This legislation authorizes the appropriation of funds for our intelligence community. It is essential that I and those who aid me in the formulation of our Nation's foreign policy make our decisions on the basis of accurate information about the capabilities and intentions of other countries and of forces that shape world events. I am pleased that the Congress has followed my recommendation and authorized sufficient funds to ensure that we continue to have the best intelligence service possible.

I am also pleased to note that this legislation contains authority for the payment of a death gratuity to the surviving dependents of intelligence personnel killed overseas as a result of hostile or terrorist activities or in connection with

an intelligence activity having a substantial element of risk. I pray that, in the future, situations will not arise that would necessitate use of this provision. It is important, however, that our intelligence officers overseas, who daily sacrifice the comforts of home to serve their country under sometimes difficult and dangerous circumstances, know that we as a nation stand behind them and will provide for the welfare of their families should tragedy strike.

In addition to providing funds for a strong intelligence service, S. 2597 also contains legislation that modifies the so-called Hughes-Ryan amendment and establishes, for the first time in statute, a comprehensive system for congressional oversight of intelligence activities. This legislation, which will help to ensure that U.S. intelligence activities are carried out effectively and in a manner that respects individual rights and liberties, was an important part of the comprehensive intelligence charter on which this administration and the Congress have worked for over 2 years. Unfortunately, the press of other legislative matters prevented passage of the charter thus far in this session.

The oversight legislation that was passed does not seek to alter the respective authorities and responsibilities of the executive and legislative branches, but rather codifies the current practice and relationship that has developed between this administration and the Senate and House intelligence committees over the past 3 years. This intent is evidenced by the language of the bill itself and the legislative history that stands behind it.

It is noteworthy that in capturing the current practice and relationship, the legislation preserves an important measure of flexibility for the President and the executive branch. It does so not only by recognizing the inherent constitutional authorities of both branches, but by recognizing that there are circumstances in which sensitive information may have to be shared only with a very limited number of executive branch officials, even though the congressional oversight committees are authorized recipients of classified information. Circumstances of this nature have been rare in the past; I would expect them to be rare in the future. The legislation creates the expectation that a sense of care and a spirit of accommodation will continue to prevail in such cases.

I wish to thank Senators Birch Bayh, Dee Huddleston, Dan Inouye, Barry Goldwater, and Mac Mathias, and Congressmen Ed Boland, Clem Zablocki, Bill Burlison, and Ken Robinson for their significant roles in the passage of this legislation.

NOTE: As enacted, S. 2597 is Public Law 96–450, approved October 14.

Interview With the President

Excerpts From a Question-and-Answer Session With John Chancellor of NBC News. October 14, 1980

JUDICIAL APPOINTMENTS

MR. CHANCELLOR. Mr. President, Ronald Reagan says if elected he's going to name a woman to the Supreme Court. What's your response to that?

THE PRESIDENT. Well, I'd say he's privileged to make that promise. I understand that when he was Governor of California he made 600 appointments to judges, and only 12 of them were women. And he made three appointments to the Supreme Court of California, and they were all white males. Also, he promised to appoint, I think, an Italian American as judge, and he's still got 3 weeks to go.

I've had a good record on appointing women, as you know, and minority groups as well. I've appointed more women by far than all the other Presidents in this Nation combined in Federal judgeships, and I'll continue that process. But I think it is a mistake for a President to promise that in the Supreme Court appointment that it would be a particular kind of American. I'll consider all of them, and I'll continue to treat women fairly.

MR. CHANCELLOR. Mr. President, it seems to me you were not surprised when I asked you that question.

1980 PRESIDENTIAL CAMPAIGN

Let me ask you about the public opinion polls and how you feel about the state of the campaign right now. In the NBC poll among decided voters you're about 10 points behind. We do see evidence in that poll that it's going to come closer to that. Can you tell me how you think it's going to go for the rest of the campaign and how it will come out?

THE PRESIDENT. I think I'll win. We have 3 weeks to go from now, almost exactly, and I think the American people, as they approach the time of making this crucial choice will determine whether their own future, the future of their families and those they love will be most beneficially affected by choosing me or Governor Reagan.

So far, the campaign has been distorted to some degree by the inevitable debate about the debates, the conjecture about who is ahead or who's not ahead, and the charges and counter-charges between candidates. I think in the future, though, the difference on the issues will be much more significant among the voters, and because of that I think I'll win.

———

MR. CHANCELLOR. Mr. President, do you think that you've had a chance to get the issues across to the people and that your opponent has dealt with issues in this campaign? My sense of the campaign to date is that there has been a great deal of talk about competence and character, that your opponent is questioning your competence and that you've been questioning his character. How would you describe the campaign so far?

THE PRESIDENT. I think it's provided an inadequate means by which the approach on the issues between myself and Governor Reagan could be addressed. We've accepted five or six different invitations, for instance, for a man-to-man debate between the nominee of the Democratic Party and the nominee of the Republican Party. Governor Reagan has refused in every instance to carry on such a debate. I challenge him now in a very constructive way, not an adversarial way, to meet me under any circumstances on a head-to-head debate so that he and I can be cross-examined on how differently we see the major issues that affect the American people now and in the future.

So far, there's been too much attention given, perhaps by the news media and others, on the conduct of the debate, the charges and counter-charges, the status of the current public opinion polls, this kind of thing, who will debate whom and under what circumstances, and not concentrating enough on the basic issues of economics, defense capability, peace in the world, and other matters of that kind.

MR. CHANCELLOR. Do you think the next 3 weeks of the campaign will be better in these terms?

THE PRESIDENT. Yes. I don't think there's any doubt about that. There's a difference in the attitude of an American voter when they finally go to the polls to choose their President, compared to what it is in the early stages of a general election campaign, and certainly sharply contrasted with the attitude of a voter in the primary campaigns when the excitement of the campaign itself is important. It's an opportunity in the primary part of the campaign to express displeasure with existing circumstances, to, so-called, send a message to Washington, and so forth. But when you get down to the point of choosing the man who will sit in this Oval Office and make decisions that affect your life for the next 4 years and the integrity of the principles of our Nation, the status of the economic circumstances within which we raise our children and prepare for the future, the relationship between our country and other nations on Earth, that is such a sobering experience that I believe the American people will focus on these issues very closely and very acutely as the time for that choice approaches.

NOTE: The interview, portions of which were shown on the "NBC Nightly News," began at 3:30 p.m. in the Oval Office at the White House.

Federal Actions in the Lake Tahoe Region
Executive Order 12247.   October 15, 1980

By the authority vested in me as President by the Constitution of the United States of America, and in order to ensure that Federal agency actions protect the extraordinary natural, scenic, recreational and ecological resources in the Lake Tahoe Region (as defined by Public Law 91–148), an area of national concern, it is hereby ordered as follows:

1–1. *Tahoe Federal Coordinating Council.*

1–101. There is established an interagency committee to be known as the Tahoe Federal Coordinating Council.

1–102. The Council shall be composed of representatives from the following Executive agencies (those of the Western Federal Regional Council, Region IX):

(a) Department of Defense.

(b) Department of the Interior.

(c) Department of Agriculture.

(d) Department of Commerce.

(e) Department of Health and Human Services.

(f) Department of Housing and Urban Development.

(g) Department of Transportation.

(h) Environmental Protection Agency.

1–103. The Council shall be chaired by the representative from the Department of Agriculture, which shall be responsible for providing administrative support.

1–104. Other agencies may be invited to designate representatives to participate in the activities of the Council from time to time.

1–2. *Environmental Thresholds.*

1–201. (a) The Council shall develop and issue environmental quality thresholds and carrying capacities for the air, water, and terrestrial components of the area known as the Lake Tahoe Region (Public Law 91–148), which lies within the States of California and Nevada.

(b) These thresholds and carrying capacities shall be developed in consultation with the States of California and Nevada, the local governments in and around the area, and the public.

(c) These thresholds and carrying capacities shall be based on a refinement and a periodic updating of the Western Federal Regional Council's "Lake Tahoe Environment Assessment" issued during February, 1980, and on other appropriate information.

1–202. The Council shall assist the State and local governments of California and Nevada in adopting and utilizing these thresholds and carrying capacities.

1–203. These thresholds and carrying capacities shall, to the extent permitted by law, be utilized by Executive agencies and the Council in determining the impact of Federal actions on the environment of the Region.

1–3. *Environmental Actions.*

1–301. An Executive agency shall, prior to authorizing any undertaking within the Region, whether by taking direct action or approving a license, permit, or financial assistance, determine if that undertaking will have a significant or potentially significant adverse effect on the environment of the Region. This determination shall be made in writing. It shall take into account the thresholds and carrying capacities developed by the Council.

1–302. The Executive agency shall transmit to the Council a copy of its determination as to the environmental impact on the Region.

1–303. (a) The Council will promptly review the agency determinations as to the environmental effect on the Region. The Council shall ensure that there is adequate opportunity for public comment on the agency determination.

(b) If the Council concludes that the action to be taken would be compatible with the environment of the Region, the

Chairman of the Council shall promptly so notify the agency.

(c) If the Council concludes that the action to be taken would have a significant adverse impact on the resources and ecological values of the Region, the Chairman of the Council shall recommend to the responsible Executive agency that the action not be undertaken or that it be modified to eliminate the adverse impact.

1–304. If the agency disagrees with the recommendations of the Council, the Chairman of the Council shall promptly refer the matter to the Council on Environmental Quality for its recommendation as to the prompt resolution of any disagreement.

1–305. Until the thresholds and carrying capacities are issued, Executive agencies shall, to the extent permitted by law, not take any direct action nor approve any license, permit, or financial assistance in the Region which would significantly (a) stimulate additional development in environmentally sensitive areas as defined by land use plans or zoning ordinances of the Region, or (b) promote automobile traffic into the Region.

1–306. Until the thresholds and carrying capacities are issued, Executive agencies shall review agency actions in the Region which may have an effect on the Region's overall waste treatment planning. This review shall determine if such actions should be deferred until waste water treatment plans, as provided by Section 208 of the Federal Water Pollution Control Act (33 U.S.C. 1288), are adopted by the States of California and Nevada and approved by the Environmental Protection Agency.

1–4. *General Provisions.*

1–401. The Chairman of the Council on Environmental Quality and the Secretary of Agriculture shall advise the President from time to time on the effectiveness of this Order. They shall recommend other administrative action which may be taken to improve the coordination of agency actions and decisions whenever such coordination would protect and enhance the Region's natural and ecological values.

1–402. Nothing in this Order shall be construed to limit, delay, or prohibit any agency action which is essential for the protection of public health or safety, for national security, or for the maintenance or rehabilitation of environmental quality within the Region.

JIMMY CARTER

The White House,
    October 15, 1980.

[Filed with the Office of the Federal Register,
    10:43 a.m., October 15, 1980]

Federal Actions in the Lake Tahoe Region

*Statement on Signing Executive Order 12247.
October 15, 1980*

I am today signing an Executive order to improve the coordination of Federal agency activities in the Lake Tahoe Basin. The issuance of this order is a result of the actions I announced on May 30, 1980. In that announcement, I affirmed that Lake Tahoe is an area of national concern and that the quality of the lake must be protected. This step we are taking today will establish a Lake Tahoe Federal Coordinating Council to see that the Federal Government does its part to meet this objective. The Council will be composed of the Departments of Defense, Interior, Agriculture, Commerce, Transportation, Health and Human Services, Housing and

Urban Development, and the Environmental Protection Agency.

The Council's purpose will be to ensure that Federal programs do not contribute to environmental degradation in the Lake Tahoe Basin. The Council will develop and issue environmental quality thresholds and carrying capacity standards for the air, water, and land resources in the region. Until these standards are adopted, the Council will recommend that proposed Federal actions having significant adverse environmental effects on the Lake Tahoe region not be approved. The Executive order also directs Federal agencies to review their programs and other actions which may affect the Lake Tahoe area and to defer action if such programs would significantly stimulate additional development in environmentally critical areas or would promote pollution from increases in auto traffic.

I am pleased that this Council already is being organized, has begun its assigned tasks, and is working in close consultation with the States, local agencies, and the public.

I am also pleased to see that California and Nevada have recently reached agreement on a revised Bi-State Tahoe Regional Planning Compact. An amended compact has been approved by both States and is now being presented to the Congress for ratification. I congratulate the Governors and legislatures of both States on this achievement. As I noted last May, it is our intention to help make this compact an effective planning instrument for Lake Tahoe. The Federal Council established today will work together with the compact agency to achieve this goal.

I am greatly encouraged by the initiatives taken thus far by the States and by the Congress as well. Pending legislation to provide for acquisition of environmentally sensitive lands at Lake Tahoe is now before the Congress. This legislation will complement the administration actions we are taking now, and it has my full support. I applaud the efforts of Congressmen Santini, Burton, and Fazio in gaining House approval of this bill, and I am hopeful that we will see this measure passed by the full Congress soon. I want to express my appreciation to all who have supported the Santini-Burton legislation, the amendment of the Tahoe Regional Planning Compact, and the establishment of the Federal Coordinating Council.

But the signing of an Executive order on the passage of a law is not a guarantee that we will protect the lake. All Americans have a stake in what we do to affect the quality of this priceless heritage. We all must be careful that the environmental stresses placed on this unique area are not exceeded. Our actions today will determine whether Lake Tahoe—a national treasure—will remain protected for future generations.

Fifth Circuit Court of Appeals Reorganization Act of 1980

Statement on Signing H.R. 7665 Into Law.
October 15, 1980

I am pleased to sign into law H.R. 7665, the Fifth Circuit Court of Appeals Reorganization Act of 1980. This legislation splits the Fifth Circuit Court of Appeals, our largest Federal appellate court, into two new circuits: the Fifth Circuit, composed of the Canal Zone, Louisiana, Mississippi, and Texas, and the Eleventh Circuit, composed of Alabama, Florida, and Georgia. There is a limit to the number of judgeships an appellate court can accommodate and still function effectively.

Some time ago it became clear that if the rapid growth in the caseload of the Fifth Circuit continued, necessitating the addition of more and more judges, an unwieldy bench would result. When the size of this court reached 26 active judges, the practical problems of having all the judges take part in a single case became unmanageable. At the same time, it became increasingly difficult to preserve consistency and predictability among the decisions of three-judge panels. The active judges of the circuit early this year unanimously petitioned the Congress requesting that the circuit be split into 2 autonomous circuits to enhance the court's ability to deliver consistent, fair, and expeditious justice.

I cannot sign this bill without noting the impact the old Fifth Circuit has had on this Nation. The Fifth Circuit has a distinguished history of judicial responsibility. This court played a key role in the long-neglected reapportionment of congressional and legislative districts, and in ending the county unit system that had denied urban Georgians equal participation in the political process.

During the dramatic and often difficult years of the 1950's and 1960's, the Fifth Circuit was charged with the actual dismantling of the system of segregation that had stood since the Civil War. In negotiating the thorny pathway that led to end of legal racial discrimination in schools, public accommodations, and other areas, many of the judges of the circuit endured personal condemnation and threats to their lives and to their families. As our Nation declared its intent to end all forms of legal discrimination based on race and color the Fifth Circuit bore the heavy burden of applying the principles laid down by the Supreme Court in a long series of landmark cases that changed the face of the Deep South.

Under the leadership of Chief Judges Richard Rives, Elbert Tuttle, and John Brown, to name just three of the chief judges known to every constitutional lawyer or student of that era, the Fifth Circuit played a crucial role in a critical period in the life of our region, holding us to the highest principles of justice on which our Nation was founded and supervising their practical application.

The enactment of this legislation represents the work and cooperation of many individuals, especially the judges of the present Fifth Circuit and the senatorial and congressional delegations from the six affected States. I commend the Congress for having acted so promptly in response to the needs of our Federal courts.

NOTE: As enacted, H.R. 7665 is Public Law 96–452, approved October 14.

Maritime Training and Appropriation Authorization Bills

Statement on Signing H.R. 5451 and H.R. 6554 Into Law. October 15, 1980

I am pleased today to sign two bills to provide continuing support for the United States-flag merchant marine: H.R. 5451, the Maritime Education and Training Act of 1980, the most comprehensive reform ever of our maritime training and education laws, and H.R. 6554, the Maritime Appropriation Authorization Act for Fiscal Year 1981.

The United States has led the world in developing technologically superior merchant vessels. However, these sophisticated vessels can be no better than the licensed officers who operate them. Therefore, in recent years, the Federal Government has increased its role in maritime education and training.

My administration has maintained the commitment of the Federal Government to the training of young men and women as licensed officers for our merchant fleet. Such training is provided at the United States Merchant Marine Academy at Kings Point, N.Y., operated by the Federal Government, and at the six State Maritime Academies—in Maine, Massachusetts, New York, Texas, California, and Michigan—that receive Federal support.

As the Maritime Education and Training Act states, "It is the policy of the United States that merchant marine vessels of the United States should be operated by highly trained and efficient citizens of the United States and that the United States Navy and the merchant marine of the United States should work closely together to promote the maximum integration of the total seapower forces of the United States."

To further this policy, the act provides more balanced Federal support of the United States Merchant Marine Academy and the six State Maritime Academies to ensure that these institutions will provide the highly specialized training required to operate United States-flag merchant vessels. Further, the act imposes certain service obligations to ensure that the graduates of our merchant marine academies will be available to operate United States merchant vessels in time of war or national emergency.

The second bill, the Maritime Appropriation Authorization Act for Fiscal Year 1981, authorizes $135 million in construction differential subsidies that will generate much needed employment in our shipyards. It provides for $347.7 million in operating differential subsidies so that U.S.-flag vessels can continue to compete in international markets with lower cost foreign operators. Further, H.R. 6554 authorizes $17 million for research and development activities, such as using coal rather than oil to run our merchant vessels.

The legislation also authorizes $32.5 million in funds for the Fiscal Year 1981 expenses of the Maritime Education and Training Act of 1980, which I have just signed. Finally, H.R. 6554 provides $38.8 million in operating expenses for the Maritime Administration. This includes funds for the preservation of vessels in the National Defense Reserve Fleet, which we have traditionally called upon in times of national emergency. Overall, this act authorizes a total of $571 million for Fiscal Year 1981, an increase of $136 million over the amount authorized last year.

I remain committed to a strong American maritime industry, as this legislation indicates. I look forward to continuing to work with the merchant marine community to achieve our common goal of a strong and vibrant U.S. merchant fleet and shipbuilding mobilization base.

NOTE: As enacted, H.R. 5451 is Public Law 96–453, and H.R. 6554 is Public Law 96–459, both approved October 15.

Household Goods Transportation Act of 1980

Statement on Signing S. 1798 Into Law.
October 15, 1980

I have today signed into law S. 1798, the Household Goods Transportation Act of 1980. This bill is an important addition to the Motor Carrier Act, which I signed only 3 months ago. While both shippers and consumers will benefit from the anti-inflationary effect of that act, this bill addresses the difficulties consumers encounter in the one circumstance that puts them in direct contact with the trucking industry—moving day.

The Household Goods Transportation Act incorporates the reforms of the Motor Carrier Act, including procompetitive changes in the areas of market entry, collective ratemaking, and rate flexibility. Beyond these, this legislation addresses three important consumer needs: improved consumer information, increased price and service alternatives, and effective remedies for poor service.

The consumer benefits of this legislation will depend in large measure on the willingness of movers to take advantage of the flexibility and freedom of these reforms. No longer will movers be subject to excessive paperwork or detailed regulations prescribing how they conduct aspects of their business. Instead, competitiveness will be the key to success. The challenge to the moving industry is great. The act gives movers every opportunity to offer improved service. No longer can regulation be blamed for poor service or consumer dissatisfaction.

This bill reduces regulation, increases competition, and provides for essential consumer protection. It furthers my regulatory goals and fulfills the commitment I made over a year ago when I proposed trucking reform legislation. I promised then to "assure that consumers receive increased protection in the household goods moving industry."

I am grateful to those Members of Congress who worked so tirelessly for this bill. Senate Commerce Committee Chair-

man Howard Cannon and Senator Bob Packwood devoted special hearings to the problems in this industry and developed the initial drafts of the bill we have today. In the House, Public Works and Transportation Committee Chairman Bizz Johnson, Subcommittee Chairman Jim Howard, and Congressmen Bill Harsha and Bud Shuster made important changes that consolidated support for the measure. Congressman Bob Eckhardt also contributed to enactment of this bill with valuable suggestions and assistance, especially in the area of dispute settlement.

Credit must also be given to the consumer representatives and household goods movers who have pressed for adoption of this legislation. Chairman Gaskins and the members of the Interstate Commerce Commission provided essential guidance for these reforms, and I look forward with confidence to the Commission's prompt implementation of this legislation.

NOTE: As enacted, S. 1798 is Public Law 96–454, approved October 15.

Judicial Councils Reform and Judicial Conduct and Disability Act of 1980

Statement on Signing S. 1873 Into Law.
October 15, 1980

I am pleased to sign into law S. 1873, the Judicial Councils Reform and Judicial Conduct and Disability Act of 1980. This legislation creates a mechanism and uniform procedures by which members of the judiciary can respond to allegations of unfitness against Federal judges. It makes a sound accommodation between two essential values—preserving the independence of the Federal judiciary, and making judges, as public servants, accountable under the law for their conduct in office.

Our Federal judiciary has a long and honorable history, one that has set a high standard for society as a whole. Almost without exception, the judges who have served in the Federal courts have conducted themselves with intellectual and personal distinction. But judges are human and have on rare occasions acted in ways that have injured the effectiveness of their courts.

The Constitution provides that Federal judges may be removed from office through the impeachment process. This procedure is cumbersome and is applied only to the most egregious cases. During the entire history of our Nation, only four Federal judges have been convicted and removed from office by impeachment. Experience has shown that if only the massive machinery of impeachment is available, some valid complaints will not be remedied. Most States have systems for dealing with unfit judges, and there is a need for a uniform, nationwide system to hear and fairly determine complaints against Federal judges.

Judicial independence—the freedom of judges to interpret and apply the law without favor or fear of retribution—is amply safeguarded by this legislation. The system created by this act is contained entirely within the judicial branch of the Government; only Federal judges are involved in the process. No judge need fear disciplinary proceedings as a result of decisions he or she has rendered, because this possibility is explicitly precluded. Furthermore, the bill assures the judges of fairness and confidentiality.

At the same time, the legislation creates uniform, known procedures for dealing with an unfit judge. Citizens can be confident that a complaint filed under this system will receive fair and serious attention throughout the process. For all these reasons the new process should increase public confidence in the quality of the Federal judiciary.

The development of this legislation has required the energy and cooperation of many individuals, particularly the Judiciary Committees of the Congress. I want to commend especially Senators Kennedy, DeConcini, Nunn, and Bayh, and Congressmen Rodino, Kastenmeier, and Railsback for their work on this important legislation.

NOTE: As enacted, S. 1873 is Public Law 96–458, approved October 15.

Federal District Court Organization Act of 1980

Statement on Signing H.R. 8178 Into Law.
October 15, 1980

I am pleased to sign into law H.R. 8178, the Federal District Court Organization Act of 1980. This legislation helps to ensure that the organizational structure of the Federal courts will reflect the needs and conditions of the areas they serve. To this end, the act creates a new place of holding court in Santa Anna, Calif., and alters somewhat the geographical boundaries of Federal courts in Iowa, Missouri, North Carolina, and Texas.

The organizational structure of the Federal courts has an impact on the overall effectiveness of our justice system. In the past, the organization of the district courts has tended to evolve in response to local pressures rather than to consideration of the long-term needs and goals of the judicial system as a whole. I commend Congress for processing district court legislation in a comprehensive manner. Congressman Robert Kastenmeier, chairman of the Judiciary Subcommittee on Courts, Civil Liberties, and the Administration of Justice, deserves special recognition for developing this approach.

NOTE: As enacted, H.R. 8178 is Public Law 96–462, approved October 15.

President's Committee on Mental Retardation

Appointment of Nine Members.
October 15, 1980

The President today announced the appointment of nine persons as members of the President's Committee on Mental Retardation. They are:

A. OMIE BROWN, of Madison, Wis., a counselor at the University of Wisconsin counseling service and a founder of the Native American Indian Children's Advocacy.

JOSEPH A. BUONOMO, of Arlington, Mass., president-elect of the National Association for Retarded Citizens and executive vice president of F. L. Putnam stockbrokers.

LEONARD G. ESPINOSA, of Albuquerque, N. Mex., an attorney who is a strong advocate of the rights of mentally retarded citizens and is active in organizations such as the National Association for Retarded Citizens.

LILIA EVANGELISTA, of the Bronx, N.Y., a pediatrician specializing in treating children with cerebral palsy, who is assistant clinical professor of pediatrics and rehabilitation at Albert Einstein College of Medicine and medical director of Lincoln Children's Evaluation and Rehabilitation Clinic.

LEIDA ILEANA COLLADO HERRELL, of Potomac, Md., an adviser on Hispanic affairs to the Montgomery County Government Department of Family Resources, previously a school psychologist.

ROBERT GREENE JORDAN, JR., of Germantown, Tenn., professor of pediatrics and child development at the University of Tennessee College of Medicine and director of the university's Child Development Center (reappointment).

WILLIAM L. McGOWAN, of Clifton Park, N.Y., president of the New York State Civil Service Employees Association and former chair of the Mental Hygiene Presidents' Association.

ANDERSON W. POLLARD, of Pasadena, Calif., community liaison officer with the child psychiatry and mental retardation program of UCLA's Neuropsychiatric Institute and a director of the American Association on Mental Deficiency and the Handicapped Early Childhood Assistance Program (reappointment).

VALAIDA SMITH WALKER, of Yeadon, Pa., an associate professor and chairperson-elect of the department of special education at Temple University, formerly commissioner of mental retardation for the southeastern region for the Pennsylvania Department of Public Welfare.

National Advisory Committee on Oceans and Atmosphere

Appointment of Seven Members.
October 15, 1980

The President today announced the appointment of seven persons as members of the National Advisory Committee on Oceans and Atmosphere. They are:

SYLVIA A. EARLE, of San Francisco, Calif., a marine botanist, curator of phycology with the California Academy of Sciences, and chief scientist on the Sea Films research vessel *Eagle*.

BURT H. KEENAN, of Lafayette, La., chairman of the board and chief executive officer of Offshore Logistics, Inc., a major transportation company serving the offshore oil industry, operating a fleet of work vessels and helicopters.

JAY G. LANZILLO, of Orleans, Mass., a working fisherman, industry representative for Chatham Seafood Cooperative and Old Harbor Fish Co., and a member of the New England Fisheries Development Task Force.

SHARRON STEWART, of Lake Jackson, Tex., director of the Texas Environmental Coalition, former chairman of the Task Force on Coastal Zone Management of the Texas Committee on Natural Resources (reappointment).

GEORGE G. TAPPER, of Port St. Joe, Fla., president of Tapper and Co. (steamship agents), Southern States Shipping Co. (customhouse brokers and freight forwarders), and St. Joe Stevedoring Co.; chairman of the Port St. Joe Port Authority, where he is working on a project to build a seafood and agriculture exporting port to use underutilized species of fish.

CHARLES H. WARREN, of Sacramento, Calif., an attorney, former Chairman of the Council on Environmental Quality, a former California State legislator.

WARREN M. WASHINGTON, of Boulder, Colo., a research scientist and director of the National Center for Atmospheric Research (reappointment).

Boston, Massachusetts

Remarks to Senior Citizens.
October 15, 1980

Senator Kennedy, Speaker O'Neill, Mayor Kevin White, my fellow workers in Washington, and those State and local officials who are here today:

It's a very great honor for me to be in this wonderful community with a man whom I've admired and heard from for a long time, Frank Manning.[1] I'm glad to hear he's going to get out of the hospital Friday. [*Laughter*] If he can do this much

---

[1] Mr. Manning, president of the Massachusetts Association of Older Americans, made one of the introductory speeches.

before he gets out of the hospital, just imagine what he can do after he gets out of the hospital.

Nothing in the world can thrill a President's heart so much as to travel around this Nation and see the wonderful spirit and the idealism and commitment and the unselfishness and the hard work and the effectiveness of the senior citizens of our country, who've learned through experience what our Nation is and what it can be for a better life in the future. There's a tremendous potential among those who've reached retirement age or who are approaching retirement age. It hasn't been long since it was a rare thing for someone to live to be 70 or 80 years old, but in the 1980's that will be the fastest growing part of the American population.

If you'll pardon my making a personal reference, my own mother, with whom I talked late last night, she said, "Don't interrupt me till the ballgame's over." [*Laughter*] She's 82 now. She just recently broke her hip. But she's dynamic and vigorous, just as young as she ever was. Each day when she wakes up, it's a new opportunity for her to stretch her mind and stretch her heart, to make more friends, to learn more about God's world, and to let her life be meaningful to those around her.

She's not much different from anyone here. Not many people when they're 68 years old volunteer for the Peace Corps and go to India and stay a couple of years and come back and start a new career. But she typifies in my own personal life the treasure of the senior citizens of this country.

And I can't help making one more personal reference about Senator Kennedy's dear mother—90 years old, recently also hospitalized, now fully on the road to recovery—and what she means to this Nation. People in every community almost in the entire world look on her, epitomizing in a highly publicized but very personal way the meaning of a family and the meaning of faith and the meaning of confidence and the meaning of deep religious convictions that never change.

Frank Manning, my mother, Mrs. Rose Kennedy are more famous than a lot of people. But they are examples of the courage and the commitment and the worth to our country of tens of millions of people just like you: men and women who, after they reach retirement age—and we've raised the mandatory retirement age, as you know, very much, and I think we might raise it some more—have a chance to start a new life in many ways, new interests, to make new friends, to continue to grow.

This election this year is a very important test in history of what our Nation will be in the future.

I grew up on a small farm in the depression years in Georgia. I remember those depression years. I remember the minimum wage fights in the Congress, when the sweat shops were put in danger by the Democrats and they advocated a 25-cent minimum wage. The Democrats were for it; the Republicans against it. My first job as a high school graduate was when the minimum wage had been raised to 40 cents an hour. That enormous increase from 25 cents to 40 cents was supported and eventually passed by the Democrats; the Republicans were against it. You might say, "Well that's just ancient history. The Republicans have changed." But do you know what my opponent says about that minimum wage? He said it's caused more unemployment and more suffering than anything since the Great Depression.

I know how a family feels when they're unemployed, when they're temporarily out of work and the children need food and clothes, need a way to go to school. Unemployment compensation is a program put into effect by the Democrats; Republicans, of course, were against it. My opponent says that "Unemployment compensation is just a prepaid vacation for freeloaders." This kind of philosophy permeates the difference between the Democrats and Republicans; it always has, it does now, and predictably it will in the future.

I remember what John F. Kennedy said about senior citizens at an older people's meeting at the White House. He said, "It's not enough for a great nation merely to have added new years to life. Our objective must also be to add new life to those years." That's still the objective of the Democratic Party. We must make sure that those opportunities for a better life are realized, because at this moment, in this election the choice will be made.

When Medicare was proposed many years ago, obviously by a Democratic President, obviously supported by a Democratic Congress, there was a man who began his political career by going around the United States from one State to another speaking against Medicare. You might guess who that man was. It's the man who's the Republican nominee for President. You might say that's ancient history to be against Medicare, but he has also has come up strongly against national health insurance.

As you know, trained by Frank Manning, supported by you, the foremost spokesman for better health care in this country, better mental health care in this country, the humane problems of having better food care in this country for the poor is your own Senator Ted Kennedy. This is the kind of opposition that we Democrats all face together.

Social security is the cornerstone of a decent life for older Americans. When Franklin Roosevelt proposed social security, the Republican opposition said this is the same as communism or socialism. Social security has been one of the greatest things that ever happened to our country.

And when I came here in 1976 to campaign for President and when I went to all the communities throughout this country to campaign for the highest office in our land, there was a general feeling then that social security was on the way toward bankruptcy. But Father Drinan, Joe Moakley, also Tip O'Neill, Senator Kennedy, all of the Democrats rallied together to put social security back on its feet, to make sure it was a sound program and free of the threat of bankruptcy that had been built up during the previous 8 years, when Republican Presidents occupied the White House. We made that change.

But if social security was ever made to be a voluntary program, so that anybody who wanted to could withdraw from it, not contribute to its trust fund any longer, but seek some other private or not have any sort of retirement system, those who depend on social security would have lost their security.

We must be sure that we keep in mind the issues that are at stake in just exactly 3 weeks from now. Our country is a great country. It's great not because of its military might, which is enormous, it's great not because of its economic might, which transcends that of all nations on Earth, it's great because of its moral principles, its ethical principles, and because, as Sen-

ator Kennedy pointed out, we've put our investment in human beings.

It's necessary for a nation to have a strong military force, but the best weapon is one that's never fired in combat, and the best soldier is one that never has to lay his life down or shed his blood on the field of battle. We've got to have a nation strong, but one at peace.

Times don't change much. When you look at history, you see a repetition of the political combat that has been in our Nation since it was first founded. My Republican opponent quite often quotes the eloquent words of Franklin D. Roosevelt. On occasion he quotes Harry Truman. On occasion he quotes John Fitzgerald Kennedy. But then a couple of months ago in an interview with Time magazine, he said, and I quote him: "If you look back, you find that those great social reforms really didn't work." And he continues to say that the compassionate programs of the New Deal were actually based on fascism. Franklin D. Roosevelt wouldn't approve of a candidate who said that quoting his own words.

There is a lot at stake in this election: minimum wage, we've improved it greatly; unemployment compensation, the Congress is now extending it an additional period of time to protect families whose incomes are in danger; Medicare, it's stronger and better than ever; social security, now sound; national health insurance, comprehensive health care, it's coming in the years ahead, and not too long, I pray. These kinds of issues, important to you, are also important to your children and my children and your grandchildren and my grandchildren. As we have been protected in our generation by the courage and conviction of Democrats in the past, it's our responsibility to be just as courageous, just as dedicated, just as unselfish, as election days approach, to protect the integrity and the quality of life of those whom we also love.

Finally, let me say to you that I'll be campaigning day and night between now and election day on November the 4th. Senator Ted Kennedy will go with me today to Pennsylvania, or to New Jersey, and we'll be campaigning together there. We'll be together next weekend in Washington, D.C., come back together to campaign in New York. He's been to California to campaign with me, to show the unity that exists in the party on which we depend.

You are partners with us. And what you do the next 3 weeks, on the telephone, in your own neighborhood, with your families, throughout this State, and perhaps throughout the Nation, can make the difference. I know from careful observation and poll results today that the election is very close. It's very close in the Commonwealth of Massachusetts. You can make the difference. The responsibility for the future of our country is on my shoulders, yes; but it's on your shoulders, as well.

We've got to make sure that we continue to have a good energy program, adequate fuel supplies, not turned over to the oil companies. We've got to give financial assistance to the elderly and the poor to pay those high energy bills. The breadth of what we must do for human beings to have a better life and for a great nation to stay at peace is very, very complicated and very broad. You understand those basic issues, just like religious beliefs, just like the love of one's own family, just like morality and ethics that guide our lives and a concern for one another. These political principles do not change.

And I ask you to join with me and with those other Democrats assembled on this stage to go all out the next 3 weeks, so that when November the 4th comes, we'll celebrate again and keep this Nation on a good path toward future progress, humaneness, compassion, and love, as the Democrats have always done. I want to see a tremendous Democratic victory in Massachusetts and throughout the Nation on November the 4th.

Thank you very much.

NOTE: The President spoke at 11:31 a.m. in the Christopher Columbus Community Center gymnasium.

Boston, Massachusetts

Remarks to Local Residents.
October 15, 1980

I want to make a deal with you. I need you to help me be elected President. And, as you know, Presidents have a limited amount of authority, but I'm asking the authorities to give all these five schools the day off tomorrow. How would you like that? [*Applause*] Now don't you forget, this is a Democratic holiday, not a Republican holiday, right?

What a beautiful day this is. Just look around you. Look at the beautiful blue sky, just breathe the fresh air. I guess the trees and the volcanoes took a day off today, right?

One thing that I'd like to say, and I'll be very brief: Young people, adults, senior citizens all have an opportunity every 4 years to shape the future of this country, to look to the years ahead to see what kind of nation we will have. One person, a few people, can make a lot of difference. Back in 1960, if 28,000 people had voted differently in Texas and if just a few thousand had voted differently in the State of Illinois, John Fitzgerald Kennedy would never have been President of this great Nation. In 1968 the contest was primarily between Hubert Humphrey, Richard Nixon, and a third candidate named George Wallace. George Wallace took a lot of votes away from the Democratic nominee. The election was very close. Had Democrats remembered the future of our Nation and had Democrats in 1968 given their support to a great man, Hubert Humphrey, Richard Nixon would never have been President of this country and we would have saved ourselves a lot of embarrassment and a major setback in the programs that are important to you and to the people that you love.

I've come here today as a Democrat in the tradition of Franklin Roosevelt, Harry Truman, John Fitzgerald Kennedy, Lyndon Baines Johnson, Hubert Humphrey to remind you of the past, to let you know that what a great nation we have today, and how much better nation we can have in the future. Don't forget to work hard, because it's an investment for yourselves and for the people who look to you whom you love.

It's also an investment in the peace of our country and the humanitarian ideals that have bound Democrats together. So, take the day off tomorrow. Between now and the next 3 weeks work hard, and let's elect Democrats from the top all the way to the bottom and show the Republicans that we can fight when the time comes.

Thank you very much. God bless you all.

NOTE: The President spoke at 11:56 a.m. outside the Christopher Columbus Community Center.

Boston, Massachusetts

Remarks at a Democratic National Committee Fundraising Luncheon. October 15, 1980

Senator Kennedy, Governor King, Speaker O'Neill, Speaker McGee,[1] distinguished public servants in State and local government, Members of the Congress, and my friends:

I'm glad to be back in this beautiful city, this exciting community.

One of the most memorable experiences that I've had as President was coming here for the dedication of the library for John Fitzgerald Kennedy. It was a day when God smiled on us. It was a day that brought back memories to my heart and to my mind that were almost overwhelming. It was a day of personal gratification for the members of the Kennedy family. And it was a day of reminder to our Nation of what a brave man had meant. To me, perhaps uniquely in that audience— and I made a brief speech—it brought back the recollection of what the Presidency means, not only to Americans but to the rest of the world.

The general election is a sobering experience in a democracy. The primary campaigns are exciting. The combatants present their views. The voters want to express their displeasure about some of the temporary, transient inconveniences in life. They want to keep the contest going. There's a chance to send a message to Washington. There's a chance to support a large number of distinguished Americans who seek the highest office in the land. But when the general election approaches it's a time of sober thought.

---

[1] Thomas McGee, speaker of the Massachusetts House of Delegates.

A President has a responsibility for the life of our country, the quality of life of people who live in it, opportunity for those who've been deprived; the quality of compassion and love expressed by our central Government; a choice between progress and retrogression; a choice between pure air and clean water and a return to pollution that has plagued our lives in days gone by; a choice between cooperation and partnership at the local level, the State level, and the Federal level of government, in accordance with our Federal system, or the driving of wedges that might separate us one from another who serve in government; a time of assessment of our Nation's strength— where it lies, the basis for it, and more importantly of all, how it will be used.

Ours is the strongest nation on Earth. We're the strongest nation militarily, and we won't let any other country become stronger than we are. Our Nation is the strongest nation on Earth economically, and we try to use our economic strength in a benevolent way—protecting our own interests, yes, but thinking about others.

Ours is the strongest nation on Earth politically. There is no nation in this whole world now, large or small, new or old, that wants to pattern its system of government after that of the Soviet Union. But in the last few years, with the heavy emphasis on human rights, a lot of countries have abandoned military or other dictatorships and totalitarian governments and have moved toward the expression, in democracies, of basic human rights. Ours is a country with unswerving moral commitments, ethical standards, religious freedom. Separation of church and state is important to us and the drawing of particular definitions, religious definitions, of what a public official must be,

contrary to the historical principles of our country.

These kinds of responsibilities are a President's. The questions that come to my desk, the problems that come to my desk are perhaps the most complicated and difficult of all. If a question can be answered in a person's private life or within an individual's home or in a city hall or a county courthouse or in a State legislature or a Governor's office, the question never comes to me. But if the question is so complicated, so difficult, involves the lives of people so intensely, it comes to the Oval Office, and I share it with Speaker O'Neill and I share it with Senator Kennedy and others and try to resolve it in a way that's acceptable to us in a historical context.

I look at the historical nature of things—what happened to John Kennedy, yes, but also what happened to Harry Truman, what happened to Dwight Eisenhower, even what happened to Richard Nixon, Gerald Ford—because I'm part of a continuum, the 39th person that's lived in the White House—the 38th that's lived in the White House, Washington wasn't President when the White House was built. But this is a time of thinking about those serious matters.

I want our country to stay at peace. I want our country to keep high the banner of human rights. I want our country not ever to forget what made us great and the crises that can evolve in the Oval Office if those questions are answered incorrectly, if there is a misjudgment, if there is an abandonment of that continuum of commitment on a bipartisan basis.

Every President since Harry Truman has strongly been an advocate of nuclear arms control. My background is in physics. I worked for Admiral Rickover as a young officer, the senior officer of one of the first two nuclear submarines ever built. I was taught then, not too many years after we used two atomic weapons, what it could mean.

Those atomic weapons pale into relative insignificance when you talk about what it is now. You see terrorism in Jerusalem, terrorism in a synagogue in Paris, where a few pounds of TNT is used to kill dozens or sometimes hundreds of people. Now we talk about megatons. A megaton is a lot of explosive. It would take—we figured on the airplane this morning—putting 50 tons of TNT in a boxcar, a train more than 200 miles long to hold 1 megaton of TNT. The control of that kind of destructive force is perhaps the most important, single responsibility on the shoulder of a President.

My opponent has said, concerning the SALT treaty which Ford, Nixon, and Carter negotiated, that he wanted to tear it up, withdraw it from consideration in the Senate. And he said that he thought the best approach to arms control was to threaten the possibility of a nuclear arms race. And he called for superiority in nuclear weaponry. On the surface it doesn't sound too bad for a proud American to say, "Superiority!" But we've always negotiated for balance, relative equality, tight controls, supervision, and then reductions.

You can imagine the reaction of Americans if Brezhnev said, "We want nuclear superiority, and on that basis we'll negotiate with you to control nuclear weapons." We wouldn't accept it; neither will they.

An arms race could cost tens of billions of dollars; Harold Brown estimated this week perhaps a hundred billion dollars. That's not what our country needs. It's a matter of judgment.

The crises that come to me—I handle them every day. I have not had a single day in the White House when problems didn't exist somewhere in the world. If I handle that problem successfully, the chances are you never know about it. But if I make a misjudgment, that potential crisis could affect your life and the life of everyone you love, perhaps everyone in this country.

I'm not omniscient. I make mistakes. I'm a human being. But to know the course of history and to understand the principles of this Nation and to have the partnership in effect, people like Tip O'Neill and Ted Kennedy and Paul Tsongas and others, and you, is the best insurance that we've got that we don't make a serious mistake.

I'm not insinuating anything underhandedly about my opponent, but there's a pattern that concerns me. There are trouble spots always in the world, and I and my predecessors, Democratic and Republican, have had to deal with those trouble spots in a diplomatic way, using America's military strength, yes, as a kind of a backup, but negotiating and talking and sitting around a peace table. That's important. My Republican opponent has called for the injection of American military forces repeatedly into trouble spots around the world—North Korea, Ecuador, Angola, Rhodesia, Cyprus. You might say that's ancient history, he's changed—this year, Cuba, Pakistan, the Middle East. The choice is a very serious one, and the American people, I think, this last 3 weeks will think about these things.

The last point I want to make is about basic equality. I'm from the South. Had it not been for Martin Luther King, Jr., I would not be standing here. Had we not been forced—against our will, I have to admit—to obey the laws and to obey the principles of the Constitution of the United States, I would not have had a chance to be the first southern President since 1844.

My State is loyal, too. I appreciate it very much what Ted Kennedy said about Massachusetts. Georgia voted for Al Smith in '28. [*Laughter*] Georgia voted for Adlai Stevenson in '52. Georgia voted for Adlai Stevenson in '56. Georgia voted for John Kennedy in '60, with a bigger margin than Massachusetts did. [*Laughter*]

So, we've been loyal Democrats, and I would like to capitalize on that partnership that exists between Georgia and Massachusetts this time. But I can tell you that the issue in Massachusetts is in doubt. I've seen the polls; so have you. And the memory and the reminder of what the Democratic Party is in that continuum is important.

I talked to Paul Tsongas last night, a great new Senator, and he said when he got back to Massachusetts from campaigning for me and others on the west coast that he's going to point out the danger of a third candidate. A few minutes ago at Christopher Columbus school, I reminded people about '68. George Wallace was a third candidate, very popular in certain States in the Nation, not just in the South. And he took away from Hubert Humphrey enough votes to put Richard Nixon in the White House.

Well, I want to remind you that it's important for you not only to help financially, which I really appreciate and which I really need, but to help with your influence and your voice and your hard work and your commitment during this next 3 weeks.

Finally, yesterday my opponent pledged, in one of his series of rapid changes, to appoint a woman as one of his first appointees to the U.S. Supreme Court. I understand why he made that statement at this point in the campaign. What he doesn't seem to realize is that equal rights for women involves more than just one job for one woman. What he doesn't seem to realize is that what's at stake here is economic justice and social justice, legal justice for a hundred million women. If he believes that, in that he ought to support the equal rights amendment, abandon that support, and substitute this for it, he's mistaken. My six predecessors in the White House supported the equal rights amendment. The Republican Party for 40 years, in its platform, supported the equal rights amendment, until this year.

I'm not going to make a campaign promise to name any particular kind of person to the Supreme Court on my first appointment. I don't think that's proper. But my record's clear. I've appointed more women to the Supreme Court than all the Presidents in the history of this country combined—I mean to the district courts, Federal courts. I've appointed more blacks, twice as many blacks to the Federal courts as all the Presidents in this country combined, more Hispanics. I'll continue that kind of approach.

But the combination of principle, continuity, historic nature of a party, a reminder of what makes our Nation great, the temptation to take an election for granted—those are the kind of thoughts that prey on my mind. I'm here with you as a partner, an American partner, a Democratic partner, trying to carry on the principles of our party and our Nation. I'll have to depend on you to help me up here. The issue is in doubt. But with your help, I have absolutely no doubt that on November the 4th we'll have a tremendous Democratic victory in Massachusetts and throughout this great land of ours.

Thank you. God bless you.

NOTE: The President spoke at 1:18 p.m. in the Boston/Lynn Room at Anthony's Pier Four Restaurant.

Yatesville, Pennsylvania

Remarks and a Question-and-Answer Session at a Town Meeting. October 15, 1980

THE PRESIDENT. Thank you, Bob Casey.

When you have a man like Bob Casey with you, you're way ahead of the game to start with, right? [*Cheers*] I'm also very glad to be in the district of Congressman Musto, who—[*applause*]—I can see you know a lot about him already, right? He's a man who gets things done and doesn't waste much time doing it. I noticed, as President, that he was sworn in one day, and the next day he announced a $1.2 million grant from the Economic Development Administration. That's the fastest work I've ever seen on Capitol Hill.

I just came from a series of Democratic rallies in Boston, Massachusetts, with Senator Ted Kennedy. And being in Boston at a political with Ted Kennedy is like being, as you know, in Veterans Stadium with Pete Rose. It's a nice arrangement to have. When you're going into the home stretch of a major contest they're the kind of people that you want to have on your team.

I know a lot of you are thinking perhaps as much or more about baseball as you are about politics. This Presidential campaign is kind of like the national pennant race. It's tight, it's going down to the wire, and if you support me the way you did the Phillies, we're going to pull this one out together. And in this race you can be a player, too—right?—not just a spectator.

Pete Rose and others are heroes in this State. I come from Georgia. If you ask almost anyone in Georgia, "Who is the greatest football player who ever played in this country?" they would say Charlie Trippi. As a matter of fact, he played at the University of Georgia when I was in college. Unfortunately, I was at Georgia Tech. They wiped us out, with his help. And I remember that he went to World War II, interrupted his college education, came back later, continued his college career, went to the Sugar Bowl, helped win a victory, threw a 67-yard pass, which I think is still the Sugar Bowl record.

Those years, during the war, the Second World War, were a time of testing for our country. Since then we have lived under the threat of a nuclear war, almost continually since World War II. Peace is not an accident. It has to be won every day, against all the forces that would gamble with the fate of the world. And that's the reason that I went to a man like Ed Muskie to ask him to be my Secretary of State, to be at my side in this daily battle for peace. I don't know if you know it or not, but Ed Muskie's father lived in Dixon City.

CAMPAIGN ISSUES

Presidents have a lot of responsibility, but the number one responsibility on the shoulder of any President is the security of our Nation and the continuing peace based on our unsurpassed strength. Our security doesn't depend just on military strength. We will never let another nation be superior to us in military strength, but there are other elements that are important to you and important to me. We must have alternative energy sources so that we are not subservient to or subject to blackmail from the OPEC oil countries. We must have a strong economy. We must rebuild our industrial base.

The spirit that turned the wilderness into the greatest industrial nation on Earth is still at work today building a new future for America.

In the past few weeks I've seen this spirit at work—a modern textile mill, like some of those you have around here; a modern steelmill, like some of those in Pennsylvania; a more productive and modern coal mine, like some of those in Pennsylvania; a fine grain terminal now shipping more American agricultural products overseas than ever before in history.

I've seen 1981 cars coming off the assembly line—the best built, best designed, safest, and most durable cars in the world. And I recommend that when you get ready to trade cars and go to the local dealers, give those American cars a chance.

Everywhere I go I see what American workers can do if American workers are given modern tools and modern plants. As has always been the case in this democracy, the future of America is in the strong hands of American workers like you in Pittston, Wilkes-Barre, Scranton. It's a good future. It's a future in which young people can make plans and older people can retire without fear. It's a future in which America will always remain strong, not only politically, militarily, and economically, but morally and ethically as well.

The election this year is extremely important to working people. On one side,

we have the Republican Party. I remember growing up during the Depression years in Georgia. The Democrats proposed a minimum wage—25 cents an hour. The Republicans were against it. My first job was as a high school graduate. By then the Democrats, over Republican opposition, had raised the minimum wage to 40 cents. I remember when Franklin Roosevelt put forward the idea of social security. The Republicans were against it; the Democrats passed it.

Times haven't changed. This time we have a Republican candidate running against me who said, *this* year, and I quote him, "The minimum wage has caused more misery and unemployment than anything since the Great Depression."

We Democrats, since I've been in office, have enacted the biggest increases in the minimum wage in history, because we believe that working people deserve decent pay for a day's hard work. That's always been the case with the Democratic Party.

In this particular metropolitan area—Pittston, Scranton, Wilkes-Barre—since I've been in office, we've got 28,000 more people at work than the day I was inaugurated, but we still have people who are unemployed.

I know from experience how a family feels when the mother or father, the breadwinner, are temporarily out of work. On one side, you've got a Republican candidate running against me who calls recipients of unemployment compensation, and I quote, "freeloaders wanting a prepaid vacation plan." We Democrats—Fritz Mondale, Ted Kennedy, Jimmy Carter, most of you—have fought to extend unemployment benefits for workers in hard-hit industries.

On one side, you've got a Republican candidate who was a major spokesman—he traveled around the country; his first introduction to politics—in a nationwide campaign against Medicare, and who now opposes national health insurance. The Republican candidate said many times that he was for making social security voluntary. This would be the end of a sound social security system. It would destroy it.

We need a President whose views on the basic integrity of the social security system are not subject to change.

We Democrats averted the collapse that faced social security 4 years ago, when I was campaigning for President in Pennsylvania after 8 years of Republican rule in the Oval Office. We're for strengthening social security and Medicare and we're for national health insurance. I'm a Democrat in the same tradition as Franklin Roosevelt and John Kennedy. We do not believe in taxing benefits from social security. We will not take away the social security beneficiary's right to have payments increase to compensate for the cost of living with inflation.

We have always understood, as Democrats, that the working people of America have built and made this Nation great. They knew it when the labor movement itself started right in the coal mines of Pennsylvania that it was not a movement of freeloaders, but of free Americans building a better life for themselves and for us, their children. They knew that if American workers have a chance with tools and modern equipment, if American workers could continue to get a fair deal, they could maintain the strength and freedom of this country and build a better world for people here and everywhere.

And finally let me say that we Democrats have pulled this country out of the recession that we faced in 1976. We've created more jobs in the last 3½ years, in spite of very serious economic problems, on a nationwide basis than ever before in any President's term in history. We still have a long way to go. If we stick together, we can do it.

The revitalization program that I have proposed will create in the next 2 years a million additional new jobs in growing and competitive industries. We'll modernize our basic industries like coal, steel, automobiles, encourage high technology industry to come into areas like yours to use the hard coal, the anthracite coal that you have to make clean-burning and easily transportable synthetic gas, synthetic oil. We'll make use of these vast coal resources for a new life for anthracite coal. I want to see OPEC oil replaced in the world energy markets with Pennsylvania coal.

We've got a long way to go. We've faced a lot of problems in the past. We'll face these that we have today and have a better life for all Americans.

And now, I want to have your questions.

QUESTIONS

PENNSYLVANIA COAL INDUSTRY

Q. Mr. President, my name is Dorothy Charge. What do you propose to do with our coal industry in Pennsylvania?

THE PRESIDENT. Fine. Let me point out to you that I've only been in office for 3½ years, but during that time we've made a lot of progress. We've finally got on the law books a new energy policy. We are making excellent progress. This year we will produce more coal in the United States than any other year in history. We also have a bright prospect for the future, because the kinds of coal in the past—some in some parts of the Nation that have had very high sulfur; coal in your part of the Nation which has low sulfur, clean burning, high BTUs, difficult to mine, expensive to mine—will now be a national treasure that we can use. And what's going to happen is that we'll take the coal mining industry with the modern, safe, productive, and convenient coal mines—much different from what they were 50 years ago or 30 years ago—combine high technology with them, create jobs that require the highest degree and level of training and pay, and let this be, as I say, a treasure of benefit to our whole country.

Another point is that we are increasing our coal exports. We can export now every bit of coal that we can transport to our sea areas and load on ships. The orders are there, and we are now beginning to put in loading facilities and improve the railroads and the highways to get that coal to port. There's no doubt in my mind that in the next 15 years, we can triple the amount of coal we are producing. This year we will produce 850 million tons of coal in this country. In the past, we have never had as much as 17 million tons of coal produced in a week. So far this year, 15 weeks we have produced over 17 million tons of coal. That's the kind of production we've got already, and we're going to triple it in the next 15 years.

Q. Hooray for Carter.

THE PRESIDENT. Thank you.

Q. Mr. Carter?

THE PRESIDENT. Yes, sir?

TAX REDUCTIONS

Q. President Carter, my name is Ed Farrell. I'm a truck driver. Now, I know that you are really trying to bring the coal industry back into the country and especially northeastern Pennsylvania, and I know that deregulation of trucking has hurt a lot of truck drivers in this valley, but that's hearsay or forgotten about as far as a lot of things are gone. All I want to know is, sir, if you are reelected, will the middle class continue bearing the burdens as far as the taxes are concerned?

THE PRESIDENT. There is no doubt in my mind that next year, Ed, we will have substantial reductions in income taxes in this country. About 50 percent of the benefits of that income tax reduction will go to modernize American factories, tools, to create those 1 million jobs that I've described to you. The other half of that income tax reduction will do two things: one is to reduce or to match the amount that social security benefits would have increased, which will be anti-inflationary in nature, and another element that I want to make sure we correct is one tax provision that has in the past served to destroy American families. Now if a man and wife live together and both work they pay much higher income taxes than a man and woman who live together who are not married, both of whom work. And I want to remove that marriage penalty, which will do two things—save people money and hold the family together.

I might point out since this is a political year, that my opponent has proposed a so-called Reagan-Kemp-Roth proposal—a massive reduction in taxes, primarily for the rich.

For instance, a family that makes $200,000 a year would have 35 times as much tax benefit as a family that made $20,000 a year. That's the kind of proposal that he has put forward, called Reagan-Kemp-Roth. It would be highly inflationary in nature. It would lead to massive Federal deficits and the elimination of a major part of the Federal Government programs that go to serve people about whom you are deeply concerned, I know.

So, a balanced tax reduction not only next year, but as a steady predictable thing in the future, would remove a major part of that unwarranted burden on the middle-income working families and, at the same time, be anti-inflationary in nature and, at the same time, create new American jobs with modern tools and modern plants to keep them at work and keep them productive. That's what I want. I believe that would suit you, too.

THE PRESIDENT. Thank you, Ed.

Q. Thank you, Mr. President.

FEDERAL EMPLOYEES RETIREMENT AND
SOCIAL SECURITY SYSTEMS

Q. Good afternoon, Mr. President. My name is Harold Spike Collins. I have a two-part question for you. If reelected, will your administration, as it has in the past, try to reduce the COLA allowance for retired Federal employees from twice a year to once a year and only allow 75 percent of it? And the second part of my question is, if reelected, will you still continue, as in the past, to try to have the Federal employees under the social security system? I think it's going to be known as universal coverage.

THE PRESIDENT. Harold, in my judgment, the COLA should apply on an annual basis, yes. The Congress has decided, for the time being, not to make a change. As far as the retirement benefits or system for Federal employees, I am not in favor of doing away with the retirement program for Federal employees and forc-

ing those employees to abandon what they've got and to move into the social security system.

I might point out, however, that those of you who are interested in the social security system should be deeply concerned about the four different times when my Republican opponent has called for the voluntary social security system. That's completely different. I'm going to keep the social security system intact, keep it sound, keep it out of bankruptcy, make sure that the payments are not taxed, make sure that the social security payments are increased when inflation goes up, and also make sure we don't change the age requirements to take away benefits that people have worked all their lives to assure. But at the same time, I'm going to protect the public employee.

AMERICAN HOSTAGES IN IRAN

Q. President Carter, I am very concerned about the present war between Iraq and Iran and how it affects our hostages. My question to you is, when was the last time you have had positive confirmation that all of the hostages are still alive and well?

THE PRESIDENT. What's your name?

Q. Joe Wallison.

THE PRESIDENT. Joe, for almost a year now, I don't believe an hour has gone by on any day that I've spent, during the hours that I was awake, that I didn't think about or even say a prayer for those hostages. We have been through several phases of trying to get the hostages released, as you know—working directly with the Iranian officials; working through intermediaries from other countries sending secret missions to Iran, meeting Iranian officials; either directly or through surrogates in other countries;

working through the United Nations; making public statements; working with the Iranian officials—the President and the Foreign Minister both of whom agreed to release the hostages back in May.

So far as we know, the best intelligence information we have from various sources, which I can't describe to you, the hostages are all alive and they're all safe. We have a way of communicating directly on occasion with three of the hostages who are being held in the foreign ministry or the department of state building in Tehran. I don't believe that the Iran-Iraq war has put the hostages' lives in danger.

I have maintained since they were first taken two basic principles that are not incompatible one with another: first, to protect the integrity and the principles and the interests of my Nation, and secondly, not to do anything as a President that would endanger the lives or the safety of the hostages or their chance to come back to freedom at the earliest possible moment.

We believe that there ought to be an end to the hostilities between Iran and Iraq and an immediate commencement of negotiations to settle the disputed boundaries between them. This reflects the long-standing policy of our country that all territorial disputes should be settled peacefully and not by aggression. The United States remains committed to the proposition that the national security and integrity of Iran is in the interest of national stability.

We oppose any effort to dismember Iran, to cut away part of it and separate it from the rest of Iran. I hope and pray that now that Iran finally has elected officials—they've got a President now; they've got a Prime Minister now; they've got a parliament elected called a Majles; and

they've got a speaker of that parliament elected—since those officials are now in office, there may be a chance for us to make some progress—I can't predict anything because they're so unpredictable—toward having someone speak for the Government of Iran and realize that they have been extremely ill-advised in keeping those hostages in their country.

So, we're doing everything we can to end the war. I don't think it's affecting the lives and safety of the hostages. We're making every effort to get those hostages home safe, and I don't believe that we—well, I can say that all of the information that we have indicates that the hostages are indeed alive and safe.

ABORTION

Q. Mr. President, my name is Ann Murphy. I'm a wife, mother, and owner of a small business. I would like to welcome you to the beautiful Pocono Northeast, and I would like to invite you to go fishing with the Murphy family at your convenience. My question, Mr. President, is: The poor women of this State have lost their freedom of choice. A woman with money has a free choice to end a pregnancy; however, a woman on welfare has no freedom to decide. What will you do to help all women have a freedom of choice?

THE PRESIDENT. Thank you, Ann. Ann, I hope you don't withdraw your invitation to go fishing.

Q. Oh, no, no. You're invited.

THE PRESIDENT. Ann, I am not in favor of abortions, and as President I have done everything I could to minimize the use of abortions in this country. When I was inaugurated I took an oath to uphold the laws of this country and the Constitution of our country, so when the

Supreme Court makes a ruling concerning abortion or concerning anything, it's my duty, regardless of my personal beliefs, to carry out the laws of this land.

You know what the Supreme Court ruling is on abortion. I have taken a firm position against the use of Federal funds to pay for abortions, because people feel so deeply and emotionally about this subject, on both sides. But it doesn't seem right to me for the Federal Government to collect taxes from those who have deep religious feelings against abortion and use that same tax money to finance abortions.

I don't want to mislead the rest of the audience. I don't see the need for a constitutional amendment on the subject. I believe that what the Supreme Court has ruled is adequate for our country.

So, my personal beliefs are deeply against the use of abortions. I will oppose the use of Federal funds to finance abortions. But, as President, I have to uphold the law the way the Congress passes it and the way the Supreme Court interprets our Constitution.

Thank you.

PENNSYLVANIA INDUSTRIES

Q. Hello, Mr. President. How are you?

THE PRESIDENT. I'm fine, great.

Q. Good. My name is Janet Pupa. There is such a lack of industry in our area that the people are moving away in order to provide for their families. Do you have any plans to bring any industry in our area when you return to the White House for the next 4 years?

THE PRESIDENT. Thank you, Janet.

One of the things that has been accomplished in this country in the last 3½ years is to add a net increase of 8½ million new jobs in this Nation, above and beyond what we had the day I was inau-

gurated. I looked at the statistics this morning and 28,000 of those jobs are in this area here, around Pittston, Wilkes-Barre, Scranton. The unemployment rate now in this area compared to when I was inaugurated has dropped about 19 percent. This has been in spite of a recession that was brought on by OPEC more than doubling the price of oil in just 12 months. As a matter of fact, in 1979 the price of oil increased more in that 1 year than oil prices had increased since oil was first discovered in Pennsylvania in the 1800's. This shock that went throughout the world has prevented adequate growth.

You might be interested in knowing that 670,000 new jobs have been created in this Nation in just the last 3 months. Housing starts have now been up for 3 consecutive months. For 6 straight weeks, we have added back 4,000 automobile workers per week. The first sales of the 1981 American cars have been extraordinarily good. All of the new, modern cars that are being produced have long waiting lists for them. The index of leading economic indicators, which is kind of a conglomerate measure of how the economy's doing, has increased more in the last 3 months than it has in the last 31 years.

So, the signs are good that the economy is improving. I can't predict for sure what's going to happen in the future. This particular part of the Nation is blessed, because you have a high level of skilled employees, you've got a broad diversity now, much better than you had 50 or 60 years ago, of different kinds of jobs that you can hold. You've got a textile industry that's benefiting from our new trade policy. In the last 2 years, we have increased American exports of textile goods by $2 billion and, at the same time, we have reduced textile imports. This is something we've not done before, to sell more of our textile goods overseas and to buy less from foreign countries.

The last thing is you've got this tremendous treasure in Pennsylvania of ore, coal, steel, and other things that God has given us. And with the new technology now available to take your coal, for instance, and to make clean-burning fuel out of it and to use it directly with the modern kinds of techniques that are much different from the ones that your parents knew or my parents knew, you can have safe mining, productive mining, high skills involved in the technology and a much brighter future.

So, I believe that in every way this particular area of our country will be blessed now and in the future, because of those reasons. I see a good next 4 years for you.

Q. Thank you very much.

COAL

Q. Mr. President, my name is Angelo Cefalo. I'm a retired international labor leader and traveled the length and breadth of this country and foreign countries, also. You are now sitting in an area which represents the most-producing, anthracite coal field in the world, including China and Wales.

THE PRESIDENT. Yes, sir.

Q. During our peak season, we employed 180,000 miners and allied workers. We mined approximately 60 million tons of coal. Your program is an excellent program, but I'm wondering about the techniques that are necessary to dewater the mines and to go into areas which are more difficult now than when the coal was virgin; whether the Government, with your assistance after January 20th, 1981, is going to be able to revitalize those who are motivated to give life to the coal industry. Are we in a position to get the

Congress to appropriate the money that is required to do this?

THE PRESIDENT. That's a good question, and I think I can answer it. Angelo, to a major degree, the Congress has already appropriated the money through what is known as the windfall profits tax. This is a tax on the unearned profits of the oil companies. In the next 10 years, just for synthetic fuels alone, it will amount to $88 billion. This program is bigger than the space program that put a man on the Moon, the Marshall plan that rebuilt Europe, and the entire interstate highway system in this country put together.

Of that $88 billion, 75 percent of it will go for getting synthetic fuels out of coal. There is no doubt that in addition to that, we'll have tremendous investments in research and development—not only how to get fuels out of coal, gas and clean-burning liquids, but also how to use the anthracite coal as it comes out of the mine with new techniques of combustion. In addition, the new mining methods will be more convenient, more profitable, and also safer.

The last point is that the rest of the world is hungry for American coal to be used in Belgium, France, Japan, China, and other places. The bottleneck now is that we have jumped into this program so quickly, and OPEC oil prices have gone up so rapidly, that we can't load and ship and put on ships for transport the coal fast enough. Now, in Hampton Roads, Virginia—Norfolk—the average ship from, say, Belgium or France has to wait 20 to 25 days after it arrives in Norfolk before it can get a load of coal.

It's just been announced this week, that in that area, tremendous improvements will be made for the storage of coal where it can be stockpiled, selected, blended to match the ship order when it comes in and to load that ship rapidly and to unload the hopper cars as they come from the mines. All of those things put together mean that the kind of mining that created a lot of problems around here with safety and also with problems with lungs would be vastly improved.

The markets are there, and they'll be steady markets. These will not be markets that come and go every year; they'll be permanent markets. A lot of these foreign nations are willing to sign contracts for 10 and 20 years in the future.

This month, in about a week, at the White House, we're going to have another conference on coal. We'll have there the railroad owners and operators, the shipping owners and operators, representatives of all the ports in our Nation on the east and west coasts, the foreign buyers, the coal mine owners and representatives of the miners themselves and, of course, the agencies of the Federal Government involved in coal production, use, and sale, just to make sure that we've got every obstacle ironed out and that those bottlenecks that I described to you, like port facilities, are eliminated very soon.

One last point. The miners are extremely important and will continue to be the root of this tremendous treasure being used properly. But the advanced technology will require scientists, engineers, plant operators, far beyond what has been required in the past just to get the coal out of the mines and put it on a hopper car. This will mean that those industries to make the final products will to a major degree be concentrated in this area. I think it's a wonderful opportunity. We are not overlooking any chance to take advantage of it.

Q. Thank you and come on back after your election.

THE PRESIDENT. I look forward to it.

PRAYERS OF DIFFERENT FAITHS

Q. Mr. President, my name is Avi Leiter. In view that you, Mr. President, are Baptist, do you agree with the head of the churches who said that God does not listen to Jewish prayers? I am a religious boy and I pray three times a day for the welfare of the Americans and Jewish people. Do you think that God does not listen to my prayers?

THE PRESIDENT. Avi—how do you pronounce your first name?

Q. Ahvee.

THE PRESIDENT. I am a deeply religious person, too. There is no doubt in my mind that God listens to your prayers, just like he does mine. Also, let me say this: It's a mistake for our country to forget about the principle of separation of church and state. This is a very emotional election year, and we have seen and heard statements made this year that cause me deep concern.

When I went to Camp David with Prime Minister Begin, a Jew, and with President Sadat, a Muslim Arab, the first day there didn't seem to be a chance in the world that we would be successful. The first thing we decided to do was to pray to God, and not only that, but to issue a statement to everyone in the world who would, to join us in praying to God that we could have success there and find peace for Israel and for her neighbors. That's what we did the first day.

We came out of Camp David, 13 days later, with a peace agreement. Do you remember that? I think that's proof. I think that's proof that God heard all our prayers, right? There's no question in my mind about it.

Thank you.

REQUEST FOR INVITATION TO WHITE HOUSE

Q. Mr. President, welcome to northeastern Pennsylvania. My name is Vincent Peperno. I'm a high school teacher from Old Forge. I think we need a little break in the routine, so I'll ask a question and I hope it isn't too funny. After you have been relected in November, will you invite me and my family to the White House? [*Laughter*]

THE PRESIDENT. What's your name?

Q. My students won't forget it. Vincent Peperno.

THE PRESIDENT. Is there anybody here that knows Vincent Peperno? What kind of fellow is he? [*Laughter*]

AUDIENCE MEMBER [*Inaudible*]—Mr. President, he's my uncle. [*Laughter*]

THE PRESIDENT. Is there anybody here that knows Vincent that's not kin to him?

AUDIENCE MEMBER. [*Inaudible*]

THE PRESIDENT. Yes, ma'am, what kind of fellow is he?

AUDIENCE MEMBER. [*Inaudible*]

THE PRESIDENT. That's all right so far. [*Laughter*] Would you invite him to your house?

AUDIENCE MEMBER. Yes.

THE PRESIDENT. Vincent, I'll invite you to my house.

DRAFT REGISTRATION

Q. Thank you very much. Thank you very much, Mr. President. Now, in a more serious vein, Mr. President, as a high school American Government teacher, my senior students are quite curious as to how you visualize the eighties in relation to the economy and the draft, as these are the things that seem to affect them? Would you please comment on that?

THE PRESIDENT. Yes, I will. I've already spelled out for you all and I need not repeat it, to save time, what I envision about job opportunities in this area, right? You think I've done okay on that?

Q. Yes.

THE PRESIDENT. Well, secondly, let me say about the registration for the draft, sometimes our Nation, a great nation, a strong nation, a peaceful nation, has threats against it from the Soviet Union or others who violate the peace. When the Soviets moved into Afghanistan I had a choice to make, as President, about how to meet that threat to peace: military action, political action, or economic action. I decided on political and economic.

So, we imposed some kind of restraints on trade with the Soviet Union that I thought would teach them a lesson and not hurt our own people. Secondly, we went to the United Nations, and 104 other countries joined with us in condemning the Soviet invasion. Also, when I checked on the registration for the draft question it became obvious to me that it would save us about 90 or 100 days, if our Nation should ever be directly threatened, to have young men already registered for the draft.

It was not a popular thing to do, as you well know. But the Congress passed the law and we put it into effect. We expected a lot of opposition to the draft, to the registration, from all over the country. But in the sign-up period, 93 percent of all of our young men 18 and 19 signed up on time, and now thousands are signing up every week to come into compliance with the law.

There is not going to be a draft. In my judgment, the registration will help us prevent having to go away from a voluntary military. My preference is to have the Army, Navy, Marines, Air Force, staffed with volunteers. We are increasing the privileges and the pay scale and the re-enlistment bonuses for them, to make sure we have a sound personnel base.

I hope that many of you young men and women who are looking for an excellent career or a patriotic thing to do will take advantage of this opportunity and volunteer to serve in the military. I did it. I served 11 years in the Navy. I went to Annapolis and I was in the submarine force. It didn't hurt my political career, as you can see, and I think it wouldn't hurt your political career.

But we have to have a strong nation, resolved, united, willing to defend ourselves if necessary. So, the registration is not going to lead to a draft.

Two more things very quickly. Fifteen percent of those young people, Vincent, who signed up for the registration, said they would like to have additional information about a career in the military. So I think it's going to help our recruitment of volunteers.

I don't have any apology to make for a strong defense. When I was inaugurated President, for 7 out of the last 8 years when the Republicans were in the White House, our defense budget went down and we were getting vulnerable and inferior, perhaps, approaching that point. Since I've been in the White House, every year we've had a steady, predictable, orderly, well-advised increase in commitment to a strong national defense, above and beyond inflation.

The last point: We've got to stay strong militarily. It's not a reflection on us to have excellent weapons and a strong military force. The best weapon is one that's never fired in combat, and the best soldier is one that never has to lay his life down or shed his blood on the field of battle.

Q. Thank you, Mr. President.

POLLUTION CONTROL AND MEDICAL CARE

Q. Hi, President.

THE PRESIDENT. Give your name; go right ahead.

Q. Okay. My name is Valencia Wilks. I'm from College Misericordia. College Misericordia sent me here with two questions to ask you. What do you propose to do about the pollution in our environment and will you increase medical aid in the medical aid area?

THE PRESIDENT. Yes. We are constantly trying to improve medical care in our country, with strong and good Medicare, with extended care for elderly citizens in particular, working for a national health insurance program to be implemented nationwide in my second term in office, and also, of course, to protect the prices that are charged to patients and others who receive medical care, with hospital cost containment.

The emphasis on the new health program will be to prevent illnesses, to concentrate on out-patient care rather than a patient going and staying in the hospital for a long time, and to hold down the costs and charges made against them.

As far as pollution is concerned, you probably noticed lately what my Republican opponent has said. I noticed that when we came into the airport, the environment was clear, the air was fresh to breathe. I guess that the trees and the volcanoes took the day off around here, because he thinks that's where all the pollution comes from. I noticed the other night right after he said that, his plane couldn't land in Los Angeles because the smog was too thick to find the airport. [*Laughter*]

But we have predicated all of our improvements—and I'm glad you brought this up, because I hadn't thought about it earlier. This is a kind of a halfway coal audience. You're interested in the future of coal. The worst thing that you could do in a coal producing region is to call for a lowering of air pollution standards. If the coal producers ever said, "You've got to have polluted air in order to burn our product," the Nation would turn against it, and you'd have the same fear built up against coal that resulted at Three Mile Island against nuclear power.

Don't let anybody ever mislead you. Every advance that I have outlined to you about the future of coal is based upon the present air pollution standards being kept. We're trying to shift, now, more than 100 electric powerplants away from oil and gas, to coal. But we're doing it maintaining the air pollution standards. You don't have to have dirty air in the United States to use coal. This is a very important point for all those interested in coal production to remember.

So, we'll maintain the quality of life in this country, better health care, a better environment, and low pollution.

One of the nicest things in my life is the all-too-infrequent times when I can come to Pennsylvania and go trout fishing in some of your beautiful streams. And it would break my heart to know that those streams, 15 years from now, 20 years from now, 50 years from now would be dead streams, with no fish there and no beauty there, because we lowered the standards of quality of our environment.

You've got precious treasures in this State in addition to deposits of minerals

that must be preserved, and I hope you'll join in with me in keeping Pennsylvania not only prosperous, but a good place to live.

INTERNATIONAL REPUTATION OF
AMERICANS AND U.S. DOLLAR

Q. Good afternoon, Mr. President. My name is Ann Marie Conroy, and I work for the Pennsylvania Welfare Department. Since this is a neighborly session, if Vincent is going to Washington to the White House, maybe you could invite his neighbors, too. I'd like to go.

Recently, I was overseas and I was very upset with the treatment of our American dollar and the American people in general. I'd like to know what you as President and we as Americans can do to improve our image abroad?

THE PRESIDENT. All right, let me try to respond to that. The dollar has been very strong, stable, and when the international financiers and bankers decide which currency they want to use as a foundation for the future security of their own banks and other institutions, they turn three times out of four to the American dollar.

The OPEC oil nations can sell their oil anywhere in the world they want to. It's a product that people avidly want. They've got a choice of getting paid in any kind of currency they choose— Deutsch marks from Germany, pounds from Great Britain, francs from France, yen from Japan. You know what they choose—United States dollars. The reason for that is that our country is looked upon in the rest of the world as being the most economically sound of all. We've not only got intelligent, well-educated people; we've always been on the cutting edge of progress. Whenever new ideas come along or technological developments, chances are they originated in the United States.

This morning in the paper I noticed five more Nobel Prize winners. If I'm not mistaken, four of them were Americans. Last year, I think almost all of them were Americans.

We've also got the blessings, which sometimes we forget, of productive land. Saudi Arabian oil is a good resource for them, but American soil is much more valuable now and in the future. And the bankers and industrialists and financiers in Switzerland and everywhere else know that a thousand years from now America is still going to be the breadbasket of the world and that we're going to be using our land in an ever more efficient way to produce food for our own selves and to sell throughout the world.

Energy. We tend to think that we have been somehow deprived and the OPEC Arab countries have been blessed. All of the Arab OPEC nations combined have about 6 percent of the world's energy reserves. The United States by itself has got 24 percent, and ours is not just oil and gas, but it's shale oil. We've got more oil in our shale than three Saudi Arabias. We've got more oil in coal than we do in shale. So our future, our present, is unbelievably attractive compared to other nations.

I've observed very closely the development of new countries. There's not a single nation on Earth that's now in the embryonic stage of development that wants its government to be like the Government of the Soviet Union. None. But a lot of nations are now turning to us as examples of the kind of government they want. Nigeria, the largest black nation in the world, has just put in a democratic government, using our Constitution as a

basis. Rhodesia, democracy; Ecuador, democracy; other countries around the world are moving toward democracy. So, in politics, in government, economically, we are a nation that is admired.

One other point: Patents are a very valuable commodity. Our country gets paid from overseas every year $5½ billion for other people to use the patents on new ideas generated in this country. The Japanese, the Germans, and everybody else have to buy the patents from us, and every year it's growing, the amount of money we earn from new patents.

The last thing is that you talk about productivity—how much can a worker produce in a day or a week? The most productive workers on Earth—where do you think they live? The United States, right? So no matter how you measure it—education, minerals, agriculture, type of government, freedom, morality, human rights, equality, new ideas, it belongs to us. And that, all put together, is what really determines the long-range value of the American dollar. It's strong now. It's the favorite currency on Earth, and my belief is, it will stay that way.

Q. Thank you very much.

AMERICAN HOSTAGES IN IRAN

Q. Welcome, Mr. President. My name is Barbara Regan. That's a name you'll remember. [*Laughter*] You didn't have to write it down.

THE PRESIDENT. I heard both names. [*Laughter*]

Q. I'm a member of the Back Mountain Jaycee-ettes. Now, the national Jaycee-ettes have designated this week as National Freedom Week, U.S.A. And what we've been doing is—well, our particular chapter has been urging the people in our beautiful Back Mountain area to wear a yellow ribbon, display a ribbon on their tree, fly their flag, and do something in support of the hostages.

We sent a letter back, presenting you with a ribbon from our club. We gave it to one of your staff members, but I guess you didn't get it yet. Do you want to borrow mine? What do you think we could do, besides this, in support, to let them know that we're there?

THE PRESIDENT. Okay. The access to 49 of our hostages is very irregular. They are permitted to receive some letters from back home and, on a few occasions, they have been permitted to make telephone calls. And also on a few occasions, the Iranians have let ministers or priests go into the compound to talk to them on special occasions.

Three of the hostages—Bruce Laingen, who was the head of the entire Embassy staff, and two others are in the state department or the foreign ministry of Tehran, and they do let diplomats from the Swiss Embassy or the Spanish Embassy or others go in and talk to them on occasion. They take them news, and they are from the outside world, and they also take them books and some magazines that have every now and then been censored.

The Iranians, so far as I know, have not mistreated in a physical abuse or endangered the lives of those hostages. As you know, not too long ago, one of the hostages got sick, and they immediately arranged for him to be returned to this country—a young man from Maine.

I think everything we can do in the way of prayer, in the way of wearing yellow ribbons—and I've got one at home that I wear on occasion, too—in the means of letting American people know that our hostages are still there, adding our support to the United Nations' effort and to efforts made through the Swiss and the

Belgians and others to reach the Iranian officials, to try to make sure this war doesn't spread to other countries—those are the kind of things all of us can do together.

Every day we have diplomatic efforts being made, directed by me, to try to reach the people in Iran who can ultimately make a decision. Even since the war began with Iraq, when Iran's security is directly threatened by Iraqi invading forces, their Majles or their parliament has still been debating how and under what circumstances to release the hostages. They've appointed, now, a committee in the parliament or congress to work out some way they could present back to the government for the hostages' release.

I can't predict to you any progress in the foreseeable future, although I pray that they'll be released every day. But I think the more we can do here to remind Americans of the hostages' plight, innocent people, the more chance that message has got to get through to them. If they don't know it, their parents know it and their husbands and wives know it and their children know it.

I would hate for those hostage families ever to believe that we didn't love them and care for them. Recently, I have signed a bill, this week I've signed a bill that the Congress passed, excluding those hostages from having to pay income taxes and giving them other special privileges for their families and, when they return, educational benefits for their children. So, I think the more we do the better off the hostage families are, and that word leaks back to the hostages, I feel sure.

It also lets other nations know that we've not forgotten them. I want the Germans and the British and the French and the Algerians and everyone else to know that we want those hostages back, so that every time a diplomat from one of those countries goes to Iran, he'll say, "You ought to let those hostages go." I think the cumulative effect of that might make the difference. And I'm very grateful to you and the Jaycee-ettes for what you are doing. I'll be glad to take your ribbon when I leave.

Let me say this in closing. I don't have time for another question; I'm really sorry. You can send it to me, and I'll answer it for you. But I'm out of time, and I promised to take just an hour. Let me say this in closing. I've had a broad range of subjects, as you know. One of the nicest things about the campaign for a President is a chance to get out among people like you and to understand your concerns and your questions and to try to respond to them.

I want to leave this message with you: I've been President now for 3½ years. I campaigned a long time before I was elected. I've studied history, as well. We dwell on, in the newspaper, radio, and television, the differences between us, the temporary inconveniences, the things that concern us, and we have a tendency to forget who we are and what we've got in this country.

If you compare our present problems with what we've experienced in the past, in the times way back in the Civil War, later with World War I, World War II, the Great Depression; the social changes that took our country apart when we gave black people full equality of rights in this country; the Vietnam war that tore our country apart again; Watergate, that was a terrible embarrassment to all Americans because of what happened in the Oval Office, itself; the CIA revelations—those kinds of things have been much more

serious problems than anything we face now.

There's no doubt in my mind that our Nation can face these problems successfully. In the past, we have always, if our Nation was unified, been able to answer any question, to solve any problem, to overcome any obstacle. That's a part of the American character. We still have a pioneering spirit, and we still have hearts filled with compassion. We still have a government directly responsible to you. And the next 3 weeks is going to be your opportunity to shape the kind of future that you want for yourself and your family and people that you love—for the next 4 years, perhaps the rest of this century.

And I hope that you won't overlook the chance that you have to shape America's future. I hope you'll be a partner with me to make sure that the greatest nation on Earth, in future years, will be even greater. Thank you very much.

NOTE: The President spoke at 3:34 p.m. in the Pittston Area Senior High School gymnasium. He was introduced by Robert Casey, former Pennsylvania State auditor general.

Lyndhurst, New Jersey

Remarks and a Question-and-Answer Session With Local Residents.   October 15, 1980

THE PRESIDENT. *Senator Bradley and Governor Brendan Byrne, Congressman Ambrosio,*[1] *friends from Lyndhurst, particularly the firemen who've just made me an honorary member of the post:*

I'm hoping no alarms for the next 30 minutes, because I would have to do my duty if we got a call. [*Laughter*]

AUDIENCE MEMBER. Can you drive the truck?

---

[1] Gabe Ambrosio, candidate for the House of Representatives.

THE PRESIDENT. I've already checked off.

AUDIENCE MEMBER. All right.

THE PRESIDENT. I'm pleased to be with you, because of several reasons. One is, it's important for me to see in America the spirit that is engendered by volunteerism, by the fact that people are willing to endanger their own safety for the love and care of others, a sense of family, because I know you have 3 minutes, I think, to get here in time of an alarm, and your families have to participate in meeting the threat to your own community.

I have had a lot of experience as a submarine officer, as an engineer officer on a submarine, the experimental submarines on which I served, going through firefighters school, and had one very serious fire which almost overcame me with acrid smoke. I also know the extreme danger of firemen. The danger to their lives is perhaps as great or greater than any other profession in our country.

I've been very interested in seeing the U.S. Fire Administration placed under the Federal Emergency Management Administration as part of our Nation's foremost defense forces against natural disaster or against a disaster from outside. And one of the things that I wanted to do when I became President is to establish a national firefighters academy to train people to be better firemen even in the future than they are in the past and to make sure that this very dangerous profession is more safe in the future.

Last week was National Firefighters Week. I called on firefighters, business, and the general public to work together to detect and to report and to prevent fires. It's the kind of cooperation that's important to a community, and of course, we need the same kind of cooperation in keeping our Nation strong—economically, socially, politically, morally, ethically—to realize the great potential that God's given us in this blessed land.

Tonight we have the time for some questions from you, and I look forward to giving the answers as best I can. And I don't know how to go about calling on the first person. If you have a question, I'll be glad to take it.

AMERICAN HOSTAGES IN IRAN

Q. I'd like to know what the state of the hostages are.

THE PRESIDENT. All right. As you know, since the hostages were taken, innocent people, by militants or terrorists in Iran, this has been a constant concern of mine. No day has gone by, no hour has gone by when I was awake that I wasn't thinking about and often praying for those hostages.

I've had two goals in mind, as your President and as their President: first of all, to protect the integrity and the principles and the interests of our own country; and secondly, and compatibly with it, not to take any action as a President that would endanger the lives or safety of those hostages or prevent their safe return to freedom as early as possible. We've been through a series of constant diplomatic, public and secret, negotiations with people in Iran who might possibly speak for that country. So far, we've not been successful except that we have protected our Nation's interests, we have served to protect the lives and safety of the hostages.

Now Iran finally has a government. They have an elected parliament, a Congress—they call it a Majles. They've elected their own speaker. They have a Prime Minister, a President, and they're putting together a Cabinet. As you know, Iran is now being attacked by Iraq, an invading nation, and their own security is at stake. They're an isolated country. They're a kind of a pariah in the international community. Their trade with us has been cut off. And they are relatively serious in their suffering, just because they still hold those 52 innocent people.

We get fairly good intelligence on Iran from varying sources. So far as I know, all 52 hostages still in Iran are safe and well. We have some ability to talk to three of them; Bruce Laingen, who was in charge of the diplomatic corps there, and two others are in the state department, or the foreign ministry of Iran. And I think that's about all I can tell you about it.

Every day from the very beginning, we have used every avenue to try to reach someone who can speak for Iran. The President of Iran and most of their public officials now say publicly that they want those hostages to be returned here safely. The parliament, or the Majles has appointed a committee to work out the mechanism by which the hostages could be released. I can't mislead you by saying that there's an immediate prospect, or a sure prospect even, that they will be released, but my hope and prayer is that they will be. And I believe that we have made as much effort as possible to secure their safe return.

So, I don't feel discouraged about it. I think we've been through worse times than we are in right now. And perhaps now that they have a government and are in danger themselves, we have a better chance to get the hostages back than before.

Yes, sir.

WATER SHORTAGE AND UNEMPLOYMENT IN NEW JERSEY

Q. Mr. President, Governor Byrne has made the statement that in April and May of next year, if we continue to have the water shortage in north Jersey— excuse me, I'm a little nervous—[laughter]—the industrial area, we may lose some jobs. At what point will the Federal Government get involved? And also, can they help subsidize the jobless?

THE PRESIDENT. I've been deeply concerned about the water shortage in New Jersey. I've talked to Governor Byrne about it, including tonight on the way in from the airport. I need to have a more direct, permanent relationship with the Governor and other officials in this State. And I will send Brendan one of my top FEMA officials to see you before this week is out to work out with you the best way to address this water shortage if it is a long-term, continuing problem.

One of the things that everyone in New Jersey can do is to comply with the conservation measures that Governor Byrne has asked, go an extra mile in saving water in every possible way. When the same thing happened in some communities, Marin County in California, they cut back water consumption in that entire county by 60 percent. It just shows what people can do if they really try. I don't want to bring up submarines too much, but I used to get by on the submarine with one quart of fresh water per day. I'm not asking you to do that, because we did have a lot of salt water— [laughter]—but I believe that you can do more yourselves.

In the long run, it's my belief that we can continue to care for those who are out of work temporarily. Now, we've asked the Congress—and I'm sure that Senator Bradley and others will continue to help us—to extend the unemployment compensation benefits if they are needed.

We've turned the corner now on the economic problems. The economic index figures for the last 3 months are the highest they have ever been in the last 31 years. For the last 4 months, we've had a steady increase in housing construction starts. And for the last 6 weeks, every week we've averaged 4,000 automobile workers going back to work, and the new American automobile models, as you know, are selling as fast as they can be produced. I believe that we've got a good prospect in the future for employment in general.

We have added, as you may know, more than a quarter of a million net new jobs in New Jersey since I've been in office. We've cut the unemployment rate in this State almost in half—because of your good work, not necessarily mine. And I think we'll continue that progress. We'll do all we can do to help you with your water shortage.

Yes, sir.

PERSIAN GULF REGION

Q. Mr. President, if this war between Iran and Iraq should escalate in the near future, will you commit American troops to that area to protect the oil pipeline?

THE PRESIDENT. In the first place, let me say that I don't believe that the war is going to escalate to any major degree in the near future. We believe that disputes between countries over boundaries, international boundaries, should be settled not by invasion or aggression but by negotiation. And we are using all of our efforts in the United Nations, working with other countries, to bring those two countries to the bargaining table to settle this dispute peacefully.

Secondly, we do not intend to inject American troops into any sort of land war in the Persian Gulf region, barring some completely unpredictable circumstances like a Soviet invasion of Iran or something of that kind, which I don't think will happen.

We will take whatever steps are necessary to keep the Strait of Hormuz open so that our country and other nations will have access to the countries on the west side of the Gulf. This is important to us, because we're getting now between 12 and 15 million barrels a day of oil—all the consuming nations together—from Saudi Arabia, Kuwait, and also from the United Arab Emirates. And that supply of oil, if interrupted for an extended period of time, would cause severe economic problems and endanger our own Nation's security.

We have a very large naval task force there, with superb fighter planes, to take care of our needs to keep that strait open. So, I believe that those forces already in place, Navy and Naval Air, will be adequate in the future. I don't see any prospect of any ground forces or troops to go in and protect our interests.

Q. Thank you.

THE PRESIDENT. Yes, sir.

UNITED STATES DEFENSE CAPABILITY

Q. Mr. President, over the past 2 months the media has reported on our defense capability. As the Commander in Chief of our military service, I'd like to know if we ought to believe that we're not in too good a shape. Are you doing anything at the present time to update our defense capability right now? [*Inaudible*]

THE PRESIDENT. Yes, of course. The readiness of our defense forces now is much higher than it was 3 or 4 years ago, when I took over.

One of the worst things that can happen in a political campaign is to demagogue an issue like the status of our Nation's defense capability. When false statements are made that the United States is weak, that we're not able to protect ourselves, we're not able to protect our interests in other parts of the world, it's a very serious and damaging false statement, for three or four reasons. One, it creates concern in the minds of you and other Americans: "Is my Nation strong? Are we vulnerable? Can we defend ourselves?" Secondly, it creates a disturbance among our own allies. And third, and perhaps most significant, it creates a false impression in the minds of potential adversaries, who might think they can take advantage of a nonexistent American weakness and in the process commit suicide for themselves.

Our Nation is strong, the strongest nation on Earth. I guarantee you that we will not let any other nation become superior to ours in military strength.

When I came into office, as a professional military background and a deep understanding of what the Commander in Chief ought to do, for 8 years before I got in the White House, 7 of those years we had gone down every year in the commitment of our budget funds for defense. It had dropped 37 percent in the 8 years before I was there, under Republican administrations.

Every year since I've been in office, we've had a steady increase in commitment of budget funds for a stronger defense—careful, planned, orderly, understood by the Congress. We've strengthened our alliances overseas. And this increase has been above and beyond inflation. I don't apologize for that. It amounts to about 5 percent of our gross national product, to keep our Nation strong enough to defend ourselves under any circumstances.

I want to remind you that our Nation has been at peace—we were talking on the way to the airport—for the first time in more than 50 years. I can sit here and tell you that I have kept our Nation at peace and I have not had to launch soldiers into combat anywhere on Earth. This is very important. But the peace has been maintained because we are strong; our weapons, the best on Earth, improving every year.

But don't forget that the best weapon is one that's never used in combat, and the best soldier is one that never lays down his life or sheds his blood on the field of battle. So, that's what I want. What I want is to keep our Nation strong and at peace. And the two go hand in hand.

Yes, I was looking for a woman. [*Laughter*]

HOUSING INDUSTRY

Q. I'd like to buy a house some day. But with the mortgage rates the way they are and the cost of the houses, it seems the more I save, the less I have. Will I ever have a house? [*Laughter*]

THE PRESIDENT. I think I'll skip the women and go back to the gentlemen. [*Laughter*]

Yes, you will. You know, we've——

Q. [*Inaudible*]

THE PRESIDENT. I'm sorry?

Q. Will you give me a loan? [*Laughter*]

THE PRESIDENT. We've done what we could to keep the housing industry strong since I've been in office, in spite of the fact that the OPEC oil prices have more than doubled last year and inflation and high interest rates have swept the world. Our interest rates, our budget deficits are much lower than most major trading countries with whom we do business. The American dollar is strong overseas. But we have had very high interest rates.

Last March, as you know, interest rates got up, the prime rate got up 19 and 20 percent. We imposed some credit restraints and put forward a much more restrictive Federal budget, and the interest rates dropped about 1 percent per week, for 6 or 7 weeks. Now they have cut back up a little bit and now leveled off—still too high.

In the meantime, we have tried to make available to the homebuilding industry kinds of loans that they didn't previously have and encouraged people to save more. What makes money available for long-range lending, like homes, is when people save. Our country, lately, has not been saving much. We've been spending about 96 percent of all we earn. Whereas a country like Germany or Japan, they save 15 to 20 percent of all they earn, we save 4 percent. That's one thing.

Another thing that we've done is to provide, through the Government, guaranteed loans, subsidized interest rates, and also, under certain programs in housing, the construction of apartments and homes to be rented. This year we'll have at least a 40-percent increase in those homes, apartments, where the Government is subsidizing or helping to construct those homes.

We've had, as I said, for the last 4 months a substantial increase each month in the number of homes being begun in this country.

I don't know how to give you any prediction about the future. My own judgment is that the interest rates in this Nation now are too high, set primarily by the banks, compared to the economic status of our country. I think they've gone too high, and I believe and hope that in the future they'll come down. I can't guarantee it, but I believe that's true.

Also, the prime rate needs to be examined, because now a lot of loans to small business people and also the homeowners are made on the basis of so many percentage points above the prime rate. The prime rate used to mean the rate that banks loaned their best customers. But now some banks set the prime rate above what they lend to their best customers and then add 1 or 2 percent or more on top of the so-called prime rate for average small business people and homeowners and so forth.

The Federal courts are now looking at that potential abuse by some banks. I'm not trying to prejudge the issue. But I think the more the American public focuses on those interest rates, to force them down to be competitive and to make sure that the banks don't abuse the public, the better off we'll be.

But we'll continue to do everything we can to increase the number of homes being built and bought in this country and to provide subsidies or help from the Government to let people like you buy a home or, if you prefer, to rent one at a reasonable rate.

The last thing is, the first 3 years I was in office we had almost—I think we averaged about 1.8 million homes per year, which was a very high rate. We are now back up to about 1½ million-homes-per-year rate, which is much better than it was before.

Yes, sir.

SOCIAL SECURITY SYSTEM

Q. Mr. President, on the problem of—[*inaudible*]—social security, and they're talking about taxing social security—[*inaudible*]—heating the homes. That seems to be a problem of—[*inaudible*]. What are you going to do about that?

THE PRESIDENT. As long as I am President, I think as long as we have a Democratic President, you will never see income from social security taxed. Also, as long as the Democrats are in the White House, you will never see the social security system be in danger of bankruptcy. When I went into the White House as President, after 8 years of Republican administrations, as you may well remember 4 years ago, everywhere I went people thought accurately that the social security system was about to go bankrupt. The Congress acted to put it back on its feet financially.

I'm running against an opponent who represents the Republican Party in its longstanding historical principles that don't change; except right before an election, sometimes those principles change.

I remember the depression years. I grew up—I was born in 1924. I remember the depression years. I remember the minimum wage that was proposed by the Democrats—25 cents an hour. The Republicans were against it; it passed. The first job I had—I got out of high school as a young man in 1941—the minimum wage then had been raised by the Democrats to 40 cents an hour. The Republicans opposed it. They called it socialism. Still, today, my Republican opponent calls the minimum wage the worst cause of unemployment and suffering since the Great Depression.

I know what it means for a family to be unemployed—temporarily, hopefully—and to depend on unemployment compensation just to keep your kids eating food and going to school and buying clothes. My opponent has said recently that unemployment compensation is only a prepaid vacation for freeloaders.

I know how important social security is. On three different occasions in recent years, my opponent has called for social security participation to be voluntary, which means that anybody that wants to withdraw from social security can do so. It would bankrupt the system within a few weeks and destroy social security. It's tied in also with Medicare. My Republican opponent got his first political experience campaigning across this Nation against Medicare. That's how he got involved in public affairs.

And finally, you mentioned the cost of heating homes for older people. We've passed the windfall profits tax, a tax on the unearned income of the oil companies. Out of that windfall profits tax will come, on a permanent basis, money to be allotted through the Governors to older people and poor families to help them pay the cost of heating their homes in the winter. My Republican opponent was against the windfall profits tax. He wants to dismantle it now, do away with it. His proposal to solve the energy crisis is to repeal the legislation that we've passed in the last 3 years, to abolish the Department of Energy, to dismantle the windfall profits tax, and to let the oil companies handle the energy crisis.

I could go on and on about the sharp basic differences that separate me from him and my party from his party that will be decided 3 weeks from now. The decision that will be made on November the

4th will affect every life in this room and your families and the people for whom you care very deeply, whether it's the elderly, the working families, our Nation's security, based on freedom from unnecessary influence by the OPEC nations, and also other basic elements like the control of nuclear weapons and the carrying out of the principles that I've outlined to you so briefly this evening.

Yes, sir.

JOHN ANDERSON AND CAMPAIGN DEBATES

Q. Mr. President, Senator Anderson has been recognized as a Presidential candidate. Are you perhaps reconsidering a public debate with yourself, Governor Reagan, and Senator Anderson?

THE PRESIDENT. Congressman.

I have repeated today, through a message directly to Governor Reagan, a challenge that he meet me in a debate, under the auspices of the League of Women Voters, at a time or forum that we can work out among ourselves. I have accepted every invitation I have gotten for a two-man debate between me as the Democratic nominee and him as the Republican nominee. He has always refused. I hope now, with just a few weeks left, that he will accept and we can go ahead and have a debate.

John Anderson, so far as I know, is a good man. I don't know him very well, but I think he's a good man. He ran for the Senate, I mean for the—you got me talking about the Senate. [*Laughter*] He ran for President as a Republican. He entered primaries and caucus States all over this country, never won the first primary, never won the first caucus, got beat in his own home State. And only then, after he was defeated in the Republican

primary, did he decide to run for President, with no party, as an Independent.

I have said before and I believe that John Anderson, as far as a Presidential candidate, is primarily a creation of the press. He doesn't have a mandate from the American people. And I think now, at least from the public opinion polls published, he seems to be sliding down.

I see nothing to be served by having a public forum where three candidates are on the stage answering questions for an hour and a half or two hours from the news media. I think it would confuse the issue and unnecessarily boost John Anderson, whom I respect, to the same status as two men who have fought a rough campaign through all the primaries and caucuses and come out with the nominations of our own party. I don't say this knocking him down, but I do believe that the best forum in this last few weeks is between me and Ronald Reagan.

The League of Women Voters set an arbitrary standard—I never did argue with it—that any candidate to be involved in the debate ought to have at least 15 percent in the public opinion polls. It was an arbitrary standard, but so be it. They were trying to exclude Barry Commoner, who is primarily an environmentalist, and, I think, Mr. Ed Clark, who is a Libertarian. And there are a hundred other candidates, you might be interested to know, in running for President. But they were trying to draw some lines. I don't think any public opinion polls now would show John Anderson to meet the League's standards that they set for themselves. I didn't have anything to do with it.

So, I think under these circumstances, this last few weeks, the proper debate that would be interesting to the American people is the debate between the two men who have a chance to be elected President and who have gone through the process of a two-party system and been nominated by our parties.

So, basically I see no prospect of my debating with John Anderson. I would take any reasonable opportunity, time or place or format to debate Governor Reagan, because I think it would be in the best interest of the people to see the sharp, stark, differences between me and him.

Thank you very much, everybody. I've got to go. I've enjoyed it.

NOTE: The President spoke at 7:01 p.m. at the Lyndhurst Volunteer Fire Department.

Secaucus, New Jersey

Remarks at a Meeting With New Jersey Labor Leaders.   October 15, 1980

That is the kind of introduction I really like. If I could just put together in New Jersey all the friends of Ted Kennedy and all the friends of Bill Bradley, I'll have it made, right? [*Applause*] That's what I want.

I want to talk to you seriously tonight about a matter that's serious to you, a matter that touches the life of every person in this room, your families, and the people that you love, and those that look to you for leadership in the trade union movement. Three weeks from tonight you will make a decision in New Jersey that will affect the future of this country.

What Ted Kennedy has pointed out as the principle and ideals and commitments of my Republican opponent is not something new. Some of you in this room are as old as I am. I was born in 1924. I grew up on a farm in south Georgia during the Depression years. I remember when Franklin D. Roosevelt put forward the

idea of social security. The Democrats passed it over enormous opposition from the Republicans. The Democrats proposed a minimum wage of 25 cents an hour, finally passed it; the Republicans opposed it. I finished high school in 1941. My first job at the minimum wage was 40 cents an hour. The Democrats approved that increase from 25 to 40 cents. The Republicans were against it. That has not changed.

As Ted Kennedy just pointed out, Ronald Reagan's attitude toward minimum wage is that the minimum wage has caused more suffering, more unemployment than anything in this country since the Great Depression. He's advocated four different times that social security be made voluntary, that anybody that wants to withdraw from social security and not pay into the social security fund could be allowed to do so. This would be the end of social security.

He got his start in politics traveling around this country, paid to do it, to fight Medicare. That hasn't changed. Now he says that national health insurance ought to be defeated. He said that labor law reform ought to be defeated, that Davis-Bacon ought to be defeated. They asked him about OSHA, to protect the safety and health of American workers. Somebody said it ought to be abolished; his response, "Amen." This is the kind of person representing a party whose principles are well known that now is challenging me and the Democratic Party and its principles to lead this Nation.

Unemployment compensation is important to a family temporarily out of work with hungry children, perhaps, and needing to meet the vital necessities of life. Ronald Reagan says that unemployment compensation is a prepaid vacation for freeloaders. In the time of Franklin

Roosevelt, in the time of Jack Kennedy, they pointed out to the American working people that for a few weeks before election day, Republicans sounded like Democrats. You know and I know what Ronald Reagan, who quotes Franklin Roosevelt quite often, says about the New Deal. He says the basis for the New Deal was fascism. These kinds of statements have been repeated down through the years, sometimes a little bit of change right before an election time, but they accurately express the principles of his party and of my opponent.

This election in New Jersey is extremely close. I don't know yet how it's going to turn out. I'm going to work as hard as I have ever worked, because I believe that major issues are at stake in the country which I love and among the people whom I love.

I've been President now for 3½ years. I sit in the same Oval Office where Jack Kennedy sat, Harry Truman, Franklin Roosevelt, Lyndon Johnson, with a heart full of understanding and compassion for working people. The decisions that come to my desk are not the easy ones. If a question can be answered easily, you answer it, yourself or in your own home, or in a county courthouse, or a city hall, or a State legislature, or a Governor's office. If it can't be answered in any of those places because it's too difficult or too complex, it comes to the President's desk, and then he has to sit down with people like Bob Roe, Bill Bradley, Ted Kennedy, and try to work it out for the country. The person in that Oval Office, however, sets the tone and the attitude of government, and as you well know, when the situs picketing bill had been passed by the Congress and Gerald Ford had committed himself to sign it, one man talked him out of it—my Republican opponent for President.

Labor is important, working people are important, but that's not all. We need to keep our Nation strong militarily, and we need to keep our Nation at peace. This is also a basic decision which a President must address every day. I have not been in office 1 day that there hasn't been a troublespot somewhere around the world. My predecessors, Democrats and Republicans, have tried to solve those troubled areas of the world peacefully, through diplomatic means, negotiation, using America's tremendous strength, yes, but using it without sending combat troops overseas.

My opponent, on many occasions in recent troubled times, has advocated sending American Armed Forces into those troubled areas in times when our country could have been involved militarily—North Korea, Ecuador, Cuba, Cyprus, Rhodesia, Angola, Pakistan, the Middle East. Three times this year he has called for the injection of American military forces into those troubled areas of the world. A sign of strength of a country is when with calm assurance we can protect our national interest without using American military forces.

For 8 years before I became President, under two Republican Presidents, 7 of those years our commitment to a strong national defense went down in American budgetary funds—37-percent drop in real dollars. Since I've been in office, we have increased our commitment to defense every year, carefully, methodically, predictably, responsibly. In real dollars we've had an increase. I make no apology for it, because in my judgment we can only keep our Nation strong and at peace together. Our country's the strongest on

Earth militarily. We're going to stay that way.

But let me close by saying two things. First of all, we've got the most outstanding weapons and the outstanding fighting men and women anywhere. But the best weapon is one that's never fired in combat, and the best soldier is one that never has to lay his life down or shed his blood on the field of battle. That is the kind of decision that must be made by a President.

I told you earlier, I don't know what New Jersey will do on November 4. There's no way I can predict it accurately, but if you have ever made a major decision in your life, this next 3 weeks you will make one. It's more important than the level of your income. It's more important than the quality of house that you have. It's more important than which college you can send your children. It's more important than the neighborhood where you and your wife might ultimately retire. The future of our country is in your hands, perhaps in this State. There is absolutely no reason why you, working with your speaker and others on every possible occasion in between five and six hundred communities in this State, can't put 25,000 workers out there in the streets, in the stores, talking to people and letting them know how crucial to the future of this country and to your State and to your families this election is.

My election can be in your hands, and what you decide the next few hours about the degree of your commitment—to raise money, you finance it; to designate workers, you do it; to lead those workers, you do it. And make sure that everybody in this State that looks to you for leadership understands the crucial issues to be involved—the quality of life of the people that you love and the status in the international community of the country that you love.

Those things are at stake. There could not possibly be a sharper difference between myself and Ronald Reagan and between the Republican Party of 1980 and the Democratic Party of 1980. You know what I believe in, you know what Ted Kennedy believes in, you know what Bill Bradley believes in, you know what John Kennedy believed in, you know what Lyndon Johnson believed in and Franklin Roosevelt and Harry Truman. That's the kind of historical perspective and the continuing commitment that is at stake. And you remember very well the times of Richard Nixon and other Republicans who turned their back on the working people of this country.

I don't want you to turn your back on the working people of New Jersey or the working people of this Nation. I'll do all I can. I need you as partners. And my question to you is: Will you join with me with an absolute total commitment to see a tremendous Democratic victory on November 4? That's my question. [*Applause*]

NOTE: The President spoke at 7:56 p.m. in the Exhibition Hall at the Meadowlands Hilton Hotel.

Secaucus, New Jersey

Remarks at a Democratic National Committee Fundraising Reception. October 15, 1980

I'm deeply grateful to Senator Kennedy for the warm words of support and the introduction that he gave to me and for a chance that I had to be with him this morning in Massachusetts and again here tonight in New Jersey. If I can just have all the support on November 4 that he got here in the primary, I will be very happy and we'll go over the top, there's no doubt about that.

As I look around this room I'm very grateful too to be here with all you candidates for Governor of New Jersey in the upcoming election. [*Laughter*] And I'm particularly glad to be with my charisma instructor—[*laughter*]—Governor Brendan Byrne, and with Bill Bradley and with Congressman Rodino, Congressman Bob Roe, and other distinguished members of your delegation.

Tonight I'd like to talk to you seriously for a few minutes about the Presidency itself and just two or three issues that I'll outline briefly that I think are important to you and important to the future of our country.

The office of President is one that's revered by the American people, in a strange, sometimes esoteric way, difficult to express. It's the highest elective office in any democracy in the world. It's an office which has tremendous power and responsibility and also very severe constitutional limitations. It's an office where troubles concentrate and where difficult questions must be answered. It's the problem that comes to my desk that can't be solved anywhere else and the questions that can't be answered anywhere else. If a problem or question can be resolved in your own life or in your family or county courthouse or city hall or State legislature or Governor's office, it doesn't come to me.

And I live in the White House, where all the Presidents except one have lived, and serve in the Oval Office, where many of my predecessors have served, and I'm reminded every day of the enormous responsibilities and support and challenge that rests on my shoulders. I share a lot

with the Presidents that Senator Kennedy has named—with Wilson, Roosevelt, Truman, Kennedy, Johnson. There's a continuity within the Presidency, and particularly within the Democratic Party, of which I'm an integral part.

I represent you in trying to shape a better life for Americans, trying to heal the differences that lie among us, trying to express as accurately as I possibly can the image that we have of ourselves, trying to protect moral commitments and family structures in the heterogeneous nature of our country built on a nation of immigrants which still is united, to try to express as best I can, on a daily basis, a certain confidence without being overconfident, a certain strength without abusing our great strength, recognizing that we have hopes and aspirations not yet realized and that we have been blessed above all people.

God has been good to us, and as we look back on previous generations, it puts in better perspective our present circumstances in life. We hear a lot on the evening news, as we read the morning papers, about the differences among us—the debates, the dissensions, the temporary and transient inconveniences that afflict any people on Earth. But we sometimes lose the overlying perspective historically of what we are and what we have. When compared with the Revolution or the War Between the States, the Second World War, the First World War, the extreme divisiveness of the Vietnam war, the Watergate embarrassments, the Great Depression, the sociological revolution that afflicted this country when we gave blacks and other minority groups equal rights, our present challenges fade into relative insignificance. But still Americans have to stop every 4 years and inventory what we are.

Ours is a nation of sound beliefs and a sure and certain future. We're not awed or fearful about the years to come, because we can look back and say what we've accomplished and the origins of the progress that we've made. We look at OPEC oil and say the Arab countries have a great lock on the economic future of the world. Collectively, they control about 6 percent of the world's energy resources. Our country alone controls 24 percent. Oil, gas wells—we'll drill more this year than ever before in history. Coal—we're producing more American coal this year than ever before in history. We've got three times as much oil in our shale alone than Saudi Arabia. And more coal than we have shale. Arab oil, yes; American soil, much more.

Ours is a country that has a certain unity of purpose that transcends the decades and generations. We make steady progress. We receive each year, in this country, over $5½ billion in payments from other modern countries just to use American patents, and that figure grows annually. The Japanese pay us untold billions of dollars just to use the new ideas that still spring forth from the ingenious minds of Americans. We say, "Well, nowadays it's a little worse." The last 3 months only, we've had a greater increase in our economic indicators than we've had in the last 31 years.

Other nations look on us with admiration. I don't know of a single nation on Earth, no matter what its basic philosophy might be, that wants to emulate the Government of the Soviet Union. But we've seen, just the short time I've been in office, keeping high the banner of human rights, that many other countries are abandoning military dictatorships and totalitarian commitments and moving toward democracy. We're opening up vast areas of the world to friendship and trade and better economic lives for us all and better peace and stability and to enhance our security.

The greatest black nation on Earth, Nigeria, 4 years ago wouldn't let the Secretary of State of the United States cross their borders. Now they're among our staunchest allies. Their President was here not long ago—elected in free and open democratic elections with a government patterned after the Constitution of the United States. And recently, we've opened up a new trade, new advice, new counsel, new cooperation, in a peaceful way, 1 billion people in the People's Republic of China, the largest nation on Earth. And we haven't lost, at the same time, trade advantages which are growing by leaps and bounds with the people of Taiwan.

We've seen a harnessing of new concepts brought about to us by the new energy challenges. That has not struck, again, awe or despair in the American people. Not too long ago, as you know, in the revolution of Iran the world lost about 4 million barrels of oil per day. We had long gas lines, and the American economic system was placed into consternation. A lot of political furor was apparent in the communities of our country. Recently, because the Congress has acted so courageously in giving us an energy policy, for the first time, we lost 4 million barrels of oil again when Iran and Iraq began their conflict. There was hardly a tremor in our country because in that short interval of time, we have slashed imported oil. In the last year alone, we have cut our oil imports over 35 percent, and today we're importing 2 million barrels of oil less per day than we did just a year ago. That's tremendous achievement.

That's tremendous achievement, brought about not by me, not by the Congress, but by you. And it gives us not only economic security, but it gives us political and strategic security, because we are less subject now to blackmail and we are much more able now to shape our own foreign policy, cementing our ties with Israel and other allies around the world, without the fear of influence by those on whom we've excessively depended in the past for their oil.

Finally, let me say this: Ours is a country where people have a chance to participate in government. The stark differences that exist between myself and my Republican opponent in my lifetime have never been equaled. Those differences exceed even the ones, in my judgment, between Barry Goldwater and Lyndon Johnson in 1964. I won't go down a litany tonight of those sharp differences concerning the minimum wage and social security and the control of nuclear weapons and the general concept of what our Nation ought to be, about afflicted people and older people and people who need health care. You've heard it before, and I've said it several times during this day. But I would like to point out to you that just a small investment of your time and effort can change the course of this country in less than 3 weeks from tonight.

In 1960 if 28,000 people had voted differently in the State of Texas and just a few thousand had changed their minds or not gone to the polls in Illinois, John Fitzgerald Kennedy would never have been President of our country. And in 1968, if just a few thousand Democrats like you around this country had given more support to a great Democrat, Hubert Humphrey, and if the issue hadn't been clouded by third party candidates or can-

didates with no party, then Richard Nixon would never have been President and Hubert Humphrey would have carried on the great tradition of Jack Kennedy and Lyndon Johnson. We've got a similar situation this year, where well-meaning people have not yet faced the awesome responsibility on the shoulders of those whose commitments and principles are compatible with the Democratic Party.

Three weeks from tonight our country will make a judgment. One of those profound judgments is the most awesome of all: What will be done with nuclear weapons? Every President since Harry Truman has moved steadily forward with SALT agreements to have equal, limited, confirmable, and gradually reducing levels of atomic arsenals.

My Republican opponent has said let's withdraw the SALT treaty that has been negotiated by myself and by Gerald Ford and by Richard Nixon, and he advocates the possibility of a nuclear arms race and the playing of a so-called card against the Soviet Union. This statement causes me deep concern, because it changes the basic attitude of American people, if implemented, from one putting a lid and a commitment to reductions of nuclear weapons into one that's a radical departure from the philosophy of every President who's served since the Second World War.

The issues are profound, and the future of our country will be affected profoundly by the decision made in just 3 weeks.

I've come here tonight to thank you for your investment in this campaign, in the future of the Democratic Party, and in the future of this country. You will help to shape the kind of life that will be lived by the people that you love and by the Nation that we all love. I'm grateful to you. You're my partners. I will do the best I can the next 3 weeks to win, but I cannot win without you. As generous as you've been tonight, that is not enough. There is not a single person in this room that can't shape the opinion and inspire the participation of hundreds, perhaps thousands, even tens of thousands of residents of this State of New Jersey in the next 3 weeks.

My hope is that you will commit yourself to this political campaign above and beyond what you've done tonight financially. Many of you have a long history of support and participation, sustaining and guiding and carrying to victory the Democratic Party. There is no doubt in my mind that if you'll do the same thing the next 3 weeks, and a few others like you around this Nation, when the returns come in on November 4, we'll have a bright future ahead of us, a future based upon the principles which you and I espouse. And we will whip the Republicans as they've never been whipped before in this general election to come.

Thank you very much. God bless you.

NOTE: The President spoke at 8:54 p.m. in the Meadowlands Ballroom at the Meadowlands Hilton Hotel.

Following the reception, the President returned to the White House.

Newington, Connecticut

Remarks and a Question-and-Answer Session With Hospital and Community Volunteers. October 16, 1980

VOLUNTARISM IN AMERICA

THE PRESIDENT. It's a pleasure to be here. I want to say, first of all, that I particularly appreciate Governor Ella Grasso and Senator Ribicoff and Chris Dodd for riding out here with me to this beautiful place.

I don't believe there's anything I could have done this morning that would start my day off better than to walk through the halls of this beautiful children's hospital and see the young people who've been afflicted with physical disabilities, some extremely serious, but who are responding with the utmost use of the talent that God's given them toward a life of hope and gratification, filled with love.

There are a lot of things that government can do, as you know, to make the afflictions of life be eased. But the most important contribution that can be made for those in need is the volunteer help that they get from hearts filled with love and from minds that understand, in a special way, the needs that can't possibly be met by any government agency, no matter how dedicated and efficient it might be.

I realize that in order for volunteers to have your effectiveness magnified, there must be facilities and tools and equipment and books and teaching aids and services. A lot of those do come from tax money paid in through the Federal, State, local governments and back, but a lot of it comes just from direct contributions from generous Americans. Our Nation is almost unique in its contributions through public service and dedication. Americans give, outside of government, about $42 billion every year to help people, quite often to help people to help other people.

It's a similar thing with a President. Your life is filled with generosity. I don't claim the same, but my life is also filled with a responsibility to help others. And the epitome of American service is through the White House and through the Oval Office and through our governments at all levels, designed to help the elderly, to help the handicapped, to help the sick, to help those who are poor, those who speak a different language, those who are newcomers to our country, those who've been suffering in the past from discrimination who want to have a better life, those who see the vision of what America can be and have not yet realized that vision.

It adds a new dimension or a different dimension to the life of a campaigner for office or a President responsible for national defense and foreign affairs, to walk through the halls of this hospital and be able to pick up in one's arms and feel the tender love of a little child who has already benefited from your generosity. I know you've come here from volunteer organizations throughout this area. Not all of you are devoting yourselves specifically to health care. That's just one element of the wide range of volunteer services that you've offered.

But on behalf of, I guess, 230 million Americans, as President, I'd like to thank you for your volunteer services on behalf of many millions of volunteers all over this Nation who can't be in this room this morning. My heart goes out to you in gratitude and my heart also goes out to you in a spirit of love and affection and a sharing of the generosity that makes our Nation such a great nation.

I have time for a few questions, if you'd like to ask them. I'll start in the back. Yes, ma'am.

QUESTIONS

WHITE HOUSE CONFERENCE ON AGING

Q. Welcome to Connecticut, Mr. President.

THE PRESIDENT. Thank you. I feel welcome.

Q. I'm very lucky to have gotten to work with older Americans, and the White House Conference on Aging is coming up in 1981. Right now, there's a grassroots effort to determine what the issues are. There are many conferences going on across the Nation, and I wondered if you could share with us what you think the issues are for older Americans for the next 10 years, and how you think government and private sector and voluntary sector can work together to address those issues.

THE PRESIDENT. First of all, I look forward to being there. [*Laughter*] I think it's been about 10 years since the last White House Conference on the Aging, and it's time now to reassess what we have done, to see what faults we've committed inadvertently, to see what omissions there are in the care for the aging.

I won't try to presuppose what the White House Conference will do, because I think the innovations coming from throughout these local meetings all over the country that will culminate with me in the White House ought not to be disturbed. I think the thrust of the program will not be specifically to government services that care for relatively incapable elderly. I think the thrust in the future will be how those who have retired voluntarily can live a more fruitful life.

I see the reservoir of the retired Americans as not yet adequately being tapped. I've seen in my mother's life, for instance—she's 82 years old. My father died in 1953. I was in the nuclear submarine program at the time and went home. And my mother was devastated for a few months because of the loss of my father, but then she actually started a new life and in 1968, she—I mean, when she was 68 years old, in 1966, she volunteered to be a Peace Corps worker, went to India, spent 2 years and came back. And she's had a broad gamut of opportunities to serve our country.

I think this is typical of what older people can do at the age of 68 or 70—now she's 82—to live a better life. I see the opening up of many part-time careers for the elderly in public service, even beyond and above what they do now—maybe in health centers like this one helping with other elderly who can't help themselves, or working as teachers' aides, working in the elements of life that relate to their former careers in local, State and Federal Governments. So, I think this is one area that can be emphasized at the White House Conference.

Another, of course, is to make doubly sure, as I have tried to do the last 3½ years, that the social security programs, the Medicare programs, are extended in the future to a broader range of services and more deeply embedded into the consciousness of America on a bipartisan basis.

Another element, and this will be the last point that I will make, is to make sure, in addition, that we have a nationwide health care service. National health insurance has not yet been adopted as a political given in our country. My Republican opponent says that he's against national health care.

It's important to me to have that program embedded in the consciousness of America and passed by the Congress and placed on the law books of our country, with the emphasis on out-patient care, an emphasis on long-term care, perhaps, in the patient's homes, with an emphasis on prevention of disease, with an emphasis on the kind of immunization programs for young people that would prevent disease in later life.

I've just signed this week, this past week as a matter of fact, the Mental Health Systems Act of 1980, which is the greatest mental health program that I've signed into law in my term, better than anything since John Kennedy and the Mental Health Programs Act of 1963. So,

these are the kind of things that I see that can be done in the future—a better life for able-bodied senior citizens, an extension of existing programs, national health care, more emphasis on prevention of disease, better treatment, for instance, in mental retardation and other mental problems, plus disabilities.

I'm looking forward to that Conference. It's going to be an exciting thing. And as you know, the former White House Conference literally transformed the attitude of Americans about the elderly, and I think it's made our whole country a better nation. I see the same thing in the future.

You might be interested in knowing that in the 1980's, the largest growing segment of the American population will be those above 70 years old. And we cannot afford to have them live a disabled life in a closet somewhere, just caring for them. They have got to be given the opportunity to contribute to a greater America, and they've got experience and sound judgment and time that can be a major contribution to our Nation's life.

I'll try to keep the other answers shorter. [*Laughter*]

PRESENTATION OF A BOOK TO THE PRESIDENT

Q. Mr. President, I am Madeline Marston, a volunteer from Newington Public Hospital. I appeal to you for the—[*inaudible*]—and for all special education programs in order to uphold the—[*inaudible*]—investment. Your help and support are essential to our investment. I would like to present you with this book, a history of Newington, which contains factual information about the development and growth of Newington and of its extraordinary—[*inaudible*].

THE PRESIDENT. Thank you. I love you. Thank you. Thank you, Madeline.

I've gotten a lot of questions. I think that's the nicest question I ever got. [*Laughter*] Thank you very much.

Yes, sir?

SOCIAL SECURITY SYSTEM

Q. I saw you about 4 years ago at the civic center with Ella Grasso, and I see you again. You're looking good. [*Laughter*]

THE PRESIDENT. Thank you. I'm feeling good.

Q. Why is it every time they have an election, they always pick on the senior citizens? [*Inaudible*]—going to cut the social security——

THE PRESIDENT. I know.

Q. ——they're going to take all your money for senior citizens. They're going to do it for that. We can't take it. We're old. We were wondering, who was that—[*inaudible*]. It must be the wrong party, or something like that. [*Laughter*]

THE PRESIDENT. That's right. You're absolutely right. I'm glad you brought that up. [*Laughter*] I'm glad you brought that up. You know, this election is one that will perhaps have the sharpest difference between two candidates that I remember in modern times. My opponent, Governor Reagan, on several occasions, for instance, in the last number of years has advocated making social security program voluntary, which means that people that want to withdraw from social security can do so, which would wipe out social security as a program.

This is nothing new, because I remember during the Depression years when Franklin Roosevelt proposed social security, the Republicans opposed it. And I remember that when the Democrats put forward a 25-cent minimum wage to eliminate the sweatshops and give working people a chance to earn a decent living, the Republicans were against it. My first job was at 40 cents an hour, minimum wage. That increase from 25 to 40 cents was put forward by Democrats. It was opposed again by the Republicans.

When Medicare was proposed to give older people some health care, my opponent, Governor Reagan, began his political career going around the Nation speaking against Medicare. And recently he's said that he's absolutely opposed to a national health care program. These kinds of sharp differences between the Democrats and Republicans and between myself and my opponent ought to be emphasized. But I can guarantee you that as long as there's a Democrat serving in the Oval Office, the senior citizens in this Nation will not be abandoned and they will not suffer.

LEAA FUNDS

Q. I'm from Women in Crisis. We're with the criminal justice system. And we would like to know, since Congress has cut funding for—well, we're funded by LEAA. And since Congress has cut the funding, is there some program that's going to be set up to fund such programs in the future in criminal justice?

THE PRESIDENT. Would you describe to me a little more specifically about what this particular program does—the Women in Crisis?

Q. Women in Crisis?

THE PRESIDENT. Yes.

Q. We are an agency of families, whose husband or son has been incarcerated.

THE PRESIDENT. I see.

Q. They are not to be penalized—the families. They are not to suffer—[*inaudible*].

THE PRESIDENT. I know. [*Inaudible*]—Senator Ribicoff could help me.

I think there has been a move in Congress to eliminate unemployment compensation when a person was in prison. Chris, do you or Senator Ribicoff know about that, or any of the Congressmen over there? Toby?

SENATOR RIBICOFF. I didn't hear the——

THE PRESIDENT. The question was about Congress attempting to eliminate funds, I think unemployment compensation or disability insurance, when a person was in prison.

Q. No, no, no.

THE PRESIDENT. No?

Q. Cutting off the LEAA funds.

SENATOR RIBICOFF. Law Enforcement Assistance——

THE PRESIDENT. I know what LEAA is. This is apparently a program for women in crisis who have a husband or a son in prison.

SENATOR RIBICOFF. That is true. I think that was a Republican-sponsored accomplishment—[*laughter*]—which, I regret to say, a number of Democrats joined in.

May I make this one comment now that I'm getting out of Congress— [*inaudible*]—I have found that year in and year out any President, be he Democrat or Republican, has been more concerned with the national interest than the Congress has been.

Now, we have a President, Jimmy Carter, who has a good, constructive record, and a real leader, who is trying to fight tooth and nail for constructive principles and constructive programs. The frustrations are congressional frustrations and not the frustrations brought about by the President of the United States.

THE PRESIDENT. Thank you.

I'll probably need to get more answers for you because I don't know. Has that cut already passed through the Congress or is it just something that has not yet passed but you're afraid will pass? Does anybody know? Is Stu Eizenstat here?

GOVERNOR GRASSO. Mr. President— [*inaudible*]—million dollars from LEAA. I think Women in Crisis is a good program. And you would have supported it, and I would have supported it. But our friends in the Congress—but I would like to say that the Connecticut delegation did not vote for it. But there were enough votes, so that it's caused great disaccommodation, a great difficulty, and it, I think, will be part of the continuing frustration. But, you see, it's so easy when people ask questions to turn to you as the President, to turn to me as the Governor— [*inaudible*]. [*Laughter*]

THE PRESIDENT. I'm not trying to avoid responsibility. I think that if cuts were made in the LEAA program it may have been proposed by me or passed by the Congress. One unique thing about the LEAA program is that a lot of the judgments about how to spend the money are made at the local and State level. So, I think that now that you've brought the thing to my attention and to the attention of your present and future Senator and also the Governor, I think we'll look into it a little more closely than we would have before, and I'll learn about this program before the day's out. [*Laughter*]

Yes, ma'am.

PROGRAMS FOR THE HANDICAPPED

Q. My name is Rachel Mosto, and my husband and I have 14 children, 11 of whom are multiple-handicapped. And I guess we see the courage and nobility with which our children tackle every day the— [*inaudible*]—born with. May we ask some of your attitudes on special education, Federal—[*inaudible*]—and advocacy for—[*inaudible*]. Can we just open it up, please for your attitude?

THE PRESIDENT. Yes. I think it's accurate to say that in the last 3½ years under my administration, with both Pat Harris and Joe Califano before her, we have done more for special education and also for the handicapped in general than has ever been done before.

We had a special White House Conference on the handicapped, as you may know. You may have been there.

Q. I was there.

THE PRESIDENT. Oh, you were there. And I participated in it personally, because it's something that has touched my life as a Governor and also my wife's life as the First Lady of Georgia and this Nation. It's very important to us.

It's one reason I wanted to come here. As President, I could have been anywhere in the Nation this morning in this last few days of a crucial campaign. I wanted to come here, not to get votes, although that may be part of it—[*laughter*]—but also to let the volunteers of this Nation all over the country know how important their work is and also to let the Nation and the national press focus on the special problems of severely disabled children who are struggling to have a fruitful life.

There is no reason for you to worry about my attitude, about continuing to carry out the programs that we're already committed to do in the future. And my judgment is that the Congress is increasingly receptive to requests for additional funds to help the severely handicapped, the emotionally disturbed children, the mentally retarded children, and others who in the past have not gotten adequate care.

There's one additional point that ought to be made: The struggle that's most important of all is going to be in the next year or two on national health insurance,

because there are various elements of that program that will be phased in year-by-year. One of the first things that we will do in phasing in national health insurance is to care for the mother during the prenatal stages and also the babies and little children in the first 2 or 3 years of their lives, to make sure that they get a good start in life and are not deprived inadvertently because the mother doesn't get the proper kind of diet and the proper kind of care before birth. That is a part of our health program in this country that is sadly lacking.

And with hospital cost containment to hold down costs, an emphasis on prevention and immunization, the care on the prenatal and early years of the child's life and the mother during those times, and the emphasis on catastrophic health insurance, where if a family's wiped out financially by extraordinary medical costs—those will be the first parts of the comprehensive national program that would go into effect.

But I can guarantee you that one of the most important elements of it will be that early prenatal and postnatal care that will prevent a lot of disabilities, and we'll continue to increase the programs for special health care and special education for the children who are disabled.

We have time for one more question. I think the lady in the back.

Q. Mr. President, I'm fortunate to work with the State Planning Council for—[*inaudible*]—and Disability. But we all have disabilities.

THE PRESIDENT. Yes, I know.

Q. I have a concern for the —[*inaudible*]—volunteer army. [*Inaudible*]—understand you are planning or considering the possibility of—[*inaudible*]—business and industry to reward the person who takes time from their job to volunteer. I find the army is—[*inaudible*]—

volunteer. I also have word you—[*inaudible*]—handle the Department of the Army. You felt that they'd give it—[*inaudible*].

THE PRESIDENT. I thank you for it. One of the things that we have had at the White House, Rosalynn sponsored it primarily, is a meeting of all the nationwide volunteer organizations. It was in the East Room. I participated by making a speech to them.

The important thing that I noticed that day was that quite often the leaders of volunteer groups are the top business executives of our country. They're the ones who are the chairman of the board or the chief executive officer of the top insurance companies or manufacturing companies and others, and I think this interrelationship between those enlightened leaders who've already made it to the pinnacle of success in their own profession, now turning toward the marshaling of additional volunteer workers, is a step in the right direction.

I think they'll be much more receptive in the future to rewarding, through time off and through extra incentives, the enlightened volunteers within their own organizations, among their own employees, who do work like you do.

Also, of course, I think the fact that we do honor outstanding volunteers is a good program. Rosalynn is very interested in seeing this expanded in the future, too—to give a few certificates of award from the President for those who typify outstanding service. It's already being done, as you know, for the outstanding teacher of the year. I think it might also be extended to the outstanding volunteer of the year in our Nation in each different category of volunteer work. I think that would be a very good thing that would publicize

what is being done. Thank you very much. I look forward to—[*inaudible*].

Q. Wow! Great! Thank you.

DIVERSITY OF SERVICES RENDERED BY VOLUNTEERS

Q. There's an 80-year-old lady who would like to ask you a question. May she?

THE PRESIDENT. No, I've got to go now. I'm sorry. I'd like to answer more questions, but—I'm *so* sorry.

Would you let her ask one more question? I don't want to referee between the ones that just want to ask one more question.

Yes, ma'am.

Q. I'm Madeleine Culver from the Commission on Aging in the city of Hartford. I would like to ask you, could you send more dollars to do something—[*inaudible*]. We need the program—the elderly service and the—[*inaudible*]—service. The city of Hartford would be very grateful—[*inaudible*]. [*Laughter*]

THE PRESIDENT. There was a question here concerning veterans. I think you can see from the breadth of the questions how important your work is and the diversity of interests in public service and how many different people you can care for—the severely disabled, the emotionally disturbed, the elderly, parents and spouses of people who are in prison, the veterans, the elderly. These are the kinds of questions that are ever present in your mind, and they're also the kinds of questions that are ever present in my mind every day that I serve as President, because I have not only to take care of common ordinary routine daily tasks, but also to look to 1981 and to 1982 as far as establishing priorities of the allocation of our limited Federal funds that you pay as taxes.

And I have to consult with Congress and consult with leaders in your groups to

see how much do we put for the handicapped, how much do we put for the
veterans, how much do we put for the elderly, how much do we put for health care
in the Federal budget? And the amount
of work that you do as volunteers, and
with people contributing through
churches and through benevolent organizations and directly to a goal that you
have in your life as important, means that
those limited Federal funds can be greatly
magnified.

There is no way to put a price tag on
the amount of volunteer work represented
in this room. If the Federal Government
had to pay every worker just the minimum wage that volunteers who work in
this Nation or in this hospital, it would
not be possible.

So, as the one in charge of the Federal
budget, I thank you, and as one responsible for the needy people in this Nation,
I thank you also.

Thank you very much.

NOTE: The President spoke at 11:14 a.m. in
the Newington Auditorium at the Newington
Children's Hospital.

Hartford, Connecticut

*Remarks at a Meeting With State, Local, and
Community Officials.   October 16, 1980*

I'm very proud to stand here with your
wonderful Governor, with Senator Ribicoff, who's made such a great record not
only for you but the entire country. And
I want to be sure that Christopher Dodd
is the Senator in January to take Ribicoff's
place and to work with me. Would you
do that, too? [*Applause*] Thank you.

I'm going inside now to make an
announcement very important to me.
I used to live in Connecticut, as you know.
I was in the submarine force. And I think

that one of the greatest things that ever
happened to the world was the development of the *Nautilus,* which gave our
Nation 25 years of good service, defended
freedom, and also kept the peace.

I'd like to point out to you that although
this was a great weapon of war, it served
its purpose well. The best weapon is one
that's never used in combat, and the best
soldier is one that never gives his life or
sheds his blood on the field of battle. The
Nautilus has performed well, and I'm
glad to see it come back home where it
belongs.

Thank you very much.

[*The President spoke at 12:55 p.m. to a crowd
assembled outside the Old State House. Following his remarks, he went to the Senate Chamber
of the Old State House, where he delivered the
following remarks.*]

THE PRESIDENT. I was standing outside
the door for a few minutes, and I thought
there were at least 2,000 people in here
from—[*laughter*]. But all of you represent
literally hundreds of thousands of people
of Connecticut, who share with me a sense
of admiration for your great Governor,
Ella Grasso, and for the congressional
delegation which has represented the
ideals and principles of your State so well.

As a President who has to face difficult
decisions every day of my life in the Oval
Office, I have a special affection for one
man who is here. I've seen him perform
when it was difficult. I've seen him make
decisions that were very close, sometimes
unpopular, but in the best interests of our
country. And I just want to express personally my deep affection, my deep admiration, and on behalf of 230 million
Americans, my gratitude to Senator Abe
Ribicoff. And I might say that after January the 20th, 1981, both I as President,
reelected, and Christopher Dodd as your
new Senator are going to call on Abe

Ribicoff for a lot of advice and counsel and hard work.

I've come here for a strictly nonpolitical task—[*laughter*]—one that's very important to me personally and as the Commander in Chief of our military forces. It's doubly significant, therefore, for me to talk to you for a few minutes about the *Nautilus* Memorial.

I recently signed the 1981 defense authorization bill, which included the authority to establish the permanent home of the U.S.S. *Nautilus,* the world's first nuclear-powered submarine or vessel of any kind, now retired, as you know, after a distinguished quarter of a century of service in keeping world peace. I considered this for a long time. I sought the advice of Ella Grasso, Christopher Dodd, the entire Congress delegation, and Abe Ribicoff. And following their advice, I decided that the best place for this submarine to stay from now on in the future is Groton, Connecticut.

I've had the honor of sharing in that history. As a young naval officer back in the early 1950's, I think 1952, I was in the nuclear propulsion program, working under Admiral Hyman Rickover. There were two submarines being built—the U.S.S. *Nautilus,* the U.S.S. *Sea Wolf.* I was the senior officer of the U.S.S. *Sea Wolf,* and I was sent over here from Schenectady, New York, to witness the laying of the keel of the *Nautilus.* Harry Truman, with a welder's outfit in his hand, made the first step.

My third son, Jeff, was born in Connecticut. We've lived here twice in my life and have always felt close to you. You probably have noticed that I and my family still speak with a Connecticut accent. [*Laughter*]

I participated in the development of the *Nautilus* at nearly every step, and I re-member vividly how excited the world was when that formidable war machine took its place underneath the oceans of the world. It's performed well, and I'm grateful that it has served its purpose as a deterrent to war, through strength, to preserve the peace.

I knew when I left that ceremony back almost 30 years ago that I had participated in a historic event. I left the Navy before the nuclear submarine *Nautilus* began its operation. I went back home to Plains, Georgia, because my father had died and I had responsibilities that I could not avoid.

I'm very grateful that Groton will be the site, the home of the *Nautilus.* People will want to come here from all over the world to be part of naval history and part of the history of the securing and the perpetuation of peace.

Ella, I'd like to present not only, to you, the right of bringing the *Nautilus* home, but last night, we called Admiral Rickover and asked him if there wasn't some memento of the *Nautilus* that he would like to share with the people of Connecticut, through you. And he took out of his own personal belongings and his own private home a tray made from teakwood from the U.S.S. *Nautilus,* and I'd like to present it to you on behalf of Admiral Rickover and Lieutenant Senior Grade Jimmy Carter.

And I might say, in closing, that this submarine itself and the symbolism of this gift from me and from Admiral Rickover is a credit to the people of this State. You have helped to make history, because of the technological capability of your people and because of your insight into the needs of our country—the need for a strong defense and the need for unity of purpose and confidence in trying times.

The first time I came here to be assigned to a submarine was when Groton Electric

Boat Company then was making refrigerator truck bodies for pickup trucks. I was assigned as the only officer on the first ship the Navy built after the Second World War, a small antisubmarine submarine called the U.S.S. *K-1*. I was the only officer there, and I helped to design it. And I saw the Electric Boat Company develop from that point ultimately into General Dynamics.

As you can see, I have a lot of fond memories of Connecticut, both in the past and even fonder expectations, politically speaking at least, for the future.

As I signed the bill for the defense construction authorization, I kept one of the fountain pens that I used, because that bill did include the permanent home establishment for the *Nautilus*. And I have a letter here that I would like to give to you, Ella Grasso, as Governor of this great State, and a fountain pen that might be used to display in the site of the *Nautilus* to remind people in the future that the Congress of the United States, representing all the people of our country, believe as I do that Groton is the proper place for this great vessel representing the spirit and ideals of our country for strength and peace.

Thank you very much.

GOVERNOR GRASSO. Thank you, Mr. President.

Windsor Locks, Connecticut

Informal Exchange With Reporters on Departure From Connecticut.
October 16, 1980

Q. We hear the hostages are nearly to be released. Is that correct?

THE PRESIDENT. I don't want to comment on it. I don't know of any immediate prospect.

Q. Well, when you say "immediate prospect", sir, are you saying just a few hours or what?

THE PRESIDENT. No, no. We've been trying to get the hostages released ever since they were taken, and we've used every possible means we can to negotiate or to send direct or indirect messages to the Iranians. But I don't have any progress——

Q. No imminent——

THE PRESIDENT. No imminent, no.

Q. Is there a potential in the arrival of the Iranian Foreign Minister here to discuss the hostage issue with the senior Iranians?

THE PRESIDENT. There's always a potential. We have not made any arrangements to meet with Mr. Rajai, but if he should be amenable to a meeting we would certainly continue to follow our practice of meeting with any Iranian official who had a possibility of speaking authoritatively for their Government.

Q. When you say "amenable to a meeting," do you mean yourself or someone else?

THE PRESIDENT. Yes, myself or Ed Muskie or Warren Christopher or whoever would be appropriate.

Q. Has Rajai suggested that he might be amenable?

THE PRESIDENT. I don't think so.

Q. You don't think so, sir?

THE PRESIDENT. No. I don't know whether he has or not. I don't have any information that he has. But we will continue to pursue, in every possible way, the possibility of having the hostages released, as we have for the last 10 or 11 months. But there is no imminent prospect, so far as I know, of the hostages being released.

Q. Would that include assisting Iran in the U.N. vis-a-vis Iraq in their dispute, supporting their position?

THE PRESIDENT. Well, we've made our position clear on the hostilities between Iran and Iraq—that they should be resolved peacefully, through negotiations; their disputes over the border should be settled in that fashion, using international intermediaries if necessary; and that disputes like this should not be settled through aggression or through invasion of another country's territory. That's our position, and I think it ought to be acceptable as our Nation's position in the U.N. Security Council.

Q. So we basically support them?

Q. Could you be meeting Rajai later today in New York?

THE PRESIDENT. No. I don't have the time.

Q. Thank you.

Q. Mr. President, could we have some more questions?

THE PRESIDENT. Thank you.

NOTE: The exchange began at approximately 1:30 p.m. at Bradley International Airport.

As printed above, the item follows the text of the White House press release.

Hempstead, New York

Remarks and a Question-and-Answer Session at a Town Meeting. October 16, 1980

THE PRESIDENT. *Senator Moynihan, Governor Hugh Carey, Lt. Governor Mario Cuomo, Congressman Tom Downey, Chairman Dominic Baranello, Stanley Harwood, Nassau County Chairman George Dempster, and others:*

I want to come to you today to make a couple brief remarks and then spend what time we have available answering your questions about matters that are important to you.

Before I came here I tried to get briefed as much as possible on what was the most important thing for Long Island in 1981 and the coming years, and the answer I got was to keep the Stanley Cup. Good luck. If you won't tell anybody else, you've got my best wishes.

For a President who came here during the last campaign and to see what is going on in Long Island, this is a very profound and secret development. The rest of the Nation doesn't quite understand what's happened here. This is not a bedroom community; it's not a suburb anymore. Seventy-five percent of the people who live in this region also work here. If you put together Nassau County and Suffolk County, yours would be 1 of the 10 most important economic communities in the United States. I won't list all the statistics, but one is interesting. If, for instance, Suffolk and Nassau counties were a State, the retail sales would be greater than one-half of all the other States in the Nation. That's unbelievable. And I think the future is going to be even brighter.

As has been my custom with townhall meetings, I want to cover two points very quickly and then let you bring up other issues of importance to you. The two I want to speak on are important to the entire country. One is the threat from pollutants, and the other one is property taxes.

CAMPAIGN ISSUES

First, we must not close our eyes to the continued pollution problems that afflict and threaten our Nation. I'm proud of the very real progress that we have made over the last several years, but contrary to what some believe, there is a continuous pollution problem in America. I noticed, as I came in on the helicopter and got off and looked around, the beauty of this countryside and the purity of the air. I'm glad to know that the trees and the volcanoes have taken a vacation for the day.

It would be a tragedy for us to turn our backs on this very serious threat. One of the great unfinished jobs of this decade, particularly for young people looking to the future, is the problem of hazardous wastes and also groundwater contamination. On Long Island your water comes from underground aquifers, which are not piped in from outside reservoirs. I know that recent incidents have caused you some concern about water quality on Long Island. I share that concern, and you have a right to be certain that the water you drink is safe. It is safe now, and I'm taking steps along with you to protect the quality of the drinking water both here and throughout the country.

First, we are providing direct technical assistance and Federal funds to a number of Long Island cities to help identify the sources of potential pollution. Second, I've signed recently a new law which tightens the standards for safe drinking water. Third, my Council of Environmental Quality right now is investigating the extent of the problem nationwide and the seriousness of the related health threats. And fourth and most important, I proposed the so-called superfund bill. This program would identify dangerous chemical dumpsites and provide the funds, largely from a kind of insurance fee on the chemical industry, to clean these dumpsites up.

This far-reaching and overdue legislation has already passed the House, and it should be passed in the Senate in the post-election session. It's an urgent priority for Long Island, for the rest of New York State, and for the entire country.

And second, property taxes. I don't need to tell you that here in Nassau County you pay the highest property taxes of any citizens in the United States. Maybe that's news to you. No? It's my goal to avoid additional pressures on your property taxes and to relieve the burdens they have to support.

Senator Moynihan, Governor Hugh Carey, and others and I have been fighting to get very substantial relief for your very high welfare burden. This is part of my welfare reform proposal which has already passed the House and is now in the Senate. In addition, the national health insurance proposal will provide further fiscal relief from Medicaid burdens. In addition, I'm increasing mass transit aid with a new formula which greatly benefits New York. The urban policy is designed to build up the local tax base and to lessen dependence on the local property taxes for the provision of basic services.

This is a political year, and I'm sure I'll get some political questions, so I'd like to point out to you that my policies that I've just outlined so briefly are diametrically opposed to those of Governor Reagan, whose positions have very serious implications for your already high property tax burdens.

After I leave, as you talk to him or his runningmate or those who represent him here in your community, you should emphasize questions about this very serious matter. First, on urban transit—an increasingly costly requirement for the future—Governor Reagan said just this year, not in ancient history, that people like yourselves—[laughter]—talking about urban transit, he said people like yourselves, and I quote, "who are going to be in charge of spending it should be responsible for raising it." This could add a great deal to your financial burdens through local property taxes.

Second, Governor Reagan said this year, "Urban aid programs, I think, are one of the biggest phonies that we have in this system and have had for a number of years." If Governor Reagan wants to dismantle our urban aid programs like Community Development Block Grants and Urban Development Action Grants, or UDAG grants, the only way I know of to make up the difference would be higher State or local taxes.

And third, because of the great massive across-the-board tax cuts proposed under the Reagan-Kemp-Roth proposal, he would need to cut over $130 billion from the Federal Government to achieve a balanced budget. If you eliminate or discount defense and entitlement programs, the total remaining Federal budget is only $150 billion. So, if you cut $130 billion out of that, the only place that these cuts could come would be from local and State taxes picking up the difference.

We should remember that he has already proposed that full responsibility for certain Federal programs like welfare and education be shifted to State and local governments. Block grants would be only a first step, he says. Suppose the $5 billion the State of New York now receives from the Federal Government for welfare and education is cut off and has to be replaced by $5 billion in new local property taxes. In that case the extra tax burden for an average family of four here would be increased more than 50 percent.

We should be moving to remove, not add, to the local property tax burdens. The Democratic Party platform reconfirms this, and I will be working with Senator Moynihan, with your Governor, with the mayors, and other local officials to achieve this goal of removing, not adding to, the local property tax burdens. Those two subjects are important.

And now I'd like to answer your questions.

QUESTIONS

EDUCATION

Q. President Carter, the cost of education is high now. What will happen to the up-and-coming generation if the cost of an education continues to rise, especially for our black children.

THE PRESIDENT. All right. One of the things that is a constant burden or responsibility for a President is to have a proper balance between the Federal role in education and the local and State role. My own philosophy, which I grew up with in Georgia—I was on the local school board and was Governor there—is to keep control of the schools, public or private, from elementary through graduate school and college, in the hands of local and State officials, not to let the Federal Government interfere in the operation of the schools, but at the same time to provide Federal funds, which are collected primarily from the income tax base and not from local property taxes, to assist those areas that need Federal assistance. In the first 3 years I was in office we increased Federal assistance for education by 73 percent.

One thing that we have done is to meet a goal of assuring that no young person in this country who's academically qualified to do college work will be deprived of a college education because of the economic circumstances of the family. And I think I can assure you now that no matter where that young man or woman might live, if they're qualified to do college work, at this moment, no matter how poor that family might be, they can get a college education.

If you find anybody that can't, you let me know, and I'll see they get in college.

NATIONAL DEFENSE

Q. First of all, Mr. President, the Hofstra ROTC program would like to welcome the Commander in Chief of the United States Armed Forces to Hofstra University. Mr. President, in May of 1981, I will be commissioned as an officer in the United States Infantry. Sir, my question is this: Since you took office in 1976, the number of active duty Army combat-ready troops has gone down. If reelected, sir, how will you change this trend?

THE PRESIDENT. What's your name? [*Laughter*]

Q. Paul Leone, Mr. President.

THE PRESIDENT. Paul.

Q. Leone.

THE PRESIDENT. Paul Leone. Paul, I'm glad to know you.

First of all, I'm very proud that you have chosen to go into the ROTC. When I was at Georgia Tech, before I went to the Naval Academy, I was also in the Naval ROTC, and I hope that many young people, in looking for a career, will take advantage of the wonderful opportunities in the volunteer military forces. No matter what your ultimate goal might be, I don't believe it would interfere in the development of your career. It didn't interrupt unnecessarily my own political progress—[*laughter*]—I became Commander in Chief. I was a lieutenant, and I think that this stands in good stead for you.

We have not had a decrease, but a real increase in the readiness of the military forces of this country in the last 3½ years. When I went into the Oval Office, for 8 years prior to my Inauguration, 7 of those years we had an actual decrease in budgeted funds going for military defense. Since I've been in office, every year above and beyond inflation, in real dollars, we've had a steady, predictable, well-planned, orderly increase in the commitment of budgeted funds to improve the military.

There's no question that now the American military forces are in better state of readiness than they were before. They are also in a better state of readiness than are equivalent divisions in the Soviet Union. We've had, as you know, threats to peace around the world. I've never been in the office of President one day that there hasn't been a troublespot somewhere in the world that might explode into combat between two nations or more nations that might affect us directly or indirectly. Because of our enormous strength militarily, politically, economically, we've been able to keep our own country at peace and encourage peace for others.

When the Soviets invaded Afghanistan I had three options as the leader of the most powerful nation on Earth: military action, political action, economic action. I decided to take the second two. We went to the United Nations. A hundred and four other countries joined us in condemning Soviet invasion and aggression. The Moslem countries united against the Soviet invasion of Afghanistan. They lost their status in the nonaligned movement. Many less developed countries who had formerly been supportive of the Soviet Union have now turned against them. The freedom-fighters in Afghanistan have been much more courageous and much more tenacious than the Soviets ever expected.

Some of the economic restraints that we've placed against the Soviet Union have borne real fruit, and my judgment is that the Soviets now see very clearly that it is not politically or economically advantageous to them to carry out any further aggressive acts. And I don't believe that Afghanistan invasion and occupation is advantageous to them either.

Finally let me say this: In all the elements of our military we will stick with our voluntary recruitment program. Barring some threat to our Nation's security that's so real and tangible that the President and Congress and the people of the United States would agree, there is not going to be any draft of young people in this country.

Let me close this answer by adding one other thing—and I say it often, because as Commander in Chief it's my responsibility to let the people know what's fact. We have a commitment for the next 5 years, not just the last 3 years, to continue this orderly increase every year in commitments for defense. It amounts to about 5 percent of our Nation's gross national product, not excessive.

I have no apology to make for it. It's a good investment. As I said this morning in Hartford, Connecticut, where the *Nautilus* will be placed in Groton in the future as a memorial, the best weapon is one that's never fired in combat, and the best soldier is one who never has to lay his life down or shed his blood on the field of battle.

So, strength, militarily, is important. It's important that the American people know we are strong and will stay strong. It's important that our allies know that we will always be strong and second to none, and it's also important that potential adversaries know that if they attack the United States of America, that they will be committing suicide.

U.S. STEEL INDUSTRY

Q. Mr. President, as you know, the U.S. steel companies are lagging far behind the Japanese. What are the Government policies concerning this issue?

THE PRESIDENT. We have, as you know, a trigger-price mechanism system now that's just being reimposed in our country that I developed since I've been in office. The purpose of this is very clear. It was hammered out by an unprecedented cooperation between steel management, the steelworkers of this country, and local communities and the Government, which I represent. It prevents dumping of foreign produced steel in this Nation at a price less than it cost them to produce it. It also makes sure that the steel industry of our country has the financial advantageous elements of making investment to modernize.

Under the revitalization program that I've already outlined that will be imposed next year, we'll have great benefits for companies whose earnings are low because they need to modernize or because they're a brand new industry, just getting started with an innovative kind of commitment. We'll let investment tax credits that formerly could only be applied to future income tax payments now be paid in cash so that if a company invests in modernization, new plants, new equipment, new tools, they'll have income tax refunds paid to them to help defray those costs to keep American workers productive.

Finally, let me say that we've got to have in this country a good working relationship between the industry, on the one hand, and the control of pollution on the other. So, we worked out an agreement with the managers of the steelplants in this Nation and the environmental community to phase very carefully over a period of years air pollution standards, provided the steel industry will agree to correct pollution problems which they've already created and have long ignored.

Not too long ago I was in New Jersey, in Perth Amboy, visiting a modern American steelplant. It's the most productive in the world. Every worker there produces more steel per year than any other plant anywhere on Earth. They take scrap steel that used to be sent overseas for processing, melt it down, and extrude steelrods. They come out of that plant at 18,000 feet per minute, almost faster than you can see. They are bound up in 1-ton bundles, and half of the total production of that plant now goes to the People's Republic of China, new friends of ours. They can produce steel, then, in New Jersey, ship it halfway around the world, and sell it to China cheaper than the best steelplants in Japan can make it and ship it just a few hundred miles over to China.

That's the kind of progress that we can realize if our industry can be revitalized. At this day, at this moment, the most productive workers on Earth are American workers. We've not been improving as much lately as some of the others.

And lastly, let me say that the innovation that comes from free people, excellent education institutions like this one, research and development, a free enterprise system, entrepreneurship, provide us with new ideas and new concepts that other people have to buy in order to use. We earn every year $5½ billion from other countries like Germany, Japan, France, Great Britain, just to pay for American patents, and those patent incomes are growing, not decreasing, every year. This is the kind of thrust forward that will keep America on the cutting edge of progress and let us prove to the rest of the world that we're not only blessed with that kind of idealism and confidence but that we have also got the natural resources on which to build that continued progress.

All the Arab OPEC nations together in the world have about 6 percent, for instance, of the energy reserves of the world—6 percent. The United States alone has 24 percent. We've also got the richest and most productive land on Earth.

So, with our people, with our attitude, with our government freedom, with the cooperation that's now building, with the good energy base derived from our new policy, and with the minerals and land with which we've been blessed, there is no doubt in my mind that the steel industry, the automobile industry, the energy industry, and other basic industries can stay competitive with any other nation no matter who it is.

MEDICAL RESEARCH LEGISLATION

Q. Hello, Mr. President. My name is Anthony Morillo. I'm a student at Hofstra University and also a member of Spinal Cord Society, which is a nationwide, nonprofit organization comprised of people who've had spinal cord injuries. We are currently interested in seeking research for curing spinal cord injuries. Currently, there are about 1 million people in this country who've had spinal cord injuries, and about 10,000 new injuries occur every year—an injury that could occur to anyone at any time.

At NYU University there are doctors who claim that they can have a cure for spinal cord injuries in 5 years if this is properly funded, and in Congress there's a bill, which is H.R. 4358, which is designating $16 million for spinal cord research. This bill has just passed the House and is going to the Senate. When it comes to your desk, sir, will you support this bill and any future centralized research program in this country?

THE PRESIDENT. Anthony, I'd rather give you a call back and see what the bill does in addition to what you say. If that's the total purpose of this bill, I would have no aversion to giving you a yes, but it might be mixed in with some things that I don't know about now in the rest of the bill that I could not possibly accept. And if I made a commitment to you ahead of time to sign that bill, no matter what was in it, God only knows what could be in it by the time it got to my desk. [*Laughter*]

But let me tell you this. Let me check on that bill when I get back, and I'll either have someone call you directly, or I'll call you and let you know what's in the bill and if I can, Anthony; I'll call you myself. If you'd give your name and phone number where you might be reached to one of my staff members, I'll give you a call and let you know. Okay? I'm in favor of it.

ASSISTANCE TO LOCAL COMMUNITIES

Q. Mr. President, I'd like to thank you for this opportunity. I'm a spokesman from the city of Long Beach, which isn't too far away from Hofstra. We're a summer resort community that has changed. But I'd like to applaud you and your administration for the Federal grants that have been made available to our community and have been used to revitalize our community. We presently have a UDAG grant application in that is vital to the central business district of our community. I would appreciate if you would continue your good policy of helping small cities to maintain their credibility and a place for young married people to exist. And only with your help can we be successful in our endeavors.

THE PRESIDENT. Thank you very much. I really appreciate that. We'll continue that program. It's a good program.

ANTHONY CASAMENTO

I might say, since the young man who just questioned me is named Anthony and

since an earlier question was in the ROTC and wanted to know about our Nation's defense, that we have a very special person in the audience today. I don't know if he's been introduced before I came in. But one of the great thrills of my life has been to give the Nation's highest award for heroism to a few people who have offered their lives in an extraordinary way for the defense of freedom and for the defense of our country. I'd like to ask Anthony Casamento to stand and let us recognize him.

Not many people in this country wear the Congressional Medal of Honor, and the ones that wear it have earned the gratitude of all Americans.

Next question.

POLITICS

Q. Good afternoon, President Carter.

THE PRESIDENT. Hello.

Q. I am Wendy Gumbs, president of Our Lady of Perpetual Hope, Lindenhurst student council. What advice would you have to any young people who are interested in entering politics?

THE PRESIDENT. Very good. Well, you know, my advice first of all would be a Democrat—[*laughter*]—because in my judgment it's important for the relationship between a public officeholder, at the local, State, or national level or in the White House, to be predicated on the principles that I'm convinced my party espouses.

The Democrats, first of all, are a broad range of people, because we represent different interests. But the underlying commitment has been expressed very accurately, I believe, by Presidents of the past. Franklin Roosevelt—I grew up in the Depression years, and I remember when the Democrats put forward social security. The Republicans opposed it, but it passed.

There was a time when sweatshops were used to abuse people of this country, including young people even younger than you. The Congress finally passed the minimum wage law, 25 cents an hour. The Democrats were for it; the Republicans were against it. My first job when I got out of high school was at 40 cents an hour, which was the new minimum wage. When it increased from 25 to 40 cents an hour the Democrats supported it, the Republicans opposed it.

We have put into effect Medicare, to give older people some help with their medical expenses after they reach retirement age. The Democrats have supported it; the Republicans opposed it. My opponent, for instance, began his political career campaigning around this Nation trying to kill Medicare. Now it's crucial to the well-being and security and hope and good life of older people. You've heard some questions raised today, over here by the young man with a spinal problem. Health insurance, which I think ought to be a nationwide commitment, is a policy that we've espoused as Democrats that's opposed by my opponent and many other Republicans.

I recognize that on occasion, even in this great community here, which is fast-growing and very prosperous, that there are families that are temporarily without income, when a factory closes because it's obsolete or when it moves to another part of the country and a family has temporary interruption of income. The unemployment compensation program is designed for a few weeks to give the mother and father, whoever's been earning a living, enough money to pay the children's hospital bills if they're sick and to buy food and drugs and so forth. My opponent has called unemployment compensation a prepaid vacation for freeloaders.

Well, the attitude that exists between someone who wants to be in politics and the public has got to be someone who wants to be not a master, but a servant. Your goal in going into politics ought to be what can I do to make the lives of the people that I love better? What can I do to make the next generation of young people have a better opportunity than I have? What can I do to keep my Nation strong with its morals and ethics, and united, and let people be free and independent? What can I do to make sure that anybody who's been a subject of discrimination because they're black or don't speak English well or because they're Jewish or because they're different from the majority or because they're women—what can we do to make sure that that discrimination is eliminated?

You also ought to be concerned about military strength of a nation, not to be used in combat, but to be used for the maintenance of peace. And if that's the kind of ideals that you have, if you express those clearly to the people around you who go to the polls and vote, there's a very good chance that you will be successful.

At this point, women don't have an equal chance. It's much more difficult for a woman now to earn a living or to be elected to office or to manage a family than it is men. If a woman and a man do the same work in this country now, if the man earns a dollar for a certain amount of work, the woman only earns 59 cents. That's why for 40 years the Republican Party has said, "We're for the equal rights amendment." The Democratic Party has said, "We're for the equal rights amendment." Six Presidents before me, and counting me, have all been for the equal rights amendment. What it says is that you cannot deprive a person of their rights, either the Federal Government or the State government, simply because of sex. That's all it says. But, again, my opponent in the race is not for the equal rights amendment.

I think that these kind of distinctions that are drawn have got to have a very important place in your life. Another thing that you have to do is to prepare yourself well with a good education, constantly studying how you can be involved in civic affairs, working with Girl Scouts, perhaps in your church or synagogue, making sure that in school that you go the second mile to improve the circumstances that are already under your control.

How old are you, Wendy?

Q. Thirteen.

THE PRESIDENT. Thirteen. You've got a good opportunity in the future. Amy's going to be 13 Sunday, and I'm very proud of her. But I hope you'll go into politics and just—this is the first time I've gotten that question—but I hope that you'll think about some of the things that I described to you.

There's a place, I might say, to be perfectly objective as President, for Republicans in our society—*[laughter]*—second place.

Thank you, sweetheart. I love you. Thank you.

Q. Thank you, Mr. President.

PRESIDENT'S ACCOMPLISHMENTS

Q. *"Dear President Carter:*

"I voted for you in 1976. I was here when you appeared here before. Since then gasoline has doubled, inflation has more than doubled, and your pledge to reduce our nuclear arsenal has been replaced by a request for a multi-billion dollar retooling of our nuclear arsenal. In view of how you've done the opposite of

what your 1976 pledges were, why should we trust you for another term in office?"

THE PRESIDENT. Hello.

Q. Mr. President?

THE PRESIDENT. Yes?

Q. That's a question composed by my son, Robert.

THE PRESIDENT. Hello, Robert. I'm glad to see you. Are you sure you voted for me in '76?

Q. I'm his mother.

THE PRESIDENT. Robert, did you vote for me in '76?

Q. *[the mother].* Yes, I did.

AUDIENCE MEMBER. *[Inaudible]*

Q. No, no, no. I disagree. I disagree. I think you're a good President.

THE PRESIDENT. I love you. Thank you.

Q. Thank you, Mr. President.

THE PRESIDENT. I love you.

Q. I think you're a good President.

THE PRESIDENT. Thank you very much.

Q. I'm from the older generation, and I believe in you. And I love your mother, Lillian. I love her. *[Laughter]*

THE PRESIDENT. Thank you very much.

Robert, I'll talk to you later, okay? I might make a brief response.

You know, our country is not perfect, and I don't claim I've never made any mistakes. Looking back on the last 3½ years, we've made some good progress. We do now have an energy policy that has taken us out from under the thumb of the OPEC Arab nations. We didn't have one before. And they have increased their price of oil enormously. They are the ones that set the price, not us.

We now are beginning to produce more American energy and also to conserve energy. This year we'll have more American oil and gas wells drilled than any year in history. This year we'll produce more American coal—this may surprise you—than any year in history. There is no limit to how much American coal we can produce and export except the rail system and how fast we can load it on ships on the eastern seaboard. We've now got ships waiting from Belgium and France and Great Britain and Japan, in Norfolk and Hampton Roads—25 days standing in line just to get American coal.

You've done well. This day, we are importing from overseas one-third less oil than we did this same day a year ago. That's great. And if we can continue that trend, there's no doubt in my mind that we'll get inflation under control.

When I was running for President here before, if I had asked you what's the number one problem, you would have said unemployment. In the last 3½ years, we've added 8½ million new jobs, hundreds of thousands of them in New York State. Never before in our history, in any President's term, in time of peace or war, have we added that many new jobs in this country.

Inflation rate is high, you're right. But our Nation has never failed. We've been through much more difficult times than this—in the Great Depression, First World War, Second World War, the divisive Vietnam war, the embarrassment of Watergate, the social revolution that swept my part of the country, and even yours, in giving black people and others an equal chance under the law. Those things have rocked our country. But whenever Americans have unified themselves and seen an issue clearly, we have never failed to answer any question, we've never failed to solve any problem, we have never failed to overcome any obstacle. And my judgment is that we are so strong in the different kinds of Americans that have come to this country that we will never fail in the future either. We're making good progress. That progress is going to continue.

I love you very much.

Q. Thank you, thank you.

AMERICAN HOSTAGES IN IRAN

Q. Um——

THE PRESIDENT. I heard you. Go ahead. [*Laughter*]

Q. Mr. President, I'd like to change the subject to foreign policy—[*laughter*]——

THE PRESIDENT. Very good.

Q. ——and ask what do you think is the next step for the United States in the hostage situation?

THE PRESIDENT. Very good. Great. What's your name?

Q. Nicholas Moyne, M-o-y-n-e. [*Laughter*]

THE PRESIDENT. Nicholas, that's a great question. Let me see if I can answer it.

In the first place, ever since our hostages have been taken—and they're all innocent people—I've had two goals in mind. One is to protect the interests of our own country and our integrity and our honor, and, secondly—and they're not in conflict—not to do anything as President that might endanger the lives or the safety or the future return of those hostages to freedom in their homeland. I've also tried to work with the families of the hostages, meeting with them personally, letting the Secretary of State meet with them, my wife's met with them, to make sure they understand that America has not forgotten them.

We've tried to negotiate with the Iranians in every possible way—directly, indirectly, through the United Nations, through secret missions, every other way. The main problem, Nicholas, has been this: There has not been any government in Iran or any leader with whom we could talk. Lately, though, the Iranians have elected a President and a Prime Minister and a speaker of their parliament, which they call a Majles, and they are putting together a cabinet. Their Prime

Minister is coming to the United States today to appear in the United Nations.

We are trying, as we have every day for the last 10 or 11 months, to work with the Iranians, to resolve the problems between us and to get the hostages back home safely. I don't know when that effort will be successful. I can't tell you that. All the information, however, that we have about the hostages is that they are today safe, they are not being abused. And three of them, who are separated from the other 49, we have a way to communicate with them every now and then, either an ambassador goes from Switzerland or Spain or some other country and to talk to them, or on occasion they can talk to someone in our country on the telephone. So, at this moment, so far as we know, the hostages are alive and well.

We don't know exactly when they'll be released. We've always maintained our hope that they would be released, and I will continue to protect our country and not to do anything as President to endanger their lives or safety and to make sure they come home free.

DIVISIONS IN AMERICAN SOCIETY

Q. Mr. President, given the existing factionalism in America today, such as developing regionalism, growing racial tensions, and the increasing influence of special interest groups, how will you combat and unite these expanding divisions in our country if reelected to a second term?

THE PRESIDENT. Okay. One of the important things to remember in our country is its heterogeneous nature. We're different. This is a nation of immigrants. We're a nation of refugees. Almost all of the families represented in this audience came here from another country. The blacks, many of them came here as slaves against their will, but they ultimately found a good life. Everyone else, from Eastern Europe or from Asia or from Latin America and so forth, came here voluntarily looking for freedom of religion, a way to have a better future.

I hope that our country will continue to preserve our own family customs, their ties of kinship with our mother countries, the commitment to religious beliefs that are perhaps different from some of others, and at the same time, join in the conglomerate American society that unifies itself, as I said in the next to the last question, when a trial or a test or an obstacle or a question or a problem comes up. I think we've made a lot of progress in doing away with the sectionalism that used to separate our country one part from another.

The last President who was elected from the Deep South, before me, for instance, was in 1844—James Polk. And it would not have been possible for me to be elected President had it not been for the civil rights movement that eliminated racial discrimination against black citizens. That changed to give people equality for blacks, made it possible for a Southern white to be considered seriously for President.

We only have now one remaining legal element of discrimination in this country. That's against women. And when we are able to get constitutional guarantees that women will not suffer from discrimination just because they're women, legally, we will have eliminated discrimination.

They'll still have prejudice; you'll still have people thinking they're better than you are or you're better than I am because of your religion or how much money your family has or what block you live on or what kind of car you have or what kind of education you've had. I think, too—and you're not going to like what I'm going to say—but we ought not to forget that we still have refugees coming here, we still have immigrants coming here.

When the Italians came to America they suffered from discrimination. When the Irish came here after the potato famine they suffered from discrimination. When the Jews came here from Eastern Europe and from Russia they suffered because of discrimination. When the first people came here from Indochina or from Asia they suffered because of discrimination. When the Cubans first came to Miami after Castro took over, they suffered from discrimination. Every time we've had a kind of a wave of immigrants who came to our Nation, they've seen what a good deal it is and what a wonderful country we've got, and they've said, "Well," in effect, "we've got it made. Let's don't let anybody else come."

There are still people who live under the boot of totalitarian governments, without freedom, without a chance to worship God, who have a hunger to come to our country, and they are different from us. When they first get there they can't speak English. Unless your parents came from England, your parents coudn't either, when they first got here. But we ought not to feel that we can erect a fence around the United States now and say no one else can come in. Our country is still growing. We are still a young country. We are still dynamic. We're still aggressive. We've still confident. We're still different from one another. That does not make us weak. That difference among us, subjugated when the interests of our country are paramount, is the source of our inherent strength.

We also benefit because our ties still go back to almost all the 150 nations on Earth. We've got special understanding of them, and they understand us. We've got relatives there, they've got relatives

here. And that's an avenue to bridge the gap that might exist between our country and theirs. When I have a problem, for instance, in a nation like Mexico or Brazil or Italy or Ireland or Israel or other countries, I turn to American citizens whose parents or ancestors came from that country and say, "I need you to help me, as President, understand how to iron out these differences in a peaceful way and honor the special beliefs and customs and religious attitudes that that country might represent." Otherwise I wouldn't have as good an education as President now as I do.

So, I think the progress that we've seen already over a period of historical time is going to continue in the next administration, and I hope that neither you nor any other young person who belongs to a minority group ever again has to suffer from either legal discrimination or prejudice from other Americans who might think they are better than you are.

SOUTH AFRICA

Q. Hello, Mr. President.

THE PRESIDENT. Hello.

Q. My name is Margaret Johnson, and I'm from Hofstra University School of Law. I would like to know, do you plan to prohibit U.S. investors from investing in South African industries? If so, how and when, and if not, why not, given your commitment to human rights?

THE PRESIDENT. If you hadn't told me what school you were in I could have guessed by the time you got through with that question.

You've got me pretty well pinned in. Let me say this: There is no authority that a President has to impose a prohibition against American citizens from investing in or going to another country.

The attitudes of the Government of South Africa, their apartheid and the deprivation of human rights in that country, are obnoxious to me. We have striven, since I've been in office, to open up the continent of Africa for the first time to the beneficial influence of American presence and American interests. It wasn't done before. Just a short time before I became President, the Secretary of State of our Nation, Henry Kissinger, tried to go on a visit to Nigeria. He was not permitted to land in Nigeria, because there was no relationship then between that largest of all black nations on Earth and our country. Last week, the new President of Nigeria came to see me. He had been freely elected, democratically, majority rule, one-man-one-vote, under a constitution patterned to a major degree after the Constitution of the United States.

Also, when I came into office, I was determined to see Rhodesia changed into Zimbabwe, to give that country a chance to be independent and to remove the blight of racial discrimination against the blacks who live there. Not too long ago, Prime Minister Mugabe came to see me in the East Room of the White House to express his appreciation to me and to the people of the country for helping his country find democracy.

Now we're working on Namibia. We and four other nations—Canada, Great Britain, France, Germany—are trying to negotiate with South Africa to release Namibia to be a free country and to let the people there make their judgments about what kind of life they want to live. Our ultimate goal is also to see the same kind of change take place in South Africa, to see apartheid eliminated and to see all people there be honored with their human rights.

Those are the basic principles on which we operate; the sooner, the better, but in the meantime we'll do the best we can working through international law, American law, and the United Nations to reach those goals which I believe you and I share.

JERUSALEM

Q. Hello, Mr. President. In your 1980 platform you stated that you would like to have a United States Embassy moved to Jerusalem. In that light I would like to ask you to sign a petition saying to the people of Israel, "You are not alone. We are united with you in proudly affirming that united Jerusalem is an integral part of the sovereign state of Israel and is its capital city. To this we pledge our complete and unswerving support. Be strong. Be strong and let us strengthen one another."

THE PRESIDENT. I have not supported that particular element of the Democratic Party platform, and I'll tell you why.

AUDIENCE MEMBER. You haven't supported Israel either.

THE PRESDENT. We have worked, as you know, with the Prime Minister of Israel and the President of Egypt, both at Camp David and subsequently, to have a peace between Israel and her major Arab nation, who's a neighbor. There is no way that any successful attempt could be made against Israel militarily absent Egypt, and now, as you know, the borders are open between the two countries, regular airplane flights go back and forth, tourism is growing every week, diplomatic relations exist, ambassadors are stationed in both capitals.

When I was at Camp David with Prime Minister Begin and Sadat, President Sadat, we, all three, agreed on a paragraph of the Camp David accords relating to Jerusalem. I know intensely the deep feelings of the Israeli people and

Jews all over the world about Jerusalem. Our commitment, agreed to by Prime Minister Begin, is that Jerusalem should forever stay undivided, that there should be free access to the holy places for all worshipers who consider that city to them to be holy, that the ultimate status of Jerusalem under international law should be resolved through negotiation, and that the final result of that negotiation would have to be acceptable to Israel.

That's my position, and I will maintain it.

MINORITIES IN THE JUDICIARY

Q. Good afternoon, Mr. President. My name is Wendella Ault, and on behalf of the African People's Organization at Hofstra University and our president, William Mayo, we'd like to extend a very hearty welcome to you.

THE PRESIDENT. Thank you.

Q. Now, we know that in our Constitution it states that all men are created equal, and you stated that you have increased minority representation in the U.S. Government. Now, I'd like to ask you, if you win the election in November, what steps do you plan on taking towards increasing that representation in the judicial government of our country?

I'd also like to say that I think you're one of the greatest Presidents we've ever had in terms of equal opportunity for the minorities of this country.

THE PRESIDENT. Thank you very much. Is your first name Wendella?

Q. Wendella, yes.

THE PRESIDENT. Wendella, as you know, our country has made fumbling or faltering steps toward giving equality of opportunity to black people and to those who speak Spanish and other newcomers to our Nation. We're not perfect, but we're struggling with that question.

When I came into office, I came in with the support of some great black leaders that I knew in Atlanta and had met in the rest of the country. I have seen at first hand as a southerner the adverse impact on me as a white person because of racial discrimination. As Governor of Georgia, I tried to eliminate that discrimination, and I've had the Ku Klux Klan marching around the Georgia Capitol as I took some of those actions, working harmoniously with my black fellow citizens of Georgia.

When I got to be President, I resolved that in filling positions in the judiciary, which is what you mentioned, that I would eliminate discrimination. We didn't have any black Federal judges in the South. With the exception of Virginia, where the Senators of that State refuse to consider anyone for a judge except white males, in every Southern State now, we will have at least one or more black Federal judges.

I have appointed twice as many black judges in the Federal system as all the other Presidents in history for the last 200 years. And I'm just getting started. I've also done it without lowering the standards of quality or professionalism or integrity, because if I should ever appoint a weak or a poor judge, who might be a woman or a black or a Hispanic, immediately those who oppose equality would say, "Look, the President lowered the standards in the judiciary." I have never done that.

So, we have not had any trouble finding excellent black judges, Hispanic judges and women judges to serve in the judiciary. I have not had a vacancy created yet, as you know, in the Supreme Court of the United States. If and when those vacancies occur, then I will follow the same policies that I've followed in the Federal judiciary on the district and circuit court levels to honor my commitment to eliminate discrimination and also to repair the remainder of discrimination that has existed so long.

Another thing that will help is for more and more representatives of the minority races and women to go through law school and to begin to prepare themselves for those kind of major responsibilities in the future. My record is good so far. I intend to improve on it in the future.

Q. I'd also like to say, I intend to.

NATIONAL DEFENSE

Q. Mr. President, my name is Tom D'Agostino. I am an electrical engineer at Underwriter's Laboratories here in Melville. First of all, I'd like to thank God for the opportunity to be here today to speak to you. It was exactly a week ago that I saw this moment. What I'd like to say is that I've read your pamphlet, your campaign pamphlet that was distributed to us. Above your photo it stated, "A glimpse of a remarkable record of achievement. A record almost unknown to most Americans and that can be read here."

I am personally troubled by the fact that the record of this administration, at this time, remains unknown, particularly with regard to the state of our national defense. I believe that many of us here, many of my peers, viewing the recent events in the Middle East, and being bombarded constantly in the media relative to the state of our defense, in our position relative to the Soviet Union, are getting to feel—it's emotional—we're getting to feel that we're moving backwards in our ability to protect ourselves and our vital interests. As our President and our Commander in Chief, I believe the American people are seeking your unequivocal assurance that our Nation can meet any

and all military crises envisioned by you and our strategic planners in Washington.

As an example, today in the New York Post, I see the Russians, it says, are geared for invasion of Poland. The reporter, Guy Hawthorn, in his second paragraph says, "The move is timed for November or December, between the U.S. Presidential election and the Inauguration, because the Soviets fear Ronald Reagan, if elected, would take a much tougher line than our President Carter." He goes on further to say that "the Kremlin believes it can depend on a relatively low-key response from President Carter once the election is over."

I would appreciate your comments on just how you would handle an invasion of a country the second time in 1980.

THE PRESIDENT. I think in every election year that I remember the question of the status of our national defenses has come up. It doesn't serve any good purpose for a candidate for President to make a false statement about the degree of competence or commitment of our military forces. It does several damaging things. It creates confusion and doubt among good Americans like you that we are able to defend ourselves. These false statements also create erroneous doubts, without foundation, among our allies and friends who depend on us to defend them and to carry on our obligation to protect the peace. And perhaps more seriously, it creates an erroneous belief in some potential adversary that they can attack us with impunity.

Our nation is at this time the strongest nation on Earth militarily. We are much more ready to defend ourselves now than we were before. When I came into office we did have some serious defects. As I told you earlier, the commitment to defense had been going down 7 out of 8 years. Now it's going steadily upward.

And at first it was difficult for me to get these defense increases through the Congress, because the American people didn't believe that we needed to do so. Now the American people and the Congress support me in these improvements in our national defense.

The Trident submarine program was bogged down when I came into office with over $2½ billion worth of lawsuits. That's been resolved, and now we've got the first Trident submarine with its new missiles now undergoing sea tests. The second one is ready to be launched. We've got a steady stream of Trident submarines coming out to help us with one leg of our so-called triad of strategic weapons.

Secondly, we were about to waste an awful lot of money, when I came into office, building a B–1 bomber, because it would have been vulnerable to the ground-placed air defenses of the Soviet Union. We changed instead to the air-launched cruise missile, a cruise missile that's a small, relatively inexpensive, very accurate, formidable new weapon that's practically invulnerable to a counter-attack from the ground air-defense forces of the Soviet Union. And now that'll be mounted on our airplanes, launched 800 or a thousand miles away. It could penetrate the Soviet Union, make an attack almost without any chances the Soviets could stop it.

The third thing was that some of our ICBM's, our intercontinental ballistic missiles, had gotten vulnerable, because the Soviets, over a period of time, had built up not only great big missiles, because they didn't have miniaturized circuits and so forth, but they started to put MIRV'd warheads on them. So, I have developed now—and I hope you'll support this—the MX missile system, which will be a smaller number of missile launchers which will be located in places where the Soviets will never know where it is. It can be moved

from one place to another, and it would take an enormous number of Soviet missiles to ever destroy those ICBM's. That's our strategic weapons—the nuclear weapons.

At the same time, we have proceeded with the control of nuclear weapons. You can't fly an airplane with just one wing on one side. You've got to have a balance. The most important single difference that I consider between myself and Governor Reagan is the approach to this defense issue.

I might repeat myself that all of our ground divisions now are in much better readiness state than they were 3½ years ago, much better than the Soviet Union equivalent divisions. We've got a strategic force now ready to move, conventional forces called rapid deployment force. We're building it up good, and in the northern part of the Indian Ocean, outside of the Persian Gulf, we've got a formidable array of Navy, with F–14 planes, each one having unbelievable electronics. They can monitor, track six targets at the same time and shoot down those six targets with just one plane. And you've seen what the Iranian F–4's have done to Iraq, and what the F–14's are doing. You've seen what the Israeli F–15's have done with the MIG–25's that have been sent against them from Syria. That's the kind of weapons we have.

Let's leave that for a moment. I can assure you that they're better than they ever were before and improving every day, second to none, but—I won't have time for another question; I want to make this point before I leave. I want you to remember what atomic weapons are.

My early Navy career was in the nuclear submarine program, working under Admiral Rickover. I had instructions on the destructive nature of atomic explosives. We dropped two atomic bombs on Japan to end the Second World War under Harry Truman. Their explosion power was about 20,000 tons of TNT. Now, we're talking about megatons or millions of tons of TNT.

It takes a few pounds of TNT, as you know, for a terrorist to blow up an automobile or to kill 100 people in a shopping center in Germany or in Jerusalem, a few pounds. A megaton, if loaded 50 tons on a box car, on a train, would take a train 200 miles long to haul that much TNT. It would take 400 railroad engines to pull it. That's how much explosive power there is in 1 megaton of a nuclear weapon.

The control of that kind of power is the most important issue before our world today. It makes energy policy and employment levels and inflation rates pale into insignificance. Every President since Harry Truman, Republican and Democrat, has committed himself to strategic arms limitations. I signed a SALT II treaty with Brezhnev in Vienna, the culmination of negotiations by President Ford and President Nixon before me. A few weeks ago Governor Reagan said that he would tear up the SALT treaty. He insisted upon nuclear superiority, and he said that the launching of a nuclear arms race would be a card to be played against the Soviet Union.

This is such a profound change in the approach to nuclear weaponry that you ought to understand it very clearly. Nuclear superiority sounds great, but put yourself on the other side. If the Soviets said, "We'll negotiate a SALT treaty with you in the future provided we have nuclear superiority," we would not negotiate with them. And we cannot expect the Soviet Union to negotiate with us on balanced, controlled, observable, and then reduced SALT agreements if one side insists on nuclear superiority. It would be an end to the arms limitation talks and a radical departure from what we've had

in the past. That's not a sign of weakness. It's a sign of strength.

The other point is this: Everybody who serves in the Oval Office knows that every day there is a troublespot somewhere in the world, sometimes three or four, and a President has to deal with problems and crises alone at times. If I address that potential crisis successfully you never know about it. If I make a misjudgment, though, that potential crisis can affect your life and the life of everyone in this country, perhaps the entire world.

In the past we've had trouble around the world. We've used our enormous military strength, economic strength, political persuasion, to resolve those differences peacefully. Governor Reagan has a very disturbing habit of proposing, as a major political figure wanting to be President, that we inject American military forces into different places around the world to resolve troubles. He has advocated that we send American military forces to Ecuador, North Korea, Cuba, Cyprus, the Mideast, Angola, Rhodesia, Pakistan, and other places, three of those proposals just this year.

When the Soviets invaded Afghanistan his proposal was, "Let's put a blockade around Cuba." This would immediately have created a major confrontation between ourselves and the Soviet Union, because every day the Soviet Union delivers to Cuba several millions of dollars worth of goods and services. This would have precipitated an international threat of war greater than any our Nation has faced since we've got peace, finally.

The tone of what my opponent uses to address nuclear arms control and the solution of problems on a peaceful basis—using our strength, yes, but not military forces—is very, very important as an issue.

I can assure you in closing that we're the strongest country on Earth militarily, and we will never be second in military strength to any other country.

Thank you very much, everybody. I've enjoyed being with you.

NOTE: The President spoke at 3:30 p.m. in the Hofstra University Physical Fitness Center.

New York, New York
Remarks at a Meeting With New York Labor Leaders. October 16, 1980

Mr. Molisani,[1] President Van Arsdale,[2] Senator Moynihan, Governor Carey, all the distinguished leaders here who represent so many thousands of working people throughout this State:

I'm very sorry that Ray Corbett[3] can't be with us because of the unfortunate death of his beloved wife, Helen, and I know that all of you will extend to him my regrets and my concerns and my prayers and the best wishes from me and from my wife, Rosalynn.

In the last 4 years I've become proud and very fond of two favorite songs. One of them is "Hail to the Chief." I want to hear it a lot more in the next 4 years. And the other one is "Look for the Union Label," and I want to hear that one a lot more as well.

This afternoon, in the brief period of time together, I'd like to remind you, as working people and as leaders of working people, how important this crucial election is, not just for me as President but for the labor movement itself and for every working man and woman and their family throughout the length and breadth of

this country. This election is not about who debates whom. The election is not about who's ahead in the polls. The election is not about who says what about the other candidate. The election in less than 3 weeks involves very serious consequences for you, for the people whom you love, and for the people whom you represent.

Sometimes we tend to forget how much this election will affect our future. The choice could not be clearer. There is a much more profound difference between me and Governor Reagan that there ever was between me and President Ford just 4 years ago. It's the sharpest possible difference in basic philosophy and commitment in public statements on issues that affect working people.

On the one side is a Republican candidate who in 1976 persuaded President Ford to reverse his solemn promise to the working people that he would not veto a common situs bill, and my opponent talked President Ford into vetoing the common situs bill. On the other side, you've got a Democratic administration that has fought for common situs and will go on fighting for it along with you until it's passed into law.

On one side is a Republican candidate who says, and I quote, about Davis-Bacon, "This is a gift of tax funds to the privileged workers." On the other side is a Democratic administration that has successfully fought off nine different times Republican attempts to repeal Davis-Bacon, and if such a bill ever gets to my desk while you've got a Democratic President in the Oval Office, I will veto it and, you can count on that.

On one side you've got a Republican candidate who said to a proposal last year to abolish the Occupational Safety and Health Administration, OSHA—his reply was, "Amen." On the other side, you've

---

[1] Secretary-Treasurer, New York AFL–CIO.

[2] President, New York State Central Labor Council, AFL–CIO.

[3] President, New York AFL–CIO.

got a Democratic administration that has strengthened OSHA and has focused its activities on the real health and safety problems of the workplace.

On one side is a Republican candidate who said this year that labor law reform, and I quote, "is a bill that should be defeated." On the other side is a Democratic administration that's fought for labor law reform, and we'll go on fighting for it, with you, until it's passed into law.

I remember, as you do, during the Depression years, when Franklin Roosevelt put forward the idea of social security. The Republicans opposed it, but a Democratic Congress and a Democratic President put it into law.

I remember back in the Depression years when a Democratic President proposed the minimum wage to eliminate the sweatshops and let working families live a decent life. At that time the minimum wage proposal was 25 cents. The Democrats put it across. The Republicans opposed it. My first job as a young high school graduate, minimum wage was 40 cents—10 hours a day. The Democrats supported it. The Republicans were against it.

I'm running against a man who hasn't changed that basic, negative Republican philosophy, because this year he said, and I quote again, "The minimum wage has caused more misery and more unemployment than anything since the Great Depression." On the other side you've got a Democratic administration, as you know, that has enacted phased, predictable, automatic increases in the minimum wage that let our lowest paid workers live a decent life now and forever more and not wait 6 years every time to get what they deserve.

I know what it means to have temporary unemployment. And I know how devastating it is to a family's life when the income is no longer there and the children are still hungry and need clothes, need to go to school. On one side you've got a Republican candidate who has called recipients of unemployment compensation, and I quote again, "freeloaders wanting a prepaid vacation plan." On the other side, you've got a Democratic administration now fighting for—and it will succeed in getting—an extension of unemployment compensation insurance for workers in hard-hit industries.

The conscience of American labor has always extended beyond even those crucial issues that affect your own members. Let me list very quickly just a few of those issues, because you ought to have these in mind every day, because they concern you, not only as labor leaders but as national leaders representing the best elements of our country.

The first is energy. The Republican candidate who fought against the windfall profits tax on the oil companies summed up his energy program this way, and I quote him again, "What needs to be done is for the Government to repeal the energy legislation. We must abolish the Department of Energy, and then turn the industry, that is, the oil companies loose to make those decisions for us."

This Democratic administration has fought successfully, as you know, for the windfall profits tax, for a massive program for better urban transportation to help develop American energy, to give us aid for poor families to pay their fuel bills, and to reduce our imports more than one-third in the last year alone. Every drop of oil that we do not have to buy from OPEC increases our economic security and our national security. We must not allow our progress on energy to be reversed.

The second item, as important perhaps to family life a. energy, is health. The Republican candidate against whom I run began his public career as a politician traveling around this country as a leader opposing Medicare. He says now, and I quote, "I am firmly opposed to national health insurance." This Democratic President shares with you a commitment to a national health plan and to all the great programs of better social life this country has adopted under Democratic Presidents since Franklin D. Roosevelt.

The third issue that affects every one of you is the cities of America. You all know that the Republican candidate used to boast about praying that the Federal Government would never bail out New York City. I'm sure the Lord heard that prayer, but like all of you, I'm glad that after due consideration, the Lord made the right decision—[laughter]—with a little help from those here below who've worked so hard on it.

The Republican candidate also said just a few months ago, and I quote him again, "Urban aid programs are one of the biggest phonies that we have in the system." There are some people in this room who might give him an argument about that, and I'm one of them. We Democrats have pushed through the first comprehensive national urban policy in our history, and we stand by our commitment to New York and to all the great cities of America.

I'm no newcomer to the object of finishing the decision on Westway. I am absolutely committed to DOT funding of that expressway. I am also committed to having the earliest possible resolution of the permits that you need to get this system expedited.

And the last subject I want to mention to you is human rights. The Republican candidate has criticized many times our human rights policy as being against the best interests of the United States. This Democratic President believes the American Government should stand up for American values. The workers of Poland have proven that human rights is a universal longing and a universal goal. As long as I am President we will hold high the banner of human rights.

Let me say this: This is a tough race. The polls say that we may be behind. The Republicans are outspending us millions of dollars. Rightwing groups are plowing tens of millions of dollars into the television, radio, newspapers, against Democratic candidates throughout this country. They are not charged against Governor Ronald Reagan's campaign. They're proposing themselves and are posing as friends of working people as they do every 4 years, before reverting to form once again as soon as the election is over. But even if the Republicans can't win the votes of labor members and working people, they are hoping to discourage it.

Governor Reagan's labor adviser told the New York Times, talking about you, and I quote again, "I don't want these people," he said, "to vote for Reagan. I don't want them to vote. I want them to stay home." We cannot let them get away with that cynical strategy. Fritz Mondale and I are going to need the help of every one of you and a lot more besides. New York is extremely important in this effort.

For the sake of everything we've done in the past, under Franklin Roosevelt, Harry Truman, Lyndon Johnson, Jack Kennedy, all the Democrats, for the sake of everything we'll do together in the future, let's get our message across to every single working family in New York. We have less than 3 weeks to go. So, let's every one of us buckle down and work together as partners. We need a victory, for myself, for Walter Mondale, for the entire New York Democratic ticket, and most of all, for the beliefs and the convictions and the ideals that we all share.

Together we can make the greatest nation on Earth even greater, but let me remind you of this: Coming to this meeting is not enough. Announcing that you are for me and Fritz Mondale is not enough. Sending out a newsletter outlining the devastating effect of Ronald Reagan's election is not enough. What we need the next 3 weeks is workers on the street, in the polling places, in public meetings, letting your voice be heard so that every person in this country that works for a living know the crucial issues at stake.

I do not intend to lose this election, and with your help, the Democrats will have a tremendous victory and whip the Republicans on November the 4th.

Thank you very much.

NOTE: The President spoke at 5:36 p.m. in Royal Ballroom "A" at the Sheraton Centre Hotel.

New York, New York

Remarks at the Alfred E. Smith Memorial Dinner. October 16, 1980

Archbishop Maguire, Mrs. Morrison, Governor and Mrs. Reagan, distinguished leaders in politics and government and public affairs, the Al Smith family members, and my good and old friend, Judge Mulligan:

You may not realize where we first met—[laughter]—but I hate to reveal a secret. It was at a Sinn Fein breakfast in Savannah—[laughter]—a few years ago. I'm sure he didn't mention it to you. [Laughter] It was one of those strange and exciting and very exuberant typical mornings, March the 17th in Savannah, Georgia. I was eating green grits, and Judge Mulligan was drinking green— well, I won't tell on you what you were drinking. [Laughter] We became good friends then, and since then I've been wanting to get together with him again.

I had understood when I was first invited and accepted the invitation that this dinner was in his honor. [Laughter] I was quite startled when I saw the program and saw that it was in the honor of Al Smith. I understand that Cardinal Cooke and Mr. Silver also made this same discovery, and that's why they didn't show up tonight. [Laughter]

I'm glad to be back at this distinguished gathering. I was here 4 years ago as a candidate for office of President of the United States of America. And I'm happy to report to you tonight that that campaign was a success. [Laughter] It's my fervent hope that I can stand here 2 or 3 years from now and make for you a similar report on the 1980 campaign. [Laughter]

For the last 3½ years I have faced the awesome pressures known only to those who occupy the Oval Office. This is a confidential assessment for Governor Reagan. Not one minute of a single one of those days, Governor Reagan, has passed without my feeling the full weight and the terrible burden and the crushing responsibility that's ever present as a companion in that office. It's a terrible experience. [Laughter] And for the rest of you, let me say, equally confidentially, how time flies when you're having fun.

I had some good help in 1976. Professor Lawrence Klein of the Wharton Economic School was the chairman of my economic advisory board. I just recently called to congratulate him, because he won the Nobel Prize in economics for his excellent advice to me on how to reduce inflation and interest rates. [*Laughter*]

And I would also like to congratulate his Eminence on the singular accomplishment this evening, although in absentia, by convincing Governor Reagan to share this platform with me. He's demonstrated a power even greater than that of the League of Women Voters. [*Laughter*] And I must confess I have listened very closely and I've observed very closely Governor Reagan and his remarks tonight. Frankly, I find him an extremely engaging, charming, and gracious man. It's hard to believe he keeps saying all those mean things about me. [*Laughter*] The fact is, I'm very proud to know and very happy to know that he is with us this evening, otherwise he might be out campaigning in some close State. [*Laughter*]

Incidentally, I gave my good friend, Mayor Koch, some advice earlier today. I told him not to get too close to Governor Reagan. It has nothing to do with politics, but on the Governor's "I love New York" button, the paint is still wet. [*Laughter*]

I would like to take advantage of this moment of good fellowship to put Governor Reagan at ease on one point. I will state publicly and for the record that I am not planning any October surprise. I can predict, however, that one of us is in for a very severe November shock. [*Laughter*]

As you all know, Governor Al Smith enjoyed the rough and tumble of politics, but he revered the art of governing fairly. His social conscience was awakened on the Lower East Side and sharpened by the unforgiving taskmasters of his alma mater, the Fulton Fish Market. Gather-

ing his natural gifts, he doggedly pursued a career that led to four terms as Governor of the most powerful State of the Union.

In those days the Federal Government was not overly responsive to human suffering. There was no social security. There was no unemployment compensation. There was no minimum wage. There was no Medicare for the elderly. There was no protection against the paralyzing effects of legalized discrimination. As Governor, Al Smith began the hammer blows of social reforms, whose reverberations echo even today.

In 1928 he decided to run for President. When the final count was in, he had not won the election. I'm proud that Georgia was a State that gave him an overwhelming victory. But a shattering heartbreak came with the realization that his own beloved New York and 39 other States had rejected him at the polls. The tide of unreasoned religious intolerance denied this country's highest office to one of the most gifted reformers of the century.

But it was a remarkable indication of this Nation's progress when, in 1960, John Fitzgerald Kennedy, Catholic, became the 35th President of the United States. Again, my State gave him a large margin of victory, greater even than his own State of Massachusetts. There were dire predictions made then that should John Kennedy become President, the Pope soon would be standing on the White House steps. And in fact, that prediction came true. The Pope did stand on the White House steps, but the year was 1979. [*Laughter*] And the President who greeted him was a Southern Baptist.

John Kennedy, a Catholic, became President with the votes of millions of Southern Baptists. And I, a Southern Baptist, became President with the votes of millions of Catholics and Jews. There is no question that we have come far in dulling the sharp pain of religious and racial intolerance.

It was on this note that I had intended to end my speech tonight, to leave you basking in the warmth of the progress exemplified in the stories of one man who did not become President and two men who did. But there have been times in my life when I, like most of you, witnessed prejudice and intolerance and should have acted or spoken out against it and did not. Something happened to me just yesterday that made me to speak a few words further to this issue.

A 12-year-old boy stood up in a public town meeting in Pittston, Pennsylvania, and asked me a question that cuts to the heart of the matter of intolerance and cut my heart as well. His name is Avi Leiter, and here is what he asked, and I quote: "In view of the fact that you, Mr. President, are Baptist, do you agree with the head of the churches who said that God should not listen to Jewish prayers? I'm a religious boy, and I pray three times a day for the welfare of the Americans and the Jewish people. Do you think that God does not listen to my prayers?"

I struggled for a moment, an awkward moment, difficult for a President or a human being, not because I was searching for the answer, but to know that such a question needs to be asked by a small boy in the United States in 1980. I told Avi that I believe God listens to his prayers just as attentively as God listens to mine. I told him about going to Camp David with Prime Minister Begin and President Sadat. On the first day we all agreed to pray to God—a Jew, a Muslim, and a Christian—and we asked the world, through a public announcement, to join us in our prayers. I told Avi that I was

sure that God heard all those prayers. Thirteen days later we surprised the world when President Sadat and Prime Minister Begin came down from Camp David with a peace agreement.

I say again, the answer I gave Avi Leiter yesterday is not nearly as important as his question. It's a question no American child should ever have to ask his President.

In our zeal to strengthen the moral character of this Nation, we must not set ourselves up as judges of whom God might hear or whom He would turn away. I understand the longing that many people have, very deeply religious, fervent people, for a sense of strong values. That longing is not exclusive to any one group, but it's shared by every person—Protestant, Catholic, or Jew—who cares deeply about the ethical standards of this Nation.

Those who originally created the promise of America were firm in their convictions. They believed in religious tolerance. They believed in tolerance for the views of others. They believed in separation of church and state. They believed that government should not decree or interfere with any person's worship or freedom of conscience. That was not because they considered religion unimportant, but because they considered it too important for government to try to influence or control.

Contrary to the pattern in all other nations, our Constitution stated in unmistakable terms that "No religious test shall ever be required as a qualification to any office of public trust under the United States." President Kennedy understood this principle clearly when he said in 1960, and I quote him: "I believe in an America where the separation of church and state is absolute, where no Catholic prelate could tell the President, should he be Catholic, how to act, and no Protestant minister would tell his parishioners for whom to vote."

My religion is an important part of my life. I've studied the Bible all my life. But nowhere in the Bible, Old or New Testament, are there instructions on how to balance the budget or how to choose between the B–1 bomber and the air-launched cruise missile. What I do find is, "Judge not that ye be not judged," and the commandment to love my neighbor.

Al Smith, a long time ago, followed those principles. It inspired the work for which we honor his memory tonight. Little Avi Leiter follows that principle. It guides him in his prayers three times every day.

We've come through difficult and bitter times in this country. We've done well. But we cannot pause on a plateau of self-congratulation while Avi Leiter and other potential future. Al Smith's of America struggle against the sheer walls of intolerance that are still all too evident.

I believe we are ready to move on. I believe that with patience and understanding and renewed effort all Americans will come to realize this: that the soul of freedom is freedom of the soul.

Thank you very much.

NOTE: The President spoke at 9:54 p.m. in the Grand Ballroom at the Waldorf-Astoria Hotel. He was introduced by Archbishop John J. Maguire.

In his opening remarks, the President referred to Lydia Morrison, hostess, Judge William Hughes Mulligan of the Second Circuit Court of Appeals, guest speaker, and Charles H. Silver, chairman, Alfred E. Smith Memorial Dinner, and Terence Cardinal Cooke.

Following the dinner, the President returned to Washington, D.C.

Federal Civilian and Military Pay Increases

Executive Order 12248. October 16, 1980

ADJUSTMENTS OF CERTAIN RATES OF PAY AND ALLOWANCES

By the authority vested in me as President by the Constitution and the laws of the United States of America, it is hereby ordered as follows:

1–1. *Adjusted Rates of Pay and Allowances.*

1–101. *Statutory Pay Systems.* Pursuant to the provisions of subchapter I of Chapter 53 of Title 5 of the United States Code, the rates of basic pay and salaries are adjusted, as set forth at the schedules attached hereto and made a part hereof, for the following statutory pay systems:

(a) The General Schedule (5 U.S.C. 5332(a)) at Schedule 1;

(b) the schedules for the Foreign Service (22 U.S.C. 867 and 870(a)) at Schedule 2;

(c) the schedules for the Department of Medicine and Surgery, Veterans Administration (38 U.S.C. 4107) at Schedule 3; and

(d) the rates of basic pay for the Senior Executive Service (5 U.S.C. 5382) at Schedule 4.

1–102. *Pay and Allowances for Members of the Uniformed Services.* Pursuant to the provisions of Section 801 of Public Law 96–342 of September 8, 1980, the rates of monthly basic pay (37 U.S.C. 203 (a) and (c)), the rates of basic allowances for subsistence (37 U.S.C. 402), and the rates of basic allowances for quarters (37 U.S.C. 403(a)) are adjusted, as set forth at Schedule 5 attached hereto and made a part hereof, for members of the uniformed services.

1–103. *Executive Salaries.* The Executive Salary Cost-of-Living Adjustment Act (Public Law 94–82, 89 Stat. 419) provides for adjustments in the rates of pay and salaries as set forth at the schedules attached hereto and made a part hereof, for the following:

(a) The Vice President (3 U.S.C. 104) and the Executive Schedule (5 U.S.C. 5312–5316) at Schedule 6; and

(b) Congressional Salaries (2 U.S.C. 31) at Schedule 7.

(c) Judicial Salaries (28 U.S.C. 5, 44 (d), 135, 173, 213, 252, 792(b), and 11 U.S.C. 68(a), and Sections 401(a), 404 (a), 404(b), and 404(d) of Public Law 95–598) at Schedule 8.

1–2. *General Provisions.*

1–201. *Effective Date.* The adjustments in rates of monthly basic pay and allowances for subsistence and quarters for members of the uniformed services shall be effective on October 1, 1980. All other adjustments of salary or pay shall be effective on the first day of the first applicable pay period beginning on or after October 1, 1980.

1–202. *Superseded Orders.* Executive Orders No. 12165 of October 12, 1979 and No. 12200 of March 12, 1980 are superseded.

JIMMY CARTER

The White House,
  October 16, 1980.

[Filed with the Office of the Federal Register,
  10:43 a.m., October 17, 1980]

NOTE: The schedules are printed in the FEDERAL REGISTER of October 20, 1980.

  The Executive order was announced by the White House on October 17.

Arrangements for the Implementation of the United States-Israel Oil Agreement

*Remarks at the Signing Ceremony.
October 17, 1980*

THE PRESIDENT. *Minister Modai and Ambassador Evron, Secretary Muskie, Mrs. Modai, and ladies and gentlemen:*

I'm very pleased to announce this morning the completion of our contingency arrangements for assuring Israel's oil supply security.

These arrangements further fulfill a promise that I made last year in connection with Israel's withdrawal from the Gulf of Suez oil fields and its conclusion of the treaty of peace with Egypt. In making peace, Israel committed itself to dependence solely on imported oil—a very bold and courageous and generous decision in this troubled time. At the time of Israel's withdrawal in 1975 from a portion of the Egyptian Sinai, the United States gave assurance that Israel would count on our help and could depend on us if it could not attain oil during its own efforts.

We renewed and extended this duration of the assurance in June of 1979, so that the establishment of peace with Egypt would not lessen Israel's long-range energy security. Now we have spelled out the emergency conditions under which the 1979 oil supply agreement may be activated. This contingency plan is a carefully defined understanding between friends, designed to ensure that all relevant concerns are taken into account. Both our nations hope this agreement will never have to be activated, but if it should become necessary, the United States will be a steadfast and dependable friend of Israel.

This agreement is one aspect of what I hope will be a broad range of cooperation in strengthening Israel's energy security. We're exploring now how we might work together further on research and development and for new energy technologies, especially shale oil extraction and the use of solar power for energy.

Our cooperation in energy and in other fields is for the cause of peace. It is against no nation. It is for the people who yearn for a secure future. It is in this spirit that I congratulate the negotiators of the oil supply understandings and invite now Secretary Muskie, representing the United States of America, and Minister Modai, representing the great nation of Israel, to proceed with the signing of the appropriate documents.

[*At this point, Secretary of State Edmund S. Muskie and Israeli Minister of Energy and Infrastructure Yitzhak Modai signed the "Contingency Implementing Arrangements for the Memorandum of Agreement of June 22, 1979 Between Israel and the United States." The President then resumed speaking.*]

I might say that Minister Modai is a very effective negotiator.

MINISTER MODAI. Thank you very much, Mr. President.

THE PRESIDENT. Mr. Minister, would you like to make a comment?

MINISTER MODAI. *Mr. President, Mr. Secretary of State, members of the administration, my Israeli colleagues:*

The peace agreement, Mr. President, between Israel and Egypt, is probably the most important event, certainly in the Middle East, but probably also in the entire world in this generation.

It came about due to the leadership of Prime Minister Ben-Gurion (Begin)[1], President Sadat, and through the devoted

---

[1] White House correction.

efforts and active participation of yourself, Mr. President.

The State of Israel, in order to achieve this peace agreement, has made very large sacrifices. A major sacrifice was the relinquishing of the Alma oil field, which we discovered and developed, and this in addition to giving up the Abu Rudeis oil field as part of the interim agreement in 1975.

Now you, Mr. President, and the Congress understood the big risk taken by the State of Israel in giving up its opportunity for oil self-sufficiency and, therefore, an agreement that guarantees oil supply to Israel was signed in June of 1979. Now, that agreement did not contain the specifications of the conditions in which that agreement could have been activated, and therefore we felt, we in Israel felt that we need to have a better definition of which are the conditions in which your guarantee will come into effect. After tedious, long negotiations—over a year—we are finally signing, here today, the specifications under which that agreement will come into effect.

That is certainly the completion of a promise, I may say, Mr. President, of an offer made by you when you were in Israel, I believe in February of 1979.

Obviously, nobody can foresee future developments in the next 15—now it's only 14—years, but we are very happy to have a document which is so clear, so detailed, and which relates to such a vital and delicate issue. I would like to thank you, Mr. President, you Mr. Secretary, and your staffs for a job so very well done.

Thank you.

THE PRESIDENT. I'd like to say to the press that following this ceremony, or perhaps already, the details of the agreement will be described. Has that been done yet? It will be done. So, your questions about the detailed agreement will be answered after this meeting.

I would like to say, informally but sincerely, on behalf of the American people, that we are very proud to have this agreement. The proposal was made voluntarily by me, on my own initiative, when I was in Jerusalem at the time when we were trying to bring to a conclusion the basic elements of the peace treaty between Israel and Egypt. Israel has taken a courageous step in bringing peace to that entire area by voluntarily giving up control of and the use of these oil wells, some of which they themselves discovered and developed.

We anticipate that Israel will continue to receive their oil from present sources, but if those supplies should be interrupted or if exorbitant prices should be imposed upon Israel, above and beyond normal marketing prices as described in this detailed document, then the United States will meet this obligation to our friend, the Government of Israel.

I consider this to be not only an investment in the security of Israel but also a very sound investment in the security of the United States of America. And it's a further demonstration of our unfaltering commitment and steady progress toward the comprehensive peace in the Middle East, which all of us so deeply desire, based upon the security of Israel, in every sense and meaning of that word.

Mr. Minister, thank you very much for your coming here to conclude this document. And I hope you'll extend my best wishes to Prime Minister Begin and to all the officials of Israel who've made this progress possible. Thank you, sir.

MINISTER MODAI. Mr. President——

THE PRESIDENT. Yes, sir?

MINISTER MODAI. I would like to wish you good luck with your endeavors.

THE PRESIDENT. Well, thank you very much. I appreciate that. That means a lot to me.

Thank you, everybody.

NOTE: The President spoke at 9:34 a.m. at the signing ceremony in the Roosevelt Room at the White House.

Veterans' Rehabilitation and Education Amendments of 1980

Remarks at the Signing Ceremony for H.R. 5288.　October 17, 1980

THE PRESIDENT. Well, I've already had a chance to meet with some of this group earlier, before I came to this ceremony. But I want to say, first of all, that this is indeed a very pleasant task that I have this afternoon, to sign into law another of a series of legislative acts that Max Cleland and the Congress and I have been able, with the help of many assembled here this afternoon, to put into practice for the well-being of the veterans of our country.

I'll call on Bill Hefner in a few minutes, but I do want to thank Chairman Alan Cranston and also Chairman Roberts for their work in passing the Veterans' Rehabiitation and Education Amendments of 1980. It provides for needed revitalization of the VA vocational rehabilitation program and is the first major reform of this program since it first began in 1943.

Along with the veterans' disability compensation and the housing benefits amendment that I signed last week, this is a major step in improving services for American veterans.

In October 1978, I sent to Congress a message on Vietnam-era veterans, which included recommendations to modernize this program, to train and to place the disabled veterans in meaningful jobs. I'm pleased that Congress has adopted many of these recommendations. Some of the major features are: an innovative pilot program to help seriously disabled veterans become self-sufficient in their daily lives; a 17-percent increase in subsistence allowance for disabled veterans in training; a 10-percent rate increase in educational allowances for veterans and their dependents who are enrolled in programs under the GI bill; and new initiatives to increase the employment of veterans, especially in federally funded programs. This includes permanent authorization of my administration's highly successful Disabled Veterans Outreach program, that was started under the initiative of Max Cleland, introduced as part of the economic stimulus program of 1977.

Despite these major improvements which I will sign into law in a few minutes, I am disappointed that Congress did not extend the delimiting date on the GI bill. This recommendation of mine would permit needy and emotionally disadvantaged veterans to pursue on-the-job training, vocational and high school courses.

As President, I have assumed personal responsibility to provide for America's veterans. The recent television dramatization of a book which I'm sure many of you have read, "A Rumor of War," was a reminder of the human toll paid by those who serve us in war and, particularly, in an unpopular war, with many American people, like Vietnam. It also implies to us, very clearly, that easing their pain is still our responsibility. It reminds us that the struggle to keep the peace in the world demands the same kind of dedication that our veterans showed in battle.

I remember the tribute that Phil Caputo wrote to his friend in "A Rumor of War." I've used this quote before. It's meant a lot to me. "Your courage," he wrote, "was an example to us, and whatever the rights and wrongs of war, nothing can diminish the rightness of what you tried to do. As I write this 11 years after your death, the country for which you died wishes to forget the war in which you died. It wishes to forget, and it has forgotten, but there are a few of us who do remember because of the small things that made us love you—your gestures, your words you spoke, the way you looked. We loved you for what you were and what you stood for."

For the past 4 years, we've worked hard to ensure that benefits and services and medical care for the veterans remain unsurpassed. We've continued to support an independent VA hospital system and have carried out a major new construction effort. We were the first administration in history to recommend annual adjustments in disability compensation. We've developed and implemented the nationwide counseling program for Vietnam veterans. We've created three major job programs and reached out to underserved veterans. And last year, I signed a proclamation establishing Vietnam Veterans Week as a special recognition of the sacrifice they made. And I've been gratified that the American public now, after too long an interval of time, is honoring those special sacrifices of young Americans who served in Vietnam.

We can be proud of this progress. I want especially to thank Max Cleland for his strong and articulate leadership of the Veterans Administration. One of the gratifying experiences of my life, as President, has been to work with Max

Cleland. He has a special insight into veterans' contributions, he's trusted by veterans of all wars, and he has a special relationship with those veterans of the Vietnam war, who too long were not appreciated adequately in America.

One of the goals that Max and I shared from the very first time I talked to him about being Veterans Administrator was to make sure that the American public, as well as the Congress, finally recognized what Vietnam veterans have suffered and how we can compensate them and give them a fruitful life—in Veterans Administrations, in job programs, and in the American public.

I also want to thank Congress for its cooperation in the last 4 years. What Max Cleland and I have requested, the Congress has been forthcoming in giving. And when the Congress has made initiatives, we've worked very closely with them.

I now take great pleasure in signing into law the Veterans' Rehabilitation and Education Amendments of 1980, following which I would like for Bill Hefner, Congressman from North Carolina, a leader in the Congress in veterans' programs, and then Max Cleland to make a few words from their two perspectives— one representing the Congress, the other one representing the Veterans Administration.

[At this point, the President signed the bill into law. He then resumed speaking.]

We've got a new law. [*Laughter*]

REPRESENTATIVE HEFNER. Thank you, Mr. President. This is a momentous occasion for me and, I would like to thank all the members of our subcommittee and the full committee of the Veterans' Affairs Committee, also for Max Cleland and all the different organizations that helped us so much. When it came to the testimony we had, we were able to arrive at what I think is a real milestone for the benefit of veterans. And it's just a start, because the Veterans' Affairs Committee will be very active in the coming years to do even more for our veterans to see that they are not second-class citizens and they get the things that they so rightly deserve.

And I want to thank you, sir, for signing this. And this is a real milestone for me, and we certainly appreciate it.

THE PRESIDENT. Thank you, Bill. It's been a good partnership.

REPRESENTATIVE HEFNER. It sure has.

THE PRESIDENT. Max?

MR. CLELAND. *Thank you. Mr. President, Congressman Hefner, ladies and gentlemen:*

I'd like to thank especially the members of the veterans' service organizations, without which this effort would have been impossible. I'd certainly like to thank the key Members of Congress who had a hand in this.

Mr. President, I think it's fair to say that without your support that this legislation on the vocational rehabilitation for disabled veterans and the expansion of benefits for Vietnam veterans would not have been possible. I want to thank you for your support, Mr. President, of this particular legislation, but I want to thank you especially for not forgetting.

THE PRESIDENT. Thank you, Max. God bless you.

And finally, let me say that I'm deeply grateful not only to those who've been recognized and who've had a chance to say a few words, but for the veterans all over the Nation and all the Members of the Congress, Bill, who worked in harmony on this good legislation. The effort, as I said, commenced 2 years ago, to bring forth this first modification of the basic legislative act which passed to initiate the programs. And I know that all of the veterans' organizations represented here are very gratified also for the leadership that has been shown by Max Cleland, by the Members of Congress, and I'm deeply grateful to all of you.

We want the veterans to have a better life in the future even than they've had before and want to make sure that the Nation remembers what our veterans contribute not only in time of war when they suffer most, but in time of peace when they prevent future disabled veterans from having to live a life of rehabilitation, when they can live a life of constructive contribution to those who have already served.

Thank you very much.

NOTE: The President spoke at 1:55 p.m. at the signing ceremony in the Cabinet Room at the White House.

As enacted, H.R. 5288 is Public Law 96–466, approved October 17.

Veterans' Rehabilitation and Education Amendments of 1980

Statement on Signing H.R. 5288 Into Law.   October 17, 1980

Today I am pleased to sign H.R. 5288, the Veterans' Rehabilitation and Education Amendments of 1980. I recently signed an unprecedented fourth consecutive cost-of-living increase for the over two and one-quarter million service disabled veterans and over 375,000 of their survivors. Taken together, these two measures will significantly improve the services and benefits provided to our disabled veterans and their families.

H.R. 5288 provides for a greatly needed modernization of the vocational rehabilitation program administered by the Veterans Administration. It also provides a 10-percent increase in education benefits for veterans and their dependents who are pursuing educational programs under the GI bill and the Survivors' Education Program.

In October 1978, I sent to the Congress a message urging that the Veterans Administration's vocational rehabilitation program be updated to provide more assistance to our disabled veterans. The administration's legislative recommendations to carry this out were sent to the Congress in the spring of 1979. I am gratified that most of the administration's proposals have been included in this measure.

The veterans' rehabilitation program, which provides disabled veterans with training to enable them to become gainfully employed, has been in existence since World War II, but has long needed modernization. Unlike the current program, which is limited to simply restoring a veteran's employability, H.R. 5288 expands the scope of services and assistance to ensure that disabled veterans actually get jobs and keep them. The new program will also place emphasis on helping severely disabled veterans who are unable to pursue a vocational objective to become self-sufficient in their daily living. In addition, H.R. 5288 increases by 17 percent the subsistence allowance benefits paid to disabled veterans in training.

My administration proposed a 10-percent rate increase effective in fiscal year 1981 in educational allowances for veterans and dependents pursuing programs of education through Veterans Administration education programs. Under the bill, half of this increase will become effective on October 1, 1980, and the balance on January 1, 1981. This well-deserved increase will help these veterans and dependents meet the increased costs of their education.

A number of other program changes are also included in the proposal I am signing today, many recommended by the administration. They include changes that will, for example, make it easier for more military service personnel to participate in the post-Vietnam educational assistance program, strengthen the administration of the GI bill program, and aid VA in improving its efforts to collect debts owed the Government.

I regret that H.R. 5288 does not include my recommendation to give educationally disadvantaged veterans an extra 2 years beyond the current 10-year limit for using their educational benefits. On the whole, however, this is an excellent bill and, I am happy to sign it into law.

NOTE: As enacted, H.R. 5288 is Public Law 96–466, approved October 17.

Interview With the President

Question-and-Answer Session with the Editorial Board of Associated Press. October 17, 1980

IRAQI-IRANIAN CONFLICT

Q. We would like to start with Iran and the situation there.

THE PRESIDENT. Fine.

Q. Does your characterization of Iraq as an aggressor and an invading nation in the war with Iran reflect a change in what you said originally was a policy of strict neutrality, and does it reflect any effort at conciliation with Iran for the sake of the release of the hostages?

THE PRESIDENT. Our policy on that has not changed. We have from the very beginning called for the honoring of international borders, the settlement of any dispute about the delineation of those borders by negotiation, not by combat.

And Saddam Husayn's own description of their ultimate goals were the Shatt-al-Arab, which is a waterway, and no Iranian territory.

It's obvious to me that the dismemberment of Iran or the carving out of a part of Iran to be separated from the rest would not be in our interest. And in any case in the world, an invasion or an aggression is something that we would condemn.

Q. So, we're still neutral, but——

THE PRESIDENT. We are neutral.

Q. ——a bit more neutral on the side of Iran now, because——

THE PRESIDENT. No.

Q. ——Iraq has moved in.

THE PRESIDENT. Well, at this moment, Iraq military forces are beyond the ultimate goal expressed by the leader of Iraq, Saddam Husayn, and I think that this is a matter of concern for us. And we would like to see any invading forces withdrawn and a settlement of the border dispute by negotiation.

We're not taking any sides in it. It's just a matter of our expressing clearly our longstanding position. This is the same position that we will take in the United Nations Security [Council] debate, if and when our time comes to speak.

AMERICAN HOSTAGES IN IRAN

Q. Is there any movement on the hostages? There's all sorts of smoke. Is it just smoke, or is there fire, too?

THE PRESIDENT. I think it would be inappropriate now to build up expectations for a breakthrough on the hostages.

We have consistently sought every possible avenue, direct or indirect to anyone who could possibly speak with authority for the Iranian militants or the Government to get our hostages released and to remove the differences between the two countries. We are observing very carefully the fact that Iran now has most of their Government intact, with a President, a Prime Minister, a Majles, or parliament, a speaker of the house, or the Majles, chosen. And there have been some indications from Iran lately among some of these leaders that they think the hostages ought to be released.

So, if we do have a possibility of negotiation, we will continue to pursue such a possibility as we have in the past.

Q. Has there been any Government contact with the Prime Minister since he's been here, any U.S. Government contact at all?

THE PRESIDENT. No.

Q. Do you anticipate any at this moment?

THE PRESIDENT. I can't respond to that, because that'll be up to him to decide, but we would be glad to make available someone to represent our Government and talk to him, he preferred it. But we don't have any indication that he has come in here for that purpose.

Q. Do you have any reason to suspect that the hostages may be released before the election?

THE PRESIDENT. No. I would like for them to be released today, but I don't have any reason to predict that they will.

CAMPAIGN DEBATES

Q. It now appears that there is going to be a one-on-one debate between you and Governor Reagan. It also appears that much of the dispute that's gone on in the past has had more to do with tactics than with anything else. What do you think, politically, you stand to gain from a debate with Governor Reagan?

THE PRESIDENT. Well, our position has been one based on principle——

Q. I was certain of that.

THE PRESIDENT. ——not expediency. We have always favored a one-on-one debate with Governor Reagan, from the very first moments that he was nominated and I was nominated, and have always been willing following the debate, if time had permitted, to have the other candidates involved in a multicandidate debate. This has been something that Governor Reagan has very carefully avoided.

Now, just less than an hour ago, I received a telegram from the League of Women Voters, inviting us to a man-to-man debate in Cleveland, Ohio, on the 28th of October. I instructed my staff immediately to accept the invitation, and we will designate someone to represent me in the negotiations for the exact format. What I want as a format is a maximum ability to respond to questions, maybe proposed by the press, but also to exchange views between myself and Governor Reagan, to pursue an issue so that the American people can see the distinct differences that separate us.

I would also like to see a followup debate, or even a preceding debate, with the Vice-Presidential candidates, with Mr. Bush and Vice President Mondale debating each other.

Q. Does that suggest that you'd like to have a debate in which you and Reagan actually talk to each other rather than going through a panel?

THE PRESIDENT. Yes. I think the League of Women Voters format that was used between myself and President Ford was better than the one they've used this year between Congressman Anderson and Governor Reagan, in that we did have a chance to have a followup question between us. I think a maximum exchange on those basic issues, raised by the press, between me and Governor Reagan would suit me best.

Q. But you didn't have an opportunity to directly question President Ford. Would you like one to directly question Governor Reagan?

THE PRESIDENT. I think that would be good. And I think that the more extensive the debate might be would be advantageous for the American people—a longer period of time.

Q. How important do you think that——

THE PRESIDENT. I'm not trying to set preconditions. We've already accepted the debate. I'm just expressing my preferences.

Q. Those are the kinds of things that your people will be negotiating for.

THE PRESIDENT. Yes, yes.

Q. How important do you think the debate will be in determining how people vote in the election, and do you think that you would win it?

THE PRESIDENT. I don't know about winning it. You know, I'm a careful enough observer to know that Governor Reagan is a professional in dealing with the media, and I say that not in derogation of him. I watched the debate that he had with Congressman Anderson, thought he did very well. He's good at expressing himself. He has addressed the same basic issues as a candidate for a number of years since he became interested in becoming President. He's articulate, and I don't underestimate him.

But I think that the result of the debate is not who's the best debater, but which of the two candidates the American people judge can resolve the issues most effectively as a President, who can deal with a crisis best, who is best able to keep our Nation strong and at peace, who can best meet the needs of Americans as a legitimate service of the American Government, who can have a more cohesive

America and better cooperation in the future with the Congress.

Those are the kinds of issues that will be discussed or debated. And I think the American people will decide whom to support for President—not who is the most eloquent or who makes the most telling debate points, but who responds to those issues most effectively in the judgment of the observer.

Q. It is a pretty high-risk operation politically, isn't it, to have a debate 5 days before the election, 5 or 6 days before, and really a one-shot occurrence, whereas in '76 the first debate didn't seem to work as much to your advantage as the latter two?

THE PRESIDENT. Well, to some extent, a Presidential campaign is a high-risk operation. A lot of people enter it; few survive. And I recognized that when I began my campaign in 1975, and I recognized it this year when I was challenged by a whole group of candidates, Democrats and Republicans. But that's part of the political process. I believe that my position on the issues, my record will stand the scrutiny to be derived from the debate.

Q. Well, given the context of the whole campaign, though, do you think this debate would be decisive?

THE PRESIDENT. No, I think not, except to the extent that it will define the issues more clearly which have not yet been defined adequately in the campaign so far.

STRATEGIC ARMS LIMITATION TREATIES

Q. One of those issues is Governor Reagan's statements, some of them made to us in our interview with him, on the SALT treaty and his statement that he'd withdraw it from the Senate.

THE PRESIDENT. Yes.

Q. You asked the Senate nearly a year ago to withhold action on the treaty because of the invasion of Afghanistan. Is there a great deal of difference between leaving it there and telling the Senate, "Don't act on it," and pulling it back to the White House from the Senate?

THE PRESIDENT. Yes, there's a great deal of difference in tearing up a treaty and saying, "Let's don't pursue it any further," and a clear statement, that I have made in the past and will make again, that we will pursue with the utmost vigor the ratification of the SALT II treaty.

There's no doubt in my mind that the SALT process itself, which has been supported by all my predecessors in this office since Harry Truman, and the SALT II treaty which we've negotiated are in the best interests of our country. To have a balanced ratio between nuclear armaments here and in the Soviet Union, to have observable and controlled limits on nuclear armaments, and to have a professed and avowed goal of massive reductions in those levels of nuclear armaments in the future is crucial. And to insinuate that a superiority in nuclear weapons would be a card that could be played to future arms control, in my opinion, is not only dangerous, but it's ridiculous.

We would not negotiate a SALT agreement in the future predicated on Soviet superiority, and the Soviet Union would be obviously unlikely to proceed with SALT negotiations predicated on American nuclear superiority. That violates the basic principle of the equal and balanced, controlled, observable in reducing levels of armaments.

UNITED STATES MILITARY STRENGTH

Q. In Boston the other day, you said that we're the strongest nation on Earth and we're going to stay that way—militarily—and in the same speech, made the same statement that you just made criticizing Reagan for suggesting nuclear superiority. Isn't there a contradiction between those two statements?

THE PRESIDENT. No, there's not, because it's not a measure of armaments alone. We're strong militarily in armaments. We have, I'd say, at least as strong a nuclear arsenal as the Soviet Union; in some respects, we are superior. Ours is more diverse, more modern, more technically advanced.

At the same time, we are protected militarily by having peaceful neighbors. The Soviets have thousands of miles of frontier with the Chinese. We've got a strong NATO alliance and other alliances around the world based on free association, without any imposition of our will on others, as is the case with the Soviet Union and the Warsaw Pact.

Ours is a free nation that's innovative. Almost every new kind of weapon, from radar to MIRV missiles and now cruise missiles, have come in their development from the democracies and not from the totalitarian governments. Our land is more productive. Our ability to innovate is best. Many countries around the world would like to emulate our form of government.

So, the totality of our Nation's strategic position, including militarily access to the oceans, warm oceans, is much superior to the Soviet Union. I would never permit our Nation to be vulnerable to a superior military force. But in balance, in my judgment, we are stronger, and in balance, we will stay stronger.

RATIFICATION OF SALT II

Q. At what point would you ask the Senate to go ahead with ratification of the Salt treaty, even if the Soviet Union remains in Afghanistan?

THE PRESIDENT. I think at the earliest possible moment after the election is over and when the new Senate is chosen. Secretary Muskie and others are already consulting with the Senate leadership. The issue is certainly in doubt, because of the uncertainty of the election outcome for a third of the Senators or more. I think once the identity of the new Senate is determined, that would be an appropriate time.

Q. Even though the condition that led you to ask for a delay in the first place persisted, that is, if the Russians remained in place in Afghanistan?

THE PRESIDENT. That's correct.

Q. What would have changed that would lead you to——

THE PRESIDENT. The likelihood or possibility of ratification.

Q. I'm not sure I understand. Do you mean that in your action of a year ago, you were concerned with the effect in the Senate, rather than the pressure upon the Russians, when you asked for a delay in the——

THE PRESIDENT. When we delayed it before, there was a certainty that had the ratification been brought to a vote, it would have been defeated. I think that that certainty of defeat has been removed. And we will continue our economic and political pressure on the Soviet Union to withdraw from Afghanistan, but as a separate commitment we will also proceed with the ratification of SALT II.

MR. POWELL.[1] Mr. President?

THE PRESIDENT. Yes.

MR. POWELL. Just let me say that if you go back and look at the statement made that we would ask that the treaty not be sent to the Floor, we made that very clear——

THE PRESIDENT. That's right.

MR. POWELL. ——that that was a step that was being made not to punish the

[1] Jody Powell, Press Secretary to the President.

Soviet Union, but based upon the climate that had been created by their action which made the ratification an impossibility.

Q. It was intended to be part of the signal that you were sending to the Russians at that time, though, wasn't it?

THE PRESIDENT. No, no. In the private confines of this room and the Oval Office, among Fritz Mondale, Secretary Muskie, Secretary Brown, Dr. Brzezinski, and others, we have never felt any doubt that the SALT II treaty is in the interest of our country, and we have never had an inclination to abandon the SALT II treaty as a means of punishing the Soviet Union.

SOVIET INVASION OF AFGHANISTAN

Q. Mr. President, your administration and you personally expended a great deal of time attempting to exert pressure on the Soviet Union to leave Afghanistan.

THE PRESIDENT. Yes.

Q. You mentioned the economic sanctions, particularly. The Soviets are still there; there appears to be very little change. Is that a failure, and if it is, can you make another run at the Soviets? What other points of pressure can we apply to prompt a withdrawal from Afghanistan?

THE PRESIDENT. Well, you know the enormous power of this country and the influence and authority of a President.

When the Soviets invaded Afghanistan, I had the options of military action, economic action, and political action. I decided not to take military action, to go to war with the Soviet Union—a wise decision, I think—but I did decide to exert a maximum amount of appropriate political pressure and economic pressure.

We took the lead in marshaling other nations of the world and condemning the Soviet Union officially through the

United Nations, and we encouraged—but they moved on their own initiative—among Moslem nations to condemn the Soviet Union as such. Thirty-four Moslem countries, some of whom had been completely friendly with the Soviet Union, even aligned with the Soviet Union, condemned the Soviets and demanded their withdrawal. I think the Soviets have hurt themselves severely in the nonaligned movement, where among some of those nations, the Soviets were looked upon as their special friend and with some degree of admiration. In addition, 104 nations joined us in the United Nations in condemning the Soviet Union as an aggressor, as an invader, and demanded their withdrawal.

We imposed economic sanctions against the Soviet Union, depriving their fishing boats of rights in this country. Fifty nations did not go to the Olympics, which was a psychological blow to the Soviet Union, both within their country and in their status among other nations. We have put restraints on the shipment of feed grains to the Soviet Union, and we've tightened up the shipment of technological equipment to the Soviet Union and have encouraged successfully our allies and other trading partners to do the same.

The most severe restraint, perhaps, on the Soviet Union has been the unanticipated courage and tenacity of the freedom-fighters of Afghanistan. The Soviets have not consolidated their strength within that country. They have run into extreme difficulty in imposing their will on the free people of Afghanistan, the freedom-loving people of Afghanistan. And I don't believe that the Soviets would consider themselves having won an assured or final victory in that country at all.

What will happen in the future, I do not know. But we've made it plain to the Soviets, we and other nations on Earth and the people who live in Afghanistan, that they have not invaded with impunity and that they have suffered very severe consequences because of their invasion.

POSSIBILITY OF FUTURE SOVIET AGGRESSION

Q. Mr. President, do you have any sense that the Soviets are in any way chastened or that this would restrain them in the future from similar actions?

THE PRESIDENT. I have a sense that that is the case, but I cannot certify.

Q. For instance, are you confident now that the Soviets would not at some point move into Poland if they felt, in fact, that the regime had been undermined by the——

THE PRESIDENT. Well, I think it wouldn't be appropriate for me to comment on that. Obviously, our country and other nations of the world believe that the Polish people should handle their own affairs to the maximum degree possible, that there should not be any increase in the influence that the Soviet Union exerts on Poland.

RONALD REAGAN

Q. Mr. President, you've said repeatedly that the trend of Governor Reagan's statements on the use of U.S. forces abroad is something that concerns you very much. Do you think that war would be more likely if Reagan were President than at this point?

THE PRESIDENT. Well, I've learned from experience not to try to make surmises of that kind, because my statements are often misinterpreted. There has been a long series of comments by Governor Reagan about the use of American military forces.

I've served in this office now almost 4 years. There hasn't been a day that's gone by that there hasn't been a troubled place in the world or several simultaneously. Both I and my predecessors have had to deal with those crises. We've tried and I've been successful in resolving some of them and dealing with others without the use of American military forces in combat.

But over a period of years, Governor Reagan does have a pattern of calling for the use of American military forces—and you know the places—in North Korea, in Ecuador, in Cuba, in Cyprus, and also in Rhodesia, Angola, Pakistan, the Mideast. There is a pattern there calling for the use of American military forces—some, this year.

One was his response to the Soviet invasion of Afghanistan calling for a blockade of Cuba. I don't have any doubt that this would have precipitated a major confrontation between us and the Soviet Union. The Soviets supply Cuba with several millions of dollars of goods and services every day. And the consequences of that proposal in itself would have been very serious. That's not ancient history; that's this year. Two other times this year, he's called for the use of American military forces.

I can't guess or conjecture what he might do if he should be in the Oval Office. But the abandonment of the SALT II treaty, the call for the use of a nuclear arms race as a card to be played against the Soviet Union, and the repeated call for the injection of American military forces into troubled areas around the world is a pattern that concerns me very much, and I think it also concerns the American people. All this is a matter of record.

Q. Well, that would seem to suggest that as a voter or a citizen you would feel that there was a danger, that this is a man who would lead us into conflict.

THE PRESIDENT. As an American citizen, I have decided to vote against Governor Reagan——

Q. On that basis?

THE PRESIDENT. ——and for myself. [*Laughter*]

PRESIDENT'S HANDLING OF CRISES

Q. Mr. President, you often have said in your campaign speeches that as President you've dealt with a lot of crises that we never know about, because they've been handled successfully, and if they hadn't been handled successfully, then we would know about them. Could you give us some specifics today of what those crises may have been?

THE PRESIDENT. Well, there always are a list of options that can be followed when you deal with a question concerning, say, Rhodesia. I could have ordered military forces into Rhodesia, as Governor Reagan proposed, to support the white supremacy government that was established there. I didn't do it. And eventually Rhodesia became Zimbabwe, with a freely elected democratic government. And I think it is now a stable nation in Africa, a friend of ours, and the rights of both the black and white citizens are being preserved.

That was a matter of judgment. And it's just one that comes to mind where Governor Reagan and I proposed a diametrically opposite approach to the same set of circumstances, which were known to the American people.

ABORTION AND SELECTION OF JUDGES

Q. You've stated consistently from the time you first began to run in 1976 that you were opposed to abortion.

THE PRESIDENT. Yes.

Q. But as President, you said that, obviously, you're sworn to uphold the laws as interpreted by the courts. Mr. President, you also have some authority over how the laws are interpreted by the courts, since——

THE PRESIDENT. That's right.

Q. ——you get to appoint judges. Considering nominees for the Federal courts and possibly for the Supreme Court, do you take into account the position of potential judges on abortion?

THE PRESIDENT. No, not on that specific issue.

I have personal opposition to abortion and to the use of Federal funds for abortion. I recognize the oath that I've taken to uphold the laws of our country as interpreted by the courts and as passed by the Congress. When the Congress authorized the expenditure of Federal funds for abortions, I've let the Department of HEW, then HHS do that. When the test was made in the courts, we defended the Congress right to proscribe the use of Federal funds, except in certain cases.

What I have tried to do is to discourage the need for abortions by improving services to unmarried pregnant women, by improving adoption services, and by encouraging family planning programs, by education of the American public with my own public statements.

But this is one of those highly emotional issues that affects people very deeply, and I have not felt that it would be advisable to have a constitutional amendment which would specifically prohibit all abortions.

Q. You say you don't take abortion into consideration as a specific issue. Are there specific issues you do routinely take into consideration in selecting judges?

THE PRESIDENT. I can't recall any. Obviously, if a proposed judge had a habit or record of racial discrimination, then I would not consider appointing that judge. But I've never gone down a judge's record on a specific issue, like abortion or others, and made a decision about who should be a judge.

INCOME TAX REDUCTION

Q. In Pennsylvania the other day, you said that there should be a balanced tax reduction not only in 1981 but as a steady, predictable thing in the future.

THE PRESIDENT. Yes.

Q. Do you envision legislation with a series of tax cuts over a——

THE PRESIDENT. No.

Q. ——period of years or——

THE PRESIDENT. No.

Q. ——action each year or——

THE PRESIDENT. I think there ought to be action at fairly regular intervals to prevent the percentage of American income being collected by the Federal Government in income taxes, but the exact form of that tax reduction ought to be predicated on existing or predictable economic circumstances at the time.

Q. But predictable intervals, so that people would know that——

THE PRESIDENT. Well, you have to make an estimate——

Q. ——that at a certain time there was going to be at least consideration of another tax cut?

THE PRESIDENT. No, no. I've put forward a revitalization program proposal to the American people that I want to see implemented next year; part of it is a tax cut. My judgment, based on next year's circumstances, is that we need about half that tax cut to go to encourage investments to create new machinery, new factories, and new jobs. In 1963 John Kennedy made a proposal for a similar tax cut; I think it was almost a hundred percent for investment in plants and machinery and new jobs.

Governor Reagan's Reagan-Kemp-Roth proposal has about 90 percent for individual tax cuts, primarily for the rich people, and about 10 percent for the stimulation of investments in new equipment, new plants, and new jobs.

My judgment is that my proposal's best. One of the reasons is that we need additional employment, we need to modernize American industrial capability, and we need to avoid inflation. His thrust would be to increase consumer spending, which would create more dollars in the marketplace for basically the same level of goods to be purchased. That would bid up the price of goods and be very inflationary in its consequence. The net result of my entire proposal would be to reduce inflation, because a part of the tax reduction for persons, the other 50 percent, would be to counterbalance the now projected increase in withholding taxes on social security.

Q. You mentioned the percentage of income in future years. Is that where the predictability would come in? I mean, would there be a guideline that said, "Okay, at this point we won't collect any more of your money"?

THE PRESIDENT. Well, we will want to hold down the percentage of income that is taken back in taxes, because if you don't make any changes in the tax laws over a period of years, as people move into higher brackets and so forth with inflation, they pay a higher rate of taxes to the Government. And so, you need to lower the tax rates in a very carefully balanced way from year to year, depending on the existing circumstances, to make sure that that percentage doesn't increase too much.

INFLATION

Q. Sir, in the 1976 campaign you voiced specific goals for reducing inflation and unemployment down to about 4 percent. Those goals weren't realized. I haven't heard you voice similar goals for a second term. Do you have any specifically in mind?

THE PRESIDENT. I think those goals would still be appropriate. We had projected, back in March of this year, a balanced budget for 1981. Recession came on us, and we are not going to be able to balance the budget. My goal is still to do so.

When you have an unemployment rate that's higher than you anticipate, the unemployment compensation payments, the welfare payments tend to unbalance the budget. As those people lose their jobs, which you did not anticipate, then they do not pay income taxes. So, you have an inevitable change in budget circumstances over which you don't have control.

No one, so far as I know, before 1979 began ever thought that the price would be more than doubled by OPEC for their oil. This inflationary wave hit the entire world, and it was something that we did not anticipate. Prior to that time we had known about the threat of inflation, obviously, but we were concentrating to a substantial degree on putting people back to work. Four years ago when I ran for President, the overwhelming concern among people about economics was unemployment, and that's why we concentrated on that subject, added an unprecedented 8½ million new jobs in the country. But with the OPEC oil price increase, the inflationary pressures built up more than we had ever anticipated.

I think we've made good judgments on economics predicated on the information we had at the time. If I knew 2 years ago what I know now and could have anticipated the OPEC price increases, we would have put more emphasis on controlling inflation. I might say that we've dealt with it properly.

We need to increase productivity of American workers; that will control inflation. We need to continue to cut down the percentage of the gross national product that is comprised by the Federal deficit, and we've cut that more than half. We need to reduce the rate of Government spending, and we've reduced that more than half since I've been in office. We also need to make sure that we reduce our dependence on foreign oil, and today we are importing a third less oil from overseas than we did just a year ago. That helps us a lot.

We need to continue to remove restraints on international trade, and with a new trade bill, we're making good progress on that. The last 2 years, we've increased, for instance as one example, textile exports by $2 billion, and at the same time, we've actually reduced the imports of textile goods—a radical departure from previous trends.

Those are the kinds of things whose cumulative effect will have a beneficial impact on inflation. None of them will stand on its own, and they will all require some degree of commitment and sometimes sacrifice on the part of the American people. But I think that now there's a consciousness in this country about the threat of inflation which is not going to be forgotten any time in the near future, and I will capitalize on that realization. And I believe I'll have better luck in controlling inflation in the years ahead.

MR. POWELL. This will have to be the last question.

DECISIVE FACTORS IN ELECTION

Q. With the campaign going down to the last 2 weeks and the debate coming up near the end of it, if you could pick up one issue that you think the campaign will hinge on—your people have said that the pendulum has swung to your side and things are now moving in your direction. If you could pick one issue, one thing that the campaign would swing on, what would it be?

THE PRESIDENT. Well, that's obviously a hypothetical question that's not sound, because the people don't single out just one issue to the exclusion of everything else. I think it would be a combination of potential crisis in its broad range and scope on the one hand, and economic circumstances in the broadest definition of the word. And I don't want crisis to be narrowly defined as just military combat. Crisis is the ability of a President to deal with unanticipated circumstances in a sound, mature way, a responsible way. And economic circumstances is whether the people think that I or Governor Reagan will do the best job to give them a stable economic future.

RALPH ABERNATHY'S ENDORSEMENT OF RONALD REAGAN

Q. Let me sneak one more, because Jody would certainly want it asked. Do you think that the Reverend Abernathy's endorsement of Governor Reagan yesterday will have a significant effect on the black vote? Are you concerned about the things that he said about your handling issues that concern the black voters?

THE PRESIDENT. Well, since we've heard the news, Jody and I and others have discussed it very thoroughly and I've decided not to withdraw from the race. [*Laughter*]

Thank you all. I enjoyed it.

Q. Thank you very much.

NOTE: The interview began at 3:28 p.m. in the Cabinet Room at the White House.

Foreign Service Act of 1980

Statement on Signing H.R. 6790 Into Law. October 17, 1980

I am today approving H.R. 6790, the Foreign Service Act of 1980. This bill provides the first comprehensive revision of personnel legislation for the United States Foreign Service in 34 years. It is an important step in the reform, simplification, and improvement of personnel administration in the Government, a top priority of my administration.

Because of its special conditions of employment, including the requirement of availability for worldwide service, the Foreign Service was exempted from most of the provisions of the Civil Service Reform Act of 1978. I recognized then, however, that the Foreign Service, operating under a 1946 act designed for a far different world, was also in need of reform, and that many of the civil service reforms, appropriately modified, would promote greater productivity and improve personnel management in the Foreign Service as well.

The Congress agreed, and we worked together to frame legislation. The Foreign Service Act of 1980 is the product of our nonpartisan collaboration.

While this bill was being drafted, events were occurring that brought home vividly to all of us the extraordinary demands placed on our Foreign Service personnel. They play an essential role in the formulation and conduct of United States foreign policy, and their service abroad often involves deprivation and danger. They are exposed to acts of terrorism and, in some places, to open hostility toward the United States and its representatives. We owe them our fullest support.

The new Foreign Service Act recognizes the professionalism and dedication required by today's Foreign Service. It sets high performance standards, provides incentive awards for outstanding service, and strengthens career development programs. It permits the President to promulgate a pay schedule that complies fully with the requirements of the Federal Pay Comparability Act. The Executive order I will sign shortly will achieve comparability between the Foreign Service and General Schedule pay systems.

When I signed the Civil Service Reform Act just 2 years ago, on October 13, 1978, I said that it would "bring efficiency and accountability and competence to the Federal Government that exceed what we have known in the past" and that it would put "incentive and reward back into the Federal system." Our experience since that law went into effect indicates that it is bringing real improvement to the civil service—and that the American taxpayers are getting a better return on their tax dollar.

I take great pride in signing this bill today. It is a modern charter, well designed to meet the needs of the dedicated, able men and women of the Foreign Service in the decades ahead. I congratulate all Members of Congress and their staffs who devoted long hours and months to preparing it and who worked closely with my administration in bringing it successfully to enactment.

NOTE: As enacted, H.R. 6790 is Public Law 96–465, approved October 17.

Import Relief for the Domestic Mushroom Industry

Letter to the Speaker of the House and the President of the Senate Transmitting a Report.   October 17, 1980

Dear Mr. Speaker: (Dear Mr. President:)

In accordance with section 203(b)(1) of the Trade Act of 1974, enclosed is a report to the Congress setting forth my decision to provide import relief on canned mushrooms in the form of increased tariffs.[1]

JIMMY CARTER

---

[1] EDITORIAL NOTE: In the letter to the Speaker, the word "duties" was substituted for "tariffs."

IMPORT RELIEF ACTION

CANNED MUSHROOMS

As required under section 203(b)(2) of the Trade Act of 1974 (the Trade Act), I am transmitting this report to Congress setting forth the action I am taking with respect to canned mushrooms covered by the affirmative finding of the U.S. International Trade Commission (USITC) on Investigation Number 201–TA–43. This action follows my receipt of the recommendation of the United States Trade Representative which takes into account the advice of the Trade Policy Committee.

After considering all relevant aspects of the case, including those considerations set forth in section 202(c) of the Trade Act, I have determined to provide three years of import relief for the domestic industry in the form of increased duties. I will issue a Presidential Proclamation, to be effective within fifteen days, increasing the current duty of 3.2 cents per pound plus 10 percent *ad valorem* on imported mushrooms, otherwise prepared or preserved, provided for in item number 144.20 of the Tariff Schedules of the United States, to:

3.2 cents per pound plus 30 percent *ad valorem* for the first year of relief;

3.2 cents per pound plus 25 percent *ad valorem* for the second year of relief; and

3.2 cents per pound plus 20 percent *ad valorem* for the third year of relief.

In addition to this import relief, I am creating a White House Task Force under the direction of Stuart Eizenstat, Assistant to the President for Domestic Affairs and Policy, that will coordinate the Administration's efforts to assist the mushroom industry in adjusting to import competition. This Task Force will include representatives from the Office of the United States Trade Representative, the Council of Economic Advisers, the Small Business Administration, the Economic Development Administration, the Farm Home Administration, and the Agricultural Marketing Service. The Task Force will work with the American Mushroom Institute and other representatives of the industry in an effort to provide the appropriate technical and financial assistance to facilitate the industry's adjustment to increased imports.

I am taking these actions to mitigate the human and social problems associated with economic adjustment. Since these actions are temporary, it is vitally important that firms within the industry take the necessary management decisions within the relief period to become more competitive or to diversify. To monitor the industry's progress, I am directing the United States Trade Representative to request under Section 203(i)(1) of the Trade Act of 1974 that the USITC report, within eighteen months of this decision, on the industry's efforts to adjust.

I have chosen to provide tariff relief rather than the quota relief recommended by the USITC because I believe it is the most appropriate form of relief in this case. Increased tariffs will enable the canning industry to become more profitable. This improvement in their financial position, which is not expected to have a significant inflationary impact, will enable the industry to implement adjustment programs which they have pledged to undertake. Tariffs are also preferable in this case because, unlike quotas, they allow the natural market forces to continue to work, thus providing relatively more incentive to the industry to adjust to foreign competition. Finally, tariffs are preferred because of the difficulty of equitably allocating quotas among countries when there are highly competitive new suppliers entering a market dominated by traditional suppliers.

NOTE: This is the text of identical letters addressed to Thomas P. O'Neill, Jr., Speaker of the House of Representatives, and Walter F. Mondale, President of the Senate.

Import Relief for the Domestic Mushroom Industry

Memorandum From the President.
October 17, 1980

Memorandum for the United States Trade Representative

Pursuant to Section 202(b)(1) of the Trade Act of 1974 (19 U.S.C. 2252), I have determined to provide import relief for the domestic mushroom industry in the form of increased duties. This action is in response to the affirmative finding of the U.S. International Trade Commission (USITC) on Investigation Number 201–TA–43. The investigation was initiated as a result of a petition by the American Mushroom Institute. The USITC's report was received on August 18, 1980. The USITC found that increased imports had been a substantial cause of serious injury, or threat thereof, to the domestic industry. It recommended the imposition of import quotas over the next three years as an appropriate remedy.

After considering all relevant aspects of the case, including those considerations set forth in section 202(c) of the Trade Act, I have determined to provide three years of import relief for the domestic industry in the form of increased duties. I will issue a Presidential Proclamation, to be effective within fifteen days, increasing the current duty of 3.2 cents per pound plus 10 percent *ad valorem* on imported mushrooms, otherwise prepared or preserved, provided for in item number 144.20 of the Tariff Schedules of the United States, to:

3.2 cents per pound plus 30 percent *ad valorem* for the first year of relief;

3.2 cents per pound plus 25 percent *ad valorem* for the second year of relief; and

3.2 cents per pound plus 20 percent *ad valorem* for the third year of relief.

In addition to this import relief, I am creating a White House Task Force under the direction of Stuart Eizenstat, Assistant to the President for Domestic Affairs and Policy, that will coordinate the Administration's efforts to assist the mushroom industry in adjusting to import competition. This Task Force will include representatives from the Office of the United States Trade Representative, the Council of Economic Advisers, the Small Business Administration, the Economic Development Administration, the Farm Home Administration, and the Agricultural Marketing Service. The Task Force will provide appropriate technical and financial assistance to facilitate the industry's adjustment to increased imports.

I am taking these actions to mitigate the human and social problems associated with economic adjustment. Since these actions are temporary, it is vitally important that firms within the industry take the necessary management decisions within the relief period to become more competitive or to diversify. To monitor the industry's progress, I am directing you as the United States Trade Representative to request under Section 203(i)(1) of the Trade Act of 1974 that the USITC report, within eighteen months of this decision, on the industry's efforts to adjust.

I have chosen to provide tariff relief rather than the quota relief recommended by the USITC because I believe it is the most appropriate form of relief in this case. Increased tariffs will enable the canning industry to become more profitable. This improvement in their financial position, which is not expected to have a significant inflationary impact, will enable the industry to implement adjustment programs which they have pledged to undertake. Tariffs are also preferable in this case because, unlike quotas, they allow the natural market forces to continue to work, thus providing relatively more incentive to the industry to adjust to foreign competition. Finally tariffs are preferred because of the difficulty of equitably allocating quotas among countries when there are highly competitive new suppliers entering a market dominated by traditional suppliers.

JIMMY CARTER

Digest of Other White House Announcements

The following listing includes the President's public schedule and other items of general interest announced by the White House Press Office and not included elsewhere in this issue.

October 12

The President returned to the White House from Camp David, Md.

October 14

The President met at the White House with:

— Zbigniew Brzezinski, Assistant to the President for National Security Affairs;
— Vice President Mohamed Hosni Moubarek of Egypt.

October 15

The President met at the White House with Dr. Brzezinski.

October 16

The President met at the White House with Dr. Brzezinski.

October 17

The President met at the White House with:

— Dr. Brzezinski;
— Secretary of State Edmund S. Muskie, Secretary of Defense Harold Brown, Deputy Secretary of State Warren M. Christopher, Lloyd N. Cutler, Counsel to the President, and Dr. Brzezinski.

The President announced the recess appointments of Laird F. Harris and Harold L. Thomas as Assistant Directors of the Community Services Administration. Both have been nominated for these positions but were not confirmed by the Senate before it adjourned.

The President left the White House for a weekend stay at Camp David.

NOMINATIONS SUBMITTED TO THE SENATE

NOTE: No nominations were submitted to the Senate during the period covered by this issue.

CHECKLIST OF WHITE HOUSE PRESS RELEASES

The following listing contains releases of the White House Press Office which are not included in this issue.

Released October 11, 1980

Announcement: Federal assistance to Miami, Fla., residents

News conference: on 1980 campaign issues— by Press Secretary Jody Powell and Stuart E. Eizenstat, Assistant to the President for Domestic Affairs and Policy

CHECKLIST—Continued

Released October 12, 1980

Advance text: radio address to the Nation on the Nation's economy

Released October 13, 1980

Advance text: remarks at a meeting with civic and community leaders in New York, N.Y.

Released October 14, 1980

Fact sheet: Privacy Protection Act of 1980

Advance text: remarks on the Nation's economy at the National Press Club

Fact sheet: Staggers Rail Act of 1980

News conference: on Jewish issues—by Vice President Walter F. Mondale

News conference: on 1980 campaign issues—by Lloyd N. Cutler, Counsel to the President, and Anne Wexler, Assistant to the President

Released October 15, 1980

Advance text: remarks to senior citizens in Boston, Mass.

Released October 16, 1980

Advance text: remarks at a meeting with New York labor leaders in New York, N.Y.

Released October 17, 1980

Fact sheet: U.S.-Israeli Agreement on Contingency Implementing Arrangements for the Memorandum of Agreement of June 22, 1979, and Oil Supply

Fact sheet: Veterans' Rehabilitation and Education Amendments of 1980

ACTS APPROVED BY THE PRESIDENT

Approved October 13, 1980

H.R. 7592_____ Public Law 96–436
Military Construction Appropriation Act, 1981.

H.R. 5546_____ Public Law 96–437
An act to amend the United States Grain Standards Act to permit grain delivered to export elevators by any means of conveyance other than barge to be transferred into such export elevators without official weighing, and for other purposes.

S. 985_____ Public Law 96–438
An act to amend the Consolidated Farm and Rural Development Act.

ACTS APPROVED—Continued

Approved October 13—Continued

H.R. 7779_____ Public Law 96–439
An act to amend the Internal Revenue Code of 1954 to authorize three additional judges for the Tax Court and to remove the age limitation on appointments to the Tax Court.

S. 1790_____ Public Law 96–440
Privacy Protection Act of 1980.

H.R. 8103_____ Public Law 96–441
An act to rename the National Collection of Fine Arts and the Museum of History and Technology of the Smithsonian Institution as the National Museum of American Art and the National Museum of American History, respectively.

H.R. 5048_____ Public Law 96–442
Manassas National Battlefield Park Amendments of 1980.

H.J. Res. 568_____ Public Law 96–443
A joint resolution to authorize and request the President to issue a proclamation designating October 12 through October 19, 1980, as "Italian-American Heritage Week".

S. 2936_____ Public Law 96–444
An act to transfer certain employees of the Architect of the Capitol to the Sergeant at Arms and Doorkeeper of the Senate.

H.R. 6440_____ Public Law 96–445
An act to establish priorities in the payment of claims against the People's Republic of China.

S. 2185_____ Public Law 96–446
An act to authorize the acceptance and use of bequests and gifts for disaster relief.

S. 2511_____ Public Law 96–447
Civil Rights Commission Authorization Act of 1980.

Approved October 14, 1980

S. 1946_____ Public Law 96–448
Staggers Rail Act of 1980.

H.R. 7085_____ Public Law 96–449
Hostage Relief Act of 1980.

S. 2597_____ Public Law 96–450
Intelligence Authorization Act for Fiscal Year 1981.

H.R. 4310_____ Public Law 96–451
An act to amend the Federal Boat Safety Act of 1971 to promote recreational boating safety through the development, administration, and financing of a national recreational boating safety improvement program, and for other purposes.

ACTS APPROVED—Continued

Approved October 14—Continued

H.R. 7665_____ Public Law 96–452
Fifth Circuit Court of Appeals Reorganization Act of 1980.

S. 2961_____ Private Law 96–62
An act for the relief of Viktor Ivanovich Belenko.

Approved October 15, 1980

H.R. 5451_____ Public Law 96–453
Maritime Education and Training Act of 1980.

S. 1798_____ Public Law 96–454
Household Goods Transportation Act of 1980.

H.R. 4273_____ Public Law 96–455
An act to amend section 17 of the Act of July 5, 1946, as amended, entitled "An Act to provide for the registration and protection of trade-marks used in commerce, to carry out the provisions of certain international conventions, and for other purposes".

S. 1482_____ Public Law 96–456
Classified Information Procedures Act.

S. 1640_____ Public Law 96–457
An act to extend certain authorities of the Secretary of the Interior with respect to water resources research and development and saline water conversion research and development programs, and for other purposes.

S. 1873_____ Public Law 96–458

ACTS APPROVED—Continued

Approved October 15—Continued

Judicial Councils Reform and Judicial Conduct and Disability Act of 1980.

H.R. 6554_____ Public Law 96–459
Maritime Appropriation Authorization Act for Fiscal Year 1981.

H.R. 4417_____ Public Law 96–460
Chesapeake Bay Research Coordination Act of 1980.

S. 2320_____ Public Law 96–461
National Bureau of Standards Authorization Act for Fiscal Years 1981 and 1982.

H.R. 8178_____ Public Law 96–462
Federal District Court Organization Act of 1980.

S. 2412_____ Public Law 96–463
Used Oil Recycling Act of 1980.

Approved October 17, 1980

S. 2622_____ Public Law 96–464
Coastal Zone Management Improvement Act of 1980.

H.R. 6790_____ Public Law 96–465
Foreign Service Act of 1980.

H.R. 5288_____ Public Law 96–466
Veterans' Rehabilitation and Education Amendments of 1980.

H.R. 3122_____ Public Law 96–467
An act relating to the tariff treatment of certain articles.

H.R. 6593_____ Public Law 96–468
Swine Health Protection Act.

S. 2043_____ Public Law 96–469
Animal Cancer Research Act.

Coastal Zone Management Improvement Act of 1980

*Statement on Signing S. 2622 Into Law.
October 18, 1980*

I have signed into law S. 2622, a bill reauthorizing and amending the Coastal Zone Management Act of 1972. The signing of this legislation fulfills a commitment I made in my 1979 environmental message to reauthorize Federal assistance to State coastal zone management programs and to strengthen the Coastal Zone Management Act by establishing a national coastal protection policy.

The importance of the Nation's coastal zone cannot be overstated. The estuaries, lagoons, beaches, bays, islands, and wetlands of the American coastline contain a wealth of natural resources and provide unlimited opportunities for outdoor recreation and the enjoyment of natural beauty. At the same time, our coasts are the site of great economic activity, including fisheries, ports, and major defense, energy, and transportation facilities. Today, nearly four out of five Americans live within 100 miles of the oceans and the Great Lakes, and it is estimated that by the end of this decade, 75 percent of the American people will reside within 50 miles of these shores.

The challenge of managing this convergence of resources, activities, and people requires a close cooperation among all levels of government and a partnership between government and the private sector. This bill provides a legislative framework for such collaboration. When I took office, only one State had an approved coastal zone management program. Today, 25 of 35 coastal States and territories have approved programs covering nearly 80 percent of our coastlines. The bill I have signed today provides for a 5-year extension of Federal financial support for these State and territorial coastal management programs. It also offers incentives to encourage the remaining coastal States to develop such programs.

Finally, section 12 of S. 2622 is designed to permit the Congress to disapprove by concurrent resolution any rule issued by the Secretary of Commerce under the Coastal Zone Management Act before the rule becomes effective. Such a provision is unconstitutional because it purports to authorize the Congress to overturn an executive action by a measure intended to have the effect of law, but which is not to be presented to the President in accordance with constitutional process regarding Acts of Congress. This section violates the presentation clauses of the Constitution, Article 1, section 7, clauses 2 and 3, and violates the separation of powers doctrine by interfering with the authorized discretion of the executive branch in administration of an ongoing program. Pursuant to my message to Congress dated June 21, 1978, I am directing the Secretary of Commerce that this requirement is to be treated as a "report-and-wait" provision and that, if such a concurrent resolution is passed, it is to be given serious consideration but not regarded as legally binding.

Passage of this bill took a year of hard work by the administration and the Congress. I want to thank all the Members of Congress who were involved in this effort. I also want to commend the outstanding work of many conservation groups, private citizens, and public bodies in commemorating 1980 as the Year of the Coast.

NOTE: As enacted, S. 2622 is Public Law 96–464, approved October 17.

Foreign Policy

Radio Address to the Nation.
October 19, 1980

This is President Jimmy Carter, speaking to you from the Oval Office of the White House.

For the past 4 years, the United States has been at peace. We've strengthened the foundations of our security. We have pursued our national interests in a dangerous and often unstable world. And we've done so without recourse to violence and war. This is no accident. It's the result of a careful exercise of the enormous strength of America.

Today I want to talk to you about what we must do together in the next 4 years to ensure our own security and to keep the peace.

The cornerstone of both security and peace is our ability to defend ourselves. In the last analysis we must be able to meet our commitments and pursue our goals peacefully, with calm assurance and confidence. That requires military strength.

We face a potential adversary, the Soviet Union, whose government has funneled much of the wealth and talents of its own people into the construction of a military machine. We would prefer to compete peacefully with Soviet farmers to feed the world, with Soviet textile workers to clothe it, with Soviet doctors to heal it, with Soviet scientists to give it new forms of energy. Those races would be a joy to run. But that is not the challenge they lay before us. Instead, we see a large buildup of Soviet military forces; we see the arming and use of client states such as Cuba; and we see the brutal Soviet invasion of Afghanistan.

This long-term challenge demands a steady, resolute response. Historically, our country has moved sharply up and down in its support for defense. After each war we have disarmed and demobilized, and then later embarked on crash buildups. Such erratic actions are always wasteful and sometimes dangerous.

My commitment has been different. It's been to provide for a steady rebuilding of our defenses. We've increased our real spending for defense—spending above and beyond inflation—every year since I became President. For 7 of the previous 8 years it had declined sharply, a 35-percent reduction in defense spending between 1969 and 1977. The effects of this long decline cannot be eliminated at a stroke. But we have made an excellent start, especially by putting our technological superiority to work.

For example, by producing a number of types of long-range cruise missiles, we can multiply the power of our existing ships and aircraft. We are doing just that. When I took office, we had no new battle tank or modern armored fighting vehicle. Now they are both in production. No answer had been found to the prospective vulnerability of our Minuteman missiles and silos. Now there's an answer—the mobile MX missile.

There was no overall plan for strengthening United States and other Allied forces in Europe. Now we have a good plan, and we are putting it into effect. We're deploying antitank missiles at a rate five times faster than the Soviets are deploying their tanks. On NATO's eastern flank, we're working to reintegrate Greece into the NATO command structure, and we attach great importance to this effort.

Our purchases of army equipment, jet fighters, and attack aircraft had dropped by some two-thirds in the 8 years before I became President. Since then, we have increased them by 50 percent.

When I came into office, I found that we had little capability for quick action in the critical Persian Gulf region. Now we have prepositioned equipment for 12,000 Marines and munitions for 500 aircraft. We've arranged for the use of five different sites in the region. We've deployed two carrier task forces in the Indian Ocean. They give us air and naval superiority to act instantly to keep open the Straits of Hormuz, through which much of the world's oil trade flows.

More will have to be done. Even further increases in pay and benefits will be needed to keep trained service men and women in our volunteer forces. Barring some unexpected decrease in Soviet military efforts, we will also need to increase our investments in the ships, aircraft, tanks, and other weapons that are the muscle of our conventional forces. Military forces give us security, but they are not an end in themselves. As I've said many times, the best weapon is one which

need never be fired in combat, and the best soldier is the one who never has to shed his blood on the field of battle.

Besides our military programs, we've devised something else, what might be called a secret weapon. This weapon will knock out about a fourth of all the Soviet long-range missiles and bombers that we project for 1985. It will eliminate thousands of nuclear bombs and warheads the Russians could otherwise have. It will enhance our intelligence-gathering capabilities to monitor what the Soviet Union is doing. It will do all this without firing a shot, without interfering with a single one of our own planned military improvements, without costing a dime. Indeed, it will save us billions of dollars.

This secret weapon, of course, is not a weapon at all. Nor is it a secret. It is SALT II, the strategic arms limitation treaty which we have signed after 7 years of negotiations with the Soviet Union, and which now awaits approval by the Senate.

This agreement strengthens our strategic position. It also strengthens peace, for what is at stake is more than a single treaty, however advantageous. What is at stake is a process, an extremely important process, the process of gradually reducing the possibility of nuclear war.

Thirty-five years after Hiroshima, the shadow of what was unleashed there still hangs over the world. We've lived with it for so long that we are in danger of becoming casual about it. We must not do that. Even a single hydrogen bomb dropped on a single major city could cause millions of deaths and injuries in the first few seconds and millions more in its wake. It is beyond the power of words to describe the horror of a nuclear holocaust. It would dwarf all the accumulated barbarities and cruelties of mankind's long history put together. More people would die in a few hours than in all the wars of all nations since the dawn of recorded history.

Most of us seldom think seriously about the possibility of nuclear war. But as the President of the United States, entrusted with the power to unleash that force, charged with the responsibility to bend every effort of mind and heart and will to see to it that it need never be unleashed, then it is something I think about every day and every night of my life.

Over the last 20 years we've taken some tentative steps away from the nuclear precipice. Now, for the first time, we are being advised to take steps that may move us toward it.

A few days ago my opponent in the current election campaign promised to scrap the nuclear arms treaty we've already signed. He said, and I quote, "The one card that's been missing in these negotiations is the possibility of an arms race." He also urges that we seek nuclear superiority. His position—and I think I state it accurately—is that by abandoning the current agreement and suggesting an all-out nuclear arms race, we could perhaps frighten the Soviets into negotiating a new agreement on the basis of American nuclear superiority.

I've had 4 years of sobering experience in this life-and-death field, and in my considered judgment this would be a very risky gamble. It is most unlikely that it would lead to any new agreement. A much more likely result would be an uncontrolled nuclear arms race and almost certainly a new rupture in Soviet-American relations. The long, slow momentum of arms control would be broken. Any future effort to negotiate arms limits—for example, on antisatellite systems, on nuclear weapons tests, on conventional and

nuclear arms in Europe—would all be imperiled.

The most important duty of a President is to defend the Nation and its vital interests. Part of that duty is to judge what course of action will diminish the possibility of nuclear war. My considered judgment, based on a very thorough knowledge of all the factors involved, is that the course I am following would do that, and that the departure recommended by my opponent would have just the opposite effect.

His argument is not with me alone. It is with our allies who, without exception, support both the SALT treaty and the continuing process of nuclear arms control. His position is a departure from the policies of President Truman, President Eisenhower, and all Democratic and Republican Presidents who have served in this office since then. Whatever their other differences, all of them saw a duty to slow the arms race and to bring the terrible weapons of nuclear annihilation under some kind of rational control.

I do not propose to turn away from that duty. I propose to lead our country in fulfilling it.

Though we must continue to work for arms control, which is in our mutual interest, we must recognize that Soviet-American relations have grown colder in the wake of the invasion of Afghanistan. The world has condemned this act of aggression, and the Soviets are being made to realize that this military occupation of a freedom-loving nation cannot be continued without severe adverse consequences. But we must not let ourselves become obsessed by fear and rivalry. If we do, we run the risk of neglecting the many other problems which are related to the Soviet Union only indirectly or not at all.

Peace is the work of many hands. It's the struggle for justice in many dark corners. It is striving to solve problems long stalemated and bitterly disputed. It's having the courage to rise above old failures and to act upon new hope. As we raise our shield against war, let us also hear the stricken voice of the homeless refugee, the cry of the hungry child, the weeping of the bereaved widow, the whispered prayer of the political prisoner. We are one with the family of all people, and the concerns to the human family are many. Around the world we've rejected the counsels of pessimism and have dared to make progress toward peace.

In the Far East, we've placed our relations with China on an honest and sensible footing. This makes the global balance of power more stable and strengthens peace both in Asia and around the world.

In the Middle East, 7 years ago this month, there was war—the fourth Arab-Israeli war in just 25 years. Today Egypt and Israel are at peace, and Israel is more secure from attack than she has ever been. We've recognized the strategic interrelationship between Israel's security and our own. When I first met President Sadat at the White House in April 1977, I told him that I intended to work for a complete peace between his country and Israel—acknowledgement of the right to exist, direct negotiations, open borders, diplomatic recognition, ambassadorial exchange, and mutual trade. He told me that he too longed for that day, but it would never happen in his lifetime. Prime Minister Begin shared his dream and his skepticism. Now that dream has come to pass, in their lifetime and in yours and mine.

We have much more work to do. But we have fundamentally changed the situation in the Middle East. The question is no longer Israel's right to exist. The

question now is the terms of a broader peace between a strong and secure Israel and her neighbors.

A bitter war is now going on in the Persian Gulf, complicating even further our efforts to obtain the release of our hostages in Iran. Think how much more dangerous that new war would be if we did not have peace between Israel and Egypt, by far the most significant military powers in the region. We will continue to consult closely with Israel and with Egypt on strategic matters of mutual interest in our common effort to preserve the peace.

In southern Africa 4 years ago, it was clear that time was running out for regimes based on the doctrine of racial supremacy. I'm proud that because we've recognized this fact, we could help with the peaceful settlement that this year brought a democratically elected government to power in Zimbabwe. We've developed excellent relations with Nigeria and other independent nations on the African Continent. There, as elsewhere, we've placed America's influence on the side of human forces that inevitably shape the future.

In Central America, a new and more just social order is emerging. We approve that struggle for justice, and at the same time we affirm our faith that economic reform can best be achieved when human rights are respected. I'm convinced that the people of Central America can find their way forward, leaving old injustices, without submitting to new tyrannies. As Americans, we all have reason to be proud of our new relationship with Panama, a relationship that has turned an isthmus of discord into a zone of peace.

I've sought to guide us in the spirit of liberty and peace. When we lose touch with that spirit, when we begin to think of our power as an end in itself, when we begin to think that the only source of respect is the threat of force, then we lose the best that is within us.

We seek a world in which the rule of law, not the threat of force, is the language of statecraft. We seek a world in which nations put aside the madness of war and nuclear arms races and turn their energies instead to the conquest of our common global enemies—dwindling resources, ecological decay, ignorance, and hunger.

No one can guarantee you a future of unvarying success. I certainly do not promise you that. Nor will I tell you that the transition from the troubled world of today to the hoped for world of tomorrow will be an easy one. I promise you only that if you entrust the responsibilities of this office to me for another 4 years, this Nation will have the strength to be secure, and I will continue to find peace by seeking solutions to the real problems, the hard problems. I will do so with both hope and realism, with both determination and restraint.

We will keep our Nation strong. But this I can say to you: Peace is my passion. And within the limits of the wisdom and opportunity God grants me, peace is my pledge.

NOTE: The President spoke at 12:10 p.m. from the Oval Office at the White House. The address was broadcast live on the Mutual Broadcasting System.

Carter/Kennedy Unity Celebration

Remarks at the Democratic Party Dinner. October 19, 1980

First of all, I want to express to Senator Kennedy my deep appreciation not only for his introduction of me and those fine words you said about my campaign and the Democratic Party but also because of his generous support that he's giving me all over the Nation. We have already been together as a campaign team in California, Massachusetts, more recently, the other night, in New Jersey and in Pennsylvania. He's been campaigning today in Michigan and other places. We'll be together tomorrow night in New York.

This is an all-out, deeply committed, extremely generous action on his part that I think will make the difference when election night comes. And from the bottom of my heart, I want to express my thanks to my friend, Ted Kennedy. Tonight, as a matter of fact, I play a supporting role to him.

There's no way I could move any further without thanking again Arthur Krim for being willing to host this wonderful evening. Arthur has been a loyal supporter and a friend for Democrats and for Democratic Presidents ever since the time of Harry Truman. His success tonight demonstrates again his leadership qualities and the trust that all of us have in him. It also bodes well for the future to know that his loyal friendship will be there in 1984 and in subsequent times when Democrats call on him to make our party great and to keep a Democratic President in the White House. Arthur Krim, we thank you very much.

I hate to do this so early, but I also want to express my thanks to Bob Strauss—[laughter]—in advance. Very seldom when it is most significant to me, do I have a chance to thank Bob Strauss. But when it comes to Democratic Party unity, Bob is the reigning world's champion. He brought the party together in 1976. Had he not done so, we would not have had a Democrat serve as President.

He's doing it again. Unity meant victory then. Unity means that we will have another victory in 1980. Bob Strauss, I thank you.

And although I'm repeating some of the things that Senator Ted Kennedy has already mentioned, I do want to express the appreciation of all of us to Lee Kling and to Steve Smith, to Bob Fitzgerald and all those in this audience who have helped to make this fundraising event and this unity dinner a success.

Before I go further, I'd like to make a presentation from me and my wife Rosalynn. Last October I joined Senator Kennedy, Joan, the Kennedy family, and others who have such deep admiration for John Kennedy in dedicating the John F. Kennedy Library in Boston, Massachusetts. It was a moving experience for us all. And now I would like to make a contribution, if someone will bring it to me.

This is a watercolor sketch of President Kennedy by Jamie Wyeth. Jamie gave the portrait to me during the 1976 campaign. It's been hanging in my home in Plains and later in the family residence of the White House ever since. Rosalynn and I want this portrait to hang where it really belongs, where others can appreciate it. We would like to offer it to Senator Kennedy for display in the John F. Kennedy Library.

For those of you who knew personally and who loved and revered Jack Kennedy and for those of us who didn't know him personally, but who respected him and admired what he stood for, there is no doubt in our mind that Ted Kennedy carries on that great tradition in the finest sense of the word.

As a spokesman for the Democratic Party, as one who's tough and effective, a superb campaigner, as one who represents the finest aspect of his own family, as one who knows the historical perspective which has made the Democratic Party the majority party in this country and kept it there, as one who loves and cares for and leads for those who are disadvantaged, who are not rich or articulate or influential, but who reach out for assistance so they can stand on their own feet and enjoy the benefits of our great society, they could not have a better friend or supporter, a more effective advocate than Senator Ted Kennedy.

And let me say something else. He proves that we Democrats know how to battle hard among ourselves. But woe be unto those who face us when we're together. When we fight side by side like Democrats, that's exactly when we win like Democrats.

We have some excellent entertainment for you here tonight, and I don't want to compete with it, certainly not with Kirk Douglas, anyway. [*Laughter*] I'm having enough trouble with members of his profession this year already. [*Laughter*] Later Kirk will introduce some absolutely superb entertainment for you—Leonard Bernstein, Carol Channing, Billy Eckstine. Just the sound of their names brings music to our ears.

This has been an historic campaign in many ways. There have been divisions and demonstrations of unity. The issues have been discussed thoroughly. And I can't say that the Democrats have had a monopoly on grasping important issues; the Republicans have done their share.

For years scientists, for instance, have been grappling with the complexity of environmental pollution, and as Senator Kennedy pointed out earlier, Ronald Reagan has found the real culprit. He did misunderstand the scientists in one way. When they said that someone needs to attack the pollution problem at its roots—[*laughter*]—unfortunately, Governor Reagan took them literally.

Many Americans are very upset at the indictment of our flowers, our woodlands, and our trees. In fact, I hear that Smokey the Bear is going to come out of retirement to join with us—[laughter]—and demand equal time from the Republicans. It's up to us to accept Smokey the Bear in our ranks and use his notable persuasive powers to bring us to a victory next month.

We unite this evening as Democrats not just in opposition to the Republicans, but we unite under the banner that we all share and in which we all believe as Democrats.

I grew up in the Depression, and I saw the change in life and the attitude and the restored hopes that Franklin Roosevelt brought to my own family. Later I served in the Navy as an ensign and a lieutenant (jg.) and then as a lieutenant under a fighting Commander in Chief, Harry Truman. Even in uniform I cheered when he gave them hell.

I worked as a farmer later on during the civil rights days, when President John Kennedy sent a ray of hope and expectation among the downtrodden and those who had been suffering from deprivation of equal legal status in our society, followed by a great President, Lyndon Johnson. I felt the pride that they instilled in me as a Democrat and an American and the love that they both inspired in the breast of those who had been excluded.

Ours is a party of strength. Ours is a party of peace. We've kept our Nation out of war. We stand for equality under the law and also equality of opportunity. We stand for freedom of religious expression. We stand for freedom of conscience. We stand for economic progress, and we stand for social progress. These goals are just as valid today as they were when Jefferson drafted the Declaration of Independence. They're just as important today. They're

just as much worth our efforts to wage a real political fight.

Ours is a nation of great achievement, and tonight, as part of our entertainment, we will prove again the superb nature of art and its achievement in our country. Among the things of which we are so proud that has transcended the obstacles of international barriers, provided cultural understanding and admiration for our country is, of course, the film industry.

It's a privilege for me now, as President of our country, a proud President of our country, to introduce one of the finest representatives of our film industry, my friend, our friend, Kirk Douglas.

NOTE: The President spoke at 7:59 p.m. in Exhibit Hall A at the Sheraton Washington Hotel.

Nuclear Arms Control Policy

Remarks to Reporters on Departure From the White House. October 20, 1980

First of all, I'd like to make a very important announcement that earlier this morning it was finally decided that Greece, after several years of absence, will be completely reintegrated back into the NATO defense structure. This culminates a very long and detailed negotiation between Greece, Turkey, and the other members of NATO. This is a great step forward to the adequate defense of the southern flank of Western Europe.

Also, I want to make a statement on perhaps one of the most important issues in this campaign and a clear distinction between myself and Governor Reagan. Yesterday both he and I discussed our views on nuclear arms control. No issue is more vital to the future of this country.

No issue more clearly demonstrates the dramatic differences between Governor Reagan and me.

After reading his speech last night, I'm concerned that he does not understand the serious consequences of what he's proposing. He talks about peace and security, but talk is not enough.

Listen carefully to his nuclear arms control policy; first, throw the existing nuclear arms limitation treaty in the wastebasket; second, threaten the Soviet Union with a nuclear arms race; third, launch a quest for so-called nuclear superiority; finally, make the naive assumption that the Soviet response to all these steps will be to agree to new concessions and reductions in their nuclear arsenal.

Can anyone seriously believe that this would actually happen? Imagine for just one moment that President Brezhnev made a speech and said, first, "The Soviet Union is renouncing its agreement with the United States on nuclear arms control;" second, "The goal of the Soviet Union is nuclear superiority;" third, "The Soviet Union is ready to launch a nuclear arms race against the United States unless the Americans make additional concessions." How would I or any President of the United States respond to that? How would any American citizen respond? The answer is obvious. We would match them missile for missile, and SALT would be replaced by a new nuclear arms race.

It is extraordinarily naive to expect that the Soviet Union would meekly accept what we would immediately and totally reject. In my judgment that sort of expectation, if it became the policy of this Nation, would have the most serious consequences for the future. It would be a devastating and perhaps fatal blow to the long-term process of nuclear arms control, a process that has been nurtured and pursued by every President of the United States, Republican and Democrat, since Harry Truman occupied this office.

Twenty-four years ago President Eisenhower made this prediction, and I quote him: "When we get to the point, as some day we will, that both sides know that [in] any outbreak of general hostilities, regardless of the element of surprise, destruction will be both reciprocal and complete, possibly we will have sense enough to meet at the conference table with the understanding that the era of nuclear armaments has ended and the human race must conform its actions to this truth or die." Surely that time described by General Eisenhower, later President Eisenhower, has now come.

Thank you very much.

NOTE: The President spoke at 7:58 a.m. on the South Lawn of the White House.

Installment Sales Revision Act of 1980

Statement on Signing H.R. 6883 Into Law. October 20, 1980

I have signed H.R. 6883, the Installment Sales Revision Act of 1980. This bill is the first step in a continuing effort to clarify and simplify our enormously complex tax laws.

The reporting of gain on sales for future payment has been a model of pointless complexity, primarily due to the lack of a coordinated taxing structure. The inexperienced were often unable to take advantage of beneficial provisions of the law because of technical difficulties, while the unscrupulous were able to exploit its ambiguity in order to avoid paying their fair share of taxes.

The new legislation specifies that unless a taxpayer otherwise elects, income from a sale will be recognized as payments are received. This general rule expands the availability of the deferred reporting privilege, does away with many of the uncertainties and confusing provisions of the present law, and eliminates much fertile ground for error, abuse, and litigation.

Congress and the administration have worked for 2 years with legal and accounting associations and with organizations representing the banking industry, farmers, cattlemen, and small businesses to revise this confusing area of tax law.

I want to thank everyone involved for their disinterested commitment to the goal of simplification and to the integrity of the income tax law. I particularly want to thank Senators Russell Long and Bob Dole and Congressmen Al Ullman, Barber Conable, Dan Rostenkowski, and John Duncan for their leadership and bipartisan cooperation in securing passage of this bill and for helping to ensure that the simplification process will continue.

NOTE: As enacted, H.R. 6883 is Public Law 96–471, approved October 19.

Congressional Reports Elimination Act of 1980

White House Statement on the Signing of H.R. 6686.   October 20, 1980

The President has signed H.R. 6686, the Congressional Reports Elimination Act.

This legislation will cut Government redtape. It eliminates over 100 reports prepared each year by Government agencies—reports that hardly anyone reads but that the taxpayers pay for. This bill will save over $8 million per year.

The key sponsors of this bill were Representatives Jack Brooks and Donald Albosta. They deserve credit for this bill and for their efforts on the broad paperwork reduction act, which has passed the House and will be before the Senate in November.

NOTE: As enacted, H.R. 6686 is Public Law 96–470, approved October 19.

Beaver Falls, Pennsylvania

Remarks to City Residents.
October 20, 1980

Thank you very much, Mr. Mayor. Mayor Campese, Congressman Atkinson, Congressman Walgren, President McBride, Chairman Donatello, Senator Ross:

This is a very famous town for me and particularly for my mother, because she's one of the greatest admirers and almost in love with Joe Namath, and I'm glad to be here for her and for me.

This morning I came into Pittsburgh, drove here to Beaver Falls, and I go from here to Youngstown, Ohio, because I want to make a talk to you this morning about some subjects that are crucially important to everyone who lives in this important region, the backbone of one of the basic industries of our Nation. It's a pleasure to be back in Beaver Valley. As you know, I've saved the best areas for last in the campaign.

I wanted to see again the beautiful land and natural area that God has given to you. In 1978, I held a town meeting not far from here, in Aliquippa, and I wanted to come back to the Valley to talk to you about some of the choices that we face in this election. This is steel country, I know, and I'm glad to be here to talk about steel.

As a preliminary, I want to talk to you about another basic industry before I get to steel, and that is coal, because in this entire region, the industrial heartland of our country, these two basic industries are important to every American.

Since January of 1977, in Beaver County, we've had an increase in employment, in spite of very serious economic problems, of 7,100—7,100 more people now are employed in your county than there were the day that I was inaugurated President.

We still have a long way to go, obviously. We've worked out for the entire country an energy policy that will help us in the future not to be threatened again by OPEC oil price increases. In 1979, the OPEC oil nations increased the price of oil more in 1 year than oil prices had increased since it was first discovered in the 1800's, not very far from here.

We have decided to expand coal production, its domestic use, and its export to other countries. So far we have been very successful. This year we will produce more American coal—over 800 million tons—than has ever been produced in any year in the history of our country. This is a good start. What we've done in energy now provides us with a superb base on which to improve the entire American industrial complex.

We have a very important and exciting future ahead of us. And we have now brought together management of the steel industry, the steel workers under Lloyd McBride, the president who's here with me this morning, and our Government agencies to revitalize the very basic industry of steel. That's good news to you; it bodes well for the future. We have an exciting number of years ahead of us.

As you know, recently the chairman of the board of United States Steel, in this area, made a statement that confirms what I've just said. We've already seen a revitalization of the steel industry commence. In 1981, we'll see a further growth in the use of steel productivity. We've now restored the trigger price mechanism for the basic steel industry, and if it's possible to do so, after we determine that there's injury to the specialty steel industry itself, we will expand the trigger price mechanism or work out equivalently for specialty steel.

It's important that this be done. But first we had to reconstitute our approach to basic steel. The revitalization program that will be put into effect next year will give special tax breaks to the steel industry to reinvest back into areas like your own, where the steel management has not done an adequate job in the past. We'll give special depreciation rules to help with reinvestments in the steel industry, and for investment credit, we will let those now be made in cash rather than on credit for future income tax payments.

We also have worked out an agreement with the help of management in the steel industry—Lloyd McBride representing the steel workers—and the Environmental Protection Agency to make sure that in the future, environmental protection rules, as we honor the quality of air and water, will have a minimal adverse impact on employment in the steel industry. This is a good agreement, never before worked out between us in this country. We now have found effective, long-term aid for the industries of this area.

I'd like to make a few remarks now to remind you of what is at stake in your own life, in the lives of your families, and in your community when you go to the polls to vote on November the 4th. This has been a strong—this is a strong Democratic area, and it shows your sound judgment based on what's best for you.

All of you remember, who are old enough, as I am, the Great Depression years of the 1930's and early 1940's. All of you remember when Franklin D. Roosevelt proposed social security. The Democratic Congress worked hard to implement social security. The Republican Party and the Republican Members of Congress opposed social security. The Democrats finally got it passed. That is not just ancient history, because my opponent in this election has several times in recent years called for making participation in social security voluntary. This would mean that anyone, if they chose, could withdraw from making payments to the Social Security Trust Fund. It would mean that social security would very quickly go into bankruptcy and would be out of commission and out of the secure, permanent, sure future that retired Americans deserve.

All of you remember during the Great Depression years the argument about the minimum wage. The Democrats proposed the first minimum wage; it was only 25 cents an hour. The Republicans opposed the minimum wage. I graduated from high school in 1941. My first job was 40 cents an hour, 10 hours a day. When we increased from 25 cents to 40 cents an hour the minimum wage, the Democrats were for it; the Republicans were against it. That seems like ancient history, but my opponent in this election, Governor Reagan, says about the minimum wage, and listen to this: "The minimum wage," he said, "has been the cause of more misery and more unemployment than anything since the Great Depression." And this year when we had high unemployment in this country, Governor Reagan said, and I quote him again, "The high

unemployment in large measure is due to the minimum wage law."

Democrats have always been interested in working families. Democrats have always been eager to see people who work for a living be given a fair wage. Some of you have been affected, your own families have been affected by unemployment. We're working hard to put people back to work. But in the meantime, we must have unemployment compensation. Let me tell you what Governor Reagan said about unemployment compensation, and I quote him again: "Unemployment compensation," he said, "is just a prepaid vacation for freeloaders."

AUDIENCE. Boo.

THE PRESIDENT. Right. That's the kind of attitude that still prevails in the Republican Party.

So, when they try to give you misleading statements about what the differences are in this election, you remember ancient history like in the Great Depression years and how Democrats under Franklin Roosevelt, later Harry Truman, later John Kennedy, later Lyndon Johnson, have helped your life. And you remember the unchanging commitment to just the opposite principles expressed by my opponent in this election and by the Republican Party.

Finally, let me say a word about perhaps the most important issue that will face your life now and in the future, and that issue is a strong national defense on the one hand, which we all support, and peace on the other. The control of nuclear weapons is one of the most important issues, *the* important issue, in this election. We have got to have a continuation of the control of atomic weapons. Every President since Harry Truman, Democrat and Republican, has worked to put a balanced control, confirmable limit on nuclear weapons between ourselves and the Soviet Union.

My opponent, Governor Reagan, has abandoned that policy. He calls for three things: One is to throw the SALT treaty, which was negotiated under Presidents Nixon, Ford, and myself with the Soviet Union, in the wastebasket; secondly, he calls for playing a trump card of a nuclear arms race against Russia; and third, he calls for nuclear superiority, which sounds good on the face of it but has a very serious defect. What would you think if President Brezhnev made a speech and said that the nuclear arms control treaty—that we have negotiated over a 7-year period— that he was going to throw it in the wastebasket; secondly, that the Soviet Union would now start an arms race and demand not balanced nuclear forces but nuclear superiority for the Soviet Union and would play this as a card against the United States in order to make us, force us, to reach some better agreement?

Obviously, we would reject that proposal and, obviously, the Soviet Union will reject that proposal. These issues—social security, minimum wage, unemployment compensation, the protection of the steel industry, the extension of protections of specialty steel, the work that our Nation must continue for nuclear arms control, for a strong defense, and for peace—these are the issues that affect this Nation in the next 2 weeks.

I'll do the best I can as a Democratic candidate to care for the issues that are important to you. But the fate of this Nation, as a result of the outcome of the election, is not in my hands. I'll do the best I can, but the fate and the decision to be made on November the 4th is in your hands.

You've always shown sound judgment in the past in supporting Democrats who ran for President. Most of the time we've been successful. But I'd like for you to remember just a moment the 1968 campaign when a lot of Democrats were confused by a third candidate, and we did not give Hubert Humphrey the support he needed. The issues had not changed. It was still a fight between Republicans on the one hand, Richard Nixon, and Democrats on the other, Hubert Humphrey. And because a lot of people didn't work the last 2 weeks of the campaign for the principles that were important to their lives, Hubert Humphrey, who would have been a great President, never served in the Oval Office, and he was replaced by Richard Nixon. Let's don't let that happen in 1980. If you help me the next 2 weeks, we'll keep a Democrat in the White House and a better life for all of you.

Thank you very much. God bless you. Thank you.

NOTE: The President spoke at 10:20 a.m. outside the Carnegie Free Library.

Youngstown, Ohio

Remarks to City Residents.
October 20, 1980

Thank you very much, Senator John Glenn. I know the people of Ohio are proud of your Senator, aren't you? [*Applause*] The whole Nation feels the same way.

Let me say, first of all, that it's a great pleasure to be back in Ohio, a State that has suffered in some areas from the economic problems brought about by OPEC price increases. But Ohio has seen, since the day I was inaugurated, 418,000 more people on the job today than in January of 1977.

We have a long way to go. My goal is to make sure that all the Ohio utility companies have a right to use Ohio coal to make electricity. Also, my goal is to make sure we continue to produce more coal. This year we will produce more United States coal than any year in history, and in the future I want to see on the international energy markets OPEC oil replaced with Ohio coal. Will you help me do that? [*Applause*]

Let me say also that John Glenn has been one of the foremost leaders in bringing about control of atomic weapons. Every President since Harry Truman has seen the advantage of controlling nuclear weapons—Democrats and Republicans. Last year we signed a treaty with the Soviet Union as a result of 7 years of negotiations, under two Republican Presidents and myself. Now my opponent, Governor Reagan, has advocated that we scrap this treaty, throw it in a wastebasket, and he calls for a nuclear arms race against the Soviet Union. This is a very serious matter of great concern to all Americans. It's important for us to prevent other nations from having atomic weapons who do not now have them. Governor Reagan's response to that is that nonproliferation is none of our business. This is a very dangerous attitude for a President to take.

We have, in this country, a real commitment in the Democratic Party for working families of this Nation. The Democrats are the ones who gave us minimum wage. My opponent, Governor Reagan, says that minimum wage has caused us more misery and more unemployment than anything since the Great Depression. Many of your families have suffered because of temporary unemployment. Governor Reagan says unemployment compensation is a prepaid vacation for freeloaders. Governor Reagan got his start in politics campaigning around this

Nation against Medicare, and he's advocated social security be made voluntary on four different occasions.

All of you know the advantages in the last 50 years when Democratic Presidents were in the White House. We made steady progress, for a better life for all Americans, a strong defense, a commitment to peace, the control of nuclear weapons, stopping the spread or proliferation of atomic weapons around the world, a strong minimum wage, unemployment compensation, increase in the use of American coal in dealing with the energy problem, bringing peace to the Middle East. Those are the kinds of issues that are at stake.

If you'll help me the next 2 weeks, we'll keep a Democratic administration in Washington, reelect John Glenn, keep a President in the White House who cares about you and have another great victory for—[*inaudible*].

Thank you very much. If you'll help me, we'll win together. Thank you.

NOTE: The President spoke at 11:35 a.m. outside the studios of WFMJ–TV.

Youngstown, Ohio

Remarks and a Question-and-Answer Session During a Live Television Broadcast.   October 20, 1980

THE PRESIDENT. First of all, let me say how delighted I am to be here in Youngstown, Mahoning Valley, back again with you after having visited here several times in the past.

CAMPAIGN ISSUES

I would like to say that this has been a time of great economic problems for the entire world, with the very unprecedented increase in OPEC oil prices foisted on the rest of the world by the OPEC nations. Last year the price of oil increased more in 1 year than it had in all the historic time since oil was first discovered in Pennsylvania in the 1800's. Most nations have been severely hurt by this unprecedented oil price increase. Our Nation has been hurt as well, but we've come through that period of trial and testing compatibly with the principles and ideals and strengths that our Nation has always shown.

Since I became President in January of 1977, there have been more than 400,000 net new jobs added in Ohio alone. In the Youngstown-Mahoning Valley area, because of your heavy dependence on steel and a general slowdown in construction, you have had to suffer a great deal. I sympathize with those families that have been placed on temporary unemployment, but would like to report to you, as you undoubtedly well know, in the last few months the steel industry leaders, both in management and in labor, the Steel Workers, have worked very closely with our administration.

We now have a strong trigger-price mechanism in effect for basic steel, and we are now exploring ways where, if possible, we will extend the trigger-price mechanism to specialty steels as well. We have also proposed a revitalization program for the steel industry, which will be very helpful with accelerated depreciation and by giving investment tax credits on a cash basis to encourage the steel management to put their profits back into the communities that have been adversely affected by changing times and some obsolescence in the steel industry.

The last thing that we've done with the steel has been to improve the relationship between the Environmental Protection Agency and the steel industry, a harmonious relationship has now been worked out, an agreement whereby, over a longer period of time, the steel industry can comply with environmental standards and at the same time have enough capital to improve their plants and to make more jobs available to steelworkers.

Lately, we've seen the economy recovering very well. I think we've bottomed out now in the recession. I think we're well on the way toward a full recovery.

In coal—this, of course, is also a very important issue for the people of Ohio. This year, because of the new energy policy, we'll have more coal produced in our country than in any year in history. That's a superb record. And my goal is to make sure that all the utility companies in Ohio have the right and the chance to use Ohio coal for the production of electricity. We have a great way to go in the future to completely revitalize industry and to put our people back to work.

As you know the election now is only about 2 weeks away, and the issues drawn, which I'm sure you'll want to discuss with me, are very sharp between myself and my opponent, Governor Reagan, and historically between the Democratic Party of this Nation and the Republican Party.

I grew up during the Depression years, where the Democrats fought for the minimum wage, the Republicans fought against it; sought it increased regularly, the Republicans were against it. My opponent thinks that the major cause of unemployment now is the minimum wage. And he also says that minimum wage has caused more misery and more unemployment than anything since the Great Depression.

Unemployment compensation is crucial for working families. We are now working to get an extension of 13 additional weeks, for those that are temporarily unemployed. My opponent says, on the other hand, that unemployment compensation is just a prepaid vacation for freeloaders.

This is the kind of difference, just to illustrate two points, that is crucial and will be decided in this election.

Later I hope we'll have a chance to discuss controlling nuclear weapons. Senator John Glenn met me this morning and is here in the studio audience with us. He's been one of the foremost proponents fighting for the control of nuclear weapons with a balanced agreement which has been the goal of every President since Harry Truman. Lately, again, as you know, my opponent has called for the scrapping of the treaty to control nuclear weapons, the initiation of a major nuclear arms race—therefore playing a trump card against the Soviet Union. This is a sharp departure from what all Presidents have done and these are the kinds of issues that I'm sure we'll be discussing this morning.

Again, let me say that I'm delighted to be with you, and now we'll welcome any questions from the audience.

QUESTIONS

EQUAL RIGHTS AMENDMENT

Q. Mr. President, Governor Reagan and the Republican Party have stated their opposition to the equal rights amendment. For what reason should the American women support your candidacy for President?

THE PRESIDENT. The last remaining legal discrimination on the lawbooks of our country is against women. Every Republican Party platform in the last 40 years has favored the equal rights amendment. Governor Reagan's position and the Republican convention this year under his leadership came out for the first time against the equal rights amendment. Six previous Presidents who served in the White House before me, Democrats and Republicans, were for the equal rights amendment.

There's been a great deal of distortion about what the equal rights amendment says. The equal rights amendment only says this: That you cannot take away a person's rights for equality by the Federal Government or the State government. That's all it says. It's the prohibition against the Federal or State government's taking away anybody's rights because of sex, because they're women.

I believe it's very important that we have the equal rights amendment passed. It'll be a major step forward and will help all Americans. Women, now, when they work an equal amount with men and the man makes a dollar for what he does, the woman only gets 59 cents. This is not right, it's not fair.

In the past, we've had women discriminated against as we have had some minority groups. I've tried to redress this in my appointments to the Cabinet offices. I've appointed more women in the Cabinet than all other Presidents combined. I've appointed more Federal judges who are women than all Presidents combined in the last 200 years.

We have a long way to go, but I think the best way to make sure that women do have a right to head families, to contribute their part to a growing society, and to have equal treatment under the law, is to ratify the equal rights amendment. It will be a major goal of mine now that we've got the extension of time for the ratification, and I believe that if I'm elected President, we will have the equal rights amendment passed. If Governor Reagan should be elected—and I hope that he won't—then equal rights for women, I think, would be dead for a long time.

U.S. GRAIN SALES

Q. As you know, the Russian grain sales, a couple of years ago, caused higher food prices and this fueled inflation. Now, we're already being told there are—higher food prices are to come, due to this pending grain sale to to China. We find this, in the grassroots, hard to rationalize, providing that it's going to cost us all this extra money, and we have to pay this little penalty. Could you respond to this and tell us what you might do to help this situation?

THE PRESIDENT. I'll try to.

As you probably remember, when Presidents Nixon and Ford were in office and Earl Butz was the Secretary of Agriculture, the Republican administration on several occasions imposed an embargo against the shipment of American grain overseas just to force down farm prices and to help economically to hold down prices artificially. We have not done that. We have tried to boost American grain sales and agricultural product sales ever since I've been in office. As a farmer myself I know the devastating effect on a farm family when grain prices and other agricultural product prices go wildly up and then wildly down after the farmers sell their crops.

We've done a couple of things. One is we've provided farm storage for American grain so that farm families can keep the grain under their control on their own farms and then market it in an orderly way to provide a smooth transition on prices and at the same time give the farmer more of the profit as prices do go up somewhat, instead of middlemen who used to buy at harvest season, hold the grain back, force the price up, and then sell at the great expense to the families who were consumers and the farmers didn't benefit at all.

When the Soviets invaded Afghanistan I had three options to use the enormous power of our country, either military options, to go into war, or to exert political persuasion and economic persuasion on the Soviets to convince them that it's not to their advantage to invade a freedom-loving country like Afghanistan. I decided to take the political and the economic steps against the Soviet Union.

We got other nations to join us in the United Nations. A hundred and four other countries condemned the Soviets' invasion and demanded their withdrawal from Afghanistan. The Moslem countries later, some of whom have been very close friends with the Soviet Union, said to the Soviet Union, "Get out of Afghanistan." We organized about 50 other countries to join us in not participating in the boycott—I mean in the Olympics in Moscow, because that would have been a demonstration of our approval of their invasion and occupation of Afghanistan.

We've tried to compensate for that interruption of grain sales with the Soviet Union. I decided that we would not sell to the Soviet Union in 1980 any extra grain above what the governments themselves had agreed to. So, we put an embargo against the sale of that extra grain to the Soviet Union. After we did that I wanted to be sure that farmers did not suffer because they couldn't sell their grain. So, we've tried to open up in foreign countries now additional new opportunities to sell American farm products.

We are producing more grain, we are storing more on farms, and we're selling more overseas. This helps our country, in my judgment, and the price of grain and other farm products has been relatively stable, compared to what it was during previous administrations. We've sold to Mexico, for instance, this year about 10 million tons of American grain. We've just signed a new agreement with China to sell them more grain. This will provide practically a negligible increase in grain prices, but it will give our Nation a much stronger dollar overseas. It will give us great exports which will build up jobs in this country for all kinds of advantages and also give the farmers a more stable income.

So, I think in the long run what we can sell in American products overseas is good for all of us and the adverse effect on us, on inflation, will be very slight, compared to the advantages that we derive.

UNEMPLOYMENT AND INFLATION

Q. Why can't all the great minds in this country sit down and work out a commonsense solution to unemployment and inflation?

THE PRESIDENT. Well, some great minds have tried to do it and with some success. You know, people tend to dwell on the temporary inconveniences and the transient problems that our Nation faces. But if you look back—you're a very young woman—but if you look back on history, just in this century, our country has faced enormous problems and challenges: the First World War, the Second World War, the Great Depression, the divisiveness of the Vietnam conflict, the social changes that took place in our society when blacks and other minorities got the rights that they had not had before, the deep embarrassment of Watergate. Our country's faced those enormous challenges successfully. Whenever the American people could understand the problems and unite together, we've been able to overcome them.

We now have severe economic challenges, but compared to most other nations on Earth, we have been blessed enormously. When we are unemployed now, because of solid Democratic commitments to working families, we have unemployment compensation. When there is a temporary inconvenience because of excessive imports, we have, as you know, a special program for the retraining of workers and for the carrying them over of a time until we can get our own industry in a competitive position.

When buying habits change, like Americans now buy the more efficient automobiles, it kind of caught the automobile industry by surprise. Now we are retooling and turning out American automobiles that are more durable, more safe, just as efficient as any cars on Earth. And I believe that American buyers now, when they go to the showrooms, will give American cars a chance in their own families' buying plans. This will keep American workers on the job.

Since I've been in office we've emphasized employment. We've added a net increase of 8½ million jobs in this country since January of 1977. We've never added that many new jobs in any President's administration before in history, even during time of war. This is a very good step forward. We also are providing better and more stable conditions for employment. A couple of years ago every time you picked up the paper, for instance, you would see a wildcat coal strike, with mines closed down and buyers who wanted to use American coal uncertain about whether they could get coal anymore. You haven't seen that since we got a good working relationship between management or the coal operators, the coal miners, and the Government. We are increasing coal production more this year than ever before in history.

Also, the inflation rate has been primarily caused to increase by OPEC more than doubling the price of oil last year. Now we are trying to put into effect a new energy policy that's paying rich dividends. We'll have more oil and gas wells drilled in this country this year than ever before in history. And compared to last year alone, every day now we import about a third less oil from overseas than we did just a year ago—a saving of about 2 million barrels of oil per day. This means that we don't import oil, we don't import inflation, we don't import unemployment. We are conserving in this country and producing more energy ourselves.

So, you watch the evening news and you see the newspaper headlines, and it's always the arguments and the divisions and the debates and the temporary disappointments and the bad news. But when you look at how our Nation compares now with what we have faced before, this unemployment and inflation level, although it's too high and we're trying to get it down, is still under control. And now if a family is suffering from temporary unemployment, you have at least not hunger and deprivation, but a government and private industry working together to make sure that the suffering is minimized.

Don't forget how great our country is. Don't forget how able we have been in the past to meet these kinds of challenges. And don't forget that the best minds and the best hearts, represented in this room, are still working to cut down even further on unemployment and inflation and give Americans an even better life than we enjoy already.

LOAN GUARANTEE FOR STEELMILL PROJECT

Q. Mr. President, since 1977 four major steelplants in the Mahoning Valley have closed permanently, and 10,000 steelworkers have lost their jobs. The only hope for regaining some of these jobs appears to be the $100 million in loan guarantees which your administration pledged to this valley in 1978 for viable steelmaking projects. A study recently completed by independent consultants under an EDA grant has concluded that the loan—with loan guarantees, a steelworker-sponsored plan to reopen the McDonald mill recently closed by U.S. Steel, and to put 750 to 1,000 steelworkers back in productive employment is feasible and within EDA guidelines.

What I would like to know is: One, do you support the worker plan to reopen these mills? Two, will you, at this time, make a public commitment to this community that EDA will immediately and without delay evaluate this proposal? Three, can the steelworkers expect a decision on their proposal before election day?

THE PRESIDENT. Yes. I will make a commitment to you that EDA will expedite this decision and make a judgment, working with the people in this community, to decide whether or not the steelmills can be put back into full operation.

As you know—as you may know, since I've been in office, we have allotted to this region, in the Mahoning Valley area, almost a quarter of a billion dollars in guaranted loans under EDA to rebuild the steelmills, to provide for possible modernization of them, and at the same time, have let EDA loans be applied to other related industries that provide jobs in this community. About $30 million in an EDA loan was recently approved for commuter aircraft, for instance, which will provide 1,500 permanent jobs of a very high quality for this region.

I can't comment to you, as much as I would like to, here on this spot, about whether or not the ultimate $100 million loan will be approved. But I can guarantee you that if the project proves feasible, as judged jointly by EDA specialists and by those who'll be responsible permanently for the financing and operations of plants, that I will certainly approve it.

I might repeat one thing that I said in my opening statement. We've made a lot of progress in the steel industry and in the automobile industry and the coal industry by trying to bring better harmony between labor and management, by making sure that the Government environmental standards are worked out very clearly now and in the future between the industry and the Environmental Protection Agency, so that there is a predictability about it, and the shocks that had formerly occurred before I became President forcing the steelmills to shut down when they did not anticipate the requirements will be el'minated. And secondly, we will put into effect next year a tax incentive that will encourage the industry itself, with great benefit to themselves, to reinvest in the communities that have in the past been dependent on steel and to modernize plants that presently exist and also to build new plants using the high technology available at this time.

So, $225 million in guaranteed loans by EDA under my administration has been or will be made available in the Mahoning Valley area to rebuild a more modern and more viable and more permanent steel industry in this area.

ABORTION

Q. Mr. President, how can you as a professed Christian take the stand you do in support of abortion?

THE PRESIDENT. I do not support abortion. I am against abortion, and I personally have done everything I could as President to minimize any need for abortion. I have never been in favor, for instance, of government financing for abortions unless the prospective mother's life was in danger or unless the pregnancy was a result of rape or incest. I am not in favor of a constitutional amendment to totally prohibit abortion.

I might point out that although my personal beliefs are as I described them to you, as President I have taken an oath to uphold the laws of the United States as interpreted by the Supreme Court of the United States. So, if the Supreme Court should rule, as they have, on abortion and other sensitive issues contrary to my own personal beliefs, I have to carry out, in accordance with my solemn oath and my duties as President, the ruling of the Supreme Court.

So, I think I've described it to you accurately. I'm personally against abortion. I'd do everything I can to minimize abortion. I do not favor any government financing for abortion. But my duties and my oath require me to carry out the ruling of the Supreme Court and the laws already in the books.

ETHICS IN GOVERNMENT

Q. Mr. President, our democracy was based on the idea of government for the people, by the people, and of the people, but nowadays, it seems that our government can be bought for the right price. How could you, as President, help change the image of America?

THE PRESIDENT. Well, there have always been, in politics, and in labor, and in all the professions, including law or education, a few people who violate their standards of morality and decency and even violate the law. I think that since the Watergate crisis, there has been a renewed and intense, investigatory attitude in the press and a very high standard of political ethics required by the American people to be sure that we don't repeat the embarrassment of Watergate.

Whenever, now, an allegation is made against anyone in my administration, for instance, the law is that a Special Prosecutor has to be appointed to investigate that particular charge. One allegation was made a few months ago against Hamilton Jordan, who was my Chief of Staff, with a very high degree of publicity. The Attorney General appointed a Special Prosecutor, an independent Republican, effective past U.S. attorney, who investigated all the charges. The findings were that the four people who accused Hamilton Jordan of having done something improper concerning drugs were all liars. They perjured themselves. Three of them are in prison now, and the other one has been acknowledged to be lying as well. But the publicity that is brought about by the investigation of these allegations and a high degree of openness in government now, I think, is very good.

We want to make sure that the standards are kept high. Recently, you've seen an additional set of stories about the so-called Abscam scandal, where a few Members of Congress did accept bribes for alleging to help some so-called sheiks from the Arab oil countries. Those investigations have gone on by the FBI, compatible with the American laws, and as you know, a maximum degree of publicity has accrued from it. And I believe, as a result of that, although it was a very embarrassing and bad situation, that again we'll have a higher standard of performance and a very careful avoidance of any repetition of bribery in the Congress.

I don't have any way to apologize to you for the things that have been done wrong. But I do point out that when something is done wrong now, it is investigated more thoroughly; more publicity is focused on the violation of standards or ethics or propriety; and all the laws now

require a public revelation of involvement of this kind that did not exist before.

So, I think that in the post-Watergate era, we will see less violation of the law, more publicity when it does occur, and a steady progress towards more ethical government.

AUTOMOBILE AND STEEL INDUSTRIES

Q. Mr. President, I was wondering why you took and bailed out Chrysler Corporation and you didn't bail out the steel industries and your saying that the steel industries were helped out and are improving, but why was Chrysler bailed out before the steel companies were?

THE PRESIDENT. I'll try to answer that. Let me say that steel is such a basic industry that what happens to automobile production in this country is vital to the steel industry. One of the reasons that we have a slowdown now in steel production in our country has been because of changed buying habits in the Nation concerning automobiles and, therefore, reduction in how many cars the American automobile manufacturers produce.

When Chrysler was threatened with bankruptcy, it was my judgment, confirmed later by the Congress, that the United States Government should guarantee loans to Chrysler. This is a very safe loan guarantee. Chrysler was required to reorganize itself to have a much more efficient plan, to have much more careful supervision of the management of the company, and to get sound loans from private banks in order for them to stay in business and avoid bankruptcy. Under those circumstances, the Federal Government agreed to guarantee some of those loans. But the loans were made not by the Federal Government, but by private banks and insurance companies and others to

Chrysler. I think this is a very good thing for our Government to do. We will not lose any money on it and Chrysler has been kept intact as a viable automobile industry, and about 225,000 jobs were saved.

I might add that when Governor Reagan was questioned about this Chrysler loan, he says, "What's wrong with bankruptcy?" I think this deep concern about my administration for the protection of an industry like Chrysler, keeping sound loans, not giving away or wasting or endangering the integrity of the taxpayers' money, is a good step.

We are working very closely with steel management now. And Lloyd McBride, who's the president, as you know, of the Steel Workers, flew in with me from Washington to Pittsburgh this morning, and he's accompanying me on this trip. The steelworkers' union knows how much we have done jointly to keep the steel industry intact. The president or chairman of the board of U.S. Steel announced recently in this area that he expected the steel production to increase steadily in the months ahead, with at least a 12-percent increase in steel production in our country next year alone.

So, I think the steel industry is sound. I think Chrysler is also sound. And keeping a viable coal industry, a viable automobile industry are both very important to steel. It's just a different proposition. We don't see any need at this time to have the Government take over part of the management of the steel industry nor provide for guaranteed Government loans. The steel industry is perfectly able to get what loans they can as a nationwide problem, but in the Mahoning Valley, where some of the steel industries do need guaranteed loans, then we are providing, as I said in an earlier answer, almost $250 billion in Government guaranteed loans for the steel industry.

We are not discriminating against steel, as we helped Chrysler. We are providing guaranteed loans for both steel and Chrysler, but the two situations are somewhat different.

Yes, sir? Back there in the pink shirt.

PROTECTION OF U.S. PERSONNEL ABROAD

Q. Mr. President, what precautions have you taken to avert a similar situation such as the takeover of our hostages in Iran happening in another country?

THE PRESIDENT. Since the wave of terrorism went across the world, not only with our hostages being taken but, as you know, other nations' hostages being taken in this hemisphere and also in the Mideast and other places, we have beefed up security at our Embassies. But I don't want to mislead you about it. It's not possible for us to station enough U.S. Marines in any capital in the world to withstand the mob action of tens of thousands or hundreds of thousands of terrorists or demonstrators, unless the host country gives us their support and adequate protection.

In all the history of diplomacy, I guess all the recorded history of diplomacy, we've never seen a case where a government like the one that existed in Iran not only did not protect the Embassies of foreign countries but actually encouraged terrorists or militants to attack the American Embassy. This is an extraordinary circumstance, and I don't believe it will be repeated. But we will continue to work closely with the governments.

When we had a threat to our Embassy in Pakistan, Islamabad, I personally called President Zia on the phone that morning, and he deployed Pakistani soldiers to protect the Embassy people there.

We had the same thing happen in Libya. We've had the same thing happen to some degree in other countries, including Colombia, with our Ambassador.

So, they are safer than they used to be. We are much more cautious. We don't have as many Embassy staff members present in areas where disharmony or violence might occur, and we have called on foreign countries to help us as a preparatory or precautionary thing to prevent a recurrence of what happened in Iran. I don't think there's any real likelihood that a government like Iran, combined with demonstrators and terrorists like occurred in Iran, will repeat itself.

Yes, ma'am—in the back row.

LILLIAN CARTER

Q. Mr. President. I would like to know how your mother is feeling?

THE PRESIDENT. Thank you very much. My mother is getting along fine. She's 82 years old. She had a very severe hip fracture, and they had to put one of those stainless steel pins in her hip and along the femur, which is the upper leg bone. She's sitting up a little bit now in the hospital room. We hope she'll be out of the hospital at the end of this week.

One time when I called her, she said, "Don't bother me now, Jimmy. I'm watching the ballgame." And I might say that—I want to be perfectly frank with you, since the Dodgers were eliminated, she's been a real strong Phillies fan, and she's been pleased last night.

But I think Mother will be out of the hospital at the end of this week. And then she'll have to be confined to a wheelchair for 2 to 3 more months before she can start to walk again. She's in good spirits. Her heart and everything are just like a young person's.

JERUSALEM

Q. Mr. President, what would be your most explicit statement on the future of Jerusalem?

THE PRESIDENT. First of all, I look upon a strong and secure Israel as an integral part of the security of our own country. And the help that we give Israel in retaining their freedom—economic aid, military aid, and a chance for security, is a direct investment in better security for my own country and yours.

Secondly, the biggest thing that's happened to provide Israel with freedom and security has been the treaty between Israel and Egypt. Egypt is by far the most powerful, strong, Arab country there is. And as you know, 7 years ago there was a war between Israel and Egypt, the fourth war in the 25 years that Israel had been in existence. Now Israel is at peace with Egypt.

Third, when we were at Camp David, we worked out between President Sadat and Prime Minister Begin, with my help, an agreement on Jerusalem, and this mirrors our position. We think that Jerusalem should be forever undivided. We think that worshipers should have free access to the holy places of Jerusalem. Third, we believe that the ultimate permanent status, legal status, of Jerusalem should be decided through negotiations, and last, that the final agreement reached in those negotiations would have to be acceptable to the Government of Israel.

INTEREST RATES

Q. Mr. President—[*inaudible*]—I am concerned with high interest rates. Homebuilding all over the country is down. The Youngstown-Mahoning County area is down 40 percent from last year. When you are reelected, what do you propose to do to lower these rates, if in fact they can be lowered? And will you be successful, and when can we hope to see some relief?

THE PRESIDENT. Obviously the interest rate is tied directly to the inflation rate. There are several ways that we can reduce the inflation rate, and we'll be working on all of them simultaneously.

First of all, we need to increase the productivity of American workers to make sure that the American worker, now the most productive on Earth, has modern tools and modern plants in which to work. That is an anti-inflationary trend.

Secondly, we need to make sure we continue to cut down on imports of foreign oil, because the amount of foreign oil we've been importing in the past has been excessive. That has been a major inflationary factor.

Third, we need to make sure we continue to reduce Federal Government spending and reduce the Federal Government deficit. We now have the Federal Government spending, growing at less than one-half the rate it was when I was elected President in 1976. And as a percentage of the gross national product, the Federal deficit now is less than one-half what it was when I was running for President in 1976. We're going to continue to work for a balanced budget.

The other thing is that—I've mentioned before—we need to have a much better working relationship among the Government, the workers and management in industry to eliminate the disharmony that exists. Let me just use the coal industry as a repetition.

In the past, we always had a continual stream of arguments and wildcat strikes in the coal industry until I became President. We sat down in the Roosevelt Room next to the Oval Office, and we worked out a procedure by which, instead of just

facing each other as enemies or antagonists or adversaries across a bargaining table when the contract was about to expire, now the coal workers, United Mine Workers, the coal mine operators, and the Government work together to make sure that we have a steady supply of coal on the market, which tends to stabilize price, and maximum emphasis on the export of American goods overseas, which helps us to control inflation.

The other point is this. It's very important for us to avoid protectionism. If we ever start trying to erect barriers between nations to prevent the free flow of trade, it would not only eliminate American jobs that produce goods that are sold overseas, including farmers and others, but it'll also mean that the products we buy here will be much more costly. I hope that Americans in the months ahead, when they get ready to buy a camera, when they get ready to buy an automobile or other products or a television set, will give American products a chance, because now we've got American automobiles, for instance, as I said earlier, that are more durable, more safe, and just as fuel-efficient as any imported cars. And I hope that Americans will give those American cars a chance, to keep American workers employed. These are the kinds of things, collectively, that will be done.

The other thing is, I think we need to continue the pressure, proper pressure on banks and other institutions not to boost their interest rates higher than economic circumstances warrant. In the past, the prime rate that banks charged was the rate they would charge their best customers, and then, for an average customer like myself who is, a farmer and a very small businessman, they would charge me maybe 1 percent or 1½ percent above the prime rate. That's the way it used to be.

Now, the banks set a prime rate artificially, and still charge me 1 to 1½ percent above the prime rate, but they charge their best customers a lot lower interest rate than the prime. So, this tends to jack up interest rates above what they ought to be. And I think the Congress and I and others need to look more closely in the future at this particular issue that I just described to you. A couple of lawsuits have been brought now in this country accusing the banks—I don't know what the ultimate result will be—accusing the banks of setting their prime rate higher than the prime ought to be. And, as you know, the prime rate affects the price of homes.

This last month, we had very good news on homebuilding. We are now at a rate of building homes more than 1½ million per year, which is very good. And general construction went up about 12 or 15 percent last month, compared to the previous month. So, the building industry, the construction industry is coming back well, but as we get inflation under control and interest rates down, it'll do much better.

U.S.-IRANIAN RELATIONS

Q. Mr. President, the hostages in Iran right now—what kind of relationship will we have with Iran once they're released?

THE PRESIDENT. You probably realize that this has been one of the most difficult things that I've ever had to face. I never go a day or even an hour without thinking about our hostages and what we can do to get them back.

I've had two guiding principles in my life, as President, since the hostages were first taken. One is to protect the integrity and the interest of my country, and secondly, not to do anything, as President, under political pressures or any other reason, that would endanger the lives or safety of the hostages or interfere with their safe return to freedom as soon as possible.

We've imposed strict prohibitions against any trade or commerce with Iran. We don't sell them oil equipment; we don't sell them spare parts for their military; we don't sell them anything that we can control under these circumstances. If Iran should release the hostages, then I would unfreeze their assets, which are several billions of dollars that were in banks here and in Europe. I would drop the embargo against trade with Iran and work toward a resumption of normal commerce with Iran in the future. It's to our advantage to have a strong Iran. It's to our advantage to have a united Iran, and we don't want to see the war that presently exists between Iraq and Iran be expanded any further in those two countries, and we don't want to see it involve other nations either.

So, we want a peaceful Iran, a united Iran, a strong Iran, with a government that they choose. And we want to restore normal commerce and trade with Iran once those hostages are released.

YOUTH EDUCATION AND EMPLOYMENT

Q. Mr. President, I am—[inaudible]—and I would like to know what programs—[inaudible]—you have planned—[inaudible]—reelected?

THE PRESIDENT. Thank you very much.

One of the goals that I had when I became President was to make sure that any young person in this country who was qualified to do college work would have a chance to go to college, no matter how poor the family might be. I believe that I can tell you that we have reached that goal. We've had now a combination of laws passed by the Congress, with Senator Glenn's help, that would give guaranteed loans or grants or work-study programs or special scholarships for young people. I don't believe now that any young person that's able to do college work is kept out of college because the family's poor.

Secondly, we've tried to increase the allocation of Federal funds for education, particularly to those students who live in poor communities or who need special help, and we've done it with a philosophy that I have of not letting the Federal Government interfere in the operation of the schools, either public or private. I think the operation of the schools, the curriculum, the hiring of teachers, and so forth ought to be strictly local and State officials, not the Federal Government.

We've improved considerably opportunities for work among young people. Now we have before the Congress a major piece of legislation—it's already passed the House; it's now in the Senate—that would provide about $2 billion over the next 2 years to add about 600,000 more jobs for young people at the junior and senior high school level on up. At the same time, I was interested in seeing these jobs provided not as government jobs, but jobs that are permanent, career jobs in the private sector, so that if a young person has a hard time getting a job, if he gets one with a TV studio or Coca Cola company or one of the automobile manufacturers or in a steelplant, the government would help provide some training for that young person, maybe in the high school or local vocational-technical school, and after a few weeks—and the young person was able to hold that job permanently—then the government would get out of it and the young person would be employed.

We have kept about a million summer youth jobs in this country ever since I've been in office. In addition to that, we have had, I think, a very good career emphasis on young people that want to go into the military. I spent 11 years in the Navy. Senator Glenn was also in the military for a long time. And I would like to encourage young people who want to go through a transition phase and have a fine career either as President of the United States or a U.S. Senator or whatever they want to do, to spend a couple years maybe in the American military, in the volunteer forces. It's a very wonderful way to see the world, to perform a patriotic duty, to get a good education, to get a good career planning. And that's the kind of opportunity that our Government would welcome and would be very helpful.

These are some of the things that come to my mind just offhand about the future. But I think our country is already the greatest nation on Earth, and I don't have any doubt that in the future it will be even greater for your generation.

NATIONAL HEALTH INSURANCE

Q. Mr. President, as a senior citizen I would like to know why countries like England and Germany have national health insurance and a great country like ours doesn't? What do you think about national health insurance?

THE PRESIDENT. I think we ought to have it. I'm strongly in favor of it. As you know, this has been one of the programs for senior citizens that has most vividly separated the Republicans from the Democratic Party.

You remember in the Depression years, when President Roosevelt came out and proposed social security. The Republicans were strongly against it. Lately, my opponent has advocated making social security voluntary, which means that people that don't want to participate in social security don't have to. It would damage social security and maybe even bring it into bankruptcy. I think it would.

Governor Reagan got his career started in politics by campaigning around the Nation against Medicare. This is a very serious threat to the security of people your age or older. We also have a real need to extend the benefits of Medicare to a nationwide comprehensive health insurance program.

I strongly support it. We've made our proposal to the Congress, and this will be a major goal for me in the future. You might be interested in knowing that Governor Reagan has come out strongly against national health insurance. We want the emphasis to be on the prevention of disease, strict hospital cost containment to hold down the cost of medical care; an emphasis on outpatient treatment rather than treating people in the hospitals; an emphasis on home care for those that have a family and can live at home; an emphasis on catastrophic health insurance, first of all, so that the family that has a very high medical bill can have help from the Government in paying those bills; and an emphasis on—this doesn't affect you directly, but I'm sure affects those you love—an emphasis on the prevention of illnesses in a little baby, both before the baby is born, when the mother is pregnant, and also in the early years of childhood, with immunization programs and the proper diet that will get that baby off to a good start. The sum total of this would be to give Americans much better health care, prevent disease, and hold down severely the extraordinary costs that Americans are paying for health care now.

So, this is a sharp distinction between the basic philosophy and commitment of the Democratic Party, that stands for social security, Medicare, national health insurance, contrasted with the Republican Party, including my opponent, whose party has been against social security,

against Medicare, and against national health insurance.

PROGRAMS FOR THE HANDICAPPED

Q. Mr. President, we have a deaf child who has to ride a bus for 1 hour and 15 minutes to the nearest school suitable for his needs. They have parents of a mentally retarded child who have to search for 8 years for a school suitable for their child's needs. My question is: What programs are presently under way to better the education of all children, handicapped and otherwise, and what, if reelected, do you plan to do for the betterment of education for elementary school age children?

THE PRESIDENT. We've had a more than 200-percent increase since I've been in office in special education, education for the disadvantaged children of all ages. Also, we've had a very difficult challenge in changing the basic law of our land for the handicapped people. Now we've made great strides. We've implemented the handicapped act, that was passed before I became President, and there's a much more clear commitment of the Government to provide special care for handicapped people of all kinds.

We had a White House conference on the handicapped. You may or may not know about it, but I attended that conference and worked on it. When I first became President, I appointed my wife as the Honorary Chairman of a special commission on mental health. She worked for 2 years. And late in 1978, early in 1979, we made a proposal to the Congress encompassing the recommendations of her mental health commission to the Congress. Recently, with Senator Kennedy's help, Senator Glenn's, and others, we passed the Mental Health Systems Act of 1980. It is landmark legislation that will provide increased funding, increased educational opportunities for young people who are emotionally disturbed, who are mentally retarded, or who have some other mental illness.

We had a signing ceremony for that only 2 weeks ago in Virginia, when my wife and Senator Kennedy and others who had worked on it were there for the ceremony. The implementation of that act will be another major step forward in the care of disadvantaged people in our society. The thrust of it is manifold, but one thing that I'm very interested in is that all of the efforts have been to give a handicapped person not only treatment and care but primarily to give them a chance to take whatever talent God gave them and to use that talent to strengthen our society and to let them be more self-sufficient and let them live normal lives.

We've also emphasized the hiring of handicapped. Max Cleland, who is the director of the Veterans Administration, had a special program for hiring handicapped veterans who were hurt, for instance, in the Vietnam war like he was. So, these are the kinds of programs that are being pursued now. The major step forward that will be realized in the future—not yet—has been the result of the Mental Health Systems Act of 1980.

THE NATION'S ECONOMY

Q. Mr. President, you have so many questions. I would localize my question though. You mentioned and concocted the misery index in 1976. You put unemployment together with inflation, and you came up with an intolerable figure of 12 percent. Right now in Mahoning Valley our misery index is 24 percent, at least. In other words, our unemployment rate is 12 percent. And when I talk to business people, they don't know whether to manufacture items for Christmas, whether to hire people for Christmastime. They don't seem to have faith in our system and in our economy. What can you do to help us? Please help.

THE PRESIDENT. I think that the last few months have shown major signs of economic recovery. For instance, every week for the last 6 weeks we've had a steady increase in the number of automobile workers employed in this country. About 4,000 automobile workers every week, on the average, have gone back to work. As you know, the new models of American cars are selling like hotcakes. There's a waiting list of 40 or 50 thousand, for instance, for the new Chrysler model.

In addition to that, the last 3 months the economic indicators—that's a conglomerate of about 9 or 10 different indicators of economic prosperity—have grown faster than they have in the last 31 years. I just gave you the results of our new information on housing starts. They've jumped substantially, back up to over 1½ million homes per year.

So, I think the severe recession that we anticipated, coming from the very high increase in OPEC oil prices, has not been nearly so severe as we thought, and we are well on the road back to recovery. I think we'll have a good Christmas. And my judgment is that the rate of employment of Americans will continue to grow very rapidly, and I believe that we'll see, because of the factors that I outlined earlier, an attenuation or reducing of the inflationary pressures in the future, too. I think the future looks very bright for us.

ANNOUNCER. Mr. President, ladies and gentlemen, we have time for just one more question.

THE PRESIDENT. I'll let you pick this one.

ANNOUNCER. All right. We'll take the lady right here in the front.

THE PRESIDENT. Okay.

TAX REFORM

Q. My husband's employed in the steel industry, and I've been employed—we've both been employed steadily. Still, with the tax rate and the inflation rate, everything seems to be getting worse and worse. The economic policies you've proposed over the past few months just don't seem to be helping. What's going to help the common man, who is carrying the heaviest part of the tax burden?

THE PRESIDENT. I had the choice to make of trying to pass an election-year tax program or waiting until after the election. I could probably have picked up some political points by putting forward a massive tax reduction proposal knowing that the Congress wouldn't pass it or knowing that the Congress would make a Christmas tree out of it, and it would cost us severely in inflation.

Governor Reagan has proposed the so-called Reagan-Kemp-Roth proposal which would cut taxes between now and 1987 about a thousand billion dollars and primarily add the tax money into consumers' hands to bid up the price for available products.

We have put forward an economic program that will be implemented next year, about half of which will go for investment in new industry, new tools, new plants, to employ American workers. Above and beyond all the other programs already— that I've outlined, this would increase employment by at least a million people by the end of next year, end of 1982.

The other thing that we've done is to have a personal income tax reduction making up about 50 percent of the total that would eliminate the increase in social security taxes that are now on the lawbooks. And we've tried to eliminate as well the so-called marriage penalty, where now if a husband and wife both work, they pay higher income taxes than if a man and woman live together and both work and they're not married.

So, we want to eliminate that marriage penalty, cut down on the impact of social security increases in taxes, and have major investments in industry to keep American workers more productive with new tools and new plants.

SOCIAL SECURITY

Q. Is the social security system in as bad a shape as they say it is?

THE PRESIDENT. The social security system is sound. It will not be bankrupt as long as a Democratic President's in the White House. You can depend on that.

NOTE: The President spoke at 12:01 p.m. in the studio of WFMJ-TV.

New York, New York
Remarks at a Meeting With the Congregation of the Concord Baptist Church and State and Local Officials.
October 20, 1980

Thank you very much, my good friends, Senator Ted Kennedy, Congresswoman Shirley Chisholm, Congressman Charlie Rangel, Dr. Taylor, and my good friend, Muhammad Ali.

Dr. Taylor, you're known both here and abroad as an eloquent and effective minister. You're not an easy man to follow in this pulpit—[*laughter*]—because I know the message of hope and glory that you expound from this place, to inspire the people in this congregation and throughout those who listen to your voice to a better life and a deeper commitment to the love of God and to our fellow human beings.

I'm also excited to share a platform with two of the greatest fighters of this century—Muhammad Ali and Shirley Chisholm. Shirley is not quite as big—[*laughter*]—but in her way, she's just as tough. [*Laughter*] And a few more weeks of training, Muhammad Ali would have been just about the size of Shirley Chisholm, I think. [*Laughter*]

I called the champion the night after the fight, and he told me that he trained too much, lost too much weight. But I think, as you know, and as Ted Kennedy has said, Muhammad Ali is the greatest.

As for Muhammad Ali, I just want to say: Float like a butterfly, sting like a bee, it's great at President to have the backing of Muhammad Ali. [*Laughter*]

I've thought a lot about this church and about what it means to you, not only in the preaching of the gospel and meeting the spiritual needs of this congregation but also the educational needs of children, the needs for housing and services for the elderly, and the overall needs of this community. One of the great Americans of all time, a man whom I am proud to call my friend, who has been with me in Massachusetts, Washington, D.C., Los Angeles, New Jersey, now here, be again with me tonight, be campaigning for me in Texas later on this week, was in Michigan earlier this week. I want to express my deep thanks to a man who carries on the true spirit and commitment of one of the greatest families who have ever lived in this country, and that's Senator Ted Kennedy. Ted, God bless you.

What he stands for is what his brother Robert stood for when he first proposed the Bedford-Stuyvesant Restoration Project. He insisted that it would have to involve the homeless and also those who owned a lot of homes; the employees and the unemployed; and also the leaders of the community and the leaders of large corporations. He wanted to be sure that jobs and housing and training and opportunity would move hand-in-hand with those who were seeking jobs and housing and training and opportunity, into areas that were sinking into deterioration and desperation. Your success in pulling all these elements into one of the most significant rehabilitation efforts in this country or, indeed, the world would have made Robert Kennedy very proud. Together, you've helped build a lasting monument to him and to his dream of an America, which his brothers shared, with a decent life for everyone.

That dream has not yet been realized. It's still in the future, but we are moving toward it. And I'm proud that in this community, my administration has been able to help in some way to give better critical health services, young people more skills to do better jobs, provide thousands of new units of subsidized housing, eight new buildings for senior citizens, and to work very closely for you and with you in making plans for a better future.

Because we've come so far, you know how far we still have to go. We've created more jobs in the last 3½ years than any other administration in history—in time of war or peace—1.3 million of the 8½ million new jobs in this country are held by black Americans, and I'm very proud of that.

But that's still not enough, and now we have as my most important domestic proposal in the Congress in 1980 the youth bill, to provide 600,000 more jobs for disadvantaged young people with an expenditure of an additional $2 billion in the next 2 years. We've got it through the House already with the help of Charlie Rangel and Shirley Chisholm, and I don't have any doubt that we're going to get it through the Senate before 1980 is over, with the help of Senator Kennedy.

In addition, it's time, now that we have an energy program in stock, to make plans for revitalizing America's industry and giving American workers new tools, new factories. It's also time to take advantage of how we can build a better social and economic life, with equality for Americans still not realized by millions of our people.

I know, after talking with Governor Hugh Carey, who's with us today, and Charlie Rangel, that we must do something about the drug program in this community and up and down this coast. I wanted to announce at this moment that we have now completed plans on a major, concentrated effort, involving millions of dollars, already available to us in five northeastern cities—New York City, Newark, Baltimore, Washington, and Philadelphia. This will involve treatment of those suffering from drug addiction, intradiction to stop drugs coming in here from the Middle East—from Afghanistan, Pakistan, Iran, through Turkey, and others—and also the prosecution of those guilty of distributing drugs. We need to put them in jail and keep them there.

These kinds of programs are typical of what Democratic Presidents have done for the disadvantaged and the afflicted people of this Nation in your lifetime and in mine. Think back in your own minds about the difference in your life, in your family's life, in the lives of those you love when people like Franklin Roosevelt were in office, or Harry Truman or John Kennedy or Lyndon Johnson, and then think about the difference when Republicans occupied the Oval Office.

Some of you are old enough, like I am, to remember the Great Depression years, when the Democrats put forward social security. The Republicans were against it. The Democrats put forward a 25-cent-an-hour minimum wage. The Republicans were against it. Later we proposed Medicare—the Democrats did.

My present opponent got his start in politics traveling around this Nation opposing Medicare, better health care for senior citizens. We believe in rebuilding our central cities, but my Republican opponent said that he prayed day and night that the Federal Government would never bail out New York City, and just recently, he has said urban aid programs are one of the biggest phonies we have in the system. He said about minimum wage, "The minimum wage has caused more misery," he said, "and more unemployment than anything since the Great Depression."

Unemployment compensation is important to a family that loses its source of income. Democrats' hearts have gone out to families who were in need. The Republican candidate says, "Unemployment compensation is a prepaid vacation for freeloaders." We believe in Medicare and social security. Senator Kennedy has been in the forefront, as you well know, for national health insurance, and I join him in that goal. But my Republican opponent says, and I quote again, "I am firmly opposed," he says, "to national health insurance."

In 1964, he called the Civil Rights Act, and I quote him again, "bad legislation." A few months before elections, Republicans try to change their spots. They put on a different cloak, and they start pretending they are for people who are aged and who need social security, or sick and need Medicare, or working and need the minimum wage, or unemployed and need unemployment compensation, or needing to have their health care insured and have been against health care.

But recently, when he was asked about his basic attitudes after changing all his positions, he said, "I'm still where I was over the past 20 years." [*Laughter*] And I predict to you that after November the 4th, he'll be right back where he's been the last 20 years—in Hollywood as a movie actor. But he'll be there only if you remember history and you recall what happens to those you love if you take the outcome of an election for granted or depend on the candidate and his public friends to do the work without your help.

You know how hard black and white leaders both worked to give black citizens of this Nation a right to vote. And you also remember in history what has happened when Democrats, who were supposed to be loyal to our party, sat back because of confusion or timidity and did not vote or did not work. One of the most vivid memories in my mind is 1968. The Republicans nominated Richard Nixon for President. The Democrats nominated Hubert Humphrey for President. Many people, as you well remember, had been for Senator Gene McCarthy, and when Hubert Humphrey got the nomination to replace Lyndon Johnson as President, a lot of Democrats said, "Hubert Humphrey's not perfect. I'm not going to help him. Let him shift for himself." So Hubert Humphrey never went to serve in the Oval Office; Richard Nixon did. [*Laughter*] It was not the fault of the Republicans who supported Richard Nixon. That was their duty, that's what we expected them to do. The fault lay in Democrats who forgot what the issues were.

Domestic issues are crucial to us, but that's not the sum total of our national character. When I came into office, the national policy of our Government was to stay away from Africa. Henry Kissinger wasn't even permitted to visit Nigeria. We were propping up the white government of Rhodesia. But I turned to a great black leader, Andy Young, and I said, "Andy, we're no longer just a nation with the big four to deal with. We've got 150 nations on Earth to deal with, and although ours is a great country with a great soul, a lot of people don't know about it because we've put on a different face outside the borders of our land." And Andy Young and now Don McHenry have the trust of people who are yellow and brown and black throughout the world. And we stood staunch in spite of tremendous political pressure against the retention of the white supremacy government in Rhodesia, and now we've got a democracy in Zimbabwe with a freely elected black Prime Minister.

Well, I don't claim that our Government is perfect. I don't claim that my administration is perfect. But you see my friends behind me on this platform. You know our record so far. You know that I've said many times, I would never have been given a chance to be elected President had it not been for Martin Luther King, Jr., and others. And many times in my own church at home we've sung the old hymn, "There is a Balm in Gilead; sometimes we get discouraged and think our work's in vain." But I tell you that together, as Democrats, we have moved forward. We're on the right road. We're making good progress.

In her statement endorsing me, Shirley Chisholm began by saying she'd made her decision based on the realities of this campaign and the state of the country at this time. And then she noted we'd not accomplished everything we'd set out to do, but that we'd only set goals on some things, but that we had also proposed specific, workable ways to reach those goals. And she pointed out that some of those goals had not yet been reached because the Congress has not yet been willing to accept them. But we'll continue to press forward the next 4 years. We've come a long way. We are not finished yet.

I'm from the Deep South, and I have seen the need to have the permanent voice of distinguished, idealistic, competent, dedicated black leaders to carry on what I believe in after I've finished my term in office. So in this first 3½ years—I haven't been President long yet—I've been able to nominate, and Senator Kennedy as the chairman of the Judiciary Committee has been able to get confirmed, twice as many black judges in the Federal district courts as all the Presidents put together in the last 200 years. And we're not through yet. And we haven't lowered the standards. Every one of those nominees has been a source of pride to me and to the Nation.

This church can prove that it makes a difference to be involved, that despite difficulties that face us, you can make a difference—in the education of your children, in the lives of senior citizens, in better houses, better blocks, better communities. The civil rights movement succeeded because thousands of people felt that they could make a difference, if they kept on until the laws of our Nation were changed, the customs of our Nation were changed. It hadn't been changed for more than a hundred years since slavery was officially eliminated from this land. Those discriminatory laws and practices fell before the marching feet of courageous, dedicated people who knew they could make a difference. You did what you could and persuaded others to join you.

In just 2 weeks, Americans must make a choice about our future. In the past, too many have stayed at home, convinced that their vote would not make a difference. I mentioned 1968 when we lost, but in 1960, if 28,000 people in Texas had voted

a different way and a few in Illinois had voted a different way, then John Fitzgerald Kennedy would never have been President of this country.

The ones who make the decision on election day are often the ones who do not work and who do not vote. It's not enough to have rights; we must use them. The next years can be a time of great progress, a time when we move past all the old prejudices and all the old past indifference, when we put our people to work—all our people to work, building a better America, economically strong, but also strong in our faith in each other, strong in our commitment to freedom, to justice, to opportunity.

So, I'd like to ask you, like Shirley Chisholm, to look at the realities of this campaign and the state of our Nation at this date and then come out and vote and help us keep our lives on the right road.

The last in what was to be his final campaign, the Presidential primary in California in 1968, Senator Robert Kennedy made a speech at Fisherman's Wharf, and in closing he said, and I quote him, "I ask you to recognize the hard and difficult road ahead to a better America, and I ask you to vote for yourselves." "The people," he said, "must decide this election and they must decide so that no leader in America has any doubt about what the people want." "For your sake and for the sake of your children vote for yourselves tomorrow," he said.

I would ask of you the exact same thing. Keep us on the road to a better America. On November the 4th, vote for your children. Vote for yourselves.

Thank you very much, and God bless you.

NOTE: The President spoke at 4:25 p.m. in the sanctuary of the church, which is located in the Bedford-Stuyvesant section of Brooklyn.

New York, New York

Remarks at an Asian Pacific American Committee Fundraising Dinner. October 20, 1980

Governor Carey, Mayor Koch, City Council President Carol Bellamy, Jimmy Ying, Kenny Yum, Danny Mark, and my friends:

It's very good for my wife to make preparations for my visit here. [*Laughter*] When she came back to Washington, she was extremely excited about the pleasure and the hospitality which you gave to her. When I arrived in front of this beautiful place this afternoon, it reminded me of a New Year's celebration. [*Laughter*] If only it were already November 5th! [*Laughter*] That would not only be the start of a new year for me, it would be the start of a new 4 years for me with your help, and I thank you for it.

I do thank you very much for your welcome, and I thank you very much for your support. Several people have said that I'm the first President ever to visit Chinatown. As a matter of fact, our first President, George Washington, lived just a few blocks from here. But that doesn't count. He was President, but this was not Chinatown, right? [*Laughter*]

George Washington could not have known that in years after his own administration, hundreds of thousands of wonderful American citizens would come here across the Pacific and have their descendents strengthen this country as greatly as you have done so. In the past 4 years alone, more than 150,000 East Asians have settled here in New York. They could not have come at a more auspicious time. More Asian Americans now serve in government, in high places, on Presidential commissions, in advisory bodies to give me

counsel on how I should perform as President, than ever before in history.

We've made a special effort to include Asian Americans in our dealings with Asian countries. Ours is a nation of immigrants. My family came here as immigrants. I presume that everyone in this room comes from a family of immigrants to our country, looking for a better life, determined to preserve the finest aspects of our heritage, our beliefs, and our customs. This is a treasure for the United States. It's one of the sources of our strength. It's one of the bases on which I, as President, can work to preserve peace. It's one of the best means that I have to use in extending the hand of friendship to hundreds of thousands, sometimes hundreds of millions of other people on Earth.

Our language skills, our cultural roots, are very precious. Yours in recent months have become especially valuable to our Nation, to help us in developing the new friendship that has now been made possible with almost a billion people who live in the People's Republic of China, and at the same time with sensitivity and understanding, to maintain our friendship with the people who live on Taiwan.

We don't know what the future will hold. Our Nation has a policy that there is one China. We realize that there are difficulties in communicating and trading between the people of Taiwan and the People's Republic of China. But I think whatever the future might hold, our Nation can play a beneficial role in strengthening the ties of peace and stability and brotherly and sisterly love among the people on the Asian Continent. As Presidents serve in years to come, you can be a great source of understanding and communication and advice and counsel, so that the decisions of our Government and the influence of the Oval Office can be beneficial in nature.

It's very important, as we have refugees trying to escape from totalitarian countries who deprive people of freedom, that we remember our own heritage—a desire for freedom, to worship as we please, and to live with the blessings of liberty. When we come to this country without giving up those precious human beliefs and possessions, we form ourselves into a united nation.

You bring to this country a tradition of hard work, of stable families, of filial and maternal love, of patriotism, of dedication, of talent; a love of beauty, respect for those who are different from you. You've helped our Nation greatly in the menial labor of building the railroads to the West, in serving in both World Wars with heroism and dedication to your land, and from enriching our own culture and our scientific knowledge and our scholarly life. And you've also learned, as I can well attest, how to receive a visitor with grace and with a welcome that warms my heart.

As President of a country comprised of 230 million people, I express my thanks to you, my admiration to you, my recognition of what you contribute to our land. You've made me feel as though I'm part of your community, just as you're part of our American community. There can be no separation among us as we strive for a better life for our children and those who look to us for leadership.

So, this afternoon as I close my remarks, let me say again how grateful I am to you for what you've meant to my wife, and now to me. And I'll pledge to you that as President, I will never forget the tremendous contribution that you have made in years gone by and the even greater contribution that you can make to a greater

America and a more peaceful world in the years to come.

Thank you very much.

NOTE: The President spoke at 7:15 p.m. at the Silver Palace Restaurant.

New York, New York

Remarks to Leaders of the Greek American Community. October 20, 1980

THE PRESIDENT. First of all, ever since I've been in office, since early 1977, we have worked almost day and night to solve the differences between Greece and Turkey, so that Greece could be reintegrated into NATO. And with the noble commitment of our Nation, I'm very pleased that Bernie Rogers, who is working, as you know, not as a representative of me directly but for the NATO alliance, was able to help work out an agreement by which the NATO leaders this morning voted unanimously to confirm Greece's commitment to NATO.

GROUP MEMBER. Greece back to NATO!

THE PRESIDENT. This is not only a great day for Greece and for the other European nations; it's also a great day for the United States of America. And I might say this is one of the most gratifying experiences of my time as President. Now, the next step, to which I am deeply committed, along with Fritz Mondale, as you well know, and all of my administration, is to resolve the question in Cyprus and to restore human rights. I need your help now.

NOTE: The President spoke at 7:15 p.m. at the Sheraton Centre Hotel.

As printed above, the item follows the text of the White House press release.

New York, New York

Remarks at a Reception With New York Jewish Community Leaders. October 20, 1980

I hope with an adequate degree of modesty, I can say that's one of the most beautiful statements I've ever heard.

The first time I came to New York City as a candidate for President I met with Mayor Beame, and after that conversation with him in the privacy of Gracie Mansion, I went back to see my wife at the end of that week's campaigning. I said, "Rosalynn, I've just met the most unselfish and dedicated public servant that I've ever known," and I can say that from the bottom of my heart.

I have never known him during that campaign and since I've been in office to make any request of me that was not for the well-being of other people, not himself, his city—which is also my city. Every person who lives in New York City is my constituent just as acutely and just as personally as it could be in the case of a mayor or Governor or member of the city council. I feel the responsibility of New York City's future on my shoulders.

After the 1976 election was over and I had been successful—with the help of many of you—Mayor Beame, Governor Carey, some of the Senate delegation and Congressmen came down to Georgia to talk to me about what we needed to do during the 4-year interval that lay ahead. We made an agenda then, because if you think back 4 years, New York was in absolutely desperate straits. We haven't succeeded in all our endeavors. The Congress has not yet adopted all the legislation we've put forward. But we have never ceased trying.

And many of the achievements have been very crucial in the life of New York City. There's a different spirit here now. There's a different confidence here now, a different unity here now, a different incorporation and appreciation among the rest of the people of this Nation for New York City now than was the case 4 years ago. I'm grateful to have played a small part in it, and after this election I intend to go through the same process to plan for the next 4 years.

I feel very heavily on my shoulders the responsibility to carry on the tradition of the brother of Senator Edward Kennedy and of Lyndon Johnson and of Franklin Roosevelt and of Harry Truman and of Woodrow Wilson and others down through the past years who have served our Nation as Democratic Presidents. All those men on occasion, and myself, have at times made mistakes, because it's easy to judge what should have been done in retrospect, but when you look to the future—an uncertain future—from the point of view of the Oval Office, you cannot always anticipate what is going to happen. Sometimes the future news is worse than you had anticipated; sometimes it's better.

The first time I met with the Prime Minister of Israel, Prime Minister Rabin, [Begin], and shortly after met with the President of Egypt, President Sadat, I outlined to them what I wanted to accomplish during my 4 years as President. "During this first term," I said, "I want to see direct negotiations, not negotiations through the United Nations or other intermediaries. I want to see the recognition of Israel's right to exist by its major Arab neighbor. I want to see a recognition that Israel must be a secure, democratic bulwark in the Mideast as an asset to the security not only of Israel, but of Egypt, her neighbor, and obviously our own country, which I lead. And I want to see open borders, and I want to see diplomatic recognition, and I want to see tourists going back and forth across those borders, and I want to see diplomats exchange at the normal trade and an end of the boycott, that at that time, as you know, stopped many timid Americans from even trading normally with Israel. And Sadat said to me, "That's a beautiful dream, my friend, but it will never happen in my lifetime."

That dream, all the elements of that dream, have come true. We still have responsibilities and duties to perform and dreams to make come true. But I tell you that the obstacles that I see ahead of me now pale into insignificance compared to the obstacles that seemed to be apparent early in 1977, when I had those first meetings. There is a new tone, a new attitude among the people of Israel and Egypt. I have walked the streets and I have ridden in parades and I have seen the love that exists and respect that exists between those neighbors, formerly filled with hatred.

Seven years ago, the fourth war was taking place between Egypt and Israel in the short span of 25 years. We haven't had war since. And the progress in carrying out the most difficult possible terms of the Camp David accords and the Mideast peace treaty, that was signed in the presence of some of you on the north side of the White House, has been remarkable. We've not had a default in carrying out those commitments. It has been very difficult for Israel to meet some of those obligations that they themselves took on.

The future is my responsibility and it's yours. I've only got one life on this Earth to live. My integrity, my honesty, my word of honor—it's precious to me. And there would be no way that I could hope for success in bringing Israel and Egypt and Israel's other neighbors to an agreement

if I ever lied. If I ever violated a commitment that I've made to Prime Minister Begin or any of his cabinet members, they would no longer trust me, and my voice would be ineffective.

And the same thing applies in my hope to bring the Arab nations, all the Arab nations into a recognition that a democratic and free, peaceful and strong Israel is necessary for their own benefit, as it is for ours. I am not going to change my policy after the election, except to renew my efforts, and anyone that claims that is not doing this Nation a good service. For someone to deliberately plant a false statement in the minds of any innocent people is bad and wrong; it's contrary to the best interests of all. It causes doubt to be engendered among people in Israel who trust me, and it causes doubt to be engendered in the minds of leaders who still look upon the United States as the only possible avenue of a common agreement that would realize the dreams that we share.

I will never recognize nor negotiate with the PLO until after they recognize Israel's right to exist and recognize Resolution 242 as the basis for the resolution of the differences in the Middle East. I do not favor a PLO state in the West Bank of Israel. I think it would be a dangerous thing. And I have told this not only to Prime Minister Begin, not only to President Sadat, but to the leaders of the other Arab nations as well, including Syria, including Lebanon, including Saudi Arabia. They know exactly where I stand. There's no reason for me to equivocate or to mislead anyone.

I know the special sensitivity of Jerusalem. When we were at Camp David, in the seclusion of those grounds, Prime Minister Begin, President Sadat, and I agreed on an acceptable paragraph to be put in the Camp David accords about

Jerusalem. Toward the end, they both agreed, mutually, that it might be better not to put it in. It was their decision, not mine. I wanted it in. I've still got a copy of it. It hasn't been lost. But I believe in an undivided Jerusalem forever, and I believe in a Jerusalem that has the right, that respects the right of worshippers to go to their own holy places. And I can tell you that no ultimate resolution of the legal status in international law concerning Jerusalem, through negotiations, will be imposed on anyone. It can only be concluded with the agreement of the Government of Israel.

These are the facts. Obviously, this is a very complicated and very delicate subject. I have never had a secret agreement with Begin or Sadat. I think it would be contrary to my status as a trusted partner with them. And I can tell you that all I've done in trying to ensure a better life for the people in Israel and for the people who love Israel has not been done out of generosity for others. It's been done because I know that it is best for the security and the strategic interests of the nation that I lead, the United States of America.

And finally, let me say that we will continue the quiet, diplomatic, military consultations that have been going on, even recently, between our Nation and Israel, searching for common ground to ensure that our mutual strategic interests in preserving a strong and secure and peaceful Israel and peace in the Middle East are carried out.

Now, to change the subject: We've only got 2 weeks left. I tell you that the election is in doubt. In many States in this country it is very close. It could go either way. Your voices, heard in Miami, in Philadelphia, in Chicago, in Cleveland and Los Angeles and San Francisco, can make the difference. And I hope that you will not be reticent in letting your voice and your influence be heard and felt. Financial contributions, yes, they're important, and your generosity will always deserve and have my thanks. But this next 2 weeks is crucial. They are crucial. And I ask you to go a second mile, to let your friends and your neighbors, other rabbis, Hasidic Jews, anyone that will listen to your voice know the importance of this election. I feel that you are my partners in accomplishing common goals of importance to the Nation that I love here and the nation that I love in Israel.

Thank you very much. God bless you.

NOTE: The President spoke at 8:05 p.m. in the Princess Ballroom at the Sheraton Centre Hotel. In his opening remarks, he referred to the introductory remarks of Theodore Mann, former chairman of the Conference of Presidents of Major American Jewish Organizations.

New York, New York

Remarks at a Democratic National Committee Fundraising Dinner. October 20, 1980

Chairman George [Weissman], who's done such a good job in helping me at this crucial time; my good friend Ted Kennedy, who has been campaigning around this Nation with me, at my side, reminding Democrats in Los Angeles and in Massachusetts, in New Jersey, in Washington, in Ohio, later in Texas, of the finest traditions of the Democratic Party, which his family represents; Governor Hugh Carey, who has been such a staunch supporter of the principles that I myself espouse, and a strong leader in every element of the life of New York State; Ed Koch, who's been a staunch defender of New York's right to exist as a viable, ongoing, happy, dynamic, and united city, and all of you who've come here tonight to make this a success:

It is really great for me to be back in New York again. I should remind some of you that I haven't stayed here full-time. I have been going back and forth. [*Laughter*] I'm sure you can tell from all these frequent visits that it's not Georgia that I have on my mind. [*Laughter*] As a matter of fact, I've been here so often lately that the FAA wants Air Force One to get a shuttle license to and from Washington. [*Laughter*]

This is a time of analysis and inventory of what the outcome of an election can mean, not just for myself but for those who represent what we believe. Liz Holtzman is not here tonight, but it's crucial to me as the future President and to your future as Americans to do everything you can the next 2 weeks to make sure that we have Pat Moynihan join with Liz Holtzman, another Democratic Senator, to represent New York State in the next 6 years.

I thought tonight since Hugh Carey and Ted Kennedy and others have outlined basically what is involved in this election, that I would speak a few minutes extemporaneously about my duties, not delineating what I've accomplished with your help in the last 4 years, but looking to the future.

It's my responsibility to make sure that this Nation is strong, that our alliances around the world are strengthened, that the integrity of our country is never in doubt, that when I speak, I speak not as a lonely voice just from the hollow shell of a room called the Oval Office, but from the hearts, as accurately as I can mirror them, of 230 million Americans. It's important for me to remember that the strength of a nation is the best guarantee of its ability to preserve the peace.

I have no apology to make about advocating a strong military force. During the 8 years before I became President, our commitments to military spending went down 37 percent—in 7 of those 8 years, down. Since then we've had an orderly, methodical, substantive, well-planned increase in real dollars, above and beyond the cost of inflation, in our Nation's defense.

I intend to maintain that record through the next 4 or 5 years and have presented my plans to the Congress. This is not militaristic in nature. It comprises about 5 percent of our gross national product as an investment in our Nation's security, my highest duty and responsibility.

I say often that Americans need not be ashamed of modern weaponry and a strong military establishment. The best weapon is one that's never fired in combat, and the best soldier is one that never is called upon to lay down his life on a field of battle. I recognize that you can't fly an airplane with only one wing. And a strong military, no matter how crucial it might be, is not an end in itself. We must combine it with a constant search for peace and settle differences, which are inevitable, through negotiation and diplomacy and a calm assurance that we need not prove America's might through combat.

I also realize the importance of controlling nuclear weapons, because here, several decades after we dropped two atomic weapons on Japan to end the Second World War, Americans are inclined to become a little callous about the power of atomic bombs. Those were 20,000 tons—20 kilotons. Now we talk about megatons—arsenals under my command, under the command of President Brezhnev in the Soviet Union. A megaton is a powerful explosive. If you put 15 tons of TNT in each one of a series of railroad cars, the train would be over 200 miles long and would require 400 diesel engines to pull it—one megaton. Some missiles that we and the Soviet Union have are several tens of megatons. That is a responsibility that I share with you.

And every president since Harry Truman has recognized that awesome power and has tried to do everything within his human capability of having a balance with the Soviet Union, controls, mutually agreed and carefully prescribed observation techniques to assure compliance with our strategic arms limitations.

Lately, that commitment has been abandoned in the heat of a Presidential campaign. I waited last night to hear the speech that Governor Reagan made. I was hoping that he would disavow his promise to tear up the SALT treaty, which, as been pointed out tonight, was negotiated under three Presidents. And I was hoping that he would disavow his previous statement that we should inject an arms race, a nuclear arms race, into our relationship with the Soviet Union. I was hoping that he would change his mind about seeking so-called nuclear superiority.

That sounds good on the surface of it, but put yourself, for a moment, in the shoes of the Soviet Union and its leaders and private citizens. Suppose Brezhnev had made a speech last week and said, "I'm going to tear up the SALT treaty that's been negotiated under three American Presidents and throw it in the wastebasket. And the Soviet Union is going to strive for nuclear superiority, and we are going to have an arms race as a possibility to threaten the United States into complying with better terms for the Soviet Union in a SALT agreement." What would our reaction be? Exactly the same as the Soviet reaction would be.

The enormous responsibility of this duty and challenge is perhaps the preeminent issue in the 1980 election, a radical departure from the policies and beliefs and commitments of Presidents who preceded me in the Oval Office ever since the Second World War.

It's important for our Nation to have an energy policy in the future that steadily removes our dependence upon and our potential subservience to the Arab OPEC nations for our oil supplies. In 1979 OPEC increased the price of oil more than the oil prices had been increased since oil was first discovered in the 1800's. Americans have reacted well, and with the help of Senator Kennedy and others, we've broken a major part of the stranglehold on our Nation's diplomacy formerly threatened at least by countries in the Persian Gulf region.

Since a year ago we've reduced our dependence on foreign oil by a third, and today we imported 2 million barrels of oil less than we imported 12 months ago. We are doing this by increasing American energy production and by stopping the waste of energy. That process must continue. This year we'll produce more coal than any year in history. We're drilling more oil and gas wells in America this year than any year in history.

But Governor Reagan says let's repeal the legislation that has been passed. Let's let the oil industry make the basic decisions about American energy policy. Let's abolish the Department of Energy. I don't know who might be the next Secretary of Energy if there is a Republican administration, but it bothers me to think how that might be an avenue to eliminate the growing independence of our country as we shape our foreign policy as it relates to the Middle East and other crucial areas of the world.

Our country must continue to strive to root out discrimination and hatred and prejudice in our own country and terrorism around the world. It's not an accident that assigning citizens secondary status has a far-reaching and adverse effect on the consciousness of human beings. My last six predecessors in the Oval Office endorsed the equal rights amendment. Forty years the Republican Party had in its platform the approval of the equal rights amendment, which says that equality of rights shall not be abridged by the Federal Government or by any State, period. That's all it says. And for us to have a President who's against that simple proposition is an issue of importance to this Nation.

We must also revitalize the American economy. American workers are now the most productive on Earth. But their productivity has not been increasing. It's been going down a little bit, and they're becoming afflicted with obsolescent plants and equipment. And it's time now to start working on that.

With the energy policy as a good base, the future opens up vast vistas of progress and achievement and excitement and a better life for all Americans. This is something that we have in store for us in the future, with increased savings by American people invested back in our ability to produce; the prohibition against protectionism, which is a constant political pressure on an incumbent officeholder in Washington; the inclination on business, management and labor, and the Government to cooperate, as we are doing in the steel industry, the automobile industry, the coal industry, the energy industry; the withdrawing of Federal intrusion into the regulation of elements of the free enterprise system, to let competition have a chance and to make sure that we don't protect the rights of corporate powers to cheat consumers; the deregulation of the rail industry, airlines, trucks, financial institutions, now communications, energy prices, is a step in the right direction. Senator Kennedy has been one of the leaders in this effort.

We also must have an end to the massive Federal deficits and excessive Federal spending. This is important to me as a basic philosophy. At the same time, we've never failed to meet the needs of those who depend on the Federal Government for a chance to have a better life.

It grieves me to see young men and women out of work. Our party in which you believe, has always had a special concern about people who had to work for a living, with their hands and fingers. Ours was the party that advocated a 25 cent minimum wage to stop the sweatshops from cheating little children and grown people, and we steadily increased that minimum wage. And now we've established a formula, with the help of Chick Chaikin and others, to make sure that in the future those lowest paid Americans had a chance to feed their children and to house their families with an aspect of decency and self-respect. That progress must continue.

It's extremely important to our Nation and our conscience and our soul to treat the most deprived in a fair way. And I believe in the principles of the Humphrey-Hawkins bill, which says that the goal of our Nation to be avidly pursued is to give all able-bodied Americans, men and women, a chance to work, because there's nothing more debilitating than to have a certain amount of talent and ability and not be able to use it and to feel an alienation from society and then turning into anger and withdrawal and hatred because of deprivation of a chance to lead a productive life.

We've made good progress in the Middle East. Everything that I've done since I've been in the White House has been oriented toward a comprehensive peace in the Middle East and the preservation of the peace and the security of Israel and honoring those mutual principles that bind us together.

As I said earlier tonight, the first time I met with Prime Minister Rabin and President Sadat, and they said, "Mr. President, what is it that you want in your term of office?" and I said, "I want direct negotiations, which we'd never had, and I want a recognition of Israel's right to exist by her major Arab nations [neighbors],[1] which we had never had. And I'd like an agreement of peace instead of war, and I would like to have open borders and diplomatic recognition and an exchange of ambassadors and free travel, for tourism and trade." And President Sadat replied, "That's a beautiful dream, but we'll never see it in my lifetime."

All of that dream that I just outlined to you has already come true, but there are additional dreams. And the obstacles that still remain to the realization of those additional dreams for a permanent peace, permanent security, permanent agreement, a permanent recognition by the entire community of nations that a peaceful and secure Israel helps to provide strategically a peaceful and secure world, just as I know that it helps to provide a peaceful and secure United States of America—that is part of the dream for the future. And the obstacle to reaching it is not nearly so great as the obstacle we faced not much more than 3 years ago.

I'd like for you to inventory in the next day or so where we stand now in our relationship to other nations; the status of Israel; the relationship with Egypt; the opening up of the continent of Africa; the strengthening of NATO; the new friends, a billion Chinese, from whom we

---

[1] White House correction.

were previously alienated; the preservation of our trade opportunities and our friendship with Taiwan; the establishment of new democracies in this hemisphere; the elimination of military dictatorships; the honoring of human rights; the establishment of new democratic nations in Africa, Nigeria, the biggest and blackest of all, and the most powerful, and the wealthiest of all black nations, and Zimbabwe too, an epitome of what can be accomplished with diplomacy. These kinds of achievements can continue in the years ahead.

And finally, let me say about New York City, it's important to me, as I told Mayor Koch tonight, as I told Pat Moynihan and Hugh Carey on the way to Hofstra College on Long Island earlier, last week, every citizen of New York is just as much my constituent as it is any of theirs.

Shortly after the '76 election, after I had been victorious and before I was inaugurated, the mayor, the Governor, and others came down to Georgia. And we sat down in the privacy of a rest area that I had chosen, and we outlined among ourselves the goals that we wanted to achieve for New York City for the coming years. For this period of my office for the first 4 years, we've achieved almost all those goals. I can't say we've got 100 percent of what we asked the Congress to do, but we're still working on the remainder.

After this election, I want to be sure that your Governor and your mayor and your two Democratic Senators and others come to meet with me in a leisurely way, but a very committed way, to inventory what we must do to make New York City be an even brighter star in the firmaments of the major metropolises of this Earth.

The welfare burden is too onerous for local government to bear. Earlier this year, Governor Reagan said, "Turn welfare back to the States"—that's a direct quote. And on the same subject, a few days later, he said, "We don't need the department of Health and Welfare." Local welfare is a crushing burden on New York City.

As we meet with the elected officials after November 4, with Senator Moynihan, who pushes this idea every time I see him, with Governor Carey, an avid proponent of the same, and with Ed Koch, who never lets me forget it, we will meet and decide how to assume the burden in accordance with the Democratic Party platform, which was drafted and approved in this same city. That's a commitment I make to you. We'll work together to achieve that goal.

And finally, let me say that I'm grateful to you. This has been a long, difficult campaign. The issues are now being drawn sharply between myself and Governor Reagan, between the Republicans and the Democrats. But as I said in my acceptance speech, it's a choice between two futures. In 23 minutes tonight, I've outlined to you my vision of the future. An outline only.

The complexities of the questions that come to the Oval Office are almost indescribable. It's not an easy job. If a question's easy to answer, you answer it yourself or in your family or at the city hall or in the State legislature or the Governor's office. If it can't be answered there, it comes to me, and I work with the Congress to try to find a good answer.

But I'd like to remind you that even though the challenges before our country are great, and even though the disappointments sometime test us, and even though there are some transient inconveniences, if you look back in history, just in our lifetime, you see much more discouraging and disparaging times than anything we face today. The Second World War, the Great Depression, the struggle

for civil rights, the embarrassment of Watergate, the divisiveness of the Vietnam war—those kinds of things have always been met by this Nation, when unified, satisfactorily.

I have absolutely no doubt that although the future is going to bring tests and disappointment and transient inconveniences, we Democrats, with the responsibility of leadership on our shoulder, you and I as partners, will never fail to make the greatest nation on Earth even greater in the future. That's my prayer. I hope you'll help me answer it.

NOTE: The President spoke at 9:39 p.m. in the Imperial Ballroom at the Sheraton Centre Hotel.

Following the dinner, the President returned to Washington, D.C.

Small Business Investment Incentive Act of 1980

Statement on Signing H.R. 7554 Into Law. October 21, 1980

I have signed into law H.R. 7554, the Small Business Investment Incentive Act of 1980. This new law will facilitate the financing of small businesses by providing needed reform of the Federal securities laws.

Small businesses are essential to economic growth and to innovation. No effort is more difficult for small businesses nor more crucial to their success than raising investment capital.

This legislation will provide a new statutory framework to streamline legal structures and encourage venture capital to invest in small businesses.

The legislation will also scale down or eliminate various paperwork and procedural requirements and reduce the regulatory and statutory constraints faced by small businesses when raising capital directly in the financial markets.

In addition, this legislation requires increased communication and, consequently, better coordination among the Federal agencies concerned with the financing of small businesses.

The act adds to the many other efforts of my administration to assist small businesses. It contributes to increased investment in our economy, to the elimination of needless and wasteful regulation, and to improved productivity through innovation.

I want to thank Senators Proxmire, Sarbanes, Nelson, Tower, and Lugar, Congressmen Staggers, Scheuer, Broyhill, and Eckhardt, and Chairman Williams and Commissioner Friedman of the Securities and Exchange Commission for their leadership and hard work in drafting and securing passage of this valuable legislation.

NOTE: As enacted, H.R. 7554 is Public Law 96–477, approved October 21.

Act to Prevent Pollution From Ships

Statement on Signing H.R. 6665 Into Law. October 21, 1980

I am pleased to sign into law H.R. 6665, the "Act to Prevent Pollution from Ships," which addresses a number of environmental issues related to intentional and accidental pollution from tankers carrying oil and chemicals. This act provides the legislation needed to implement the Protocol of 1978 Relating to the International Convention for the Prevention of Pollution from Ships of 1973.

Since my message on oil pollution to the Congress in March of 1977—following a series of tanker casualties during the winter of 1976–77 in and near the coastal waters of the United States—this administration has emphasized the need for international cooperation as a primary means of reducing the risks of tanker operation.

At the request of the United States, the International Conference on Tanker Safety and Pollution Prevention was held in London in 1978. At this conference, the United States presented a detailed set of proposals related to new design, construction, and equipment standards, as well as new procedures for vessel inspection and certification. After extensive technical meetings and consultations, the United States was successful in obtaining two protocols, one of which, the 1978 Marine Pollution Protocol, is the subject of the legislation being signed today.

The Port and Tanker Safety Act was signed into law on October 17, 1978. It was the first major step in implementing the results of the Tanker Safety Conference. The present act completes the legislative implementation of the 1978 Marine Pollution Protocol. It will become effective upon the date of enactment or on the date the Protocol becomes effective for the United States, whichever is later. This ensures that U.S.-flag shipping will not be placed in an uncompetitive position vis-a-vis foreign shipping prior to the entry into force of the Protocol and will enable the Secretary of Transportation to prepare the necessary regulations prior to the entry into force of the Protocol.

The United States has been and will continue to be a leader in urging the adoption of international maritime safety and environmental standards. My signing this legislation today is a mark of our determination to protect the marine environment from pollution.

NOTE: As enacted, H.R. 6665 is Public Law 96–478, approved October 21.

Stevenson-Wydler Technology Innovation Act of 1980

Statement on Signing S. 1250 Into Law.
October 21, 1980

I am pleased to sign S. 1250, the Stevenson-Wydler Technology Act.

Throughout this administration, I have been concerned with maintaining the strength of America's economy and the competitiveness of our industry. I have announced several initiatives addressing such vital national questions as productivity growth, innovation, trade development, new energy technologies, as well as specific programs for the steel, auto, textile, and shoe industries, which provide jobs for millions of Americans.

An essential element in each of these initiatives is an emphasis upon technological advancement, which is critical to increasing productivity and ensuring our long-term competitiveness.

The legislation I am signing today establishes a clear Federal mandate to promote industrial technology. It also offers an opportunity for enhanced government-business cooperation to achieve our national goals.

The Stevenson-Wydler Technology Innovation Act of 1980 is designed to foster a new era of government-industry cooperation. The best inventive minds from government, industry, and universities will work together at technology centers on innovative processes to increase productivity in a large number of industries. For example, they will investigate ways to make industrial machinery more efficient by reducing friction and improving welding. Improvements in metal processing will increase productivity in every manufacturing industry, but especially in the automobile and business machine industries.

These technology centers can be established almost immediately after congressional approval of appropriations later this year. Although they will initially be funded jointly by government and industry, the centers are expected to become completely self-supporting within 5 years.

This legislation also establishes a Center for the Utilization of Federal Technology (CUFT), which I called for in my industrial innovation message of last year. This center will be a clearinghouse for technological information—a one-stop shopping center for industries, universities, and State and local governments.

The Stevenson-Wydler Technology Act is of course only the first step in a major innovative effort.

We have much more to do in this crucial area, and currently the Congress is considering legislation that would reform our patent policy while encouraging industry to take the financial risks involved in developing inventions. We are also moving ahead to implement another recommendation—Corporations for Innovation and Development, to provide risk capital for start-up funding of new inventions. This program will involve State governments as well as the Federal Government, and during the past month we have contacted all 50 Governors to seek their participation in this program.

Improvements in technology and productivity are essential if our efforts to maintain a leading position in domestic and world markets are to succeed. To meet the challenges posed by an increasingly competitive world, we must marshal all the creative genius and all the vision we have available in government, industry, and labor.

Senator Stevenson and Congressman Wydler have shown such vision in producing this legislation. Their efforts were given bipartisan support by other Members of both Houses of Congress, notably Senator Cannon of Nevada, Congressman Brown of California, and Congressman Fuqua of Florida. I want to thank all of them for their hard work and leadership.

NOTE: As enacted, S. 1250 is Public Law 96–480, approved October 21.

Small Business Legislation

Statement on Signing H.R. 5612 Into Law. October 21, 1980

In 1980 we have done more to expand opportunities for small businesses than in any year in the past. Together with the Congress, my administration has discarded the traditional practice of ceremonial support for small business in favor of meaningful changes in policy that actually improve the competitive climate for small business.

Today, I will sign yet another piece of legislation of direct benefit to millions of small business men and women, H.R. 5612. This new law will help small business people pay the cost of a successful defense against an action brought by the Government. This new law will also direct more Federal purchasing to small firms owned by minorities. Finally, this new law will help small businesses win a greater share of our export market.

I have made it a personal goal to see that companies owned by minorities and women get their fair share of Federal procurement. Under my administration, purchasing from these groups has increased markedly, as recommended by the White House Conference on Small Business. However, minority procurement contracts have tended to be short-lived and are often restricted to the service area— such as janitorial and food service work.

So, I am particularly pleased that this new law continues for another year the 8(a) pilot program designed to direct more Federal contracts of a long-range and technically sophisticated nature to minority companies—contracts which only recently went almost exclusively to larger companies.

Another section of this legislation provides small businesses with "equal access to justice"—another high priority of the White House Conference on Small Business.

Many small businesses have learned from bitter experience that when an unfair action is brought against it by a Government agency it may be cheaper and easier to pay a fine than to fight for vindication.

This new law will change that. My administration has consistently endorsed the principle that financial relief be available to small businesses that prevail in litigation when the Government's position is found to be arbitrary. Some of the proposals previously advanced were too broad in their application and too expensive, but this legislation strikes a fair balance between the Government's obligation to enforce the law and the need to encourage business people with limited resources to resist unreasonable Government conduct.

Another problem small businesses have long faced is finding ways to sell goods and services abroad. Thousands of small companies want to sell their goods and services overseas, but lack the experience and the capital to do so.

This new law provides a range of export assistance. Some of this assistance will be in the form of loans or loan guarantees from the Small Business Administration. Technical aid will be made available by the SBA and the Department of Commerce. Export promotion centers will be organized to help familiarize small businesses with export sales opportunities and assistance.

I am proud of what my administration has done for our millions of small businesses. The actions we have taken with the Congress and with small business leaders themselves—through the White House Conference on Small Business—will result in a healthier small business community and, consequently, in a more vigorous national economy.

In signing H.R. 5612, I want to congratulate Senators Nelson, Culver, Morgan, Levin, DeConcini, and Stevenson and Representatives Smith, Addabbo, LaFalce, Mitchell, Ireland, Kastenmeier, and Zablocki, as well as Arthur Levitt, Jr., and the other leaders of the White House Conference on Small Business for their work with my administration on behalf of our Nation's small businesses.

NOTE: As enacted, H.R. 5612 is Public Law 96–481, approved October 21.

Solid Waste Disposal Act Amendments of 1980

Statement on Signing S. 1156 Into Law. October 21, 1980

I am pleased today to sign the Solid Waste Disposal Act Amendments of 1980, which will significantly strengthen our power to stop illegal hazardous waste practices. Senator Culver, Congressman Staggers, and Congressman Florio are to be particularly congratulated for shepherding these important amendments through the Congress.

My administration has moved with all the tools at its command to address the critical environmental problem of hazardous waste disposal:

—An aggressive program was mounted to take action against those responsible for dangerous hazardous waste dumping. Hazardous waste task forces were formed at the Environmental Protection Agency and at the Justice Department. Over 1,300 possible hazardous waste sites have been investigated. As a result, 51 enforcement actions have been filed, and 40 emergency-response actions have been taken. The Environmental Protection Agency is also assisting the States to strengthen their programs with grants of $30 million.

—The Environmental Protection Agency has issued regulations designed to prevent continued dumping of toxic wastes. These regulations take effect on November 19, just 5 weeks from now. They set stringent requirements for all handlers of hazardous waste, and establish a system to choke off so-called midnight dumpers. They will help our Nation to manage wastes safely and prevent the creation of new Love Canals.

—Finally, over 16 months ago I proposed enactment of superfund legislation. The superfund law will allow the Environmental Protection Agency to respond immediately to hazardous situations by providing authority to clean up old dumpsites first and then argue in court as to who should pay the cost. It will also create a fund to pay for cleanup where no responsible party can be identified. This vital bill has passed the House and is pending in the Senate. I will make every effort to enact the superfund law during the postelection session of Congress that begins November 12.

The cost of adequately handling and disposing of hazardous waste sites runs into the billions of dollars. But the costs of ignoring the problem would be far higher. The legislation that I am signing today is an important step toward meeting our responsibilities to the American public.

NOTE: As enacted, S. 1156 is Public Law 96–482, approved October 21.

Miami, Florida
Remarks and a Question-and-Answer Session at a Town Meeting.   October 21, 1980

THE PRESIDENT. *Senator [Representative] Claude Pepper, Senator Chiles, Congressman Dante Fascell, Ms. Athalie Range, other friends:*

It's a real pleasure to be here in the home of the Red Raiders. And I hear you're going to be State champions again next year. Is that right? [*Cheers*] As you know, Miami Edison has a tradition of winning, all the way from journalism to basketball. As you know, Democrats have a similar tradition. And I wholeheartedly endorse traditions like these.

Before I take your questions I want to say just a couple of things very briefly.

CUBAN AND HAITIAN REFUGEES

Two weeks ago I was in Florida again, in Tallahassee, in your State capital, signing a bill called the Refugee Education Assistance Act. By that act Congress and my administration, with the help of your distinguished congressional leaders here, recognized the Federal responsibility to resettle the Cubans and the Haitians who've come here this year. This has been a nationwide problem. Floridians have performed superbly in the finest tradition of the United States of America.

But I have felt a special responsibility as President for the financing of this extra cost on you. The Congress has made available $100 million, and I had the judgment about how much of that would be paid, 75, 85, 90 percent of your cost. I have de-

cided, as I announced in Tallahassee, that the Federal Government will pay 100 percent of the cost of this settlement.

I hear a few boos over here on my left about the Cuban refugees. I presume that your families didn't immigrate to this country. You must be native American Indians. The rest of us have all come here later.

Let me say this. This is a political year. One of the most difficult human problems I've ever had to face as President has been the refugees that have come here from Cuba and from Haiti this year, sometimes, a few days, in an uncontrollable stream. We didn't anticipate it. Our laws were not designed to accommodate three or four thousand refugees coming here per day. Our laws were designed for people to be screened in a foreign country, carefully cataloged, and brought here a few at a time. This just didn't happen.

All over the world there are refugees searching for freedom. And whenever you think back on the history of our country you'll recognize that our Nation is a nation of immigrants, we're a nation of refugees.

When the Jews came from Eastern Europe, when the Italians and Greeks came here, when people came here from Africa even, against their will, when my ancestors came here from Ireland and Scotland and England, when others came from Latin America, each time our families were looking for freedom for the right to worship as we choose, outside of an atheistic control of a person's religious beliefs, and we came here looking for a better life. And we found it.

But once people get here and realize all the tremendous advantages of freedom and a good life and a great country and a better opportunity for our children than we had, there's a natural human tendency to say, "Don't let anybody else come in.

We've got it made. Let's forget about refugees. Let's forget about immigrants in the future." I'm glad that the early settlers of this country didn't stop my ancestors when they wanted to come to the United States.

We have done all we could to enforce the law. I've stationed a flotilla of Coast Guard and Navy ships between here and Mariel Harbor to make sure we could control the flow of those who came here against our laws. We've been very forceful in trying to stop the boats going to Cuba to pick up people to come here against our laws. But once those boats were loaded, as President I had a choice to treat them as human beings with a precious life or to see their lives lost at sea. And I did what was right. And I'm glad the Floridians did what was right, too.

And finally, let me say that I want to make sure that even in the future Florida doesn't suffer because of the refugees who've settled here. The flow is pretty well under control now, as you know. But in the taking of a census, for instance, the allotment of Federal funds for different things, for housing, for revenue sharing, and so forth, comes to a State or a city in accordance with its population. And I'm instructing the Department of Commerce, the Census Bureau, in accordance with its so-called Lawton Chiles amendment, to make it possible for Cuban and Haitian refugees to be accommodated or accounted for in determining all Federal funding formulas. So, you won't suffer now and in the future.

VIEWS ON THE PRESIDENCY

I'd like to say one other thing. The duties of a President are very broad. A President can't avoid tough questions, and I don't believe a candidate for President should try to avoid the tough questions. President Kennedy once said, "It's a lot easier to make speeches than to solve the problems." I think every President who's been in the Oval Office finds that to be true.

I have to admit that my opponent is very good at making speeches. A lot of people say he's a better one at making speeches than I am, and I guess they're right. But when you're in the Oval Office dealing with a crisis or when you're in an international forum, when unanticipated things present themselves to you for response, or when you're sitting across the negotiating table with President Brezhnev trying to guarantee the future of our Nation and the peace of the world, you can't rely on 3 by 5 cards and you can't read a teleprompter.

I think you've judged during this campaign where every time I have a chance, I meet with people like you to take any question you ask, do the same thing with the press—answer any question—that I'm prepared to meet those issues, think on my feet, make proper responses. That hasn't been the case in the other camp.

You know the terrible flap that occurred when there was a new debate, that I thought had been resolved by President Nixon, President Ford, and me about how many Chinas there would be. It created an international incident, and Mr. Reagan had to back down on what he had professed to believe. And I know he didn't think before he spoke when he said pollution was mostly caused by trees. I'm not sure it was a coincidence when that night he tried to fly back home to California, and his plane couldn't land at the airport because of the smog. [*Laughter*]

Well, these are the kinds of statements that are sometimes humorous and sometimes can be repaired very quickly by others speaking for you in a political campaign. But in a time of crisis, when every word and every thought counts, it's a different proposition. And that's why I think it's good training for me to come here to be with you this morning.

And I'm very glad, at Miami Edison, to answer any question you ask to the best of my ability—don't know all the answers. If I don't know the answer when you ask the question, I'll get the answer, call you personally on the phone, and respond to your question that way.

Now I'll take the first question.

QUESTIONS

SOCIAL SECURITY PAYMENTS AND UNEMPLOYMENT COMPENSATION

Q. Mr. President, my name is Henrietta Schulman. I live in Miami—Florida, of course. [*Laughter*] Why has a law been passed, very quietly, to deprive senior citizens on social security who work full or part time to augment their social security benefits—are deprived of their unemployment benefits if they are laid off? Who benefits [from] this? The employers, of course. They don't have to pay the tax on the unemployed senior citizens. I would like to know, very much, who thought up this law, what was the purpose of it, and where you stand on this issue. My friends and fellow citizen workers are very much interested in a law that affects them so drastically.

Thank you.

THE PRESIDENT. Thank you, Henrietta. Henrietta, right?

I never heard of the law before—[*laughter*]—but let me say this. I'll find out in a minute, because I've got an expert, two experts here on my left—Senator Chiles and Congressman Pepper.

The only law that I recall that we've used concerning earnings of retired people drawing social security was they raised the amount of earnings that you could receive without losing your social security benefits. When I was elected President, the limit was $3,200. We've raised that limit up to $5,000. In addition, we have indexed social security payments so that as the cost of inflation goes up, your social security benefits go up at least as much, so you won't lose your purchasing power.

Let me pause just a minute and ask either Senator Chiles or Congressman Pepper if they know anything about the law to which you refer. Lawton?

SENATOR CHILES. [*Inaudible*]

THE PRESIDENT. I see. Senator Chiles points out that under the law you take the larger of the two. If your unemployment compensation would be higher than your social security payments, then you take unemployment compensation, because you benefit most. If your social security payments, however, are higher than your unemployment compensation would amount to, according to Senator Chiles, you would take the highest of the two figures.

Q. Well, I question that, because the minimum is $50 a week, supposedly. That's where they take the figure from, from what I understand. Very few people knew about this law. Those I questioned knew nothing about it at all. It was quietly put in as of July 1st. Up till then, we were collecting unemployment when we were laid off, particularly on seasonal jobs, which a good many of us work.

THE PRESIDENT. Yes. Let me ask—Stu Eizenstat, would you go and talk to Miss Henrietta? And if you can't give her the full answer, let me talk to her personally afterwards, and I'll get you a further answer.

Q. Right.

THE PRESIDENT. We tried. I guess the law calls for you to get the highest of the two benefits. If that's not the way it's administered, we'll try to do something about it.

Q. Right. Thank you.

THE PRESIDENT. Thank you, ma'am.

FEDERAL ASSISTANCE FOR MIAMI

Q. I'm Timothy Roundtree, Cutler Ridge area. Mr. President, distinguished guests, fellow citizens, this question is concerning the flow of money coming down for the disaster areas, or more or less, to be more specific, supposingly being for the blacks to aid us in recovering things that were lost during riots and other things. The money that comes down, I'm wondering now why it never really reaches the ones that it is due to come to. It always stops a little bit above the head, and it never comes down to the people that are in need.

And one second portion of that: Being a Christian, I'm also wondering why there's not a greater force towards protecting the rights of Christians within our community.

THE PRESIDENT. Since the riots did take place in the Miami area, in Liberty City, as you know, I came down and I met with 65 or 75 leaders there to try to let them tell me what they needed most in that area, both to repair the damage that had been done, physical damage, and also to make sure that we had the allotment specifically of Federal funds—and I think the amount is about $60 million that we've made available—to make sure it was focused on those that needed it most.

We've tried to to set up training programs there for young people to make sure they could hold a job. We've tried to provide jobs there. We are now trying to encourage new industry to come in there and provide jobs for people. We're also making loans available and sometimes grants available to minority business leaders—

and in your area, it would be black business leaders—to establish their own small industries if they wanted to or their small businesses.

And I believe that we're doing the best we can, from the Federal point of view, to make sure that those funds are going where they're supposed to go. In this community, I presume that there are leaders here in the local government, perhaps some of the State agencies, that join in the responsibility for allotting those funds.

If you know of specific instances, however, where the funds that have been allotted by me through Small Business Administration, Economic Development Administration, and minority affairs branch of the Commerce Department or other agencies, that you think are not getting to the people that I intend for the money to get to, if you'd give me those specific examples after this meeting, I'll look into it myself today and make sure that the problem is straightened out.

As far as persecution or abuse of Christians is concerned, it's hard for me to know what instance you might be mentioning. My own hope and my own belief is that in this community as well as throughout the Nation, we do have an adequate degree of protection for persons because of their race or because of their religious beliefs.

There again, if you know of specific instances where people are being abused because of their Christian beliefs, I'd like very much to know about it so that I can join in with the Governor and the local officials, including the police officials, to make sure that that aura or threat of discrimination or abuse is removed.

RELIGIOUS FREEDOM

Q. Mr. President, on the issue of Christian rights, we're speaking now of—there are human rights that are written on the law, there are rights for the minorities, and et cetera that is in law. But there are no rights to protect the Christians as such. What I mean by this—this Nation was built on a Christian foundation, and it can be moved time after time after time and completely being diminished, little by little. There's no law written to keep the rights of a Christian, to give us the rights, to guarantee the rights of assembly, the rights of assembling in homes, and things like this, speaking on the streets, et cetera. There's nothing to guarantee the rights. They can be changed today or tomorrow. And this is what I mean by making laws specifically concerning these things.

THE PRESIDENT. Timothy, as a Christian and a Baptist myself, I can tell you that this Nation was not founded just on the Christian religion. This Nation was founded on the proposition that there would be no special religion designated by the Congress or the United States—this is in the Constitution of the United States— either by the Congress or any State respecting the establishment of religion or singling out a particular religion as being favored over any other.

So, I don't think it would be, in fact, I know it would not be appropriate for the Congress to pass a law or for the State of Florida or Georgia to pass a law that said that Christians have a special privilege above and beyond those who worship in a different way from we do or those who choose not to worship at all. That's part of the Constitution, not to give special privilege to any particular religion.

Q. Thank you.

THE PRESIDENT. Thank you very much.

I might say, Timothy, that that's a good question, because in our Nation now, there are those who are trying to define an acceptable definition of who can serve this country and to define, by law or through the political persuasion, the definition of a Christian. To me, the Bible doesn't say whether there's one or two Chinas, and the Bible doesn't say how you balance the Federal budget, and the Bible doesn't say what causes pollution, and the Bible doesn't say whether or not we could have a B–1 bomber or whether we could have air-launched cruise missiles.

You know, this is the kind of statements lately, which has never been done to this extent before, that some religious groups are trying to say is a definition of what a Christian is. And I know you agree with me that that's wrong. Right?

Q. I agree.

THE PRESIDENT. I agree with you. Thank you, Timothy.

RELIGION AND GOVERNMENT

Q. Mr. President, my name is Connie Skinner, and I live in unincorporated south Dade County. As a Christian and as a Southern Baptist myself, I don't feel like the words "duty" and "self-discipline" and "responsibility" are out of date. And I think the American public is willing to do what is necessary to help bring down the spiral of inflation, to solve our problems. "Just give us something to do," I think, is what we want to say. As President of the United States, what do you regard as our greatest need now, and how can I meet that need, besides voting, I mean?

THE PRESIDENT. Thank you, Connie. I'll try to answer that.

The Bible and the study of it is a very important part of my life, on an absolutely daily basis, I never miss. And I try to understand God's guidance to me, expressed in the Old Testament and the New Testament.

The Bible says many times that you should respect a manmade government. And as you know, in the Old Testament

God specifically annointed through his prophets, some of the leaders of Israel and perhaps other countries—Judah, certainly.

The Bible also specifies and other religions, do as well—the Moslem religion has very strict ethical and moral standards about "Judge not that ye be not judged" and "Love your neighbor as yourself." And one Bible verse, the first one I ever learned, in the New Testament says, "God is love." Self-discipline is another element of religious teachings that I think probably permeate all beliefs in God, no matter what country where one might dwell or what one might profess as the "definition," of God. [Not] to control one's own urgings that might gratify oneself and hurt another person is obviously contrary to God's teachings.

And I think to strengthen a nation, a nation under God, so that its own purposes and commitments and ideals and hopes and dreams can be expressed clearly and in substantive terms is good. To alleviate hunger, suffering, deprivation, discrimination, hatred, to me, is compatible with God's teachings. To promote peace for ourselves and around the world, to me, is part of Biblical admonition and teaching. Also, human rights in the broadest sense of that word, to me, is in accordance with God's teaching.

I think that this kind of standards of human ethics, human performance, concern about others, unselfishness, generosity, love, harnessing one's efforts in a common purpose when those ideals are compatible with your understanding of God's teachings—all that is a legitimate part of politics and government.

I have prayed more since I've been President than I ever did before in my life, because I feel the need for it more. And I have never found any incompati-

bility between my religious beliefs and my duties as a public official. I believe the same could be said among the 435 Members of Congress and the 100 Members of the Senate who represent, probably, all possible religious beliefs in our country. So, this is important.

Finally, let me say this. There have been some statements made, as you know, about what kind of believers God can hear. I believe that God hears all those who pray to him from one's heart.

When I got to Camp David with Prime Minister Begin and President Sadat, the prospects for a peace settlement were fairly hopeless. We didn't know what to do. We didn't know each other well. We stayed there 13 days. And the first day, we all three decided that we would pray to God, and we issued a press release, the only one we issued, and asked that people all over the world to join in with us, in their own way, to pray for peace. I'm not going to decide what caused us to reach a peace settlement, but I don't believe those prayers hurt. And I believe God heard all three of us.

Thank you.

CUBAN AND HAITIAN REFUGEES

Q. My name is Amy Rosichan, and I'm from Miami, Florida. I live in what used to be a very nice part of Miami called East Buena Vista. The last several years, thousands of illegal immigrants have moved into our neighborhood, and it has become badly overcrowded, run down, and full of illegal rooming houses. Your administration let all these people in. My question is, if you are reelected, what will you do to settle these people and to help make our neighborhood as nice as it used to be?

THE PRESIDENT. Thank you very much.

So far, as you know, this year we've had, I think, about 125,000 Cubans, plus the Haitians, come here to this country. We've settled now in permanent locations, with sponsors and in most all cases with jobs, 91 percent of them. We still have a few that still have not been settled. The ones that haven't been moved from the settlement camps are all now in Arkansas. Some have found sponsors and found jobs, and the sponsors and the refugees didn't get along or either they lost their job, and they still are a problem for us.

We're doing the best we can to find a suitable community for those kinds of refugees, preferably outside of Florida. We're doing the best we can, since Florida has been so heavily burdened with refugees, to find other places around the Nation where the unemployment rate is low—as it is, by the way, in metropolitan Miami—but where the community has not been overburdened so far. I think that we'll continue that.

In my second term I intend, first of all, to have a correction in the U.S. law, passed by Congress, to prepare for large numbers of refugees who come here illegally. The laws so far don't cover that proposition or that problem. I think the Congress will move now to correct that defect in the law. And I'll continue to make sure, using the Navy, the Coast Guard, all of my resources in the future— and we've learned from this experience— to minimize that flow of refugees so that Florida will not be impacted again with this large number coming in here so fast that the settlement process didn't work well.

We've got literally dozens and dozens of church groups, community groups, Jaycees, Lion's Clubs, Rotary Clubs, and others all around the Nation who are trying to help settle these refugees. We are making good progress, and I think by the end of this year we'll have the problem solved.

Thank you, Amy, very much.

UNITED STATES ARMED FORCES

Q. Mr. President, sir, my name is Frank Sierer, and I'm from Homestead, Florida. My question deals with the current retention problems being experienced today by all branches of the Armed Forces. Sir, if you are to be reelected, what leadership will you display to the Congress as well as to those persons pursuing military careers to continue their present course. And will you also exert a maximum effort to bring military pay and benefits parallel with those of the private sector, sir?

THE PRESIDENT. Yes. The answer to your last question, Frank, is yes. We signed a major bill just a month or two ago, as you know, sponsored by Senators Nunn and Warner, a Democrat and Republican, to bring a major step toward making sure that the pay and privileges, the travel expenses, the housing expenses, the resettlement expenses, and the reenlistment bonuses were substantially more attractive to Armed Forces personnel than they had been in the past, to correct the defect that had existed. This is not the first time that we've improved pay and allowances since I've been in office, and it won't be the last time. We'll continue this process.

Another thing that we have done is to institute registration for the draft in order to keep the draft from being necessary in the future. We had 93 percent of our young people that signed up during the first period required. Fifteen percent of those, Frank, said they would like to have more information about a career in the military. There's no doubt that those 15 percent, who will now be contacted, will give us a vast reservoir of recruitment that we didn't have before.

Also, I think we can all point out to our young people the advantageous development in their lives of possible military service. I went into the Navy when I was 18, and I stayed in there for 11 years. I was a submarine officer, went to the Naval Academy. And I can tell you that that 11 years out of my life that went into the military did not interfere with my political success. I went on to occupy one of the political offices in this country.

And I would guess that a young person who wants to see the world, who wants to have a stable future, good retirement at a fairly early age, as you know, an education, unexcelled anywhere, in the basic trades, and a good career, in and out of the military, can go in for 2, 3, 4 years or for 20 years and have a very good life. I think the surge of patriotism that I have seen in this country in the last few months will help us with that as well.

The last thing is that we must have a military where no other nation can successfully challenge us. I'm determined that our Nation will be second to none in basic military strength, in weapons, and the quality of military personnel, as well.

A lot of people complain that we spend too much on our military. We spend about 5 percent of our gross national product. The 8 years before I came into office, Frank, under Republican administrations, two of them, defense spending dropped 37 percent. It went down 7 years out of 8.

Ever since I've been in office, we've had a steady, planned, effective increase, above and beyond inflation, in our military budget. I don't have any apology to make for that. I think in order to keep the peace, we must have a strong military. And as I say many times, the best weapon is the one that need never be fired in combat, and the best soldier is one that never has to lay his life down on the field of bat-

tle to die. That's what we'll continue to do.

Q. Thank you, sir.

THE PRESIDENT. Thank you.

REQUEST TO VISIT THE PRESIDENT

Q. Mr. President, I'm Chip Turri, and I'm from Miami. And I was wondering, well, my social studies class is going on a trip to Washington, D.C., over the Thanksgiving holidays.

THE PRESIDENT. Yes.

Q. And we were hoping that maybe we could come and visit you and congratulate you on your reelection. [*Laughter*]

THE PRESIDENT. Chip, that's the kind of question I love. [*Laughter*] I'm a little hesitant, though, even to make a commitment to you. I don't know exactly where I will be on Thanksgiving weekend. But let me promise you this: When you come to Washington, we will welcome you on a visit to the White House, and if I'm in Washington, I'll be glad to stand there personally and let you all congratulate me. If I'm not, maybe Amy or somebody could substitute for me. Okay? [*Laughter*]

Q. Okay. Thank you.

THE PRESIDENT. I'll look forward to it.

PREPARATION FOR THE PRESIDENCY

Q. I am Robert Roman from North Miami. Mr. President, I have a strong desire to someday become President of this great country. What advice would you give me to perform this job? And would a visit to the White House help me to understand my responsibilities? [*Laughter*] If so, would you extend an invitation to me? [*Laughter*] I promise to take notes and do all my homework. [*Laughter*]

THE PRESIDENT. Robert, I'm afraid that if you had followed me around yesterday, you would change your mind.

[*Laughter*] I can tell you right now it is a terrible job, but later on, you know, maybe it'll get better by the time you get ready to run.

I was with Governor Reagan the other night, and I pointed out to him all the difficulties and the burdens and so forth. [*Laughter*] And then I told the audience, "It's amazing how time flies when you're having so much fun." [*Laughter*]

My advice to you, if you ever want to become President or a high elected official, is first of all to be a Democrat. And let me very briefly tell you why. I'm not a Democrat by accident.

I grew up as a small boy during the Great Depression. I was born in 1924. I saw the Democrats, under Franklin Roosevelt, change my life. Our family didn't have electricity on the farm. Franklin Roosevelt was for the REA; the Republicans were against it. I saw old people in so-called poor folks homes. Franklin Roosevelt and the Democrats thought we ought to have Social Security; Republicans were against it.

There used to be sweatshops, where people could work little tiny kids without any protection. The Democrats, under Roosevelt, thought we ought to have a minimum wage, at least 25 cents an hour; Republicans were against it. My first job when I got out of high school in 1941 was at the minimum wage—10 hours a day, 40 cents an hour. When it jumped from 25 to 40 cents an hour, the Democrats supported it; Republicans were against it.

That sounds like ancient history, but it's not. Now the man who's the Republican nominee for President says the minimum wage has caused more misery and more unemployment than anything since the Great Depression.

I believe that when a family is temporarily unemployed, when a mother and father can't take care of their little kids and feed them and buy them clothes and and send them to school, that there ought to be some unemployment compensation. My opponent, Governor Reagan, says unemployment compensation is a prepaid vacation for freeloaders.

I remember when I got a little bit older, we thought that elderly citizens ought to have some health care. I believe Harry Truman put forward Medicare; Republicans were against it. My opponent, Governor Reagan, got started in politics traveling around the country almost professionally speaking out against Medicare. He said that to give medical care for the aged—let me read you exact quote. "Medical care for the aged," Ronald Reagan said, "is a foot in the door of the Government takeover of all medicine."

Later he professed four times to be in favor of making social security voluntary. This would be the end of social security.

Now what we need is a national health insurance program for preventive health care and for catastrophic insurance, so that a family won't be wiped out if they have high medical bills, for the control of hospital costs, for prenatal care and care for little tiny children and mothers at the time of birth of a child. These are the kinds of things that Democrats are for—national health insurance. This is what Governor Reagan says about that: "I am firmly opposed," he said, "to national health insurance."

Well, I could go on and on, but nowadays, this month, and all the way back to the first part of the depression, there has been a steady pattern. People who are old, people who are sick, people who are newcomers to this Nation, people who are deprived of their civil and human rights, women, minorities, the temporarily unemployed have got a friend, the Democratic Party, and they've almost always got an enemy, the Republican Party. After those bills are passed and work for a while, the Republicans then go back and say, "Yes, that's a pretty good bill." But that's the basic element.

If you want to become involved in public life—I'm not trying to brag on myself; leave me out of it—you pretty well need to forget about yourself. Don't say, "How can I be a boss, a Member of Congress, or a Governor, or a President." Say, "What can I do among the people around me to give them a better life? How can I be a servant for them?" And then if there's a lot of work to do, do more than anybody else. And pretty soon, people will turn to you and say, "Help me with this," or "Write a letter to the Governor for me," or "Put in a good word with the Congressman." You will become a leader because you're a better servant. I think this is a way also into public service.

Finally, if you come up to Washington, stop by the Oval Office. I'll be glad to see you, show you where your future job will be held. [*Laughter*]

Q. You promise, don't you?

THE PRESIDENT. I promise, yes.

Q. I'll be up there soon. Thank you.

THE PRESIDENT. Thank you.

[*At this point, there was a disturbance in the audience.*]

THE PRESIDENT. Go ahead.

UNITED NATIONS

Q. Mr. President, my name is Bennett Bramson. I'm student activities director at Lehrman Day School in Miami Beach, and I live there as well. And I hope you won't mind if I emulate you, because it's hot as heck over here.

THE PRESIDENT. It is hot. Thank you, Bennett, go ahead.

Q. Mr. President, I was wondering, why have we continued to support the United Nations in lieu of the fact that it seems to be a stage for Third World and terrorist theatrics, rather than a true forum for world peace?

THE PRESIDENT. Bennett, I agree with you in many ways, because the United Nations can be one of the most aggravating and disappointing organizations that I've ever known.

When it was originally conceived by Franklin Roosevelt and other leaders in the Western World and later put into effect when Harry Truman was President, it was a major step toward giving nations a forum within which they could address disputes instead of going to war in an isolated regional part of the world, and the other nations on Earth may not know anything about it.

Since then, we've had the number of nations on Earth almost triple. We now have probably more than 150—I've forgotten the exact number. And those nations are small. Their people are yellow or brown or black. Their governments are sometimes fumbling, sometimes insecure. The country is poverty stricken. Sometimes they don't know their status in the international community. They use the United Nations to learn and to let their voice be heard.

Since I've been in the White House, there has never been a day that there wasn't a problem area somewhere in the world, sometimes two or three. And almost always, after a few weeks go by or sometimes just a few days, the nations who were involved in that dispute will take their case to the United Nations. Recently, Iran brought its case against Iraq to the Security Council of the United Nations. I think it might lead eventually to a resolution of that dispute without further spreading that war.

But we retain under the U.N. Charter, as you know, a veto power in the Security

Council, ourselves and four other major nations. If the United Nations should propose some action that we can see would be contrary to the best interests of our Nation, then we can exercise the veto. I've done it on occasion; so has my predecessors.

If the United Nations were abolished, I think the world would start trying to find a way to establish another forum. I don't know if it'd be any better.

Also, through the United Nations there is a great provision of benefits for refugees around the world that we don't give ourselves, and it kind of encourages other countries, the Communist nations included, to contribute to those problems, sometimes which they caused themselves.

So, I think in balance that the United Nations is good. It ought to be reformed, the debate ought to be limited. The constant harping and criticism about Israel, for instance, is contrary to the basic Charter of the United Nations and the basic intention.

Sometimes, if you get a majority of a certain ethnic group like the Arabs, you could take a terrorist organization like the PLO, and they can stir up a lot of trouble and kind of blackmail people into voting their way. This is not good. But the United States, Israel, and other nations so far have been able to prevail.

A recent move was threatened—Syria started it—to expel Israel, for instance, from the General Assembly, not to accept their credentials. And I announced without delay that this was contrary to the Charter and principles of the United Nations, that we would not permit it, we would veto such a move in the Security Council if it came to that body, and if Israel should be deprived of their credentials to sit as a part of the General Assembly, that I could see no way that we could participate in the deliberations of that body any longer.

Q. Thank you very much.

THE PRESIDENT. Thank you.

[*At this point, the disturbance in the audience continued.*]

AMERICAN HOSTAGES IN IRAN

Q. Mr. President, my name is Adam Chotiner, and I live in Miami, Florida. My question is, if the Iraq-Iran war gets to be a bigger problem, would we be forced to enter because of the American hostages still in Iran?

THE PRESIDENT. Adam—it's Adam?

Q. Yes.

THE PRESIDENT. It's hard for me to hear you. That's a very good question.

In the first place, Adam, we have done and are doing all we can to bring the Iran-Iraq war to an end and to make sure that it doesn't spread any further and to try to make sure that no other nations get involved in it. So far, we don't detect any additional threat to the American hostages because of the war affecting Iran.

Ever since our hostages were taken, we've had two principles in mind that I have tried to carry out: first, is to protect the interests of our own country, my country and yours, and to make sure that we didn't have our principles violated, we were not embarrassed, and we stood up for our rights; and secondly, to make sure that I didn't do anything as President, for political advantage or by mistake, that might endanger the lives or the safety of our hostages or interfere with their ultimate return back to freedom in this country.

So far, we've been successful in both those efforts, although we've been very disappointed that the hostages didn't come back earlier. I can't predict to you that the hostages will come back soon. I don't know yet. It's not completely in our hands, of course.

But in the past, up until just recently, we've not had anybody in Iran that could speak with authority for their country. At first, it was just militants and terrorists who took our innocent hostages. Later there was just a mass of confusion. But now Iran has elected a President, a Prime Minister, a parliament—they call it a Majles—and that Majles has now organized itself. They've got a speaker of the parliament, and they've elected a seven-person committee to work out how to release the hostages.

In the past, we've had one agreement all worked out with the President of Iran, the Foreign Minister of Iran, Mr. Ghotbzadeh, with the militants themselves, who were ready to release the hostages. And at the last minute, the President announced in Iran that everything had been worked out; we announced it over here that it had been worked out. And then because of timidity and delay, those hopes were dashed.

So, I don't want to build up in your mind any new hopes that might be dashed, just to get some political advantage. We're working literally every day to get the hostages home. But I can tell you that I don't believe that the war has put the hostages in any greater danger, and I do believe that the hostages will come home safely before it's over.

Q. Thank you.

THE PRESIDENT. Thank you.

This will have to be the last question. Yes, ma'am?

CUBAN AND HAITIAN REFUGEES

Q. My name is Michelle Bruton, and I live in Opa-Locka, Florida. And I'd like to ask you, what are you planning to do, if and when you are elected, about the homeless refugees and other people that are roaming the streets and creating disturbances and problems in our community?

THE PRESIDENT. Thank you, Michelle.

Michelle, we have been fairly successful so far, under the most difficult possible circumstances, in finding a place for those hostages to be relocated. Now all the hostages still in settlement camps, as I said earlier, have been moved out of Florida and into Arkansas. There are still, I guess, 7,500 or so of the hostages that have not yet found a home. We're trying to find them a place—I mean, excuse me, the refugees. We're trying to find those refugees a place outside of Florida. We've done the best we could to make sure that your costs, money costs in settling the hostages—the refugees, excuse me—were paid by the Federal Government.

We also will help in the future to make sure that we don't have another massive flood of refugees coming here, and this is a very important thing for us. The refugee situation is much better now than it was. Florida has responded well to a very difficult challenge. I'm extremely proud of what has been done in Florida concerning the refugees. But we will minimize in the future and use the legal authority that I have, including the Navy and the Coast Guard, to be sure that the rest of the refugees that come here are coming in accordance with United States law. There are going to be some problems in the future.

And as those refugees that have already come here have to be resettled, we're doing everything we can to find them a good home some place in the country outside of Florida, where the unemployment level is relatively good and where it won't interfere and cause a very high unemployment rate. That's the best we can do.

Let me say in closing that it's been a very good pleasure for me to come here, to have your questions about a series of issues, about the disaster areas, about religious ethics, about the retention of people in our Armed Forces, about the refugees who've come here from Cuba and from Haiti, about the status of a President and what a public servant ought to be, about the United Nations, about Iran, Iraq, and our hostages being held there, a broad range of issues that we've had a chance to discuss.

One of the most interesting, I think, was concerning religious freedom and what it means to protect people in their right to worship as they choose without abuse and without human beings trying to define what God is or what a true believer might be. This exchange of ideas has been very helpful to me. I've learned a lot from you.

Let me say this in closing. Ours is a great country. Every day in the news we hear about the arguments, the debates, the differences, the temporary inconveniences, the disappointments, the challenges. And we fail sometimes to remember how great our blessings are.

If you think back in history, those of you who are as old as I, you'll remember the Great Depression, and you'll remember the First World and Second World War, which my father was in. And you'll remember the divisiveness of the civil rights demonstrations and the burnings that took place when we were trying to find a way to treat black citizens equally when they'd been suffering from discrimination so long. And you'll remember the Vietnam war and how it almost tore our country apart. And you'll remember the embarrassment of Watergate and other serious problems where our Nation was challenged, much more serious than anything we face now.

And when the American people could understand what the challenge was, no matter how serious the question or the obstacle or the challenge, we've never failed to answer the question, to solve the problem, to overcome the obstacle, or to meet the challenge.

Ours is a great country, and one of the reasons it's so great is that we are different from one another. We've come here from all over the world. And this doesn't make us weak; it makes us stronger. Your community, yes, in Miami, has been through tough times. I don't deny that. And I regret that you've had to suffer, perhaps more than anyone else in this Nation, because of the refugees who've come here in a flood.

When I was sworn in as President, the unemployment rate in the Miami metro area was 11 percent. It's been cut now by 40 percent, and there are 88,000 more people in this metropolitan area now holding jobs than there were in January of 1977. There are still some people unemployed; it concerns me. The inflation rate is too high; it concerns me. Our Nation's not perfect; that concerns me.

But don't forget what a great Nation we have, and don't forget that in a free society, where everyone has a chance to speak and to make your voices heard, particularly less than 2 weeks from now in the general election, we'll make the greatest Nation on Earth even greater in the years ahead. That's my prayer. You join me, and it'll come true.

NOTE: The President spoke at 11:03 a.m. in the Miami Edison Senior High School gymnasium.

Miami, Florida

Remarks at a Reception With Dade County Democrats.   October 21, 1980

Senator Chiles and Chairman Whitehead, Congressman Lehman, Senator [Representative] Claude Pepper, my good friend,

Vice Mayor—[inaudible]—Senator Jack Gordon, Gwen Margolis who will soon be Senator—[laughter]—I know, you don't have to tell me, I know—Bob Shevin, and Speaker pro tempore-elect Larry—[inaudible]—and others:

Let me say this, I've got a question to ask you: How many of you believe that in less than 2 weeks from now, we're going to whip the Republicans in Florida? [*Applause*] Right on. Okay. Any opposed, by like sign. That's real democracy in action. That makes me feel good.

We had a good townhall meeting this morning of some very difficult questions. And as I stood there and saw the unique nature of the concerns here in southern Florida, I recognized the breadth of responsibility of a President. I'm not going to go down a delineation of all the issues in this campaign; they're too multitudinous to cover. But there are a few that are important—one is the care that the Democratic Party has always had for a working family, for the elderly, for people who lack adequate care and respect, people who lack equality of treatment and opportunity, people who've suffered from legal and other discriminations, people who were deprived, people who didn't speak good English, people who might be temporarily unemployed, people who were poverty stricken, people like myself that grew up in the Depression in a house that didn't have running water or electricity. And we've seen our lives transformed for the better under Roosevelt and Truman and Johnson and Kennedy.

And when you think about the times when they had those long pauses— [*laughter*]—it's a sobering thought. When the housing program of our Nation was absolutely destroyed, when civil rights progress came to a screeching halt, whose fault was it?

I'm not sure. [*Laughter*] It's their fault

once they get in office, but their actions are predictable. Republicans don't change spots, and although Republicans historically were against Medicare, against social security, against the minimum wage, against unemployment compensation, against the care for the aged, they haven't changed. The issues are still clear.

In 1948, nobody thought Truman would win. But the working people saw that he had stood strong for them and, at the last minute, because of over-confidence on the Republican side, he won reelection. That's a good story. In 1960, if 28,000 people in Texas had changed their vote and a few thousand in Illinois, John Kennedy would never have been President of this country. That's a good story. In 1968, a lot of people were for Gene McCarthy. Hubert Humphrey got the nomination. The McCarthy Democrats said, "Hubert Humphrey's not perfect. He served in the Lyndon Johnson administration. We can't vote for him."

George Wallace was a third party candidate. Republicans, predictably, supported Richard Nixon. He was elected. Hubert Humphrey never had a chance to serve as our Persident. What a great president he would have been. What a great president he would have been. I don't blame the Republicans because Richard Nixon was elected. It was kind of their duty, being Republicans, being mistaken in other things, to make a mistake in that way. [*Laughter*] But Democrats put Richard Nixon in the White House.

There's a parallel this year, a parallel this year. The issues between me and Governor Reagan are as sharply drawn as any time that I remember in my lifetime, perhaps even stronger differences than existed between Barry Goldwater and Lyndon Johnson in 1964. But there's a lot of confusion. This State is close. All the public opinion polls say that this State is close. Our own analyses show that the State is close. We've got less than 2 weeks to go. I'll do the best I can.

I'll try to come back to Florida; my wife will be back in Florida; Fritz Mondale will be back in Florida; these people on the platform with me will be working hard. But the difference will be up to you. I'm not trying to make, particularly, a pep talk, but I'm just trying to tell you from the bottom of my heart that in this next 10 or 12 days, I need you not to be satisfied with what you've already done, and God knows how much I appreciate what you've done. I see the teachers in front who helped put me over the top at the convention. I know all of you have helped me now, regardless of what you have done in the past.

Senator Kennedy is campaigning hard for me, trying to pull his people into an enthusiastic support for the Democratic ticket. But a lot of his supporters are not making the sacrificial effort that he himself is making. He was with me last night late, early yesterday, night before last, last week on the weekend when he could have been resting, he was in Michigan campaigning for me, he's on the way to southern Texas to campaign among the Hispanic-Americans there. He's been with me in Los Angeles, in Boston, in New Jersey.

The point is we've got a few days left. The issues are so important to you, to the quality of your life, to the lives of people that you love, to the people who look to you for leadership, to the principles that have made our Nation and our party great. And I hope this next 10 days or so that you will make an extra sacrificial commitment, above and beyond anything you've done.

I'm not talking about money; I'm talking about time. There's not a single person in this room that cannot contact a thousand people between now and election day. In your own home even, on the telephone, you can contact a thousand people. I know, because as busy as I am some days, I call 120 different people. Tough job, but you can do it. And some of you can reach more than 10,000 people with your enormous influence, because people trust you. You're the one that's interested in politics and government. You're the one that comes into the same room with the United States Senator and two Congress Members and with the United States President. People turn to you. Say, "These are the issues at stake." I'm not going to delineate the issues now.

I believe if we do form that Democratic team with the fervor and commitment and the hard work and the sacrifice that is required, there is no doubt that we'll have a victory on November the 4th and a continuation of the progress we've made toward peace, toward unity, toward the honoring of human hunger of all kinds, toward the enhancement of self-respect, better education, better care for the elderly, better chances for peace and continuation of the stability of Israel, a closer tie between our two countries, the sharing of a strategic responsibility, the rooting out of religious discrimination which we now see raising its ugly head on the horizons in this country. Those kinds of things are important to everyone. And what happens in Florida could very well made the difference. What happens with you could very well make the difference.

In closing, let me say that I'm grateful to you. The President's job is a tough job. As Lawton pointed out, a lot of times the questions that come to my desk are difficult ones. But I don't feel lonely because in the past, now, and in the future, I'll have the partnership of people like you whose sound judgment helps me to make the right decisions, whose interest helps to guide me to matters that I might very well overlook, but who share with me a commitment to make the most beautiful, the greatest nation on Earth even better in the future. Let's do it together. We'll work hard.

NOTE: The President spoke at 12:40 p.m. in the Galeria Ballroom at the Sheraton River House.

Orlando, Florida

Exchange With Reporters Upon Arrival at Orlando International Airport. October 21, 1980

Q. Mr. President, Governor Reagan says the United States has been humiliated and embarrassed by the hostage crisis, which he says your foreign policy helped to create.

THE PRESIDENT. Well, the fate of the hostages is too important, to the hostages, to their families, and to our country, to be made a political football. I will not make any statement that would tend to complicate an already very sensitive situation. Throughout this year candidates have tried to refrain from this temptation.

In September, I believe it was, September 13th, Governor Reagan pledged to the American people that he would not inject the negotiations for the hostages into the political campaign. I regret that he has broken his pledge, but I am not going to depart from the past commitment that we have made to continue to do everything we could to preserve the lives and safety of the hostages.

Q. But he says he has some ideas for solving the crisis, though he says he can't discuss them. Would you like to know what they are?

THE PRESIDENT. I think I won't comment on that until I see exactly what he had to say.

Q. Would you address yourself to his charge that it was your weak foreign policy which caused the kidnaping of the hostages in the first place?

THE PRESIDENT. No.

NOTE: The exchange began at 3 p.m. at the West Terminal area.

Orlando, Florida

Remarks at the 1980 Democratic Victory Fund Barbecue.   October 21, 1980

Governor Bob Graham, Senator Lawton Chiles, Bill Gunter, who's the next U.S. Senator from Florida, distinguished members of Congress and State government, and my good friends and neighbors from Florida:

It's always good to come home, and as you know, I feel at home here with you. Doyle Conner once told me when I ran for Governor of Georgia in 1970 that I did so well in south Georgia that I carried four counties across the State line. [*Laughter*] And since then, I've felt like I'm part of your State.

I've come home to remind you that we've only got less than 2 weeks to decide what kind of nation we'll have in the future and on November the 4th to whip the Republicans from the courthouse all the way to the White House. That means getting out the votes for me and for Bill Gunter and for your next Congressman from the Fifth District, Dave Best—you think you can do that?—for Congressman Bill Nelson. And I know that all of you believe and know that we will have Claude Pepper there to help us all do a better job for the people of Florida.

I'll never forget what Florida did for me in 1976. As I told a small group a few minutes ago, we came to your State, our neighbors, when I didn't have any friends in this country, very few people knew who

I was or had ever heard of me. And we went from one courthouse to another and one small radio station to another, one of your homes to another, met with just a few friends, visited in your churches, in your Lion's Clubs, in your schools, talked to you, and learned and listened. I went in one direction; my wife went in another. And that was the basis for my success later on in 1976.

The contest here in your primary, I think, was the turning point in the entire election. It focused attention not only on you Floridians and your judgment but also on the fact that my campaign did have some strength. It made a great impact on the rest of the Nation. 1976 in the primary was a very gratifying gift that Florida people made to me. Later it was generally assumed that Florida, because of some of your past voting mistakes, might go Republican in November. [*Laughter*] But when the returns came in, the Florida electors went to Jimmy Carter and to Fritz Mondale. That was in '76 in November.

Again this year, if you remember back in November, it was generally thought throughout the country that if Senator Kennedy announced that he was a candidate for President that Florida would certainly go for him. We campaigned down here among you. You had confidence in me again. When the returns came in, you were in my column.

I'm a southerner, and I believe in tradition. You've established a good tradition of supporting Jimmy Carter for President. I want you to help me again on November the 4th. Okay? [*Applause*]

There are a few things that I want to mention to you. You've been very gracious and very generous to come out here today to meet with me. As we approach the last few days of the campaign there are some memories that ought to be impressed on our minds.

I grew up not far from the Florida line on a farm. I was born in 1924. When the Great Depression came, I was a young, impressionable man, a boy. I remember what Franklin Roosevelt and the Democratic Party did to change my life and the life of my family. We didn't have running water in our house. We didn't have electricity. The Democrats thought that REA would be good for farmers; the Republicans were against it. They called it socialism for the Federal Government to help build dams and generate electricity for farmers.

There were a lot of sweatshops in our country, and young people about Amy's age, 13 years old and younger, boys and girls, were working under uncontrollable and embarrassing conditions. Working families didn't have a right to earn a decent living to finance their homes. And the Democrats proposed a minimum wage, 25 cents an hour; the Republicans opposed it. The Democrats finally prevailed and gave working people of this Nation a better life.

I graduated from high school in 1941, my first job at a minimum wage, 40 cents by then. That increase from 25 to 40 cents was a great thing in our lives. Democrats sponsored it; Republicans, they were against it.

Democrats saw that older people were living in poor folks homes, we called them, without any self-dignity, without any security, having slaved away all their lives to make this a better country. So, the Democrats said, "We need something to give that security to older people," and put forward the idea of social security; Republicans were against it. Social security passed.

Later, I won't go into all the details, but Democrats, again, put forward Medicare to give older people a chance to have a better health care after their retirement age. My opponent, Governor Reagan, got his start in politics working for the American Medical Association, traveling around this country speaking against Medicare.

You might say minimum wage is ancient history, but he says the minimum wage has caused more misery and more unemployment than anything since the Great Depression. Democrats have always been interested in people that were temporarily out of work and need a way, during those trying times, to feed their families, to keep their children in school. Unemployment compensation was devised by Democrats. Recently, my opponent said that unemployment compensation was just a prepaid vacation for freeloaders.

This general sense, that started in the 1930's or before and has come all the way up to this time, to modern days, separates one party from another. I've had major responsibilities on my shoulders as a President to honor your expectations to keep our Nation as you want it.

The 8 years before I became President, under two Republican administrations, spending for defense went down 7 of those years. Defense budgets went down 37 percent the 8 years before I went into the Oval Office.

Since then, we've had a steady increase, predictable increase, sound increase every year in defense expenditures. I don't have any apology to make for it. I'm a military man. My background is as a naval officer. I was a submarine officer, as some of you know. And I believe that the best way to keep our Nation at peace is to keep it militarily strong. As long as I'm in the White House, we're going to do that.

Those of you who are deeply committed to peace, don't worry about that, about military strength. Our weapons, our military forces, men and women, will never be excelled by any other nation on Earth. We're in the cutting edge of prog-

ress. And our strategic nuclear weapons and our conventional weapons, our Navy, our men and women, are strong, and they're going to stay strong. But an airplane doesn't fly on just one wing. With that powerful military strength, you've got to have two more things.

One is a commitment to arms control, because we don't want to have a nuclear arms race in this world. Every President since Harry Truman has insisted upon balanced, equivalently equal, controlled, observable arms control treaties. Recently, as you know, my opponent said, let's throw the arms control treaty in the trash, and let's start an arms race or threaten an arms race against the Soviet Union, to play a trump card against them. That's a radical departure from what all Presidents have done, Democratic and Republican, since the Second World War.

It's important to us as a nation, it's important to our allies and friends, like Israel and the Middle East, to make sure that Iraq and other countries of a radical nature do not have military weapons that are nuclear explosives. We've had a very strong nonproliferation policy under Democrats and Republicans, but Governor Reagan says that nonproliferation is none of our business.

The issues are clearly drawn, not only about the past and present but also about the future. We now have a sound energy policy to give us a basis on which to revitalize American industry, to have modern tools and modern plants for American workers, to put all our people to work; to have better health care for our citizens, more preventive health care, catastrophic health insurance, better care for pregnant women and little babies, better care for elderly citizens, more outpatient care rather than inpatient, the holding down of hospital costs. These changes in our health program can be implemented with a national health insurance plan. I'm for it, Democrats are for it; Governor Reagan's against it.

And the last two points I want to make are these.

My background since I got out of the Navy has been as a farmer. I'm very proud that you have given me some good, well-trained Florida leaders to come and help me.

Reubin Askew is one of the best public servants I've ever known, and he's our Special Trade Representative. Since he's been there, we've made remarkable progress. This year we'll have $40 billion worth of American agricultural products sold overseas. That's an $8 billion increase over last year, and 1979 set world records. 1978 set world records. 1977 set world records.

Another man you've given me is Jim Williams. We will have these first 3 years, with the help of him and others, the highest gross income and the highest net income for farmers in our Nation's history.

We've made good progress in getting Government's nose out of the private affairs of American citizens. We've deregulated the airlines, the railroads, the financial institutions, trucking, working on communications. And those of you who live in the Orlando area know that airline deregulation has been good for you. Before it took place, there were 4 flights coming in here; now 15. That increase has been very good for the entire country. It's put the competition back in the free enterprise system, let our Government work like it ought to.

And finally, let me remind you about the importance of you as an American citizen. Your coming here and contributing financially is very beneficial to us. We couldn't get along without it. We've been counting on you, and you haven't disappointed us. Richard Swann's done a su-

perb job, and all of you've joined in. But I'd like to remind you that that's not enough.

If you believe in the greatness of our Nation, if you believe in the principles of our party, if you believe in the importance of democracy and the partnership that must exist between the White House, the Oval Office, the President, and you personally, if you care about your own family and the people that you love outside your family, I'd like for you this next 10 days to work as hard as you've ever worked before to try to shape this election so that we can be victorious.

You might say one person can't make much difference. I remember in 1960 if 28,000 people had changed their votes in Texas and a few thousand in Illinois, John Kennedy would never have been President.

In 1968 if all of the people assembled here and a few like you around the country had had the confidence in the Democratic candidate to go out and work hard for him, Richard Nixon would never have served in the White House, and we would have had a great Democratic President, Hubert Humphrey, to carry on the principles that I've described to you.

But when you think back on Roosevelt, Harry Truman, Johnson, Kennedy, those memories, for working people, for people who believe in a strong defense and for peace, for people who believe in a brighter future for our country, better education for our children, self-respect for the elderly, dignity for those who are black or who don't speak English well, but might speak Spanish, are very important.

And our country has taken the leadership in recent years in trying to bring peace not only to our own Nation but to others. I've been proud to represent you in negotiating with President Sadat and Prime Minister Begin to bring peace to

Israel. And I see this not just as an achievement for Israel, to make sure that they are secure and strong and democratic and free and at peace, but that investment there by the people of our Nation, with me as your leader, has given our own Nation more stability, more security, more chance for freedom and for peace, and has stabilized a very troubled area of the world. These kind of strategic common relationships that bind us together with foreign countries are important to us all.

I'm grateful to you for what you mean to me in the past and in the present, and I'm even more grateful for what you're going to mean to me 2 weeks from now when you have helped to elect me and Fritz Mondale to another term in office.

Thank you very much. I love you all. God bless you.

NOTE: The President spoke at 4:39 p.m. in the main picnic area at Turkey Lake Park.

New Orleans, Louisiana
Remarks at a Rally With Local Residents. October 21, 1980

Mayor Morial, who has done so much to keep this beautiful and ancient and precious city, with a very calm and strong leadership, moving into the 1980's and toward the 21st century, with progress and determination and confidence and, at the same time, preserving the special heritage which has always been greatest for those who live in New Orleans, you have a good partner in Moon Landrieu. As a matter of fact, that partnership is so close that I have to guard the other cities' interests, as Moon and your own Mayor Morial plan for the future. So, Moon, be nice to the other cities. Keep what you want for New Orleans. Let the rest of them have a chance. What bothers me is

that Russell Long gives him advice on what to do. [*Laughter*]

And I might say that I have a secret—but not so secret—love affair with a certain woman in New Orleans, and that's Lindy Boggs. She has the special qualities of a southern woman—beautiful, strong, idealistic, deeply committed—which all of us admire. And I first fell for her, I have to say, when she managed the 1976 Democratic Convention so well and chose the same nominee that I was supporting myself.

And I'm also very proud to have as my Louisiana State chairman a man who led this State with good humor, with courage, with confidence, with the utmost in fashion in clothes, with a certain debonair attitude, and who came out of office with the highest support, I guess, that any Governor ever left office with. And also, I'm very proud to have him supporting me. I would much rather have Edwin Edwards leading my campaign than to be in Governor Reagan's shoes with the Republican Governor leading his. That gives me great confidence in the future.

So, I don't want the people of Louisiana to let me down. I don't want the people of Louisiana to let Fritz Mondale down, and I don't want the people of Louisiana to let Governor Edwin Edwards down either.

We've got some good people in our Cabinet from Louisiana, in addition to Moon Landrieu. Ray Marshall, as you know, is from Oak Grove, Louisiana. Jack Watson, my Chief of Staff, is from Shreveport, Louisiana. And I'm very grateful to come down here on this same historic site that I believe turned the tide not only in Louisiana in 1976 in the general election, but also gave the Nation a new belief which just narrowly came to pass, that I could be elected President of the United States.

As Lindy Boggs pointed out, Thomas Jefferson and Andrew Jackson are the two founders of the Democratic Party. Thomas Jefferson did a lot of great things, but the Louisiana Purchase is by far the wisest decision that he or any other President ever made. And I'm very glad that you mentioned Andy Jackson, too, who fought the British here, in Louisiana, in New Orleans, and beat them so bad that no foreign invader has ever dared come to this place since then, unless you might call Admiral Farragut and Ben Butler invaders from a foreign country.

But now that we've got our Nation all back together, we southerners know that although no southern President has served, from the Deep South, since 1844 when James Polk was elected, we're going to keep the hands on the reins in Washington, with southerners who brought our Nation together in a unified way and have a better future for us all.

When I came here in 1976, I made a few promises to you. First of all, I promised that the extremely high unemployment rate that prevailed in many parts of our land would be brought down. We've added in the last 4 years 8½ million new jobs in this country, a record never before achieved by any President who's served in the White House in time of peace or war.

We promised, also, the elderly citizens of New Orleans, of Louisiana, and this country, that we would make sure that the prospective bankruptcy of the social security system was corrected. And with the help of Russell Long, Bennett Johnston, Gillis Long, and other members of your delegation, we have now got social security back on a sound basis, and we're going to keep it that way as long as a Democrat serves in the White House.

At the urging then of Bennett Johnston and Russell Long—they told me to mention that we were going to get a north-south highway started. I didn't know what I was talking about, but I promised it, and the I–49 connector is now underway to being a reality. And let me point out to you that this list of things would not be complete in Louisiana if I didn't say that I promised also to pass a law through Congress, if they would cooperate, to decontrol the prices of oil and natural gas.

We moved too fast for some; we didn't move fast enough for others. But that new law had never been passable since the days of Harry Truman, under Democrats or Republicans. And now we're seeing rich dividends, because this year in the United States of America, we'll have more oil wells, more gas wells drilled than any year in the history of this land.

And I might also point it out to you— and it affects your community very deeply—and this may be a surprise: The United States of America will produce more coal in 1980 than any other year in history. And the only thing that keeps us from tripling coal production is that we don't have the port facilities and the transportation facilities to load American coal to replace OPEC oil on the energy markets of the world. I see a real need to improve the channels and to improve the loading facilities in great ports like New Orleans, which will let you be one of the coal shipping centers of this land.

I might point out that for Louisiana farmers and for others around this land we set world records in grain exports in 1977. We set new world records in 1978. We set new world records in 1979. And in 1980, in spite of restraints on shipments of grain to the Soviet Union, with new markets in China, Mexico, and other places, we'll have $40 billion of American agricultural exports going overseas—a lot of it through New Orleans. This is $8 billion more than last year; a new world's record and the biggest increase in any year in the history of our country.

And now, I'd like to close my remarks by saying just a few things about what are involved in your decisions to be made on November the 4th.

I grew up, like many of you, during the Great Depression. I lived on a farm in south Georgia. My father and his father and others before him had never had a chance to finish high school. We didn't have electricity on our farm; we didn't have running water inside the house. And we turned to Franklin Roosevelt and to other great Democratic leaders to help us have a better life.

Franklin Roosevelt proposed the REA; the Republicans opposed it. Franklin Roosevelt and the Democrats proposed that our senior citizens would have social security; the Republicans opposed it. Many people were working in sweatshops, little children 9, 10 years old, boys and girls working in sweatshops all day. The Democrats proposed a minimum wage to give working people in this Nation a chance to live a decent life, to meet the needs of their family, and to have some self-dignity—25 cents an hour. The Republicans opposed it.

My first job when I finished high school in 1941 was at the minimum wage. It had been increased by the Democrats from 25 cents to 40 cents an hour. The Republicans opposed that increase. This is the kind of record that was set during those years when I was a young man growing up.

Later, Harry Truman said we ought to have Medicare to give older people a chance for some health insurance when they reached their retirement age. The Republicans, of course, opposed it. My opponent in this election got started with his public career campaigning around this Nation against Medicare. He has said that the minimum wage has caused more misery and more unemployment than anything since the Great Depression. And he has said unemployment compensation for families who are temporarily out of work is just a prepaid vacation for freeloaders.

The differences that historically have been the case between Democrats and Republicans to give the poor, the elderly, the children, the sick, the working families, the farmers a better chance in life—those differences between our two parties still prevail. Major issues are at stake on November the 4th. Those decisions cannot be made by candidates. I'll be working day and night, political leaders on this stage will be helping me, but the issue is in your hands.

There is no way that Republican voters can carry New Orleans or Louisiana on November the 4th. The only possibility for a Republican victory here is a Democratic Party that's divided, which we do not have—it's united now—and [if] Democrats who believe that their families and themselves and those they love ought to have a surer, more secure, more peaceful, more prosperous life in the future, don't work between now and November the 4th and get your friends and neighbors to go out and vote.

If you will help me, if you will dedicate yourselves to the principles that have made our party and our Nation strong, if you'll remember the heritage of Louisiana and what's given you a better life and will give your children an even better life, then there's no doubt in my mind that with your help, as partners, we will have a tremendous victory, we'll keep a Democrat, Jimmy Carter, with your help, in the White House for the next 4 years.

Thank you very much. I love you all.

NOTE: The President spoke at 7:17 p.m. from the stage in Jackson Square.

New Orleans, Louisiana

Remarks at a Democratic National Committee Fundraising Dinner.　October 21, 1980

Now I see how David Treen feels. It's awful difficult to follow Edwin Edwards. [*Laughter*] You might think this is a campaign between me and Governor Reagan. As a matter of fact, we are just surrogates. The contest in Louisiana, and I'm thankful for it, is between Edwin Edwards and the Republican Governor who took his place temporarily. And I don't want you friends of Edwin's and mine to let him and me down. Right? [*Applause*]

When I ran for President in 1976, the chairman of my campaign here was Bennett Johnston. And we had a tremendous rally in Jackson Square shortly before the election. Not many people thought I had a chance. It's very difficult to defeat an incumbent President who took over and brought the Nation out of the embarrassment of Watergate. That rally, I think, showed the Nation that my strength was a little greater than had been thought and, for the first time since James Polk was elected in 1844, a President went to Washington from the Deep South.

Edwin was quoting Harry Truman. A lot of people looked on me with suspicion when I went north to campaign. I went to Illinois to try to get Adlai Stevenson and others to support me there, and I made a speech one night. They were worried about southern loyalty to the Democratic Party and what it stands for. Adlai introduced me. He had some little sly things to say about southerners, and they weren't quite in the mainstream of the Democratic Party, you know. And I said, "Adlai, I remember in 1952 when your father ran for President. Illinois didn't vote for him, but Georgia did." And in 1956 when Adlai Stevenson ran for President as a Democrat, Illinois didn't vote for him, but Georgia did.

And the other night I was at the Al Smith dinner. And I pointed out that in 1928, when he ran and he was killed politically because he was a Catholic, and there was a lot of prejudice against him, Georgia voted for Al Smith; New York didn't. And when I went to Massachusetts in 1976, there were a lot of people who said, "Well, is this Deep South Democrat in the mainstream of our party? Does he know what the Democratic Party stands for?" And I pointed out to them that when John Kennedy ran for President of the United States, he got a bigger majority in Georgia than he did in Massachusetts.

We've understood down here what it means to be a Democrat. I think we represent some of the finest elements of the Democratic Party. Sometimes those principles have been betrayed, and we have had in the public's mind an image as Democrats that were not compatible in the national party with southern beliefs. I'm not prejudiced, but I think maybe the national party made some mistakes, and we were always right.

And the other night I was at the Al Smith dinner, as I mentioned earlier. Governor Reagan was there. It's the first time I've seen him since we were Governors. And I told him that the burdens of the Presidency are very heavy. It's an onerous job. The trials and tribulations of the Oval Office are almost unbearable for a human being. It's difficult, it breaks you down—always worrying. He listened very carefully. But I can tell you that 3½ years sure passes fast when you're having a lot of fun. [*Laughter*]

We in Georgia and Louisiana and other parts of the Nation remember what the Democratic Party has done for us. I mentioned a few things at Jackson Square tonight, personal things, things that are important. My father was a farmer. Our people moved to this country over 300 years ago—all been farmers, every one; none of my family ever finished high school until I came along—looking for a better life and found it, because Democratic leaders had confidence in human beings.

They saw a certain worth in farmers that didn't have running water, didn't have electricity and needed it. The Republicans, when the REA was founded, called it socialism and communism, because the Government was going to help farmers have a better life.

People who had to work for a living have always been a special concern of Democrats. I worked in the field when I was a boy. It didn't hurt me. But we went to work before daybreak and quit when the sun went down and went and pumped water and fed the livestock—went to bed after dark, got up at 4:30 in the morning. It was normal routine for my family and for maybe some of yours. And those who worked in the nearby shirt factory, the women folks whose husbands couldn't make a living on a small farm with a couple of mules, couple of plows, didn't get paid fairly. The folks that owned the factories weren't southerners; they were from up north.

And the Democrats saw something wrong with that and proposed a minimum wage—25 cents an hour, a radical proposal. Republicans opposed it. But it gave the working people a new dignity, a new self-respect, a new chance in life they'd never had before. And then slowly and methodically, always over Republican opposition, the minimum wage was gradually increased, just to let average people have a chance in life.

And I'm not going to dwell any further on social security, on the rural free delivery of mail a little bit earlier, on Medicare, on Medicaid, on better education, housing programs, a stable farm economy where the farmers themselves had a little control over the marketing of their own crops, stable prices. Those kinds of things all came from the Democrats, and every one of them were opposed by Republicans. I don't want to dwell on that anymore.

What I want to point out is the other aspect of a Democratic Party, a Democratic Party of stability, of management competence, of the understanding of American industry and the strength that is inherent in our country not only because of human beings whom we love, but because of the stewardship that God's given us over natural resources.

I've only been in office 3½ years. I saw some real needs when I was elected. My background is in the military, and the way I got a college education was because my daddy supported a Congressman who was elected, Mr. Steve Pace, and I got an appointment to Annapolis. It's all I wanted to do from the time I was 5 years old. I served in the submarine force. And when I went in the Oval Office, I was concerned because our national defense under 8 years of Republican administration was going down. Defense spending went down 7 out of 8 of those years and dropped 37 percent between 1959—between 1969 and the time I came in office—37 percent.

We've increased defense spending every year to give your country a better chance to defend itself. And because of military preparedness, worked out methodically, carefully, in advance, with businesslike principles of management, we've had a chance to keep our Nation at peace. I've not had to send our military forces into combat since I've been in the White House, and I hope I can go out of office at the end of 4 more years with that record still intact.

I'm the first President that can say that in more than 50 years. But the reason for it is that we've not only kept a strong defense, but we've worked for peace. We've used American strength to protect our interests and to extend the beneficial impact of America around the world.

We had never entered the great continent of Africa, with 50 or more nations, until I was inaugurated President. And now we have relationships with those countries that are paying rich dividends. Henry Kissinger, the last year he was Secretary of State, wasn't permitted to go into Nigeria. Now Nigeria, the largest and strongest and most economically sound and the most democratic black nation on Earth, is a staunch ally of the United States—tremendous trade potential there. It had never been done before. We didn't fire a shot; we didn't push anybody around. But we've opened up that vista of a better life not only for those people but for us, for our farmers and our merchants, those who work in the factories producing American goods. A billion people in China now are friends, allies, not in a military way, but providing tremendous stability and strategic strength to keep eastern Asia at peace.

Not long ago I was in a little steel plant in Perth Amboy, New Jersey. The workers in that plant produce more steel per year per worker than in any plant on Earth. They take scrap metal that used to go overseas and they make steel rods. I asked the manager of it, "Where does this steel go?" He said, "Half of it goes to China." They make steel cheaper in New Jersey and ship it halfway around the world and beat the price of the Japanese right next door. But we've got a

market there that's giving us a bright future.

We've got 44,000 fewer employees in the Federal Government now, full-time employees, than we had the day I came in office. But we're giving better service to our people, better housing programs under Moon Landrieu, better education for our children. In the United States today, there is not a single child, boy or girl, who finishes high school who's able to do college work that cannot get a college education because their family is too poor. That's a human achievement, but it also strengthens our country.

Agriculture is important to me. We've tried to get government's nose out of the free enterprise system of this country. Republicans have talked that way for generations, but with the help of your congressional delegation and others, we've finally done it. We have not only decontrolled the price of oil and gas, which every Republican President has always promised, and which will give us this year, in 1980, the largest number of oil and gas wells being drilled than any year in history, but the United States is also producing more coal this year than any year in history. And we can sell all the American coal we can transport to a port and load on a ship. There're ships in Hampton Roads, Virginia, right now, waiting 25 days to come alongside the pier and load. This is the result of a new energy policy, sound business principles, looking to the future, recognizing our natural resources, that a Democratic administration has put into effect. The Republicans have talked about it ever since many of us were born; the Democrats have finally done it.

We've not just deregulated a major element of the energy industry, we've also deregulated the railroads. We've deregulated the airlines; we've deregulated the trucking industry; we've deregulated financial institutions; we're working on the deregulation of communications, to let the free enterprise system of our country—which the Republicans always claim is theirs—be free of government intrusion and let the competitive spirit of America prove once again that economically, America is great. We've got the most productive workers on Earth at this moment. Their productivity's not been increasing as rapidly as it has in some other countries, but now that we have an energy policy to give us a base, we are ready to move ahead with major investments to modernize our plants.

I've been in a textile mill not long ago in Spartanburg, South Carolina—an old, dilapidated building, but a very modern plant. In the last 2 years, we have increased American textile exports—exports—$2 billion. At the same time, we have reduced American textile imports. That's a remarkable achievement by a Democratic administration who believes that it's a better for our country to sell goods overseas than unnecessarily to buy goods overseas and import them to this country to put American workers out of their jobs.

OPEC oil is a great strategic possession. The Arab OPEC countries have about 6 percent of the nation's—of the world's reserves—6 percent. The United States alone has 24 percent. That's important, too, particularly to Louisiana and to Oklahoma and to Texas and a few other States. But American soil is perhaps the greatest natural resource that we have. And I would guess that 100 years from now or 1,000 years from now, our country will still be the breadbasket of the world.

We imposed sales restraints on the Soviet Union when they invaded Afghanistan. I had to either take military action, or economic and political action. I decided to take the latter two, to impose

some restraints on them. Everybody knows it was not a political thing to do. It was about a week before the Iowa caucuses. We didn't want the American farmers to suffer.

I believe we ought to continue to build the markets for American products overseas. Democrats—in 1977, we set a world record on agricultural exports from this country. A lot came through here, New Orleans. In 1978, we set another world's record—agricultural exports. In 1979, we set another world's record in agricultural exports. This year with the Soviet restraints on, we opened up six marketing centers in the major buying points around the world and tried to set a new record.

This year we will export to other overseas countries $40 billion of American agricultural products—new record—$8 billion more than last year we increased this year, more than we've ever increased before in any year in history. We've tripled our sales to Mexico in the last 4 years, and we will sign tonight, in 30 more minutes, in the People's Republic of China and here, a new agricultural agreement on a long-term basis for a major annual sale of American grain. This is the kind of approach that pays rich dividends.

So, you've got a combination in the Democratic Party of sensitivity to human beings, the guarantee of a better life for Americans, the honoring of basic civil rights to give black people and Spanish-speaking people and others an equal chance in life and, at the same time, a competence in management and an improvement in the business climate of this Nation, a freeing of the free enterprise system, an expansion of exports, a revitalization of industry, more profits—not under Republicans, but Democrats. The combination of those is extremely important.

And finally, let me say that military strength is not enough. We've worked for peace not only for ourselves, but for others—in the Middle East; we've stabilized the eastern Asian area. We're striving forward to make sure that we control the horrible threat of nuclear weapons.

I'm not going to stand here tonight and berate my Republican opponent. But all those elements of a better life that the Democrats espouse—I could quote to you verbatim what he has said in condemnation of those programs—social security, minimum wage, Medicare, unemployment compensation, better health care in the future, housing programs, all. But the most important single issue on which he and I stand apart is the control of nuclear weapons. Every single President since Harry Truman, Democrats and Republicans, have worked hard to control nuclear weapons, to have balanced, controlled, confirmable agreements between our two countries, with the goal in mind of lowering the arsenals of nuclear weaponry as a clear prospect for the future.

Governor Reagan has said, "Let's scrap the nuclear arms control treaty. Let's play a trump card against the Soviet Union. The prospect of a nuclear arms race," he said, "might contribute to more stability in the future." Nuclear superiority sounds good to a proud American, but it destroys the basis on which nuclear arms control can be enforced and on which agreements can be reached.

There is no way that an American President or an American citizen would sit quiet and subservient if Brezhnev made the same speech and said, "I'm going to tear up the treaty that has been negotiated under two Republican and one Democratic President. We're going to work for Soviet nuclear superiority. We're going to start an arms race. And we believe that now the United States will be more amenable to an agreement." What would our reply be? Our reply would be the same as theirs: "We'll match you missile for missile," and an arms race is the result.

Well, there are a lot of issues at stake on November the 4th—old, ancient, historical issues that have always divided our party, modern issues that are in the daily newspaper now, and issues for the future that might be even more significant to the lives of those who look to you for leadership in this State. My plea to you is that this next 10 days that you use every bit of influence you can to bring about a Democratic victory in Louisiana. It's crucial for us to win. I believe a lot is at stake, not just a job for me, but because the things in which we believe, the things that have made America great, will be decided on a future course as a result of November 4th.

We've got problems in this country, yes. I've made mistakes in the White House, yes; every President has. But the principles that have guided me have been the same as the ones that guided you. This next election will show what kind of country we have. We are a strong country, we are a prosperous country, we are a country blessed by God. We're the greatest nation on Earth, and with your help, we'll make it even greater in the future.

Thank you very much.

NOTE: The President spoke at 9:10 p.m. in the Imperial Ballroom at the Fairmont Hotel.

Beaumont, Texas

Remarks Upon Arrival at Jefferson County Airport. October 22, 1980

Mayor Myers, my good friend, Jack Brooks, Congressman Charlie Wilson:

I'm really grateful for these stomping boots. And I want to ask you, how many of you are going to help me stomp the Republicans on November 4? [*Cheers*]

We've done that a lot of times in Texas. Whenever the Democrats in this State were united, working toward a common goal, recognizing the intense issues that affect the quality of life for the working people of this Nation, for the ones who are the backbone of the greatness of our country, Democrats have never been defeated.

Ten days from now, we have a sharp difference between myself and Governor Reagan, between the Democrats and Republicans, what we've always stood for, and in the quality of life that you will enjoy in the years ahead. I'll do the best I can. I need your help. This is a crucial election. Having Ralph Yarborough here helps me a lot. I'll be meeting Lloyd Bentsen at my next stop. And I believe that Bill Hobby here and other Democrats show you the depth of importance of this election.

All of you remember the longstanding differences between the Democrats and Republicans. In the Great Depression years, I grew up as a boy on a farm. Democrats were for the REA and electricity for farmers; Republicans were against it. Democrats were for a minimum wage. It was only 25 cents an hour then. Republicans were against it. Democrats raised the minimum wage to 40 cents when I got my first job, working for the Government; Republicans were against it. Franklin Roosevelt and the Democrats were for social security; the Republicans were against it. Governor Reagan got his start in politics campaigning around this country, for the American Medical Association, against Medicare to give old-age people better health care. He hasn't changed his spots, neither have the Republicans. They still feel the same way about the working people of this Nation.

Democrats have always been in the forefront of giving us a better life in our State. Agricultural income, oil and gas production, coal production, better security, more commitment to peace now and in the future—all of these issues are very important to you and to me. You'll help me, as partners; we'll have a greater life in our great country in the next 4 years, and we will whip the Republicans on election day on November the 4th.

Thank you very much. God bless you.

I'm very proud of these stomping boots. Thank you for making them for me.

Good luck.

NOTE: The President spoke at 10:50 a.m. at Hangar No. 1 in the general aviation area.

Beaumont, Texas

Remarks to Employees of the Bethlehem Steel Corporation.   October 22, 1980

Congressman Brooks, Congressman Charlie Wilson, Senator Parker, Senator Yarborough, Lieutenant Governor Bill Hobby, representatives of both management of this fine Bethlehem Steel plant and also, of course, my friends who do the work here that's so crucial to our country:

I have had a chance to participate in the dedication and the launching of great warships for our country, nuclear cruisers, I've visited nuclear aircraft carriers, I've served in submarines, and I can tell you that the work you do here is no more [less] important to the security of the United States of America than is the work of those who produce the warships that protect our land and the armed forces themselves.

The first responsibility of any President is to guarantee the security of the United States. From the moment that I took office as President and as Commander in Chief of our military forces, I set two vital goals.

One was reversing the decline in our military strength that had occurred the 8 years before I became President. Seven of those years we had gone down in budgeting funds for the military forces of our country. Since then, we've had a steady, annual, carefully planned, and effective increase above and beyond the inflation rate in the allotment of United States Government budget money for a stronger defense.

The other thing that I decided to do as President was to make sure that we corrected an equal threat to our national security by reducing our dependence on foreign oil. Military security and energy security are both vital to our national security. I fought long and hard for the first comprehensive energy policy that this country's ever had. We've won a great victory, a victory that had eluded other Presidents before me, both Democrats and Republicans.

We're at the end of a 12,000-mile supply line, a very uncertain supply line. At the other end is danger, turmoil, uncertainty, sometimes the desire to bring this Nation to its knees. As you remember, the last time there was a crisis in the Persian Gulf, with the Iranian revolution, we lost about 4 million barrels of oil per day. America was thrown into confusion. It was a severe damage to our economic security. Long waiting lines at gas stations took place.

This time, with a new energy policy now in the law books of our Nation, when the war between Iran and Iraq took place and we lost another 4 million barrels of oil per day, our Nation was able to withstand that shock without any damage to the quality of life or the security or confidence of the American people.

The reason for that, of course, is complicated. But a large part of the credit belongs to you and other Americans around this country who recognized that the only way to reduce our excessive dependence on foreign oil is two things: One is to conserve energy, not to waste it; and the other one is to produce more American energy here at home.

The OPEC oil nations have 6 percent of the world's energy reserve—6. The United States by itself has 24 percent. But in the past, the oil and gas industry was hamstrung by excessive Government regulation. We were successful finally under this administration, working with a Democratic Congress, to pass the laws deregulating the production and a phased deregulation of the pricing of natural gas and oil from this country.

Last night, I got some figures that showed how successful we have been. Now the number of drilling rigs operating in the United States, many of them made by you right here, was at an all-time high— 3,164 drill rigs running now in the country, a record never before achieved in this country. Also, the number of oil and gas wells to be drilled in 1980 will be the highest number in the history of our country.

This is part of the achievement of which we are so proud, but in matters that don't relate directly to you, but affect your lives, we're doing equally well. Our country—this may be a surprise—is producing more American coal this year, from the coal mines, than any year in history. And we can export as much coal to eager foreign buyers as we can pass through the waterways, railroads, and over the highways, and load on ships. In Hampton Roads, Virginia, at this moment, ships are waiting 25 days to come alongside the pier to pick up American coal.

This is the kind of progress of which we Democrats and we Americans can be truly proud. As you also know, this is a step forward in a better life for you.

I came into office in January of 1977. Since then, the number of jobs available in Texas, the number of people that work in Texas have increased over 900,-000. The per capita income of Texans on the average has gone up more than 40 percent, and the unemployment rate has been slashed enormously in your State. There's a new recognition that on the agricultural farms, among farm families, in exports of American products, we're making good progress now.

And with the new energy policy now in place, we can revitalize American industry in the years ahead. The American worker is the most productive worker in the world, but lately that productivity per worker has not been going up as rapidly as it ought to be. It's been about steady. Other countries are going up. But we need to give the American workers new plants, new machinery, new tools, to be sure we're never second to the workers in any country. We're making good progress now, and with a sound economy, a good, level-headed administration to make sure that tax programs and laws on the books are effective, we can have that kind of future ahead of us.

I'm from the Deep South, from Georgia. My philosophy in government is probably about the same as yours. I don't believe that government ought to stick its nose in the affairs of private citizens, and I don't believe that government ought to stick its nose in the minds and hearts and jobs of people in the private enterprise system. A lot of people talk about that, for a long time, ever since I remember anything about politics, but nobody's been able to do anything until the last 3½ years.

We have now not only deregulated oil and gas, we've also deregulated the United States railroads, trucking, airlines, financial institutions. We're working on the communications industry next. And this means that in the future we'll let the free enterprise system function the way it ought to be and let competition, which you are very eager and able to meet, give America not only better production, not only higher exports but also more inexpensive and finer things to buy.

We've formed a new relationship between business and management and the government in our troubled steel industry, in coal industry, in automobiles. You may remember 3 years ago, every time you picked up a newspaper there were headlines about wildcat strikes in the coal mines. You haven't seen those in the last 2 years, because now the coal workers, mine workers, and management are sitting down together and saying, "What can we do to make sure our industry stays sound, the mines are producing coal, and the workers are fully employed?" Doing the same thing in steel—it's helped Bethlehem Steel and its corporate structure as much as anything in the past has done. We can meet foreign competition.

Not long ago, I was in a little steel plant in Perth Amboy, New Jersey, a modern plant. They use scrap steel that used to be sent overseas. Now it's produced in the United States into steel rods. Every worker in that plant produces more steel per year than in any other steel plant in the world. And I ask them where their product goes. Like yours, it's an international market. They said half the steel produced in that plant goes to the People's Republic of China. They're making steel in New Jersey, shipping it halfway around the world, 12,000 miles, and selling it to China cheaper than Japan, right across an inland waterway, can make it and sell it in competition. That's the kind of thing that we're trying to do all over this Nation.

And finally, I'd like to say this to you. This election of 1980 is important to you and to your families, to the people that you care about, and to the true opportunities for future years that mean so much to individual human beings in this country.

My background is a lot like yours. I grew up on a farm in south Georgia. My people have lived in this country for a long time. Nobody in my family before me—my father, my grandfather, or anyone else—had ever had a chance to finish high school until I came along. I remember the Great Depression years, when people were starving and a lot of people were hungry. The elderly had no security. And then the Democrats came along, under Franklin Roosevelt, later followed by Harry Truman, Lyndon Johnson, John Kennedy, gave us a better life. This was a very important thing for us.

I remember when they didn't have a minimum wage. The Democrats said at least we ought to pay American workers and their families 25 cents an hour. The Democrats were for it; Republicans were against it. I'm older than most of you, but I got my first job in 1941 when I finished high school. The minimum wage then was 40 cents. When it was raised from 25 to 40 cents, the Democrats pushed it through Congress; Republicans, of course, were against it. It's been a steady pattern ever since and the same issues being drawn in this election, when my opponent says the minimum wage has caused more misery and unemployment since anything since the Great Depression.

I know that some of you, on occasion, are unemployed, maybe not at this particular plant, but some of those that you care about, working people of our country. The Democrats have put into effect unemployment compensation to tide you over, so your wives and children can have something to eat, send your kids to school, during those times when plants changed locations or when models changed in automobiles. My Republican opponent says that unemployment compensation is a prepaid vacation for freeloaders.

There's always been a difference in the way Democrats look toward people and Republicans look toward people. I remember when old folks had to live in poor folks homes. The Democrats put forward social security; Republicans, of course, were against it.

My opponent started his career in politics speaking around this country, paid by the American Medical Association, against Medicare. It just gives some medical care for retired people. He's against national health insurance, of course. And he believes that the same structure that's always characterized the Republican Party ought to be kept intact. You all know that these issues don't change.

When Lyndon Johnson ran for President, he gave the working people of this country a better life, gave minority people a better life, gave older people a better life, provided better education for your children, a better chance for you to organize, to present your case to management and negotiate a settlement that would give working families a better quality of existence in the greatest land on Earth.

Finally, let me say this. I'm indebted to you. What you do for this country, you can afford to be proud of it, because you contribute as much to our national security as anyone I know.

There's a bright future for this country, a secure America, America that's strong militarily, America at peace, an America where nuclear weapons are controlled and where we don't let other nations that don't have them now build them and threaten others against them with terrorist acts. Governor Reagan says that nonproliferation is none of our business. It is our business. You think for a few moments about what it would mean if Libya or Iraq had atomic bombs. The threat of terrorism is enormous. And those are the kinds of issues that will affect your life, your safety, and the quality of existence of those you love in the years ahead.

I come here as a President, yes. I come here as Commander in Chief of military forces of this country, yes. I also come here as a candidate running for reelection. I ask you to help me. It'll mean a lot to me. I think it'll mean a lot to the country, a lot to the future. I don't claim to know all the answers. Like yourselves, sometimes I make mistakes. But there's a tide of history that I've tried to point out to you in just the few minutes we've had together.

It's been an exciting thing for me to come here. I want people all over this Nation, through the television cameras and otherwise, to see what you're doing, because it's a reassuring thing. It means that all Americans, no matter where they might live, in Iowa, in California, in Georgia, in Maine, can say, "Well, those folks down in Beaumont, Texas, are producing a product that will go all over the world. It'll give us a better life, a more secure life, a better future." That's what I want. With God's help, we'll have it together.

Thank you very much.

NOTE: The President spoke at 11:30 a.m. outside the Bethlehem Steel Corporation plant, which he toured prior to his remarks.

Waco, Texas

Remarks at a Rally With Local Residents. October 22, 1980

Thank you very much, Lloyd Bentsen, for your introduction. Lloyd Bentsen is the man that asked me to work with him to eliminate the tax on the small royalty owners of Texas and Oklahoma and Louisiana, and I agreed to do it. We're going to do it when the Congress reconvenes. That's the kind of leadership you've got in Washington, Lloyd Bentsen.

And I'm also glad to be with Congressman Marvin Leath, one of the finest new Members of Congress, with Charlie Wilson, who was with me earlier in Beaumont, Senator David Pryor, and others that I won't name this morning. But I particularly want to mention Congressman Bob Poage, who represented the people of this district for 42 years and who also represented the people of the Third District of Georgia, where I live, because he knew what farm families needed, he knew what Americans needed—a strong defense, unity among the oil people, and a bright vision of the future. That's what Bob Poage gave us when he was in the Congress, and that's what he still gives us this day.

And I also want to be sure to point out to you the great honor always paid to me when I can be in the same congregation, the same audience, on the same platform with Lady Bird Johnson, one of the finest people who ever lived on Earth. I know that I'm not only in the geographic heart of Texas; I'm also in the Democratic heart of Texas, right? [*Applause*] You might say I came here for the purpose of getting votes for the Presidency, and that's partially true, but this is also the biggest airport close to one of my favorite towns in the United States, and that's Abbott, Texas, because any town that can produce

Willie Nelson will always be close to my heart.

Not too long ago I was in Beaumont, earlier today, and they gave me a new pair of boots. Congressman Jack Brooks said they were stomping boots—to stomp Republicans on November the 4th.

But let me say this: I grew up on a farm, and I know you need high-top boots for things besides stomping Republicans. As you well know—and I see a few carriers out here in the audience—Republicans have a habit of spreading a lot of horse manure around right before an election. And lately, as you also know, it's getting pretty deep all over this country.

I noticed the other day in the news that former President Richard Nixon, one of the great Republican Presidents, as you know, has been writing campaign advisory memos for Ronald Reagan. When I saw where Ronald Reagan was getting his advice, I began to understand a few of the things he'd been saying a little bit better.

Yesterday, I noticed in the news also that Governor Reagan announced that he has a secret plan to get the hostages back. Those of you who remember past elections when Richard Nixon ran against Hubert Humphrey probably find that sounding familiar. Do you remember when Richard Nixon said just before an election in 1968 that he had a secret plan to win the war in Vietnam? You all remember that?

AUDIENCE. Yes!

THE PRESIDENT. Well, here it is 12 years later, and we still don't know what Mr. Nixon's secret plan was to win the Vietnam war. Now, how many of you Texans with sound judgment, familiar with history, believe that Ronald Reagan has a secret plan to get the hostages back? How many of you think that?

AUDIENCE. No!

THE PRESIDENT. Governor Reagan, so far, has had a good opportunity, and he's done pretty well in keeping his plan secret. He's got a secret plan for providing for the well-being of retired Americans by calling four times to make social security voluntary. If there's any one plan I know that would put social security instantly into bankruptcy, it's to let people who want to withdraw from paying social security to do so. Voluntary social security would be the end of it. But Mr. Reagan says he's got a secret plan for correcting that defect.

Mr. Reagan has a secret plan for providing good health care for senior citizens by being against Medicare. He traveled all over this Nation, his first time in public life, working for the American Medical Association, campaigning against Medicare.

Mr. Reagan also has a secret plan for helping working families by being against the minimum wage. He said the minimum wage has caused more misery and more unemployment in America than anything since the Great Depression. I remember when we didn't have a minimum wage, and the Democrats proposed that it be 25 cents an hour. The Republicans were against it, said it was socialism or communism. Later, the Democrats proposed the minimum wage of 40 cents an hour. That's when I got my first job. The Republicans were against that enormous increase, and they said that a working man or a working woman trying to support a family wasn't worth 40 cents an hour.

Mr. Reagan also has a secret plan to take care of working families who are temporarily unemployed without unemployment compensation. He says that unemployment compensation is just a prepaid vacation for freeloaders. That's the kind of secret plan that's still being put into effect. And as you know, Mr.

Reagan has already revealed one of his secret plans for curing pollution. He wants to cut down all the trees in the United States. He said that's where the pollution comes from.

Well, there's one more thing that the Republicans are covering up, perhaps a little more deeply than most, and that is a crucial issue to you, even more important, perhaps, than social security, Medicare, minimum wage, unemployment compensation, and that's our Nation's defense. As long as I'm President of the United States and Commander in Chief of the military forces, we're going to have a strong nation, because I know that only through strength can we stay at peace.

In the 7 years before I became President, when Republicans were in the White House, in 7 of the 8 years, we had a decrease—a decrease—under the Republicans, in real funds for our Nation's defense. That, ladies and gentlemen, is not compatible with the philosophy of Texas Democrats, to cut defense spending in 8 years, under Republicans, 37 percent. Since I've been in office, we've had an orderly, steady, effective increase, above and beyond inflation, every single year. And with the help of Democrats in the Congress, we're going to keep that steady, upward progress as long as I serve in the White House.

The state of our Nation's defense is a legitimate issue for a congressional and also a Presidential election, but there's no place in this campaign for false charges.

The latest example is my opponent's charge, for instance, that we are not involved in the Iran-Iraq war because we're weak. Obviously, that charge is untrue and false. Our country is strong. In fact, we have the most powerful naval force ever assembled in the Indian Ocean, with two carrier task forces in that region. We have overwhelming naval and air

superiority to protect our interests there. We've prepositioned equipment for 12,000 Marines and munitions for 500 American aircraft, and we've arranged, recently, for facilities to be used at five different sites in that crucial region. When I took office, we had virtually no defense at all, under Republican Presidents, in that region. Today, we've acted to keep the straits open and to protect our vital interests. I can tell you, ladies and gentlemen in Texas, we're ready.

Let me say, also, that we had no battle tank being built; now we've got one. We had no new armored personnel carrier being developed; now we've got one. The Trident missiles and the Trident submarine were in a stalemate; now they're being built and produced and launched and tested. We didn't have any way to defend our silo missiles; now the MX missile will give us that capability. We didn't have any air-launched cruise missiles then; now we'll produce 3,000 of them in the next year. We're making sure that throughout the world American defenses are strong, because that's compatible with the American character. Those defenses were weakened under Republicans, but under Democrats we're putting our Nation strong, and that's the way it's going to stay to keep the peace.

I want to cover one more issue which you may not hear much about here in Waco, but Bob Poage knows about it, Lloyd Bentsen knows about it, and others on this stage know about it, and that's international affairs. Sometimes a President and a Member of Congress have to make a difficult decision. Two years ago, my administration established diplomatic relations with the People's Republic of China. Some of the Republicans thought it was a mistake. A billion people live there. That may not sound like it has anything to do with you, but listen to this about farm exports. Agriculture is a major element of the life of Texas. The fact is that since I became President, in that one nation alone, annual United States farm products exports to China have gone from zero to over $2 billion. The number one customer in the world for Texas cotton is the People's Republic of China.

We have quadrupled our sales of agricultural products to China in the last 2 years, and now, because of an agreement that we signed just last night in Beijing and in Washington, we'll be able to expand that trade even further. Under this agreement the Chinese will buy at least 6 million tons of American wheat and corn during each of the next 4 years. They can buy up to 9 million metric tons if they choose. Our best estimate is that next year they'll buy about 7.2 million metric tons of United States grain, and their purchase of Texas grain and cotton will continue to go up.

That's a lot of wheat. It may not be easy to understand how much 7 million tons is, but that's enough to make 15 loaves of bread for every man, woman, and child in the nation of China. This is good news for American farmers. It's good news for all Americans. As a matter of fact, in the last 3½ years we've had the highest gross income of farmers in history, we've had the highest increase in net farm income in history. This year we are drilling more oil and gas wells in the United States than any year in history. We're producing more American coal than any year in history. And we've set records under Bob Poage's leadership; now we're following along.

In 1977 we set a world record in farm product exports—1978, a new world's record; 1979, a new world's record; 1980, the highest of all, $40 billion worth of American farm products going overseas to foreign customers. That's what we're doing for the people of Texas.

I might say in closing that this election year is a very crucial year for you, for your families, and for people that you love. The issues are sharply drawn. You remember the past history and the differences between the Democratic Party and the Republican Party. I remember growing up on a farm. Franklin Roosevelt, the great Democratic President, said, "We ought to give the farmers an equal chance and start the REA and turn on electricity in the farmhouses of America." The Republicans, as you may remember, were against it.

Franklin Roosevelt thought that older people ought to be taken off the po' farms, as we called them, and given social security and some human decency and self-respect and security in their older years. He proposed social security. The Republicans were against it. I've already mentioned the minimum wage. Democrats have always been for it; Republicans were against it.

The working families of this Nation have always been foremost in the minds of Democratic leaders. Your great leader, Lyndon Johnson, proved that when he was in office. You might think that your vote doesn't matter in a national election, but if just 28,000 people had changed their minds in Texas in 1960, John Kennedy and Lyndon Johnson would never have been able to serve this great country. This is how close it is. And in 1968, if just a few Democrats had been more enthusiastic in supporting our ticket, Richard Nixon would never have served in the Oval Office in Washington; we would have had Hubert Humphrey instead.

So, think about your families, think about your future, think about the defense of this country, think about the industrial complex of our Nation. I share the same philosophy you do and that Democrats have shared down through the generations. We believe in human beings and making sure that our people have a better life. We believe in self-respect for those who might be old or afflicted or poor or not well educated, who can't speak English well or who might be black.

We believe in giving people a better chance in life, more security—let them stand on their own feet, manage their own affairs, live a good life. That's what Democrats have always believed. But we also believe that the Government should not interfere in the private lives of human beings, and the free enterprise system should compete and be truly free. The Republicans talk big, but they talk to big business mostly. The profits to them are more important.

Let me tell you in closing what we've done the last 3½ years. We have deregulated the price of oil and natural gas. Every President for many years has promised this, Democrats and Republicans. President Eisenhower vetoed a bill when he was in office, in 1956 I believe, that would have accomplished this purpose. We did it under a Democratic administration. Some thought we did it too fast; some thought we did it too slow. But the fact is that this has resulted in a great boon to the people of Texas. You've got in this State alone, compared to January of 1977, 914,000 people more holding jobs now. That's a good progress.

The unemployment rate in Texas since January of 1977, when I took over from a Republican President, is down 30 percent. Per capita income, that's how much the average Texan makes every year, has gone up over 40 percent in 3½ years. We've taken the Government's nose out of the industrial system of our country. We've deregulated not only the oil and natural gas, we've deregulated the railroads, deregulated the airlines, deregulated the trucks, deregulated the financial institutions, working on the communication systems to let us have competition, good products, good sales overseas, good jobs for Americans, good competition, and let the people of this Nation have a better life.

That's what the Democratic Party has done for you now and in the past. And the Democratic Party, with your help when we whip the Republicans on November the 4th, you're going to have a better life for this country in the future.

Thank you very much. Go to work. God bless you all.

NOTE: The President spoke at 1:41 p.m. at the James Connally Airfield at Texas State Technical Institute.

Texarkana, Arkansas

Exchange With Reporters Upon Arrival at Texarkana Municipal Airport.
October 22, 1980

Q. Mr. President, there is a new poll showing you up on Ronald Reagan by a point or two.

THE PRESIDENT. Oh, really? I haven't paid much attention to polls when I was behind. I don't think I'll start now.

Q. What do you think put you up?

THE PRESIDENT. It's hard to say whether we're up or down. But I think the American people, here a few days before the election, are beginning to pay much more attention to the issues between me and Governor Reagan and not so much to the debate format or whether there are two or three on the stage together or what the poll results say or what who said about whom. But the seriousness of this campaign and the effect on the future, I believe, is going to have a beneficial effect in the coming days for me.

Q. Any fear you'll peak too soon?

THE PRESIDENT. No, not with just a one point difference. That's not much.

Q. Do you think you have the momentum now?

THE PRESIDENT. I hope so.

Q. You come back.

THE PRESIDENT. I'll be back.

NOTE: The exchange began at 5 p.m.

As printed above, this item follows the text of the White House press release.

Texarkana, U.S.A.

Remarks at a Rally With Local Residents. October 22, 1980

Governor Bill Clinton, Senator Lloyd Bentsen, Governor George Nigh, Lieutenant Governor Bobby Freeman, Congressman Sam Hall, Congressman Beryl Anthony, other distinguished Democrats on this stage:

Hello, everybody from Arkansas. How you doing? [*Cheers*] Hello, everybody from Texas. How you doing? [*Cheers*] And as you know, we have people here from Oklahoma and from Louisiana as well.

This is a very important day for me, because I stand here on a spot which has historic memories for Democrats and for Southerners. I look across this square and I see a monument to the heroes of the Confederacy, and I think back in history about that. And I realize that not only did John Kennedy stand here where I am, with one foot in Texas and one in Arkansas, but that Lyndon Baines Johnson stood here, too. And I remember that it was you who put me on the road to the White House to represent the finest

elements of the South and the entire region and the finest elements of the Democratic Party, and I thank you from the bottom of my heart.

I was a farmer. My family have lived in this Nation more than 300 years. All of us have been farmers. I grew up on a farm as a boy during the depression years. My father or his father or none before him ever had a chance to finish high school, but I did. And the reason I did it was because we had a better life, because we had Democrats in the White House in Washington and a Democratic Congress that cared about human beings and believed in the alleviation of suffering and gave us a better chance than we would otherwise have had.

And I come from the part of the Nation, as you do, too, that believes in hard work, self-sacrifice, trust in our families, strong communities, a deep belief in God. And I pray that we never forget those values, which never change.

Today I want to talk to you just for a few minutes about the decision that you will be making on the 4th day of November. There is a great difference between myself and Governor Reagan. There's a great difference between the Republicans and the Democrats. But what we're talking about in this election, as the last days draw to a close, is the difference in the futures that we will have.

But as we plan for the years ahead, it's very important that we recognize the differences that do exist, because the Republicans would have you believe, in these last few days, that there's not much difference between us. On one side, we've got Franklin Delano Roosevelt, Harry Truman, John Fitzgerald Kennedy, and Lyndon Baines Johnson and what they mean to us in changing this Nation for the better. On the other side, we've got Herbert Hoover and we've got Richard

Nixon and we've got Gerald Ford, and now we've got Ronald Reagan, the same tradition. And don't you forget it for a moment when you go to vote on election day.

And let's now talk about senior citizens for a moment. On the one side, you've got a party under Franklin Roosevelt that saw that it was not good for retired people to live on po' farms, as we called them in south Georgia, where they could no longer earn their own living. The Democrats wanted the senior citizens to have some decency in life and some security and some self-respect, so he proposed social security. The Republicans were against it.

Later on, we have seen my opponent, Governor Reagan, on four different occasions say he believes that social security program ought to be voluntary. A voluntary social security program would instantly face bankruptcy, and that would be the end of social security. And don't you forget this sharp difference that's going to be decided on November the 4th.

Let's talk about the working families of this country. Most people in this Nation have to work for a living. They're not rich, but they want to earn their own living.

I remember how it was, not too long ago, during the depression years: little boys and girls, not as big as my daughter Amy, who's now 13, working in sweatshops 18 hours a day and grown men and women slaving all day long from sunup to sundown, with no decent wage to buy their families something to eat and clothes to wear and shelter over their heads. And the Democrats proposed a minimum wage. It was only 25 cents an hour. The Republicans opposed it. Later, when I got my first job as a high school graduate, the minimum had been raised by the Democrats from 25 cents to 40

cents an hour. The Republicans were against it. The Republicans said the minimum wage was socialism, communism.

That's not ancient history, because let me tell you what Governor Reagan says about the minimum wage. He says that the minimum wage has caused more misery and more unemployment than anything in this Nation since the Great Depression—a difference that's very important when you make a decision on November the 4th if you care about working families.

Sometimes in our society we have changes take place: factories close down, move to another community; sometimes buying habits of people change and you no longer have people building buggies and other things, there's a shift to automobiles—temporary unemployment. Democrats know that during those times, Americans who want jobs don't draw a paycheck for a few weeks. So, the Democrats put forward the idea of unemployment compensation. It's paid for by the workers and employees. It's kind of an insurance program.

Governor Reagan says that unemployment compensation is a prepaid vacation for freeloaders. We're not talking about freeloaders. We're talking about people who want to work, who have been working, who've paid their own insurance, but want their families to eat, if they are temporarily unemployed.

Let's talk about Medicare. Medicare is a Democratic program put forward under Harry Truman, so that when you reach your retirement age, in addition to social security—and the payments are taken out of your social security, as you know— it provides health care for senior citizens. Democrats are very proud of this program. It was opposed by the Republicans. They thought it was socialism again.

And Ronald Reagan, who's running

against me for President, said that he was against Medicare, that it was a program that would let the Government of the United States take over the medical system of this Nation and take away the freedom of our people. As the representative of the American Medical Association, he traveled all over this Nation trying to kill Medicare. A great difference is going to take place on election day depending on your decision.

I see this statue. I'm a southerner, and I'm proud of it. And I'm going to talk to you just a moment about something that's very important to southerners, and that's civil rights.

There was a time in our Nation, in our part of the country, when the laws were passed to prevent black people from having their constitutional rights or even the right to vote in an election. I look out over this audience, and I see black and white southerners here together, sharing a common life, better under the Democrats, rights guaranteed. The man responsible for that change was your neighbor from Texas, Lyndon Baines Johnson. And when the civil rights legislation was passed, it made us proud. But Governor Ronald Reagan said that the civil rights legislation was bad legislation. Those are the kind of things that will be decided by you in 10 days from now, on November the 4th.

Let's talk about employment. In the last 3½ years, as Lloyd Bentsen said, we've added almost 9 million new jobs in this Nation, in spite of OPEC oil prices and international problems that were created all over the world in the economy. In Texas alone, compared to the day I was inaugurated in 1977, there are 914,-000 more people holding jobs today than there were 3½ years ago, and in Arkansas 195,000 more people on the job than the

day I was inaugurated President. That's the kind of record the Democrats have.

If you'll pardon me, let me mention Governor Reagan one more time, because we're looking to the future. He's for the so-called Reagan-Kemp-Roth tax program, a big giveaway program for rich people that'll saddle the Americans with enormous inflation. That's not just my opinion. President Ford, a Republican, who supports Reagan in this election, refuses to endorse that ridiculous tax proposal. Even the Wall Street Journal and Business Week said it won't work. And Mr. Reagan's own Vice-Presidential candidate, George Bush, said if the Reagan-Kemp-Roth proposal is put into effect, it'll cause a 30-percent inflation rate. As a matter of fact, George Bush said then it was "voodoo economics." That's the kind of approach that Democrats want to prevent, that's at stake with your jobs and with inflation in the future.

I want to mention a couple of other things. One is that the Democrats believe that our air ought to be pure and that our water ought to be clean and that the land God gave us over which to be stewards would still be productive and not spoiled by poisons. Scientists have searched for a solution to the pollution problem for a long time. Governor Reagan has found the solution. He says pollution's caused by trees. [*Laughter*] Well, that's a pretty sharp difference from what I believe, because not too long ago I signed a reforestation bill that will make provisions for this whole area through here to reseed our forests and to build more trees. And God's going to help us, right? [*Cheers*]

So, if you want to see the trees destroyed to control inflation [pollution], vote Republican. If you want to see the trees planted to make the air purer and deal with inflation [pollution] at its source, vote Democratic, a very good choice.

I know very clearly that this area here is interested in the production of energy. The small royalty owners are now being hurt by the new law passed under my administration. With the help of these men here, George Nigh in Oklahoma, the people in Louisiana, Lloyd Bentsen in Texas, all of you, we've now decided to change the law—it's already been done in the Senate, it'll be done soon—to exempt those small royalty owners from that tax.

We have a new energy policy that this country's never had before, one that's really serving well. Republicans in the long run have said, "Let's decontrol the price of oil and gas to increase the production of American energy." In 1956 a law was passed along those lines. I don't know the details. It was vetoed by President Eisenhower. But we knew that we had to address this in a way that would help the energy-producing States and also be fair to those who consume energy, in your State and around the Nation. So, we passed a new energy bill. It now provides that over a period of time, energy prices will be decontrolled. Already it's having great impact.

We've got more oil drillrigs running right now and gas drillrigs right now than ever before in history—3,164 as of midnight last night. And this year we'll have more oil wells and gas wells drilled in this country than in any year in history. You might be also interested in knowing that we're producing more coal this year than ever before in history.

On the other hand, we've got a Republican administration that wants to dismantle what we've done. Governor Reagan says the best approach to the energy problem is to repeal everything we've done, to dismantle the Department of Energy, and let the oil companies make all

the decisions for our life in the future on energy. That's the decision you've got to make on November the 4th.

One other thing I want to say that's most important of all, more important than inflation, more important than how many jobs we've created in the last 3½ years, and that is our defense capabilities and the preservation of peace.

Eight years before I became President, seven of those years expenditures for American defense went down. Under two Republican Presidents, the defense budget decreased by 37 percent. When I took over the Oval Office, the responsibilities of Commander in Chief, we began a steady, well-planned, sure increase every year, above and beyond inflation, to give us a strong defense. And as long as I'm in the White House, we'll have a strong defense, second to none on Earth in military equipment and in our Armed Forces personnel.

But at the same time, a President has to decide how to use that enormous power. You can't fly an airplane with just one wing, and having a tremendous defense establishment is just part of the job. That defense capability has got to be used to keep the peace. We've got to control nuclear weapons. Governor Reagan says, throw the nuclear weapons control treaty in the wastebasket. Let's start a nuclear arms race as a trump card to be played against the Soviet Union. We're trying to keep other nations around the world, like Libya and Iraq, from having atomic weapons. Our nonproliferation program is extremely important to every person who values life in this audience. Governor Reagan says that nonproliferation is none of our business.

Every President who's served in the Oval Office before me, Democrats and Republicans, have been faced with troubled times around the world, troubled places. Not a day has gone by that that wasn't the case. We've known that we had an enormous military structure in this country, but we've tried to deal with those problems peacefully.

Governor Reagan, on the other hand, when he's seen trouble spots around the world, is advocating sending in American military forces, in North Korea, in Ecuador, in Cuba, Cyprus, the Middle East, Rhodesia, Angola, Pakistan. Those trouble spots have been resolved diplomatically by other Presidents, but, while he still hoped to be President, he has said, "Let's send in American military forces."

These kinds of issues affect you and they affect me and they affect every person in this Nation and on Earth. I stand here needing your help. The issues are clearly drawn. A great deal is at stake, in your life, in the lives of those who live in the same home with you and those whom you love and who look to you for leadership. We've only got 10 days to go. It's going to be a close race in Louisiana. It's going to be a close race in Texas. It's going to be a close race in Arkansas. And we're behind right now, I would guess, in Oklahoma. And what you do the next 10 days will make a decision about what kind of nation we'll have in the years ahead.

Will we preserve the tradition of the Democratic Party? Will we have commitments made to a better life for working people of this land? Will we have older people having security in their declining years, give them a full, fruitful life, to honor them for what they've given this country? Will we have a better education for our children, better housing for our families, better jobs, better social security, better minimum wage? Will we have a strong defense? Will it be used for peace? These are the kinds of issues that face you, and the judgment is in your hands.

I would guess that most of you here are Democrats and will support me. But let me ask you to do this in the next 10 days: Get on the telephone, talk to those you see. There's no one in this audience that can't contact between now and election day 500 or 1,000 people, some of you maybe more, because the sound of your voice can be heard. If you'll help me, be partners in the future as you have been in the past, then we'll win on November the 4th; we'll stomp the Republicans and keep this Nation on the road to future progress.

Thank you very much. God bless you all.

NOTE: The President spoke at 5:40 p.m. outside the United States Post Office Federal Building. The podium from which he spoke straddled the Arkansas-Texas State line.

Following his remarks, the President returned to the White House.

White House Conference on Families

Statement on Receiving the Conference's Final Report. October 22, 1980

I have received the report of the White House Conference on Families, and I want to thank the 125,000 Americans who helped to produce it. I am determined that their efforts will lead to real improvement in policies and programs to strengthen and support the American family as an institution.

This Conference has reaffirmed the central role that families play in our national life. It has documented the ways in which our major institutions, including government, ignore and even undermine families. With unprecedented openness and broad participation, the Conference has produced a mandate and an agenda for action.

The consensus on the major recommendations is a remarkable achievement and shows how Americans of different backgrounds and beliefs can unite around a specific program. The delegates' principal recommendations lay out a practical, moderate, and sensible agenda to combat the insensitivity that so often characterizes the attitude of our major institutions toward the family.

When I addressed the Conference in Baltimore, I said "I will do all I can to make sure your report does not sit on the shelves." We are already working to implement the recommendations of the White House Conference on Families:

1) We are today bringing into the White House leaders of major corporations to discuss the Conference recommendation dealing with family-oriented personnel policies. This meeting will be followed by an intensive seminar for personnel decisionmakers on how to institute and expand upon policies in the workplace that reduce conflict between work and family responsibilities.

2) I have recently proposed a change in our tax laws to reduce the "marriage tax penalty." Enactment of this deduction will lessen the most obvious form of tax discrimination against families.

3) I have established an Office for Families in the Department of Health and Human Services to help ensure a voice for families and to follow up on these recommendations.

4) I am directing all Federal departments and key agencies to undertake a thorough analysis of their policies and programs in light of the recommendations contained in the final report of the White House Conference on Families and to develop detailed plans for implementing Conference proposals.

5) Within the White House, I am asking the Domestic Policy Staff to make Conference recommendations an invariable criterion for the evaluation of policies and programs.

6) We will continue to work with the National Advisory Committee of the White House Conference on Families, its Chairperson, Jim Guy Tucker, and its Director, John Carr, who have done a superb job in making this Conference a success.

7) We will also continue to work with the private and voluntary organizations that represent and serve American families. Since many of the recommendations are directed not at government, but at business, labor, religious groups, social services, media, and other private groups, their involvement in implementation is crucial.

These steps are only the beginning of a long-term effort to enhance family strengths and to reverse the neglect of families that characterizes all too many of the decisions and actions undertaken in our society.

I am proud of the way this Conference listened to and involved so many American families, of the way it has put families at the center of national discussion, of the way it has found consensus and agreement where many predicted only conflict. The White House Conference on Families has brought us from rhetoric to action, from principles to programs, from a vision to an actual plan for strengthening and supporting the families of our Nation.

United States-People's Republic of China Grain Agreement

White House Statement.   October 22, 1980

Today, we signed in Beijing a grain agreement with the People's Republic of

China which accomplishes two important things. First, it will promote the sale of U.S. grain to a large and growing market. Second, it will further the process of building a long-term structure for U.S.-China relations.

Under the terms of this agreement, China will purchase at least 6 million metric tons (MMT) of U.S. wheat and corn annually for a 4-year period beginning January 1, 1981. The Chinese may purchase up to 9 MMT without prior notice.

Since the establishment of diplomatic relations in January 1979, U.S. agricultural exports to China have expanded rapidly and will reach a record $2 billion in 1980. China is now our most important customer for cotton and one of the most important for other farm products.

The agreement grew out of a dialog dating back to Secretary Bergland's visit to the People's Republic of China in 1978. It will provide important benefits for both U.S. farmers and consumers. It will help to moderate the wide swing in grain prices that are often associated with annual fluctuations in agricultural exports. The agreement will also provide further stimulus to our dynamic agricultural export sector and contribute to our growing surplus in agricultural trade, which will reach $22 billion in 1980.

The President takes great personal pride in the fact that in his administration he was able to take the difficult but enormously successful step of establishing full diplomatic relations with China, the largest country in the world.

The establishment of diplomatic relations with China almost 2 years ago made it possible for us to move ahead to build a new relationship which truly enriches us in knowledge, trade, and culture:

—Trade more than doubled from $1.1 billion in 1978 to $2.3 billion in 1979. This year we estimated it will almost double again to $4 billion.

—About 25 cultural and sports delegations from China visit our country every 6 months, and we are reciprocating with visits by orchestras and other cultural groups as well as our Olympic athletes.

—We have 13 separate working agreements in science and technology, which not only give us current and future commercial benefits but make it possible for our scientists and technicians to share in China's research in medicine, earthquake prediction, and agriculture.

Important as they are, there is more to our relationship than trade and cultural ties. We have also begun carefully and deliberately to build a consultative relationship which will enable us to work together to identify and cooperate on issues of common interest, such as the Soviet invasion of Afghanistan.

This effort to construct a long-term strategic relationship is still new and therefore fragile. It is based on carefully written and painstakingly negotiated understandings set down in the joint communique establishing diplomatic relations between the United States and China. This administration has consistently made clear its resolve to honor those understandings.

We have come a long way since that day almost 2 years ago when the President announced that we had reached agreement with the Chinese on the establishment of diplomatic relations. Thirty years of mutual isolation and hostility have been replaced with a deepening consultative relationship which is already contributing significantly to American security and to the peace and stability in East Asia and the world beyond.

White House Reception for Black Ministers

Remarks at the Reception.   October 23, 1980

I understand you've had a good day so far. If there's one thing I don't relish, it's trying to substitute for Coretta King and Andy Young and Jessie Jackson as a speaker. I might let Reverend Moss take my place up here; I know he'd do a better job. One thing that I think is good about people who lead congregations and lead larger groups than that, congregations of congregations, is that you have a chance to take your activism, your deep commitment, your experience and turn it into advice for people—a very precious possession that you have.

I tried to think of a story to illustrate this point. The only one I could think of was one that my pastor told not long ago about a young, very proud, very arrogant new preacher. His name was Reverend Quail. And he had a bishop whose name was Bishop Rice that he admired very much, and he wanted to make an impression on the bishop. So he went to see him and said, "Bishop Rice, I've noticed how revered you are by all those who know you, and I know how wonderful a man you are, and I just want to know how you get your knowledge and your experience, and the advice you give people is so profoundly important." And Bishop Rice recognized that the young man wanted a good assignment the next time change took place. [*Laughter*] So he said, "Young man, I'll tell you what I do." He said, "When I get a little bit down in the dumps and need some revelation, I remember that God made this world. And I try to escape from human beings' influence as much as I can and forget about human beings and go out and just be alone with God." And he said, "The best

thing I've ever found is I can go out and just walk in the rain." He said, "I like to go out by myself alone, and not many people on the street, and I just turn my eyes up to the heaven and let the rain fall on my face." "Well," the Reverend Quail said, "I think I'll try that the next time it rains, Bishop Rice." [*Laughter*]

So 3 or 4 days later came a big heavy rain. It was kind of cold out there, and Reverend Quail went out and stood in the rain and looked up and it rained on him. He stood there a long time, not much happened. [*Laughter*] So he went back to see the bishop. He said, "Bishop Rice, I took your advice." And he said, "Ordinarily, your advice is very good, but I don't think it worked this time." He said, "Well, what happened?" He said, "I went out in the rain. I stood there and turned my face up to the heavens. It just beat on my face. I got cold. It ran all down my neck." He said, "I felt like a fool." And Bishop Rice said, "Well, how many revelations you want out of one rain?" [*Laughter*] Well, if you don't get anything else out of this meeting, you can take that story home and use it as you see fit.

This is a time for advice. It's time for turning to those who have leadership. It's a time for remembering what you mean to this country. As I have said many times, some of you have heard me say this before, I know of no other group in this Nation any more capable of combining God's will and your lifetime commitment with the education and the inspiration and the leadership of others than the black ministers of this land. When you see a hungry child, when you see a homeless family, when you see a lonely and destitute senior citizen, when you see a mind's not being developed, when you see deprivation around you, you remember the teachings of Christ. But you go further than that. You try to do something about it. And the activism that transformed the Southland and raised the spirits of this entire Nation and set an example for the whole world came from you, in my judgment.

And I've said also many times that had it not been for the courage of Rosa Parks and had it not been that Martin Luther King, Jr., was a minister who believed in the same principles that you espouse and exemplify in your own lives and transform this Nation, I would not be standing here as President, because you recognize the significance of change and the need for our Nation to look anew at itself. Our principles, our ideals, our Constitution are very good, but the practicalities of life and how judgments made by those in high places affected the people that you loved and who looked to you for leadership and guidance, not only spiritually but in a very closely related thing, in the human values of life which were also the teachings of Christ, that's what has made this country improve so much. It hasn't come far enough.

I've had your advice; it's been good advice, and I've taken it. In many cases the judgments that I've made, the decisions that I've made have originated with you and a few others like you around this country whom I trust and who have been partners with me. We've made some progress. I've had a chance to appoint judges to the Federal bench, places that had been closed after more than 200 years to black people. And we've got a long way to go. I've appointed twice as many black judges as all the other Presidents put together in the history of this country. But that's not enough. And when I look on what John Kennedy wanted and what Lyndon Johnson wanted, had the times permitted, I'm sure they would have done just as much or more.

And I look to the future, too, because we've now got food stamps so people don't have to have cash money to buy them. That was an idea that came from you all. And it's made it easier for those who've starved to eat. And we've had some economic setbacks in the last few years. The whole world has been shocked by high inflationary pressures. And we've added 8½ million new jobs; 1.3 million of those that weren't available on January 20th, 1977, are now held by black people in this country; another million by Hispanic American people. We've tried to focus our job programs for a change on permanent career jobs in the private sector of our economy and also on those who were chronically prohibited, by various factors that ought not have been there, from having full employment.

We've still got a long way to go. The unemployment rate is too high, but we're working on it with your guidance. We've now got a youth bill, as you well know, through the House of Representatives. It's now in the Senate. And I believe that after the partisanship of this campaign election is gone, we'll see those $2 billion added on to the programs we've already got, and we'll see 600,000 young people put to work that have been wanting jobs and show they can be good citizens of this country.

In 1968, we passed an open housing law. You were the ones that initiated it, and I know you breathed a sigh of relief when it was passed. It hasn't meant 2 cents, because we have not yet been able to get through the Congress authority to enforce the law of the United States. And now we've gotten through the House of Representatives the amendments to the open housing law to give our executive department the right, the authority, the legal status to enforce the law. That is a project for the future, building on what you've done in the past.

I'm worried about the status of social security. I'm worried about the status of the minimum wage. I'm worried about the status of youth employment programs. I'm worried about the status of housing programs for the poor and the elderly. I'm worried about the status of the criminal justice system in this country that needs to be improved steadily, because it's not good enough yet. And you think back to the 8 years before I came in this office and what was happening to those programs, what was happening to the Equal Employment Opportunity Commission now headed by Eleanor Holmes Norton, what was happening to our foreign policy concerning Africa before Andy Young and before Don McHenry transformed this Nation and its image in the eyes of the Third World. We don't want to go back to that.

There's a lot at stake. And one of the things that has changed the lives of people that you care about has been the new program for our cities. You know, one of the brightest spots in black American achievement has been in the management, as mayors, of some of our major cities. It has proved the effectiveness of black Americans to manage a complicated and very desperately needed improvement in the lives of black and white citizens, because those ghetto areas of the deteriorating central cities, when I campaigned around this country in 1976, were in danger. Everywhere I went, there was a feeling of despair and hopelessness and discouragement and trouble. It's been improved tremendously. And I believe that the mayors of this country, Democratic and Republican, would overwhelmingly tell you that what I've just said is true.

We've got a long way to go, but we've now begun to focus all the programs—education programs, health programs, welfare programs, transportation programs, housing programs, rebuilding programs, with EDA—on those areas that formerly were deprived, when under a previous administration those kind of funds were kind of channeled out into the rich suburbs where the influence is greater, where the citizens might have been better organized, and where deprived people very seldom live and benefit from Federal programs. This is the kind of change that has been made so far. We want to keep that progress underway.

I've been deeply disturbed lately at the attacks that have been made by depraved human beings on black citizens in our country, in Buffalo, New York, and Atlanta, Georgia. I've talked to the Attorney General about it. I've talked to Judge Webster about it; Drew Days about it. Jack Watson on my staff in the White House is monitoring this program to root out those criminals, day and night. It's a blight on our economy, it's a blight on our society, it's a blight on our country to have this done. And those kinds of people and the Ku Klux Klan have got to be caught, brought to justice, proved that they violated the law, and put under the jail where they belong.

Not long ago, I read Daddy King's autobiography. And he went through part of his book and pointed out the troubles he's seen. And as a leader in a great family, one of the greatest families our Nation has ever seen, he's had his suffering and his disappointment, his pain, his anguish, and his sorrow. But he said every now and then he reminds himself of an old saying, "I was put here on a purpose." And there's no doubt in my mind that Daddy King was put here on a purpose. What his life meant, his communion with his wife, his offspring, and his own family, his influence, that of his family has inspired me; I'm sure it's inspired a lot of you. And I might add that as President of this country, I think the United States of America was created by God with a purpose—on a purpose. We're beginning to set an example for the rest of the world with human rights, with basic decency, with equality of opportunity.

And I can tell you this: that had it not been for the Constitution of the United States, we would not have the largest and most influential and perhaps the most economically sound black nation on Earth, Nigeria, now a democracy, an ally of ours, whereas shortly before I became President, the Secretary of State of the United States was not permitted to come into that country on an official visit. And it was done with the influence of the people there. I don't want to claim credit for it. But when they got ready to have a change from a military government, one of the kindest and best and most unselfish military governments I ever saw, into a freely elected assembly, with a Prime Minister that visited me in this room not long ago, they used the United States Constitution as a pattern after which they could predicate their own government.

And I went there on an official visit, the first time in 200 years—I hate to say this—that an American President had ever made an official visit to a black African country. No credit to me. I point out to you that it took us too long to do it. All the other Presidents should have been going over there, because it's not just only a benevolent thing to show equality, but it's good for our country. And we're selling rice from Arkansas in Nigeria now, and we're buying a lot of oil from them; got good trade going. It didn't hurt us. [*Laughter*] It helped us,

right? And also, now we've got an opportunity to invest there, not only have a sale for American products but a good, sound future to stabilize the continent of Africa in order to continue to make progress.

And we've seen the same thing happen in a country formerly known as Rhodesia. You all know the situation when I came in this office. We were trying desperately to see majority rule invoked and to give black people a right to vote and to have a democratic government elected there. And had it not been for Andrew Young working with all those leaders involved who laid the groundwork for the British success—and we were partners with them—we would not have had standing here not too long ago, the Prime Minister, Mugabe—black leader, great new democracy in Africa.

This is the kind of thing that our country can do, because God, I think, created it on a purpose. That doesn't mean that we've done enough, but we're on the road toward the promised land. This, to me, is where you and I share a responsibility for the future we are facing now with economic problems. Inflation pressures are too high. And the judgment on what kind of tax program we'll have next year, and what kind of job programs we'll have next year, and what kind of rebuilding of American industry we'll have next year, will decide what kind of life we'll have next year among the people about whom you care and about whom I care.

The so-called Reagan-Kemp-Roth proposal is a tax proposal for the rich, which will not build new jobs and new industry and new tools and new factories. It'll have a tremendous benefit for some at the expense of the others. And we'll have inflationary pressures build up in this country that'll make what we've seen in the past pale into insignificance. Those are the kinds of issues that are hard to understand. But the underlying thrust of what the Democratic Party has always stood for and what the Republican Party has always stood for is exemplified by that change.

I know you've had a long, hard day. I just want to say one more thing. A lot of people to whom you speak and a lot of people to whom I speak say this is a big country, 230 million people. Over a hundred million will probably vote. What can one person do? What can one congregation do?

In 1960 if 28,000 people in Texas had changed their vote and just a few thousand in Illinois, John Kennedy would never have been President, Lyndon Johnson would never have been Vice President, and the change that's taken place in your life with voting rights, civil rights, new opportunities might never have come to pass in this Nation in our lifetime. That was a good story. It had a good ending.

In 1968 we had another story. We had a good Democratic nominee, Hubert Humphrey. And they had somebody to represent the Republican Party; his name was Richard Nixon. I've thought a lot about who put Richard Nixon in the White House. It wasn't Republicans, because once they choose their nominee, you can expect them to vote for him. It wasn't the Republicans that put Richard Nixon in the Oval Office. It was the Democrats who didn't vote.

Some of them were for Gene McCarthy. And they said, "Well, Hubert Humphrey is not a perfect man." And the main thing they had against him was that he served

as Vice President under Lyndon Johnson. That was the mark they put on him, and they wouldn't support him. And George Wallace, who had support in some States, was a third candidate. And folks said, "Well, I don't think I'll vote." The Republicans voted, and Hubert Humphrey lost. And perhaps one of the best Presidents this country would ever have seen did not have a chance to serve.

I don't want to see the same thing happen in 1980. I didn't get in this race to lose. I believe I was put here on a purpose, and I believe you all came to the White House this afternoon on a purpose. And if you and I can get together, I guarantee you that the Republicans will not sit in the Oval Office for the next 8 years. Right? [*Applause*] I'm with you.

Thank you. God bless you.

NOTE: The President spoke at 3:11 p.m. in the East Room at the White House.

Corporation for Public Broadcasting

Nomination of Melba Beals To Be a Member of the Board of Directors. October 23, 1980

The President today announced that he will nominate Melba Beals, of San Francisco, Calif., to be a member of the board of directors of the Corporation for Public Broadcasting. She would replace Lucius Perry Gregg, Jr., whose term has expired.

Beals, 38, is a freelance writer, consultant, and lecturer. She was a reporter with KQED–TV in 1971 and with KRON–TV from 1972 to 1977. She has published articles in newspapers and magazines in San Francisco and has ghostwritten two books.

Health and Medical Care for Love Canal Area Residents

Statement on a Request to Congress for Appropriations.   October 24, 1980

I have sent to the Congress a budget amendment to provide more than $3.8 million for medical examinations and health studies for the people exposed to contamination in the Love Canal area of Niagara Falls, N.Y. This request supplements some $640,000 in funds from the Center for Disease Control and the Environmental Protection Agency.

Last May, because of concern about the potential health effects from exposure to chemical wastes, I declared an emergency for the Love Canal neighborhood and authorized relocation of about 700 families to temporary quarters. At the same time, I committed Federal resources to conduct further health and environmental studies in the area.

This appropriation request will make available funds for the Center for Disease Control in conjunction with the State University of New York at Buffalo, to carry out my commitment to residents of the area.

These funds will provide for a complete medical examination for each of the approximately 4,000 adults and children who lived in the area as of June 1978. These examinations will consist of medical history interviews, laboratory tests at a clinic to be established near the area, physical examination, and clinical followup. Funds for special chromosome, nerve conduction, and psychological studies are included in this request.

Related environmental analyses will be carried out by the Environmental Protection Agency.

I urge the Congress to act quickly on the measure when it reconvenes on November 12.

Interview With the President

Question-and-Answer Session With Clifford Evans of RKO General Broadcasting.   October 24, 1980

ISRAEL

MR. EVANS. There is much concern about the anti-Israel resolutions, UNESCO and in the General Assembly, and other attempts to isolate Israel in the world community. Now, what are we, what is the United States doing about this?

THE PRESIDENT. Well, I am very disturbed by the efforts of the enemies of Israel to isolate Israel in the world community. We will not permit this to happen. Not only is Israel our friend and our ally, but attempts to isolate Israel are also intended to weaken this country and also to destroy the progress that we have made already with the Camp David accords and the peace treaty between Israel and Egypt.

We are committed to the Camp David accords, and we are committed to the peace effort that is continuing, all based on the proposition of honoring U.N. 242, passed earlier in the General Assembly and in the Security Council. We have made it clear, for instance, that we will veto any change in U.N. Resolution 242.

We oppose the creation of an independent Palestinian state. As I have repeatedly said, we oppose a PLO state. But I want to go even further. Whenever in the future the United Nations is misused or abused on Israeli-Arab issues with malicious and unfair and one-sided resolutions, we will oppose them, and in the Security Council we will veto them. Secretary Muskie gave fair warning that this would be our policy, on August the 20th when he spoke at the General Assembly or Security Council. Now I want to say it emphatically and clearly, so there can be no misunderstanding in anyone's mind.

Also, I want to make it clear again that we will not permit any isolation of Israel in other United Nations organizations, nor will we allow the United Nations to be used as a propaganda organ for the PLO. That is the reason we voted against the Women's Plan in Copenhagen this summer. It contained anti-Israeli language and called for the diversion of funds out of the United Nations funds to the PLO.

For this same reason I personally intervened with various heads of government to obtain their support to prevent the PLO becoming an observer in the recent deliberations of the World Bank and the International Monetary Fund. We were successful in this effort after a massive attempt by the other side to change this longstanding policy.

When two Islamic nations introduced a resolution to reject Israel's credentials at UNESCO's General Assembly in Belgrade just last month, in September, I again intervened and got other nations to help us stop it. And earlier this week I instructed our delegation at the UNESCO conference not to participate nor to be present even in any session at which Yassir Arafat appeared.

We took similar strong action at the national tourism conference in Manila when another effort was made early this month to drive Israel out. We stopped that effort, too.

We have successfully opposed every effort to reject Israel's credentials at the current session of the U.N. General Assembly, and I have made our position clear. If such an effort should be successful, and I don't believe it would, then I see no way that we could continue even to participate in the deliberations of that body.

Well, these are a few examples that come to mind offhand about our staunch support for Israel and our staunch commitment not to permit the isolation of Israel nor to permit Israel to be driven out of the General Assembly or embarrassed nor to use the General Assembly or United Nations bodies to promote the PLO.

MILITARY SALES TO SAUDI ARABIA

MR. EVANS. Let me throw you a curve, Mr. President. What about the recent story that the Department of Defense is considering changing our commitment of 1978 and now is prepared to sell to Saudi Arabia, for their F–15's, equipment that would give them offensive capability against Israel. I am speaking about such things as bomb racks. Now, lay it out. Just what is that situation?

THE PRESIDENT. That is not a curve. I welcome that question, as a matter of fact.

There will be absolutely no change in the assurance given to the Congress in 1978 by Secretary Harold Brown, acting under my instructions, on the sale of F–15's to the Saudi Arabians. In accordance with those assurances, we will not agree to provide offensive capabilities for the planes that might be used against Israel, and that obviously includes bomb racks.

FINANCIAL ASSISTANCE FOR NEW YORK CITY

MR. EVANS. I am a New Yorker, Mr. President, so I ask you this: Are you truly serious when you say that you want to help New York City with its staggering financial problems of welfare costs and the costs of Medicaid?

THE PRESIDENT. We have had a consistently good record in dealing closely with the mayor of New York, both Mayor Beame and now Ed Koch. The Governor of New York, the congressional delegation of New York, shortly after the 1976 election was over, they came down to Georgia and met with me. We spelled out a 4-year agenda to keep New York from going into bankruptcy, and we have been successful. We have channeled massive funds into New York City and in other cities in the State that are in trouble since that time.

The Democratic National Convention in its platform this year gave a commitment to assume, for the Federal Government to assume the costs of welfare. I announced the other night in New York that I support this Democratic platform. I also announced that after the 1980 election I will sit down with the mayor, the Governor, and the congressional delegation, and we will work out again a 4-year agenda to carry out the commitments that we have made.

PRESIDENT'S HEALTH

MR. EVANS. Your voice sounds a little scratchy, Mr. President, between the rigors of campaigning and the responsibility of being the President. How do you feel?

THE PRESIDENT. I feel very good. Obviously, when you make 12 or 13 speeches a day and don't get much rest in between, your voice gets a little tired. But I feel very good, very confident, looking forward to the next 10 days and, I hope after that, the next 4 years.

CAMPAIGN DEBATE

MR. EVANS. And Tuesday evening, of course, as that debate is just around the corner, the debate with Ronald Reagan. The American people have been looking forward to this for some time. Are you ready to cross verbal swords with Ronald Reagan?

THE PRESIDENT. It is something I have been looking forward to for a long time,

also. We have accepted five or six individual invitations to have a two-man debate with Governor Reagan. This is what I have been waiting for. I am looking forward to it.

MR. EVANS. There you have the views of the President. From the Oval Office here in the White House, Clifford Evans, RKO General Broadcasting.

NOTE: The interview began at 1:20 p.m. in the Oval Office at the White House.

As printed above, the interview follows the text of the White House press release.

Gloucester City, New Jersey

Remarks and a Question-and-Answer Session With Area Residents.
October 24, 1980

CAMPAIGN ISSUES

THE PRESIDENT. Well, to Cass and Jim and all the family, I want to say, first of all, thank you, and particularly to Eilene. [*Laughter*] She pointed out that the Phillies did the country a great service, recently, because, you know, nobody pays any attention to the Presidential election until after the World Series is over. [*Laughter*] And their getting through in 6 games saves us a little time, right? [*Applause*] Also, she pointed out that historically, whenever the National League wins the World Series, do you know what happens in the Presidential election? What happens? [*Applause*] The Democrats win, right? [*Applause*] The Democrats win, too. So thank you, Eilene, that's a good reminder.

Also, my mother has just about paid her hospital and doctor bills betting on the Phillies this last—[*laughter*]. She's taken all—the first time anybody ever took money from the doctors in the hospital. She did it this time.

Well, I'm very grateful to have a chance to come here to this Knights of Columbus Hall. It reminds me very deeply and personally that President Kennedy was active, as you know, in his own local Knights of Columbus, and that's where he learned, I think, to represent the true ideals and the principles of the Democratic Party— one of public service, community service in a generous and unselfish way, and that typifies what all of you feel in your own hearts.

This is a time of service. It's a time when our Nation's principles are tested. And every 4 years when we have a chance to present to the American people the record of an incumbent administration like ours, which is Democratic, to point out that we are in the history and the theme and commitment and principles and ideals and tradition of Franklin Roosevelt, Harry Truman, John Kennedy, Lyndon Johnson, it's kind of a reassuring thing to remind us every now and then of the sharp differences.

One of those differences, obviously, is to deal effectively with the economic affairs of our country. As you know, we were hit very severely last year by economics that endangered the well-being of the working families of our country, when OPEC Arab nations raised the price of oil more in 1 year than the price of oil had increased since it was first discovered in Pennsylvania in the 1800's. As you know, the inflation rate got up around 20 percent for a while, and we started taking action, tightening up on the Federal budget spending, working for a higher productivity of workers. And for the last 3 months, we've had the average down around 7 percent for the last 3 months. The figures we got today were a sharp reminder that now and in the future we've got to deal with inflation in a very effective and very firm way.

The proposal that we have advocated for next year—after the election, not during an election year—to have a tax stimulus to create new tools, new factories, new jobs for American workers, is anti-inflationary in its impact. It will not only give us a better life, better jobs, but will cut down inflation. Governor Reagan, on the other hand, has proposed the so-called Reagan-Kemp-Roth proposal, which gives great awards to rich people but saddles the rest of us with enormous inflationary pressures. It's just like pouring gasoline on a fire, to add the Reagan-Kemp-Roth proposal to high inflationary pressures. Governor Reagan's own running mate, George Bush, said it would cause inflation rates up to 30 percent, and he called it "voodoo economics." And we Democrats don't want any "voodoo economics." And so just like the Phillies won, Eilene, Democrats have got to win to keep this country on a stable basis, to keep our folks working good, okay?

Now I think it's good for me to answer questions that you might have and, I'm very eager to.

QUESTIONS

TAX REDUCTION PROPOSALS

Q. In view of what you've just said, do you think considering the independence of Congress during the recent years that you or any President can deal with them to put through a program in order to deal with our economic ills?

THE PRESIDENT. Yes, ma'am, I do. We've had very good success in dealing with the Congress the last 3½ years. We've passed about 80 percent of all the legislation we've sent to the Democratic Congress. And on this particular tax proposal, we've consulted very closely with the leaders on the House and Senate side.

I don't say that we'll come out 100 percent with what we advocate, but the basic thrust of it will be similar to what President Kennedy did back in 1963.

He put forward a proposal then, which you may remember; I do. It was 100 percent designed to let American industries reinvest their profits into new factories, new tools, new jobs to keep our people at work. At that time, the inflation rate was only about 1 percent; now it's much higher. And it's more important now than it was then even, not to have a highly inflationary tax proposal.

So, over 50 percent of our tax proposal will be designed to create those new tools, new factories, and new jobs for American workers. And the other part of it, which will help families and those who are wage earners, will compensate for the increases in social security taxes already on the law books; it'll give you a tax refund so you won't have to pay any more money. And it does one other thing which I think is important, long overdue. Now, when a husband and wife work and both have some income, they pay a higher income tax than a man and woman who both work and who live together who are not married. This is called a "marriage penalty," and so we are going to advocate that we remove that marriage penalty, which will be a tax reduction for married families that have more than one working and also remove the penalty on people for getting married.

So, with those two exceptions—on social security offsets and the marriage penalty—the rest of our tax reduction will go toward new jobs, new plants, and new tools. And the total effect of our tax proposal will be to cut down inflation rather than to make inflation higher.

Governor Reagan's proposal, 90 percent of it, goes for personal income taxes which will primarily reward the very rich.

If you make $200,000 a year, any of you that are here that make that, you will probably be for Governor Reagan. [*Laughter*] And only 10 percent of it goes to create those new tools and new jobs for Americans. And it'll be highly inflationary, because it will dump, between now and 1987, a trillion dollars, which is a thousand billion dollars, into purchasing power to bid up the cost of a limited amount of goods because industry won't be producing more because they won't have that tax privilege.

So, mine doesn't go quite as far as President Kennedy's does, since almost 100 percent of his went for business investment and new jobs, but it goes along that line. So, yes, it will be anti-inflationary in nature, not inflationary in nature.

I can't overlook you.

AMERICAN HOSTAGES IN IRAN

Q. Do you know when the American hostages are going to be released yet?

THE PRESIDENT. No, I don't.

You know, one thing that concerns me a lot lately has been a buildup in the American press—the television, radio, and newspapers—of expectations that the hostages are going to come home early, that I don't think are justified. I don't have any way to know when the hostages might come home. And I think for us to expect that they're going to come home this weekend or next week or the following week is going to lead to very bitter disappointments in our country if they don't come home when we think they might.

What we have done, since the very first day they were taken, is to protect their lives and their safety and make sure that someday they could come home to freedom and, also, not to violate our Nation's principles and our Nation's honor. But I think it would be a mistake for anyone to start trying to put a time schedule on when they're coming home. We've been disappointed too many times. So, let's just hope and pray they come home safely someday and don't plan on any particular date at this point.

Don't forget to pray for them, okay? Good.

ABORTION

Q. Mr. President, what is your stand on abortion, and how does it compare to Governor Reagan's?

THE PRESIDENT. I have a very deep, personal opposition to abortion. I don't think that the Federal Government ought to spend any money to pay for abortions, unless the mother's life is directly in danger or unless the pregnancy is a result of rape or incest and she reports that rape or incest very quickly after becoming pregnant. This has been my position for a long time, and I believe that that's the best approach to it.

As you know, an incumbent President has to take an oath of office, Joey, that if the Congress passes a law or if the Supreme Court rules on the matter of abortion, I have to carry out the law. And so that's my belief. I don't think we need a constitutional amendment on it, but I'll do everything I can, as I have in the past, not to let Federal funds be used to pay for abortions and to minimize any need for abortion in this country.

PRESIDENT'S PROUDEST ACHIEVEMENT

Q. What's your proudest achievement since you've been President?

THE PRESIDENT. Well, it's hard to know—well, you say what's your proudest achievement? Every President has to deal on a daily basis with crises, with trouble-spots around the world, and every President has available to him the enormous power of the United States—military weapons, troops, and so forth. I think my proudest achievement is having kept our Nation at peace, because it's a temptation, when there is a troubled area in the world, to want to stick American military forces in there to try to resolve it. I've not had to do that, and I believe that this is the most important, single thing that I've done.

My first responsibility is to keep our Nation secure and to have a strong defense. And all of the 8 years before I became President, the Republicans had let defense spending go down 37 percent, and I felt our Nation was in danger of not being the strongest nation on Earth. We have reversed that in every year. We have built up and will continue to build up our commitment to defense. I've said many times—I know the press here has heard me say a lot of times—that the best weapon is one that's never used in combat, and the best soldier is one that never has to lay his life down on the field of battle.

So, to keep our Nation strong and at peace, that's my proudest achievement. And I pray God that I'll have that record when I go out of office.

SOCIAL SECURITY SYSTEM

Q. Mr. President, I'd like to know what you and your administration's doing about the social security situation in this country right now. There's a lot of hullaballoo in the newspapers and television that it's going broke.

THE PRESIDENT. Yes.

Q. I'd like to know just what your position is on keeping it strong and saving a lot of people in this country that depend on it.

THE PRESIDENT. Yes, I'd like to answer that. You may or may not remember in 1976, almost exactly 4 years ago, when I was campaigning around the country and so was President Ford, the biggest concern that people had when I went to a group like this was, "The social security system is on the way to bankruptcy." But I and the Democratic Congress, particularly Jim Florio, Bill Bradley, and others, have worked to get the social security system back on a sound basis. And it will be kept sound and free of bankruptcy as long as you have a Democrat in the White House. We will not permit any taxation of social security benefits, and we will continue to have social security benefits increased enough to compensate for the rise in inflation.

I just read today a Wall Street Journal article. As you know, the Wall Street Journal is a strong Republican newspaper and a strong supporter of Governor Reagan. It had an article on the front page—maybe somebody's got it here—"Reagan's 23 Teams Feed Him Hot Ideas on How to Run the United States." One of the things that they propose is that they do away with the minimum wage. Another one is that they reduce social security payments and a whole series of things that accurately mirror what Governor Reagan has said in the past, even after he began running for President, and which he later says he's changed his mind about.

But I think this kind of article, in a paper that supports Mr. Reagan, shows what we might expect if he should go in office. And there are a lot of other things in here like that, too—that they would cut off Federal funding for any city, for instance, that had rent control and not permit any more housing funds coming in, and would let States do away with food stamps if they want to, and let States have their own kind of welfare programs and not let the Federal Government support them. And another thing that I know you all are concerned about—property taxes—

Governor Reagan has also proposed that the cost of education, for instance, and the cost of welfare, be put on the States and local governments.

Those are the kind of things that concern me very deeply, and so far we've not been able to get Governor Reagan to be specific on how he's going to cut the budget so deeply. But I think this kind of shows who's going to get cut. But don't worry about social security being sound and maintained as I told you it was, as long as a Democrat is in the White House.

AID FOR PAROCHIAL SCHOOLS

Q. How do you feel about aid to parochial schools?

THE PRESIDENT. We have given, as you know, an increasing amount of aid to parochial schools, and we'll continue to do that. We've worked especially strongly on going along with the guarantee that every young child who finishes high school, regardless of how poor the family might be, to be guaranteed of a college education, either for direct grants, or Government-guaranteed loans, for work-study programs, and sometimes for scholarships. The only thing that I've disagreed with is the tax credit. But I believe that we will go ahead and continue to increase the allotment of Federal funds for the parochial and for the public schools.

PROSPECTS FOR HOME BUYERS

Q. Mr. President, first of all, I'd like to thank you very much for honoring Gloucester City—first of all, it's a great town—and secondly, for honoring our family. I would like to ask—I think one of the American dreams in our society today is for people to own a home. Many people in the age group around 21 to 35 are having a problem fulfilling this dream.

Now, the mortgage rates approximately 6 months ago were very, very high; fortunately, the last few months, they have been lower. When you elect a President, you hope that these rates will stay down, and how would you try to make sure that they will stay down?

THE PRESIDENT. Well, obviously the best way to hold down mortgage rates is to control inflation. And I think another way is to make sure that the policies of banks are exposed to the public to analyze if they are or are not charging interest rates that are higher than the economic circumstances warrant. The American dollar has strengthened tremendously overseas. We've got a good sound economy. And the figures from last month showed that the housing starts in this country have jumped up substantially above 1½ million home units per year, as you know. Interest rates are too high. And I'll continue to work on them. I think the main thing is what I've already described—is the tax policies for the future.

If you make American workers more productive—we're already the highest producing workers in the world, but we haven't been gaining as much lately—and if you may have good harmony between management and labor—you probably noticed a couple years ago, almost every headline showed that there were wildcat strikes in the coal mines. You haven't seen that in the last 2 years, because the mineworkers and the management have been cooperating on how we could produce more American coal. You might be interested in knowing that this year we'll produce more American coal than any year in the history of our Nation. And we've done the same thing in the steel industry, the same thing in the automobile industry, to get those industries working together toward the future,

with government on the one hand, and with management and labor on the other.

Also, we've begun to work more closely with industry now, which we hadn't done before, on environmental protection laws, to make sure that the steel industry could put its investments back in their own modernized plants and still not cause a deterioration in the quality of our air.

The final point is this: We have a good working relationship with Congress. Jim Florio has been a very strong adviser for me and a good partner with me. He worked with me, for instance, to get approval for the Camden Veterans' Hospital that we're going to build—$75 million there—to serve several hundred thousand veterans in this area. That's part of a better life for people who have homes in this area. We've got a senior citizens home that's going to be built; I think it's got 90 units. And of course, we're also providing ways for people to buy their own homes by bringing the *Saratoga* in here to get it repaired, and which has created, as you know, about 8 or 9,000 jobs.

So, the combination of productive workers, holding down inflation, planning for the future, giving people a better life where they live, all will contribute to increased housing in this area. And we've had enormous increases in the number of home units allocated for New Jersey—I think much more on a per capita basis than have the average States had.

Yes, sir? In the back row.

ENERGY SOURCES

Q. Mr. President, the oil so critical to our national defense—have you considered the acceleration of conversion of our oil-fired electric generator units over to coal, and also increased their speeding up the licensing of those nuclear powerplants that are basically fully completed right now since the Three Mile Island incident?

THE PRESIDENT. Yes. We have identified over 100 oil-burning powerplants, mostly on the east coast—a few burn natural gas—all of which can be converted over to coal without lowering our air pollution standards. And we've asked the Congress to move expeditiously and already got the bill through the Senate, by the way. It's called oil back-out legislation. It will let a utility convert over to coal, help them pay for the cost of the conversion—sometimes with loans, sometimes with grants—and also gives them an extra allotment of funds when necessary to put in the air exhaust scrubbers to make sure that the air pollution standards are not lowered.

In addition to that, after the Three Mile Island incident, we had the so-called Kemeny report, that made recommendations on how the existing and planned nuclear powerplants could be made more standard in their design, constructed so they'd be more safe, operated more uniformly, and also have the personnel in them trained better. And we are now beginning to give licenses again to those atomic powerplants that had been held up for so long. The first licenses are going to those powerplants that are almost an exact copy of a powerplant that's working now successfully. And the Nuclear Regulatory Agency [Commission] is moving on that item to let those atomic powerplants start producing power and to let new ones be licensed.

So, I think that combination of backing out utilities from using oil and natural gas, shifting to coal, plus the licensing of nuclear powerplants, will help to meet the goals you described. Both of those are well on the way, and I hope this oil back-out legislation can now get through the House.

I know Jim Florio's for it. He'll be helping us with it. It's already passed the Senate.

INFLATION

Q. Mr. President, I deal in the fresh food business all the time. And I come in contact every day with people that, through inflation, are having trouble getting the food on the table—every day, you know, and that's not just once a month or anything. And I was wondering if your economic advisers have ever come to you and said there is a possibility someday of a zero inflation rate?

THE PRESIDENT. In July we had a zero inflation rate, and I hope you enjoyed that month—[laughter]—because it's the first time we'd had one, I think in 13 years, and obviously we haven't had one since. That was kind of an aberration. But at that time, food prices had pretty well leveled off.

The high inflation rate that we've got today was to a large extent due to increased food prices. As you know, on a worldwide basis, grain prospects are very low. The Soviet Union will produce about 20 million tons of grain less than we thought they would a week or two ago. Our grain harvest is going to be down because of drought in some areas, including New Jersey. Argentina is having a poor grain year and also Australia and Canada. So all those nations—really the only ones that export any appreciable amount of grain; the Soviets import—have a short crop in prospect, and that tends to drive up the price of feed grain. The feed grain tends to drive up the price of beef and pork and poultry that eat the grain and milk cows that give milk.

So I think that those food price pressures have driven up the cost of living. As I pointed out, though, in the last 3 months we have had an inflation rate down to 7 percent, but these new figures—which is about 12 percent a year for this 1 month—show us that we've got to be extremely careful about inflation as the number one economic threat in the months ahead. We can't have a massive Federal deficit, we can't have a massive election year tax cut, we cannot have a lowering of our ability to control government spending. These are exactly the things that Governor Reagan has proposed with his Reagan-Kemp-Roth bill, to give people a massive election year tax cut which would fan the fires of inflation. So that's a basic difference between us on economics, and I hope the American people will understand it. Controlling inflation is our number one domestic commitment.

NATIONAL DEFENSE

Q. Mr. President, I've been reading for a couple of years now, in the press, that our defense, our general defense stature, is not what it's supposed to be, and yet I hear from the Federal Government that it is. Are we—is our defense in order, or is there much room for improvement?

THE PRESIDENT. Yes, our defense is in good condition. We are the strongest nation on Earth militarily, and we've taken steps since I've been in office to correct a downward trend. For the last 15 years, the Soviets have had a steady upward increase, every year, in their expenditures for defense, for armaments. Seven of the eight years when Presidents Nixon and Ford were in the White House, we had a decrease in American expenditure for defense. Over that 8-year period, our expenditures for defense went down 37 percent in real dollars.

Since I've been in the White House, I have every year increased our commitment to defense, above and beyond the inflationary cost. And for the next 5 years,

I've presented to the Congress a projection of continued annual increases in our defense expenditures.

We've corrected a lot of things. You live near a shipyard and you probably have kept up with it, but before I came in office we didn't have any Trident submarine and Trident missile program ongoing. It was tied up with $2.4 billion of lawsuits, and the construction had almost come to a screeching start [halt]. Now the Trident submarine program and its missile are well on the way. We did not have any air-launched or ground-launched cruise missile program. This next year, we'll manufacture about 3,000 of those and have them put into effect. We didn't have any way to defend our fixed silo missiles, which were becoming vulnerable to Soviet attack. Now we have the MX missile system that we've proposed to the Congress, and I predict it will be approved and will go into production. That's just in the nuclear weaponry alone.

We also didn't have any military presence in the Persian Gulf region. That was a very serious defect in our defense capability. That's a troubled part of the world. And now we have two major aircraft carrier task forces in the northern Indian Ocean around the Persian Gulf region, and we've made arrangements for facilities to be used in case of an emergency in five different locations in that region. We've now begun to build up our rapid deployment force, because it's something that we can send overseas in a hurry to any troublespot in the world. We have pre-positioned materiel for 10,000 marines to use if we need to bring them into that troubled region of the world, and 500 airplanes already have pre-positioned; fuel and armaments to use if we have to.

We've worked out with our NATO Allies a 15-year plan now. NATO was in the doldrums when I took office and was kind of dispirited. Now there's a new spirit, a new sense of communication and commitment in NATO. We've got a 15-year plan for steady increases in our buildup of forces there.

Some other things that have helped us, too, militarily. For instance, we've now formed a friendship with a fourth of the people on Earth, in China, with normal diplomatic relations which will help to stabilize the Asian continent in the future. We don't have a military treaty with them, but now we're working with them to help keep that strategic area calm. We still have maintained our good trade relationships with Taiwan, as you know. And in Japan and South Korea and Australia and New Zealand, where we have alliances, we've strengthened those as well.

The point is that all these things have been done in the last 3½ years. And we've worked so that the Congress, and I, and the public who want to study it, know that this is what we've done, and this is what we're going to do over a full 8-year period, which keeps us strong, lets us meet any challenge, and lets us protect our interests. And by using those military strengths in a calm, carefully considered and effective way, we have kept our Nation at peace. We haven't had to prove that our military forces were all-powerful; we just want to make sure that people know it.

The last point is that in any election year, you're going to hear those who are outside the White House complaining because our country has been permitted to get too weak. I was down in Tampa, Florida, this past week, and I read a statement made by Governor Reagan. It said that the incumbent President and the Secretary of State had seriously let this Nation's defense capabilities deteriorate, so that now we were second in strength to the Soviet Union. That was a statement he made in 1976, by the way, when President Ford

was in office. So, you always hear that in an election year, but I can tell you, our Nation is the strongest, and we'll never be second to any nation in military strength.

AID TO EDUCATION

Q. Could you explain to me about this: Why financial aid for nursing students was cut in the budget?

THE PRESIDENT. Why financial aid was cut——

Q. Financial aid for nursing students?

THE PRESIDENT. Well, the overall commitment for financial aid to students has been increased tremendously since I've been in office. I don't know which particular program you're talking about. David, do you know any that we've cut?

MR. RUBENSTEIN. There haven't been any cuts. [*Inaudible*]—the average—about a 73-percent increase.

THE PRESIDENT. There may have been some proposal that an individual person made that we couldn't finance. But since I've been in office, in just 3½ years, we've increased Federal expenditures for education by 73 percent in that short period of time. And as I said earlier, there is no reason, now, for any student in this country who's able to do college work not to go to college, no matter how poor the family might be. If you know of any student like that, you let me know and I can guarantee you that that student can either get a loan or a scholarship or a grant or a work-study program, so they can go through college. That's one thing that we have done successfully since I've been in office—a lot of other things, too. [*Laughter*]

POLITICAL ENDORSEMENTS BY BLACK LEADERS

Q. Mr. President, recently several black leaders have come out for Reagan. Do you think this is going to significantly affect your campaign?

THE PRESIDENT. No, sir. I considered that very carefully and decided not to withdraw from the campaign. [*Laughter*]

That's just a tiny minority of black—actually former black leaders, they're not black leaders now. I'm not trying to knock them or anything, but Ralph Abernathy is the main one. He used to be the head of SCLC, and all of the people who were associated with Martin Luther King, Jr., including the present president of the SCLC, the Southern Christian Leadership Conference, have all endorsed me for President. I'm not trying to low-rate Ralph Abernathy, but that's a tiny minority among the black community who've endorsed Governor Reagan.

Well, I wish I could stay and take more. I'm sorry. I'm sorry. I've got two or three more places to go before I get back home tomorrow.

AUDIENCE. Put on the hat!

THE PRESIDENT. Jody,[1] should I put on the hat? How's that look? [*Applause*] There goes Kansas City. [*Laughter*]

Well, let me say how proud I am to be with you. I'm very proud to be with you. This is the first time I've had a session like this when we depended on one family, primarily, just to arrange a little get-together and invite their friends and relatives in. But I think your questions have been extraordinarily good, ranging from housing to student aid and to inflation and to defense. Matters of that kind—and social security—are very important to me and to you, too. And I hope that after this session, that you'll remember the heritage of the Democratic Party, the differences that exist between me and Governor Reagan,

---

[1] Jody Powell, Press Secretary to the President.

and help me as much as you can to get elected.

God bless you all. Thank you again.

NOTE: The President spoke at 3:04 p.m. at the Knights of Columbus Hall.

Wyoming, Michigan

Remarks to Area Residents.
October 24, 1980

It's good to be in Wyoming, a beautiful town. Thank you very much—[*inaudible*]—everybody. And I really wanted to have a chance to say just a word. It's sure fine to have—[*inaudible*]—here with me. How many of you would like to have Dale Sprik go to Congress next year? [*Applause*]

This is a wonderful occasion for me. I've just come here from New Jersey, where I had a chance to meet with a group, a large crowd like this group, to listen to questions that were important to private families. One of the great things about the Democratic Party—we've had the heritage from Franklin Roosevelt to Harry Truman to John F. Kennedy to Lyndon Johnson and now to me—is to remember what has been accomplished in your life, when Democrats have pulled together—[*inaudible*]—of this Nation, both in the White House and and also in the Congress.

I remember having grown up on a farm in south Georgia. And under Franklin Roosevelt, during the Great Depression years, we got for ourselves a new life. At that time, there was no social security. The Democrats were for it; the Republicans were against it. As you know—[*inaudible*]—children, 9 and 10 years old, were working in sweatshops, and adults were working at a wage that couldn't support their own families. The Democrats put forward a minimum wage of 25 cents an hour; the Republicans were against it. My first job was when the minimum wage went up from 25 cents to 40 cents, when I finished high school in 1941. The Democrats got that bill through; the Republicans were against it. They didn't figure the working families were worth 25 cents and then 40 cents an hour. The Democrats have always had their confidence in, and have always had their hearts go out to the working families of this country.

This hasn't changed. There is still a great threat in my Republican opponent to those same principles. He says the minimum wage has caused more misery and more unemployment than anything since the Great Depression. And he also refers to people who are drawing unemployment compensation as having a prepaid vacation for freeloaders. Democrats have always understood that with changing times there are going to be people who want to work, who are eager for a job, but who are temporarily unemployed.

Also, as you well know, it's important that our Nation be kept strong militarily, and that's what we've done in the last 3½ years. For 8 years before I came to the White House, we had a steady decrease in the Nation's commitment to a strong defense. It went down 37 percent. Seven years out of eight, we had lower budget allocations for a strong defense. But you all have to remember that it takes two wings on an airplane for it to fly. Not only must we be strong militarily—*[inaudible]*—use that strength to maintain peace. The best weapon is one that never has to be fired in anger, and the best soldier is one who never has to lay his life down or shed his blood on a field of battle.

Let me make just one other comment to you. As you know, we don't have very long to go before November the 4th. I'll do the best I can. Dale Sprik will do the best he

can. Fritz Mondale will do the best he can, to make sure that we preserve the principles of the Democratic Party and give a better life to the senior citizens, to those who are afflicted, to the working families of this country, to maintaining strong families, to keep our Nation strong, but at the same time to keep it at peace. Those are the kinds of issues that affect every one of you now and for the next 15 or 20 years. So, think on these things— what's best for your family, what's best for the people that you love.

We're going all out these next 6 or 7 days in preparing for the last few days before the election. There's no one listening to my voice who cannot contact at least 500 people in the next 8 or 10 days and urge them to vote for a better future for this great country and a better future for the citizens in it, who have benefited in the past from the heartfelt concern of Democrats. And we want to keep Republicans out of the Oval Office and out of the Congress for the next 40 years. Help me. We'll win together.

Thank you very much.

NOTE: The President spoke at 7:40 p.m. outside the Wyoming Public Library.

Wyoming, Michigan

Remarks and a Question-and-Answer Session With High School Students. October 24, 1980

THE PRESIDENT. Ms. Schooley may or may not have known it, but my first public job after I came home from the Navy was to be a member of the Sumter County Library Board, and I was very proud of it. They put me on the board because I read more books than anybody else in the county—*[laughter]*—and my library card number in Sumter County is 005. So, I got in on the ground floor.

And my second job in public life was as a member of the Sumter County School Board, and then I ran for the State senate. And when I got to the senate, I only had one request, and that was that I be appointed to the Education Committee. And later I got to be secretary of the committee and chairman of the Higher Education Committee. Then I ran for Governor, got defeated once, ran again and won, and then got this job—[*laughter*]— which I'm planning on keeping for a while. [*Laughter*]

I'm very delighted to be here tonight. I think it's especially fitting for me to come to meet the parents of Roger Chaffee. As the Commander in Chief of our military forces and as the President of maybe 230 million Americans, it's always important to recognize great achievement and the pioneering spirit and superb heroism and courage. And I was delighted to receive a book about their son from them outside. It touched my heart, and I look forward to reading it, because I know it will be an inspiration to me as it has been to so many people.

CAMPAIGN ISSUES

Also, I read about your community here, both Wyoming and Cedar [Grand] Rapids, to think about what our country has been and how it was formed. We are a nation of refugees, a nation of immigrants. Possibly everyone's family represented in this room came here from a foreign country, looking for a better life, expecting to have freedom, to worship as we please, to be innovative if we chose, to preserve our heritage and our background, our beliefs, to take pride in our own families, to make them strong and cohesive, to build communities all the way

across the vast expanse of this Nation; at the same time, not to let that diversity in our Nation weaken us.

We have somehow or another, in a democratic system where each person is precious and respected, taken that diverse makeup of what is the American population and welded it together in a beautiful mosaic, at the same time very strong.

We have difficult times. In the past we've been through some terrible times, beginning with the Revolution, going through the Civil War, later the First World War; the Second World War, in my lifetime; the Great Depression, which I mentioned outside; the change that we've taken in social affairs to give black people and those who speak Spanish, finally, full citizenship rights, and that was a shock to our country; the divisiveness of the Vietnam war, when Americans were hungering for peace; and then later on, of course, the embarrassment of Watergate.

Our country has been tested many times over, with economic deprivation, with the divisions among our people, with the great challenge to the security of our Nation. But no matter how difficult those problems have been, no matter how serious the questions that have been put to us, no matter how high the obstacles that we've had to face, this country when united has never failed: We have never failed to answer a question; we've never failed to solve a problem; we've never failed to overcome an obstacle.

And now there are problems in this area. In Michigan the unemployment rate is very high, because inevitable changes that take place with the rapid increase in the price of oil has shocked the American customer, who in the past have preferred a certain kind of automobile and now, because of very high prices foisted on us from overseas, prefer a different kind of automobile. But as fast as America can retool and rebuild and put out a product to meet changing times, those cars are selling like hotcakes, long waiting lists for the new automobiles in America.

But we go through this transient period. The function of government is to make sure that those families that are adversely affected by those changing times, which are inevitable, don't suffer to an extraordinary degree, that there's no actual hunger or actual loss of the family structure. And that's a part of a democratic society. That's why we care about people. And that's why I'm very glad to come here tonight to meet with young people and also to meet particularly in the library.

Socrates, as you know, was a great teacher, and there was a kind of give and take. So, if you ask me questions tonight that I can't answer, I'll go with the reference section—[*laughter*]—and find the answer very quick, and I'll scuttle back and I'll ask Ms. Schooley to help me.

Do you all have any question? I was hoping maybe one question or two. Okay, great.

QUESTIONS

VALIDITY OF GOVERNMENT ECONOMIC REPORTS

Q. My name is Dave—[*inaudible*].

THE PRESIDENT. Dave.

Q. Mr. President, in recent weeks there have been reports by the media that your administration has juggled Government figures to try and make the economy look better than it is, and that only today it has been reported that the Consumer Price Index was manipulated to make inflation appear not too much as bad as it is. In the past, data from Government agencies has always been insulated from politics, but it is apparently not so in the final days of your election campaign. How do you respond to these reports?

THE PRESIDENT. They're all false, of course. The reports are put out by an absolutely independent Government agency, both dealing with unemployment, with inflation, with the change in the gross national product. Those kind of statistical data that come out on economics are derived from interviews with— like on employment—40,000 families and also an inventory among businesses around the Nation about how many people they have employed, whether they're working 40 hours a week or an average of 38½ hours a week. And all that information is put together completely independently of me or anyone who works for me in the campaign or in my own direct administration.

Those allegations are completely false. If I could control the figures on the Consumer Price Index, it would have been better today than it came out. [*Laughter*]

I would like to say that the last 3 months, we have had an inflation rate of about 7 percent. Early this year, as you know, it was up approaching 20 percent. But it's still too high, and I think this 12-percent figure we got today sends us a clear signal that we cannot forget about the threat of inflation.

Last year the price of OPEC oil and oil all over the world increased more in 1 year than it had all the other times since oil was discovered in the 1800's. And all the nations on Earth have been shocked by this change, and we're trying to accommodate those changes. Our Nation is strong enough to withstand it. And we are suffering some temporary inconvenience, and it's very serious to some people and of great concern about the future.

But there would be no way to doctor those figures, because there are many independent groups with computerized facilities, like the Chase Manhattan Bank and the great universities and, of course, the Congressional Budget Office, that corroborates those figures with their own independent data. And if it was ever shown that anybody distorted those figures, it would be just a devastating indictment and would destroy the fabric of our country. It's not true.

POSSIBILITY OF THIRD WORLD WAR

Q. Mr. President, my name is Mike Williams, and I go to Godwin High School. And I'd like to know if you think I will see a third world war in my time and what you can do to prevent a major world war if you're reelected.

THE PRESIDENT. Thank you. That's an excellent question.

In the last 50 years no President has been able to say that they did not send American troops into combat, until this last 3½ years that I've been in office. We'd lost eight brave young men who went into Iran to try to save the hostages, but they were not sent into combat.

The attitude of a nation is determined pretty much by the people's desires and also by the character of the President and the restraints that are placed on a President by Congress and other factors in an international basis. I've not been in office a single day since I have been President that there wasn't a serious trouble spot somewhere in the world or sometimes several trouble spots at the same time.

I have built up the Nation's defense capability since I've been in office. For 7 of the previous 8 years before I got in office, our commitment for defense went down every year; there was a 37-percent reduction. But since then, since I've been there, we have increased it steadily, in a very carefully planned way, in a very orderly way, and we've encouraged our allies in Europe to do the same thing so that we won't be vulnerable.

The best way for a nation to stay at peace is to be strong militarily, economically, and politically, and for our own people to know we're strong, for our allies to know we are strong, and for our potential adversaries to know that we are strong.

Also, all of my predecessors in the White House have believed very deeply that when there is a troubled place in the world that the best way to resolve it is through political means and diplomatic means, not by the use of American military forces to be injected into some place which might erupt into combat and get us in a larger war.

There are two factors involved that are perhaps even more important than that. One is the control of nuclear weapons. Every President since Harry Truman has worked hard to control nuclear weapons, to have equivalent or balanced nuclear forces between ourselves and the Soviet Union, with tight controls on them, a way to monitor whether or not we were both complying with a treaty or an agreement, and with the ultimate goal to reduce those nuclear arsenals.

Lately, however, there has been a threat to that commitment. Governor Reagan, my opponent, has said that he wants to tear up the SALT treaty that was negotiated under President Nixon, President Ford, and myself. He has threatened the possibility of a nuclear arms race as a trump card to be played against the Soviet Union to try to force them into more favorable terms on a possible future nuclear agreement. This won't work.

If President Brezhnev announced that he was tearing up the treaty that had been negotiated over a 7-year period, was going to insist on the Soviets being superior to us, not equal, but superior to us in nuclear capability, and would start an arms race in order to force us to comply with not so favorable terms, we would reject that, obviously, would we not? And we would say, we'll match you missile for missile, and all of a sudden we'd be embarked in a major nuclear arms race.

Several times in the past number of years, some three or four times this year, Governor Reagan has also advocated the injection of American military forces into one of those troubled areas around the world. A few that come to mind where he's advocated this is North Korea; Ecuador, when there was a little fishing dispute; this year he advocated putting a blockade around Cuba; earlier, send in American military forces to Cyprus, to the Middle East, to Angola, to Rhodesia to prop a white supremacy government, to Pakistan. Those kinds of statements by him, I believe all since he's been wanting to be President, concern me very much.

So, I'm not saying that any President would want our Nation to get into war, but there has to be a calm, moderate, reasonable approach, insisting on diplomacy, not having to show that we've got the strongest nation on Earth by using military force, and a calm approach also to controlling nuclear weapons. This is the kind of thing that I believe we will do. And the American people are quite concerned about these two issues.

I think I can predict to you that you will not see a third world war. My judgment is that the Soviet leaders also want to avoid a nuclear war. And with constant communication with them, with our allies, with our friends around the world, an insistence on human rights, the honoring of the natural inclinations of people to be free, not injecting ourselves into the internal affairs of another country, dealing with crises, like the capture of our hostages or the Middle East, with a benevolent attitude, insisting that other countries move toward democracy if it's their will, like in

the recent, the formed country of Zimbabwe—those are the kind of ways to use America's enormous strength, not to push people around, but to let them realize the ideals and hopes that have nurtured and inspired us, and do it all peacefully.

I believe we can keep this Nation at peace.

Q. Thank you.

THE PRESIDENT. I promise.

REGISTRATION FOR THE DRAFT

Q. Hi. I'm Missy Stewart. I'm from Godwin High School, also. Since you pardoned the Vietnam draft dodgers, are you also planning on pardoning the 19-year-olds who did not register, and if not, what will their punishment be?

THE PRESIDENT. Thank you.

I hope they'll register. [*Laughter*] We had a very good sign-up. And the last time we had a draft registration, in the first period that it was required I think about 75 percent signed up. This time, although there was some displeasure expressed, we had about 93 percent sign up. Of those 93 percent, 15 percent of them said they wanted more information about a career in the military forces. So, I think it's going to encourage recruitment.

It would not be appropriate for me ahead of time to say that I would excuse or pardon a violation of the American laws. My oath is to carry out the law, to enforce the law, and to enforce the United States Constitution.

I think as the young people who opposed the registration realize that we're not going to have a draft—no law permits a draft in this country. The only way we would ever propose a possible draft of young people in this Nation is if our security was directly threatened and if the President and the Congress agreed that we needed a new law, which we don't have now, passed to let people actually be drafted.

We're not even going to examine young people, you know, physically and so forth to get them ready. It's just a matter of having people put their name on the list, their age, if they want to get information about the military, if they're a conscientious objector or not, so that if we do have to marshal our forces in the future, it'll save us about 90 or 100 days in getting our Nation ready.

So, I can't answer your question directly about if I will or will not pardon them. They'll have to comply with the law, and I hope now that they know there won't be a draft, but just registration, that they'll comply with it. So, you encourage your boyfriends to register. [*Laughter*]

Q. Okay.

THE PRESIDENT. I'm sure you've got a lot of them. [*Laughter*]

Yes, sir, in the back. Yes.

UNITED STATES MILITARY PREPAREDNESS

Q. My name is John—[*inaudible*]—from Godwin High School. Last spring a Navy—[*inaudible*]—did not meet its deployment schedule, because of undermanning and critical ratings. In September of 1980, the New York Times reported only 6 of our 13 aircraft carriers were combat ready. The same article reported naval air squadrons were in a poor state of readiness. Assuming your reelection, how would you attempt to resolve these problems, strictly in manpower and materiel ready.

THE PRESIDENT. Our military forces are much closer to full readiness now than they were when I took over. There are always fighting units that are not fully ready.

One thing is that we deployed very rapidly when the Persian Gulf threats arose,

when our hostages were captured and when it became obvious that there was a disturbance there because of the revolution in Iran a little earlier, we deployed two major aircraft carrier task forces into the northern part of the Indian Ocean. And we have now pre-positioned equipment and materiel for about 10,000 marines and enough to operate 500 of our airplanes, and we've got five different places over there in that region now that we can use not as permanent bases, but as facilities.

And we've also begun to develop a rapid deployment force that we can send to a troubled area in the world quickly if we need to to protect our interests. We have a much higher percentage of our ground divisions, our regular land forces in a state of readiness, for instance, than do the Soviet Union. All of our divisions that are stationed overseas, like in Europe or South Korea and so forth, are at a full state of readiness. But some of those that we keep in this country. would only be brought up to a full state of readiness if we had to marshal additional forces, and then you would call up the Reserves or call up the National Guard on a temporary basis until we could get more permanent military people marshaled.

We've made a lot of progress, I think, in improving the military forces with a steady buildup, a very predictable buildup in budget allocations. And I think this also ought to be pointed out. We are still and always will be on the cutting edge of technological developments in our nuclear weaponry, which we pray God we'll never have to use, in our airplanes, and so forth.

You probably have noticed that some of the American planes that we have sold to Israel, the F–15's, when they have used them and they've been challenged by the MIG–25's from Syria, the MIG–25's went down. And lately, even when Iran has some F–4's, which are not the most modern planes of our own, those planes are so formidable that in the war between Iran and Iraq, when those F–4's attacked the capital city of Iraq, Baghdad, the Iraqis don't even put up planes to try to stop them.

So, that just shows that the best the Soviets can build, that is the MIG–25's, and the best that we can build, even not the most modern planes of all—we stand up very well. So, we're going to stay strong, keep at an adequate state of readiness.

And I believe that we can always stick in the forseeable future with a fully voluntary military force. I don't see any reason for us to go to a draft. But as I pointed out earlier, we have had about 15 percent of our 18- and 19-year-olds who've registered saying, "We would like to have more information about a career in the military services." I wish that all of you young people, men and women, would carefully consider the possibility of serving in the military for a couple of years or 3 years, whatever suits you.

I went into the Navy when I was 18, and I stayed 11 years. I went to the Naval Academy, and then I did graduate work, and I was on submarines. And as you can see, it didn't hurt my political career very much. [*Laughter*] And no matter what career you're going to take up, politics or medicine or being a lawyer or being a teacher or whatever, this is a good way to serve your country, to do a patriotic thing, to see the world, to have an exciting life, to learn a career, to get experience, and to mature a little bit before you finally make a permanent decision about what you want to do in your lives. So, I would hope that everyone who's listening to my voice would seriously consider getting information about serving in the military.

We will see a buildup, all volunteer— I'm not talking about draft—we'll see a buildup very rapidly in young women who are serving in the military. And 95 percent of all the billets or positions in the military now can be filled by women. Only a very few, in actual combat roles, are not using women.

So, I would like to put in a plug for my military forces and yours while I have a chance. Thank you.

Yes, ma'am.

AMERICAN HOSTAGES IN IRAN

Q. Jo Weaver, Lee High School. I'd like to know, is it true that the American hostages in Iran are going to be released on Sunday or Monday?

THE PRESIDENT. Jo, I wouldn't get my hopes up. I hate to be discouraging. But I've been involved in this now for more than 11 months, and we've had private messages and also some public statements time after time after time that the hostages were going to be released imminently, soon. We've always been disappointed. And I think it's good for the American people to be very cautious about building up expectations about an early release of the hostages.

I have literally prayed every day, sometimes several times during the day, that our hostages would be safe, would not lose their lives, and would come back to freedom, and I've always wished they would come back that day.

But I don't want to build up your hopes too much. We don't have any clear signal from the Iranian leaders about when the hostages will or will not be released, and we don't know their terms, because the Majles, or parliament, committee still has not reported their terms.

I have an additional responsibility on my shoulders above and beyond or at least equal to the safety of the hostages, and that is not to betray my country, not to do anything that would bring discredit on my country or violate our honor or interfere with the interests of my Nation. I have never found those two things to be incompatible, protecting my Nation and protecting the hostages. But I cannot predict to you that they'll be released anytime soon. I wish I could.

Yes, ma'am.

VIEWS ON THE PRESIDENCY

Q. Mr. President, my name is Pam Cramer, and I'm from Lee High School. I was wondering how you feel [about] having a 6-year term of Presidency, instead of a 4-year where a person could get reelected twice, and what you feel your greatest achievement is as President.

THE PRESIDENT. Fine. I could probably answer your question a little bit better November the 5th. [*Laughter*] If I'm successful, the 8 years might look a little bit better.

I have said several times since I've been in the White House that I thought one 6-year term would be preferable, because as soon as I got into the Oval Office to serve, I hadn't been in there more than a year when the general presumption in the press and among others was that everything I did was designed just to get reelected. And I can't deny that sometimes I think about reelection, certainly lately. [*Laughter*] But it takes away the stature of the office.

And I've seen in other countries, like Mexico and Venezuela and, to some degree, in France, that a longer term for President is better. I doubt if the Congress and the people will ever change the Constitution, but if they did, I think it would serve the country well.

Let me say one other thing about the greatest achievement. It's hard to know. I think the first question I got exemplifies my greatest achievement—to keep this Nation strong and secure and at peace. And another prayer that I have is that when I go out of office, hopefully January of '85, that I can say that I never had to send a young man or woman into combat. That's what I hope. That's my best achievement so far, and I think maybe be extended peace to others, as well.

I think history might look back on this administration and say that the Mideast peace agreement between Israel and Egypt was a notable thing. I think they might say that the opening up of Africa to beneficial influence and trade and understanding with our country was an innovation that will pay rich dividends in the future. And I would guess the normalizing of relationships with China, with a billion new people there who are now our friends, will help to stabilize the situation in Asia, preserve the peace over there, and give us wonderful opportunities to sell American products and to have new and exciting relationships with the people of China.

There are a few things that come back fondly to me, and I think the maintenance of peace is the most important.

Thank you, Pam.

One more? Let me have one more question.

Yes, sir.

MINIMUM WAGE AND UNEMPLOYMENT COMPENSATION

Q. My name is Larry Hibel from Rogers High School.

THE PRESIDENT. Larry? Is that right?

Q. Larry.

THE PRESIDENT. Larry.

Q. Right. And the Republican candidate has attacked the minimum wage as inflationary——

THE PRESIDENT. Yes.

Q.——and the cause of teenage unemployment.

THE PRESIDENT. I know.

Q. What is your position of the issue?

THE PRESIDENT. All right. If you don't mind, let me elaborate on that a little bit, because what you've asked vividly demonstrates the difference between the thrust of the Democratic Party and the Republican Party. I don't want to alienate Republicans who might be inclined to support me, but you know this attitude on the minimum wage is important.

The first minimum wage law, that I mentioned outside, was for 25 cents an hour. The Democrats were for it, and the Republicans were against it. And the next one was 40 cents an hour. That's when I got my first job. The Democrats were for it; Republicans were against it.

I think all the way down through the years, Democrats have been more inclined to care about the working family and what it means for a husband or a wife to bring an adequate paycheck home to give the children a better life than they had themselves. Now we look back on the 25-cent-an-hour wage, it doesn't seem like much, but then it was a lot. Around where I live in Georgia, a lot of people, particularly women, work for the minimum wage now in the textile mills. The minimum wage is pretty much the prevailing wage there for many people. Governor Reagan has said, not too long ago, that the minimum wage has caused more misery and unemployment than anything since the Great Depression.

And I know that in this area, where many hard-working, dedicated people, because of change in buying habits for automobiles, are temporarily out of work. I feel very strongly that we need to have an unemployment compensation program. Governor Reagan says, not too long ago, that unemployment compensation is just a prepaid vacation for freeloaders. Well, you know, I don't believe that it's right for a person who wants to be President to say that a temporarily unemployed automobile worker is a freeloader, because that unemployment compensation is partially paid, as you know, by the employer and costs the employee also directly or indirectly, kind of an insurance program.

These are the kinds of issues that I believe are at stake in the election. It's not a matter of liberal or conservative. On fiscal matters, I consider myself to be reasonably conservative. In the tax program that I put forth for next year, for instance, it's anti-inflationary in nature.

The so-called Reagan-Kemp-Roth proposal would mean a reduction in taxes between now and 1987 of a thousand billion dollars, heavily oriented toward very rich people, that would flood this country with excessive money and create high inflation. George Bush, the Republican Vice-Presidential candidate, said that the Reagan-Kemp-Roth proposal would create 30 percent inflation or more, and he called it "voodoo economics."

So, the thing is that a stable, mature, responsible approach to the betterment of working families, the protection of people if they are unemployed, an adequate social security program to give people security in their older age, a responsible approach toward inflation—these are things that are at stake in this session.

One of the good achievements of my administration has been to put minimum wage tied to the average prevailing industrial wage paid in industry, so that as the other wages go up the minimum wage goes up, almost always behind it, but along with it. In the past the minimum wage sometimes would lag behind 6 years, and you'd have to have a real fight in the Congress to get the minimum wage built up so that the family wouldn't suffer severely with the impact of inflation. We've indexed, in effect, minimum wage, not to the Consumer Price Index, but to the average prevailing industrial wage.

That's my attitude toward the minimum wage. I don't think it's caused more misery and unemployment than anything since the Great Depression, and I don't think unemployment compensation is a prepaid vacation for freeloaders. That's a profound difference that's going to be decided by the voters on November the 4th.

Let me say this in closing. I wish I had more time. I've got one more event tonight, and I've had a long day. I'm going to go to Toledo, Ohio, tomorrow. I'll have a town meeting like this with 2 or 3,000 people, and I'll have good questions like you asked. I try to do that every day when I'm out, several times. And I'll also be making a major speech tomorrow on agriculture. I'm a farmer, before I ran for Governor, and my family have always been farmers, and I'm interested in that subject.

But it's been a delight to be with you. You've asked some very good questions, and I think that your questions will carry throughout the Nation, because the national press is here to report not only your questions but my answers. And to have these questions from young people gives me a different perspective than what I would have gotten had I not come to be with you.

Thank you again. It's been an honor for me to be with you. I thank you very much.

NOTE: The President spoke at 7:50 p.m. in the Main Reading Room of the Wyoming Public Library. He was introduced by Edna Schooley, librarian of the Wyoming Public Library.

Wyoming, Michigan

Informal Exchange With Reporters.
October 24, 1980

Q. Do you know if the hostages will be released on Sunday?

THE PRESIDENT. I don't have any information if that's true. I think it would be a mistake to build up expectations like that, because we have no idea what the Iranians are going to demand, whether or not we can accept their demands, or if they'll even make any demands. I think it's just a mistake for us to assume that the hostages will be released.

Q. So you don't have any new information?

THE PRESIDENT. No, I don't.

Q. Thank you.

NOTE: The exchange began at 8:20 p.m. outside the Wyoming Public Library.

Grand Rapids, Michigan

Remarks at an AFL–CIO Fundraising
Reception for Dale Sprik.   October 24, 1980

I was just holding Tricia in my arms. Tricia, right? Tricia and I want to work for, contribute to, and vote for Dale Sprik. Okay? [*Cheers*]

I'm not going to hold up your party very long, but I would like to say just a few things.

I've come here just to talk to a group that I know are already for Dale. You've come here to have a good time, but also to express your commitment to the Democratic Party, to the principles that have made our Nation great, and also to give your support to a very heroic and hardworking campaigner who ought to be in Congress and I believe will be there next January.

When Tricia grows up, I want to be sure that she has a good life. I want to be sure that we have someone in Congress from this district who cares about the family structure, who cares about average people, who believes in the finest things in life for all of us, no matter how rich we might be, who wants Tricia to have a better life perhaps even than her parents, who wants to have a good environment, who's concerned about consumers, who are all of us, who want to protect the integrity of the social security system, who want to have good wages for people that are employed, who want to have good housing programs, who'd like to have a protection for Medicare and would like to have a national health insurance program put into effect with an emphasis on prevention of disease and outpatient care and a cheaper and more inexpensive hospital care and some attention being given to pregnant mothers and their little babies when they're born.

I'd like to have somebody in the Congress who believes in a strong nation, but also someone who believes in the maintenance of peace. Our country is strong and at peace.

I know what it is to run a campaign. I ran for State senate, almost had it stolen from me; ran for State senate for reelection; ran for Governor, got beat, 1966. In 1970 I ran again for Governor, and I was elected. And I began to run for President in 1975, and I ran for 2 solid years. I know what it means to have friends.

Well, tonight you've come here as a friend for Dale Sprik, but you haven't done enough. Coming here is not enough. There's not a single person here this next 8 or 10 days that couldn't contact at least 500 people on the telephone. I have done my duties and also made more than 100 calls a day long distance. And all of you've got telephones, and you've got phone books.

And there's no one here that can't raise a few hundred dollars for him. Some of you have access to organized money, to the tax system. Some of you have influence in unions and other sources of money. And some of you may not be able to give but $5, but you could call 20 more people and say, "Can't you give a good, future Congressman $5?"

I'd just like to ask you to kind of start a crusade tonight so that my visit here, which is enjoyable for me, will have a beneficial impact for him and his campaign. I'd like for him to join me next January in Washington.

And there's one other candidate that I'd like to ask you to support. I'm not going to mention myself tonight. But we have an outstanding man running for election in this country, one of the finest people I have ever known, almost like a brother to me, an absolutely close partner, and that's Fritz Mondale. And I want you to support him for Vice President. [*Laughter*] Okay? [*Applause*]

Thank you very much. I love you all. Work hard, and we'll win together and give Tricia a better life in the future.

NOTE: The President spoke at 8:40 p.m. at Local 1165 of the Laborers' International Union of North America.

Digest of Other White House Announcements

The following listing includes the President's public schedule and other items of general interest announced by the White House Press Office and not included elsewhere in this issue.

October 19

The President returned to the White House from Camp David, Md.

October 20

The President has declared an emergency for the State of New Jersey as a result of a water shortage.

October 23

The President met at the White House with:

—Zbigniew Brzezinski, Assistant to the President for National Security Affairs;

—representatives of the Service Employees International Union;

—representatives of the New York Board of Rabbis;

—George Boyer, an employee at Cavanaugh's Restaurant in Philadelphia, Pa.;

—Rev. Joseph Lowery, national president of the Southern Christian Leadership Conference.

The President announced the recess appointments of two individuals. They are:

ALEX P. MERCURE, of Albuquerque, N. Mex., to be Under Secretary of Agriculture for Small Community and Rural Development;

JOHN TRUESDALE, of Maryland, to be a member of the National Labor Relations Board for a term expiring August 27, 1985.

October 24

The President met at the White House with:

—Dr. Brzezinski;

—Vice President Walter F. Mondale, Secretary of State Edmund S. Muskie, Secretary of Defense Harold Brown, Deputy Secretary of State Warren M. Christopher, Jack H. Watson, Jr., Assistant of the President, Dr. Brzezinski, and Lloyd N. Cutler, Counsel to the President;

—Larry Holmes, world heavyweight boxing champion.

The President left the White House for a trip to New Jersey, Michigan, and Ohio. Releases and announcements issued after the cutoff date of this issue begin on page 2455.

NOMINATIONS SUBMITTED TO THE SENATE

NOTE: No nominations were submitted to the Senate during the period covered by this issue.

CHECKLIST OF WHITE HOUSE PRESS RELEASES

The following listing contains releases of the White House Press Office which are not included in this issue.

Released October 19, 1980

Advance text: radio address on foreign policy

Released October 20, 1980

Advance text: remarks to reporters on nuclear arms control policy

Released October 22, 1980

Fact sheet: United States-People's Republic of China grain agreement

Released October 24, 1980

Advance text: opening remarks to area residents in Gloucester City, N.J.

ACTS APPROVED BY THE PRESIDENT

Approved October 19, 1980

H.R. 6686_____ Public Law 96–470 Congressional Reports Elimination Act of 1980.

H.R. 6883_____ Public Law 96–471 Installment Sales Revision Act of 1980.

S. 1393_____ Public Law 96–472 An act to amend the Earthquake Hazards Reduction Act of 1977 and the Federal Fire Prevention and Control Act of 1974 to authorize the appropriation of funds to the Director of the Federal Emergency Management Agency to carry out the earthquake hazards reduction program and the fire pre-

ACTS APPROVED—Continued

Approved October 19—Continued

vention and control program, and for other purposes.

H.R. 5295_____ Public Law 96–473
An act to amend the Social Security Act with respect to the retirement test, to reduce spending under title II of the Social Security Act, and for other purposes.

H.R. 5326_____ Public Law 96–474
An act to authorize the Secretary of Agriculture to convey certain Government-owned property in the Kisatchie National Forest to the State of Louisiana in exchange for certain property at old Camp Livingston, Louisiana.

H.R. 6816_____ Public Law 96–475
An act to provide for the exchange of certain Federal coal leases in the State of New Mexico for other Federal coal leases in that State.

S. 3072_____ Public Law 96–476
Rattlesnake National Recreation Area and Wilderness Act of 1980.

S. 707_____ Private Law 96–63
An act for the relief of certain aliens.

ACTS APPROVED—Continued

Approved October 21, 1980

H.R. 7554_____ Public Law 96–477
Small Business Investment Incentive Act of 1980.

H.R. 6665_____ Public Law 96–478
Act to Prevent Pollution from Ships.

H.R. 2743_____ Public Law 96–479
National Materials and Minerals Policy, Research and Development Act of 1980.

S. 1250_____ Public Law 96–480
Stevenson-Wydler Technology Innovation Act of 1980.

H.R. 5612_____ Public Law 96–481
An act to amend the Small Business Act, to provide for the payment of the United States of certain fees and costs incurred by prevailing parties in Federal agency adjudications and in civil actions in courts of the United States, and for other purposes.

S. 1156_____ Public Law 96–482
Solid Waste Disposal Act Amendments of 1980.

S. 2725_____ Public Law 96–483
An act to extend certain authorizations in the Clean Water Act, and for other purposes.

Toledo, Ohio

Remarks and a Question-and-Answer Session at a Town Meeting.
October 25, 1980

THE PRESIDENT. Thank you very much, my good friend Lud Ashley, Senator John Glenn, Senator Metzenbaum, Congressman Pease, Mayor DeGood, and all my friends, both Republicans and Democrats, who've come here—especially Democrats. I'm glad to be with you.

It's a pleasure to be introduced by one of our Nation's greatest Members of the Congress, who's left his mark not only in this community, which has seen so much progress lately, but also on our Nation's progress in energy and urban affairs. When the Congress addressed the energy issue, perhaps the most difficult issue the Congress has ever had to deal with, Lud Ashley was chosen by the Speaker and by his fellow Members of the House to head up the comprehensive committee, to put together this very successful program.

I'm glad to be here in the home of the Spartans. I understand you have a tradition of championships. And there's another very famous Toledo athletic team that I understand has been knocked lately by the Republican Vice-Presidential candidate, the Mud Hens. I'm for the Mud Hens. I think they've done a great job. There are some people in the so-called Bush league, but not the Mud Hens. [*Laughter*]

I really share your pride in the revitalization here of Toledo. The Chamber of Commerce says that over a quarter of a billion dollars has been invested in your great community in the last 2 years in partnership with the Federal programs that have been hammered out with the Democratic congressional leaders and my own administration. That's the kind of partnership that I think is crucial to our Nation. Now that we have an energy policy in place for the first time in the history of our Nation, it's time for us to completely revitalize the industrial complex of the United States.

I will be going from here to a nearby farm in one of the richest agricultural regions of the world to make my single major farm speech of the campaign. This speech will be recorded. It'll be played later on on radio stations and television stations around the Nation. But I wanted to come here to your area—a dynamic, progressive, unified community with industry and agriculture—to make sure that I had this impact in the last 10 days, to make Lud Ashley's prediction come true.

We have now about 35 more minutes. I'm not going to make my remarks any longer. I'd like to start with the questions, beginning on my left. I'll try to keep my answers pertinent, brief, and to the point.

PROGRAMS FOR THE ELDERLY

Q. Mr. President? Is the mike on?

THE PRESIDENT. I can hear you. I don't know if the audience can.

Q. I am Eleanor Kahle, a representative of the most rapidly increasing segment of population in the United States today, the senior citizens.

THE PRESIDENT. Yes.

Q. We are also the group most adversely affected by inflation. We are concerned about allocations for programs affecting seniors, primarily those programs that focus on keeping seniors out of institutions as long as possible. As the need and numbers increase, being granted the same amount of funding as in the past is in reality a cut decreasing the reduction of services that we are able to give to our seniors.

What are your plans for the continuation or the increase of funding in the areas of nutrition, transportation, housing, health care for senior citizens? What is your commitment to us?

THE PRESIDENT. Thank you, Mrs. Kahle. Since this is an election year, I think it's incumbent on a candidate to point out what has been done, what will be done, and the contrast between me and my Republican opponent.

When I was campaigning in Toledo 4 years ago, the biggest single concern of senior citizens was the prospective bankruptcy of the social security system. With the help of Howard Metzenbaum, John Glenn, Lud Ashley, Don Pease, and other Democrats, we were able to put the social security system back in a sound financial condition. And I can guarantee you that as long as a Democrat is in the White House, the social security system will never be threatened with bankruptcy again. That's the first thing.

Secondly, concerning social security, it's very important to realize that over a period of years, my opponent, Governor Reagan, has called for the voluntary participation in the social security system on at least four different occasions. This would mean the end of a sound social security system. If you could let anybody who wants to, who's paying into the social security fund, withdraw anytime they

wanted and make it voluntary, obviously the social security system would be dead.

Closely associated with social security in the past is the future. I read yesterday a Wall Street Journal analysis—as you know, that's a very strong Republican paper, very strong, supportive of Governor Reagan—front page article saying that Governor Reagan's advisers were asking him to eliminate the increases in social security that will go to pay senior citizens as inflation builds up in order to keep their purchasing power intact. If I am reelected, we will continue those annual increases for social security benefits so that you will not have any reduction in your buying power in the years ahead. Also, I am adamantly opposed to any sort of taxation of social security benefits, and I will not change the eligibility requirements for social security beneficiaries either.

Another thing that's very closely associated with social security is Medicare. As you know, this was a Democratic program. It was opposed by the Republicans. As a matter of fact, Governor Reagan got his start in politics working for the American Medical Association, traveling around the Nation speaking against Medicare. And of course, we want to have national health insurance with an emphasis on prevention of disease; a lid on hospital costs so they don't charge you too much for your medical care; an emphasis on outpatient care, the care for senior citizens and others in their own homes, not in very expensive hospital rooms; an emphasis on the prevention of illness among very tiny babies and little children, starting at the prenatal stage, where mothers and babies in the first few years of their existence on Earth can have good medical care; and also a catastrophic health insurance program so that if a family is affected by unexpectedly high health costs, then you would have a Government insurance program to help them pay those very high bills. Those are the kind of things that are in the national health insurance program that I've put to the Congress. Governor Reagan says he's absolutely opposed to any such program, if he should become President.

So, we will continue our very steady growth in housing programs, improving programs for social security, and health insurance. And I might point out that the health insurance emphasis is not toward a massive spending program, but would probably actually reduce the cost of health care because you'd be preventing disease and preventing those chronic things that take place in a person's life. because they didn't get adequate care when they were little tiny babies, a lid on hospital costs, and an emphasis on outpatient treatment. All those things will reduce medical care costs and give us better medical care.

So, from housing to social security, Medicare to health insurance, I think my programs are very good, sound, already presented to the Congress, making good progress through the Congress. Governor Reagan would be just the opposite. I suggest you vote Democratic.

EMPLOYMENT; ENERGY

Q. My name is Anne Zanville. Mr. President, I would like to ask you what are you going to do about the unemployment in this country and the energy crisis?

THE PRESIDENT. Thank you very much, Anne.

Since I've been in office, we have emphasized employment perhaps as successfully as anything that we've done. In the last 3½ years, we have added almost 9 million new jobs above and beyond the Americans who were employed when I was inaugurated President. I noticed the figures this morning, for instance, for Ohio. There has been an increase in employment in Ohio of 417,000 people in the last 3½ years. In other words, today, in full-time jobs, there are 417,000 more Ohioans at work than there were when I came into office. And in the Toledo metropolitan area, although right now you are suffering from the changes taking place in the automobile industry, there are 17,000 more people at work now than when I was inaugurated. That's as of last month. So, we've made good progress. Unemployment is still too high.

We have formed a very close working relationship in some of our basic industries between the Government, management, and labor. You probably remember 2 or 3 years ago, almost every headline showed that there were wildcat coal strikes and the mines were shut down. You have not seen one of those headlines, I don't believe, in the last couple of years, except very rarely. And this year, we'll have more American coal produced than any year in history. We'll also have more oil wells and gas wells drilled this year than any year in history. Today we are importing from overseas one-third less oil than we did just a year ago. This shows the effectiveness of the other part of your question, the energy program. And it also helps greatly with employment in the automobile industry.

With a very high increase in oil prices—OPEC raised the oil prices last year, in 1 year, more than oil prices had increased since oil was first discovered in the 1800's, and our economy has had to accept that shock along with nations all over the world. I think we've done very well in accommodating that. And as you know, the inflation rate was up around 20 percent earlier this year because of that. The last 3 months, we've gotten the inflation rate average down to about 7 percent—still pressures—we must guard against increased inflation. In the steel industry, the same thing—the workers, management, and the Government are working together. So, I see for us now a great opportunity to completely reindustrialize this country.

After the Second World War the United States rebuilt industry in Germany, we rebuilt industry in Japan, and now it's time to rebuild industry in the United States of America. That's what we're going to do.

HAITIAN AND CUBAN REFUGEES

Q. Mr. President, Shirley Flanner, foreign language department here at Start High School. *Bienvenido.* [Welcome.]

THE PRESIDENT. *Gracias. Es un placer para mí estar aquí.* [Thank you. It's a pleasure for me to be here.]

Q. Mr. President, in Florida and Texas many problems are developing due to the non-English-speaking refugees who need schooling, medical care, et cetera. Some of the city officials there say that the Government has bailed out and left them financially in the pits. Number one, have we bailed out, and number two, do you think we should help them financially?

THE PRESIDENT. I've just come from Florida early this week and had a townhall meeting in Miami, which has been the most heavily impacted city in the Nation, as you know, with the refugees escaping from Cuba. The Congress has passed a law, which I support, so that those refugees that have come here and put an extra burden financially on the communities where they've settled, the Federal Government will pay 100 percent of those extra costs.

It's very difficult for me to deal with this issue, because from Haiti and from Cuba people have come to our country in a flood that we did not anticipate and

which the American laws did not anticipate either. A lot of people said, "Let the boats sink. Stop them. Don't let them come on our shores." We did the best we could with a flotilla of Navy and Coast Guard ships to try to prevent those boats going from Florida down to Cuba to pick them up, and now we've got the flow stopped.

But I think it's good for all of us to remember that ours is a country of refugees. Ours is a country of immigrants. Unless there are a few American Native Indians in this audience, all of our families came from foreign countries. We've come here, sometimes against our will, as was the case with the black slaves early in our history, but we've come here most of the time looking for a better life, looking for religious freedom, looking to escape from persecution, looking for a chance that our children could have more freedom and more opportunity than we had. It's not weakened our country to have those immigrants come in. It's strengthened our country.

When the European Jews came here, there was an opposition to it among those already here. When the potato famine in Ireland occurred and the Irish came here, they were despised by some who had been here a little longer. And when the Europeans came here from Poland or from Italy or from Holland, there was an inclination on the part of some Americans to say, "We've got it made in this great country. Now no more immigrants ought to come." But that's not part of the consciousness and the character of our Nation.

So, we will, in accordance with American immigration laws, continue to strengthen ourselves with immigrants. And when there is a special unanticipated flood of refugees that nobody ever thought would take place, the Federal Government has acted to alleviate the financial burden on local people and on State governments. And we've done it very effectively in Florida. Florida, particularly, and other places, maybe like some in Toledo, have performed superbly. I'm very proud of the way Americans have reacted. Our country is not weakened because of it.

My judgment is that our country will be even stronger because of the freedom-loving immigrants who've come here and also because of the way Americans have reaffirmed the principles and the ideals which have been the root of our progress in years gone by.

PROGRAMS FOR THE ELDERLY

Q. Good morning, sir, Mike Clemmer.
THE PRESIDENT. Mike.

Q. I'm a student at the University of Michigan, and I would like to join— [*laughter*]—sorry about that, gang, Ohio country. I would like to join Anne in asking you about your plans for programing to the aged.

During your administration, the United States seems to have become increasingly hostile and cruel as a place for older adults to live. Last winter older adults froze to death in the winter, because they could not afford heating fuel. Hundreds of older adults died last summer, because they could not afford air conditioners or even fans as protection against the heat. The aged have suffered from both hypothermia and hyperthermia as their reward for their efforts to conserve energy.

The price of fuel and other utilities as well as increasing tax burdens have forced too many older adults to give up their homes and move to the senior highrises, nursing homes, or worse, in these inner-city ghettos of the aged. When the price of fuel has forced cuts in public transportation and increases in fares where

public transit is available, older adults are forced to abandon their private automobiles because of fuel and oil prices.

THE PRESIDENT. Mike, do you have a question?

Q. Yeah, I do.

THE PRESIDENT. When you get through reading the Republican brochure, I'd like to have the question. [*Laughter*]

Q. Sir, I'm not a Republican.

THE PRESIDENT. I didn't say you were. I said you were reading the Republican brochure.

Q. Well, unfortunately, I'm calling it as I see it, and I've talked with quite a few older adults in preparing this.

THE PRESIDENT. I doubt if you'd find that those statements are true, but go ahead if you insist.

Q. Okay. The energy relief program was too little too late, and transportation programs seemed stonewalled. The Older Americans Act has thrown services to the aged into a confused and miserly retrenchment.

AUDIENCE MEMBERS. Question!

Q. You'll get the question.

The legislation assuring the barrier-free access to——

THE PRESIDENT. We've only got 45 minutes.

Q. I know it. The mainstream of our society is commonly circumvented.

If you are reelected, sir—and this is my question, because it's very important to my career plans, because my concern is the older adults—what new initiatives do you plan to undertake to make our Nation a more hospitable place for our older adults and those millions of others, the handicapped and the poor, who share some or all of the aged's needlessly difficult circumstances?

THE PRESIDENT. Mike, I don't know if it's necessary for me to repeat the answer

I gave Anne over here earlier. But I'll try to add one or two more points.

The Congress, at my urging, not only put social security back on its feet, but we also increased each year social security payments to more than compensate for the inflationary pressures. Just a couple months ago, I think in May, we increased social security payments 14.3 percent, which is at least as much and a little bit more than the inflation rate's increase because of OPEC oil price increases.

In addition to that, we've got an extraordinary revitalization of elderly housing programs, whereas under Nixon and Ford, as you may remember, the housing program was completely killed. There was a moratorium placed on any Federal Government housing for the elderly.

In addition to that, in the same Wall Street Journal article that I just read—the superb Democratic program, financed already out of general revenue funds, and in the future to be financed out of windfall profits tax funds, have been allotted directly to State governments, to be transferred to older citizens who are poor to pay for the increase in their heating bills—and a new amendment will let them help pay their air-conditioning bills in extraordinarily warm weather in the summer—so that they won't be afflicted with adverse cold in their own homes.

We have also increased, by several billions of dollars, the new allocation of funds to let senior citizens and poor citizens insulate their homes, so that they can have cheaper fuel bills. And then if the fuel bills do go up, we'll pay them cash money—as we have 2 years now, 3, as a matter of fact—and we'll do it again this year, so they will not suffer.

Yesterday, in the same Wall Street Journal, which I'm sure you read on occasion, Mr. Reagan's advisers advocated the doing away with the special alloca-

tion of funds for senior citizens to pay their heat bills. As long as I'm in the White House, we will protect the senior citizens, continue to improve their living conditions, social security, health care, housing, transportation, and the ability to pay increasing heat bills. That's what my plans are for the future.

THE MIDDLE EAST

Q. First of all, Mr. President, I'd like to add my welcome to the welcomes that you've just heard from the other people.

THE PRESIDENT. Thank you, sir.

Q. My name is James Epstein. I'm a teacher at Start High School, however my question has nothing to do with Start High School. Mr. President, earlier in your administration, when you met with President Sadat and Prime Minister Begin, you gave Israel and Jewry the world over great confidence that the U.S. would be supportive of a just peace for Israel and the Near East. Since then, some of that confidence seems to have waned, and especially as a result of an apparent slip-up in communication between the White House and the U.N. Representative at one time. Can you give us some idea of how our former confidence can be restored?

THE PRESIDENT. Yes. I'll try.

When I first met with the Prime Minister of Israel it was Mr. Rabin, and just 2 or 3 weeks later I met with President Sadat. At that time they had just completed the fourth war between Israel and Egypt in the 25 or so years, 30 years, of Israel's existence. I told the Prime Minister and the President that my ultimate goal for the Mideast was that the major Arab nation, Egypt, should start to recognize, first of all, Israel's right to exist, which no Arab nation had been willing to do; secondly, that there should be direct negotiations between Egypt and Israel; third, that Israel's security should be guaranteed in an agreement; fourth, that there should be open borders between the two nations, there should be diplomatic recognition between the two nations, there should be exchange of ambassadors between the two nations, and also trade and tourism between the two nations.

President Sadat replied to me, "That's my dream also, Mr. President, but it'll never come into realization in my lifetime." All of those dreams have already been realized.

We are still engaged in the negotiations between Israel and Egypt to try to bring about a comprehensive peace. There are some difficult issues. If I should ever mislead the leaders or people of Israel or Egypt in any way, my value as an intermediary or mediator would be destroyed. I have got to keep the trust of both sides by being honest and open. I do not have any secret agreements or understandings with Israel that's not known by the world and certainly not known by President Sadat or vice-versa. I'll maintain that.

I know there are some very sensitive issues with the Israeli people and also with American Jews. I will never support a PLO state or a Palestinian independent state. I'll never negotiate or recognize the PLO until after they announce that they support Israel's right to exist, to live in peace, and support U.N. 242 as a basis for a Mideast settlement.

I will continue to protect Israel in international councils, in UNESCO, the ILO, in trade missions, and in the General Assembly. I've since announced that if the constant Syrian and other effort is ever successful—which I don't think it will be—to expel Israel from the General Assembly or to reject their credentials, that I see no way our Nation would continue to participate in the deliberations of that body. If there are resolutions in the future in the Security Council, where we have a veto, I will continue to protect Israel, and if those are frivolous resolutions designed to damage Israel or to damage the peace process that we initiated at Camp David, I will direct that a veto be exerted by the United States to kill such a resolution.

Another point that ought to be made is this though. I cannot always promise you that I will agree with Israel—unless it's the desire of the American Jewish community to terminate the peace process—when Israel takes a unilateral step, say on Jerusalem, with a proposal that the headquarters be moved into east Jerusalem, I cannot approve that as an unbiased negotiator or mediator between the two. The agreement that I have with the Israelis and the Egyptians is that Jerusalem will remain an undivided city, that the holy places will be freely acceptable (accessible) [1] to all those who want to worship there, and that the ultimate legal status of Jerusalem will be determined through negotiations, understanding that the final terms of that negotiation would have to be acceptable to the Government of Israel. That's the American position, well understood by Mr. Begin and all his fellow workers, well understood by President Sadat and all his fellow workers, and I think it's a sound position.

I might add that we are very much aware that our aid programs and our support for Israel is not a benevolent act. My duty is to the United States. And when I see a strong, united, secure, democratic Israel, that is a direct benefit to the security of my own Nation. And I'm very proud of the fact that in just 3½ years, the Congress and I together have provided more military and economic aid to

---

[1] White House correction.

Israel than in all the other almost 30 years of Israel's existence. This is a good investment for us in our own security. And it will continue.

TAX CUTS

Q. Mr. President, my name is Joe Guerrero. Governor Reagan has proposed tax cuts which he says will benefit the American people. However, many experts say these would benefit only the wealthy while they would take away money used to fund Federal programs for the aged, the poor, black, and Hispanics. Don't you feel that this would be counterproductive?

THE PRESIDENT. Yes. [*Laughter*] Joe, let me explain to you why.

We have been afflicted in our Nation and all over the world this last 12 or 18 months with the unanticipated and enormous increase in oil prices. It's created a change in buying habits for Americans concerning what kind of automobiles they want, as you know. They want the smaller, more efficient cars now with high-priced gasoline. It's also created inflationary pressures for all countries. The inflationff rate in Israel is probably almost 200 percent, and ours, as I say, this quarter has been about 7 percent. It's still too high, but the inflationary pressures are there.

Governor Reagan has come out here, in an election year, with a massive tax reduction proposal called Reagan-Kemp-Roth. Its primary benefits would be for rich people—and maybe there are some in the audience—[*laughter*]—because a person making $200,000 a year, under Reagan's proposal, would get 35 times more tax benefits than a family making $20,000 a year. This would create a flood of money into the American economy, if it ever should be put into effect, that meant that for a given level of products,

as they were bid for, with that flood of money, inflation would go sky high. It would just be like pouring gasoline on a fire.

My tax proposal, which we will put into effect next year, is anti-inflationary in nature. Most of it will go to encourage industry to create new tools and new plants, to encourage American workers to be more productive and to increase jobs. There are two other elements of it. One is to offset the increase in social security payments next year, to keep the social security system sound. And the other element is to eliminate the so-called marriage penalty, because now, as you know, a man and woman who are married and who are living together and both working pay higher income taxes than a man and woman who are living together, both working, who are not married, and that to me is destructive to the family system of our country. So, we're going to change that.

And finally let me say that Governor Reagan's proposals are absolutely ridiculous. There's no way for him to cut taxes 30 percent the next 3 years, have a massive increase in the Federal spending for defense above and beyond a large increase that's been put into effect by me, without eliminating almost completely all the Federal programs that are precious and dear to the people who need help most.

His attitude is expressed pretty accurately when he refers to the minimum wage. And the Wall Street Journal article yesterday said that his advisers will urge him to completely eliminate the minimum wage. He has said about it, "The minimum wage has caused more misery and more unemployment than anything since the Great Depression."

And I know in Toledo at this time with the automobile industry changing, taking place, there are people, hard-working families, who are temporarily unemployed. That situation is improving lately, but still you have that. Governor Reagan says that unemployment compensation is a prepaid vacation for freeloaders. I'm quoting him exactly. That's the attitude that might be expressed from the Oval Office if Governor Reagan should be in office. It's not only his tax program but it's his historic, long-term, and most recent statements and attitudes that concern me very deeply.

So, I agree with your premise and your question.

VIEWS ON GOVERNMENT

Q. Mr. President, my name is Pete Ganzel. I'm 18 years old, and this is my first time voting in the Presidential election.

First of all, I want to say I feel very alienated from our Government. And the question I have is, how can you bring the Government down to reach me personally? And also, as a youth I feel that there's really no one in the Government who will sit down, listen to my criticism, listen to my suggestions, listen to my ideas, and give us some straight answers, no traditional political doubletalk, which we hear so much in the past, and we also hear it in the elections going on now.

For instance, if you are elected and if I would come to Washington, D.C., would you give up 3 hours of your time, sit down, and talk to me? [*Laughter*]

THE PRESIDENT. No. Steve, I couldn't promise you that I could give you 3 hours of my time. There are 230 million people in this Nation, and if I gave everybody 3 hours I wouldn't have any way to deal with the problems that you and I discuss. But one thing that I have done is to come to places like this.

I had two of these kinds of sessions yesterday with smaller groups, one in the Grand Rapids area, a little town called Wyoming, just high school students, where the five high schools chose their five outstanding students and they came and cross-examined me in front of the local television, radio news media and also the national press, and earlier with a group in Gloucester City, New Jersey, where one Catholic family in the Knights of Columbus Hall brought all the members—about 60 of their family and friends and they asked me questions about government issues that affected them. And I answered those questions in public, and I'm doing the same thing today. I'll go from here out to a farm nearby, to talk about agriculture.

I've done this all during the campaign. I have to say that Governor Reagan has not. He's not had a town meeting, and he's not going to have a town meeting. He very seldom has even a press interview, because, as you know, when he has made a statement, quite often it's been very embarrassing. I'm eager to have my views known clearly to you and otherwise.

Lud Ashley, I presume, is your Congressman. It's much easier for him to deal directly with you or a small group of your classmates. If you have—and I'm sure Lud would be glad to. Lud, is that right? And to a large degree, Steve, I get my instructions from people like Lud Ashley and Don Pease and Howard Metzenbaum and John Glenn about what I ought to do for Ohio. But our system of government is such that you, dealing with Mayor DeGood, if you live in Toledo, or dealing with your own Congressman, Lud Ashley, or with your Senator, can present your views to me indirectly. And in a system like this, a session like this, you can present your views to me directly.

I might say one other thing. There's no reason for you to be alienated from your government. Are you 18 now?

Q. Yes.

THE PRESIDENT. So you'll be able to vote on November the 4th. That vote is crucial. You've heard us discuss today matters of inflation, employment, the aged. You've heard discussion about taxation, about Israel, about peace. Those kinds of things are important to you and to all Americans.

So, I will continue to let my views be known, as clearly as I can. I'll honor the views of your own local elected officials, and also I'm very interested in your views as well. So, you can write to me, call me, and if you come by Washington, I'll be glad to see you briefly. But I can't promise you the 3 hours, okay?

Q. Thank you.

Q. Mr. President, my name is John Drolshagen. I'm an unemployed, disabled vet. It's kind of a redundancy, I think. My question is why the veterans, disabled and the rest of us, are treated as third-class citizens, and why the Agent Orange syndrome from Vietnam is being pushed under the carpet? And who comes out with the figures of what is acceptable for catching cancer from this—what percentage? I'd like to know who says it's okay that an "x" amount of us have Agent Orange and that's to be accepted?

THE PRESIDENT. I'll try to answer that—John, is that right?

Q. Yes, sir.

THE PRESIDENT. John, when I became President, I was very concerned about the situation with veterans, and particularly Vietnam veterans. There was no screening process for veterans from the Vietnam war who had either psychological problems or physical problems as a result of any debilitating or damaging experience in the war. I searched this country over to find the best person possible to head up the Veterans Administration, who had a special insight into Vietnam veteran problems, and I chose Max Cleland who's the Veterans Administration Administrator. He's a triple paraplegic. He was injured in Vietnam. He's a very strong and able person. He was a senior staff member of the Senate Veteran's Committee, working along with John Glenn, Howard Metzenbaum, and others who are especially interested in veterans.

We've established now several thousand screening centers around the Nation where Vietnam veterans, in particular, can come and get a special insight into their own problems and get treatment. We've had special job programs created for Vietnam veterans since I've been in office. It never existed before. We've extended the time within which the GI bill can be honored for Vietnam veterans.

In addition to that, we've had a very good increase annually, for the first time, in veterans benefits. No President's ever done that before, but every year we've increased veterans benefits at least to try to stay up with the cost of inflation. We've done that four times since I've been in office.

On the Agent Orange question, it's a very serious problem. Max Cleland, with a staff of both scientists and doctors, is trying as best he can to find out the facts about the Agent Orange effect on people's lives and health. And if you have a special problem for that, I hope that you will call Max Cleland. I'll have my staff tell him to wait for your call, and he can refer you to specifically the people in his agency and the Veterans Administration that can answer your question. So, if you would just give my staff members your name and address and telephone number. And if you wish, I'll have Max Cleland give you a call personally about it.

Keech LeGrand[2] says that's all the questions I can take. Can I take one more, Keech? I'm going to be late.

Thank you, ma'am. I'll take it.

PRESIDENT'S INCUMBENCY

Q. Mr. President, this will be brief. Everybody knows, everybody should know that the problems that beset this Nation today are not the doing of one man, nor will they be undone by one man. Yet a second term offers you greater understanding, experience, greater strength, greater freedom, conviction to act. Why is this not more positive in your campaign?

THE PRESIDENT. Thank you, ma'am. Well, as you know, in the heat of a campaign it's often very difficult for a candidate to make those points as well as you just made it then. We've not had a President who's served two full terms since Dwight Eisenhower, because of different circumstances, assassination, resignation, and other tragedies. And I believe that it is to the advantage of the American people to understand the continuity that is valuable to us.

If you were managing a major corporation or trying to determine the affairs of a major city, obviously someone who had been in that office for 3 or 4 years would be much more knowledgeable about the interest groups and the challenges and the problems and their possible solutions; also the intricacies of the Federal Government bureaucracy, just a knowledge about other nations on Earth and their leaders, their characteristics, their hopes and their dreams, and the problem, troubled areas. But in the heat of a campaign, charges are made against an incumbent administration that quite often steal the headlines.

---

[2] White House staff advance person.

I was in Orlando, Florida, this week. And I noticed, for instance, the headlines, "Reagan Charges United States Has Lost Military Supremacy"—big headline. And it went on to say that we have now, because of the maladministration of the incumbent President become, and I quote Mr. Reagan, "This administration has allowed the United States to become number two in military power." And it went on to say, "collapse of the American will and the retreat of American power." The date on that is September 1976. He was talking about President Ford, and it's hard for me to understand how, if President Ford and Kissinger let the Nation become the number two military power, how I have let the Nation become a number two military power.

This kind of rhetoric and exaggeration in a political campaign tends to cover up what actually is the circumstance in our country. Our country is not second to any in military power; it will never be. And just to continue the tradition, I'd like to read to you the response that President Ford's spokesman made. He said, referring to Governor Reagan's comment, he said, "This is the kind of thing you could read in every right-wing magazine in the last 5 years." I'm not making that comment, I'm just quoting President Ford 4 years ago about Governor Reagan.

The point is that the people of this Nation in a political campaign have to stop and consider what is our Nation's circumstance, what has been accomplished in energy, in the number of jobs built, in how Toledo itself has changed in the last 2 or 3 years, whether senior citizens are now more secure, whether we are reducing oil imports, whether peace has been brought to the Middle East, whether we've opened up new friendships with a billion people on Earth in China, whether our defense establishment is strong, whether our Nation has stayed at peace. These are the kinds of issues that I think are proof of what has been done under this administration and gives a good preview of what will be done if an experienced President, knowing how to work with the Congress, knowing how to deal with these issues, can stay in office another 4 years. I'm glad you asked the question. It gave me a chance to answer it.

Thank you very much, everybody. God bless you.

NOTE: The President spoke at 10:03 a.m. in the Roy Start High School gymnasium.

Waterville Township, Ohio

Remarks to Area Residents.
October 25, 1980

Thank you, Governor John Glenn. [*Laughter*] Senator Glenn is one of the great leaders of our Nation, a hero who has put the brightest feature of our country before the eyes of the entire world, as you know, in the military and now in the Senate. It's indeed an honor for me to be introduced by him. He's a man who is familiar with Ohio problems and international problems as well. I'm also grateful that Senator Howard Metzenbaum is here, another great leader. You are indeed well represented in the United States Senate.

I was with Lud Ashley and Don Pease earlier, and I'm very grateful today to be with two people that at this moment are even more important to me and that's Don and Carolyn Schaller and their family.

Bob Bergland, a great Secretary of Agriculture, is also here, and after my speech he will be available to answer questions from the farm organizations and the farm

reporters, because what I've decided to do here on this beautiful farm is to make a more formal address, not only to this group assembled here but for the entire Nation, on one of the most important subjects that could possibly be discussed by any President and particularly during a campaign season, and that's on agriculture.

This is a story that hasn't been adequately told. And this speech will be recorded, and later it will be replayed in all the great agricultural States of the Nation. You might be interested in knowing, for instance, that the number one industry in New York State is agriculture, and, of course, I come from an agricultural State as well. I have to admit, looking out at this beautiful black soil, that we could use it as fertilizer on my farm—[*laughter*]—and make a better crop.

But today I want to make this speech verbatim so I will refer to my notes. And I wish you'd listen very carefully, because this message, that comes to you directly from me, will be going to literally millions of others in this Nation, both in the cities and on the farms, who believe that God has given us a great gift in our land over which we have a responsibility to exercise proper stewardship.

You have an important choice to make on November the 4th, not just between two candidates and two parties, but your choice could be between two different futures, for you and for your children and for your country. Nowhere is that choice more clear than in the future of our Nation's agriculture.

The farm programs of the last five decades, 50 years, came originally from Franklin D. Roosevelt in the New Deal. Democratic Presidents and Democrats in Congress have supported and have improved these programs. For 8 years before

I took office, Republican Presidents mismanaged the affairs of American farmers. They repeatedly vetoed needed price support legislation. Four times in 1973, 1974, and 1975, the two Republican Presidents embargoed farm exports, including those to some of our most important international trading partners, not to protect our Nation's strategic and security interests, but for the express purpose of driving American farm prices down. There was no real effort to develop new farm markets such as those in Mexico and in China.

The Republicans imposed price controls on food and cut off food aid to hungry nations while production costs on the farms soared. Poorly managed grain inspection as you well remember allowed substandard shipments of American grain overseas to tarnish the reputation of American farmers. Domestic markets were flooded with imported meat at the worst time for our farmers and our ranchers. Import quotas for dairy products went up five times in one year alone. By the time I took office, grain prices were in a tailspin.

Think back to 1976 and early 1977. Cattle producers were liquidating herds after 4 years of heavy losses. Farm income was dropping fast. Consumers and producers were in open confrontation. And our Nation's reputation as a reliable exporter of farm products had been severely damaged. In short, the farm policy that I inherited was an unholy mess.

I came into office with a lifetime of experience in farming. As a boy, I got up at 4 o'clock in the morning, as many of you did, to catch the mules and be in the field, waiting for it to be light enough so I would know how to plow the rows of cotton and corn and peanuts so that I would not plow up the crops as we tried to control the bermuda grass. And we got back to the house after sundown and then had

to feed and water the livestock without electricity on the farm to help. I grew up learning the hard way about the hard work and the complex economics of farming, and how valuable and how vulnerable farm families are to distant economic events over which we had very little control or influence in those days.

I learned the value of listening to other farmers. That's why I appointed Bob Bergland, a farmer, as my Secretary of Agriculture. That was a radical departure from the Republican policy of recruiting from the boardrooms of large agribusiness corporations, from large banks, and from commodity exchanges, the Secretaries of Agriculture who served under Republicans' administration. That may explain the Republican indifference to the ordinary farmer, but I changed that, and this is how. And I hope you'll listen carefully.

First, we set out to reduce government interference and to return production and marketing decisions to farmers. The cornerstone of this policy is a farmer-owned grain reserve, which has taken government out of the grain business. The grain reserve has become one of the most effective farm marketing tools ever devised. Just look at the results. In the last 4 years, we've had several record large crops; in wheat and corn there have been back-to-back record years. In 1979 we saw record yields unequaled in history in six major crops. Yet the bottom did not fall out of the market, thanks to the grain reserve. When prices began to weaken, enough farmers put their grain into the reserve on their own farms to cushion the market. They were able to hold off selling when prices dipped. And when prices rose, the farmers, not the middlemen, cashed in.

At the same time we began the reserve, we increased aid for building on-farm storage. Since 1976 farmers built

1.8 billion more bushels of on-the-farm grain storage capacity. And last month, I approved legislation to help build even more.

We did away with the out-dated and the rigid acreage allotment system, which you remember. Farmers were freed to make planting decisions based on market conditions, rather than on Federal bureaucratic conditions.

There were other accomplishments, too.

Beginning with the Food and Agriculture Act of 1977, which many of you helped to draft, I acted to bring price supports and loan rates in line with production costs. I sought price levels to keep pace with rapidly rising production costs and adjusted them higher again within the last 3 months. We adopted a formula for target prices based on the cost of production for each crop. When that formula failed to adjust rapidly enough, we corrected it with new legislation.

In contrast to Republican vetoes, I moved quickly to restore health to the dairy industry. Within weeks of taking office, I increased the support level. And then, we worked with Congress to enact an 80-percent-of-parity minimum. Last year we extended this authority.

I moved quickly to improve our inadequate promotion of agricultural exports. We lowered overseas barriers to our farm exports with the new trade treaty concluded last year. We opened trade offices, under Bob Bergland's leadership, in key importing countries. We greatly increased export credits and have worked hand in hand with the private sector through the cooperator program. Perhaps most important, we carefully laid the foundation for opening important new markets in foreign countries, like in China.

To protect and preserve our basic soil and water resources, I signed into law the landmark Soil and Water Resources Conservation Act. The Republicans attempted to weaken the agricultural conservation program. I strengthened it. I increased support for agricultural research by nearly 50 percent in just 3 years. I also moved quickly with special help to farmers who suffered from natural disasters like this summer's heat and drought. We expanded to $6 billion the economic emergency loan program we began in 1978, and I just signed into law a new crop insurance program to protect farmers against weather, crop disease, and insect losses.

My administration has also supported farmer cooperatives. We defended the Capper-Volstead Act against those who wanted to gut it. We kept the administration of this vital authority in the hands of the Secretary of Agriculture where it belongs. We supported export ventures by farm cooperatives and got rid of regulations that kept cooperatives from participating fully in commodity loan programs. We also expanded and modernized farm credit programs, including a special program for beginning farmers. Of all the funds loaned by the Farmers Home Administration in its 45 years, nearly half have been loaned by this administration.

My administration has been especially sensitive both to agriculture's unique energy needs and to the opportunity for farmers to become producers of energy. I assigned the highest priority allocation of all during energy shortages to agriculture.

We passed the windfall profits tax over Republican opposition, and I established a program to provide over $10 billion during this decade to produce gasohol from the crops of American farms. When I took office production of gasohol was barely measurable. I set a production capacity target of 500 million gallons of alcohol by the end of next year, enough so that gasohol will amount to 10 percent of all unleaded gasoline sold in America. Secretary Bergland has just approved guarantees for 15 new plants to produce 246 million gallons of alcohol. The result of all this speaks for itself.

In the 4 years of my administration, total gross farm income, total net farm income, total production, total consumption, and total farm exports topped any previous record of any period in the history of this Nation. Farm exports, in dollars and in volume, have set new records in every single year of my administration. We'll set another record with an $8 billion increase in exports this year for a total $40 billion, the biggest annual gain in history.

We have broadened and diversified our exports so that markets will be more sound in the future, with changing circumstances. We've more than tripled sales to Mexico. We've increased our feed grain exports to Japan and Italy. We are now selling almost 7 times as much to China and to Taiwan as we did in 1976. In fact, China is now the world's largest single buyer of American cotton and one of the largest buyers of American grain.

The sharp drop in farm prices that we inherited in 1977—and think back on those years—has reversed. Despite record production, which ordinarily would drive farm prices down, prices have risen steadily in the last 4 years. Corn has gone from $1.60 in 1977 to over $3. Wheat has gone from $2 to over $4. Cattle prices have doubled, from $32 to $64. Milk that sold for less than $10 in 1977 now sells for more than $13.

I'm not completely satisfied with the record I've outlined to you. The cost freeze and squeeze on farmers has been severe and has limited net farm income too long. But we've made good progress, working with you as partners, and more progress is still to come.

In contrast to this, my Republican opponent does not understand the complex reality of our farm economy. Just a few months ago he said that he was not familiar with parity. He said farm price supports, and I quote him, "subsidize the inefficient." He said, and I quote again, "Dairy subsidies are subsidizing those who could not compete." To be fair, my opponent recently dropped a lifetime of opposition to government farm programs. He now says he would keep the basic elements of my programs in effect. And why not? The farm programs of this administration work. American farmers will have to decide how confident they are of Governor Reagan's election year conversion.

For the next 4 years I will propose even more forward-looking farm programs. We'll use the experience of the last 4 years to draft the 1981 farm bill—as you know, it's up for repassage next year—that responds to various farm needs, but most of all to the family farm. As before, we'll work with farmers and with your own organizations in developing the new proposals as we did in 1977 which will shape your economic lives.

We're going to continue to reduce government regulation in our economy, including agriculture. We'll push ahead on fuel conservation, gasohol, solar innovations. We need to improve transportation systems for getting farm products to market, and to that end I've authorized an effort to create farmer-run transportation co-ops much like rural electric co-ops. We're going to help farmers export even more, improving the links between market development and assistance to developing nations, and increasing promotion of value added products like meat, poultry, breeding animals, and soy bean products. We'll continue to protect our farmland and the productivity of its soil. And we'll continue our efforts to expand research and education.

Before closing, I want to say a few words about the most controversial farm issue of this election year—the suspension of grain sales to the Soviet Union.

In 1976 I promised America's farmers that I would resort to an embargo only if our national security or foreign policy interests were threatened, and never just to keep prices down. I kept my word.

When the Soviets invaded Afghanistan earlier this year, last year in winter, I saw this for what it was: brutal aggression with ominous implications for the security of that region and, indeed, the world.

As your President, I took immediate action. I curtailed Russian fishing rights in our waters. I stopped the sale of many high-technology products that the Soviets needed. I stopped phosphate sales to the Soviet Union. And I suspended the shipment of grain beyond that included under our official Government agreement with the Soviets, 8 million bushels (tons)[1] per year.

When I announced this, shortly before the Iowa caucuses, as a matter of fact, I told the American farmers we all would bear the costs—not just the farmers. I don't have any doubt that the farmers have borne the heaviest load. I recognize that. But we used tax dollars to remove from the market more grain than was originally scheduled to be sold to the Soviets. The net budget cost was less than $600 (million).[2]

I imposed restraints on trade with the Soviet Union for one simple reason. Their invasion of Afghanistan was brutal aggression which threatened the interests of the United States and the free world. These restrictions have hurt the Soviets, and

---

[1] White House correction.
[2] White House correction.

they are going to continue to hurt as long as they are fighting and killing the people of Afghanistan.

The people of the Soviet Union are eating even less meat now than they did 5 years ago. They have less meat to eat in the Soviet Union than any other nation in all of Europe. Even their satellite countries are better off, and the Soviet situation is getting worse. This crop year they face a shortage of up to 60 million tons of grain, and they will not come close to making that up so long as the United States stands firm. And so long as Soviet aggression continues and the security threat exists, we will stand firm. We will continue to find more permanent and dependable customers for farm products to ensure that the American farmer does not suffer because of a lack of export opportunities.

My Republican opponent has tried to make political hay out of this decision. He claims to be opposed to the embargo. I think it's about time we look at the facts. The fact of the matter is that Governor Reagan publicly and directly opposed selling any grain whatsoever to the Soviet Union until he saw a chance to benefit politically from the decision that I had to make.

In 1975 he suggested using a grain embargo to force the Soviets out of Angola. In 1979 he threatened a similar grain embargo against Nigeria, the largest, most prosperous, and most influential country in Africa.

Three months before the invasion of Afghanistan, he said, and I quote, "If the Russians want to buy wheat from us, I would not sell it to them." The truth is that he never once raised his voice in opposition to the embargoes imposed under Mr. Nixon and Ford. And those embargoes were not imposed to protect our national interests. They were not directed against an aggressor nation. They were designed to do one thing and one thing only: to force down the prices American farmers get for your crops.

American farmers can decide now how much credit Mr. Reagan should get for reversing 5 years of public, unqualified support for food embargoes just in time for the election.

As I said at the beginning of this talk, the differences between me and my opponent, between the Democratic Party and the Republican Party are great. They are not just differences in degree. They are deep differences that will affect the life of everyone listening to my voice. They pose to you an important question: Do you want to place the critical questions facing American agriculture—energy, price supports, export development, soil conservation, cooperatives, science, education—in the hands of a man who has not shown a basic grasp of our farm economy? Or do you choose another like future, guided by the steady and experienced leadership of someone like you, a farmer, working with Bob Bergland, a farmer, and with farm organizations and you, the farmers of this Nation, who understand the problems and opportunities which are existing now before other American farmers who are not here today?

I want to strengthen our farm economy—for your sake, yes, but also for the sake of all the American people. I'm asking you for another 4 years as your President to continue to accomplish that worthy goal. I need your help on November 4.

Thank you very much. God bless you all.

NOTE: The President spoke at 11:58 a.m. in the Schaller residence.

Foreign Service Salary Schedule

Executive Order 12249.   October 25, 1980

By the authority vested in me as President of the United States of America under Section 403 of the Foreign Service Act of 1980 (Public Law 96–465 approved October 17, 1980), and in order to establish a new Foreign Service Schedule, it is hereby ordered as follows:

1–101. Salary classes for certain members of the Foreign Service are established as set forth in the Foreign Service Schedule attached hereto and made a part hereof.

1–102. Notwithstanding the provisions of Executive Order No. 12248, and pursuant to the provisions of Section 2101 of the Foreign Service Act of 1980, the salary rates set forth in the attached Foreign Service Schedule shall take effect on the first day of the first pay period which begins on or after October 1, 1980.

JIMMY CARTER

The White House,
    October 25, 1980.

[Filed with the Office of the Federal Register, 11:31 a.m., October 27, 1980]

NOTE: The schedule is printed in the FEDERAL REGISTER of October 28, 1980.

The text of the Executive order was released on October 27.

Trade With the Soviet Union

Letter to Senator Henry Jackson Concerning the Jackson-Vanik Amendment to the Trade Act of 1974.   October 25, 1980

Dear Senator Jackson:

You wrote to ask my views about section 402 of the Trade Act of 1974, the Jackson-Vanik amendment.

From the beginning of my Presidency I emphasized our commitment as a nation to human rights as a fundamental tenet on which our foreign policy would be based. That commitment of mine is as deep and as important to me today as it was then.

You have always been a pioneer in the area of human rights and your leadership and support have been instrumental in our success. I am sure that the record will show that American words and actions in the last period have left their mark on the rest of the world. Because of our leadership the defense of human rights has its rightful place on the world agenda for everyone to see.

The Jackson-Vanik amendment, which you authored, represents an important statement of our nation's commitment to the free emigration of Soviet Jewry. As you well know, I, along with you, have been specifically concerned about Jewish emigration from the Soviet Union. The year before I became President, Jewish emigration was about 14,000. Last year it was up to 50,000—the highest level in more than 10 years. The lower rate this year in the wake of the Soviet invasion of Afghanistan is of great concern. We will continue to register our strong concern about this low level of emigration at the Review Conference on Security and Cooperation which will meet in Madrid next month. The Soviet Union has an obligation to honor its Helsinki commitment.

After the Afghanistan invasion, I took a number of steps, including the suspension of grain sales and the restriction of high-technology exports to the Soviet Union, to make quite clear to the Soviets that we cannot conduct business-as-usual with them while their troops are occupying another country.

With the Soviet troops still in Afghanistan and with unacceptable denials of free emigration, it is totally inappropriate to consider any changes to section 402 of the Trade Act of 1974, and I have no intention of doing so. Furthermore, I can assure you that the U.S. delegation under the leadership of Ambassadors Griffin Bell and Max Kampelman at the CSCE Conference in Madrid will take every opportunity to make clear to the Soviet Union that their record of emigration is a violation of the Helsinki accords.

I value your views on this subject and I look forward to working closely with you on these very vital issues.

Sincerely,

JIMMY CARTER

NOTE: The text of the letter was released on October 27.

Wayne County, West Virginia

Remarks at a Rally With Area Residents.   October 27, 1980

THE PRESIDENT. Thank you very much, Governor Jay Rockefeller, who is destined, I believe, because of the deep appreciation of the West Virginia people for what he is and what he has been and what he will do, to be the next Governor of your great State. And I look forward to working with him during the next 4 years.

And I'm also grateful to Jennings Randolph, a man who sets a standard for public service that is an inspiration to us all. As Wendell Ford and Carl Perkins and Nick Joe Rahall and all of us who've served in Washington together know, most of the new ideas that come forward for us to address have already been understood and proposed by Jennings Randolph, because he has his heart close to the people of this Nation. And when there's a real need for better housing, better transportation, better use of coal, better life for the working families of this Nation, Jennings Randolph seems to have a special sensitivity to understand that need and to lead the rest of us in meeting those needs for all.

I'm grateful, too, to have a chance to come here to meet with people from Ohio, particularly Kentucky, because they are represented here by a great Governor and also by a great Senator. And Carl Perkins, a Congressman from across the river, is one of my greatest friends of all.

Let me say that I've spent the last few days thinking about the upcoming debate tomorrow night. As Wendell Ford pointed out, my opponent is not out campaigning among the people; he's trying to decide what role he's going to play in the debate tomorrow night. The problem that I've had in preparing myself for the debate is, which Ronald Reagan am I going to face tomorrow evening on television? Because as the election has progressed and as we get closer and closer to the voting time, he has flip-flopped on almost every conceivable issue depending upon what audience happens to be listening to him at the particular time.

He's been strongly against, even prayed against, aid for New York City, but lately he's been in New York, telling them how much he loves New York. He was against many things for which he now professes to support. Not too long ago, as a matter of fact this October, to the automobile workers in the Chrysler plant, he was telling them how proud he was that the Federal Government, with the help of the people on this stage, had helped Chrysler stay solvent. But that contrasts with the Ronald Reagan of last October, who said he didn't see anything wrong with Chrysler going bankrupt.

I don't know if I'll be debating the Ronald Reagan who now professes to be for safety and health of workers, or one who replied not long ago when somebody said that OSHA, the Occupational Safety and Health Administration, ought to be abolished, who stood there and said, "Amen." I don't know if I'll be debating a man of this election campaign who now professes to be for improving the social security system, or one who on at least four different occasions has suggested making social security voluntary, a proposal that would mean the end of a strong and viable social security system.

I don't know if I'm running against a man who opposed selling grain to the Soviet Union last year, or the one who declined this year to support the grain embargo after the Soviets had invaded Afghanistan. I don't know if I'm debating a Ronald Reagan who now professes to be for working families, but who's against labor law reform, who's against the Davis-Bacon Act, who said about the minimum wage that it's caused more misery and more unemployment than anything since the Great Depression, and who said just this year again that the primary cause of unemployment was the minimum wage.

I don't know if I'm debating against a man who now professes to be for working families who are temporarily unemployed, or one who said not too long ago that unemployment compensation was just a prepaid vacation for freeloaders. I don't know if I'm debating a man who lately professes to be almost in the image of Franklin Roosevelt, or one who a little earlier said that the foundation for the New Deal was fascism.

I may be having difficulty predicting what Governor Reagan will be saying in this debate, but we all know which Ronald Reagan would sit in the Oval Office if the Republicans win this election.

It'll be the same Ronald Reagan who said just a few weeks ago that he hasn't changed his position in the last 20 years, the Ronald Reagan who worked to kill Medicare, who opposes national health insurance, who rejects a decade of progress in nuclear arms control, who wants to scrap the synthetic fuels program, which will take coal from this region and convert it into synthetic fuel, that's the key to breaking the OPEC stranglehold which they formerly had on us.

There's one thing in this election that is certain, though, and I want you to listen very carefully to this, because you've got a good voting record in this area. Republicans always campaign like Democrats. You've heard them. They quote Franklin D. Roosevelt; they quote Harry Truman; they quote John Kennedy; they quote Lyndon Johnson. But think about this question: Have you ever heard a Republican candidate for President quoting a Republican President?

AUDIENCE. No!

THE PRESIDENT. No. Never, never. But when they get in the Oval Office, they're just like all the Republican Presidents that have caused hardship and trial and tribulation and forgotten the working families of this country, but they try to mislead you the last few days before the election. That's one thing you can count on. Republicans will govern like Republicans. Don't you forget it on election day.

I want to say just a word about coal. I'm proud to have been able in my administration, working with your Democratic Governors, United States Senators, the Members of Congress, to do more for the coal industry than ever before in the history of this country. Listen to this: We will produce more coal in 1980 than has ever before been produced in the United States of America. We will exceed 800 million tons for the first time, and the trend is in the right direction. This is the first year in our history in which more than 50 percent of all our Nation's electricity has been produced from coal.

Our exports of coal to foreign countries will set an alltime record this year. And we could load millions more tons of coal on ships to be sold overseas if we just had the transportation system and the port loading facilities available for this new demand for coal that's been brought about by the policies of our administration.

In the near future, as you know, you will have an exciting, new, bright life ahead of you as we begin to produce synthetic liquids and gaseous fuels from your coal. We can triple—*triple*—United States coal production in the next 15 years if we keep Democrats in office to help you. That's where we need your help.

As you know, over the past several weeks, since the Congress has finally passed our new energy policy into law, we've begun to move on our new synthetic fuels program. We've signed historic agreements to help finance and to guarantee the construction of synthetic facilities, including the SRC–1 program in Kentucky and the SRC–2 plant in West Virginia. These major plants will be the forerunner of others in this Nation and will show why 75 percent of the $88 billion in windfall profits tax will go to produce synthetic fuels out of coal.

The American people have to understand, though, and this is an important thing for you to remember, that coal is both a clean fuel and also a safe fuel. If we are ever to achieve our goal for energy security, do not let anyone try to convince you that the best way to produce and use more American coal is to lower air quality standards or water quality standards. To do that will turn the

American people and the world against coal.

What these men on the platform and I have done, working with Sam Church, the president of the United Mine Workers, is to try to make sure that all the projected increases that I've described to you, all of them, include maintaining the quality of our environment. We do not have to make people choose between jobs and prosperity on one hand and good health and a beautiful America on the other. We can burn coal, let it be the bright new vision of an independent policy in the future, and still keep our air clean and our water clean and our land productive. Do not let anyone mislead you about that, because the best way to turn people against coal is for them to think that we have to lower those standards for air and water quality.

Last week the Environmental Protection Agency extended a plan in Ohio which will allow greater use of coal. This plan sets limits on average emissions over a 30-day period, rather than a daily average. And this will continue on into 1982. This would allow much greater use of Ohio coal.

Also last week the EPA and Armco Steel Company reached agreement on an innovative approach to control air pollution of the Armco plant in Middletown, Ohio. Instead of controlling each individual source, it limits the total pollution emitted from an imaginary bubble over the entire plant. This allows the company to concentrate its cleanup efforts on sources that are the least costly to control. The result is more pollution control per dollar spent. This is the first practical application of this new principle. And now other steel companies throughout the Nation can do the same, reducing pollution control costs and thus raising capital or money to modernize their facilities and to put more people to work.

Just last Friday we announced a grant to finance a coke production plant in Canova, West Virginia. This would not only mean new jobs at the plant when it's finished, but 300 construction jobs and 1,500 miners will go to work now in West Virginia, in Virginia, and in Kentucky.

In order to meet export demand we are going to rebuild our railroads; we are going to improve our highways; we are going to improve our loading facilities at our major seaports. In international energy markets my goal is to replace OPEC oil with West Virginia, Ohio, and Kentucky coal.

And finally, let me say this: Coal is important for the security of our Nation. Many of you have spent your lives in the coal mines and in the communities surrounded by the mines. You've contributed a lot to the quality of life of other Americans. But it's important, too, to remember the well-being and the health and the safety of the miners and the miners' families, to protect the interests of the mineworkers. Working with President Sam Church and your representatives, we have broadened black lung protection, we've guaranteed mineworkers' pensions, and I've requested extensions of trade adjustment assistance and unemployment benefits so that workers do not have to bear all the hardships as our Nation faces up to rapidly changing economic circumstances and prepares for a brighter economic future.

If American workers have the tools and the training, they can out-produce any workers on Earth. And we're going to give them the tools and training. With a new energy policy as a foundation, we're ready to move into the future and rebuild opportunities for jobs and a brighter and more prosperous life for Americans. At the end of the Second World War, America rebuilt the industry of Germany; America rebuilt the industrial complex of Japan. And now it's time for us to rebuild the industrial complex of the United States of America, and that's what we're going to do. You help me, I'll help you; we'll have a better future in the years ahead if Democrats are in office.

Thank you very much. I'm counting on you. Work this last week.

NOTE: The President spoke at 1:24 p.m. at the Tri-State Airport.

Convention on the Elimination of All Forms of Discrimination Against Women

Announcement of President's Intention To Transmit the Convention to the Senate. October 28, 1980

The President has indicated his intention to send the Convention on the Elimination of All Forms of Discrimination Against Women to the Senate when it reconvenes on November 12, 1980. This treaty was adopted by the General Assembly of the United Nations on December 18, 1979, and signed by Sarah Weddington, Assistant to the President, on behalf of the United States, on July 17, 1980, at the World Conference on the U.N. Decade for Women in Copenhagen.

Adoption of the agreement was the culmination of several years of negotiations at the United Nations. The Convention defines discrimination against women as "any distinction, exclusion or restriction made on the basis of sex which has the effect or purpose of impairing or nullifying the recognition, enjoyment or exercise by women, irrespective of their marital status, on a basis of equality of men and women, of human rights and funda-

mental freedoms in the political, economic, social, cultural, civil or any other field."

The Convention requires parties to take all appropriate measures to eliminate discrimination against women in political and public life, law, education, employment, health care, commercial transactions, and domestic relations.

The Convention also establishes a committee of 23 nongovernmental experts who will review compliance with the Convention.

The President will recommend that U.S. ratification of the treaty be accompanied by a reservation preserving the prerogative of the State governments, since some of the subjects covered by the Convention are matters currently under State jurisdiction.

Other areas of concern with respect to conformity of U.S. law with the Convention will be addressed through implementing legislation or through reservations and understandings accompanying U.S. ratification of the Convention.

Cleveland, Ohio

Remarks at the 1980 Presidential Campaign Debate.   October 28, 1980

MRS. HINERFELD. Good evening.

I'm Ruth Hinerfeld of the League of Women Voters Education Fund. Next Tuesday is election day. Before going to the polls, voters want to understand the issues and know the candidates' positions. Tonight, voters will have an opportunity to see and hear the major party candidates for the Presidency state their views on issues that affect us all. The League of Women Voters is proud to present this Presidential debate.

Our moderator is Howard K. Smith.

MR. SMITH. Thank you, Mrs. Hinerfeld.

The League of Women Voters is pleased to welcome to the Cleveland, Ohio, Convention Center Music Hall President Jimmy Carter, the Democratic Party's candidate for reelection to the Presidency, and Governor Ronald Reagan of California, the Republican Party's candidate for the Presidency. The candidates will debate questions on domestic, economic, foreign policy, and national security issues.

The questions are going to be posed by a panel of distinguished journalists who are here with me. They are: Marvin Stone, the editor of U.S. News and World Report; Harry Ellis, national correspondent of the Christian Science Monitor; William Hilliard, assistant managing editor of the Portland Oregonian; Barbara Walters, correspondent, ABC News.

The ground rules for this, as agreed by you gentlemen, are these: Each panelist down here will ask a question, the same question, to each of the two candidates. After the two candidates have answered, a panelist will ask followup questions to try to sharpen the answers. The candidates will then have an opportunity each to make a rebuttal. That will constitute the first half of the debate, and I will state the rules for the second half later on.

Some other rules: The candidates are not permitted to bring prepared notes to the podium, but are permitted to make notes during the debate. If the candidates exceed the allotted time agreed on, I will reluctantly but certainly interrupt. We ask the Convention Center audience here to abide by one ground rule: Please do not applaud or express approval or disapproval during the debate.

Now, based on a toss of the coin, Governor Reagan will respond to the first question from Marvin Stone.

QUESTIONS

U.S. ARMED FORCES

MR. STONE. Governor, as you're well aware, the question of war and peace has emerged as a central issue in this campaign in the give-and-take of recent weeks. President Carter's been criticized for responding late to aggressive Soviet impulses, for insufficient buildup of our Armed Forces, and a paralysis in dealing with Afghanistan and Iran. You have been criticized for being all too quick to advocate the use of lots of muscle, military action, to deal with foreign crises. Specifically, what are the differences between the two of you on the uses of American military power?

GOVERNOR REAGAN. I don't know what the differences might be, because I don't know what Mr. Carter's policies are. I do know what he has said about mine. And I'm only here to tell you that I believe with all my heart that our first priority must be world peace, and that use of force is always and only a last resort, when everything else has failed, and then only with regard to our national security.

Now, I believe, also that this meeting, this mission, this responsibility for preserving the peace, which I believe is a responsibility peculiar to our country, that we cannot shirk our responsibility as the leader of the Free World, because we're the only one that can do it. And therefore, the burden of maintaining the peace falls on us. And to maintain that peace requires strength. America has never gotten in a war because we were too strong. We can get into a war by letting events get out of hand, as they have in the last 3½ years under the foreign policies of this administration of Mr. Carter's, until we're faced each time with a crisis. And good management in preserving the peace requires that we control the events and try to intercept before they become a crisis.

But I have seen four wars in my lifetime. I'm a father of sons; I have a grandson. I don't ever want to see another generation of young Americans bleed their lives into sandy beachheads in the Pacific, or rice paddies and jungles in Asia, or the muddy, bloody battlefields of Europe.

MR. SMITH. Mr. Stone, do you have a followup question for the Governor?

MR. STONE. Yes. Governor, we've been hearing that the defense buildup that you would associate yourself with would cost tens of billions of dollars more than is now contemplated. In assuming that the American people are ready to bear this cost, they nevertheless keep asking the following question: How do you reconcile huge increases in military outlays with your promise of substantial tax cuts and of balancing the budget, which in this fiscal year, the one that just ended, ran more than $60 billion in the red?

GOVERNOR REAGAN. Mr. Stone, I have submitted an economic plan that I've worked out in concert with a number of fine economists in this country, all of whom approve it, and believe that over a 5-year projection, this plan can permit the extra spending for needed refurbishing of our defensive posture, that it can provide for a balanced budget by 1983, if not earlier, and that we can afford—along with the cuts that I have proposed in Government spending—we can afford the tax cuts I have proposed—and probably, mainly because Mr. Carter's economic policy has built into the next 5 years, and on beyond that, a tax increase that will be taking $86 billion more next year out of the people's pockets than was taken this year. And my tax cut does not come close to eliminating that $86

billion increase. I'm only reducing the amount of the increase.

In other words, what I'm talking about is not putting Government back to getting less money than Government's been getting, but simply cutting the increase in spending.

MR. SMITH. The same question now goes to President Carter. President Carter, would you like to have the question repeated?

THE PRESIDENT. Yes.

MR. STONE. Yes, President Carter, the question of war and peace, a central issue in this campaign. You've been criticized in the give-and-take for responding late to aggressive Soviet impulses, for an insufficient buildup of our Armed Forces, and a paralysis in dealing with Afghanistan and Iran. Governor Reagan, on the other hand, has been criticized for being all too quick to advocate the use of lots of muscle, military action, to deal with foreign crises such as I mentioned. Specifically, what are the differences between the two of you on the uses of American military power?

THE PRESIDENT. Mr. Stone, I've had to make thousands of decisions since I've been President, serving in the Oval Office. And with each one of those decisions that affect the future of my country, I have learned in the process. I think I'm a much wiser and more experienced man than I was when I debated 4 years ago against President Ford. I've also learned that there are no simple answers to complicated questions. H. L. Mencken said that for every problem there's a simple answer. It would be neat and plausible—and wrong.

The fact is that this Nation, in the 8 years before I became President, had its own military strength decreased. Seven out of eight years, the budget commitments for defense went down, 37 percent, in all. Since I've been in office, we've had a steady, carefully planned, methodical but very effective increase in our commitment for defense.

But what we've done is to use that enormous power and prestige and military strength of the United States to preserve the peace. We've not only kept peace for our own country, but we've been able to extend the benefits of peace to others. In the Middle East, we've worked for a peace treaty between Israel and Egypt, successfully, and have tied ourselves together with Israel and Egypt in a common defense capability. This is a very good step forward for our Nation's security, and we'll continue to do as we've done in the past.

I might also add that there are decisions that are made in the Oval Office by every President which are profound in nature. There are always troublespots in the world, and how those troubled areas are addressed by a President, alone in that Oval Office, affects our Nation directly, the involvement of the United States and also our American interests. That is a basic decision that has to be made so frequently by every President who serves. That's what I've tried to do, successfully, by keeping our country at peace.

MR. SMITH. Mr. Stone, do you have a followup on——

MR. STONE. Yes. I would like to be a little more specific on the use of military power, and let's talk about one area for a moment.

Under what circumstances would you use military forces to deal with, for example, a shutoff of Persian Oil Gulf, if that should occur, or to counter Russian expansion beyond Afghanistan into either Iran or Pakistan? I ask this question in view of charges that we are woefully unprepared to project sustained—and I emphasize the word "sustained"—power in that part of the world.

THE PRESIDENT. Mr. Stone, in my State of the Union address earlier this year, I pointed out that any threat to the stability or security of the Persian Gulf would be a threat to the security of our own country. In the past, we've not had an adequate military presence in that region. Now we have two major carrier task forces. We have access to facilities in five different areas of that region. And we've made it clear that working with our allies and others, that we are prepared to address any foreseeable eventuality which might interrupt commerce with that crucial area of the world.

But in doing this, we have made sure that we address this question peacefully, not injecting American military forces into combat, but letting the strength of our Nation be felt in a beneficial way. This, I believe, has assured that our interests will be protected in the Persian Gulf region, as we've done in the Middle East and throughout the world.

MR. SMITH. Governor Reagan, you have a minute to comment or rebut.

GOVERNOR REAGAN. Well, yes, I question the figure about the decline in defense spending under the two previous administrations, in the preceding 8 years to this administration. I would call to your attention that we were in a war that wound down during those 8 years, which of course made a change in military spending because of turning from war to peace. I also would like to point out that Republican Presidents in those years, faced with a Democratic majority in both Houses of the Congress, found that their requests for defense budgets were very often cut.

Now, Gerald Ford left a 5-year projected plan for a military buildup to restore our defenses, and President Carter's administration reduced that by 38 percent, cut 60 ships out of the Navy building program that had been proposed, and stopped the B–1, delayed the cruise missile, stopped the production line for the Minuteman missiles, delayed the Trident submarine, and now is planning a mobile military force that can be delivered to various spots in the world—which does make me question his assaults on whether I am the one that is quick to look for use of force.

MR. SMITH. President Carter, you have the last word on this question.

THE PRESIDENT. Well, there are various elements of defense. One is to control nuclear weapons, which I hope we'll get to later on, because that's the most important single issue in this campaign. Another one is how to address troubled areas of the world. I think, habitually, Governor Reagan has advocated the injection of military forces into troubled areas, when I and my predecessors—both Democrats and Republicans—have advocated resolving those troubles and those difficult areas of the world peacefully, diplomatically, and through negotiation.

In addition to that, the buildup of military forces is good for our country, because we've got to have military strength in order to preserve the peace. But I'll always remember that the best weapons are the ones that are never fired in combat, and the best soldier is one who never has to lay his life down on the field of battle. Strength is imperative for peace, but the two must go hand in hand.

MR. SMITH. Thank you, gentlemen. The next question is from Harry Ellis to President Carter.

THE NATION'S ECONOMY

MR. ELLIS. Mr. President, when you were elected in 1976, the Consumer Price Index stood at 4.8 percent. It now stands at more than 12 percent. Perhaps more significantly, the Nation's broader, under-lying inflation rate has gone up from 7 to 9 percent. Now, a part of that was due to external factors beyond U.S. control, notably the more than doubling of oil prices by OPEC last year.

Because the United States remains vulnerable to such external shocks, can inflation in fact be controlled? If so, what measures would you pursue in a second term?

THE PRESIDENT. Again it's important to put the situation into perspective. In 1974 we had a so-called oil shock, wherein the price of OPEC oil was raised to an extraordinary degree. We had an even worse oil shock in 1979. In 1974 we had the worst recession, the deepest and most penetrating recession since the Second World War. The recession that resulted this time was the briefest we've had since the Second World War.

In addition, we've brought down inflation. Earlier this year, the first quarter, we did have a very severe inflation pressure, brought about by the OPEC price increase. It averaged about 18 percent the first quarter of this year. The second quarter, we had dropped it down to about 13 percent. The most recent figures, the last 3 months, or the third quarter of this year, the inflation rate is 7 percent—still too high, but it illustrates very vividly that in addition to providing an enormous number of jobs—9 million new jobs in the last 3½ years—that the inflationary threat is still urgent on us.

I noticed that Governor Reagan recently mentioned the Reagan-Kemp-Roth proposal, which his own running mate, George Bush, described as voodoo economics, and said that it would result in a 30-percent inflation rate. And Business Week, which is not a Democratic publication, said that this Reagan-Kemp-Roth proposal—and I quote them, I think—was completely irresponsible and would result in inflationary pressures which would destroy this Nation.

So, our proposals are very sound and very carefully considered to stimulate jobs, to improve the industrial complex of this country, to create tools for American workers, and at the same time would be anti-inflationary in nature. So, to add 9 million new jobs, to control inflation, and to plan for the future with the energy policy now intact as a foundation is our plan for the years ahead.

MR. SMITH. Mr. Ellis, do you have a followup question for Mr. Carter?

MR. ELLIS. Yes, Mr. President. You have mentioned the creation of 9 million new jobs.

THE PRESIDENT. Yes.

MR. ELLIS. At the same time, the unemployment rate still hangs high, as does the inflation rate. Now, I wonder, can you tell us what additional policies you would pursue in a second administration in order to try to bring down that inflation rate? And would it be an act of leadership to tell the American people they're going to have to sacrifice to adopt a leaner lifestyle for some time to come?

THE PRESIDENT. Yes. We have demanded that the American people sacrifice, and they've done very well. As a matter of fact, we're importing today about one-third less oil from overseas than we did just a year ago. We've had a 25-percent reduction since the first year I was in office. At the same time, as I said earlier, we have added about 9 million net new jobs in that period of time—a record never before achieved.

Also, the new energy policy has been predicated on two factors: One, conservation, which requires sacrifice, and the other one, increase in production of American energy, which is going along very well—more coal this year than ever before in history, more oil and gas wells drilled this year than ever before in history.

The new economic revitalization program that we have in mind, which will be implemented next year, would result in tax credits which would let business invest in new tools and new factories to create even more new jobs—about a million in the next 2 years. And we also have planned a youth employment program which would encompass 600,000 jobs for young people. This has already passed the House; now has an excellent prospect to pass the Senate.

MR. SMITH. Now, the same question goes to Governor Reagan. Governor Reagan, would you like to have the question repeated?

GOVERNOR REAGAN. Yes, please.

MR. ELLIS. Governor Reagan, during the past 4 years, the Consumer Price Index has risen from 4.8 percent to currently over 12 percent. And perhaps more significantly, the Nation's broader, underlying rate of inflation has gone up from 7 to 9 percent. Now, a part of that has been due to external factors beyond U.S. control, and notably, the more than doubling of OPEC oil prices last year, which leads me to ask you whether, since the United States remains vulnerable to such external shocks, can inflation in fact be controlled? If so, specifically what measures would you pursue?

GOVERNOR REAGAN. Mr. Ellis, I think this idea that has been spawned here in our country, that inflation somehow came upon us like a plague and therefore it's uncontrollable and no one can do anything about it, is entirely spurious, and it's dangerous to say this to the people. When Mr. Carter became President, inflation was 4.8 percent, as you said. It had been cut in two by President Gerald Ford. It is now running at 12.7 percent.

President Carter also has spoken of the new jobs created. Well, we always, with the normal growth in our country and increase in population, increase the number of jobs. But that can't hide the fact that there are 8 million men and women out of work in America today, and 2 million of those lost their jobs in just the last few months. Mr. Carter had also promised that he would not use unemployment as a tool to fight against inflation. And yet, his 1980 economic message stated that we would reduce productivity and gross national product and increase unemployment in order to get a handle on inflation, because in January, at the beginning of the year, it was more than 18 percent.

Since then, he has blamed to the people for inflation, OPEC, he's blamed the Federal Reserve System, he has blamed the lack of productivity of the American people, he has then accused the people of living too well and that we must share in scarcity, we must sacrifice and get used to doing with less. We don't have inflation because the people are living too well. We have inflation because the Government is living too well.

And the last statement, just a few days ago, was a speech to the effect that we have inflation because Government revenues have not kept pace with Government spending. I see my time is running out here. I'll have to get this down very fast.

Yes, you can lick inflation by increasing productivity and by decreasing the cost of Government to the place that we have balanced budgets and are no longer grinding out printing press money, flooding the market with it because the Government is spending more than it takes in. And my economic plan calls for that.

The President's economic plan calls for increasing the taxes to the point that we finally take so much money away from the people that we can balance the budget in

that way. But we'll have a very poor nation and a very unsound economy if we follow that path.

MR. SMITH. A followup, Mr. Ellis?

MR. ELLIS. Yes, you have centered on cutting Government spending in what you have just said about your own policies. You have also said that you would increase defense spending. Specifically, where would you cut Government spending if you were to increase defense spending and also cut taxes, so that, presumably, Federal revenues would shrink?

GOVERNOR REAGAN. Well, most people, when they think about cutting Government spending, they think in terms of eliminating necessary programs or wiping out something, some service that Government is supposed to perform. I believe that there is enough extravagance and fat in Government. As a matter of fact, one of the Secretaries of HEW under Mr. Carter testified that he thought there was $7 billion worth of fraud and waste in welfare and in the medical programs associated with it. We've had the General Accounting Office estimate that there is probably tens of billions of dollars that is lost in fraud alone, and they have added that waste adds even more to that.

We have a program for a gradual reduction of Government spending based on these theories, and I have a task force now that has been working on where those cuts could be made. I'm confident that it can be done and that it will reduce inflation, because I did it in California. And inflation went down below the national average in California when we returned money to the people and reduced government spending.

MR. SMITH. President Carter.

THE PRESIDENT. Governor Reagan's proposal, the Reagan-Kemp-Roth proposal, is one of the most highly inflationary ideas that ever has been presented to the American public. He would actually have to cut Government spending by at least $130 billion in order to balance the budget under this ridiculous proposal.

I noticed that his task force that's working for his future plans had some of their ideas revealed in the Wall Street Journal this week. One of those ideas was to repeal the minimum wage, and several times this year, Governor Reagan has said that the major cause of unemployment is the minimum wage. This is a heartless kind of approach to the working families of our country which is typical of many Republican leaders in the past, but I think has been accentuated under Governor Reagan.

In California—I'm surprised Governor Reagan brought this up—he had the three largest tax increases in the history of that State under his administration. He more than doubled State spending while he was Governor—122-percent increase—and had between a 20- and 30-percent increase in the number of employees——

Mr. Smith. Sorry to interrupt——

The President. ——in California.

Mr. Smith. ——Mr. Carter.

The President. Thank you, sir.

Mr. Smith. Governor Reagan has the last word on this question.

Governor Reagan. Yes. The figures that the President has just used about California is a distortion of the situation there, because while I was Governor of California, our spending in California increased less per capita than the spending in Georgia while Mr. Carter was Governor of Georgia in the same 4 years. The size of government increased only one-sixth in California of what it increased in proportion to population in Georgia.

And the idea that my tax-cut proposal is inflationary: I would like to ask the President, why is it inflationary to let the people keep more of their money and spend it the way they'd like, and it isn't inflationary to let him take that money and spend it the way he wants?

Mr. Smith. I wish that question need not be rhetorical, but it must be because we've run out of time on that. [*Laughter*] Now, the third question to Governor Reagan from William Hilliard.

URBAN POLICIES

Mr. Hilliard. Yes, Governor Reagan, the decline of our cities has been hastened by the continual rise in crime, strained race relations, the fall in the quality of public education, the persistence of abnormal poverty in a rich nation, and a decline in the services to the public. The signs seem to point toward a deterioration that could lead to the establishment of a permanent underclass in the cities. What, specifically, would you do in the next 4 years to reverse this trend?

Governor Reagan. I have been talking to a number of Congressmen who have much the same idea that I have, and that is that in the inner-city areas, that in cooperation with local government and with National Government, and using tax incentives and with cooperation with the private sector, that we have development zones. Let the local entity, the city, declare this particular area, based on the standards of the percentage of people on welfare, unemployed, and so forth, in that area. And then, through tax incentives, induce the creation of businesses providing jobs and so forth in those areas.

The elements of government through these tax incentives—for example, a business that would not have, for a period of time, an increase in the property tax reflecting its development of the unused property that it was making wouldn't be any loss to the city, because the city isn't getting any tax from that now. And there would simply be a delay, and on the other hand, many of the people that would then be given jobs are presently wards of the Government, and it wouldn't hurt to give them a tax incentive, because that wouldn't be costing Government anything either.

I think there are things to do in this regard. I stood in the South Bronx on the exact spot that President Carter stood on in 1977. You have to see it to believe it. It looks like a bombed-out city—great, gaunt skeletons of buildings, windows smashed out, painted on one of them "Unkept promises," on another, "Despair." And this was the spot at which President Carter had promised that he was going to bring in a vast program to rebuild this area. There are whole blocks of land that are left bare, just bulldozed down flat, and nothing has been done. And they are now charging to take tourists through there to see this terrible desolation.

I talked to a man just briefly there who asked me one simple question: "Do I have reason to hope that I can someday take care of my family again? Nothing has been done."

MR. SMITH. Followup, Mr. Hilliard?

MR. HILLIARD. Yes, Governor Reagan. Blacks and other nonwhites are increasing in numbers in our cities. Many of them feel that they are facing a hostility from whites that prevents them from joining the economic mainstream of our society. There is racial confrontation in the schools, on jobs, and in housing, as nonwhites seek to reap the benefits of a free society. What do you think is the Nation's future as a multiracial society?

GOVERNOR REAGAN. I believe in it. I am eternally optimistic, and I happen to believe that we've made great progress from the days when I was young and when this country didn't even know it had a racial problem. I know those things can grow

out of despair in an inner city, when there's hopelessness at home, lack of work, and so forth. But I believe that all of us together—and I believe the Presidency is what Teddy Roosevelt said it was; it's a bully pulpit—and I think that something can be done from there, because the goal for all of us should be that one day, things will be done neither because of nor in spite of any of the differences between us— ethnic differences or racial differences, whatever they may be—that we will have total equal opportunity for all people. And I would do everything I could in my power to bring that about.

MR. SMITH. Mr. Hilliard, would you repeat your question for President Carter?

MR. HILLIARD. President Carter, the decline of our cities has been hastened by the continual rise in crime, strained race relations, the fall in the quality of public education, the persistence of abnormal poverty in a rich nation, and a decline in services to the public. The signs seem to point toward a deterioration that could lead to the establishment of a permanent underclass in the cities. What, specifically, would you do in the next 4 years to reverse this trend?

THE PRESIDENT. Thank you, Mr. Hilliard.

When I was campaigning in 1976, everywhere I went the mayors and local officials were in despair about the rapidly deteriorating central cities of our Nation. We initiated a very fine urban renewal program, working with the mayors, the Governors, and other interested officials. This has been a very successful effort. That's one of the main reasons that we've had such an increase in the number of people employed. Of the 9 million people put to work in new jobs since I've been in office, 1.3 million of those has been among black Americans and another million among those who speak Spanish.

We now are planning to continue the revitalization program with increased commitments of rapid transit, mass transit. Under the windfall profits tax, we expect to spend about $43 billion in the next 10 years to rebuild the transportation systems of our country. We also are pursuing housing programs. We've had a 73-percent increase in the allotment of Federal funds for improved education. These are the kinds of efforts worked on a joint basis with community leaders, particularly in the minority areas of the central cities that had been deteriorating so rapidly in the past.

It's very important to us that this be done with the full involvement of minority citizens. I've brought into the top levels of Government—into the White House, into administrative offices of the executive branch, into the judicial system—highly qualified black and Spanish citizens and women who in the past had been excluded.

I noticed that Governor Reagan said that when he was a younger man that there was no knowledge of a racial problem in this country. Those who suffered from discrimination because of race or sex certainly knew we had a racial problem. We have gone a long way toward correcting these problems, but we still have a long way to go.

MR. SMITH. A followup question?

MR. HILLIARD. Yes, President Carter, I'd like to repeat the same followup to you. Blacks and other nonwhites are increasing in numbers in our cities. Many of them feel that they are facing a hostility from whites that prevents them from joining the economic mainstream of our society. There is racial confrontation in the schools, on jobs, and in housing, as nonwhites seek to reap the benefits of a free society. What is your assessment of the Nation's future in a multiracial society?

THE PRESIDENT. Ours is a nation of refugees, a nation of immigrants. Almost all of our citizens came here from other lands and now have hopes, which are being realized, for a better life, preserving their ethnic commitments, their family structures, their religious beliefs, preserving their relationships with their relatives in foreign countries, but still forming themselves together in a very coherent society, which gives our Nation its strength.

In the past, those minority groups have often been excluded from participation in the affairs of government. Since I've been President, I've appointed, for instance, more than twice as many black Federal judges as all previous Presidents in the history of this country. I've done the same thing in the appointment of women, and also Spanish-speaking Americans. To involve them in administration of government and a feeling that they belong to the societal structure that makes decisions in the judiciary and in executive branch is a very important commitment which I am trying to realize and will continue to do so in the future.

MR. SMITH. Governor Reagan, you have a minute for rebuttal.

GOVERNOR REAGAN. Yes. The President talks of Government programs, and they have their place. But as Governor, when I was at that end of the line and receiving some of these grants for Government programs, I saw that so many of them were dead-end. They were public employment for these people who really want to get out into the private job market, where there are jobs with a future.

Now, the President spoke a moment ago about—that I was against the minimum wage. I wish he could have been with me when I sat with a group of teenagers who were black and who were telling me about their unemployment problems, and that it was the minimum wage that had done away with the jobs that they once could get. And indeed, every time it has increased you will find there is an increase in minority unemployment among young people. And therefore, I have been in favor of a separate minimum for them.

With regard to the great progress that has been made with this Government spending, the rate of black unemployment in Detroit, Michigan, is 56 percent.

MR. SMITH. President Carter, you have the last word on this question.

THE PRESIDENT. Well, it's obvious that we still have a long way to go in fully incorporating the minority groups into the mainstream of American life. We have made good progress, and there's no doubt in my mind that the commitment to unemployment compensation, the minimum wage, welfare, national health insurance, those kinds of commitments that have typified the Democratic Party since ancient history in this country's political life are a very important element of the future. In all those elements, Governor Reagan has repeatedly spoken out against them, which, to me, shows a very great insensitivity to giving deprived families a better chance in life. This, to me, is a very important difference between him and me in this election, and I believe the American people will judge accordingly.

There is no doubt in my mind that in the downtown, central cities, with the new commitment on an energy policy, with a chance to revitalize homes and to make them more fuel-efficient, with a chance for a synthetic fuels program, solar power, this will give us an additional opportunity for jobs which will pay rich dividends.

MR. SMITH. Thank you, gentlemen.

Now for the fourth question, to President Carter from Barbara Walters.

INTERNATIONAL TERRORISM

Ms. WALTERS. Mr. President, the eyes of the country tonight are on the hostages in Iran. I realize this is a sensitive area, but the question of how we respond to acts of terrorism goes beyond this current crisis. Other countries have policies that determine how they will respond. Israel, for example, considers hostages like soldiers and will not negotiate with terrorists.

For the future, Mr. President, the country has the right to know, do you have a policy for dealing with terrorism wherever it might happen, and what have we learned from this experience in Iran that might cause us to do things differently if this or something similar happens again?

THE PRESIDENT. Barbara, one of the blights on this world is the threat and the activities of terrorists. At one of the recent economic summit conferences between myself and the other leaders of the Western world, we committed ourselves to take strong action against terrorism. Airplane hijacking was one of the elements of that commitment. There is no doubt that we have seen in recent years, in recent months, additional acts of violence against Jews in France and, of course, against those who live in Israel by the PLO and other terrorist organizations.

Ultimately, the most serious terrorist threat is if one of those radical nations, who believe in terrorism as a policy, should have atomic weapons. Both I and all my predecessors have had a deep commitment to controlling the proliferation of nuclear weapons in countries like Libya or Iraq. We have even alienated some of our closest trade partners, because we have insisted upon the control of the spread of nuclear weapons to those potentially terrorist countries.

When Governor Reagan has been asked about that, he makes a very disturbing comment that nonproliferation, or the control of the spread of nuclear weapons, is none of our business. And when he was asked specifically, recently, about Iraq, he said there's nothing we can do about it.

This ultimate terrorist threat is the most fearsome of all, and it's part of a pattern where our country must stand firm to control terrorism of all kinds.

MR. SMITH. Ms. Walters, a followup?

MS. WALTERS. Yes. While we are discussing policy, had Iran not taken American hostages, I assume that, in order to preserve our neutrality, we would have stopped the flow of spare parts and vital war materiels once war broke out between Iraq and Iran. Now, we're offering to lift the ban on such goods if they let our people come home. Doesn't this reward terrorism, compromise our neutrality, and possibly antagonize nations now friendly to us in the Middle East?

THE PRESIDENT. We will maintain our position of neutrality in the Iran and Iraq war. We have no plans to sell additional materiel or goods to Iran that might be of a warlike nature. When I made my decision to stop all trade with Iran as a result of the taking of our hostages, I announced then and have consistently maintained since then that if the hostages are released safely, that we would make delivery on those items which Iran owns, which they have bought and paid for—also, that the frozen Iranian assets would be released. That's been a consistent policy, one I intend to carry out.

MR. SMITH. Would you repeat the question now for Governor Reagan, please, Ms. Walters?

MS. WALTERS. Yes. Governor, the eyes of the country tonight remain on the hostages in Iran, but the question of how we respond to acts of terrorism goes beyond this current crisis. There are other countries that have policies that determine how they will respond. Israel, for example, considers hostages like soldiers and will not negotiate with terrorists.

For the future, the country has the right to know, do you have a policy for dealing with terrorism wherever it might happen, and what have we learned from this experience in Iran that might cause us to do things differently if this, or something similar, should happen again?

GOVERNOR REAGAN. Well, Barbara, you've asked that question twice. I think you ought to have at least one answer to it. [*Laughter*]

I have been accused lately of having a secret plan with regard to the hostages. Now, this comes from an answer that I've made at least 50 times during this campaign to the press. The question would be, "Have you any ideas of what you would do if you were there?" And I said, well, yes. And I think that anyone that's seeking this position, as well as other people, probably, have thought to themselves, "What about this, what about that?" These are just ideas of what I would think of if I were in that position and had access to the information, in which I would know all the options that were open to me. I have never answered the question, however. Second—the one that says, "Well, tell me, what are some of those ideas?" First of all, I would be fearful that I might say something that was presently under way or in negotiations, and thus expose it and endanger the hostages. And sometimes, I think some of my ideas might involve quiet diplomacy, where you don't say in advance or say to anyone what it is you're thinking of doing.

Your question is difficult to answer, because, in the situation right now, no one wants to say anything that would inadvertently delay, in any way, the return of those hostages if there is a chance of their coming home soon, or that might cause them harm.

What I do think should be done, once they are safely here with their families and that tragedy is over—and we've endured this humiliation for just lacking 1 week of a year now—then, I think, it is time for us to have a complete investigation as to the diplomatic efforts that were made in the beginning, why they have been there so long, and when they come home, what did we have to do in order to bring that about, what arrangements were made? And I would suggest that Congress should hold such an investigation.

In the meantime, I'm going to continue praying that they'll come home.

MR. SMITH. Followup question.

MS. WALTERS. Well, I would like to say that neither candidate answered specifically the question of a specific policy for dealing with terrorism, but I will ask Governor Reagan a different followup question. You have suggested that there would be no Iranian crisis had you been President, because we would have given firmer support to the Shah. But Iran is a country of 37 million people who were resisting a government they regarded as dictatorial.

My question is not whether the Shah's regime was preferable to the Ayatollah's, but whether the United States has the power or the right to try to determine what form of government any country will have, and do we back unpopular regimes whose major merit is that they are friendly to the United States?

GOVERNOR REAGAN. The degree of unpopularity of a regime when the choice is total authoritarianism—totalitarianism, I should say, in the alternative government, makes one wonder whether you are being helpful to the people. And we've been guilty of that. Because someone didn't meet exactly our standards of human rights, even though they were an ally of ours, instead of trying patiently to persuade them to change their ways, we have, in a number of instances, aided a revolutionary overthrow which results in complete totalitarianism, instead, for those people. And I think that this is a kind of a hypocritical policy when, at the same time, we're maintaining a détente with the one nation in the world where there are no human rights at all—the Soviet Union.

Now, there was a second phase in the Iranian affair in which we had something to do with that. And that was, we had adequate warning that there was a threat to our Embassy, and we could have done what other Embassies did—either strengthen our security there or remove our personnel before the kidnap and the takeover took place.

MR. SMITH. Governor, I'm sorry, I must interrupt. President Carter, you have a minute for rebuttal.

THE PRESIDENT. I didn't hear any comment from Governor Reagan about what he would do to stop or to reduce terrorism in the future. What the Western allies did decide to do is to stop all air flights—commercial air flights—to any nation involved in terrorism or the hijacking of airplanes, or the harboring of hijackers. Secondly, we all committed ourselves, as have all my predecessors in the Oval Office, not to permit the spread of nuclear weapons to a terrorist nation or to any other nation that does not presently have those weapons or capabilities for explosives. Third, not to make any sales of materiel or weapons to a nation which is involved in terrorist activities. And, lastly, not to deal with the PLO until and unless the PLO recognizes Israel's right to exist and recognizes U.N. Resolution 242 as a basis for a Middle East peace.

These are a few of the things to which our Nation is committed, and we will continue with these commitments.

MR. SMITH. Governor Reagan, you have the last word on that question.

GOVERNOR REAGAN. Yes. I have no quarrel whatsoever with the things that have been done, because I believe it is high time that the civilized countries of the world made it plain that there is no room worldwide for terrorism; there will be no negotiation with terrorists of any kind. And while I have a last word here, I would like to correct a misstatement of fact by the President. I have never made the statement that he suggested about nuclear proliferation, and nuclear proliferation, or the trying to halt it, would be a major part of a foreign policy of mine.

MR. SMITH. Thank you, gentlemen. That is the first half of the debate.

Now, the rules for the second half, quite simple. They're only complicated when I explain them. [*Laughter*] In the second half, the panelists with me will have no followup questions. Instead, after the panelists have asked a question the candidates have answered, each of the candidates will have two opportunities to follow up, to question, to rebut, or just to comment on his opponent's statement.

Governor Reagan will respond, in this section, to the first question from Marvin Stone.

STRATEGIC ARMS LIMITATION

MR. STONE. Governor Reagan, arms control: The President said it was the single most important issue. Both of you have expressed the desire to end the nuclear arms race with Russia, but by methods that are vastly different. You suggest that we scrap the SALT II treaty, already negotiated, and intensify the buildup of American power to induce the Soviets to sign a new treaty, one more favorable to us.

GOVERNOR REAGAN. Yes.

MR. STONE. President Carter, on the other hand, says he will again try to convince a reluctant Congress to ratify the present treaty on the grounds it's the best we can hope to get.

Now, both of you cannot be right. Will you tell us why you think you are?

GOVERNOR REAGAN. Yes. I think I'm right, because I believe that we must have a consistent foreign policy, a strong America, and a strong economy. And then, as we build up our national security, to restore our margin of safety, we at the same time try to restrain the Soviet buildup, which has been going forward at a rapid pace and for quite some time.

The SALT II treaty was the result of negotiations that Mr. Carter's team entered into after he had asked the Soviet Union for a discussion of actual reduction of nuclear strategic weapons, and his emissary, I think, came home in 12 hours having heard a very definite *nyet*. But taking that one no from the Soviet Union, we then went back into negotiations on their terms, because Mr. Carter had canceled the B–1 bomber, delayed the MX, delayed the Trident submarine, delayed the cruise missile, shut down the Minuteman missile production line, and whatever other things that might have been done. The Soviet Union sat at the table knowing that we had gone forward with unilateral concessions without any reciprocation from them whatsoever.

Now, I have not blocked the SALT II treaty, as Mr. Carter and Mr. Mondale suggest that I have. It has been blocked by a Senate in which there is a Democratic majority. Indeed, the Senate Armed Services Committee voted 10 to 0, with 7 abstentions, against the SALT II treaty, and declared that it was not in the national security interests of the United States—besides which, it is illegal, because the law of the land, passed by Congress, says we cannot accept a treaty in which we are not equal. And we're not equal in this treaty for one reason alone: Our B–52 bombers are considered to be strategic weapons; their Backfire bombers are not.

MR. SMITH. Governor, I have to interrupt you at that point. The time is up for that. But the same question now to President Carter.

MR. STONE. Yes, President Carter. Both of you have expressed the desire to end the nuclear arms race with Russia, but through vastly different methods. The Governor suggests we scrap the SALT II treaty, which you signed in Vienna—intensify the buildup of American power to induce the Soviets to sign a new treaty, one more favorable to us. You, on the other hand, say you will again try to convince a reluctant Congress to ratify the present treaty on the grounds it is the best we can hope to get from the Russians.

You cannot both be right. Will you tell us why you think you are?

THE PRESIDENT. Yes, I'd be glad to.

Inflation, unemployment, the cities—all very important issues, but they pale into insignificance in the life and duties of a President when compared with the control of nuclear weapons. Every President who has served in the Oval Office since Harry Truman has been dedicated to the proposition of controlling nuclear weapons, to negotiate with the Soviet Union—balanced, controlled, observable, and then reducing levels of atomic weaponry.

There is a disturbing pattern in the attitude of Governor Reagan. He has never supported any of those arms control agreements—the limited test ban, SALT I, nor the antiballistic missile treaty, nor the Vladivostok Treaty negotiated with the Soviet Union by President Ford—and now he wants to throw into the wastebasket a treaty to control nuclear weapons on a balanced and equal basis between ourselves and the Soviet Union, negotiated over a 7-year period, by myself and my two Republican predecessors.

The Senate has not voted yet on the strategic arms limitation treaty. There have been preliminary skirmishings in the committees of the Senate, but the treaty has never come to the floor of the Senate for either a debate or a vote. It's understandable that a Senator in the preliminary debates can make an irresponsible statement, or, maybe, an ill-advised statement. You've got 99 other Senators to correct that mistake, if it is a mistake. But when a man who hopes to be President says, "Take this treaty, discard it, do not vote, do not debate, do not explore the issues, do not finally capitalize on this long negotiation"—that is a very dangerous and disturbing thing.

MR. SMITH. Governor Reagan, you have an opportunity to rebut that.

GOVERNOR REAGAN. Yes, I'd like to respond very much.

First of all, the Soviet Union—if I have been critical of some of the previous agreements, it's because we've been outnegotiated for quite a long time. And they have managed, in spite of all of our attempts at arms limitation, to go forward with the biggest military buildup in the history of man.

Now, to suggest that because two Republican Presidents tried to pass the SALT treaty—that puts them on its side—I would like to say that President Ford, who was within 90 percent of a treaty that we could be in agreement with when he left office, is emphatically against this SALT treaty. I would like to point out also that Senators like Henry Jackson and Hollings of South Carolina—they are taking the lead in the fight against this particular treaty.

I am not talking of scrapping; I am talking of taking the treaty back and going back into negotiations. And I would say to the Soviet Union, we will sit and negotiate with you as long as it takes, to have not only legitimate arms limitation but to have a reduction of these nuclear weapons to the point that neither one of us represents a threat to the other. That is hardly throwing away a treaty and being opposed to arms limitation.

MR. SMITH. President Carter?

THE PRESIDENT. Yes. Governor Reagan is making some very misleading and disturbing statements. He not only advocates the scrapping of this treaty—and I don't know that these men that he quotes are against the treaty in its final form—but he also advocates the possibility—he said it's been a missing element—of playing a trump card against the Soviet Union of a nuclear arms race and insisting upon nuclear superiority by our own Nation as a predication for negotiation in the future with the Soviet Union.

If President Brezhnev said, "We will scrap this treaty, negotiated under three American presidents over a 7-year period of time; we insist upon nuclear superiority as a basis for future negotiations; and we believe that the launching of a nuclear arms race is a good basis for future negotiations," it's obvious that I, as President, and all Americans would reject such a proposition. This would mean the resumption of a very dangerous nuclear arms race.

It would be very disturbing to American people. It would change the basic tone and commitment that our Nation

has experienced ever since the Second World War, with all Presidents, Democratic and Republican, and would also be very disturbing to our allies, all of whom support this nuclear arms treaty. In addition to that, the adversarial relationship between ourselves and the Soviet Union would undoubtedly deteriorate very rapidly.

This attitude is extremely dangerous and belligerent in its tone, although it's said with a quiet voice.

MR. SMITH. Governor Reagan?

GOVERNOR REAGAN. I know the President's supposed to be replying to me, but sometimes, I have a hard time in connecting what he's saying with what I have said or what my positions are. I sometimes think he's like the witch doctor that gets mad when a good doctor comes along with a cure that'll work.

My point I have made already, Mr. President, with regard to negotiating. It does not call for nuclear superiority on the part of the United States; it calls for a mutual reduction of these weapons, as I say, that neither of us can represent a threat to the other. And to suggest that the SALT II treaty that your negotiators negotiated was just a continuation, and based on all of the preceding efforts by two previous Presidents, is just not true. It was a new negotiation, because, as I say, President Ford was within about 10 percent of having a solution that could be acceptable. And I think our allies would be very happy to go along with a fair and verifiable SALT agreement.

MR. SMITH. President Carter, you have the last word on this question.

THE PRESIDENT. I think, to close out this discussion, it would be better to put into perspective what we're talking about.

I had a discussion with my daughter, Amy, the other day, before I came here, to ask her what the most important issue was. She said she thought nuclear weaponry and the control of nuclear arms.

This is a formidable force. Some of these weapons have 10 megatons of explosion. If you put 50 tons of TNT in each one of railroad cars, you would have a trainload of TNT stretching across this Nation. That's one major war explosion in a warhead. We have thousands, equivalent of megaton, or million tons, of TNT warheads. The control of these weapons is the single major responsibility of a President, and to cast out this commitment of all Presidents, because of some slight technicalities that can be corrected, is a very dangerous approach.

MR. SMITH. We have to go to another question now, from Harry Ellis to President Carter.

ENERGY

MR. ELLIS. Mr. President, as you have said, Americans, through conservation, are importing much less oil today than we were even a year ago. Yet U.S. dependence on Arab oil as a percentage of total imports is today much higher than it was at the time of the 1973 Arab oil embargo. And for some time to come, the loss of substantial amounts of Arab oil could plunge the U.S. into depression. Now, this means that a bridge must be built out of this dependence.

Can the United States develop synthetic fuels and other alternative energy sources without damage to the environment, and will this process mean steadily higher fuel bills for American families?

THE PRESIDENT. I don't think there's any doubt that, in the future, the cost of oil is going to go up. What I've had as a basic commitment since I've been President is to reduce our dependence on foreign oil. It can only be done in two ways: one, to conserve energy, to stop the waste of energy, and secondly, to produce more American energy.

We've been very successful in both cases. We've now reduced the importing of foreign oil in the last year alone by one-third. We imported today 2 million barrels of oil less than we did the same day just a year ago.

This commitment has been opening up a very bright vista for our Nation in the future, because with the windfall profits tax as a base, we now have an opportunity to use American technology and American ability and American natural resources to expand rapidly the production of synthetic fuels, yes; to expand rapidly the production of solar energy, yes; and also to produce the conventional kinds of American energy. We will drill more oil and gas wells this year than any year in history. We'll produce more coal this year than any year in history. We're exporting more coal this year than any year in history. And we have an opportunity now, with improved transportation systems and improved loading facilities in our ports, to see a very good opportunity on the world international market, to replace OPEC oil with American coal as a basic energy source.

This exciting future will not only give us more energy security but will also open up vast opportunities for Americans to live a better life and to have millions of new jobs associated with this new and very dynamic industry now in prospect because of the new energy policy that we've put into effect.

MR. SMITH. Would you repeat the question now for Governor Reagan?

MR. ELLIS. Governor Reagan, Americans, through conservation, are importing much less oil today than we were even a year ago. And yet, U.S. reliance on Arab oil as a percentage of total imports is much higher today than it was during the 1973 Arab oil embargo. And the substantial loss of Arab oil could plunge the United States into depression.

The question is whether the development of alternative energy sources, in order to reduce this dependence, can be done without damaging the environment, and will it mean for American families steadily higher fuel bills?

GOVERNOR REAGAN. I'm not sure that it means steadily higher fuel costs, but I do believe that this Nation has been portrayed for too long a time to the people as being energy-poor when it is energy-rich. The coal that the President mentioned: Yes, we have it, and yet one-eighth of our total coal resources is not being utilized at all right now. The mines are closed down; there are 22,000 miners out of work. Most of this is due to regulations which either interfere with the mining of it or prevent the burning of it. With our modern technology, yes, we can burn our coal within the limits of the Clean Air Act. I think, as technology improves, we'll be able to do even better with that.

The other thing is that we have only leased out and begun to explore 2 percent of our Outer Continental Shelf for oil, where it is believed by everyone familiar with that fuel and that source of energy that there are vast supplies yet to be found. Our Government has, in the last year or so, taken out of multiple use millions of acres of public lands that once were—well, they were public lands subject to multiple-use exploration for minerals and so forth. It is believed that probably 70 percent of the potential oil in the United States is probably hidden in those lands, and no one is allowed to even go and explore to find out if it is there. This is particularly true of the recent efforts to shut down part of Alaska.

Nuclear power: There were 36 powerplants planned in this country—and let me add the word "safety"; it must be done with the utmost of safety. But 32 of those have given up and canceled their plans to build, and again, because Government

regulations and permits and so forth make it take more than twice as long to build a nuclear plant in the United States as it does to build one in Japan or in Western Europe.

We have the sources here. We are energy-rich, and coal is one of the great potentials we have.

MR. SMITH. President Carter, your comment?

THE PRESIDENT. Yes, sir. To repeat myself, we have this year the opportunity, which we'll realize, to produce 800 million tons of coal—an unequaled record in the history of our country. Governor Reagan says that this is not a good achievement, and he blames restraints on coal production on regulations—regulations that affect the life and the health and safety of miners and also regulations that protect the purity of our air and the quality of our water and our land. We cannot cast aside those regulations. We have a chance in the next 15 years, insisting upon the health and safety of workers in the mines, and also preserving the same high air and water pollution standards, to triple the amount of coal we produce.

Governor Reagan's approach to our energy policy, which has already proven its effectiveness, is to repeal or to change substantially the windfall profits tax, to return a major portion of $227 billion back to the oil companies, to do away with the Department of Energy, to short-circuit our synthetic fuels program, to put a minimal emphasis on solar power, to emphasize strongly nuclear powerplants as a major source of energy in the future. He wants to put all our eggs in one basket and give that basket to the major oil companies.

MR. SMITH. Governor Reagan.

GOVERNOR REAGAN. That is a misstatement, of course, of my position. I just happen to believe that free enterprise can do a better job of producing the things that people need than Government can. The Department of Energy has a multi-billion-dollar budget, in excess of $10 billion. It hasn't produced a quart of oil or a lump of coal or anything else in the line of energy.

And for Mr. Carter to suggest that I want to do away with the safety laws and with the laws that pertain to clean water and clean air, and so forth—as Governor of California, I took charge of passing the strictest air pollution laws in the United States—the strictest air quality law that has ever been adopted in the United States. And we created an OSHA, an occupational safety and health agency, for the protection of employees before the Federal Government had one in place. And to this day, not one of its decisions or rulings has ever been challenged.

So, I think some of those charges are missing the point. I am suggesting that there are literally thousands of *unnecessary* regulations that invade every facet of business, and indeed, very much of our personal lives, that are unnecessary; that Government can do without; that have added $130 billion to the cost of production in this country; and that are contributing their part to inflation. And I would like to see us a little more free, as we once were.

Mr. SMITH. President Carter, another crack at that?

THE PRESIDENT. Sure. As a matter of fact, the air pollution standard laws that were passed in California were passed over the objections of Governor Reagan, and this is a very well known fact. Also, recently, when someone suggested that the Occupational Safety and Health Act should be abolished, Governor Reagan responded, "Amen."

The offshore drilling rights is a question that Governor Reagan raises often.

As a matter of fact, in the proposal for the Alaska lands legislation, 100 percent of all the offshore lands would be open for exploration, and 95 percent of all the Alaska lands where it is suspected or believed that minerals might exist. We have, with our 5-year plan for the leasing of offshore lands, proposed more land to be drilled than has been opened up for drilling since this program first started in 1954.

So, we're not putting restraints on American exploration; we're encouraging it in every way we can.

Mr. SMITH. Governor Reagan, you have the last word on this question.

GOVERNOR REAGAN. Yes. If it is a well-known fact that I opposed air pollution laws in California, the only thing I can possibly think of is that the President must be suggesting the law that the Federal Government tried to impose on the State of California—not a law, regulations that would have made it impossible to drive an automobile within the city limits of any California city, or have a place to put it if you did drive it against their regulations. It would have destroyed the economy of California, and, I must say, we had the support of Congress when we pointed out how ridiculous this attempt was by the Environmental Protection Agency. We still have the strictest air control or air pollution laws in the country.

As for offshore oiling, only 2 percent now is so leased and is producing oil. The rest, as to whether the lands are going to be opened in the next 5 years or so—we're already 5 years behind in what we should be doing. There is more oil now in the wells that have been drilled than has been taken out in the 121 years that they've been drilled.

Mr. SMITH. Thank you, Governor. Thank you, Mr. President.

The next question goes to Governor Reagan from William Hilliard.

SOCIAL SECURITY

MR. HILLIARD. Governor Reagan, wage earners in this country—especially the young—are supporting a social security system that continues to affect their income drastically. The system is fostering a struggle between the young and the old, and is drifting the country toward a polarization of these two groups. How much longer can the young wage earner expect to bear the ever-increasing burden of the social security system?

GOVERNOR REAGAN. The social security system was based on a false premise, with regard to how fast the number of workers would increase and how fast the number of retirees would increase. It is actuarially out of balance, and this first became evident about 16 years ago, and some of us were voicing warnings then. Now, it is trillions of dollars out of balance, and the only answer that has come so far is the biggest single tax increase in our Nation's history, the payroll tax increase for social security, which will only put a Band-aid on this and postpone the day of reckoning by a few years at most.

What is needed is a study that I have proposed by a task force of experts to look into this entire problem as to how it can be reformed and made actuarially sound, but with the premise that no one presently dependent on social security is going to have the rug pulled out from under them and not get their check. We cannot frighten, as we have with the threats and the campaign rhetoric that has gone on in this campaign, our senior citizens, leave them thinking that in some way they're endangered and they would have no place to turn. They must continue to get those checks, and I believe that the system can

be put on a sound actuarial basis. But it's going to take some study and some work, and not just passing a tax increase to let the roof fall in on the next administration.

MR. SMITH. Would you repeat that question for President Carter?

MR. HILLIARD. Yes, President Carter. Wage earners in this country, especially the young, are supporting a social security system that continues to affect their income drastically. The system is fostering a struggle between young and old and is drifting the country toward a polarization of these two groups. How much longer can the young wage earner expect to bear the ever-increasing burden of the social security system?

THE PRESIDENT. As long as there's a Democratic President in the White House, we will have a strong and viable social security system, free of the threat of bankruptcy. Although Governor Reagan has changed his position lately, on four different occasions he has advocated making social security a voluntary system, which would, in effect, very quickly bankrupt it. I noticed also in the Wall Street Journal earlier this week that a preliminary report of his task force advocates making social security more sound by reducing the adjustments in social security for the retired people to compensate for the impact of inflation. These kinds of approaches are very dangerous to the security and the well-being, and the peace of mind of the retired people of this country and those approaching retirement age.

But no matter what it takes in the future to keep social security sound, it must be kept that way. And although there was a serious threat to the social security system and its integrity during the 1976 campaign and when I became President, the action of the Democratic Congress, working with me, has been to put social security back on a sound financial basis. That's the way it will stay.

Mr. Smith. Governor Reagan.

Governor Reagan. Well, that just isn't true. It has, as I said, delayed the actuarial imbalance falling on us for just a few years with that increase in taxes. And I don't believe we can go on increasing the tax, because the problem for the young people today is that they're paying in far more than they can ever expect to get out.

Now, again this statement that somehow I wanted to destroy it, and I just changed my tune, that I am for voluntary social security, which would mean the ruin of it. Mr. President, the voluntary thing that I suggested many years ago was that a young man, orphaned and raised by an aunt who died, his aunt was ineligible for social security insurance, because she was not his mother. And I suggested that if this is an insurance program, certainly the person who's paying in should be able to name his own beneficiaries. And that's the closest I've ever come to anything voluntary with social security. I, too, am pledged to a social security program that will reassure these senior citizens of ours they're going to continue to get their money.

There are some changes I'd like to make. I would like to make a change that discriminates in the regulations against a wife who works and finds that she then is faced with a choice between her husband's benefits, if he dies first, or what she has paid in; but it does not recognize that she has also been paying in herself, and she is entitled to more than she presently can get. I'd like to change that.

Mr. Smith. President Carter's rebuttal now.

The President. Fine. These constant suggestions that the basic social security system should be changed does cause concern and consternation among the aged of our country. It's obvious that we should have a commitment to them, that social security benefits should not be taxed, and that there would be no peremptory change in the standards by which social security payments are made to the retired people. We also need to continue to index the social security payments so that if inflation rises, the social security payments would rise a commensurate degree to let the buying power of the social security check continue intact.

In the past, the relationship between social security and Medicare has been very important to provide some modicum of aid for senior citizens in the retention of health benefits. Governor Reagan, as a matter of fact, began his political career campaigning around this Nation against Medicare. Now we have an opportunity to move toward national health insurance, with an emphasis on the prevention of disease; an emphasis on outpatient care, not inpatient care; an emphasis on hospital cost containment to hold down the cost of hospital care for those who are ill; an emphasis on catastrophic health insurance, so that if a family is threatened with being wiped out economically because of a very high medical bill, then the insurance would help pay for it. These are the kind of elements of a national health insurance, important to the American people. Governor Reagan, again, typically is against such a proposal.

Mr. Smith. Governor.

Governor Reagan. There you go again. [*Laughter*]

When I opposed Medicare, there was another piece of legislation meeting the same problem before the Congress. I happened to favor the other piece of legislation and thought that it would be better for the senior citizens and provide better care than the one that was finally passed.

I was not opposing the principle of providing care for them. I was opposing one piece of legislation as versus another.

There is something else about social security—of course, that doesn't come out of the payroll tax; it comes out of the general fund—that something should be done about. I think it's disgraceful that the Disability Insurance Fund in social security finds checks going every month to tens of thousands of people who are locked up in our institutions for crime or for mental illness, and they are receiving disability checks from social security every month while a State institution provides for all of their needs and their care.

Mr. SMITH. President Carter, you have the last word on this question.

THE PRESIDENT. I think this debate on social security, Medicare, national health insurance typifies as vividly as any other subject tonight the basic historical differences between the Democratic Party and the Republican Party. The allusions to basic changes in the minimum wage is another, and the deleterious comments that Governor Reagan has made about unemployment compensation. These commitments that the Democratic Party has historically made to the working families of this Nation have been extremely important to the growth in their stature and in a better quality of life for them.

I noticed recently that Governor Reagan frequently quotes Democratic Presidents, in his acceptance address and otherwise. I have never heard a candidate for President, who is a Republican, quote a Republican President, but when they get in office, they try to govern like Republicans. So, its good for the American people to remember there is a sharp basic historical difference between Governor Reagan and me on these crucial issues—also, between the two parties that we represent.

Mr. SMITH. Thank you, Mr. President, Governor Reagan.

We now go to another question, a question to President Carter by Barbara Walters.

ASSESSMENTS OF OPPONENT

Ms. WALTERS. Thank you.

You have addressed some of the major issues tonight, but the biggest issue in the minds of American voters is yourselves, your ability to lead this country. When many voters go into that booth just a week from today, they will be voting their gut instinct about you men.

You've already given us your reasons why people should vote for you. Now would you please tell us for this your final question, why they should not vote for your opponent, why his Presidency could be harmful to the Nation and, having examined both your opponent's record and the man himself, tell us his greatest weakness.

THE PRESIDENT. Barbara, reluctant as I am to say anything critical about Governor Reagan, I will try to answer your question. [*Laughter*]

First of all, there's the historical perspective that I just described. This is a contest between a Democrat in the mainstream of my party, as exemplified by the actions that I've taken in the Oval Office the last 4 years, as contrasted with Governor Reagan, who in most cases does typify his party, but in some cases, there is a radical departure by him from the heritage of Eisenhower and others. The most important crucial difference in this election campaign, in my judgment, is the approach to the control of nuclear weaponry and the inclination to control or not to control the spread of atomic weapons to other nations that don't presently have it, particularly the terrorist nations.

The inclination that Governor Reagan has exemplified in many troubled times since he's been running for President—I think since 1968—to inject American military forces in places like North Korea, to put a blockade around Cuba this year, or in some instances, to project American forces into a fishing dispute against the small nation of Ecuador on the west coast of South America—this is typical of his longstanding inclination, on the use of American power, not to resolve disputes diplomatically and peacefully, but to show that the exercise of military power is best proven by the actual use of it.

Obviously, no President wants war, and I certainly do not believe that Governor Reagan, if he were President, would want war. But a President in the Oval Office has to make a judgment on almost a daily basis about how to exercise the enormous power of our country for peace, through diplomacy, or in a careless way, in a belligerent attitude which has exemplified his attitudes in the past.

MR. SMITH. Barbara, would you repeat the question for Governor Reagan?

MS. WALTERS. Yes, thank you. Realizing that you may be equally reluctant to speak ill of your opponent, may I ask why people should not vote for your opponent, why his Presidency could be harmful to the Nation? And having examined both your opponent's record and the man himself, could you tell us his greatest weakness?

GOVERNOR REAGAN. Well, Barbara, I believe that there is a fundamental difference—and I think it has been evident in most of the answers that Mr. Carter has given tonight—that he seeks the solution to anything as another opportunity for a Federal Government program. I happen to believe that the Federal Government has usurped powers and autonomy and authority that belongs back at the State and local level—it has imposed on the individual freedoms of the people—and that there are more of these things that could be solved by the people themselves, if they were given a chance, or by the levels of government that were closer to them.

Now, as to why I should be and he shouldn't be, when he was a candidate in 1976, President Carter invented a thing he called the misery index. He added the rate of unemployment and the rate of inflation, and it came, at that time, to 12.5 under President Ford. And he said that no man with that size misery index had a right to seek reelection to the Presidency. Today, by his own decision, the misery index is in excess of 20 percent, and I think this must suggest something.

But when I have quoted a Democrat President, as the President says, I was a Democrat. I said many foolish things back in those days. [*Laughter*] But the President that I quoted had made a promise, a Democrat promise, and I quoted him because it was never kept. And today, you would find that that promise is at the very heart of what Republicanism represents in this country today. And that's why I believe there are going to be millions of Democrats that are going to vote with us this time around, because they too want that promise kept. It was a promise for less government and less taxes and more freedom for the people.

MR. SMITH. President Carter.

THE PRESIDENT. Yes. I mentioned the radical departure of Governor Reagan from the principles or ideals or historical perspective of his own party. I don't think this can be better illustrated than in the case with guaranteeing women equal rights under the Constitution of our Nation. For 40 years, the Republican Party platforms called for guaranteeing women equal rights with a constitutional amendment. Six predecessors of mine who served in the Oval Office called for this guarantee of women's rights. Governor Reagan and the new Republican Party has departed from this commitment—a very severe blow to the opportunity for women finally to correct discrimination under which they have suffered.

When a man and a woman do the same amount of work, a man gets paid a dollar; a woman only gets paid 59 cents. And the equal rights amendment only says that equality of rights shall not be abridged for women by the Federal Government or by the State governments. That's all it says—a simple guarantee of equality of opportunity which typifies the Democratic Party and which is a very important commitment of mine, as contrasted with Governor Reagan's radical departure from the longstanding policy of his own party.

MR. SMITH. Governor Reagan.

GOVERNOR REAGAN. Yes. Mr. President, once again, I happen to be against the amendment, because I think the amendment will take this problem out of the hands of elected legislators and put it in the hands of unelected judges. I am for equal rights, and while you have been in office for 4 years, and not one single State—and most of them have a majority of Democratic legislators—has added to the ratification or voted to ratify the equal rights amendment.

While I was Governor, more than 8 years ago, I found 14 separate instances where women were discriminated against in the body of California law, and I had passed and signed into law 14 statutes that eliminated those discriminations, including the economic ones that you have just mentioned, equal pay and so forth. I believe that if in all these years that we've spent trying to get the amendment, that we'd spent as much time correcting these laws, as we did in California—and we were the first to do it.

If I were President, I would also now take a look at the hundreds of Federal regulations which discriminate against women and which go right on while everyone is looking for an amendment. I would have someone ride herd on those regulations, and we'd start eliminating those discriminations in the Federal Government against women.

MR. SMITH. President Carter.

THE PRESIDENT. Yes. Howard, I'm a southerner, and I share the basic beliefs of my region about an excessive government intrusion into the private affairs of American citizens and also into the private affairs of the free enterprise system. One of the commitments that I made was to deregulate the major industries of this country. We've been remarkably successful, with the help of the Democratic Congress. We've deregulated the air industry, the rail industry, the trucking industry, financial institutions; now working on the communications industry.

In addition to that, I believe this element of discrimination is something that the South has seen so vividly as a blight on our region of the country which has now been corrected—not only racial discrimination but discrimination against people that have to work for a living—because we have been trying to pick ourselves up by our bootstraps since the long Depression years and lead a full and useful life in the affairs of this country. We've made remarkable success. It's part of my consciousness and of my commitment to continue this progress.

So, my heritage as a southerner, my experience in the Oval Office, convinces me that what I've just described is a proper course for the future.

MR. SMITH. Governor Reagan, yours is the last word.

GOVERNOR REAGAN. Well, my last word is again to say that we were talking about this very simple amendment and women's rights. And I make it plain again: I am for women's rights. But I would like to call the attention of the people to the fact that so-called simple amendment could be used by mischievous men to destroy discriminations that properly belong, by law, to women, respecting the physical differences between the two sexes, labor laws that protect them against doing things that would be physically harmful to them. Those could all be challenged by men. And the same would be true with regard to combat service in the military and so forth.

I thought that was the subject we were supposed to be on. But, if we're talking about how much we think about the working people and so forth, I'm the only fellow that ever ran for this job who was six times president of his own union and still has a lifetime membership in that union.

MR. SMITH. Gentlemen, each of you now have 3 minutes for a closing statement. President Carter, you're first.

CLOSING STATEMENTS

THE PRESIDENT. First of all, I'd like to thank the League of Women Voters for making this debate possible. I think it's been a very constructive debate, and I hope it's helped to acquaint the American people with the sharp differences between myself and Governor Reagan. Also, I want to thank the people of Cleveland and Ohio for being such hospitable hosts during this last few hours in my life.

I've been President now for almost 4 years. I've had to make thousands of decisions, and each one of those decisions has been a learning process. I've seen the strength of my Nation, and I've seen the crises that it approached in a tentative way. And I've had to deal with those crises as best I could.

As I've studied the record between myself and Governor Reagan, I've been impressed with the stark differences that exist between us. I think the results of this debate indicate that that fact is true. I consider myself in the mainstream of my party. I consider myself in the mainstream even of the bipartisan list of Presidents who've served before me. The United States must be a nation strong; the United States must be a nation secure. We must have a society that's just and fair. And we must extend the benefits of our own commitment to peace, to create a peaceful world.

I believe that since I've been in office, there've been six or eight areas of combat evolve in other parts of the world. In each case, I alone have had to determine the interests of my country and the degree of involvement of my country. I've done that with moderation, with care, with thoughtfulness; sometimes consulting experts. But I've learned in this last 3½ years that when an issue is extremely difficult, when the call is very close, the chances are the experts will be divided almost 50–50. And the final judgment about the future of our Nation—war, peace, involvement, reticence, thoughtfulness, care, consideration, concern—has to be made by the man in the Oval Office. It's a lonely job, but with the involvement of the American people in the process, with an open government, the job is a very gratifying one.

The American people now are facing, next Tuesday, a lonely decision. Those listening to my voice will have to make a judgment about the future of this country. And I think they ought to remember that one vote can make a lot of difference. If one vote per precinct had changed in 1960, John Kennedy would never have been President of this Nation. And if a few more people had gone to the polls and voted in 1968, Hubert Humphrey would have been President; Richard Nixon would not.

There is a partnership involved. And our Nation, to stay strong, to stay at peace, to raise high the banner of human rights, to set an example for the rest of the world, to let our deep beliefs and commitments be felt by others in all other nations is my plan for the future. I ask the American people to join me in this partnership.

Mr. SMITH. Governor Reagan.

GOVERNOR REAGAN. Yes, I would like to add my words of thanks, too, to the ladies of the League of Women Voters for making these debates possible. I'm sorry that we couldn't persuade the bringing in of the third candidate, so that he could have been seen also in these debates. But still, it's good that at least once, all three of us were heard by the people of this country.

Next Tuesday is election day. Next Tuesday all of you will go to the polls; you'll stand there in the polling place and make a decision. I think when you make that decision, it might be well if you would ask yourself, are you better off than you were 4 years ago? Is it easier for you to go and buy things in the stores than it was 4 years ago? Is there more or less unemployment in the country than there was 4 years ago? Is America as respected throughout the world as it was? Do you feel that our security is as safe, that we're as strong as we were 4 years ago? And if you answer all of those questions yes, why then, I think your choice is very obvious as to who you'll vote for. If you don't agree, if you don't think that this course that we've been on for the last 4 years is what you would like to see us follow for the next 4, then I could suggest another choice that you have.

This country doesn't have to be in the shape that it is in. We do not have to go on sharing in scarcity, with the country getting worse off, with unemployment growing. We talk about the unemployment lines. If all of the unemployed today were in a single line allowing 2 feet for each one of them, that line would reach from New York City to Los Angeles, California. All of this can be cured, and all of it can be solved.

I have not had the experience the President has had in holding that office, but I think in being Governor of California, the most populous State in the Union—if it were a nation, it would be the seventh-ranking economic power in the world—I, too, had some lonely moments and decisions to make. I know that the economic program that I have proposed for this Nation in the next few years can resolve many of the problems that trouble us today. I know because we did it there. We cut the cost—the increased cost of government—the increase in half over the 8 years. We returned $5.7 billion in tax rebates, credits, and cuts to our people. We, as I've said earlier, fell below the national average in inflation when we did that. And I know that we did give back authority and autonomy to the people.

I would like to have a crusade today, and I would like to lead that crusade with your help. And it would be one to take government off the backs of the great people of this country and turn you loose again to do those things that I know you can do so well, because you did them and made this country great.

Thank you.

MR. SMITH. Gentlemen, ladies and gentlemen, for 60 years the League of Women Voters has been committed to citizen education and effective participation of Americans in governmental and political affairs. The most critical element of all in that process is an informed citizen who goes to the polls and who votes.

On behalf of the League of Women Voters, now, I would like to thank President Carter and Governor Reagan for being with us in Cleveland tonight. And, ladies and gentlemen, thank you and good night.

NOTE: The debate began at 9:30 p.m. in the Cleveland Convention Center Music Hall. It was broadcast live on radio and television.

Ruth J. Hinerfeld is chair of the League of Women Voters Education Fund, and Howard K. Smith is a correspondent with ABC News.

Cleveland, Ohio

Informal Exchange With Reporters Following the 1980 Presidential Campaign Debate.   October 28, 1980

Q. How do you think it went?

THE PRESIDENT. Very good. I thought the issues were discussed very thoroughly. I thought it was an excellent debate, and it drew the sharpest possible differences accurately between the basic commitments of Governor Reagan and myself. So, I thought the debate served a very useful purpose.

Q. Did you get in all of the points that you wanted to make?

THE PRESIDENT. Well, not all of them. I had a few more points I could have made, but we only had about 45 minutes for each one of us to talk. And within that time frame, I think I did pretty well in getting our points across.

Thank you.

Q. Are you prepared to claim victory? Did you win it?

NOTE: The exchange began at 11:09 p.m. in the Cleveland Convention Center Music Hall.

Cleveland, Ohio

Remarks at a Carter/Mondale Rally. October 28, 1980

Unaccustomed as I am to public speaking—[*laughter*]—I find myself called upon tonight to substitute for my good friends, John Glenn and Bob Strauss, who are out educating the press about what took place in the debate just a few minutes ago. [*Laughter*] I thought it was a very fine opportunity for me and Governor Reagan to sharply draw a distinction between the Republicans and Democrats—history, and a distortion of history; the control of nuclear weapons, and an absence of commitment to control of nuclear weapons. Equal rights for all Americans, a secure nation, peace—these are the kinds of things that were discussed quite thoroughly.

Now, as I said in my closing statement, we've got another week to go. Next Tuesday the decision will be not in the hands of debate judges or the League of Women Voters or the press, the decision will be in the hands of millions of Americans, like you, around this Nation. And I want to ask you: Are you with me? [*Applause and cheers*] Are we going to win? [*Applause and cheers*] Are you going to work this next week? [*Applause and cheers*] We'll have a tremendous victory on November the 4th. Thanks to you, I don't have any doubt about it.

Good luck. God bless you for a greater America.

NOTE: The President spoke at 11:30 p.m. in the Grand Ballroom at the Bond Court Hotel.

Pittsburgh, Pennsylvania

*Remarks and a Question-and-Answer
Session at a Town Meeting.
October 29, 1980*

THE PRESIDENT. *Mayor Caliguiri, Bishop
Appleyard:*

I want to thank also Dean Werner for
allowing us to use this beautiful place for
a public discussion of issues that are important to the people of this country. It's
historic; it's popular. It's been used, I
know, for many fora. It's a meeting place
where ideas are exchanged that have been
beneficial not only to this community and
to the Commonwealth of Pennsylvania
but to the entire Nation. You've made this
a vital concourse for the exchange of ideas
and hopes and dreams and expression of
concern and commitment about years to
come, building upon the history of the
past.

CAMPAIGN ISSUES

Pennsylvania was founded, as you
know, almost 300 years ago, more than a
century before the Constitution and the
Bill of Rights. This Commonwealth was
the forerunner in protecting many of the
individual rights which all Americans now
hold dear, sometimes even take for
granted—freedom of religion, trial by
jury, the right to petition, rule by law,
democracy itself.

Today Pittsburgh in a special way, I
think, carries on the tradition of tolerance
and respect for individuals, no matter
how different a particular individual
might be from the majority of the population. You've even named one of your
thoroughfares "Value of the Person
Street." You're a city proud of its neighborhoods and its ethnic variety. You're a
city of champions in more ways than one.
I'm confident that you will always reject
those who try to incite division and who

do not understand what America stands
for.

Next Tuesday our Nation honors its
most precious freedom, the right for the
people of this country to chart the future
of this country. I'm confident about that
future. We can keep the peace. We can
keep our Nation secure. We can keep our
Nation on the road to social justice, to
equal economic opportunity for all Americans, women as well as men.

Last night, as you may have heard, we
had a debate between myself and Governor Reagan, which I thought was a
very fine opportunity for us to draw as
sharply as we could, under the format
provided, the differences between us as
men, as candidates, as representatives of
the Republican and the Democratic
Party, and our sharply contrasting vision
of the future. I thought it was a constructive debate.

The time limit constrained us from
getting into some of the areas of life that
I would like to have discussed—steel, agriculture, some of the domestic issues. But
I think the panelists decided that in this
particular time the discussion of nuclear
arms, nonproliferation, peace, war, the
proper use of America's strength—those
kinds of issues were preeminent in the
minds of the questioners, and of course,
they were mirrored in the responses that
we gave.

Obviously, we had a chance to discuss the values of human beings, minimum wage, Medicare, social security,
equality of opportunity, whether any
citizens should be paid a lower wage because they happened to be black. That
kind of issue is still, unfortunately, a part
of the political dialog of today. But the
thrust of America has always been to
eliminate those discrepancies and to remove discrimination and to move to the

future in a spirit of harmony and equality of opportunity.

Got a great nation—part of its greatness will be demonstrated here this morning when you ask me, the President of our country, questions and I give you the best answers I can. And now I'd like to have the first question.

Yes.

QUESTIONS

SOCIAL SECURITY; WAR AND PEACE

Q. I have a question. What I would like to know—I'm speaking for the senior citizens. Now, in the social security we'll get a raise, and after you get a raise, your rent goes up, the food goes up, Medicare goes up. Is it possible that when you get this raise, that the senior citizens wouldn't have to pay more rent, more for food, and more for living quarters? Why is it that when we get this raise, that everything else should go up? Now, I'm not speaking for myself. I'm one of the senior citizens quite fortunate that I have lived better since I've been a senior citizen than I was. But there is so many that's suffering.

Is it possible that the Government or the State can do anything that the older folks won't have to suffer when they go to the store to buy something, or when their check goes up, that the rent won't go up or the Medicare? Can't it be on the level that when they get their raise that they won't have to go up?

Now, this question you don't have to answer if you don't want to. [*Laughter*]

THE PRESIDENT. I'll try. [*Laughter*]

Q. The next part that I was going to say—please keep our boys out of war. Can't we have peace without sending our boys to the war?

THE PRESIDENT. I'll try to answer both questions. [*Laughter*]

I think you've noticed that in recent days in the Wall Street Journal, which is hardly a Democratic newspaper, they quoted Governor Reagan's task force of advisers, about whom he brags quite frequently, as advocating some basic changes in social security. One change that he proposed, at least his advisers have announced that they would propose, is to do away with the indexing of social security.

As you know, a few weeks ago we had a 14.2-percent increase in social security checks, to try to compensate people like you for the increase in the cost of living—food, housing, and other goods. We'll continue this, I guarantee you, as long as we have a Democrat in the White House, because the social security system has been a product of the Democratic Party.

I remember during the Depression years when Franklin Roosevelt put forward the idea of social security. You may remember that the Republicans were against it, but it was put into effect. And since then, the social security system has constantly been improved for the benefit of those who retire and also—something that Governor Reagan forgot last night—for the benefit of young couples who might die and leave a widow and children or who might become disabled.

He made a very serious statement last night which was an error, and that is that the amount of money that young people pay into social security is more than the benefits they ever get out. This is exactly contrary to the facts, because no matter what kind of income you might have, even the highest paid executive officer in a major corporation, a recent analysis has shown, gets more benefits back in insurance coverage, for only's family if one becomes disabled, or retirement benefits if you do reach retirement age, than you ever put into it.

So, this threat to the social security system still exists. As you know, it's now sound; it will not go into bankruptcy. And I guarantee you that in the future we'll continue to increase social security payments to make up for the increase in cost of things that a senior citizen has to buy.

I don't want to mislead you, because it may be that in a particular community, housing goes up a lot more than, say, on a national average, and the social security payments are figured out for the national average. So, there will be an occasion, at times, when you might not get exactly enough increase to pay for those increased in cost. But perhaps if housing goes up, you might have your own home or that may not be an extra cost, and you get that extra pay.

But anyhow, we don't want social security to be changed, we don't want social security benefits to be taxed, and we do not want social security to be voluntary. We do not want young people who are contributing to the social security system now to be able to withdraw, which would bring social security into bankruptcy. Those things must be guarded against, and that is a crucial issue which was discussed last night in the debate.

The other part is about war. My fondest hope and my most fervent prayer is that I can go out of office, hopefully at the end of 4 more years, having kept our Nation at peace. I think it's been 50 years since we've had an administration serve in the White House without our Nation being at war.

We've got enormous power in this country. Our military forces are second to none. Our influence around the world is very great. And I have to make a judgment, literally several times a week, when a troubled spot develops in the world: What are American interests, and what should the degree of American involve-

ment be; how deeply should we become involved?

I have always tried to use America's strength with great caution and care and tolerance and thoughtfulness and prayer, because once we inject our military forces into combat, as happened in Vietnam, it's hard to control it from then on, because your country loses prestige if you don't ultimately go ahead and win. I think all the Presidents in the Oval Office before me have had that sense of moderation. Some have not been successful in keeping our Nation at peace. But I will continue to work and to pray that neither your boys nor my boys nor my future grandchildren will have to go to war.

So, social security and war—two good points.

Yes.

RELIGION AND POLITICS

Q. Mr. President, my name is James Disantis, and I'm a born-again Christian who's supporting you for the second time, although I've seen many evangelical leaders endorse Ronald Reagan rather than your candidacy. Could you comment on this and tell me why you think this has happened, considering your exemplary public witness on domestic issues involving the poor and on international issues as a peacemaker in the Middle East, an area of great sensitivity for most evangelical Christians.

THE PRESIDENT. Well, I think it would be a mistake, James, to assume that evangelical Christians would be any more homogenous in their political preferences than would other groups in our Nation. I would hope that all Americans would support me unanimously, but I know that that's asking for too much.

There has been a high degree of publicity given in recent months to the so-called Moral Majority. As a matter of fact, Reverend Jerry Falwell, the leader of the Moral Majority, habitually and weekly, even more often, during the 1976 campaign castigated me severely and was one of my most difficult opponents or critics. He hasn't changed.

There are some issues on which I disagree strongly with his basic philosophy or approach to government or religion. I don't think there ought to be any religious test for political acceptability, and I don't think there ought to be any political test for religious fellowship. I believe that the people will make a sound judgment, recognizing the necessity for the separation of church and state.

I have never found any incompatibility between my religious convictions and my duties as a President. Every night I read a chapter in the Bible, with my wife when we're together; we read the same chapter when we're separated. It's part of my existence. I've done it for years.

And I have never found anything in the Bible, in the Old or New Testament, that specifies whether or not we should have a Department of Education in the Federal Government or whether you should have a B–1 bomber or the air-launched cruise missiles—[*laughter*]—or whether we should share with Panama, the rest of this century, operation of the Panama Canal or whether we should be able to guard it in the next century as has been worked out. Those kinds of measuring rods to define what is an acceptable Christian are contrary to my own beliefs.

So, I'm willing to keep my faith in God, of course, and I'm willing to put my faith in an election year, in the hands of the people of this country. And I believe most Americans want to preserve that proper separation of church and state.

I ought to close by saying that I respect the right even of Reverend Falwell to express his views, even from the pulpit. But when you start putting a measuring stick on a political figure and saying he is or is not an acceptable person in the eyes of God, I remember the admonition in the New Testament: "Judge not that ye be judged" and "God is love." So, it's not a big problem for me.

Thank you very much. That's a good question.

Yes, ma'am.

NUCLEAR ARMS CONTROL

Q. Mr. President, I have a question about last night's discussion about nuclear arms control. Governor Reagan seemed to be saying that we should renegotiate the SALT II treaty after first obtaining nuclear superiority. My question is, doesn't this position effectively rule out an arms agreement? First of all, it would be very difficult to determine an actual point of nuclear superiority. And number two, would this not accelerate the arms race as never before?

THE PRESIDENT. Yes, there's no doubt about that.

What's your name?

Q. Jane Kuczynski.

THE PRESIDENT. Jane Kuczynski.

Jane, of all the issues we discussed last night, I consider this to be by far the most important, and I tried to express myself in the limited time. I only had two minutes and then a minute followup on most of the rebuttal times.

Governor Reagan's position on nuclear arms control is a radical departure from what all Presidents have done, including President Eisenhower, Johnson, Kennedy, Nixon, Ford, and myself.

The concept has been to negotiate with the Soviet Union a balance and then tight controls and then an assured way to monitor whether or not those controls or those agreements were honored and then, with the firm commitment by ourselves and the Soviet Union, as circumstances warrant, to reduce the level of the nuclear arsenals.

The treaty that I have negotiated was begun by President Nixon, and it was continued by President Ford and finally concluded by me. It was a continuum there. Governor Reagan says, "Let's throw that treaty away. Let's do not consider it. Let's don't let the Senate debate it. Let's don't let the American people become familiar with its issues. Let's don't see whether it is a fair and balanced treaty worthy of Senate ratification."

As I mentioned last night, you can have individual Members of the Senate who take a very radical approach or an ill-advised approach or a new approach or propose some relatively insignificant amendment which is important to them. Their view, which is a departure from the best interests of our country, in my judgment, can be moderated or changed by the other 99 Senators. But when a President or a Presidential candidate says, "We will not even consider this treaty," that short circuits the whole process.

That treaty has now come out of the Armed Services Committee. It was considered by the Senate Armed Services Committee and the Foreign Relations Committee, and now it's ready for a decision on the Senate floor.

Governor Reagan last night said another thing that's of great concern concerning nuclear weapons. The arms limitation treaties are negotiated only between ourselves and the Soviet Union. When the limited test ban treaty was negotiated by President Johnson, Governor Reagan at that time did not support it. When President Nixon negotiated the antiballistic missile treaty and SALT I treaty, Governor Reagan did not support it. When President Ford negotiated an agreement at Vladivostok, which was the basis for the current treaty, Governor Reagan did not support that agreement. And now the final agreement on this particular SALT treaty, he still does not support it.

Perhaps even more interesting from last night, it was the first time a major issue had been presented to the American public. I've been discussing it, but I'm glad that 80 or 100 million Americans last night could see that Governor Reagan has another extremely dangerous approach, and that is not concerning the Soviet Union but concerning radical or terrorist nations who don't yet have atomic bombs.

His position has been that if Libya, a terrorist nation, or Iraq or other countries like Pakistan, South Africa want to have an atomic bomb, it's none of our business. He last night insinuated that he had not said this. But I had my people look it up again this morning. And the New York Times of February 1st, this year, said: "Ronald Reagan indicated today he believed the United States should not stand in the way of countries developing their own nuclear weapons," saying, and I quote, "I just don't think it's any of our business."

For people who care about controlling terrorism, that is the ultimate terrorist threat. Just imagine what would happen if the PLO or Qadhafi in Libya had an atomic bomb. They could threaten the ultimate terrorist act. Also, in the Middle East in particular, some of those countries are extremely rich in dollars, because they have massive amounts of oil to sell. There's no doubt that they could buy the services of qualified scientists and engineers, machinery, equipment in order to build atomic weapons.

So, I think the combination of rejecting not just this particular treaty, but all the previous treaties negotiated by four different Presidents and rejecting the influence of the United States to prevent radical or terrorist nations from having atomic bombs, those two things combined are the single, most important issue in the 1980 election.

And every American ought to stop and think what will happen to this world if we have no control over nuclear weapons between ourselves and the Soviet Union, if we launch, as Governor Reagan has proposed, an arms race, and if we take the position it's none of our business if terrorist nations have atomic weapons. That is the single, most important issue in this campaign, and I'm glad last night it had a chance to come out.

Thank you.

AMERICAN HOSTAGES IN IRAN

Q. First of all, Mr. Carter, my name is Cathy Faloon, and I'd like to welcome you to Pittsburgh. We're really proud to have you here in our city of champs.

THE PRESIDENT. Thank you.

Q. I was wondering if you really feel in your heart that the hostages know that you're trying to do your best to have their release?

THE PRESIDENT. I'm not sure. There's no way for me to know what the hostages know.

When Richard Queen came home after he was released because he was ill, I had a private conversation with him and his mother and father and his brother in the Oval Office. And I didn't cross-examine him, but it was obvious to me that he had been misled by his captors and was convinced in a way that the American people had forgotten the hostages.

Obviously, by the time he had a few days of rest in Germany and got here, we had sent State Department officials over to show him some newsreels and newspapers and thousands of letters and the heartbreak that existed among the American people of all kinds since the hostages were taken.

But my guess is that the hostages have no idea how many prayers have gone up for them, how many yellow ribbons have been tied on trees, how many times the American news stories have been about them, and how our hearts have gone out to their families. I don't believe they know it.

I don't have any way to predict when the hostages will come home. This has been a very difficult issue for me and for the American people; more difficult, obviously, for the hostages and their families.

But we've had two basic principles that have guided me in everything I've done, and they haven't ever changed. One is that I as President should protect the honor and the integrity and the interest of my Nation, and secondly, and tied in with it, is that I should never do anything as a President that would endanger the lives or safety of the hostages or interfere with their earliest possible return to freedom and to their families. We've never deviated from those policies. The understanding that we now have with Iranian officials, with the United Nations, has been put forward to the public since last January or February. We've not changed.

And my hope and prayer is that the Government which Iran finally has—a President, a Prime Minister, a parliament, a speaker of the parliament, a Cabinet—that they are approaching a time of making a decision about the hostages.

I found out early this morning, 7 o'clock our time, that they had completed about a 4-hour closed debate this morning, and tomorrow they'll have their first open debate on the hostage issue. What that indicates I do not know. But all we can do is to continue to protect the interest of the hostages, protect the interest of our Nation, and pray that they'll be released.

My guess is that when they are released, they would have a few days of rest and physical examination and proper diet, in Germany or some acceptable place, and then come home to the welcome that I hope they'll be prepared to receive. And at that time I have no doubt that they will know how much we love them.

Q. Thank you.

RONALD REAGAN

Q. Mr. President, my name is Anthony Calura. I'm an elected constable in the second ward in the city of Pittsburgh and also vice chairman. My question is, what's been running through my mind, why Ronald Reagan, a candidate for President of the United States, at the age of 70 would be allowed to run. If my memory serves me right, I read some time ago in, I believe it was one of the New York newspapers, that he was 72 years old. I don't believe that a man that old should be running my country and your country.

THE PRESIDENT. Anthony, I'm thankful that you didn't ask a question. [*Laughter*]

That's an issue that hasn't been raised in the campaign, one that I would not want to raise. I think the American people know the age of myself and Governor Reagan. And I've seen in the polls, in the public opinion polls, a fairly good indication that the American people are not particularly concerned about Governor Reagan's age.

I did notice last night, when I faced him across the stage, that he's a very strong and very capable campaigner, very sure of himself, very vigorous, and I would not want to insinuate in any way that he was not qualified because of age to be President. I hope the American people will make a judgment on other issues.

But I thank you for your comment.

VIETNAM VETERANS AND AGENT ORANGE

Q. Mr. President, my name is Rachel Hobson, and I'm from McKeesport, Pennsylvania. And I wondered, what words of hope and benefit can you offer to the Vietnam veterans who were sprayed with Agent Orange?

THE PRESIDENT. Fine.

Rachel, as you probably know, until I became President and until Max Cleland became the director [Administrator] of the Veterans Administration, very little had been done about investigating the impact on individual persons of the use of Agent Orange and also the recruitment of people who think they may have been injured to come forward and let their case be examined.

When I was elected President, I was deeply concerned and said many times during 1975 and '76 that the most unappreciated group in this Nation were the young men who went to Vietnam to fight in an unpopular war. Even the veterans organizations, at that time, had not felt the impact of leadership that was available from the Vietnam veterans. That was a 15-year war, but they were not appreciated adequately by the American people.

We've changed that, the main way that we have changed it is by my recruiting Max Cleland to head up the Veterans Administration. He's a young man of great dynamism and personal integrity and sensitivity. I happen to have known him as a Georgia State senator when I was Governor of Georgia. He left Georgia after I was no longer Governor and took a position as one of the leading staff members of the Senate Veterans' Affairs Committee under Alan Cranston. And as you know, he's a triple amputee, injured in Vietnam, who has to spend his life in a wheelchair, but who has retained in his own personal commitments the finest aspect toward deprivation because of injury.

He has a special interest in the Agent Orange question and personally monitors not only the inventory or the listing of all our servicemen who may have been injured by Agent Orange but the medical examination of every person involved and also the research that's going into the physical characteristics of someone who has been exposed to this defoliant spray.

So, I can't tell you any more than that. I don't know what the ultimate outcome will be for an individual case. But it's a matter that's very close to me. It's one that is a burning issue with Max Cleland. And you can be assured that it will not be ignored and that those who have been injured by Agent Orange, when their case is confirmed, will be adequately cared for.

Q. Thank you.

THE PRESIDENT. Thank you.

GOVERNMENT REGULATION OF PRIVATE INDUSTRY

Q. Mr. President, thank you for coming to Pittsburgh. We appreciate it.

THE PRESIDENT. Thank you.

Q. My name is Charlie Datz, and I'm from Westmoreland County, which is just a little way away from here.

THE PRESIDENT. Right.

Q. My question today is about the controversy which has emerged regarding the Government regulation of private industry, particularly as it impacts upon environmental protection standards. If reelected, could you kind of share with us the joint strategies which you would employ to bolster employment on one hand, while making significant progress on the other hand in protecting the environment that we need to protect and in preventing Government overregulation of business in the meantime?

THE PRESIDENT. Yes.

Q. Thank you.

THE PRESIDENT. The essence of a successful Presidency or other management leader is to be able to balance conflicting forces or conflicting ideas or conflicting circumstances or facts.

I guess one of the most difficult jobs in the world is the Presidency, because you're in the Oval Office, you receive issues on your desk that can't be resolved anywhere else. If an issue can be resolved easily, it's probably done in your own private life or within the confines of your home or in a city hall or a Governor's office or a State legislature. If none of those places can solve a difficult problem, it comes to me, and I work with the Congress or with my administration to try to resolve it.

There are some basic differences. You've put your finger on a very important one. How do you balance the quality of Americans' lives on the one hand versus economic progress, which involves jobs, which is a part of the quality of a person's life? I think we've done a good job in this respect.

Coal is important to me and to our Nation, to Pennsylvania and the other States near you. In my judgment, the worst thing we could do for the future job opportunities for coal miners or for the production of American coal is to lower air and water pollution standards so that we can use more coal right now. I'll tell you why.

You know better than any other people in this country, those of you who live in Pennsylvania, the impact of the Three Mile Island incident on the consciousness of people. It caused a shock wave to go around the world, of concern about nuclear power. If people who presently are turning to coal as a fuel believe that the only way they can burn coal as a fuel is to have dirty air and destroy our streams and to make our land less productive, they will turn away from coal, and the opportunities for increased production of coal would be gone.

Now, without lowering the standards on air pollution, working with President Sam Church of the United Mine Workers, who's with me today, and with Governor Jay Rockefeller and others from Pennsylvania, we have kept our standards high on air pollution quality. At the same time, we have increased coal production so that this year we'll produce more American coal than has ever been produced in history.

We now have an opportunity to triple the present production of coal in the next 15 years without lowering environmental standards. That's an important consideration to be made.

Last night I noticed that Governor Reagan said that we would have much better production of coal—it's what he used as an example—if we didn't have all those so-called regulations. The regulations not only apply to air and water quality, but they also apply to mine safety and health. In the past when someone has said we ought to abolish the Occupational Safety and Health Administration, OSHA, Governor Reagan's response was, "Amen."

This is a law designed to protect mineworkers, and it does increase the cost of coal a little bit per ton for the miners to be free of the constant threat of black lung disease and death. Sam Church told me this morning, only yesterday three miners lost their lives in Kentucky. So, you can't eliminate Government regulation that protects the quality of our life, the safety and health of workers just to have a little bit of an increase in productivity.

We have tried to work with the steel industry in Pennsylvania, in Ohio, and other places to improve the relationship between EPA, or Environmental Protection Agency, and the production of steel. We've come up now and just worked out with Armco Steel a so-called bubble concept, where you in effect have a theoretical bubble over the entire plant. This lets the steel industry control air quality at a much lower cost. We've also had a 30-day averaging period for coal utility plant emissions, which will increase the amount of coal that will be burned in the future in the production of electricity.

These kinds of changes have been worked out very carefully with mine operators, steelplant owners, mineworkers, steelworkers, and the Environmental Protection Agency so that we can have continued progress on economic growth and new jobs without destroying the quality of the earth and air and water God gave us.

Finally, let me say this: We'll continue this process. Now that we have an energy policy in place in this country, we've got a base on which to revitalize the entire system of industry in our country. We had good news this week on productivity; that is, how much can an average American worker produce in a week's work or a day's work. But in general other countries' productivity has been going up faster than ours.

We rebuilt German industry after the Second World War. We rebuilt Japanese industry after the Second World War. Now that we've got an energy policy in place, it's time, in my judgment, to rebuild American industry, and that's what we're going to do.

Q. Thank you very much.

THE PRESIDENT. Thank you. I might add a personal note, Charlie.

Q. Mr. President, my name is——

THE PRESIDENT. Just a minute. Let me add a personal note. You all may not be interested, but I'm going to add it anyway. [*Laughter*]

Every time I get a chance to go to Camp David, I do so. And we're right across the line from Pennsylvania and only 16 miles from Gettysburg. And not too far from Camp David, there's a nice, beautiful trout stream on a dairy farm, and the dairy farmer happens to be a very close friend of mine. And nothing would grieve me more than to see that beautiful stream some day destroyed by acid rain and be sterile and have no life and no beauty.

And I have a deep sense that our country is strong enough and technologically advanced enough and wise enough to have both good jobs, good progress, good industry, good worldwide leadership, and also have a good environment. I don't think the two are incompatible.

Yes, sir.

SPECIALTY STEEL INDUSTRY

Q. Mr. President, my name is Gene Salvadore. And I'd like to ask a question on behalf of the specialty steel industry, which I'm sure you're aware is primarily centered in western Pennsylvania. With currently thousands of specialty steelworkers unemployed, why will you not now commit to support specialty steel products being included in the trigger price system?

THE PRESIDENT. All right. As you know, early in my administration we established the trigger price mechanism, which had not been in existence before, working with the steel industry leaders, both management and labor, under the auspices of the Treasury Department of my administration. It worked out very well. Earlier this year United States Steel filed a law suit claiming that Japanese and mostly European steel manufacturers had dumped their products on our market. So now, after careful negotiations which took several months, we have reimposed the trigger price mechanism as it was before and as the steel industry had requested.

I'm very much aware of the threat to the specialty steel industry. In this neighborhood there are about 30,000 steelworkers who are involved in the production of specialty steel. We're now investigating the situation to see if there is a need for the trigger price mechanism to apply to specialty steel. Obviously, if we've stopped dumping on basic steel products and if the Europeans or Japanese being blocked there try to make up the difference by concentrating on specialty steel items and dump those products on our market, obviously we would have to extend the trigger price mechanism to protect specialty steel.

We're now investigating the situation as rapidly as we possibly can, working with the steelworkers, the steel industry leaders, Treasury Department, investigating foreign marketing, production costs, and the sales policies. So, all I can tell you is that I believe November 10th is when they will make their report to me. Is that the right date, Stu? [1] November the 10th. When I get that report, if I determine that there is a threat to the specialty steel industry of our country from unwarranted dumping, then I would impose the trigger price mechanism to protect that threatened elements of the specialty steel industry.

TRIGGER PRICE MECHANISM LOOPHOLES

Q. Mr. President, my name is Guy Bubb. I'm from Turner Heights, Pennsylvania. And all of us in Pittsburgh are interested in the steel industry because it's such a vital part of our economy. On trigger pricing, again, one of the things we've heard just this week is that there's a very serious problem with a loophole in the trigger pricing mechanism having to do with offshore incorporation. If you're familiar with that, sir, would you comment on that subject?

THE PRESIDENT. I'm not familiar with it. Just a minute. Stu, are you familiar with it?

Q. This was reported this week by one of our economists in Pittsburgh, sir.

THE PRESIDENT. Does that mean that if there should be a steelplant, say, in the Caribbean or somewhere other than in Europe and Japan, they might be able to dump steel here?

Q. Yes, sir.

THE PRESIDENT. I've never heard about that before. Guy, if you would go over and see Mr. Eizenstat, who's standing just on my left, and give him your name and your telephone number, I'll check that out, and he can call you back later on today or perhaps tomorrow.

Q. Thank you very much, sir.

---

[1] Stuart E. Eizenstat, Assistant to the President for Domestic Affairs and Policy.

THE PRESIDENT. Thank you. It's something that I need to know about. Stu, you might want to come over and get his address.

Yes, ma'am.

INFLATION

Q. President Carter, I'm concerned as a housewife and mother about the rate of inflation. What do you plan to do about stabilizing it?

THE PRESIDENT. Thank you. What's your name?

Q. I'm Betty Deceder from Ambridge.

THE PRESIDENT. Thank you.

Betty, this is probably the most persistent and difficult issue that I have to face, along with the Prime Minister of Israel, where the inflation rate is about 200 percent, many Latin American countries, where it's 75 to 100 percent, Japan and Germany, where the inflation rate has doubled in the last 12 months. It's a worldwide problem of inflation, and the primary root of it, not the only cause, has been the unprecedented increase in the price of oil imposed on the world by the OPEC nations.

We had a larger increase in 1979 in oil prices than the total increase in oil prices since it was first discovered in Pennsylvania in the 1800's. This shock wave of increased energy costs rocked the whole world economy. We've tried to deal with it as best we could.

The first quarter of this year, the first 3 months, the inflation rate was up to 18 percent. The second 3 months, it had dropped down to 13 percent. The last 3 months, it's averaged 7 percent. One month it got down to zero, that was in July; but this last month, up around 12 percent. The average has been 7 percent—still too high.

I would say the underlying inflation rate now was within the neighborhood of 9 percent. What can be done about it? That's a good question. There are several reasons that we have high inflation, and let me list them all very quickly. I may forget a few.

One is, how much does the American worker produce per hour worked? We need modern tools and modern plants, and that's the main thrust of our revitalization program that will be put into effect next year if I'm reelected. We'll have a substantial tax reduction. The thrust of it will be, though, to encourage industry to build new plants and to remodel existing plants in the steel industry, the automobile industry, the basic industries that are so important to our people. That's one thing—to increase the productivity of American workers.

Another is to reduce unwarranted growth in Federal spending and the collection of taxes. We've been pretty successful since 1976. The rate of growth of Federal spending is only half what it was when I took office as President, and our deficit, the Federal deficit, compared to the gross national product—how much our Nation produces—is only half what it was, or less than half, when I came in office. We'll continue to be restrained on how much the Federal Government collects and spends, and we'll have a substantial tax reduction next year to carry this out.

Another thing, of course, is to have good relationships between management and labor. You probably remember, 3 years ago you hardly ever picked up a newspaper in Ohio or Kentucky or Pennsylvania or West Virginia that wildcat coal strikes hadn't shut down the mines. You haven't seen those headlines in the last couple of years. This is a very good and constructive new relationship, because in the past, in the steel industry, the automobile industry, the coal industry, and others, about the only time that management and labor faced each other was when they were negotiating a new contract and they were bargaining to see who could get the best advantage against one another.

Now we've changed that. A part of the credit is mine, but most of it is in the industries themselves. Now management and labor say, "What can we do to have workers safer, better paid, more constantly employed, better product, more competition against foreign imports or other competition that might be based elsewhere?" That's a very good thing to bring down inflationary pressures.

Another one is to export as much as we can, because when American workers produce a good product and sell it overseas, it really contributes to a much better market for us and it makes the products that we buy in our country cost less. If you can build two things and then sell one of them overseas, you can sell the one at home cheaper than you could if you only built one thing. Right? So, this is what we've tried to do. We've had world records set in 1977, '78, '79, and the beginning of '80 in agricultural exports, and we're much better off than we were before in the export of manufactured goods as well.

The last point I want to make is this. I could go on; it's a long list. But this is an important one, and that is to get the Government's nose out of the unwarranted regulation of the free enterprise system, because when regulatory agencies were first set up they were designed to protect consumers. But over a period of years, in almost every instance the industry regulated became so influential in Washington, because the consumers weren't organized and didn't much know what was going on, didn't have high-paid lawyers, those regulatory agencies began to protect not the consumers but the industry they were supposed to regulate.

So, we have deregulated the airlines; we've deregulated the trucking industry; we've deregulated the rail industry; we've deregulated the financial institutions, the banks and so forth; we're working now to deregulate the communications industry. And we have also been able to get Government regulation and paperwork reduced by 15 percent.

So, the inflation question is so complicated that you can't just deal with one part of it to the exclusion of all the others. I've just mentioned to you four or five of the elements in reducing inflation. There's something that all of you can do, and this is the final point I'll make.

In Germany and Japan when people earn a paycheck, they generally save about 15 or 20 percent of what they earn. They save their money; they put it in a bank. It's invested in new homes, new industry, new jobs, new tools. In the United States when we earn a dollar, we only save about 4 cents, the lowest saving rate of any nation, I think, on Earth.

So Americans can think about how much obligation you have to save money, which helps your own security, and to invest it back in the future of your country. It's contrary to international agreements for me to urge Americans just to buy American products. But as you go to the store to purchase products or to the automobile showroom to purchase a new car, you ought to think about the consequences of your decision.

When the OPEC oil prices hit us, American manufacturers were still building big, inefficient automobiles, because that's what you wanted. When the price of gasoline jumped up to above a dollar, all of a sudden the American people wanted the smaller, more efficient automobiles. The Germans and Japanese, that have always been paying $2 a gallon for gasoline, they've been making the small cars.

The American manufacturers are now changing to produce exactly those kinds of cars that the American buyers want. They're more durable. You've seen the test on television; they're more safe. And they're just as efficient. So, now Chrysler, Ford, General Motors, American Motors, Volkswagen in America, they're producing the cars that Americans want.

So, you might think about the advantage in holding down inflation to buying American products when the competitive relationship between two cameras or two automobiles is about the same, to give the advantage to your neighbors who work and manufacture those products in our own country. Those are a few things that I think are important.

Good question. I might point out that one of the advantages of a town meeting like this is that it's impossible for me to answer a question like that in a debate, when you've got 2 minutes. But I think it's good for the American news media and for audiences like you to understand some of the elements involved in the inflationary picture. And there are some things we can do. It's not a hopeless case, if we all work together, if we understand it, and if we're persistent and don't give up.

Yes.

EMPLOYMENT AND TRAINING PROGRAMS

Q. President Carter, my name is Frankie Mae Getu. I'm executive director of the Welfare Rights Organization of Allegheny County and committeewoman in the 16th ward, the 15th district. And I'd like to congratulate you on your debate last night. You were great.

THE PRESIDENT. Thank you.

Q. I have a request I'd like to ask you before I go on to my questioning. I see every time there's a problem or a crisis in the country that you invite men from across the country, black, white, indifferent, but you never invite any women.

THE PRESIDENT. Oh, now, that's not true, Frankie Mae.

Q. Well, you haven't invited any poor women.

THE PRESIDENT. I haven't invited you yet, but I'll invite you next time. Maybe that would help. [*Laughter*] Go ahead, Frankie Mae.

Q. When I see the cameras, I see all men. So, I'm an advocate of the ERA, and so, I would like to put that in.

THE PRESIDENT. Well, thank you. Maybe it's because too many of the cameramen are men. [*Laughter*]

Q. Maybe so.

THE PRESIDENT. But go ahead.

Q. My question is—CETA has helped a lot of people get jobs, but in my area over 80 percent of people are on some kind of dole—welfare, SSI, or whatever. When I send young men and young women down to the CETA office, the guidelines, they tell me, are very hard. I would like those guidelines simplified, and I'd like to see Pennsylvania get more PSE jobs for people to go to work.

Another question I have—I have two questions.

THE PRESIDENT. All right.

Q. One's concerning public housing. We have a great executive director here named Danny Petrogelli, but he can only

do so much. And we heard there were cutbacks, you know, for money. Projects have virtually become slums. We would like a little bit more money allocated to Pennsylvania, you know, to clean our projects up.

Thank you.

THE PRESIDENT. Thank you, Frankie Mae.

It would be helpful to me—I see that you are the kind of person who is concerned about those you serve and, also, you know how well the Government services get delivered in the neighborhood. So, I'll ask one of my staff members to get your name and address. Next time we have a meeting on housing or on CETA, I'll make sure you come and participate. I'm sure you'll be speaking out just like you did this morning.

Q. I'll be waiting.

THE PRESIDENT. All right.

Q. Also, there's a young lady. I'd like to divide my time. I'm used to trying to do this. Miss Ross, she said no one was here representing the senior citizen. I would like to spare some of my time to her.

THE PRESIDENT. Well, I think this is the last question we'll have a chance to answer, because our hour is up. But the first question I got, you remember, was about senior citizens, so I think her question may have been covered. But let me respond briefly to those two.

We tried to administer the CETA program in a fair and objective way. At first, when the CETA program was put into effect, there were some abuses. I don't know what happened in Pittsburgh; I don't remember. So far as I know, it was okay. But in some cities around the country, the local officials took advantage of the CETA program and put people on CETA that should not have been there.

Also, they used CETA workers to replace regular workers who should have been full-time employed and were supporting a family.

So, because of that we did, in our new CETA legislation, propose a few restrictions that weren't there before, and I have to tell you that over my objection the Congress added some additional restrictions on CETA jobs, because of a reaction against some abuses that had taken place in some highly publicized occasions around the country.

So, even though it takes a little more time, I believe that in general the CETA program is better administered now, and the abuses have been eliminated, and the jobs go where they deserve to go.

Q. No, they're not. That's why I'm here, because you say put welfare recipients to work. I represent welfare recipients in western Pennsylvania. I've sent kids down there; there are four and five applications. Now, if you want us to work, give us the jobs, you know. And that way, we can get skills and go out into the private sector. That is why I brought the question up.

THE PRESIDENT. There's a limit to what you can do with Government jobs.

Q. But we're not getting them to do anything with, President——

THE PRESIDENT. Yes, but let me say this. I'm glad you brought it up, and I'm glad you're persistent. But what we've tried to do, and I maybe look at it different from you, Frankie Mae, as a basic philosophy—I think the best jobs are the permanent jobs that the young people can have for a full-time life's career and not just a temporary job under the CETA program, except as a transition phase. So, we're not putting all our eggs in the CETA basket.

Q. I understand that.

THE PRESIDENT. Now, I believe I can make you and me both happy with this next statement. We've been deeply concerned about job opportunities for young people, the very ones that you mentioned. I noticed that in Pennsylvania, even though we have had serious economic setbacks because of the OPEC price increases and a brief recession, today there are 338,000 more people at work in this State than there were the day I was inaugurated as President. And in the Pittsburgh metropolitan area we've increased employment by almost 74,000. So, more people are in full-time jobs than there were 3½ years ago—still have a long way to go.

We have now gotten through the House of Representatives in Washington, ready to be voted on in the Senate, a major new program, the only major domestic program I've put forward this year, and that is for youth employment. It will add about a $2-billion commitment for young people at the junior and senior high school years on up. It will provide jobs in the private sector.

It also ties the Labor Department and the Education Department together so that if a young man or woman is offered a job at a local grocery store or a Coca-Cola company or an automobile dealership and they don't quite know how to hold a job because they can't read and write quite well enough or they don't know how to add or subtract, then the local school system will work with that employer and say, "These are the things that this young person needs to do to hold a job permanent."

During the first few weeks when that young person is on the job, the Government will pay part of the salary, and as that young person is able to do the full-time work, then the employer takes over the full-time salary. We're talking about $2 billion, which is a lot of money, and we're talking about 600,000 jobs, just for young people of the kind that you are concerned about. That's part of it.

Additionally, with our revitalization program that I talked about earlier to build new planes and new factories and so forth, we anticipate an increase, just next year alone, of 500,000 more jobs and by the end of the following year a total of a million new jobs. That's above and beyond what we have been discussing before.

So, the chance for us to revitalize American industry and to concentrate on youth employment, particularly disadvantaged youth that have been excluded, because of discrimination, from opportunities in the past, I think are compatible with what you want and what I want. So, we're making some progress.

And I predict to you that after this election is over next Tuesday and the Congress comes back into session that the youth act is one of the bills that they will indeed pass, and we'll have that law on the books and the money appropriated for it this year.

Thank you.

Q. Thank you, President Carter. I'll see you in the White House in '81.

THE PRESIDENT. Right on.

I can take one more question.

HANDICAPPED VENDORS AT FEDERAL FACILITIES

Q. Mr. President, I'm Bob Redman from Dormon, suburban Pittsburgh, and it is my pleasure to welcome you, among the many thousands who could not make it here. The one comment my wife made was, when the phone rang, "Doesn't it pay to live nice?"

A comment and/or question: As a political liaison representative of the blind vendors at the time, I wrote a letter to Joseph Califano opening a law which is now Randolph-Shepherd. All right? My question is this: On Federal properties now, every landlord seems to interpret the law to suit himself. What can you do about that?

THE PRESIDENT. Your name is Mr. Redman, right?

Q. Yes, Bob.

THE PRESIDENT. Right. Well, my hope is that the special programs that we've put into effect for disadvantaged people—I presume you are blind. Correct?

Q. That is correct. Partially.

THE PRESIDENT. Partially blind—have been an improvement. The new disability act has been implemented, and under Joe Califano and Pat Harris, the Department of Health and Human Services is now giving much more attention to the problems of the disadvantaged than before.

If there are specific cases where a landlord is not complying with the new regulations and the new law, if that violation is made known to me or to Secretary Pat Harris, then we will move immediately to enforce the law. But without knowing the specific case, it would be difficult for me to give you an adequate response.

VIEWS ON THE PRESIDENCY

Q. One more short one, if I might.

THE PRESIDENT. All right, sir.

Q. In conjunction with the office that you maintain, executively speaking, as opposite from House and Senate which is elected, what can we do whereby to help yourself and future Presidents forthwith to regain the ability and/or powers that they had in the days of Harry Truman?

THE PRESIDENT. Well, I think it's probably a mistaken idea that the relationship between the Congress and the President has changed very much. The President's powers are limited by the Constitution and haven't been changed appreciably. The President is strengthened in his influence to the extent that citizens participate in making judgments. The President is a person who has to cut through the influence of lobbyists and powerful persons on Capitol Hill in the shaping of legislation.

Q. How well I know.

THE PRESIDENT. The President is the only person that can reach the attention and the comprehension of the public, because, as you say, it's a bully pulpit. So, I think that the degree to which private citizens participate in the shaping of laws, the protection of rights, the progress of our Nation, in that way a President's hand can be strengthened. Also, through this kind of meeting, through press conferences, and, I think, through the electoral process now going on, a President's hands can be strengthened.

The only restraint that I know about—two restraints, that have been a result of Vietnam and Watergate, is more openness in government, and I approve of that very strongly, and a role that Congress can play in the prevention of an unwarranted involvement in war, and I don't disapprove of that either.

So, I think with those two exceptions, the balance between the President and the Congress is roughly the same as it has been down in history. As a completely unprejudiced observer, I think the President needs a little more power. [*Laughter*]

And if you would give me that support and involvement, I think we'll get it.

Q. Thank you.

THE PRESIDENT. Thank you, sir.

Let me say one other thing. Let me make one other brief comment in closing. I think you all see from the questions that I received the breadth of interest that the American people have in the job of a President and how beneficial it is for me to come and share these experiences with you.

We had a problem with social security and the benefits of the aged, a hope that we could stay out of war, a question about the Moral Majority and about nuclear arms control, about terrorists having atomic bombs, about the age of candidates, about Agent Orange, about Government regulations as they relate to the environment, about specialty steel and what we could do to eliminate any possible loopholes, about how to control inflation, about jobs for young people, housing programs for the deprived or low-income families, and about blind vendors from a blind American who has a special interest in the problem, and the relationship between a President and the Congress. These are the kinds of issues and kinds of questions that are important to me.

We tend, I think, to underestimate what we've got. I don't look on this Presidential election or the debate last night as an onerous chore. It's an opportunity for Americans to stop and to inventory where we are, what God's given us, what have we done with it, what is our future, how severe are our inconveniences, how able are we to deal with challenges and answer questions and overcome obstacles.

If you think back, just in my lifetime, you know, I've seen a Great Depression. I grew up in it on a farm in Georgia. And I've seen the Second World War and the Korean war and the divisiveness of the Vietnam war. And I've seen the shock to the Southland and to the Nation when we changed our whole social pattern and gave blacks and other minorities full citizenship rights. It shook our country. And I've seen the embarrassment of Watergate and other challenges that have confronted the American people. And I might say that all of those I named are worse than anything we face now.

Sure, I agree with you that inflation is too high, unemployment is too high. Sure, I agree with you that there are troubled areas around the world. But our Nation is strong, able, united, at peace, dynamic, aggressive, innovative, free. This country has never had a question that it couldn't answer, and we have never had a problem we couldn't solve, we've never had an obstacle we couldn't overcome, if we were united in our commitment.

We're a nation of diversity, different families, different ethnic backgrounds, different religious beliefs, different commitments, different interests, but we weld ourselves together in a cohesive nation of great strength and great promise and great purpose. And the principles that I outlined that existed among your ancestors 300 years ago haven't changed—religious freedom, proper respect one for another, worth of a human being, no matter how low their income might be or what their status in life might be, socially speaking, opportunities to improve, children a better life than their parents, good stewards over the earth and land and water that God gave us.

Those are the kinds of things that have always been important to Americans. They're still important to us. And I predict to you that the greatest nation on Earth, which God's given us, will be even greater in the future.

Thank you very much.

NOTE: The President spoke at 11:02 a.m. at Trinity Episcopal Cathedral.

Pittsburgh, Pennsylvania

Remarks to Area Residents.
October 29, 1980

Good morning, everybody. I've come back to Pittsburgh, the city of champions, to remind all of you that we have less than a week to go before you make a judgment and cast a vote that will shape the future of this country.

I know that many of you observed the debate last night, when the issues between me and Governor Reagan, between the Democratic Party and the Republican Party, were sharply drawn. There's hardly a person in this great audience that can't remember how your lives were benefited under the administrations of great Democratic Presidents of the past. President Truman, President Roosevelt, President Kennedy, President Johnson have all taken action, working with Democratic Members of the Congress, to give better lives to the aged, for those who are afflicted and disabled, for those who are deprived of basic rights, and for the working people of this Nation. They've also been very eager and have always been successful in giving us a better chance for jobs and for progress and for peace.

I ask you this next week not to forget your heritage, not to forget the past differences between Republicans and Democrats, to join with me as full partners, so on November the 4th, we'll whip the Republicans from the courthouse all the way to the White House. I need you, and I'll be depending on you.

Thank you, and God bless you.

NOTE: The President spoke at 12:25 p.m. outside Trinity Episcopal Cathedral.

As printed above, the item follows the text of the White House press release.

Rochester, New York

Remarks at a Rally With Area Residents. October 29, 1980

Governor Hugh Carey, Mayor Tom Ryan, Mayor Jim Griffin, County Chairman Larry Kirwin, my good friends from northern and eastern New York:

How many of you believe we're going to whip the Republicans next Tuesday? [*Applause*]

I've come here to form with you a partnership during these next few days to give the Democrats a tremendous victory, which this Nation needs and which our people earned. There are a lot of cities that I could have been visiting today during these last few moments before the election, but I said to myself, "I would rather be in Rochester." You voted for me in 1976. You voted for me this year in the primary, and I want you to keep up that great tradition on November the 4th, okay? [*Applause*]

I'm glad to come here to John F. Kennedy Square, with a sculpture built in his memory, because it's important during these last few days before a great election when you, in the solitude of the voting place, will decide the future of our country, to remind yourselves and each other of the great tradition of the Democratic Party, which has meant so much to this country. We are a party of builders; we are a party of partnership. We're a party which believes in the future of this Nation and never doubts it. We're a party that believes in unity; we're a party that believes in strength; and we are a party that has proven that we believe and can maintain peace in this country and around the world.

As I'm sure you all know from watching the debate last night, that the choice next Tuesday is not just between me and Governor Reagan, it's not just between the Democratic Party and the Republican Party; it's a choice between two vastly different concepts or beliefs concerning what this Nation must be. It's a choice between two vastly different futures for America. The meaning of that choice is not just in what he and I say but in the consequences of our words, the consequences of what we believe, the consequences of what we will do. The choice is crucial, and the consequences to your life, to the lives of the members of your family, and to those that you love, are very grave.

The President of the United States is not just a servant of the present, he's also the guardian of the future. His actions echo down through the ages in the judges he appoints, the regulatory board members he names, the legislation he gets passed through Congress, the ideals established in the hearts and minds of the American people, and the agenda which he sets for the Nation's future. When he sits as one negotiator at the head of state with other national leaders from around the world, he must be careful, because his words weigh heavily on the hearts and minds of people everywhere. He represents what this Nation is and what this Nation can be. He must be sensitive to the concerns and the ideals of America, and he must be adamant in his protection of America's interests.

Never does a day go by, in my duties in the Oval Office, when there is not some serious trouble somewhere on Earth. A President must decide, sometimes alone, what are America's interests, what degree of involvement should be our role. As Commander in Chief, the President of this country has within his power to unleash the most awesome, destructive military force in the history of the world. If he is skillful, if he is wise, if he is thoughtful, if he is moderate, if he is careful, if he is courageous, if he remembers America's beliefs and character, it's a task which I pray God will never have to be performed. We must not get ourselves in a situation where the horrible power of atomic weaponry is unleashed on this world.

As President I have had to make some difficult decisions, thousands of them, and as I said last night, with each one of those decisions, I learn. I learn about this Nation, its strengths, its needs. I learn about our people and the possibilities for an improved life for them. I expect to make many more decisions. I've fought some bitter fights, as you know, against special interests. I carry some political scars because of those fights, and I carry those scars with pride. I've made some mistakes, and I've taken the heat for them, and I've learned from them. And because I have learned I'm a better President now, and I'll be a better President in the next 4 years.

A President in these modern times must have patience. A President in these modern times must have compassion. When the toughest decisions are made, a President cannot rely upon advisers, because the most difficult decisions will often find advisers divided 50–50 on both sides of an issue. He cannot rely on ideology, and he cannot rely on maxims or sayings or memories from the distant past. He must have sound judgment to act, when necessary, alone, and that's why this campaign must focus on the real issues and their consequences for the future for every human being on Earth.

We have got serious problems these days, problems that involve economics, but the outlook is improving, as you well know. The shocks that hit this Nation in 1974 because of OPEC oil price increases caused the deepest recession since the Second World War. We've just been through the smallest and the shortest recession, because we had planned for this eventuality. In 1979 oil price increases were greater in one year than they had been since oil was first discovered in the 1800's. The inflation rate has been high lately, yes—earlier in this year, 18 percent, and then later, the second quarter, 13 percent; the most recent quarter just ended, 7 percent. Inflation is still too high, but I'd like to remind you that in the past when our Nation has been tested we have never failed the test.

Just in my lifetime I remember the Great Depression. I remember the Second World War, the Korean war. I remember the social changes that took place in our Nation, very difficult changes, when we gave equality of opportunity and voting rights to our black citizens and others. And I remember the divisiveness of the Vietnam war, the tragedy and the embarrassment of Watergate. All those problems that I've just named were much greater in scope than anything we face today. But when our Nation is united, when we analyze our blessings, when we remember what God gave us, this Nation has never failed to answer any questions. This Nation has never failed to solve any problems, and this Nation has never failed to overcome any obstacle, no matter how great it might be. We've got a great nation, the greatest on Earth, and in my belief, we'll have a greater nation in the future.

Let me comment on just one other specific thing that was covered really for the first time in the debate last night. It involved the most important issue of all— lifting the shadow of nuclear terror from this Earth. Last night Mr. Reagan flatly denied that he had ever made the statement that nuclear proliferation is none of our business. Let me read you something verbatim from the New York Times of February 1st this year, and I quote, "Ronald Reagan indicated today that he believed the United States should not stand in the way of countries developing their own nuclear weapons, saying, and we quote Mr. Reagan, 'I just don't think it's any of our business.' "

This issue is the most important single issue in the campaign this year. Inflation is important. Unemployment is important. The progress of our Nation economically is important. Education is important. But the most important single issue is the control of nuclear weapons. Every President since Harry Truman has worked under the most difficult circumstances to negotiate with the Soviet Union balanced, controlled, observable agreements to limit atomic weapons with the hope of reducing those weapons in the future.

The treaty that I have negotiated was begun by President Nixon and continued by President Ford. It's now before the Senate. It's not yet come to the floor for a debate or a vote. Governor Reagan has said, let's throw that treaty in the trash and not let the Senate debate this important issue. Let's put forward a nuclear arms race and demand nuclear superior-

ity in hopes that we can get some better deal from the Soviet Union.

This approach of his is a radical departure from the most serious commitment that all my predecessors in the Oval Office have had since the Second World War. And combined with his belief that it's none of our business if a radical and terrorist nation like Libya has the atomic weapon, this particular issue on nuclear arms, nuclear weapons, atomic bombs, is the most serious of all.

In closing let me say this: I've described the election of 1980 to you as a choice between two futures. Here's what I see in the future that we are fighting for together. I see a nation strong and at peace. I see a nation secure in the pursuit of progress for all people; a nation where everyone can have the dignity of a decent job, where new industries create a new generation of American buildings and American vehicles that will house us and move us in comfort with a lot less energy, and that energy that we use coming from America itself; a nation where children are educated to their maximum potential, where the elderly are treated with respect, which they've earned, where families are strong and intact and secure. I have a vision of a nation free enough to attract and strong enough to welcome the deprived from other parts of the world, a nation of liberty and justice and love.

I need your help to make this vision a reality. Together let us make the greatest nation on Earth even greater in the future. You help me and we will do that together.

Thank you very much. God bless you all.

NOTE: The President spoke at 3:35 p.m. at John F. Kennedy Square.

Newark, New Jersey

*Remarks to Local Ministers and
Community Leaders.   October 29, 1980*

Thank you, Governor Byrne.

Senator Bradley, Congressman Rodino, Congressman Minish, Mayor Kenneth Gibson, Dr. Scott, my good friend Reverend Howard Woodson, brothers and sisters:

I've always known I had the little people of the Nation with me, but it's real good also to have one of the really big people of this country with me and that's Rosie Grier. [*Laughter*] And I'm not talking about just physical size. I'm talking about heart. I'm talking about soul. And it's good to be in a town run by a long-distance runner.

It's good to be in a church that's in a beautiful new building, but it's one of the oldest places to worship God in this country and one of the oldest communities in this Nation, filled not only with political leaders, mayor of East Orange and other great cities, but also filled with ministers of the Gospel, who bear so much of the responsibilities on your shoulders to decide the outcome of elections, to decide the daily and weekly lives of your people, to hold people to their true beliefs that never change, the best instincts that sometimes have to resist temptation with your help, of sustaining people in times of need, of giving guidance, not only to those who are poor or meek or black or who don't speak English well but also giving guidance to those who lead who might forget those who are poor or black or who don't speak English well. And I don't know any other group in this Nation that has done such a good job during the last years in which I've lived, in the last 30 or 40 years, than the black ministers of this Nation, who have kept in the forefront of what our Nation stands for.

The civil rights movement changed the South, it changed this Nation, and after we got to the point of having people like Andrew Young and Don McHenry speak for our Nation, it's changed the image of this country in the eyes of the entire world. And a lot of that credit goes to people like you throughout this Nation, the black ministers of America, and I thank you for it. And I might say also that our Nation has also got to keep its eyes upward and forward.

Sometimes we stumble. Sometimes we go through disappointments, trials, tribulations. Sometimes we have temporary inconveniences. Sometimes we have frustrations. Sometimes things don't move as fast as we'd like for them to move. And it takes an inner spirit and an inner faith and an inner commitment and some deep, personal courage to retain leadership in times like that. I think that Howard Woodson is a man of that kind.

Not too long ago he was in the White House with me. He flew back with us on Air Force One to Philadelphia. He's been an adviser for me not only in a spiritual way but also when he was Speaker, now working with the Governor. And many of you, like him, have kept a proper balance between a deep religious faith, the service of those who look to you for leadership, and a direct involvement in politics, particularly when election day approaches. And that is one reason that I came tonight—to talk to you about that.

Newark, Essex County represent the kind of challenges that I share as President of this country, serving in the Oval Office, looking at its hopes and its potentials, its needs and its problems, because many of the programs that my administration has initiated has been targeted to the needs of this very city and other cities in this county.

Newark, for instance, has received the second highest number of Urban Development Action Grants, UDAG grants, of any city in this Nation, regardless of size. Essex County has received the single largest grant in the country under my new urban parks program, and Essex is second only to Cook County, where Chicago's located, in the total urban parks funding. But I know and you know that we ought not to stand here and brag on what has been done. Let's look to the future about what we're going to do together. And I want to make a personal pledge—not under any pressure, because nobody asked me to to do it—to enter into a new and a full and a greater partnership with the city of Newark, with the county of Essex, with the State of New Jersey, so that we can make a real difference here in the years ahead.

Ken Gibson, Brendan Byrne, representatives of the private sector, officials such as Peter Shapiro, Peter Rodino, Joe Minish, who are here, Senator Bradley, and others are working together in a constructive way in this city. And they've come to me with a coordinated plan, a concept whereby the Federal Government, the State government, the local government, the private employers, and the people who work here spell out for this community a much better and a brighter life. I'm not going to list for you all the different projects and programs that are already underway, but if you think back 4 years ago when Brendan Byrne was beginning to change the concept of New Jersey about itself and build a new sense of pride and partnership and progress

and idealism and confidence, I'm very proud to have been part of that change.

I want this group to come to Washington after the election and work, to meet to see what we can do in the future as an even stronger team, because I see a determination here on the part of the mayor and the Governor and others, and I'm determined that my administration will be a genuine part of this effort.

The other things at stake in this election, in addition to a better life, better jobs, more employment, less suffering, better education, better housing, better transportation, better cohesion among people who are different from one another, better understanding, better progress, more equality—these kinds of things are part of our national consciousness. But also at stake in this election is whether we'll continue to build social justice in our country. It's clear that there's a sharp difference between the longstanding, historical commitment of the Democratic Party, on the one hand, and the very sharp, differing commitment or lack of commitment in the Republican Party.

All you've got to do is sit here in the quietness of this sanctuary and think about the changes that took place under Franklin Roosevelt and Harry Truman and John Fitzgerald Kennedy and Lyndon Johnson. And I think the last 3½ years is part of that Democratic mainstream of progress and compassion and concern and good management. And I think about the other times when Democrats were not in the White House and what the cause of the outcome of those elections was. I'll mention that in a few minutes.

But I think you know that Democrats and I stand for vigorous enforcement of our civil rights laws; for open housing amendments to make sure that we do not have any longer discrimination in where people have a right to live; for the equal rights amendment, to give women a chance for equality under the Constitution of the United States; for national health insurance; for the strengthening of social security; for the preservation of minimum wage to apply equally to all people; for aid to cities, where the central part of the cities might have been deteriorating in the past; for aid to our public schools; for the youth bill that will give 600,000 new young people jobs at a cost of $2 billion over the next 2 years; for tough standards of quality for environment; and for strong protection for consumers of all kinds. That's what I stand for. That's what the Democratic Party stands for. But my opponent's positions are just as clear, and they could not be more different from mine.

I didn't come here tonight to spend my time criticizing him. But I think it's important to remember that 16 years ago, he launched his political career, contrary to some of the comments that he made last night, as a spokesman for the American Medical Association and the anti-Medicare lobby. He campaigned all over this Nation trying to kill Medicare. And he has called repeatedly for making social security a voluntary program. Last night he stated—I don't know if you noticed it—that for a young person to contribute to social security is a bad investment. That's not true, and that's typical of what he has been saying over many years. It's an outstanding investment, no matter what the level of income of an American citizen might be.

Today he says, and I quote him, "I am firmly opposed to national health insur-

ance." What we want is a health insurance program that will have an emphasis on prevention of disease, an emphasis on treating of patients outside the hospital whenever possible instead of inside the hospital, a commitment to controlling hospital costs so they don't go up so high that people can't afford them, an emphasis on medical care and proper diet for women who are about to have little babies and for those little babies once they are born, for catastrophic health insurance to make sure that a family doesn't get wiped out economically with an unexpectedly high medical bill. Those commitments, as part of this program, will be an·extension of social security, an extension of Medicare, and will give the American people better health care at a much reduced cost.

Fifteen years ago he said that the Civil Rights Act was, and I quote, "a bad piece of legislation." And this year he says, and I quote him again, "Urban aid programs are one of the biggest phonies that we have in the system." This year, as you know, he blamed pollution on trees and volcanoes, and then after taking three or four different positions in the same day, he flew home to Los Angeles to rest. And as you know, his plane couldn't land at the airport, because the smog was too thick. [*Laughter*]

Well, the pattern that I've just outlined—a few examples shows the difference. The choice on November the 4th is not just between me and Governor Reagan, it's not just between the Democratic Party and the Republican Party. The choice is between two clear beliefs about what America is, two clear commitments, sharp, different, about what America ought to be, two vastly different futures for our country. And as the time for the election approaches next Tuesday, it's important on every one of you as a leader in your own right, who can reach a thousand or perhaps 10,000 people between now and election day to think about how this difference might affect you personally, the members of your own family, the people that you love, or the people who love you.

The consequences of what Governor Reagan believes, what he says, what he will do in the Oval Office is what makes the choice so crucial. Governor Reagan said last night in the debate that when he was young, and I quote, "This country didn't even know it had a racial problem."

AUDIENCE MEMBER. He had to be real young. [*Laughter*]

THE PRESIDENT. Well, Governor Reagan may not have known, but to millions and millions of Americans, including some in this congregation, who suffered racial prejudice and racial injustice for 300 years, it was not simply a problem; it was a lifelong disaster.

I don't know what you're going to do the next 5 days. It may be that you'll go back to your home or to your church and say, "I went to a rally at Bethany Baptist, and I think I've done enough because my presence there added esteem or prestige to the congregation." And you might say, "I'm sure the rest of those ministers and the rest of those public officials are going to take care of the election. And if they work hard, New Jersey will be in the Democratic column, so I don't need to do very much." Or it may be that you'll say, "This is the most important decision that's been made politically in my lifetime, and what I do might make the difference between who is elected President, who will serve the next 8 years or perhaps the rest of this century, which party will be in power in the Oval Office."

I believe in the Democratic Party myself. I believe in the legacy that I've inherited from the Presidents that have served there before me. I believe in the mission of the Democratic Party. Every great advance that's taken place in this country in this century that has affected your lives, from collective bargaining to the minimum wage, to social security, to Medicare, to Medicaid, to civil rights legislation—every single one of those has been made possible by Democrats, almost invariably over the opposition of Republicans.

Our party stands for progress. Our party stands for justice. When workers sought to organize, they looked to the Democrats. When older citizens said they needed security in their retirement years, they called on the Democrats. When Americans wanted justice and opportunity and basic rights, they turned to the Democrats and the Democrats always came through.

Today Americans are once again looking for the Democrats, not in the past, not even in the present, but in the years ahead, for national health insurance, for jobs and training for our young people, for a strong, new economic future, for human rights and equal rights. And with your help the Democrats are going to come through on November the 4th, and we're going to whip the Republicans again in New Jersey.

You might say one person can't make a difference. I want to repeat something I said last night, because I would like for you to carry it away in your mind and in your heart. One person can make a difference. In 1960 if 28,000 people had voted different in Texas and just a few thousand had voted differently in Illinois, John Kennedy would never have been

President; likely, Lyndon Johnson would never have been Vice President or President. The Voting Rights Act, the Civil Rights Act, would never have come into being in this law of the land, and our country would have been a different land, for you and for your families. That's a story with a good ending.

In 1968, if just a few more Democrats had done our duty, things would have been different. Who put Richard Nixon in the Oval Office in January of '69? It was not the Republicans, because they are supposed to and they're expected to vote for their nominee. The people that put Richard Nixon in the Oval Office instead of Hubert Humphrey were the Democrats, not the ones who voted, but the ones who didn't vote and didn't work.

You remember that year, and Rosie Grier remembers vividly the personal tragedies of that year. The election returns were one of those personal tragedies, but I remember that Senator Robert Kennedy made a speech on the last day of what was to be his final campaign, in the Presidential primary in California, in 1968. And I would like to share with you, to close my remarks, the closing lines of that speech that you can carry away from here in your hearts, and I quote Robert Kennedy. He said, "I ask you to recognize the hard and difficult road ahead to a better America, and I ask you to vote for yourselves. The people," he said, "must decide this election, and they must decide so that no leader in America has any doubt about what the people want. For your sake and for your children," he said, "vote for yourselves."

You devote your time and your talents and every last measure of your strength to show them that you as children of God, as leaders who are trusted, who are put here for a purpose, that each one of you has a precious life to contribute to the service of others. Every Sunday morning you preach to those who will listen. Every one of those people who listen to you counts, and it matters to you and to all of us if they're weak or if they're strong, if they're blessed or if they suffer. But it's in our hands about what kind of life they will have on this Earth in the future.

I need you to be my partners in this next 5 days, to make an effort, above and beyond what you intended to make when you came here. It's not enough to just be a Democrat. It's not enough just to have a good voting record. It's not enough just to preach a sermon on Sunday outlining the differences that will be decided on Tuesday. I'd like to ask you to leave here with the commitment in your heart and mind to do everything you possibly can to make sure that every single registered person votes on November the 4th. And if you do, we'll have a better life in this Nation; we'll continue the progress that you've seen under Democratic Presidents. And we'll have a nation not only great, as we've seen it already, but even greater in the years ahead. That's what I want from you.

Will you do it for me? [*Applause*]

NOTE: The President spoke at 7:01 p.m. in the sanctuary of Bethany Baptist Church.

Newark, New Jersey

Remarks at the Essex County Democratic Committee Gala Dinner. October 29, 1980

Chairman Ray Durkin, County Executive Peter Shapiro, Senator Bradley, Congressman Rodino, Joe Minish and Mrs. Minish, Bob Roe, Mr. Speaker, Governor Brendan Byrne:

It's a shame for me to come here and interfere with the thing that all politicians like most of all, and that is to have his home folks give a testimonial banquet to him before the funeral services are called. Brendan, alive and well, knows how much you think of him. And I know that although his relationships have not always been perfectly harmonious with Essex County, this was your chance to show what you think of one of the greatest Governors that this Nation has ever seen. I'm glad to be part of it.

Lately Brendan has had so much experience introducing me that he's got it down to kind of like playing a tape. He just punches a button and out it comes. And I hope to give his successor just as many opportunities to practice the same speech in the next 4 years.

Today I started off in Cleveland. I was in Cleveland last night. [*Laughter*] I went to Pittsburgh for several events and then to Rochester for rallies and then to Newark and now here with you. I go from here to Philadelphia. It's been a long day. I particularly wanted to be in Essex County, because I remembered what happened in 1960, when the Essex County votes put John Fitzgerald Kennedy in the White House. And I came to ask you to do the same thing for me in 1980.

When Democrats go into Governors' offices and when Democrats go into the White House following a Republican administration, we have a lot of extra hard work to do. I tried to think of a story to illustrate the point. The only one I could think of was one I'm sure you've heard a lot of times before, because it's one of my favorites. It's about an old man who was arrested and taken before the judge for being drunk and setting a bed on fire. And he said, "Judge, I plead guilty to being drunk, but the bed was on fire when I got in it." [*Laughter*] Well, the same thing happens to Democrats who go into office following a long Republican administration. And I think tonight in the next 8 or 10 minutes that I'll spend with you, it would be incumbent on me as a Democratic President to remind you of the differences that have been made in your own lives, in my life, in the lives of people that you love and who look to you for leadership by the Democratic Party.

Last night was a good and sharp debate which drew distinctions which perhaps had not been recognized adequately between me and Governor Reagan. But this campaign is not just one between two men. It is not just one between two parties, as a matter of fact; it's between two futures, two commitments, two ideals, two concepts of what this Nation is.

But tonight I want to look back just a few minutes at my own life as a young farmboy in the south Georgia area, small town—and perhaps the same changes took place in your life if you have the same age roughly as mine. I remember the Great Depression when I grew up— I was born in 1924—and the fact that people then had no hope for the future. We had suffered under a Republican administration, Herbert Hoover. Hoover wasn't a bad man, but he represented what the Republican Party was then and what the Republican still is. That's a fact. It hasn't changed in the last 50 or more years.

Franklin Roosevelt came into the office bringing a message of hope—not just to bring order out of chaos in our Nation's banking system and our esteem for one another and to eliminate the fear of fear, but he also had a compassion for people, along with a good administrative capability in the White House in Washington. He was a cripple. He understood what it meant to overcome disability. And he looked on the farmers throughout this country who didn't have electricity and who had to work from 4 o'clock in the morning until dark, and then come in from the field and hand-pump water for livestock. He proposed the REA. The Democrats supported him. The Republicans were against it.

Roosevelt was a rich man from a wealthy family with influence. But he saw the little children working in the sweatshops, and he saw grown men and women being paid wages that wouldn't give their loved ones adequate food or shelter or clothing, and certainly no chance for advancement in life. And he put forward the radical concept of a minimum wage, 25 cents an hour. The Republicans called it socialism, communism. How could the Government possibly interfere in the private enterprise system and pay a grown man or a woman 25 cents an hour? The Democrats prevailed. I finished high school in 1941. I got my first job at a minimum wage—10 hours a day, 40 cents an hour. That radical increase from 25 cents to 40 cents was put through the Congress by the Democrats. The Republicans, of course, opposed it.

When I grew up, once people got to a senior year in life, if they didn't have a family to support them, they went to what we call the po' folks farm—no security, deprivation, no self-respect. Franklin Roosevelt put forward the idea of social security. Republicans opposed it, predictably, but it went into effect, and the program has been expanded since then to give a better life for senior citizens who finance through their own contributions at work, insurance for their senior years. Every single advance has been opposed by the Republican Party. It is not an accident. These kinds of concepts for the poor, the working families, the deprived, the aged, are still the commitments of our party.

As a young man in the South, having served 11 years in the Navy, I went back home. I served on the local school board. And it took me a while to realize that the white children were riding to school in buses and the black children were walking. It took me a while to realize that the only books that the black kids had in school were the ones that the white kids had already worn out and discarded. We had, then, under our law, separate but equal ruling by the Supreme Court. The Democrats in the White House, that you helped to elect, thought that after 300 years it was time for our Nation to provide equality of opportunity and an end to official deprivation and discrimination. It was a radical change that swept my part of the country, and it made it possible for a man like me, ultimately, following along behind Martin Luther King, Jr., and others, to be considered as President of our country. We had not had a President from the Deep South since 1844.

But it opened up a time for us to see ourselves as human beings, yes, but to see our neighbors as human beings with equal rights—a radical departure from what had been accepted in our great Nation; a radical departure proposed by Democrats, John Kennedy, Lyndon Johnson, in the mainstream of our party, to transform the lives of people for the better.

Governor Reagan said at the time that the civil rights laws were bad legislation. Democrats wanted older people to have better health care and put forward Medicare. Governor Reagan worked full time as an employee or a lobbyist for the American Medical Association, going around this country pointing out that Medicare was a radical proposal involving socialistic tendencies and the intrusion of the Federal Government into the private affairs of patients and their doctors.

Several times in recent years he's advocated that social security ought to be voluntary and just last night he said that when a young person invests in social security it's a bad investment. The policies, the attitudes, the concerns of the Democrats toward people have not changed, and these same concerns that have exemplified what the Republican Party has done in bygone years still exist.

When I took over as President, my greatest concern was that for the last 50 years no President had served without our Nation being at war. I saw our Nation's defense in danger, because 7 out of the last 8 years under Republican administrations we had had a decrease in budget commitments for defense, 37-percent decrease in our commitment to a strong defense. We've changed that. The Democrats have changed that, because we realize that only through a strong nation can we keep the peace, and we've kept peace not only for ourselves but for others around the world.

We have worked hard as a strong, leading nation to open up the continent of Africa for the beneficial impact of American principles and ideals and commitments. There are 4 billion people on Earth. A billion of them live in China, and now they are our new friends, and we've doubled our trade with Taiwan in the process.

And we've seen President Sadat and Prime Minister Begin come together with a new peace treaty and the recognition of Israel's right to exist, direct negotiations, open borders, diplomatic recognition, exchange of ambassadors, and now a prospect for Israel to be secure and to be at peace. And we recognize there too that what we've done for Israel, half the total aid that Israel has received in 32 years has come in the last 3½ years as an investment in our Nation's own security, a typical commitment of the Democrats, begun by Harry Truman, who 12 minutes after Israel declared their independence recognized them as an independent nation—a tide and a thrust and a commitment of our party that's a source of pride to me. And which we sometimes tend to forget, there's a sharply differing concept with the Republicans.

I remember in 1973 when Israel was struggling with a major war, the last one, the fourth one in 25 years. There was an official hesitation or reassessment in order to force Israel to take action desired by a Republican President and a Republican Secretary of State, in Washington, completely contrary to what the Democrats have always done and the way we have always felt, because we see that a strong and independent democracy, at peace in the Middle East, is the best thing for our security in that troubled region of the world. And we also see very clearly that to be overly dependent on OPEC Arab oil is a threat to our own Nation's energy security. And we've moved to take action, with the help of your superb congressional delegation, and we now have an energy policy that was hammered out over the most difficult possible circumstances, new, only recently completed, but we already see great benefits.

We are importing now one-third less oil from overseas than we did 1 year ago. And we'll have more oil and gas wells drilled in the United States this year, in 1980, than in any year in history. And we are producing more coal in this country this year than any year in history.

And we believe that we ought to get the Government's nose out of the private enterprise of this country. We've deregulated rail, deregulated trucking, deregulated airlines, deregulated financial institutions, working on communications, to make sure that we have a free enterprise system that's competitive, that's competitive so that the customers get a better deal and the business community gets a better deal as well, completely contrary to the philosophy of and the commitment of and the record of the Republican Party.

And the final point I want to make is this: We're a nation that believes in the use of American strength for the benefit of others, and we're also a nation that represents and recognizes the hunger in the peoples' minds throughout the world for freedom from the threat of nuclear terror. I spent a large part of my time as President continuing the work that was done by my predecessors ever since Truman to have balanced, controlled, observable, confirmable agreements with the Soviet Union to limit and then reduce nuclear arsenals.

The destructive power is beyond the comprehension of the human mind. I described last night what one of our large warheads is, very briefly. It would take a train 2,500 miles long with 50 tons of TNT per car to have the equivalent of one major warhead, 10 megatons, and we've got literally thousands of megatons in this country and in the Soviet Union. And the control of that destruction is the single most important issue in this race, because Governor Reagan, in a radical departure from all past experience of Presidents,

Democratic or Republican, said, "Let's scrap the treaty. Let's play a trump card against the Soviet Union. Let's insist upon superiority, not equality and balance and reduction, and let's not overlook the opportunity of the missing thing and that is a nuclear arms race."

And the threat to the world from terrorism is something that Democrats recognize. Just think what a few pounds of TNT do in Jerusalem on the streets or in Germany in a beer hall when 100 people were killed—a few pounds. Think what a terrorist country like Libya could do with an atomic bomb. And when Governor Reagan was asked about this in New York by the New York Times, as published in the February 1st edition this year, he said, "the control of the spread of nuclear weapons to terrorist organizations or any other country is none of our business"—none of our business.

This is the issue, and I want to remind you of this in this Democratic county at this fundraising event, just a few days before the election, to think on these things. Think about the minimum wage, think about social security, think about energy policy, think about our relationship with our allies and friends around the world, think about strength, think about peace, think about nuclear weapons, think about yourself, your children, your family, the people who know you are a leader and the people whom you lead. Think on those things and decide whether or not this next 5 days you've got the time to invest in the outcome of this election.

I won't see the White House again until after the election. My wife and my boys, my Cabinet, my Vice President, many people around this Nation are working full time. This group in here, if you were dedicated, commensurate with the issues at stake, could spend at least 5 hours a day, not working on your own business or your own law firm, but working to make sure that New Jersey casts its vote on November the 4th in the Democratic column, because the issue is so close—one or two percentage points. The difference is, who is the likely voter, whether or not the Democrats will go to vote.

It wasn't the Republicans who put Richard Nixon in the Oval Office in 1969 in January and kept Hubert Humphrey, one of the great men of all times, from serving as President; it was the Democrats. It was the Democrats who did not vote. It was the Democrats who did not work, because you have to expect the Republicans to support their nominee. Can't blame them. And the Gene McCarthy group who said Hubert Humphrey is not worthy to be our President because he served with Lyndon Johnson cost him the election. But a few more Democrats, working with a deep commitment based on the differences between our parties, recognizing the issues at stake, could have prevented a national tragedy.

I tell you that the differences between me and Ronald Reagan that I have outlined tonight are more deep and more penetrating differences even than those I've outlined to you about basic Democratic and Republican philosophy. And I ask you this next 5 days to make a sacrificial effort, not waiting to see what your neighbors would do, not judging by what you did in 1976, not judging by what other Democrats might expect you to do, but individually, alone, decide what you can do the next 5 days, and exert your maximum effort—because I believe it's worth it to you, to your children, and to those you love, and to those who love you. If you'll help me, we'll win together on November the 4th.

Thank you very much and, God bless you.

NOTE: The President spoke at 8:13 p.m. in the Grand Ballroom at the Robert Treat Hotel.

President's Commission on Executive Exchange

Appointment of Four Members.
October 29, 1980

The President today announced that he will appoint four persons as members of the President's Commission on Executive Exchange. They are:

J. J. SIMMONS III, of Muskogee, Okla., vice president and assistant to the chairman of the board of Amerada Hess Corp. He was with the Interior Department for 9 years, where he served in positions including Administrator of the Oil Import Administration (reappointment).

GERALD M. TABENKEN, of Bangor, Maine, president and chief executive officer of H. Tabenken & Co., a wholesale beer, wine, and beverage distribution firm, and president of the National Beer Wholesalers Association of America.

MAURICE B. TOBIN, a Washington, D.C., attorney who is active in civic affairs, former counsel to the Congressional Committee on Public Works and Transportation.

PHILIP F. ZEIDMAN, a Washington, D.C., attorney who served previously as General Counsel of the Small Business Administration and special assistant to Vice President Hubert H. Humphrey and is Vice Chairman of this Commission (reappointment).

Federal Council on the Aging

Nomination of Six Members.
October 29, 1980

The President has announced his intention to nominate for reappointment four members and nominate two new members to the Federal Council on the Aging to fill expiring terms.

The new members to be nominated are:

JESSE M. UNRUH, State treasurer of California, will be nominated for a term expiring June 5, 1983, vice Dr. Fernando Manuel Torres-Gil.

HERBERT H. SHORE, executive vice president of the Dallas, Tex., Home for Jewish Aged, will be nominated for a term expiring June 5, 1982, vice Walter L. Moffett.

Those to be nominated for reappointment are:

MARY A. MARSHALL, of Virginia, for a term expiring June 5, 1983.

BERNICE L. NEUGARTEN, of Illinois, for a term expiring June 5, 1983.

JAMES T. SYKES, of Wisconsin, for a term expiring June 5, 1983.

WESLEY C. UHLMAN, of Washington, for a term expiring June 5, 1983.

Situation in Iran

White House Statement on Remarks Attributed to the Assistant to the President for Congressional Liaison. October 29, 1980

We have seen the remarks attributed by the Shreveport Journal to Frank Moore, but have not been able to reach Mr. Moore to see whether or not the newspaper report corresponds to comments he actually made.

In the meantime, three points should be noted:

1. Mr. Moore is not a spokesman for the administration on matters relating to Iran;

2. The administration has no information suggesting that the Ayatollah Khomeini is terminally ill; and

3. As a matter of policy, the administration does not speculate on the course of internal developments in Iran.

Philadelphia, Pennsylvania

Remarks to Members of the Polish Community.   October 30, 1980

Thank you, Representative Bill Borski, for your warm introduction. It's an honor for me to be with you. I was informed by my distinguished escorts on the way from the Fairmont Hotel here that I'm the first President who's ever been to Polonia, and it's a great honor for me to come and be with you this morning.

I've had a good time in my visits to Philadelphia lately, meeting with Mayor Bill Green, and having my wife come here, and my son, Chip, come here, and the Vice President come to Philadelphia. It's a wonderful year to congratulate Philadelphia, because you've won it all, I think. The Phillies won the World Series, the Eagles are doing okay. You've won the *Saratoga.* The *Forrestal* is next. It's just a good year all around.

There's one more victory that I want to see you win, not only for Philadelphia but for Pennsylvania and the whole country. Does anybody know what that is? [*Applause and cheers*] Right on. Next November the 4th, next Tuesday, you will make a decision that will affect your own lives, the lives of your families, the life of this Nation.

I also want to thank another guest, Stanley Walesa, who's here with me this morning. As you know, he too is associated very closely with the recent victory, a human victory in Poland for all mankind. I know you are very proud of what his son has accomplished. His commitment to the rights of working people has been and is an inspiration to the entire world.

As you know, the Republican leaders have criticized my commitment on behalf of this Nation to the principle of protecting human rights, not only in our own country but in other nations. This is a deep commitment of mine, but they seem to think it's naive for America to stand up for freedom and to stand up for democracy. I disagree with that very strongly. If we in the land of freedom do not stand up for human rights, then what is it, what is the meaning of America? What should we stand for? What should our commitment be? Just ask the Polish workers who are struggling for human progress. Ask them if America should stand up for human rights.

I come to you today in Philadelphia, the city where our American rights were first ratified. I come to you as a leader of the Democratic Party, a party that has embraced human rights since the time of Thomas Jefferson. I come to ask your support on November 4th, because we share the same values and the same commitments. For almost two centuries the Democratic Party has opened its arms, as you know, to every American of every culture, every background, every religion. When I form the policies of our Nation in international affairs these days, my two closest advisers represent families who came here from Poland, Secretary of State Ed Muskie and National Security Adviser Zbigniew Brzezinski.

It's important that we remind ourselves that ours is a nation of immigrants; we're a nation of refugees. And when every new wave of refugees or immigrants came to this country it was the Democratic Party that opened its arms and its hearts to them, gave them a role to play in shaping

of our country and in the hammering out for all Americans strength, but the preservation of those precious, individualistic commitments of religion and family and heritage and blood kinship.

The Democratic Party has been on the cutting edge of change and tolerance. When people said that no Roman Catholic could be President, ours is the party, the Democratic Party, that nominated and then elected John Fitzgerald Kennedy. We've come a long way since 1960. Twenty years ago the enemies of that Roman Catholic Democratic candidate said that if John Fitzgerald Kennedy were ever elected President, the Pope would someday stand on the steps of the White House. Those critics were right. They were a little off on their timing, though— [*laughter*]—because Pope John Paul II arrived at the White House in 1979, and I'm proud to say that he was welcomed there by a Southern Baptist.

We have come a long way. America has a Southern Baptist as a President, now elected with the support of northern Catholics, and the world at last has a Polish Pope. Who would have predicted either of these things 20 years ago?

It's important for us to consider, too, in this election year some special characteristics that are important for us all to remember. I've been listening to the Republican candidate. Then, you know, he's trying to wrap himself in the mantle of great Democratic Presidents. But it happens every election year. Here's what Franklin Roosevelt said back in 1944 about how Republicans change their tune at election time. I quote President Roosevelt: "The whole purpose of Republican oratory these days seems to be to switch labels," he said. "Now imitation may be the sincerest form of flattery, but I'm afraid that in this case it's the most obvious common garden variety of fraud."

And now the Republicans have the nerve to quote Franklin Roosevelt himself.

John Kennedy predicted it back in 1960, when he said of the Republicans, and I quote John Kennedy, "They're even beginning to say a few kind words about Franklin Roosevelt. Twenty years from now, they might even speak a good word for Harry Truman, but he won't say anything good about them." [*Laughter*]

As you know that prediction has come true. And I predict that 20 years from now, Republican candidates might even be saying nice things about Jimmy Carter's second term.

For working families, there is a special message in this election. Five decades, 50 years, the Democrats have fought for the rights of working people. We enacted the minimum wage over Republican opposition. We enacted unemployment compensation over Republican opposition. We enacted social security over Republican opposition. We enacted laws that gave the right of people to form unions and participate in collective bargaining over the opposition of Republicans. In the last 3½ years, we've fought together for common situs, for labor law reform, and against the repeal of Davis-Bacon—in each case over the opposition of Republicans.

My opponent's views are a matter of record. He described people drawing unemployment compensation as, and I quote, "freeloaders wanting a prepaid vacation plan." And last year when it was proposed that the Occupational Safety and Health Administration be abolished, that protects the safety and health of workers, his reply was, "Amen." This year he said, and I quote, "The minimum wage has caused more misery and unemployment than anything since the Great Depression."

These issues are extremely important. He says he wants to abolish the minimum wage, and if he can't do that, then, as he said in our debate, he wants to exempt young workers from the minimum wage. That would threaten the jobs of adults, as you know, who now rely on the minimum wage for protection, for a basic standard of decency with displacement by a new subclass of workers without the protection of the minimum wage. We Democrats oppose that. We've not lowered the minimum wage; we've raised it.

The man who said these things is proclaiming himself now a friend of the working families. He likes to put on a hardhat and quote Franklin Roosevelt. It's a new script, but to Republicans in election years, it's an old part. As you know, this is the candidate who is my opponent who says that the basis for the New Deal was fascism.

In an election year it's important for us to remember not just current events, not just the sharp differences that exist between two candidates—and the differences between myself and Governor Reagan are extremely sharp and accurately, now, defined—but the historical perspective of what our Nation is, what it has been, points very clearly to what it can be. You who are as old as I am, who remember the Great Depression years, the great changes that took place in our lives under Democrats, under Democratic leaders, have a clearer concept, perhaps, than some of our younger children, who haven't known those difficult days and seen a new life open up for us all.

Now I want to point out in final terms some special things about Poland. We have a good friendship with Poland. When I became President, my first [state] [1] visit outside this Nation was to Poland. We have strong ties of understanding, and the connections which exist between families like you and the homeland of your ancestors or, perhaps, the homeland of you yourselves are very strong.

Recently I ordered quick approval of Poland's request for new credit guarantees for American grain. It was the largest such guarantee ever made by our country to any other nation. I wanted to demonstrate our admiration for the way the Polish nation is conducting itself in this time of change. I wanted to show our desire for better relations between our people, to strengthen even further the human ties between our two countries. The shipyard workers in Gdansk, the coalminers in Silesia, the store workers in Warsaw, have sent a powerful message around the world. Poland has reminded us that the desire for human rights and human dignity is universal. I want the people of Poland to know that we heard their message, that we observed and admired their courage. I want the people of Poland to know that the human rights in America is a commitment which is still alive and that we hold the banner of human rights high, as a nation with deep and unchanging commitments.

This morning I pledge to you that as long as I am President, this Nation will stand up for its beliefs, will stand up for our ideals, will stand up for our values, because my values, as President, are the same as yours. And in this last few days of the Presidential election of 1980, I'd like for you to think on those values, what

_____
[1] White House correction.

they've meant to you in your lives, what you want them to mean to your children and your grandchildren, the historic thrust of our Nation, what it has been in the past and is now, what it can be in the future.

In many ways my political future is in your hands, but even more importantly, the political future of our Nation, its ties with Poland and with other ancestral countries that are so important to us— those ties that bind us together can be preserved by you. And I ask you in this next few days to make a sacrificial effort to show your commitment to our Nation, what it stands for, what it has been, and even more importantly, what it will be in the years ahead.

Thank you very much. God bless you.

NOTE: The President spoke at 8:35 a.m. in the main hall of the Pilsudski Club.

Philadelphia, Pennsylvania

Remarks to Members of the Young Men's Hebrew Association and Area Residents. October 30, 1980

Mayor Green, Mayor Koch, Bill Badoff:

First of all, I would like to join in with all of you in welcoming to this city the mayor of the Big Apple. I think it's appropriate to say, Mr. Mayor, welcome to the new city of champions.

And also, I want to express my deep thanks to Ted Mann, not only for his warm introduction, but what he's meant to me in the last 4 years, expressing very clearly and sincerely and from the bottom of his heart the commitment to our own Nation's interests, our security interests, our interests in peace, stability in the world, humanitarian commitments which we share. The breadth of his understanding and the breadth of his commitments have been an inspiration to me as President.

Next Tuesday the American people will make a profound judgment. They will decide which candidate, which party, which philosophy will guide our great Nation, not only in the next 4 years but perhaps for the remaining years in this century. I cannot think of a more important choice. As I've said many times, it's not just a choice between two candidates or two parties, but between two futures, the future of your own lives, the lives of your family members, the lives of those you love, the life of those you love in other nations.

And I've come here this morning to ask you for your help between now and next Tuesday. You have a strong voice in your own community, and this group collectively and individually has a strong voice that can be heard in every community of this country. I'd like for your voice to spread the word that I give you this morning, on what is at stake for our country. I'd like for you to be side by side with me and with Fritz Mondale, your friend, as we lead the Democratic Party to victory on November 4th. I want you on my side because we believe, together, in those deepest values which epitomize the Democratic Party down through the years.

Three centuries ago a young English Quaker by the name of William Penn had a very prophetic notion. He believed that a people of diverse backgrounds and beliefs could live and could work together. He believed that a society might be founded on the basis of full freedom of conscience, where religious liberty would not only be protected but would be respected as well. His belief in tolerance was not some abstract formulation or some theoretical commitment. He had felt the weight of religious repression, he had seen the price of religious intolerance, and he was resolved to do something about it.

William Penn set a new standard to govern the New World. It's a standard and an ideal that we still respect. He said no men nor number of men on Earth has power or authority to rule over men's consciences in religious matters. It's my privilege to lead a party, a political party that has perfected this spirit of religious and cultural tolerance. The Democratic Party not only allows diversity; it embraces diversity.

We are not a rich man's party by any stretch of the imagination, but we are rich in our diversity, rich in representing the diversity which is America itself and the source of a great portion of our strength. The Democratic Party has always had room for East European Jews, for Italians, for Poles, for Irish, for blacks, even Baptists from the rural South. [*Laughter*]

William Penn set a new standard to govern a New World, and it's a standard and an ideal that we still respect. We have a party that has fought and has had to fight for civil rights for minorities. We had to fight for them and have to fight today for equal rights for women. And the disturbing thing about civil rights and equal rights for women is that we've had to fight for them. It has not been a shared commitment by both parties.

Ours is a party that champions human rights abroad and faces opposition to this policy on the domestic political battlefield this year. The Democratic Party has fought for social justice because so many of us know too well the sting of social injustice.

We're a compassionate party because we can identify personally with those Americans who need help. We are a party that champions progressive causes because we ourselves have benefited from our Nation's social progress. We've come a long way together as a party and as a country, and we're going to go even further, because we are honest with ourselves about how far we have come and also how far we still have to go.

Recently a 12-year-old boy stood up in a town meeting that I was holding in Pittston here in the Commonwealth of Pennsylvania. What he asked cuts to the very heart of intolerance, which has reared its head in this country just in recent weeks. His name was Avi Leiter, and here's what he said: "In view of the fact that you, Mr. President, are Baptist, do you agree with the head of the churches who said God should not listen to Jewish prayers? I'm a religious boy," he said, "and I pray three times a day for the welfare of the Americans and the Jewish people. Do you think that God does not listen to my prayers?"

I told Avi that I believed God listens to his prayers just as I believe he listens to mine. I told him about being at Camp David with Prime Minister Begin and President Sadat. I told him that the world held little hope for peace when we secluded ourselves there, because those two nations had been torn by four wars in just 25 years.

And I told him that on the first day of our meetings, there was little on which we could agree, but we did agree to pray together. And we asked the entire world to join us in our prayers—a Jew, Moslem, and a Christian—and the world prayed with us. I told Avi that after 13 days we came out of Camp David with a peace agreement, and I told him that in my opinion that was proof enough, at least for me, that God heard all our prayers.

I bring this story up this morning, not to arouse emotions, but because it illustrates how far we still have to go in ridding our Nation of religious intolerance. It also illustrates how important it is for all of us to stand up for what we believe and to exercise our beliefs in the most tangible possible terms, within the limits of our constitutional rights, on election day and in our influence as we approach choice that will be made, to let people know what we believe in a loud and clear, unequivocal manner.

Today I want to outline for you my own position on a number of critical issues. I will be blunt, brief, to the point. It's time for us to look at the facts at the so-called bottom line.

First, the energy challenge. Before I took office, as you well know, our Nation did not even have an energy program, except one that had been forged under the Republicans by the oil companies themselves, working with the Arab OPEC nations, their partners. Three years after the Arab oil embargo, we were still trying to ignore the challenge that presented itself to our country. Most Americans were led to believe that there was not even an energy crisis at all. Two Republican administrations did little to correct this dangerous delusion.

This year, for the first time in history, we have an energy policy and we've actually reduced our dependence on foreign oil by 25 percent, 2 million barrels a day less than we have to buy from overseas. Congress has passed a historic synthetic fuels program and a windfall profits tax to pay for it. We're drilling more oil and gas wells than any time in our history.

We're producing more coal this year than any time in history.

The bottom line is that the United States is today far less vulnerable to oil blackmail. Some of you may remember the Arab boycott against American businesses who traded with Israel, which we eliminated by law when I became President. We are much better able now to support our friends and to protect American ideals and principles and independence of friends like Israel, to stand up for what we believe.

Recently I signed with Minister Modai, in the Roosevelt Room at the White House, an agreement which Prime Minister Begin and I and President Sadat had all proposed jointly; that is, to guarantee to Israel that if their supply of oil should be interrupted in the future or if they should be charged exorbitant prices for oil that would wreak an economic problem for them, then the United States would make up that oil supply. And that agreement extends for the next 14 years.

Look, on the other hand, at what the Republicans are offering: no conservation program at all. They even want to eliminate the 55-mile-per-hour speed limit. They want to throw out all or part of the windfall profits tax. They want us to rely solely on the oil companies to meet the energy challenge. And I think it's incumbent on you and me to think for a moment on who might be the next Secretary of Energy and who might be the next Secretary of State. The Republican bottom line: vulnerability, impotence in defending our friends and our principles.

Just for a few moments I'd like to talk specifically about Israel and the Jewish people. As Ted Mann pointed out, the United States has given aid to Israel since 1977 more than all previous administra-

tions combined. The year before I became President, Jewish emigration from the Soviet Union was down to 14,000. Last year it was up to 50,000, the highest level in a decade, because we've put it as a top priority of my administration. And I have never met with President Brezhnev or with Gromyko and neither have the Secretaries of State of our Nation ever met with any Soviet leader that this question of Soviet Jews and their right to emigrate was not at the top of our list of agenda items.

And despite the fact that the Soviets have invaded Afghanistan, been condemned by the world, and that interruption of emigration has occurred, it is still higher now than it was when I took office. But we will not rest until every Soviet Jew who wants to leave the Soviet Union can do so.

Israel has been at war with Egypt, as you know, four times since 1948. Egypt is the strongest, most powerful, most influential of all Arab nations. Under my administration, Israel is at peace with this most powerful Arab neighbor. Today there are commercial flights between the two countries. The borders are open. They are cooperating on joint regional concerns, full diplomatic relations, Ambassadors assigned to represent each country in the other. There's tourism today, and today an Israeli tourist can buy the Jerusalem Post in the Cairo newsstands.

Just this week, the President of Israel paid a state visit, an official state visit, to Egypt. It was the first such visit by an Israeli head of state to any Arab country in history.

Let's talk just a moment, in closing, about American policy toward Israel.

Fact: The United States stands shoulder to shoulder with Israel against all her enemies, not as a favor to Israel, but as a direct investment in better peace and more security for our own Nation. We face these enemies whether they be a PLO terrorist carrying a bomb or a smooth-voiced diplomat at the United Nations.

Let me be very clear on one point: If there is any move to expel Israel from the United Nations, the United States will veto that action in the Security Council. And also, should Israel be deprived of its credentials in the General Assembly, through whatever means or whatever trick or procedure, I see no way whatever that the United States could continue its own participation in that body.

Referring to the PLO, let me say that the United States will never recognize nor negotiate with the PLO as long as it refuses to recognize Israel's right to exist and refuses to accept United Nations Resolution 242 as a basis for Mideast peace. The United States does not deal with organizations which try to accomplish their objectives by means of terrorism.

Terrorism is a crime against decency and humanity. We condemn it wherever it occurs, either on the streets of Paris or on the streets of Jerusalem, whether those responsible are neo-Nazis or members of the PLO.

And I think the most disturbing single incident that came up in the debate night before last was the fact, confirmed since the debate by the press, that the Republican candidate for President said that he thought it was none of the United States business if any other nation decides to develop nuclear weapons for themselves. Think for a moment what it would mean to our country, to Israel, or to other nations who might be subject to threats of terrorism, if some of Israel's neighbors or

a country like Libya had an atomic bomb developed while the United States official policy was to look the other way.

The United States has a moral commitment to Israel because we share so many things in common. A strong, independent, democratic nation committed to peace in the Middle East is a major asset for our country, and we share these strategic understandings and consultations, looking toward the future. A strong Israel is not just in Israel's interest or the United States; it's in the interests of the entire free world.

Under my administration, as you well know, the United States has never used economic or military aid as a lever against Israel. We have never had a suspicion of a thought of doing this. We've not done it in the last 4 years. And we will never do it as long as there is a Democratic President in the Oval Office.

You remember in 1973 when Israel was in the throes of a war. The Republican administration announced quietly that we would reassess America's relationship with Israel. And in effect, there was a cutoff of arms and a freeze on relationships in an attempt to force Israel to succumb to the will of the Republican President. It's good for us to think on these things.

We are committed to the defense of Israel's security. We are also committed to defend its place in the world community. The United States will not permit Israel to be isolated. We are committed to the Camp David accords. We'll veto any change in the United Nations Resolution 242. We oppose the creation of an independent Palestinian state. And we will go even further: Whenever the United Nations is misused with malicious, unfair, and one-sided anti-Israeli resolutions, we will oppose them and we will veto them in the United Nations Security Council.

Your President and your country believes in an undivided Jerusalem. We believe, with Prime Minister Begin and, I might also add, President Sadat, that the future of Jerusalem will be decided, among all nations, through negotiations, negotiations whose conclusion must be confirmed with the concurrence and the agreement of the Government of Israel.

You in this city need to remember one other point. You're concerned about Israel's neighbors, and so are we. It's good for our country to have friendly relationships with the moderate Arab countries. In 1978 Secretary Harold Brown assured the Congress that our country would not provide Saudi Arabia F–15 offensive equipment, equipment that would give them an offensive capability against Israel. That assurance stands today.

Let me say in closing that you live in a city dedicated to tolerance. You're a city that, because of that, has remembered the Holocaust. You've erected a monument to 6 million martyrs. I'm proud to say that under my administration, with the help of Ted Mann, Ed Koch, and others, the United States Government has set into motion the development of a similar national memorial. That's what the Holocaust Commission will do. It will design a suitable memorial to this historic crime, and we will study the constant memory of its victims.

But the greatest memorial that I'm committed to offer is an active one. It is our unflagging, constant, untiring support of the results of the world's abhorrence of the Holocaust, and that is the formation, the protection, and the perpetuation of a strong and free state of Israel.

I feel deeply that you and I share many beliefs and commitments, a permanent commitment to human rights, a commitment to progress, to humanitarian action, commitments to the deprived, to those who are persecuted, to those who are in the minority, to those who need a strong voice and don't have the numbers to exert their voice, to the protection of newcomers, haven for refugees, commitment to peace, a sacred conviction that an affront to just one person's belief is an affront to all humanity. And I pledge to you that as long as I am President of the United States, that commitment which you and I share will be kept.

Thank you very much.

NOTE: The President spoke at 9:43 a.m. at the Young Men's Hebrew Association. He was introduced by Theodore Mann, former chairman of the Conference of Presidents of Major American Jewish Organizations.

New York, New York
Remarks at the International Ladies' Garment Workers Union Rally.
October 30, 1980

Thank you very much, my good friend, Chick Chaikin. I am proud to be in the heart of the greatest city on Earth, New York. I love New York and I love all of you. New York's heart is a big heart, and it's also a Democratic heart. Right? [*Cheers*] This is the State and the city that gave us Al Smith and the greatest President of the 20th century, Franklin Delano Roosevelt, and the Governors like Herbert Lehmann and Averell Harriman, and United States Senators like Robert Wagner, Sr., and Robert Kennedy, and mayors like Robert Wagner, Jr., and Abe Beame. And I'm proud to be here with the inheritors of that great Democratic tradition, your courageous Governor, Hugh Carey, your outspoken, fighting mayor, Ed Koch—how am I doing, Ed?—your wise and your humane Lieutenant Governor, my friend Mario Cuomo, and your brilliant United States Senator, Daniel Patrick Moynihan, and your next United States Senator, Liz Holtzman.

Today we're together, we're determined, and we are united. And next Tuesday we're going to whip the Republicans like they've never been whipped before. It's up to you and me together to roll up a Democratic victory from Staten Island to Niagara Falls and all across this land. The lines are sharply drawn. The choice is crucial, and especially for New Yorkers. If you ride the bus or the subway, then you know how Governor Reagan used to pray every day that the Nation would never extend a helping hand to New York.

I'm sure the Lord heard that prayer, as he hears all prayers, but after due consideration and with a little help from below, he decided to answer some other prayers instead—that is, mine and yours, to revitalize New York. And that's what we've done together. Here's something else that Mr. Reagan said. Quote: "Real Americans," he said, "just plain don't like New York." All right, how many of you are real Americans? [*Cheers*] How many of you love New York? [*Cheers*] That's right. I've got real news for Mr. Reagan. There are some real Americans here on Seventh Avenue, from Manhattan and Brooklyn and Queens and the Bronx and Staten Island, and from Georgia, who just plain don't like Republicans.

And here's something else that my Republican opponent said about our cities. Just a few months ago he said, and I quote again, "Urban aid programs are one of the biggest phonies that we have in this

system." I disagree. I think urban aid programs are one of the biggest necessities we have in this system. In 1978, down in city hall, I stood with Hugh Carey, Ed Koch, Pat Moynihan, and I signed a bill granting $1.6 billion in loan guarantees for New York City. It hasn't cost our Nation a dime, because New York is a great city, growing, strong, prosperous, with a bright future ahead of all of you. Under the new Urban Development Action Grant program, New York has received more grants than any other city in the Nation. We've put $600 million into economic development for New York, for community development. We changed the formula that determines how much money is allotted. It was a tough fight, but we won it together. And the result is that the city is getting an extra $110 million a year, and now we're fighting to change the formula to give you that kind of benefit for your mass transit program.

But urban America is just one of the areas of crucial choice, and in just a few minutes, I'd like to outline for you a few key basic issues that separate me from my Republican opponent. On one side, you've got a Republican candidate who promises ideological loyalty tests for possible Federal judges, including members of the Supreme Court. On the other side, you've got a Democratic administration pledged to an independent qualified judiciary. I've been faithful to that pledge, as you know, for the last 4 years, and I will remain faithful to it if and when I'm called upon to appoint members of the United States Supreme Court.

Another basic issue. On one side is a Republican candidate who launched his political career as a traveling salesman for the anti-Medicare lobby. Now he says, and I quote, "I am firmly opposed to national health insurance." On the other side, you've got a Democratic administration committed to the enactment of national health insurance. And I'll work with Senator Kennedy, with Pat Moynihan, and your congressional delegation and other Democrats around this land to give the $200,000 burden a lift off the shoulders of New York that now costs you for Medicaid and make sure that the taxpayers of New York have the break that you deserve and that you will get under a Democratic administration.

And there's another basic issue I'd like to mention. On one side, you've got a Republican candidate who's turned his back on 40 years of support for the equal rights amendment. And on the other side, you've got a Democratic administration and a Democratic President who has pledged to fight for the rights of women, like the rights of men, and inscribe them in the Constitution of the United States with the equal rights amendment.

And there's another basic issue. On one side, you've got a Republican candidate who said this year—listen to this—that the minimum wage has caused more unemployment than anything since the Great Depression. He's on record this year as favoring the abolition of the minimum wage, and if he can't abolish it, then he wants to lower it by the backdoor route of a so-called subminimum wage for minority and other young people. That's what he proposed during the debate just this week. On the other side, you've got a Democratic administration that supports the minimum wage, just as Democrats have supported it against Republican opposition ever since Franklin D. Roosevelt first got it enacted, when it was only 25 cents an hour, and the Republicans were against giving working men and women 25 cents an hour for their hard labor.

We Democrats know that the minimum wage has given a decent life and made it possible for millions of Americans. We Democrats know that it's wrong to tell a 25- or 30-year-old mother or father that he or she can't have a job because it's been filled by someone who's being paid a special sub-minimum and sub-standard wage. We Democrats raised the minimum wage, not lowered it, and that's a basic difference between me and my Republican administration [opponent].

There is another basic difference. On one side, you've got a Republican candidate who says, and I quote again, "What needs to be done for the government is to repeal the energy legislation we've passed and turn the oil industry loose." And on the other side, you've got a Democratic administration that fought successfully for the windfall profits tax and for the massive new energy program that has already reduced our oil imports by one-third compared to what it was only 12 months ago.

Every drop of oil that we do not have to buy from OPEC increases our economic security and our national security. We must not allow our progress to be reversed by letting a Republican back in the White House.

Let me mention one other basic issue, and Governor Reagan says that this is the foundation of his economic program. On one side is a Republican candidate who bases his entire program on Reagan-Kemp-Roth—a massive tax cut for the rich—huge increases in defense spending, and a balanced budget all at once. His own running mate, George Bush, said that this would cause a 30-percent inflation rate. He called it "voodoo economics."

Many of you read Business Week magazine. It's hardly a Democratic publication.

And here's what Business Week said about Reagan-Kemp-Roth, the foundation for Governor Reagan's economic program. Business Week said it's completely irresponsible, it will touch off an inflationary explosion that would wreck this country and impoverish everyone on a fixed income. That's what Business Week thinks about Governor Reagan's economic program.

We Democrats know that unemployment is still too high, but in America today a higher percentage of our people have jobs than ever before in history. We've created almost 9 million new jobs, and 200,000 of those jobs are right here in the New York metropolitan area. Unemployment here is down 22 percent since the day I was inaugurated President.

Most of all, there's another basic issue that you ought to be reminded of every day, and that is that we Democrats dare to fight for peace, and the Republican candidate for President is utterly without any foreign policy experience. He has repeatedly called for us to send American military forces to intervene in trouble spots around the world. In 1975 he called for the use of American military forces in Ecuador in a fishing dispute; later, in Angola; in 1976, in Rhodesia and Cyprus. This year, so far, he's called for the use of American military forces in Cuba, in Pakistan, and in the Middle East. Let's make sure that we don't have to find out whether he'll call for the use of American military forces next year by sending him back to Hollywood and California, where the American military forces won't listen to his voice.

As you know, the American Democratic administration has kept this Nation strong and also kept this Nation at peace, and we have extended American peaceful inclinations and influence to other troubled areas around the world. That's what we did in the Middle East, where we helped bring a treaty of peace between Israel and Egypt, the first ever peace between Israel and one of her Arab neighbors.

The Democratic Party is committed, and I am committed, to a strong and secure Israel, an Israel safe from the threats of terrorism, an Israel that has a strong strategic partner in the United States. Let there be no mistake about it, the Democratic Party and this Democratic President have stood by Israel's side for 32 years, and we always will.

And there's something else we Democrats stand for, and that's basic human rights. America should always stand for human liberty and human dignity. As long as I'm President, we will hold high the banner of human rights.

Now, let me touch on one final basic issue, the most important issue of all. The Republican candidate says that the best approach to nuclear arms negotiations would be to threaten the possibility of an arms race. The possibility of a nuclear arms race is what the Republican candidate proposes. We Democrats disagree. We're committed to mutual and balanced controls on the terrible weapons of nuclear annihilation. I consider this to be the overriding issue of this campaign. The New York Times of February 1st, 1980, reported this about Governor Reagan and his attitude toward letting other nations have atomic bombs. Think for a moment what it would mean to us and to Israel and other peace-loving nations if Libya and other terrorist governments had the atomic bomb. All Presidents in the past have tried to prevent the extension of nuclear explosives from going to these kinds of nations. This is what the New York

Times said: "Governor Reagan indicated today that he believes the United States should not stand in the way of countries developing their own nuclear weapons, saying, 'I just don't think it's any of our business.'"

Over the last 20 years, we've taken the first long step away from the nuclear precipice. We must stay on that road until the shadow of a nuclear holocaust is lifted from the people of this Earth. On issue after issue, the choice is clear, and the stakes for our country are very high. This is a tough race. It's going right down to the wire. The Republicans are out-spending us by millions of dollars.

Fritz Mondale and I are going to need the help of every one of you. New York is absolutely vital to our victory. For the sake of everything that we've done together in the past, for the sake of everything the Democratic Party has meant to you, to New York City, to New York State and this Nation, for the sake of everything we're pledged to do together in the future to give us a strong and peaceful nation, let's win a victory not just for Jimmy Carter and Fritz Mondale, but for the whole Democratic Party and the whole Democratic ticket and, most important of all, for the beliefs and the conviction and the ideals we share.

Will you help me next Tuesday? [*Applause and cheers*] Are we going to have a great victory next Tuesday? [*Applause and cheers*]

Thank you very much. God bless all of you.

NOTE: The President spoke at 12:34 p.m. at the intersection of Thirty-Seventh Street and Seventh Avenue. He was introduced by Sol C. Chaikin, president of the International Ladies' Garment Workers Union.

Saginaw, Michigan

*Remarks at a Rally With Area
Residents.   October 30, 1980*

THE PRESIDENT. As you may know——
AUDIENCE MEMBER. [*Inaudible*]
THE PRESIDENT. Amy's just fine.

As you may know, Plains, Georgia, has a lot in common with you. We are both very close to I–75. I think I'll just move up and stay with you all for a while. So, if you want to see Amy in 1986, just get on I–75 and come on down to Plains. We'll be there.

Let me say first of all, Senator Riegle, Senator Levin, Congressman Bob Traxler, who introduced me so well, Congressman Albosta, Congressman Dale Kildee, and all of you, my friends, it's a great pleasure to be with you. This has been a good Democratic day for me. I started out this morning with Polish Americans in Philadelphia, and just came from a tremendous rally in the garment district of New York. And I go from here to St. Louis, Missouri, and tonight I'll be in South Carolina, right, and tomorrow in Florida and Texas. And I'll wind up the last day of the campaign on the west coast, in California and in Oregon and Washington, and I'll be back in Plains to vote on Tuesday. And Tuesday, I want to tell you that I'll be looking to this area of Michigan and the State of Michigan and the Nation to give use a tremendous victory over the Republicans. Okay? [*Applause*]

This afternoon I want to talk to you about a few things that are quite serious to me and to you, to your families, to the people that you love, and to the nation about which you care so deeply. This is troubled times in many places of the world, and we've been faced with many very serious challenges in the last 4 years. But Democrats are builders, just as the people of Michigan and the workers of our automobile industry are builders. We have never been afraid to face change. We have never been afraid to face any question; we've never failed to answer it. We've never faced any challenge that we could not meet; we've never faced any problem we could not solve; we've never faced any obstacle we could not overcome. Americans are like that, we are builders. Democrats are builders. That's why you and I are Democrats. That's why we're going to win next week.

In recent weeks, I've had a chance to travel around this country to see what is going on in America. One of the things I've seen that has thrilled my heart: I've seen the best, the most durable, the safest, the most fuel-efficient automobiles in the world rolling off the assembly lines in Michigan. And they're going to replace those foreign cars on the market, and you can depend on that. And as you well know, they're built by the best automobile workers in the world, right?

We have faced rapidly changing times because last year, in 1979, the OPEC oil companies and countries increased the price of oil more than the oil prices had increased since it was first discovered in the 1800's. Our Nation changed its buying habits and very quickly the automobile industry of our country—the automobile workers, management—and government got together to plan for the future. The new cars now being assembled in this Nation are the highest quality of all. And, as you know, there are long waiting lists for the new model cars. This change has been a traumatic experience for some of us, for you and for me. As President, I have felt a personal responsibility to play a leading role in shaping the future of the automobile industry.

One of the things that we have done is to spell out the very clear new tax incentives to encourage reinvestment by saved tax monies into modern tools and plants so that the American workers can continue to be the most productive in the world. We've worked out a very good relationship now between the Environmental Protection Agency and the automobile industry, so that we could understand one another and work in harmony to continue the progress that has been made.

We've obviously had to deal with temporary unemployment. We have been true to the principles of the Democratic Party in making sure that unemployment compensation was paid to workers when they are unemployed because of a changed desire and the changing models. This is quite in contrast to my Republican opponent who says that unemployment compensation is a prepaid vacation for freeloaders.

Throughout this campaign, for the last 4 years, we have said that it's important for our Nation to be strong, vibrant, and dynamic in meeting inevitable change. We've had some tough and historic obstacles, but I promise you this, as long as I am President, the Government of the United States will play its rightful role in making American cars the cars of the future. I believe in that goal, and with your help, we'll carry it out.

We've backed up Chrysler when they needed help most. We've backed them up with $1½ billion in sound loan guarantees. We've backed up a 100,000 Chrysler workers, and we've backed up a total of 250,000 other employees in the automobile industry in this Nation who depend upon Chrysler being a viable organization for their livelihood. And because we did, there's a K-car today, 40,000 back orders for it. Chrysler's building fuel-efficient automobiles, and Chrysler's building for the future.

Again there was a sharp difference shown between the basic philosophy of the Democratic Party, that I've just outlined to you, and the attitude of my own opponent who represents the Republican Party, who, when faced earlier this year with the question of guaranteed loans for Chrysler, said, and I quote him, "What's wrong with bankruptcy?"

I feel this direct responsibility to expedite the ITC determination about how imports are affecting the automobile industry, and after this election is over, I will continue my efforts along those lines. When I was in Venice in May, I met with the Japanese leaders there, their Foreign Minister, and I expressed the great concern that I had about alleged plans in Japan to expand their automobile capacity. They've now assured me and they have urged their manufacturers to exercise prudence and predict a decline in their exports to the United States in the final months of this year.

The last time I was in Michigan, I said I was going to talk to the Japanese about their automobile exports to this country. And I can announce today that I will be meeting with the Japanese Prime Minister soon after the election to discuss the automobile issue and a whole range of other issues of importance to their country and to our own.

It's good for you to remember—many of you are young—to remember what is so important about the basic philosophy of our two parties down through the years.

I grew up as a young boy on a farm during the Depression years. I was born in 1924. And the Depression years saw a great change in our life. We faced a life of despair. We didn't have electricity on our farm. There was no guarantee of an equitable payment for hard work done.

The Democrats proposed the REA to put electricity on the farms. Republicans opposed it. The Democrats felt that there should be an end to sweatshops and that grown men and women should have a chance to earn enough with their honest labor to feed and to clothe and to house their family. So, the Democrats put forward the idea of a minimum wage, 25 cents an hour. The Republicans opposed it. Later the Democrats raised it.

When I finished high school, I got my first job—40 cents an hour. That increase from 25 cents to 40 cents was supported by the Democrats. The Republicans said it was socialism and the unwarranted injection of the government into the affairs of the private enterprise system. Later, of course, Roosevelt thought that the older people in our country ought to have some security in their old age. So, the Democrats put forward the idea of social security. The Republicans opposed it.

Years later, under a Democratic administration, it was proposed that we have Medicare to give our retired citizens some modicum of health care. The Republicans opposed it. Governor Reagan, as a matter of fact, got his start in political life working for the American Medical Association, traveling around this country speaking against Medicare, calling it socialized medicine and the injection of socialism into the system of our country.

The Government has a proper role to play in helping people have a better life. The Democratic government philosophy has always been that government ought to take people who want to work for themselves, stand on their own feet, have a better life, have self-respect, have better health care, have better education, and give them a boost to be more self-sufficient, to take whatever talent or ability God might have given that individual person and let that talent and ability be expanded. Education programs, public education has always been supported strongly by Democrats, as you well know.

There's a basic difference in philosophy that still permeates the consciousness of Americans on both parties and the two candidates running for President this year. I reject the negative approach. I know that the American people will reject it too. And I come today to you to offer you a choice, and the clearest possible choice, about our Nation's future.

For decades Walter Reuther and the United Automobile Workers stood with Harry Truman and with John Kennedy and with Lyndon Johnson. They fought for Medicare. They fought for national health insurance. Ronald Reagan called that socialism, again. He ridiculed Walter Reuther for proposing, and I quote, "socialized medicine." Governor Reagan can call this dream whatever he wants, but we're going to make it a reality.

This time we're going to make good on all the promises that Harry Truman and Walter Reuther and John Kennedy and Lyndon Johnson and Franklin Roosevelt were fighting for. This time we're going to realize our dream. With the help of those assembled behind me, who are serving in the Congress, we're going to reach that dream and make national health insurance a reality, because what it will do for us is to give us a chance to prevent disease. It'll give us a chance to

control hospital costs. It'll give us a chance to emphasize at-home care and outpatient care, not the incarceration for long periods in a hospital as the only way to get adequate medical care. It'll give us catastrophic health insurance. If a family's wiped out financially by high medical costs, the insurance will help pay for it. It'll give special care to women, pregnant women and newborn babies during the first few months or years of their lives. This is the kind of thing that must be done.

On one side in this campaign you've got a Republican candidate who's turned his back on 40 years of commitment, his own party's commitment, to the equal rights amendment. Six predecessors of mine in the Oval Office have believed that there must be a guarantee for the rights of women, like the rights of men, inscribed in the Constitution of the United States. This is not a radical proposal. What it says, very simply, is this: that equality of rights cannot be abridged for women by the Federal Government or the government of any State. That's it. That's it in its totality, and that's what we mean when we say we're going to give equal rights.

On one side is a Republican candidate who's repeatedly called for sending American military forces to troublespots around the world. In 1975, Governor Reagan——

[Interruption from the audience.]

Okay, listen, and I'll talk. In 1975 Governor Reagan wanted to send American military forces to Ecuador and to Angola. In 1976 he said let's send military forces to Rhodesia and Cyprus. This year, so far, he's wanted to send American military forces to Cuba, to Pakistan, and the Middle East. On the other side, you've got an experienced Democratic administration which has strengthened our Nation's defenses. It's strengthened our Nation's alliances, and it's built a new and a fruitful relationship with one-fourth the total population of the world, in China, and doubled our trade in the meantime with the people of Taiwan.

We've been interested in having peace for ourselves, yes. But we have also used our peaceful influence to help other people around the world, including, of course, the Israelis and the Egyptians, and now we're trying to extend that peace to Israel's other neighbors. This is the kind of commitment that the Democrats have exemplified down through the ages.

On one side is a Republican candidate who's criticized our human rights policy as being against the best interests of the United States. When I spoke this morning to the Polish Americans, I had Mr. Walesa with me, the father of the labor leader in Poland, who has hammered out in that country a new approach and a new dream of the rights of Polish workers. And I told the Polish Americans this morning that as long as I'm President of our country, we will hold high the banner of human rights.

I've outlined to you a few issues that I think are very important, because there is a sharp distinction between the Democratic Party and the Republican Party, and between the two candidates who represent those parties this year. The other thing, though, is perhaps even more important of all: On one side, you've got a Republican candidate who says in this year, 1980, in a time of growing concern about nations like Iraq or Libya, terrorist nations, that they might be developing nuclear weapons, that nuclear proliferation, as Governor Reagan says, is none of our business.

On the other side, you've got a Democratic administration pledged to halting the dangerous spread of nuclear weapons to the nations that do not now have them, nations that might be highly unstable and irresponsible. That's the business not only of everyone in government in the United States but of every government and of every human being on Earth. The most important single commitment that a President can have is to keep our Nation strong, yes, but at peace, and to control the horrible possible blight of atomic weapons that threatens this world.

I mentioned to you the other night on television that one nuclear warhead on one of our major missiles has about 10 megatons of explosive power. I'd like to remind you again what that means. If you put 50 tons of TNT in every railroad car—50 tons—it would stretch 2,500 miles long and take a thousand diesel locomotives to move it. That's just one warhead, and we've got literally hundreds of equivalent warheads to that explosive power. To control that terrible destructive force has been the preeminent commitment of every President, Democratic or Republican, since Harry Truman.

Governor Reagan would abandon that commitment, a treaty negotiated under three Presidents—two Republicans and myself—over a 7-year period to have a balanced, controlled, confirmable agreement with the concept of lowering the arsenals in both nations. Governor Reagan said recently the one thing that's been missing from the nuclear arms negotiations is a nuclear arms race. I hope you'll remember that if you forget everything else I'll say this afternoon, because it is the most important single issue.

Two other points and then I'd like to be coming to a close. Two other points. On one side you've got a Republican

Presidential candidate who said this year that the minimum wage has caused more unemployment and more misery than anything since the Great Depression. He's on record this year as favoring the abolition of the minimum wage. If he can't abolish it he plans to lower it by the backdoor route of a so-called subminimum wage for minority or other youth. That's what he proposed during the debate night before last. On the other side you've got a Democratic administration carrying on the tradition of strengthening the minimum wage, just as Democrats have supported and strengthened that commitment to the lowest paid, hard-working American families ever since Franklin Roosevelt. We know that the minimum wage has made a decent life possible for millions of Americans, and we Democrats know it's wrong to tell a 25- or a 35-year-old man or woman, a mother or father, that he or she can no longer have a job because it's been filled by someone much younger who's working for substandard wages. This is extremely important to me and to the working people of our country.

And finally, let me say that I'm a farmer. My people have lived in this country for a long time. All of my ancestors—my father, my grandfather, and others—have been farmers. One of the greatest commitments that I've made as President is to strengthen the life and the economy of farmers, ranchers in this Nation. Under my own administration, in spite of very severe blows, as you know, on a worldwide basis, we've had the highest gross income for farmers, the highest net income for farm families, the highest exports in history. As a matter of fact, this year, in spite of restraints on sales to the Soviet Union after they invaded Afghanistan, we will sell overseas to permanent customers $40 billion worth of American

agricultural products, an $8 billion increase over last year, the largest single increase in history. And when we developed our farm program in 1977 we did it with the closest possible cooperation of farmers themselves and of organizations representing them.

If you've been listening to the Republican candidate, then you know he's trying to wrap himself in the mantle of great Democratic Presidents. But it happens every election year. Here's what Franklin Roosevelt said back in 1944 about how Republicans change their tune at election time. "The sole purpose of Republican oratory these days," he said, "seems to be to switch labels. Now, imitation may be the sincerest form of flattery, but I'm afraid in this case it's the most obvious, common, garden variety of fraud." And now the Republicans have the nerve to quote Franklin Roosevelt himself.

John Kennedy predicted it back in 1960, when he said of the Republicans, "They are even beginning to say a few kind words about Franklin Roosevelt. Twenty years from now, who knows. They might even speak a good word for Harry Truman. But he won't ever say a good word about them." [*Laughter*] As you know, that prediction came true. And I predict that 20 years from now Republican candidates will even be saying good things about Jimmy Carter's second term, if you will let me.

Well, in closing let me say that I've described the election of 1980 as the choice between two futures as quickly and as briefly as I can, covering a fairly broad range of issues. Here's what I see in the future that we are fighting for together. I see a nation strong and at peace. I see a nation secure in its pursuit of progress, equity, and justice for our people, a nation where everyone can have the dignity of a decent job, where new industries create a new generation of American buildings and vehicles that will house and move us in comfort on a lot less energy, and that energy coming from America, a nation where children are educated to their maximum potential, where the elderly are treated with the respect that they have earned, where families are intact, loving and secure. I have a vision of a nation free enough to attract and strong enough to welcome the deprived from other parts of the world as we have welcomed the Jews from Eastern Europe and the immigrants here from Germany and from Poland and from Italy and from other nations from which almost all of us have come, a nation of liberty and of justice and of compassion and of concern, a nation of confidence, a nation of commitment, a nation of unity, a nation of strength.

I need your help to make this vision a reality. Together you and I can make the greatest nation on Earth even greater in the future. That's my pledge. Will you help me? [*Cheers*] Thank you very much. I need you to work now. Okay? [*Cheers*]

Thank you very much.

NOTE: The President spoke at 4:34 p.m. in the Athletic Center gymnasium, Saginaw Valley State College, University Center.

St. Louis, Missouri

Remarks at a Rally With Area Residents.
October 30, 1980

THE PRESIDENT. *Senator Tom Eagleton, Congressman Young, Congressman Volkmer, Governor Teasdale, Mrs. Teasdale, Mayor Conway, all of my friends who've come here:*

Do you think we're going to whip the Republicans next Tuesday? [*Cheers*] Right on. This is a beautiful crowd.

Yesterday, 4 years ago, I stood here in this same shopping center, and I talked to you about the problems that faced our Nation. One of the most serious problems at that time was that we had a Republican President in the Oval Office. You got rid of him. I thank you for that great improvement.

It is good to be back with you. I promised you then that if you would send me to Washington as President, we would have a foreign policy that represents the character and the high moral standards and the common sense and the sound judgment of the American people—I'm quoting myself—and that we would have a government that would not embarrass nor shame you. I tried to be honest with you about what I was and what I would try to do, and that's what I've done the last 4 years. I've kept my promise, and I hope now that you'll help me next Tuesday.

And I also told you that I did not know all the answers, but the changes that we needed to make in this Nation at that time would not be easy. You sent me to Washington, and you set me to work on making those beneficial changes. If it had been anywhere but Missouri, it would have been a close election. But you gave me a bigger majority than you had given any Presidential candidate since Harry Truman, and I thank you very much. You've got a good tradition. Do the same thing next week.

I have been very lucky to have your own Senator Tom Eagleton there to help me in the important fight for the rights of labor and for the cities and for young and old people who've been put to work.

He was there in the fight against the ridiculous Reagan-Kemp-Roth tax proposal, which is the foundation, it's the foundation of Ronald Reagan's future economic policy. Business Week, which, as you know, is not a Democratic publication, said Ronald Reagan's Kemp-Roth proposal is completely irresponsible. It would result in an inflationary explosion that could wreck this country and would impoverish all Americans living on a fixed income.

Is that the kind of leadership you want in the White House for the next 4 years?

AUDIENCE. No!

THE PRESIDENT. You're right. We don't want tax breaks for the rich instead of creating jobs and giving American workers the tools to compete.

We've tried to build not just for today and tomorrow but for the rest of this century, for your children and mine, for your grandchildren and mine, so that we can have a prosperous city here and a prosperous nation, a city and a nation of which we can be proud.

We've been able to project for you, working closely with your congressional leadership and your mayor and others, fighting for economic improvement in mass transit, so that this historic city can take advantage of the great traditions that you have here. And I am extremely proud of what is happening in St. Louis and this metropolitan area. You've done a great job.

We've had some economic setbacks brought about because OPEC oil nations increased the price of energy last year more than oil prices had increased since oil was first discovered in the 1800's. But because of what you have been able to do, 26,000 people in St. Louis have jobs today who did not have jobs when I was here and made my speech just 4 years ago.

That's the kind of progress we'll continue for the next 4 years.

I believe, like all Democrats have believed, that working families know who is on their side in this election. From Franklin Roosevelt to Harry Truman, Lyndon Johnson, John Kennedy, the Democratic Party is on the side of the working people of this Nation, and don't you ever forget it. For more than 50 years, the Democrats in the White House and in the Congress have fought for the rights of working people.

We enacted the minimum wage; the Republicans opposed it even when it was down to 25 cents an hour. We then raised it to 40 cents an hour—the first job I had; the Republicans did not think that working people, men and women, were worth 40 cents an hour. We have put into effect unemployment compensation. The Democrats were for it; the Republicans were against it. The Democrats were for social security; the Republicans were against it. The Democrats were for the REA, for electrification of farms; the Republicans, of course, were against it.

The Democrats were for Medicare; the Republicans were against it. And the man who led the fight against Medicare was Ronald Reagan, and he wants to be in the White House now. You've got to keep him out.

For the last 3½ years, we have fought together for common situs, for labor law reform, and against the repeal of Davis-Bacon.

My opponent's views are changing very rapidly as the election day approaches, but they're a matter of record.

He describes people drawing unemployment compensation, and I quote him—listen—freeloaders wanting a prepaid vacation plan. That's the way he describes mothers and fathers who want to work, who had a job, who lose their jobs temporarily and compensate themselves by contributing to unemployment insurance—freeloaders wanting a prepaid vacation plan.

Last year when it was proposed to do away with the Occupational Safety and Health Administration which protects workers safety and health, when somebody said, "Let's do away with it," Ronald Reagan said, "Amen."

This year he said, and I quote: "The minimum wage has caused more misery and more unemployment than anything since the Great Depression."

If you've been listening to the Republican candidate, then you know he's trying to wrap himself up in the mantle of great Democratic Presidents. But it happens every election year. Here's what Franklin Roosevelt said back in 1944 about how Republicans change their tune at election time. Listen to Franklin Roosevelt's words: "The whole purpose of Republican oratory these days seems to be to switch labels. Now, imitation may be the sincerest form of flattery," Roosevelt said, "but I'm afraid in this case, it's the most obvious common or garden variety of fraud."

And now the Republicans have the nerve to quote Franklin D. Roosevelt himself. John Kennedy predicted it back in 1960, when he said of the Republicans, and I'm quoting John Kennedy: "They're even beginning to say a few kind words about Franklin Roosevelt. Twenty years from now," Kennedy said, "they might even speak a good word about Harry Truman, but Harry Truman will never say a good word about the Republicans, and you can count on that." As you well know, John Kennedy's prediction came true.

And I want to predict another thing for you tonight, that 20 years from now Republican candidates will even be saying nice things about Jimmy Carter's second term.

I don't want to leave this subject too quick, because I kind of enjoy talking about it.

This year, in 1980, Ronald Reagan said, and I quote again: "Fascism was really the basis for the New Deal." Do you think that Franklin Roosevelt, the father of the New Deal, would want to be quoted by a man who said that about his program?

The Republican candidate also said in 1980, this year, and I quote him again: "I'm opposed to national health insurance. There is no health crisis in America." Do you think that Harry Truman, who first proposed national health insurance, would be rooting for that candidate today?

AUDIENCE. No!

THE PRESIDENT. The Republican candidate in 1980 calls the food stamp program, and I quote, "a massive rip-off." Would Lyndon Johnson have liked the sound of that?

AUDIENCE. No!

THE PRESIDENT. And the Republican candidate of 1980 says that we should threaten a nuclear arms race. Do you imagine that John Fitzgerald Kennedy, who negotiated the nuclear test ban treaty, would have agreed with a statement like that?

AUDIENCE. No!

THE PRESIDENT. Of course not. And neither would any of our Presidents since Harry Truman, Republican or Democratic, because all of us Presidents have known that our primary responsibility in this world is to control the terrible weapons of nuclear annihilation.

The most important issue of this campaign is the issue of peace. I'm committed to using America's great strength, yes, but not to get this Nation in armed conflict, but in the service of peace.

And I'm proud that we were able to bring peace between Israel and Egypt, the first peace between Israel and an Arab nation. And I am also proud that for the first time in half a century, for a full 4 years the United States of America has been at peace. And we're going to keep it that way the next 4 years with a Democrat in the White House.

No issue is more important, and no issue demonstrates so vividly the difference between my vision of what this Nation ought to be and that of Governor Ronald Reagan. Of course, I know that every American wants peace, and I'm sure my opponent does. But you must carefully consider the consequences of his habit of calling for the use of armed force. Every President who's served in the Oval Office has to serve during times of trouble somewhere in the world, challenges from one country to another. Since I've been in the White House, six or eight times armed conflict has broken out somewhere in the world.

In 1975 Ronald Reagan called for sending United States military forces to Ecuador and then to Angola later on. In 1976 it was Rhodesia and Cyprus. This year, so far, it's Cuba, Pakistan, and the Middle East. Let's make sure we don't have to find out what his choices are for starting armed conflict, with American forces, next year.

Let me comment here on the most important issue of all. Every President since World War II has sought agreement to limit nuclear arms—the test ban treaty

under President Kennedy, the antiballistic missile treaty under President Nixon, the Vladivostok accords under President Ford, the nuclear arms limitation agreement negotiated over 7 years by my two predecessors and myself. Governor Reagan has never supported a single one of these agreements. Instead, he proposes to tear up the existing agreement and threaten a massive new arms race.

And he also says that when other countries like Libya try to develop their own nuclear weapons, that it's none of our business. During the debate this week, he flatly denied that he had ever said that. Yet the New York Times, the Washington Post, and the Washington Star all reported what he said. Here's what the New York Times said on February 1st, 1980, and I quote: "Ronald Reagan indicated today that he believed the United States should not stand in the way of countries developing their own nuclear weapons, saying," and I quote Mr. Reagan, "'I just don't think it's any of our business.'"

I say that's wrong, and I believe that halting the spread of nuclear weapons to all nations, and especially to nations that harbor terrorists or may even engage in terrorism themselves, is our business. And with your help and support, our Nation will maintain that commitment to control nuclear weapons in the years ahead.

While we're here tonight let's continue to get the record straight. Governor Reagan is trying to blur other parts of his record too, because when that record is examined very closely by the American people, it's embarrassing for him.

On several occasions he strongly opposed grain sales to the Soviet Union. Then at the moment of truth, as Soviet troops marched in Afghanistan, he buckled, he shifted his position, he opposed the embargo. Overnight Governor Reagan became an election-year supporter of gain sales to Russia. This week we've seen him make some similar shifts.

All this year he made it crystal clear that he opposes the minimum wage, he wants it repealed. This week in the debate he tried to shift his position again. He still wants to undercut the protections of the minimum wage, but he's found a new way to go about it, by exempting millions of young workers from its coverage, by exposing millions of more workers to a new form of competition from a new subclass of workers working at substandard wages.

Let's look at what Governor Reagan is saying about social security this week. For years he had a habit of suggesting that the system be made voluntary. Now he denies this. Now he says, as he said in the debate this week, that social security is a bad investment for young people. That is absolutely untrue. In fact, a typical married worker with dependents, starting out this year at the age of 22, would get back 3½ times more than they pay in and at the same time be covered for disability. And if the husband should die, the wife and the children would be covered, as you know, until the children reach the age of 18. That's an outstanding investment for Americans, and it's been the foundation of security for our people.

For years Governor Reagan opposed Medicare. He started in politics as a traveling salesman for the anti-Medicare lobby. All across this country he said that Medicare was socialism. That should not be too surprising. After all, he's the same person who said that the New Deal was based on fascism, who said that the minimum wage was the main cause of unemployment, who said that trees are the number one cause of air pollution. [*Laughter*]

This week in the debate he said that he never really meant to oppose Medicare. He said he just thought there was a better approach. That's a good excuse, as you know. But that's all it is, just an excuse.

Governor Reagan has become an expert in rewriting the history of his own record. This campaign scheme, as a last-minute operation, is political plastic surgery, and it's not going to work.

And finally, let me say this about the Presidency itself, because Missouri knows what the Presidency means. You know because you observed Harry Truman serve in the Oval Office under some of the most trying and difficult times in the history of this Nation.

The President of the United States is not only the servant of the present, but he's also the guardian of the future. His actions echo down through the years, in the judges he appoints, the regulatory board members he chooses, the agenda that he sets for the Nation, the tone and attitude that is engendered in the hearts and minds of the American people.

When he sits down as head of state with other national leaders, he must always be aware that his every word is weighed and measured, because his voice is the voice of America. He must be sensitive to the needs of other people, yes, around the world, yet adamant always in the protection of America's interests.

As Commander in Chief, the President has within his power to unleash the most awesome, destructive military force in the history of the world. If he's skillful and wise and moderate, it's a task, pray God, he will never have to perform.

I've been President now for almost 4 years, and I've made thousands of decisions, and each one of those decisions has been a learning process for me. Every decision I make leaves me better prepared to make the next one. What I've learned has made me a better President and will make me a better President in a second term. I consider myself to be in the mainstream of the Democratic Party and also in the mainstream of the bipartisan list of Presidents who served in the Oval Office before me.

Let me point out to you, like them, I believe that the United States must be a nation strong. The United States must be a nation secure. We must have a society that's just and fair. We must dare to struggle always, every day, for a peaceful world.

There have been many times of crisis and conflict during these years. In each case, I've had to make a decision as President, often alone. What are the interests of my country? What is the degree of involvement of my country? I've learned that the more difficult the decisions might be, the more likely it is that advisers and experts will be split. Some will advise, do this. Some will advise, do that. The final judgment must be made by the man in the Oval Office.

Sometimes it's a lonely job, yes; but with the involvement of the American people, like you, it's a gratifying job.

Each one of you faces a lonely decision next Tuesday in that voting booth. Your decision makes a difference. Remember, as I said on the debate night, if just one voter per precinct had changed in 1960, John Fitzgerald Kennedy would never have served as President of our country. If just a few more people, a few more Democrats had gone to the polls in 1968, Hubert Humphrey would have been President; Richard Nixon would never have served in the Oval Office.

And you in Missouri remember vividly how close the election was in 1948. If just a few Democrats, a few members of labor unions, a few students who were enlightened about the future, a few aged who were concerned about social security, a few working families who were interested in the minimum wage, had not gone to the polls in 1948, then Harry Truman would never have served his term as a President of this country.

I say, let's go on building a partnership, to stay strong, to stay secure, to raise high the banner of human rights and to keep our Nation at peace. For the sake of all we've done together in the past as Democrats, for the sake of all we can do in the future for a greater country, let's win a tremendous victory on Tuesday not just for me and Fritz Mondale, not just for the Democratic Party but for the ideals and the beliefs and the vision and the hopes and the dreams and the confidence in the strength of the Nation we love. If you help me, we'll have a great future together.

Thank you very much.

NOTE: The President spoke at 7:20 p.m. at the North West Plaza Shopping Center.

Department of Justice Investigation of Billy Carter

White House Statement.   October 30, 1980

No one at the White House has seen the report which the Office of Professional Responsibility in the Department of Justice has submitted to the subcommittee of the Committee on the Judiciary, concerning the conduct of the Justice Department proceedings against Billy Carter. Accordingly, we cannot comment on press accounts of what is said to be contained in the report.

We believe there is no basis for press accounts that the report makes a statement as to any lack of cooperation by the President or the White House staff.

The President and the White House staff have cooperated fully in Mr. Shaheen's investigation. All depositions requested from members of the White House staff have been taken, and access has been provided to their relevant records.

The President himself has also agreed to the interview requested by Mr. Shaheen. By mutual agreement, the holding of this interview has been deferred until the production and examination of all relevant White House records, including those of the President, have been completed.

It is true that arrangements were made to schedule the interview with the President on three dates in October, but each of these dates had to be postponed because the production and examination of relevant White House records had not been completed. When this is done, the interview with the President will be promptly scheduled.

Human Services, and four State insurance commissioners, who are public members, appointed by the President.

The four public members are:

JOSEPH C. MIKE, of Hartford, Conn., who has served as State insurance commissioner since 1977 and was deputy insurance commissioner prior to that time. He also serves on the Connecticut Commission on Hospitals and Health Care and is a member of the executive committee of the National Association of Insurance Commissioners.

SUSAN MITCHELL, of Madison, Wis., who was appointed commissioner of insurance in 1979. Prior to her appointment, she headed the department of regulation and licensing. She is the only female State insurance commissioner in the country.

WILLIAM WOODYARD, of Little Rock, Ark., who was appointed insurance commissioner in 1976 and served as deputy insurance commissioner and chief counsel prior to his appointment. He is president-elect of the National Association of Insurance Commissioners.

ROGER DAY, of Salt Lake City, Utah, who was appointed insurance commissioner in 1977. Previously, he served as administrative assistant to the executive director of the Utah Group Health Plan. He represents the western States on the executive committee of the National Association of Insurance Commissioners.

Supplemental Health Insurance Panel

Appointment of Four Public Members.
October 30, 1980

The President has announced his intention to appoint four public members to the Supplemental Health Insurance Panel. The Panel was created by Congress in June 1980 to evaluate State regulatory programs regarding Medicare supplemental health insurance policies.

The Panel is composed of five ex-officio members, the Secretary of Health and

National Council on Adult Education

Appointment of Five Members.
October 30, 1980

The President has announced his intention to reappoint one member and appoint four new members to the National Council on Adult Education.

The new members to be appointed are:

LOUIS R. SMERLING, of Minneapolis, Minn., a member and past president of both the Minnesota State Board of Education and the National School Boards Association. He is a retired businessman.

LILA C. TASI, of Queens, N.Y., special assistant to the Commissioner of Employment, City of New York. She is a former education specialist and teacher.

PERNELL SWETT, of Pembroke, N.C., superintendent of schools, Robeson County. He is a former adult education specialist at HEW in Washington.

ANN R. SHARRY, of Boston, Mass., director of counseling and career services at Emanuel College. She is active with the Sisters of Notre Dame and in civic affairs.

The member to be reappointed is:

MAXIE C. JACKSON, of East Lansing, Mich., director of the Center for Urban Affairs at Michigan State University. He has served as a member and Vice Chairman of the Council for 1 year.

Advisory Committee on Housing

Appointment of Chairman and 48 Members. October 30, 1980

The President has announced the appointment of 48 members to the Advisory Committee on Housing. The Committee, composed of private citizens representing all segments of the housing industry and related interests, will assure that the administration housing task force, created earlier this month, will have a broad and informed perspective on housing issues.

The task force includes representatives of the Departments of Housing and Urban Development and Treasury, the Council of Economic Advisers, the Office of Management and Budget, the Domestic Policy Staff, the Federal Home Loan Bank Board, the Federal Reserve Board, the Comptroller of the Currency, and the Federal Deposit Insurance Corporation.

The Chairman of the Advisory Committee will be Robert Weaver, of New York, who served as the first Secretary of Housing and Urban Development under President Lyndon B. Johnson.

In addition to Mr. Weaver, the new members of the Advisory Committee are:

PAZELL JACKSON, of New York, N.Y., vice president, Bowery Savings Bank;

HAL GREENWOOD, of Minneapolis, Minn., chairman, Midwest Federal;

MARIAN SANDLER, of San Francisco, Calif., vice chairman, Golden West Financial Group;

BOB BOUCHER, of Denver, Colo., president, Mortgage Bankers;

JESS HAY, of Dallas, Tex., president, Lomas & Nettleton;

ALDEN McDONALD, of New Orleans, La., president, Liberty Bank;

PETER SHAPIRO, of Essex County, N.J., county official;

BERTHA GILKEY, of St. Louis, Mo., president, Cochran Tenant Organization;

LEON FINNEY, of Chicago, Ill., executive director, the Woodlawn Organization;

BOB GEORGINE, of Washington, D.C., president, Building Trades;

CARL HOLMAN, of Washington, D.C., National Urban Coalition;

FRANCISCO LUGOVINA, of The Bronx, N.Y., chairman, Hispanic Housing Coalition;

CHARLES HAAR, of Cambridge, Mass., professor, Harvard University;

JIM HAYNES, of Cleveland, Ohio, president, National Association of Real Estate Brokers;

ARTHUR DECIO, of Elkhart, Ind., chairman, Skyline Corp.;

ANNA HERNANDEZ, of Santa Clara, Calif., executive director, Santa Clara County Housing Authority;

CUSHING DOLBEARE, of Washington, D.C., executive director, National Low Income Housing Coalition;

PHIL BROWNSTEIN, of Washington, D.C., attorney, former FHA Commissioner;

MARILYN MELKONIAN, of San Francisco, Calif., counsel, Lucas Films, former Deputy Assistant Secretary of Housing and Urban Development;

JACK CREIGHTON, of Tacoma, Wash., vice president of Weyerhaeuser;

PEDRO AGUIRRE, of Dallas, Tex., architect;

AMANZIO CHAPA, of San Juan, P.R., president, Colonias del Valle, president, Housing Assistance Council;

DAVE CROWLEY, of Washington, D.C., executive director, American Association of Homes for Aging;

ROBERT O'CONNOR, of Hartford, Conn., executive director, Connecticut State Housing Finance Agency;

BOB DALL, of New York, N.Y., partner, Salomon Brothers;

MAX KARL, of Milwaukee, Wis., chairman, Mortgage Guarantee Insurance;

MARY WIDENER, of Oakland, Calif., executive vice president, Neighborhood Housing Service;

KATHERINE LYALL, of Baltimore, Md., professor, Johns Hopkins University, former Deputy Assistant Secretary of Housing and Urban Development;

PAUL MASVIDAL, of Miami, Fla., president, Biscayne National Bank;

ANITA MILLER, of New York, N.Y., Ford Foundation, south Bronx project specialist;

VONDAL GRAVLEE, of Birmingham, Ala., former president, National Association of Home Builders;

MERRILL BUTLER, of Orange County, Calif., president, National Association of Home Builders;

LEON WEINER, of Wilmington, Del., president, National Housing Conference;

RAY NASHER, of Dallas, Tex., Ray Nasher Co.;

JIM ROUSE, of Columbia, Md., chairman, the Rouse Co.;

HENRY MAIER, of Milwaukee, Wis., mayor of Milwaukee;

DONALD MANES, of New York, N.Y., Queens Borough president;

BETTY BOGOSIAN, of Warwick, R.I., Harwol Properties;

HERMAN SMITH, of Fort Worth, Tex., president-elect, National Association of Home Builders;

KEITH JOHNSON, of Portland, Oreg., president, International Woodworkers of America;

A. CARLTON DUKESS, of New York, N.Y., executive vice president, Wingate Development Corp.;

STANLEY TAUBE, of Minneapolis, Minn., president, National Apartment Association;

HARRY ALBRIGHT, of New York, N.Y., chairman, Dime Savings Bank;

GREGORY W. FRAZIER, of Denver, Colo., chief executive, National Urban Indian Council;

CHARLES ROYER, of Seattle, Wash., mayor of Seattle;

BRENDAN BYRNE, Governor of New Jersey;

ROBERT McKINNEY, of Indianapolis, Ind., chairman of the board, Jefferson Corp.;

GAYLE CINCOTTA, of Chicago, Ill., chairperson, National People's Action.

Foreign Produced Alcohol Fuel

Letter to the Secretary of the Treasury. October 30, 1980

To Secretary Bill Miller

Foreign produced alcohol should not benefit from the exemption granted to gasohol from the four cent a gallon gasoline tax. This exemption should be applied only to domestically produced alcohol fuel, to encourage the growth of our domestic industry.

I would like this corrected immediately by administrative means if possible, by legislation if necessary.

Sincerely,

JIMMY CARTER

Meeting With Prime Minister Suzuki of Japan

White House Statement. October 30, 1980

The President announced today that he will meet with Japanese Prime Minister Suzuki after the election to discuss bilateral and multilateral issues of mutual concern, including the automobile import question.

In making the announcement in Saginaw, Mich., the President said that American and Japanese leaders have customarily met after national elections and that his meeting with Prime Minister Suzuki would continue this pattern. He pointed out that while the two leaders have not yet set the time or agenda for this meeting, automobile imports would figure in the discussions. The President said earlier this month that it was his intention to consult with Japanese leaders about the automobile import question soon after the U.S. International Trade Commission rules on the case in November.

The President stressed again the importance of a strong U.S. automobile industry to the Nation's economy and indicated that he has already taken a number of steps to restore the health of this key industry and to enable it to meet competition from abroad. The ITC investigation, already underway, will determine whether imports have caused injury to our domestic industry. The ITC will submit its findings and recommendations to the President in November regarding the possible need for import relief. The President repeated his pledge to take action on those recommendations immediately after receiving them.

International Bank for Reconstruction and Development

Announcement of U.S. Recommendation of A. W. Clausen To Be President.
October 30, 1980

The White House today confirmed press reports that the United States has proposed to other member governments the election of A. W. Clausen to succeed Robert McNamara as President of the World Bank.

Mr. McNamara, who has been President of the Bank since 1968, has recently announced his intention to retire effective July 1, 1981.

Mr. Clausen, 57, is president and chief executive officer of the Bank of America and its parent, BankAmerica Corp. He is a resident of San Francisco, Calif.

For more than a decade Robert McNamara has provided the extraordinary leadership and sense of vision which have enhanced the role of the World Bank as our most effective international instrument of economic and social development. After reviewing the qualifications of numerous potential successors, the President concluded that Mr. Clausen is the individual best qualified to continue the Bank's strong leadership in the 1980's.

As chief executive of one of the largest American commercial banks with offices throughout the world, Mr. Clausen has acquired extensive international experience. He has the stature to maintain the confidence of the Bank's member governments and the trust of the international capital market, as well as a proven record of commitment to international economic development and assistance to poorer nations.

The Bank's President is elected by its Board of Executive Directors. The Executive Directors are selected by the member governments and cast weighted votes in proportion to their capital contributions to the Bank. The United States Director casts about 21 percent of the total vote. The term of the President is 5 years.

Since the organization of the Bank and the International Monetary Fund in 1946, it has been customary for the Bank's President to be an American, and for the Managing Director of the IMF to be a citizen of another member nation. The present Managing Director of the IMF is J. de Larosiere of France.

Mr. Clausen presently serves as one of the President's appointees on the Japan-United States Economic Relations Group.

He is a past chairman of the Japan-California Association, a member of the National Council for United States-China Trade, a member of the Business Council and the Business Roundtable, and a trustee of the Harvard Business School.

Import Relief for the Domestic Mushroom Industry

Proclamation 4801.   October 29, 1980

TEMPORARY DUTY INCREASE ON THE IMPORTATION INTO THE UNITED STATES OF CERTAIN MUSHROOMS

By the President of the United States of America

A Proclamation

1. Pursuant to Section 201(d)(1) of the Trade Act of 1974 (the Trade Act) (19 U.S.C. 2251(d)(1)), the United States International Trade Commission (USITC), on August 18, 1980, reported to the President (USITC Report 201–43) the results of its investigation under section 201(b) of the Trade Act (19 U.S.C. 2251(b)). The USITC determined that mushrooms, prepared or preserved, provided for in item 144.20 of the Tariff Schedules of the United States (TSUS) (19 U.S.C. 1202), are being imported into the United States in such increased quantities as to be a substantial cause of serious injury, or the threat thereof, to the domestic industry producing an article like or directly competitive with the imported article. The USITC recommended the imposition of quantitative restrictions on imports of the above specified mushrooms.

2. On October 17, 1980, pursuant to section 202(b)(1) of the Trade Act (19 U.S.C. 2252(b)(1)), and after taking into account the considerations specified in section 202(c) of the Trade Act (19 U.S.C. 2252(c)), I determined to remedy the injury, or threat thereof, found to exist by the USITC by proclaiming a temporary duty increase. On October 17, 1980, in accordance with section 203 (b)(1) of the Trade Act (19 U.S.C. 2253 (b)(1)), I transmitted a report to the Congress setting forth my determination and intention to proclaim a temporary duty increase and stating the reason why my decision differed from the action recommended by the USITC.

3. Section 203(e)(1) of the Trade Act (19 U.S.C. 2253(e)(1)) requires that import relief be proclaimed and take effect within 15 days after the import relief determination date.

4. Pursuant to sections 203(a)(1) and 203(e)(1) of the Trade Act (19 U.S.C. 2253(a)(1) and 2253(e)(1)), I am providing import relief through the temporary increase of the import duty on the subject mushrooms.

Now, THEREFORE, I, JIMMY CARTER, President of the United States of America, acting under the authority vested in me by the Constitution and the statutes of the United States, including sections 604 and 203 of the Trade Act (19 U.S.C. 2483 and 2253), and in accordance with Article XIX of the General Agreement on Tariffs and Trade (GATT) (61 Stat. (pt. 5) A58; 8 UST (pt. 2) 1786), do proclaim that—

(1) Part I of Schedule XX to the GATT is modified to conform to the actions taken in the Annex to this Proclamation.

(2) Subpart A, part 2 of the Appendix to the TSUS is modified as set forth in the Annex to this Proclamation.

(3) This Proclamation shall be effective as to articles entered, or withdrawn

from warehouse for consumption on or after November 1, 1980, and before the close of October 31, 1983, unless the period of its effectiveness is earlier expressly suspended, modified or terminated.

IN WITNESS WHEREOF, I have hereunto set my hand this twenty-ninth day of October, in the year of our Lord nineteen hundred and eighty, and of the Independence of the United States of America the two hundred and fifth.

JIMMY CARTER

[Filed with the Office of the Federal Register, 11:23 a.m., October 31, 1980]

NOTE: The text of the proclamation was released on October 31.

Columbia, South Carolina

Remarks and a Question-and-Answer Session at a Town Meeting.
October 31, 1980

THE PRESIDENT. *My good friend, Dick Riley, and Senator Fritz Hollings, distinguished Members of the Congress who are here, State and local leaders, students, teachers, parents:*

I'm glad to be here in the Southland, back home, where I belong and where I'm going to return—and I'm intending to come back down here to stay in 1985 after I finish my second term in the White House.

CAMPAIGN ISSUES

To be serious for a few minutes before I take the questions, I want to say that I come here at a time when one of the great questions dividing the South is about to be decided. I've tried never to shirk the tough questions, never to shrink from speaking out on issues that people care about deeply, and I will not do that today. Even though I am from Georgia, I honestly believe that the Gamecocks have a chance against the Bulldogs tomorrow. And aside from football teams, there's also a contest between two men. One, of course, is Hershel Walker from Wrightsville and the other Georgian is George Rodgers from Duluth. If Georgia's made two contributions to what's best for the lives of South Carolinians, I'll say George Rodgers maybe comes first, but I hope Jimmy Carter comes second. Okay? [*Applause*]

If this had been anywhere else, I would have said it was too early to have alert people come to discuss affairs of our Nation. But here in Columbia, in South Carolina, I know that a lot of you have already done a half a day's work before you came to the meeting, and I base that assumption on how hard your great Governor, Dick Riley, works on anything that's good for South Carolina. You can be proud of him.

It's always a special pleasure for me to talk to students. I talk to Amy quite often about matters of great importance to our Nation. [*Laughter*] Amy's only 13 years old, but she knows what atomic bombs would do to the world. And I also was serving on the local school board as my first public position back in the 1950's, approaching the early 1960's when the great decision was made in the South, and later throughout the Nation, about equality of rights, the elimination of discrimination, the honoring of the principles of our Constitution—one of the greatest changes ever having taken place in the world. It's helped all of us, black and white, and I'm very proud to be part of a nation—a region of that kind.

When those changes were taking place, there were two reasons that one of the older members of the school board always gave why we couldn't do what was better. The first was, "We've never done it that way before." And the other one was, "We've already tried it." So when you're caught between those two things—never done it before and already tried it—it opened up an avenue for young minds to address the crucial issues of our time.

This is a season for inventory. As we approach the 4-year election for a President, it's good for us to look at the nation God's given us—the land, the freedom, the individual hope that exists in the hearts and minds of people, a search for equality of opportunity, the elimination of doubt and division and fear and trepidation, and the engendering of hope and confidence in the future and our lives. This part of our Nation, the South, has suffered in the past. There were times when we had a very poor educational system. There were times when our people worked for starvation wages. There were times when our land was depleted with soil erosion because the poverty that swept this part of our Nation didn't permit good cultivation techniques and good fertilizing techniques.

This is a time when we can look back on those years with a great deal of gratitude. And a lot of that gratitude, in my judgment, goes to the principles and the ideals of the Democratic Party, because I grew up like many of you my age during the Depression years. And I saw Franklin Roosevelt and other great Democrats like Harry Truman come along in those years of despair and raise the banner of hope and do away with the affliction of older people and put forward social security. Republicans were against it. Minimum wage—Republicans were against it; the REA to put electricity on our farms—the Republicans were against it. Later, Medicare to give our older people a good

chance for health care—the Republicans were against it.

And now we look to the future, a change that must take place to give our Nation even brighter years ahead. The Democrats have their hearts with the working people of this Nation. It hasn't changed, never will change. That is a basic issue of this year.

And of course, to keep our Nation strong is a part of the Southern character. We are not a belligerent people. We recognize that only through strength can we have assured peace. And I'm proud to say that for the last 4 years, for the first time in a half a century, the United States has been a nation at peace. We have not had any war, and I pray to God that for the next 4 years, through strength, we'll keep our great Nation at peace.

It's a crucial time in our lives. We've faced them before. And before I take the first question, I'd like to remind you that when our Nation has been tested in the past, we've never failed the test. We've never failed to answer a question, no matter how difficult it might have been. We've never failed in this Nation to solve a problem, no matter how complex. We have never failed in this Nation to overcome an obstacle, no matter how high. And the problems that we face now, the temporary inconveniences, pale into insignificance when we look back on some of the experiences that we've had, with the Great Depression, the World Wars, the divisiveness of Vietnam, the shame of Watergate. What we face now are tests of our national strength and will, but I guarantee you that we will not fail in this great Nation.

And now I'd like to have the first question, and I'll try to keep my answers brief.

QUESTIONS

THE SOVIET UNION

Q. Mr. President, I want to know, okay, when we started in Vietnam——

THE PRESIDENT. Yes?

Q. ——in 1963 with Kennedy, okay, and the Russians started sending weapons over there, that was all fine and dandy. We had to fight with the Russians and the Communist Chinese. All right. Now that the Russians have taken Afghanistan they ask for our help. We don't give it to them. We might send small arms over there but we're trying to please the Russians. The Russians have been taking from us since World War II. And like the next war, well, it's going to be fought by people like me. And I for one am sick and tired of people pushing us around. I'd like to see us start pushing the Russians around—or not pushing them around but standing up for our rights.

THE PRESIDENT. The first American entry into Vietnam was under Dwight Eisenhower, but it was pursued by John Kennedy, and then later by Lyndon Johnson, then by Nixon and later we wound up that war unsuccessfully, as you know, under Gerald Ford. I think it would be an improper assumption that either Democrats or Republicans were responsible for it. It was one of those tragedies that existed, the first time our Nation has ever gotten into a war that we did not win. And we were there, in my judgment, trying to protect freedom, but the Nation was divided because of it. I think we learned a lesson from it, and that is not to inject ourselves into the internal affairs of another country unless our own direct security was involved.

I'd like to point out to you that in recent years, we have not fared poorly in our contests with the Soviet Union. When the Soviets went into their neighboring nation, Afghanistan, this was not a triumph for communism, it was an indication of the failure of communism. If the Soviets' friendship and their form of government had been attractive to the Afghan people, the Soviets would not have had to send 80,000 troops into that small, freedom-loving country in order to try to impose their will on it. And there are now 900,000 people, at least, or more, who have left Afghanistan to escape to freedom, now living in Pakistan; several hundred thousand perhaps in Iran. The same thing's happened in Cuba. If Castro should open the doors of Cuba, the people would escape from totalitarian government to freedom. The same thing's happening in Cambodia.

But if you look back in the last 10 to 15 years, you'll see that the Soviets have lost out around the world in their claim on the friendship and influence of people who are very strong. Egypt was formerly a Soviet ally; now Egypt is one of our strongest allies. Nigeria, the biggest and most powerful, most influential, wealthiest black nation on Earth—80 million people in Africa. A year before I became President, the Secretary of State, Henry Kissinger, was not permitted to land his plane in Nigeria. Now they're our strong ally and friend. Just a few weeks ago, the new democratically elected President of Nigeria was over here to recement the friendship between our two countries.

Also, for the first time in my memory, perhaps in history, we are strong allies and friends now, not military allies, but friends and trading partners with both Japan and China. Four billion people live on Earth; 1 billion of them live in China. Not too long ago, the Chinese and the Russians were military allies. Now we have a good working relationship with the Chinese, and the Soviets, basically, have been frozen out—a major loss by the Soviet Union in their strategic influence, and a major gain for us. We're not exchanging military alliances with China, but having their friendship helps to stabilize that whole Asian region.

In NATO, lately, we have revitalized that relationship. We've got a 15-year progressive plan now, where we're increasing our own defense expenditures with the help of Fritz Hollings in the Senate, and we are also calling upon our allies to increase their expenditures, putting in new tactical nuclear weapons, so that we can defend ourselves.

I think it's important for us to remember that the best way to deal with a question like Afghanistan is not to send American military forces halfway around the world to fight in a neighboring country, when the Soviets have millions of troops just a few miles away. The best way for us to address those kinds of issues is through moderation, strength, political, diplomatic, and economic means.

Just one final point. No President serves in the Oval Office without there being a problem area in the world somewhere, every day, sometimes two or three. Since I've been President, there have been six or eight times when armed conflict has broken out somewhere on Earth. I've had to make a judgment about how to address that threat to world peace.

When the Soviets went into Afghanistan, I had military options, economic options, political options. I decided—no one else decided—I decided that our options should be political and economic. We marshaled 104 other nations with us to condemn the Soviet Union, the first time that it had ever been done. The Moslem countries, 34 of them, some of them former, very close allies and de-

pendent on the Soviet Union, condemned the Soviet Union, demanded that they withdraw from Afghanistan. We have supported, publicly and otherwise, the freedom fighters in Afghanistan, giving them the strength of world opinion to say, "You can keep your freedom." And the Soviets have been bogged down in Afghanistan, unable to impose their will on those people, and they've suffered accordingly.

The Soviets are relatively isolated. We've prevented Soviet Union ships from fishing in American waters. We've cut off the shipment of feed grains to the Soviets, and now in the Soviet Union they have a lower meat allotment and food allotment than any other nation in Eastern Europe, much lower even than their satellite countries. They're suffering because they don't get our grain. They are not going to get it until they get out of Afghanistan, until they change their policy. And we've also cut off the shipment of technological, advanced items to the Soviet Union.

So, the thing that we're trying to do now is to restrain the Soviet Union from further aggression and to prove to them once and for all that aggression does not pay. But the failure of communism has been demonstrated vividly by the fact that the Soviets don't have a single nation on Earth, out of 150 nations, that want to have the same kind of government that exists in the Soviet Union. But there are dozens of nations now shifting over to the American form of government, which shows that in the long run, we'll prevail.

Good question. I'll try to keep my other answers shorter, but that's a darned good question.

Yes, sir?

FEDERAL EMPLOYEES

Q. Yes, sir, Mr. President. I have really a two-part question I would like to ask you this morning. First of all, I would like to know your position on the merger of the civil service retirement system with social security and, second of all, are you for or against the repeal of the Hatch Act for Federal employees?

THE PRESIDENT. I am for the modification of the Hatch Act to give them more influence without their being subservient to the elected political leaders, like myself, who might interfere in their freedom of choice in the election campaign. I'm not in favor of the elimination of the civil service retirement system for any person; force them into the social security system.

Q. Thank you, sir.

THE PRESIDENT. Thank you, sir.

THE ECONOMY AND ENERGY

Q. President Carter, I would like to ask you, how do you propose to work out the problem of unemployment, taking into consideration inflation, which has, in other words, closed down many important, large corporations like Chrysler, and other places like that?

THE PRESIDENT. Okay. Let me point out, first of all, that because of the action of the Congress and me, Chrysler has not been closed down. As a matter of fact, we decided in our Government to guarantee loans to Chrysler from the private banks and insurance companies, at no risk to the taxpayers, to let Chrysler stay a strong and viable company. They have about 100,000 people that work directly for Chrysler and another 250,000 that supply Chrysler with important items in making their automobiles. Chrysler has now come out with a K-car, as you know, and the first day that car rolled off the assembly line they had 40,000 people waiting to buy it.

The American automobiles now, by the way, are more durable, safer, and just as fuel-efficient as any cars on Earth. And I hope that when Americans go to the car dealers in the future to buy automobiles that if all things are equal, they'll remember that American workers are making those American cars.

Secondly, on inflation, we were hit in '79 by OPEC, the oil producing nations, mostly Arab nations, with an increase in the price of oil greater than the total increase in oil price since oil was discovered back in the 1800's. We had a similar impact in 1974, when we had extremely high unemployment and much higher inflation in '74 than we've had in the last 6 months of this year. We've added, since I've been in office, in spite of that shock, almost 9 million new jobs in this country, above and beyond what we had the day I was inaugurated in January of '77—1.3 million of those jobs went to black citizens, and another million went to Spanish-speaking citizens. So, we've had a good growth in employment. Also, the last few months, unemployment rate has been going down, not going up.

The first quarter of this year, when we had the worst shock of the OPEC price increases, the inflation rate averaged about 18 percent. The second 3 months, the inflation rate averaged about 13 percent. In this last 3 months, the inflation rate averaged 7 percent, varying from zero to about 12 percent. The average was 7 percent. That's still too high, and we're working on it.

But my own commitment has been to create jobs, not in the government but in the private sector of our economy. It's very important to remember that we've got now 44,000 fewer full-time Federal Government workers than we had when I was inaugurated President. We're giving better services with a more efficient Government, but we have permitted people to be employed in the private sector.

And we now have a youth bill before the Congress—it's already passed the House; I think it'll pass the Senate—that will provide 600,000 jobs for young people at the junior, senior year in high school and above, combined with corrective education in vocational technical schools in the high schools to let those young people hold jobs.

In addition, we've got a revitalization program that's going to be put into effect next year that gives tax incentives to businesses to invest in new tools and new plants to keep the American workers more productive. This will add another million jobs in the next 2 years.

And of course, with our new energy policy, where we've cut down our imports of oil from overseas by one-third just in the last 12 months, we've got a base now to provide an exciting new future for Americans in the production of synthetic fuels, in the repair or weatherization of homes to make them more efficient, the use of solar power, the building of a public transportation system, aid to poor families that have to pay higher heat bills. These kinds of things are now on the law books and will give us a bright new future, using American energy to propel our vehicles more efficiently, to heat our homes more efficiently, and to give us a technological opportunity that this Nation has never experienced.

The size of this is important for all of you to remember. What we will do in the next 10 years, based on our new energy technology, is bigger than the Marshall plan that rebuilt Europe after the Second World War, plus the total space program that put men on the Moon, plus the entire Interstate Highway System in this Nation. That's how big it is. So that gives us a wonderful opportunity in the future for more jobs, an exciting, better life, more security because we're not depending on OPEC oil, and a chance for young people like you to go into new kinds of careers without the impact of discouragement or danger to our Nation that we've experienced in the past.

All those things have happened. I might point out this. This election year is very important to all of you. Governor Reagan has taken positions just the opposite from what I've described. On his tax program, which is the basis for his future economic development—it's called the Reagan-Kemp-Roth bill—this would give tremendous tax breaks to the rich and would result in uncontrollable inflation.

Business Week magazine, which is hardly a Democratic publication—it's kind of a conservative business publication—said that Governor Reagan's proposal was completely irresponsible and would result in an inflationary explosion in this Nation that would destroy our economy and rob or impoverish everyone living on a fixed income. That's his proposal there. On energy, his proposal is to repeal what we've done, that I just described to you, abolish the Department of Energy, and turn over the responsibility for the future on energy to the oil companies. His attitude on the minimum wage is to repeal the minimum wage. He's been against the minimum wage from the very beginning, and his proposal is to do away with it. As a matter of fact, just this year, he said that the minimum wage has caused more unemployment than anything since the Great Depression.

So, on energy, on economics, on job security, on social security, on Medicare, on the control of nuclear weapons, on many very important issues, the decision about your life's future will be made next Tuesday. And that's why I'm here to ask you all to help me and to keep intact the things that I've described, that'll give you a better life.

Thank you.

SALT II TREATY

Q. Mr. President, on behalf of myself and the mighty W. J. Kenner Raiders, we welcome you to South Carolina. And my question is, in a recent newspaper article, our own Senator from South Carolina, a Democrat and chairman of the Senate budget, has come out against the SALT II treaty. Also, Senator Henry Jackson, a Democrat, has stated his opposition to SALT II. In face of growing opposition from your own party, why do you still support the SALT II treaty which would place us in a position of military inferiority to the Soviet Union?

THE PRESIDENT. Okay. I'll be glad to answer that. There's no guarantee that among Democrats there'll be unanimity about an issue of that kind. And there's a difference in perspective between a Senator and a President. The Senate has only just begun to consider the strategic arms limitation treaty. This treaty is a continuation of what Presidents have attempted to do ever since Harry Truman was in office.

Under the limited test ban treaty, under the SALT I treaty, under the antiballistic missile treaty, under the Vladivostok agreement under President Ford, and now, after 7 years of negotiation under Presidents Ford, Nixon, and myself, we've come up with this treaty.

This treaty has now begun to be considered by the committees in the Senate. It has not yet reached the Senate floor for either a debate or a final vote. My belief is that the treaty, as negotiated, is good. It's a treaty that's balanced. It's a treaty that will control nuclear weapons. It's a treaty that can be confirmed by observation from satellites and from other places. It's a treaty which will lead to a lowering of the arsenals of our Nation and the Soviet Union in the future. In my judgment, it's a necessary step toward much more drastic reductions in nuclear weapons, which I think you'd find that your own Senator Hollings and also Senator Jackson would prefer.

The thing is, a Senator can disagree and can express his own opinion, which is part of our system. But a President must be in the leadership for our Nation's attitude and tone. A President has to deal with other nations around the world. Every one of our allies around the world is in favor of the ratification of this treaty.

I don't claim the treaty is perfect. But this treaty would require the Soviet Union, immediately, to dismantle 10 percent of all its nuclear launchers. It would restrain the Soviet Union between now and 1985, when the treaty expires, to reduce their planned increase by at least a third in the number of nuclear launchers they will have. This treaty will also permit us to move ahead on every single plan that we have for improving our own strategic forces—the Trident submarine, the Trident missiles, the air-launched cruise missiles, the ground-launched cruise missiles, the MX missile, located in mobile sites. It will permit us to move ahead on every single plan that we have.

There's no way to negotiate a treaty that's perfect for a given country, because you've got to negotiate with another nation. But the balance here has been retained and, in my judgment, only with the ratification of SALT II can we then move on to additional engagements with the Soviet Union to have that balanced, reduced, controlled, and confirmable arrangement. If we don't have this treaty, then the Soviets are under no restrictions whatsoever, either about building new missiles, putting more warheads per missile, concealing from the world, including is what they are doing. This is very important element of the agreement.

The Soviets have gone to enormous missiles, like the SS–18, because they didn't have miniaturized circuits and didn't have as good a propellant system as we do. Our missiles are basically smaller, more accurate. We've been in the forefront of technological progress. We're the first nation that MIRVed missiles, put more than one warhead on a single missile. If the Soviets are unrestrained, they could put 25 or 30 warheads on a single missile. Under this agreement that we worked out, they are limited to only 10. If we didn't have the treaty, they could immediately move toward 40, 20, 30 warheads per missile. In my judgment, there is no doubt that this treaty is for the best interests of our country and the entire world.

The last point is, if this treaty is withdrawn by the President—if Governor Reagan should be elected and the treaty is withdrawn—then there will be no debate on the Senate floor, there will be no debate that the American people can observe, there will be no chance to modify this treaty within the Senate to make it more acceptable to the American position and perhaps to be accepted by the Soviet Union. There'll be no base for control of nuclear weapons, and there'll be no base for a further negotiation on SALT III, which will be the next treaty that would be even lower in its limit on our country

and theirs. So, to abandon this treaty would be a major setback for our Nation, in my judgment, a major advantage for the Soviet Union, in my judgment, and an elimination of the progress toward the control of nuclear weapons which, in my judgment, is the most important single issue facing this Nation and the world in the next few years.

Governor Reagan was not for the limited test ban treaty. Governor Reagan was not for the anti-ballistic missile treaty. Governor Reagan was not for the SALT I treaty, now in effect. Governor Reagan was not for the Vladivostok agreement negotiated by President Ford. And Governor Reagan, still, is not for this treaty.

There's another element of nuclear threat that ought to be mentioned in passing that's very important, and that is the proliferation of nuclear weapons among nations that don't presently have them. Our country has been in the forefront of trying to restrain the spread of nuclear weapons, atomic bombs, to other countries. All Presidents have done that until Governor Reagan came along as a candidate for President. He was asked a couple of times this year, "Suppose another nation like Pakistan or Iraq or Libya wanted to develop their own atomic weapon?" Governor Reagan said, "That's none of our business." He thinks that each nation ought to have a right, if they choose, to develop their own atomic weapons. And the threat to us from a terrorist nation like Libya, if they had an atomic bomb, would be an overwhelming terrorist threat.

So, the attitude toward the control of nuclear weapons is something on which Senator Hollings, Senator Jackson, and others agree. Governor Reagan's position is a radical departure—on the control of all nuclear weapons, past, present, and future agreements, the control of the spread of nuclear weapons to those that don't have them.

I think this issue is the most important that will be decided next Tuesday. Thank you.

VERIFICATION PROVISIONS OF SALT II

Q. Mr. President, I'm the parent of a child at Drare High School. I'm a teacher at C. A. Johnson High School here in the city. I went into the military during the Korean war, along with my brother. I flew 95 combat missions in Vietnam; I did three tours over there. My last one was in target intelligence at Eighth Air Force on Guam, choosing targets for B–52s. In both wars, strange things happened. We gave up a defensive position at the negotiating table and came back to the 38th parallel, which is indefensible, and apparently the North Vietnamese— the North Koreans rather, are simply waiting for an opportunity to charge across that line. And, as a matter of fact, that battle has never been resolved. We're still meeting at the negotiating table there.

In Vietnam, as a chooser of targets, all sorts of strange things were happening to us. We got a message in one day that said, "You cannot bomb a military target within 1 kilometer of any foreign embassy." Within 24 hours, we got a new list of addresses of foreign embassies. And, of course, what the North Vietnamese did was they gave new embassies to their friends, which included military targets, and we still couldn't strike those military targets. And we said, "Why?", and they said, "Well, the United States State Department said we cannot."

THE PRESIDENT. What's your question?

Q. Okay. Just a minute. I'm trying to give you some background. I'm not sure that you understand.

THE PRESIDENT. I understand. Go ahead.

Q. Let me tell you another thing that was very, very strange. At target intelligence, we chose some targets for our B–52s that we felt would have stopped the flow of military goods down the Ho Chi Minh trail within a week, by bombing the dikes and dams around Hanoi and the harbor. We were told that we could not do this, we could not put the people of Hanoi and Haiphong up to their hips in muddy water and stop the flow of military goods down the Ho Chi Minh trail, which was killing our people, because the State Department said, "What would the world think of us?" Okay?

Now, this bothered me greatly at the time, and it still bothers me. And I look at some of the things that you want to do. For instance, you want to sign a treaty with the Soviet Union that cannot be verified. They will not let our people go on their territory and count what they've got. You want to do it from satellites.

THE PRESIDENT. I have signed the treaty. There is nothing in the treaty that cannot be verified by us.

Q. Can we send people on their territory and actually count their weapons on the ground?

THE PRESIDENT. No. I can assure you on my word of honor as a gentleman and a southerner and a President that there is nothing in that treaty that we cannot verify, with our own means.

Q. Apparently, Senator Hollings agrees with me that we cannot do it. We're dealing with people——

THE PRESIDENT. I don't believe that.

Q. ——whom lying, cheating, and stealing is their main——

THE PRESIDENT. I think, really, that we're about to run out of time.

Q. ——point, is their main philosophy. Okay. I really haven't got to my question yet, for goodness sake.

THE PRESIDENT. I noticed that. I noticed that. Maybe after I have to leave, you would want to continue your explanation, but I really would like to have a question, and I'll try to answer it.

COUNCIL ON FOREIGN RELATIONS

Q. Okay. In both conflicts, I was told that I was fighting to hold back world socialism. And now I discover that there is a semi-secret organization, based in New York, whose avowed purpose is world socialism and you belong to it—the Council on Foreign Relations. Your top 17 advisers are members of the Council on Foreign Relations. Can you explain your relationship with the Council on Foreign Relations? And then I'll sit down.

THE PRESIDENT. Sure. I don't have any relationship with the Council on Foreign Relations.

Q. The minute you became elected you didn't, because it was written into the bylaws. But before that, were you a member of the Council on Foreign Relations?

THE PRESIDENT. I don't believe I've ever been a member of it. No, I don't think I have ever been a member of any such organization as the Council on Foreign Relations.

Q. I'm surprised. All right. I stand corrected.

THE PRESIDENT. Thank you. Let me point out that the Vietnam war was over when I became President. There were some restraints placed on American fighting men during the Vietnam war and during the Korean war that were very disturbing to many Americans. Those restraints were imposed by President Ford, President Nixon, also by President Johnson, President Kennedy, and President Eisenhower, and Truman before him, in the Korean war.

Sometimes a President has to place restraints on the activities of our country. I have available at my fingertips, literally, the most awesome destructive force on Earth. I described the other night in the debate what a 1-megaton warhead was, and we've got the equivalent of several thousand megaton warheads. And a President has to exercise moderation and restraint. A President has to assess the consequences of actions. A President has to retain the confidence of one's own people. A President has to understand what the exchange of a few megaton warheads would do in this country. It would result in 100 million Americans being killed. And it's all right for us to say we are the strongest nation in the world, let us push around everybody else, but that's not what a President can do. You've got to have sound judgment and an even temperament and a careful consideration in the White House.

This will have to be the last question.

AID FOR THE HANDICAPPED

Q. Good morning, Mr. President.

THE PRESIDENT. Good morning.

Q. My name is Walter Smith. I'm from Columbia. My daughter's in the public schools here in Columbia, South Carolina.

I'd like to ask you one question. Can you help, nationally, deaf people, black and white relationships, handicapped, the education of these people, equality in education for these people, for minorities—trades, work, and technological improvements? Most of the government agencies are not helping handicapped people. We're on very low levels. We are very far behind educationally. I would like to ask you to help us better our future, so that our people can look to you and possibly vote for you.

THE PRESIDENT. One of the most gratifying things for me as President has been the ability to implement the special sections in the laws relating to disabled or handicapped people. We've had a special emphasis on special education and also a new commitment to the prevention of handicaps early in a child's life, so that they won't follow them through their years as an adult. We've increased, for instance, the Federal allocation of funds for public education by 73 percent since I've been in the White House and, at the same time, we have committed ourselves not to let the Federal Government interfere in the operation of or the management of the school systems themselves. That should be left at the local level and the State level, and that's part of my philosophy as a southerner and as a former school board member in Sumter County, Georgia.

I might say that we still have a long way to go, because many handicapped people in this Nation don't know about the new changes and the new financing programs that have been put through the Congress since I've been in office to give young people and older senior citizens a chance—who are handicapped—to learn a trade and to have a better chance in life.

I have put into office, as the Admin-istrator of the Veterans Administration, a young man who happens to be from Georgia, Max Cleland, who was an officer in the Vietnam war. He's a triple amputee, having lost both his legs and one arm in the Vietnam war. But he has a special knowledge of how handicapped people suffer but also a special knowledge of how they can overcome those handicaps and live an almost normal, fully productive life. This is a major commitment of mine.

I think your question is very well-placed, and I think that it would be good for this audience to learn this morning one symbol, so that you can talk to a handicapped or a deaf person in the future, and that's the symbol like this [signing]. How about everybody trying it? It means, "I love you." So whenever you meet someone who can't hear and who might be mute and who can't speak, if you'll go like this [signing], it means "I love you."

And I'd like to tell the audience from the bottom of my heart, as your President, as your next-door neighbor, and as one who's enjoyed being with you this morning, I love you all. Thank you very much.

NOTE: The President spoke at 8:10 a.m. in the Township Auditorium.

Columbia, South Carolina
Remarks at a Meeting With State and Local Democratic Leaders. October 31, 1980

Mr. Mayor, my good friend Governor Riley, Fritz Hollings, the fine Members of the Congress, Butler and Ken, Mendel—it means a lot to me to be here with you—Bob McNair, my old friend, who was one of the leading Governors along with Fritz Hollings, that set a standard for me to try to follow when I became Governor.

I'm very glad to be in South Carolina. I just have been concerned, as I told the students, that this Saturday, South Carolina and Georgia are going to be playing against each other and—[laughter]—I'd like to remind you that no matter how it comes out, I need your support on Tuesday—Okay?—[laughter]—because when the Heismann Trophy comes to Columbia, to your Gamecocks, don't forget that your Heismann Trophy winner come from Duluth, Georgia. [Laughter]

We've got a lot in common. When Ann Williams was singing, I remembered my years when I was 9, 10, 11, 12 years old, I always came every summer to spend a week or two down by Abbeyville, Greenwood, Ninety-Six with my grandmother's people, the Pratts. There was a little railroad stop there, and it was named Pratt. And when anybody asked me where I went to South Carolina, I just said, "We went to Pratt, South Carolina." [Laughter] There was only one family that lived there, but—[laughter]—it's about the same size as Archery, Georgia, where I grew up.

I thought a lot about what to talk about this morning, because I want to be brief. I'm not going to make a political speech as such. But I tried to think back in my own lifetime about things that might be interesting or important to you. I did grow up during the Depression years on the farm, and I saw how my own life was transformed by a Federal Government that I felt cared about us. We didn't have running water. We didn't have electricity.

I grew up like many of you. The bell rang on our farm at 4 o'clock in the morning Sun time. And we caught the mules in the barn lot, and we were in the field waiting till it got bright enough to see how to plow and not plow up the cotton and corn and peanuts before the Sun ever rose. And we got home after sundown, and then had to pump water and feed the livestock before we went to bed that night quite early. We had a battery radio—that was it—to keep track of the outside world. And then the REA program came along, and later the minimum wage for the workers in the factories to do away with the sweatshops, and then social security. And people in the South began to have a better life.

My daddy got involved in politics, because he was on the Sumter Electorate Membership Board. He was the first board member. I think it was in 1937, when I was 13 years old. And it kind of opened up a better life for us. And then I was like a lot of you, my family came to this country in the early 1600's, 1630's, and went from Virginia to the Carolinas, North Carolina, then down to Georgia before the Revolution.

All of us have been farmers—not a single one from me back to that first settler that didn't farm. My daddy didn't finish high school. Neither did his father nor any of our ancestors. I was the first boy that ever finished high school. And my daddy was in the military in the First World War, first lieutenant, and his ambition for me from the time I was 5 years old was to go to the Naval Academy, and I did. But the military, West Point and Annapolis, to us was the ultimate in what a southern young man could achieve. And to get a college education was something that was a dream that very few people realized.

When I came home from the Navy after 11 years, I was still filled with my southern heritage and my southern commitments. We were approaching a time of testing of this Nation and this Southland, more severe than anything since the War Between the States, because at that time, black people couldn't vote. And a lot of people didn't see the devastation that was being wreaked on white and black by racial discrimination in an absence of equality of opportunity. I served on a local school board, went on there in 1954 and went off in 1962. It was worse than being President. [*Laughter*] Tough years.

A lot of you remember it, because the Governors and the State legislators and others right then didn't want to touch school integration. And the school board members had to do it. And when it was HEW saying, "Do it," a lot of southern white people didn't do it. But when the Federal courts and the Constitution of the United States was put before us, as is the case with the southern character, we revered our Constitution, and we complied with the law that transformed our life for the better. And it opened up a new era for the Southland.

My service there on the local government taught me a lot about what needed to be done, and I ran for the State senate, because I wanted to continue some progress in Georgia to have a better school system. You all had a better one than we did when I was elected to the State senate. And when I got to the State senate, I only wanted one assignment. And that was to be put on the education committee, because I saw that as the biggest challenge for the South, to give our young people's minds a chance to grow and to develop and to give our children a better chance in life than we had had, even, and to see the grandchildren come along even better. And I served on the education committee; I was the secretary of it, and I was chairman of the university committee in the Georgia senate, served two terms, then ran for Governor.

I was defeated in 1966. I was a newcomer to statewide politics; nobody knew who I was. I came close, but I was defeated. I learned a lot out of that defeat. I went around the State of Georgia for 4 years. I shook hands with 600,000 people. My wife went one direction, I went another. I learned a lot about politics. And I learned to tie my own political future with a direct contact between me and an individual voter. And I went to the voters who quite often felt that they didn't have a chance to let their voices be heard. And then I became Governor and served along with John West and other great southerners and people from all over the country, and got—to know about this Nation. And then, of course, I was elected President.

But I've had a chance as a school board member, as a State senator, as a Governor, as your neighbor, as a President to see the necessity for a partnership, not just between the Federal, State, and local governments but among organizations that represent people outside of government, and among those individual human beings in this Nation who ought to be part of and who are part of the history, the present, and the future development of our country.

I've won some political victories that people didn't think I could win. I was not predicted to win in 1976, as you know.

South Carolina gave me a great victory here, and it was crucial in the very close election between myself and an incumbent President, Gerald Ford, who had repaired the damage that Richard Nixon and Watergate had done. A lot of people felt obligated to him because he had done a good job. And it was a difficult thing, but I think the overriding feeling in that '76 election was the choice between what the Democratic Party stands for and what the Republican Party stands for. It doesn't change much.

You can go back during those years that I described to you earlier. The Republicans were against social security. The Republicans said that REA was a socialist plot to inject the Federal Government into the private enterprise system of this country. When the Democrats put forward a 25-cent minimum wage, Republicans were against it. They said that a grown man and a grown woman trying to feed children and pay rent, buy food, wasn't worth 25 cents an hour. I got out of high school in '41. My first job was working for the government, measuring land 10 hours a day, 40 cents an hour. I had to furnish my own car and pay the expenses. But that was a lot of money for me, $28 a week, I got. That was the minimum wage then. Republicans were against the 40-cent minimum wage. It hasn't changed much. Medicare, a program that provided older people with a modicum, at least, of health care: Democrats put it forward; Republicans were against it.

The South is looked upon as a conservative region of the Nation, and I don't disparage the word "conservative," because conservative in a way means to conserve precious things. But the connotation of conservative to mean the preservation of power and the deprivation of equality of opportunity is something that I turn against.

The South's been always interested in a strong defense—always. Whenever our Nation's been tested in war, the battleground casualty figures and those lost in prison camps have always shown that the South came forward, quick, patriotically, and first. But at the same time we know the value of peace. No part of the Nation has suffered so much from the ravages of war as Georgia and South Carolina. But we know that the preservation of peace is dependent on strength—not only strength militarily but strength of character, unity, confidence, respect for one another. And I got elected President because the Nation was ready to change.

The last President from the Deep South was James Polk, who was elected in 1844, and between 1844 and 1976, there was not a chance for anyone from the Deep South to be elected President. But the country's changed, and I think there's now a realization that we're one nation and that some of the things that have stirred in the South—progress, technology, better education, more equality, harmony, friendship among people who are different—has been an inspiration to the rest of the country.

Well, next Tuesday the Nation will make a decision about who will lead our country the next 4 years, yes, between two men, between two parties, but also between two futures. And I hope that this next few days you'll think back on our past, blacks and whites, what we've done together, what the Democratic Party's meant to us. Our country's at peace. It's been 50 years since a President could stand before any audience and say, "We haven't had a war since I've been in the White House." And I hope we can go 4

PHOTOGRAPHIC PORTFOLIO

President Jimmy Carter

Overleaf: Addressing the 10th Regular Session of the Organization of American States at the OAS Building in Washington, D.C., November 19. *Above left*: With Nigerian President Alhagi Shehu Shagari on the South Lawn of the White House, October 7. *Above right*: Meeting with Chancellor Helmut Schmidt of the Federal Republic of Germany in the Oval Office, November 20. *Below*: Greeting local Brownie troop and gifted children from Texarkana, Texas and Arkansas, at Texarkana Municipal Airport, October 22.

Above left: At a White House
reception for Robert Strauss in the
East Room, December 9. *Below left*:
Receiving a certificate of appreciation
from the National Association of
Women Judges in the East Room,
October 3. *Above right*: At signing
ceremony for the Martin Luther
King, Jr., and Boston African
American National Historical Sites in
the Cabinet Room, October 10. *Below
right*: Casting vote at Plains High
School, Plains, Georgia, November 4.

Above left: Greeting Mikhail Baryshnikov and other Kennedy Center honorees at the White House, December 7. *Below left*: Meeting with President's Advisory Committee on Women in the Cabinet Room, December 16. *Above right*: Signing Paperwork Reduction Act of 1980 in the Cabinet Room, December 11. *Below right*: Meeting with past and present American Nobel Prize winners in the Oval Office, November 19.

Above: With Mrs. Carter during White House visit of President-elect and Mrs. Reagan, November 20. *Left*: With President-elect Reagan at the White House, November 20.

more years, through strength, keep our Nation at peace.

So, to conclude my rambling remarks, I'd like to say this: I've come here as a friend and as a neighbor, kin to some of you, to ask you for your help, because the election is going to be very close. And I believe that the issues at stake are important to you, important to your family, to those you love, and to those who look to you for leadership. You've been invited here to the Governor's Mansion because you are leaders. And there's no one in this group that can't reach 500 or a thousand people, maybe even 10,000 people through the radio and so forth between now and November the 4th, next Tuesday.

And I'd like to ask you as a special favor, as a neighbor, as a southerner, as an incumbent President, as a Democrat, as a friend, to go a second mile for me this last few days. It's important that I and the Democratic candidates who are running with me on the same ticket in South Carolina be elected. We'll try to continue the heritage that's made us a great part of the world. We'll try to bind ourselves closer together in the spirit of common belief in liberty, in freedom, in human rights, in respect for one another, in the characteristics of which I'm very proud as an American.

Thank you very much.

NOTE: The President spoke at 9:20 a.m. on the lawn of the Governor's Mansion.

Medicare and Social Security

Statement by the President.   October 31, 1980

None of the great achievements of our past 50 years is more important to the people of this country than social security and Medicare. They provide earned benefits to millions of retired people and disabled Americans, and they protect all of us from living in fear of a future of poverty, dependence, and despair. These great initiatives are the pride of the Democratic Party. Their history illustrates the basic differences between Democrats and Republicans in American public life.

We Democrats believe in a strong social security system. We fought for it and we enacted it over Republican opposition. We Democrats believe in affordable health care for all Americans. Under Harry Truman and Jack Kennedy and Lyndon Johnson, we fought for Medicare over Republican opposition. And we are fighting Republican opposition today to enact an affordable national health plan that will improve Medicare for the elderly, extend protection against catastrophic medical expenses to all of us, improve health coverage for the poor, and provide special benefits to expectant mothers and children in the first years of life. That is the Democratic agenda and the agenda for the next 4 years of the Carter administration.

Where do the Republicans stand in this election? Governor Reagan's first major experience in public life was to engage in an active, hard-fought campaign against Medicare. If he had his way, our seniors would have little protection against health costs today. Last Tuesday night in the debate, he tried to tell us he just supported an alternate approach, but the record speaks for itself. That so-called alternate approach, the Kerr bill, was simply a welfare bill which would have helped only those who had already spent their life savings, sold off their assets, and sacrificed their economic security to pay their medical bills.

The truth is that Governor Reagan worked to convince the American people that Medicare, which protects all of us against medical expenses when we retire or are disabled, was socialism. He made that charge in a phonograph record which was the main organizing tool of the American Medical Association's anti-Medicare campaign. He also charged that Medicare would lead to the Government's telling people where to live and where to work and that if Medicare passed, "you and I are going to spend our sunset years telling our children and our children's children what it once was like in America when men were free."

The truth is, it took Democratic Presidents and Democratic Congresses to pass Medicare over the opposition of Ronald Reagan and the Republican Party, just as it will take a Democratic President and a Democratic Congress to enact a national health plan over that same opposition.

Nor is Governor Reagan's opposition to Medicare and Medicaid a matter of ancient history. He wrote in his syndicated newspaper column for April 5, 1979, that "those who claimed during the debates over Medicare-Medicaid in the 1960's that these programs would be the first foot in the door to massive Government interference in health care have been proved totally correct."

Tuesday night we saw the same Ronald Reagan who posed as a friend of Medicare assume the role of lifelong defender of the social security system. He actually told us he had never advocated making the social security system voluntary. Everyone knows that if we let wealthy people who can afford elaborate private pensions leave the social security system, the cost to those Americans who would be left would rise to prohibitive levels. But before Ronald Reagan began to aspire to higher office, that is exactly what he pro-

posed. Because of his denial, it is important to set the record straight.

For example, in October of 1964 in a local speech, he said this: "Can't we introduce voluntary features that would benefit a citizen to do better on his own, to be excused upon presentation of evidence that he had made provisions in nonearning years?" And this was not a single flight of fancy; it was a consistent Reagan theme for several years.

Governor Reagan has a right to change his mind. He does not have a right to rewrite history on subjects as important as social security and Medicare. Last Tuesday night he showed not just a desire to revise the past but also a fundamental failure to understand the value of the social security system as it exists today.

Mr. Reagan told the Nation: "The problem for young people today is that they are paying into social security far more than they can ever expect to get out." If those of us who listened to Governor Reagan believed him, then it could do great damage to public confidence in the social security system. But Governor Reagan was flat wrong. The average young worker with dependents will receive benefits $3\frac{1}{2}$ times the amount of his payments and $1\frac{3}{4}$ the amount paid by himself and his employer together.

Contrary to Governor Reagan's misinformed opinion, social security is and will remain a sound investment. It protects almost all of us from disability and provides a hedge against dependency as we grow older. I want to see that it stays that way. I think it is important when the same Governor Reagan who did favor a voluntary social security system years ago, just as he did fight against the enactment of Medicare, believes, mistakenly, that social security is a poor investment for the young people of our country.

The positions of Mr. Reagan's past are important not because we seek to debate history but because their echoes are heard in the positions he and his advisers are taking today.

I listened carefully to Mr. Reagan's comments Tuesday night, and this is what he said about the future of social security. "What is needed," he said, "is a study I have proposed by a task force of experts to look into this entire problem as to how it can be reformed and made actuarially sound, but with the premise that no one presently dependent on social security is going to have the rug pulled out from under them and not get their check."

What will emerge from this study directed by "experts" who will see that no one "presently" in social security loses benefits? Does Governor Reagan propose to reduce benefits for those Americans now paying into the social security system not yet dependent on its benefits? Does he intend to reduce the cost-of-living allowance for retirees, as his advisers suggested last Friday in the Wall Street Journal? Does he intend to let affluent Americans who can afford large private pensions "opt out" of the system, leaving far higher tax burdens on those who remain? What does he have in mind? I find little to comfort the American people in the record of Mr. Reagan, the record of the Republican Party, or the reports from behind the closed doors of his advisers.

Mr. Reagan has a habit of saying that we are distorting his position. But it was Governor Reagan who built a record of opposition to Medicare and a national health plan; it was Governor Reagan who once proposed a voluntary social security system; and it was Governor Reagan who carefully hedged his answers last Tuesday and told us then that social security is a poor investment for young Americans.

My own position is clear. I oppose taxation of social security benefits. I support the indexing of benefits to keep pace with inflation. I oppose cutting back basic social security and disability provisions on which most Americans rely. As I have in the past, I will insist on the financial integrity of the system. The social security reforms enacted 2 years ago have fundamentally assured the integrity of the system through the first quarter of the 21st century. If adjustments are needed, we will see that they are fair. And I will seek to assure, as with the 8-percent social security tax credit I proposed in the economic renewal program, that social security taxes are relieved in ways which are consistent with the health and integrity of the system as a whole.

Social security and Medicare have immeasurably improved the lives of senior citizens in this country. Governor Reagan can remember, as I can, when older Americans lived in constant fear of financial disaster, when men and women who had worked hard all their lives had to face a retirement without dignity. I am proud to stand for social security and for decent health care, and I propose to continue the great fight for social justice in our country.

Let's win this election and get on with our work of building a secure future for our Nation.

NOTE: The statement was released in Columbia, S.C.

Lakeland, Florida

Remarks at a Rally With Area Residents.
October 31, 1980

First of all let me express my thanks to Senator Lawton Chiles, to Governor Bob Graham, Ambassador Askew, Congressman Allen, Mayor Oldham, and all the mayors who've come here from the surrounding territories. And from the bottom of my heart let me thank my neighbors, the Floridians, who gave me an overwhelming victory in '76 twice, early this spring, and who are going to give me a big victory on November the 4th over Ronald Reagan.

As you know, in the last 4 years I've been to a lot of places, and I've seen a lot of people. But I just want to say how great it is for me to be back down here in the South, at home, where I belong and where I'll be in 1985.

I grew up on a farm in south Georgia not far from the Florida line, and I've never forgotten those early values that were important to me—hard work, self-sacrifice, trust in our families, closeness with our neighbors, and trust in our God. And I pray that we in the South and the people of this Nation will never get away from those ideals and commitments which although other things change, those ideals and commitments never change.

Most of you have the same background, the same kind of families, the same kind of upbringing that I have had in my own life. You share with me the values and my love of this country. It was you who put me on the road to the highest honor that any American can have, to serve as your President. It was you, the people of Florida, who launched my campaign in 1975 and 1976, who kept me on the road early this year, in the spring, when I had a tough opposition. It's you who stood with me all the time in the past. You've got a great political tradition of supporting Jimmy Carter. We are people of traditions. Let's don't change it. Okay? [*Applause*]

I want to be frank and honest with you. I've come back to my part of this country to ask you to join with me once again in a great and a noble campaign. It's a campaign for peace. It's a campaign for jobs. It's a campaign for a secure and prosperous and progressive and united future for the country that we love. Without your help I cannot win. If the election were held today, the issue would be very much in doubt. It's a close election.

Throughout the Nation—and as you know it's a close election in Florida itself—we must not allow a defeat for the Democratic Party, its candidates, and for all we stand for. There's too much at stake. This is not just a matter of personality between myself and Governor Reagan. It's not just an issue of whether or not a Democrat sits in the Oval Office. The question is, are we going to finish the work we've begun on energy security, on revitalizing our economy, on an effective, steady, carefully planned rebuilding of our Nation's military forces, on peace for our country, on peace for the Middle East, and on control of the most powerful weapon that ever has been known or envisioned in the history of mankind?

I have confidence in the American people, and I have confidence in their judgment. I have confidence in you. When it comes down to a time of decision, when you go into the voting booth next Tuesday, Americans will choose wisely. They will choose continuity. They'll choose to get on with the job that we've set for ourselves.

Many questions have been raised in this campaign. The hardest questions of all is the one American people must ask yourselves: Who should serve in the Oval Office? Who should hold power over peace and war? Who should hold the power to lead our Nation into the future? If you've been listening to the Republican candidate in recent weeks, then you know he's trying to wrap himself in the mantle of great Democratic Presidents. It happens every election year. Let me read you what Franklin D. Roosevelt said back in 1944 about how Republicans changed their tune in the few weeks before an election. This is Roosevelt's words: "The whole purpose of Republican oratory these days seems to be to switch labels. Now imitation may be the sincerest form of flattery, but I'm afraid that in this case, it's the most obvious common or garden variety of fraud." And now the Republicans have the nerve to come back and quote Franklin D. Roosevelt himself.

John Kennedy said in 1960 about the Republicans: "They're even beginning to say a few kind words about Franklin Roosevelt. Twenty years from now, they might even speak a good word for Harry Truman. But Harry Truman will never say a good word about Republicans." You can depend on that. And I make this prediction about the future myself. I predict that 20 years from now, Republican candidates for President will be saying nice things about Jimmy Carter's second term.

The Republican candidate, Governor Reagan, said this year, 1980, "Fascism was really the basis of the New Deal." Do you think that Franklin Roosevelt, the father of the New Deal, who brought us the minimum wage, who brought us social security, who brought us the REA, who brought us the first steps to a good medical care for our people would have wanted to be quoted by that candidate?

The Republican candidate, in 1980, this year, said, and I quote, "I'm opposed to national health insurance. There is no health crisis in America." Do you think that Harry Truman, who first proposed national health insurance, would be rooting for that candidate today? The Republican candidate, this year, said that we could threaten a nuclear arms race. Do you imagine that John Fitzgerald Kennedy, who negotiated the nuclear test ban treaty, would have agreed with that? Of course not. Of course not. History doesn't change. There's a thrust of history that separates the Democratic Party and Democratic Presidents from those of the Republicans.

Many of you grew up like I did in the South. You saw your lives changed by Dmocratic administrations. They faced difficult issues. They made tough decisions. And almost always the Republicans were there in opposition to the Democrats giving the working people of this Nation, the elderly people of this Nation, a good life. Republicans were against the minimum wage when it was 25 cents an hour. Republicans were against social security. They called it socialism or even communism. Republicans were against the rural electrification program. They said that the power companies themselves ought not to have any competition from those TVA dams that gave our farmers a better life. The Republicans have always been against those programs that give people of this country a better life.

Let me say this too: Guess what Governor Reagan said about social security this week? For years he had a habit of suggesting that social security ought to be voluntary. But as the election time approached, he began to change his tune, but not very much. This week, in the debate, he said that social security is a bad investment. That is absolutely untrue. As a matter of fact, a typical married worker with dependents, starting out paying even the age of 22, will get back $3\frac{1}{2}$ times more than he's paid into social security. And all those years, when that young person is getting toward retirement age, he has the protection, if he becomes disabled—or if a husband dies, as you know the wife and the children until they're 18 years old are covered by social security. But Governor Reagan has a commitment to change that program established by Democrats which means so much to the people of this country.

For years, Governor Reagan opposed Medicare. He started in politics as a traveling salesman for the anti-Medicare lobby. All across this country he said that Medicare was socialism. That should not be too surprising. After all this is the same person who said the New Deal was based on fascism. It is the same person who said, just this year, that the minimum wage was the primary cause of unemployment. And this is also the same person who said that trees are the number-one cause of pollution. [*Laughter*]

Let me say a few words about the Presidency. Last night I was in Missouri before I went to Columbia, South Carolina. We had a rally like this in St. Louis, and the memory of everyone in that audience was about Harry Truman. Harry Truman understood what the Presidency is. So did Franklin Roosevelt. So did Lyndon Johnson, and so did John Kennedy. There is a continuity in serving in the White House, almost always shared among Democrats, often by Republicans as well. We must have a strong nation, and as long as I'm President we will have a strong military force, because Democrats have known, and especially those of us from the South, that only through strength can we keep our Nation at peace.

In 7 of the last 8 years before I became President, when Republicans were in the White House, we had a decrease in real funds allotted in the Federal budget for our Nation's defense. Since I've been in office, we've had a steady, orderly, and effective increase above and beyond in-

flation every single year. When I came into office there was no long-range cruise missile program. Now we have one. There was no new battle tank or modern, armored personnel carrier. Now they're in production. There was no answer to the potential vulnerability of our ICBM's and silos to protect our Nation from strategic attack. Now there is an answer, the mobile MX missiles. Our purchases of Army equipment, jet fighters and aircraft, had dropped by two-thirds in the 8 years before I became President. Since then we've increased them by 50 percent.

I'm not trying to point out these changes since I've been in office in a deeper commitment for our national defense to frighten anyone. The point is that the only way to keep our Nation at peace is to keep our Nation militarily strong, to let the American people know it, to let our allies know it, and to let any potential adversary know that if they attack the United States of America, they will be committing national suicide.

I can stand here before you today, the first President in 50 years who can, and say that since I've been in the Oval Office, this Nation that we love has not been at war. We have been at peace. Every American wants peace. I'm sure my opponent wants peace. But you must carefully consider the consequences of his habit of calling for the use of armed forces. In 1975 he called for sending U.S. military forces to Ecuador and to Angola. In 1976 it was Rhodesia and Cyprus. This year, so far, Governor Reagan has advocated sending military forces of our country to Cuba, to Pakistan, and to the Middle East. It's important for you and me to make sure Tuesday that we don't have to find out in 1981 where he wants to send American military forces next year.

Another very important subject, more important than social security, more important than the minimum wage, more important than medicare, more important than any other issue that's before us this year, and that is how to limit atomic weapons, nuclear arms.

Every President since World War II, Democrats and Republicans, has sought agreements with the Soviet Union, balanced controls, confirmed agreement to limit nuclear weapons with a commitment to lower the level of nuclear arms in both countries in the future. The test ban treaty, under President Kennedy, the antiballistic missile or ABM treaty, under President Nixon, the Vladivostok agreement, under President Ford, the nuclear arms limitation agreement that I signed earlier in my administration, last year, negotiated 7 years by three Presidents, Governor Ronald Reagan has never supported a single one of these agreements to limit nuclear weapons. Instead, he proposes to tear up the existing agreement and threaten a massive, new nuclear arms race.

Also he says—and this is almost equally disturbing—that when other countries, like Iraq or Libya, try to develop and to build their own nuclear weapon, it's none of our business. During the debate this week, Governor Reagan flatly denied that he had ever said that, yet the New York Times, the Washington Post, the Washing Star, and other news media around this country quoted him when he said it—not once, but more than once. Here's what the New York Times said February 1st, 1980: "Ronald Reagan indicated today that he believes the United States should not stand in the way of countries developing their own nuclear weapons." Governor Reagan said, and I quote him, " 'I just don't think it's any of our business.' "

It'll be too late to ask Governor Reagan what he meant by that statement after he gets in the Oval Office, if he should be elected. Now is the time for every American to stop and think about the consequences of casting aside nuclear arms limitation agreements and opening up the way for terrorist countries to have atomic weapons. The spread of nuclear weapons to all nations, and especially to those who harbor terrorists or even engage in terrorism themselves, is our business. And with your help and support, we will keep the commitment of this Nation, which has been the commitment of all Presidents, Democratic and Republican, to control those nuclear weapons and to avoid the threat of nuclear destruction which might come if a deviation from that policy should occur.

And finally let me say this: The President of the United States is not just the servant of the present, but he's also in many ways the guardian of the future. His actions echo down through the years in the judges he appoints, in the regulatory board members he chooses, the agenda he sets for this Nation. When he sits as a head of state with other leaders from around the world, he must always be aware that his every word is weighed and measured because his voice is the voice of America. He must be sensitive to other nations' concerns, but he must be adamant in the protection of American interests.

As Commander in Chief the President has within his power the unleashing of the most awesome destructive military force the world has ever seen. If he's skillful and wise, if he's understanding and tolerant, if he's moderate in his actions and committed to carrying out the desires of the American people, he'll never have to order that unleashing of great destructive power.

I know that you believe that we have a major task before us, and I know that you believe that the President of this country has a major responsibility on his shoulders. I'd like to point out in closing that November the 4th you'll have to make a judgment about what this Nation will be. A President represents himself, yes. A President represents his party, the Democratic Party, the mainstream of it. A President has to make judgments, when times of trouble or crisis or armed conflict arise in the world, about the level of our Nation's interest and what our Nation's involvement ought to be. A President can have advisers to come into the Oval Office and to sit with him and to consider what ought to be done. But my experience with advisers is that when the issue is very close, when the decision is very great and profound, the President must make that judgment alone. He must share with the American people the commitment of his life, the experience that he has, his knowledge of our country.

You will make a decision on November the 4th in a similar way. You'll be alone, and you'll decide between now and then how deeply your feelings will persist as you cast your votes. I presume that you'll be here and will be helping me as you go to the polls and vote, but I want to ask you to do this: Think about the future during these next few days. Think about your family members. Think about the people that you love and those who love you. Think about the severity of the consequences of the election day: peace, war, employment, civil rights, minimum wage, social security, protection of consumers, an energy policy, the stature of our Nation, moderation, progress. These are the kinds of issues that are important to every

person who listens to my voice. And I ask you to go to the polls on November the 4th and between now and then to make a sacrificial effort to get all those over whom you have influence or listen to you to join with us in a noble crusade to make the greatest nation on Earth even greater in the future.

Thank you very much. I love you. God bless you.

NOTE: The President spoke at 11:59 a.m. at the Lakeland Civic Center.

Lakeland, Florida

Remarks to Reporters Concerning Medicare and Social Security.   October 31, 1980

We have what I consider to be a very important matter to discuss with the American people through the press.

One of the most striking aspects of the debate this week between Governor Reagan and me was his attempt to misrepresent his long-held views and his record on a number of important issues. Two of those areas are social security and Medicare. As everyone in this Nation knows, social security and Medicare are among the greatest advances for simple humanity and decency in our country's history. They're also the pride of the Democratic Party.

In the debate Governor Reagan flatly denied that he had ever advocated making participation in the social security system voluntary. But, in fact, he did advocate exactly that on a number of occasions. This has been amply documented.

In addition, Mr. Reagan stated that young people today are paying in far more than they can ever expect to get out of social security. This is categorically untrue. The facts are that a typical young mother or father entering the system today will ultimately receive 3½ times what he or she puts in, and that is taking inflation into account. But social security provides not only retirement benefits but disability insurance and survivor's benefits for widows and for children as well.

On Medicare, Mr. Reagan said in the debate that he never opposed the principles of Medicare. The facts are that he did indeed oppose Medicare, both in principle and in application. As a traveling salesman for the American Medical Association's campaign against Medicare, he sowed the fear that Medicare would mean socialism and that it would lead to the destruction of our freedoms. This is an album that was put out as a result of Mr. Reagan's campaign against Medicare, a professionally prepared effort on his part to kill Medicare.

This was the issue at stake. He traveled around this country, as he well knows, in an attempt to kill Medicare. Now he flatly denies that he did so. Just last year, Mr. Reagan wrote, presumably referring to himself, and I quote his words, that "those who claimed during the debates over Medicare or Medicaid in the 1960's that these programs would be the first foot in the door to massive Government interference in health care have been proven totally correct." Those are the words of Governor Reagan this year. Because social security and Medicare are so vital to the lives of our people, it's crucially important to set the record straight and to correct the misstatements that Governor Reagan made.

Because the misinformation which Mr. Reagan presented to a hundred million people during our debate can easily cause a totally unwarranted loss of confidence in the social security system, it's important to set the record straight, because no politician should be allowed to get away with rewriting history, even his own history. It's important to set the record straight.

I would like now to introduce two men who can give you a much more detailed analysis of these crucial issues. They're as well equipped to do that as any two people in our country. They have the confidence and trust of Members of the Congress and of leaders in the role in our country to give secure lives to the retired people of our Nation and to protect Medicare and social security. Wilbur Cohen. His intimate knowledge of the social security system dates back even further than the formal beginning of the system itself.

In 1934, as a research assistant to the special Cabinet committee appointed by President Franklin D. Roosevelt, Mr. Cohen actually helped to draft the original Social Security Act. Later, he served as Director of Research and Statistics for the Social Security Administration. As an Assistant Secretary of Health, Education, and Welfare under President Kennedy, Mr. Cohen helped to draft and to secure the passage of Medicare. And as Secretary of HEW, in the Cabinet of President Johnson, he was in charge of the overall administration of both social security and Medicare. He now serves on the National Commission on Social Security, appointed by the Speaker of the House of Representatives, Tip O'Neill.

The other man is Robert Ball. Robert Ball served as Commissioner of Social Security under three administrations. He was responsible for the administrative implementation of Medicare. He started in the local social security office and rose to the highest position in the Social Security Administration as a recognition of his merit. He's the author of a definitive book on social security, published by the Columbia University Press about 2 years ago, and now serves on the Advisory Council on Social Security.

Mr. Cohen and Mr. Ball have between them some three-quarters of a century of knowledge and experience concerning social security and Medicare. They share my concern about setting the record straight and correcting the misstatements that Governor Reagan has made. I am proud to introduce them to you now. They will give you the benefit of their knowledge and their analysis.

NOTE: The President spoke at 1:11 p.m. at Lakeland Municipal Airport.

Memphis, Tennessee
Remarks and a Question-and-Answer Session at a Town Meeting.   October 31, 1980

THE PRESIDENT. *Senator Sasser, Congressman Jones, Congressman Ford, Congressman Alexander from Arkansas, Speaker MacWhirter, a special visitor, Bill Winter from Mississippi, and my good friend Johnny Cash and my cousin, June Carter Cash:*

I haven't just recently claimed her as a cousin. She's been my cousin for a long time.

I'm here today because I believe the people of Memphis and the mid-South should get a chance to question or to listen or to be with at least one of the Presidential candidates this week. Also, I believe in beauty, and I wanted to come to the city, among all the major cities in the Nation, that's been chosen the cleanest of all. That's great; that's great.

Anyone who's familiar with geography or familiar with history or familiar with the South or familiar with the technological changes that are going to take place in this Nation the next few years has to look on Memphis with great admiration and anticipation. The confluence here of major highways, railroads, tremendous opportunities for barge traffic, coal in the future, synthetic fuels, technology, new ideas, cohesion of your people, competence—gee, you've got a lot to be thankful for. After 1985, maybe, when I come South, I'll spend some time with you again.

CAMPAIGN ISSUES

You've had to make some tough decisions in recent years, but you've made good ones. I notice that since the day I was sworn in as President, you've added 24,300 new jobs in the Memphis metropolitan area alone.

And as President, I know something about decisions as well. I've had to make literally thousands of them in the Oval Office. One of the most important and meaningful ones was one of the most difficult, and I'd like to mention it because it affects you and your life, and that is to establish full diplomatic relations with the People's Republic of China. You might say, "How does a decision like that made by a President in the Oval Office affect my life?" Well, as a result of this historic step, we've got a billion new friends, a billion new customers for products that you make and products that you grow on the productive land that God's given us in this country.

Earlier this month we signed the grain agreement with China guaranteeing that we'll sell them between 6 million and 9 million tons of American grain every year. And we still have an opportunity to sell them steel, coal, other products that we manufacture. This means, too, that rice production in this region, a rapidly growing crop, will have new opportunities for export sales. Korea will buy more rice this year perhaps than ever before in history. And we've got new possibilities of major rice sales to Nigeria, the largest and also the most influential and also the largest and the most economically sound black nation on Earth; 80 million people live in Nigeria.

We have also tripled our trade with Mexico in the last 4 years. And all the time we were improving our relationships with China, we have doubled trade with Taiwan.

At this moment China is the biggest customer in the world for American cotton. And we've had a good opportunity, short of any sort of military relationship, to join with China in keeping stability in the Western Pacific, to make sure that we could keep the world at peace.

I'm very grateful that for the first time in 50 years—50 years—I can say, as President, since I've served in the Oval Office the United States has not been at war and I pray that the next 4 years we'll keep our Nation at peace.

The last point I want to make before I answer questions is this: Being a southerner, I'm proud of my heritage. And I think you've done a superb job in this region to preserve the finest aspects of the past, like the revitalization by the preservation of Beale Street area, and also to look to the future with your $800 million coal gasification plant. And you have also been able to balance in this region the proper economic growth with industry and with agriculture.

A lot of people say OPEC oil is a special blessing that God gave to the Arab countries. All the Arab nations together have about 6 percent of the world's energy reserves—6. The United States by itself has 24 percent. And if I had a choice between Arab oil and American soil, I'll take the good land that God gave us.

And now we've got a solid 30 minutes for questions, and I'll start on my right.

QUESTIONS

AGRICULTURAL POLICIES

Q. Mr. President, I'm Marlin Jackson, from a small country town in Paragould, Arkansas, the First Congressional District. I'm president of a small country bank, and I've served for the past year as chairman of the agricultural division of the American Bankers Association. My question, sir, is, there was a conspicuous absence in the national debate of a discussion of agriculture and farming. And I would like for you to discuss with us this evening the basic difference between your farm policies and those farm policies as proposed by Governor Reagan. And more importantly, do you understand what parity is? [*Laughter*]

THE PRESIDENT. The only comment that I recall that Governor Reagan has made about agriculture this past year is that he did not know what parity meant. I grew up as a farmer. My people have lived in this Nation since long before the Revolution. We have all been farmers. And I've been extremely interested in a good agriculture policy for our country.

The farmers ought to think back. You've had a terrible drought in this area, as we have in Georgia. But think back to 1977 and compare what existed then with what has happened since that time. Net farm income for farmers in the last 3½ years is the highest under any President who ever served; gross farm income, the highest under any President who ever served. Exports of farm products set a new world's record in 1977, a higher record in '78, a higher record in '79.

In '80, early this year when the Soviets went into Afghanistan, we restricted grain sales to the Soviet Union, and we started looking around to make sure that we did not let the full suffering for that action fall on the shoulders of farmers. So, we explored for new customers.

Last year we exported $32 billion worth of American farm products—$32 billion. We will increase that this year by 25 percent, the biggest increase in the history of this Nation. We will export to foreign countries this year $40 billion worth of American farm products.

Also, it's good to point out that the price of corn now compared to 4 years ago, early in '77: twice as high. Meat prices have doubled. Soybean prices have doubled. Wheat prices have doubled.

We've got a long way to go in agriculture. In 1981 we'll have a new farm bill coming up to replace the one that we passed in 1977. We'll do the same thing we did before. We'll use a farmer as the Secretary of Agriculture, Bob Bergland, and not some paid representative or lawyer that represents the main grain trading companies that in the past took the profits away from farmers who had to sell their crops in the harvest season.

One other point. We have gotten the Government's nose out of the affairs of the American farm family, and we've let the farm family build on their farms 2.8 billion bushels of storage so that the farmers, when they harvest their crops—corn, soy-beans, wheat, oats, barley, rye, rice—can store those crops on the farm, wait until the price reaches an acceptable level for them, and then sell the crops.

As you know, in the past farmers quite often had to sell their crops during harvest season. That's when the middlemen put the price down as low as possible to buy the crops cheap, and then they would hold the crops in major grain elevators until the price went up, sell them, and the consumer had to pay a lot more. The farmers didn't get any profit. That has been changed, and that will continue to be changed.

And the last point is that we have opened up to the farmers a bright new prospect for using new technology. Two years ago we produced hardly any gasohol from crops grown in this Nation. This year we'll produce 135 million gallons. Next year we will reach our goal of producing 500 million gallons of fuel from the farms, not from OPEC, which I think is a very good step forward and will give us 10 percent of our fuel from it.

Thank you, sir.

I might add one postscript. Ed Jones is here. He's one of the most knowledgeable members of the Congress about agriculture. He helps guide me in the right direction. Ed? And Bill Alexander has formed on his own initiative, with a group of interested people, the Mississippi Valley International Trade Center, which is promoting the sale of American farm products, particularly those grown in your big region here, three States, to foreign countries.

So, a lot's going on good for the American farmers and others interested in agriculture in the years ahead. Now, the second question.

ENVIRONMENTAL PROTECTION

Q. Mr. President, I'm Sue Jankey, from Bartlett, Tennessee, and I'm very much concerned about America's natural resources. Considering this country's energy needs, what role will the protection of the environment play in the policies of your second administration?

THE PRESIDENT. Sue, I think that's an outstanding question, because that's one of those balances that has to be drawn that I mentioned earlier.

We've finally passed, after 3 years, a new energy policy for our country. We never had one before.

In 1974 the OPEC oil companies— OPEC oil countries increased the price of oil much more than anyone ever thought they would. We had a terrible recession, the worst recession since the Second World War. The unemployment rate went much higher than it's been any time this year, and the inflation rate was much higher even than it's been in the last 6 months.

In '79 we had an even worse increase in the price of oil. As a matter of fact, the price of oil last year went up more than since oil was first discovered in the 1800's. We were partially ready for it with our new energy legislation. We held unemployment down. As a matter of fact, unemployment here is lower than it was when I went into office. We've added 9 million new jobs in our country, a net increase of 9 million new jobs, 24,000 of them right here in the Memphis metropolitan area. The last few months, the unemployment rate's been going down. We were hit hard with inflation—18 percent the first quarter this year, 13 percent the second quarter, 7 percent average this quarter.

And in that balance we've tried to make sure that as we produce new energy that we protect the quality of our environment. We haven't destroyed America's beauty and the purity of our air and the cleanliness of our water, and the productivity of our land in giving us this new energy achievement. Compared to a year ago, we're importing one-third less oil from overseas, 2 million barrels every day less than before. That's good, because as you import oil from overseas, you also import inflation and you import unemployment.

There was a temptation to say, well, let's do away with environmental laws in order to expedite production. But we've worked with the coal companies, the United Mine Workers, with the steel industry, and the steelworkers, we've worked with the automobile industry and the automobile workers, we've worked with agriculture, to make sure that we do not lower environmental standards in order to increase production.

This year, in the United States we've got more oil drillrigs running today, over 3,100, than ever before in history. We'll produce more oil and gas wells this year than any year in history. We're producing more coal in the United States this year, over 800 million tons, than ever before in history. We're exporting more coal than ever before in history. And our environmental laws are being enforced as well. We're protecting the beauty of the precious part of our Nation that ought not to ever be destroyed.

But in Alaska, for instance, all of the offshore areas would be open for oil and gas exploration, 95 percent of all the land in Alaska that's got mineral potential will be open for exploration, and we've opened up in our continental United

States, south of Alaska, more land for exploration for oil and gas in a 5-year period than has been opened up since 1954, when the offshore leasing program started.

The point is that we have made all this progress, and between now and 15 years in the future, we will triple coal production, and we have not lowered environmental standards one bit, and we're not going to.

And this is one more point I'd like to add: If Americans are ever told that the only way you can burn American coal is to have dirty air and filthy water and destroy the cleanliness of our land, then people would be very reluctant to use coal. But as long as we keep our standards high on environmental quality, then the American people can say we can use coal with confidence. And my goal is, using Memphis as one of the major ports, by the way, on the international energy markets to replace OPEC oil with American coal.

RELIGION AND POLITICS

Q. Mr. President, I'm Peggy Reynolds, from Memphis. It seems to be the popular thing these days for your opponent on those of us that support our new Department of Education to be charged with being immoral. As a mother and a teacher, I think it's the best thing that's happened for children and education since peanut butter. How are you reacting to these charges from our moral opponent?

THE PRESIDENT. Well, this is a question I've never answered before, but I think this morning, here among my friends and my neighbors, in a State that houses the headquarters of the Southern Baptist Convention, I'd like to answer the question.

We're kind of one family here in the South. We share a common background. We share a common upbringing. We share a common set of values about patriotism, about family, about hard work, about neighborliness, and we share, many of us, a common religious faith. We worship in different ways, but in the South we've always respected another person's religious beliefs.

I grew up as a little boy who went to Sunday school every Sunday morning. From the time I was 3 years old, I never missed going to Sunday school. When I went to the U.S. Naval Academy as a midshipman for 3 years, I taught Sunday school. It was an extra chore for me, but it was one that I enjoyed. I taught the little children of the officers and enlisted men who worked full time at Annapolis. When I got on a submarine, on a ship, quite often Sunday mornings, certainly on Easter Sunday and so forth, I would hold religious services for other crew members on the ship, who wanted me, as a young officer, to tell them about Christ, about my religion.

When I was elected Governor, the first day I moved to Atlanta I shifted my church membership to a nearby church. And I became a deacon in the church, taught Sunday school to a senior citizens group. When I moved to Washington as a President, immediately I joined a church, First Baptist Church in Washington. And about one out of four Sundays when I'm there at the church—I travel a good bit on weekends—I teach Sunday school still.

My religious beliefs are very precious to me, and I've never tried to criticize those who worshiped differently from me. But until this year, I have never had anybody question the sincerity of my belief in

God and my commitment of my life as a Christian believing in Jesus Christ as my savior.

Lately I have heard about—I have not seen them—some very vicious television advertisements questioning my religious beliefs, insinuating all kind of damaging things to me within the region that I love so much. I'm not going to dignify these attacks by answering them specifically.

But I feel sure about my own relationship to God. And I hope and I pray that the people who know me so well, including Johnny Cash, who came to Atlanta when he had just finished making a beautiful movie in Israel, and I joined him in the premiere showing of that movie, not to get publicity, but because it was part of my life. And here the last few days of an election to have my opponent and those who support my opponent allege that I have a false belief or that I would twist my beliefs against the teachings, as I understand them, from the Bible is very, very disturbing to me.

I'm not trying to say this in a bragging way, because it's maybe not appropriate for a President, but this is important. For years my wife and I have closed each day, never missed, reading a chapter in the Bible, Old Testament and New Testament. When she and I were apart last night, we read the same chapter. And quite often we call each other on the phone and kind of share what we read about. We both study Spanish, and for the last 2 or 3 years, each evening we read the chapter in Spanish just to kind of get two birds with one stone. I don't believe God minds it. [*Laughter*] I don't quite understand it quite as well.

But, you know, I believe and hope that those listening to my voice on television,

radio, or in this audience will share with me a belief that in our country we ought to be able to separate church and state. It's the way I was raised.

Peggy, one other point, just to summarize: I'm not in favor of a religious definition of an acceptable politician, and I'm not in favor of a political definition for Christian fellowship or for religious fellowship. I don't see anything in the Bible that says whether or not we should have a Department of Education, or whether we should build a B–1 bomber or the air-launched cruise missile, or whether we should share the responsibility for the operation of the Panama Canal. These are the kinds of things that have been injected, for the first time in my memory, in a major way into the political arena, tied in with religion.

The last point is anyone who believes differently from me has a perfect right to express themselves privately or publicly or even from a religious pulpit, but I have a right to explain myself. And I appreciate your having given me that opportunity.

EQUAL RIGHTS AMENDMENT

Q. Mr. President, I'm Caroline Graves, from Immaculate Conception High School here in Memphis. Seeing how ERA ratification is at a standstill right now, if you're reelected what would you do to ensure that the progress that has been made in this direction so far will not be eroded by the time I or even my children enter the business world?

THE PRESIDENT. Thank you, Caroline.

You know, the equal rights amendment is one of those very divisive issues on which people have strong feelings both ways.

Again, to repeat myself, I grew up in the South, and I grew up in a time when there was a lot of discrimination against people because they were black. My first job after I came home from the Navy was on a local school board, and we had so-called separate but equal rulings from the Supreme Court. It took me a few days, a few weeks on the school board to realize that the white kids were riding school buses to school, the black kids were walking, and that the books that the black kids used in their schools were the ones that the white kids had worn out.

The South made a change. It was very difficult to give equality of opportunity to all of our citizens. It was the best thing, in my judgment, that's happened to the South in my lifetime.

I come from a working family. My mother helped support our family during the Depression years. She was a registered nurse, which was quite an achievement back in those days, in the twenties, early thirties. She worked either 12 hours a day for $4 or 20 hours a day for $6. And the cash money that she brought home during the depression years was very important to us.

Nowadays in this country we've eliminated a lot of discrimination, but there is still discrimination against women. When a man and a woman work the same job, the same amount of time, on an average throughout the country if the man gets paid a dollar, the woman only gets paid 59 cents. That's not right, because quite often, as you know, about a fourth of the households or families in this country, a woman is the head of the household, and that means that the children only are getting 59 percent as much food, clothing, shelter, and an opportunity in life.

There've been a lot of distortions about the equal rights amendment. Let me tell you exactly what the equal rights amendment says. It doesn't say anything about bathrooms. It doesn't say anything about women being drafted. It doesn't say anything about homosexual families. Here's what the equal rights amendment says: that equality of rights shall not be abridged by the Federal Government nor any State government because of sex, because somebody's a woman. That's all. That's the amendment. It says that the Federal Government nor a State government shall not take away equal rights from a person because they're a woman. That's all it says.

We've extended, since I've been in the White House, the time for the ratification of that constitutional amendment by 3 years. It runs out, I think, in March of 1982. Thirty-five States have ratified the amendment, got 3 States to go. I don't know what those States will do, because States are independent of me and State legislators are the ones that have to vote on it.

But I believe that we should guarantee women equal rights in the Constitution of the United States, and I'll do all I can to get that amendment ratified.

Caroline, I'm kind of long on postscripts today, but let me say that this is not a partisan issue. The first party to include the equal rights amendment in its platform was the Republican Party, 40 years ago. For 40 solid years the Republican Party under Eisenhower, Goldwater, Nixon, Ford have always supported the equal rights amendment, until this year when Governor Reagan changed it. Six Presidents before me, Ford, Nixon, Johnson, Kennedy, Eisenhower, Truman, have all favored the equal rights amendment. Governor Reagan's opposition to the equal rights amendment is a radical departure from the mainstream of other Presidents and also his own party.

I don't think it's liberal or conservative when you guarantee women that you won't cheat them. And that's what the amendment says: you can't cheat women.

EDUCATION

Q. Mr. President, my name is Pat Ostrander. I am president-elect of the Memphis Education Association and first and foremost a teacher of first grade. As a teacher I am particularly pleased about the establishment of the new Department of Education and about its potential. And I would like to know from you, sir, what do you see as the major focus of the Department of Education during the next 4 years of your Presidency?

THE PRESIDENT. Okay. Thank you, Pat.

I think I said earlier that my first job was on a board of education. And when I ran for the Georgia Senate back in '62, I only had one request when I got to Atlanta, and that was to be on the Committee on Education. When I was Governor, I spent about 25 percent of my time trying to improve the education system in Georgia, because it was in bad shape and it was important to me, as a young person who got a good education, to give the same opportunity to others.

My family lived in this Nation for a long time. My father didn't finish high school; neither did his father. Nobody before me ever finished high school. And I could see that the future of the South lay in its children.

When I got to Washington, it was obvious to me there that almost all of the relationships between the "E" part, the education part of HEW—education was down here, health and welfare were on top—was just arguing and squabbling with the States and local board members in the Federal courts.

There was no way for a Congressman or a Governor or a member of the school board or a teacher or a school superintendent or a parent to go to Washington and know exactly where to go to get the answer to a question about education. You went to the Department of Health, Education, and Welfare, and there was nobody there who could really speak for education.

Now we've got a Secretary of Education that sits with me in the Cabinet Room in Washington. And if anybody in this Nation has any question about education, from kindergarten all the way up to graduate school, there's one person, Secretary Shirley Hufstedler, responsible for education.

We have increased Federal funds for education 73 percent since I've been in the White House, and we've done it with a commitment that's very dear to me. I do not want to see the Federal Government's nose in the affairs of the local school systems. That ought to be by the local people and the State legislatures and the State Governors. We need to preserve that, but at the same time there are areas of our Nation that are in need and that allotment of funds for special education, for retarded children of all ages, the correction of defects in an education system run by and controlled by the local people is important.

I had another goal in mind that we have reached. Most of the time a President can't reach his goals. But one that we've reached is this: There is no need in the United States of America for any young person who finishes high school, who's able to do college work, to be deprived of a college education because of the poverty of a family.

I guarantee you that for the first time in the history of our Nation, any young person who's academically able to do college work can get a college education—I don't care how poor that little kid's family might be—through grants, scholarships, loans, or work-study programs. Now, I'm not claiming that if a young person refuses to work at all on a part-time job that they're going to have their way paid through college. But through a work-study program, loans, grants, or scholarships, every single child in the United States can now get a college education. That's a good achievement, and we've got a lot more to do.

SOVIET BRIGADE IN CUBA

Q. Mr. President, I'm Mike Leahy, from Christian Brothers High School here in Memphis, and I'd like to ask this question. Concerning the Soviet brigade that still remains in Cuba, you promised extensive military maneuvers in the Caribbean and in Guantanamo Bay. Does the poor showing we made during these maneuvers reflect our present military capability, and if so, why hasn't anything been done to alleviate this problem?

THE PRESIDENT. All right.

As you know, about a year or two ago, there was a great deal of publicity about the fact that a Soviet brigade did exist in Cuba. As a matter of fact, when John Kennedy was President, early in the 1960's, I think 1962, the Soviets had a ma-

jor military force in Cuba. They began to put into Cuba missiles that could reach and attack our Nation. John Kennedy demanded that the Soviets remove those weapons—they had nuclear warheads—and the Soviets did so.

At that time, they left in Cuba a brigade, maybe more than one, but they've cut it down lately to about 1,500 men. We monitor that brigade very closely, almost on a daily basis, from our satellite observation stations that go around the Earth all the time or from other means. We know what the brigade consists of; we know what its capability is. That brigade of Soviet soldiers ought not to be in Cuba. Like the Berlin wall, like the Soviet presence in Afghanistan, it's not acceptable to us. We'll never say that it's acceptable to have that brigade in Cuba.

The brigade has no offensive capability that could threaten us. It has no missiles that could reach our shores. It has no ships or amphibious forces that could launch an attack against the United States. It has no airplanes, nothing that could reach us. It's there primarily, I believe, for two reasons. One is to make sure that Castro, who receives several million dollars worth of aid from the Soviet Union every day, is watched by the Soviets in Cuba. And secondly, I think it's there, maybe from the beginning of Castro's administration, his regime, to support Castro if his people started to turn against him. That's not a likely prospect now, but it's there.

We will continue to monitor the Soviet brigade, and we will not permit that brigade to mount any threat, any possible threat of an attack on us. We have formidable naval forces, we have strike forces in our country, in Florida, in Tennessee, Georgia, Alabama, Mississippi, that could attack that region if we had to defend ourselves. We do mount major naval exercises in the Caribbean region regularly, sometimes secretly, sometimes in a highly publicized way. We have had a major amphibious landing force exercise in Guantanamo itself, as you know, since this high-publicity item became aware in the American people's consciousness.

And so, we're doing the best we can to protect our interests, to reassure America, to let the Soviets know that they cannot mount for even locate an attack force in Cuba against us. That would not be something that we would abide. And the Soviets have agreed that they will not increase the force in Cuba in such a way that it would comprise an offensive threat to us.

But I don't want to mislead you, Mike. It would require, I think, a very serious misjudgment on the part of any President to try to send American soldiers into Cuba to try to root out a small brigade of Soviet troops that don't harm us. We don't have that legal right. But we do have the right to defend ourselves and to protect us against any threats, and we will honor that right to protect our Nation and its interests.

Thank you very much.

ISRAEL

Q. Mr. President, my name is Mark Levine. I'm the rabbi of the—[*inaudible*]—congregation here in Memphis, Tennessee. Mr. President, the American people know that there is only one country in the Middle East that is not a totalitarian dictatorship or a fragile feudal monarchy. American people know that there is only one state in the Middle East that shares our own American democratic ideals, our democratic form of government, our democratic institutions, including exciting elections like the one we're presently engaged in. That state is the state of Israel.

The highlight of your Middle East policy was the Camp David agreement, which resulted in the peace between Egypt and Israel, for which we're extremely grateful and thankful. However, we are concerned and confused by signals that have emerged from your administration that have signaled the Arabs that in a second Carter administration you would be more forthcoming in pressuring Israel to make a concession that would be detrimental to its very existence, that would result in the emergence of another Palestinian terrorist state, a platform for Soviet intentions in the Middle East, and ultimately harmful to our own aspirations in the Middle East as Americans.

My question to you is: These concerns have been reinforced by reports emanating from Arab capitals that your signals, either through your failure to veto in the United Nations votes that were detrimental to Israel as well as private assurances received from your emissaries, that indeed in a second administration you would bear down hard on Israel. Mr. President, can you assure us, either way?

THE PRESIDENT. Yes, I'd be glad to. This will be the last question I'll have a chance for, but let me reply very briefly.

The first time I met with the Prime Minister of Israel, Mr. Rabin led the Government there. Just 2 or 3 weeks later I met with President Sadat. I told them both that the dream that I had as President was to have a major Arab nation, Egypt, recognize Israel's right to exist— none ever had; engage in direct negotiations with Israel—none ever had; recognize Israel's right to be secure—none ever had; to work for a peace treaty possibly, with open borders, exchange of tourism, recognition diplomatically, and exchange of Ambassadors.

President Sadat said, "That's a good dream. It'll never happen in my lifetime." All those dreams have now come true. And although Israel and Egypt had four wars in 25 years, the latest one in 1973, they now engage in discussions not about war, but about peace. They face each other not across barbed wire with bullets and tanks, but across a table, through negotiators. We've been a part of it.

In 1973 when Israel was in danger because of the Arab invasion, a Republican administration announced that we were reassessing our policy toward Israel and withheld, as you know, crucial military aid which Israel needed. We've never done that, and that will never be done as long as a Democrat serves in the White House.

We have one thing to contribute in pursuing peace in the Middle East, and that is the trust that the Arabs and the Israelis have in me. If I should ever betray that trust, if I should ever tell a lie, if I should ever make a misleading statement to them or go back on a promise, then my role as a mediator would be gone. I could not serve any more in that good office.

I look on the Mideast peace agreement not as a favor to Egypt and Israel, but as an investment in the security of my own country, because I see the fact that Israel is there, is secure, is democratic, is committed to peace, is strong, as a direct bulwark in the strength and the peace of my own Nation.

I will never support a PLO state. I will never negotiate with nor recognize the PLO until after they recognize Israel's right to exist and assume that 242 resolution is the basis for Middle East peace.

I will never cause any reassessment of our policy toward Israel in military or economic aid, as was done under the last Republican administration. As a matter of fact, in the last 3½ years the amount of military and economic aid that we have given to Israel, with the support of Congress, has been as much as all the previous administrations in history since Israel first became a state.

I will never permit the other nations of the world, including the Arab nations, to isolate Israel in the world community. And if in the United Nations Security Council there should be an effort to expel Israel, I will veto such a resolution, if there's a resolution passed in the General Assembly to withhold the credentials of Israel. I see no way that my country would participate any further in the deliberations of the United Nations General Assembly.

Another point that I would like to make in closing is this: We've not sent any signals to the Arab countries. I don't deal with other nations in that fashion. Every posture that I have maintained in the Middle East has been well understood by the Jews in Israel and around the world, well understood by the Arabs in Egypt and the other countries. I don't have any secrets with Begin against Sadat. I don't have any secrets with Sadat against Begin.

We'll continue to work for a Mideast peace, for a secure Israel, for a Jerusalem that's undivided. And the ultimate legal status of Jerusalem in the community of nations will be determined by negotiations, and the conclusion of those negotiations will have to be acceptable to the Government of Israel. That's my assurance to you. I will not violate the commitment that I make.

That's a good question.

One other comment, and I'd like to close. I've enjoyed having the questions. They've been very interesting and, I think, very stimulating—one on religion was the first time I've had. I'm glad that I had the chance in the South to reply.

Keep this in mind: There's a lot at stake next Tuesday. Many of your lives have been changed by what Franklin Roosevelt did in the Depression years with TVA, REA, over the opposition of the Republicans. Many of your lives have been changed by the establishment of the minimum wage, 25 cents only. Republicans opposed it, called it socialism. Many senior citizens lives have been changed by social security. Republicans were against it. Medicare, Republicans were against it. The change in the tone of relationships among white and black citizens has helped the people in the South.

A commitment to strong defense has been a habit of southerners, who've always been the first ones to volunteer, have been willing to lay down their lives for the defense of our country.

When I went into the Oval Office, as a professional military officer, having served 11 years in the Navy, in the submarine force, for 7 of the previous 8 years our defense commitments had gone down, 37-percent reduction in the 8 years before I got there. We've had a steady deep commitment to an increase above and beyond inflation ever since the day I was in office. I've used the strong military capability not to inject our military forces into war, but to maintain the peace. And that issue is important next Tuesday.

Every President since Harry Truman has committed himself to controlling nu-

clear weapons with balanced, controlled, confirmable agreements between ourselves and the Soviet Union. Governor Reagan has abandoned that policy. Our Nation has always been in favor of keeping the radical nations, Libya, Iraq, and others, from having atomic weapons. This year Governor Reagan said if one of those other nations wants to have an atomic weapon, it's none of our business.

Those issues are very important to you and to your families, to the people that you love, to the people who look to you for leadership. That's what's at stake next Tuesday.

I believe in a strong country, a country that's fair and just, a country that gives our children a better chance in life than we had, a country that's united, where people share experiences and share confidences and share commitments in the years to come. And I believe in a strong defense. But I also believe, as I said in the debate the other night, that the best weapons are the ones that are never fired in combat, and the best soldier is one that never has to shed his blood or give his life in battle. Remember that when you go to the polls next Tuesday.

Thank you. God bless you.

NOTE: The President spoke at 2:52 p.m. in Hangar 6 of the Federal Express Complex at Memphis International Airport.

Jackson, Mississippi
Remarks at a Rally With Area Residents. October 31, 1980

Governor Bill Winter, former Senator Jim Eastland, Mayor Dale Banks, Mr. Speaker, Mr. Chairman, my friends from Mississippi:

Last night about this time I was in St. Louis, Missouri, talking to people who remembered the great Presidency of Harry Truman. Early this morning I was in Columbia, South Carolina. Later I was in the central part of the State of Florida. Then I went up to Memphis, Tennessee, and now I've come here to Jackson, Mississippi. And tonight I'll be in Houston, Texas. Tonight I want to talk to you for a few minutes about the Southland, about what it means to be a southerner and about what Mississippi has meant in my own campaign to become President of the United States, the first President from the Deep South since James Polk was elected in 1844.

I remember election night of 1976, when the issue was in doubt: the choice between a Republican President for 4 more years and a southern Democrat, who'd be in the White House for 8 years. Mississippi came through then. You've set a good tradition. I'm counting on you Tuesday night.

First I want to clear up a very important point. Last night in Missouri I was reminded of the fact that when Harry Truman ran in 1948 they said he ran a mean campaign. Some people say that I've run a mean campaign, but I have not. I want to tell the truth about the Republicans, and when I do, they always say it's mean.

I grew up on a farm in deep south Georgia, very similar to the lives of many of you or at least your mothers and fathers during the Depression years. I remember what it meant to live in a house that didn't have electricity or running water. We worked from early in the morning till late at night. To plow—a mule; we didn't have tractors. We didn't have electricity on our farm. And we had a lot of needs in our lives. And then Herbert Hoover, a typical Republican, was replaced by Franklin D. Roosevelt in the White House. Franklin Roosevelt proposed the TVA, the REA, to transform the lives of all southerners. The Republicans were against TVA. They were against REA. They said it was socialism or communism for the Government to bring electricity to rural farms in Mississippi and in Georgia.

My mother had to work for a living. She was a registered nurse. She worked 12 hours a day. She was paid $4. Sometimes she worked 20-hour-a-day duty. Then she was paid $6. The Democrats thought that men and women who were grown and who had to support a family were worth at least a minimum wage. They put forth 25-cent-an-hour minimum wage. It was quite a struggle, because the Republicans were against it. They didn't believe that an able-bodied man or woman was worth 25 cents an hour. Later, as I approached the age to finish high school, I got my first job measuring land for the Government, 10 hours a day, furnished my own car and paid all expenses; 40 cents an hour, which was the minimum wage then. The Democrats were for increasing the minimum wage to 40 cents. The Republicans, predictably, were against it.

Franklin Roosevelt felt that the senior citizens, the elderly in our country, ought to get out of po' folks homes, and they ought to have social security. So, Franklin Roosevelt put forward the idea of social security. The Democrats supported him. The Republicans said it was socialism, communism. They opposed it. But the Democrats prevailed, and now our senior citizens in this Nation, nationwide, have some respect in their old age, and they have a security that they didn't have before.

Later, in 1961, Democrats proposed Medicare to give senior citizens some chance for good medical attention. Obviously, the Republicans were against it. Democrats prevailed, and now we have a better life. Those kinds of things are typical of what has taken place between the party of the working people, the party of the elderly, the party of the young, the party of equality on the one hand, and the party of privilege on the other.

You've been listening lately to the Republican candidate, Governor Reagan, who's running against me, and you know he's been trying to wrap himself in the mantle of Democratic Presidents.

[Interruption from the audience.]

I'm trying to tell the truth, but they don't want to hear it back there.

Every time a Republican starts running for President, you always notice they quote Democratic Presidents. Have you every heard a Republican candidate quote a Republican President?

AUDIENCE. No!

THE PRESIDENT. No. And you never will. Here's what Franklin Roosevelt said in 1944, and I quote Franklin Roosevelt. He said, "The whole purpose of Republican oratory these days seems to be to switch labels just before an election. Now, imitation," he said, "may be the sincerest form of flattery, but I'm afraid that in this case, it's the most obvious common or garden variety of fraud." And I might say that Roosevelt wasn't the only one who observed this phenomenon. Republicans have now taken to quoting Franklin D. Roosevelt himself.

John Kennedy in 1960 said this: "The Republicans are even beginning to say a few kind words about Franklin Roosevelt. Twenty years from now," Kennedy said, "they might even speak a good word for Harry Truman. But I guarantee you that Harry Truman will never say a good word about Republicans." Now, you all know that that prediction of John Kennedy came true. And I want to make a prediction to you tonight. Twenty years from now, Republican candidates are going to be saying nice things about Jimmy Carter's second term.

Presidents have a lot of duties to perform, and I'm talking about the South tonight. I came from a family; my father didn't finish high school. Neither did his father. Nobody in our family had ever finished high school in 300 years in this country until I came along and got an appointment to the U.S. Naval Academy.

Southerners know what it means to protect our Nation. We've always been in the forefront of volunteering to go to war, to give our lives, if necessary, to defend our Nation. The honor roll of those who lose their lives is always headed by southerners, who know what it means to defend basic rights. But we also know what it means to have a strong defense. When I got to the Oval Office as President, as an ex-submarine officer, for 8 years Republicans had let the Americans' defenses go down. Seven of those 8 years, we had had a decrease in the commitment of Federal budget dollars for defense. Since I've been in the Oval Office, with the help of John Stennis, who was speaking for me last night in Columbus, we know that we have had a steady increase in defense expenditures above and beyond the cost of inflation. That's the kind of commitment that we've made for defense.

We'll continue to do it, but it's important to remember, it's important to remember that the reason to have a strong defense is to keep our Nation at peace. When I came into office, there was no long-range cruise missile program. Now we have one. There was no battle tank. Now we have one. There was no modern armored fighting vehicle. Now they're in production. There was no answer to the potential vulnerability of our silo-based ICBM's. Now there's an answer—the mobile MX missiles. Our purchases of Army equipment—listen to this—jetfighters and attack aircraft had dropped by two-thirds in the 8 years before I became President. Since then, we've increased them by 50 percent.

I'm not here to tell you that the end in itself is to have major military forces, but I can say this—and no President has been able to say this for the last 50 years: Since I have been in office, this country has been at peace. We have not had a war, and I'm determined to have—[*applause*].

Every President faces difficult decisions. The Oval Office is sometimes a lonely place, but the judgment, the moderation, the careful, prayerful consideration of basic issues in a time of crisis is the important function of a President who serves you.

I said earlier I grew up on a farm. I want to say just a word about agriculture. I know something about farmers. I even know what parity means. [*Laughter*] When I was growing up, farmers had a difficult life. There was no price support for agricultural products, there was no stability in our lives. It was boom one year

and bust the next—mostly bust—because when the farmers made a good crop, they sold at harvest time, and the middlemen bought our products, and when the price went up later on, maybe because they held grain from the market or cotton from the market, the farmers didn't get the profit. Now that's been changed under a Democratic administration. And we've got a policy that's been in effect since I've been in office, with Bob Bergland, a farmer, as the Secretary of Argiculture, that has transformed the lives of many farmers in this Nation.

Since I've been in office, we've had the highest gross income in history, the biggest increase in net income in history, the biggest exports of American farm products in history. Now we've got the most onfarm storage in history—2.8 billion bushels of grain are now being stored by the farmers on their farms so that they can market their grain when the markets are good. This not only helps farm families—it costs the middlemen, yes—but it helps consumers as well, because you don't have the wild fluctuations in wheat, corn, oats, milk, and other products that we had before under the Republicans, as you know.

We had Secretaries of Agriculture, not who were farmers, but we had Secretaries of Agriculture who were employees or executives of the very middlemen who had been responsible for keeping farmers impoverished for many years. It's better to have a Secretary of Agriculture who's a dirt farmer, and that's what we'll have as long as I'm in the White House.

I want to say a word to you about an issue that you may not ever have thought about much before and that's China—the People's Republic of China. One of the difficult decisions that I've had to make, as President, has been to normalize relationships with one-fourth of the total population of this Earth—a billion people in China. You might say what has that got to do with someone who lives in Jackson, Mississippi, or who lives on a farm in southern Mississippi? I'll tell you what it's got to do with it. Right now, as Jim Eastland knows, the number-one customer in the world for American cotton is China, and we've only had normal relationships with them 2 years. We just signed an agreement where they will buy every year between 6 million and 9 million tons of American grain.

In Mexico—we have tripled trade with Mexico in just 4 years, and now we have a good contract and a good ability to sell American rice, Mississippi rice, to countries like Korea. They'll have their biggest orders with us this year ever. And recently when I met with the new, democratically elected President of Nigeria—the biggest, most powerful, and newest democracy in Africa—they agreed to open up their markets for American rice. These are the kinds of things that have helped us to make good progress.

I know what it means to be able to sell things we grow on the farm, not just to American consumers but to consumers around the world. In 1977 we set a world record for farm exports. In 1978 we broke the record. In 1979 we broke it again. And this year we'll have an $8 billion increase in American exports overseas, up to a total now of $40 billion, a new record again.

When Ronald Reagan was asked about subsidies, he said he wasn't familiar with the subject. [*Laughter*] And only recently he's heard about the Tennessee-Tombigbee, which is going to take those farm products to market. Recently he said, and I quote him, which may be mean—[*laughter*]—here's what he said about price supports: "You subsidize the inefficient," he said, "when you put a floor under the price for farmers." And again he said at a later time, he said, farmers should start planning for an end to Government assistance in production and in the marketplace.

Well, people of Mississippi, I know what it means to have a stabilized price for farmers, because you can have a devastating drought that wipes you out one year. You can have the highest production in the world the next year. Farmers don't want a handout. Farmers want to stand on their own feet, but they want to have markets that are stable and predictable, because they can't control the weather. And almost all of our programs that we have don't cost America anything. They help the farmer, yes, but they help our consumers as well. It's the best investment I know in the economy of this country.

Just a word about energy, because, as you know, most of American energy comes here from the South in oil and gas. I believe, like you southerners, that we ought to have a minimum of interference by the Federal Government in the private affairs of American citizens and in the free enterprise system of our country. Republican Presidents have been promising for a decade to deregulate the price of oil and natural gas. The Democratic Congress, working with me, has done that, careful and projected to the future so everyone can understand the benefits of it.

This year we will have more oil and gas wells drilled in the United States than any year in history. Right now we've got over 3,100 drillrigs running in the United States, never before that many in history. And this year, ladies and gentlemen—this may be a surprise to you—we'll produce more coal in the United States than any year in history. We are exporting more coal than any year in our history, and in the next 15 years, keeping our same, rigid standards, on air pollution and water pollution, we will triple the production of American coal. What I want to see on the international markets is to replace OPEC oil with American coal and American energy, and we're going to do it.

And finally let me say, looking to the future, I've talked to you about this election not just as a contest between two men who disagree on every major issue that I've described to you, but it's a campaign to decide the future of this Nation, the rest of this century and perhaps beyond.

Think on things that are important to you—agriculture, trade, stability. Think about the minimum wage, which Ronald Reagan wants to repeal. Think about peace. Think about a strong defense. Think about social security. Think about Medicare. Think about the things that are important in your life now and in the future. I see a nation in the future strong. I see a nation at peace. I see a nation secure. I see a nation in the pursuit of progress for all its people. I see a nation where everyone can have the dignity of a decent job, where new industries create a new generation of American buildings and vehicles that will house us and move us in comfort on a lot less energy, and what energy we use coming from America, not overseas.

I see a nation where our children are better educated to their maximum potential that God's given them, where the elderly are treated with the respect, which they have earned with their life's work, where families are secure and intact and respect one another. I have a vision of a nation free enough to attract the deprived from other parts of the world, a nation of liberty and justice and love.

I need your help this next few days, because, as you know, the election is not very far off. I've been President now for almost 4 years. I've made thousands of decisions. In each one of those decisions in the Oval Office, I have been learning about this country. Every decision I make leaves me better qualified to make the next decision. What I've learned has made me a better President over a 4-year period, and it'll make me a better President in my second term.

I consider myself to be in the mainstream of the Democratic Party. I consider myself to be a true southerner, representing the ideals and commitments that have made us proud of our own region of this land. I also consider myself in the mainstream of bipartisan Presidents, Democrats and Republicans, who've had tremendous repsonsibilities on our shoulders and who've tried to represent our Nation well. Like them, I believe that our Nation must be strong, yes. The Nation must be secure. We must have a society that's just and fair. We must dare to struggle for a peaceful world.

There have been times of crisis and conflict during these years. In each case I alone have had to determine what are the interests of my Nation, what degree of involvement should we put forward? Should we try to resolve problems diplomatically or politically, or should we send American soldiers to die overseas? I've learned that the more difficult the decision is, the more likely it is that my advisers and experts will be divided almost equally. The final judgment has to be made by the man in the Oval Office.

Sometimes it is a lonely job, but with the involvement of the American people like you and the heritage that I've gotten from you it's a gratifying job. Now each one of you faces a similar lonely decision next Tuesday in the voting booth. Your decision will make a difference. It's made a difference in the past. Think how few votes would have changed in 1948 and Harry Truman would never have been President. Think how few votes would have been changed in 1960 and John Kennedy would never have served this Nation, and think how few votes would have been changed in 1968 to put another Democrat in the White House and Richard Nixon would never have served and embarrassed our Nation.

So, my final word is I need you to go on with me to build a partnership, to stay strong, to stay secure, to raise high the banner of human rights, and to keep our Nation at peace. For the sake of all we've done in the past, the things that have made us proud of Mississippi, proud of Georgia, proud of this Nation, for the sake of all we can do in the future together to make us even prouder of a life that we can have, let's win a victory next Tuesday, not just for me and Fritz Mondale, not just for the Democratic Party, but let's win a victory for the South, for the ideals and beliefs that we have, the vision that we share for a greater nation even than we've had before.

You join me. We'll have a partnership. We'll whip the Republicans and have a great nation.

Thank you very much. God bless you.

NOTE: The President spoke at 5:25 p.m. outside the Governor's Mansion.

Houston, Texas
Remarks at a Rally With Area Residents.
October 31, 1980

THE PRESIDENT. Thank you. Right on.

AUDIENCE [*chanting*]. Four more years!

THE PRESIDENT. Thank you. You've got me convinced. I'll take it.

First of all, let me say that it's really great to be in your wonderful State of Texas. At least you have got a real southern gentleman for your Lieutenant Governor. [*Laughter*] To Congressman Mickey Leland, Congressman Bob Eckhardt, one of the great leaders, not only of Texas but of the entire Nation and who needs to stay in the Congress and who needs your help, all of you help him. Jack Brooks already won his election overwhelmingly, as you know. Mike Andrews is going to be your next Congressman from the 22nd District, Bob Hutchins, next Congressman from the District 7. And I want to say that it's good to be in a city that can produce a baseball team like the Astros. You can really be proud of them. The whole Nation was, and I'm very glad that Joe Sambito and Joe Niekro are here tonight. And I noticed the Houston Oilers are right up there at the top, right? [*Applause*]

It's always good to come back to Houston, because you run out of great things to say about it—the biggest city in the biggest county in the biggest continental State—a city, by the way, that since the day I was sworn in as President, has added 240,000 new jobs for Houston citizens. That's great.

Last night about this time I was in St. Louis, Missouri, and I was speaking to an audience that remembered very clearly the time of Harry Truman, a great President who understood what our Nation was all about, a man who made some difficult decisions, a man who was castigated by the Republicans because they said he was too mean when he ran his campaign. [*Laughter*] Sometimes they say the same thing about me. All I do is tell the truth about Ronald Reagan, and the truth sounds mean.

If you've been listening to the campaign lately you've probably noticed that the Republican candidate, everywhere he goes, quotes Democratic Presidents. Have you ever heard a Republican candidate for President quoting a Republican President?

AUDIENCE. No!

THE PRESIDENT. No. And there's a good reason for it, because every time an election approaches they like to forget about their record. It happens every election year. As a matter of fact, Franklin Roosevelt said in 1944—and I'd like to quote that great President about how the Republicans change their tune when election day approaches—he said, "The whole purpose of Republican oratory these days seems to be to switch labels. Now, imitation," he said, "may be the sincerest form of flattery, but I'm afraid that in this case it's the most obvious garden or common variety of fraud."

Now, that didn't stop with Franklin Roosevelt. It happened, the same thing, when John Kennedy ran for President in 1960. He said about the Republicans, "They're even beginning to say a few kind

words about Franklin Roosevelt. Twenty years from now," Kennedy said, "they might even say a good word about Harry Truman. But," he said, "I guarantee you that Harry Truman will never say a good word about a Republican." [*Laughter*] And I want to make a prediction to you tonight. Twenty years from now I predict that Republican candidates are even going to be saying good things about Jimmy Carter's second term.

You're the State that has provided great leaders in Washington for the Democratic Party and for our Nation. Sam Rayburn was a man who led the Congress of the United States, who knew what it meant to be a Democrat, to be proud to be part of the South, to take the heritage that is part of our own consciousness and let it be beneficial for the rest of the country. And when the New Deal came along there were people like you and me who were waiting for a change in life. And I think it's time, with just 3 or 4 days to go before you make a great decision, to think back on those days. Some of you are quite young, Larry Gatlin's age, who's a great friend of mine. Some of you, old as I am. I was born in 1924, but I remember how things have changed, in my life, because of the Democrats.

I grew up on a farm in south Georgia, where everybody worked from before daybreak until after sundown and then had to plow, put the plow in the barn, pump water for the mules, and then go to bed after dark. My mother was a registered nurse. She worked 12 hours a day for $4 or either she worked 20 hours a day for $6. We didn't have electricity on our farm. And old people when they got past retirement age, if they didn't have a family that was rich, had to go to what we called the po' folks farm. Maybe some of you remember those days.

Roosevelt came along, and as a young man Lyndon Johnson helped Franklin D. Roosevelt. As is the case with Democrats, they cared about working people. And they looked upon old people and said, "We need to make sure that when they reach retirement age, they have some self respect." So, Roosevelt proposed, along with Democrats, that we have social security. The Republicans opposed it. They called it socialism, even called it communism. Franklin Roosevelt thought that the American farmers ought to have electricity, proposed TVA, REA. The Republicans opposed it, called it socialism, even communism.

Roosevelt even was radical enough to believe that a grown man or a grown woman ought to be paid living wages; 25 cents an hour was the first proposed minimum wage. Republicans were against it. They called it socialism, communism, the interference of government in the private affairs of big business. I got my first job when I finished high school in 1941. I worked 10 hours a day for the minimum wage, which at that time was 40 cents. I had to furnish my own car and pay all the expenses to measure land for the government. Republicans opposed that radical increase from 25 cents to 40 cents an hour. This has been the typical continuing struggle between the party you and I represent and the Republicans who always imitate Democrats just before elections to get in office.

Later in 1961, Medicare was proposed to give our senior citizens a chance for some medical care when they reached the retirement age if they didn't have much money. My Republican opponent, Ronald Reagan, an employee of the anti-Medicare lobby, went around this Nation making speeches, and he referred to Medicare as socialism—"socialized medicine," he said. Now he's against national health insurance.

He's proposed several times lately that social security be voluntary. This year he proposed that the minimum wage be abolished. He said that the thing that's caused more misery and more unemployment in this country than anything since the Great Depression was the minimum wage. And he said the other night in the debate— you probably heard it—that social security was a bad investment for a young person. The fact is that a young man, a husband, or a young mother with children, if they start at the age of 22 and put their money into social security, they'll get back 3½ times more than they put in. And all that time they're working they have the protection of disability, or if one of them dies, survivor's benefits for the other spouse and all the children until they're 18. That's the kind of program that Ronald Reagan is still against. He can't change his spots just before election, although he's trying very desperately to do so. And it's important for us to remember these basic truths as we approach the time for a decision.

My people have lived in this country for a long time, since the 1600's. They've all been farmers, every one of them. My father never had a chance to finish high school; neither did his father. Nobody in my family ever finished high school until me. And I had an ambition when I was a child to go to the Naval Academy, to get a college education. It was a wild dream. Nobody ever thought I could ever do it. But I was lucky enough to go. I served in the Navy for 11 years and when I got out of the submarine force, I went back home and saw the changes take place in the Southland, when black people and those who speak Spanish were finally given equal rights, a right to vote, a right to be holding a job, a right to have a chance in life.

And let me ask you a question. Let me ask you a question, those of you who might speak Spanish, those of you who might be black, those of you who might be women. Which party has always been in favor of helping those who felt the scourge of discrimination? The Democrats. The Democrats. And it has not changed. It has not changed. We would never have had the civil rights bill, the voting rights bill, had Roosevelt, Johnson, Kennedy not been elected. Never would have happened.

Another thing—let me say this—[*applause*]—I agree with you. And let me say this, when the civil rights act and the voting rights act was passed——

[*Interruption from the audience.*]

You're for me. Be quiet, man.

AUDIENCE [*chanting*]. Four more years!

THE PRESIDENT. He's for me. Let me finish. That's good. Okay, let me talk. And when the voting rights act and the civil rights act passed, Ronald Reagan said that's bad legislation. So, what we need to do is to remember as election day approaches, which party is best for our country.

I went in the Oval Office as a young President, remembering that our Nation had to be strong. I went into the Oval Office, after I was elected, as a young military officer concerned about what had happened to our Nation's defense the last 8 years before I became President. In those

8 years, 7 of them under Republicans— the Republicans——

[*Interruption from the audience.*]

AUDIENCE [*chanting*]. Four more years!

THE PRESIDENT. Okay, you got me. Thank you.

The Republicans have a lot of money. They have enough money to back—to pay a few people to work for them.

I want to cover three more points to you, because these are important because they affect your lives. One is, concerning defense. When I was elected President the Republican administration 8 years before I was elected cut spending for defense every year except one. We had a reduction of 37 percent below what it was a year before when Nixon became President, in 8 years—37-percent reduction. Every year since I've been in office, as a Democratic President, we have added to our defense spending to give our country strength in our military forces. This will continue for the next 5 years, because I know, like other people know, that we can only have peace in our Nation if our Nation is strong. And I can make another statement that no other President can make in the last 50 years. Since I have been in the Oval Office, our Nation has not known war; we have been at peace. And I'm going to keep this Nation at peace.

I know I'm in the State of Texas, and I want to say something about land and I want to say something about oil. First of all, all the Republican Presidents have always promised that when they got in the Oval Office that they were going to decontrol the price of oil and gas to let our Nation produce more energy. Who has been able to do it? A Democratic President, working with a Democratic Congress, and we've already seen rich results for our Nation. This year we will have more new oil wells and gas wells producing in this country than any year in history. We've got more oil drillrigs running right now than the Nation has ever had in history. We're producing more American coal than we've ever produced in history, and we're cutting every day the amount of oil we buy from overseas.

In economics Democrats have always been those in favor of the investment in new jobs, new plants, new opportunities for our people. Ronald Reagan has a basic approach to taxation and economics called the Reagan-Kemp-Roth proposal.

[Boo's from the audience.]

You understand it very well.

You all know that Business Week is a magazine that's not particularly a Democratic publication. But Business Week said that Ronald Reagan's tax proposal was completely irresponsible, that it would cause an inflationary explosion that would destroy this Nation's economy, and it would impoverish every person in this country living on a fixed income. That's what Business Week thinks about Ronald Reagan's tax proposal. And George Bush, who was a temporary Texan, said that Ronald Reagan's proposal was "voodoo economics" and would cause 30-percent inflation. At least one time George Bush was right.

And the final point I want to make is this, about land, about agriculture. As I said earlier, I grew up on a farm, and I was very interested when I got to be President to have a Secretary of Agriculture who was a dirt farmer. In the past, as you know, the Republicans have chosen for Secretary of Agriculture a lobbyist or an executive in the major food-process-

ing companies or the middlemen who handle large quantities of grain after the farmers sell it cheap at harvest time. I wanted to be sure I had somebody in there like Bob Bergland who understood the life of an American farm family. We've changed.

We've had a lot of progress made already. Look back on what happened to the farmers in 1977 before we passed our new farm bill. Corn prices have doubled. Wheat prices have doubled. Beef prices have doubled. In the last 3½ years gross income of farmers in this Nation have grown faster than ever before in history. Net farm income has gone up more than ever before in history. On exports—Texas is a very important State—we've had more exports and set a new record in 1977, a higher record in '78, an even higher record in '79. And this year we had the biggest increase in exports in the history of our Nation, $8 billion. We'll export $40 billion overseas this year.

And I want to mention a word to you that you might not think about concerning farm families, and that's China. There are 4 billion people who live on this Earth. A billion of them live in China. We've normalized relationships now with that country about 2 years ago. This year we just signed an agreement—as a matter of fact last week—to sell China between 6 million tons and 9 million tons of American grain every year. The number one customer for American cotton right now is the People's Republic of China. We've tripled trade with Mexico in the last 4 years. We've opened up the sale of our products to Korea, to Nigeria, to other countries. The American farmers have never been better off. That's a very important commitment, an historic commitment of the Democratic Party.

And finally let me say this: I may not have mentioned it earlier, but I need your help this next few days. November the 4th is the day. A President has sometimes a difficult job, but he has to face problems that affect your life. I've made thousands of decisions since I've been in the Oval Office, and every time I've made a decision I've learned in the process. I became a better President with every decision, and I'll be a better President than I have already in the second term.

I've never served one day as President that there wasn't a crisis or a troublespot somewhere in the world. There have been six or eight armed conflicts that broke out in the world since I've been President. I've had to make a judgment about our Nation's interests and about the depth of our Nation's involvement, whether to handle that problem through politics or diplomacy, or through the injection of American military forces into those troubled areas. A President has good advice, but I know from experience that when the difficult times come and the issue is sharply divided and the decision is very important, that advisers tend to split about 50–50. A President has to make a decision based on sound judgment, based on prayer, based on the understanding of the conscience of this country, about peace, or war. And I believe in peace.

I have to make some difficult and some lonely decisions. In the next few days, 100 million Americans have to make a difficult and a lonely decision. That decision will affect your life, the life of your family, the life of people that you love, the ones that look to you for leadership. You would not have come here tonight if you weren't interested in politics and government, but you have a responsibility like I do, the next few days, to make those judgments about the future of our Nation.

You might say, well, one person can't make much difference, but think back on 1948. If just a few people had voted differently, Harry Truman would never have been President. In 1960, if 28,000 people had changed their vote in Texas and a few thousand in Illnois, then John Kennedy and Lyndon Johnson would never have served this Nation as President. If just a few people had gone out and worked a little harder in 1968, Hubert Humphrey would have been President and Richard Nixon would never had embarrassed this Nation in the White House.

So, you've got a choice to make, between the Herbert Hoover to Richard Nixon Republican Party, or the Franklin Roosevelt, Lyndon Johnson, Harry Truman, John Kennedy, and Jimmy Carter Democratic Party. I need your help. Will you help me? We'll win together. We'll win together. Four more years, right. [*Applause and cheers*]

NOTE: The President spoke at 8:33 p.m. at the Miller Outdoor Theater at Hermann Park.

Board of Foreign Scholarships

Appointment of Four Members.
October 31, 1980

The President has announced the appointment of four members to the Board of Foreign Scholarships for terms expiring September 22, 1983. They are:

MARIO A. ANGLADA, of New York, vice Tomas Rivera, term expired.

H. BRANDT AYERS, of Alabama, vice Elbert Benjamin Smith, term expired.

ADELAIDE CROMWELL GULLIVER, of Massachusetts, vice Monroe D. Donsker, term expired.

HARRISON E. SALISBURY, of Connecticut, vice Bartle Bull, term expired.

Advisory Committee for Trade Negotiations

Appointment of Three Members.
October 31, 1980

The President today announced the appointment of three members of the Advisory Committee for Trade Negotiations for 3-year terms. They are:

LEE L. MORGAN, of Peoria, Ill., chairman and chief executive officer of Caterpillar Tractor Co.;

RUDOLPH A. OSWALD, of Potomac, Md., director of the AFL–CIO's Department of Research, former assistant director of the Department of Education of the AFL–CIO, and former director of research with the Service Employees International Union;

GLENN E. WATTS, of Chevy Chase, Md., president of the Communications Workers of America and a member of the executive council of the AFL–CIO.

National Commission on Alcoholism and Other Alcohol-Related Problems

Appointment of 12 Members.
October 31, 1980

The President has announced his intention to appoint 12 members of the National Commission on Alcoholism and Other Alcohol-Related Problems.

Harold Hughes, former United States Senator and Governor of Iowa, will be Chairman of the Commission. Dr. Jean Harris, Secretary of Human Resources of Virginia, will be the Vice Chairperson.

In addition to Mr. Hughes and Dr. Harris, other public members of the Commission will be:

FLOYD E. BLOOM, of California, director of the Davis Center for Behavioral Neurobiology, the Salk Institute;

SHEILA BIERMAN BLUME, of New York, director, New York State Division on Alcoholism and Alcohol Abuse and president of the American Medical Society on Alcoholism;

JANIE SALINAS FARRIS, of Texas, assistant director of the Adult Mental Health/Mental Retardation Services of Harris County;

MELVIN ALLAN GLASSER, of Michigan, director, Social Security Department, United Auto Workers;

JAMES S. KEMPER, JR., of Illinois, chairman of the board of the Kemper Insurance Co.;

JOSEPH A. PURSCH, of California, medical director of the Comprehensive Care Corp., and former Director of the Navy Alcohol Rehabilitation Service of the Naval Regional Medical Center in Long Beach.

The President also appointed four nonvoting members of the Commission from the Federal Government. They are:

MAX CLELAND, Administrator of Veterans Affairs;

JOAN B. CLAYBROOK, Administrator, National Highway Safety Administration;

JOHN R. DeLUCA, Director, National Institute on Alcohol Abuse and Alcoholism, Department of Health and Human Services;

BRIG. GEN. WILLIAM CHARLES LOUISELL, Deputy Assistant Secretary of Health Affairs, Department of Defense.

In addition, eight members of the Commission will be appointed from the Congress.

National Advisory Council on Economic Opportunity

Appointment of Five Members.
October 31, 1980

The President has announced his intention to appoint one new member and to reappoint four members of the National Advisory Council on Economic Opportunity for terms expiring August 15, 1983.

The new member is Henry Mateo Mestre, Jr., of California, vice Ralph Ochoa, term expired. Mr. Mestre is executive director, Spanish Speaking Unity Council, a community development corporation. He is also a member of the Private Industry Council of Oakland and a member of the National Urban Coalition.

Those being reappointed are:

EDWARD F. FEIGHAN, of Ohio, Cuyahoga County commissioner and former Ohio State representative;

LINDA HADLEY, of Arizona, assistant director, Navajo mental health program;

JUAN J. MALDONADO, of Texas, mayor, city of San Juan, Tex.;

EVELYN WATTS, of Florida, a member of the boards of the National Association for the Advancement of Colored People, Council on Human Relations, Pinnelas County Opportunity Council, Gulf Coast Health Systems, South Pinellas Senior Citizens Group.

President's Export Council

Appointment of Three Members.
October 31, 1980

The President has announced his intention to appoint three members to the President's Export Council. The new members are:

THOMAS F. BARNUM, of Lake Forest, Ill., president and chief executive officer, Consolidated Foods—Frozen Food Group. He is also senior vice president of Consolidated Foods.

FRANK DROZAK, of New Jersey, president, Seafarer's International Union of North America. He is also president of the AFL–CIO Maritime Trades Department.

STEPHEN P. YOKICH, of Detroit, Mich., vice president, United Auto Workers. He is also a member of the U.A.W. International Skilled Trades Advisory Committee.

Housing and Services for the Handicapped

Announcement of an Interagency Initiative.
October 31, 1980

The White House today announced the launching of a new interagency independent living initiative designed to foster the development of community-based housing and services that will enable handicapped persons to live more independently outside of institutional-type facilities.

The initiative, promised by the President in a speech last spring before the President's Committee on Employment of the Handicapped, will utilize funds from existing Federal programs not previously targeted on independent living. Through the combined resources of seven agencies, over $80 million in ongoing program funds will be available to expand current independent living capability for the physically, developmentally, and mentally disabled.

ACTION, the Community Services Administration, the Department of Education, the Department of Health and Human Services, the Department of Housing and Urban Development, the Department of Labor, and the Department of Transportation will each be participating in this initiative.

The President is inviting each Governor to submit comprehensive letters of intent describing resource commitments and activities within their State devoted to independent living. On the basis of these letters, up to 15 States will be selected for participation in the initiative.

Within the selected States, project proposals will be solicited from local and State groups involved in addressing the needs of the handicapped. These proposals will describe how independent living projects would tap agencies' existing generic programs to meet independent living needs. The proposals will be reviewed first by a State panel, then by a Federal coordinating task force responsible for final selections.

Stuart E. Eizenstat, Assistant to the President for Domestic Affairs and Policy, described the initiative as a "highly significant example of interagency coordination designed to encourage more effective utilization of existing program resources to serve handicapped persons."

Self-Government for Mid-Pacific Islands

Announcement of an Agreement Between the United States, the Marshall Islands, and the Federated States of Micronesia.
October 31, 1980

Representatives of the United States, the Marshall Islands Government, and the Federated States of Micronesia today initialed a Compact of Free Association, a basic document which will, when finally approved, authorize self-government for the 120,000 inhabitants of hundreds of islands ranged across 3,000 miles of the mid-Pacific and will also establish the terms of a unique, continuing, close relationship with the United States. The initialing also advances President Carter's goal, announced in 1977, of terminating in 1981 the United Nations Trusteeship Agreement under which the United States has administered the Trust Territory of the Pacific Islands since 1947. The islands, formerly ruled by Spain and Germany, became a Japanese League of Nations mandate as a result of World War I and were captured by United States military forces during World War II.

Initialing for the United States was Ambassador Peter R. Rosenblatt, who has served since 1977 as President Carter's Personal Representative for Micronesian Status Negotiations. He was joined by Anton A. deBrun, Secretary of Foreign Affairs of the Marshall Islands, and Andon L. Amaraich, Secretary of External Affairs of the Federated States of Micronesia and Chairman of its Commission on Future Political Status and Transition.

Today's initialing represents the virtual completion of a negotiating process that began in 1969. The Compact provides that the United States will retain plenary authority in defense and security matters and that three Micronesian entities—the Marshall Islands, the Federated States of Micronesia, and Palau—will acquire full internal self-government and authority over all aspects of their foreign relations other than those which the United States determines to be defense- and security-related. The Compact also sets forth the financial and other types of assistance which the United States will provide over a 15-year period and covers the many other realms—including environmental regulations, trade, finance, and taxation—in which the United States and Micronesia will remain linked. The Compact's aid and defense provisions continue for 15 years and thereafter, as may be mutually agreed. It also provides each of the Micronesian entities the option of unilateral termination should any of them later decide to seek full independence or any other political status. However, such unilateral termination would be subject to continuation of U.S. defense rights and economic assistance for their full terms.

During several months following to-day's initialing ceremony, negotiators for all of the governments involved will conclude their work on a dozen or more detailed subsidiary agreements covering such subjects as telecommunications, extradition, and military land-use and operating rights. Once these subsidiary agreements have been completed, the Compact of Free Association will be formally signed. At that point the Compact will be presented to the voters of Micronesia for approval by plebiscite and submitted to the United States Congress as a joint resolution for enactment into law. If the Compact is approved, the United States will present the completed arrangements to the United Nations and seek termination of the Trusteeship Agreement. The United States strategic trusteeship in Micronesia is the last of the 11 U.N. trusteeships established after World War II.

Palau, the fourth party to the current negotiations, was unable to send a delegation to Washington this week, because the voters of this small island group in the Western Carolines go to the polls on November 4 to elect their first national government. That government will take office on January 1, 1981, whereas elected governments took office in the Marshall Islands and the Federated States of Micronesia in May 1979. In a letter dated October 25, however, the Palauan negotiators informed Ambassador Rosenblatt that they would meet with him in Washington on November 6 and 7 with a view to concluding negotiations and initiating the Compact and several closely related agreements.

Marshallese President Amata Kabua had initialed an earlier version of the Compact with Ambassador Rosenblatt at Kona, Hawaii, on January 14, 1980, but the document initialed today contains numerous changes from the January version, several of which were introduced by the Marshallese themselves.

Another district of the Trust Territory, the Northern Mariana Islands, in 1975 approved an agreement establishing an even closer relationship with the United States through commonwealth status. Residents of the Northern Marianas have since elected their own Governor and legislature, but the Commonwealth will come into full legal existence only upon termination of the Trusteeship Agreement.

There is no exact precedent in international law or U.S. constitutional practice for the free association status which the three Micronesian entities have chosen. The autonomy which the Micronesian states will exercise exceeds that of U.S. territories, while U.S. defense authority in the freely associated states is comprehensive and therefore of a different nature from the treaty relationships with even America's closest allies.

National Institute of Justice

Appointment of 18 Members to the Advisory Board.   October 31, 1980

The President has announced his intention to appoint 18 members to the National Institute of Justice Advisory Board. All are new positions.

The committee will recommend the policies and priorities of the National Institute of Justice. The members to be appointed are:

SHIRLEY SCHLANGER ABRAHAMSON, of Wisconsin, justice, Supreme Court of Wisconsin, representing the courts.

CARLOS HUMBERTO ARCE, of Michigan, study director, National Chicano Research Network, University of Michigan, representing research interests.

OTTO BEATTY, JR., of Ohio, State representative from Columbus, Ohio, representing State and local governments.

F. T. DAVIS, JR., of Georgia, attorney, former general counsel, President's Reorganization Project, representing defense attorneys.

DAVID FOGEL, of Illinois, professor at the University of Illinois (Chicago Circle Campus) criminal justice department, representing the academic community.

DON M. GOTTFREDSON, of New Jersey, dean, school of criminal justice, Rutgers State University, and director, National Council on Crime and Delinquency Research Center, representing the academic community.

STANLEY HARWOOD, of New York, partner in the firm of Shayne, Dachs, Weiss, Kolbreuer, Stauisci and Harwood, representing the general public.

ALAN I. KLINEMAN, of Indiana, senior partner in the firm of Klineman, Rose, and Wolf of Indianapolis, representing defense attorneys.

WILLIAM DENT LEEKE, of South Carolina, commissioner, South Carolina Department of Corrections, and former president, American Correctional Association, representing corrections interests.

GORDON A. MARTIN, JR., of Massachusetts, attorney at law, representing the general public.

PATRICK VINCENT MURPHY, of Maryland, former commander, New York City Police Department, Detroit Police Department, and District of Columbia Police Department, representing professional organizations.

LLOYD EDGAR OHLIN, of Massachusetts, professor, Center for Criminal Justice, Harvard Law School, representing academic interests.

LORENZO E. PATINO, of California, municipal court judge, Sacramento, representing State and local governments.

MIMI HALPER SILBERT, of California, president, Delancy Street Foundation, representing community and neighborhood organizations.

JAMES CLOUDIS SMITH, of Florida, attorney General, State of Florida, representing prosecutors.

PATRICIA McGOWAN WALD, of Maryland, judge, United States Court of Appeals, representing the courts.

BILLY L. WAYSON, of Virginia, president, Institute for Economic and Policy Studies, representing research interests.

HUBERT WILLIAMS, of New Jersey, director of police, Newark, and adjunct professor, Rutgers University Graduate School of Criminal Justice, representing police.

United States Naval Academy

Appointment of Evelyn Gandy as a Member of the Board of Visitors.
October 31, 1980

The President has announced his intention to appoint Evelyn Gandy, of Jackson, Miss., as a member of the Board of Visitors of the United States Naval Academy for a term expiring December 31, 1983.

Ms. Gandy, a former Lieutenant Governor of Mississippi, is deputy for Human Resource Planning and Development for the State of Mississippi.

Other positions in State government held by Ms. Gandy include member of the Mississippi State Legislature, assistant attorney general, commissioner of public welfare, commissioner of insurance, and State treasurer for two terms.

National Advisory Community Investment Board

Appointment of 13 Members.
October 31, 1980

The President has announced his intention to appoint 13 new members to the National Advisory Community Investment Board.

The Board was established to promote cooperation between private investors and businesses and community development corporation projects.

The new members are:

RICHARD C. BLUM, of San Francisco, Calif., vice chairman, board of directors, U.R.S. Corp. in San Francisco;

CLANZEL THORNTON BROWN, of Jacksonville, Fla., president of the Jacksonville Urban League, Inc.;

ANDY CAMACHO, of Los Angeles, Calif., a partner in the law firm of Fonner, Kunkel & Camacho in Los Angeles;

JUDITH ANN KOCH CATALINO, of Menomonee, Wis., executive director, Mitchell Street Center in Milwaukee;

DONALD PHILIP GALLOP, of St. Louis, Mo., a partner in the law firm of Johnston, Gallop, Creep & Newman in St. Louis;

GUADALUPE INIGUEZ, of Phoenix, Ariz., a tax attorney for Wales and Plattner, P.C., in Phoenix;

JOHN OLIVER LESLIE, of Oxford, Miss., mayor of the city of Oxford;

MCLAIN T. O'FARRALL, JR., of Richmond, Va., an investment banker and head of municipal operation for the Southeastern Region of U.S., Alex Brown & Sons in Richmond;

MALCOLM D. PRYOR, of Philadelphia, Pa., a senior consultant, Liberty Government Securities Group, New York City;

ANTHONY VINCENT MILANO, of Bridgeport, Conn., secretary for Connecticut Office of Policy and Management;

LEON RICHTER STRAUSS, of St. Louis, Mo., founder and president of the Pantheon Corp. in St. Louis;

HENRY TOPEL, of Wilmington, Del., president of Henry Topel & Co., real estate broker in Wilmington;

NELLIE MAE VARNER, of Detroit, Mich., vice president and partner of Strather-Varner Properties in Detroit.

Digest of Other White House Announcements

The following listing includes the President's public schedule and other items of general interest announced by the White House Press Office and not included elsewhere in this issue.

October 25

Following campaign appearances in Ohio, the President went to Camp David, Md., for a weekend stay.

October 27

The President returned to the White House from Camp David.

The President left the White House for a week of campaign activities throughout 16 States. Releases and announcements issued after the cut-off date of this issue begin on page 2617.

October 31

The President has announced his intention to appoint two persons to be Government members of the Board of Directors of the National Consumer Cooperative Bank. The members are:

JAMES A. JOSEPH, Under Secretary of the Interior;

RICHARD JOHN RIOS, Director of the Community Services Administration.

NOMINATIONS SUBMITTED TO THE SENATE

NOTE: No nominations were submitted to the Senate during the period covered by this issue.

CHECKLIST OF WHITE HOUSE PRESS RELEASES

The following listing contains releases of the White House Press Office which are not included in this issue.

Released October 25, 1980

Advance text: remarks to area residents in Waterville Township, Ohio

CHECKLIST—Continued

Released October 25—Continued

News conference: on agricultural issues—by Secretary of Agriculture Bob Bergland in Waterville Township, Ohio

Advance text: remarks to the Council on Foreign Relations in Denver, Colo.—by Zbigniew Brzezinski, Assistant to the President for National Security Affairs

Released October 31, 1980

Transcript: remarks on social security and Medicare programs—by former Secretary of

CHECKLIST—Continued

Released October 31—Continued

Health, Education, and Welfare Wilbur Cohen and former Commissioner of Social Security Robert Ball

---

ACTS APPROVED BY THE PRESIDENT

NOTE: No acts approved by the President were received by the Office of the Federal Register during the period covered by this issue.

Brownsville, Texas

Remarks at a Rally With Area Residents.
November 1, 1980

THE PRESIDENT. *Mayor Hernandez, Congressman Kika de la Garza, Lieutenant Governor Bill Hobby, my many friends here in Brownsville:*

It's a great honor to be with you. I'm happy to be here, because in the next few days you will make a decision that will affect the future of your own lives, the future of your families, and the future of this great Nation.

I'm happy to be the first President who has ever visited Brownsville. Thank you for your great welcome.

As you know, Zachary Taylor was here before, but that doesn't count because he came as a general. [*Laughter*] And I understand he built these buildings, some of them, these historic buildings, as an army post. But we've come a long way since then, and now this is a center of great education for some of the finest people in the United States. This is a college where a great man, the late Dr. Arnulfo Oliveria was president. Dr. Oliveria will be sorely missed. And I'm very grateful to know that his wife Eloisa is here with us this morning. We're glad to have you here.

As you know, this great man's life was dedicated to better education for the people that he loved. For decades he worked for progress and for enlightenment. He inspired a generation of students with his fine example. And he also did much to improve the quality of education throughout the State of Texas, in part by help-ing to ensure equal access to educational opportunity for children and for young people from Spanish-speaking homes.

As you know, one of the issues at stake in this election is equality of education. The Democratic Party has always been the party of better education for those who were poor and whose families didn't have a good chance, but we believe that the children, with the gift of God of intelligence and ability, ought to have a chance in an educational system to expand that intelligence and to use that ability for their own selves and for this country. The Republican record has always been just exactly the opposite.

Governor Reagan, who's running against me, does not share Dr. Oliveria's commitment and my own to better education. We have doubled, since I've been in the White House, funds for student aid programs. And now there should be no child in the United States who finishes high school, no matter how poor their family might be, who cannot, through loans or grants, through scholarships or work-study programs, get a college education. And you can depend that we will continue that policy as long as the Democrats are in the White House.

We've expanded greatly the program called Head Start, and we've expanded it to include migrant children. We're working hard right now with Senator Bentsen and with Kika de la Garza to make as much as $45 million available in Federal money in the border districts to help with the increase in school construction for the number of Mexican school children

2617

who reside here legally, because decent education is not just a border issue, it is a national issue. And I won't forget it.

Governor Reagan's only commitment on education is this. He says, "If I am elected President, I will abolish the Department of Education."

There are other areas, too, where the sharp issues are drawn that will affect your lives. We could not have more different views, Governor Reagan and I, than we have in health. Governor Reagan says, and I quote him: "Virtually all Americans have access to medical care today." Yet in south Texas I know that 13 counties with 22 percent of the population of this great State have only 3 percent of the physicians.

That's why, in the tradition of great Presidents like Roosevelt, Truman, Kennedy, and Lyndon Johnson and also Vice President Humphrey and Senator Ted Kennedy, I am committed to national health insurance, which will provide a cost-saving emphasis on the prevention of disease, on catastrophic health insurance if a family's wiped out economically with high medical costs, on the control of hospital costs so they can't go too high on you, on outpatient treatment instead of inpatient treatment, and also to include, as you know, an additional three-quarters of a million people in south Texas who presently do not qualify for that kind of health care. That's why we've funded seven new consumer-run primary care centers in south Texas.

There's something else I'm committed to, and it's expressed by the Spanish saying: *Dime con quien andas y te diré quien eres.* [Tell me who you walk with, and I'll tell you who you are.] And you know who I walk with, right? [*Cheers*]

I am proud that I've been able in just 3½ years to appoint more than 200 His-

panic Americans to senior Government positions, more than any other previous administration in history. And I know the concern of all Americans with equal justice. I'm very proud to have appointed three times as many Hispanic judges as all the Presidents combined in 200 years, since this Nation was formed, and they have been the highest possible quality.

I'll only mention one of them, because there's something special about him that perhaps you didn't know. One of them is Reynaldo Garza. He now sits as a judge on the Fifth Circuit Court of Appeals. But many of you may not know about the first job I offered to Judge Garza in January of 1977, shortly before I was inaugurated President. I called Judge Garza, and I offered him the position as Attorney General of the United States.

I regret very much that because of personal considerations in his own family, that the United States did not have the benefit of his service in that Cabinet post as Attorney General. He would have been the first Hispanic Attorney General in the history of our country. But I am proud of the job that he's now doing on the Federal bench.

We flew in this morning from Houston, maintained a low altitude, and we had a chance to look at the absolutely beautiful farming country that you have here. And I wanted to say a word about agriculture, because it's important to me as a farmer, I know it's important to this district. You've been blessed by God with productive land, and you've utilized it to the highest as good stewards of what God has given you. I even know what parity means. [*Laughter*]

When I was growing up, like many of you, I worked in the times before Franklin Roosevelt was able to change the attitude of this Nation's Government toward agriculture and toward farm families. We worked from dark in the morning till dark at night, getting ready to produce crops that quite often were stolen from us at the time of harvest. We didn't have electricity on our farms. And we didn't have any security for the aged who slaved all their lives away on the farm and wound up with nothing to show for it when they reached retirement age.

The Democrats changed all that. I remember when we put electricity on the farm, and I remember when we tried to stabilize the market so farmers could have a better life. That's why I'm very glad to come here to the State that produced a great President like Lyndon Baines Johnson, because he understood also the plight of American farmers and also the great contribution that agriculture makes to the economic life's blood of our Nation.

I began by appointing the Secretary of Agriculture, a dirt farmer, one who understands the special needs of farm families, Bob Bergland. He's been an outstanding man. And in the past, as you know, when Republican Presidents have chosen a Secretary of Agriculture, they've always chosen a bigshot executive in some company that buys products from farmers at a cheap price and sells those same products to consumers at a high price. We don't want another Earl Butz back in the Secretary's office. We want Bob Bergland.

Bob Bergland and I knew from experience that most often farmers, when they produce their grain, other products, had to put those products to market in the rush of the harvest season when prices were low. So, we figured it would be good to provide storage on farmers' farms. We've created 2.8 billion bushels of storage and now farmers can store their own crops. They can decide for themselves when to take those crops to market.

And that policy has paid rich dividends in two or three ways. One, we've increased prices a great deal that the farmers receive. Since 1977 the price of corn has almost doubled; the price of wheat has almost doubled; the price of beef has also doubled. And the consumers have benefited from it. The consumers have now stable policies in agriculture, and as you well know, we have a steady supply of good grain.

We've had in this last 3 years the biggest increase in gross income for America's farmers in history, the biggest increase in net income for American farm families in history. And on exports we have used great ports like Brownsville and great production areas like your own to increase the sale of products overseas. In 1977 we set a world's record on American farm exports; '78, broke that record; '79, broke it again. And this year we'll increase exports $8 billion to a new record of $40 billion worth of American farm products being sold overseas. That's the kind of program we've had for American farmers.

You might be interested in knowing that since 1977 we have tripled trade with Mexico, and this year we'll sell to Mexico 10 million tons of American grain.

We've opened up vast new opportunities for sales in the future with the People's Republic of China, where one-fourth of the people on Earth live. China has already become the number one customer for American cotton, and we've just recently signed an agreement with China where they will buy between 6 and 10 million tons of grain every year for the next 5 years. These opportunities have helped our country. They've also helped people like you. And I might say that Brownsville is one of the special ports designated by the Chinese through which that vast stream of grain will flow to feed those billion people. It's an average of 15 loaves of bread per year per person in China, coming from American farms.

As you may know, the State of Georgia has a wonderful fishing industry, shrimp boats. And I don't want to pass without pointing out to you that Kika de la Garza and I have a great interest in those who own shrimp boats and the crews that work on them, and we're going to make sure that your opportunities to serve this Nation are honored in the years ahead as well.

In closing my remarks, I want to point out to you some considerations that must be important to you in the next few days. Tuesday will be a time of great decision, and I know you've observed, maybe some with intense interest, some with casual interest, what's gone on in this campaign so far.

If you've been listening to the Republican candidate, Governor Reagan, then you know he's trying to wrap himself in the mantle of great Democratic Presidents. But this happens every election year. Have you ever heard a Republican candidate quoting a Republican President?

AUDIENCE. No!

THE PRESIDENT. You haven't heard Governor Reagan talking about Herbert Hoover, have you?

AUDIENCE. No!

THE PRESIDENT. Have you heard Governor Reagan quoting Richard Nixon?

AUDIENCE. No!

THE PRESIDENT. No. But he talks a lot about Franklin Roosevelt.

AUDIENCE. Yes!

THE PRESIDENT. But then he turns around and says that the foundation for the New Deal is fascism; it's fascism.

And now the Republicans continue to quote Franklin D. Roosevelt. John Kennedy predicted back in 1960—let me quote him. This is what John Kennedy said about the Republicans: "They're even beginning to say a few kind words about Franklin Roosevelt. Twenty years from now," Kennedy said, "the Republicans might even speak a good word about Harry Truman. But I guarantee you that Harry Truman will never say a good word about Republicans."

As you know, that prediction came true. And I want to make another prediction for you, that 20 years from now Republican candidates for President will even say good words about Jimmy Carter's second term.

AUDIENCE [*chanting*]. We want Carter! We want Jimmy!

THE PRESIDENT. You've got me. Thank you. You've got me. Thank you.

Let me say that I believe in the Democratic Party, and I hope that you'll think back in history, recent history and even as far back as I remember, about what the Democratic Party has meant to you. I believe in the mission of the Democratic Party. Every great advance that's been made in the lives of working people for the last 50 years has come under the Democratic administrations. Collective bargaining for workers, to the minimum wage, social security, Medicaid, Medicare—every single one of these has been made possible by Democrats, always over the opposition of Republicans.

I'm proud to be a Democrat, because our party stands for progress and it also stands for justice. When workers sought the right to organize, they looked to the Democrats. When older Americans needed security with their retirement, they called on the Democrats. When Americans have wanted justice and opportunity and basic rights, they've always counted on the Democrats and the Democrats have always come through.

Today Americans are still looking for the Democrats to provide national health insurance, for jobs and training for our young people, for a strong economic future, for human rights and equal rights, a strong defense, and peace. With your help, the Democrats will come through on November the 4th.

I've described the election of 1980 as a choice between two futures, and this is what I see in the future to which we're looking. I see a nation at peace; a nation strong enough to be secure in its pursuit of progress for all our people; a nation where everyone has the dignity of a decent job, where new industries create a new generation of American buildings and American vehicles that will provide us with houses and will move us using less energy, that energy that we do use coming from our own Nation; a nation where children are educated to their maximum potential, where the elderly are treated with the respect that they've earned, where families are close and intact and secure. I have a vision of a nation free enough to attract and strong enough to welcome the deprived from other parts of the world; a nation of liberty, of justice, and of love. I need your help to make this vision a reality.

I've been President now for almost 4 years. I've made thousands of decisions, and each one of those decisions has been a learning process for me. Every decision I make leaves me better prepared to make the next one. What I've learned has made me a better President, and I believe I'll be an even better President in the second term, because I understand now much more closely your needs, the strength of our Nation, and the future available to us all.

I consider myself to be in the mainstream of the Democratic Party and also in the mainstream of the bipartisan Presidents, Republican and Democrat, who have insisted on controlling nuclear weapons and wanting to keep our Nation at peace. I believe that the United States must be a nation strong. I believe the Nation must be secure. We must have a society that's just and fair. We must dare to struggle for a peaceful world.

There have been many times of crisis and conflict during these last few years. In each case, I alone have had to make a judgment about the interest of my Nation and about the involvement of my Nation. In each case, I've had to decide what to do to keep our Nation, its interests protected and to keep our boys from having to give their lives on the field of battle. And I'm proud that I can make a statement that no President in the last 50 years has been able to make: Since I have been in the Oval Office, our Nation has been at peace; we have not been at war.

I've learned one other thing, and that is that the more difficult the decisions are, the more important the issue is, the more likely that the advisers will be split roughly 50–50, and the President has to make the final judgment in the loneliness of the Oval Office. Sometimes it has been a lonely job, but with the involvement of the American people, it's also a gratifying job.

Now each one of you, in the next few days, faces the same kind of decision, a lonely decision, because you'll go in the voting booth alone. But even before election day next Tuesday, you have a decision to make. Are the issues important enough to you, to your family, to the people that you love, to work the next few days in a sacrificial way? There's no one here, no matter how poor or how lacking in influence, that can't reach several hundred people between now and election day. Some of you have enough influence to reach a thousand or 10,000.

And I hope you'll consider very carefully what will be the circumstances in your life Wednesday morning if you wake up to find that a Republican will be in the White House the next 4 years.

AUDIENCE. No!

THE PRESIDENT. The issue is up to you. Just think back in 1948. If a few people had not voted or changed their mind, Harry Truman would never have been President. And think back in 1960. If 28,000 people in Texas had voted differently and just a few thousand in Illinois, John Kennedy would never have been President, and the likelihood is that Lyndon Baines Johnson would never have been President.

Those are good stories. Listen to what happened in 1968. If just a few more people like you had worked those last few days, had urged people to go to the polls, Hubert Humphrey would have been a great President, and Richard Nixon would never have been in the Oval Office.

Those elections ought to be ever present in your mind as you face Sunday, Monday, and then election day. It's not enough for you just to vote. I'm asking you to encourage everyone in the sound of your voice to work hard this next few days and on Tuesday to vote with us and give a great victory for your lives, for those you love, and for the greatest nation on Earth. Together, we Democrats will whip the Republicans and have a greater future.

AUDIENCE [*chanting*]. We want Carter!

THE PRESIDENT. *Muchas gracias a todos. Necesito sus votas, su trabajo. Gracias a todos para su ayuda.* [Thank you, everyone. I need your votes, your work. Thank you for your help.]

NOTE: The President spoke at 10 a.m. on the front lawn of Gorgas Hall at Texas Southmost College.

San Antonio, Texas
Remarks at a Rally With Area Residents.
November 1, 1980

Senator Bentsen, Congressman Henry Gonzalez, Congressman Kazen, distinguished friends from San Antonio and around this part of Texas:

I am very glad to be back here, because I never am permitted to forget about this district and what it means to the rest of the Nation, because Henry Gonzalez and Chick Kazen just won't let me forget about you.

In the best Democratic tradition, Henry Gonzalez has worked to improve the quality of life for all people in San Antonio, and while he's done very much for the business of this community, by bringing it the world's fair in 1968, helping to keep it crowded with conventions today, he's done even more to bring dignity to the lives of all Americans and to gain equality of opportunity for all our citizens. And I thank him on behalf of the people of this Nation. And I also want to express my thanks to Congressman Kazen, who comes from a Lebanese-American family, who spoke Spanish before he did English, because he represents the fact that this area is rich in its diversity, it's rich in its patriotism, it's rich in its commitment to a better life for all Americans, and I thank him too.

It's always good to be introduced by Lloyd Bentsen, a great Texan and a great American, a man who understands the past, present, and future of our Democratic Party and of our country, but it's particularly pleasing to me to be introduced in this historic site, a site which exemplifies not only the history of our Nation and its development but also epitomizes basic human courage. As a matter of fact, this historic site is a tourist attraction that helps to keep San Antonio prosperous and gives the world a chance to see what you have to offer here. But the Alamo will soon be seeing new action, redevelopment. It'll be linked to another historic site, the San Antonio River.

As you know, with a grant of $6 million from my Urban Development Action Grant program, we have been able to bring $48 million in private money to San Antonio. More than 800 permanent jobs will be created here in addition to many small businesses. And I'm very glad to say that there have been tens of thousands of new jobs created in San Antonio, almost a million new jobs created in the State of Texas since I was inaugurated President, and we're going to keep that progress going.

Lloyd Bentsen mentioned Republicans who try to masquerade as Democrats just before election day. If you've been listening to the Republican candidate for President, then you know he is trying to wrap himself in the mantle of great Democratic Presidents. Let me ask you a question: Have you ever heard a Republican candidate for President quote a Republican President?

AUDIENCE. No!

THE PRESIDENT. No. And there's a good reason for it, because their past record which will be the same as their future record if they get in the Oval Office, is not something to brag about.

Can you imagine Ronald Reagan, making a speech at the Republican Convention, when he quoted Franklin D. Roosevelt, quoting Herbert Hoover and Richard Nixon?

AUDIENCE. No!

THE PRESIDENT. It always happens.

Here's what Franklin D. Roosevelt said about that back in 1944. He said about the Republicans that change their tune late in October, early November: "The whole purpose," he said, "of Republican oratory these days seems to be to switch labels." Sound familiar? "Now imitation," he said, "may be the sincerest form of flattery, but I'm afraid that in this case what it is is just common or garden variety of fraud." And Roosevelt was not the only one that said something about that.

John Kennedy predicted back in 1960—here's what John Kennedy said: "They're even beginning to say a few kind words about Franklin Roosevelt." And Kennedy said, "Twenty years from now, the Republicans might even speak a good word about Harry Truman, but I guarantee you that Harry Truman will not say a good word about Republicans." As you know, that prediction came true. And I want to make a prediction to you today here in front of the Alamo. I predict that 20 years from now, Republican candidates will be saying nice things about Jimmy Carter's second term.

Standing here reminds me of courage. Standing here reminds me of the dedication of brave men. Standing here as Commander in Chief, it would be inappropriate for me not to comment on the Kelly Air Force Base, which has the largest concentration of Air Force personnel anywhere in the world.

My background, my training, is as a professional military officer. I went to the Naval Academy, and I served 11 years in the Navy. I was an officer in the submarine force. I want to point out to you what has happened about defense in recent years. As long as I'm President, we will have a strong nation, because I know that only through strength can we have peace. In the last 50 years, no President has been able to make the statement that I'm going to make now. In my term of office, we have not had war. We have stayed at peace.

AUDIENCE. Four more years!

THE PRESIDENT. Thank you. Okay. I accept. [*Laughter*]

And the reason that we're going to have 4 more years and also 4 more years at peace, is that we have corrected the neglect of our Nation's defense establishment that I inherited after 8 years of Republican misrule. In 7 of those 8 years, under Nixon and Ford, when Republicans were in the White House, we had a decrease in real terms for our Nation's defense. Since I've been in office, though, with the help of Lloyd Bentsen and the Members of the Congress, we've had a steady, orderly, and effective increase above and beyond inflation every single year for a strong defense for the strongest nation on Earth, and we're going to keep that up.

When I came into office, there was no long-range cruise missile program. Now we have one. We'll be producing 40 highly accurate, advanced cruise missiles per month. When I came into office, there was no new battle tank. Now we have one. There was no modern armored fighting vehicle to carry personnel; now they're in production. There was no answer to the potential vulnerability of our ICBM's, our missiles located in silos. Now we have an answer, the mobile MX missile. And listen to this: Under those Republican Presidents, our purchases of Army equipment, jet fighters, and attack aircraft had dropped by two-thirds in the 8 years before I became President. Since then, we have increased those purchases by 50 percent.

We know that the purpose of a strong defense is to keep our Nation at peace and to protect American interests and the interests of our allies around the world. Every day that I've been in office, we've

had trouble places somewhere in the world. Armed conflict has broken out in different locations between nations six or eight times since I've been President. The judgment that has to be made is what are America's interests? What degree of involvement should we exercise? How should we use our tremendous strength?

We'll keep the most modern weapons. We'll keep the highest trained military men and women to serve our Nation. But I'm a father of young sons, and I have grandchildren coming along as well, and I always will remember, as President, that the best weapon is one that does not have to be fired in combat, and the best soldier is one that doesn't have to lay his life down or shed his blood on a field of battle.

I believe the mothers and fathers of this Nation and I believe the young men and women of this Nation will remember Tuesday, when they go to the polls to vote, that Presidents, in dealing with difficult times, have been contradicted by Governor Reagan on several occasions. He has called for the sending of American military forces to fight in many areas around the world in recent years, not just since I've been President, when this year he called for the sending of American troops to Cuba and to Angola and to other countries, Pakistan, but in the past to North Korea, to settle a fishing dispute in Ecuador. This year he wanted to send American military forces to establish a blockade around the island of Cuba. He wanted also to send American military forces to Cyprus, to Rhodesia, and to the Middle East.

Presidents have to make a judgment when troubled times arise, when crises come to the Oval Office. If a President handles them well our Nation's interest can be protected, and you may not even know how serious that crisis might have been. But if a President makes a misjudgment that crisis can affect your life, and it can affect the life of this Nation and perhaps the peace and security of everyone on Earth.

Peace, war, crisis are important issues in the lives of every person. But there are other humane things at stake as well. Think back on the difference between the Democratic and Republican Parties. When has your life been benefited? Where did the great progress come from? Just since I've been old enough to remember—I grew up on a farm—we got REA, the TVA program, electricity on the farms, by Democrats, over Republican opposition. We got the minimum wage, which at first was only 25 cents an hour. The Republicans opposed it, because they didn't think that an able-bodied man or an able-bodied woman was worth 25 cents an hour. I got my first job as a high school graduate working 10 hours a day at the new minimum wage of 40 cents. I had to furnish a car and pay all the expenses in the process. But that 40-cent wage, guaranteed by the Democrats, was opposed by the Republicans.

Social security—the Democrats put it forward; the Republicans called it socialism, communism. Medicare, a Democratic program—my opponent got his start in politics campaigning all around the country speaking against Medicare, calling it socialized medicine.

The Republicans and the Democrats historically have had a different attitude toward progress or lack of progress. One of the key issues in this election is concerning social justice. At stake is whether we continue to build a society committed to equality of opportunity and social justice. I stand for vigorous enforcement of our civil rights laws. When Lyndon Johnson and the Democratic Congress were passing the Civil Rights Act, Ronald Reagan said, "That's bad legislation."

I'm for the open housing amendment now before Congress, and I'm for the equal rights amendment to give women equal treatment in this country. And I might add that for 40 years, for 40 years, the Republican Party platform always supported equal rights for women until Ronald Reagan came along. Six Presidents before me in the White House supported equal rights for women. My mother was a working woman. She was a registered nurse. She worked 12 hours a day when I was a child for $4, and sometimes she nursed 20 hours a day in order to earn $6. Nowadays when a man and woman do the same work a man gets paid a dollar; a woman only gets paid 59 cents.

What the equal rights amendment says is this: that equality of rights—this is the whole thing—equality of rights shall not be abridged or taken away by the Federal Government nor any other State government because a person is a woman. What it says, in effect, is quit cheating women.

I might add in closing that I'm for a strong public school system. I'm for the youth bill now before the Congress, already passed the House, that will provide 600,000 jobs for our young people. I'm for tough safeguards to protect our environment. I'm for protecting consumers so you won't be cheated. Those are the kinds of positions that Democrats have always supported and Republicans now and in the past have always opposed.

I've described this election in 1980 as a choice between two futures. Now, this is what I see in the future that we are fighting for together: I see a nation at peace. I see a nation strong. I see a nation secure. I see a nation dedicated in its pursuit of equality of opportunity and progress for all people. I see a nation where everyone can have the dignity of a decent job, where new industries create a new generation of American buildings and American vehicles that will house us and move us with less energy, but energy that comes from the United States and not overseas.

And I see a nation where children are educated to the maximum potential that God gave them, where elderly people are treated with the respect that they've earned with a dedicated life, where families are strong and secure and intact. I have a vision of a nation free enough to attract and strong enough to welcome the deprived from other parts of the world, a nation of liberty, of justice, and of love.

I've been President now for almost 4 years. I've made thousands of decisions, and each one of those decisions has been a learning process for me. Every decision I make leaves me better prepared for the next one. What I've learned has made me a better President and will make me a better President in my second term. I consider myself——

AUDIENCE [*chanting*]. We want Jimmy!

THE PRESIDENT. You got me. Thank you.

I consider myself to be in the mainstream of the Democratic Party and also in the mainstream of the bipartisan Presidents who have served [before] [1] me. There is a radical difference, a sharp difference between myself and Governor Reagan on most every major issue that will affect your life. The Presidency is a good job, but it's a lonely job. But, with the involvement of the American people as partners under our democratic system, it's a gratifying job.

—————
[1] White House correction.

Now, I face lonely decisions, but so do you. At this moment, looking for the last few hours before election day on November the 4th, you've got a decision to make. Your coming here is good. Your voting for me on November the 4th is good, but there's a lot more that you can do. Between now and then, there's nobody in this crowd that can't contact 100 people, some of you 1,000 people, maybe those with more influence, 10,000 people. Think about the consequences in your own life if Wednesday morning you wake up and you face the prospect of a Republican being in the Oval Office for the next 4 years.

You might say one person can't make much difference, but just remember in 1948 that a few votes changed would have meant that Harry Truman would never have been President. And in 1960, if 28,000 people in Texas had voted differently and just a few in Illinois, then John Kennedy would never have served as President, and perhaps Lyndon Johnson would never have been President either. Those elections came out well. But 1968 is another example when Democrats didn't work hard for the nominee the last few days. If you and I had worked a little more and recognized the consequences, Hubert Humphrey would have been President, and Richard Nixon would never have served in the Oval Office.

To close my remarks, I want to quote from another Democrat who never became President, because he was killed a few days before the end of the primary season. Senator Robert Kennedy made a speech on his last day of what was to be his final campaign. It was in the Presidential primary in California in 1968. And I would like to share his closing lines with you. He said, "I ask you to recognize the hard and the difficult road to a better America. I ask you to vote for yourselves.

The people must decide this election. They must decide so that no leader has any doubt about what the people want. For your sake and for the sake of your children, vote for yourselves."

Thank you very much. I need you. ¡Viva San Antonio!

NOTE: The President spoke at 12:57 p.m. outside the Alamo.

Abilene, Texas

Remarks at a Rally With Area Residents. November 1, 1980

Senator Lloyd Bentsen, Congressman Omar Burleson, Henry Gonzalez, Lieutenant Governor Hobby:

You have turned out this afternoon in such tremendous crowd that I think after 1985 when I'm through in the White House I might come out here and spend a long time with all of you. Okay?

I rode in on the airplane with Charlie Stenholm, and I realized where I went wrong. He raises cotton and hogs instead of peanuts, and he wound up without any opposition. [*Laughter*] So, it looks like peanut farmers are the ones that have to face a formidable opponent. But I'll say this: At least in the Abilene area peanut farmers have a lot of friends, and I thank you for it.

Lloyd Bentsen mentioned one thing that's important, and that is the right of American people to have a decent job. I was looking at the statistics before I came to Texas this time. You know, the world has suffered a great deal economically the last few years because of the OPEC price increases, and a lot of

unemployment exists still in our country and other places too. We have added 9 million new jobs, and I notice that since I was sworn in as President in January of 1977, 914,000 more people have jobs in Texas. That's a pretty good record.

A lot of good Texans have come out to welcome me. I notice that your illustrious Governor was not here to see me. [*Laughter*] I asked some of the students at your great colleges nearby where he might be. They said, "He might be home reading the Third Commandment." Now, for those of you who don't know what the Third Commandment is, I suggest that when you get home, you get your Bible if you've got one—I'm sure you have—turn to Exodus 20 and read the Third Commandment. And I believe that your Governor's there thinking about not only the Commandment, but the warning that goes with it.

Well, don't forget now when you get home, read the Bible, okay? [*Laughter*] How many of you will look it up? [*Applause*] Okay. Keep your promise.

I know I've come to the right part of Texas, and I understand a little bit better since I've read about Abilene and this area why you've turned out so well. Not too far from here, there's a town called Albany, Texas. It was named after Albany, Georgia, not too far from my home. [*Laughter*] And I understand that there's a county northeast of here where Albany is the county seat, I believe, named Shackleford County. Shackleford County is named after a Georgia doctor, Captain John Shackleford, who let a group of volunteers from Georgia, who came here to fight when Texas was seeking your independence. And there's one Georgian who does grow peanuts for a living who's still fighting for Texas, and this time I need your help, okay? [*Applause*]

2627

This has been a long, difficult campaign, and I think you've noticed the trends that take place during the political season. It's hard to keep labels on people, because there's a great effort at pretense, particularly among Republicans. I'm sure you've been listening to my Republican opponent, and you know that he's tried to wrap himself in the mantle of great Democrats. Let me ask you a question. Some of you have seen a lot of Presidential elections. Have you ever heard a Republican candidate for President quoting a Republican President?

AUDIENCE. No!

THE PRESIDENT. Have you ever thought of why? Because when Republicans are running for office, they like to sound like Democrats, but when they get in office, they act like Republicans, and they never do anything or say anything that's worthy of quotation later on.

Now, it'll be good for you to remember that when you think about where it came—social security—Republicans were against it. Minimum wage. Republicans were against it. REA. Republicans were against it. Even rural free delivery of mail. Republicans were against it. Medicare. Republicans were against it. Basic civil rights, put into effect by your great President, Lyndon Baines Johnson, the Republicans were against it. Think on those things.

Franklin Roosevelt saw this political phenomenon way back in 1944. I'd like to quote what Franklin Roosevelt said. "The whole purpose of Republican oratory these days seems to be to switch labels. Now, imitation may be the sincerest form of flattery," he said, "but I'm afraid in this case, it's the most obvious common or garden variety of fraud." That wasn't the case just in 1944, because in 1960,

when Kennedy and Johnson were running for office, Kennedy said of the Republicans, "They're even beginning to say a few kind words about Franklin Roosevelt. Twenty years from now," Kennedy said, "they might even speak a good word for Harry Truman, but I guarantee you that Harry Truman will never say a good word about Republicans."

As you know, that prediction came true. And I want to make a prediction to you now. I predict that 20 years from now, Republican candidates will even be saying nice things about Jimmy Carter's second term.

This afternoon, I'm going to make a different speech from the one I've been making for the last week. A political rally is a good place to talk about things that will inspire you for enthusiasm and to point out the differences between Republicans and Democrats. But I want to make a little more serious talk about one particular issue that's important here in this deeply religious educational center, and then I want to spell out for you, in just a few words, not the differences between me and my Republican opponent, but about the future, because it will affect your life.

We who live in this region of the Nation almost like one family, we share common background, a common upbringing, a common set of values about the importance of patriotism, families, hard work, neighborliness. Many of you also share with me a common religious faith. I'm sure that some of you have seen campaign advertisements and mailings that attack my religious faith and also my character in a very ugly way. You may see even more in the next few days. I'm not going to dignify these attacks by counterbalancing each one and denying what they've alleged, which are all false. I don't intend to debate the sincerity of my own religious convictions in a political campaign. I have to depend on you who know me, know what I stand for, to speak up for me. But I believe in the separation of church and state. And I don't believe in religious tests for political acceptance, and I don't believe in political tests for religious fellowship.

Now, I'm very deeply grateful for your welcome and for this tremendous crowd. Somebody told me it's the largest one they've ever seen in west Texas. And I'm deeply grateful also for a chance now for the next 7 or 8 minutes—and I'll be relatively brief—to give you a special political speech that I've never made before. In this long election campaign the past records and statements of the candidates have been thoroughly debated, thoroughly scrutinized, but more important than what has been said or done in the past is what will be done in the future, what must be done to build the kind of future that you would like to have for yourselves, your family and for those you love. So, I want to talk to you about my hopes and plans for the next 4 years, building on what we've already accomplished together since I've been in office, about a common agenda for the second term of office which I hope to serve as your President.

First, I want to say that I'm confident about the future of our Nation. The next 4 years can be very good years. The major reason for confidence is that we have learned. We've learned so much about the challenges that have confronted us the last few months, and we've laid the foundation now to meet those challenges in the future. We know we face dangers in the world, but we've learned to use our strength wisely, in the service of our real interests, and our real values.

We know we face problems at home. We've learned a great deal also about the causes and the nature of some of those problems and about the courage and determination necessary to solve them. In 4 years as President, I've learned a great deal about myself, and I've learned a great deal about this country. I've learned that it's not always enough just to be right. We must set priorities on the most important work, [or] it may not ever be done.

We need to make sure that the people understand our programs and our policies and our commitments and then build a consensus among the people of this Nation to get your support. We've learned to do that, and the best example, I think, of our success is in energy, which has been the most serious domestic challenge that I have had to face. Four years ago, think back: Most people were led to doubt that there even was an energy problem. Today we lead the world in dealing with this severe challenge.

There's another reason for confidence in addition to energy, and that is that during my term in office we've been able to address many other challenges—economic deregulation, where we ended regulation after many, many Presidents, Republicans and Democrats, had promised to do so, and brought competition to the airline, railroad, trucking, banking, and finance industries. We've cut Government paperwork by 15 percent. In education, where we've made a 73-percent increase in our investment in the next generation of Americans, we've kept the Federal Government's nose out of the local schools, public and private. And we now have a situation in the United States where no young American who's able to do college work will ever again be deprived of a college education, no matter how poor their family might be.

And in defense we reversed a 7-year decline under Republican administrations and began a steady, balanced, well-planned increase in our ability to defend our country and defend our interests. In these and other areas, then, we've laid a foundation for further progress. We've paid a short-term price, for that's the nature of investing in our Nation's future. Today's sacrifice will bring tomorrow's security. Our investment will begin to pay rich dividends over the next 4 years if we stay on course.

My broad objectives, then, in my second term, can be stated quite simply: Security at home. We'll continue to have a nation whose national defense capability is second to none. Second is peace aboard. I'm the first President in 50 years who can make this statement: Since I've been in the White House our Nation has been at peace. We have not had war. And my commitment for the next 4 years, with God's help, is to continue that record.

These goals are more difficult to attain than they are to state, but attain them we shall. Security at home also means energy security. It means economic security for our Nation, for each of us, and our families. It means the security of knowing that our rights as Americans are guaranteed. We've put into place the first comprehensive energy program in our history. It's already helped us to reduce imports of foreign oil by one-third in the last year alone. This day we have more oil drillrigs running in the United States than ever before in history. This year we'll bring in more oil and gas wells than any year in history. This year we will produce more American coal than

any year in history, and we will also export more coal than any year in history. We are making good progress. That's the kind of base on which we can build for the future.

And I'm glad to say that Americans are now conserving more energy. And as I look at this beautiful farmland around me, I can tell you that part of the production of fuel in the future will come directly or indirectly from the Sun. Two years ago we had no gasohol production in this country to speak of. This year we'll have 135 million gallons, and by the end of 1981 we'll produce in our Nation 500 million gallons of gasohol from growing crops of the rich land that God gave us to take care of.

This commitment to the future, to continue the progress we've made, using the great technology and the natural resources of our country are very important to you and to me. The inflationary forces that have swept the world are far from vanquished, as you know. Last year OPEC oil prices went up more in one year than oil had increased in price since oil was first discovered in the 1800's. The first quarter this year the inflation rate was 18 percent; Second quarter, 13 percent; this quarter just completed, down to 7 percent—still too high, still too high. We must build on the progress that we've made in deregulation, in cutting government spending growth.

We've cut the rate of increase of government spending more than 50 percent since I've been in office, and as a part of the gross national product we've also cut the Federal deficit by 50 percent since I've been in office. And we've changed the relationship between labor and management in the basic steel industry, the coal industry, the automobile industry, and others, where now instead of just arguing with each other every 3 years about the terms of a labor contract, now government, management, labor work together to strengthen those basic elements of the prosperity of our country in the future.

I want to continue the economic revitalization effort that I've already proposed and started to increase the productivity of our economy and sharpen our technological edge in the world marketplace. One of the greatest allies that any President could have in Washington in forging for the future a successful industrial complex, to increase American productivity with sound tax programs, good investment in new tools and new plants, new jobs, is Senator Lloyd Bentsen. He's my ally in Congress. His proposals will be put into effect. He and I work closely as partners to give you and all of our families a better life. This is the only way I know to fight inflation and to put Americans to work by the millions, in new jobs, with new tools, new factories, in fact, in entire new industries that many Americans cannot even envision yet.

We've also made great strides in the last 4 years in the protection of the quality of our air, to keep it pure, our water, to keep it clean, and our land, to keep it unspoiled and productive, in safety of workers and the healthfulness of workers. In the next 4 years we must tackle and solve another problem that hasn't been addressed yet, and that's the long-neglected and increasingly serious environmental problem of toxic wastes, poisons that have in the past been dumped in our soils and in our streams, both nuclear materials and also others that must be controlled. We can do it. And we've already made progress now in making plans for the future. A superfund bill has

passed the House and is now before the Senate for consideration. There are few things that we could do that would have a more beneficial effect on the long-term health of our people.

I want to increase the productivity of our land and expand the agricultural markets around the world, to honor the stewardship of our farm families, and to enrich our own people and others with America's bountiful harvest. I'm a farmer. My people have lived in this country since the early 1600's. Every generation of my family have been farmers—my father was a farmer, his father, and all the way back since they first came to this Nation as settlers.

I've chosen as the Secretary of Agriculture a man who's also a dirt farmer, and one difference between Republicans and Democrats is who they choose to be the Secretary of Agriculture. I didn't choose, as Republicans have done, a member of the board of directors of a major processing plant that buys farmers' products cheap at harvest season and sells them high to consumers later on. I chose a man who knows what it means to plow a mule and to plow a tractor and has given you a better life.

And if you'll allow me one more minute I'd like to point this out. I've seen in my early days and also since I've been home from the Navy, as a farmer, that quite often we've had to sell our crops at harvest time at whatever price prevailed. Later the middleman made a lot of profit and cheated the consumers in the process. But Bob Bergland and I have seen the difference that ought to be made, and we've increased farm storage by 2.8 billion bushels to encourage farmers to take their grain at harvest time, to store it and to keep it and then to sell it when the market was right. This has paid rich dividends already.

In just 3½ years we've seen the greatest increase in gross income for farmers in the history of this country, the greatest increase in net income for farmers in the history of this country, and we've opened up overseas markets that our Nation never dreamed would be. As a matter of fact, we set a world record on exports in 1977. We broke that record in 1978. We broke it again in 1979, and this year we've had the greatest increase in exports in history, $8 billion increase. This year we'll sell $40 billion worth of American farm products overseas. That's a great record. We're going to continue it in the next 4 years.

I'd like to mention a word that you might think strange around Abilene, Texas, but it affects your life, and that's China. We opened up diplomatic relations with China 2 years ago, a billion people, one-fourth of the total population of the world. We've doubled trade with Taiwan since it happened. But let me tell you just a minute about China. Recently we sold enough wheat to China every year to produce 15 loaves of bread for every one of those billion people every year. Six to nine million tons of grain will go to China every year for the next 5 years.

Texas produces a lot of cotton. You know what nation is the biggest and best customer for the United States in the world today? China. Already. And they're just getting started in demanding products from us. Mexico is your neighbor. In the last 4 years we have tripled trade with Mexico. This year we'll sell Mexico 10 million tons of American grain. Those programs were hammered out not with agricultural specialists from major colleges. They were hammered out by Bob Bergland and me working with farmers

and with organizations of farmers to make sure that agriculture remains the basis for the economy and the economic growth of America in the future.

Another thing I want to say about the future is this: In the next 4 years I want to help our country achieve a long-deferred dream of the Democratic Party and the American people, a national health plan, a plan that emphasizes prevention of disease, a plan that gives care for mothers, both before and after their babies are born, that protects families with catastrophic health insurance from being financially destroyed if a family member is sick for a long time, a plan that would put a limit on how much hospital costs can increase. These kinds of commitments would give America better health and would cost much less than health care costs today.

In the next 4 years I want to see equal rights for American women guaranteed where the rights of Americans are supposed to be guaranteed, in the Constitution of the United States.

I'd like to stop and say a word about that. It might make my speech a little longer, but I think it's important, because I come from a very conservative region of our Nation. A lot of people have been misled about the equal rights amendment, but let me tell you just in a few words what it means. My mother, Lillian, is a working woman. During the Depression years, she was a registered nurse. She worked 12 hours a day for $4 a day. And sometimes when she was lucky she worked 20 hours a day and got paid $6 for it. She helped our family a lot during the Depression years.

Nowadays, a third of our families are headed by women who have to bring home a paycheck to buy food and clothing and shelter for the whole family. Now when a man and woman do the same amount of work, a man gets paid a dollar, and a woman gets paid 59 cents on the average. That's not right. And what the equal rights amendment says is this—it's a very simple amendment. It says: Equality of rights cannot be abridged by the Federal Government or any State government just because the person's a woman. That's all it says. It doesn't say anything about bathrooms. It doesn't say anything about homosexuals. It doesn't say anything about being drafted. It just says that the Federal Government and the State governments have got to stop cheating women. That's all it says.

And the last thing I want to mention to you about the future is this: Security at home is obviously important, but it will avail us little if we don't have continued progress toward our other great goal, and that is peace in the world. Real peace is more than just the absence of war. There's something that must be constructed brick by brick through a strong defense and a wise and restrained foreign policy. During the next 4 years, in cooperation with our allies, we will continue the steady strengthening of our conventional and our strategic military forces. We'll strengthen our presence in the vital Persian Gulf and the Indian Ocean region, building a system of regional security in that part of the world through diplomacy as well as military strength. That's a major task for the early 1980's.

In the Middle East, I want to continue to use our country's good offices to help achieve the dream of a strong and secure Israel living in peace with all her neighbors. This is an ambitious goal, I know, but 4 years ago, no one believed that by 1980 there would be a treaty of peace between Israel and the most powerful Arab country in the world, Egypt. The Camp David process works, and we'll stay with it. The thing is that we're not just doing Israel a favor, because it's a great contribution to our own security to have a strong, secure, democratic, peace-loving Israel in the Middle East.

One of the least noticed changes in the last 4 years and one of the most important has been our tremendous improvement in our relationship with the so-called Third World countries, the home of the vast majority of the human race. We've built positive relationships, that I've already mentioned with China, with Nigeria, and other African countries, and with Central and South America. Just to point out the importance of better relations with the Third World, let me remind you that every American who has been killed in action since World War II has died on the soil of a Third World country. In my second term, I want to help our Nation solidify these new relationships by working with them and with their people in promoting economic development, political stability, and basic human rights.

Most important of all, during these next 4 years, I want to continue our Nation's efforts to lift the shadow of nuclear annihilation from this Earth. I'm determined to move ahead with balanced and verifiable nuclear arms control. This is crucial to our national security, to our leadership of the Western Alliance, to our efforts to halt the spread of nuclear bombs to unstable or terrorist regimes and organizations. Our ultimate goal is nothing less than to turn the attention of the whole world from the works of war to the works of peace.

When Americans went to the Moon and turned their eyes back to Earth, we saw our planet for what it is: a beautiful, fragile spaceship in which all of us, all 4 billion of us, must travel together. In the coming decade, all the people of the Earth, increasingly, will face problems like environmental decay, resource depletion, and hunger. There are going to be conflicts, tensions, pressures, and they'll be intense. The sooner we stop fighting each other and start fighting these common enemies of all human beings, the more likely it will be that we can survive and to prosper.

All these efforts to build security at home and peace abroad will be affected by your choice next Tuesday. I appreciate what you've done in the last few years. I congratulate you and I thank you. You've given this party, the Democratic Party, your contributions in your hearts, but none of us can walk away satisfied that we've fulfilled our obligations. The job is not yet over. You still must have a willingness to contribute your leadership, your dedication, your energy, and your spirit. We've only got a few days now to make a decision. It will affect your life. It'll affect the future of your family; it'll affect the future of the people that you love. It'll affect the future of the country that you love.

It's nice and I appreciate your coming out here this afternoon. Many of you have made financial contributions, maybe worked in campaign organizations for candidates who are Democrats, and I thank you for that too. But now, these next few hours, as we approach the final deadline for deciding the future, I'd like to ask you to do more. I'd like to ask you to stop and think about the consequences to you and your family if you should wake up Wednesday morning and find that a Republican will be in the Oval Office the next 4 years. Think about it. The choice will be yours. The choice will be yours.

Think back in 1948, how just a few votes if they had changed would have prevented Harry Truman from ever serving as President in his term. Just think back to 1960, when John Kennedy and Lyndon Johnson were on the Democratic ticket. If 28,000 people in Texas had voted differently and just a few thousand in Illinois, John Kennedy would never have been President, and Lyndon Johnson, perhaps, never would have had a chance to serve this country either. Those two stories came out well. But think about 1968. If just a few Democrats the last few hours had done a little more work, we would have had a great Democratic President and Richard Nixon would never have embarrassed this country in the White House.

So, now it's up to you. There's not a single person in this great audience that can't reach at least a hundred other people between now and Tuesday. Some of you might reach a thousand. Some might reach as many as 10,000 through the media and so forth. But I'd like to ask you to make a sacrificial effort these next few days to make sure that you and I can remember the past when the Democratic Party served us so well and think about those things in the future that I've outlined to you this afternoon.

I thank you for your partnership. God bless you for your past efforts. Let's get together and win on Tuesday and keep this country on the road to peace and prosperity.

NOTE: The President spoke at 3:53 p.m. at Abilene Municipal Airport.

Fort Worth, Texas

Remarks at a Rally With Area Residents.
November 1, 1980

My good friend Jim Wright, Senator Lloyd Bentsen, Lieutenant Governor Bill Hobby, Congressman Martin Frost, Congressman Charles Stenholm, Congressman Henry Gonzalez, Ralph Yarborough, a great Senator from the past, but still with us in the present:

I'm very grateful to be here with Louis Zapata and all of you, and I'd like to ask you a question. Are we going to whip the Republicans next Tuesday? [*Applause*] Right.

It's a great honor for any American to come here to Fort Worth, which was so important in establishing in the consciousness of all people the pioneer spirit of our land, the strength of those who never faltered in the face of danger, who exemplified human courage, the ability to explore for a better life, starting right here, the starting point of the Chisholm Trail, on the way to Chicago and the great markets. And I'm very glad to see that you're still on the cutting edge of American industry and business and progress in Fort Worth. This historic area is now being rebuilt and preserved by the close cooperation of my administration, Jim Wright, the local officials. It's typical of what Fort Worth has been in the past and the greater future you have ahead of you in the years ahead, and I'm glad to be part of it.

You know, the world has suffered the last 4 years since I've been President. We've had terrible ravages of inflation in almost every nation on Earth. In Israel the inflation rate is 200 percent. A lot of communities around the world have inflation rates over 100 percent. Unemployment, very high. They've had no employment growth in Germany, France, Great Britain. But I notice in this Nation in the last 4 years we've added almost 9 million new jobs for American workers, in Texas alone, 914,000 new jobs, in Dallas and Fort Worth area, 294,400 brand new jobs, in the Fort Worth city limits, 46,000. That's the kind of country we've got.

God has blessed us in this Nation. You might look back on past times and just think about how they were, compared to what we experience now, with the blessings God's given us. What's happened right here, in kind of a revitalization of the historic treasure of our country, is typical of what has happened.

I was born in 1924. I grew up on a farm in south Georgia, and I remember what happened in my own life in those last 50 years since Democrats were in the cutting edge of helping working families and the poor and the elderly and those that didn't have good education. My family have lived in this country since the 1600's. Every one of us have been farmers. My father never had a chance to finish high school. Neither did his father. As a matter of fact, I'm the first one in my family that ever had a chance to finish high school.

I grew up on a farm, as I say, and when Franklin Roosevelt came into office, we were facing despair and poverty. He thought that working families ought to be treated in a decent way, and he put electric lights in our farmhouse. Republicans were against the REA, the TVA program. They said it was socialism, communism. Franklin Roosevelt thought that a working man or a working woman ought to have a decent wage to buy food, clothing, shelter for their children, so he put forward the first minimum wage, 25 cents an hour. The Republicans were against it. They didn't think that a working man or woman was worth 25 cents an hour. They said it was communism, socialism, to have the Government tell an employer to pay a man or woman 25 cents. I got my first job as high school graduate in 1941. Minimum wage, 10 hours a day, I had to furnish my own car and pay the expenses, 40 cents an hour. The Democrats put it forward. It was a great advance. Republicans were against it.

Franklin Roosevelt thought that older people when they reached retirement age ought to have some security in life, ought to have some chance for self-respect, so he proposed social security. Republicans said it was communism, socialism. Democrats passed it into law. Later on in 1961 the Democrats thought that older people ought to have Medicare, put forward the program. Republicans opposed it.

My opponent in this election, Governor Reagan, got his start in politics working for the medical lobby, traveling around this country telling people that Medicare was socialized medicine, and this country was going to be taken over by socialists. This kind of historic background I tell at the beginning of my talk, because I think it's good for you—remember that things don't change very much. You're approaching a major decision next Tuesday. And I don't want you to forget historically what has happened.

You've been listening lately to Governor Reagan speak, and you know, if you saw the Republican Convention, that he's been trying to wrap himself in the mantle of great Democratic Presidents. Let me ask you a question. Have you ever in your life heard a Republican candidate for President quote a Republican President?

AUDIENCE. No!

THE PRESIDENT. No, you haven't. No, you haven't, and I'll tell you why.

They talk like Democrats just before election day and try to mislead the voters of this Nation. And then when they get in office, they act like all the other Republicans have always acted, and so they never do anything or say anything that's worthy of quoting later on.

It's surprising how many working people in this country get misled every 4 years by the high-paid song and dance Republicans put on. Franklin Roosevelt understood it. I'd like to read you what he said in 1944—listen to this—Roosevelt's words: "The whole purpose of Republican oratory these days seems to be to switch labels." "Now, imitation," he said, "may be the sincerest form of flattery, but I'm afraid that in this case, it's the most obvious common or garden variety of fraud." Roosevelt knew what he was talking about.

The same thing happened in 1960. You remember it, when John Kennedy and Lyndon Johnson were heading the Democratic ticket, Republicans doing the same thing, here's what John Kennedy said of the Republicans: "They're even beginning to say a few kind words about Franklin Roosevelt. Twenty years from now, they may even speak a good word for Harry Truman, but I guarantee you that Truman will never say a good word about Republicans." As you know, that prediction came true. The Republicans almost fooled Democratic voters in 1960, It was that close. You remember it. If 28,000 people in Texas had voted differently and a few thousand in Illinois, John Kennedy would never have been President. Likely, Lyndon Johnson may never have been

President, and this country would have suffered because of it.

Now, I'll make a prediction to you now. I predict that 20 years from now the Republican candidates will even be saying nice things about Jimmy Carter's second term.

Let me quote a few things that Governor Reagan has said. I didn't come here tonight to criticize him particularly, but I just want to quote his words. The Republican candidate said this year, 1980, fascism was really the basis for the New Deal. Now, do you think Roosevelt would have liked that?

AUDIENCE. No!

THE PRESIDENT. The Republican candidate this year, 1980, said, "I'm opposed to national health insurance. There is no health crisis in America." And the Republican also said this year about the minimum wage, "The minimum wage has caused more misery and more unemployment than anything since the Great Depression."

And the Republican candidate this year says that in 1980, that we should threaten a nuclear arms race against the Soviet Union. John Kennedy negotiated the nuclear test ban treaty, and every President since Harry Truman, Republican and Democratic, have known that the awesome power of nuclear destruction and the control of it was a major responsibility of a President until Ronald Reagan changed the policy.

Well, you notice that I like to quote Governor Reagan. I would also like to quote your Governor. [*Laughter*] But I'm afraid that if I did, my mother might wash my mouth out with soap, so I won't do it.

Now, I'd like to remind you of this: You've all seen the polls. The election is close. As a candidate for reelection I'll fight all the way to the wire. This campaign does mean a lot to me personally, because I've invested a lot of years of my life in building a foundation now for a greater future for our country. But what matters most is not what it means to the candidates, but it's what it means to millions of Americans around this country just like you. Think about the consequences for a moment in your own life if you wake up Wednesday morning and discover that we'll have a Republican administration for the next 4 years. Think about it.

Think about the consequences if they are successful in repealing the minimum wage law. Think about the consequences for working people of an administration hostile to their very basic rights to organize, the consequences to working women of an administration that would deny constitutional protections of the right to equal pay when women do equal work. Think about the consequences to older Americans if Mr. Reagan should be successful in his often-made proposal to make social security voluntary. It would mean the end of social security. And the other night in the debate I notice he said again that for a young person social security payments were a bad investment. The fact is that for a young father or mother starting at the age of 22, making social security payments, they'll get back $3\frac{1}{2}$ times more than they put in by the retirement age. And in addition, as a bonus, they get disability benefits if something happens to them, and if one of them dies the survivor benefits, as you know, help the surviving spouse and all the children till they're 18. Now, the spreading of word by a President (candidate)[1] that so-

---

[1] White House correction.

cial security is a bad investment is a direct threat to the security of the aged people of this country.

Think about minorities. I'm from the Deep South. I saw what happened to us in the South with the passage of the voting rights bill, civil rights bill under Lyndon Johnson. It's the best thing that ever happened to the Southland. And at the time it passed, Governor Reagan said, "The Civil Rights Act is bad legislation." We would not be having the enormous economic growth, the technological advances, prosperous farms, a better life, if we had still around us the stigma of racial discrimination. Think about minorities; what might happen to you Wednesday morning if a bad dream comes true.

Think about the threat to the American environment. God's given us a beautiful land. I've been flying all over Texas this morning, from Houston to Beaumont, San Antonio, Abilene, and now to here, and I've seen what you've got—clear air, beautiful streams, good, productive land. The Democrats believe that we can have technological advances and economic development and still keep good stewardship over the precious things that God gave us.

Think what it'll mean to the philosophy of the Supreme Court if you have a strict theological or philosophical requirement before a person can be considered to interpret the Constitution of the United States. Think about the consequences to our control of nuclear weapons, to our ability to control their spread to terrorist countries. Think about the consequences to our children and our grandchildren. Think about American agriculture that's grown so well the last few years with a farmer as the Secretary of Agriculture. We've never before seen so

much increase in gross income. We've doubled the prices of corn, wheat, beef. We've never had so much of an increase in history in net farm income. We've set a world's record in '77 on exports of American farm products, broke that record in '78, broke it again in '79. This year the biggest increase in history, $8 billion more than last year, $40 billion worth of American farm products going overseas.

And I might tell you this: I'd like to mention one word. You don't think about it often. The word is "China." We've just signed a contract with China to send them every year enough wheat to make 15 loaves of bread for every one of the 1 billion people who live in that country. And I might point out to you Texans that already China is the number one customer of American cotton. We have tripled trade with Mexico since I've been in the White House. This year we'll sell to Mexico 10 million tons of American grain. Think what will happen to those programs and those commitments and the involvement of American farmers in the next farm bill that'll be written in 1981 if we don't have Democrats there to protect you along with a Democratic Congress.

We also must have a strong defense, and this is an important issue on which I will close my remarks. As long as I'm President we'll have a nation with a defense strong enough so it'll be second to none, and you can count on that. Now, here again the Republicans talk big and they mislead people. But let me tell you what happened the 8 years before I became President. We had two Republican Presidents in the Oval Office. In 7 of those years—listen to this—7 out of 8 years our Federal budget for defense went down, in over an 8-year period we had a reduction of 37 percent in American invest-ment in defense.

Since I've been in office, with the help of Jim Wright, Lloyd Bentsen, and other members of the Texas delegation, we've had a steady increase every year above and beyond inflation in our Nation's de-fense. We've got a strong defense now, and as long as we have a Democrat in the Oval Office we'll keep it strong. But we'll also remember that having powerful, advanced, destructive weapons and highly trained men and women in our Armed Forces is not enough. It's how you use America's defense capability that counts.

My philosophy is this: We keep the peace with a strong America. And I can say something to you that no President has been able to say in the last 50 years: Since I have been in the White House we have not been at war. We have been at peace. The best weapon is one that never has to be fired in combat, and the best soldier is one that doesn't have to lay his life down or shed his blood on the field of battle. That's what I believe.

When I came into office there was no long-range cruise missile program. Now we have one. We're building 40 every month. When I came into office there was no battle tank being built. Now they're in production. When I came into office there was no modern personnel armored fight-ing vehicle. Now we're making them. There was no answer to our potential vul-nerability of our ICBM missiles located in silos. Now we have an answer, the mobile MX missile. Listen to this: When I came into office our purchases, under the Re-publicans, of Army equipment, jet fighters aircraft, attack aircraft, had dropped by two-thirds in 8 years before I became President. Since then we've increased ex-penditures for those items by 50 percent.

Now, I've described to you a few items which are used by the Republicans every 4 years to confuse people. I've described the election of 1980 as a choice between two futures. Here's what I see in the fu-ture that you and I are fighting for to-gether. I do see a nation at peace. I see a nation strong enough to be secure. I see a nation in the pursuit of progress for all its people. I see a nation where everyone can have the dignity of a decent job, where new industries create a new genera-tion of American buildings and vehicles to house us and to move us, using less energy, yes, but the energy that we use coming from America, not from overseas.

I see a nation where children are edu-cated better than we've been educated, to their maximum potential given them by God, where the elderly are treated fairly and with the respect that they've earned with a productive life, where families are close and intact and secure. I have a vi-sion of a nation free enough to attract and strong enough to welcome the de-prived from other parts of the world seek-ing liberty and justice and love. And I need your help to make this vision a reality.

Think just one more moment with me. You've been great to come out this eve-ning. I'm sure you've supported Demo-cratic candidates this election and in the past. Some of you maybe make financial contributions to help the Democratic Party pay for advertising and all, and that's good. But think about the possibili-ties next Wednesday morning, and I want you all to resolve in your hearts to do the best you can these last few hours for your-self, for your family, for the people that you love.

Think back in history what great Demo-crats have meant—Franklin Roosevelt,

Lyndon Johnson, Harry Truman, John Kennedy. Think about the Republicans all the way from Herbert Hoover to Richard Nixon, how they've changed your lives, and how Republicans have been elected by misleading people the last few days before an election. I'd like for all of you to resolve in your hearts to do something about it, not just to vote.

There's not a single person listening to my voice that cannot contact at least a hundred other people between now and next Tuesday. Some of you might contact a thousand, and some even, through the electronic media or otherwise, 10,000. But I ask you to join in with me in a crusade to keep this Nation on the road to peace, keep this Nation on the road to progress, to make sure we have equality of opportunity, to keep our working families strong, to give our children a better education, to keep our Nation respected around the world, to look forward with confidence and with unity and deep commitment, because you're partners with me, as a candidate. And I hope you'll be partners with me in the next 4 years, if you'll do what I ask you between now and Tuesday.

Thank you very much. God bless all of you.

NOTE: The President spoke at 5:54 p.m. outside the Fort Worth Livestock Exchange.

Milwaukee, Wisconsin

Remarks to Supporters of Representative John B. Anderson. November 1, 1980

THE PRESIDENT. Let me say, first of all, how thankful I am to you for having come out here tonight on this meeting just a few hours before we have the election. I'm sure when John Anderson comes somewhere to speak, the Carter supporters let him talk. Thank you very much. You support a good man. I'm sure he'd want me to speak.

First of all, let me say that we've only got a few hours now before the American people go to the polls to make a major decision. I'm going to be speaking inside to the crowd, and you can hear my voice. When I come back out, I'd like to have a chance to shake hands with a few of you that I could reach.

But the point is that I'll make all the decisions as President, in the Oval Office, with your help. Between now and November the 4th, next Tuesday, the decisions will be in your hands. And I'd like for you to think about the consequences to you and your family, to those that you love, if we wake up Wednesday morning and find that a Republican, Ronald Reagan, will be President for the next 4 years.

AUDIENCE. No!

THE PRESIDENT. And that could happen, because it is so close a contest throughout the Nation.

In 1948, as you know, just a few votes less would have meant that Harry Truman would never have been our President. And in 1960 if only 28,000 people in Texas and a few thousand in Illinois had voted differently, John Kennedy and Lyndon Johnson would never have led this country. And in 1968 if just a few more Democrats the last few hours had done their work, we would have had a great President named Hubert Humphrey, and Richard Nixon would never have served in the Oval Office. That's what a few voters can mean in this country.

So, I'll be speaking inside about some issues that are important to you. When I come out, if you're still here, I'd like to shake your hand and thank you for the help you're going to give me between now and next Tuesday.

Thank you. God bless you all.

NOTE: The President spoke at 9:04 p.m. outside the Red Carpet Inn.

Milwaukee, Wisconsin

Remarks at a Reception With Carter/Mondale Supporters.   November 1, 1980

THE PRESIDENT. *Senator Nelson, Congressman Zablocki, Mayor Henry Maier, Secretary of State Bill Phillips, former Governor Martin Schreiber, Speaker Ed Jackamonis—[inaudible]—Bob Freibert, ladies and gentlemen:*

This is the culmination of a very exciting campaign day for me. I started out this morning in Houston, Texas, and then went to Brownsville, Texas, for an outdoor rally. Then I went to San Antonio, Texas, for an outdoor rally, to Abilene for an outdoor rally, to Forth Worth for an outdoor rally, and now here to Milwaukee. And tonight I go to Chicago. And I might say that I believe this has been a fruitful day.

And I want to ask you, do you believe we're going to whip the Republicans Tuesday? [*Cheers*]

I've been to a lot of good places. I saved the best till last, and that's why I'm here tonight.

The outcome of this election is crucial. And I want to ask you especially this next few hours to work for a man that's important to Georgia just as much as he is to Wisconsin, and that's Gaylord Nelson. We have got to have him in the Senate. He's a man of special courage and integrity, you know that. But on issue after issue, in my judgment as President, Gaylord Nelson has been ahead of the trend of public opinion and opinion in the Senate—the Ethics Code, the environment, bringing the Vietnam war to an end, helping small business, dairy price supports, agriculture, the automobile industry.

Gaylord Nelson has not only stood by you, but because of his national stature he's been able to do you a better job, because he gets small business leaders from all over the Nation to support the programs that are good for the small business people of Wisconsin. The same way with agriculture—he gets farmers all over the Nation to work with him in order to implement programs that are better for the farm families of Wisconsin.

And I want every Democrat in this State to realize that the Republican Party is not our enemy in this election. Republicans can't beat us. Democrats are the only ones that can beat ourselves, by not voting. A low turnout Tuesday by the working families of this Nation, by the minority citizens of this Nation, by the elderly citizens of this Nation, by the farmers of this Nation, by those who've been deprived in life and have been given a better life by the Democrats—that's the only thing that might cause a defeat for us.

I've been campaigning a long time, and I've seen the issues drawn between me and Governor Reagan very clearly. You've seen them, too. But you probably have been listening to Republican candidates. Some of you are as old as I am, and you've been through former Presidential elections. What you know is that Governor Reagan is doing the same thing that Republican candidates for President always do. They wrap themselves in the cloak of Democrats and claim to be just like Democrats just before an election takes place.

Let me ask you this: Have you ever heard a Republican candidate for President quoting a Republican President?

AUDIENCE. No!

THE PRESIDENT. You haven't. And the reason is that they talk like Democrats until election day and then inauguration day, and then they get in the Oval Office and they act like all the Republicans have done. They don't have anything to talk about or brag about after their terms are over. But their commitment is to mislead the people of this Nation, and they get away with it because they raise false issues and people fall for them.

Think about how ridiculous it would have been even at the Republican National Convention, in his acceptance speech, if Ronald Reagan had got up there and quoted one word of Richard Nixon or Herbert Hoover.

AUDIENCE. No!

THE PRESIDENT. Obviously he didn't do it; obviously he didn't do it.

But the mainstream of the two parties year after year, decade after decade, generation after generation, does not change. Franklin Roosevelt saw it very clearly, and I'd like to read to you what he said in 1944 about how the Republicans changed their tune at election time. This is what he said: "The whole purpose of Republican oratory these days seems to be to switch labels. Now, imitation may be the sincerest form of flattery, but I'm afraid that in this case it's the most obvious common or garden variety of fraud." Fraud.

Now, he's not the only one that observed this phenomenon. In 1960 John Fitzgerald Kennedy said about the same Republican tactic, this is what John Kennedy said: "Those Republicans are even beginning to say a few kind words about Franklin Roosevelt. Twenty years from now," Kennedy said, "they might even speak a good word about Harry Truman." [*Laughter*] "But," he said, "I guarantee you that Harry Truman will never say a good word about Republicans."

And I'd like to make a prediction for you tonight. I predict that 20 years from now some Republican candidates for President are going to be saying a good word about Jimmy Carter's second term.

Let me remind you of a few things. No man who says that the New Deal was based on fascism has a right to quote Franklin D. Roosevelt. No man who opposes the minimum wage and says it has caused more misery and more unemployment than anything since the Great Depression has a right to quote Harry Truman.

And no man who has failed to support every single nuclear arms limitation agreement since the Second World War has the right to quote John Fitzgerald Kennedy. And no man who has professed several times to be in favor of a voluntary social security and who campaigned around this Nation in opposition to Medicare, calling it socialism and communism, has the right to quote Lyndon Baines Johnson.

And no man has a right to come to Wisconsin and claim to be a friend of the farmers who says, and I quote Reagan: "You subsidize the inefficient when you put a floor under the price." And he also said, at a separate time, "Farmers should start planning for an end to Government assistance in production and in the marketplace."

It's important for me to point out to you, as an incumbent President in the mainstream of my party, the consequences to you and to your families and to the people that you love if you should wake up Wednesday morning and find that Ronald Reagan will be occupying the Oval Office for the next 4 years.

AUDIENCE. No!

THE PRESIDENT. I believe that the working families of this country understand who's on their side in this election—the Democratic Party. For five decades we have fought for the rights of working people. We enacted the minimum wage; the Republicans were against it. We enacted unemployment compensation; the Republicans, against it. Ronald Reagan said that unemployment compensation is a prepaid vacation for freeloaders.

We enacted the right of working people to belong to a union; the Republican Party opposed it. And for the last 3½ years, we've fought together for common situs, for labor law reform, and against the repeal of Davis-Bacon. And as Gaylord Nelson knows, the Republicans have been on the opposite side of all those issues.

My opponent's views are a matter of record. I'm quoting his words exactly. Last year when somebody proposed that the Occupational Safety and Health Administration should be abolished and the protection of workers' rights to health and to safety should be abandoned, Ronald Reagan stood there and said, "Amen." This is the kind of opponent that's now claiming to be a friend of the working families.

I just saw the headline in one of your local papers, and this is the candidate who's going all over this country claiming that there's really no difference between himself and me and there's really no difference between the Democratic Party and the Republican Party. Every 4 years, they almost, or they do, get away with it. And then later the people wake up in

January or February of the next year and realize what's happened. And for 4 years we have maladministration under Republicans, where the working people's rights are slowly taken away and older people have to fight to keep what they've gotten under Democrats, until the next election comes along.

These kinds of issues are important to you. But I think, I believe that the most important single issue in this election is the issue of peace. No President in the last 50 years can make the statement I'm going to make to you now: Since I have been in the Oval Office, this Nation has not been at war; we have been at peace.

Now, I give him credit. I believe that every American wants peace. I believe my opponent wants peace. But's it's important on you as American voters to consider carefully the consequences of his habit of calling for the use of American military forces in time of crisis or time of trouble.

I've not been in the Oval Office a single day since I've been President that somewhere in the world there was not some kind of armed conflict. And I've had to make a judgment by myself about the degree of America's interest and how we should be involved, whether to resolve that issue, to protect ourselves diplomatically, politically, or by going to war. The judgment is a President's. The judgment is a President's.

In 1975 Ronald Reagan called for sending U.S. military forces to Ecuador and to Angola. In Ecuador we had a small dispute over fishing rights. He advocated sending the Navy, to go to war—[*laughter*]—perhaps, with Ecuador. In 1976 it was Rhodesia and Cyprus. This year, so far, it's been Cuba, Pakistan, and the Middle East. And what I want you to do is to help me make sure that in 1981 we don't have to see which part of the world he wants to send American military forces to fight in.

Gaylord Nelson put his finger on an even more important issue than war and peace, an even more important issue than the minimum wage or social security, an even more important issue on the well-being of American farmers. Every President since World War II has sought agreements to limit nuclear arms. Listen to this. The test ban treaty under President John Kennedy, the antiballistic missile treaty under President Richard Nixon, the Vladivostok accords under President Ford, the nuclear arms limitation agreement, finally negotiated by me after 7 years of constant negotiation, including my two Republican predecessors—listen—Governor Reagan never supported a single one of these agreements. Instead, he proposes to tear up the existing agreement and threaten a massive, new nuclear arms race. It's a sobering thought.

And you might say, well, nobody in his right mind could propose that. But listen. [*Laughter*] Now's the time to think about those things and how important it is to you, because I believe that halting the spread of nuclear weapons to all nations and controlling those weapons that we and the Soviets already have is the most important single duty of an American President. We don't want Libya to have an atomic bomb. When recently Governor Reagan was asked on two occasions this year, not in ancient history, what he thought about nations getting atomic bombs of their own who presently do not have them, his reply was, "That is none of our business." This issue is one that we don't want to have to analyze with this man in the Oval Office.

I've described the election of 1980 as a choice between two futures. Here's

what I see in the future that we are fighting for together, you and I. I see a nation at peace. I see a nation strong. I see a nation sure of itself because it is secure.

I see a nation dedicated to the pursuit of progress for all people, all people; a nation where everyone can have the dignity of a decent job, where new industries create a whole new generation of American buildings and vehicles that will house us and move us with less energy, yes, and that energy coming from the United States and not overseas.

I see a nation where children are educated to their maximum potential that God gives them, where the elderly are treated with the respect that they have earned with a life of hard work and dedication, where families are strong and intact and secure. I have a vision of a nation free enough to attract and strong enough to welcome the deprived from other parts of the world; a nation of liberty and justice and love.

It's important for you to think about this vision that I've outlined so briefly.

I've been President now for almost 4 years. I've made thousands of decisions, and each one of those decisions has been difficult. But it's been a learning process. Every decision I make leaves me better qualified to make the next one, because I learn a little bit about this country, about its people, about its limitations, about its opportunities, about other nations around the world and their leaders and the interrelationship among us. What I've learned makes me a better President.

I consider myself to be in the mainstream of my party and also in the mainstream, on most major issues, of the bipartisan list of Presidents who've served before me.

I know and you know that the United States as a nation must be strong militarily, and we'll keep it strong. The United States must be a nation secure, and we'll keep it secure. And we must have a society that's just and fair. We must dare to struggle for a peaceful world. There've been many times of crisis and conflict during these years; six or eight times, armed conflict has broken out somewhere in the world. In each case, I alone, as your President, have had to determine what are our interests and what should be our action.

I've got good advisers, as good as ever served. But I know from experience that when the issue is so sharply drawn and the differences are so extreme among the people of this country and the issue is so important, that quite often my advisers split almost exactly on both sides of the issue. At that time a President, in the loneliness of the Oval Office, has to make the decision. So, sometimes it is a lonely job, but with the involvement of the American people, there's a partnership formed and the job becomes very gratifying.

Now, those lonely decisions are not easy. All of you and those that you can influence will make a similar lonely decision on Tuesday. That's probably an easy one for you. I would assume that most of you are Democrats and will support me and Gaylord Nelson and the other Democrats. That's not enough. Some of you may even have contributed financially to keep the Democratic Party going, to pay for advertisements and the cost of campaigns. If so, we appreciate it, but that's not enough.

I've outlined to you as briefly as I could in 19 minutes some things that I consider to be important to you individually, to your families, to the people that you love, to the people who love you. There's no one in this room between now and Tuesday morning that can't reach at least a hundred people, most of you could reach a thousand people, some perhaps, through the use of news media and because you have positions of leadership, can reach 10,000 people, to give them basically the same message that I've just given to you.

You might say, "Well, what difference does it make, because I'm just one person and Wisconsin is just one State. So, if we don't do our job, maybe my neighbors will do a little more and make up for my laxity in shaping my own life."

In 1948 it made a difference. This time, 2 nights ago I was in St. Louis, Missouri, talking about Harry Truman. And if just a few people had voted differently in 1948, Harry Truman would never have been our President.

I just came from Texas. And I know that in 1960, and you remember, that John Kennedy and Lyndon Johnson won by the narrowest of margins. If only 28,000 people in Texas had changed their minds and voted the other way, just a few thousand in Illinois, John Kennedy would never have been President, and Lyndon Johnson, the Civil Rights Act and all the changes that took place would never have come into being.

Those stories had a happy ending. But you in Wisconsin, in particular, remember 1968, when the Democratic Party was divided and Gene McCarthy's supporters, many of them, said, "Well, it doesn't make much difference, Hubert Humphrey has been tainted because he served in the White House with Lyndon Johnson." And people didn't go to the polls and didn't work the last few hours before the election took place. If we had worked, if we had given that great man Hubert Humphrey our support, he would have been President, and Richard Nixon would never have embarrassed this Nation in the White House.

Now the decision is up to you. I'll do all I can. I've made seven or eight speeches today. I'll make a lot of them tomorrow. We're going to Chicago and to Detroit and to Philadelphia and other places. But really the thing is in your hands. I've done all I could. And I'd like to ask all of you tonight when you leave here and everybody listening to my voice to make a sacrificial effort the next few days, to do much more than you ever thought you would do, to contact as many people as will listen to your voice, and remember the great issues at stake, because what we are doing here is shaping the future of our Nation and the future of your families and the future of people that you care about.

It's in your hands. And I'd like to ask you to join me in a partnership so that Tuesday when the returns come in, we will continue to have a Democrat in the Oval Office and a nation even greater every year.

Thank you very much.

NOTE: The President spoke at 9:12 p.m. in the New Orleans Room at the Red Carpet Inn.

Chicago, Illinois

Remarks at the Italian-American Sports Hall of Fame Dinner. November 1, 1980

I hope you'll forgive me for interrupting your banquet, but I heard about all the famous people here tonight and I wanted to come and see them. [*Laughter*] As a matter of fact, I've been a great admirer and a fan of some of the great Italian American athletes, the heroes that you are recognizing tonight. And I've come here not at all to talk about politics, but to shake hands with some of these famous people.

When I was a young naval officer just learning how to be a submarine engineer, one of my great heroes was Phil Rizzuto, and Mickey Mantle and Joe DiMaggio. I've always wanted to shake his hand, and I hope I can tonight. And Tommy Lasorda is one of my mother's sweethearts. I don't know if you know it or not— [*laughter*]—my mother adopted the Dodgers many years ago, and she's kind of a mascot of theirs. As a matter of fact, she's got a full Dodger uniform in Plains, including cleats, the gloves, and everything else. And of course, as a long-time racing fan, Donatelli has always been a name that's been important in my life.

Also, I would like to point out that Andy Robustelli—is he here tonight? I want to meet him, too. That's just great. And also Andy Varipapa. It's just unbelievable that I could have a chance to know him. Let them come on up, if they don't mind. I know you've already recognized them, but I want you to see me shake their hand. And is Joy Piccolo here, too? Is Joy here? It's a great honor for me. Thank you very much. Mr. Varipapa, God bless you. Thank you very much. Andy Granatelli? How you doing? And Joy, Joy Piccolo? Hi, Joy. Well, they're coming up here.

This is a very great thrill for me. When I heard about this banquet and the names of those that you were honoring, I wanted to come not only as a sports fan all my life, but also as President of a great nation. And I wanted to be here on behalf of 230 million people to let you know that the whole world understands the great contribution that these men and women and the Italian Americans have made to our country.

This is a time for reassessment, to recognize the blessings that God's given us. We've come here from all over the world. Ours is a nation, as you know, of refugees or immigrants. Almost all of our families have come here from foreign nations. We've tried to keep together our heritage, our religious beliefs, the strength of our families, our blood ties with our mother countries. At the same time, we've formed together an extremely close and strong bond of friendship and mutual commitment to freedom, to the value of human beings, to the concept that all should have an equal opportunity. And I know that all of you have shared with me, since I've been Commander in Chief, the realization that not only have we contributed a lot in sports and greatness and personal courage and commitment and sacrifice in time of peace, but in time of war, Americans from all over the world, whose families have come here, have been willing to offer their very lives for the preservation of freedom.

So, it's an honor for me to be with you. It's a thrill for me to meet these heroes of mine and to share with you a moment of greatness with them for Italian Americans, for all Americans, and for the greatest nation in the world.

Thank you very much.

NOTE: The President spoke at 11:45 p.m. in the Rosemont Room at the Hyatt Regency O'Hare Hotel.

Department of Justice Investigation of Billy Carter

White House Statement.   *November 1, 1980*

The subcommittee of the Senate Committee on the Judiciary has now made public a confidential report from the Department of Justice's Office of Professional Responsibility (OPR) on its investigation of certain aspects of the Billy Carter matter.

As stated in the memorandum of the subcommittee's counsel, Judge Phillip W. Tone and Michael Davidson, the OPR report "contains no information of any significance which adds to or subtracts from the subcommittee's own report." The subcommittee's own report was released to the public on October 2, 1980.

The subcommittee's counsel also points out that, contrary to the transmittal letter from OPR counsel, the OPR report is not in response to any request from the subcommittee.

Chairman Birch Bayh's statement adds: "Even more puzzling is why Mr. Shaheen (OPR counsel) would provide this type of information to the subcommittee if he truly did not want to make it public. His conclusions and his dealings with the White House are sensitive only as they impact on current politics."

Since the OPR report was delivered to the subcommittee, there have been press reports mischaracterizing the content of the report based on unauthorized leaks. These press accounts characterized the President's response to the investigation as being "uncooperative" or "unresponsive." Neither of these words appears in the OPR report and the report does not so characterize the President's response.

The President has at all times stated his intention to cooperate fully in all legitimate inquiries into the Billy Carter matter and to comply with OPR's request to take a sworn verbatim statement from him. To date OPR has not scheduled a firm date for interviewing the President nor at any time indicated to White House counsel that it felt that the President or any member of his staff was not cooperating fully with the OPR in its investigation.

The facts as to the President's full cooperation are as follows:

OPR informed the President's counsel of its investigation by memorandum dated August 8, 1980. In this memorandum OPR requested access to the appointment and telephone logs of the President and other White House personnel as well as copies of materials forwarded by the President or his staff to the congressional committees reviewing the Billy Carter matter. OPR also stated its intention to take sworn verbatim statements of the President and members of his staff after the requested materials had been collected and reviewed.

The President and most of his staff were absent from Washington the week of August 10, attending the Democratic National Convention in New York City. Upon their return, counsel for the President informed OPR in writing of the President's intention to cooperate fully with the investigation. The President had given the same assurances to the congressional committees investigating the Billy Carter matter. The Senate subcommittee investigation was completed early in October and its report was released to the public on October 2.

All non-classified material furnished by the White House to the congressional committees was delivered to OPR on September 8, 1980, and the classified documents were delivered on October 9, 1980.

On August 26, 1980, counsel for the President met with OPR attorneys to review the names of those persons OPR wished to examine and to identify White House records, in addition to telephone and appointment logs, that OPR wanted to review.

Over the course of the next several weeks, OPR took sworn statements from seven members of the White House staff including Dr. Brzezinski and Mr. Cutler. OPR was also given full access to the appointment and telephone logs maintained by these persons.

Because the President's telephone logs and appointment schedules contain detailed information relating to calls and meetings involving confidential foreign policy and national security matters not relevant to OPR's investigation, it was mutually agreed that OPR would specify those individuals it was interested in, and the White House diarist would extract from the logs all entries responsive to this request. A list of 32 names was furnished by OPR on October 10 and the diarist's review of the logs was completed on October 16 and furnished to OPR.

During its investigation, OPR also asked to review all of the President's private evening notes over a 2-year period. The President makes these notes for his own personal use, and they cover a vast range of events, opinions and observations about various individuals that are highly confidential and wholly irrelevant to the subject matters involved in OPR's investigation. The President had voluntarily furnished to the Senate subcommittee all items in these notes referring to Billy Carter and Libya. These items were supplied to OPR and OPR was also permitted to review all other items relating either to Billy Carter and all remotely pertinent items relating to Libya. Agreed extracts of three such notes were furnished to the Department on October 22.

On October 22, the Department of Justice requested permission to review in their entirety the President's private notes for 43 days. On Monday morning, October 27, officials of the Department of Justice met with counsel for the President, at the latter's request, to discuss this matter. Because of the private and confidential nature of some of the material in the President's notes and the fact that no such material not previously furnished was relevant to OPR's investigation, it was suggested by White House counsel that the Department designate the specific portions of the notes it wanted to review; this might be done by reference to specific events, identified persons, or the like. The OPR attorneys appeared to accept this proposal as reasonable and agreed to furnish such designations. When they are furnished all such items will be made available. It should be noted that the offer to produce these items from the President's private notes goes well beyond what OPR would be entitled to examine under compulsory process.

Suggestions were made from time to time in discussions among counsel concerning agreeable dates for the interview of the President. Although three dates when it was thought the President would be in Washington were suggested, no firm date was set. Counsel for the President offered to arrange an interview in mid-October, on the basis of the material furnished up to that time, but the Department made clear that it did not want to interview the President until it had completed its document review. A similar offer was made on October 27 and rejected by OPR.

The President stated at the outset his willingness to respond under oath to questions relating to Billy Carter and Libya. At no time has any attempt been made by the President, or any member of his staff, to delay the completion of the Department's investigation or to defer the date for the interview of the President beyond the date of the election.

American Hostages in Iran

Statement by the White House Press Secretary.   November 2, 1980

As you know, the Majles has acted. They have stated that their decision is compatible with the four points previously announced by the Ayatollah Khomeini. At this point, we don't have a completely accurate translation. We're attempting to get one and also to obtain clarification of the action by the Majles. The decision is now in the hands of the executive officers of Iran and the United States—their legislative branch having acted.

The President will be consulting with his senior foreign policy advisers in Washington. We will respond to the Iranian action in accordance with American law and the two principles that have guided our actions throughout; namely, the national interest of this country and our concern for the safe and early release of the hostages. We will keep the press and public informed of developments to the maximum extent possible and of the full details of any actions taken by the United States Government.

The President was notified of the action of the Majles shortly before 4 a.m. CST by Deputy Secretary of State Warren Christopher. The decision to return to Washington was in effect reconfirmed at that time. It had been our view since the beginning of this latest phase that the President ought to return to Washington if there was a prospect that major decisions had to be made, simply because of the greater access to his advisers and the advantages in communications afforded by the White House.

The President also instructed Secretary of State Muskie shortly after 4 o'clock to begin briefing the congressional leadership and to begin briefing Governor Reagan and Congressman Anderson.

NOTE: Press Secretary Jody Powell read the statement to reporters on board Air Force One during the flight from Chicago to Washington, D.C. The text of the statement was not issued as a White House press release.

American Hostages in Iran

Remarks on the Iranian Parliament's Decision Concerning the Hostages. November 2, 1980

THE PRESIDENT. The Iranian parliament today has finally taken a position on the release of our hostages. This is a significant development. We have long been aware that there would be no resolution of this problem until the new Iranian Government was in place and the Parliament had acted.

Many months ago we made clear the steps that we would be prepared to take when the hostages are released. Ever since the American hostages were illegally seized in Iran, I have affirmed that our policy is based on two fundamental objectives: protecting the honor and the vital interests of the United States and working to ensure the earliest possible safe release of the hostages. As we understand the Parliament's proposals, they appear to offer a positive basis for achieving both of these objectives. We are pursuing the matter through diplomatic channels. Any action taken by our Government will be in full accordance with our laws and with our Constitution.

I know that I share with the hostages, with their families, and with the people of this country the desire for a prompt return of those for whom we have waited so long. I know also that all Americans will want that return to be on a proper basis, which is worthy of the suffering and sacrifice which the hostages have endured.

Let me conclude with a final comment. We are within 2 days of an important national election. Let me assure you that my decisions on this crucial matter will not be affected by the calendar. We are in contact with the bipartisan leadership of the Congress, with Governor Reagan, with Congressman Anderson, and we will keep the American people informed.

I wish that I could predict when the hostages will return. I cannot. But whether our hostages come home before or after the election, and regardless of the outcome of the election, the Iranian Government and the world community will find our country, its people, and the leaders of both political parties united in desiring the early and safe return of the hostages to their homes, but only on a basis that preserves our national honor and our national integrity.

Thank you very much.

Q. Mr. President, are you encouraged with the developments? Do you see a new hope?

THE PRESIDENT. I think the comment I made expresses how I feel.

Q. Mr. President, do you think the Iranians are trying to take advantage of our elections?

NOTE: The President spoke at 6:23 p.m. to reporters assembled in the Briefing Room at the White House. His remarks were broadcast live on radio and television.

During the day, the President held meetings with his advisers to assess the situation and consider appropriate steps in response to the action taken by the Iranian Parliament.

U.S.-China and U.S.-London Air Service

Letter to the Chairman of the Civil Aeronautics Board. November 2, 1980

To Chairman Marvin Cohen

I have reviewed the following orders proposed by the Civil Aeronautics Board:

United States-London Case (1981)

Docket 37937

United States-People's Republic of China Service Proceeding

Docket 38629

The first of these cases selects Pittsburgh and Baltimore as new "gateway" cities for non-stop air service between the United States and London; the new services will commence in April 1981. This expansion of opportunities for our travelers, our air carriers, and for the geographic areas they serve was made possible by the new agreement my Administration reached in March of this year with the government of Great Britain; the agreement reduced restrictions on air service between our two nations, authorizing the designation of ten new U.S. gateways to London from 1981 to 1985.

The second decision selects Pan American World Airways as the first United States air carrier to provide scheduled commercial air service between the United States and the People's Republic of China. This selection has been made possible by one of the four agreements I signed on September 17, 1980, which together completed the process of normalizing the U.S.-P.R.C. relations. Flights will begin later this year. The agreement resumes scheduled air service between our country and mainland China after a gap of 31 years. Under the agreement, a second U.S. carrier will be selected to provide additional

U.S.-P.R.C. service in 1982. The route covered by the first carrier will connect New York, San Francisco, Los Angeles and Honolulu, with Beijing and Shanghai, and can include an immediate stop in Japan.

I do not intend to disapprove the Board's orders within the 60 days allowed by statute. In order to preserve the opportunity for interested parties to secure judicial review, I affirm that no foreign policy or national defense reason underlies my actions.

Both these decisions are especially pleasing to me, as I am sure they are to you, since they carry forward policy initiatives for which we have worked together: expanding service and cutting consumer costs through the elimination of anticompetitive regulation, and building a framework for strong and lasting relations between the people of the United States and the people of the People's Republic of China.

Sincerely,

JIMMY CARTER

[The Honorable Marvin S. Cohen, Chairman, Civil Aeronautics Board, Washington, D.C. 20428]

Leadership and Coordination of Nondiscrimination Laws

Statement on Signing Executive Order 12250. November 2, 1980

Today, I take great pride in signing an Executive order that will give the Department of Justice leadership and coordination responsibilities for fighting illegal discrimination in Federal programs.

On May 1, 1980, I announced that I would be issuing an Executive order to strengthen the participation of the handicapped in Federal and federally assisted programs. In the course of developing that Executive order, I determined that it afforded an excellent opportunity to strengthen across the board implementation of statutes banning discrimination based not only on handicap but also on race, color, religion, national origin, and sex in federally assisted programs. Accordingly, the Executive order I am signing today is an important step toward a comprehensive, coherent approach to the goal of distributing Federal aid on a nondiscriminatory basis.

Under this Executive order, primary enforcement responsibility will remain with the agencies for their own programs, while coordination responsibility, in areas other than employment, will be vested in the Department of Justice. This will complement the Equal Employment Opportunity Commission's leadership responsibility in the equal employment area.

I am delegating to the Attorney General, through this Executive order, authority to approve regulations implementing laws prohibiting discrimination. Within the limits of regulatory discretion under the governing statute, the Attorney General should continue this administration's practice of balancing competing national goals to determine the general public interest. I am also instructing him to bring to my attention regulations that raise particularly difficult policy issues.

The Attorney General will be developing procedures to end duplication, inconsistency, and conflict in this crucial area. He will oversee the development of basic standards for such key elements of a compliance program as data collection, complaint investigations, cooperation with State and local human rights agencies, and the imposition of sanctions. The order also calls for the Attorney General to prepare a plan for carrying out the responsibilities assigned to him under this order. The Attorney General already has such a plan in draft form.

I believe that the action I am taking today will make it easier for those jurisdictions which wish to comply with Federal nondiscrimination statutes and much harder for those who seek to violate those provisions. It is an outgrowth of my determination to prevent Federal dollars from being used to perpetuate patterns of conduct which inhibit the full enjoyment of Federal financial assistance by all groups within our society.

Leadership and Coordination of Nondiscrimination Laws

Executive Order 12250. November 2, 1980

By the authority vested in me as President by the Constitution and statutes of the United States of America, including section 602 of the Civil Rights Act of 1964 (42 U.S.C. 2000d–1), Section 902 of the Education Amendments of 1972 (20 U.S.C. 1682), and Section 301 of Title 3 of the United States Code, and in order to provide, under the leadership of the Attorney General, for the consistent and effective implementation of various laws prohibiting discriminatory practices in Federal programs and programs receiving Federal financial assistance, it is hereby ordered as follows:

1–1. *Delegation of Function.*

1–101. The function vested in the President by Section 602 of the Civil Rights Act of 1964 (42 U.S.C. 2000d–1), relating to the approval of rules, regulations, and orders of general applicability, is hereby delegated to the Attorney General.

1–102. The function vested in the President by Section 902 of the Education Amendments of 1972 (20 U.S.C. 1682), relating to the approval of rules, regulations, and orders of general applicability, is hereby delegated to the Attorney General.

1–2. *Coordination of Nondiscrimination Provisions.*

1–201. The Attorney General shall coordinate the implementation and enforcement by Executive agencies of various nondiscrimination provisions of the following laws:

(a) Title VI of the Civil Rights Act of 1964 (42 U.S.C. 2000d *et seq.*).

(b) Title IX of the Education Amendments of 1972 (20 U.S.C. 1681 *et seq.*).

(c) Section 504 of the Rehabilitation Act of 1973, as amended (29 U.S.C. 794).

(d) Any other provision of Federal statutory law which provides, in whole or in part, that no person in the United States shall, on the ground of race, color, national origin, handicap, religion, or sex, be excluded from participation in, be denied the benefits of, or be subject to discrimination under any program or activity receiving Federal financial assistance.

1–202. In furtherance of the Attorney General's responsibility for the coordination of the implementation and enforcement of the nondiscrimination provisions of laws covered by this Order, the Attorney General shall review the existing and proposed rules, regulations, and orders of general applicability of the Executive agencies in order to identify those which are inadequate, unclear or unnecessarily inconsistent.

1–203. The Attorney General shall develop standards and procedures for taking enforcement actions and for conducting investigations and compliance reviews.

1–204. The Attorney General shall issue guidelines for establishing reasonable time limits on efforts to secure voluntary compliance, on the initiation of sanctions, and for referral to the Department of Justice for enforcement where there is noncompliance.

1–205. The Attorney General shall establish and implement a schedule for the review of the agencies' regulations which implement the various nondiscrimination laws covered by this Order.

1–206. The Attorney General shall establish guidelines and standards for the development of consistent and effective recordkeeping and reporting requirements by Executive agencies; for the sharing and exchange by agencies of compliance records, findings, and supporting documentation; for the development of comprehensive employee training programs; for the development of effective information programs; and for the development of cooperative programs with State and local agencies, including sharing of information, deferring of enforcement activities, and providing technical assistance.

1–207. The Attorney General shall initiate cooperative programs between and among agencies, including the development of sample memoranda of understanding, designed to improve the coordination of the laws covered by this Order.

1–3. *Implementation by the Attorney General.*

1–301. In consultation with the affected agencies, the Attorney General shall promptly prepare a plan for the implementation of this Order. This plan shall be submitted to the Director of the Office of Management and Budget.

1–302. The Attorney General shall periodically evaluate the implementation of the nondiscrimination provisions of the laws covered by this Order, and advise the heads of the agencies concerned on the results of such evaluations as to recommendations for needed improvement in implementation or enforcement.

1–303. The Attorney General shall carry out his functions under this Order, including the issuance of such regulations as he deems necessary, in consultation with affected agencies.

1–304. The Attorney General shall annually report to the President through the Director of the Office of Management and Budget on the progress in achieving the purposes of this Order. This report shall include any recommendations for changes in the implementation or enforcement of the nondiscrimination provisions of the laws covered by this Order.

1–305. The Attorney General shall chair the Interagency Coordinating Council established by Section 507 of the Rehabilitation Act of 1973, as amended (29 U.S.C. 794c).

1–4. *Agency Implementation.*

1–401. Each Executive agency shall cooperate with the Attorney General in the performance of the Attorney General's functions under this Order and shall, unless prohibited by law, furnish such reports and information as the Attorney General may request.

1–402. Each Executive agency responsible for implementing a nondiscrimination provision of a law covered by this Order shall issue appropriate implementing directives (whether in the nature of

regulations or policy guidance). To the extent permitted by law, they shall be consistent with the requirements prescribed by the Attorney General pursuant to this Order and shall be subject to the approval of the Attorney General, who may require that some or all of them be submitted for approval before taking effect.

1–403. Within 60 days after a date set by the Attorney General, Executive agencies shall submit to the Attorney General their plans for implementing their responsibilities under this Order.

1–5. *General Provisions.*

1–501. Executive Order No. 11764 is revoked. The present regulations of the Attorney General relating to the coordination of enforcement of Title VI of the Civil Rights Act of 1964 shall continue in effect until revoked or modified (28 CFR 42.401 to 42.415).

1–502. Executive Order No. 11914 is revoked. The present regulations of the Secretary of Health and Human Services relating to the coordination of the implementation of Section 504 of the Rehabilitation Act of 1973, as amended, shall be deemed to have been issued by the Attorney General pursuant to this Order and shall continue in effect until revoked or modified by the Attorney General.

1–503. Nothing in this Order shall vest the Attorney General with the authority to coordinate the implementation and enforcement by Executive agencies of statutory provisions relating to equal employment.

1–504. Existing agency regulations implementing the nondiscrimination provisions of laws covered by this Order shall continue in effect until revoked or modified.

JIMMY CARTER

The White House,
   November 2, 1980.

[Filed with the Office of the Federal Register, 11:33 a.m., November 3, 1980]

NOTE: The Executive order was released on November 3.

Akron, Ohio

Remarks at a Rally With Northeast Ohio Carter/Mondale Supporters.
November 3, 1980

THE PRESIDENT. Thank you very much, everybody. I feel great.
Vice President Mondale, Senator Glenn, Senator Howard Metzenbaum, Congressman Seiberling, Congressman Pease, Congressman Mary Rose Oakar, and distinguished friends from the Akron and Canton region:

Let me say this, and I don't want you ever to forget it: Fritz Mondale is the best Vice President any President has ever had. We faced a lot of problems together. We've worked together. We've prayed together pretty often, and tomorrow with your help we're going to win together.

This is the first time that Fritz and I have been together to campaign at the same location since the Democratic National Convention, and it's fitting that we should come here in beautiful Ohio, the heartland of the greatest nation on Earth. But let me give you a sober reminder. Tomorrow you will decide what kind of America it will be. I know you've considered the consequences of this election. The vote you cast tomorrow will echo throughout the next 4 years—as a matter of fact, throughout the rest of this cen-

tury, and nowhere will that echo be more clear than how it affects your lives, the lives of your family, those you love here in the Akron-Canton area.

I know there are problems here. We've faced them together. But working with dynamic leaders like John Glenn, Howard Metzenbaum, John Seiberling, and others, we have made a good start on solving these problems. I'm very grateful, for instance, in looking at the statistics, to know that in Ohio we have had, since I've been in the Oval Office as President, an increase in total employment—just in Ohio, 558,000 more people now at work than there were January 1977; in Akron, metropolitan area of Akron, 20,400 people more on the job now than 3½ years ago; in Canton, 18,300 more people at work than there were 3½ years ago. And that's in spite of the fact the last few months, we have had some economic setbacks.

We've faced inflation together. The first quarter of this year, because of OPEC price increases, we had an 18-percent inflation rate. The second quarter, we cut it down to 13 percent. This quarter just ended, the average was 7 percent, still too high. But the point is that we're working together to make this a better nation and to make your own community a better place to live. This is important to remember also, because we've had some specific projects that we've worked out together for you—a private government investment of $86 million to build a Goodyear Technical Center, where workers of this area can be trained and retrained for meaningful, good paying jobs. These kind of projects will continue.

Tomorrow we honor the Nation's most precious freedom, the right to chart the future of our own country. I'm confident that the Democratic Party can continue to give America the future it deserves. I want to ask you a question. How many of you believe that tomorrow we're going to whip the Republicans all the way across this Nation? [*Applause*]

Let me give you a reminder of something. There is no way that Republicans can beat us, because there are not enough of them to do it. But we Democrats are the only ones that can beat ourselves by not voting. A low turnout by the working families of this Nation, a low turnout by the farmers of this Nation, a low turnout by those who've been deprived in life and given a better chance by the Democratic Party down through the generations—that's the only thing that can hurt us.

If you've been listening to the Republican candidate the last few months, you wouldn't be able to tell what party he belongs to. [*Laughter*] He's tried to wrap himself in the mantle of great Democratic Presidents. Let me ask you a question. Have you ever heard a Republican candidate for President quote a Republican President?

AUDIENCE. No!

THE PRESIDENT. Do you know why?

AUDIENCE. Why?

THE PRESIDENT. Because every year— you think back on it—I've been watching Presidential elections since the 1930's— every time when the last few months come before an election, the Republican candidate starts trying to act like a Democrat. They comment, they quote Democratic Presidents, but once they get in office, they govern like Republicans, they talk like Republicans, they act like Republicans, they mistreat American citizens like Republicans. So when they go out of office, they haven't left anything there to talk about, they haven't said anything that you want to quote. [*Laughter*]

I heard the last part of Ronald Reagan's speech when he accepted the nomination at the Republican Convention. He quoted Franklin D. Roosevelt. Can you imagine Ronald Reagan standing up there and quoting Herbert Hoover or Richard Nixon? [*Laughter*] Of course not. And I'll say this, too. I don't like it much because no man who says the New Deal was based on fascism has a right to quote Franklin D. Roosevelt. And no man who has always been and still is in favor of abolishing the minimum wage has a right to quote Harry Truman. And no man who has failed to support every single nuclear arms limitation agreement since the Second World War has a right to quote John Fitzgerald Kennedy. And no man who calls Medicare socialism and communism has a right to quote Lyndon Baines Johnson.

Now, you can rewrite the record in some professions or in some businesses, but you can't, with a discerning American electorate, rewrite 20 years of ultra-conservatism under the Republican banner in the last few months before an election takes place. John Kennedy, back in 1960, sized it up pretty well. He saw the same phenomenon then, same thing in '64, '68, '72, '76, same thing today. This is what John Kennedy said. "They're even beginning," he said about the Republicans, "to say a few kind words about Franklin Roosevelt. Twenty years from now," Kennedy said, "they might even speak a good word about Harry Truman, but I guarantee you that Harry Truman won't say anything good about Republicans." [*Laughter*] Now, that prediction came true, and I want to make another prediction now. Twenty years from now, I predict that the Republicans are going to be saying good things about Jimmy Carter's second term.

I'm proud to be a Democrat. I believe in the heritage and the mission of the Democratic Party. I grew up on a farm during the Depression years, and I saw how the Democrats changed my life. Democrats have been for the progressive changes for the working people of this Nation, every decade, every election, every generation. Don't be misled by Republicans who try to change their spots just before election day. Remember the heritage of Franklin D. Roosevelt. Think for a moment. Remember the heritage of Harry Truman. Remember the heritage of John Fitzgerald Kennedy. Remember the heritage of Lyndon Baines Johnson. Remember the heritage of Hubert Humphrey. Every great advance in our country the last half century, from collective bargaining to the minimum wage, from social security to Medicare, civil rights, quality of life—every single one of them has been made by the Democratic Party. And the Democrats have always been opposed by the same basic Republican commitment and philosophy, quite often the same people in every one of these progressive issues.

But we in the Democratic Party are not just a party of past accomplishments. We are the party of the future. The Democratic Party is the party that fights for the interests of working people. The Democratic Party is one that fights to protect the quality of our life, that protects the health and security and the self-respect of elderly Americans, that supports national health insurance for all Americans, that supports human rights for people in this country and around the world, including equal rights for women guaranteed in the Constitution of the United States. And we are also the party that's strong enough and sure enough to dare to work for peace.

Now, those are our goals as Democrats, and we're going to fight for them together for the next 4 years. For the last 50 years, no President has been able to make this next statement that I'm going to make to you. For the last 4 years since I have been in office, our Nation has not been at war. We have been at peace; and with your help we will keep this Nation at peace for the next 4 years. But peace is something that must be built, step by step, brick by brick. Every day that I've been in office there've been dangers, there have been conflicts, there have been serious problems or troubled areas somewhere in the world. Each time I've had to make critical judgments: What are America's real interests? What degree of involvement should our Nation have in resolving those troubles or those crises? How should we use our Nation's tremendous strength?

I'm a father. I'm a grandfather. And as President, I will always remember to keep our Nation strong militarily, yes, second to none, but I also will always remember that the best weapon is one that never must be fired in battle and the best soldier is one that need never lay his life down or shed his blood on the field of battle.

Presidents have to make judgments when troubles come. If the crisis is well-handled, our Nation's interests are protected, the crisis passes, perhaps sometimes without your even knowing about it. But if a President makes a misjudgment, it can affect your lives and the life of everyone on Earth. I'm proud that our Nation has helped to achieve a treaty of peace between Israel and her most powerful Arab neighbor—the first peace ever between Israel and an Arab country. That's a commitment of the Democratic Party, to keep our Nation at peace and extend the benefits of peace to others.

Our greatest commitment above all other things, above the minimum wage, national health insurance, is to prevent nuclear war. We must continue our progress in a careful, balanced, verifiable control of nuclear arms. That's the great overriding issue of this campaign. The greatest legacy that we can leave our children is a world at peace. Peace is my passion, and with your support for the next 4 years, maintaining this Nation at peace is my pledge to you.

In closing, I want to make a special statement that I've not made before in this campaign. I want to say a few words directly to those citizens in this country who share the goals that I've just described to you, but who are considering a vote tomorrow for Congressman John Anderson. Obviously, there are some differences between us. But on many of the key issues of this campaign, like the need for energy conservation, pure air, clean water, controlling the spread of nuclear weapons, keeping our Nation at peace, the equal rights amendment, our views are very close. And the most overriding issue of all, the issue of peace and the control of nuclear weapons and preventing the spread of nuclear weapons to terrorist countries and to other nations that don't now have the atomic bomb—on this great fundamental issue, all of the candidates are on one side except that Governor Reagan is on the other side.

I ask you to consider the consequences to your lives if you should wake up Wednesday morning and find a new administration ready to take over the Oval Office, not committed to these goals, if they can control our country for the next 4 years. I appeal to you for your support tomorrow for Fritz Mondale and me, not just for your sake or mine but for the sake of these crucial goals that we share. The election of 1980 is a choice between two futures, and let me talk very briefly in closing about the two futures that you and I can have together.

In the next 4 years we can build a nation at peace, a building that can stand for many years in the future; a nation secure, secure in its defense, secure in its energy needs; a nation of new technology, new factories, new jobs, new tools—whole new industries that many of us don't even envision at this time; a nation of new energy sources, where American coal, including that from Ohio, replaces OPEC oil; a nation that stands for human rights, a nation that stands for these things and is not afraid to say so. These goals are not dreams; they can and they must be achieved. They will be on my agenda and on yours. As long as I'm President, we can work together to achieve these practical, vital goals. I need your help to make these goals a reality.

You might say, "Well, I've done a lot this morning, the day before election, to get up early, to come out to the airport to participate in a Democratic rally." Maybe some of you have even given a small financial contribution to Democratic candidates to pay for advertising and so forth. I tell you now that's not enough. It's not even enough for you to go and vote tomorrow, because all of you have shown a special interest in politics by coming out here. There's not a single person listening to my voice that can't contact at least a hundred people between now and the time the polls close tomorrow. A hundred people can make a lot of difference.

Remember 1948, when just a few Democratic votes, if they had changed, would have meant Harry Truman would never have served as President. Remember 1960: If 28,000 people in Texas had voted differently and just a few thousand in Illinois, John Kennedy would never have been President, and Lyndon Johnson, and the Civil Rights Act and the great progress that was made might never have come to pass. Those are two stories that ended with a happy ending. But think about 1968: Because some of us, divided because of Gene McCarthy and the Chicago convention, didn't give our support to a great American, Hubert Humphrey never had a chance to serve as President and Richard Nixon, if we had just worked a little bit, would never have served as the last Republican President to be elected to serve in this country. Think about those things, how important they were to you.

Let's remember not national affairs, remember your own personal lives, the lives of people in your family, your children. I was playing last night with my two grandchildren at home. Think about those things and remember the events tomorrow will also remind us of the last words of a great American who was killed in the heat of a campaign back in 1968. On the last day of his campaign, Robert Kennedy said, and I'd like to leave you with these words, they're the last thing I'll say. I'm quoting him. "I ask you to recognize the hard and difficult road to a better America. I ask you to vote for yourselves. The people must decide this election," he said. "For your sake and for the sake of your children, vote. Vote for yourselves."

Thank you.

NOTE: The President spoke at 10:36 a.m. at the Akron-Canton Airport.

Akron, Ohio

Informal Exchange With Reporters on Departure From Akron.　November 3, 1980

Q. Are you going to revise your timetable on the hostages? I know you're not going to—[*inaudible*]. Do things look better?

THE PRESIDENT. Well, I just read the news reports this morning, and I think they stand for themselves. And what I said yesterday, I think is the best summary I can make.

Q. Are you encouraged, though, this morning, Mr. President?

Q. Are you going to win this election?

Q. You two are going together, with your arms around each other and so forth.

THE PRESIDENT [*laughing*]. We don't get to see each other very often.

Q. Do you really think you're going to win today—tomorrow?

THE PRESIDENT. I feel good about it.

Q. I didn't expect you to say no.

THE PRESIDENT. Well, I feel good about it.

Q. Are you going to get those Anderson voters?

THE PRESIDENT. I hope so. Some. They're fine people. We need them.

Q. Will you get them—the Anderson voters?

THE PRESIDENT. I hope so. See you later.

NOTE: The exchange began at 11:10 a.m. at Akron-Canton Airport.

The press release includes a reporter's question on news about the hostages, which was asked of the President upon his arrival at the airport prior to the rally. The President did not comment on the situation at that time.

Granite City, Illinois

Remarks at a Rally With Area Residents. November 3, 1980

THE PRESIDENT. What a tremendous welcome, I thank you very much. It makes me especially proud that I'm the first Democratic nominee to come to Granite City since John Fitzgerald Kennedy. You helped him. I'm counting on you.

I particularly want to express my admiration, my appreciation as Commander in Chief of our military forces, and on behalf of 230 million Americans, for the wonderful job that has been done for the years past and many years in the future by your great Congressman, Mel Price. And I also want to thank Mayor Paul Schuller, Chairman Chris Costoff, Committeeman Bruce Cook, and Dave Robinson, your next Congressman from the adjacent district.

Also let me say that it's a pleasure for me to be in the soccer capital of Illinois. Since I've been President, you've been the State champion 4 years, and I want us to have 4 more years together.

As you know, we are now standing in the heartland of America's industrial district. At the end of the Second World War, we rebuilt Japan. At the end of the Second World War, we rebuilt Western Europe. Now it's time to rebuild the United States of America, and that's what we're going to do.

Not long ago, last summer, I was delighted to take a trip down the Mississippi. And not far from here, with the help of Mel Price and others, we've now recommitted ourselves to the rapid rebuilding and the expansion of Lock and Dam 26. That will help you. It'll help all of the people of the whole Nation.

And as you know, my administration has also been very concerned about and interested in the steel industry. We've now put a plan in effect nationwide, with management, with the steelworkers, and with my administration, to help this industry and all those who work in it. It's already making great progress.

Granite City has seen this at firsthand. Your steelplants are now committed, as you know, to major expansion in the months and years ahead, and EPA has just reached an agreement with Granite City Steel that will protect the quality of our environment and at the same time will protect the jobs of thousands of workers here, now and in the future. That's the kind of progress that we're going to make in the years ahead.

Let me ask you one question. How many of you know that tomorrow we're going to whip the Republicans? [*Applause*] There is no way that the Republicans can win an election. There's not enough of them. But there is a way the Democrats can lose an election—by not going out between now and the end of the voting time tomorrow and using your influence and your voice and your vote to make sure that we have a victory. We're the ones, as working families, that can lose the election. We're the ones, as farmers, that can lose the election. We're the ones, as senior citizens, who might lose this election. We're the ones, who have been deprived of a good life in the past, but given one by Democratic leaders in years gone by, who might lose the election.

Republicans cannot beat us, but if we don't work hard these last few hours, we might very well beat ourselves. And I'd like to remind you of how the working families will feel, how the elderly will feel, how the farmers will feel if we wake up Wednesday morning and find that for the next 4 years we'll have Republicans in the White House. That would be the worst thing that can happen. Let's don't let it happen.

If you've noticed, lately my Republican opponent, Ronald Reagan, has been doing the best he could to sound like a Democrat. I want to ask you a question. Have you ever heard a Republican candidate for President quote a Republican President?

AUDIENCE. No!

THE PRESIDENT. No, you haven't. Some of you watched the Republican convention, and you heard Ronald Reagan quoting Franklin D. Roosevelt. Can you imagine Ronald Reagan standing there and quoting Herbert Hoover and Richard Nixon?

AUDIENCE. No!

THE PRESIDENT. Okay, there's a reason for it, because it happens every 4 years. Every 4 years, the Republican candidates for President try to make the working families, the farmers, the elderly, and others forget the difference between Democrats and Republicans. This has caused America several times to make serious mistakes until it's too late, after election day, to realize what's happened.

A man who says that the New Deal was based on fascism hasn't got any right to quote Franklin Delano Roosevelt. A man who opposes and has always opposed, and who now suggests that it be repealed, the minimum wage has no right to quote Harry Truman. And no man who failed to support the limited arms agreement, the antiballistic missile agreement, the limited test ban agreement, SALT I, the Vladivostok agreement, every single nuclear arms limit—no man who opposed all of those has any right to quote John Fitzgerald Kennedy. And no man who campaigned all over this Nation, as Governor Reagan did, fighting against Medicare, calling it socialism, has any right to quote Lyndon Baines Johnson.

Now, you can rewrite the lines in motion picture scripts, and you can rewrite the lines in the records sometimes in business or professions, but there's no way that a rightwing Republican with a 20-year record in public affairs, his statements on the record, can change his spots the last 3 or 4 months before election and get away with it. But they always try.

Back in 1960, this is what John Kennedy said about this exact same thing, and I'd like to quote John Kennedy. This is what he said about the Republicans: "They're even beginning to say a few kind words about Franklin Roosevelt. Twenty years from now," Kennedy said, "they might even speak a good word about Harry Truman. But I guarantee you that Harry Truman won't say a good word about Republicans." As you well know, that prediction came true.

And I'd like to make a prediction to you this afternoon. I predict that 20 years from now the Republican candidates for President are going to be saying nice things about Jimmy Carter's second term.

Like many of you, I grew up during the Depression years. I lived on a farm. My mother was a registered nurse. She had two different kinds of jobs during the Depression. One was 12 hours a day on duty; she made $4. The other times, when she was a little more fortunate, she worked 20 hours a day on duty, away from home, and she brought home $6. The Democrats cared about people like my mother, and so they proposed a minimum wage, 25 cents an hour. The Republicans were against it. They said it was socialism, communism for the Federal Government to interfere between employees in the sweatshops and employers who owned the companies.

Later, when I finished high school in 1941, I got my first job working for the Government, measuring land. I got paid 40 cents an hour, a big increase from 25 cents up to 40 cents. The Republicans were against it, but the Democrats prevailed. My life was like a lot of yours.

When senior citizens reached the retirement age, if they didn't have a family that could support them, they went to what was called the po' folks farm. Franklin Roosevelt and the Democrats cared about senior citizens, and they put forward the idea of social security. The Republicans were against it. They called it socialism, communism to have an insurance program paid for by working people to give them some security in their retired age and some sense of self-respect and human dignity.

My father never had a chance to finish high school; neither did his father nor any other man in my family before I came along. My daddy had to work from before daylight until dark, because we didn't have electricity on our farm. The Democrats felt that farmers ought to have a better life and put forward the idea of the TVA and the REA. The Republicans were against it. They called it socialism, communism, and an interference in the free enterprise system and the major companies that sold power in those days.

This has not changed down through the years, but every time before an election year Republicans try to make us forget those things. I see some young people over here on the side with signs holding up for Governor Reagan. They don't remember those years, and they don't know the historical difference between Democrats and Republicans that never change. They don't know how many times the Republicans have tried to mislead Democrats just before election year.

Governor Reagan hasn't changed. He says the minimum wage has caused more misery and more unemployment than anything in this Nation since the Great Depression. He says that unemployment compensation is a prepaid vacation for freeloaders. He says, just like he did about Medicare, that national health insurance is a symbol of socialism, and he's against it. And as you know, this policy of his is typical of the Republicans.

But we are also a nation that believes in a strong military, and the Democrats have put forward in the last 4 years, with the help of Mel Price and others, a repair of our Nation's defense. I believe in a strong defense, but let me tell you this. In the last 50 years no President has been able to make the next statement that I'm going to make to you: For the last 4 years, since I have been in office, our Nation has not been at war; we have been at peace. And with your help, we'll keep our Nation strong and at peace for the next 4 years. But peace is not something that comes automatically; it has to be built piece by piece, brick by brick.

Every day that I've been in office, somewhere in the world there has been a crisis, there has been armed conflict, there's been a trouble spot. There've been dangers, yes. But I have known, as many of you, that the President of the United States is the one that must make a decision. What are the real interests of America? How should we protect those interests? What degree of involvement should we pursue? Should we try to solve those troubles peacefully, politically, diplomatically, or should we inject our military forces in the war?

I'm a father; I'm a grandfather. And as President I'll always remember this: Keep our Nation strong, yes; but the best weapon is one that need never be fired in battle, and the best soldier is one that need never shed his blood on the field of battle.

And I'm proud that our Nation, not only keeping ourselves at peace, has been able to spread the benefits of peace to others. We brought finally a treaty of peace between Israel and Egypt—the first time ever that Israel has been at peace with any of her Arab neighbors. That's a commitment of the Democratic Party, to bring peace. But I think that you ought to be reminded that the major commitment, the strongest responsibility on the shoulders of every President since Harry Truman, Democratic and Republican, has been to prevent nuclear war.

We must continue our progress in the careful, balanced, verifiable control of nuclear weapons. It's the greatest overriding issue of this campaign. The greatest legacy that we can leave our children is a world at peace. Peace is my passion. And with your support for the next 4 years, we'll control nuclear weapons, we'll prevent the radical countries like Libya from having atomic bombs, and we will keep our Nation at peace. That's my pledge to you.

And finally, let me say that I'm proud to be a Democrat. I believe in the heritage and I believe in the mission of the Democratic Party, the heritage and the mission of Franklin D. Roosevelt—think back—the heritage and mission of Harry Truman, the heritage and the mission of John Fitzgerald Kennedy, the heritage and the mission of Lyndon Baines Johnson, the heritage and the mission of Hubert Humphrey. Every great advance in our Nation, in your lives, for the last half century, from the collective bargaining to the minimum wage, from social security to Medicare, every single one of them has come under Democratic administrations over the opposition of Republicans. Don't forget that for a minute.

But the Democratic Party is not just a party of achievement in the past. The Democratic Party has been an organization, with you part of it, that's always looked to the future. The Democratic Party is the party that fights for the interests of working people, that fights to protect the quality of our lives, that protects the health and the security of senior citizens, that supports national health insurance for all Americans, that supports human rights for all people in this country and around the world, and the Democratic Party is a party that supports equal rights

for women guaranteed in the Constitution of the United States. These are our goals, and we'll work together for them for the next 4 years.

Now, today I'd like to say a special word directly to those citizens of this country who share these goals that I've just outlined to you, but who are considering a vote for Congressman John Anderson. Obviously, there are some differences between me and him, but on many of the key issues of this campaign, like the need for energy conservation, pure air, and clean water, controlling the spread of nuclear weapons, equal rights amendment, our views are very similar one to another. And on the one most important issue of all, the control of nuclear weapons and preventing the spread of nuclear weapons to other countries, on this great fundamental issue, all of the other candidates agree on one side; on the other side is Governor Ronald Reagan.

I ask you to consider the consequences of a new administration that is not committed to these goals if they should control our country for the next 4 years. I appeal to you for your dedicated support, your deep commitment during these next few hours as people approach the time to cast their ballots. You might say, "Well, one person can't make a difference. I've come here today, and I've added my voice to the crowd. Maybe I've been involved in the Democratic Party in the past. Maybe I've even been part of a Democratic organization or made campaign contributions. That's enough." But that's not enough.

The other night I was over in St. Louis at a rally where I reminded people primarily about Harry Truman. In 1948 there was an election, very close. If just a few thousand people around the country had voted differently or had not gone to the polls, Harry Truman would never have been President. In 1960—think back very carefully—if 28,000 people in Texas had voted the other way and a few thousand people in Illinois had voted differently, John Kennedy would never have been President, and Lyndon Johnson, the Civil Rights Act, and the great progress we've made under those two great men would never have come to pass.

Those two stories wind up with a happy ending, but let me remind you of another campaign, in 1968, where a few Democrats, maybe some of you and me, didn't work as hard as we should for the Democratic nominee. Hubert Humphrey, a great American with a great heart, never was able to serve as President of this country. And instead we had the last Republican President ever elected to serve in the Oval Office, Richard Nixon. That's the difference that we want to prevent this time.

Let's remember these events that I've just outlined to you as you leave this great rally. Let's remember also the words of another Democrat who might have been President, but who died on his last day of campaigning, and that's Robert Kennedy. In 1968, on the last day before he was killed, he made a speech, and this is what he said. And I'd like to conclude my remarks just by quoting him, because the message that he gave to you is the one I'd like to give to you today. Robert Kennedy's words: "I ask you to recognize the hard and the difficult road to a better America. I ask you to vote for yourselves. The people must decide this election. For your sake and for the sake of your children, vote, vote, vote for yourselves. Vote for yourselves."

Thank you very much. God bless you. Don't forget to vote for yourselves.

NOTE: The President spoke at 12:37 p.m. from a stage outside Granite City South High School.

East St. Louis, Illinois

Remarks at a Rally With Area Residents.
November 3, 1980

THE PRESIDENT. Good morning—good afternoon. Mayor Officer and all of you, are there any Democrats here?

AUDIENCE. Yes!

THE PRESIDENT. Are you going to help us tomorrow?

AUDIENCE. Yes!

THE PRESIDENT. Are we going to whip the Republicans?

AUDIENCE. Yes!

THE PRESIDENT. It's a great pleasure for me to be here in East St. Louis to see the great strides forward that you're making under the leadership of your fine new mayor. He and I have formed a good partnership in looking down the road to the months and years ahead.

I know that all of you realize the basic differences between the Democrats and Republicans and how important it is to all of you, on election day, to get out and work for your own lives, for a better future for you and for your families and for people that you care about. In the past you've always noticed that when Republicans approach election day they start trying to talk and act like Democrats. But don't let them fool you, okay?

I want to remind you that every vote counts. You all remember in 1948, if just a few people had voted differently, Harry Truman would never have been President. And in 1960, when John Kennedy and Lyndon Johnson were running as President and Vice President, if only 28,000 people had voted differently in Texas and a few thousand in Illinois, then John Kennedy would never have been President, Lyndon Johnson, and the Civil Rights Act and the Voting Rights Act might never have taken place and Richard Nixon would have been President then. You, with your votes, can make a difference.

And think back on 1968, when we lost the opportunity to have a great President and we wound up with Richard Nixon. Hubert Humphrey would have been one of the greatest leaders that this Nation had ever seen, but because a few Democrats, like yourselves, didn't get out and work for him and vote for him on election day, the last Republican President to be elected in this Nation, Richard Nixon, took his place in the Oval Office. We do not want that to happen after tomorrow, right?

I need your help. I think all of you realize that all of the great strides forward in your own lives have been made under Democratic administrations over the opposition of Republicans. Social security was put into effect by Democrats, the Republicans called it socialism, communism. The minimum wage was started out 25 cents an hour, was put into effect by Democrats. The Republicans were against it. As you well know, the Civil Rights Act and the Voting Rights Act were put into effect by Democrats. The Republicans opposed it. As a matter of fact, my opponent, Governor Reagan, said when the Civil Rights Act was passed, that it was bad legislation.

We don't want to see the Oval Office taken over by a bad result that you learn about when you wake up Wednesday morning. The difference might very well be in the hands of those of you listening here to my voice in East St. Louis. So, in this last few hours, I'd like to ask you not only to vote yourselves, but to contact as many people as you possibly can. There's no one here that I can see who can't reach at least 100 people between now and tomorrow night when the polls close.

So, if you believe in a better future for our country, if you believe in a better fu-

ture for your own lives, if you believe in a better future for the people in your family and for those that you care about and love, then I ask you to work hard this last few hours. Make sure we have a Democratic victory, have a better life in the future for East St. Louis and for our Nation that we love so much. Let's keep a Democrat in the White House; whip Ronald Reagan. You help me; we'll do it together.

Thank you very much. God bless you all. Work hard.

NOTE: The President spoke at 1:30 p.m. at the corner of Missouri and Collinsville Avenues.

Springfield, Missouri
Remarks at a Rally With Area Residents. November 3, 1980

Well, as you know, the pollsters were wrong in 1948. They've been saying there's no way I could carry southwest Missouri, but we're going to show them wrong again in 1980, right? [*Applause*] There's no doubt that as Harry Truman said many times, the people make a decision in this Nation, and the people's strength is the strength that made him such a great leader, admired now through history as one of the greatest Presidents who ever served this country since its original founding.

I want to thank Governor Teasdale and Tom Eagleton for making me feel at home, along with all of you here in Springfield. It's fitting to wind up my campaign on the final day of the election in the home State of this great man, Harry Truman. Missouri has given our Nation a wealth of great leaders, and Senator Tom Eagleton, as you well know, carries on that proud tradition. I'm proud to be his friend on the same ticket with him. I place a great reliance on his support and also on his advice and counsel, and I look forward to working with him for you during the next 4 years.

Now, today I come to Springfield for a special reason. In the quiet moment that we have together here, I come to ask you for your support. This has been a long campaign. A lot of people have been confused about what's at stake. As you well know, down through the ages, since before 1948, there's a few months before election time Republican candidates for President always pretend to be Democrats. And if you've been listening to my Republican opponent, Governor Reagan, you know that he's tried to wrap himself in the mantle of great Democratic Presidents.

I want to ask you a question, and think about this: Have you ever heard a Republican candidate for President quote a Republican President?

AUDIENCE. No!

THE PRESIDENT. You never have. Some of you may have watched the Republican convention, when Governor Reagan got the nomination. He quoted Franklin D. Roosevelt. Can you imagine Governor Reagan standing there and quoting Herbert Hoover or Richard Nixon? [*Laughter*] Of course not. And there's a reason. There's a reason.

Some of you are as old as I am. You grew up during the Great Depression. You've seen many 4-year periods come and go, many campaigns for President come and go. Republicans always run like Democrats. But once they're in office in the Oval Office, they govern like Republicans, and by the time their 4 years is over, after they have misled the people enough to get elected, they never have done anything worth remembering and they never have said anything worth quoting.

No man who, on four different occasions, has called for the destruction of the social security system, by calling for it to be voluntary, or who in the debate last week said that social security was a bad investment for a young man, has a right to quote Franklin D. Roosevelt. And no man who opposes the minimum wage and called it the most severe contributor to misery and unemployment since anything from the Great Depression has a right to quote Harry Truman. And no person who's failed to support every single nuclear arms limitation agreement has a right to quote John Fitzgerald Kennedy. And no man who campaigned around this Nation against Medicare and called it socialism has any right to quote Lyndon Baines Johnson.

You can rewrite the lines in the movie industry, and you can rewrite the lines in the history in some businesses. But there's no way to wipe out 20 years of rightwing Republicanism exemplified by Governor Reagan in just a few months before the election time. But this has always been what the Republicans have tried. Everybody's recognized it. Back in 1960, this is what John Kennedy had to say about the Republicans. Let me quote him. "They're even beginning to say a few kind words about Franklin Roosevelt. Twenty years from now, the Republicans might even speak a good word about Harry Truman. But he'll never say a good word about the Republicans." As you know, that prediction about Harry Truman has come true.

And I'd like to make a prediction to you now. I predict that 20 years from now the Republicans are going to even say a good word about Jimmy Carter's second term.

I come here to you as a Democrat, a man proud to be a Democrat. I believe in the heritage and the mission of the Democratic Party, the heritage and the mission of Franklin Delano Roosevelt, the heritage and the mission of Harry S. Truman, the heritage and the mission of John Fitzgerald Kennedy, the heritage and the mission of Lyndon Baines Johnson. Think back in your own lives what these men have meant to you.

I grew up on a farm during the Depression years. I was born in 1924. My father had to work for a living. He never had a chance to finish high school. Neither did his father nor anyone in my family ever finish high school before I was able to do so. My mother was a registered nurse. She had two kinds of duties that she had to perform. One was 12 hours a day. She got paid $4. The other was 20 hours a day. She got paid $6 for that—it was a lot of money for her and for a working family during the Depression. I remember that Franklin Roosevelt and the Democrats came forward with the idea of a minimum wage, 25 cents an hour. They thought that a grown man or a grown woman trying to care for a family, to buy food, clothing, pay for housing deserved 25 cents an hour. Republicans were against it. They called it socialism, some said communism, for the Government to try to say that a sweatshop was not proper in the free enterprise system.

I remember that older people, when I was young, that didn't have a rich family went to what we called the po' folks farm and lived in embarrassment and abject poverty the rest of their lives. Franklin Roosevelt felt, along with Harry Truman, that the older people who had served our country with a great life and dedicated work ought to have some security in their old age. They ought to have some self-respect, ought to have some human dignity. So, the Democrats put forward the idea of social security. Republicans were against it. They said it was socialism, some said communism, to let the Government interfere in the private right of citizens to be poor when they're old.

We didn't have electricity on my farm. We didn't have running water, till I was

13 or 14 years old. Franklin Roosevelt felt that the farmers deserved an equal break. He put forward the idea of the TVA and the REA. Finally, we got electricity on our farm in 1937. Republicans were against it. They said it was socialism, communism, for the Federal Government to interfere in the right of the private power companies to have a monopoly on the distribution of power.

Later on, in the early 1960's, Democrats came forward with Medicare. My opponent Governor Reagan got his start in politics campaigning around this country against Medicare. He called it socialized medicine, socialism. Some even said, communism. Republicans were against it. The Democrats put in that guarantee that at least older people could have some rights to decent health care.

Down through the ages, for the last 50 years at least, every great advance has been made for working people, for farmers, for the elderly, for young people to get a better education, from social security to Medicare, from collective bargaining to the minimum wage, every time the Republicans have been against it. They haven't changed. Not at all. But they tend to mislead the people just before an election, and because they have enormous campaign contributions from the rich, they can dominate the radio and the television, and they can send out a false message which quite often misleads people. And a lot of times the people don't wake up until the morning after the election and realize that next January there's going to be another Republican sitting in the Oval Office.

There is no way that Republicans can win an election in this country. There are only about 30 percent of them. What costs the Democrats the election: the Democrats who forget history and who forget how their own lives and the lives of their families, and the lives of people you love are affected by the outcome of an election. This is a very important thing for us to remember during these last few hours before election time.

Democrats have always believed in a strong defense. We've always believed that that strong defense capability should be recognized in order to preserve the peace. For the last 8 years before I became President, Republicans let our defense establishment go down 7 out of 8 of those years—37 percent reduction in budgeted funds for defense. But we have kept our Nation strong and we've also kept our Nation as all Americans want it.

In the last 50 years, no president can make the statement that I'm just now going to make to you: For the last 4 years, since I have been in office, our Nation has not been at war; our Nation has been at peace.

My background is as a trained military officer. I served 11 years in the Navy. I went to the Naval Academy. I was a submarine officer. And when I got in the Oval Office I was dedicated to restoring to our Nation its military strength. But I'm also a father and I'm a grandfather, and as President I'll always remember this: The best weapon is one that never has to be fired in battle; the best soldier is one that never has to shed his blood on the field of battle. We'll keep our Nation strong, but we'll keep it at peace.

As you know from having observed Harry Truman in office, and other Democratic Presidents, that Presidents have to make decisions in times of trouble and in times of crisis. I've not served in the Oval Office a single day that there wasn't trouble somewhere on Earth, armed conflict, the possibility of war. But I've had to make a judgment in each instance about what are our Nation's interests, what degree of involvement should I order in order to use the tremendous strength of our Nation? Should I try to resolve those difficulties peacefully with strength, diplomatically, politically, or should I try to resolve them by sending American boys into war? That judgment has to be made by a President, with the strength of belief in our Nation's honor, with an understanding of what our Nation's desires are, and with a calm assurance and a careful, moderate approach to potential crises.

If a President deals with a crisis properly the chances are that you never know about it. But if a President makes a misjudgement, that crisis can affect your life and affect the life, perhaps, of every human being on Earth. Our greatest commitment, ever since Harry Truman was in office, by Presidents, Democratic and Republican, has been to control nuclear war, prevent the spread of nuclear weapons to radical nations like Libya and Iraq and others, to have a careful, balanced, verifiable control of nuclear arms. It's the greatest overriding issue of this campaign. The greatest legacy we can leave our children is a nation more peaceful, more dedicated to the pursuit of peace. The election of 1980 is really a choice not just between two candidates or even two parties but a choice between two futures.

Let me talk very briefly in closing about the kind of future that you and I can have. In the next 4 years, together we can build a nation strong and keep it strong, but also keep our Nation at peace. And we can also build peace far beyond the next administration in the years and the decades and the generations ahead, a nation that's secure, confident of itself, secure in its defense, secure in its energy needs, a nation of new technology, new factories, new tools, new jobs, whole new industries based on a new energy program about which we cannot even dream yet, a nation of new energy sources, where Americans can house themselves and propel themselves down the highways, through the skies, over the rails, with energy efficiency, yes, but with energy derived from the farms and the mines of America, a nation that stands for human rights here at home and throughout the world. These goals that I've described to you so briefly are not just dreams. They're the things that we can accomplish.

My background is as a farmer. All the generations of my family since they first came to this country in the late 1600's have been farmers. And I'm very proud of what we've done. I can't pass by a visit to Missouri without mentioning agriculture.

When I became President I saw the mistakes that had been made under Nixon, Ford, and Earl Butz. I was determined to bring in the Secretary of Agriculture, a dirt farmer, Bob Bergland, who understood, as I did, how farmers needed a new life. I remember when we used to have to sell our crops at harvest time, when the prices were at the bottom. Our crops, our grain, our cotton, and everything else, was bought at that time when the prices were low and the middle-man, the bigshot processors, made all the profits. When a Republican President's elected his Secretary of Agriculture almost invariably is some representative of the food processors, of the middleman. The agriculture farmer gets left behind. We've changed that. We've built on our farms since I've been in office 2.8 billion bushels of storage space. Now the farmers at harvest time can keep their crops, can watch the market, can sell the crops when it's best for them. This helps the consumer too. It presents [prevents] [1] the wild fluctuations up and down in the price of basic grains.

What's been the result? In the last 3½

---

[1] White House correction.

years we've had bumper crops. One year we had record crops in five different categories. But we've not had the farmers suffer. The prices in 1977 for feed grains were just about double; price for beef, just about double. Gross income in the last 4 years has increased more than ever before in history. Net income for farm families the last 4 years has increased more than it ever has in history. We set a record in 1977 in exports to foreign countries of American farm crops; 1978, we broke that record; 1979, we broke it again. This year we've had the biggest increase in history, $8 billion increase over last year. We'll export $40 billion worth of American farm products to foreign countries. This is the kind of record we've had. And as we approach 1981 to write a new farm bill to replace the 4-year bill of 1977, I want to be sure that we have a farmer in the White House, a farmer in the Secretary of Agriculture's office, and we work with farmers and farm organizations as we did in 1977 to give agriculture a new boost in the future. That's what we've got to do.

And I know Missouri is also a great industrial State now. After 1945, at the end of the Second World War, when Harry Truman was President, the United States rebuilt the industry of Western Europe. We rebuilt the industry of Germany, and I tell you now that we've got an energy policy in place it's time for us to rebuild the industry of the United States of America, and that's what we're going to do.

Well, I think I need not pursue any further the difference between our two parties and our vision of the future. Let me remind you once again that the responsibility is in your hands. I know all of you have contributed a lot by coming here this afternoon to meet with me on this last day of the campaign. You've done it at a sacrifice, I know. And some of you have been actively involved in Democratic Party affairs, maybe for a long time. Maybe some of you have even given a financial contribution to pay for the campaigns of some Democratic candidates. That's not enough.

Think for a few minutes about what Democrats have meant to you down through the years—Roosevelt, Truman, Kennedy, Johnson, and others. Think how your lives have been changed and how different it would have been had those great men not ever have served. Think about yourself, your family members, the people that you love, the ones who look to you for leadership, and in this next few days—next few hours—make sure that you do even more than you had anticipated when you came here. There's no one in the sound of my voice that can't reach a hundred people between now and tomorrow when the polling places close. Please do the best you can.

You might say, well, one person can't make a difference, but that's not true. Remember those headlines you just saw from the Chicago Tribune. Had just a few people throughout this country voted differently, Harry Truman would never have been reelected President and never have done the great things he did in his full second term. Think about 1960 when John Kennedy and Lyndon Johnson were on the Democratic ticket. If 28,000 people in Texas had changed their vote and a few thousand had voted differently in Illinois, John Kennedy would never have served as President. Lyndon Johnson, likely, would never have served as President. Those stories wound up well. But think about 1968. If a few more Democrats like you and me had done a little extra work the last 24 hours, had realized what it meant to them, we would have had a great President, as you well know: Hubert Humphrey. And the last Republi-

can President to be elected, Richard Nixon, would never have embarrassed our country in the Oval Office.

So, let's remember these things tomorrow. I appreciate your great support and the welcome that you've given me here, but I want to quote a man in closing that never had a chance to serve as President because he was killed. The last day he campaigned in 1968 Robert Kennedy had a vision of what this country ought to be. And in Los Angeles he made this speech the last day he lived. He said to the voters on that day, and I quote him, "I ask you to recognize the hard and difficult road to a better America. The people must decide this election. I ask you to vote for yourselves. For your sake, and for the sake of your children, vote. Vote for yourselves."

Thank you very much.

NOTE: The President spoke at 3:16 p.m. at the Springfield Regional Airport.

Detroit, Michigan
Remarks at a Rally With Area Residents.
November 3, 1980

Senator Riegle, Senator Levin, Mayor Coleman Young, distinguished Members of the Congress:

Let me say first of all, that I wanted to come back here to Detroit, to Michigan, because I had to be in Washington yesterday and miss my long anticipated visit, and I heard the Republicans claimed they were going to carry Michigan. I came here to show them they're wrong. They're wrong. *We'll* carry Michigan.

As you know, Democrats have always been builders. People in your State have always been builders. And lately, with the changes taking place all around the world in energy prices, changed buying habits, we've been eager to face the future, forming a new partnership between the automobile industry—its leaders in labor and in management—and government. And one of the most delightful experiences I've had as President has been to see the new, modern, efficient, safe, durable automobiles coming out of Michigan, that are going to put those foreign cars off the market, and you can depend on that.

Also, it's very important—since Michigan is such a great labor State—it's very important for us to remember, as these last few hours approach before election, the sharp and historical differences that exist between the two parties. Every election year, shortly before the voting comes, the Republican candidates begin to act like Democrats. They try to mislead the American voters with highly financed campaigns from rich people. But all of you know that you have never heard a Republican candidate for President quote a Republican President. They all quote John Kennedy or they all quote Franklin Roosevelt, and there's a reason for it. Because once Republicans get in the Oval Office, they govern like and they act like Presidents [Republicans].[1] They don't do anything to be remembered later. They don't say anything to be quoted later. We want to keep a Democrat in the White House for the working people of this country.

Think back in your own lives. Think now on the current events and the future that will affect your lives, your family lives, and those you care about. When Chrysler was facing bankruptcy, the Democratic administration and the Democratic Congress moved forward to protect almost 300,000 jobs. My Republican opponent said, "What's wrong with bankruptcy?" Think what it means for

---

[1] White House correction.

minimum wage. My opponent is against minimum wage, would like to repeal it. He's always been against it. Democrats have initiated it and have protected it. Davis-Bacon, labor law reform, every element that's important to you or to your families, are Democratic issues. They've been opposed by Republicans. Social security, Medicare, looking to the future, national health insurance, all of these issues, very important to the working people of this Nation, must be remembered by you in these last few hours.

It's important what you do. Your coming here is obviously a very important factor. It makes me feel better to be welcomed this way in Detroit. But the next few hours you've got to do more than that, because think back: In 1948, just a few votes difference and Harry Truman would never have been reelected President. In 1960, if 28,000 people had voted differently in Texas and a few thousand in Illinois, John Kennedy, Lyndon Johnson would never have been President. And think in 1968 what happened when perhaps some of you and I didn't help Hubert Humphrey enough. We had the last elected Republican President, Richard Nixon, who betrayed his office and embarrassed our country. We cannot afford to let that happen again. We have got to win tomorrow. The vote depends on you. You help me; I'll help you. We'll have a great country in the future.

One last comment I'd like to make. Obviously the race is between me and Ronald Reagan, but I'd like to make a special appeal to the people this year who have been supporting John Anderson. Obviously we disagree on some issues. There's no doubt about that. But on the basic issues, on progress for the future, on the equal rights amendment, controlling nuclear weapons, keeping our country moving, protecting the minimum wage, working for the working people of this Nation, there's a lot in common between us. And I'd like to ask you these last few hours not to waste a vote. Make sure you cast your vote so that we can prevent an administration being in the Oval Office who disagrees with those basic issues that combine the efforts and the common beliefs of the Anderson supporters and the other minor candidates and my own.

We cannot afford to wake up Wednesday morning and discover that we've got a rightwing Republican administration in the Oval Office for the next 4 years. Let's don't let that happen. Let's win together. God bless you. Work hard. We'll win.

NOTE: The President spoke at 6:31 p.m. in the terminal at the Detroit Metropolitan Airport.

Portland, Oregon

*Remarks at a Rally With Area Residents.
November 3, 1980*

THE PRESIDENT. Thank you very much.
AUDIENCE [*chanting*]. "We want Jimmy!"
THE PRESIDENT. You've got me.

To Neil Goldschmidt, let me say first of all that I want you to express personally my deep thanks to Mrs. Wayne Morse, because anyone in this Nation who admires courage, who admires the ability of a man of great stature to express himself under difficult circumstances for the best interest of our Nation, that person must indeed appreciate the straightforward endorsement and support of the widow of a great man, Wayne Morse.

I'd like to say to Les AuCoin, who has been helpful to me from the very beginning, to Jim Weaver, to Ron Weiden, who'll be the next Congressman, and to Teddy Kulongoski, whom you're going to

support for the U.S. Senate, right? [*Applause*]

But I'm very glad to come out here to Oregon tonight, because I remember very distinctly what happened here in 1975. I also am very deeply grateful to you for three members of my Cabinet whom you trained for me and let me use in Washington. We've never had a better Secretary of Agriculture than the man that you trained here and sent to Minnesota for a little fine tuning. Bob Bergland has been one who was a radical departure from what the Republicans have done in the past. They've always chosen some executive secretary or some lawyer who represented grain speculators or either processors of food who bought grain and products from farmers cheap during harvest season, and then sold it to consumers high after they manipulated the market. But Bob Bergland has put the farmer of America back in the driver's seat on marketing grain and helping make it possible for us to make all-time records of grain exports, a lot of it shipped from the west coast to China. China is now our number one customer of American cotton and, as you know, the next 5 years we'll be selling China between 6 and 9 million tons of grain from the United States, enough for 15 loaves of bread for every man, woman, and child in the billion people who live in China. That's the kind of Secretary of Agriculture you trained for me.

And of course, Cecil Andrus has been a great Secretary of Interior, a good Governor of Idaho, well-trained in Eugene, at the same high school, I understand, that Neil Goldschmidt attended himself. And there's no way to say too good a thing about Neil Goldschmidt, particularly with him sitting here. But you've made a great contribution to the Nation.

I might say also that Oregon is important to me because you've been innovators in energy conservation, in urban revitalization, in the conservation of our natural resources, and in standing up for the rights of women. As a matter of fact, Oregon is the only State that's ratified the equal rights amendment, not once, but twice.

Recently, when I've been in South Carolina, Mississippi, Tennessee, Florida, I've reminded the people there the real meaning of the equal rights amendment. Our country for 200 years has tried to remove the legal impediments to equal opportunity for all people, and I've told them very frankly what the equal rights amendment means. It doesn't have anything to do with restrooms, doesn't have anything to do with drafting people, doesn't have anything to do with homosexuality. It just says very simply, as you well know, that equality of rights shall not be abridged by the Federal Government nor by any State government because a person is a woman or because of sex. That's all it says. All the equal rights amendment says, in effect, is neither the Federal Government nor the State government any longer will have a right to cheat women. We're going to stop that if I'm elected, but if Ronald Reagan's elected, we'll never have the equal rights amendment. We have got to have it. With your help, we'll do it.

Now, I'm also glad to come to Oregon because you're a State that loves trees. Now Ronald Reagan has provided a lot of opportunity for jokes about trees. I'm going to spare you tonight. I'm not going to tell a joke abut trees. But there's nothing funny about Ronald Reagan's candidacy, nor is there anything funny about what he stands for. You know that very well here in Oregon. And here in your State, you might very well hold the key to this election. All the poll results I've seen show that here in this State the issue is in doubt. The outcome of the election hangs in the balance, with just a few votes one way or the other making a difference. And that's why I've crossed this continent tonight, to make my last appearances here and a little bit later tonight in Seattle, before I fly back home to vote in Plains. I asked Jody Powell, my secretary, early this morning, "Where are we going to spend the night?" He said, "Mr. President, this night, there's not any tonight." So we'll be leaving, flying back home for that purpose.

I know you've been listening a lot to the campaign lately. It's been a highly publicized campaign. You've been listening to the Republican candidate, and you know now that he's trying to wrap himself in the mantle of great Democrats. If you've been listening to him the last 3 or 4 months, you would think that he's a very moderate, or maybe even a liberal Democrat. Let me ask you if you remember back in history. Have you ever heard a Republican candidate for President quoting a Republican President? [*Shouts*] You never heard it. Some of you watched the Republican Convention and heard the acceptance speech by Ronald Reagan. He quoted Franklin Roosevelt. Can you imagine him standing up there and quoting Herbert Hoover or Richard Nixon? [*Shouts*] It's ludicrous, isn't it? Because when Republicans are running for President, they deliberately try to mislead Democrats around this country about their true beliefs on issues that are important to the working people of this country, the farmers of this Nation, the elderly people of this Nation, those who've been deprived in life and given a better chance in life by Democrats.

This has been the case all down through history. As a matter of fact, as you know, when John Kennedy was running in 1960, he pointed this out very clearly. Let me quote what he said. "The Republicans are even beginning to say a few kind words about Franklin Roosevelt. Twenty years from now, they might even speak a good word for Harry Truman. But I guarantee you that Harry Truman will never say a good word about Republicans." Now I'm going to make a prediction to you tonight. I predict that 20 years from now, Republican candidates for President are even going to be saying good things about Jimmy Carter's second term.

We need to think about the consequences Wednesday morning, if the people of this Nation wake up and find that there will be in the White House for the next 4 years a rightwing Republican governing this Nation. Think about your own lives, think about the lives of your families, think about the lives of those that you love. Think about a man who says that the minimum wage has caused more misery and unemployment than anything since the Great Depression. Think about a man who started his political career campaigning around this Nation in 1961 against Medicare, calling it socialism. Think about a man who has been against the limited test ban treaty, a man who's been against the anti-ballistic missile treaty, the man who's been against the SALT I treaty, a man who's been against the treaty or agreement signed in Vladivostok under Gerald Ford, a man who's now against a limitation on nuclear arms treaty, SALT II, negotiated by me and two Republican Presidents over a period of 7 years, a man who has never supported a single one of these agreements that control nuclear weapons. Think about a man who said twice this year, when questioned about the possibility of third world nations, those who don't now have atomic weapons, getting them, like Pakistan, Iraq, and Libya, saying it's none

of our business, it's none of the business of the American Government.

The consequences of this election are very dear and very important to all of you. Everything the Democratic Party has stood for in the last 50 years has been beneficial for the working people of this country, and in every instance, the Republicans have been against it. They've never changed. Collective bargaining for working people of this country—the Democrats supported it; Republicans were against it. Social security—the Democrats were for it; Republicans were against it. Minimum wage—the Democrats were for it; Republicans were against it. Civil rights, the Voting Rights Act—the Democrats were for it; Republicans were against it. Governor Ronald Reagan said about the Civil Rights Act, it's bad legislation. Medicare—Democrats were for it; Republicans were against it. And now national health insurance—another commitment that the Democratic Party has made to you. Equal rights amendment—Democrats are for it; Republicans are against it.

These are the kinds of things, in their totality and individually, that affect not just generalities about what's good or bad for a whole nation, but what's good or bad for you and your family—better education, better life, better working conditions, better environment, better economy.

I served in the Navy for 11 years. I'm a Naval Academy graduate, submarine officer. When I got to the Oval Office I was determined to strengthen our Nation's defense, because in the 8 years before I became President commitments for defense expenditures had gone down 37 percent. So I worked hard, along with the Democratic Congress, to repair that damage and to make our Nation strong. There's a reason for it. And you need not be frightened about the fact that our

Nation is strong, because I'm able to say for the first time of any President in 50 years, for the last 4 years since I have been in office, our Nation has not been at war; we have been at peace.

And we've been at peace because we've kept our Nation strong and because we've addressed the difficult issues that affect our country with caution, with moderation, with determination, and with a calm assurance of our own strength. I'm a father, I'm also a grandfather. And as President, I'll always remember that the best weapon is one that's never fired in battle and the best soldier is one that never has to shed his blood on the field of battle.

It's good for you to remember, too, that in the loneliness of the Oval Office a President has to make many crucial decisions. I've not served a single day in the last 3½ years that somewhere on Earth there hasn't been serious trouble, most often armed conflict. Many potential crises come to the man elected to serve this Nation as President. If that issue is handled properly, then the crisis perhaps passes without your ever knowing about it. But if a misjudgment is made, then the crisis becomes important and may affect your life or the lives of everyone who lives on Earth.

I'm proud that we've been able to extend peace not just for our own people but to others around the world. But my most important single commitment, the greatest commitment of this Nation, is to prevent nuclear war. We must continue our progress in careful, balanced, verifiable control of nuclear arms. That's the great overriding issue of this campaign. The greatest legacy we can leave our children is a world at peace. Peace is my passion, and with your support and for the next 4 years, peace is my pledge to you.

I want to say just a word about our stewardship of air and water and land. Because we've made a commitment as Democrats, we've been able to have a strong and a viable nation, a carefully considered harvesting of our timber and other resources, the improvement of the quality of our land, and productivity—the highest productivity in the history of our country, the highest gross and net income increase of farmers, the highest exports in history. Our lakes and our rivers are cleaner than they were. The air is more fit to breathe. We've tripled our investment in solar energy. We've doubled the size of our national park system. We've strengthened the Endangered Species Act. We've created more wilderness areas than in any other administration.

By contrast, Governor Reagan scorns energy conservation. He dismisses solar energy as, quote, "exotic." He wants to weaken the Clean Air Act and undercut our efforts to promote health and safety in the workplace. Recently, someone said let's do away with OSHA, the Occupational Safety and Health Administration. Governor Reagan said, "Amen."

It's a clear choice. Only the Democrats will continue and strengthen that commitment to a decent environment. Only the Democrats recognize that we can have jobs for our people through our economic revitalization program without sacrificing the air we breathe and the water we drink.

The election of 1980 is a choice between two futures. Let me close my remarks by saying very briefly what kind of future you and I can have. In the next 4 years, together, we can build a nation at peace— a building of a peace for the future, not just 4 years, but for the rest of this century; a nation secure, secure in its defense, secure in its energy needs; a nation of new technology, new factories, new tools, whole new industries that we may not have even dreamed about yet; a nation of new energy sources where American coal and the production of American land replaces OPEC oil; a nation that stands for human rights and is not afraid to say so. These goals are not just idle dreams, they can and must be an agenda for the Democrats and for this Nation. And as long as I'm President, that's the agenda that we will follow.

I'm proud to be a Democrat. I believe in the heritage and the mission of the Democratic Party. Some of you here are as old as I am, and you remember how your lives were changed beneficially by the heritage and the mission of Franklin Delano Roosevelt, by the heritage and the mission of Harry Truman, by the heritage and the mission of John Fitzgerald Kennedy, by the heritage and the mission of Lyndon Baines Johnson, and by the heritage and the mission of Hubert Humphrey.

Every great advance in our country for half a century, from collective bargaining to the minimum wage, from social security to Medicare, every single one of them has been made possible by the Democratic Party. Now, with the election just a few hours away, now it's clearer than ever to me that the winner tomorrow will be either myself or Ronald Reagan.

Tonight I want to say a word directly to those Oregonians who might still be considering a vote for John Anderson. On many of the key issues, on many of the key issues, I'm sure that you, young people in college and others, issues like energy conservation, equal rights for women, protecting our air and water and, above all, the overriding issue of nuclear arms control and preventing the spread of nuclear weapons to countries that don't have them—on all these central issues, you and I are basically in agreement. It would be a tragedy if a split among those of us who are committed to these goals results in

handing over the White House to those who oppose these directly. I know what I'm talking about, because here in Oregon in 1976 the Gene McCarthy candidacy got 40,000 votes, and as a result the Republicans won this State by just 1,700 votes. So, tonight I appeal to all those who support Mr. Anderson: Consider the consequences of a Ronald Reagan Republican victory. Vote for Fritz Mondale and me not just for his sake and mine, but for your own sake and for the sake of the goals and ideals that you and I share.

You might say that one person can't make a difference. Let me cast my vote as a protest or let me just relax because I'm sure other people will vote. It's been good of all of you to come out here tonight—late at night, yes. You may have been involved in other Democratic campaigns in the past. You may have even contributed money so those campaigns could be financed, through advertisement and through other efforts. But remember 1948 when just a few Democratic votes made a difference, and Harry Truman was re-elected President. And think about 1960, when if 28,000 people in Texas had changed their vote and a few thousand in Illinois had not voted at all, John Kennedy would never have been elected President, and Lyndon Baines Johnson, and the Civil Rights Act, the Voting Rights Act that changed the social consciousness of this Nation might never have been recorded in history. Those stories ended well, but think also about 1968 when perhaps some of you did not support Hubert Humphrey, and we sat back and didn't give our full commitment to a man who would have been a great President of this Nation, and the last time this Nation elected a Republican President would never have happened. Richard Nixon would never have been President and disgraced our country in the Oval Office.

Think on those things. Think on those things.

I know tonight as you leave this place it's important for you to do everything you can to affect the outcome of this election. Don't just vote yourselves. There's no one here that can't get on the telephone tomorrow and call fifty or maybe a hundred people to urge them to go and vote, along with you, to support the principles and the ideals that have made our Democratic Party and made our Nation great. Let's remember what's happened in past elections as we approach the election tomorrow.

Let me just close my remarks by quoting another Democrat, an idealist, yes, a courageous young man, yes, a young man who was killed the last day he campaigned, who might have been President himself, Senator Robert Kennedy. This is what he said to a group of supporters in Los Angeles just before he died, and this will be the last thing I say to you. These are his words. "I ask you to recognize," he said, "the hard and the difficult road to a better America. I ask you to vote for yourselves. The people must decide this election. For your sake and for the sake of your children, vote. Vote for yourselves."

Thank you very much. I'm depending on you. Thank you very much. Work hard between now and tomorrow night. I need you. I need you. Let's win together.

NOTE: The President spoke at 9:27 p.m. at the Federal Express ramp at Portland International Airport. He was introduced by Secretary of Transportation Neil Goldschmidt.

Seattle, Washington

Remarks at a Rally With Area Residents. November 3, 1980

THE PRESIDENT. How many of you believe we're going to whip the Republicans tomorrow? [*Applause*] Right. You don't know what it does to a man who's been campaigning since early this morning—I got up at 5 o'clock Washington time. When I asked Jody Powell, "Where do we spend the night?" he said, "Governor, this evening there ain't no tonight." We're going to leave here and fly back to Plains to vote. But I want to say that I thank you all for coming out. I love all of you. It's great to be here with so many Democrats, and particularly a man who has fought all his life—and still has a long time to fight—for all Americans, throughout all his career, and knows how to get things done for the United States of America and for the State of Washington, Warren G. Magnuson.

And I want to mention another man, too. In 1972 as the Governor of Georgia, I had one of the greatest honors of my life at the Democratic National Convention in Miami to nominate a man for President, a man who's done more in public life to keep our Nation strong and secure and at peace than anyone I know, Senator Scoop Jackson, my friend.

And I want to mention, too, your next Governor and my friend Jim McDermott. The only thing wrong with Jim McDermott is I have trouble with that first name. It kind of slips my mind on occasion. But I would like to say that all the Jims and all the Jimmys and all the Teds this year are working for a great Democratic victory tomorrow with your help.

You're blessed in this State with a fine Democratic delegation who will all be on the ticket tomorrow—Alan Swift, Don Bonker, Norman Dicks, Mike Lowry. This is a State, as you know, with a great future. You're the home of Boeing, the largest exporting corporation in America. You can really be proud of that. And your port is the closest one to China. It may be that you haven't yet realized the tremendous change that will take place in the life of all those in Oregon, Washington, California, and particularly throughout our Nation, when we see what will occur with the wonderful trade with China.

The normalization of relations with that great country has already meant that China is the number one buyer of American cotton. And lately we've signed a trade agreement—between 6 and 9 million tons of American grain that will be shipped to China every year for the next 5 years, enough grain for 15 loaves of bread for every one of the 1 billion people who live in China. You've indeed got a wonderful future if you keep this wonderfull Democratic ticket in office, and that includes me as well as the men behind me.

All of us are now working on the northwest fisheries bill to stock your salmon fisheries. In the past, one of the most important bills ever introduced for the fisheries industry, the American Fisheries Promotion Act, which will strengthen your industry and give our American fishermen greater rights within the 200-mile fishing zone than foreign fishermen have. We're going to pass that bill if I'm reelected, Maggie's reelected, the congressional delegation is sent back to Washington to represent you.

I've come here to the State of Washington many times in the last 4 years. As a matter of fact, I've been here twice as much since I've been in office as President as any previous President has ever been to see you—more than any Presidential candidate. It's because I love the State of Washington and because I've been so eager to work with you when you've made grat progress or when you've faced great potential difficulties. I came here when Mt. St. Helens erupted and traveled that area with Warren Magnuson, went back to Washington, worked with him and your delegation, to make sure that we took care of this tremendous trial for the peo-

ple of the State of Washington. And I'm very important to you in coming here as a candidate, because I represent, I believe, the image and the commitment and the ideals of the party down through the last half century that has meant so much to the lives of you and your families and those you love.

It's not a coincidence that I've come here on the last stop of my long campaign trail. I leave here tonight in a few minutes and fly back to Plains, Georgia. I'll arrive there just in time to vote in the morning, visit my mother who's in the hospital—she'll be out tomorrow—then we'll go back to Washington to listen to the returns. I've crossed a half a continent to be with you.

Let me tell you this in the utmost seriousness. The Republicans cannot beat us. There are not enough Republicans in this Nation to win an election. But the Democrats can beat ourselves. A low turnout by the working families of this Nation, a low turnout by the elderly citizens of this Nation, a low turnout by the teachers and students of this Nation, a low turnout by those who've been disabled and have been given a better life by the Democratic Party, a low turnout by those who share the ideals that have made you and me, together, partners in this election—those are the very things that can hurt us and put a Republican in the White House for the next 4 years. And after we wake up, Wednesday morning, and find that we've got a rightwing Republican leading this country, it's too late for us to decide we should have worked harder. You've been listening to this campaign for the last—more than a year, and you've heard the Republican candidate wrap himself in the mantle of the Democratic Party. It's not an accident. It happens every 4 years. It's happened that way all my life.

Have you ever heard a Republican candidate for President quote a Republican President?

AUDIENCE. No!

THE PRESIDENT. And you never will. You never will. Republicans campaign the last few months as Democrats, but once they get in office, they govern like Republicans. And after 4 years of incumbency, a Republican President has not left anything to be remembered favorably and he's not said anything to be quoted in the future. Now, some of you watched the Republican convention. You heard Ronald Reagan quoting Franklin D. Roosevelt. It would have been inconceivable for Ronald Reagan to quote Herbert Hoover or Richard Nixon, right?

AUDIENCE. Right!

THE PRESIDENT. It's important for the people of Washington to think very seriously about the consequences of this election and the differences between us. No man who says that the New Deal was based on fascism has a right to quote Franklin D. Roosevelt. No man who opposes the minimum wage has a right to quote Harry Truman. And no man who opposed the limited test ban agreement, SALT I, the Vladivostok agreement, the antiballistic missile treaty, has the right to quote John Fitzgerald Kennedy. And no man who campaigned around this country as a full-time employee of the anti-Medicare lobby, calling that legislation socialism, has the right to quote Lyndon Baines Johnson.

Now, you can rewrite the lines in a movie script. You can change the advertising posture of a major corporation, but in the last 3 months of a campaign, you cannot change the lifetime commitment of a man dedicated to the most reactionary element of the Republican Party. Think in your own lives what has happened to you under Democrats. Think how they

change just before an election. We recognize it now because we see it in person, but it's been that way for a long time. Let me read you what John Kennedy said about the Republicans in the campaign of 1960.

He said, "They're even beginning to say a few kind words about Franklin Roosevelt. Twenty years from now they might even speak a good word for Harry Truman. But I guarantee you that Harry Truman will not say a good word about Republicans." As you know, that prediction has come true, and now tonight I'd like to make a new prediction to you. I predict that 20 years from now Republican candidates for President will even be saying good things about Jimmy Carter's second term.

I'm proud to be a Democrat because I believe in the heritage and the mission of the Democratic Party. It's changed my life. It's changed the life of my mother. It changed the life of my father. The Democratic Party's given my children a better chance for a better life. I believe in the heritage and the mission of Franklin D. Roosevelt. I believe in the heritage and the mission of John Fitzgerald Kennedy. I believe in the heritage and mission of Harry Truman. And I believe in the heritage and the mission of Lyndon Baines Johnson. And I believe also in the heritage and the mission of Hubert Humphrey. Every great advance, every single great advance in our Nation, in the private lives of our citizens, for the last half century, from collective bargaining to the minimum wage, from social security to Medicare—every single one of them has been made possible by Democrats, over the opposition of Republicans.

Ever since Franklin Roosevelt the pattern has been the same. Collective bargaining—Democrats supported it; Republicans opposed it. Social security—Democrats supported it; Republicans opposed it. Ronald Reagan said four times that social security should be voluntary, which would destroy it. In the debate last week he said that for a young person, social security was a bad investment. The minimum wage—Democrats supported it; Republicans opposed it. Ronald Reagan has suggested this year, proposed, that the minimum wage be repealed. Civil rights—the Democrats supported the Voting Rights bill, the Civil Rights Act. Ronald Reagan said it was bad legislation. Medicare—Democrats supported it; Republicans opposed it. I've described Ronald Reagan's support for the opposition, calling it socialized medicine. National health insurance, other moves in the future—Democrats support it; Republicans oppose it. Ronald Reagan says there will be no national health insurance if he becomes President.

We believe also in a strong defense. I'm a southerner. I'm a graduate of the Naval Academy, a submarine officer. I used to come to Seattle and tie up at your pier on my first submarine. When I got into the Oval Office, in 7 of the last 8 years under Republican administrations, we had had an actual reduction in the commitment of our Nation's budget funds for defense, a 37-percent reduction over a period of 8 years. Since then, with the help of Scoop Jackson, Warren Magnuson, and others, we've had a steady, planned increase in commitment, above and beyond inflation, for a strong defense. That's why our Nation has been strong. That's why we've been influential. And that's why tonight I can stand here and, for the first time in 50 years, make a statement that no other President has been able to make, and that is, for the last 4 years, since I have been in office, our Nation has not been at war, we have been at peace. And with your help—with your help we will keep this Nation strong and at peace.

I'm a father and I'm a grandfather and I know the tremendous power available at the fingertips of an American President. But as President, I'll always remember that the best weapon is one that's never fired in battle and the best soldier is one that never has to shed his blood or give his life in war.

All Presidents, Democratic and Republican, have had to face troubled times. There's never been a day since I've been in that office that there hasn't been a crisis somewhere in the world, armed conflict between other nations. I have had to make the judgment in each instance—what is the interest of my country? How can I protect those interests? How can I protect the honor of my Nation? How can I protect our commitment to our allies? What is the degree of involvement? Can I resolve this problem disploniatically, politically, through persuasion, through the exercise of strength, without war? Those are the judgments that a President must make. If I handle those kinds of crises properly, with sound judgment, a sure strength, self-confidence, moderation, recognizing the ideals and commitments of the American people, then quite often you never know about the crisis that I faced for you. But if a President makes a misjudgment, any one of those crises can affect your life or perhaps the life of every person who lives on Earth.

I'm very much aware of the fact that the greatest commitment that I have is to prevent nuclear war. We must continue our progress in the careful, balanced, verifiable control of nuclear arms. This is the greatest overriding issue of this campaign. Governor Reagan has said—when asked about nuclear weapons or nuclear bombs for Pakistan, Iraq, Libya, his reply was, "That's none of our business."

It's very important that every American consider the consequences of that election. The election of 1980 is an election not just between two men, not just between two parties, but between two futures.

Let me talk very briefly in closing about the future that you and I together can have. In the next 4 years, we can build a nation at peace, peace not just for 4 years, but a nation with a commitment to peace so deep and a foundation so strong it'll last the rest of this century or beyond; a nation secure, secure in our military defense, yes, also secure in our energy needs; a nation of new technology, new tools, new factories, new industries that many of us have never even dreamed; a nation of new energy sources where American coal and American fuel derived from growing crops and from the Sun replace OPEC oil; a nation that stands for human rights and decency and self-respect for individual human beings, not just here but around the world.

These goals are not just dreams. They can and they must be our real agenda. As long as I'm President, working with you, that will be my commitment. But I need your help in a sacrificial way. With the election just hours away, it's now clearer than ever that the winner tomorrow will be either Governor Reagan or myself.

Tonight, I want to say a word directly to the Washingtonians who have been considering a vote for Congressman John Anderson. On many of the key issues, like energy conservation, equal rights for women, protecting our air and water, a better life for working people, the overriding issue of nuclear arms control, preventing the spread of nuclear weapons to radical and other countries—on all these central issues, the young people, primarily, and others who support John Anderson, agree with me. But it would be a tragedy if a split among those of us committed to these goals results in handing over the White House to those who oppose all these goals. I know what I'm

talking about, because in the adjacent state of Oregon last time, Gene McCarthy got 40,000 votes and Oregon went to the Republicans by 1,700.

Consider the consequences of a Republican victory. Think about it deeply. You might say, "Well, one vote can't make a difference." Or you might say, "I've come here tonight in the middle of the night. I've done enough for the Democratic Party because I'm going to go tomorrow and vote for the entire Democratic ticket." You might have even helped with the campaign or made a financial contribution. I tell you that's not enough, because the issue of this election is so close nationwide that what you do personally might be the difference between victory and defeat. It might be the difference between a good life for you and those you love and a challenge to the things in which you believe so deeply.

The other night I was in St. Louis talking about and listening to the people respond about Harry Truman. Remember the election in '48. If a few people had changed their votes, then Harry Truman would never have been reelected. Think about 1960 when John Kennedy and Lyndon Johnson were on our ticket. If 28,000 people in Texas had changed their vote and just a few thousand in Illinois had not voted, John Kennedy would never have served this Nation as President, Lyndon Johnson likely would never have been elected President; the Civil Rights Act, the Voting Rights Act, the great changes that have taken place for the betterment of your lives, might never have occurred.

Both those stories had a good ending, but think about another election in 1968 when the Democratic Party was divided. Some of the Gene McCarthy voters said, "Hubert Humphrey hasn't measured up to our 100-percent standard," and they didn't give him the support. A great man, a heart full of love, a great idealist, a great Democrat, never had a chance to serve this Nation as President. And what happened? The last Republican that this country has elected, Richard Nixon, was elected President, disgraced the White House, because Democrats, not Republicans, determined the outcome of that election.

So tomorrow, the issue's in your hands. Let's remember these events that I've just outlined to you. There's not a single person listening to my voice that can't contact at least 50 or 100 people between now and the time the polls close tomorrow. Let's remember in closing, the words of another Democrat—and this is the last thing I'll say to you. This is a Democrat who died in the midst of a campaign. He was a good, idealistic Democrat, never had a chance to serve as President. I don't know if he'd have been elected or not. His name was Robert Kennedy. This is what he said to his supporters in Los Angeles. He said, "I ask you to recognize the hard and difficult road to a better America. I ask you to vote for yourselves. The people must decide this election. For your sake and for the sake of your children, vote. Vote for yourselves."

Tomorrow vote for yourselves. Vote Democratic. Help us. God be with you.

NOTE: The President spoke at 11 p.m. at the Flightcraft Hangar at Boeing Field International Airport.

Plains, Georgia

Informal Exchange With Reporters After Voting. November 4, 1980

Q. Do you think you're going to win, Jimmy?

Q. Mr. President, how do you feel?

THE PRESIDENT. Well, I think I got two votes.

Q. Who did you vote for?

THE PRESIDENT. I voted for the one I consider to be the best candidate.

Q. Who was that?

THE PRESIDENT. That was myself.

Q. What are your prospects, Mr. President? What do you think?

THE PRESIDENT. I think good. It depends on the turnout and how well our organization works. It's a very close election. But I have confidence in the American people, always have, and they've never disappointed me so far.

Q. What do you think you would do if you lost this election today?

THE PRESIDENT. Well, I obviously would abide by the American people's judgment, whether I won or lost.

Q. But I mean your future plans.

THE PRESIDENT. Oh, well, I'm counting on winning.

Q. Have you got some late polling information that encourages you?

THE PRESIDENT. Well, I haven't gotten any late polling information. I think the polls have been published and pretty well closed 24 hours ago, most of them within the bounds of error. And it really depends on the turnout, on the attitude of the people, the weather across the country, how well the organizations work.

Q. Does it look neck-and-neck right now?

THE PRESIDENT. I think it's very close.

Q. Governor Reagan got a surge from that debate, but some polls showed that it began to dissipate. What gives you the confidence that perhaps you're going to go over the top today?

THE PRESIDENT. Well, I really have to wait till the returns come in. But I think the judgment of the American people will be good.

Q. What about the hostages? Any late information?

THE PRESIDENT. No. All of the information we had about the hostages has been steady, that they will be turned over by the militants to the Government, that Algeria will be an intermediary, may play a larger role. We've been in touch with the Algerians not only now, but for a long time. Even before the five United Nations members went to Iran, months ago, the Algerians were working very closely with us—Mr. Majawi was. We've had meetings in Washington with Ambassador Malek, who represents Algeria in our country. So, I think the Iranians couldn't have chosen a better intermediary than they did, in choosing the Algerians.

Q. Well, we have a report this morning that Tehran has asked for certain clarifications. Do you know anything about that?

THE PRESIDENT. No. I talked to the State Department this morning about an hour before we came in to Warner-Robins. And we will exchange documents with them, probably through the Algerians. What we will propose will be to uphold our Nation's honor and integrity. It'll be made public at the proper time, and I think the American people will be pleased.

Q. Do you expect to have the [*inaudible*]—to be released?

THE PRESIDENT. I feel more encouraged about the hostages now than I have in the past, but the time schedule for their release is something I can't predict.

Q. Did the hostage issue handicap you in your reelection bid?

THE PRESIDENT. Well, obviously the last year, you know, the concern about the hostages, the frustrations that all Americans have felt, I think have obviously been a negative political factor. But we've acted properly. In retrospect, I see no

way we could have done any differently, because I wanted to protect the lives and the safety of the hostages under every condition and also protect the honor of my country, and we've done both things.

Q. There were references in the news media to saying that you had become a hostage of sorts because of the hostage issue. Did you ever feel that way?

THE PRESIDENT. No. No. Obviously, my judgment has been made consistently in what I considered to be better for the country, first of all, and commensurately with that, and not in conflict with it, what's best for the hostages. The only failure we've had, so far as I know, has been the delay in the hostages being released. But there were times, as you well remember, when we feared for the lives of the hostages, and I think the way we have handled the matter has been best under the difficult circumstances.

Q. Mr. President, in your last day on the campaign trail you made an explicit pitch to the John Anderson supporters. Do you think you reached them?

THE PRESIDENT. Well, I hope so. I'll see you downtown.

Q. Mr. President, would you do anything different on the campaign this time from what you did?

THE PRESIDENT. We've done the best we could. I'll see you downtown.

NOTE: The exchange began shortly after 8 a.m. outside Plains High School, where the President and Mrs. Carter voted.

Plains, Georgia

Remarks to Area Residents.
November 4, 1980

Good morning, everybody. I hope some of you got to bed last night. I didn't. [*Laughter*]

As you all know, 4 years and—you can't hear? As you all know, 4 years and 1 day ago I came back the day after the election just as the Sun was rising in the east. And I thanked all of you for having helped me be elected to the highest office available in the free world.

I've had now a chance to serve for 4 years the greatest nation on Earth and the greatest people in the world. We've made some very difficult decisions, and every time I've made a judgment in a time of crisis or a time of solitude about the future of our country or the future of your lives, I've done it with the memory of my upbringing here in Plains, the fact that I'm a southerner, the fact that I'm an American. I've offered my life, as many of you have done, in time of war, to preserve freedom and to preserve the things in which we all believe.

We've made some difficult decisions. Some of them have not been politically popular. Some of them have been highly publicized. Some of the crises with which I've dealt you've never known about them, because they didn't develop into something that affected your life or the lives of people around the world. We've tried to deal fairly with all people, with black people, with those who speak Spanish, with women, for those who've been deprived in life. We've done this in every instance. Sometimes it's aroused the displeasure of others, and sometimes it's been politically costly.

Some of the most difficult decisions that have ever been made by the Congress or a President have been made in the last 4 years. We've been afflicted with the shock of more than a doubling in the price of oil in 1979, but our country was ready for it. Our people responded well. We've had unbelievable inflation the early part of this year. It's begun to come down, because you've responded. And we're now importing, as you know, 2 million barrels of oil a day less than we did just a year ago. We've cut it 30 percent in less than 12 months, because of you, not because of me. It was difficult for the Congress to take this action, but they did it, and they aroused the animosity of some who thought we moved too fast, didn't move fast enough.

The Panama Canal treaty was one of the things that I think is a courageous judgment that we've made. We acted in a way that was fair and decent. We did away with the colonial atmosphere of our country. We've formed a partnership with Panama. Now we share with them the responsibility for opening that canal, keeping it operating properly. After the year 2000 we'll still have a full right to defend it. This was a decision not easy to make, perhaps one of the most difficult judgments that an individual United States Senator has ever had to make.

We've kept our Nation strong, kept our Nation at peace. Sometimes it has not been easy to make a judgment in times of crisis overseas, but I can say to you something that no President has been able to say for the last 50 years. Our Nation has not been at war. We've been at peace.

And as you well know, the economic news has not always been good. I've noticed that we've had drought here in Georgia. We've had very difficult increases in energy prices. We've tried to handle these issues as you would have me handle them. In balance, our Nation has made good progress. We've honored the principles that are important to my life and yours. I think we've enhanced the freedom of people around the world. We've kept high the banner of human rights. We've not only kept our Nation at peace, we've extended peace to the people who live in the Middle East, with the exercise of the proper influence of our great country.

We've opened up government to people that in the past have been excluded. I've appointed more black judges, for instance, than all the other Presidents combined in 200 years—twice as many, as a matter of fact—more women judges than all the Presidents in 200 years put together; more judges that speak Spanish than all the Presidents combined in 200 years. This has not hurt our country. It's let those people, formerly deprived, formerly having been suffering from discrimination, be part of the decisionmaking process of our country.

Today is a great day in the life of a democracy. It's when the President and all of his challengers can cast a vote that counts the same as yours, and it's a time when you'll make a judgment about the Nation's future. I've always had confidence in the American people. I've never been disappointed, and at the conclusion of this day of voting I'll be willing to abide by the judgment. My belief is that I'll be reelected. I'll do the best I can to serve you. And I'm grateful from the bottom of my heart for the confidence that you've had in me.

Many people from Plains, from Americus, from Richland, from Preston, from Schley County, from around this area, have gone all over the Nation to speak for me and shake hands with people in other States, to tell them that you have confidence in me and that I would not disappoint them if I became President. I've tried to honor your commitment to those other people. In the process I've tried to honor my commitment to you. God bless you. Thank you.

Don't forget to vote, everybody.

NOTE: The President spoke at 8:15 a.m. at the Plains Depot.

1980 Presidential Election

Remarks on Return to the White House Following the Campaign.   November 4, 1980

Don't you know it's raining?

Well, let me say first of all that I'm very grateful and surprised to see you all out here in the rain. It means a lot to me to know that as we have been partners for the last 4 years that we still have the same relationship. We've made a good record for ourselves; we've tackled every tough issue that the Nation has faced without flinching; we made the right decisions. I think we have served our Nation well. We can be proud of what we have achieved.

The election this day is one that's part of a democratic process that'll give the American people a chance to express their opinion about what the future ought to hold. I feel confident about the outcome. I want to make sure that all of you don't forget to vote. This is your privilege and also your duty.

It may be a long night. We don't know yet what the returns will be. But I understand there's a heavy turnout so far in the areas that have been reported in. We have a long way to go. This is a very important day for me and for you both, I think for our country.

So, let me close by saying from the bottom of my heart no matter what the outcome is today I still feel very confident. You've got my eternal gratitude and my eternal friendship—and not only mine but the Nation's, because you've done a superb job. And I look forward to doing the same superb job with you the next 4 years.

God bless you. Thank you very much.

NOTE: The President spoke at 11:50 a.m. to a group of campaign supporters and members of the White House staff who had gathered on the South Lawn of the White House for the President's return.

Domestic Policy Review on Nonfuel Minerals

Memorandum From the President.
November 4, 1980

Memorandum for the Secretary of the Interior, the Secretary of Commerce, the Secretary of the Treasury, the Secretary of State, the Secretary of Labor, the United States Trade Representative, the Director of the Federal Emergency Management Agency, the Administrator of the Environmental Protection Agency, the Chairman of the Regulatory Council

At my direction and under the chairmanship of the Secretary of the Interior, a Domestic Policy Review on Nonfuel Minerals was undertaken to advise me on the nature and extent of foreseeable problems in the supply, availability, and price of certain minerals. One important conclusion of this review was that nonfuel mineral data gathering and analysis in many cases should be stronger and more cohesive to support the formulation of policies affecting nonfuel minerals.

Improvements should begin by strengthening current capabilities. To assure there is a focal point for minerals data and analysis, I am designating the Bureau of Mines in the Department of the Interior as the principal Federal agency for nonfuel mineral data gathering and analysis. My proposed FY 1981 budget for the Bureau of Mines provides the basis for upgrading certain minerals data and analysis. Each of you, however, has certain responsibilities for the collection, analysis, and presentation of nonfuel minerals information. It is essential that these responsibilities be executed in a manner that achieves the following objectives:

- Development of information and analysis necessary to support existing policies of Federal agencies with nonfuel minerals responsibilities.
- Coordination of information gathering and analysis to avoid duplication and overlap.
- Anticipation of future information requirements, including those of the minerals industries.
- Timely publication of nonclassified information in a manner that will meet public needs.

To meet these objectives, the Secretary of the Interior, through the Bureau of Mines, shall convene an Information Coordinating Committee. Each of you is to participate in this group, providing your assistance and support.

The Committee's initial tasks will include:

- Publication of an inventory of all minerals data sources in the Federal government.
- Development of standards of compatibility among data bases.
- Identification of significant gaps in data categories, and duplication in existing programs, and recommendations for termination of unnecessary data programs.
- Identification of analytical information systems capable of supporting nonfuel mineral policy analyses in such areas as national security, economic stability and growth, international trade, national and international stockpiles, public land management, environmental assessment, and regulatory policy. The development of an appropriate program to improve existing systems and recommend establishment of new systems, when needed, will be part of this process.
- Examination of the possible approaches to strengthen national and

international nonfuel minerals information exchange.

The Secretary of the Interior should convene this Committee as soon as possible and establish reporting requirements. In addition, the Secretary of the Interior shall report on the activities of the Committee as part of his Annual Report to Congress under the Mining and Minerals Policy Act.

You should give these assignments your immediate attention.

JIMMY CARTER

1980 Presidential Election

Remarks on the Outcome of the Election.
November 4, 1980

I promised you 4 years ago that I would never lie to you. So, I can't stand here tonight and say it doesn't hurt.

The people of the United States have made their choice, and, of course, I accept that decision but, I have to admit, not with the same enthusiasm that I accepted the decision 4 years ago. I have a deep appreciation of the system, however, that lets people make the free choice about who will lead them for the next 4 years.

About an hour ago I called Governor Reagan in California, and I told him that I congratulated him for a fine victory. I look forward to working closely with him during the next few weeks. We'll have a very fine transition period. I told him I wanted the best one in history. And I then sent him this telegram, and I'll read it to you. "It's now apparent that the American people have chosen you as the next President. I congratulate you and pledge to you our fullest support and cooperation in bringing about an orderly transition of government in the weeks ahead. My best

wishes are with you and your family as you undertake the responsibilities that lie before you." And I signed it Jimmy Carter.

I have been blessed as only a few people ever have, to help shape the destiny of this Nation. In that effort I've had your faithful support. In some ways I've been the most fortunate of Presidents, because I've had the daily aid of a wise man and a good man at my side, in my judgment the best Vice President anybody ever had, Fritz Mondale.

I've not achieved all I set out to do; perhaps no one ever does. But we have faced the tough issues. We've stood for and we've fought for and we have achieved some very important goals for our country. These efforts will not end with this administration. The effort must go on. Nor will the progress that we have made be lost when we leave office. The great principles that have guided this Nation since its very founding will continue to guide America through the challenges of the future.

This has been a long and hard-fought campaign, as you well know. But we must now come together as a united and a unified people to solve the problems that are still before us, to meet the challenges of a new decade. And I urge all of you to join in with me in a sincere and fruitful effort to support my successor when he undertakes this great responsibility as President of the greatest nation on Earth.

Ours is a special country, because our vast economic and military strength give us a special responsibility for seeking solutions to the problems that confront the world. But our influence will always be greater when we live up to those principles of freedom, of justice, of human rights, for all people.

God has been good to me, and God has been good to this country, and I'm truly thankful. I'm thankful for having been able to serve you in this capacity, thankful for the successes that we have had, thankful that to the end you were with me and every good thing that I tried to do.

There's an old Yiddish proverb that I've often thought of in the days and months that I've held this office. It says simply, "God gives burdens; also shoulders." In all the days and months when I have served you and served this country, you've readily given me your shoulders, your faith, and your prayers. No man could ask any more of his friends.

I've wanted to serve as President because I love this country and because I love the people of this Nation. Finally, let me say that I am disappointed tonight, but I have not lost either love.

Thank you very much.

NOTE: The President spoke at 9:54 p.m. at the Sheraton Washington Hotel. His remarks were broadcast live on nationwide television.

1980 Presidential Election

Remarks With Reporters on the Results of the Election.   November 5, 1980

Q. Is it true that you and Jody [1] are getting in that Volkswagen headed for Iowa? [*Laughter*] Next week?

THE PRESIDENT. Well, I thought you all would——

Q. Next week?

THE PRESIDENT. I thought you all would want something to do the rest of this week, so we thought we'd just go around and thank a few people that helped us so much.

Q. Well, maybe it's worth coming out. You can't get started too early.

_____
[1] Jody Powell, Press Secretary to the President.

THE PRESIDENT. Well, I know you all have been through a hard time these last 36 or 48 hours campaigning. I slept late this morning, feel good.

What'd you say, Helen [Helen Thomas, United Press International]?

Q. When did you first know that you were going to be defeated?

THE PRESIDENT. Monday night. Saturday evening we thought that we were well ahead in the polls, 2 or 3 points. Pat's [2] polls have always been unbelievably accurate. Monday night Pat sent word to us that we had dropped precipitously and were down, I think, 6 or 7 percentage points, which is landslide proportions, as you know.

Q. But the only thing that happened between Saturday night and Monday was the events in Iran and the news from Iran. So, would you say that that was the cause?

THE PRESIDENT. I don't know. I haven't seen the detailed analysis. I think Pat and the pollsters could probably tell you more about that.

Q. Mr. President, what are your long-range plans? Have you made any?

THE PRESIDENT. Well, I don't know yet. I'm going to go up to Camp David and spend 2 or 3 days with Rosalynn, and I think we'll have a chance then to talk about what we want to do.

Q. How is she?

THE PRESIDENT. She's good. She's feeling well. I told her Monday night that we were going to lose and all the indications pointed to that. She's been campaigning even longer and harder than I have, as you know. And none of us looked on this as a pleasant experience, but she's remarkably calm and looking to the future.

Q. What are your thoughts more in the

_____
[2] Pat Caddell, the President's pollster.

long term, Mr. President, about whether you'll write your memoirs and do that from Plains or Atlanta?

THE PRESIDENT. Well, that's my plans. We obviously have voluminous files; any President does. They'll eventually have to go into a proper library or repository somewhere. I'll have to have access to those. So, wherever I can keep those records and documents, that will really belong to the public eventually, is where I'll do most of the writing. But I think it's appropriate for a person who served in this office to make a report to the public, and in general that's been done through——

Q. How will history judge you?

THE PRESIDENT. I don't know yet. I've, you know, not had a chance to assess the conclusion of the administration. I've really been hoping that history could judge with a two successive term administration so that some of these things that we have worked on could be consummated. I think in general that the opening of access into Africa, the normalization of relations with China, the Mideast peace efforts, the maintaining of our Nation's peace, in international affairs it will look on us well. That remains to be seen.

Q. What confidence do you have, Mr. President, that the gains that you made under your Presidency, as you see them, will be retained by your successor?

THE PRESIDENT. Well, all of my comments are quite subjective in nature. From my perspective, in each instance when I've made the literally thousands of decisions, they've been shaped by, ultimately, my analysis of the confluence of events and circumstances and factors, and I've made judgments, I think, that led to a constructive ultimate resolution of the issues. And I think the same kind of events will mold the decisions of Gov-

ernor Reagan and his advisers in the future. There are some unpredictable things about the international circumstances that we don't know.

I also will go ahead, of course, and do the best I can to continue the peace momentum in the Middle East. I'll certainly be meeting with Prime Minister Begin——

Q. When?

THE PRESIDENT. ——in a week or so; I think the 13th of this month. And following that meeting I'll have a good analysis, probably, of the intention of his government, and I'm sure I'll be in contact directly or otherwise with President Sadat to see what his desires are.

It's important for the world to realize and for the American public to realize that I'll be the President for the next 2½ months. Governor Reagan and I had a very clear discussion of this, as did President Ford and myself 4 years ago. We will keep him informed, but the full constitutional responsibilities and authority, obviously, will be mine. I don't want to put that burden on him.

We will work very closely with his transition team that they've put together. Jack Watson, by the way—I asked Jack a few minutes ago to head up my own transition effort, and he's quite willing to do it. He represented me before when I took over this office, so Jack's familiar with both the successive and——

Q. Well, as a lameduck, do you think that you could, I mean, really do anything in foreign affairs? Will you still meet with the Japanese?

THE PRESIDENT. Yes, my intention is to do so. I think the foreign leaders will certainly want to understand the continuity of our system of government, and I think the continuity will be obvious to them all. My own inclination, although no final decision has been made, is that

Secretary Muskie would go ahead with his plans for his Latin American tour, because I think those leaders need to know that we are working very harmoniously with my successors in office and Ed Muskie's successors. We have current challenges on a daily basis in our relationship with a hundred and fifty other countries, and we'll deal with those——

Q. How about the hostages?

THE PRESIDENT. Well, I had a long meeting this morning with Christopher and Muskie, Brzezinski on the hostage issue. We'll continue to deal with it using the principles that I've outlined to you before, which we will certainly honor, to protect the hostages, their lives and safety, to work for their earliest possible release, but not to do anything that would violate the honor and integrity of our country. Any action that we take will have to be compatible with American law, the American Constitution.

Q. Mr. President, where do you feel your failures lie? Do you think there was a failure in too much loyalty to too few individuals?

THE PRESIDENT. No, I don't think that's a factor at all. I think in the, you know, post-Watergate era the press and the public are legitimately interested in personal fallibilities.

The allegations that I cheated by borrowing money from Bert Lance's bank and, in effect, channeling money through my warehouse into my campaign fund in 1976 received headline treatment for weeks. I had to spend tens of thousands of dollars of my own personal money just for C.P.A.'s and lawyer fees. Obviously, all of those allegations were false, and they were finally announced to be completely false. But that series of charges, headlines, news stories about my cheating as a candidate in 1976 obviously

made a small impression on the American consciousness.

The same allegations that Hamilton Jordan did something that was illegal in the use of drugs was ultimately shown to be made by three convicted felons who lied, but, you know, the impression still exists. Rosalynn saw one of the Moral Majority preachers this morning saying that Hamilton Jordan's use of drugs is something that the American electorate answered last night by putting a true Christian in the Oval Office.

But those kinds of things, you know, have come up, and they are inevitable. And they're part of the American consciousness, and I'm sure they made an impression on some people. But I think that in general my administration has been open. I think my loyalty has not been misplaced at all. And I think the ultimate analysis of these charges and countercharges will show that there have been some human fallibilities, but they are inevitable, and there's been certainly no, there's no instance where anybody in my administration has benefited at the expense of our Nation, financially or otherwise.

Q. Mr. President, last night Bob Strauss told me that the Ayatollah had accomplished his goal and he was tired of that point. Would you reflect on that?

THE PRESIDENT. Well, it's hard to say. I think Khomeini's professed public animosity against the Shah and against me the last 12 months has been obvious, and that included his statements this weekend. But I don't have any way to know what the Ayatollah's goals were.

I doubt if any successor of mine, including Governor Reagan, would materially change the posture that we are maintaining, and I doubt that anybody in my position the last 12 months would have done substantially different from what I did. I don't know anything that could have been done better or differently.

But obviously the hostage issue, coming as it did with the anniversary publicity and so forth, was a factor. But I can't say it was more important than the high interest rates or other factors that would influence the American people.

Q. You don't think Khomeini aimed at the election time to target——

THE PRESIDENT. No. I think that we have a tendency over here to greatly exaggerate the importance of the American election in the minds of the Iranian people. Their Government is still in its embryonic stage. They're struggling for political power and authority. Their country is endangered with an armed invasion. Their life's blood economically, with oil and the Abadan refinery, have been lost. They are still isolated among the community of nations. And for us to exalt, you know, the outcome of an election here, when the facts are that policies won't be basically changed toward Iran and the hostages, into something important for the Iranians I think is just a mistake.

Q. Apparently a lot of people voted a protest against changes that have occurred——

THE PRESIDENT. Yes.

Q. ——changes in our economy and the world economy, the change in the scarcity of resources, in our own lifestyles that perhaps have diminished because of that, and America's inability to continue to rule the world from the standpoint of military power.

THE PRESIDENT. Yes.

Q. Do you believe that under Governor Reagan that somehow a change in policies can reverse or somehow return this country to the point where people may have been voting to returning to?

THE PRESIDENT. That's hard to say. I don't want to predict what might happen in the future. I'm sure that Governor Reagan will do the best he can to carry out his campaign commitments, which are deeply felt by him, I'm sure, and to restore as much as possible our Nation's preeminence in some areas where we have not been able to exert our will to dominate others. But the inexorable historical movements are that we don't have control over some things that we formerly did.

We have become very dependent, for instance, on foreign oil supplies, and I've done the best I could, one of our notable domestic successes, in changing our basic policy toward energy, establishing one, finally, that would result in a decreased dependence on that oil. Whether anybody could do more in the future, I can't say. I hope that now that those policies are established in law that the benefits of them will accrue to our country under Governor Reagan. This is one element that has shown that we are somewhat dependent upon decisions made overseas.

I think one of the major elements in the outcome of the election was the doubling of oil prices last year. It was unanticipated, and this wreaked havoc with the international economy. Germany, Italy, France, Great Britain have had zero increase in employment in their nations. We've had a substantial increase, 10 percent, in total employment in our country during the same period of time. The inflation rate has doubled in Germany, doubled in Japan. And inflationary pressures in Great Britain, interest rates, are much higher; in Israel, 200-percent inflation rate. Some of the economies of other nations have almost been destroyed, some of the Latin American countries, Caribbean countries, independent countries.

So, I think we've assimilated these economic shocks as well as any country on Earth. The one thing that has hurt has been the inflation rate, because we started out at such an extremely low base of price, for instance, for gasoline, whereas the other countries were approaching $2 a gallon for gasoline before these prices were doubled. Ours were very low, and we had to go up. So, on a percentage basis ours went up much higher.

So, I'd say that kind of outside event—the capturing of our hostages, the increase of OPEC oil prices—is the kind of inevitable occurrence that we experienced that no one could have prevented. Whether we change the events in the future, I don't know.

But the opening up of China to normal relations is something that I don't think any President would want to endanger. I'm not trying to speak for Governor Reagan. The fact is that we've doubled our trade with Taiwan at the same time. And I think we've got a stable relationship there with the Shanghai Communique decision by Nixon and the normalization by me. We have a good relationship with our NATO Allies.

The budget restraints are going to be equally severe on Governor Reagan as they would have been on me. The conflicting demands by interest groups have to be met, with always disappointment by some because they have to share the restraints with others.

I would hope that we could have embedded in the consciousness of our people, through the media and otherwise, some of the benefits that we've derived, with energy, the new policy in Africa, new policy in Latin America, new policy with China, the progress towards peace in the Middle East, strengthening of NATO. I think that those things are helpful.

The big unmet decision is: What about strategic arms limitation? And I will do everything I can to contribute to that control. If Governor Reagan's professed desire to withdraw the SALT II treaty from consideration, to start with a fresh approach proves to be acceptable to the Soviets, then Governor Reagan can expect my full support of whatever effort he makes.

Q. There's a Republican Senate now.

THE PRESIDENT. I understand.

Q. Mr. President, going back to this whole question of the political climate, we have this extraordinary scrutiny of public officials and Presidents, you have an independent Congress, you have this post-Watergate syndrome, as we call it, and you have the fact that public officials have to campaign for years and years to get to an office, such as you. What's the future of the Presidency, as you see it? Are we in for a series of one-term Presidents? Can you just talk about the office a little bit?

THE PRESIDENT. I notice that there are a lot of political leaders out of work, and I'm going to be competing with a lot of folks for a job. [*Laughter*]

Well, I think you know the attrition in the Presidency since Eisenhower, and there were different circumstances. But the fact is that it's very difficult for someone to serve in this office and meet the difficult issues in a proper and courageous way and still maintain a combination of interest group approval that will provide a clear majority in an election time. I don't say that in derogation of the process.

And I know there's been some analysis that I haven't been a good enough politician, but, you know, I hope that history will show that I have never flinched in dealing with issues that some of my predecessors have postponed.

The Panama Canal treaty was, in my

judgment, a necessary step. It probably encompassed the most courageous votes ever cast in the United States Senate. The outcome of it was favorable to our country, but the political aftermath was obviously a very strong negative reaction, particularly among those who were opposed to the treaty. They became fervent in their desire to defeat all those who had supported the Panama Canal treaty.

Among some groups the appointment of minorities to judgeships, you know, didn't go over well, because it was a highly publicized effort. Women's rights is clouded by all kinds of, I think, distorted analyses of what the equal rights amendment means. My judgment is that the pursuit of those two goals, basically encompassing civil rights, ought to be continued. But that arouses another negative element, who are very highly financed, very highly motivated, to determine the outcome of public elections for the Presidency and otherwise.

I hope that one of the things to come out of the election is a realization of the difficult decisions made here, the need for maybe a closer cooperation and coordination between the President and the congressional leadership. And the fact that constituency groups, when they're disappointed because they don't get 100 percent of what they realize, needs to be balanced with basic support and approval for the 90 percent they get. You know, that's obviously a factor in an election year.

I think there was some down side to the Mideast agreement. It's necessary for a President, in negotiating between Arabs and Israelis, to be balanced in one's approach. It would have been easy for me to demagog this issue, referring to Israel's territorial future and the status of Jerusalem. You know, there are dozens of facets of that that I could have used for political advantage, but it would have, I think, short-circuited any future involvement of Sadat and other Arab leaders in reaching the comprehensive peace that I hope is still to come.

So, I think that the Presidency itself is still strong and intact. I've read a lot of history since I've been in this office. And my relation with the press, my relationship with the public at this moment is, I think, good compared to what Truman's was when he was in the heat of the political battles, in dealing with the labor unions, with railroad strikes, with other elements that were so difficult to handle.

So, I don't have any concern about the status of the Presidency. If we have failed, I think it's in not getting across to the public the significance of these key issues that we have addressed. I've just mentioned two or three of them to you for illustrative purposes.

The refugee question has hurt us badly. It wasn't just in Florida, but it was throughout the country. It was a burning issue. It made us look impotent when we received these refugees from Cuba. I think in retrospect we handled the situation properly. We took them in. We tried to restrict the flow and enforce the American law. We finally got through Congress some financial recompense for the communities that had to bear the financial burden. But, you know, looking back on this last 6 months, I don't see anything we could have done differently or better, but there was a political cost to how we handled it.

I'm not saying all these things in a tone of regret or excuse; I'm just trying to answer your question about some of the factors that go into an electorate's decision. And I think this last few hours before the election took place, the dominating news story of the hostages not coming home immediately, the mobs in the street, Khomeini's statement, just kind of reconfirmed America's concern about our lost dominance of world affairs and our preeminence in economic affairs.

You know, face the facts. I don't think there's any indication in the polls that there was a personal turning against me, although you can ask Pat about that. I haven't talked to Pat, but Jody says that the number of people that thought I handled the hostage question right went up; the number of people who thought I used it for political manipulation went down. There was not an aversion to me. It was just a frustration that there are some unresolved challenges and problems. And the natural tendency is to vote against incumbents in the U.S. Senate, the Congress, and, I guess, Governors as well.

Q. What do you think happened to the Senate?

THE PRESIDENT. I think the same thing that I've discussed with you applied nationwide. I still haven't seen any sort of breakdown regionally. But there was a kind of across-the-board, literally, a 10-percent drop in political approval from Saturday until Monday night, and I think it was just a kind of a floodgate opening of people.

Q. Mr. President, do you anticipate after you leave office that you'll continue to speak out on public affairs, be very visible in the public eye, or will you rather become a historian and a scholar and look to your memoirs as your major activity?

THE PRESIDENT. I don't know yet. You know, I really haven't thought through that. I haven't even talked to Jody or Rosalynn or any of my other advisers. I would guess, though, that those matters that are very important to me, for which

I've worked for 4 years, that I would defend them in a proper way.

I hope that I can keep my commitment to be very constructive in my relationship with Governor Reagan when he's in office. I don't think I'll comment on the relationship that I've had with my predecessors, but I would like to have a good, positive relationship with Governor Reagan. I know vividly how much support could be forthcoming from an ex-President who understands these issues.

And although I might disagree with him on approach on some things, the SALT issue as an example, if he makes a positive move to control nuclear weapons using his tactics, I'm not going to condemn him for it. I'll be in there helping him anyway he asks me to, to bring about the consummation of the same goals that I'm sure he wants, that is, to control nuclear weapons. And the fact that we have to abandon my approach and adopt his, that's a prerogative he'll make. I'll support it. I want to be very constructive.

Q. When Lyndon Johnson went out of office, the stories say that he felt the greatest sense of relief despite the loss. Will you be feeling any relief? Do you feel like a great load has been lifted off your shoulders?

THE PRESIDENT. Well, I've still got the full load for the next 2½ months. [*Laughter*]

Q. I understand that. But is there any statement that you're looking forward?

THE PRESIDENT. Well, in a way. You all can see it first hand—the constancy of the responsibility on a President. There's no way to escape, day or night. Somewhere in the world, something's going on about which you have to be concerned. And the way our Government is structured, a Cabinet officer can't act, you know, without direct authority from a President on matters of a crucial nature. I have not found it to be onerous. It's been a very gratifying experience for me. I've looked forward to each day with anticipation. I've never approached even the most serious crisis with a sense of dread.

But obviously, for someone else to be dealing with the routine duties will be a relief. And I'd like to contemplate about history and perspective and where our Nation goes from now. Still, as I said last night in my closing sentence—it wasn't in the text that I had ahead of time—I love this country and its people, and the outcome of the election hasn't affected that feeling at all.

Q. Mr. President, Governor Reagan will be the sixth President in 21 years, the second one to come into this office without any Washington experience.

THE PRESIDENT. Yes.

Q. What do you think about that, the Washington experience, knowing people and the system? I mean, is there anything you would have done differently? Is there any advice you would give him? He's in the same situation.

THE PRESIDENT. Well, it's hard to say. I think Governor Reagan will have the same things to learn that I had to learn.

Most people have excessively limited their analysis of my advisers to those that came here with me from Georgia. And I think if you look at the Cabinet makeup, both the original Cabinet and the present Cabinet, you'll see the breadth of their experience, geographically and their background, their knowledge of Washington, their knowledge of international affairs. It's very broad and very impressive. So, I have not felt limited in understanding the international or the national scene excessively.

Obviously, I have grown in the job. I

understand much better now who in the Congress is dependable, who is effective, who works hard, who can be constructive, what their personal district needs are. Those are the kind of things that I have learned in the process.

Also, I spent the first couple of years in this office as a student. You know, it's my nature to learn things, and I studied in the most meticulous detail the makeup of the budget, the role of the hundreds and hundreds of little tiny Government entities and agencies in a relationship. I didn't know those things well before I came here. I've also studied history. I've also studied the makup of, roughly, the hundred and fifty nations, their relationship with one another, the characteristics of the leaders of the nations that are important to us. Those are the kinds of facts that I, myself, have felt I needed personally.

And I've governed this country as a strong President. I think any of my Cabinet officers would tell you that the ultimate decisions have been mine.

I don't know what Governor Reagan's philosophy will be. He may want to do the same thing, or he might want to devolve a much greater authority to his Secretary of State or to his Secretary of the Treasury or to his budget officers. I don't really know how he will address the office. I think each President is different.

Q. You say you've governed this country as a strong President.

THE PRESIDENT. I hope so.

Q. The perception seems to have been you were a weak President. Why do you believe there was a failure in the country to perceive you as you perceive yourself?

THE PRESIDENT. Well, Sam [Sam Donaldson, ABC News], what I meant was that I have never avoided the ultimate responsibility of making the difficult decision. I think that Secretary Vance or Muskie or Christopher or Brzezinski or Bill Miller or even the ones who've gone, Califano, Blumenthal, would tell you that when the final judgment came, I made it, and I tried to acquaint myself with all the factors. And that's what I meant by governing as a strong leader. I didn't try to put the responsibilities off on anyone else. When a mistake was made, I tried to take the blame.

On the image part, anyone who sits in this office would have to refer, without being repetitious, to the question that was asked earlier. There are international events—refugees, oil prices, the capturing of an Embassy in Iran—over which a President has no direct control, and the fact that we don't have control and our Nation is not able to dominate world affairs to suit our own inclinations reflects adversely on the image of a President.

On those issues that I could decide—should we go ahead with the Panama Canal treaty or not, should we normalize relationships with China or not, should we deal with the Mideast peace treaty in a highly speculative way by going to Camp David and then later going to Jerusalem and Cairo or not—I don't think I've failed, in those respects when the issues were in my hands, to act with a proper degree of boldness. And I've done it after very careful consultations. I'm not trying to brag on being bold or courageous and so forth. I'm trying to keep an analytical judgment of how I see myself. History will—[*inaudible*].

Q. Mr. President, since the ship is so small and the sea is so large, do you feel that the Presidency should be a 6-year term?

THE PRESIDENT. Yes, if I could just in a stroke of the pen change the Constitution, I would personally prefer a single 6-year term. I think the adverse consequences of a potential lameduck Presidency toward the end is relatively minor compared to the removal of the, quote, stigma or insinuation that everything is done for political reasons. I hadn't been in this office a year before almost every decision I made was tainted with the allegation, at least by some, that an element of sincerity or objectivity was missing and was replaced by a grasping for political advantage. There are some other factors. But I think that between those two, the single 6-year term, I think, would add to the stature of the Presidency.

And you have always faced the possibility of the lameduck. The lameduck thing comes and goes, unfortunately, with public opinion polls. When a President is strong in the public opinion polls, like immediately after Camp David, I found that I had a much easier success in getting my will implemented in Congress. When it looked like I was faltering and Kennedy might sweep me out of office, you know, after he announced as a candidate last October or November, I found that I had more difficulty in the Congress. But I think in balance you'll find, when the analyses are finally concluded, that our success in the Congress has been very good.

Q. Mr. President, can we talk about the Democratic Party for a moment? How bad shape is it in, what needs to be done to restore it, and what role would you play in——

THE PRESIDENT. I don't know yet. That's one question I really haven't thought about it.

Q. Mr. President, how big a factor was Senator Kennedy's furious assault on you during the primary and the somewhat lukewarm endorsement he gave you at the convention and afterward? How big a factor was that?

THE PRESIDENT. Well, let me say that afterward has been very good, superb. I talked to Senator Kennedy last night, and he expressed his great admiration for the campaign we've run, for the announcement last night congratulating Governor Reagan. When I couldn't go out to campaign Sunday because of the hostage issue, he graciously cancelled his afternoon's activities and went out to represent me. I think that it's been very helpful.

I have no criticism of Senator Kennedy's running for the nomination, because among him and his advisers, I think it was obvious a year ago that he would capture the nomination. I would guess that every one of you thought that. Go back and look at the writings of the political columnists. It was a generally accepted fact.

There's no doubt that the very heated campaign in the spring months crippled me politically with some constituency groups, and we had to spend a lot of time reestablishing my credentials among the minority citizens, women, the poor, the elderly, and others that are very dear to me and very important to me. I think after the convention Senator Kennedy did his part to try to repair that damage, but the damage was obviously there.

Q. Did you recover from it?

THE PRESIDENT. Not completely.

Q. Does it hurt that the South rejected you?

THE PRESIDENT. Well, I don't look on it as a rejection. I would rather have carried the South and the rest of the Nation, but I have nothing but fond feelings toward the South.

Q. Mr. President, do you think that Governor Reagan is as much a threat to world peace and a lot of other things that your campaign rhetoric indicated?

THE PRESIDENT. I have a firm belief that Governor Reagan will do his utmost to maintain the peace.

Q. Mr. President, is there any possibility that you would consider running again?

THE PRESIDENT. That's a question that I hadn't even dreamed about.

Q. When will you meet with Reagan?

THE PRESIDENT. Will I meet with Reagan?

Q. When?

THE PRESIDENT. Whenever's convenient for him. I think the first time I met with President Ford was, the first time I ever came in this office was the 3d of December. But I'm going to be kind of busy for the next couple of weeks. I'm sure Governor Reagan's going to want to get some rest. It's been strenuous for him, too.

We'll let our transition teams be working with each other. I asked Governor Reagan last night if there was ever any semblance of incompatibility between our transition groups for him to call me immediately, and personally that I would resolve it; I was determined to have this be the best transition that's ever taken place in history. I'll go a second mile to accommodate him and to provide him with an administration that would be best for our country.

And I'll have the full responsibility and authority of the Presidency until the day he takes the oath of office. He understands that, and he agrees. We'll give him absolute access to all security briefings. I've already met this morning with Admiral Turner and instructed him accordingly, and we'll be providing Ed Meese, who I understand will represent him, with every possible assistance.

I've got to go.

Q. Mr. President, on the previous question did you mean to leave open the possibility that you might run for national office again?

THE PRESIDENT. I really haven't thought about that and don't want to comment on it.

Q. Any advice for Reagan? Ford had advice for you. He said meet with Giscard and Schmidt as fast as you can. Do you have any advice for him?

THE PRESIDENT. No, I haven't thought about that.

MR. WISE.[3] Let's go to Camp David, Mr. President.

Q. Do it in Guadeloupe.

Q. Have you had any contact, any word from any foreign leader, calls?

THE PRESIDENT. Yes, some have come in expressing their friendship.

Q. Brezhnev?

THE PRESIDENT. I haven't seen an inventory on that. I just got a small—[*inaudible*]. I'll probably get them tomorrow.

Q. Are you going to go on vacation after Camp David?

THE PRESIDENT. No, I don't think so. I'm going to stay at Camp David off and on probably for about a week, but I imagine I'll come down here several times just to meet with some of my advisers.

What we're doing now is to make a kind of an inventory, an agenda of the responsibilities that we have to pursue this next 2½ months. I met with Ed Muskie and Christopher and Brzezinski this morning. They'll be doing that for me in international affairs. But we're keeping current at the same time. And I've instructed Jack Watson and Stu Eizenstat to do the same thing on domestic issues.

We have the congressional session to approach. We've pretty well got the agenda

---

[3] Phillip J. Wise, Jr., Appointments Secretary to the President.

there. We'll establish priorities for the pursuit of those congressional decisions.

But I feel at ease.

Q. You won't resubmit SALT, then, or anything like that?

THE PRESIDENT. No, I think that would probably not be well advised. It's not a matter of resubmission. SALT is still on the congressional calendar. It never has been withdrawn, as you know.

But I feel very much at ease and look forward to getting a few days rest. And I want to go out of this office in 2½ months and make this, hopefully, the best 2½ months of the whole administration.

Thank you.

Q. You'll stay a week at Camp David?

THE PRESIDENT. Rosalynn will stay a week. I'll be back before.

Q. Good luck.

THE PRESIDENT. Thank you all.

Q. Good luck, sir.

THE PRESIDENT. Well, I've enjoyed being with you this morning and the last 4 years.

NOTE: The exchange began at 11:30 a.m. in the Oval Office at the White House.

Digest of Other White House Announcements

The following listing includes the President's public schedule and other items of general interest announced by the White House Press Office and not included elsewhere in this issue.

November 3

The White House announced that the President met with his advisers at 8 a.m. for about 45 minutes. The recent developments in Iran were thoroughly analyzed. The Preident and his advisers felt that if the hostages were transferred to Government control, this would be a significant step. They also viewed favorably the prospect of a role for the Algerians in the situation.

November 5

The President left the White House for a stay at Camp David, Md.

NOMINATIONS SUBMITTED TO THE SENATE

NOTE: No nominations were submitted to the Senate during the period covered by this issue.

CHECKLIST OF WHITE HOUSE PRESS RELEASES

The following listing contains releases of the White House Press Office which are not included in this issue.

Released November 1, 1980

Advance text: remarks at a rally with area residents in Abilene, Tex.

CHECKLIST—Continued

Released November 2, 1980

Announcement: President's return to the White House to discuss with advisers the situation in Iran

News conference: on the President's report to the Nation on the situation in Iran—by Press Secretary Jody Powell

Released November 3, 1980

Fact sheet: Executive Order 12250, leadership and coordination of nondiscrimination laws

Released November 6, 1980

News conference: on transition arrangements for the new administration—by Jack H. Watson, Jr., Assistant to the President, and Mr. Powell

---

ACTS APPROVED BY THE PRESIDENT

NOTE: No acts approved by the President were received by the Office of the Federal Register during the period covered by this issue.

Commission on Fine Arts

Appointment of Five Members and Designation of Chairman. November 10, 1980

The President today announced the appointment of five persons as members of the Commission on Fine Arts for 4-year terms. They are:

JOHN CARTER BROWN, of Washington, D.C., who has been Chairman of this Commission since 1976. He is Director of the National Gallery of Art, a member of the National Trust for Historic Preservation, and treasurer of the White House Historical Association. He has been redesignated Chairman.

JOHN S. CHASE, of Houston, Tex., president of the John S. Chase architectural firm, a fellow of the American Institute of Architects, and a member of the National Office of Minority Architects.

SONDRA GELB MYERS, of Scranton, Pa., chair of the Commission on Architecture and Urban Design for the city of Scranton, and former vice chair of the Public Committee for the Humanities in Pennsylvania.

WALTER A. NETSCH, of Chicago, Ill., a partner in the architectural firm of Skidmore, Owings & Merrill. He has won several architectural awards and is a fellow of the American Institute of Architects.

EDWARD DURELL STONE, JR., of Fort Lauderdale, Fla., a landscape architect with the El Morro resort in Venezuela. He has won several architectural awards and has been a member of this Commission since 1971.

National Institute of Justice

Appointment of Terry Q. Alarcon as a Member of the Advisory Board. November 10, 1980

The President today announced the appointment of Terry Q. Alarcon, of New Orleans, La., as a member of the National Institute of Justice Advisory Board.

Alarcon, 32, is administrative assistant to the sheriff in the Orleans Parish Criminal Sheriff's Office.

Council on Wage and Price Stability

Message to the Congress Transmitting a Report. November 12, 1980

To the Congress of the United States:

In accordance with Section 5 of the Council on Wage and Price Stability Act, as amended, I hereby transmit to the Congress the twenty-second quarterly report of the Council on Wage and Price Stability. The report describes the Council's activities during the first quarter of 1980. These include the monitoring of prices and wages in the private sector as well as of various Federal Government activities that could lead to higher costs and prices without creating commensurate benefits. The report discusses the Council's activities before Federal regulatory agencies and its role in my anti-inflation program.

The Council on Wage and Price Stability will continue to play an important role in our efforts to fight inflation. Its work supplements fiscal and monetary policies by calling public attention to wage and price developments and to actions by the Government that should be of concern to American consumers.

JIMMY CARTER

The White House,
November 12, 1980.

Science and Technology

*Message to the Congress Transmitting a
Report.   November 12, 1980*

To the Congress of the United States:

I am pleased to submit to the Congress
the Second Annual Science and Technology Report as required by the National
Science and Technology Policy, Organization, and Priorities Act of 1976.

The events and issues discussed in this
report—and in its companion report, the
*Five-Year Outlook on Science and Tech-
nology*—show how closely government
policies and developments in science and
technology are connected. Careful and
systematic assessment of scientific and
technological developments remains crucial to the formation of effective public
policy.

I hope that this report, like its predecessor, will contribute to the informed discussion so necessary to the maintenance
of our scientific and technological
capabilities.

JIMMY CARTER

The White House,
    November 12, 1980.

NOTE: The report is entitled "Science and
Technology: Annual Report to the Congress,"
National Science Foundation, June 1980 (Gov-
ernment Printing Office, 87 pages).

and submitted to me by Secretary
Duncan.

The Report describes actions taken by
Federal agencies pursuant to Executive
Order 12217, which I issued on June 18,
1980, to increase the conversion of Federal facilities now burning oil or natural
gas to coal or other alternate fuels. All
Federal agencies must survey and identify
facilities subject to the Act and submit
annual plans for funding their conversions beginning in Fiscal Year 1982. Five
major Federal installations are now in the
process of converting twelve units to coal.
These conversions will displace 920,000
barrels of oil per year.

The Report also discusses the results of
Executive Order 12185, in which I directed all Federal agencies to establish
rules to encourage conservation of petroleum and natural gas by recipients of Federal financial assistance. Agencies published final rules and guidelines to
implement this Executive Order on August 29, 1980.

JIMMY CARTER

The White House,
    November 12, 1980.

NOTE: The report is entitled "Implementation
of Section 403 of the Fuel Use Act: Federal
Facilities and Financial Assistance Annual
Report."

Powerplant and Industrial Fuel Use

*Message to the Congress Transmitting a
Report.   November 12, 1980*

To the Congress of the United States:

I am pleased to transmit the first Annual Report on the implementation of
Section 403 of the Powerplant and Industrial Fuel Use Act of 1978, which was
prepared by the Department of Energy

The Presidential Transition and Domestic and Foreign Policy Issues

*Remarks in a Question-and-Answer Session
With Reporters.   November 12, 1980*

Q. What did we do wrong?

THE PRESIDENT. Nothing. It's Jody
that's been doing it wrong. [*Laughter*] I
thought since Jody hadn't done so well
with his job, I'd come down and see if I
could do it any better. [*Laughter*] I don't

have any announcement to make, I'll just answer your questions.

AMERICAN HOSTAGES IN IRAN

Q. Mr. President, we want to know about the Christopher mission. What can you tell us about the discussions with the—[*inaudible*]?

THE PRESIDENT. Mr. Christopher reported a successful mission to me. He went there to relate to the Algerians our basic response to the Iranian proposals. The Algerians accepted the outline of response and have already relayed to the Iranians the response. So Christopher believes it was a successful mission.

Q. Have you heard anything back from the Iranians?

THE PRESIDENT. No.

Q. Do you think after the Christopher mission you're any closer to a resolution of the hostage crisis?

THE PRESIDENT. It's up to the Iranians. I think it would certainly be to their advantage and to ours to resolve this issue without any further delay. I think our answers are adequate, and I believe that the Iranian proposal was a basis for resolution of the differences.

Q. Mr. President, are you able to describe the United States answer to the——

THE PRESIDENT. No. No, I think it's better not to get into any sort of specificity at all about our response.

NUCLEAR NONPROLIFERATION AND ARMS CONTROL

Q. Mr. President, do you have any comment on the wisdom and the likely success of President-elect Reagan's strategy of dealing with the Soviet Union based on linkage?

THE PRESIDENT. Well, as I said, I think the day after the election to a group of

reporters, I'll be very constructive and very helpful to Governor Reagan in his new effort or different effort to control nuclear weapons. If his tactic has any chance of success, although it's different from mine—and I hope it will have every success—then he will have my full support.

Q. Mr. President, will you be meeting with Mr. Reagan soon?

THE PRESIDENT. Yes. I intend to meet with him maybe sometime next week, whenever is convenient for him. I have not quite so heavy a schedule these days as I have have had in the past.

Q. Have you spoken to him recently? Have you been——

THE PRESIDENT. No, I've not spoken to him personally since the night of the election, but I have sent word to him through Mr. Meese, his liaison designee, that I would be glad to meet with Governor Reagan whenever it's convenient. And I have heard from Jack Watson that next week might be appropriate, but that's a judgment for Governor Reagan to make. Whenever it's convenient.

Q. Mr. President, after all you said on the campaign trail about Governor Reagan's views on arms control, the possibility of an arms race, the likelihood—his advocacy of an arms race, how can you in good conscience now say that you would support that?

THE PRESIDENT. Well, I think my approach is best. And I would much prefer that SALT II be ratified or at least amended minimally by the United States Senate and then ratified, and then let the Soviets reject or accept the minimal amendments. But Governor Reagan will be President next January. And after he is President and assumes the responsibility for negotiating arms control limitations on behalf of our Nation, I will abandon my own approach—which I still believe is preferable—but I will abandon my own approach and support his, as long as I can do it in good conscience.

The fact is that we need to limit and control, control and limit nuclear arms between ourselves and the Soviet Union. We need to keep adequate flexibility for our own country, reduce substantially the Soviet arsenals, have a system of monitoring, using our own technical means, the compliance with the treaty. All those things are built into SALT II, and if Governor Reagan can find an alternative means to reach the same goals, I will be supportive.

Q. The other?

THE PRESIDENT. The other part is on nonproliferation. I think our Nation must continue to be the world leader in preventing the proliferation of nuclear explosives among nations that don't presently have them. And I will give every support to that proposition, hopefully supporting Governor Reagan's commitment to the same goal.

MIDDLE EAST PEACE NEGOTIATIONS

Q. Can you make progress on Palestinian autonomy tomorrow in your talks to Mr. Begin. What do you hope to accomplish?

THE PRESIDENT. I don't really know until I talk to him. The basic responsibility is now and has been and will be in the future on the shoulders of the parties directly involved. The two national leaders, President Sadat and Prime Minister Begin, obviously must continue their efforts. My independent report from both of them is that they are determined to do so. There is another negotiating session scheduled later this year between Sol Linowitz, representing me, and the representatives of President Sadat and Prime Minister Begin. I presume that will go forward. I'll urge them to do so. That was supposed to be a pre-summit conference.

If that session is constructive, there would be a possibility—unlikely possibility that a summit would take place prior to inauguration. I doubt that that would be the case. But if I inform Governor Reagan before he becomes President that this is the situation so far and that Prime Minister Begin and President Sadat both would like to have a meeting with him subsequently, it would be his judgment about whether he thought it was advisable. But I hope that the Camp David process will be kept intact to a major degree and don't know precisely what Governor Reagan's position will be on that.

Q. So there could be a summit.

POSSIBILITY OF A TAX CUT

Q. Mr. President, could you go along with a tax cut this year——

THE PRESIDENT. No.

Q. ——if the Congress passed it?

THE PRESIDENT. No.

Q. You would veto those bills?

THE PRESIDENT. I don't think that'll be necessary. The Senate Democratic Caucus today decided that they didn't think it would be advisable. I've talked to the Speaker and to Majority Leader Wright and to Danny Rostenkowski and others in the House. They agree that it would not be advisable.

The Congress has all it can handle with the present, very heavily loaded agenda. I think for them to take on the new task of trying to hammer out a major tax cut would be inappropriate, and I would do everything I could to discourage it.

THE PRESIDENTIAL TRANSITION

Q. Mr. President, Mr. Meese apparently gave you—or presented your administration with a list of things that Governor Reagan does not want done between now and inauguration. Could you tell us in your own words what it is that you want to see accomplished between now and inauguration and what you're willing to pass on right now and leave to his administration?

THE PRESIDENT. That will have to be a judgment made by me. Obviously, we'll try to accommodate Governor Reagan as much as we can, but the ultimate judgment about what I do and what I don't do will have to be made by me unilaterally. We'll have a meeting tomorrow morning with the Democratic congressional leadership—a routine meeting that's been scheduled for a long time— to go down the list of agenda items to see which are the ones that have a chance for adequate support to pass and which ones are a high enough priority to pass. I don't want to start making a list, because I'm afraid that if I fail to name something, people might think I deliberately excluded it. But obviously the Alaska lands bill, the appropriations bills, the reconciliation legislation, the second budget resolution— those kind of things are highly valuable to the Nation and also have a good chance to pass and, I think, have an adequate degree of bipartisan support.

The youth employment bill, to me, is very important. The superfund is another item on which there might be a bipartisan agreement. That still has to be explored. But obviously, executive decisions would have to be made by me until the day I go out of office, and then the next day would be made by Governor Reagan.

On long-term things—national health insurance, welfare reform—these are obviously matters that would have to wait for the subsequent administration. So I'll just have to make a judgment on individual items—what to pursue and what not to pursue.

Q. Mr. President, the Reagan transition people say they've identified 6 percent of the Federal budget that they say amounts to waste and fillout and so forth that could conceivably be eliminated.

Does that surprise you that they've been able to identify such a large percentage of——

THE PRESIDENT. You ask—you made one predication that they said they had identified that, and your second predication was that they had identified that. They're not necessarily the same. It's easy—[*laughter*]—it's easy to say that you can eliminate 6 percent, but you can't eliminate 6 percent of veterans' benefits, retirement benefits, disability benefits; you can't eliminate 6 percent of social security payments; you can't eliminate 6 percent of the commitment of our Nation to defense capability. It's easier to say 6 percent, but there are some parts in there that can't be cut. So if you talk about 6 percent of the total, you're talking about 35 or 40 percent of things that can be cut, and that's an extraordinary reduction in items like Headstart or food stamps or special programs for the elderly like Meals on Wheels. You know, when you leave out defense and entitlement programs, you've really got only about 25 or 30 percent left. So I would doubt the accuracy of that figure.

I notice that the second budget resolution from the House committee does encompass a 2-percent reduction. I think that's within the realm of feasibility. Whether it's practical, I don't know. But I think a 6-percent across-the-board cut would be very, very excessive.

PRESIDENT'S FUTURE PLANS

Q. Mr. President, could you be any more specific about your own plans for the future?

THE PRESIDENT. Yes, I'd be glad to. I'm going to go out of office on Inauguration Day. I intend to go to Plains that day, and I'll be living in Plains for the foreseeable future, certainly a number of months, maybe longer. I'll set up a transition office in Georgia, likely in Atlanta.

And as you know, the transition time runs either for 6 months, or some of the transition funds can be expended up to the end of the fiscal year, which is the 30th of September.

And then following that, I'll be living the life of a former President under routine budgetary funding. I'll be responsible for my documents and records, which belong to a President, and I'll transfer those around Inauguration Day—some ahead of time, some afterwards—down to an appropriate place in Georgia. They'll have to be catalogued, filed. I guess over the period of months ahead, I'll probably do some writing. I intend to play a fairly low profile role during the foreseeable months ahead, and we'll probably go back and forth between Plains and Atlanta during that period. That's basically what I have in mind.

THE DEMOCRATIC PARTY

Q. Would you like to play a role, Mr. President, would you like to play any kind of a serious role in sort of the rebuilding of the Democratic Party after——

THE PRESIDENT. Well, eventually. I think it's obvious that the Democratic Party needs to be strengthened. I don't think it matters who the identity of the chairman might be, as far as any candidates are concerned. I've seen a lot of speculation about Vice President Mondale and Senator Kennedy and John Glenn and others. I think the identity of the next chairman should be decided, hopefully, on a consensus basis. There will be two major roles to play. One is to raise funds, to get the Democratic Party on a sound financial base—we've made a lot of progress on that since I've been in office—and secondly, to organize the party with identifying candidates to support for Congress, Governor, and so forth, and re-

pairing the damage that's been caused by this recent defeat.

My own role would be not a minority party critic. I'd like to play a constructive role. I'll reserve the right to speak out on issues that are important to me that I've espoused so far, but I intend to be very helpful to the new President when he's in office.

Q. Do you see yourself as the leader of the Democratic Party?

THE PRESIDENT. No, not necessarily.

Q. Well, then, as the titular head?

THE PRESIDENT. Well, it depends.

THE PRESIDENT'S FUTURE PLANS

Q. Some people say that you might run for Governor of Georgia again.

THE PRESIDENT. No way. [*Laughter*]

Q. You say it depends, sir. Could you expand on that?

THE PRESIDENT. Well, I'm interested in environment. I'm interested in consumers. I'm interested in the rights of minorities, human rights. I'm interested in problems concerning employment, working families. I'm interested in matters that relate to women's rights and control of nuclear weapons. On matters of that kind, I reserve the right to speak out as forcefully as I consider it to be appropriate.

But as far as being the leader of the Democratic Party or trying to organize the party structure or trying to decide who is or who is not the chairman of the party and mounting a nationwide campaign, I don't intend to do that.

Q. Would you like to run for President again?

THE PRESIDENT. No, I don't have any desire to do that, along that line at all.

ADMINISTRATION'S ACHIEVEMENTS

Q. Mr. President, looking back, now, do you see any obvious mistakes of the last

2 months which have led to the events of now?

THE PRESIDENT. Well, I obviously didn't get enough votes. [*Laughter*]

No, I don't think I want to comment on the reasons for the election defeat. That's a counterproductive effort, when you lost like I did, to try to justify it. I think that it's good now for the press to engage itself in an analysis of the election results and the reasons for them and the result of them. I think that we'll go through a phase of analyzing what the next administration will bring to the country, which is appropriate. I'll try to be constructive in my role with the transition and also with the new administration's goals when I do share them. And most of the goals, obviously, I do share—peace and prosperity and controlling inflation, that sort of thing.

And then eventually, I think history will judge me and my own administration. There are obviously a lot of very difficult issues which we addressed. One of the, I guess anomalies, is that the things on which I worked hardest were the ones that were politically counterproductive. My most serious political challenge ever was the ratification of the Panama Canal treaty. I think it was necessary, it was important, it was a chore, a job that other Presidents had passed on to their successors. I decided to address it. We did it successfully by the narrowest of margins. It was obviously a very costly political thing to do.

And I think some of our policies on the Third World nations, opening up Africa or maybe the China decision, even the Mideast thing caused me very serious political problems with certain constituency groups. But dealing with the energy problem, there's no way to make friends or get votes that way. I'm not saying this in a complaining sense, but I think the issues

that we addressed finally, most of them that were most difficult were not politically advantageous. So I believe that it will just have to be a long historical analysis of what we did well and didn't do well.

VICE PRESIDENT MONDALE

Q. [*Inaudible*]—to encourage Fritz Mondale to start laying the groundwork for a race in '84?

THE PRESIDENT. No, I don't want to encourage or discourage him. I could not possibly think higher of Fritz Mondale than I do. No President has ever been blessed, as I have, with a better Vice President. Fritz and I are actually almost as close as brothers. We share the intimacies of the responsibilities officially, politically. Our families are close. We've never had a serious disagreement, although Fritz has been absolutely free to disagree with me on policy and to put his views forward strongly. As far as I know, our staffs have never had a disagreement that was serious. So, I have the highest regard for Fritz, but as far as trying to influence what he does in the future, I will not do that.

He's coming back from vacation Thursday night. I'll be meeting with him Friday morning, but the purpose of the meeting will not be for me to determine his political future.

TIMING OF PRESIDENT'S CONCESSION SPEECH

Q. Mr. President, in light of some of the criticism after your concession statement coming before the polls closed, do you have any other feelings today as to whether or not you should have delayed your concession until after all the polls were closed?

THE PRESIDENT. Well, we discussed that—Jody and I and others—I think it was all right. I don't think anybody who observed the political scene at 9:30 or whenever it was, at 9, 10 o'clock when I conceded, was in doubt about the outcome of the election and——

Q. There have been some reports of people leaving the polling lines as soon as they heard that you were going to concede.

THE PRESIDENT. I don't believe it was because I conceded. They may have left the polls because they didn't want to vote in the congressional race or the Senate race or the Governor's race and did want to vote for or against me. But obviously, to me, it was obvious that I had lost the election. I certainly would not have conceded otherwise. I don't think it was a mistake.

THE PRESIDENT'S PAPERS

Q. What will happen to your papers, Mr. President, after you finish?

THE PRESIDENT. They'll be transferred to Georgia, and they'll be placed in a library. I will help organize the building of a library to store both mementos of my term in office and also——

Q. Where would they likely be?

THE PRESIDENT. I don't know for sure. At this time, I would say the more likely place would be Atlanta, but I'll have to consult with other people. But it will be in Georgia for sure. And I'd say—Atlanta has 25 or 30 colleges, and I'd like for it to be so that the papers—the papers are unbelievably voluminous. And under the present law and even the new law that'll go into effect with the next term, those papers are the property of the President.

My desire is to deed a substantial portion of the papers, at least, to the United States Government, so that I don't derive any financial benefit from that part of it. But then I will retain custody of them, depending on the sensitivity of the individual paper, for a certain period of time.

I've really not gone through that, although my lawyers and other advisers are now preparing briefings for me so I'll understand it. But the papers will be moved down in trailer trucks to Georgia, deposited in a library, and be available under restrictions that I described for scholars and others to peruse.

THE PRESIDENTIAL TRANSITION

Q. Mr. President, through meetings next week with Governor Reagan, do you plan to consult with him on approaches to such things as the hostage issue, the Palestinian autonomy talks, so that it can be somewhat of a joint approach?

THE PRESIDENT. Yes. I'm not trying to put any responsibility on him. I will inform him; I think that's a better word than consult.

We have kept Governor Reagan informed to the limit of what he desired up till now. Sometimes he designates someone on his staff to be briefed. Sometimes he gets a briefing in person. Sometimes George Bush gets a briefing. But we have made every attempt, I think successfully, to accommodate him on that. But he and I had a clear understanding that—on election night—that until the oath of office was taken by him, that I would have the full responsibility and authority of the Presidency, and that any information given to him would be for that purpose only and not to involve him in the decisionmaking process itself.

I have sent word to him and told him that if he had any ideas or thoughts or advice, that I would be glad to receive those, but that I'd have to retain full control of the Government and its authority.

Q. Have you received any?

THE PRESIDENT. Well, indirectly. I think Mr. Meese and Watson have a good working relationship, and I think they have, for instance, consulted on some items in the Congress that might be pursued aggressively or let die for this term. There will be consultations concerning some appointments that I have made that have not yet been confirmed. I think, for instance, that Congress, the Senate has probably confirmed 250 judges that I've appointed since I've been in office. I think there are probably less than 20 still up there. Whether the Senate leadership will go ahead with those, I don't know. But that's kind of out of my hands and out of Governor Reagan's hands.

So far as I know, so far the relationship has been very good and constructive, with my keeping the authority and responsibility and his being informed. But I will certainly keep him informed, as we do daily, on the hostage question. And after I meet with Prime Minister Begin, I'll probably communicate in some way with President Sadat, and then give Governor Reagan a report on the status of their desires to proceed with any negotiations.

DEMOCRATIC NATIONAL COMMITTEE CHAIRMAN

Q. Mr. President, should John White step down as DNC chairman?

THE PRESIDENT. No, I think John ought to be considered along with others. I would like to talk to him about his desires first. My understanding is that John wants to have an orderly transition and wants to avoid any breach or divisiveness in the party, because of the selection of the next chairman. That's my desire. I don't have any candidates, but I'll add my voice and influence, if necessary, just to create harmony and get a chairman that can do the role that I described earlier.

AMERICAN HOSTAGES IN IRAN

Q. Mr. President, how hopeful are you on the Iranian situation?

THE PRESIDENT. It's hard to say.

Q. Do you have any timetable in mind?

THE PRESIDENT. No. I've had a timetable in mind for more than a year now, and it never has been reached. I can't predict.

THE PRESIDENTIAL TRANSITION

Q. Mr. President, as an outgoing—in the interest of the Nation, I'm wondering, as an outgoing President to an incoming President, can you share with us a thought, a measure of guidance, a measure of advice that you would offer your successor?

THE PRESIDENT. I had a lot more advice when I came in than I do going out. [*Laughter*]

Q. Seriously.

THE PRESIDENT. No, I think I won't answer that. When I meet with him privately, I'll have some things to talk with him about—not advice on his conduct, but things that I learned the hard way. I know that when I first met with President Ford, he said the most difficult task he had was the foreign aid bills in the Congress—getting them passed in an acceptable form. It's obviously of great advantage to our country to have an adequate foreign aid program, and that's one of the items on which I might comment to Governor Reagan. That's one of the remaining items on the agenda, but, no, I think I'll avoid your question of what kind of advice I'd give him.

LIBERALISM AND CONSERVATISM

Q. Mr. President, what do you think about this rising tide of conservatism in the country? Where do you think the country is going to be 4 years from now?

THE PRESIDENT. I don't know. It's hard to—it's hard for me to answer that question, because you have to define the issue. There's a duality of responsibility, at least a duality of responsibility that a President has. One is a fiscal responsibility and that's one aspect of liberalism and conservatism. I've considered myself to be conservative or cautious or responsible fiscally. I noticed in a governmental report that was covered in the paper this morning, newspaper, that for the first time in 50 years, under my administration, the Government expenditures per capita have turned downward. We've had a very restrained Government expenditure since I've been in office, in real dollars. We now have 55,000 fewer full-time employees in Government than we did when I came in office. We have had a hiring freeze on constantly since last March. We'll continue it on until the end of this term. And that is a very tight restraint.

We've tried to deal with inflation as best we could, which is a part of the other aspect of a President's responsibility, and that's to be concerned or compassionate about those who do need special consideration, to have a chance to have a constructive and productive life, and to overcome handicaps of different kinds—the elderly, women, the poor, the afflicted, the minority groups. Those kinds of people who just want to be self-supportive and want to have an element of human decency and self-respect sometimes need special consideration from the Government. So there, I guess you could encompass that under the word "concern" or "compassion."

So, fiscal responsibility on the one hand and concern or compassion on the other is something that is a duality. In many cases they meld; sometimes they're in conflict. In my own highly biased judgment, we have managed those two reasonably well. And I hope in the wave of conservatism, to use your word, that the concern or compassionate element is not lost in the future. There are obviously some ancillary questions concerning consumers' rights and concerning the quality of the environment and concerning arms control and concerning human rights. Is that liberal or conservative? Who knows? I don't know how to characterize it, but those are the kinds of issues that can't be blanketed under a single word or a single simplistic phrase or a single simplistic philosophy.

I've been a very strong proponent of civil rights, of human rights, of arms control, of environmental quality, of the protection of the afflicted. At the same time, I think my record is almost unmatched in fiscal restraint or responsibility.

Q. Can you see the country getting away from that? This new Republican administration coming in and maybe not being as sensitive about civil rights, about human rights, about the poor, about the elderly, and about other social programs that may affect a lot of people in this country? That seems to be the platform they ran on.

THE PRESIDENT. I hope that's not going to be the case. But I think that was the clear indication during the campaign, that there was a distinction drawn there, obviously. You know some of the issues that were so cutting during the campaign. The grain embargo against the Soviet Union—I felt that it was a necessary action for me to take in order to exert maximum economic pressure on the Soviet Union after they invaded Afghanistan. I had to take the action just a few days before the Iowa caucus, when I genuinely believed it would cost me the election in

Iowa. And I still believe it would be a serious mistake for us to lift the grain embargo, which would be a reward to the Soviet Union above and beyond what the public generally knows.

It's been a very serious restraint on them. Also, there's a worldwide, a relative worldwide shortage of grain now, and to open up that additional market demand from the Soviet Union, of limited grain stocks, would be doubly inflationary. That's the kind of issue that we had to address during the campaign.

I felt that we needed a Department of Education, a Department of Energy. I think we ought to be very cautious about an inflationary tax cut. Those are issues—I'm not trying to resurrect them, but those were the kind of things that we had to deal with, and I think it would be difficult to characterize those individual items as conservative or liberal. Is it conservative to have a grain embargo against the Soviet Union, or liberal?

Q. Mr. President, do you agree with Senator McGovern that the so-called rightwing group had a disproportionate influence on the election results and that a group should be formed to combat their influence?

THE PRESIDENT. I think—that's not my approach to politics.

NATO

Q. One of the hallmarks of your administration that you liked to boast about most was the 3-percent increase in NATO spending that you managed to push through for some time. You thought it was vital and important. But now it appears that our chief European ally, the West Germans, are not going to come anywhere near that. You're going to meet Mr. Schmidt next week. Do you think Americans should be asked to pay the 3 percent if the Europeans won't pay the 3 percent themselves?

THE PRESIDENT. The Americans are the leaders in the free world. I don't say that minimizing the importance of our allies, but sometimes we have to take action more than or ahead of others. This was the case with the Soviet invasion of Afghanistan. It was the case with revitalizing NATO.

My hope is that the Germans, including Chancellor Schmidt, will keep their commitment to the 3-percent growth. It's the same with the other NATO Allies. All of them have not complied up until now. The Germans have. Harold Brown is pursuing this commitment with the NATO military leaders; I'll be pursuing it with Chancellor Schmidt. If our allies don't comply with their commitment, then I think we should go ahead and do our part independently, to maintain an adequate defense for ourselves and to be sure that we can meet our obligations to our allies.

We've got a special role to play in Southwest Asia in the Persian Gulf region. It's above and beyond what the European allies will join on an equal basis. And as you know, the Germans are restricted by their Constitution from activities outside Western Europe. But we've got our own responsibilities to bear, and this has been a constant problem for me. I'm not bemoaning that, but we've had to take action. If we move more forcefully, sometimes our European allies say we don't consult adequately or we don't act adequately in harmony. If we are more cautious in our actions, sometimes the Western allies say we're too timid. But in my judgment we've done what was right. We've consulted more than has been the case in the past in peacetime, and I've had a very good relationship, I think, with the Western European leaders.

In my judgment, those countries are blessed with outstanding leaders, and we've had a good and constructive progress made already. If we have problems now with their placement of the theater nuclear force weapons or with their meeting the 3-percent growth, that's a temporary setback. But I believe their public opinion will bring them along to comply.

GRAIN EMBARGO AGAINST THE SOVIET UNION

Q. Mr. President on the grain embargo: There are stories that Governor Reagan's advisers say that he may reconsider his position on that, and that a person ought not to be held to campaign promises when real time situations develop. You do agree with that?

THE PRESIDENT. I think the policy that I've maintained is a proper one. And if Governor Reagan, because of changing circumstances or changing awareness on his part, should comply with what I think is best for our country, I would be pleased.

Q. Should he keep his campaign promises or——

THE PRESIDENT. That's a judgment for him to make, Sam [Sam Donaldson, ABC News].

THE PRESIDENT'S MEMOIRS

Q. You said during the campaign that there were crises that nobody knew about because you handled them properly, and I'm wondering whether there are going to be any big surprises in your memoirs——

THE PRESIDENT. Well, I hope so. [*Laughter*]

Q. Buy the book. [*Laughter*]

THE PRESIDENT. Yes, buy the book. [*Laughter*]

Q. If you send us all free copies. [*Laughter*]

THE PRESIDENT. A lot of big surprises.

GRAIN EMBARGO AGAINST THE SOVIET UNION

Q. Do you think the grain embargo has really hurt the Russians?

THE PRESIDENT. Yes, ma'am. Yes, it certainly has. It would be good for Jody to get from the Secretary of Agriculture or from the CIA, an analysis of what has been caused in the Soviet economy by the American grain embargo. And you can analyze it yourself, take it or leave it, if you believe it to be accurate.

There's no doubt in my mind that it has hurt them severely. The Soviets have the lowest meat consumption of any of their satellite countries, lower than any of their satellite countries. They have had a sharply reduced ability to produce milk or meats of all kinds. They've cut back on their herd sizes. They have a very low grain harvest this year—20 or 30 million tons lower than they had anticipated. And the grain that they have bought from some sources, not us, in recent months, has been at a high price and in relatively small ships, which increases their difficulty of loading. I think this has been a very severe element in the Soviet economy, and I think they deserve it, because their invasion of Afghanistan was unforgiveable, unacceptable in international circles. And I think that they have to be shown that that kind of aggression is not profitable for them.

Maybe one more question.

THE PRESIDENT'S FUTURE PLANS

Q. Mr. President, can you tell us what your personal hopes are for this last 2 months in the office? Whether you have a couple of points that you want to get across either to the American people or even a wider audience? Whether you're going to do any traveling? I wonder, the human rights conference in Madrid, is that anything?

THE PRESIDENT. No. I don't intend to do any major traveling. I've got a lot of things to do to get ready to change my life and to transfer authority to Governor Reagan, and I'm responsible for an orderly transition, along with him.

That's going to be very time-consuming. I've already discovered that. In addition, we've got the Congress, to conclude the preparation of the 1982 budget, which is my responsibility and is a major undertaking at best. I'll try to put forward a budget on which I would be glad to govern if I were to be in office. I'm not going to try to embarrass Governor Reagan. It'll be a practical budget and a responsible budget. In addition to that, I have a lot of just routine expressions of thanks and appreciation to people that I'd like to pursue, including the press. And you're all invited to a Christmas party at the White House, and I'll be looking forward to seeing you there. So, I think the time will be very full.

Q. Mr. President, could you say just a word or two more about your future? Will you indeed write your memoirs?

THE PRESIDENT. Yes.

Q. Would you ever get back into business again?

THE PRESIDENT. You mean commercial business?

Q. In the commercial business——

THE PRESIDENT. No, I don't think so. I don't want to be bound on my oath, you know, because if my family is starving, I'll have to make some money for them. But I don't intend—I think it's inappropriate for an ex-President to be involved in the commercial world.

There may be some kinds of benevolent or nonprofit corporations in which I would let my influence and my ability be used, but not in a profit-making way.

But I intend to do some teaching, maybe, some lecturing. I'll make some speeches. I'll write my—I intend to write more than one book, as a matter of fact. And I'll try to husband, carefully, for future use, my documents and library materials, the mementos that would go into a museum-type presentation, hopefully in the same location. There's plenty to be done, but that would be about the limit of it.

Q. At one point——

THE PRESIDENT. I intend to become a good fly-fisherman—[*laughter*].

Q. No celebrity golf tournaments?

Q. Mr. President, at one point you told people in your church here in Washington that one of the things that you might do as a former President was to be a missionary abroad.

THE PRESIDENT. I never did tell anybody that. That was a misquote.

Q. That is not something that you——

THE PRESIDENT. I don't want to foreclose anything like that. It's a matter of—I might do some work for my church, or I might do some work for the Lion's Club in Plains, or I might work for other nonprofit groups or Boy Scouts or something like that. But no, I'm not trying to foreclose anything.

I think I've told you about all I know right now.

Q. Thank you very much.

Q. Does this count as a news conference? [*Laughter*]

THE PRESIDENT. I won't count it.

Q. There are no cameras, you see.

Q. Come back soon.

THE PRESIDENT. No cameras.

Q. Come back soon.

Q. Yes, every day.

THE PRESIDENT. Oh, really? I'll come back maybe again soon.

Q. You're much better than Jody.

THE PRESIDENT. I enjoyed it. You all are much nicer to Jody than you are to me in a news conference. [*Laughter*]

Q. Oh, you read the transcript. You know better than that.

NOTE: The question-and-answer session began at 3:52 p.m. in the Briefing Room at the White House. The transcript released by the White House includes Press Secretary Jody Powell's briefing for reporters which followed the President's departure.

Situation In Iran

Notice Extending the National Emergency. November 12, 1980

On November 14, 1979, by Executive Order No. 12170 I declared a national emergency to deal with the threat to the national security, foreign policy and economy of the United States constituted by the situation in Iran. Since that situation continues, the national emergency declared on November 14, 1979, must continue in effect after November 14, 1980. Therefore, pursuant to section 202(d) of the National Emergencies Act (50 U.S.C. Sec. 1622(d)) I am signing this notice of the continuance of the national emergency and causing this notice to be published in the FEDERAL REGISTER and transmitted to the Congress.

JIMMY CARTER

The White House,
   November 12, 1980.

[Filed with the Office of the Federal Register, 4:13 p.m., November 12, 1980]

United States-Egypt Convention on Taxation and Fiscal Evasion

Message to the Senate Transmitting the Convention.   November 12, 1980

To the Senate of the United States:

I transmit herewith, for Senate advice and consent to ratification, a Convention between the Government of the United States of America and the Government of the Arab Republic of Egypt for the avoidance of double taxation and the prevention of fiscal evasion with respect to taxes on income, (the Convention) signed at Cairo on August 24, 1980. I transmit also the report of the Department of State with respect to the Convention.

The Convention will replace the income tax convention with Egypt which was signed in 1975. I therefore, desire to withdraw from the Senate the following treaty, removing it from the Treaty Calendar:

Convention between the Government of the United States of America and the Arab Republic of Egypt for the avoidance of double taxation and the prevention of fiscal evasion with respect to taxes on income, signed at Washington on October 28, 1975 (Executive D, 94th Cong., 2d Sess.).

The Convention is similar to the United States model in major respects although different in form and pattern as the model was published after the negotiations of the convention had begun. As in the model, business profits of a resident of one country may be taxed by the other only if such profits are attributable to a permanent establishment in the other country. Similarly, with respect to independent personal service income, an individual who is a resident of one State may be taxed by the other State only if certain tests are met. In the Convention, the time threshold is shorter than in the United States model, and, with respect to entertainers, the dollar threshold is lower.

Maximum rates of tax are established on a reciprocal basis for the taxation by the source country of dividends, interest, and royalties. In general, these maximum rates in the Convention exceed the rates specified in the United States model. The rates in the Convention are, however, consistent with those established in other

United States tax conventions with developing countries.

I recommend that the Senate give early and favorable consideration to the Convention.

JIMMY CARTER

The White House,
    November 12, 1980.

United States-Canada Convention on Taxes

Message to the Senate Transmitting the Convention. November 12, 1980

To the Senate of the United States:

I transmit herewith, for Senate advice and consent to ratification, a Convention between the United States of America and Canada with respect to Taxes on Income and Capital (the Convention), signed at Washington on September 26, 1980, and a related exchange of notes for the information of the Senate. I also transmit the report of the Department of State with respect to the Convention.

The Convention will replace the existing tax convention with Canada, signed in 1942, as amended by supplementary conventions signed in 1950, 1956 and 1966. It is based, in general, on the United States and OECD model conventions but deviates from the models in a number of important respects in order to take account of particular features of Canadian law and its interaction with United States law, the unique economic relationship between the United States and Canada, and the provisions of the existing convention.

As in the existing convention, the new Convention provides that the business profits of a resident of one Contracting State will not be subject to tax by the other State except to the extent that they are attributable to a permanent establishment which the resident has in the other State. The definition of a permanent establishment in the Convention is more comprehensive than that in the existing convention and is very similar to the definition in the United States model.

The Convention establishes maximum reciprocal rates of withholding at source for dividends, interest, and royalties. Although the rates exceed those in the United States model for several types of income, there are a number of significant reductions in withholding rates in comparison with the existing convention.

I recommend that the Senate give early and favorable consideration to the Convention and give advice and consent to its ratification.

JIMMY CARTER

The White House,
    November 12, 1980.

Convention on the Elimination of All Forms of Discrimination Against Women

Message to the Senate Transmitting the Convention. November 12, 1980

To the Senate of the United States:

With a view to receiving the advice and consent of the Senate to ratification (subject to certain qualifications and possibly to appropriate implementing legislation), I transmit herewith a copy of the Convention on the Elimination of All Forms of Discrimination against Women. The Convention was adopted by the United Nations General Assembly on December 18, 1979 and signed on behalf of the United States of America on July 17, 1980. The report of the Department of State with respect to the Convention is also transmitted for the information of the Senate.

Adoption of this Convention by the General Assembly at the conclusion of its

34th Session in December, 1979, was the culmination of a negotiating process that lasted several years. Throughout this process, the United States was an active participant and a vigorous supporter of a comprehensive and effective international instrument to achieve the elimination of discrimination against women. Although certain earlier human rights treaties relate to the rights of women, none of these previous instruments attempted to deal with women's rights in as comprehensive a manner as this Convention. The wide scope of the Convention is particularly noteworthy and commendable in that it calls upon States Parties to take "all appropriate measures" to eliminate discrimination against women in such diverse fields of human endeavor as politics, law, employment, education, health care, commercial transactions, and domestic relations. Moreover, the Convention establishes a Committee on the Elimination of Discrimination against Women to review periodically the progress being made by States Parties.

Ratification of the Convention on the Political Rights of Women in 1976 was a recent express affirmation by the Executive and Legislative branches of the U.S. Government that human rights in general and women's rights in particular are matters of legitimate concern to the international community and are not subjects with exclusively domestic ramifications. U.S. ratification of the Convention at hand, the newest of the international human rights instruments, would be consistent with this affirmation and would make clear at home and abroad the commitment of the United States to eliminate discrimination against women.

The great majority of the substantive provisions of the Convention are consistent with the letter and spirit of the United States Constitution and existing laws.

However, certain provisions of the Convention raise questions of conformity to current United States law. Nevertheless, the Departments of State and Justice and other interested agencies of the Federal Government concur in the judgment that, with the adoption of certain qualifications and, possibly, appropriate implementing legislation, there are no constitutional or other legal obstacles to United States ratification. The report of the Department of State on the Convention and an attached legal memorandum describe the provisions of the Convention and identify those areas of concern that will require further discussion and treatment.

This Convention is a significant new element in the development of the international law of human rights. By giving its advice and consent to ratification of the Convention, the Senate will confirm our country's traditional commitment to the promotion and protection of human rights and will enhance our nation's ability to achieve progress throughout the world. I hope that all States will become Parties to the Convention, and that it will be applied universally. I recommend that the Senate give early and favorable consideration to this Convention.

JIMMY CARTER

The White House,
    November 12, 1980.

Interim Convention on Conservation of North Pacific Fur Seals

Message to the Senate Transmitting a Protocol. November 12, 1980

To the Senate of the United States:

I am pleased to transmit the Protocol Amending the Interim Convention on

Conservation of North Pacific Fur Seals between the United States, Canada, Japan, and the Soviet Union, signed in Washington on October 9, 1980.

The Interim Convention was signed in 1957; it replaced an earlier convention on North Pacific fur seals dating back to 1911. Under the two conventions, the herds of fur seals have been protected and managed, and the population has increased from 300,000 animals to approximately 1.7 million. The Interim Convention was extended in 1936 and 1969. A 1976 Protocol further extended the Convention and amended it in order to provide greater protection for fur seals. This Protocol extends the Interim Convention for an additional four years, until 1984. It also reflects the four signatory nations' recognition of the extensions of fisheries jurisdictions which have occurred since the entry into force of the 1976 Protocol.

I transmit also for the information of the Senate the report of the Department of State with respect to the Protocol.

I urge the Senate to act favorably at an early date on this Protocol.

JIMMY CARTER

The White House,
November 12, 1980.

Wright Brothers Day, 1980

Proclamation 4802.   November 12, 1980

By the President of the United States of America

A Proclamation

Seventy-seven years ago on December 17, at Kitty Hawk, North Carolina, the Wright Brothers launched man into the age of powered flight. Though their historic first flight lasted but 12 seconds, inventors Orville and Wilbur Wright accomplished what mankind had dreamed of for centuries.

The development of the airplane is one of the most remarkable achievements of the Twentieth Century. Because of it, barriers of time and distance have lost much of their social and political significance to the world family of nations.

In the three generations since that historic flight in 1903, aviation has grown to become one of America's greatest enterprises; one of its largest employers; a fundamental ingredient in the national economy; a mighty deterrent against aggression and a prime defender of peace. Our air transportation system is the greatest in the world and the primary public carrier in the United States. Moreover, some eighty-five percent of the aircraft in use throughout the world are of United States manufacture, and the free world's seven largest airlines are United States flag carriers.

To commemorate the historic achievement of the Wright Brothers, the Congress, by joint resolution of December 17, 1963 (77 Stat. 402; 36 U.S.C. 169), designated the seventeenth day of December of each year as Wright Brothers Day and requested the President to issue annually a proclamation inviting the people of the United States to observe that day with appropriate ceremonies and activities.

NOW, THEREFORE, I, JIMMY CARTER, President of the United States of America, do hereby call upon the people of this Nation, and their local and national government officials, to observe Wright Brothers Day on December 17, 1980, both to perpetuate the memory of the Wright Brothers' signal achievement and to stimulate American pride in the furtherance of this Nation's aeronautical progress.

IN WITNESS WHEREOF, I have hereunto set my hand this twelfth day of November in the year of our Lord nineteen hundred and eighty, and of the Independence of the United States of America the two hundred and fifth.

JIMMY CARTER

[Filed with the Office of the Federal Register, 10:50 a.m., November 13, 1980]

Ambassador at Large

Exchange of Letters on the Resignation of Gerard C. Smith.   November 10, 1980

To Gerry Smith

I reluctantly accept your resignation as my Ambassador at Large, United States Special Representative for Non-Proliferation Matters and Special Representative to the International Atomic Energy Agency.

As you know, one of my major objectives as President has been to exert the influence of the United States to prevent the proliferation of nuclear weapons. You have rendered an enormous service to this worthy cause.

This is the latest—and I hope not the last—of your many contributions to the public interest as one of the nation's true citizen-statesmen. As our Ambassador for the successful SALT I negotiations, as the Director of the State Department's Policy Planning Staff and, in your younger days, at the Atomic Energy Commission, you had already made your place in our modern history. As the first Chairman of the Trilateral Commission, where you were one of my early mentors in foreign policy, you forged one of the most valuable private links we have to bring the leaders of the free world together.

I regret your departure from public service. I am consoled that we will remain friends and colleagues.

Sincerely,

JIMMY CARTER

[The Honorable Gerard C. Smith, Ambassador at Large, Department of State, Washington, D.C. 20520]

> *Gerry, you have my greatest admiration and appreciation. It is personally gratifying to me that you & I share common goals in arms control—*
>
> *J*

October 20, 1980

Dear Mr. President:

When I earlier advised you of my wish to return to private life, you asked me to remain in your Administration for a further period. I would now like to offer my resignation to be effective November 4. It has been a privilege and a great experience to wrestle with the grave problems of non-proliferation under your inspiring leadership. Historians will, I think, find you made a large contribution to world security in forcing attention on the central danger of the cancerous spread of nuclear explosives. I regret not having been able to do more to help reduce this danger.

If I can be of any use to you as a private citizen, I hope you will call on me.

With respect and admiration and best wishes for the years to come.

Respectfully,

GERRY
Gerard   Smith

[The President, The White House, Washington, D.C.]

NOTE: The texts of the letters were released on November 13.

Alaska Lands Conservation Bill

Statement on House Approval of the Legislation.   November 13, 1980

I am pleased and gratified with the approval yesterday by the House of Representatives of the Alaska National Interest Lands Conservation Act. Both Houses of Congress have now endorsed the greatest land conservation legislation of the century, thus assuring that the "crown jewels" of the Alaskan natural wonders are afforded protection. It is a victory in the long struggle to resolve this issue and is truly an historic event in our Nation's history. The passage of a balanced Alaska lands bill has been my highest environmental priority since the beginning of my administration, and the bill approved yesterday closely resembles the proposals I sent to the Congress more than 3 years ago.

At stake in this debate over Alaskan lands has been the fate of millions of acres of irreplaceable natural wonders, unique wildlife populations, continuation of native cultures, and the opportunity to ensure that future generations of Americans will be able to experience and benefit from these nationally significant resources. And, beyond the protection of Alaskan lands, has been the need to provide for the development of the economic and energy potential that is available in Alaska and that is important to this Nation's future.

Today's action designates more than 43 million acres of national park system lands, 54 million acres of national wildlife refuges, and classifies a total of 56 million acres of Federal lands as wilderness. At the same time, the bill provides for development of Alaska's oil, gas, mineral, and timber resources while conveying to the State and native communities lands of interest to them. The bill produces a balance between protection and development that will help keep our Nation both energy strong and environmentally rich.

I want to commend the Congress, particularly Senator Paul Tsongas and Congressman Mo Udall, and all those associated with the Alaska lands question, for their hard work and tireless devotion over the last 2 years to the passage of this bill. All Americans can be proud of this achievement.

Meeting With Prime Minister Menahem Begin of Israel

Remarks Following the Meeting. November 13, 1980

THE PRESIDENT. Well, to continue a long and very fruitful series of meetings between myself and Prime Minister Begin, we've had a chance this morning to review the progress that has been made, both in our bilateral relationships in bringing peace to the Middle East. This has been one of the most difficult, time-consuming, but one of the most gratifying experiences that I've had as President.

In my judgment there is a general recognition in our two countries and, indeed, around the world, of the close interrelationship between our two nations that is unshakable. It's predicated not on the identity of particular leaders, but on the strong feelings shared among the people of the two countries. Also, in our Nation I think there has been a greatly enhanced realization of the strategic value to our country of a strong and a peaceful and a democratic nation in Israel in a troubled region of the Middle East. Internationally, also, the end of 30 or 32 years of war between Israel and Egypt has been a very gratifying development.

We have assessed this morning the prospects for future progress. Prime Minister Begin and I have shared the reminder to ourselves and, hopefully, to expand to the world that the Camp David accords and the peace treaty between Israel and Egypt are solemn documents, committed on the honor of our Nation, on a permanent basis, signed by the leaders of the three nations with ourselves as witnesses, and we consider these to be permanently binding on us as a prospect for peace unfolds in the future. We also are well aware that there is no viable alternative extant to the continuation of the Camp David peace talks, and we are committed to that prospect and to that process.

There is no doubt that there will be delays in the future and frustrations, problems to be faced. I think the extreme political and personal courage exhibited by Prime Minister Begin and by President Sadat has been the foundation of the progress that we have made, and I'm deeply grateful to Prime Minister Begin for that exhibition of leadership on his part.

We have a permanent commitment to the peace and security of Israel. The ties that bind our two nations together are very strong, and I'm doubly grateful for the contributions that Prime Minister Begin has made to this process and to this achievement.

I'd like to ask Prime Minister Begin to comment briefly if he would, expressing, again, my sincere gratitude to him and on behalf of the American people my gratitude and my commitment to the further enhancement of the relationships that exist between our two countries, which are already very strong and mutually beneficial.

Prime Minister Begin?

THE PRIME MINISTER. Thank you, Mr. President.

I am very grateful to the President for his invitation to come and meet with him in the White House, although my visit to the United States this time is of a private character. We had a friendly discussion, as always, and may I share with you my personal feeling this time.

I am deeply impressed by this shining example of a true democrat given by the President. He proved what is the beauty of democracy, and how he took the deci-

sion by his free people, the citizens of the United States—I am still under the impression of this gracious acceptance of the decision of the American people. And it will be an example not only for future generations in this country but also for many other nations.

At the same time as I cabled to the President after the election I expressed to him on behalf of the people and Government of Israel our gratitude for all he has done during the tenure to strengthen and fortify the security of Israel and his incessant efforts to bring about peace between Israel and its Arab neighbors, which were crowned by the Camp David agreement and the peace treaty between Israel and Egypt, a turning point in the annals of the Middle East.

Now, both the President and I share the same view that the Camp David agreement is a binding treaty which should be carried out. We believe that it is a commitment, a sacred trust. We found a way to make peace between the two countries, Egypt and Israel. We have to find a way to bring into realization the agreement on the full autonomy for the Palestinian Arabs in Judea, Samaria, and the Gaza district. It took some time. It may take some time. We have to be patient, because it's an historic conflict; it didn't start yesterday; it may not finish tomorrow. We made great progress; we shall make it also in the future. And therefore in this direction we shall continue our efforts, namely to be faithful to what we achieved, written, and signed at Camp David and carry out the commitments all the three countries took upon themselves in accordance with that international treaty.

Thank you, ladies and gentlemen. Thank you, Mr. President.

THE PRESIDENT. Fine. Thank you.

Have a good visit in our country. Call

me anytime I can be of help, particularly the next 2 months.

NOTE: The President spoke at 12:07 p.m. on the South Grounds of the White House.

Convention on Higher Education

Message to the Senate Transmitting the Convention. November 13, 1980

To the Senate of the United States:

With a view to receiving the advice and consent of the Senate to ratification, I transmit herewith a copy of the Convention on the Recognition of Studies, Diplomas and Degrees Concerning Higher Education in the States Belonging to the Europe Region.

This instrument was adopted on December 21, 1979 by the International Conference of States for Adoption of the Convention convened by the United Nations Educational, Scientific and Cultural Organization (UNESCO), and signed on behalf of the United States on December 21, 1979. I also transmit, for the information of the Senate, the report of the Department of State on the Convention.

The Convention is open for signature and ratification only by States of UNESCO's Europe Region (which includes the United States), as well as the Holy See. Other States which are members of the United Nations, of one of its Specialized Agencies or of the International Atomic Energy Agency, or which are Parties to the Statute of the International Court of Justice may be authorized to accede to the Convention by a two-thirds vote of an *ad hoc* committee comprised of at least twenty Contracting States from the Europe Region of UNESCO.

The United States participated actively and effectively in the negotiation of this Convention to ensure that its provisions are compatible with the Constitution, laws, and policies of the United States and do not infringe on the powers and responsibilities of local governmental and nongovernmental educational or professional authorities. Thus, while promoting the objectives of the Final Act of the Helsinki Conference to facilitate the recognition of academic credentials and to improve the mobility of students, teachers and scholars, the Convention acknowledges the pluralistic, decentralized and frequently nongovernmental nature of the decision-making process pertaining to education and entry into the practice of professions in the United States. The Convention establishes an implementation mechanism to achieve international and domestic cooperation and coordination in carrying out its terms.

The report of the Department of State summarizes the Convention's provisions and concludes that no reservations, understandings or declarations are necessary.

By giving its advice and consent to ratification of this Convention, the Senate will advance the cause of higher education within and among the States Parties to the Convention. I recommend that the Senate give prompt consideration to the Convention and advise and consent to its ratification.

JIMMY CARTER

The White House,
November 13, 1980.

Employment and Training Programs

Message to the Congress Transmitting a Report. November 13, 1980

To the Congress of the United States:

I am transmitting to you the 18th annual report on employment and occupational requirements, resources, uses, and training, as required by section 127(a) of the Comprehensive Employment and Training Act (CETA) of 1973, as amended. This report features a discussion of the serious unemployment problems experienced by many youth today, especially minority teenagers, and summarizes the Administration's proposals for a youth education, training, and employment initiative for the 1980's.

Also included in this volume are a report on services for veterans, as required by the Vietnam Era Veterans' Readjustment Assistance Act; a report from the Secretary of Health and Human Services on cooperative program linkages with CETA programs, as required by section 127(b) of the 1978 CETA Amendments; a review of recently completed research and evaluation findings concerning employment and training programs, as required by section 313 (d) and (e) of CETA; a number of additional reports responding to requirements in the amended CETA and the Full Employment and Balanced Growth Act of 1978; and a statistical appendix, containing information about the labor force and employment and training programs.

JIMMY CARTER

The White House,
November 13, 1980.

NOTE: The report is entitled "Employment and Training Report of the President—Transmitted to the Congress 1980" (Government Printing Office, 393 pages).

Regulatory Commission as required by Section 307(c) of the Energy Reorganization Act of 1974. This report covers the Commission's activities from October 1, 1978 to September 30, 1979, and also briefly describes additional actions taken later that year and in 1980.

This report highlights the March 1979 incident at Three Mile Island and details the Nuclear Regulatory Commission's response to the accident—and its shortcomings in acting.

In October of 1979, the President's Commission on the Accident at Three Mile Island submitted recommendations for extensive reform and reorganization of the Nuclear Regulatory Commission, many of which were outlined in my response to this report on December 7, 1979. The Administration is currently implementing a Nuclear Regulatory Commission reorganization plan, that will improve the management of the agency and enhance its ability to respond to emergency situations. I have also established through Executive order the Nuclear Safety Oversight Committee which will help me make sure that the Nuclear Regulatory Commission and industry are taking the necessary steps to improve nuclear safety.

JIMMY CARTER

The White House,
November 13, 1980.

NOTE: The report is entitled "U.S. Nuclear Regulatory Commission, 1979 Annual Report" (Government Printing Office, 319 pages).

Nuclear Regulatory Commission

Message to the Congress Transmitting a Report. November 13, 1980

To the Congress of the United States:

I hereby transmit the Fifth Annual Report of the United States Nuclear

Federal Energy Conservation Programs

Message to the Congress Transmitting a Report. November 13, 1980

To the Congress of the United States:

I herewith transmit to the Congress the

third annual report required under Section 381(c) of the Energy Policy and Conservation Act (P.L. 94–163; 420 U.S.C. 6361(c)).

This report covers the energy conservation activities undertaken by Federal agencies during Fiscal Year 1979. These include the establishment of conservation policies and efficiency standards in Federal procurement and the development of a ten-year plan for energy conservation in Federally-owned or leased buildings. The report also describes programs for carrying out a public education program to encourage energy conservation and to promote vanpooling and carpooling arrangements.

JIMMY CARTER

The White House,
November 13, 1980.

NOTE: The 65-page report is entitled "Federal Energy Conservation Programs—Annual Report to the Congress from the President of the United States, Fiscal Year 1979."

National Climate Program

Message to the Congress Transmitting a 5-Year Plan. November 13, 1980

To the Congress of the United States:

I hereby transmit to Congress the Five-Year Plan for the National Climate Program as prepared by the Department of Commerce. This Five-Year Plan, to establish goals and priorities and to clarify various agencies' roles, is in accordance with section 5 of the National Climate Program Act of 1978.

The plan is divided in three major parts: introducing and developing of the Five-Year Plan, the projects and activities to be emphasized over the five years, and the administration of the program and future directives.

The National Climate Program is in-

tended to aid our Nation in understanding the climate processes and to make such information widely available.

JIMMY CARTER

The White House,
November 13, 1980.

NOTE: The plan is entitled "National Climate Program—Five-Year Plan, September 1980."

Thanksgiving Day, 1980

Proclamation 4803. November 13, 1980

By the President of the United States of America

A Proclamation

The greatest bounty of our Nation is the bounty of our heritage—our diversity as immigrants and descendants of immigrants, our common identity as Americans.

We have set aside one day a year to give thanks for all that we have. Yet Thanksgiving is more than just a day of celebration. It is also a commemoration—of the day America's earliest inhabitants sat down to table with European colonists.

That occasion was historic not only because it established a national holiday, but because it marked the start of a national tradition of cooperation, unity and tolerance.

Even in times of trial and frustration we have much to be thankful for, in our personal lives and in our Nation. As we pause on Thanksgiving to offer thanks to God, we should not forget that we also owe thanks to this country's forefathers who had the vision to join together in Thanksgiving, and who gave us so much of the vision of brotherhood that is ours today.

Now, THEREFORE, I, JIMMY CARTER, President of the United States of America, do proclaim Thursday, the 27th of November, 1980 as Thanksgiving Day. I call upon all the people of our Nation to give thanks on that day for the blessings Almighty God has bestowed upon us, and to join the fervent prayer of George Washington who as President asked God to ". . . impart all the blessings we possess, or ask for ourselves to the whole family of mankind."

IN WITNESS WHEREOF, I have hereunto set my hand this thirteenth day of November, in the year of our Lord nineteen hundred and eighty, and of the Independence of the United States of America the two hundred and fifth.

JIMMY CARTER

[Filed with the Office of the Federal Register, 10:25 a.m., November 14, 1980]

Bill of Rights Day, Human Rights Day and Week, 1980

Proclamation 4804. November 14, 1980

By the President of the United States of America

A Proclamation

On December 15, 1791, the Bill of Rights became part of the Constitution of the United States. On December 10, 1948, the United Nations General Assembly adopted the Universal Declaration of Human Rights. Marking these anniversaries together gives us an opportunity to renew our dedication both to our own liberties and to the promotion of human rights everywhere.

The Bill of Rights carries with it an implied responsibility for the governed as well as for the governing. No American citizen can rest satisfied until the Bill of Rights is a living reality for every person in the United States, irrespective of race, religion, sex, national or ethnic origin. We cannot simply rely on the decency of government or the alertness of an active free press. Each individual must shoulder his or her share of the responsibility for seeing that our freedoms will survive.

The Universal Declaration of Human Rights is the cornerstone of a developing international consensus on human rights. Through it, the members of the United Nations undertake to promote, respect and observe human rights and fundamental freedoms for all without discrimination. We must continuously monitor the progress of this effort and the records of governments around the world.

The promise of the Declaration is remote to all those who suffer summary executions and torture, acts of genocide, arbitrary arrest and imprisonment, banishment, internal exile, forced labor, and confinement for political cause. It is remote to the countless refugees who flee their lands in response to the elimination of their human rights. It is remote to those subjected to armed invasions or to military coups that destroy democratic processes. The Declaration will ring hollow to that segment of a population discriminated against by laws of *apartheid* or by restrictions on religious freedom. It will ring hollow to those threatened by violations of freedom of assembly, association, expression and movement, and by the suppression of trade unions.

The Declaration must also ring hollow to the members of the U.S. Embassy staff who have been held captive for more than a year by the Government of Iran.

The cause of human rights is embattled throughout the world. Recent events make it imperative that we, as Americans, stand firm in our insistence that the values embodied in the Bill of Rights, and contained in the Universal Declaration, be enjoyed by all.

I urge all Americans to support ratification of the Genocide Convention, the Convention on the Elimination of all Forms of Racial Discrimination, the Covenant on Economic, Social and Cultural Rights, the Covenant on Civil and Political Rights, and the American Convention on Human Rights. I renew my request to the Senate to give its advice and consent to these important treaties.

Now, THEREFORE, I, JIMMY CARTER, President of the United States of America, do hereby proclaim December 10, 1980, as Human Rights Day and December 15, 1980, as Bill of Rights Day, and call on all Americans to observe Human Rights Week beginning December 10, 1980. It should be a time set apart for the study of our own rights, so basic to the working of our society, and for a renewal of our efforts on behalf of the human rights of all peoples everywhere.

IN WITNESS WHEREOF, I have hereunto set my hand this fourteenth day of November, in the year of our Lord nineteen hundred and eighty, and of the Independence of the United States of America the two hundred and fifth.

JIMMY CARTER

[Filed with the Office of the Federal Register, 12:15 p.m., November 14, 1980]

World Weather Program Plan

Message to the Congress Transmitting the Plan. November 14, 1980

To the Congress of the United States:

I am pleased to transmit to Congress, in accordance with the Senate Concurrent Resolution 67 (1968), the World Weather Program Plan. The plan details the activities of Federal agencies in FY 1980 and 1981 toward developing improved world-wide weather observations and services and the United States effort to conduct a comprehensive program of research to further the development of the World Weather Program.

Our ability to forecast the weather and understand the dynamics of climate is an important aspect of developing and executing effective policies in many areas of national endeavor. Events over the last year have demonstrated how interwoven are our national goals with those of other countries. This is essentially true with respect to international meteorology. The World Weather Program was formulated so that the United States could join with other countries to establish goals to better understand and forecast the global weather. The sharing of resources data and ideas to attain these goals is accomplished through the Global Atmospheric Research Programs sponsored by the World Meteorological Organization and the International Council of Scientific Unions and the operation of the World Weather Watch.

I commend to your attention and review this important plan.

JIMMY CARTER

The White House,
November 14, 1980.

NOTE: The plan is entitled "World Weather Program—Plan for Fiscal Years 1980 and 1981" (Government Printing Office, 48 pages).

Digest of Other White House Announcements

The following listing includes the President's public schedule and other items of general interest announced by the White House Press Office and not included elsewhere in this issue.

November 10

Late in the afternoon, the President returned to the White House from Camp David, Md.

November 12

The President met at the White House with:

—David L. Aaron, Deputy Assistant for National Security Affairs;

—Senior White House staff members;

—Secretary Edmund S. Muskie and Deputy Secretary Warren M. Christopher, Department of State, Secretary of Defense Harold Brown, and Zbigniew Brzezinski, Assistant to the President for National Security Affairs.

The White House announced that the President has designated Charles L. Schultze as Chairman of the Council on Wage and Price Stability. He replaces Alfred E. Kahn, who has resigned.

The President announced the appointment of Robert Pitofsky as a member of the Council of the Administrative Conference of the United States. He is a Commissioner of the Federal Trade Commission.

The President transmitted to the Senate nominations for persons who received recess appointments while the Congress was in recess. They are:

JOHN C. SAWHILL, to be Chairman of the Board of Directors of the United States Synthetic Fuels Corporation;

CATHERINE CLEARY, JOHN DeBUTTS, LANE KIRKLAND, and FRANK SAVAGE, to be Members of the Board of Directors of the United States Synthetic Fuels Corporation;

LAIRD F. HARRIS and HAROLD L. THOMAS, to be Assistant Directors of the Community Services Administration;

ALEX P. MERCURE, to be Under Secretary of Agriculture for Small Community and Rural Development;

JOHN C. TRUESDALE, to be a member of the National Labor Relations Board;

HANNAH D. ATKINS, DONALD F. McHENRY, and WILLIAM J. vanDEN HEUVEL, to be Representatives of the United States to the 35th Session of the General Assembly of the United Nations;

NATHAN LANDOW, H. CARL McCALL, BARBARA NEWSOM, and RICHARD W. PETREE, to be Alternate Representatives of the United States to the 35th Session of the United Nations General Assembly.

The President transmitted to the Congress the annual report on space and aeronautics and the annual report on the Alaska Railroad.

November 13

The President met at the White House with:

—Dr. Brzezinski;

—Frank B. Moore, Assistant to the President for Congressional Liaison;

—the Democratic congressional leadership;

—Senator Howard H. Baker of Tennessee.

The President transmitted to the Congress the annual report of the Office of Alien Property, Department of Justice, and the annual Report of Activities Conducted on Behalf of Handicapped Persons Under the Rehabilitation Act of 1973.

November 14

The President met at the White House with:

—Mr. Aaron;

—Vice President Walter F. Mondale;

—Mr. Moore;

—Representative Carl D. Perkins of Kentucky.

NOMINATIONS SUBMITTED TO THE SENATE

The following list does not include promotions of members of the Uniformed Services,

NOMINATIONS—Continued

nominations to the Service Academies, or nominations of Foreign Service officers.

Submitted November 12, 1980

The following-named persons to the positions indicated to which they were appointed during the last recess of the Senate:

To be Representatives of the United States of America to the Thirty-fifth Session of the General Assembly of the United Nations:

DONALD F. McHENRY, of Illinois

WILLIAM J. VANDEN HEUVEL, of New York

HANNAH D. ATKINS, of Oklahoma

To be Alternate Representatives of the United States of America to the Thirty-fifth Session of the General Assembly of the United Nations:

NATHAN LANDOW, of Maryland

BARBARA NEWSOM, of California

RICHARD W. PETREE, of Virginia

H. CARL McCALL, of New York

MELBA PATTILLO BEALS, of California, to be a member of the Board of Directors of the Corporation for Public Broadcasting for a term expiring March 26, 1986, vice Lucius Perry Gregg, Jr., term expired.

JOHN C. SAWHILL, of the District of Columbia, to be Chairman of the Board of Directors of the United States Synthetic Fuels Corporation for a term of 7 years (new position), to which office he was appointed during the last recess of the Senate.

The following-named persons to the positions indicated to which they were appointed during the last recess of the Senate:

To be members of the Board of Directors of the United States Synthetic Fuels Corporation for the terms indicated:

JOHN D. DeBUTTS, of Virginia, for a term of 1 year (new position).

CATHERINE BLANCHARD CLEARY, of Wisconsin, for a term of 2 years (new position).

FRANK SAVAGE, of New York, for a term of 3 years (new position).

JOSEPH LANE KIRKLAND, of the District of Columbia, for a term of 5 years (new position).

JOHN C. TRUESDALE, of Maryland, to be a member of the National Labor Relations Board for the term of 5 years expiring August 27, 1985 (reappointment), to which office he was appointed during the last recess of the Senate.

NOMINATIONS—Continued
Submitted November 12—Continued

HAROLD LAFAYETTE THOMAS, of the District of Columbia, to be an Assistant Director of the Community Services Administration, vice John B. Gabusi, resigned, to which office he was appointed during the last recess of the Senate.

LAIRD F. HARRIS, of Michigan, to be an Assistant Director of the Community Services Administration, vice Frank Jones, resigned, to which office he was appointed during the last recess of the Senate.

ALEX P. MERCURE, of New Mexico, to be Under Secretary of Agriculture for Small Community and Rural Development (new position), to which office he was appointed during the last recess of the Senate.

Submitted November 13, 1980

STEPHEN G. BREYER, of Massachusetts, to be United States Circuit Judge for the First Circuit vice a new position created by P.L. 95–486, approved October 20, 1978.

CHECKLIST OF WHITE HOUSE PRESS RELEASES

The following listing contains releases of the White House Press Office which are not included in this issue.

Released November 12, 1980

Announcement: initiation of formal transition efforts and information on the transition officers

Released November 13, 1980

Announcement: nomination of Stephen G. Breyer to be a United States Circuit Judge for the First Circuit Court of Appeals

Released November 14, 1980

Announcement: transfer of funds from the 1977 Inaugural Committee to the 1981 Inaugural Committee

---

ACTS APPROVED BY THE PRESIDENT

NOTE: No acts approved by the President were received by the Office of the Federal Register during the period covered by this issue.

Cuban and Haitian Entrants

Executive Order 12251.   November 15, 1980

By the authority vested in me as President of the United States of America by Section 501 of the Refugee Education Assistance Act of 1980 (Public Law 96–422), Chapter III of Title I of the Supplemental Appropriations and Rescission Act, 1980 (94 Stat. 865; Public Law 96–304), and Section 301 of Title 3 of the United States Code, and in order to provide for assistance to be made available relating to Cuban and Haitian entrants, it is hereby ordered as follows:

1–101. The Secretary of Health and Human Services is delegated the authorities vested in the President pursuant to Sections 501(a) and (b) of the Refugee Education Assistance Act.

1–102. The funds appropriated to the President for Special Migration and Refugee Assistance in Chapter III of Title I of the Supplemental Appropriations and Rescission Act, 1980, are hereby made available to the Secretary of Health and Human Services to reimburse State and local governments for cash and medical assistance and social services pursuant to Section 1–101 of this Order.

1–103. All the functions vested in the President by Section 501(c) of the Refugee Education Assistance Act of 1980, are hereby delegated to the Secretary of Health and Human Services.

1–104. In carrying out the functions delegated to him by Section 1–103 of this Order, the Secretary of Health and Human Services shall ensure that among the actions he takes or directs from time to time, he shall promptly take action which provides assistance for those Cuban and Haitian entrants located or to be located at Fort Indiantown Gap, Fort McCoy, Fort Chaffee, Fort Allen, existing processing and reception sites in Florida, and such other sites as he may designate.

1–105. Executive Order No. 12246 of October 10, 1980, is revoked.

1–106. This Order is effective November 15, 1980.

JIMMY CARTER

The White House,
    November 15, 1980.

[Filed with the Office of the Federal Register, 11:06 a.m., November 17, 1980]

NOTE: The text of the Executive order was released on November 17.

Federal Civilian and Military Pay Increases

Report to the Congress.   November 18, 1980

To the Congress of the United States:

In accordance with the provisions of section 5305 of Title 5 of the United States Code, I hereby report on the pay adjustment I ordered for the Federal statutory pay systems in October 1980.

The Secretary of Labor, the Director of the Office of Management and Budget, and the Director of the Office of Personnel Management, who serve jointly as my agent for Federal pay, found that an overall increase of 13.46 percent in General

Schedule rates of pay would be appropriate if comparability with private enterprise salary rates for the same levels of work were to be achieved. The Advisory Committee on Federal Pay recommended that the findings of my agent be implemented.

After considering the findings of my agent and the recommendation of the Advisory Committee on Federal Pay, I determined that economic conditions affecting the general welfare necessitated a lesser increase in accordance with the alternative plan provisions of section 5305 (c) of Title 5 of the United States Code. Accordingly, on August 29 I sent to the Congress an alternative plan which called for an increase of 9.1 percent at each grade, except that the full comparability increase would take effect to the extent that it did not increase a rate of pay to more than $9,069 per year. Neither House of Congress disapproved this alternative plan so on October 16, I signed Executive Order No. 12248 implementing it.

Under this Executive Order:

—The scheduled rates of pay under the General Schedule were increased by an overall 9.11 percentage in accordance with the alternative plan. (This is a correction of the overall percentage figure forwarded to Congress on August 29, 1980.)

—The scheduled rates of pay under the other statutory pay systems, the Foreign Service and the Department of Medicine and Surgery of the Veterans Administration, were increased by an overall 9.10 percentage in accordance with the alternative plan.

—The scheduled rates of pay for the Vice President and the Executive Schedule and Congressional and Judicial salaries were increased under the provisions of Public Law 94–82, based on the overall 9.11 percentage increase in the rates of pay under the General Schedule.

—The scheduled rates of pay for the Senior Executive Service were increased under the provisions of section 5382 of Title 5 of the United States Code based on the new rate of pay for GS–16, step 1, of the General Schedule and the new rate of pay for level IV of the Executive Schedule. (The rates included in this Order are a correction of the rates forwarded to Congress on August 29, 1980.)

—The scheduled rates of pay and allowances for members of the Uniformed Services were increased 11.7 percent in accordance with the provisions of section 801 of Public Law 96–342, approved September 8, 1980.

I am transmitting herewith copies of the reports of my Pay Agent and the Advisory Committee on Federal Pay, the alternative plan, and the Executive Order I promulgated to put this pay adjustment into effect. Also included is Executive Order 12249 which puts into effect a new Foreign Service Schedule authorized by section 403 of the Foreign Service Act of 1980 (Public Law 96–465, approved October 17, 1980), in accordance with the provisions of section 5305 of Title 5 of the United States Code.

JIMMY CARTER

The White House,
    November 18, 1980.

Architectural and Transportation Barriers Compliance Board

Reappointment of Three Members.
November 18, 1980

The President today announced the reappointment of three persons as members of the Architectural and Transportation Barriers Compliance Board. They are:

PAUL MULDAWER, of Atlanta, Ga., an architect and urban designer who has won awards for making buildings accessible to the handicapped;

WILLIAM R. RALLS, of Okemos, Mich., a partner in the Lansing firm of Doyle, Carruthers, Hess & Ralls, P.C., and a former commissioner of the Michigan Public Service Commission;

HALE J. ZUKAS, of Berkeley, Calif., coordinator of community affairs for the Center for Independent Living in Berkeley, where he has worked to eliminate architectural and transportation barriers to the disabled.

the United Nations Commission on Transnational Corporations.

As members of the Panel of Arbitrators

MYRES SMITH McDOUGAL, a professor of law at Yale University, a former member of the U.S. Panel on Permanent Court Arbitration;

SOIA MENTSCHIKOFF, dean of the University of Miami (Florida) Law School;

OSCAR SCHACHTER, a professor of law at Columbia University School of Law, a specialist in international law;

DETLEV FREDERICK VAGTS, a professor at Harvard University Law School, who has served as a counselor on international law to the State Department.

International Centre for the Settlement of Investment Disputes

Appointment of Four Members of the Panel of Conciliators and Four Members of the Panel of Arbitrators.   November 18, 1980

The President today announced the appointment of four persons as members of the Panel of Conciliators and four persons as members of the Panel of Arbitrators of the International Centre for the Settlement of Investment Disputes (ICSID). ICSID is a World Bank affiliate which provides facilities for the arbitration and conciliation of investment disputes between foreign investors and host governments. The persons appointed today are:

As members of the Panel of Conciliators

JAMES COFFIN GREENE, a partner in the Los Angeles law firm of O'Melveny & Myers;

PETER H. KAMINER, senior managing partner in the New York law firm of Winthrop, Stimson, Putnam & Roberts;

BAYLESS ANDREW MANNING, a partner in the New York law firm of Paul, Weiss, Rifkind, Wharton & Garrison, former dean of Stanford Law School;

SEYMOUR JEFFREY RUBIN, a professor of law at American University, former General Counsel of the Agency for International Development, and U.S. representative on

Motor Carrier Ratemaking Study Commission

Appointment of Four Members.
November 18, 1980

The President today announced the appointment of four persons as members of the Motor Carrier Ratemaking Study Commission. This Commission was created by the Motor Carrier Act of 1980 to examine the collective ratemaking process and determine whether antitrust immunity should be eliminated. The members appointed today are:

JAMES H. EDLER, of North Ridgeville, Ohio, corporate director of traffic for American Greetings Corp. and second vice president of the National Small Shipments Traffic Conference;

STEPHEN P. MURPHY, of Kansas City, Mo., senior vice president and general counsel of Yellow Freight System, Inc., and a member of the American Trucking Association;

MICHAEL C. THOMETZ, of Chicago, Ill., vice president and general manager of Badger Freightways, Inc.;

RICHARD WARREN, of Westfield, N.J., distribution operations manager of Lever Brothers Co. and chairman of the motor carrier reform task force of the National Association of Manufacturers.

Woodrow Wilson International Center for Scholars

Appointment of Two Members of the Board of Trustees.   November 18, 1980

The President today announced the appointment of two persons as members of the Board of Trustees of the Woodrow Wilson International Center for Scholars. They are:

JESSE H. OPPENHEIMER, of San Antonio, Tex., an attorney, member of the Chancellors Council of the University of Texas, and a national committee member of the Harvard University Center for Jewish Studies (reappointment);

KENNETH B. CLARK, of Hastings-on-Hudson, N.Y., president of a personnel consulting firm, distinguished professor of psychology emeritus of the City College of the City University of New York, and author of several books and articles.

Department of State Reception Honoring Cyrus R. Vance

Remarks at the Reception for the Former Secretary of State.   November 18, 1980

I'm delighted to be here this evening in my good place in the program between the chest [1] and Cy Vance. [*Laughter*] This is wonderful for me. And I felt it completely appropriate, as I walked in the door, when Ed Muskie said that this is a meeting of friends, a kind of a family.

Ever since I asked Ed Muskie to be Secretary of State, he's been trying to act

---

[1] Prior to the President's remarks, Secretary of State Edmund S. Muskie unveiled a Chippendale chest, contributed by Department of State employees and their families, to be placed in the State Department's Diplomatic Reception Room, in honor of Secretary Vance.

more statesmanlike than Cy Vance. [*Laughter*] Cy, I can't say that he's succeeded at all. [*Laughter*]

It's also appropriate for us to be bound together with a common tie. With very few exceptions, all of us have served with Cy Vance in a time of crisis and achievement, a time of disappointment, a time of frustration, a time of sorrow, and a time of joy.

And it's also appropriate to honor this evening not just Cy Vance but Gay Vance. I've had an excellent relationship with my Cabinet members. I think the strongest personal ties that we have has been with Cy and Gay. We've been on the tennis court together. We've been in the trout streams together. We've been on cross-country skis together. We've been up all night together. We've sweated through crises together. We've traveled together. When Rosalynn has been on trips by herself, Gay was there.

And it's always been an inspiration to me to see on the evening television in a time of intense importance to our country Cy Vance come down the ladder from an airplane with the "United States of America" on it and to see Gay Vance at his side. The diplomatic service, the Foreign Service is one of sharing, and there is not a husband or a wife here, employed in the State Department in the service of our Nation, whose spouse does not share in the fullest sense of the word that common dedication to a great nation.

Ed covered a lot of points that I wanted to make in my remarks about Vance. I think it's appropriate for me, though, as a President who has sat with Cy Vance during 13 days at Camp David, sometimes he and I alone representing our Nation, speaking either to Prime Minister Begin or to President Sadat or, most often, I might say, to their subordinates, where we negotiated the details of the Camp David accords, to know the worth and the virtue of this man, his depth of integrity and also his calmness and his patience and his perceptiveness, and a kind of sense about him so that when he told me something or told a foreign leader something or told one of his fellow workers in the State Department something, there was no doubt about its accuracy and about the soundness of his judgment.

I think Cy had this same relationship with the Members of Congress, who in times of cross-examination or doubt, when secret negotiations were going on, were reassured by the depth of his knowledge of detail and about the breadth of his statesmanship and about his own integrity.

I won't enumerate again, because Ed has covered it very well, some of the things that have bound us together. Most of the things Ed mentioned were achievements, triumphs. We also shared the greatest personal sorrow when our American hostages were taken and we went through weeks and then months of frustrating, constant efforts to protect their lives and their safety and at the same time protect the integrity and honor of our Nation and work for their early release. We accomplished all those goals except the last one, and of course, our commitments are still as deep and as fervent now as they have been in any one of those days when they were separated from us.

I'm very proud to have served with Cy Vance. He was the Cabinet officer about whom there was no debate during this time 4 years ago. There was an absolute unanimity among all those who advised me: "The best man you can get under any circumstances to be Secretary of State is Cy Vance." And all those multiple sources of advice were accurate. I'm very grateful to him personally.

I tried to think of some notable expression to sum up Cy's work, and the one that I think is most appropriate is a quotation from Oliver Wendell Holmes. He made this in 1913, trying to describe at a graduation ceremony, I believe, what was the measure of one's service to one's country and to oneself. And I'll just quote it in closing.

This is what Oliver Wendell Holmes said about Cy Vance: "To see so far as one may and to feel the great forces that are behind every detail, to hammer out as compact and solid a piece of work as one can, to try to make it first rate, and to leave it unadvertised."

I intend to spend a lot of my time in the future advertising what Cy Vance has done for our country.

NOTE: The President spoke at 7:15 p.m. in the Diplomatic Reception Room at the Department of State.

Organization of American States

Remarks at the 10th Regular Session of the General Assembly.   November 19, 1980

Mr. President, first of all let me thank you for those gracious words.

Mr. Secretary General and distinguished Foreign Ministers, Ambassadors, ladies and gentlemen:

I speak to you today for the fifth time in an important forum in this hall and, despite considerable efforts to the contrary, I'm afraid, also for the last time as President of the United States. I want to say how grateful I am for the privilege of working with all of you and the leaders of your nations, and I want to take a few minutes to assess what we have done together and to describe my own hopes for the future.

On my first visit to the Organization of American States in April of 1977, I said that no single policy, no single slogan could encompass a region as diverse as ours. I spoke instead of certain principles—a belief in nonintervention and in the sovereignty of nations, a determination to work for human rights and for democracy, a common commitment to deal with global economic issues and to resolve regional political disputes. These principles have helped the United States make its contribution to the new and more balanced relationships that are emerging in our hemisphere.

After 4 years of practical experience, I'm more convinced than ever that the future we desire lies in recognizing yearnings that are common to individuals and to nations alike. As individuals the peoples of the Americas yearn for basic human rights; they desire personal liberty, to be free from torture and arbitrary arrest, to participate in making the basic decisions that shape their own future, to have adequate food, health care, and education. And as part of the global community, every nation of the Americas has a desire and a right to help shape the future, not only of our own hemisphere but indeed the entire world.

Some would ignore or resist these treasured rights, the rights of individuals and the rights of nations, but the future lies with those who cherish them and who are willing to defend them.

Let me speak briefly of the last 4 years.

Many here assisted in the negotiation and the ratification of the Panama Canal treaties. These treaties and their far-reaching impact will endure. They will endure because they are based on the mutual trust and the mutual respect that have been carefully and sometimes painfully forged by the people of a small na-

tion and the people of a large nation. They will endure because they serve the interests of all who rely on the Panama Canal. They will endure because they epitomize the broadest possible commitment of my country to a new and a better relationship with the developing nations of the world. They will endure because the treaties serve the cause of peace.

Last month El Salvador and Honduras served the cause of harmony and progress, resolving their decades-old border dispute. These two countries, working with former President Bustamante of Peru and with their own Secretary-General, have earned the admiration and respect of all those who love peace.

The treaty of Tlatelolco, when completed, will forever ban nuclear weapons from Latin America. I'm proud to have signed protocol I of this treaty on behalf of the United States of America. It's imperative that the remaining nations of our hemisphere put aside their hesitation and join in this vital commitment to ban the spread of nuclear weapons and to set an example for other nations in other regions of the world.

In Nicaragua many of us have been working together to help that country heal its wounds. It's in the interest of all who care about freedom to help the Nicaraguan people chart a pluralistic course that ends bloodshed, respects human rights, and furthers democracy.

El Salvador continues to struggle against terrorists on the right who seek to restore an old tyranny and terrorists on the left who seek to create a new one. That struggle of theirs is ours as well. Their path, the peaceful path of stability and moderation, is precarious, but it's the only path that can lead to both liberty and justice.

We must insist upon a strict policy of nonintervention as the people of these two nations design their own future.

For too long, the United States seemed wedded to the status quo, even when that meant a continuation of poverty, social injustice, and even political repression. That attitude betrayed my Nation's dynamism and our faith and confidence in the future. And that, thank God, has now been changed. We understand and support the necessity of peaceful and moderate political progress in Central America and elsewhere in this hemisphere.

Your governments throughout the hemisphere have also worked to improve the prospects for economic development. We've strengthened the Inter-American Development Bank and the World Bank. We've reduced trade barriers by expanding generalized tariff preferences and eliminating the discriminatory provision against Venezuela and Ecuador. We've worked to stabilize commodity prices by a common fund and individual commodity agreements on sugar and coffee and cocoa. Regional cooperation has been invigorated, in the Andean Pact, with the Caribbean group, and most dramatically with Venezuelan-Mexican assistance for the Caribbean basin.

Through my own personal participation and through the influence of my country, we have worked to strengthen and to expand the beneficial influence of this Organization of American States.

As all of you know, the cause that has been closest to my own heart is the cause of human rights. I'm convinced that a new conscience has been awakened. That conscience serves a concept of human rights that is not unique to any country nor even just to this hemisphere, but is universal. In this hemisphere, since 1977 13 countries have ratified the embodi-

ment of that concept, the American Convention of Human Rights. This has brought the convention into force and has created an inter-American court to judge human rights violations. In addition, the Inter-American Commission on Human Rights is more effective today than it was 4 years ago. It deserves our strongest continuing moral and financial support.

Today no government in this hemisphere can expect silent assent from its neighbors if it tramples the rights of its own citizens. The costs of repression have increased, but so have the benefits of respecting human rights. I pray that this progress will continue, although I know from experience that progress is not always easy as we defend human rights.

Some claim, as the President has mentioned, that Jimmy Carter elevated human rights and democracy on the inter-American agenda and that the agenda will change when I leave my office. They are wrong. Hemispheric support for human rights is a historic movement, a movement that has been recognized this year in the Nobel Peace Prize. I take pride in being part of that movement.

The cause of human rights will be all the stronger if it remains at the service of humanity, rather than at the service of ideological or partisan ends, and if it condemns both terrorism and repression. In the phrase "human rights," the "rights" are important; the "human" is *very* important.

As a citizen of the Americas, I'm deeply encouraged by the trend toward greater democratization. I'm heartened that in many countries thousands of people who were political prisoners just 4 years ago are now free. Those who see a contradiction between our security and our humanitarian interests forget that the basis for a secure and a stable society is the bond of trust between a government and its own people.

The future of our hemisphere is not to be found in authoritarianism that wears the mask of common consent, nor totalitarianism that wears the mask of justice. Instead, let us find our future in the human face of democracy, the human voice of individual liberty, and the human hand of economic development. If we build on the best of what we have begun, we can see a better time at the end of this decade.

We can see a time when longstanding disputes like Belize, Bolivian access to the sea, and the Beagle Channel dispute between Argentina and Chile have been settled in a spirit of cooperation and justice. We can see a time when the treaty of Tlatelolco has come into force and other regions have followed the lead of Latin America in banning nuclear weapons.

We can see a time when human rights are no longer threatened by the violence of either governments or terrorists and when every government responds to the will of its people expressed through democratic institutions. We can see a time when nations have cooperated, in the OAS and elsewhere, to develop just and fair ways of dealing with the migration of people, a time when no nation disregards the immigration laws of its neighbor and many nations offer a haven to the few who still need such a place to dwell.

And we can see a time when today's aspirations for greater economic development and cooperation have become living realities through common action inspired by this body and its experts.

Let me conclude on a personal note. My interest in Latin America and the Caribbean and in human rights and in democracy did not begin 4 years ago, and

my interest will not end on January the 20th, next year. I will continue to speak out for the universal ideals which are embodied in our hearts and in the American Convention on Human Rights. I will continue to work with you, my friends, to make this hemisphere and the world more just, more secure, and more free.

Thank you very much.

NOTE: The President spoke at 10:43 a.m. in the main auditorium at the Organization of American States Building.

President's Export Council

Appointment of Roger Gettys Hill as a Member.   November 19, 1980

The President today announced the appointment of Roger Gettys Hill, of Racine, Wis., as a member of the President's Export Council.

Hill is president and founder of Gettys Manufacturing, a firm manufacturing electronic control systems for industry. He is a member of the Independent Business Association of Wisconsin and served on the international trade subcommittee of the Chamber of Commerce of the United States.

Meeting With Chancellor Helmut Schmidt of the Federal Republic of Germany

Remarks to Reporters Following the Meeting.   November 20, 1980

THE PRESIDENT. To the American and the German press and to the people that you inform, I'd like to say that we are very delighted again to have Chancellor

Helmut Schmidt coming here representing the Federal Republic of Germany, along with Hans-Dietrich Genscher and other members of his party who have meant so much to us during these recent years.

Although quite often the differences that exist between democratic nations and governments are highly publicized and receive a great deal of attention, it's good at a time like this to reemphasize the common basis on which we deal with international problems, the common approach that we have to these problems, the common goals that we seek to achieve, and the ties that bind our countries together and our people together in an unbreakable fashion. We share our commitment to democracy, to freedom, to peace, to the strength of our alliances, to unrestrained international trade, to the enhancement of the ideals that we share.

And I would like to point out today that during this last 4 years since I have been President, we've had a very fruitful and constructive relationship between myself and Chancellor Schmidt and between the two Governments of our great nations.

This is a time of looking to the future: the control of nuclear weapons, the bringing of peace to the Middle East, the proper dealing with the less developed nations of the world, the enhancement of international trade, the control of inflation, the management of the energy problem, the elimination of the waste of energy, and the construction of facilities for producing alternative forms of energy. All these kinds of questions we share, and the ultimate goals and, on almost every occasion, the means to reach those goals are a common commitment of our two people.

I'm very grateful that we've had the honor and the privilege and the assistance of this visit by Chancellor Schmidt, who's come here to receive a well-deserved award in New York, and I'm also grateful for the personal advice that he's always given to me and the common commitments that we represent among our people.

Chancellor Schmidt, it's an honor to have you in our country again. We look forward to many fruitful years of close cooperation with you and your Government, between our two nations, and we are very grateful for the common goals that we share and have done so well between our countries for the benefit of our people and the world.

Thank you very much. And I'd like to ask Chancellor Schmidt if he would say a few words.

THE CHANCELLOR. This time, Mr. President, I would like to use a little sheet of paper in answering your kind words, a sheet of paper which I've, myself, been working upon this morning.

I would like to thank you very much for what you said this morning, right now, here, and for the long period of cooperation that you and your administration had with our Government and with myself. To listen to you and to talk to you has always been, as much as today, a pleasure and has confirmed to us how close we are to each other, namely, the Federal Republic of Germany on the one hand and the United States of America, their two Governments, and last, but not least, the President and the German Chancellor as persons.

Ladies and gentlemen, I've often called our friendship unshakable, and I want to repeat this here and today in this place that embodies American power and American elegance and also at this time of change in the American Capital.

Your contribution toward the strengthening of the ties which bind us together has been and is significant. You have given the Atlantic relationship a high priority in the policies of your administration, Mr. President, from the very beginning, and you have kept it that way. Of course, the German-American friendship is a very essential ingredient of the Atlantic relationship. We have trusted each other in the past; we have relied upon each other in the past; in the present we shall, and will continue to do so in the future as well. And as long as this remains so, we do not need to lose confidence in our joint future.

Let me thank you, Mr. President, for what you have done and still do. Let me thank you for your friendship, for your trust, your help, your candor. And I would like to, in saluting to the American President, include his aides, secretaries, diplomats, soldiers, armed forces, all those Americans with whom we have worked together over the last 4 years, over the last 30 years, and will work together over the next 4 years and over the next 30 years.

I wish you very heartily all the best, Mr. President.

THE PRESIDENT. Thank you, Chancellor Schmidt.

NOTE: The President spoke at 1:40 p.m. on the South Lawn of the White House.

Meeting With Chancellor Schmidt of the Federal Republic of Germany

White House Statement.   November 20, 1980

President Carter and the Chancellor of the Federal Republic of Germany, Hel-

mut Schmidt, held a thorough conversation in Washington, November 20, during the Chancellor's visit to the United States, November 18 through 21. The President hosted a White House luncheon for the Chancellor and Foreign Minister Hans-Dietrich Genscher on November 20 in which Secretary of State Muskie, National Security Adviser Brzezinski, and senior officials also participated.

The conversation between the President and the Chancellor covered a wide range of political, security, and economic issues of mutual interest to the two countries. The President and the Chancellor agreed on the necessity of continuing these close consultations, including during the transition period, in order to assure continuing full coordination of the policies followed by the two countries on major international issues.

In their conversation the President and the Chancellor agreed on the continued importance of improving NATO's defense posture and of efforts aimed at reaching arms control agreements with the Soviet Union and its Warsaw Pact allies in order to ensure a stable military balance.

In their discussion of East-West relations, both sides welcomed the continuation of the CSCE process at the Madrid review conference, to which both Governments remain committed. In this context they stressed the right of each country, irrespective of its political or social system, to resolve its problems in free exercise of its sovereignty and without intervention from any quarter. Moreover, they reiterated, with reference to the resolution of the General Assembly of the United Nations, their regret that there is no evidence of Soviet readiness to withdraw its forces from Afghanistan and to seek a political solution of the Afghanistan crisis.

The President and the Chancellor discussed the latest developments in the Middle East. They reviewed the ongoing negotiations in the Camp David framework and stressed the urgent need for progress toward a comprehensive peace settlement.

Secretary Muskie and Foreign Minister Genscher also held a separate meeting earlier in the day.

Meeting With President-Elect Ronald Reagan

Remarks to Reporters Following the Meeting. November 20, 1980

THE PRESIDENT. I would like to say while the press are here that we've had a very enjoyable and a very productive hour or so together, not only describing to one another the commitment that we share for a good transition period, but also I've outlined to Governor Reagan some of the issues that I've faced as President that will be shared with him in the transition period and inherited by him on Inauguration Day.

One of the wonderful things about our country, being a democracy, is the orderly transition of authority and responsibility. He and I understand very well that I will be the President in the fullest sense of the word until Inauguration Day, and then instantly at the time he takes the oath of office, he will have the full responsibilities. We have a very good working relationship personally and also a very fine transition commitment, which has been in effect for several weeks now.

I understand that Rosalynn and Nancy have had a good visit, too, and Mrs.

Reagan has had a chance to look at the White House and the place where they will be living in the future.

But I'm very grateful to Governor Reagan for having come this afternoon and permitted me to share with him some of the common commitments we have as the President and the future President of our Nation. It's been a delightful experience for me and very gratifying.

Governor Reagan?

THE PRESIDENT-ELECT. I want to express my appreciation to the President. He has been most gracious and most cooperative, he and his people, with regard to this transition and has certainly made it a much easier time than it could otherwise have been. And we're deeply grateful, appreciate it very much.

THE PRESIDENT. Thank you, sir. Good luck. I'll be seeing you in the future often.

THE PRESIDENT-ELECT. Thanks very much. I hope so.

MRS. REAGAN. Thank you so much.

NOTE: The President spoke at 3:26 p.m. in the Oval Office at the White House.

The Cyprus Conflict

Letter to the Speaker of the House and the Chairman of the Senate Foreign Relations Committee. November 20, 1980

Dear Mr. Speaker: (Dear Mr. Chairman:)

In accordance with the provisions of Public Law 95–384, I am submitting the following report on progress made during the past 60 days toward a negotiated settlement of the Cyprus problem.

As was noted in my last report, intercommunal talks between representatives of the Greek and Turkish Cypriots resumed on August 9 under the aegis of

United Nations Special Representative Ambassador Hugo Gobbi. Systematic substantive examination of the essential problems dividing the communities began on September 16. The parties have been examining the following general subjects, on the basis of one topic each meeting:

(A) Resettlement of Varosha under United Nations auspices;

(B) Promotion of goodwill, mutual confidence and normal conditions;

(C) Constitutional problems;

(D) Territorial divisions.

Meetings were held on September 24, October 1, 8, 15, and 31 and November 5 and 12. We are encouraged by the fact that the negotiators at these sessions have engaged in serious examinations of their differences and are seeking mutually acceptable solutions. The negotiating atmosphere between the parties has remained congenial.

I am hopeful that the good start achieved by these meetings will develop into sustained negotiations leading to a comprehensive solution. Serious, sustained talks provide the best opportunity for reaching a just and lasting settlement of the issues that face Cyprus.

Sincerely,

JIMMY CARTER

NOTE: This is the text of identical letters addressed to Thomas P. O'Neill, Speaker of the House of Representatives, and Frank Church, chairman of the Senate Foreign Relations Committee.

Digest of Other White House Announcements

The following listing includes the President's public schedule and other items of general interest announced by the White House Press Office and not included elsewhere in this issue.

November 15

The President met at the White House with David L. Aaron, Deputy Assistant for National Security Affairs.

November 17

The President met at the White House with:

—Zbigniew Brzezinski, Assistant to the President for National Security Affairs;

—Charles L. Schultze, Chairman of the Council of Economic Advisers.

November 18

The President met at the White House with:

—Dr. Brzezinski;

—Secretary of Defense Harold Brown, Secretary of State Edmund S. Muskie, Deputy Secretary of State Warren M. Christopher, Lloyd N. Cutler, Counsel to the President, and Dr. Brzezinski;

—Senator Daniel K. Inouye of Hawaii.

November 19

The President met at the White House with:

—Dr. Brzezinski;

—Frank B. Moore, Assistant to the President for Congressional Liaison;

—1980 American Nobel Prize winners Baruj Benacerraf, James W. Cronin, and Val L. Fitch, previous American winners in the sciences, and Ambassador Wilhelm H. Wachtmeister of Sweden.

November 20

The President met at the White House with:

—Dr. Brzezinski;

—Governor Hugh Gallen of New Hampshire.

The President left the White House for a stay at Camp David, Md.

CHECKLIST OF WHITE HOUSE PRESS RELEASES

The following listing contains releases of the White House Press Office which are not included in this issue.

Released November 19, 1980

Advance text: remarks at the 10th regular session of the General Assembly of the Organization of American States

NOMINATIONS SUBMITTED TO THE SENATE

NOTE: No nominations were submitted to the Senate during the period covered by this issue.

ACTS APPROVED BY THE PRESIDENT

NOTE: No acts approved by the President were received by the Office of the Federal Register during the period covered by this issue.

The Honorable John William McCormack

Statement on the Death of the Former Speaker of the House of Representatives.
November 22, 1980

I am saddened to learn of the death of Speaker John McCormack. He was a dedicated and distinguished Speaker of the House of Representatives, and throughout his 42 years in the House served with distinction and a strong, heartfelt belief in the Democratic Party.

John McCormack was a man of strong character and remained actively devoted to his constituents through the last months of his life.

Rosalynn and I extend our deepest sympathies to his family and many friends.

The Honorable John William McCormack

Executive Order 12252. November 24, 1980

As a mark of respect to the memory of the Honorable John William McCormack, former Speaker of the United States House of Representatives and a Representative of the State of Massachusetts, it is hereby ordered, pursuant to the provisions of Section 4 of Proclamation 3044 of March 1, 1954, as amended, that until interment, the flag of the United States shall be flown at half-staff on all buildings, grounds and naval vessels of the Federal Government in the District of Columbia and throughout the United States and its Territories and possessions. I also direct that the flag shall be flown at half-staff for the same length of time at all United States embassies, legations, consular offices, and other facilities abroad, including all military facilities and naval vessels and stations.

JIMMY CARTER

The White House,
     November 24, 1980.

[Filed with the Office of the Federal Register, 2:55 p.m., November 24, 1980]

Death of John Pennington

Statement by the President.
November 24, 1980

With the death of John Pennington, journalism has lost one of its most dedicated and effective practitioners. He was a resourceful and courageous investigative reporter, yet scrupulously honest and fair. The sensitivity and compassion reflected in his writing were in the highest tradition of southern journalism.

He was my good friend. Rosalynn and I are saddened by his passing and extend our deepest sympathy to his family.

United States-Canada Convention for the Protection of Migratory Birds

Message to the Senate Transmitting a Protocol to the Convention. November 24, 1980

To the Senate of the United States:

I transmit herewith, for Senate advice and consent to ratification, the Protocol

2743

Amending the Convention of August 16, 1916 for the Protection of Migratory Birds in Canada and the United States of America. The Protocol modernizes and adds flexibility to the subsistence taking provisions of the Canada convention by allowing the contracting parties to authorize the taking of migratory birds and the collection of their eggs by the indigenous inhabitants of the State of Alaska and the Indians and Inuit of Canada for their own nutritional and other essential needs, during seasons established so as to provide for the preservation and maintenance of stocks of migratory birds. The report of the Department of State is enclosed for the information of the Senate in connection with its consideration of the Protocol.

The 1916 Convention pertaining to Canada was the first of our migratory bird conventions and reflected the knowledge of ornithology and migratory bird management at the time. The Convention makes a valuable contribution to the conservation of migratory birds by establishing for migratory game birds, migratory insectivorous birds, and other migratory nongame birds, closed seasons during which no hunting is permitted except for scientific or propagating purposes under permits issued by proper authorities. The taking of nests or eggs of such birds is also prohibited except for scientific or propagating purposes under laws or regulations.

The Convention has very narrow exceptions which permit the taking by Alaskan Eskimos and Indians of a few sea birds and eggs for subsistence purposes. These narrow exceptions present two problems, however. They do not recognize the centuries old historical use of other species of migratory birds by Alaskan natives. In addition, they do not recognize and permit needed subsistence taking by other local rural residents of bush Alaska who are neither Indian, Aleut, nor Eskimo. As a result, the provisions of the Convention have been widely ignored by the rural subsistence inhabitants of Alaska. Further, there has been considerable friction among different user groups, and between user groups and law enforcement and management officials. The conclusion of the Department of the Interior is that the existing subsistence provisions of the Convention are "unworkable, unenforceable, and incapable of responding to the legitimate subsistence needs of many rural Alaskans."

The provisions of the Protocol adequately respond to the subsistence needs of the State of Alaska, while at the same time protecting our migratory bird resources. The Protocol does not abrogate the limited rights granted to Indians and Eskimos in the 1916 Convention, but broadens subsistence taking rights to all "indigenous inhabitants of the State of Alaska" so as to respond to subsistence needs of rural Alaska in a racially non-discriminatory way. Excessive exploitation of the birds is guarded against by reserving to the competent authorities of the two countries the right respectively to determine what constitutes legitimate subsistence needs, and to establish hunting seasons so as to provide for the preservation and maintenance of stocks of migratory birds.

I am confident that this Protocol will enhance our ability to manage and conserve a valuable natural resource. I urge the Senate to act favorably on this Convention at an early date by giving its advice and consent to ratification.

JIMMY CARTER

The White House,
November 24, 1980.

Import Quota for Upland Cotton

Proclamation 4805.   November 24, 1980

SPECIAL LIMITED GLOBAL IMPORT QUOTA
FOR UPLAND COTTON

*By the President of the United States
of America*

A Proclamation

1. Section 103(f)(1) of the Agricultural
Act of 1949, as added by Section 602 of
the Food and Agriculture Act of 1977
(the Act) (91 Stat. 913, 934; 7 U.S.C.
1444(f)(1)), provides that whenever the
Secretary of Agriculture determines that
the average price of Strict Low Middling
one and one-sixteenth inch cotton (micro-
naire 3.5 through 4.9), hereinafter referred to as "Strict Low Middling Cotton," in the designated United States spot
markets for a month exceed 130 per centum of the average price of such quality of
cotton in such markets for the preceding
thirty-six months, notwithstanding any
other provisions of law, the President shall
immediately establish and proclaim a special limited global import quota for upland cotton. A quota, effective from April
3 through July 2, 1980, was placed in
effect by Proclamation No. 4742.

2. When a special quota has been established during the preceding twelve
months, the amount of the next quota is
to be the smaller of twenty-one days of
domestic mill consumption of upland cotton at the seasonally adjusted average rate
of the most recent three months for which
data are available or the amount required
to increase the supply to 130 percent of
the demand. The quota is to remain in
effect for a ninety-day period.

3. The Secretary of Agriculture has
informed me that he has determined that
the average price of Strict Low Middling
Cotton in the designated spot markets for
the month of September 1980 has exceeded 130 per centum of the average
price of such cotton in such markets for
the preceding thirty-six months. The Secretary's determination was based upon the
following data:

(a) The average price of Strict Low
Middling Cotton in the designated spot
markets for the month of September 1980
was 87.1 cents per pound.

(b) The average price of Strict Low
Middling Cotton in the designated spot
markets for the thirty-six months preceding the month of September 1980 (September 1977 through August 1980) was
62.85 cents per pound.

4. Twenty-one days of domestic mill
consumption of upland cotton, which is
any variety of the Gossypium hirsutum
species of cotton, at the seasonally adjusted
rate of the most recent three months for
which data are available (June 1980
through August 1980) is 238,633,920
pounds.

5. On the basis of computations made
in accordance with Section 103(f)(1) of
the Act, a quantity of 261,757,920
pounds of upland cotton is required to increase the supply of such cotton to 130
percent of the demand therefor.

Now, THEREFORE, I, JIMMY CARTER,
President of the United States of America,
by the authority vested in me by the Constitution and Statutes of the United States
of America, including Section 103(f)(1)
of the Agricultural Act of 1949, as added
by Section 602 of the Food and Agriculture Act of 1977, and in order to establish
a special ninety-day limited global import
quota for 238,633,920 pounds of upland
cotton, do proclaim that the temporary

2745

provision set forth in item 955.07 of Part 3 of the Appendix to the Tariff Schedules of the United States is hereby amended to read as follows:

"Item	Article	Quota Quantity (in pounds)
955.07	Notwithstanding any other quantitative limitations on the importation of cotton, upland cotton, if accompanied by an original certificate of an official of a government agency of the country in which the cotton was produced attesting to the fact that cotton is a variety of the Gossypium hirsutum species of cotton, may be entered during the 90-day period November 28, 1980 through February 25, 1981......................	238,633,920 pounds".

IN WITNESS WHEREOF, I have hereunto set my hand this 24th day of November, in the year of our Lord nineteen hundred and eighty, and of the Independence of the United States of America the two hundred and fifth.

                                    JIMMY CARTER

[Filed with the Office of the Federal Register, 10:39 a.m., November 25, 1980]

Earthquake in Southern Italy

Message to President Alessandro Pertini. November 24, 1980

Dear Mr. President:

I was saddened to learn of the devastation wrought by the recent earthquake which struck southern Italy. The hearts of the American people go out to your countrymen at this tragic time. We share in your profound grief and we stand ready to be of assistance. Our Embassy in Rome is prepared to help in every possible way.

Please extend our deepest sympathy to the families and friends of the victims of this tragedy.

                    Sincerely,

                                    JIMMY CARTER

NOTE: The text of the message was released on November 25. The press release contained the following information on U.S. assistance to Italy:

At the request of the Italian Government, the United States is providing an initial fund of $1.5 million to aid the victims of the earthquake. The fund includes 1,000 tents from U.S. Defense Department stockpiles in Europe and six military helicopters for reconnaissance and relief operations from the nearby U.S. military installations. Additionally, U.S. military installations in the vicinity are providing the Italian Government with tractors and other equipment as well as military personnel.

The Agency for International Development's Office of Foreign Disaster Assistance (OFDA) is coordinating all U.S. Government disaster assistance to Italy.

National Oceanic and Atmospheric Administration

Nomination of Capt. Kelly E. Taggart To Be Director of the Commissioned Officer Corps. November 25, 1980

The President today announced that he will nominate Capt. Kelly E. Taggart to be Director of the Commissioned Officer Corps, National Oceanic and Atmospheric Administration (NOAA).

Taggart is Deputy Associate Director of NOAA's Office of Fleet Operations. He has been with NOAA and its predecessor agency, the U.S. Coast and Geodetic Survey, since 1955. He has served as Commanding Officer of a NOAA survey vessel and on aerial photographic mapping missions.

Canadian River Commission

Appointment of James A. Bradley as Federal Representative and Chairman.
November 25, 1980

The President today announced the appointment of James A. Bradley, of Amarillo, Tex., as Federal Representative and Chairman of the Canadian River Commission. This Commission represents a water compact between the States of New Mexico, Texas, and Oklahoma.

Bradley retired in 1977 as Director of the Water and Power Resources Service's Southwest Region after 30 years with the Water and Power Resources Service and its predecessor agency.

National Bible Week

Remarks at a White House Reception for Ministers and Religious Leaders.
November 25, 1980

THE PRESIDENT. After all I've read in the news media the last few months, it's a remarkable sight to see so many people who believe in God in the same room without physical combat. [*Laughter*]

There are two reasons for that, obviously. One is that we have so much for which we can be thankful. The blessings of God, the gifts of God in this country are so overwhelming that it doesn't take just Thanksgiving season to remind us of them and of the things for which we are constantly thankful. And the other one is our common commitment to the principles expressed in the Bible. This is a time for

reassessment, in my judgment, for those who have very deep religious convictions, in a nation where freedom of expression is guaranteed as a constitutional right. Sometimes freedom of expression can be abused. Sometimes its free use can cause controversy. Sometimes that controversy is well-advised, sometimes perhaps we might judge it not to be well-advised. But I think at the conclusion of this difficult year, in religious circles—not just political circles—it's a time for those of us who do believe in the Bible, who study it as part of our lives, who look upon it as a foundation for everything we believe, to reassess how we've come together in a spirit of love and mutual understanding and a common commitment to serve Christ, those among us who are Christians, and the Supreme God for us all.

Diversity is an integral part of life, in a democracy in particular. Diversity is not something of which we need to be afraid. Our Nation has grown strong, not in spite of it, but perhaps because of it, and the pluralistic elements of our society in every respect give it strength.

I don't know what would happen if there was complete homogeneity among religious believers, whether we would have a stronger religious community or not. I'm not qualified to judge. But the point I'm making is that we need not fear debate, exploration, or argument.

I remember that one of the things Arnold Toynbee said was that religion is a search for truth about man's existence and his relationship to God. And he went on to say that when we stop searching, that we become like the Pharisee who is proud of being superior and not like the publican who said, "Lord have mercy on me, a sinner." So, as we approach the future, I think it's good for us to recognize the need for diversity and the search through God for a common ground on which we can serve Him best and enhance His kingdom on Earth.

I'm very grateful to be President of a great nation where deep religious belief is an integral part of the fabric of our society. And I hope that we can put aside the condemnation of one another and the exaltation of ourselves, the belief that we are superior, the Pharisaic attitude, and through humility and a recommitment to compassion and love can heal the wounds that have concerned us all this year.

I'd like to say that I'm very grateful to be part of this National Bible Week. It's a development in our national life that reminds us of the things that I've described, plus many others that I haven't mentioned. And it's an honor for me to introduce to you now the chairman of National Bible Week, Mr. Howard Kauffmann, who I will ask to come to the stage for some comments.

MR. KAUFFMANN. Thank you very much, Mr. President. It is indeed a privilege to be here this afternoon. I reckon that few, if any, Americans could be invited into this house without feeling a sense of awe, and certainly nobody in my line of work could. So, I went to my favorite book for guidance and recalled something that Paul wrote to the Corinthians—that God loves a cheerful giver. And that helped me put things back into perspective.

From all over this country, we are getting stories about the success of the 40th annual interfaith National Bible Week. More clubs and organizations are taking part than ever before in rediscovering the inexhaustible riches that we find in the Scriptures. Churches and synagogues, the Boy Scouts, Kiwanis groups, libraries and bookstores, in labor unions and in business—all are participating this year in much greater numbers than ever before.

In Amarillo, Texas, for example, folks are taking turns in a televised reading of the entire Bible, from Genesis right through Revelations. And in Boston, a similar Bible-reading marathon is underway right at this moment.

Mr. President, your message in support of the importance of National Bible Week has been a great boost to our campaign, and we thank you for focusing attention on the Good Book and how it can help guide us in these complex times. And we'd like to express our appreciation for the example you have set, as a layman who knows and uses his Bible, by presenting you with a very special version. This is the new Washburn College Bible. Obviously, it's not the pocket-sized edition. [*Laughter*]

It contains what many consider to be the most important change in Bible design since Gutenberg. Every page, in fact every line was redesigned to enhance the readability and the poetic qualities of this greatest of all books. And this monumental task took 10 years of work by the renowned graphic designer Bradbury Thompson, who I believe is scheduled to be here today. And then this work has been further enhanced by reproductions of religious art masterpieces chosen by Carter Brown, the Director of the National Gallery of Art.

We trust that you'll enjoy this new edition as well as you have the traditional manuscripts. Day after tomorrow, all of us will pause and give thanks for all that we have received. So this is truly a most appropriate time for us all to reflect on the value of the Bible to us.

Thank you, Mr. and Mrs. Carter, for inviting us today.

THE PRESIDENT. This gives Rosalynn and me something to do the next few months. [*Laughter*] Well, I want to thank Chairman Robinson [1] and Howard Kauffmann for this gift. Is Bradbury Thompson

---

[1] Gilbert Robinson, vice president, National Laymen's Bible Committee, Inc.

here? Professor Thompson—at Yale, I believe. Stand up. Come here. Come on up. [*Applause*] Professor Thompson, come on up.

Bradbury Thompson, the noted designer, spent 10 years working on the new format for the Bible, and as you know, J. Carter Brown—I don't believe J. Carter Brown, my cousin, is here—[*laughter*]— but I think this kind of dedication to a new and exciting presentation of God's word is very exciting to us all.

And now I'd like to ask Clamma Dale, one of our favorite and most brilliant singers and artists in this Nation, to close our program here with selections. She's been here before at a state dinner, and I was very excited today earlier, to find that she was going to come and give us a rendition. Clam, I'll let you introduce your own selection. Would you like to do that? Thank you very much. She's not only a delightful and exciting singer, but also very beautiful, as you can see.

NOTE: The President spoke at 4:23 p.m. in the East Room at the White House.

Central Intelligence Agency Retirement and Disability System

Executive Order 12253. November 25, 1980

By the authority vested in me as President of the United States of America by Section 292 of the Central Intelligence Agency Retirement Act of 1964 for Certain Employees, as amended (50 U.S.C. 403 note), and in order to conform the Central Intelligence Agency Retirement and Disability System to certain amendments to the Civil Service Retirement and Disability System (Public Law 96–179), it is hereby ordered as follows:

1–101. The Director of Central Intelligence shall maintain the Central Intelligence Agency Retirement and Disability System in accordance with the following:

(a) Eliminate the "living with" requirement in the case of recognized natural children.

(b) Add a requirement of dependency to the definition of child and define "dependent" as follows:

"Dependent," in the case of any child, means that the participant involved was, at the time of the participant's death, either living with or contributing to the support of such child, as determined in accordance with such regulations as the Director shall prescribe.

1–102. The provisions of Section 1–101 are effective as of January 2, 1980.

1–103. The Director of Central Intelligence is authorized to prescribe such regulations as are necessary to carry out the provisions of this Order.

JIMMY CARTER

The White House,
November 25, 1980.

[Filed with the Office of the Federal Register, 11:14 a.m., November 26, 1980]

NOTE: The Executive order was announced by the White House on November 26.

National Family Week, 1980

Proclamation 4806. November 26, 1980

By the President of the United States of America

A Proclamation

The American family has been the most resilient, dynamic force in the growth and development of our Nation. Yet its influence is so subtle that we tend to take for granted the vital functions it performs as the source of love, support, and guidance, the wellspring of courage, determination and inspiration.

National Family Week gives us a chance to highlight the special contributions and needs of the family, to acknowledge the new challenges that American families now face, and to act on the many significant recommendations generated by the White House Conference on Families.

It is a time to seek ways to strengthen and support the family—a time to renew the realization that the fundamental integrity and vitality of the Nation relies on the underlying health of the American family.

Now, THEREFORE, I, JIMMY CARTER, President of the United States of America, in accordance with Senate Joint Resolution 156, do hereby request that the week of November 23, 1980, be designated National Family Week and call upon the people of the United States to observe this week with appropriate activities in their communities.

IN WITNESS WHEREOF, I have hereunto set my hand this twenty-sixth day of November, in the year of our Lord nineteen hundred and eighty, and of the Independence of the United States of America the two hundred and fifth.

JIMMY CARTER

[Filed with the Office of the Federal Register, 11:15 a.m., November 26, 1980]

Counsel to the President

Announcement of the Resignation of Lloyd N. Cutler.   November 26, 1980

The President has accepted the resignation of Lloyd N. Cutler as Counsel to the President, effective November 30.

At the President's request, Mr. Cutler will continue to serve as an unpaid consultant on a number of pending matters, including the legal aspects of the negotiations for the return of hostages held in Iran, the disposition of the President's papers, and the President's actions on legislation completed by the 94th Congress.

Mr. Cutler, who was appointed Counsel on October 1, 1979, had planned to stay only 1 year.

The President said that he accepted Mr. Cutler's resignation "with deep appreciation to you for having performed your difficult tasks so superbly and for having helped me so much during some trying times."

Meat Imports

Notice of Intention To Suspend Import Limitations.   November 28, 1980

INTENT TO SUSPEND MEAT IMPORT LIMITATIONS FOR CALENDAR YEAR 1981

The Act of August 22, 1964, as amended (78 Stat. 594; 93 Stat. 1291; 19 U.S.C. 1202 note) (the "Act"), requires the imposition of limitations on imports of certain meat articles if expected imports in any calendar year exceed 110 percent of the allowable import level as defined by the Act. However, the Act further provides that the President may, after giving 30 days notice and opportunity for public comment, suspend the import limitations if certain controlling factors specified in the Act are present.

On November 26, 1980, the Secretary of Agriculture published in the FEDERAL REGISTER (45 FR 78740) his estimate of (1) the allowable level of imports of fresh, chilled or frozen cattle meat (TSUS 106.10), fresh, chilled or frozen meat of goats and sheep, except lambs (TSUS 106.22 and 106.25), and prepared fresh, chilled or frozen, but not otherwise preserved, beef and veal, except sausage (TSUS 107.55 and 107.62), calculated according to the formula provided in the Act, and (2) the level of imports of those articles in the absence of imposition of import limitations. The allowable level of imports announced is 1,315 million pounds. The expected level of imports announced is 1,458 million pounds. Since the expected level of imports is more than 110 percent of the allowable level of imports, Section 2(f)(1) of the Act requires the imposition of import limitations.

The Act permits the President to suspend the import limitations on meat when the supply of meat articles will be inadequate to meet domestic demand at reasonable prices if the quotient determined in accordance with Section 2(d) of the Act is equal to or greater than 1.0. The Secretary has calculated this quotient for calendar year 1981 to be 1.16.

Information has been submitted to me which indicates that the supply of meat in the United States for calendar year 1981 will be inadequate to meet domestic demand at reasonable prices.

Therefore, in accordance with Section 2(g) of the Act, I, Jimmy Carter, President of the United States of America, hereby give notice that I intend to suspend the import limitations ordinarily required by the Act, such suspension to remain in effect for the calendar year 1981 unless changed circumstances necessitate further action under the Act.

Comments may be submitted within 30 days to the Under Secretary for International Affairs and Commodity Programs, U.S. Department of Agriculture, Room 6616, 14th and Independence Avenue, S.W., Washington, D.C. 20250, Attention of Mr. R. E. Anderson, for analysis and referral for my consideration. The Draft Impact Statement analyzing this action is available on request from the same person.

JIMMY CARTER

[Filed with the Office of the Federal Register, 12:12 p.m., November 28, 1980]

National Commission on Student Financial Assistance

Appointment of Four Members and Designation of Chairman.   November 28, 1980

The President has appointed four members to the National Commission on Student Financial Assistance, a new commission created by the Education Amendments of 1980 to study a wide range of issues dealing with financial aid for postsecondary education.

The Commission will submit recommendations to the President and Congress on matters such as appropriate means of student loan subsidization, the relationship between differing forms of aid, and the general impact of Federal student aid programs.

The President designated Congressman William D. Ford, of Michigan, as Chairman of the Commission. Mr. Ford is chairman of the House Subcommittee on Postsecondary Education. He was instrumental in writing and passing the Education Amendments.

The other members appointed by the President are:

ALPHONSE JACKSON, JR., of Louisiana, a member of the State legislature and president of a public relations and advertising firm. A former classroom teacher, Mr. Jackson was the first black from Louisiana to serve on the board of the National Education Association.

MARCELLA MAXWELL, of New York, dean of Continuing Education and Community Outreach at Medgar Evers College. She is also chairperson of the New York City Commission on the Status of Women.

JOSEPH B. MONTOYA, of California, a State senator. He is vice chair of the Senate Education Committee, chairman of the Select Committee on Occupational Preparation and Placement, and a former member of the California Advisory Committee on Vocational Education.

Four other members of the Commission will be selected by the President pro tempore of the Senate and four by the Speaker of the House.

Digest of Other White House Announcements

The following listing includes the President's public schedule and other items of general interest announced by the White House Press Office and not included elsewhere in this issue.

November 23

The President returned to the White House from Camp David, Md.

November 24

The President met at the White House with:

—Zbigniew Brzezinski, Assistant to the President for National Security Affairs;

—Frank B. Moore, Assistant to the President for Congressional Liaison;

—Representative Tim Lee Carter of Kentucky.

In a ceremony in the Oval Office, the President received diplomatic credentials from Ambassadors Stoyan Iliev Zhulev of Bulgaria, Daw San Myint of Burma, K. R. Narayanan of India, Abdallah Ould Daddah of Mauritania, and Rita Delia Casco Montenegro of Nicaragua.

The President transmitted to the Congress the fiscal year 1979 annual report of ACTION.

The White House announced that the President has designated the Secretary of Energy as Chairman and the Secretary of the Treasury as Vice Chairman of the Advisory Committee to the Board of Directors of the United States Synthetic Fuels Corporation.

The President announced that he will nominate Fernando E. Rondon, of Alexandria, Va., now Ambassador to the Democratic Republic of Madagascar, to serve concurrently as Ambassador to the Federal and Islamic Republic of Comoros. Rondon has been Ambassador to Madagascar since earlier this year and a Foreign Service officer since 1961.

The President announced that he will nominate Henry Reiter Webb, Jr., of McLean, Va., for the rank of Ambassador while he serves as United States Negotiator on Textile Matters.

The President announced that he will nominate Alice Coig McDonald, of Prospect, Ky., to be a member of the National Council on Educational Research. McDonald is deputy superintendent of education for the State of Kentucky.

November 25

The President met at the White House with:

—Dr. Brzezinski;

—Governor Jerry Brown of California;

—Mr. Moore;

—Governor Brendan Byrne of New Jersey;

—a group of his advisers for a budget overview session.

November 26

The President met at the White House with:

—Dr. Brzezinski;

—Mr. Moore;

—Senator Bill Bradley of New Jersey.

The President left the White House for Camp David, Md., where he stayed for Thanksgiving and the holiday weekend.

November 28

The President has declared a major disaster for the Commonwealth of the Northern Mariana Islands as a result of Typhoon Dinah, beginning about November 23, which caused extensive property damage.

The President has declared a major disaster for the State of California as a result of major fires and high winds, beginning on or about November 15, which caused extensive property damage.

NOMINATIONS SUBMITTED TO THE SENATE

The following list does not include promotions of members of the Uniformed Services, nominations to the Service Academies, or nominations of Foreign Service officers.

Submitted November 24, 1980

FERNANDO E. RONDON, of Virginia, a Foreign Service officer of Class two, now Ambassador Extraordinary and Plenipotentiary of the United States of America to the Democratic Republic of Madagascar, to serve concurrently and without additional compensation as Ambassador Extraordinary and Plenipotentiary of the United States of America to the Federal and Islamic Republic of the Comoros.

HENRY REITER WEBB, JR., of Virginia, for the rank of Ambassador during his tenure of service as United States Negotiator on Textile Matters.

ALICE COIG MCDONALD, of Kentucky, to be a member of the National Council on Educational Research for a term expiring September 30, 1982, vice John Corbally, term expired.

CHECKLIST OF WHITE HOUSE PRESS RELEASES

The following listing contains releases of the White House Press Office which are not included in this issue.

Released November 25, 1980

Announcement: report to the President and the Congress on "Health Hazards Associated with Alcohol and Methods to Inform the General Public of These Hazards" by the Departments of Treasury and Health and Human Services

---

ACTS APPROVED BY THE PRESIDENT

Approved November 24, 1980

H.R. 7212_____ Public Law 96–484
An act to ratify a settlement agreement in a land dispute between the Pamunkey Indian Tribe and the Southern Railway Company, and for other purposes.

Approved November 26, 1980

S.J. Res. 156_____ Public Law 96–485
A joint resolution to authorize the President to issue a proclamation designating the week of November 23 through 29, 1980, as "National Family Week".

H.R. 7764_____ Private Law 96–64
An act for the relief of Doctor Eric George Six, Ann Elizabeth Six, and Karen Elizabeth Mary Six.

H.R. 1762_____ Private Law 96–65
An act to convey all interests of the United States in certain real property in Sandoval County, New Mexico, to Walter Hernandez.

H.R. 3459_____ Private Law 96–66
An act to waive the statute of limitations with regard to the claim of Eazor Express, Incorporated, of Pittsburgh, Pennsylvania, against the United States.

Earthquake in Southern Italy

Statement on United States Assistance.
December 1, 1980

The earthquake which struck southern Italy on the evening of Sunday, November 23, was the worst natural disaster to strike Western Europe in half a century. Human suffering—from the anguish of those with families buried under the rubble to the misery of survivors without shelter in the face of cruel winter storms—is incalculable.

The death toll mounts as the missing become confirmed dead. Well over 3,000 have died, and at least 200,000 are homeless. The Italian Government and its people have mobilized their resources. Army, police, firemen, and volunteers work to the limit of their strength in rescue efforts.

But the Italian effort is not enough. The international community must help and is doing so. The United States is doing its part. I have asked our Agency for International Development office of foreign disaster assistance to respond swiftly to Italian requests, and it has already made available more than $3.5 million in relief supplies. U.S. military personnel in Italy are cooperating closely with international donors and Italian officials. An American delegation will be sent to Italy.

Congress moved quickly and generously in 1976 following a serious earthquake in Italy's northeast. Last week's disaster was far more tragic and destructive. The reconstruction effort will be enormous. The Italian Government will need help in meeting the burden, and the United States must join with others in providing that help. Therefore, I fully encourage congressional initiative to provide up to $50 million for Italian earthquake relief and to support reconstruction. I urge swift passage of the appropriate legislation. This U.S. aid will be made available when an adequate system for accepting and distributing the funds is established.

United States-Portugal Fishery Agreement

Message to the Congress Transmitting the Agreement. December 1, 1980

To the Congress of the United States:

In accordance with the Fishery Conservation and Management Act of 1976 (Public Law 94–265; 16 U.S.C. 1801), I transmit herewith a governing international fishery agreement between the United States and Portugal, signed at Washington on October 16, 1980.

This agreement is one of a series to be negotiated in accordance with that legislation. I urge that the Congress give favorable consideration to this agreement at an early date. Since 60 calendar days of continuous session, as required by the legislation, may not be available, I recommend that the Congress consider issuance of a joint resolution to bring this agreement into force.

JIMMY CARTER

The White House,
    December 1, 1980.

NOTE: The message was announced by the White House Press Office on December 2.

Alaska National Interest Lands Conservation Act

Remarks on Signing H.R. 39 Into Law.
December 2, 1980

THE PRESIDENT. I see this simple little bill lying on the table here. [*Laughter*]

This is indeed a proud day for me and for the Congress and for all of you who've worked so hard to help create and enact this legislation. To Mo Udall, to John Seiberling, to Senator Jackson, to Phil Burton, Paul Tsongas—who can't be here today because of the death of his father— Alan Cranston, Ted Stevens, to the Alaska coalition, not to be confused with the entire Alaska delegation—[*laughter*]— both of which deserve credit for the passage of the legislation, and for Secretary Andrus and others, I am deeply grateful.

For nearly a quarter of a century, really, since even before 1958, thousands of dedicated Americans have worked for this historic moment. The bill before me now, the Alaska National Interest Lands Conservation Act, without a doubt is one of the most important pieces of conservation legislation ever passed in this Nation. I was going over this morning early the comparison between what this bill is and the original administration proposal that we submitted to the Congress, and they are remarkably similar. Never before have we seized the opportunity to preserve so

much of America's natural and cultural heritage on so grand a scale.

We are setting aside for conservation an area of land larger than the State of California. By designating more than 97 million acres for new parks and refuges, we are doubling the size of our National Park and Wildlife Refuge System. By protecting 25 free-flowing Alaskan rivers in their natural state, we are almost doubling the size of our Wild and Scenic Rivers System. By classifying 56 million acres of some of the most magnificent land in our Federal estate as wilderness, we are tripling the size of our Wilderness System.

We've preserved the unparalleled beauty of areas like the Misty Fiords and Admiralty Island National Monuments in southeast Alaska. And we've ensured that Alaska's Eskimos and Indians and Aleuts can continue their traditional way of life. And we've given the State of Alaska, finally, the opportunity to choose the land which will be theirs through eternity.

I've been fortunate. I've seen firsthand some of the splendors of Alaska. But many Americans have not. Now, whenever they or their children or their grandchildren choose to visit Alaska, they'll have the opportunity to see much of its splendid beauty undiminished and its majesty untarnished.

This act of Congress reaffirms our commitment to the environment. It strikes a balance between protecting areas of great beauty and value and allowing development of Alaska's vital oil and gas and mineral and timber resources. A hundred percent of the offshore areas and 95 percent of the potentially productive oil and mineral areas will be available for exploration or for drilling. With this bill we are acknowledging that Alaska's wilderness areas are truly this country's crown jewels and that Alaska's resources are treasures of another sort. How to tap these resources is a challenge that we can now face in the decade ahead.

As a nation, we have been blessed with an abundance of natural resources. We've also been blessed with an abundance of natural wonders—from the Grand Canyon to the gates of the Arctic, from the Everglades to Yellowstone—we're only just now learning how to use the one without abusing the other. We must not let the pressures of the day interfere with these efforts to enhance the quality of our lives. We cannot let our eagerness for progress in energy and in technology outstrip our care for our land, for our water and for air, and for the plants and animals that share all of these precious vital resources with us. Every time we dig out minerals or drill wells, every time we ignore erosion or destroy a sand dune or dam a wild river or dump garbage or create pollution, we're changing the living Earth.

Sometimes this change might be beneficial, but we should always change the world in which we live with great care. We are affecting the air we breathe and the water we drink. We have nothing more precious than life itself, nothing more valuable to us than health. We must not forfeit these in the pursuit of progress. We must face the fact that these threats to the quality of life will mount inexorably in the years ahead.

We've tried to look forward to the year 2000, and we've been very concerned at what we've seen. We must face the fact that these threats to the quality of life will perhaps be the greatest challenges which this Nation must face. None of us can afford to relax our vigilance, and we certainly cannot afford to rely on government alone to be vigilant for us. Each of us has a responsibility to the environment that nurtures all of us.

Years ago, Americans used to feel secure surrounded by wide oceans, but today, we have a different world view and different kinds of oceans to contemplate. Today, we know that all of us, the globe over, belong to the same, very small world, adrift in the vast areas of space. We see more clearly that we have a duty—to ourselves and to our descendants, to the environment and to the world itself—to conserve, to preserve, to use, but to think before we act, and always to care.

We Americans have a history of viewing the environment as wilderness and wilderness as something that must be conquered. But we must never forget that as vast and dark and forbidding as the forests may seem, they are very fragile; and as wide and as boundless as the oceans may seem, they're quite vulnerable. For all that the Earth has given us, we owe it our respect and, more importantly, our understanding. We're the stewards of an irreplaceable environment. That's an awesome task as well as a precious gift.

In the decade past we've worked hard to build strong programs to protect the environment and, where there was damage, to clean our skies and waterways. We have made some progress. It has not been easy. Human greed is not an easy foe to conquer. As Governor and as President, this has been one of my most difficult political challenges, and throughout my life in the future, it's a challenge that I will continue to meet.

In the last 4 years, we've strengthened the Clean Air and Clean Water Acts and the Coastal Zone Management Act. We've established strict Federal environmental standards for coal mining, provided for better control of pesticides and toxic chemicals. We have at least continued our protection of endangered species. Outside of Alaska, we've made vast additions to our National Park System. We've created new wilderness areas and designated new Wild and Scenic Rivers. We cannot afford to retreat from these efforts now. We cannot afford to look at the immediate financial profits and ignore the long-term costs of misusing the environment.

Protecting our environment also brings immediate results to our health and to the development of new technology, new areas of understanding, new knowledge that benefits us all. It brings us some financial costs as well, but these costs, compared to the benefits, are very modest indeed. The price of not protecting the environment would be far greater and far more lasting. Much of the damage cannot possibly be repaired at any price. We protect it today, or we lose it for all time.

In tackling our challenges—the problems of hazardous waste disposal and eroding beaches, extinction of plant and animal species, and human overpopulation—we have our forebears to emulate. When they came to these shores they faced challenges beyond any they had known previously, and they had to think and they had to fight their way through. Their success is our legacy now. Their triumphs and their mistakes have much to teach us.

We've learned the hard way, in some cases, that we cannot, without consequence, take from the land without giving. We've learned, too, that what we need as we enter the 1980's is the same thing the pioneers had when they first entered the wilderness of this country— determination, courage, daring.

We were determined to preserve portions of Alaska. Fifty-six million acres of that State can now stand pristine. We dared to act with foresight, instead of hindsight, and with an understanding that Alaska will help keep our Nation both energy-strong and environmentally rich.

As our descendants look back on the 1980's, I hope it will be said by them that we kept our commitment to the restoration of environmental quality; that we protected the public health from the continuing dangers of toxic chemicals, from pollution, from hazardous and radioactive wastes; that we put this Nation on a path to a sustainable energy future, one based increasingly on renewable resources and on the elimination of waste.

Let it be said that we moved to protect America's countryside, that this year, the Year of the Coast, was perhaps the turning point in protecting, finally, our coastland from mismanagement; that we redirected the management of the Nation's water resources toward water conservation and environmental protection; that we've faced squarely such worldwide problems as deforestation, acid rain, toxic waste disposal, carbon dioxide buildup, and nuclear proliferation.

That all of us have won so much in Alaska is all the more reason to continue our fight for our other environmental concerns. That we've struck a balance between Alaska's economic interests and its natural beauty, its industry and its ecology, is all the more reason to try now to strike similar balances elsewhere in our Nation. This act of Congress gives us both the knowledge and the impetus and inspiration.

For today, in closing, let me say, let us celebrate. The mountains that rim the Misty Fjords and rise above Admiralty Island, the tracks of man's past along the Bering Strait, the rivers and lakes that harbor salmon and trout, the game trails of caribou and grizzly in the Brooks Range, the marshes where our waterfowl summer—all these are now preserved, now and, I pray, for all time to come. I thank God that you have helped to make it possible for me to sign this bill.

After I sign the bill, I'd like to call on John Seiberling and Mo Udall and Scoop Jackson and Ted Stevens and Secretary Andrus to say a few words. But they will speak not only for me and our Nation but for all of you who've been so instrumental in this tremendous achievement.

Thank you very much.

[*At this point, the President signed the bill.*]

REPRESENTATIVE SEIBERLING. Mr. President and guests, as one who spent several months, in fact, several years on the long trail to this day, this is one of the great thrills of my life.

When I was in Alaska it occurred to me that there are very few places in this country where you can see vast sweeps of land and myriads of wildlife just as they were when the Creator made them. And to save part of that heritage that thrilled the pioneers of old required thinking big and thinking long. Many thousands of people worked on this legislation, but if there are any people who were absolutely indispensable to it, those people are President Carter and Cecil Andrus, and we are going to be eternally indebted to them.

I remember in 1977, in one of our village hearings, in the village of Togiak, Alaska, one of the old natives there said that if we fail to save the land, God may forgive us, but our children won't. Mr. President, our children will be eternally indebted to you.

REPRESENTATIVE UDALL. Where in the heck were all these folks out in Arizona when I needed it? [*Laughter*]

The fall of even-numbered years is hazardous for political figures and for football coaches, and I remember Winston Churchill, or some great thinker, maybe it was I—[*laughter*]—said the most exhilarating experience is to be shot at and missed. [*Laughter*] I remember, Mr. President, up in Fairbanks, last summer, they had a fair and exhibits and booths. And the Junior Chamber of Commerce got 2,000 empty beer bottles, and they had four pictures on the wall that you could pay a quarter and throw a beer bottle at— Jimmy Carter, Cecil Andrus, Mo Udall, and the Ayatollah—number one. [*Laughter*] And so here we are, just a couple of— [*laughter*]. They said 1 minute. I'll abuse it, but not very much.

Americans have been really poor judges of our contemporary Presidents, as witness the revival of Harry Truman in recent years—the Republicans have discovered him and his greatness. We've been pretty harsh on our contemporary Presidents, and I don't pretend to read history, but I'll tell you one thing: This President, Jimmy Carter, and his administration are going to rank big among the Presidents in conservation. No one has done more, no President has done more, with the possible exception of Theodore Roosevelt, to do things in conservation that need being done, and nobody can ever take that away from you, Mr. President.

I'm joyous. I'm glad today for the people of Alaska. They can get on with building a great State. They're a great people. And this matter is settled and put to rest, and the development of Alaska can go forward with balance. I feel a sense of joy for the American people who've waited a long time for this great day. And I'm happy about all of us that the conservation movement has been bipartisan over the years, going back to Roosevelt and Pinchot and all the great Presidents.

Einstein once said when congratulated on his scientific work, he said, "We all stand on the shoulders of great men of the past." And in bringing this legislation about, we ought to remember that there are people like John Saylor, who's no longer with us—our amendment in 1971 was Section D–2 of this bill; it was the Udall-Saylor Amendment—other good Interior Secretaries like Cecil Andrus, and one whose name I've forgotten, a relative of mine. [*Laughter*] But we ride on, we stand on the shoulders, as we make this great achievement, of some of the giants of the past, and I'm proud to be a part of it.

One of the things I like about my country, and there are a lot of them, is that we love the land. There's a deep feeling for the beaches and the mountains and the wilderness areas. We love the land, and we're going to protect the land. And I think the old song put it best: "This land is your land, this land is my land, from the redwood forests to the New York Island," and so on. "This land belongs to you and me." And that's what we've done here today. I'm proud to be a part of it.

Thank you very much.

SENATOR JACKSON. Thank you, Mr. President, and thank you, Cece, for the great leadership that you gave us in this long endeavor.

We're here as the result of a section that was placed in the Native Claims Settlement Act, all related to settling the issue with the Aleuts, the Eskimos, and the Indians of Alaska, and we put in a little section called D–2. And that's where the title came, D–2 of the Native Claims Settlement Act. That was 1971. It took 9 years of effort really to make this possible.

And two things I think that stand out:

One is perseverance, which was always present with humor—after all, without Mo Udall—[*laughter*]—where would we be? But I think it's also a tribute to the best in the art of compromise, and with patience and compromise and bipartisanship, because Senator Stevens, in particular, stuck his neck out over and over again, kept us together on the Senate side, when it was said over and over again, "It's dead." And in all of this, we had the backing and the support of the President of the United States and Cece Andrus moving around the various offices when it was dead, only to be revived again.

So, this is a great day. It's not what everyone wanted on either side of the issue, but I believe it will be indeed a lasting monument in striking a balance between development on one hand, and preservation and conservation on the other. We salute you, Mr. President.

SENATOR STEVENS. Thank you very much, Mr. President, Mrs. Carter.

You're very gracious to offer me the opportunity to make some remarks here. They've got to be short, because I've got an election I hope to win in about 5 minutes if I'm going to be the Assistant Majority Leader next year. It starts at 10 o'clock, so I won't be long. [*Laughter*]

Mr. President, this is a historic bill. I want you to know that there are people at home, as Scoop Jackson has said, who believe that we've made a mistake. I'm one who's very proud of my State and proud of the heritage and its great attractions that have brought all of you to this room and have committed so many people to try and preserve a portion of Alaska. We have not disagreed on goals; we have disagreed on the means to attain those goals, and we've disagreed from the point of view of the half million people who live there 365 days a year trying to protect our rights when we see the avalanche of 225 million people who want to prevent us from making the mistakes that their predecessors made with regard to their lands.

We believe that the American system is one that evolves and that we can learn from mistakes of others. I do believe there's balance in this bill, because it will fulfill the commitment of the Statehood Act. And we will have to go into Alaskan ownership, an area, Mr. President, the size of California or a little bit larger, and the rights of our Alaskan native people will be protected by virtue of the additional amendments that are in this bill to the Alaskan Native Land Claims Settlement Act.

I'm indebted to my good friend Scoop Jackson and to Senator Hatfield, Mark Hatfield, and others who worked so long on our side to keep up this good humor and to keep us moving towards the goal of trying to get a bill that would fulfill our hopes and aspirations and meet the goals of all of you here. This bill did not do that for us, and I think for some of you, it didn't meet all of your goals either. So, we're not finished, Mr. President; we've just really started.

Over half of the Federal lands that will remain under the control of the Department of Interior will be in Alaska after the passage of this bill. Over half of the hydrocarbon resources of the United States are in Alaska's lands. We know that the time will come when those resources will be demanded by other Americans. And we seek to protect our freedoms, to try to prevent us from becoming a "permit society" where we have to have a permit to do everything; and at the same time, be able to contribute to the nation that we all love so well.

The other day, a friend of mine crashed an airplane in a national monument, Mr. President, and he was told that he better get that out of there. And then, when he started to get it out, he was told he couldn't get it out because he was going to use a helicopter to lift it out and he didn't have a permit to fly a helicopter in a national monument. Now, that may not seem to be oppressive to you, but to us, freedom is the essence of living on the frontier, and I've done my best to try and protect those freedoms with the help of all these gentlemen here, and I too congratulate you for a milestone in conservation legislation.

THE PRESIDENT. Thank you.

SECRETARY ANDRUS. Thank you very much, ladies and gentlemen.

Mr. President, Mrs. Carter, distinguished Members of the Congress:

I will be brief so Ted can make his election. But I would hope, Mr. President, that we would recognize that in these times of need for energy and minerals that the American people have spoken through their elected Members of the Congress that, yes, they're concerned, but they are also concerned about the environment in which they live and that they feel that we too have to leave a legacy for future generations. And this we have done, Mr. President. At least they have the opportunity to make a difficult decision in the future if they must.

But we wouldn't be here today without the characteristic tenacity of yourself, Mr. President, and the total willingness of you to meet at any time and to work on this bill. There are many people in this room that deserve the credit, and if we started the list would be longer than the bill that the President just signed. But Mo Udall mentioned John Saylor. I think too of

Lee Metcalf. I think too of my predecessor, Rogers Morton, and other people that have worked on this. Those three men are no longer with us, but I'm certain that they're looking down upon us today saying, "Well done," to the Congress of the United States, to the President, the executive branch, the people who've proven that you can collectively continue to resolve difficult problems.

We in America have spent too many years in salvage operations, protecting the last little remnant of redwoods or a short stretch of free-flowing river. Now, here in Alaska we have indeed done it the first time, and the Alaskan native that John Seiberling spoke of will not have to ask forgiveness of his grandchildren. They will be pleased. And so we're all proud today, those of us that are here, me, you, the audience. But I think the beneficiaries are those generations yet unborn who will have the opportunity to visit, as the President described, those unique areas.

I'm pleased to have been a part of it, Mr. President, and as history writes about this administration, I think it will be one of the hallmarks, of course, the landmark legislation that you helped pass. My appreciation goes to all those people that have worked with me. And in closing let me be just a tiny bit provincial in that obviously Bob Bergland's department, my department, the White House staff, congressional staff, everybody worked on it, but the Department of the Interior personnel worked long and hard, day and night, weekends, without time off, and I appreciate it.

NOTE: The President spoke at 9:34 a.m. at the signing ceremony in the East Room at the White House.

As enacted, H.R. 39 is Public Law 96–487, approved December 2.

United States-Bangladesh Convention on Taxation and Fiscal Evasion

Message to the Senate Transmitting the Convention.   December 2, 1980

To the Senate of the United States:

I transmit herewith, for Senate advice and consent to ratification, the Convention between the Government of the United States of America and the Government of the People's Republic of Bangladesh for the Avoidance of Double Taxation and the Prevention of Fiscal Evasion with Respect to Taxes on Income (the Convention), together with a related exchange of notes, signed at Dacca on October 6, 1980.

The Convention, in general, follows the pattern of the United States model income tax convention, with a few departures from the model to accommodate Bangladesh's status as a developing country.

The Convention differs in one major respect from other recent United States tax treaties, including those with developing countries. In most of these treaties a source country exemption is provided for shipping and aircraft operating income. The convention with Bangladesh, however, provides exemption for aircraft income only; shipping income is taxable under the internal laws of the two Contracting States.

The exchange of notes sets out certain understandings between the two governments.

I recommend that the Senate give early and favorable consideration to the Convention and give advice and consent to ratification.

JIMMY CARTER

The White House,
　December 2, 1980.

United States-Norway Convention on Taxation

Message to the Senate Transmitting a Protocol.　December 2, 1980

To the Senate of the United States:

I transmit herewith, for Senate advice and consent to ratification, a Protocol amending the Convention between the United States of America and the Kingdom of Norway signed at Oslo on December 3, 1971, which Protocol was signed at Oslo on September 19, 1980. I also enclose, for the information of the Senate, the report of the Department of State.

The Protocol modifies the existing convention between the United States and Norway. It takes into account changes in Norway's tax system during the years since the Convention was negotiated and otherwise brings it up to date.

In 1975, Norway amended its corporate tax in several ways to increase the burden of that tax on corporations deriving income from the extraction of offshore oil and gas. The 1975 legislation also added a special tax on income from submarine petroleum resources. Article I of the Protocol clarifies certain questions arising from these changes by providing foreign tax credits with respect to the corporate tax and the special tax, with a limitation for taxpayers subject to the special tax to the amount necessary to offset United States tax on the petroleum income from sources within Norway. This limitation is similar to that contained in the Third Protocol to the income tax convention between the United States and the United Kingdom.

The Convention does not provide specific rules to determine when a country has the right to tax income resulting from the exploration or exploitation of its continental shelf and its natural resources. Article II of the Protocol allows Norway and the United States to impose a tax on income derived from the exploitation or exploration of natural resources on their respective continental shelves after such activities have existed for more than 30 days in a twelve month period. With respect to income from employment in such activities, however, an exemption is provided for wages attributable to sixty days of personal services performed in the taxable year.

In addition, the Protocol modifies the rate of withholding tax at source on dividends and interest and allows the United States to tax gains from the sale of shares in companies whose assets consist principally of United States real property. It also contains other provisions, including a new provision on the tax treatment of entertainers and athletes and clarifies provisions on administrative cooperation.

I recommend that the Senate give early and favorable consideration to the Protocol and give advice and consent to its ratification.

JIMMY CARTER

The White House,
　December 2, 1980.

Budget Deferrals

Message to the Congress.　December 2, 1980

To the Congress of the United States:

In accordance with the Impoundment Control Act of 1974, I herewith report four new deferrals of budget authority totalling $2,770.8 million and three revisions to previously transmitted deferrals increasing the amount deferred by $846.2 million.

The new deferrals involve programs related to International Security Assistance, Department of Defense military construction programs, and the Tennessee Valley Authority.

The revisions to existing deferrals involve programs in the Departments of Defense, Transportation, and the Treasury.

The details of the deferrals are contained in the attached reports.

JIMMY CARTER

The White House,

December 2, 1980.

NOTE: The attachments detailing the deferrals are printed in the FEDERAL REGISTER of December 5, 1980.

Christmas 1980

Statement by the President.
December 2, 1980

Rosalynn and I send special greetings and good wishes to those of our fellow citizens who join us in the joyous celebration of Christmas.

Together let us thank God for all the blessings He has given us and ask Him to sustain and strengthen us as individuals and as a nation. Let us also offer our prayers for those who live where there is strife, hunger, persecution, or injustice. May the year ahead be better for them and for their families and loved ones.

We hope that this hoiday season will be a very happy and satisfying one for all Americans and that 1981 will bring us closer to the realization of our hopes and dreams.

Meeting With Vice President Muhammad Husni Mubarak of Egypt

Remarks Following the Meeting.
December 2, 1980

THE PRESIDENT. I'd like to say for the people of our country and to the people of Egypt how delighted we are and honored to have Vice President Mubarak come here to visit with me personally and to deliver a very important message to me from President Sadat.

One of the most gratifying things about my own service as President of our country has been the close and personal relationship that has existed between me and President Sadat and Vice President Mubarak and the other leaders of Egypt. It's been the courage and the good vision of the future that has enabled the initiative by President Sadat in going to Jerusalem and in opening up the possibility of peace to be successful. Also, in this troubled time when the Middle Eastern region and the area around the Persian Gulf is a great challenge to the rest of the world and a threat to peace, the indissoluble ties between the United States and Egypt, based upon the peace treaty which has been consummated, gives a stabilizing effect that is valuable to us all.

I've expressed to President Sadat through Vice President Mubarak my deep appreciation, my admiration, and my commitment on behalf of the American people, I'm sure, speaking accurately for the next administration, that these ties of friendship and mutual purpose will continue, and the efforts for a comprehensive peace in the Middle East will also continue. This is a hope and a dream of mine, the leaders of Egypt and the leaders of Israel, and I'm sure the other neighbors of Israel in that region and indeed the entire northern part of Africa as well—desire for peace and stability for themselves and for the world.

So, to Prime Minister Mubarak, welcome. Thank you for this additional visit, and my best wishes to President Sadat and to the people of your great country.

THE VICE PRESIDENT. I am very pleased to meet with President Carter once again and to convey to him President Sadat's message. I also conveyed to the President the appreciation of the Egyptian people for the cooperation and understanding we always found here. For 4 years the friendship and the cooperation between our two nations grew steadily. We look forward to continuing this warm relation with the American people and their leadership.

As you know, President Sadat and the entire Egyptian people value this friendship with the American people very highly. President Carter has made a great contribution to the cause of peace in the Middle East. We are determined to pursue the goal of establishing comprehensive peace in the region. We are certain that the American people will continue to lend us their support.

I have extended an invitation to President Carter on behalf of President Sadat to visit Egypt soon. He is held with the greatest esteem and affection. He laid a solid foundation for a historic transformation in the Middle East.

Our respect to the President; our admiration, of President Sadat, me, and the Egyptian people, to President Carter and his administration. Thank you.

THE PRESIDENT. Thank you again. It's a pleasure to have you here.

THE VICE PRESIDENT. Thank you very much.

NOTE: The President spoke at 11:58 a.m. on the South Grounds of the White House.

Convention on the Conservation of Antarctic Marine Living Resources

Message to the Senate Transmitting the Convention.   December 2, 1980

To the Senate of the United States:

I transmit herewith, for the advice and consent of the Senate to ratification, the Convention on the Conservation of Antarctic Marine Living Resources. I also transmit for the information of the Senate the report of the Department of State with respect to this treaty.

The Convention on the Conservation of Antarctic Marine Living Resources will establish international mechanisms and create legal obligations necessary for the protection and conservation of the marine living resources found in the waters surrounding Antarctica. The Convention incorporates an ecosystem approach to the management of those resources, including standards designed to enable mankind to conserve the individual populations and species and to maintain the health of the Antarctic marine ecosystem as a whole. Implementation of this Convention offers a welcome and unusual opportunity to apply to shared resources an effective regulatory framework prior to the emergence of large-scale commercial harvesting of those resources.

The significance of this Convention lies not only in its environmental and resource management provisions and objectives. It also represents an important example of international cooperation among the Consultative Parties of the Antarctic Treaty. The system established by the Antarctic Treaty two decades ago has permitted its Parties, who maintain differences of position concerning claims to territorial sovereignty in Antarctica, to work together to further scientific research and to ensure that Antarctica does not become the scene or object of international discord. This new Convention, which extends this unique pattern of international cooperation into the area of resource management, is thus also important as an international legal and political undertaking.

The United States played a leading role in the negotiation of the Convention on the Conservation of Antarctic Marine Living Resources. The Convention reflects our concern for the protection of the Antarctic marine ecosystem—including the whales, penguins and seals which are components of it. It is my hope that the United States will also play a leading role in the effective implementation of the Convention. To this end, it is important that the United States be represented at the first meeting of the Commission which will be held within a year of the entry into force of the Convention following the deposit of the eighth instrument of ratification.

I recommend that the Senate give early and favorable consideration to this treaty and give its advice and consent to ratification.

JIMMY CARTER

The White House,
  December 2, 1980.

State of Israel Bond Organization

Remarks at a Dinner Honoring AFL–CIO President Lane Kirkland. December 2, 1980

I have to admit that the applause sounds better now than it did a year ago. [*Laughter*]

Ambassador Evron, President Lane Kirkland, Tom Donahue,[1] members of

---
[1] Secretary-treasurer, AFL–CIO.

the AFL–CIO executive council, members of great independent labor unions, and other friends of Israel who've come to join me in honoring Lane tonight:

I want to begin by offering my congratulations to the Israel Bond Organization on their 30th anniversary and on having just passed the $5 billion mark. That's how much this organization has raised for Israel's economic development. And I've also been very eager to join with you tonight in saluting a man who has won my deepest admiration. My feeling for Lane Kirkland extends beyond either politics or party. I want Lane to know in the presence of those he loves and respects that in me he has a friend for life.

Lane and I have a lot in common. We're both Democrats; we're both southerners. Both of us are proud of what we've been able to accomplish together. Each of us has been elected to one term in office—[*laughter*]—as President. But I have a strong feeling that the similarity ends right there. [*Laughter*] Fortunately for organized labor, fortunately for all the people of our great country, fortunately for all people around the world who honor and cherish human rights, we expect Lane Kirkland to be heading the American labor movement for many years to come.

As many of you know, the AFL–CIO has its main office on 16th Street, right across from Pennsylvania Avenue. You might say that they are within shouting distance of the White House. This is a little fact of which I've been reminded from time to time when I heard the voices coming across the street toward my office. I know this great labor organization is proud of its close proximity to the seat of the executive power of our country. I've been told that President George Meany enjoyed taking friends to his office window and pointing out to them how his office looked down on the White House. [*Laughter*] And I wouldn't be surprised if Lane Kirkland carries on a similar ritual as some of his friends who visit him up there.

In a few weeks I'll be leaving my office on Pennsylvania Avenue, but there is, of course, a positive side of the transition. Lane Kirkland, those who work with him, will be staying behind, and it's nice to know that a good friend of mine will be looking after our neighborhood in the years ahead.

Tonight I've come to help you in honoring a great American in a special way.

Golda Meir, in her lifetime, became a symbol of Israel, but she was more than a symbol. I first met Golda Meir when I was Governor of Georgia, making a very important trip for me to Israel. She received me and my wife in her office for extended conversations about religion, politics, her own nation, our Nation, the close ties that bind us together. I knew her to be a living, breathing, loving, human example of what Israel is all about.

Golda Meir embodied the finest qualities of her own nation. She was strong, yet compassionate. She was tough-minded, but also an idealist. She had a bright vision of the future, but she lived in the real world. She was defiant to her enemies, but she still found humor in life's adversities. She was a lover of democracy and of peace, she was a champion of working people, she was a fighter for the rights of labor. Most of all she was a real leader. As a leader, she could distinguish from the permanent from the transient. She was a fighter who always knew the reason for her own struggle.

In October of 1972 she told a conference of American women, "I doubt if I will live long enough to see an Arab leader who wants peace with Israel." At the time she spoke, her doubts were well founded.

When I first met with President Sadat, early in 1977, he shared the same basic sentiments about the unlikely prospects of finding an Israeli leader and an Arab leader, at the same time, who jointly shared the commitment to peace adequately, to search for it. But 5 years after Golda Meir made her remarks, as President Anwar Sadat of Egypt arrived on his peace mission in Jerusalem, and the world both held its breath and then breathed a sigh of relief, she saw the breakthrough for what it was.

Here's what she said to President Sadat, in her very emotional welcome to him: "When I was asked many years ago when I thought peace would come," she said, "I said the date I do not know. But I know under what conditions it will come: when there will be a great leader of an Arab country. He will wake up one morning and feel sorry for his own people, and for his sons who have fallen in battle. That day will be the beginning of peace." And then she said this to President Sadat: "You've come to us for the sake of your sons as well as for the sake of ours."

Of all mothers who mourn their sons that fell in battle, Golda Meir could get to the heart of a matter—as you can see from these brief remarks—and so can Lane Kirkland. Where there's controversy, Lane is able to strip the matter down to its basic elements. He sees what is essential and what is not. He also sees what is negotiable and what is not and never can be negotiable. Lane and I have fought side by side for many good causes these past 4 years, but I've never doubted Lane's strength and his will to keep right on fighting until ultimately the goal is won or will be won.

His commitment to economic and social justice does not stop with those questions narrowly defined as so-called "labor issues." I'll never forget something that Lane said to me in a small group in the summer of 1979. We were at Camp David, wrestling with the challenge of foreign oil dependency, trying to arouse our Nation and to turn it around on this urgent matter. Lane Kirkland sized up the situation perfectly. No one put the whole question better than he. "Mr. President," he said, "the issue is freedom."

When we raised the issue of human rights around the world, many people did not then and still do not see the significance of it, the profound significance of the issue of human rights. The people in Africa see it. The people in Asia see it. The people in Latin America see it. The people in Eastern Europe understand it. Many of the people in Western Europe and in this country still do not see the profound significance of the issue of human rights. But to Lane Kirkland the issue has always been clear. Human rights is what the United States of America should stand for in the world.

When the United States and Israel and her major Arab neighbor began their first fumbling steps toward progress for a much desired peace, Lane Kirkland knew the importance of that struggle, and he joined it. To him the issue was clear—not just peace for the Middle East but peace also for the United States of America.

Lane Kirkland is being honored here tonight with the Golda Meir Leadership Award for, quote, "Leadership, service, and dedication in the spirit and measure of the founders of the State of Israel." Like the founders of Israel, like Golda Meir, Lane is committed to the rights of working people. He's dedicated his life to protecting and expanding those rights. Like the founders of Israel, Lane is committed to human rights. To him, labor rights and human rights are indivisible.

Lane is also committed to Israel itself, to its security, to its development, to its long-term prosperity. That commitment is in the great tradition of the American trade unionism. It was in 1917 that the American Federation of Labor voiced its official support for the claim of the Jewish people for a national homeland in Palestine. For more than six decades of challenge and diversity and adversity in Israel and outside Israel among Jewish people, that commitment of the American labor movement has never wavered.

It's a commitment shared today by America as a whole. We Americans support Israel, because we identify with its struggle. It's a struggle for freedom, it's a struggle for democracy, it's a struggle, itself, for the protection of human rights. We identify with Israel's courage, its unwavering, unswerving determination. We Americans, as individuals, care about Israel. We care about Israel's people, but our support for that great country is not just a case of a big nation looking out for a smaller one. It is and it ought to be recognized by everyone as a true partnership.

I've been privileged to help, as President, in forging that true partnership between the United States and Israel: a partnership built not on the superiority of one of the partners, but on the common interests, on common goals, on common values of both nations and both peoples.

In March of last year, I went to Jerusalem to help bring the Camp David accords to fruition. While there, I had the opportunity to speak at one of the most democratic political assemblies in the world: the Israeli Knesset. And I certainly found it to be the most lively organization that I've ever addressed.

Here's a nation that has fought four wars in which its very survival, in each instance, has been at stake. Here's a nation that has been under attack since the very day of its founding. Yet Israel has never lost sight of its democratic foundations. For more than 30 years, in spite of war, in spite of terrorism, in spite of every kind of international harassment, the people of Israel have clung tightly and fiercely to their own liberty. And Israel has proven that democracy need not be something that a nation honors only when its own security is certain.

That's always a temptation—when a nation's security is threatened—to turn from democracy. Israel has never been tempted to do so. Administrations change. Policies are modified. People disagree. Governments have differences. But the values which the United States and Israel hold in common must and they will endure.

Israel has never known peace, not complete peace. It's always faced the dangers of terrorism, the dangers of neighbors who threaten its very survival. But through the good will of many people, these three great nations have now taken a major first step. We've begun the process. We've turned two great peoples from the posture of war to the embrace of friendship. We've been peacemakers. And our three nations have been something else. We have been teachers. The United States, Israel, and Egypt have indeed shown the world that enmity and hatred are not irreversible, that peoples can, if they choose, learn to live together, learn to work together.

Tonight we've come here to pay honor to a man who has shared this commitment, again, to Israel and to the ideals for which it stands—democracy, human rights, and the love for peace.

In closing I would like to say a brief word about the future. This evening Jews everywhere begin their annual celebration of freedom and dedication. There's much to celebrate this Chanukah. Since the first Chanukah candle was lit we have seen 2,000 years of preservation and continuity in the Jewish faith. And for the first time in that 2,000-year history or more, an independent, secure Israel has seen that peace is possible, that peace is not just a dream. The process we've undertaken, the lesson that has been learned, can be the beginning of a full and lasting peace. That goal can be won by carrying on what has been begun. It must be won through negotiation, not through terrorism, and not through a continued state of belligerence. The road to full peace will not be easy, but the direction has now been clearly marked.

Recently I met with Prime Minister Begin, who expressed to me since the election in our own country a deep desire and a deep commitment to continue the Camp David process toward a full and complete peace in the Middle East. And today, through the Vice President, Mubarak, Egypt, I received a personal request from President Sadat that this peace process be pursued by the United States and Israel and Egypt in the months ahead.

I'm very proud of what we've started. I'm proud, too, of our commitment to Israel. For me that commitment has been a personal one, deeply personal for me. I came to the Presidency of this great country determined that the security of Israel would never be threatened by another war. I leave office having helped in forging the only recognized and formal peace that Israel has ever known. This is a precious thing, not to be abandoned.

In a few weeks my own public duties will pass to my successor. But my commitment to Israel, to its peace with Egypt and with its other neighbors, to the peace it deserves, to the peace it cherishes, to the peace so valuable to the people of my country, this commitment to Israel and to peace will remain with me for the rest of my life.

Thank you very much.

NOTE: The President spoke at 9:17 p.m. in the International Ballroom at the Washington Hilton Hotel.

Agricultural Act of 1980

Statement on Signing H.R. 3765 Into Law. December 3, 1980

Four years ago, one of the chief priorities of my administration was the establishment of an International Food Security Reserve, a reserve of food grain to be held by the Government to help alleviate hunger around the world. Today, I am pleased to sign into law H.R. 3765, which establishes this Reserve.

For the past three decades, our Government has appropriated funds each year to buy grain and other foods to ship to needy people overseas. That program has helped millions, but when crops were poor and grain prices increasing, the amount of grain our dollars could buy declined just when help was needed most.

This new authority will make our dollars more effective. We can purchase when production is abundant and hold them until needed. These stock purchases will strengthen markets for our farmers during the periods of low farm prices. And they will help assure needy people and nations around the world that American food aid will be sufficient when they are needed most.

This bill also authorizes a new program of special loan rates for 1980 and 1981 crop wheat and feed grains in the farmer-owned reserve. These provisions should significantly strengthen this important program. And it changes the market order rules to facilitate the use of private funds by growers to promote the use of California walnuts and olives.

There are two troublesome features in the bill. It requires waiver of all interest due the Government on 1980 and 1981 crop wheat and feed grains in the farmer-owned reserve. I believe this requirement is needlessly expensive and is unnecessary for the effective operation of the program. I hope the Congress will delete this provision during the next year's review of farm legislation.

The second troublesome feature authorizes a commodity loan program for alcohol processors. Such a program would duplicate programs already available to processors of alcohol. It would divert to alcohol processors programs intended to provide price support for farm commodities. And it would be costly. Because the establishment of such a reserve is not required by the law, I do not intend to request funds to implement that program. I hope the Congress will delete this provision as well during next year's consideration of farm legislation.

NOTE: As enacted, H.R. 3765 is Public Law 96–494, approved December 3.

National Advisory Community Investment Board

Executive Order 12254. December 3, 1980

By the authority vested in me as President of the United States of America by Section 704 of the Economic Opportunity Act of 1964, as amended (42 U.S.C. 2981c), and in order to establish a National Advisory Community Investment Board, in accord with the Federal Advisory Committee Act, as amended (5

U.S.C. App. I), it is hereby ordered as follows:

1-101. There is established a National Advisory Community Investment Board which shall be composed of fifteen members in accord with Section 704 of the Economic Opportunity Act of 1964, as amended (42 U.S.C. 2981c).

1-102. The Board shall perform the functions and carry out its activities as provided by Section 704 of the Economic Opportunity Act of 1964, as amended (42 U.S.C. 2981c).

1-103. The Director of the Community Services Administration shall provide the Board with such administrative services and support as may be necessary.

1-104. Notwithstanding the provisions of any other Executive order, the functions of the President under the Federal Advisory Committee Act (5 U.S.C. App. I), except that of reporting annually to the Congress, which are applicable to the Board, shall be performed by the Director of the Community Services Administration in accordance with guidelines and procedures established by the Administrator of General Services.

1-105. The Board shall terminate on December 31, 1981, unless sooner extended.

JIMMY CARTER

The White House,
    December 3, 1980.

[Filed with the Office of the Federal Register,
    11:04 a.m., December 4, 1980]

Middle East Peace Negotiations

Announcement of Trip by Ambassador Sol M. Linowitz to Egypt and Israel. December 3, 1980

The President has asked Ambassador Sol M. Linowitz to travel to both Egypt and Israel to consult with President Sadat and Prime Minister Begin and their colleagues on how to ensure continued momentum and progress in the Middle East peace process.

Throughout his administration, the President has accorded the highest priority to furthering peace efforts in the Middle East and, therefore, to maintaining momentum in the Camp David process.

Both President Carter and President-elect Reagan have pledged themselves to ensure continuity and an effective transition in foreign policy matters.

Upon his return, Ambassador Linowitz will report to the President so that the President can ensure that the President-elect will be fully informed and prepared with respect to the United States effort to attain comprehensive peace in the Middle East.

Situation in Poland

Statement by the President. December 3, 1980

The United States is watching with growing concern the unprecedented building of Soviet forces along the Polish border and the closing of certain frontier regions along the border. The United States has also taken note of Soviet references to alleged "anti-Socialist" forces within Poland. We know from postwar history that such allegations have sometimes preceded military intervention.

The United States continues to believe that the Polish people and authorities should be free to work out their internal difficulties without outside interference. The United States, as well as some Western governments, and also the Soviet Union, have pledged economic assistance to Poland in order to alleviate internal Polish difficulties. The United States has no interest in exploiting in any fashion the Polish difficulties for its political ends.

Foreign military intervention in Poland would have most negative consequences for East-West relations in general and U.S.-Soviet relations in particular. The Charter of the United Nations establishes the right of all states, both large and small, to exist free of foreign interference, regardless of ideology, alliances, or geographic location. I want all countries to know that the attitude and future policies of the United States toward the Soviet Union would be directly and very adversely affected by any Soviet use of force in Poland.

Import Controls on Peanuts

Memorandum From the President. December 3, 1980

Memorandum for the United States Trade Representative

By the authority vested in me as President by the Constitution and statutes of the United States, including Section 301 of Title 3 of the United States Code, I hereby authorize you to perform on my behalf, with respect to the importation of peanuts only, all functions vested in me by Section 22 of the Agriculture Adjustment Act of 1933, as amended (7 U.S.C. 624).

This delegation of authority shall expire on January 20, 1981.

This memorandum shall be published in the FEDERAL REGISTER.

JIMMY CARTER

[Filed with the Office of the Federal Register, 11:05 a.m., December 4, 1980]

NOTE: The memorandum was announced by the White House Press Office on December 4.

Governor Ella Grasso of Connecticut

Statement on the Governor's Resignation From Office.   December 4, 1980

I am deeply sorry to learn that Governor Ella Grasso's health has forced her to announce her resignation from office.

In her quarter century of public service to the people of Connecticut and the Nation, Ella Grasso has demonstrated and fulfilled the great potential of democratic government—integrity, compassion, and responsibility.

As State legislator, Connecticut's secretary of state, Member of Congress, and for 6 years as Governor, Ella Grasso has fought to improve the lives of those most vulnerable in our society.

Her career stands as a testament to the good that government can do, and to the difference one person can make.

I have valued her hard work and support during my own period of national service. I will continue to treasure her as a friend.

Governor Grasso, the gratitude and prayers of all of us go with you.

International Emergency Economic Powers Act

Message to the Congress Reporting on Administration Actions.   December 4, 1980

To the Congress of the United States:

On November 14, 1979, in Executive Order No. 12170 I declared a national emergency to deal with the threat to the national security, foreign policy and economy of the United States constituted by the situation in Iran. That declaration was made pursuant to the authority vested in me as President by the Constitution and statutes of the United States, including the International Emergency Economic Powers Act (50 U.S.C. 1701 *et seq.*) and the National Emergencies Act (50 U.S.C. 1601 *et seq.*). I reported that declaration to the Congress on November 14, 1979, pursuant to Section 204(b) of the International Emergency Economic Powers Act (the Act).

On April 7, 1980, I issued Executive Order No. 12205, pursuant to the November 14, 1979, declaration of national emergency, which provided for certain trade, financial and other measures against Iran and its nationals. I reported that action to the Congress on April 7, 1980, pursuant to Section 204(b) of the Act.

On April 17, 1980, in Executive Order No. 12211 I declared a national emergency to deal with the threat to the national security, foreign policy and economy of the United States that was referred to in Executive Order No. 12170 and Executive Order No. 12205 and to deal with the added unusual and extraordinary threat to the national security, foreign policy and economy of the United States created by subsequent events in Iran and neighboring countries, including the Soviet invasion of Afghanistan. That declaration was made pursuant to the authority vested in me as President by the Constitution and statutes of the United States, including the Act, and the National Emergencies Act. I reported that declaration to the Congress on April 17, 1980, pursuant to Section 204(b) of the Act.

Pursuant to Section 204(c) of the Act (50 U.S.C. 1703(c)), I hereby report to the Congress with respect to action that I have taken since April 17, 1980, pursuant to Executive Orders Nos. 12170, 12205 and 12211 and with respect to such changes as have occurred concerning the information previously reported to the Congress.

1. Pursuant to the three Executive Orders, the Department of the Treasury, acting under my delegation of authority to the Secretary of the Treasury, has issued a series of regulations that prohibit imports of goods and services from Iran or of Iranian origin (other than for news dissemination), payments or transfers of funds or other property to any person in Iran (except for news-gathering activities and family remittances) and payments and transactions in support of travel to or travel and maintenance within Iran of U.S. citizens and U.S. permanent resident aliens.

2. As I directed in Executive Order No. 12211, prior licenses for transactions by persons subject to the jurisdiction of the United States with Iran Air, the National Iranian Oil Company and the National Iranian Gas Company have been revoked with the effect that their offices in the United States have been closed down.

3. Pursuant to Executive Orders Nos. 12170 and 12211, the Department of the Treasury, acting under my delegation of authority to the Secretary of the Treasury, issued on July 2, 1980, a proposed rule which would require that certain types of blocked Iranian property be held in interest-bearing status. Comments have been received on the proposed rule, but a final rule has not yet been issued.

4. The Justice Department has filed Suggestions of Interest with all courts considering litigation involving the Government of Iran, its agencies and instrumentalities asking those courts to stay proceedings for ninety days in cases pending before them in light of the serious foreign policy consequences of further proceedings at this time. A number of courts have granted this request, including the only two Courts of Appeals to rule on the

requested stay. Other courts have denied the request and are proceeding to consider the merits of the cases pending before them.

5. A census of blocked Iranian assets and claims against Iran and Iranian entities, which was provided for in regulations issued by the Department of the Treasury on April 9, 1980, has been undertaken.

6. On November 2, 1980, the Iranian Parliament adopted a resolution establishing its terms for the release of the hostages. Since that time various messages have been transmitted between the Government of Iran and the Government of the United States using the Government of Algeria as an intermediary.

7. On November 12, 1980, I transmitted to the Congress a Notice of the continuance after November 14, 1980, of the national emergency which I declared in Executive Order No. 12170.

8. The national emergencies which I declared in connection with the threat to the national security, foreign policy and economy of the United States arising from events in Iran during November 1979, and subsequent events in Iran and neighboring countries, including the Soviet invasion of Afghanistan, continue to exist. Those threats and the rationale for taking steps under the Act continue to the present time. I shall continue to exercise the powers at my disposal to deal with those threats.

9. I am transmitting herewith regulations issued since April 17, 1980, pursuant to the three Executive Orders referred to above, together with the proposed rule requiring that certain types of blocked Iranian property be held in interest-bearing status.

JIMMY CARTER

The White House,
December 4, 1980.

International North Pacific Fisheries Commission

Appointment of Dayton L. Alverson as a Commissioner of the U.S. Section. December 4, 1980

The President today announced the appointment of Dayton L. Alverson, of Seattle, Wash., as a Commissioner of the United States Section of the International North Pacific Fisheries Commission.

Alverson was special assistant to the Assistant Administrator for Fisheries of the National Marine Fisheries Service until his retirement in 1980. He was with the Bureau of Commercial Fisheries for 14 years and served as Acting Director of the Bureau in 1969.

Alverson has served as a consultant to the State Department's Bureau of Oceans and International Environmental and Scientific Affairs and as chairman of the Advisory Committee for Marine Resources Research of the Food and Agricultural Organization of the United Nations. He is the author of numerous scientific and technical articles.

Appropriations Bill for the Departments of State, Justice, and Commerce, the Judiciary, and Related Agencies

Letter to Senate Majority Leader Robert C. Byrd.   December 4, 1980

Dear Senator Byrd:

I have decided that I will veto H.R. 7584, the State-Justice-Commerce Appropriations Act of 1980. A provision in this Act, the Helms-Collins amendment, would impose an unprecedented prohibition on the ability of the President of the United States and the Attorney General to use the Federal courts to ensure that our Constitution and laws are faithfully executed.

Throughout my Administration, I have been committed to the enhancement and strong enforcement of our civil rights laws. Such laws are the backbone of our commitment to equal justice. I cannot allow a law to be enacted which so impairs the government's ability to enforce our Constitution and civil rights acts.

I have often stated my belief that busing should only be used as a last resort in school desegregation cases. But busing is not the real issue here. The real issue is whether it is proper for the Congress to prevent the President from carrying out his constitutional responsibility to enforce the Constitution and laws of the United States.

The precedent that would be established if this legislation became law is dangerous. It would effectively allow the Congress to tell a President that there are certain constitutional remedies that he cannot ask the courts to apply. If a President can be barred from going to the courts on this issue, a future Congress could by the same reasoning prevent a President from asking the courts to rule on the constitutionality of other matters upon which the President and the Congress disagree.

For any President to accept this precedent would permit a serious encroachment on the powers of this office. I have a responsibility to my successors and to the American people not to permit that encroachment to take place. I intend to discharge that responsibility to the best of my ability.

The purpose of this letter is to ensure that there is no doubt about my opposition to the objectionable provision in the State-Justice-Commerce Appropriations Act. My opposition also applies to the inclusion of such a provision in the Continuing Resolution.

I would of course prefer to avoid a veto of the Resolution. I recognize the difficulties such a veto could impose on critically important operations of the government and on the Congressional schedule. But I would be shirking my constitutional responsibilities if I allowed this unprecedented and unwarranted encroachment on Executive authority and responsibility to prevail.

Sincerely,

JIMMY CARTER

[The Honorable Robert C. Byrd, Majority Leader, United States Senate, Washington, D.C. 20510]

Import Controls on Peanuts
Proclamation 4807. December 4, 1980

MODIFICATION OF IMPORT CONTROLS ON PEANUTS

On Behalf of the President of the United States of America

A Proclamation

1. Item 951.00 of Part 3 of the Appendix to the Tariff Schedules of the United States provides that no more than 1,709,-000 pounds of peanuts described therein may be imported into the United States during any 12 month period beginning August 1 in any year. This limitation was proclaimed by the President in Proclamation No. 3019 of June 8, 1953 (18 FR

3361) and was amended in subsequent proclamations, under the authority of Section 22 of the Agricultural Adjustment Act of 1933, as amended (7 U.S.C. 624).

2. The President has delegated his authority under Section 22 of the Agricultural Adjustment Act of 1933, as amended, with respect to peanuts, to me as United States Trade Representative by memorandum dated December 3, 1980.

3. I have been advised by the Secretary of Agriculture that there is a substantial deficit in the domestic supply of peanuts, of the type and physical description described below, which are suitable for edible use. I have been further advised by the Secretary of Agriculture that he has reason to believe that an additional quantity of the peanuts described below may be imported without rendering or tending to render ineffective, or materially interfering with, the price support program of the Department of Agriculture with respect to peanuts, or reducing substantially the amount of any product processed in the United States from peanuts with respect to which such program is being undertaken.

4. I agree that there is reason for such belief by the Secretary of Agriculture. Therefore, I am requesting the United States International Trade Commission to make an immediate investigation with respect to this matter pursuant to Section 22 of the Agricultural Adjustment Act of 1933, as amended (7 U.S.C. 624), and to report its findings and recommendations to me as soon as possible.

5. The Secretary of Agriculture has also determined and reported to me that a condition exists with respect to peanuts which requires emergency treatment, and

that the modification in the quantitative import limitations hereinafter proclaimed should be imposed without awaiting the report and recommendations of the United States International Trade Commission.

6. I find and declare that a condition exists which requires emergency treatment and that, without awaiting the recommendations of the United States International Trade Commission with respect to such action, an additional quantity of peanuts should be permitted entry, as hereinafter proclaimed, in order to meet domestic requirements for peanuts suitable for edible use, until supplies become available from the 1981 domestic crop. I also find and declare that the entry of such quantities of peanuts, under the conditions hereinafter proclaimed, will not render or tend to render ineffective, or materially interfere with, the price support operations now being conducted by the Department of Agriculture for peanuts, or reduce substantially the amount of any product processed in the United States from domestic peanuts.

Now, THEREFORE, I, REUBIN O'D. ASKEW, United States Trade Representative, acting pursuant to the authority vested in the President of the United States of America by the Constitution and Statutes of the United States of America, including section 22 of the Agricultural Adjustment Act of 1933, as amended, and delegated to me by memorandum dated December 3, 1980, do hereby proclaim:

(1) Part 3 of the Appendix to the Tariff Schedules of the United States is hereby modified by inserting in numerical sequence the following temporary provision:

Item	Articles	Quota quantity
951.01	Notwithstanding the quantitative limitation on the importation of peanuts described in item 951.00, an additional quantity of such peanuts, within the scope of such quota, may be entered during the period December 4, 1980 through June 30, 1981: *Provided*, That the following certificates (or a bond for their production) for such peanuts shall be filed with the appropriate customs officer at the time of entry (except that such peanuts, blanched or otherwise prepared or preserved shall not require such certificates):	
	(a) a certificate issued by the U.S. Department of Agriculture attesting to the fact that the peanuts meet the requirements as to quality, size, and wholesomeness that are specified in the Outgoing Quality Regulations of the Marketing Agreement for peanuts No. 146 (45 FR 41675–83 (June 20, 1980)) and	
	(b) a certificate issued by the U.S. Department of Agriculture laboratories or designated laboratories approved by the Peanut Administrative Committee attesting to the fact that the peanuts tested "negative" as to aflatoxin	200,000,000 pounds: Provided, That peanuts in the shell shall be charged against this quota on the basis of 75 pounds for each 100 pounds of peanuts in the shell.

(2) The temporary provision added to Part 3 of the Appendix to the Tariff Schedules of the United States by paragraph (1) of this proclamation shall be deleted therefrom on July 1, 1981.

Signed this 4th day of December, 1980.

REUBIN O'D. ASKEW

[Filed with the Office of the Federal Register, 11:42 a.m., December 5, 1980]

NOTE: For the text of the memorandum authorizing the United States Trade Representative to issue Proclamation 4807, see p. 2772 of this volume.

Holiday for Federal Employees

Executive Order 12255.   December 5, 1980

PROVIDING FOR THE CLOSING OF GOVERNMENT DEPARTMENTS AND AGENCIES ON FRIDAY, DECEMBER 26, 1980

By virtue of the authority vested in me as President of the United States, it is hereby ordered as follows:

SECTION 1–1. *General Provisions.*

1–101. All Executive departments and agencies shall be closed and their employees excused from duty on Friday, December 26, 1980, the day following Christmas Day, except as provided by Section 1–102 below.

1–102. The heads of Executive departments and agencies may determine that certain offices and installations of their organizations, or parts thereof, must remain open and that certain employees must report for duty on December 26, 1980, for reasons of national security or defense or for other public reasons.

SECTION 1–2. *Pay and Leave for Employees.*

1–201. Friday, December 26, 1980, shall be considered a holiday for the purposes of the pay and leave of employees of the United States.

JIMMY CARTER

The White House,
    December 5, 1980.

[Filed with the Office of the Federal Register, 10:42 a.m., December 5, 1980]

Omnibus Reconciliation Act of 1980

*Remarks on Signing H.R. 7765 Into Law.
December 5, 1980*

THE PRESIDENT. This is the kind of legislation that's very gratifying for me to sign. This is an unprecedented act on the part of the Congress to pursue even further than it has been in the past the advantages of the budget procedure. There have been times this year, because of the strict discipline that we've placed on the budget process, when we were doubtful about whether the budget procedure itself could be preserved. But the Reconciliation Act of 1980, which I am going to sign in a few minutes, is a vivid demonstration of the courage of the Congress in dealing with

very difficult questions in exercising budget restraint.

Many of the items that contribute to a budget deficit are not covered automatically each year when the Congress considers the appropriations bills and other related processes. For instance, the tax code, the major entitlement programs, are not ordinarily reviewed. But this year, beginning in March, when the congressional leadership in both Houses, both parties, and I, worked together to see what could be done to reduce the Federal deficit and restrain the inflationary pressures, the Congress in its first budget resolution directed all the committees to give a list, aided by us in the administration, of things that could be done to increase revenues by expedited and more equitable collection of taxes of all kinds, and also to reduce expenditures which were above and beyond the normal legislative process. This has resulted in substantial savings. And I would estimate that this bill here, when I sign it into law, will result in a decrease in the budget deficit in excess of 8 billions of dollars, roughly $5 billion in reduced spending, roughly $3 billion or more in expedited or increased revenue collections.

I'm very much indebted to the Congress, which in an election year, when it's very difficult to exercise this sort of discipline, has done so, so superbly. Bob Giaimo, the Budget Committee leader in the House, Fritz Hollings and his predecessor Ed Muskie in the Senate, working with Leon Panetta and with Senator Bellmon, with Senator Long and others— I need not name the whole list—have done a superb job. It's with a great deal of pleasure that I sign this bill into law.

In addition to that, we have tried through every possible process to restrict the expenditure of unnecessary funds and to control inflation. We have had a personnel freeze in effect since March, and when I go out of office next month we will have between 55 and 60,000 fewer full-time employees than we had when I was sworn into office in January of 1977. But the combined total of the exercising of fiscal discipline, I think, is paying rich dividends for our Nation in restraining an already too high inflation rate and a budget deficit that is of concern to all of us.

I would like to sign this bill into law, and then call on, first, Congressman Bob Giaimo, representing the House Budget Committee, and then Senator Fritz Hollings, representing the Senate Budget Committee to make remarks.

[At this point, the President signed the bill.]

Gentlemen, I thank you very much.

Everybody assembled here, on this side of the table at least, knows that this was not an easy task. *[Laughter]* It was one of the most difficult legislative processes I've ever witnessed, and Bob Giaimo and Fritz Hollings and all those who worked with them deserve credit and a great deal of thanks from all the people of our Nation. Bob Giaimo.

REPRESENTATIVE GIAIMO. Thank you. Mr. President, this is really a historic event in the legislative process which you initiated back in the early spring or the late winter, in fact in March, when you and your people met with the congressional leadership, both House and Senate, and you hammered out certain economic measures which had to be taken in order to try to correct this terrible economy and this high inflation rate. And one of these suggested remedies was a new legislative vehicle which we all call reconciliation, but which in simple terms is a savings package in reducing Federal expenditures.

Now, Presidents have traditionally sent up legislative reform packages to the Congress, and usually, as you know, Mr. Presi-

dent, nothing much ever happens to them. Until this year, I think, the highest amount of legislative reform that was ever enacted on a President's suggested package of reforms was $200 million. This bill this year took your legislative reform suggestions and effected about $4.6 billion of them in direct spending, plus the revenue savings, as you know, of about $3.5 billion. But more than that, it's $4.6 billion for this year; it's over $21 billion over the next 5-year period.

And what we've done here with your direction and drive and help and with the help of the leadership in the Congress, I think, is to fashion a new legislative tool for the future years, to begin to look at the entitlement programs, where 75 percent of the Federal dollars are spent, and we have a tool and a vehicle for beginning to look at them, change them, correct them, modify them, and begin to make some effective savings. And I think this has happened through your leadership, and I thank you.

THE PRESIDENT. Let me say one word. When Ed Muskie came to join me in the administration as Secretary of State, his successor, Fritz Hollings, took over this project in a very difficult time. And no one can imagine the tremendous pressure from lobbying groups and others to protect unwarranted expenditure programs better than those that have been involved in the infighting that has taken place to protect the interest of our country. And in a very courageous fashion, Fritz Hollings has not only been able to bring together a harmonious group of Senate leaders but also has been able, under difficult circumstances and working harmoniously with Bob Giaimo and the House leadership and my own administration—and Fritz, I want to congratulate you on the ability that you have exhibited in leadership in making this possible.

SENATOR HOLLINGS. Well, thank you, Mr. President.

We really are, in the Senate, very grateful to you, because had you not led the way here in the early spring, we wouldn't be here today signing any kind of reconciliation measure.

I think the significance of this particular occasion is, on the one hand, that discipline had to be worked out between the executive and the legislative branches. Our friends sometimes always think government is a true-false quiz and whether or not we have a balanced budget is going to depend on the constitutional provision. You're looking at a gentleman who took the oath of office back in 1959, where in its constitution, the State had provided for a balanced budget back in 1895, and they gave it to me in the absolute red. So, I know better than any about constitutional provisions. It's going to happen only by working together, particularly developing the discipline within the legislative branch. And significantly, in other words, rather that just balancing the budget, we have aimed it in the right direction.

Adlai Stevenson, once asked whether he was a conservative or a liberal, said, "That's not the important question. The important question is, am I headed in the right direction?" [*Laughter*] So, today we've headed the Government's finances in the right direction. You've cut back on the employees, and we have proved that you can get us back in the black in a disciplined, deliberate manner. You can't do it overnight, but to come from a $60 billion deficit down in the realm of, what would it be, 18 without a tax cut and 27 with a tax cut, is quite an accomplishment.

It has been a magnificent pleasure working with Bob Giaimo and the House colleagues, and particularly now we've

woven in even Russell Long, who's right in behind here—[*laughter*]—and the chairmen of the substantive committees in the Congress. We get nowhere unless the Congress themselves appreciates this as their process and their accomplishment.

REPRESENTATIVE GIAIMO. And Mr. President, we have here the man who I think's going to be the next chairman of the Ways and Means Committee. [*Laughter*]

THE PRESIDENT. I would like to say in closing that as Fritz and Bob pointed out, there is an inherent competition between the Appropriations Committees, the Budget Committees, the Ways and Means Committee, and the Finance Committee in the Congress, and this is a healthy competition. In this particular respect, though, we have seen a remarkable degree of cooperation. Had that not been obvious this year, I would not be signing this bill today.

We made additional recommendations for savings. I believe that they changed to an annualized indexing of entitlement programs—needs to extend further, for instance. It's not a politically attractive concept. It's been a good step forward already taken. And I hope and trust that under the leadership of Fritz Hollings and Bob Giaimo's successor and others that we'll see this process continued and even expanded in the future. It's a good step in the right direction, and I'd like to express not only my thanks to Henry Bellmon—I wish he was here—but also to Congressman Panetta and of course to Russell Long, to Danny Rostenkowski, and others in the Congress who've worked on this, and also, of course, to the leadership—Tip O'Neill, Bob Byrd, and the Republican leadership as well, have been so good.

Thank you all very much.

My omission of the House Rules Committee chairman was inadvertent—[*laughter*]—because as all of us know, the strong leadership of Dick Bolling in a crucial time is what made the difference. And I thank you all from the bottom of my heart.

NOTE: The President spoke at 9:34 a.m. at the signing ceremony in the Cabinet Room at the White House.

As enacted, H.R. 7765 is Public Law 96–499, approved December 5.

Moapa Band of Paiutes

Statement on Signing S. 1135 Into Law.
December 5, 1980

I am pleased to sign into law S. 1135, which provides for approximately 70,500 acres of public land in Nevada to be held in trust for the Moapa Band of Paiutes.

The people of the Moapa Band have, with outstanding initiative and dedication, developed the resources of their small reservation and the knowledge and skills needed to sustain their community. Since 1968 the Moapa Band has established successful farming operations, including a greenhouse tomato-growing project; a leather manufacturing company; a construction company, which has built homes and a community center on the reservation; and a number of social and educational programs.

I congratulate the Moapa Band on these significant achievements and Senator Howard Cannon, who worked so hard for passage of this historic legislation. This bill will provide the Moapa Band with the increased land base it needs in order for its people to continue their economic and social growth. It is my hope that this land will serve as a foundation on which the people of the Moapa Band can build a community in which both economic development and the traditions of their tribal culture will continue to flourish.

NOTE: As enacted, S. 1135 is Public Law 96–491, approved December 2.

United States Postal Service

Nomination of Wallace Nathaniel Hyde
To Be a Governor.   December 5, 1980

The President today announced that he will nominate Wallace Nathaniel Hyde, of Asheville, N.C., to be a member of the Board of Governors of the U.S. Postal Service.

Hyde, 57, is president of Hyde Insurance Associates and former vice president of First Citizens Bank and Trust.

Digest of Other
White House Announcements

The following listing includes the President's public schedule and other items of general interest announced by the White House Press Office and not included elsewhere in this issue.

November 30

The President returned to the White House from Camp David, Md.

December 1

The President met at the White House with:

—Zbigniew Brzezinski, Assistant to the President for National Security Affairs;

—Frank B. Moore, Assistant to the President for Congressional Liaison;

—President Rodrigo Carazo Odio of Costa Rica.

December 2

The President met at the White House with:

—Dr. Brzezinski;
—the Democratic congressional leadership;
—Mr. Moore.

December 3

The President met at the White House with:

—Dr. Brzezinski;
—Mr. Moore;
—the Cabinet;
—James T. McIntyre, Jr., Director of the Office of Management and Budget.

The President has transmitted to the Congress the annual report on White House personnel required by the White House authorization bill.

December 4

The President met at the White House with:

—Dr. Brzezinski;
—Mr. and Mrs. Olen Range of Justin, Tex., whose farm the President had visited on July 21 to view the effects of the summer drought;
—Representative Marty Russo of Illinois;
—Mr. Moore.

December 5

The President met at the White House with:

—Dr. Brzezinski;
—Vice President Walter F. Mondale, Secretary of Defense Harold Brown, Deputy Secretary of State Warren M. Christopher, Jack H. Watson, Jr., Assistant to the President, and Dr. Brzezinski;
—Mr. Moore.

The President left the White House for a weekend stay at Camp David.

NOMINATIONS SUBMITTED TO THE SENATE

The following list does not include promotions of members of the Uniformed Services, nominations to the Service Academies, or nominations of Foreign Service officers.

Submitted December 1, 1980

CAPTAIN KELLY E. TAGGART to be Director of the Commissioned Officer Corps, National Oceanic and Atmospheric Administration, with the grade of rear admiral (upper half).

Submitted December 5, 1980

WALLACE NATHANIEL HYDE, of North Carolina, to be a Governor of the United States Postal Service for the term expiring December 8, 1989, vice M. A. Wright, term expiring.

JOSEPH S. BRACEWELL, of Texas, to be President of the Solar Energy and Energy Conservation Bank (new position).

CHECKLIST OF WHITE HOUSE PRESS RELEASES

The following listing contains releases of the White House Press Office which are not included in this issue.

Released December 2, 1980

Fact sheet: H.R. 39, Alaska National Interest Lands Conservation Act
Advance text: remarks on signing the Alaska National Interest Lands Conservation Act
Advance text: remarks at the State of Israel Bond Organization dinner

Released December 3, 1980

Text: report to the Congress on White House personnel

Released December 5, 1980

Fact sheet: H.R. 7765, the Omnibus Reconciliation Act of 1980
Text: remarks to the Canadian Club of Montreal in Montreal, Canada—by Zbigniew Brzezinski, Assistant to the President for National Security Affairs

ACTS APPROVED BY THE PRESIDENT

Approved December 1, 1980

S. 2357_____ Public Law 96–486
Federal Question Jurisdictional Amendments Act of 1980.

Approved December 2, 1980

H.R. 39_____ Public Law 96–487
Alaska National Interest Lands Conservation Act.

H.R. 8329_____ Public Law 96–488
An act to allow the obsolete aircraft carrier United States ship Intrepid to be transferred to the Intrepid Museum Foundation, Incorporated, before the expiration of the otherwise applicable sixty-day congressional review period.

S. 43_____ Public Law 96–489
An act to promote safety and health in skiing and other outdoor winter recreational activities.

H.R. 7942_____ Public Law 96–490
An act to approve and implement the protocol to the trade agreement relating to customs valuation, and for other purposes.

S. 1135_____ Public Law 96–491
An act to provide for certain lands to be held in trust for the Moapa Band of Paiutes and to be considered to be part of the Moapa Indian Reservation.

H.R. 8112_____ Public Law 96–492
An act to require the Secretary of the Interior to convey a parcel of land located in Colorado and certain mineral interests to the Ute Mountain Ute Tribe and to pay an amount to such tribe for energy development.

S. 2251_____ Public Law 96–493
Gasohol Competition Act of 1980.

Approved December 3, 1980

H.R. 3765_____ Public Law 96–494
Agricultural Act of 1980.

H.R. 4084_____ Public Law 96–495
Suisun Marsh Preservation and Restoration Act of 1979.

Approved December 4, 1980

S. 1386_____ Public Law 96–496
Arts and Humanities Act of 1980.

S. 1179_____ Public Law 96–497
An act to incorporate the Gold Star Wives of America.

ACTS APPROVED—Continued

Approved December 4—Continued

S. 3193_____ Public Law 96–498
An act to designate the Jacob K. Javits Federal Building.

Approved December 5, 1980

H.R. 7765_____ Public Law 96–499
Omnibus Reconciliation Act of 1980.

H.R. 2510_____ Public Law 96–500
An act to amend title 5, United States Code, to permit Federal employees to obtain review of certain disability determinations made by the Office of Personnel Management under the civil service retirement and disability system.

S. 885_____ Public Law 96–501
Pacific Northwest Electric Power Planning and Conservation Act.

H.R. 8117_____ Public Law 96–502
An act to amend the Safe Drinking Water Act, and for other purposes.

H.J. Res. 634_____ Public Law 96–503
A joint resolution to authorize the United States Secret Service to continue to furnish protection to the former Vice President or his spouse.

H.R. 2583_____ Public Law 96–504
An act to amend chapter 83 of title 5, United States Code, to discontinue civil service annuity payments for periods of employment as a justice or judge of the United States, and for other purposes.

H.R. 5108_____ Public Law 96–505
Metlakatla Indian Community Enrollment Act of 1980.

H.R. 7698_____ Private Law 96–67
An act for the relief of two mining claimants.

H.R. 7960_____ Private Law 96–68
An act to provide for the setting aside in special trust lands and interests within the Winema National Forest to Edison Chiloquin and for the transfer of moneys otherwise available to Mr. Chiloquin from the Klamath Indian Settlement to the Secretary of Agriculture for the acquisition of replacement lands or interests.

S. 1578_____ Private Law 96–69
An act for the relief of Doctor Halla Brown.

S. 1828_____ Private Law 96–70
An act to exempt the existing facilities of the Milner Dam from section 14 of the Federal Power Act, and for other purposes.

Week Ending Friday, December 12, 1980

Situation in Poland

White House Statement.   December 7, 1980

Preparations for possible Soviet intervention in Poland appear to have been completed. It is our hope that no such intervention will take place. The United States Government reiterates its statement of December 3, regarding the very adverse consequences for U.S.-Soviet relations of Soviet military intervention in Poland.

Kennedy Center Honors

Remarks at a White House Reception for the Honorees.   December 7, 1980

Only Fritz Mondale can fully appreciate the gratification of defeated political candidates being associated with these famous and popular and successful people. [*Laughter*]

Tonight we come to the White House not just to honor five wonderful artists and the art that they represent, but we really come here to acknowledge the progress and the commitment to the arts and the famous and unfamous artists throughout our country. There's no doubt that there is an intensification of the interest of Americans in the arts, and there's a constant broadening of the number of Americans who are appreciative of and directly involved in the arts.

It's a very fine thing to have people throughout our country, in New York and Washington and also in Plains and other places between, who can observe and appreciate and also participate in the finer things of life. The number who go to concerts and to theaters, to museums, and who can appreciate the fine artists' performances on television are constantly growing. This is exemplified in some ways by the fact that in the last 4 years we've had a greater commitment from the Federal Government itself to the National Endowment for the Arts than in the previous 12 years. And I would like to point out hastily that this is not a particular achievement of me or my administration; it's an accurate representation, through the Congress, of the relative interest of the American people in this common commitment.

Only a very few people have lived in this home and served as President. It's a gratifying and exhilarating experience. But one of the finest aspects of it is not just being part of history but being able to participate in this room and on the South Lawn in the performances that have been very exciting to me and to Rosalynn as some of these and other famous Americans have come here to perform in such a superlative way. In our Sunday afternoon concerts, which have been broadcast afterward, through Public Broadcasting, to literally millions of people, and through the evening performances that have been so exciting for us all, Americans and famous foreign visitors, this has been one of the most important and also one of the most interesting and exciting elements of serving as President.

This evening I'm not going to repeat all of the words of praise and the accolades that have been heaped on these five recipients of the award, but I would like to say just a few words about each one of them.

Leonard Bernstein singlehandedly, or I might say, with both hands and his entire body, as a matter of fact—[*laughter*]—has brought great music as a vital part of the personal lives of literally millions of Americans and people throughout the world with his deep commitment, his knowledge of communication, his ability as a teacher, and the inner commitment that makes his words and his attitudes a kind of a burning inspiration to those who have admired his own works and the way he interprets and explains the fine works of others. In motion pictures, on Broadway, in the concert hall, and, I am thankful to say, here in the White House, he's been a favorite of us and of millions of his fellow Americans.

I had a delightful time this afternoon with Leonard Bernstein. He talked to me for a while and then enjoyed the hospitality of the Lincoln Bedroom, where he could remember the "Lincoln Suite," I'm sure. Good luck to you.

And James Cagney, who has ranged all the way from public enemy—[*laughter*]— to Yankee doodle dandy—[*laughter*]—all the way from Mr. Roberts to Shakespeare, has come here, crossing the ocean, to be with us and to be honored as one of the great performers, who has been a frequent guest in the movie theater in the room below us here in the White House. I think almost every American has a Jimmy Cagney impression. [*Laughter*] As he came through the receiving line, he and I agreed that we would not exchange Jimmy impressions this evening. [*Laughter*] So, we'll spare you that.

But I would like to say that in a special way James Cagney has touched the heart of many Americans who admire him for what he is and the stirring and breadth of the performances that he has made famous.

Those who've seen the choreography in "Oklahoma" and "Rodeo" know that it represents the heart and the soul of the American experience, and to have Agnes DeMille here tonight is indeed a thrill for me and I know for all of you.

A few days ago we honored Aaron Copland on his birthday, and the association that she has had with him and with many other great composers has been almost a unique experience in American artistic life. There are many very fine and famous people who can epitomize what makes our Nation great, but if you think back on all the things that she's done for us, she's kind of captured the spirit of Americans in a special way. When you think of "One Touch of Venus," of "Carousel," which was the first Broadway play I ever saw in my life, of "Allegro" and "Gentlemen Prefer Blondes," "Brigadoon," "Paint Your Wagon," and many others, this is the kind of thing that she's given us, and we are deeply grateful to you and the wonderful life that she's made available to us.

These are all truly Americans, but perhaps the most significant American of all is Lynn Fontaine, because she came here as an immigrant. And that's a special part of America's life, because we are a nation of immigrants. And perhaps one of the bases for the strength of American art is the breadth of the scope and the inherited values which have been brought here and epitomized by these artists and others from all over the world.

She indeed came and set a performance standard for American actresses throughout the 20th century and with her husband, Alfred Lunt, shared a career that has been described as matchless in America and perhaps throughout the world. I understand that the first time they appeared together on the stage was here in Washington, D.C., in "A Young Man's Fancy." Is that correct? Close to correct? And then 50 years later they came back to the White House for another performance when they received from the President the Medal of Freedom. And between that first appearance on a Washington, D.C., stage and receiving the highest award that a President can give, they created together and also individually a legend of artistic excellence, an inspiration to us all, and we love you.

And I've deliberately saved Leontyne Price till last. She's been described as the Stradivarius of singers—[*laughter*]—and I think of all the performances that I've heard in the White House, the greatest thrill of mine was when Leontyne Price came here to perform. And I realize that Vladimir Horowitz is here—has been here—and Baryshnikov is here tonight. The only single exception that I can think of was the first time that Amy got her violin and played "Twinkle, Twinkle, Little Star." [*Laughter*]

But I remember the shock that swept through an audience at a funeral service when Leontyne Price sang, "The Lord's Prayer." It was almost like a blow in the solar plexus, and a gasp of emotion and exhilaration went through that group. And when she came and sang when the Pope was here and the other performances that I've heard, she's been truly an inspiration to us all. She's won 15 Grammy Awards. I won't go down the list of awards that others have won, but all the way from "Porgy and Bess" to "Cleopatra" she has exemplified the finest in superlative performance. When she made her debut at the Met the ovation lasted 42 minutes, and that's an example of performance above and beyond the exemplary performances of those others who perform in the Metropolitan in such a fine

way. But I'm grateful to her not only for what she does in the performing arts but for what she means in insisting upon the finest values of our country, human rights, equality of opportunity, the commitment to overcome handicap and the deep concern about others who are struggling to achieve the same degree of realization of the American dream.

These five honorees share superb talent, but they also share something special, and that is the gift of creation, an ability to exceed what is normally expected from a talented person, to look at the daily struggle that all of us human beings experience, and to give to us as a constant reminder the ideal of perfection. As President of a great country, I'd like to say again that we are honored to have them here, because they epitomize the finest elements of the character of the people of the finest nation on Earth.

Thank you, and God bless you all. We'll see you at the Kennedy Center.

Thank you.

NOTE: The President spoke at 6:30 p.m. in the East Room at the White House.

Following the reception, the President and Mrs. Carter attended the awards ceremony at the John F. Kennedy Center for the Performing Arts.

Juvenile Justice Amendments of 1980

Statement on Signing S. 2441 Into Law. December 8, 1980

On July 1st of this year, I sent a message to Congress indicating my deep commitment to the goals and objectives of the Juvenile Justice and Delinquency Prevention Act. I am pleased to reiterate that commitment by signing S. 2441, the Juvenile Justice Amendments of 1980. This legislation will continue the authorizations of both the Juvenile Justice and Delinquency Prevention Act and the Runaway and Homeless Youth Act for 4 years.

The children of America are our most precious resource. One negative experience with the justice system can permanently mar a young person's future. The Juvenile Justice and Delinquency Prevention Act is particularly important, because it establishes a program to prevent young people from having that first negative experience with the criminal justice system, rather than reacting to incidents after their occurrence. Six years after its enactment, we can take great pride in its accomplishments. It has demonstrated many new alternatives to traditional methods of dealing with children in the juvenile justice system and contributed to substantial progress in providing fair and effective treatment for our young people.

The report of the House Committee on Labor and Education found that since passage of the original act, the proportion of serious crimes committed by juveniles has steadily dropped.

The major share of funds under the act is allocated to the States to implement the programs each State decides are most appropriate and effective for that particular State. I am particularly pleased that Congress accepted an amendment advocated by the administration which will result in the removal of juveniles from adult jails and lockups. This provision will go a long way toward addressing what the Deputy Attorney General termed a "national catastrophe" when testifying before Congress last March.

It is also satisfying that provisions of the law which call for the coordination of Federal juvenile delinquency programing have been strengthened. The Coordinating Council on Juvenile Justice and Delinquency Prevention has provided Federal agencies with an effective means of marshaling their forces and acting in a unified and consistent manner. These efforts to reduce duplication and promote interagency cooperation should serve as a model for all levels of government.

Other provisions of S. 2441 authorize assistance for children who have run away from home or who are otherwise homeless, establish a separate Office of Juvenile Justice and Delinquency Prevention within the Justice Department assuring the independence necessary to effectively do its job, and reduce redtape at the local level.

Since first enacted in 1974, the Juvenile Justice and Delinquency Prevention Act has enjoyed a broad base of support from public agencies and private organizations and strong bipartisan support in the Congress. I would like to give particular credit to Senator Birch Bayh, an author of the original 1974 legislation. The children of the country will lose an effective advocate when he leaves the Congress. I would like to thank Senator Strom Thurmond, Congressman Ike Andrews, and Congressman E. Thomas Coleman, who managed the bill and were instrumental in assuring that the legislation was not ignored in the closing days of the congressional session.

NOTE: As enacted, S. 2441 is Public Law 96–509, approved December 8.

Death of John Lennon

Statement by the President.
December 9, 1980

John Lennon helped create the music and the mood of our time. His spirit, the spirit of the Beatles—brash and earnest, ironic and idealistic all at once—became the spirit of a whole generation.

In the 1960's, John Lennon and the Beatles captured the imagination of the world. Their greatest success came when they conquered America; and in recent years, it was in America that John Lennon chose to live, because he valued the atmosphere of freedom and ferment he found here. His work as an artist and musician was far from done, but in the songs he composed, both in partnership with Paul McCartney and in his own right, he leaves an extraordinary and permanent legacy.

I know that I speak for many millions of Americans when I say that I am saddened by his death, and distressed by the senseless manner of it. It is especially poignant that John Lennon has died by violence, though he had long campaigned for peace.

Rosalynn and I extend our deepest sympathy to Mr. Lennon's wife, Yoko, and to their young son, Sean.

NOTE: Mr. Lennon was shot and killed outside his apartment house in New York City on December 8.

Council on Wage and Price Stability

Statement on Signing S. 2352 Into Law. December 9, 1980

I have signed into law, S. 2352 which extends authority for the Council on Wage and Price Stability through September 30, 1981, and authorizes appropriations of $9,770,000 for that period.

The bill also includes a provision which allows the powers granted the President under the Credit Control Act of 1969 to expire on June 30, 1982. Under that act the President, in a period of serious inflationary threat stemming from excessive credit expansion, may authorize the Board of Governors of the Federal Reserve to impose various kinds of controls over the extension of credit. I believe that abolishing the authorization granted to the President under the act is highly unwise, because many of the act's provisions can be extremely helpful at critical periods in the fight against inflation. This is no time to strip a President of inflation-fighting powers. At the same time, I recognize that certain improvements to the Credit Control Act may be desirable. It is my hope that during the next 18 months Congress will enact a new Credit Control Act that saves the essential inflation-fighting powers that the act makes available.

NOTE: As enacted, S. 2352 is Public Law 96–508, approved December 8.

Pension Benefit Guaranty Corporation

Appointment of Two Members of the Advisory Committee, and Designation of Chairman. December 9, 1980

The President today announced the appointments of two persons to be members of the Advisory Committee to the Pension Benefit Guaranty Corporation. The appointments are for terms expiring February 19, 1983. They are:

ROBERT TILOVE, of Brooklyn, N.Y., a senior vice president with Martin & Segal. This is a reappointment.

DEENE G. SOLOMON, of San Francisco, Calif., an attorney with Heller, Ehrman, White & McAuliffe, a visiting associate professor at Hastings College of Law, and author of numerous publications on ERISA law and pension benefits.

The President has also designated Phyllis Speilman, currently a member, to be Chairman of the Corporation.

Robert S. Strauss

Remarks at a White House Reception
Honoring the Ambassador.   December 9, 1980

THE PRESIDENT. I know that assembled in this room are some of the closest friends of Robert Strauss. As you may know, Bob Strauss was involved in the Presidential campaign this year—[*laughter*]—despite what he would tell you now. [*Laughter*] You know I'm just kidding. Bob is a very loyal friend. I noticed that he waited a whole week after the election before he had dinner with Ronald Reagan. [*Laughter*] I'm not going to make a long speech. I have a lot of other very nice things to say about Robert Strauss— [*laughter*]—at the banquet this evening, but among this group of close friends of mine and Bob's, I would like to make a special presentation to him.

He's done a lot of memorable things to me—I mean, for me. [*Laughter*] At one of my earliest Cabinet meetings, when I was very nervous as a new President trying to don the aura of a distinguished statesman and a new President, Bob was nice enough to give me a very large picture as a gift. The staff was very excited, and the Cabinet was very interested. It was a beautiful photograph of me with a big black fly on the end of my nose. [*Laughter*] And now in the future when anyone asks me where I got that portrait, if they need an answer, I would, of course, say, "Oh, that one. Bob Strauss, of course, gave it to me." Well, this evening I want to return the favor. [*Laughter*]

Let me begin by saying that some of Bob's comments during the last few weeks remind me of something that President John Kennedy said. I think it was right after the Bay of Pigs—[*laughter*]—along the lines that victory has a hundred fathers, but defeat is always an orphan. I was reminded of that recently when some-body said they saw Bob Strauss on the television and one of the newsmen asked him about me. He said, "Well, I understand he did a fair job as President. Of course, I never knew the man personally." [*Laughter*] I just want to make sure that Bob Strauss never forgets the great and the noble effort that he and I shared this year.

I asked a great man, Lee Kling, to choose an appropriate gift that might be memorable and also evoke memories of the experience that we've had. And I want him to have this beautiful painting by Norman Rockwell. [*Laughter*] It's entitled, as you may know, those that are close enough to see it, it's entitled, "The Defeated Candidate." And I intend to inscribe it after this ceremony: "To Bob Strauss, thanks for making it all possible." [*Laughter*]

Well, I'm sure that you would agree, Bob, that this would make a very good conversation piece. Your friends, maybe even some of your clients—[*laughter*]—will look up on the wall in your office and say, "That's a wonderful picture, Bob. Where'd you get it anyway?" And I'm sure that Bob will say, I hope with a touch of pride, "President Jimmy Carter gave me that picture." And then when his guests say, "Well, why would he give you a picture like this?" I'd just like to be there to hear what Bob would say. [*Laughter*]

In closing, let me say that, Bob, this beautiful picture is yours, and you have certainly earned it.

AMBASSADOR STRAUSS. You know, I believe for the first time in my life I'm going to say I have nothing to say. [*Laughter*]

Mr. President, Rosalynn, Mrs. Johnson, and all of my friends:

I know of nothing that could give anybody more pride than to be in the White

House surrounded by family and good friends and to have let the whole world see the warmth and friendship that exists between Helen and myself and a splendid President and a gracious and lovely First Lady.

Thank you very much.

NOTE: The President spoke at 6:37 p.m. in the East Room at the White House.

Robert S. Strauss

Remarks at a Dinner Honoring the Ambassador.　December 9, 1980

THE PRESIDENT. *Senator Bentsen, my good friend Vice President Mondale, Joan, Ambassador Bush, soon to be Vice President of this great country, Senator Baker, Speaker O'Neill, Lady Bird Johnson, Gene Rostow, George Bristoe, who will follow me, other friends of Bob Strauss:*

As I sat in the audience tonight I was grieved at some of the light and disrespectful remarks made about Bob Strauss. [*Laughter*] Sometimes there is an occasion for levity; sometimes there's an occasion for serious analysis of a man's career and what he's meant to the people who come to honor him. And I don't believe there's anyone here tonight that hasn't been helped in a tangible and specific way by Bob Strauss to reach the ambitions that we have had in our own private lives, sometimes in our public life as well. I can't say that everything Bob Strauss has attempted that he's achieved for himself or for us. No one could do that as a human being. But if you think in your own lives, Bob has meant a lot to all of us.

This past 12 months I've had ambition. My hope was to serve a second term as President and then go back to Plains and retire. Bob has helped me achieve one of those ambitions. [*Laughter*] And as I leave next month for Plains, Bob Strauss will be in the forefront of my mind. [*Laughter*]

Bob is also very good with advice. Not long before I left the Oval Office this afternoon I read a last-minute letter from Bob Strauss. This is an absolutely true story, of course. The last paragraph—to the President of the United States, mind you—was: "Mr. President, wash your face and put on a clean shirt." [*Laughter*] "This new crowd will be a little bit more classy than the ones with which you're familiar." [*Laughter*]

During the tough days of the campaign Bob was always eager to say to me, "Mr. President, your real problem is public relations. You've never been able to let the American people know about your own great successes. What they know and what they remember are the things that you attempted and didn't quite achieve." No one has ever accused Bob Strauss of having that problem. [*Laughter*] So, tonight, I want to share part of my problem with my friend Bob Strauss.

When we think of Bob we remember very vividly the wonderful achievements of his public career. We think of the great roles he's played in shaping our Nation's present, our Nation's future. We think of the man who pulled the Democratic Party back together in a very difficult time in 1972. We think of the man who worked miracles, literally miracles, in putting together the Multilateral Trade Negotiations when everyone had given it up for dead. We think of the man who worked to keep the Camp David process on track. And there was, of course, the other Bob Strauss that wore the hat of the main adviser for the President on controlling inflation. [*Laughter*] But as Bob approaches you for a job, I wish you good luck in finding that particular item on Bob's current résumé. [*Laughter*]

I'm glad, along with you, that Bob has great achievements. And I'm also glad that the people of our Nation have become aware of them, because as the great Dizzy Dean expressed it—and Bob quotes him quite often—"It ain't bragging if you've done it." Right, Bob? [*Laughter*]

When I think of Bob, two words come to my mind. One is "Democrat" and the other one is "loyalty." Since I see a few unfamiliar faces here tonight who will be more familiar to the American people in the future, I'll skip right over to the second one of those. I won't talk about Democrats tonight. Bob Strauss is loyal in the deepest and most durable sense of the word. He's loyal to his beliefs, and he's loyal to his friends. And when you are lucky, as I have been, to share both his beliefs and his friendship, then you're a lucky man indeed.

Bob has fought many good fights during his life. He's faced some of the most tough, iron-willed, and effective bargainers in the world. Prime Minister Ohira, Japan, during the Multilateral Trade Negotiations, I know how tough a bargainer he is; our Western allies with whom Bob had to deal on some very difficult questions of importance to all of you; President Sadat, a noble man of deep convictions, tough, effective bargainer; Prime Minister Begin, a deeply dedicated man, tough and effective bargainer, iron-willed; the bureaucrats in the State Department— [*laughter*]—tough, iron-willed, as Bob Strauss would well agree; Helen Strauss— [*laughter*]—tough, iron-willed, difficult bargainer, but a beautiful and wonderful helpmate who has meant as much to this Nation as has her honored husband.

Bob has of course won some; he's lost some. And through it all he shared some great and noble causes over the years. He's fought for his party, and he's fought for his country. And through all those fights and long afterwards, he's always been a loyalist, loyalist to his cause and loyal to his friends.

Bob Strauss believed in President Lyndon Johnson, and everybody knows it. He never lets anyone forget it, because he's proud of that loyalty. Bob Strauss fought for Hubert Humphrey, and he will not let anyone forget that either, because he's proud of that loyalty. And he fought for Jimmy Carter, and I personally will never forget it. I will never forget it, because I'm proud of that loyalty.

And so, tonight I join you in returning at least part of the favor, part of the loyalty that Bob Strauss has given to us and to his country. When he served as President, Lyndon Johnson used to say that all the brains in our country did not come from a few prestigious old schools. A lot of people figured when he said that that he had one particular school in mind. And now there's another one to which his name and his influence is dedicated. Lyndon Johnson believed in education, as Fritz Mondale has said. It was his burning commitment throughout his lifetime. He believed that our country was full of talent. He believed that in every region of the country there were people with a sense of public duty and the talent for politics. He wanted to make sure that young people with a concern for government and public affairs had a chance to nourish that concern, to fulfill their dreams, to understand what our system of government was all about. And he wanted them to know the "how" of democracy and the "why" of it also, and that is the founding principle of the Lyndon Johnson School at the University of Texas.

I'd like to join in the salutes that have already been given, but since I am President I want to say these words myself, a salute to the person who's been the guiding light to the Lyndon Johnson School and to the LBJ Library and to her husband and to millions of admirers in this country, Lady Bird Johnson. We love you, Lady Bird Johnson.

I almost agree with everything that Lady Bird Johnson says, but it would be difficult, if not impossible, for the Robert S. Strauss fellowship or the entire LBJ School for that matter, to produce one more Lyndon Baines Johnson or one more Robert S. Strauss. What it can do though is to give many young men and women, who have a desire to serve, training in the field of service. They will have an opportunity now to let their country be the beneficiaries of the legacy of that great family.

And I would like to end my remarks tonight with something that Lyndon Baines Johnson said, and might have said about the man we honor tonight if he were here. "The American people," he said, "are tired of wrecking crews. They want builders; they want people who construct." We are blessed to live in a free country, a country of free expression, a country of free political action. But it takes more than just freedom as important as it is, to make democracy work. It takes commitment. It takes dedication. It takes tenacity. It takes a knowledge of other people. In other words, it takes politics in the best and the noblest sense of that word. Our political system has a lot of critics. We have commentators of every ideological stripe who cite the inadequacies of our two political parties and how they relate one to the other. But both parties can be thankful that in this Nation of ours there is one Robert Strauss.

So, tonight in the town where there are so many people who believe so firmly in one particular cause that they've lost sight of how we make decisions in this great pluralistic society, through debate, through bargaining, through tolerance, through politics, tonight we honor a builder, a man who knows how to bring people together, who sees what unites people when all that many can see is what divides people.

A half century ago a man who I suspect had a lot in common with Bob Strauss left us these well-known words—every Democrat's heard them a thousand times—"I belong to no organized political party, I'm a Democrat." But tonight we honor a Democrat who spent a good part of his life knowing in his heart that Will Rogers was right, but trying to convince the rest of us that Will Rogers was wrong, and loving every minute of the effort to convince us that democracy and our party and our Nation has the inner strength, the foundation of principle and commitment, the acknowledgment of differences among us, and the high ideals that never change, to be successful, no matter how great the problem, how difficult the adversity, how serious the obstacle in our lives.

So, tonight it's my great pleasure to salute and to introduce a great American, a Democrat, a loyal friend, a builder of a better life for us all, my true friend, Robert Strauss.

AMBASSADOR STRAUSS. Fellow Democrats and Republicans, I accept your nomination. [*Laughter*] Before I speak for 2 or 3 minutes, let me remind you, Mr. President and Mr. Vice President, Mr. Speaker, Mr. Majority Leader-designate, Mr. Vice President-designate, and let me remind those in this room that these fellows have had people working for a week on their material, and I just started thinking of mine the last 2 or 3 minutes. [*Laughter*]

President Carter, as I said to Rosalynn when you commented that I had helped you achieve one-half of your goal, and I also said to her that you, when I suggested it in that note—and it is true, I sent that note that he wash his face and wear a clean shirt—that he took half of my advice tonight. [*Laughter*] He never took it off. [*Laughter*]

I must say to you that I think we each have strengths and weaknesses, and one of my strengths has been my ability to recognize my weaknesses—[*laughter*]—and one of the things I've always been able to do is take what I was doing seriously, but not myself too seriously. But tonight I think I'm beginning to lose that capacity. I began to get disturbed about myself when just before I came up here, my mind was wandering a bit, and even though the President was speaking, I leaned over and said to Helen, "You know, Helen, I think that what Brezhnev said to Senator Percy that hasn't yet been reported was, 'Be sure and give my regards to Bob Strauss.'" [*Laughter*] You know, that's pretty good for just the last 2 or 3 minutes. [*Laughter*]

It's getting late, and let me conclude more seriously if I can for a moment by saying to you first, Mrs. Johnson, how proud that Helen and I are and the members of our family are that our names will be associated with the school. I think the former President would be very pleased at that, and we are very proud of that association.

Let me also say that in all seriousness that I was thinking tonight as I sat there, what a truly magnificent Nation this is. You think of Afghanistan, and you think of Poland, and one can't avoid thinking of the Middle East, and we even think of what happens in a stable society like Great Britain when the government changes with dramatic shifts. And here we are with a change of government, with a transition, and here we are in this room

that's truly a montage of America—corporate leaders, politicians, young and old, some jaded and some just beginning—but all of us, all of us, absolutely convinced that this process can work and all of us tonight in this joyous, happy, positive room knowing that we are participating right at the halfway point of a change of government, and things go on with stability and with soundness.

And my friend Abe Ribicoff just returned a couple of days ago from Europe, and he said, "The one thing I thought of as Casey and I flew home, Bob, was all I heard about just before I left this Nation was what was wrong with America. But all I heard about in Europe where they saw us from afar was how they could become a part of this great Nation, how they could bring their companies here, how they could bring their families here, how they could bring their security here, all wanting to be a part of this great Nation."

And so, it is tonight that I would conclude by briefly saying to you that this process serves us well. This evening, I think, is a moment of reminder, a pause at midpoint in the transition to say that it works. God bless it and preserve it, and each of you.

Thank you so much.

NOTE: The President spoke at 10:38 p.m. in the Grand Ballroom at the Sheraton Washington Hotel.

Paperwork Reduction Act of 1980

Remarks on Signing H.R. 6410 Into Law. December 11, 1980

THE PRESIDENT. This is the kind of bill when at least everybody in the room is smiling. [*Laughter*] And a lot of people who are not here are not very pleased with this legislation, but I think it's very important to our country.

I'm very delighted to have Senator Chiles and Chairman Jack Brooks, Frank Horton, and others who've worked so hard on this legislation, and after I've signed the bill I'd like to ask them to make a comment.

This legislation, which is known as the Paperwork Reduction Act of 1980, is the latest and one of the most important steps that we have taken to eliminate wasteful and unnecessary Federal paperwork and also to eliminate unnecessary Federal regulations. In the first meeting that I had in this room in 1977 with my Cabinet, I directed all of the members of the Cabinet and major agency leaders to cut down on the amount of paperwork that the Federal Government placed upon the American people as an extraordinary and unnecessary burden. Two years later, because of that effort, we had cut the amount of time that Americans spend on Federal paperwork by 15 percent and had also created some new tools in the executive decision alone which could restrict any further increase in the paperwork burden. The Office of Management and Budget was given this responsibility.

We began, for instance, a paperwork budget, the first one that our Nation had ever seen, which meant that an agency had to justify to the Office of Management and Budget and to me as President any increase in the information that they derived from American citizens or the American free-enterprise members. This had to be approved ahead of time, just as approval was achieved for the expenditure of Federal moneys.

We set up this new budget in the Office of Management and Budget, this new unit, in order to cut paperwork again and to continue to eliminate unnecessary regulations. Last year, in order to establish this procedure firmly into the laws of our Nation as an extension to an Executive order, and also to expand it and to make it more effective, we asked the Congress to strengthen the Federal Reports Act by requiring that all Federal agencies clear their paperwork requirements with the Office of Management and Budget. We found ready support on the Hill, particularly among those who will speak after I'm finished.

The act I'm signing today will not only regulate the regulators, but it will also allow the President, through the Office of Management and Budget, to gain better control over the Federal Government's appetite for information from the public. For the first time it allows OMB to have the final word on many of the regulations issued by our Government. It also ensures that the public need not fill out forms nor keep records which are not previously approved by OMB.

This legislation is another important step in our efforts to trim waste from the Federal Government and to see to it that the Government operates more efficiently for all our citizens. In scope, it stands with the civil service reform and the deregulation of trucking and rails and airlines and other industries. And in spirit, it stands with the designation of the Inspectors General to attack waste and with the requirement that agencies write their rules in understandable English and study the impact of these regulations on small businesses.

We have made a great deal of progress through executive action over a 4-year period. This new action, embedding my own philosophy and the philosophy of those behind me into the laws of our Nation, will perpetuate this progress and will enhance the progress even further in the future.

I'm very delighted now to sign this legislation, following which I would like to ask Chairman Jack Brooks to make a few remarks, if he's willing to do so.

[*The President signed the bill as Representative Brooks spoke.*]

REPRESENTATIVE BROOKS. I'd be honored, Mr. President, and to say first that certainly you ought to be commended for your courage in presenting this program—in working on it, in encouraging it, and in signing it in spite of solid opposition from the usual bureaucrats who are against—[*laughter*]—any management proposals. In 1965, with the ADP proposition on computers, that has saved the Government billions of dollars, we had the same pressure from some of the same bureaucrats just fighting President Johnson—and they've fought you. But you had the courage to do it, because you know that this bill is a landmark of your administration and will help to get a handle on 10 to 15 percent of the Federal budget that we spend on information and paper processing.

It is the most important legislation that you have passed and that we have been able to work on. It will help this Government run the information upon which decisions are made that cost billions of dollars a year.

Thank you, sir.

THE PRESIDENT. Lawton Chiles.

SENATOR CHILES. Mr. President, you mentioned that this was one of the first things that you talked about in your Cabinet meeting. It was also one of the things that you talked about on the stump all over the country when you were campaigning. I think this is certainly a promise fulfilled, and I'm delighted to have had a chance to participate in that.

Frank Horton and Tom McIntyre

headed up a Paperwork Commission, and this was the cornerstone of the recommendations from the Paperwork Commission. Elmer Staats in the GAO has been tremendous support to us as we fought some of those bureaucrats, Senator Danforth, working with me on our House side, and I also want to compliment the staffs of Jack Brooks and my staff and all the staffs that worked on this, because they did a yeoman's task too. And I'm delighted to participate with Jack Brooks. When you get him working on something, you know he's going to take care of his side. You've just got to worry about your side. [*Laughter*]

I think we've got a good bill, and I think what now we have is the framework that is there for an administration to really implement it, and really do something about paperwork.

THE PRESIDENT. I'll always remember the day that Frank Horton and Tom McIntyre and Elmer Staats and others brought the paperwork report into my office, which was a very good and reassuring report and one that's been a basis of this legislation. Frank, I'd like to ask you to say a word.

REPRESENTATIVE HORTON. Mr. President, this is an honor for me to participate in this ceremony, and as one of the original authors of the bill it's a great pleasure to be here and to see you sign your name to this very important piece of legislation, which as you point out is going to be a very landmark piece of legislation in your administration.

It is true that in October of 1977 as the Chairman of the Paperwork Commission, I presented to you the report of the Paperwork Commission. Many of those people are here. Tom McIntyre, as you pointed out, was a member of the Commission from the Senate. Senator Bill Brock was also a member, and then when he left the Senate, Senator Hatfield was a member. On the House side, Tom Steed was a great support and was a member of the Commission also, and I'm sorry he's not here. I think he did have an invitation but he's just not here, but he did a lot too.

Mr. Staats and other members of the Commission, people who are in this room now worked with the Commission, and I might say parenthetically, it's one Commission that self-destructed. It was to be in existence for 2 years. It did self-destruct in those 2 years. It started October 1975. It went out of existence in 1977, and furthermore, we turned back $1.4 million that we didn't spend that had been appropriated. But from the outset, Bert Lance as your OMB Director, his successor, Jim McIntyre, and then of course, with your tremendous support, this legislation has been now signed into law.

We said in 1977 that the cost of paperwork was $100 billion a year to the Federal Government and business, small business and large business, and this is the culmination, really, of the work of the Paperwork Commission—is this legislation which is going to put in place an office which can carry on the thing that you've started, namely to try to cut back on this tremendous amount of paperwork. And, Mr. President, in this you have completely succeeded, and I want to congratulate you and thank you for your leadership in this field.

THE PRESIDENT. With you as partners, there's no way I could have failed. Thank you very much. As you say, we've addressed the bureaucrats, and we've won, right? [*Laughter*]

NOTE: The President spoke at 9:15 a.m. at the signing ceremony in the Cabinet Room at the White House.

As enacted, H.R. 6410 is Public Law 96–511, approved December 11.

Comprehensive Environmental Response, Compensation, and Liability Act of 1980

Remarks on Signing H.R. 7020 Into Law. December 11, 1980

THE PRESIDENT. Although it's impossible to single out all of the people who've been responsible for this legislation, I would like particularly to thank the ones who were responsible for its drafting and later call on a few to say a word after I finish with the signing ceremony.

Congressman Jim Florio, Senator Jennings Randolph, Senator Bob Stafford, and many others worked on this important bill in its drafting phase, and those others that I'll mention later on worked in a very concerted and effective way in getting the legislation through the Congress.

I would like to express my thanks to Howard Baker, to John Rhodes, on both sides of the Hill, of the Capitol, for making this a bipartisan project, succeeding in their effort even after the election of this year. And if I had time I would thank all eight committees who were responsible for the legislation—[*laughter*]—three committees in the Senate and five committees in the House who had direct responsibility over terms of this legislation itself. And, of course, Senator Bill Bradley and Congressman Mario Biaggi, Congressman Biz Johnson, although I stole him from the Senate later on, former Senator Ed Muskie, Congressman Gore, and in the public sector I would like particularly to thank Irving Shapiro, who, on behalf of the leaders of the free enterprise system of our country, were instrumental in pushing this bill to a final conclusion. This directly affects the chemical industry, and the enlightened attitude of the executives of that industry was a very constructive element.

Almost 1½ years ago I sent to the Congress the original proposal for this landmark legislation, landmark in its scope and in its impact on preserving the environmental quality of our country. It was known as a superfund bill, which began a massive and a needed cleanup of hazardous wastes in our country, a problem that had been neglected for decades or even generations. It fills a major gap in the existing laws of our country and also will tend to focus the attention of the public on this very crucial problem that must be resolved. It provides adequate funding, coming primarily from industry, but also from government, and it establishes certain standards for liability if toxic chemicals are damaging to people or to property.

We responded directly and quickly to some of the highly publicized problems with toxic wastes that are just representative of many similar challenges and problems throughout the country. Love Canal and Valley of the Drums come to my memory right this moment. They are stark reminders of the neglect in our society to deal with a growing problem.

We've created in this country great prosperity and a leadership in the entire world with our chemical industry and with the energy industries, but we had neglected to pay part of the cost of that development. And now, of course, we must face that responsibility. The result here is a bill that substantially meets the criteria that I set out in the original proposal that I made to the Congress a year and a half ago. Most important, it enables the Government to recover from responsible parties the costs of their actions in the disposal of toxic wastes. While it does not deal with oil pollution in the way that I did propose, I understand that the Congress intends to act on a comprehensive oil pollution superfund similar to this in scope next year.

In my 4 years as President I think everyone who knows me understands that one of my greatest pleasures has been to strengthen the protection of our environment. Along with the Alaska lands bill and other major legislation, this superfund bill represents a fine achievement for the Congress and for my own administration and for the whole Nation.

I now take great pleasure in signing into law H.R. 7020, and I'm proud that the Congress and my administration have come together to produce this timely and urgently needed response. Following the signature I'd like to ask Congressman Florio to speak first, and I'll call on a few others to follow him.

[*At this point, the President signed the bill.*]

SENATOR RANDOLPH. Why don't we cheer you, Mr. President, while you sign? [*Applause*]

REPRESENTATIVE FLORIO. I appreciate that applause. [*Laughter*]

Let me just say that I and the other Members of the Congress, as well as the President and this administration, I think can all be very proud of what we've done in this very crucial area, not just this legislation but really to address the whole problem of the inappropriate disposal of toxic materials. Really, that's a two-part problem. Prospectively we have a new regulatory system which is just going into effect now, the Resource Conservation and Recovery Act, and therefore we should have no new Love Canals being created. And this bill, of course, is the second part, which is to go back and clean up what, unfortunately, has been done over the last number of years.

So, this is a very important piece of legislation. The administration should be very proud—and I know they are—of what they've done to bring to the public's attention this problem and the remedial actions that we're taking. I'm very pleased to be part of it as well.

THE PRESIDENT. Thank you, Jim. Senator Randolph?

I'd like to say just a word before Senator Randolph speaks, not because he led the applause for me but——[*laughter*]. Over a 4-year period, the term of any President, there is a series of achievements of which a President and a nation can be proud. And it's an extraordinary thing for me, as I look back on my own administration here, to recall the unbelievably large number of times when basic legislation like this has been sponsored by and supported by and husbanded through the Congress by Jennings Randolph.

A lot of these problems that arose, he very early—long before I got involved in politics at all—could see the threat to our country, and to see the culmination of his longstanding effort is indeed an inspiration to a President and also an inspiration to all those who admire you.

Senator Randolph.

SENATOR RANDOLPH. Thank you very much, Mr. President.

You have been innovative, you've been creative, you've been well reasoned in what you have done so many times as President of the United States. You were very supportive; in fact you brought in a sense this legislation to the Hill. I will say for our committee—and I mention not by name but all members of our committee on Environment and Public Works— I thank them all, many who are here today, because we have never permitted in that committee the so-called mere partisanship and politics to surface. We've had our differences, to be sure, but we have worked together, and we believe that that's necessary.

So, I thank Bob Stafford, I thank all of the members, and Bob, of course, is moving up. [*Laughter*]

THE PRESIDENT. Because of that I want him to speak in a minute. [*Laughter*]

SENATOR RANDOLPH. I don't have this opportunity often enough—captive audiences. [*Laughter*] But I want to thank all the Members on the Hill and Doug Costle—here's Doug—and all of the people who are here that have been so helpful as individuals and through their organizations to bringing this good day. It is a good day.

I wish to add this, that for a long time we've been at this in our committee. We started 3 years ago, and we began to work and churn our way through the many problems that seemed unsolvable, at least in part. Now what you, Mr. President, and others have done is to bring to fruition not the final conclusion, but certainly a bold step forward in this effort to clean up the waste materials, the hazardous waste materials of this country that have afflicted the body politic and made our life less than the quality we hope will sometime come into being.

And so, I'd like to add this: We've been very haphazard over the years, as the American people, in handling and in the disposition of these hazardous wastes. So, again, I'm just so grateful for your words and for the opportunity to have worked with you and all others, all in this room, working towards something that calls for the best from the American people.

THE PRESIDENT. Well, I'd like to call now on the man who helped to resurrect this bill when we thought it might be doomed after the election returns came in, but, Senator Stafford, if you would say a few words.

SENATOR STAFFORD. Thank you very much, Mr. President.

A few months ago I didn't really think that we could achieve this moment, and getting this bill passed reminded me often of something like the "Perils of Pauline" as we tried to steer it from one crisis to another. But thanks to your help and everybody on the committees on both sides of the aisle, we now, I think, have an effective way of coping with the toxic releases in this country. And I'm just elated, as all of us are, that we've been able together to reach this point.

Thank you, sir.

THE PRESIDENT. Thank you.

There are many others on the various committees that I should designate for deserved recognition, but I'd like to call on Al Gore, who I think as far as the leadership in the House, really came to the forefront in the last few days, and on Rules Committee influence and others he performed a very notable function. Would you say a word, Congressman Gore?

REPRESENTATIVE GORE. Thank you very much, Mr. President.

Just briefly I'd like to personally thank you for those who worked hard on this legislation. It was of invaluable assistance to have the President of the United States on the telephone personally calling Members of the House and Senate, bending their ear on a regular basis, saying, "Vote for this legislation." It wouldn't have been passed without your help. I'd also like to thank the enthusiastic men and women that you brought to this city who worked tirelessly to get this legislation enacted, and they're in the Justice Department and in the EPA and on the White House staff. We couldn't have done it without them either.

Thank you, Mr. President.

THE PRESIDENT. Thank you.

And finally, I rarely call on any of my own Cabinet officers or agency heads to make a comment, but I would particularly like for Doug Costle to say a word or two. He doesn't know I'm going to call on him but——

MR. COSTLE. Thank you, Mr. President.

I think this bill is, in fact, very strong testimony to what has been a truly bipartisan effort in the last year, and I feel really undeserving to be here. The people who've done the work at EPA and on the Hill, the Members of the Congress, who have, in the face of a lot of pressures to go a different direction, who've stuck with it—it just takes an enormous amount of effort and energy to get something like this to happen, and I just feel very moved this morning that it finally came to pass.

Thank you, Mr. President.

THE PRESIDENT. I'd like to say one other word before I leave, and that is that I've noticed some analyses in the press and otherwise that the so-called lame-duck Congress has not been productive. The legislation that has been passed in this last month has been truly extraordinary.

When I went down the list of key bills that I wanted to see put into law before I leave this office, back early in November, the list included things that we thought were highly doubtful: The reconciliation legislation, that not only saves more than $8 billion in deficits but also sets a precedent for the future, the paperwork bill, that I signed a few minutes ago, the Alaska lands bill, this bill on superfund, and others is a real testimony to a dynamic, hardworking, and very effective 96th Congress. And on behalf of my administration and the entire Nation, I want to express both my admiration for you and my appreciation to all the Members of the Congress for a superb achievement.

Thank you very much.

NOTE: The President spoke at 9:45 a.m. at the signing ceremony in the Cabinet Room at the White House.

As enacted, H.R. 7020 is Public 96–510, approved December 11.

Administrative Conference of the United States

Appointment of Ronald B. Lewis as a Member of the Council.   December 11, 1980

The President today announced the appointment of Ronald B. Lewis as a member of the Council of the Administrative Conference of the United States.

Lewis is a Washington attorney who was previously Deputy Adviser for Regulatory Policies at the Council on Wage and Price Stability.

National Commission on Alcoholism and Other Alcohol-Related Problems

Appointment of Laura Wittstock as a Member.   December 11, 1980

The President today announced the appointment of Laura Wittstock, of Minneapolis, as a member of the National Commission on Alcoholism and Other Alcohol-Related Problems.

Wittstock is director of the development office for fundraising of the American Indian Alcohol Treatment Program and former executive director of the American Indian Press Association.

Tariff Concessions on Live Cattle Imports

Proclamation 4808.   December 11, 1980

PROCLAMATION TO IMPLEMENT CERTAIN TARIFF CONCESSIONS ON LIVE CATTLE IMPORTS

By the President of the United States

A Proclamation

1. On September 17, 1979, under the authority of section 101(a)(1) of the Trade Act of 1974 (the Trade Act) (19 U.S.C. 2111(a)(1)), the United States entered into a trade agreement with Canada containing concessions by the United States on five tariff items regarding imports of live cattle. Section G of Annex III of Proclamation No. 4707 of December 11, 1979, provided for the staged reductions in the rates of duty for four of the tariff items on cattle. Those staged reductions were subsequently implemented by a notice published in the FEDERAL REGISTER (45 Fed. Reg. 20603 (1980)). Implementation of the concession on a fifth tariff item was made contingent upon the conclusion of certain trade negotiations with the United Mexican States. Those negotiations were concluded on March 18, 1980.

NOW, THEREFORE, I, JIMMY CARTER, President of the United States of America, acting under the authority vested in me by the Constitution and the statutes of the United States, including but not limited to Title I and section 604 of the Trade Act (19 U.S.C. 2483), do proclaim that:

(1) Section G of Annex III of Proclamation No. 4707 of December 11, 1979, is amended, as provided in the Annex to this proclamation, to notify and publish the effective dates, as required by Proc-

lamation No. 4707, and to add an additional tariff item.

(2) The aforesaid amendment shall be effective with respect to articles entered, or withdrawn from warehouse for consumption, on or after January 1, 1980, and as to which the liquidation of entries or withdrawals has not become final and conclusive under section 514 of the Tariff Act of 1930 (19 U.S.C. 1514). If applicable, reliquidation under 19 U.S.C. 1520 is authorized.

IN WITNESS WHEREOF, I have hereunto set my hand this eleventh day of December, in the year of our Lord nineteen hundred and eighty and of the Independence of the United States of America the two hundred and fifth.

JIMMY CARTER

[Filed with the Office of the Federal Register, 11:46 a.m., December 12, 1980]

NOTE: The annex is printed in the FEDERAL REGISTER of December 15, 1980.

The proclamation was announced by the White House Press Office on December 12.

United States Air Force Academy

Appointment of Governor Edmund G. Brown, Jr., as a Member of the Board of Visitors. December 12, 1980

The President today announced that he will appoint Edmund G. Brown, Jr., Governor of California, as a member of the Board of Visitors to the United States Air Force Academy.

This 15-member board meets annually to inquire into the morale and discipline, curriculum, instruction, physical equipment, fiscal affairs, academic methods, and other matters relating to the Academy.

National Historic Preservation Act Amendments of 1980

Statement on Signing H.R. 5496 Into Law. December 12, 1980

I am pleased today to sign into law H.R. 5496, the National Historic Preservation Act Amendments of 1980.

This landmark historic preservation legislation—the first major amendment to the National Historic Preservation Act since 1966—will provide better definition and guidance for programs at all levels of government. The bill clarifies the responsibilities of all Federal agencies with respect to historic preservation, provides a statutory basis for State historic preservation programs, and gives local governments a specific role in the preservation effort. Local governments will be included in the process of reviewing nominations to the National Register of Historic Places and will be eligible to receive grant money from the Historic Preservation Fund. This legislation also provides mechanisms to increase private sector involvement in historic preservation activities, and it reauthorizes the Historic Preservation Fund through 1987 at an annual level of $150 million. These features will strengthen this highly successful program by increasing public participation and by encouraging more decentralization in decisions affecting historic properties.

Although this bill greatly improves our Nation's historic preservation program, it contains other provisions that I find troubling.

The bill provides that certain executive functions be performed by the Advisory Council on Historic Preservation, not all of whose members are appointed by the President in conformity with the appointments clause of the Constitution. To avoid a constitutional conflict, individuals not so appointed should participate only in the Council's advisory activities.

The bill also raises certain constitutional questions about the authority of the Council to conduct litigation on its own behalf. While I believe the bill can be construed so as to avoid constitutional infringement, I have asked the Attorney General to study the matter and advise the Council regarding his conclusions.

Finally, the bill raises the question of whether Congress may, by concurrent resolution not presented to the President for his approval or disapproval, veto regulations issued by an executive agency. As I have noted on prior occasions, I oppose this legislative veto device, and pursuant to my message to Congress of June 21, 1978, I will treat these legislative vetoes as report-and-wait provisions.

This administration has actively supported legislation to protect our historical heritage, and I salute the Members of Congress—particularly Senator Bumpers and Congressman Seiberling—and the historic preservation organizations who have worked so diligently to secure the passage of this bill.

NOTE: As enacted, H.R. 5496 is Public Law 96–515, approved December 12.

Patent and Trademark System Reform

Statement on Signing H.R. 6933 Into Law. December 12, 1980

I have today signed H.R. 6933, a bill which makes several major reforms in the patent and trademark system.

One of my administration's major concerns has been the role of industrial innovation in promoting this Nation's economic health. More than 2½ years ago, I initiated a review of industrial innovation to identify ways in which the Federal Government could improve the innovation process. We were assisted by hundreds of individuals from private industry, organized labor, the universities, and public interest groups.

As a result of these efforts, in October of 1979 I sent to the Congress an industrial innovation message proposing initiatives in nine critical areas relevant to innovation, including legislation to strengthen our patent system. I am pleased to sign this bill, which embodies many of my proposals.

We have already taken other steps to revitalize our patent system, including the application of modern methods of management and computer technology in the Patent and Trademark Office.

The legislation I am signing today does not eliminate all the problems we identified. It does not establish a comprehensive governmentwide policy for the allocation of rights in inventions made with Federal support. This legislation leaves in place the existing, often inconsistent array of statutory and nonstatutory patent policies governing individual agencies. Also left uncovered are large business contractors who perform more than 90 percent of the government's research and development work.

I am persuaded, however, that the present package of reforms goes far toward strengthening the effectiveness of the patent incentive in stimulating innovation in the United States.

The patent reexamination procedures established by this legislation constitute the most significant improvement in our patent laws in more than a century. Under these procedures, during the life of an issued patent any interested person—for example, a patent owner, a potential licensee, or a competitor—may obtain a prompt and relatively inexpensive reevaluation of its validity by the Patent and Trademark Office. Patent reexamination will make it possible to focus extra attention on the most commercially significant patents. This legislation will improve the reliability of reexamined patents, thereby reducing the costs and uncertainties of testing patent validity in the courts. The provisions of this legislation will result in less cost to the public for patent reexamination.

This legislation also authorizes the Commissioner of Patents and Trademarks to set fees at levels that recover a greater portion of the Office's operating costs. A new system of fees for maintaining patents in force will further shift some of the burden of supporting the patent system away from the public to the commercial users of inventions. This feature will be helpful to small businesses and individual inventors by keeping initial patent fees low.

In the area of Government patent policy, this legislation enables small businesses and nonprofit organizations to obtain title to inventions made with Federal support. I hope that this measure will benefit the public in some measure by making the fruits of federally supported research and development more widely available. While I regret that it was not possible to enact comprehensive legislation, I am pleased with the progress we have made.

The enactment of this legislation promises some real benefits to the Nation's economic health by stimulating our people's innovative activity. It now becomes the responsibility of the Government and industry to work together to realize that promise.

NOTE: As enacted, H.R. 6933 is Public Law 96–517, approved December 12.

Earthquake in Southern Italy

Statement on Signing H.R. 8388 Into Law.
December 12, 1980

I am today signing legislation that will enable the United States to provide $50 million in assistance to the unfortunate victims of the earthquakes that have devastated southern Italy.

This disaster—the worst natural catastrophe in Western Europe in half a century—has killed more than 3,000 people and left more than 200,000 homeless. Whole villages have been wiped off the map. We in the United States are deeply sympathetic to the Italian people and their government in this time of great sorrow and great need.

The funds provided by this legislation will, I hope, provide some measure of immediate relief to the stricken area and help a courageous people to overcome the effects of disaster.

I know my feelings are shared by all Americans—whose spontaneous contributions to private voluntary agencies are already aiding in the relief efforts—in praying that the worst is now over and that the suffering of southern Italy will now give way to hope as the rebuilding process begins.

NOTE: As enacted, H.R. 8388 is Public Law 96–525, approved December 12.

National Science Foundation Authorization and Science and Technology Equal Opportunities Act

Statement on Signing S. 568 Into Law.
December 12, 1980

I have today signed into law S. 568, which authorizes appropriations for the

National Science Foundation for fiscal year 1981 and provides support for efforts to bring women and minorities into full participation in science and engineering.

It is gratifying to join Congress in devoting increased attention to the under-involvement of women and minorities in the scientific and technical professions. More than half the population of the United States is made up of women and members of minority groups, yet relatively few of them pursue careers in science, engineering, and technology. This bill will help to correct that inequity and prevent the waste of a vast pool of potential talent.

There are nevertheless deficiencies in this legislation that cause me to sign it with reservations.

The bill contains an unprecedented level of detailed funding specification and administrative direction. These provisions are an incursion on executive management responsibility, distort program balance, impede program management, and would be a serious problem for any agency. They are particularly serious in the case of the National Science Foundation.

This unique agency was established to extend the enormously effective scientific effort mounted by the United States during World War II. That effort was led by scientists themselves and by their perceptions of how scientific research and endeavor could best contribute to the war effort. To build on the success of that approach, the National Science Foundation was established with a unique structure and an independent, nonpolitical scientific leadership. To this day, moreover, it draws very heavily on advice from scientists and engineers outside the Government in selecting, by standards of scientific merit, the programs it should pursue and the projects it should support. The success of the Foundation and the spectacular achievements of American science

attest to the wisdom of this approach to Federal support of science.

The National Science Foundation is not and should not be free from responsibility to the people and their representatives. But if the Foundation and the scientific enterprises it supports are to contribute effectively to meeting the needs of the people and the concerns of the country, then the Foundation must continue to be led and directed by scientists. The level of detailed political direction in this legislation represents a trend in the wrong direction.

I am also disturbed by the number and nature of instructions given in committee reports accompanying this legislation. Expressions such as "the Committee *directs* the Foundation to develop an experimental pilot program . . .", "the Committee *directs* the Foundation to provide continued strong support for scientific instrumentation and equipment", and "members of (an advisory group) *shall* serve for three year terms" abound in these reports.

To be sure, the occasional use of committee reports to send informal congressional messages to executive agencies is a time-honored and often desirable practice. It has a number of advantages for both branches precisely because committee reports are not law, need not clear all the legislative and constitutional hurdles a law must clear, and lack the force of law.

But when a committee *directs* in such a report that an agency of the executive act in a specific way, with the apparent expectation that the agency will take the direction as having something like the force of law, the practice takes a dangerous turn. Moreover, when such directions multiply as they have in the case of this legislation, they can easily become an instrument for detailed management of the agency by a few Members of Congress or by committee staffs. This should concern the Congress as much as it concerns the executive.

I am therefore reminding the Director of the National Science Foundation that committee reports are not law and should not be treated as though they were.

NOTE: As enacted, S. 568 is Public Law 96–516, approved December 12.

Warren Grant Magnuson Clinical Center

Statement on Signing S.J. Res. 213 Into Law. December 12, 1980

I have today signed S.J. Res. 213, a bill designating the Clinical Center of the National Institutes of Health as the "Warren Grant Magnuson Clinical Center."

This act is an appropriate tribute to the long and distinguished career of Senator Magnuson, who has been a leader in the cause of better health care for Americans. He has been called the "Commander in Chief" of the war against cancer and heart disease. In 1937 as a freshman Member of the House of Representatives, he sponsored the legislation creating the National Cancer Institute. He has had an unwavering commitment to the idea that progress in health care depends on research and has through his many years of public office contributed substantially to the excellence of health research in the United States.

NOTE: As enacted, S.J. Res. 213 is Public Law 96–518, approved December 12.

Digest of Other White House Announcements

The following listing includes the President's public schedule and other items of general interest announced by the White House Press Office and not included elsewhere in this issue.

December 7

The President returned to the White House from Camp David, Md.

The President met at the White House with:

—foreign policy advisers;

—the National Security Council.

December 8

The President met at the White House with:

—Zbigniew Brzezinski, Assistant to the President for National Security Affairs;

—Frank B. Moore, Assistant to the President for Congressional Liaison;

—administration officials to review the fiscal year 1982 budget.

December 9

The President met at the White House with:

—Dr. Brzezinski;

—Mr. Moore;

—Philip Henry Alston, Jr., U.S. Ambassador to Australia;

—Lew R. Wasserman, president of Music Corporation of America, Inc., and Mrs. Wasserman;

—the executive committee of the Democratic National Committee.

December 10

The President met at the White House with:

—Dr. Brzezinski;

—Mr. Moore;

—administration officials to discuss the fiscal year 1982 budget.

December 11

The President met at the White House with:

—Dr. Brzezinski;

—administration officials to discuss the fiscal year 1982 budget.

In a ceremony in the Oval Office, the President received diplomatic credentials from Ambassadors Jorge Mario Eastman of Colombia, Federico Edmundo Poujol of Honduras, Moteane John Melamu of Botswana, Fernando Schwalb Lopez Aldana of Peru, and Kubulan Los of Papua New Guinea.

The President today announced that he has designated John Dalton as Chairman of the Federal Home Loan Bank Board. Dalton has been a member of this Board since earlier this year and is former president of the Government National Mortgage Association.

The President has designated Mr. Jeno Paulucci as his personal representative to lead a delegation to Italy on Saturday, December 13. Mr. Paulucci and the members of his delegation will confer with Italian Government officials and others involved in providing relief to victims of the recent earthquake. The primary objective of the delegation's mission will be to express United States sympathy and concern and to explore ways in which the United States can most usefully augment the assistance it has already provided for earthquake victims and their communities. The delegation is expected to complete its mission late next week and will report to the President upon return to Washington. In addition to Mr. Paulucci, who served as President Ford's special representative during the recovery from the 1976 Friuli earthquake, the Presidential delegation will comprise:

MARIO BIAGGI, Member of Congress, New York;

SILVIO CONTE, Member of Congress, Massachusetts;

MARIO CUOMO, Lieutenant Governor of New York;

GERALDINE FERRARO, Member of Congress, New York;

ROBERT GEORGINE, president, Building and Construction Trade Unions;

BENJAMIN L. PALUMBO, director, Federal Government relations, Philip Morris Inc.; and

NANCY PELOSI, chairperson, Northern California Democratic Party, San Francisco.

December 12

The President met at the White House with:

—Dr. Brzezinski;

—Vice President Walter F. Mondale, Deputy Secretary of State Warren M. Christopher, and Dr. Brzezinski;

—Representative Dan Glickman of Kansas;

—Mr. Moore.

The White House announced that the President has received a report from Secretary of State Edmund S. Muskie on the recently completed NATO Foreign Ministers meeting.

The President today announced that he will designate Georgiana Sheldon as Acting Chairman of the Federal Energy Regulatory Commission effective January 2, 1981. Sheldon has been a member of this Commission since it was established in 1977.

The President left the White House for a weekend stay at Camp David.

NOMINATIONS SUBMITTED TO THE SENATE

NOTE: No nominations were submitted to the Senate during the period covered by this issue.

CHECKLIST OF WHITE HOUSE PRESS RELEASES

The following listing contains releases of the White House Press Office which are not included in this issue.

Released December 11, 1980

Fact sheet: H.R. 6410, Paperwork Reduction Act of 1980

Fact sheet: H.R. 7020, Comprehensive Environmental Response, Compensation, and Liability Act of 1980

ACTS APPROVED BY THE PRESIDENT

Approved December 8, 1980

S. 3152_____Public Law 96–506
An act to amend the Public Works and Economic Development Act of 1965 and the Appalachian Regional Development Act of 1965 to extend the authorization for such Acts for two additional years.

H.R. 4892_____Public Law 96–507
An act to repeal section 506 of the Communications Act of 1934.

S. 2352_____Public Law 96–508
An act to increase the authorization for the Council on Wage and Price Stability, to extend the duration of such Council, and for other purposes.

S. 2441_____Public Law 96–509
Juvenile Justice Amendments of 1980.

Approved December 11, 1980

H.R. 7020_____ Public Law 96–510
Comprehensive Environmental Response, Compensation, and Liability Act of 1980.

H.R. 6410_____Public Law 96–511
Paperwork Reduction Act of 1980.

Approved December 12, 1980

H.R. 6889_____Public Law 96–512
Methane Transportation Research, Development, and Demonstration Act of 1980.

S. 1918_____ Public Law 96–513
Defense Officer Personnel Management Act.

H.R. 7724_____ Public Law 96–514
An act making appropriations for the Department of the Interior and related agencies for the fiscal year ending September 30, 1981, and for other purposes.

H.R. 5496_____ Public Law 96–515
National Historic Preservation Act Amendments of 1980.

S. 568_____ Public Law 96–516
National Science Foundation Authorization and Science and Technology Equal Opportunities Act.

H.R. 6933_____ Public Law 96–517
An act to amend the patent and trademark laws.

S.J. Res. 213_____ Public Law 96–518
A joint resolution to designate the Clinical Center of the National Institutes of Health located in Montgomery County, Maryland,

ACTS APPROVED—Continued

Approved December 12—Continued

as the "Warren Grant Magnuson Clinical Center of the National Institutes of Health".

H.R. 6086_____ Public Law 96–519
An act to provide for the settlement and payment of claims of United States civilian and military personnel against the United States for losses resulting from acts of violence directed against the United States Government or its representatives in a foreign country or from an authorized evacuation of personnel from a foreign country.

H.R. 8228_____ Public Law 96–520
An act to provide that a certain portion of Lake Erie shall be declared nonnavigable.

H.R. 6211_____ Public Law 96–521
An act to authorize the Secretary of the Interior to issue certain patents under the Color of Title Act.

H.R. 7805_____ Public Law 96–522
An act to authorize appropriations for the American Folklife Center for fiscal years 1982, 1983, and 1984.

H.R. 7466_____ Public Law 96–523
An act to amend section 8102 of title 5, United States Code, and section 7 of the Federal Advisory Committee Act to permit the employment of personal assistants for handicapped Federal employees both at their regular duty station and while on travel status.

H.R. 7815_____ Public Law 96–524
An act to recognize the meritorious achievements of certain individuals by providing for the designation of certain post offices in their honor, and for other purposes.

H.R. 8388_____ Public Law 96–525
An act to amend the Foreign Assistance Act of 1961 to authorize appropriations for international disaster assistance for the victims of the recent earthquakes in southern Italy.

H.R. 6258_____ Private Law 96–71
An act providing for reinstatement and validation of United States oil and gas leases numbered C–9496, C–9711, C–11600, C–11621, C–11622, C–11630, C–11631, C–11597, C–11599, C–13774, C–14197, C–17049, C–18262, C–26048, C–13532, C–11581, C–11585, C–11590, C–11591, C–11595.

Appropriations Bill for the Departments of State, Justice, and Commerce, the Judiciary, and Related Agencies

Message to the House of Representatives Returning H.R. 7584 Without Approval. December 13, 1980

To the House of Representatives:

I am returning without my signature H.R. 7584, the State-Justice-Commerce Appropriations Act of 1980. A provision in this Act, the Helms-Collins Amendment, would impose an unprecedented prohibition on the power of the President of the United States and the Attorney General to seek a particular remedy in the Federal courts that in some cases may be necessary to ensure that our Constitution and laws are faithfully executed.

Throughout my Administration, I have been committed to the vigorous enforcement of the Fourteenth Amendment to our Constitution and of our civil rights laws. They are the backbone of our commitment to equal justice. All Americans are the beneficiaries of over two decades of progress since the Supreme Court upheld the constitutional right of all races to equal educational opportunity and the Congress passed landmark civil rights legislation to end discrimination in voting, housing, employment, education and public accommodations. We should not turn back the clock to an era when the Department of Justice stood passive and the en-

tire burden of seeking a remedy for the infringement of constitutional rights fell on the victims of discrimination themselves.

I have often stated my belief that busing should only be used as a last resort in school desegregation cases. But busing even as a last resort is not the real issue here. The real issue is whether it is proper for the Congress to prevent the President from carrying out his constitutional responsibility under Article II to enforce the Constitution and other laws of the United States.

The precedent that would be established if this legislation became law is dangerous. It would effectively allow the Congress to tell a President that there are certain constitutionally-mandated remedies for the invasion of constitutional rights that he cannot ask the courts to apply. If a President can be barred from going to the courts on this issue, a future Congress could by similar reasoning prevent a President from asking the courts to rule on the constitutionality of other laws and the constitutional necessity of other remedies upon which the President and the Congress disagree. That would be a most undesirable interference with the constitutional separation of powers.

For any President to accept this precedent would gravely encroach on the powers of his office. I have a responsibility to my successors and to the American people not to permit that encroachment to take place. I intend to discharge that responsibility to the best of my ability.

JIMMY CARTER

The White House,
    December 13, 1980.

NOTE: The House of Representatives reconsidered H.R. 7584 on December 13, and the bill was referred to committee.

White House Conference on Coal Exports

Remarks to Industry Representatives.
December 15, 1980

First of all, I want to welcome all of you to the White House to a very important conference. This is a labor of love for me.

One of the major commitments that I had when I began my own campaign for President several years ago was to try to evolve for my country a national energy policy that would help us to reduce our excessive dependence on imported oil. We've made good progress with a very farsighted and courageous Congress, and I think the other nations in the world are also realizing that we are quite vulnerable so long as we have no substantive alternatives to a dependence on an uncertain supply of oil from the Persian Gulf region. We don't want to break away completely from the purchase of this OPEC oil, but at least we've got to lessen the competition for limited supplies of oil, help to restrain the price to hold down inflationary pressures, and to give us security with alternative supplies of energy.

Today we have assembled here buyers, for whom we are thankful, the producers, for whom we are thankful, also those who are involved in transportation. Leaders in government are also present, because this is a continuing program that will require the removal of obstacles that have existed in the past to the production and the exporting and the use of coal in our own country.

National security is, of course, paramount for all those who hold public office, and I consider an adequate national and international energy policy to be vital our Nation's security. When I was at the economic summit in Venice earlier this year, the main subject that addressed us in economic matters was how to change our commitment concerning energy in the future.

One of the goals that all of us set, the other seven leaders of the Western nations and myself, was first of all to reduce the amount of energy expended in total terms compared to economic growth that each nation experienced—in other words, to have a more efficient use of all kinds of energy collectively; secondly, to reduce the percentage of our total energy used, which was comprised of oil, from 51 percent, 53 percent, down to about 40 percent—all these goals by 1990; third, to reduce in real terms the total amount of oil that all the nations consumed; and, of course, additionally, to increase the amount of alternative forms of energy to be developed, both the advanced forms of energy, the more exotic ways to use solar energy, magneto hydrodynamics, and the use of fuels derived from the Sun indirectly from growing crops, and perhaps even the use, in an increasing degree, of waste products to produce consumable energy, methane and other products. These obviously are important goals, but I think the root of every measure of substantive progress, at least in our country, is coal.

Many Americans were surprised this year to find that we have set a record in this country this year in the production of coal. Our Nation will produce about 800 million tons of coal in 1980. Our country has never produced 17 million tons of coal in 1 week before, but this year 18 different weeks, we have produced more than 17 million tons of coal. A lot of that's because of the new energy policy. A lot of that is because of an awakening interest in reducing oil imports. But I would say one of the major elements that has made it possible for this sustained high production has been the good relationship between management and labor.

Historically in our country, ever since even before Harry Truman's time, the coal industry has been plagued with excessive disruption in sustained coal production because of wildcat strikes and the inability of management and labor to work together toward long-range common problems. That has been changed. And I'm very grateful for it, because it not only gives management and labor a better prospect for future profits and future income for working families, it also enhances the opportunity for labor and management to work together harmoniously other than the times in the past when difficult controversial contracts were being negotiated. Now labor and management, government, buyers, sellers, transporters can work together, as in this conference, to make sure that the supplies of coal are adequate, that they are sure and dependable, and that prices are kept reasonable.

The last thing I'd like to say is this: We have great opportunities in foreign countries for the sale of American coal. We want our coal to be of high quality. We want it to be delivered on time. We want the supply to be certain. We want the prices to be reasonable, and we want there to be a good relationship between the purchasers of American coal and the American suppliers. These goals are not impos-

sible to achieve. We feel that by 1990, in Europe alone, there is an excellent opportunity for more than tripling the purchase of American coal. Total imports will increase that much, and in Japan and other nations in the western Pacific, imports of coal will very likely increase by 700 percent during the next 10 years.

American suppliers cannot take this market for granted. We, in this country, are going to have to work hard; we're going to have to be highly competitive with other suppliers; we're going to have to give good service. We've already made plans under my administration for the next administration to expedite decisions to be made on increased dredging of American ports and improving the transportation system to get coal from the mines to the ports themselves. The rapidly increasing demand for coal has proven vividly to us that the transportation and loading facilities in our country have to be improved. I don't think anyone in a position of authority in this country doubts that any longer.

We welcome the investment by foreign buyers in this improvement in transport, loading, and handling facilities. And we believe that the American laws that protect the interest of members of a contractual arrangement are as good as those anywhere in the world to make sure that when a contract is made for the delivery of coal to a foreign buyer, that the foreign buyer will be adequately protected. We are very much interested in improving this protection, which is already existent.

Well, let me say again that I deeply appreciate this group coming to the White House area here to discuss one of the very important elements of national and international existence. And I think what we have done in the last 3 or 4 years to prove to the world not only the present value of coal but to the greatly enhanced potential value of coal in years ahead has been very beneficial indeed.

You have a large responsibility on your hands, because you represent not only our own Nation's interests and its national energy policy but also the interests of the free world and making sure that all varied forms of energy can be used to the maximum in most efficient degree possible. These are some of the points I wanted to make to you.

Again, I'm deeply grateful to those leaders in this room who have made it possible for us to make the progress we have so far, and I turn over the program now to you for a very beneficial interrelationship among one another, because we share a mutual opportunity and the mutual advantages to the enhanced production, consumption in this country and export of our precious American coal to foreign buyers in the years ahead.

Thank you very much.

NOTE: The President spoke at 2:30 p.m. in Room 450 of the Old Executive Office Building.

National Commission on Student Financial Assistance

Appointment of Robert J. McKenna as a Member. December 15, 1980

The President today announced that he will appoint Robert J. McKenna, of Newport, R.I., to be a member of the National Commission on Student Financial Assistance.

McKenna is an associate professor of political science and director of college and community relations at the Newport College. He is a Rhode Island State senator and serves on the Senate Health, Education and Welfare Committee. McKenna

was selected Outstanding Educator in America in 1970 and is active in postsecondary education matters.

Census Statistics on Legal Immigrants

Executive Order 12256.   December 15, 1980

By the authority vested in me as President of the United States of America, I hereby determine that States, counties and local units of general purpose government have been significantly affected by major population changes within the meaning of Section 118 of Public Law 96–369 if there reside within such jurisdictions at least fifty legal immigrants from Cuba or Haiti who arrived between April 1, 1980, and September 30, 1980. Pursuant to Section 118 of Public Law 96–369 and other applicable law, it is hereby ordered as follows:

1–101. The Bureau of the Census shall designate, as of September 30, 1980, those affected States, counties, or local units of general purpose government described above and shall supply estimates of the total number of such Cuban and Haitian immigrants to the President and to all departments and agencies of the Executive Branch which administer laws which authorize benefits according to population or population characteristics. The Bureau of the Census and the Department of Commerce shall designate the estimates so supplied as official statistics.

1–102. Beginning with fiscal year 1981, all departments and agencies of the Executive Branch shall utilize the estimates furnished under Sec. 1–101 for all formulas affecting the allocation of funds in the administration of laws distributing benefits according to population or other population characteristics, unless such utilization would be contrary to law.

1–103. The Bureau of the Census shall supply the estimates required by Sec. 1–101 for States within 30 days of the issuance of this Order and shall supply all other estimates as soon as is practicable.

1–104. To the extent permitted by law, all departments and agencies of the Executive Branch shall cooperate with the Bureau of the Census in discharging the functions under this Order.

1–105. This Order shall expire when the Bureau of the Census issues 1981 population estimates.

JIMMY CARTER

The White House,
   December 15, 1980.

[Filed with the Office of the Federal Register,
   2:07 p.m., December 16, 1980]

NOTE: The Executive order was announced by the White House Press Office on December 16.

International Security and Development Cooperation Act of 1980

Statement on Signing H.R. 6942 Into Law. December 16, 1980

Today I am signing H.R. 6942, the International Security and Development Cooperation Act of 1980. This act authorizes appropriations for fiscal year 1981 security and development assistance programs and related activities and makes certain substantive changes in the statutory standards, procedures, and requirements governing such programs.

The programs and activities made possible by this legislation are vital to United States foreign policy interests. They are our principal means of helping our friends and allies meet their defense needs and of contributing to the economic development of countries less favored than our own.

In requesting these authorizations, my administration drew the attention of the Congress to the fact that the legislation governing these programs is sadly in need of reform. Over the years, this legislation has grown increasingly complex and cumbersome. In many cases, it has made it more difficult for the United States to respond promptly and effectively to unforeseen emergencies and to changes in international circumstances. As a result, we proposed several carefully selected changes to the law. While the bill that I am approving today differs in a number of respects from the proposals put forth by the administration, I am nonetheless pleased to note that the Congress has responded to my concern over the rigidity of the statutory bases for our security and development assistance programs.

Nevertheless, I am seriously concerned about sections 107 and 202 of H.R. 6942. Section 107 amends section 36(c) of the Arms Export Control Act to permit the Congress to disapprove, by adoption of a concurrent resolution, proposed major commercial exports of defense articles and services to any country except NATO members, Japan, Australia, and New Zealand. This provision conflicts with Article I, section 7 of the Constitution, which states that legislative measures having the force and effect of law must be presented to the President for approval. Because of its potential for involving the Congress in the day-to-day implementation of the law, this responsibility was allocated solely to the President under the Constitution. Moreover, this is the first time that the Congress has sought to impose such a legislative veto on private transactions regulated by the Arms Export Control Act. Not only will this veto power inject an unnecessarily disruptive element into legitimate commercial enterprise by subjecting proposed exports to disapproval even after they have been approved by the executive branch, but it may also erode the position of U.S. industry abroad and cause legal action to be taken against the U.S. Government should the Congress disapprove a proposed export.

Section 202 extends the Congress authority to disapprove, by concurrent resolution, the use of economic support funds for the Middle East.

While I am signing H.R. 6942 into law because of its overall importance to the foreign policy and national security of the United States, I must express my deep reservations about sections 107 and 202. My action today does not mean that I accept the constitutional validity of these provisions.

The ultimate importance to the United States of our security and development assistance programs cannot be exaggerated. The programs and activities provided for in H.R. 6942 will enable the United States to continue its contribution to the achievement of a secure and stable world.

NOTE: As enacted, H.R. 6942 is Public Law 96–533, approved December 16.

Federal-State-Local Government Funding Simplification

Statement on Signing S. 1835 Into Law. December 16, 1980

I have today signed into law S. 1835, which extends for 5 more years the authority of the Joint Funding Simplification Act of 1974.

I am pleased that the Congress has continued this authority to assist State and local governments obtain and use Federal assistance from a number of Federal programs in a more coordinated and simplified process.

In the past 5 years, for example, the joint funding process has assisted the States of Arizona, Kentucky, and Rhode Island, along with a number of cities, regional organizations, counties, and Indian tribal governments to develop or improve service delivery and economic and community development programs.

Joint funding is a proven management tool that has enabled the Federal agencies and State and local governments to work together to reduce administrative paperwork and achieve a more timely delivery of funds to meet the needs of our people.

I urge both the Federal agencies and State and local governments to take full advantage of the joint funding authority.

NOTE: As enacted, S. 1835 is Public Law 96–534, approved December 16.

Federal Insecticide, Fungicide, and Rodenticide Act Extension

Statement on Signing H.R. 7018 Into Law. December 17, 1980

I have today signed H.R. 7018, a bill to extend the Federal Insecticide, Fungicide, and Rodenticide Act until September 30, 1981.

In approving this bill, I want to emphasize my view, and that of the Attorney General, that section 4 is unconstitutional. Section 4 purports to allow Congress to disapprove agency regulations issued under the Federal Insecticide, Fungicide, and Rodenticide Act by a concurrent resolution not submitted to the President for his approval. For that reason, section 4 violates Article I, section 7 of the Constitution. Relatedly, section 4 violates the constitutional separation of powers by purporting to give Congress a role in administering substantive statutory programs. In accordance with my June 21, 1978, message to Congress, the executive branch will treat section 4 as a "report and wait" provision and will not consider a congressional expression of disapproval under section 4 to be legally binding.

NOTE: As enacted, H.R. 7018 is Public Law 96–539, approved December 17.

Commission on Presidential Scholars

Appointment of Moctesuma Diaz Esparza as a Member.   December 17, 1980

The President today announced the appointment of Moctesuma Diaz Esparza, of Los Angeles, as a member of the Commission on Presidential Scholars.

Esparza is a producer of award-winning films and vice president of the Euclid Foundation. He is a member of the Los Angeles Bicentennial Committee and served on the National Endowment for the Humanities Review Panel on Public Media.

National Highway Safety Advisory Committee

Appointment of Nicholas Figueroa as a Member.   December 17, 1980

The President today announced the appointment of Nicholas Figueroa, of New York City, as a member of the National Highway Safety Advisory Committee.

Figueroa is deputy commissioner in charge of trials with the New York Police Department and a former assistant U.S. attorney for the Southern District of New York.

Modification of Tariff Schedules

Memorandum From the President. December 17, 1980

Memorandum for the United States Trade Representative

I have signed into law an Act "To approve and implement the protocol to the trade agreement relating to customs valuation, and for other purposes" (P.L. 96–490). That action enables you to exercise delegated authority to accept for the United States the Protocol to the Agreement on Implementation of Article VII of the General Agreement on Tariffs and Trade. Following such acceptance, that portion of the above-mentioned Act implementing the Protocol may become effective when the European Economic Community also implements the Protocol. I hereby delegate to you the authority to make that determination as required by section 2 of the Act.

This document shall be published in the FEDERAL REGISTER.

JIMMY CARTER

[Filed with the Office of the Federal Register, 10:45 a.m., December 18, 1980]

Modification of Tariff Schedules

Proclamation 4809.   December 17, 1980

PROCLAMATION TO MAKE EFFECTIVE THE AMENDMENTS OF SECTION 3(b) OF PUBLIC LAW 96–490 AND FOR OTHER PURPOSES

By the President of the United States

A Proclamation

1. Proclamation No. 4768 of June 28, 1980, implementing the Customs Valuation Code, made numerous changes to the

Tariff Schedules of the United States (TSUS) (19 U.S.C. 1202) and established staged reductions in the rates of duty proclaimed therein, pursuant to the General Agreement on Tariffs and Trade and other trade agreements.

2. Pursuant to the authority of sections 503(a)(1) and 503(a)(2)(A) of the Trade Agreements Act of 1979 (93 Stat. 251), and by Proclamation No. 4768, I designated certain articles, identified by specific TSUS item numbers, to receive advanced staging of reductions in the rates of duty applicable to such items.

3. Section 3 of the Act to Approve and Implement the Protocol to the Trade Agreement relating to Customs Valuation, and for Other Purposes (Public Law 96–490 of December 2, 1980) made a number of technical amendments to schedule 4 of the TSUS and authorized the President to proclaim the effective date for certain of those amendments.

4. In order to continue the previously proclaimed staged reductions and the provisions for advanced staging established pursuant to sections 503(a)(1) and 503(a)(2)(A) of the Trade Agreements Act of 1979 for those products affected by the technical amendments made by P.L. 96–490, it is necessary to make certain conforming modifications to the TSUS.

Now, THEREFORE, I, JIMMY CARTER, President of the United States of America, acting under the authority vested in me by the Constitution and the statutes, including but not limited to Section 604 of the Trade Act of 1974, Titles II and V of the Trade Agreements Act of 1979, and Section 3(b) of P.L. 96–490, do proclaim that:

(1) The amendments to the TSUS set forth in section 3(b) of P.L. 96–490 shall be effective on the date of this Proclamation and shall be effective as to articles exported to the United States on or after the date of this Proclamation;

(2) Schedule 4, part 1C of the TSUS is modified by deleting items 411.40 (as amended by P.L. 96–490) and 411.42 and by substituting the following in lieu thereof:

	"Papaverine and its salts:			
411. 40	Products provided for in the Chemical Appendix to the Tariff Schedules	26.9% ad val.	11.6% ad val.	7¢ per lb. + 104% ad val.
411. 42	Other	11.6% ad val.		7¢ per lb. + 104% ad val.";

(3) The rates of duty established for products of least developed developing countries (LDDC's) by Proclamation No. 4768 for item numbers 404.32, 406.36, and 408.24 of the TSUS shall be the rates inserted in the column entitled "LDDC" for items 403.74, 406.73, and 408.31, respectively, as added by section 3(a) of P.L. 96–490;

(4) The rates of duty, including rates in the column entitled "LDDC", and the staged reductions in those rates, established by Proclamation No. 4768 for item numbers 403.76, 408.32, 411.40, and 411.42, shall continue to apply to such item numbers, whether the provisions of the TSUS referred to by these item numbers were amended by P.L. 96–490 or modified by this Proclamation;

(5) The amendments made by paragraphs 2, 3, and 4 of this Proclamation shall be effective on the date of this Proc-

lamation and shall be effective with respect to articles exported on or after the date of this Proclamation.

IN WITNESS WHEREOF, I have hereunto set my hand this seventeenth day of December, in the year of our Lord nineteen hundred and eighty, and of the Independence of the United States of America the two hundred and fifth.

JIMMY CARTER

[Filed with the Office of the Federal Register, 10:46 a.m., December 18, 1980]

NOTE: The proclamation was announced by the White House Press Office on December 18.

National Advisory Council on Continuing Education

Appointment of Five Members.
December 18, 1980

The President has appointed the following persons to be members of the National Advisory Council on Continuing Education for terms expiring September 30, 1983:

WILLIAM L. BLOCKSTEIN, of Madison, Wis., director of the Health Sciences Unit, professor of pharmacy, and clinical professor of preventative medicine at the University of Wisconsin;

CHARLES J. O'LEARY, of Orono, Maine, president of the Maine AFL–CIO and member of the Governor's Task Force on the Economics of Higher Education and the Title I Advisory Committee;

RAJENDRA PRASAD, of Los Altos, Calif., assistant superintendent of San Mateo schools; and

CONSTANCE H. TIMBERLAKE, of Syracuse, N.Y., chairperson and associate professor in the community services department of the University of Syracuse.

The President has also appointed Constance M. Carroll, of Novato, Calif., to be a member of the National Advisory Council on Continuing Education for the term expiring September 30, 1982. She is president of Indian Valley Colleges in the Marin Community College District of California.

National Advisory Council on Vocational Education

Appointment of Six Members.
December 18, 1980

The President has appointed the following persons to be members of the National Advisory Council on Vocational Education for terms expiring January 17, 1983:

SAMUEL BERNSTEIN, of University City, Mo., executive director of the Jewish Employment and Vocational Service;

ROSE FONG CHAO, of Flushing, N.Y., manager of Capital Investors and Management Corp.;

ROGER ALLAN EMMERT, of Silver Spring, Md., coordinator of Federal and State educational programs, Archdiocese of Baltimore, Washington and Wilmington;

ROY ROSAVIO ESCARCEGA, of Los Angeles, Calif., vice president, social services division, the East Los Angeles Community Union;

RAY MARIE LEVIS, of Wayne, Mich., assistant superintendent, Wayne County Intermediate School District; and

HOPE M. ROBERTS, of Reno, Nev., chairman, Nevada Council for Vocational Education.

Christmas Pageant of Peace

Remarks on Lighting the National Community Christmas Tree.   December 18, 1980

THE PRESIDENT. Merry Christmas, everybody.

AUDIENCE. Merry Christmas.

THE PRESIDENT. Come on. *Merry Christmas,* everybody.

AUDIENCE. Merry Christmas!

THE PRESIDENT. Much better.

This is my fourth Christmas that, as President of our great country, I've been privileged to participate in the Pageant of Peace. Last year, we had a very sober Christmas, and we all were hoping that there would be an early release of the American hostages. And along with that, we prayed that their lives would be spared, that they would stay in touch with all Americans who love them, and that we would not be forced to give up either our hope or our faith in God.

Our American hostages have not yet come home. But most of our prayers have been answered. They have stayed in touch with their families. So far as we know, they are safe and their lives have been spared.

Last weekend the families of the American hostages met here in Washington again to have a briefing by the State Department officials, including the Secretary of State, about the status of the negotiations for their release and to receive the information that we have about how those hostages are getting along. I asked the families of the hostages whether or not they wanted all the lights on the Christmas tree to be lit tonight, or whether they wanted us to light just the Star of Hope on top of the tree and then all Americans to pray that the hostages would come home. At that time, we might light the other lights on the tree and celebrate their safe return. The hostage families asked me to do this year the same thing we did last year. And that is just to light the Star of Hope and to hold the other lights unlit until the hostages come home. And they also asked me to ask all Americans to continue to pray for the lives and safety of our hostages and for their early return to freedom.

And now I would like to ask us just for about half a minute to pray to God fervently for our hostages, their lives, their safety, and their early freedom. If everyone would join me just for a half minute.

[Pause for silent prayer.]

Amen. And I want to ask all those who listen to my voice to continue to pray fervently that our prayers tonight for the hostages will be answered.

I am a Christian. I'm very proud of my faith. It's the most important element of my life. But I'm also President of a nation that has a wide range of kinds of religions, and also a President of a nation that believes very fervently in the separation of church and state, which means, to put it in simple terms, that the Government cannot tell any American how to worship. We know down through history that many people's lives have been lost, much blood has been shed, much hatred has been engendered because of religion. People have turned against one another, and even in recent years in the Middle East, the basis for the hatred and the misunderstanding, the bloodshed and the continued wars has been founded in a difference in religious belief.

Ours is a nation of immigrants, a nation of refugees, a nation of freedom, a nation of diversity. We don't understand exactly how God works. God doesn't always answer our prayers exactly the way we want Him to, and that's the reason why this year, the Pageant of Peace has as its theme, Faith, because it requires faith on someone who believes in God to trust God to answer our prayers as He sees fit.

In the first Christmas, the people who lived in the land of the Jews were hoping for a Messiah. They prayed God to send them that savior, and when the shepherds arrived at the place to see their prayers answered they didn't find a king, they found a little baby. And I'm sure they were very disappointed to see that God had not answered their prayers properly, but we Christians know that the prayers had been answered in a very wonderful way. God knew how to answer prayer. The people who offered prayers in a very narrow and human way didn't understand how their prayers should be answered.

There was also a particular characteristic of that first Christmas, and that is gentleness, simplicity, love, a relationship between people who didn't understand each other very well, but who came to have their lives changed because of a simple faith.

My background is as a farmer and farmers have to have a lot of faith in order to keep on every year, planting a crop, not having control over what's going to happen next. You might think that cold winter, frozen land, snow, sleet, rain would not be a part of a successful farming operation. But God knows that in the wintertime the land has to lie fallow; there has to be a period of cold in order for the crops to grow when the Sun shines. A simple act of faith has been built up in farmers because of experience, yes, but because of their trust in God and in the future.

I noticed that our lovely Girl Scout's name is Lillian Smith. Is that right? One of the very famous Georgia writers is named Lillian Smith, and she wrote a small book called, "Memory of a Large Christmas." And to close my talk, let me tell you about that book.

Lillian Smith—a very famous writer—when she was a young child had a rich father. The family lived not very far from Plains, Georgia, and in that early part of her life, every Christmas they had a lot of presents, a big house, a lot of kinfolks, a lot of neighbors that came, and the Christmas was very happy. When she became a little older, her father lost everything he had, was absolutely bankrupt—the only thing he had left was a little tiny cottage in the mountains of north Georgia that they used to use as a game, for a summer camping place. That's all they had.

So, they moved up to the north Georgia mountains in the wintertime, and they thought it was going to be the worst Christmas ever. They didn't have any money. Their kinfolks were in south Georgia, they didn't know their neighbors, and they approached the Christmas with a great deal of dread and trepidation. And as the Christmas day approached there was a chain gang working nearby. How many of you know what a chain gang is—or was? A chain gang used to be prisoners who had chains on their legs and on their arms and had to do hard labor, and the chain gang members were murderers, bank robbers, one of them had burned down a barn—they were despised people. And Lillian Smith's father said, "Let's have a great Christmas. Let's invite the chain gang members to come and have Christmas with us."

They didn't have much to eat, nothing fancy, but they had enough to feed those despised, outcast people. And those chain gang members came in, the prisoners came into their little, tiny hut, and they began to laugh and sing songs and tell stories and eat the food heartily. They cleaned up the cabin, they washed the dishes, and they went back to a little railroad car that they were living in. It was very cold. And when they got through, Lillian Smith and her brothers and sisters and her parents agreed it was the greatest Christmas they ever had. It was a Christmas of simplicity, gentleness, understanding, and love among people who were quite different one from the other.

So, as we approach this Christmas, in a time of concern, trepidation, not knowing what the future is going to bring, let's have faith that God will answer our prayers. And let's not just have a faith that sits down and doesn't move and waits for good things to happen, but a faith like the farmers have and like Lillian Smith's father had, to reach out and use the gentleness and the love that we know about to encompass others in our hearts. That will warm us inside. That will tell us again what the birth of the Christ Child meant to us and be an expression of Christmas. And that kind of Christmas, filled with love for one another, is a Christmas that we all want and the world really needs.

It's wonderful to be President of a great country like ours. And I wish you, and Rosalynn and Amy and all of us wish you a very, very merry Christmas.

Thank you very much.

[At this point, the Carter family moved from the stage to the lighting stand.]

Is anybody ready to light the tree?

AUDIENCE. Yes!

THE PRESIDENT. Is anybody ready to light the tree?

AUDIENCE. *Yes!*

THE PRESIDENT. Okay. I'm going to ask this Christmas not Amy, but my oldest grandson, Jason, to throw the switch and light the tree.

[The President's grandson threw the switch, lighting the Star of Hope and 59 smaller trees.]

And you probably noticed that in addition to the Star of Hope on top of the tree that there are 59 trees around the outside. Have they already explained what they are? Well, 50 for the States, 7 terri-

tories, 1 for senior citizens, and 1 for those who are missing in action, that we pray also will be alive and well if they still exist alive. And so, those are the 59 trees, and we all will continue to pray that we can turn the rest of the lights on when the hostages come home.

Goodby, thank you very much, and merry Christmas again.

NOTE: The President spoke at 5:47 p.m. on the Ellipse.

Civil Service Status for CETA Participants

Executive Order 12257.   December 18, 1980

NONCOMPETITIVE CONVERSION OF CETA PARTICIPANTS TO CAREER OR CAREER-CONDITIONAL CIVIL SERVICE STATUS

By the authority vested in me as President of the United States of America by Sections 3301 and 3302 of Title 5 of the United States Code, and to provide opportunities for unemployed or disadvantaged persons to enter the Federal Civil Service, it is hereby ordered as follows:

1–101. Subject to the Civil Service laws, rules, and regulations, Executive agencies may, subject to approval by the Director of the Office of Personnel Management, give excepted appointments to qualified persons who have successfully completed job training funded through the Comprehensive Employment and Training Act, as amended (29 U.S.C. 801 *et seq.*) or a work experience program hosted by an Executive agency under this statute.

1–102. Such appointments may be to any position up to and including GS–3, or the equivalent thereof, for which the appointee is otherwise qualified under the Civil Service laws, rules, and regulations.

1–103. No one shall be eligible for such an appointment if more than three months have expired since the successful completion of the job training or work experience program.

1–104. Excepted appointments under the authority of this Order are only authorized pursuant to an employment training program developed by an agency in accordance with guidelines established by the Office of Personnel Management. These guidelines will provide for due credit for training acquired during a hosted work experience program. Continued employment under such excepted appointments is subject to the satisfactory performance of assigned duties and satisfactory participation in such employment training program.

1–105. An agency may noncompetitively convert an excepted appointment under this authority to career or career-conditional appointment, provided the appointee satisfactorily completes at least six months of continuous service, and otherwise meets the qualifications and other requirements established by the Director of the Office of Personnel Management. Prior to an individual being converted to a career or career-conditional appointment, each agency shall conduct a careful and formal evaluation of the individual's performance.

1–106. The Director of the Office of Personnel Management shall issue employment training program guidelines which shall include procedures for periodically evaluating the performance of such appointees and for the prompt separation of those who do not satisfactorily perform assigned duties. The Director shall also prescribe such regulations as may be necessary to implement this Order.

JIMMY CARTER

The White House,
    December 18, 1980.

[Filed with the Office of the Federal Register, 10:31 a.m., December 19, 1980]

NOTE: The Executive order was announced by the White House Press Office on December 19.

Wood Residue Utilization Act of 1980

Statement on Signing S. 1996 Into Law. December 19, 1980

I have today approved the enrolled bill, S. 1996, providing for a pilot program to encourage the efficient utilization of wood residues. The objective of the pilot program is to develop, evaluate, and demonstrate new and innovative means of wood utilization. The activities carried out will be applicable to both private forest lands and the lands of the National Forest System.

There is a significant opportunity to more efficiently utilize our timber resources. Annually, some 190 million dry tons of wood and wood residues are left on timber harvest areas in the Nation. Use of material now left in the forest and resulting from the manufacturing process will benefit local economies by providing the raw material for expanded or new processing facilities. It will benefit the environment by reducing the need to burn this material in order to prepare the site for the next crop of trees. And it will benefit the Nation's long-term timber supply. The legislation has special application to developing uses of wood residues as an alternative energy source.

It is appropriate that the Federal Government engage in this 5-year pilot effort. By providing incentives—both financial and technical—we can encourage testing of various approaches and gain knowledge of the costs involved in such approaches. With this information, private concerns will be encouraged to initiate practices to improve wood utilization. I appreciate the support of many Members of Congress who worked diligently to fashion a bill which provides for strong teamwork between the private and public sectors in improving utilization.

I congratulate the private organizations who aided in the development of this measure, and in particular, the American Forestry Association. A continuing interest by a broad representation of interest groups is important to a successful application of the pilot program.

Finally, I want to emphasize that efforts to improve utilization of the forest resource will be carried out in an environmentally sound manner. Pressure on our renewable resources as a result of accelerated utilization must not be allowed to jeopardize the perpetuation of those resources.

NOTE: As enacted, S. 1996 is Public Law 96–554, approved December 19.

Digest of Other White House Announcements

The following listing includes the President's public schedule and other items of general interest announced by the White House Press Office and not included elsewhere in this issue.

December 14

The President returned to the White House from Camp David, Md.

December 15

The President met at the White House with:

— Zbigniew Brzezinski, Assistant to the President for National Security Affairs;

— Frank B. Moore, Assistant to the President for Congressional Liaison;

— Alonzo L. McDonald, Jr., Assistant to the President, James T. McIntyre, Jr., Director of the Office of Management and Budget, and William J. McGill, Chairman of the President's Commission for a National Agenda for the Eighties;

— Mayor Steven Pawlings of Utica, N.Y;

— Mr. McIntyre.

The President and Mrs. Carter hosted a dinner for members of the Cabinet and senior White House staff on the State Floor of the White House.

December 16

The President met at the White House with:

— Dr. Brzezinski;

— Mr. Moore;

— Sam Brown, Director of ACTION;

— the President's Advisory Committee on Women.

In separate telephone calls, the President spoke first with House Majority Leader John Brademas and House Minority Leader John J. Rhodes, and then with Senate Majority Leader Robert C. Byrd and Senate Minority Leader Howard H. Baker, Jr., on the occasion of the adjournment of the 96th Congress.

December 17

The President met at the White House with:

— Dr. Brzezinski;

—the Vincent Peperno family, who had been invited to the White House during a townhall meeting at the Pittston Area Senior High School in Yatesville, Pa., on October 15;

—Frank Press, Director of the Office of Science and Technology Policy;

—Mr. Moore;

—John W. Gardner, former chairman of Common Cause.

The President and Mrs. Carter hosted a Christmas reception in the afternoon for Residence staff on the State Floor of the White House.

The President and Mrs. Carter hosted a Christmas party in the evening for White House correspondents on the State Floor of the White House.

December 18

The President met at the White House with:

—Dr. Brzezinski;

—Richard F. Celeste, Director of the Peace Corps;

—Mr. Moore;

—administration officials to review the fiscal year 1982 budget.

The President and Mrs. Carter hosted the Congressional Christmas Ball on the State Floor of the White House.

December 19

The President met at the White House with:

—Dr. Brzezinski;

—Vice President Walter F. Mondale, Secretary of State Edmund S. Muskie, Secretary of Defense Harold Brown, Deputy Secretary of State Warren M. Christopher, Jack H. Watson, Jr., Assistant to the President, and Dr. Brzezinski;

—Mr. Moore.

The President left the White House for a weekend stay at Camp David.

NOMINATIONS SUBMITTED TO THE SENATE

NOTE: The Congress having adjourned *sine die* on Tuesday, December 16, no nominations were submitted during the period covered by this issue. The first session of the 97th Congress will convene on Monday, January 5, 1981.

CHECKLIST OF WHITE HOUSE PRESS RELEASES

NOTE: All releases of the White House Press Office have been included in this issue.

ACTS APPROVED BY THE PRESIDENT

Approved December 15, 1980

H.R. 7631_____Public Law 96–526
Department of Housing and Urban Development—Independent Agencies Appropriation Act, 1981.

H.R. 8105_____Public Law 96–527
Department of Defense Appropriations Act, 1981.

H.R. 7591_____Public Law 96–528
An act making appropriations for Agriculture, Rural Development, and Related Agencies programs for the fiscal year ending September 30, 1981, and for other purposes.

H.J. Res. 205_____Public Law 96–529
A joint resolution authorizing appropriation of funds for acquisition of a monument to Doctor Ralph J. Bunche and installation of such monument in Ralph J. Bunche Park in New York City.

H.R. 8061_____Public Law 96–530
District of Columbia Appropriation Act.

H.R. 6243_____Public Law 96–531
An act to provide that the park referred to as the East Lake Park located within the West Point Lake project on the Chattahoochee River, Georgia, shall hereafter be known and designated as the "R. Shaefer Heard Park".

S. 2134_____Public Law 96–532
An act to provide for the acquisition of certain property in square 758 in the District of Columbia as an addition to the grounds of the United States Supreme Court Building.

H.R. 927_____Private Law 96–72
An act for the relief of Doctor Ka Chun Wong, and his wife, Marilyn Wong.

ACTS APPROVED—Continued

Approved December 16, 1980

H.R. 6942_____ Public Law 96–533
International Security and Development
Cooperation Act of 1980.

S. 1835_____ Public Law 96–534
An act to extend the Joint Funding Simplification Act of 1974.

H.R. 5856_____ Public Law 96–535
An act to amend title 32, United States
Code, to allow Federal recognition as officers of the National Guard of members of
the National Guard of the Virgin Islands in
grades above the grade of colonel.

H.J. Res. 644_____ Public Law 96–536
A joint resolution making further continuing
appropriations for the fiscal year 1981, and
for other purposes.

S. 576_____ Private Law 96–73
An act for the relief of Larry Grathwohl.

Approved December 17, 1980

S. 2728_____ Public Law 96–537
Indian Health Care Amendments of 1980.

S. 988_____ Public Law 96–538
Health Programs Extension Act of 1980.

H.R. 7018_____ Public Law 96–539
An act to extend the Federal Insecticide,
Fungicide, and Rodenticide Act until Sep-
tember 30, 1981, and for other purposes.

S. 3074_____ Public Law 96–540
Department of Energy National Security
and Military Applications of Nuclear Energy Authorization Act of 1981.

H.R. 6975_____ Public Law 96–541
An act to extend certain temporary tax provisions, and for other purposes.

S. 3235_____ Public Law 96–542
An act to clarify certain effective date provisions of the Customs Courts Act of 1980.

H.R. 7385_____ Public Law 96–543
An act to authorize the Secretary of the Interior to transfer certain land and facilities
used by the Bureau of Mines, and for other
purposes.

H.J. Res. 601_____ Public Law 96–544
A joint resolution making an appropriation
for the International Monetary Fund for the
fiscal year ending September 30, 1981.

Approved December 18, 1980

H.R. 1298 _____ Public Law 96–545
An act to designate the United States Post
Office and Federal Building in Huntington,
West Virginia, as the "Sidney L. Christie
Federal Building".

ACTS APPROVED—Continued

Approved December 18—Continued

H.R. 8173_____ Public Law 96–546
An act to provide for distribution in the
United States of certain International Communication Agency films relating to President Lyndon Baines Johnson.

S. 1391_____ Public Law 96–547
An act to amend section 9 of the National
Climate Program Act to extend the authorization for appropriations for fiscal year
1981, and for other purposes.

H.R. 8404_____ Public Law 96–548
An act to designate the Federal Building-
United States Courthouse in Sacramento,
California, the "John E. Moss Federal Build-
ing-United States Courthouse".

S. 1972_____ Public Law 96–549
An act to authorize the Secretary of the Interior to reimburse certain purchasers of
subleases from, and creditors of, the Sangre
de Cristo Development Company, Incorporated, and for other purposes.

S. 444_____ Private Law 96–74
An act for the relief of the Jewish Employment Vocational Services, Saint Louis, Missouri.

S. 453_____ Private Law 96–75
An act for the relief of Joe L. Frazier of
Elko, Nevada.

S. 1307_____ Private Law 96–76
An act for the relief of Gerald W. Frye.

S. 1615_____ Private Law 96–77
An act for the relief of James R. Thornwell.

H.R. 4522_____ Private Law 96–78
An act for the relief of Annette Jutta Wohrle.

H.R. 5687_____Private Law 96–79
An act for the relief of Michael G. Mac-
donald.

H.R. 5788_____ Private Law 96–80
An act for the relief of Jun Ae Hee.

H.R. 8386_____ Private Law 96–81
An act for the relief of Roy P. Benavidez.

Approved December 19, 1980

H.R. 8298_____ Public Law 96–550
An act to designate certain National Forest
System lands in the State of New Mexico for
inclusion in the National Wilderness Preservation System, and for other purposes.

H.R. 8235_____ Public Law 96–551
An act to grant the consent of the Congress
to the Tahoe Regional Planning Compact,
and to authorize the Secretary of Agriculture
and others to cooperate with the planning
agency thereby created.

ACTS APPROVED—Continued

Approved December 19—Continued

H.R. 3351_____ Public Law 96–552
An act to amend chapter 55 of title 10, United States Code, to authorize dependents of members of the uniformed services serving on active duty to use CHAMPUS inpatient cost-sharing rates for certain surgery performed on an outpatient basis.

S. 2318_____ Public Law 96–553
An act to revise the boundary of Crater Lake National Park in the State of Oregon, and for other purposes.

S. 1996_____ Public Law 96–554
Wood Residue Utilization Act of 1980.

H.R. 5182_____ Public Law 96–555
An act to amend the Chesapeake and Ohio Canal Development Act to change the termination date of the Chesapeake and Ohio Canal National Historical Park Commission from the date ten years after the effective date of such Act to the date twenty years after such effective date.

H.J. Res. 570_____ Public Law 96–556
A joint resolution to provide for a temporary increase in the public debt limit.

H.R. 7147_____ Public Law 96–557
An act to provide that certain land of the United States shall be held by the United States in trust for certain communities of the Mdewakanton Sioux in Minnesota.

S. 2069_____ Public Law 96–558
An act to authorize the Architect of the Capitol to contract for personal services with individuals, firms, partnerships, corporations, associations, and other legal entities.

H.R. 1316_____ Private Law 96–82
An act for the relief of Kuo-Yao Cheng.

H.R. 3869_____ Private Law 96–83
An act for the relief of Eileen Angella Crosdale.

ACTS APPROVED—Continued

Approved December 19—Continued

H.R. 4139_____ Private Law 96–84
An act for the relief of Feeronaih Abbosh.

H.R. 4778_____ Private Law 96–85
An act for the relief of Sada Kim.

H.R. 5067_____ Private Law 96–86
An act for the relief of Doctor Toomas Eisler and Carmen Elizabeth Eisler.

H.R. 5157_____ Private Law 96–87
An act for the relief of Lilia Ester Cantu.

H.R. 5379_____ Private Law 96–88
An act for the relief of Jaramporn Sermsri and Akharata Sermsri.

S. 551_____ Private Law 96–89
An act for the relief of Fred W. Sloat of Salt Lake City, Utah.

H.R. 935_____ Private Law 96–90
An act for the relief of Jesse Kuo Tang and Sharon Kuo Tang.

H.R. 936_____ Private Law 96–91
An act for the relief of Kit Tung.

H.R. 2433_____ Private Law 96–92
An act for the relief of Zora Singh Sunga.

H.R. 2872_____ Private Law 96–93
An act for the relief of Olivia Manaois Abrasaldo.

H.R. 3096_____ Private Law 96–94
An act for the relief of Raymond M. Gee.

H.R. 3138_____ Private Law 96–95
An act for the relief of Surip Karmowiredjo.

H.R. 3707_____ Private Law 96–96
An act for the relief of Joy Marsia Dehaney.

H.R. 5745_____ Private Law 96–97
An act for the relief of Michael Chinwen Ke.

H.R. 6030_____ Private Law 96–98
An act for the relief of Elena Patricia Mattos.

S. 1772_____ Private Law 96–99
An act for the relief of Min-Zen Lin.

S. 2849_____ Private Law 96–100
An act for the relief of Charles Jeffrey Greene.

Eisenhower Battle Group

Message on the Battle Group's Return to the United States. December 20, 1980

Welcome home.

This is a great day—a proud day for our nation and our navy.

As the Eisenhower Battle Group represents the naval power of our country, you, individually, represent the moral power of free men. You have represented your country to everyone in the world. Embodying the dauntless spirit of America, your battle group has made manifest the resolve of the United States to stand firm in support of our nation's basic principles. You have shown our strength and our will to meet any challenge.

Deployed to the Indian Ocean, you have reassured our nation, our allies and the entire world that the United States dedicates its power to the preservation of peace.

Well done from a grateful nation. Best wishes for a joyous reunion with your families and loved ones.

Sincerely,

JIMMY CARTER

NOTE: The message was sent to the officers and men of the U.S.S. *Eisenhower,* U.S.S. *South Carolina,* U.S.S. *Virginia,* and Carrier Wing Seven.

The text of the message was released on December 22.

President's Export Council

Remarks on Receiving the Council's Final Report. December 22, 1980

MR. JONES. Mr. President, it's a great pleasure for me and also a privilege to present to you this two-volume report from your Export Council. We have some two dozen members of the Export Council here, and after 17 months of work, they've produced this report which I think is appropriately entitled "The Export Imperative."

It's interesting that this is the fifth effort over the last 17 years to do something in this country about developing an export policy and an export program. This Council did not spend its time working assiduously to develop a report that would contain all the new things that could be done in terms of solutions to problems that didn't exist. Rather, this was an active working council working with your executive branch of Government, working assiduously on the Hill with the House Export Caucus and the Senate Export Caucus. I'm pleased to say that during the 17 months of its existence not a single piece of legislation, not a single executive branch action was taken that in any way impeded our improvement of exports. Rather, we had several significant victories that will, we believe, enhance our exports.

We concentrated our activities on, one, increasing national export consciousness so that the public would understand the need for improved exports. We felt that was vital at a time when we sensed this growing protectionism. And we must ward off protectionism. Secondly, we worked very hard at finding solutions to the so-called disincentives to exports. They're very practical, pragmatic, and politically feasible moves that we've suggested. And then finally, we worked at improving the incentives for exports, but not at cost to the Federal Treasury. There are things that can be done in line of incentives that we feel will be extraordinarily helpful.

And so, on behalf of the Council, Mr. President, may I present you with this report.

THE PRESIDENT. Thank you very much, Reg. I appreciate it.

Let me say first of all to Reg Jones and to Phil Klutznick, to all the members of the Export Council how deeply grateful I am for the work they've done. There's no doubt that when an assessment is made of what has been accomplished with their help, it's impressive and gratifying to me as President and beneficial to our Nation.

When I first went to meet with the other Western leaders I had long conversations with Chancellor Schmidt, with President Giscard d'Estaing, and with then Prime Minister Callaghan. Their belief was that the Multilateral Trade Negotiations were dead. But ultimately, because of the help of these men and women and the very deep commitment of the Congress, the good work of the Special Trade Representative, we have a Multilateral Trade Agreement that will bring rich dividends to our Nation, and indeed the entire world trade picture.

We have assiduously fought against protectionism, even though in every single instance, it's politically attractive to

certain very powerful political groups to erect trade barriers to protect a particular community in our Nation or a particular community of workers or business. We have not done that. And I'm very thankful for it. We have, with the help of Phil Klutznick and others, reorganized the trade functions of the Federal Government so they are much more effective, much more efficient, much more clearly understandable by workers and by management in how the Federal Government can assist in the enhancement of export and trade.

We have aroused, I think perhaps more significantly, the interest of American business leaders, the free enterprise system, and also the trade union leaders in the advantages of exports. And at every level of government, the Governors, with George Busbee's great help, the key mayors around our Nation, as well as the Federal Government, has now realized that American exports are crucial to the well-being of our own economy. Agricultural exports have set world records every year since I've been in office. In spite of the restraint on trade with the Soviet Union, we have still set exemplary records in increasing new customers and the volume of trade with countries around the world.

One of the most significant developments now and potentially in the future is the new trade relationships that will be evolved with the People's Republic of China; a quarter of a billion people, one-fourth of the total population on Earth, now are good, potential customers for us now and in the future. At the same time, since I've been in office we've almost tripled trade with the people of Taiwan. Mexico, Canada have become increasingly great trade partners for us. This Council has been playing a leadership role in the multiple relationships with

Congress in how to enhance trade and how to enhance exports. This past quarter's record on our trade balance, current accounts balance, shows that it's the highest since 1975, the second highest favorable balance in the history of our Nation. And we will probably wind up this year, 1980, with a positive trade balance in spite of excessive imports of oil from overseas.

The last thing that I'd like to say is that I'm very grateful to these men and women for the dedicated work that they performed. This is a good report. I'm particularly eager to see a continuity guaranteed between my own administration and that of the next President. So, I will, through Executive order, extend the life of this Council for several months to give Governor Reagan a chance with his own administration to see the value of what has been accomplished in the past and the value, even more importantly, of what can be accomplished by this Council in the months ahead.

I'm deeply grateful to all the members who've served, particularly the Chairman, Reginald Jones. It's been a great boon for our Nation, in every community, so far as I know, in the entire country. And thank you all very much for being such an integral part of this tremendous progress both in attitude and tone and commitment and also the tangible results that have been so profoundly gratifying to me as President. Thank you very much.

I might comment as a postscript, I noticed that Senator Roth has come in representing the Senate and also Ed Muskie has come in. We had not only State and Commerce but also Agriculture, Labor, Treasury, Special Trade Representative, Export-Import Bank—the agencies of the Federal Government were brought together in a very close and cooperative fashion to work together, and I think this guaranteed that we spoke with a clear and single voice, guided by the Council members in a very effective way. And I want to thank all the members of my administration, Phil and you and Ed Muskie particularly, for the great work you've done. Ed, thank you.

NOTE: The President spoke at approximately 11 a.m. in the Cabinet Room at the White House.

White House Reception for Secret Service and Military Aides Office Employees

Remarks at the Reception.
December 22, 1980

Merry Christmas.

First of all, let me say that Rosalynn and I want to welcome you to the White House to an old-fashioned Christmas party. We had anticipated having a very warm day today, but Pat Caddell's survey was not exactly accurate. But I hope you won't be too cold, because the entertainment we have is going to warm everybody up.

We've got snow in the background, and after the show is over we've got refreshments and also sleighrides for those—or rather, hayrides for those who want to enjoy them, and if you would like to go inside the White House to get warm and enjoy the beauty of the tree which is one of the most beautiful I've ever seen. The decorations are in the Victorian style.

This is the, I think, 181st Christmas at the White House, and it's the 80th Christmas since the Secret Service began to protect the President. Through, I think, 14 administrations and something like 17 campaigns the Secret Service has provided safety and protection and security for the First Family and those who sought the Presidency. And as we approach this holiday season, Rosalynn and Amy and I and all our boys and grandchildren want to express our deep appreciation to all of you for being so wonderful to us, for keeping us safe, sometimes at the danger of your own lives, and we just want to say, God bless you, Merry Christmas to you. Have a good time this afternoon.

You have performed like true Olympians, and this afternoon to entertain you, I would like to introduce a real Olympic star, someone who's soon to show you that she's poetry on ice, a young woman who is a gold medal winner in the winter Olympics, who comes here as part of the only cabaret ice show this side of Las Vegas, the Urban Hilton on Ice. And now I'd like to introduce to you, Peggy Fleming and a wonderful show for your entertainment. We're grateful to you.

Merry Christmas. God bless all of you. Thank you.

NOTE: The President spoke at 2:30 p.m. on the South Lawn of the White House.

Rail Worker Pension Benefits

Statement on Signing H.R. 8195 Into Law.
December 23, 1980

I am today signing H.R. 8195, a bill which provides a cost-of-living increase in the industry pension benefits of retired rail workers next year and directs rail labor and management to report jointly their recommendations for sound long-term financing of their pension system by March 1, 1981.

The report requirement and deadline imposed by this bill are especially important since the rail industry pension system is seriously underfunded and could run out of money within 2 years. To help address this problem, my administration has proposed the rail pension assurance amendments to protect railroad workers, retirees, and their families by restoring the railroad pension fund to solvency. We have also invited rail labor and management to submit long-term financing proposals.

The seriousness of the railroad retirement financing crisis cannot be overemphasized. I urge that the report required by H.R. 8195 be submitted within the statutory deadline, so that the affected parties and the Congress will have sufficient time to develop and agree on an industry-financed solution to this financial crisis without added Federal subsidies.

Any reluctance I have in signing H.R. 8195 arises from the fact that the bill does not provide revenues to finance the cost-of-living payment increases that it mandates. The effect of this omission is to increase the cash deficit of the rail industry pension by approximately $40 million a year. This shortcoming in the bill makes it all the more essential that railroad labor, management, and the Congress act quickly to provide additional financing before the railroad retirement trust fund is further depleted.

NOTE: As enacted, H.R. 8195 is Public Law 96–582, approved December 23.

Special Federal Employee Death Benefit

Memorandum of Disapproval of H.R. 5888.
December 23, 1980

I am withholding my approval of H.R. 5888, a bill that provides for payment of a $50,000 lump-sum death benefit to survivors of Federal law enforcement officers, firefighters and certain other employees killed in the line of duty. This benefit would be paid in addition to the regular death benefits available to all Federal employees, and would be retroactive to September 26, 1976.

I am not approving H.R. 5888 because the special benefits it would provide are preferential and unwarranted, and because the bill would become a precedent for extension of similar benefits to other Federal employees.

My disapproval of this bill in no way reflects on the bravery and dedication of Federal employees in law enforcement and firefighting occupations. Nor does it in any way diminish the gratitude that I and this Nation feel for those who sacrifice their lives in the performance of their duty.

H.R. 5888 is objectionable because it would single out certain groups of employees for preferential treatment under the Federal employee workers' compensation law (FECA). Survivor benefits provided by the Federal Government should be adequate in all instances to ease the financial burden resulting from an employee's death, regardless of occupation. Moreover, there are many civilian employees outside the areas of law enforcement and firefighting who are also exposed to special hazards in their work. It is inequitable and unfair to provide a greater benefit to a select group of Federal employees based only on the nature of their employment. Such preferred treatment is directly contrary to the evenhandedness that must be basic to a workers' compensation system.

Under the existing FECA program, the Federal Government already pays generous death benefits to survivors of employees who die on the job. These benefits are tax-free and are adjusted annually for increases in the cost of living. Depending on family size, such benefits can be as high as 75% of the employee's salary while alive, and are limited in total amount and duration only by changed family circumstances. The Government's Group Life Insurance Program, which was recently liberalized for younger employees, also provides substantial protection in the event of an employee's death.

The proponents of H.R. 5888 argue that this legislation is needed to assure parity with State and local police and firefighters, who receive a $50,000 death benefit under a law passed in 1976. However, one of the main reasons for enactment of that law was that States and localities' compensation systems were inadequate or nonexistent and that life insurance coverage was often unavailable. The Congress at that time expressly decided against granting the $50,000 death benefit to Federal firefighters and law enforcement officers because the benefits provided under FECA are comparatively generous and would in many cases exceed the $50,000 payment authorized for State-local public safety officers.

Although the costs entailed in H.R. 5888 are not large, the special treatment provided by the bill would inevitably set a precedent for extension of its benefits to other, if not all, Federal employees who die in the line of duty. This would result in an unwarranted and costly added burden on the taxpayers of this Nation.

Finally, the retroactive provision in the bill is objectionable by arbitrarily excluding employees whose deaths occurred before the effective date.

For all of these reasons, I cannot approve H.R. 5888.

JIMMY CARTER

The White House,
    December 23, 1980.

National Patriotism Week

Proclamation 4810. December 23, 1980

By the President of the United States of America

A Proclamation

We are a Nation with many blessings. We have liberties enjoyed by no other Nation on Earth. We have a government admired by many. We have fought hard to preserve our independence and the independence of others, and to gain equal rights and responsibilities for all our citizens. We have much to be thankful for and much to be proud of.

Together we have built a great Nation, a Nation founded on freedom, a Nation forged by patriots. We have made America strong with our strength. We have made America a Nation at peace with our love of peace.

We live in a Nation we all care about deeply. It is important that we continue to care, that we continue to respect ourselves and each other, and that we honor our past and present by reaffirming our commitment to the greatness that is ours.

To recognize our freedoms and honor this great Nation, the Congress, by joint resolution of October 10, 1980 (P.L. 96–421), designated the week commencing with the third Monday in February of 1981 as "National Patriotism Week" and requested the President to issue a proclamation calling upon the people of the United States to commemorate that week with appropriate celebrations and observances.

Now, THEREFORE, I, JIMMY CARTER, President of the United States of America, do hereby call upon the people of the United States to observe the week beginning with the third Monday in February 1981 as National Patriotism Week.

I call upon all primary and secondary schools to adopt an appropriate curriculum for that week which should include such elements as the study of the Pledge of Allegiance and the national anthem, national symbols, seals and mottos, and national monuments, heroes, and accomplishments.

I request each Federal agency recognize that week by taking such action as it may deem appropriate.

IN WITNESS WHEREOF, I have hereunto set my hand this twenty-third day of December, in the year of our Lord nineteen hundred and eighty, and of the Independence of the United States of America the two hundred and fifth.

JIMMY CARTER

[Filed with the Office of the Federal Register, 3:27 p.m., December 23, 1980]

Advisory Committee for Trade Negotiations

Appointment of Robert Barrie as a Member. December 23, 1980

The President today appointed Robert Barrie, of Washington, D.C., as a member of the Advisory Committee for Trade Negotiations for a term of 2 years.

Barrie is the manager of the Federal legislative relations operation of General Electric and was formerly an adviser to Senator Hubert Humphrey.

Plains, Georgia

Informal Exchange With Reporters. December 24, 1980

THE PRESIDENT. Hello.

Q. How's it feel to be back, Mr. President?

THE PRESIDENT. Oh, it feels good.

Q. Sir, what do you think the chances are that the hostages could be gotten out before January 20th. At this point, is there much chance of that, do you think?

THE PRESIDENT. Well, I don't want to be overly optimistic. We've always been disappointed in dealing with the Iranians, as you know. But we'll continue to try to deal with the Iranians, as we have in the past, both protecting the honor of our country and also trying to do everything we can to protect the lives and safety of the hostages.

We will not pay any ransom. We never have been willing to even consider that. What we have tried to do is to deal with the Iranians through the Algerians, not negotiating directly, so that the possibility of restoring the situation as it was before the hostages were taken. But the prospects for their early release, I think, is unfortunately quite dim.

Q. Were you disappointed by the latest response suggesting, as it did, that they didn't understand there are things you can't do, Mr. President?

THE PRESIDENT. Yes. We explained our position very clearly to the Iranians through the Algerians, and either they just ignored what we told them we could or would do or else they deliberately made demands that they knew we couldn't meet.

Q. Are you more concerned now, Mr. President, about the prospect of trials?

THE PRESIDENT. When the revolution took place in Iran there were 50,000 Americans there, and ever since those early days when literally thousands of people in Iran have been killed, my deepest personal concern about human beings has been to keep Americans alive. We extracted all the Americans without loss of life. And of course, my concern the last 13 or 14 months has been the safety of the

hostages and their well-being, and we'll continue to do everything we can to preserve both their safety and well-being.

Q. They're talking once again about putting the hostages on trial. The Majles addressed itself to that in the conditions it set down.

THE PRESIDENT. Well, more than a year ago we let the Iranians know the consequences of any trial, and I don't think it's necessary for me to repeat that.

Q. This is also the anniversary of the Soviet invasion of Afghanistan.

THE PRESIDENT. Yes, I know.

Q. Do you have any comment?

THE PRESIDENT. I think the Soviets made a serious mistake in going into Afghanistan. They've not been able to establish any government in Afghanistan that was supported by the people themselves. The Afghan army, on which the Soviets thought they could rely, has now been almost completely dissipated by desertions, because the Afghan people don't support the Soviet invasion. The Soviets have suffered very severely by worldwide public condemnation of their aggression and the occupation. And, of course, the economic constraints that we've placed on the Soviets with the grain embargo, I think, has hurt them very badly.

So, the Soviets made a serious mistake in going into Afghanistan. I don't see any signs that they've made any progress in the last year.

Q. Economic news was really pretty bad, the CPI yesterday, and Reagan's talking about meeting with Federal Reserve Board Chairman Volcker. Is that appropriate for him to do?

THE PRESIDENT. Sure. I meet with Mr. Volcker regularly. We have a regular scheduled meeting. It's a luncheon, as a matter of fact, every month, with me and the Chairman of the Federal Reserve and the Secretary of the Treasury and a couple of my advisers, including Charles Schultze, and we discuss how best we can handle the inflation process and constrain it and keep economic growth up and employment high. But, of course, the Federal Reserve, under the law, is completely independent of the President's influence, and I can't demand that the Federal Reserve do this or that.

But I think the overall economic status of our country is very healthy. The value of the dollar's high. We've had the highest trade balance this past quarter of any in history, except one in 1975. We'll have a positive trade balance this year in spite of imports of oil. Employment is the highest it's ever been in the history of our country. The percentage of the labor force that is employed is the highest it's ever been in history.

So, we have a lot to be thankful for in this country. Inflation is excessively high because of OPEC oil price increases, and, of course, the interest rates are too high also. But you can't have everything perfect. But in general we have a strong economy and have set alltime records in many elements of economic prosperity and benefits to our people, and I'm very proud of what we've done.

Q. Were you surprised at the surge in the growth rate last month?

THE PRESIDENT. In the growth rate?

Q. In the GNP.

THE PRESIDENT. Yes. It was higher than we had anticipated. We thought it would be less than 1 percent, but it was up about 2½ percent. And of course, the American people's income has been higher than has the inflation rate, which is another encouraging factor. But there's still room for improvement. I don't deny that.

Q. Is it time for an economic emergency to be declared?

THE PRESIDENT. No. I think for anyone to declare an emergency would arouse a psychological reaction that would very likely damage the economy and the growth and enhance inflation. I don't think that ought to be done; don't think it will be done.

Q. By raising expectations, you mean, unnecessarily?

THE PRESIDENT. Just by creating a semblance of panic. I think for any public official who has authority to say that there's an emergency and so forth would naturally tend to cause excessive reaction which might exacerbate the situation.

Q. Mr. President, what do you think of Henry Kissinger's travel plans? He says he's going to the Middle East to meet with foreign leaders with Ronald Reagan's approval.

THE PRESIDENT. Well, I think that would be good. I hope that and I expect that Governor Reagan will continue the Camp David process to try to bring peace to the Mideast and to let there be a continued search for peace by the Egyptians and the Israelis. And I think that when I go out of office and Sol Linowitz is no longer the special ambassador for the peace process that Secretary Kissinger or anyone else who speaks with authority for the President would do a good job there.

Q. Has he consulted with you or will he be in touch with you, so far as you know?

THE PRESIDENT. Well, the transition process is going on as best we can manage it, and both Secretary Muskie, dealing with General Haig, and Harold Brown, dealing with Cap Weinberger, have tried to provide continuity. And I have no doubt that Sol Linowitz will make a special report both to me and to the representatives of Governor Reagan before we go out of office.

Q. What's your view of the Reagan Cabinet?

THE PRESIDENT. I don't want to comment on the Cabinet. I'll let the Senate assess the quality of those appointees.

I would like to say that there was an event yesterday that I considered to have perhaps the most profound significance constitutionally of anything that's happened in my 4 years. The Ninth Circuit Court of Appeals ruled that the congressional veto over executive decisions was unconstitutional. This is a struggle in which we've been engaged for the last 4 years. In fact, it's a 40-year struggle between the President and his executive branch of Government, on the one hand, and the legislative on the other.

I've never signed a bill that had a legislative veto in it that I didn't express my own opinion that it was unconstitutional. And yesterday the Ninth Circuit Court of Appeals, in San Francisco, ruled that the legislative veto was, indeed, unconstitutional. I'll be issuing an Executive order soon to all executive officers telling them to act accordingly, and I'll be consulting with the Attorney General within the next few days to see whether or not we should go directly to the Supreme Court and let the Supreme Court confirm the finality of the victory that we won in San Francisco in the Circuit Court.

Q. I take it you'll be telling the department and agency heads to ignore such congressional vetoes.

THE PRESIDENT. Exactly.

REPORTER. Thank you, sir.

NOTE: The exchange began at 11:30 a.m. outside Hugh Carter's antiques store.

Soviet Intervention in Afghanistan

Statement by the President.
December 24, 1980

One year has passed since the Soviet Union launched its brutal assault on its small, nonaligned neighbor, Afghanistan. On December 27, 1979, Soviet paratroopers seized key Afghan institutions in Kabul, including the Presidential Palace, where President Amin was then killed. The Soviets installed a puppet government under the nominal leadership of Babrak Karmal, who was in the Soviet Union at the time.

The tragedy that has continued to unfold in Afghanistan over the past 12 months weighs heavily on all Americans. We have watched the Soviet armed forces employ massive firepower and increasingly brutal tactics. We have seen the ranks of Afghan refugees fleeing devastation and political and religious oppression at home swell to more than 1.2 million in Pakistan alone. And amid this grim spectacle, we have been heartened to witness the brave resistance of the Afghan people, who have continued their struggle for independence and the right to determine their own political future.

The Soviet invasion of Afghanistan and attempted forceful occupation of that fiercely independent, nonaligned, Moslem nation has had a profoundly negative impact on the international community. An overwhelming majority of member states of the United Nations demanded the immediate withdrawal of foreign troops from Afghanistan in a special General Assembly session in January 1980. An increased majority reiterated this demand following careful General Assembly consideration of the Afghanistan issue last month. The 40-member Islamic Conference has been particularly forceful in condemning Soviet actions and in seeking an appropriate political solution. If the Soviet leaders expected that the world would avert its eyes and quickly forget their aggression in Afghanistan, they have been disappointed.

We urge the Soviet Union to respond to those nations urging withdrawal of Soviet military forces and inviting Soviet cooperation in the search for a political solution to the Afghan crisis. For our part, we have offered to join in the effort to find a political solution involving a Soviet withdrawal, and we repeat that offer today. The suffering of the Afghan people must be brought to an end.

The Afghan people and their struggle have not been forgotten and will not be forgotten by the rest of the world. We call on the Soviet Union to work with us and others in finding a way to bring peace to that tormented nation.

NOTE: The statement was released at Plains, Ga.

Chadha v. Immigration and Naturalization Service

Statement on the Ninth Circuit Court of Appeals Decision.   December 24, 1980

I am very pleased to learn of a very important decision Monday by the Ninth Circuit Court of Appeals in San Francisco. The court ruled that a legislative veto of an executive branch action is an unconstitutional intrusion on the separation of powers. This ruling sustains the position that I and many of my predecessors have taken in signing into law otherwise meritorious bills containing a legislative veto provision under which a resolution of one or both Houses can nullify an executive branch action.

The Senate and House submitted briefs in this case supporting the constitutionality of the legislative veto, and the Department of Justice successfully argued against its constitutionality. The Attorney General informs me this is truly a landmark decision.

I have asked the Attorney General to examine the possibility of seeking Supreme Court review of the decision as soon as possible, so that this important issue—debated for more than 40 years—can be finally resolved. I trust that the Congress will agree that a decision by the Supreme Court on this important issue is in the best interest of the Government as a whole.

NOTE: The statement was released at Plains, Ga.

Inland Navigational Rules Act of 1980

Statement on Signing H.R. 6671 Into Law. December 24, 1980

I have signed H.R. 6671, the Inland Navigational Rules Act of 1980.

Traditionally, the United States has had three different systems of navigation rules—one for the Great Lakes, one for western rivers, and a third for other inland waters. International law created yet another. H.R. 6671 eliminates confusing inconsistencies by combining the three United States navigation rules systems into one and ensuring that the unified rules conform as closely as possible with the international rules to which this Nation agreed in 1972. These unified navigation rules will reduce the potential for confusion and thus lessen the danger of collision.

Credit for this achievement is deservedly shared by many. Members of the Coast Guard's Rules of the Road Advisory Committee, who represent a cross section of maritime interests, have worked selflessly for several years on a totally voluntary basis to reach this result. I would like to thank the members of the Committee for their dedication and make special note of the efforts of its Chairman, Gordon W. Paulsen, who tirelessly and effectively shepherded the development of these rules.

I wish also to congratulate the Congress, and especially Congressman Mario Biaggi, chairman of the Subcommittee on Coast Guard and Navigation. I am proud to sign this bill into law.

NOTE: As enacted, H.R. 6671 is Public Law 96–591, approved December 24.

The statement was released at Plains, Ga.

Farm Credit Act Amendments of 1980

Statement on Signing S. 1465 Into Law. December 24, 1980

I am today signing S. 1465, the Farm Credit Act Amendments of 1980.

For over 60 years the Farm Credit System has ably serviced the credit needs of farmers and ranchers, and more recently, those of aquatic producers and harvesters. S. 1465 represents the culmination of an effort, begun in 1978, to update and improve the Farm Credit System's authorities so that it can continue to efficiently and effectively make its significant contribution in meeting the credit-related needs of agriculture throughout the 1980's. Among its more noteworthy features, the enrolled bill:

—lowers the percentage of voting members of rural utility and service cooperatives and some farm supply cooperatives who must be farmers in order for these cooperatives to be eligible for loans from a bank for cooperatives;

—authorizes the banks for cooperatives to provide export credit and related services to cooperatives;

—provides special authority to aid young, beginning, and small farmers;

—authorizes the provision of loan funds from Federal intermediate credit banks to rural commercial banks; and

—enables Federal land banks to extend to commercial fishermen the same range of services which are currently available to farmers and ranchers.

Finally, in signing this bill, I want to emphasize my view, and that of the Attorney General, that section 508 is unconstitutional insofar as it would permit Congress to disapprove certain Farm Credit Administration regulations by passing a concurrent resolution. This provision violates Article I, section 7, of the Constitution, which requires congressional action that has the effect of law to be submitted to the President for his possible veto. Moreover, by granting Congress an extra legislative role in administering substantive statutory programs, this provision of section 508 violates separation of powers principles. In accordance with my June 21, 1978, message to Congress, the executive branch will treat section 508 as a "report and wait" provision and will not consider a congressional expression of disapproval under section 508 to be legally binding.

NOTE: As enacted, S. 1465 is Public Law 96–592, approved December 24.

The statement was released at Plains, Ga.

National Tourism Policy Bill

Memorandum of Disapproval of S. 1097.
December 24, 1980

I am withholding my approval from enrolled bill S. 1097, "The National Tourism Policy Act."

Among other provisions, this bill would establish a United States Travel and Tourism Administration (USTTA) as an independent agency, create a Travel and Tourism Advisory Board, and abolish the United States Travel Service of the Department of Commerce.

My Administration has proposed that the Federal government's role concentrate on development and coordination of policies conducive to tourism, collection of information, and selected promotional activities. Because tourism is an integral part of other trade promotion activities, we also recommended to Congress that the Travel Service be incorporated into the Commerce Department's International Trade Administration, where overseas tourism activities would be carried out by the Foreign Commercial Service.

By contrast, S. 1097 would separate the government's travel and tourism activities from other international trade functions. This is a seriously flawed management approach. The establishment of independent agencies to promote individual aspects of international trade would only impede the efficient management and coordination of important related functions.

Furthermore, the bill would create an agency not only independent of a Cabinet department but also virtually independent of Presidential direction. The principal initial function of the USTTA would be to develop a detailed and comprehensive tourism development plan, including estimates of funding and personnel needed to carry it out. The plan would be submitted by April 15, 1982 to the House and Senate Commerce Committees. Under the bill, that plan and any budget requests or legislative recommendations by the USTTA would have to be submitted concurrently to the President and Congress, and no Federal officer or agency would be permitted to review or approve them before their submission to Congress. I consider this to be an unacceptable derogation of the President's executive authority and responsibility.

In addition, the Travel and Tourism Advisory Board—14 of the 17 members of which would be senior executives of the travel and tourism industry—would be given extraordinary powers of oversight. It would monitor the activities of the USTTA and report to Congress on the agency's preliminary plans and final budget requests. The composition of the Board and its functions would almost certainly ensure that the USTTA would be more responsive to special industry interests than to the need for a coordinated Federal approach that will balance the needs of tourism against other national priorities.

Finally, the USTTA would be authorized to establish branch offices in foreign countries, consult with foreign governments, and represent U.S. travel and tourist interests at international meetings, conferences, and expositions. In this way, the USTTA would become an independent foreign office in miniature. It would be highly undesirable to grant such an agency the ability and mission to deal with foreign governments directly, and independently of the Department of State. The proper conduct of foreign relations requires that the central role be played by the Department of State, under the direction of the President, and that contacts with foreign governments by

Federal agencies be undertaken only in close cooperation with the Department of State.

For these reasons, and because S. 1097 is deficient or objectionable in several other respects, I am withholding my approval from the bill.

JIMMY CARTER

The White House,
    December 24, 1980.

NOTE: The text of the memorandum of disapproval was released at Plains, Ga.

Relief Bill for Mr. and Mrs. Clarence Oveson

Memorandum of Disapproval of H.R. 4386.
December 24, 1980

I am withholding my approval from H.R. 4386, a bill "For the relief of Mr. and Mrs. Clarence Oveson."

H.R. 4386 would direct the Secretary of the Treasury to pay $50,000 to Mr. and Mrs. Clarence Oveson of Saint Louis and Koochiching Counties, Minnesota. The payment would be for full settlement of the Ovesons' claims arising from the assumption of management by the United States of certain real property owned by the United States but occupied by the Ovesons. The payment would not affect any claims that the Ovesons might have arising from the loss of any structures affixed to the land. The Ovesons apparently purchased the land in question from another individual in good faith though title to the land actually rests with the U.S. Government as part of the Voyageurs National Park.

I am withholding my approval from H.R. 4386 because it would provide compensation to individuals who have occupied Federal lands without authority.

Approval of this legislation would set a precedent of rewarding unauthorized users of Federal lands. It would not only undermine ongoing efforts by all Federal land management agencies to eliminate such uses but could also invite additional unauthorized use.

While I sympathize with the plight of the Ovesons, I cannot support the payment of taxpayers funds to them to remedy a problem they have with other private individuals in a situation in which the United States Government was in no way at fault. I understand that there may be legal remedies available to the Ovesons against the person who improperly sold them land to which he did not have clear title.

JIMMY CARTER

The White House,
    December 24, 1980.

NOTE: The text of the memorandum of disapproval was released at Plains, Ga.

Plains, Georgia

Informal Exchange With Reporters Following a Visit With Allie Smith. December 25, 1980

THE PRESIDENT. We're sorry all of you can't be with your families. But we're going to go back to Washington tomorrow.

Q. Do you have any Christmas morning thoughts, Mr. President?

THE PRESIDENT. Well, we're very happy to be in a nation that's at peace, and where brotherly love prevails, and we're very glad to be with our family, at home in Plains. We'll be going back to Washington tomorrow so all of the press can be with your families.

Q. Tomorrow?

THE PRESIDENT. Yes, tomorrow. Tomorrow afternoon.

Q. What did you get for Christmas?

THE PRESIDENT. Well, I got a lot for Christmas. Shirts, books, tools.

Q. What did Mrs. Carter give you?

MRS. CARTER. Books. I gave him books and we gave him—the children and I gave him—[*inaudible*]—[a bicycle]—and he gave me a television set, because we don't have a television set. [*Laughter*]

THE PRESIDENT. Good luck to all of you.

Q. You might be better off without it. [*Laughter*]

THE PRESIDENT. Maybe so. I don't know.

Q. What do you plan to do for the rest of the day, Mr. President?

THE PRESIDENT. We're going to eat lunch around here with Rosalynn's folks and go down and see Billy and let Amy see her new school. That's about it.

Q. Do you have any pangs of regret vetoing that bill? The poor Ovesons aren't going to get their $50,000 on Christmas Eve? The bill you vetoed yesterday.

THE PRESIDENT. No pangs. [*Laughter*]

NOTE: The exchange began at 9:40 a.m. outside the home of Allie Smith, Mrs. Carter's mother.

Plains, Georgia
Informal Exchange With Reporters.
December 26, 1980

Q. Mr. President, did you get a chance to see the tape of the hostages, the Christmas tape?

THE PRESIDENT. Yes, I saw it.

Q. What did you think of it?

THE PRESIDENT. Well, they have a longer tape that we're going to look at today, the State Department will, but we were glad to see those 15 or so hostages, and they seemed to be doing fairly well. But what they need is freedom.

REPORTER. Thank you.

NOTE: The exchange began at 9 a.m. outside Carters Warehouse.

Plains, Georgia
Informal Exchange With Reporters.
December 26, 1980

Q. I just wondered whether you've seen the tape and what your impression was?

THE PRESIDENT. I've just seen the brief tape—[*inaudible*]—going to have a longer one now. And we got a message this morning—yesterday, rather, from the Algerians that they have seen all 52 hostages and that they all seemed to be well, and we're very pleased at that. We'll be getting a more complete report from the Algerians, who have seen the hostages.

Q. Do we know more about where they're being held now and under what circumstances?

THE PRESIDENT. Yes, this is known.

Q. Is it luxury or is it——

THE PRESIDENT. No, not luxury.

Q. Very adverse conditions?

THE PRESIDENT. Well, it's still imprisonment. They are not free. That's the most important single thing. It's a criminal act, has been from the very beginning. We'll continue, as best we can, to acquire their freedom, but we don't know what the future holds.

Q. Do you see the pictures as a comfort, to have seen pictures of them more recently, or as an insult?

THE PRESIDENT. Well, it's still insulting to see them being held as prisoners. Obviously, the families of the 50 men and women are pleased to know that they are up and around and seem to be in relatively good health. But we'll have a complete report later on this week from the Algerians who have seen all 52 of them. We are pleased that they are, finally, observed by someone in whom we have confidence, and I'll be getting a report on that.

Q. What's next, sir? What's next?

THE PRESIDENT. We'll continue to protect our Nation's honor, to work for the hostages' release and make sure that we do everything we can to protect them from any abuse, and to make sure they stay alive and well.

Q. Is there encouragement in the fact that they have now been seen and all accounted for?

THE PRESIDENT. That's encouraging to me, because there were three or four that we had not had confirmed as being well since last April, I believe. And now if this report is true—and I believe it to be true—then that is reassuring to know that they are all alive and well.

Q. Do we know that all 49 are actually staying at the spot where the pictures were taken?

THE PRESIDENT. It is now known where all 49 of them were, at least at the one time this week, and we believe that they were observed where they are staying.

REPORTER. Thank you, sir.

NOTE: The exchange began at 10:55 a.m. outside Lillian Carter's town home.

Digest of Other White House Announcements

The following listing includes the President's public schedule and other items of general interest announced by the White House Press Office and not included elsewhere in this issue.

December 21

The President returned to the White House from Camp David, Md.

December 22

The President met at the White House with:

— Zbigniew Brzezinski, Assistant to the President for National Security Affairs;

— Frank B. Moore, Assistant to the President for Congressional Liaison;

— Most Reverend James B. Hickey, Archbishop of Washington, D.C., and Most Reverend Thomas C. Kelly, secretary general of the U.S. Catholic Conference.

The President and Mrs. Carter hosted a Christmas party in the evening for members of the White House staff on the South Lawn of the White House.

December 23

The President met at the White House with Dr. Brzezinski.

The President left the White House to spend the Christmas holiday in Plains, Ga.

The President, in a recess appointment, named Lynn R. Coleman as Deputy Secretary of Energy, replacing John Sawhill, who has resigned. Coleman is currently General Counsel of the Department of Energy.

The President has signed an order designating Marvin Cohen to be Chairman of the Civil Aeronautics Board for a term expiring December 31, 1981.

December 26

The President went to Camp David following his return to Andrews Air Force Base, Md., from the visit to Plains.

NOMINATIONS SUBMITTED TO THE SENATE

NOTE: The Congress having adjourned *sine die* on Tuesday, December 16, no nominations were submitted during the period covered by this issue. The first session of the 97th Congress will convene on Monday, January 5, 1981.

CHECKLIST OF WHITE HOUSE PRESS RELEASES

The following listing contains releases of the White House Press Office which are not included in this issue.

Released December 24, 1980

Fact sheet: *Chadha v. Immigration and Naturalization Service*

ACTS APPROVED BY THE PRESIDENT

Approved December 22, 1980

H.R. 2170_____ Public Law 96–559
An act to provide for the reimbursement of legal expenses incurred by the city of Fairfax with respect to a 1971 entry and search by employees of the Federal Government.

H.R. 5487_____ Public Law 96–560
An act to designate certain National Forest System lands in the States of Colorado, South Dakota, Missouri, South Carolina, and Louisiana for inclusion in the National Wilderness Preservation System, and for other purposes.

S. 2163_____ Public Law 96–561
An act to provide for the conservation and enhancement of the salmon and steelhead resources of the United States, assistance to treaty and nontreaty harvesters of those resources, and for other purposes.

S. 1824_____ Public Law 96–562
An act to designate the "John D. Larkins, Jr., Federal Building."

H.J. Res. 615_____ Public Law 96–563
A joint resolution providing for appointment of David C. Acheson as a citizen regent of the Board of Regents of the Smithsonian Institution.

S. 2227_____ Public Law 96–564
An act to grant the consent of the United States to the Red River Compact among the States of Arkansas, Louisiana, Oklahoma, and Texas.

ACTS APPROVED—Continued

Approved December 22—Continued

H.R. 7217_____ Public Law 96–565
An act to establish the Kalaupapa National Historical Park in the the State of Hawaii, and for other purposes.

H.J. Res. 642_____ Public Law 96–566
A joint resolution providing for convening of the first regular session of the Ninety-seventh Congress on January 5, 1981, and for other purposes.

H.R. 7865_____ Public Law 96–567
Nuclear Safety Research, Development, and Demonstration Act of 1980.

S. 3027_____ Public Law 96–568
Disaster Relief Act Amendments of 1980.

S. 2726_____ Public Law 96–569
Environmental Research, Development, and Demonstration Authorization Act of 1981.

H.R. 2111_____ Public Law 96–570
An act to extend the service area for the Sacramento Valley Canals, Central Valley project, California, and for other purposes.

S. 1784_____ Public Law 96–571
Alaska Federal-Civilian Energy Efficiency Swap Act of 1980.

S. 1148_____ Public Law 96–572
An act to reauthorize title I of the Marine Protection, Research, and Sanctuaries Act, and for other purposes.

S. 2189_____ Public Law 96–573
Low-Level Radioactive Waste Policy Act.

H.R. 999_____ Public Law 96–574
An act to amend the Plant Variety Protection Act (7 U.S.C. 2321 et seq.) to clarify its provisions, and for other purposes.

H.R. 4941_____ Public Law 96–575
An act to name a dam and reservoir on the San Gabriel River, Texas, as the "North San Gabriel Dam" and "Lake Georgetown", respectively.

H.R. 8345_____ Public Law 96–576
An act to name the United States Customs House in Ogdensburg, New York, the "Robert C. McEwen United States Customs House".

H.J. Res. 337_____ Public Law 96–577
A joint resolution designating February 11, 1981, "National Inventors' Day".

Approved December 23, 1980

H.R. 7709_____ Public Law 96–578
An act to amend the Tariff Schedules of the United States to increase the quantity of cigarettes that may be accorded duty-free treatment if acquired in the insular possessions and entered by returning United States residents.

ACTS APPROVED—Continued

Approved December 23—Continued

H.R. 7626_____ Public Law 96–579
Military Pay and Allowances Benefits Act of 1980.

S. 3096_____ Public Law 96–580
An act to amend the Wild and Scenic Rivers Act to authorize the acquisition of certain lands in Douglas County, Wisconsin.

S. 1985_____ Public Law 96–581
An act to authorize the Secretary of Agriculture to convey certain lands in the State of Arizona, to authorize the Secretary of the Interior to convey certain interests in lands in the State of Arizona, to amend the Act of March 14, 1978 (92 Stat. 154), and for other purposes.

H.R. 8195_____ Public Law 96–582
An act to amend the Railroad Retirement Act of 1974 to extend certain cost-of-living increases.

H.R. 6796_____ Public Law 96–583
An act to amend and extend title VII of the Comprehensive Employment and Training Act.

H.R. 7682_____ Public Law 96–584
An act to amend title 10, United States Code, to provide greater flexibility for the Armed Forces in ordering Reserves to active duty, and for other purposes.

H.R. 7814_____ Public Law 96–585
An act to designate certain lands of the Fire Island National Seashore as the "Otis Pike Fire Island High Dune Wilderness", and for other purposes.

H.R. 7306_____ Public Law 96–586
An act to provide for the orderly disposal of certain Federal lands in Nevada and for the acquisition of certain other lands in the Lake Tahoe Basin, and for other purposes.

S. 1142_____ Public Law 96–587
An act authorizing appropriations to the Secretary of the Interior for services necessary to the nonperforming arts functions of the John F. Kennedy Center for the Performing Arts, and for other purposes.

Approved December 24, 1980

S. 3212_____ Public Law 96–588
An act to designate the "Thomas J. McIntyre Federal Building".

H.R. 5043_____ Public Law 96–589
Bankruptcy Tax Act of 1980.

S. 3261_____ Public Law 96–590
An act to amend section 222 of the Communications Act of 1934 in order to include Hawaii in the same category as other States for the purposes of such section.

ACTS APPROVED—Continued

Approved December 24—Continued

H.R. 6671_____ Public Law 96–591
Inland Navigational Rules Act of 1980.

S. 1465_____ Public Law 96–592
Farm Credit Act Amendments of 1980.

H.R. 4774_____ Public Law 96–593
An act to amend the National Labor Relations Act to provide that any employee who is a member of a religion or sect historically holding conscientious objection to joining or financially supporting a labor organization shall not be required to do so.

H.R. 1196_____ Public Law 96–594
An act to revise and improve the laws relating to the documentation of vessels, and for other purposes.

H.R. 4968_____ Public Law 96–595
An act to amend the Internal Revenue Code of 1954 with respect to net operating loss carryovers of taxpayers who cease to be real estate investment trusts, to increase interest rates on certain United States retirement bonds, and for other purposes.

H.R. 5391_____ Public Law 96–596
An act to amend the Internal Revenue Code of 1954 with respect to the determination of second tier taxes, and for other purposes.

H.R. 8444_____ Public Law 96–597
An act to authorize appropriations for certain insular areas of the United States, and for other purposes.

H.R. 3317_____ Public Law 96–598
An act to amend the Internal Revenue Code of 1954 with respect to excise tax refunds in the case of certain uses of tread rubber, and for other purposes.

H.R. 3637_____ Public Law 96–599
International Coffee Agreement Act of 1980.

H.R. 7694_____ Public Law 96–600
An act to authorize the Secretary of Defense to provide civilian career employees of the Department of Defense who are residents of Guam, the Virgin Islands, or the Commonwealth of Puerto Rico the same relative rotation rights as apply to other career employees, to authorize the Delegates in Congress from Guam and the Virgin Islands to have two appointments at a time, rather than one appointment, to each of the service academies, and to authorize the establishment of a National Guard of Guam.

H.R. 5505_____ Public Law 96–601
An act to simplify certain provisions of the Internal Revenue Code of 1954, and for other purposes.

National Forest Lands Bill

Memorandum of Disapproval of H.R. 6257.
December 28, 1980

I am withholding my approval of H.R. 6257, a bill to authorize the Secretary of Agriculture to convey certain National Forest System lands and for other purposes. As originally introduced in Congress, this was a noncontroversial bill providing a simplified procedure for conveying small parcels of land within the National Forest System. Sections one through seven of the bill would accomplish this purpose. However, during the closing hours of the 96th Congress, a new section 8 was added that would adversely affect the Alaska Railroad, an agency of the Department of Transportation.

Section 8 would require the Secretary of Transportation to issue regulations for the rental of Alaska Railroad lands under terms that would result in a loss of revenue to the Railroad, provide for inequitable treatment of different tenants, and create a complicated method for determining rents that would be extremely difficult to administer. It would further delay the Railroad's effort to raise its lease land rents to fair market value, and it would lock into statute past practices that have been criticized by the General Accounting Office and the Department of Transportation. It would also inhibit the Railroad's ability to establish a modern lease land development program consistent with normal commercial practice.

The Railroad is operated as a self-sustaining business by the Federal Government, to the benefit of the State of Alaska and its citizens. Rental income from rail lands is used to pay part of its operating costs. The loss of revenue resulting from this bill may force the Railroad to curtail service or require a new federal operating subsidy to make up the difference. A curtailment of service would injure those shippers and residents of Alaska who use the Railroad, and an increase in federal funds for the Railroad is unacceptable.

For these reasons, I am vetoing H.R. 6257. However, I support those provisions in the bill that would give the Secretary of Agriculture authority to dispose of small tracts of National Forest lands that have become difficult to administer efficiently. This authority, which the Department of Agriculture has been seeking for several years, would greatly facilitate the disposal of approximately 200,000 acres of National Forest lands that present special management problems and would eliminate the need for a case-by-case authorization from the Congress before such lands can be sold or exchanged. Therefore, I urge the 97th Congress to enact similar authority early next year.

JIMMY CARTER

The White House,
December 28, 1980.

NOTE: The text of the memorandum of disapproval was released on December 29.

Relief Bill for Isaac Hulver

Memorandum of Disapproval of S. 442.
December 28, 1980

I am withholding my approval of S. 442, a bill which would provide for the private relief of Mr. Isaac Hulver of Kansas City, Missouri. The United States court of appeals ruled against the claim of Mr. Hulver on the basis that the 2-year statute had expired before suit was filed, thus barring any tort action against the United States. Application for review was made to the United States Supreme Court, which declined, without comment, to hear the case.

Objection to this bill is two-fold, as expressed to me by the Department of Justice and the Veterans Administration. First, in 1979 the Supreme Court held that the statute of limitations was not merely a technicality, but that it was one of the conditions on which the traditional sovereign immunity of the United States has been waived to suit in tort, and that the period of limitations is as important to operation of the Federal Tort Claims Act as are the substantive rights created by that law. Second, this bill constitutes unwarranted preferential treatment which would defeat the goal of uniform application of the law. The federal courts have determined that this claim is forever barred as a tort claim against the United States. Having been afforded due process of the law in the courts, it would be unwise for Mr. Hulver to be singled out for special consideration beyond what the law provides for all persons in similar circumstances.

I am not unmindful of the significant contributions made by Mr. Hulver to his country in wartime, or the seriousness of his injuries, for which service connected disability compensation has been awarded since his discharge from the armed forces in 1945. These considerations do not justify preferential treatment in this case.

JIMMY CARTER

The White House,
    December 28, 1980.

NOTE: The text of the memorandum of disapproval was released on December 29.

Cheese Imports

Proclamation 4811.   December 30, 1980

PROCLAMATION TO AMEND THE TARIFF SCHEDULES OF THE UNITED STATES WITH RESPECT TO THE QUANTITATIVE LIMITATIONS OF CERTAIN CHEESES

By the President of the United States of America

A Proclamation

1. Import limitations have been imposed on certain cheeses pursuant to the provisions of Section 22 of the Agricultural Adjustment Act, as amended, 7 U.S.C. 624. Section 701 of the Trade Agreements Act of 1979, P.L. 96–39 (the "Act"), requires that the President proclaim limitations on the quantity of cheese of the types specified therein, which may enter the United States in any calendar year after 1979. The Act provides that the annual aggregate quantity of such types of cheese entered shall not exceed 111,000 metric tons. Such quantitative limitations appear in Part 3 of the Appendix to the Tariff Schedules of the United States (TSUS) (19 U.S.C. 1202). The present limitations became effective on January 1, 1980, pursuant to Proclamation 4708 of December 11, 1979.

2. In order to permit imports at a level

more nearly in line with current trade requirements, the quantitative limitations set forth in the Appendix to the TSUS must be modified.

Now, THEREFORE, I, JIMMY CARTER, President of the United States of America, acting under the authority vested in me by the Constitution and the statutes of the United States, including the provisions of Section 22 of the Agricultural Adjustment Act of 1933, as amended, and the Trade Agreements Act of 1979, do hereby proclaim that Part 3 of the Appendix to the Tariff Schedules of the United States is modified effective January 1, 1981, as set forth in the Annex to this Proclamation.

IN WITNESS WHEREOF, I have hereunto set my hand this thirtieth day of December, in the year of our Lord nineteen hundred and eighty, and of the Independence of the United States of America the two hundred and fifth.

JIMMY CARTER

[Filed with the Office of the Federal Register, 10:40 a.m., December 31, 1980]

NOTE: The annex is printed in the FEDERAL REGISTER of January 2, 1981.

The proclamation was released by the White House Press Office on December 31.

United States Naval Academy

Appointment of Austin H. Middleton as a Member of the Board of Visitors.
December 31, 1980

The President today announced the appointment of Austin H. Middleton, of Butte, Mont., as a member of the Board of Visitors to the United States Naval Academy.

Middleton is deputy director of Montana Energy and MHD Research and Development Institute, Inc. He graduated from the Naval Academy in 1946 and served in the Marine Corps until 1969.

American Hostages in Iran

Informal Exchange With Reporters.
December 31, 1980

Q. Mr. President, do you think we're close to a deal on the hostages?

THE PRESIDENT. No, I can't predict that. But we've made a reasonable proposal through the Algerians, and I think that it would be to the advantage of the Iranians and, certainly, to the advantage of our imperiled hostages, if they would accept what we have proposed.

Q. But the latest statement from Iran, however, seemed to suggest they might want to look at this one; they might want to soften their opposition.

THE PRESIDENT. Any prediction of a favorable response from the Iranians has always been mistaken, but I hope they will go ahead and resolve this.

Q. What's your hunch?

THE PRESIDENT. Wait and see.

Q. How are you feeling?

THE PRESIDENT. Very good. I feel fine. It's just a strap on my shoulder. No problem.

NOTE: The exchange began at 2:40 p.m. at the South Portico of the White House, following the President's return by helicopter from Camp David, Md.

New Year's Day

Informal Exchange With Reporters.
January 1, 1981

Q. Mr. President?

THE PRESIDENT. Helen [Helen Thomas, United Press International], where have you been lately? Good to see you.

Q. [*Laughter*] Have you got any message for the world on New Year's or do you have any New Year's resolutions?

THE PRESIDENT. Well, we're going to have a good transition and try to turn over the Nation and the Government in good condition and just pray that we'll continue to have peace and prosperity for the American people.

Q. What about the game?

THE PRESIDENT. It's hard for me to stay neutral when Georgia is playing.

Q. Are you feeling better?

THE PRESIDENT. I feel fine.

Q. I'll be around.

THE PRESIDENT. I'll look forward to seeing you again. See you all later.

NOTE: The exchange began at 9:40 a.m. on the South Lawn of the White House as the President departed Washington, D.C., to attend the Sugar Bowl football game between the University of Georgia and Notre Dame in New Orleans, La.

Temporary Tariff Concessions

Proclamation 4812.   December 31, 1980

By the President of the United States of America

A Proclamation

1. On July 26, 1978, the President, pursuant to his authority in section 101 (a) of the Trade Act of 1974 (Trade Act) (19 U.S.C. 2111(a)), entered into a temporary trade agreement with India. This agreement provided for temporary modifications in the rates of duty for certain products to be implemented in stages. The agreement further provided for its termination upon initial implementation of an overall agreement on tariffs pursuant to the Multilateral Trade Negotiations (MTN).

2. On September 21, 1978, the President issued Proclamation No. 4600 implementing the July 26 temporary trade

agreement, which proclamation modified the Tariff Schedules of the United States (TSUS) by inserting the necessary rates of duty in the appendix thereto and provided for further staged reductions of such rates.

3. On January 1, 1980, the United States, by Proclamation No. 4707, of December 11, 1979, initially implemented its overall agreement on tariffs reached during the MTN as provided in Schedule XX to the Geneva (1979) Protocol to the General Agreement on Tariffs and Trade. Pursuant to section 125(e) of the Trade Act (19 U.S.C. 2135(e)), the tariff concessions granted in the temporary agreement have continued in force for a one-year period which will terminate at the close of December 31, 1980.

4. After complying with the requirements of section 125(f) of the Trade Act (19 U.S.C. 2135(f)), I have decided to terminate Proclamation No. 4600, pursuant to the authority of section 125(b) of the Trade Act (19 U.S.C. 2135(b)), effective January 1, 1981.

Now, THEREFORE, I, JIMMY CARTER, President of the United States of America, acting under the authority vested in me by the Constitution and the statutes of the United States, including Title I and section 604 of the Trade Act (19 U.S.C. 2483), do proclaim that:

(1) Proclamation No. 4600, identified in the second recital of this proclamation, is terminated at the close of December 31, 1980.

(2) Part 2C of the Appendix to the Tariff Schedules of the United States (TSUS) is deleted, with the result that articles presently subject to the column 1 rates of duty provided in Part 2C of the Appendix to the TSUS shall be subject to the rates of duty established for such articles in schedules 1–7 of the TSUS by Proclamation No. 4707 of December 11,

1979. These rates shall apply with respect to articles entered, or withdrawn from warehouse for consumption, on or after January 1, 1981.

IN WITNESS WHEREOF, I have hereunto set my hand this thirty-first day of December, in the year of our Lord nineteen hundred and eighty, and of the Independence of the United States of America the two hundred and fifth.

JIMMY CARTER

[Filed with the Office of the Federal Register, 3:07 p.m., January 2, 1981]

NOTE: The proclamation was released by the White House Press Office on January 2, 1981.

Continuance of Certain Federal Advisory Committees

Executive Order 12258. December 31, 1980

By the authority vested in me as President by the Constitution and statutes of the United States of America, and in accordance with the provisions of the Federal Advisory Committee Act, as amended (5 U.S.C. App. I), it is hereby ordered as follows:

1–101. Each advisory committee listed below is continued until December 31, 1982.

(a) Committee for the Preservation of the White House; Executive Order No. 11145, as amended (Department of the Interior).

(b) President's Commission on White House Fellowships; Executive Order No. 11183, as amended (Office of Personnel Management).

(c) President's Committee on the National Medal of Science; Executive Order No. 11287, as amended (National Science Foundation).

(d) President's Council on Physical Fitness and Sports; Executive Order No. 11562, as amended (Department of Health and Human Services).

(e) President's Committee on Mental Retardation; Executive Order No. 11776 (Department of Health and Human Services).

(f) Presidential Advisory Board on Ambassadorial Appointments; Executive Order No. 11970 (Department of State).

(g) Committee on Selection of Federal Judicial Officers; Executive Order No. 11992 (Department of Justice).

(h) President's Advisory Committee for Women; Executive Order No. 12050 (Department of Labor).

(i) United States Circuit Judge Nominating Commission; Executive Order No. 12059, as amended (Department of Justice).

(j) United States Tax Court Nominating Commission; Executive Order No. 12064 (Department of the Treasury).

(k) Judicial Nominating Commission for the District of Puerto Rico; Executive Order No. 12084 (Department of Justice).

(l) President's Export Council; Executive Order No. 12131 (Department of Commerce).

(m) Peace Corps Advisory Council; Executive Order No. 12137 (Peace Corps).

(n) Advisory Committee on Small and Minority Business Ownership; Executive Order No. 12190 (Small Business Administration).

(o) Federal Advisory Council on Occupational Safety and Health; Executive Order No. 12196 (Department of Labor).

(p) President's Committee on the International Labor Organization; Executive Order No. 12216 (Department of Labor).

1-102. Notwithstanding the provisions of any other Executive order, the functions of the President under the Federal Advisory Committee Act which are applicable to the committees listed in Section 1-101 of this Order, except that of reporting annually to Congress, shall be performed by the head of the department or agency designated after each committee, in accordance with guidelines and procedures established by the Administrator of General Services.

1-103. The following Executive Orders, that established committees which have terminated or whose work is completed, are revoked:

(a) Executive Order No. 12022, as amended, establishing the National Commission for the Review of Antitrust Laws and Procedures.

(b) Executive Order No. 12054, as amended, establishing the President's Commission on Foreign Language and International Studies.

(c) Executive Order No. 12061, as amended, establishing the Small Business Conference Commission.

(d) Executive Order No. 12063, establishing the United States Court of Military Appeals Nominating Commission.

(e) Executive Order No. 12078, as amended, establishing the President's Commission on World Hunger.

(f) Executive Order No. 12093, as amended, establishing the President's Commission on the Holocaust.

(g) Executive Order No. 12103, as amended, establishing the President's Commission on the Coal Industry.

(h) Executive Order No. 12130, establishing the President's Commission on the Accident at Three Mile Island.

(i) Executive Order No. 12157, establishing the President's Management Improvement Council.

(j) Executive Order No. 12195, establishing the President's Commission on United States-Liberian Relations.

1-104. Executive Order No. 12110 is superseded.

1-105. This Order shall be effective December 31, 1980.

JIMMY CARTER

The White House,
    December 31, 1980.

[Filed with the Office of the Federal Register,
    3:08 p.m., January 2, 1981]

NOTE: The Executive order was released by the White House Press Office on January 2, 1981.

Leadership and Coordination of Fair Housing in Federal Programs

Executive Order 12259.   December 31, 1980

By the authority vested in me as President by the Constitution of the United States of America, and in order to provide under the leadership of the Secretary of Housing and Urban Development, in accordance with Section 808 of the Act of April 11, 1968, as amended (sometimes referred to as the Federal Fair Housing Act or as Title VIII of the Civil Rights Act of 1968), 42 U.S.C. 3608, for the administration of all Federal programs and activities relating to housing and urban development in a manner affirmatively to further fair housing throughout the United States, it is hereby ordered as follows:

1-1. Administration of Programs and Activities Relating to Housing and Urban Development.

1-101. All programs and activities of Executive agencies, including agencies which exercise regulatory responsibility, relating to housing and urban development shall be administered in a manner affirmatively to further fair housing.

1–2. Responsibilities of Executive Agencies.

1–201. The authority and responsibility for administering the Federal Fair Housing Act is vested in the Secretary of Housing and Urban Development.

1–202. The head of each Executive agency is responsible for ensuring that its programs and activities relating to housing and urban development are administered in a manner affirmatively to further the goal of fair housing as required by Section 808 of the Act of April 11, 1968, as amended (Title VIII of the Civil Rights Act of 1968), and for cooperating with the Secretary of Housing and Urban Development who shall be responsible for exercising leadership in furthering the purposes of the Act. As used in this Order, the terms "programs and activities" include programs and activities operated, administered or undertaken by the Federal government; grants; loans; contracts; insurance; guarantees; and Federal supervision or exercise of regulatory responsibility.

1–203. In carrying out the responsibilities in this Order the head of each Executive agency shall take appropriate steps to require that all persons or other entities who are applicants for, or participants in, or who are supervised or regulated under, agency programs and activities relating to housing and urban development comply with this Order.

1–3. Specific Responsibilities.

1–301. In implementing the responsibilities under Section 1–2 the Secretary of Housing and Urban Development shall:

(a) Develop guidelines for determining the categories of programs and activities relating to housing and urban development which are operated, administered, undertaken, controlled or regulated by Executive agencies.

(b) Promulgate regulations regarding programs and activities of Executive agencies related to housing and urban development which shall:

(1) describe an institutionalized method for analyzing the impact of housing and urban development programs and activities in promoting the goal of fair housing;

(2) describe the responsibilities and obligations in assuring that programs and activities are administered and executed in a manner affirmatively to further fair housing; and

(3) describe the responsibilities and obligations of applicants, participants and other persons and entities involved in housing and urban development programs and activities affirmatively to further the goal of fair housing.

(c) Coordinate Executive agency implementation of the requirements of this Order and issue standards and procedures regarding the administration of programs and activities relating to housing and urban development in a manner affirmatively to further fair housing.

1–302. Upon publication of guidelines by the Secretary of Housing and Urban Development under Section 1–301(a), each Executive agency shall provide the Secretary with a description of all programs and activities relating to housing and urban development within its jurisdiction.

1–303. Within 180 days of the publication of final regulations by the Secretary of Housing and Urban Development under Section 1–301(a) the head of each

Executive agency shall publish proposed regulations providing for the administration of programs and activities relating to housing and urban development in a manner affirmatively to further fair housing, consistent with the Secretary of Housing and Urban Development regulations, and with the standards and procedures issued pursuant to Section 1–301(c). As soon as practicable, each Executive agency shall issue its final regulations. All Executive agencies shall formally submit all such proposed and final regulations, and any related issuances or standards to the Secretary of Housing and Urban Development at least 30 days prior to public announcement.

1–304. The Secretary of Housing and Urban Development shall review regulations, standards and actions under Sections 1–302 and 1–303 to ensure conformity with the purposes of the Federal Fair Housing Act and consistency among the operations of the various Executive agencies and shall make any comments with respect thereto on a timely basis.

1–305. In addition to the regulations and guidelines described in Section 1–301, the Secretary of Housing and Urban Development shall implement the Secretary's authority and responsibility for administering the Federal Fair Housing Act by promulgating regulations describing the nature and scope of coverage and the conduct prohibited.

1–4. Cooperative Efforts.

1–401. The Secretary of Housing and Urban Development shall:

(a) Cooperate with, and render assistance to, the heads of all Executive agencies in the formulation of policies and procedures to implement this Order and to provide information and guidance on the affirmative administration of programs and activities relating to housing and urban development and the protection of

rights accorded persons by the Federal Fair Housing Act; and

(b) initiate cooperative efforts, including the development of memoranda of understanding between Executive agencies designed to provide for consultation and the coordination of Federal efforts to further fair housing through the affirmative administration of programs and activities relating to housing and urban development.

1–402. In connection with carrying out functions under this Order the Secretary of Housing and Urban Development is authorized to request from any Executive agency such information and assistance deemed necessary. Each agency shall, to the extent permitted by law, furnish such information and assistance to the Secretary.

1–5. Administrative Enforcement.

1–501. Each Executive agency shall be responsible for enforcement of this Order and, to the extent permitted by law, shall cooperate and provide records, data and documentation in connection with any other agency's investigation of compliance with provisions of this Order.

1–502. If any Executive agency concludes that any person or entity (including any State or local public agency) applying for or participating in, or supervised or regulated under, a program or activity relating to housing and urban development has not complied with this Order or any applicable rule, regulation or procedure issued or adopted pursuant to this Order, it shall endeavor to end and remedy such violation by informal means, including conference, conciliation and persuasion. An Executive agency need not pursue informal resolution of matters where similar efforts made by another Executive agency have been unsuccessful. In event of failure of such informal means, the Executive agency, in conformity with rules, regulations, procedures or policies issued or adopted by it pursuant to Section 1–3 hereof, shall impose such sanctions as may be authorized by law. To the extent authorized by law, such sanctions may include:

(a) cancellation or termination of agreements or contracts with such person, entity, or State or local public agency;

(b) refusal to extend any further aid under any program or activity administered by it and affected by this Order until it is satisfied that the affected person, entity, or State or local public agency will comply with the rules, regulations, and procedures issued or adopted pursuant to this Order;

(c) refusal to grant supervisory or regulatory approval to such person, entity, or State or local public agency under any program or activity administered by it which is affected by this Order or revoke such approval if previously given;

(d) any other action as may be appropriate under its governing laws.

1–503. Findings of any violation under Section 1–502 shall be promptly reported to the Secretary of Housing and Urban Development. The Secretary of Housing and Urban Development shall forward this information to all other Executive agencies.

1–504. Any Executive agency shall also consider invoking appropriate sanctions against any person or entity where any other Executive department or agency has initiated action against that person or entity pursuant to Section 1–502 of this Order.

1–505. Each Executive agency shall seek the advice of the Secretary of Housing and Urban Development in this regard prior to a decision to initiate actions to invoke sanctions. Each such decision and the reasons therefor, shall be documented and shall be provided to the Secretary of Housing and Urban Development in a timely manner.

1–6. General Provisions.

1–601. Nothing in this Order shall limit the authority of the Attorney General to provide for the coordinated enforcement of nondiscrimination requirements in Federal assistance programs under Executive Order No. 12250.

1–602. All provisions of regulations, guidelines and procedures proposed to be issued by Executive agencies pursuant to this Order which implement nondiscrimination requirements of laws covered by Executive Order No. 12250 shall be submitted to the Attorney General for review in accordance with that Executive Order. In addition, the Secretary will consult with the Attorney General regarding all regulations, guidelines and procedures proposed to be issued under Sections 1–301, 1–302 and 1–303 of this Order to assure consistency with coordinated Federal efforts to enforce nondiscrimination requirements in programs of Federal financial assistance pursuant to Executive Order No. 12250.

1–603. Nothing in this Order shall affect the authority and responsibility of the Attorney General to commence civil actions in cases involving a pattern or practice of discrimination or raising an issue of general public importance under the Federal Fair Housing Act.

1–604. (a) Part IV and Sections 501 and 503 of Executive Order No. 11063 are revoked. The activities and functions of the President's Commission on Equal Opportunity in Housing described in that Executive Order shall be performed by the Secretary of Housing and Urban Development.

(b) Sections 101 and 502(a) of Executive Order No. 11063 are revised to apply to discrimination because of "race, color, religion (creed), sex or national origin." All departments and agencies shall revise regulations, guidelines and procedures issued pursuant to Part II of Executive Order No. 11063 to reflect this amendment to coverage.

(c) Section 102 of Executive Order No. 11063 is revised by deleting the term "Housing and Home Finance Agency" and inserting in lieu thereof the term "Department of Housing and Urban Development."

1–605. Nothing in this Order shall affect any requirement imposed under the Equal Credit Opportunity Act (15 U.S.C. 1691 *et seq.*), the Home Mortgage Disclosure Act (12 U.S.C. 2901 *et seq.*) or the Community Reinvestment Act (12 U.S.C. 2810 *et seq.*).

1–7. Report.

1–701. The Secretary of Housing and Urban Development shall submit to the President an annual report commenting on the progress the Department of Housing and Urban Development and other Executive agencies have made in carrying out requirements and responsibilities under this Executive Order.

JIMMY CARTER

The White House,
  December 31, 1980.

[Filed with the Office of the Federal Register,
  3:09 p.m., January 2, 1981]

NOTE: The text of the Executive order was released by the White House on January 2, 1981.

Agreement on Government Procurement

Executive Order 12260.   December 31, 1980

By the authority vested in me as President by the Constitution and statutes of the United States of America, including Title III of the Trade Agreements Act of 1979 (19 U.S.C. 2511–2518), and Section 301 of Title 3 of the United States Code, and in order to implement the Agreement on Government Procurement, as defined in 19 U.S.C. 2518(1), it is hereby ordered as follows:

1–1. *Responsibilities.*

1–101. The obligations of the Agreement on Government Procurement (Agreement on Government Procurement, General Agreement on Tariffs and Trade, 12 April 1979, Geneva (GATT 1979)) apply to any procurement of eligible products by the Executive agencies listed in the Annex to this Order (eligible products are defined in Section 308 of the Trade Agreements Act of 1979; 19 U.S.C. 2518(4)). Such procurement shall be in accord with the policies and procedures of the Office of Federal Procurement Policy (41 U.S.C. 401 *et seq.*).

1–102. The United States Trade Representative, hereinafter referred to as the Trade Representative, shall be responsible for interpretation of the Agreement. The Trade Representative shall seek the advice of the interagency organization established under Section 242(a) of the Trade Expansion Act of 1962 (19 U.S.C. 1872(a)) and consult with affected Executive agencies, including the Office of Federal Procurement Policy.

1–103. The interpretation of Article VIII:1 of the Agreement shall be subject to the concurrence of the Secretary of Defense.

1–104. The Trade Representative shall determine, from time to time, the dollar equivalent of 150,000 Special Drawing Right units and shall publish that determination in the FEDERAL REGISTER. Procurement of less than 150,000 Special Drawing Right units is not subject to the Agreement or this Order (Article I:1(b) of the Agreement).

1–105. In order to ensure coordination of international trade policy with regard to the implementation of the Agreement, agencies shall consult in advance with the Trade Representative about negotiations with foreign governments or instrumentalities which concern government procurement.

1–2. *Delegations and Authorization.*

1–201. The functions vested in the President by Sections 301, 302, 304, 305(c) and 306 of the Trade Agreements Act of 1979 (19 U.S.C. 2511, 2512, 2514, 2515(c) and 2516) are delegated to the Trade Representative.

1–202. Notwithstanding the delegation in Section 1–201, the Secretary of Defense is authorized, in accord with Section 302(b)(3) of the Trade Agreements Act of 1979 (19 U.S.C. 2512(b)(3)), to waive the prohibitions specified therein.

JIMMY CARTER

The White House,
   December 31, 1980.

[Filed with the Office of the Federal Register,
   3:10 p.m., January 2, 1981]

NOTE: The annex is printed in the FEDERAL REGISTER of January 6, 1981.

The Executive order was released by the White House Press Office on January 2, 1981.

Leadership and Coordination of Fair Housing in Federal Programs

Statement on Executive Order 12259.
January 2, 1981

In my urban policy report to the Congress, I promised to issue an Executive order concerning Title VIII of the Civil Rights Act of 1968, the Fair Housing Act. I am fulfilling this promise today. This Executive order will strengthen the abil-

ity of each executive agency to administer its Federal programs and activities in such a way as to promote fair housing. This Executive order:

• reemphasizes HUD's authority and responsibility to administer the Fair Housing Act;

• stipulates the leadership and coordination role of HUD and the responsibilities of all other agencies with respect to the preparation and implementation of regulations and procedures which will further fair housing;

• requires all agencies to use informal and formal means to remedy violations of regulations or procedures adopted pursuant to the order;

• sets a timetable for implementation of these requirements by all Federal agencies;

• directs HUD to submit an annual report to the President noting the progress made by the Federal Government in furthering fair housing objectives.

This order will not by itself close the gap between the present reality and the national fair housing objectives set by Congress in the Civil Rights Act of 1968. That gap can truly be narrowed only by a heightened enforcement program such as the one that would have gone into effect had Congress adopted the Fair Housing Amendments of 1980. Yet this order will help. It will then be the task of the 97th Congress to strengthen the Federal Government's ability to secure prompt and equitable compliance with Title VIII fair housing provisions by enacting the amendments to the Civil Rights Act of 1968 supported so vigorously by this administration.

This is the third in a series of Executive orders I have issued to improve the Federal Government's ability to enforce our Nation's civil rights laws.

Executive Order 12067 was issued to clarify to the leadership responsibility of

2855

the Equal Employment Opportunity Commission where job discrimination was concerned. Executive Order 12250 defined the leadership responsibility of the Department of Justice in programs involving Federal financial assistance. The present Executive order sets out the leadership responsibilities of the Department of Housing and Urban Development in administering programs and activities relating to housing and urban development in such a way as to promote the cause of fair housing.

NOTE: The President signed Executive Order 12259 on December 31, 1980.

National Labor Relations Act Amendments Bill

Statement on Signing H.R. 4774 Into Law. January 2, 1981

I have signed into law H.R. 4774, a bill amending the National Labor Relations Act to provide, among other things, that employees who have conscientious objections to joining or financially supporting a labor organization shall not be required to do so.

In signing H.R. 4774, I want to emphasize that the language in this bill defining conscientious objection is not to be construed in such a way as to discriminate among religions or to favor religious views over other views that are constitutionally entitled to the same status. To put any other construction on this definition would, in my view, create serious constitutional difficulties. I have invited the Chairman of the National Labor Relations Board to consult with the Attorney General on the proper interpretation of this language.

NOTE: As enacted, H.R. 4774 is Public Law 96–593, approved December 24, 1980.

Federal Election Commission

Recess Appointment of Vernon Thomson as a Member.   January 2, 1981

The President today announced the recess appointment of Vernon Thomson as a member of the Federal Election Commission. He replaces Max L. Friedersdorf, who is resigning.

Thomson, 75, was a member of the FEC from 1976 until 1979, when he retired. He was a Member of the House of Representatives from 1961 to 1974 and Governor of Wisconsin from 1956 to 1958.

Digest of Other White House Announcements

The following listing includes the President's public schedule and other items of general interest announced by the White House Press Office and not included elsewhere in this issue.

December 28, 1980

The White House announced that the President will receive the Algerian delegation at Camp David early this afternoon. The meeting will give the President the opportunity to express the appreciation of the American people to the Algerian delegation for their work as intermediaries between the United States and Iran and to be informed about the condition of the hostages.

December 31, 1980

The President announced the recess appointments of three persons who were nominated for positions but not confirmed before the Senate adjourned. They are:

JOSEPH S. BRACEWELL, to be President of the Solar Energy and Energy Conservation Bank;

WALLACE N. HYDE, to be a member of the Board of Governors of the U.S. Postal Service;

RALPH W. EMERSON, to be a member of the Foreign Claims Settlement Commission.

January 2, 1981

The President met at the White House with Vice President Walter F. Mondale, Secretary of State Edmund S. Muskie, Secretary of Defense Harold Brown, Zbigniew Brzezinski, Assistant to the President for National Security Affairs, and Jack H. Watson, Jr., Assistant to the President.

NOMINATIONS SUBMITTED TO THE SENATE

NOTE: The Congress having adjourned *sine die* on Tuesday, December 16, 1980, no nominations were submitted during the period covered by this issue. The first session of the 97th Congress will convene on Monday, January 5, 1981.

CHECKLIST OF WHITE HOUSE PRESS RELEASES

The following listing contains releases of the White House Press Office which are not included in this issue.

Released January 2, 1981

Announcement: Recess appointment of Walter Meheula to serve as United States District Judge for the District of Hawaii

ACTS APPROVED BY THE PRESIDENT

Approved December 28, 1980

S. 1803_____ Public Law 96–602
An act to modify the boundary of the Cibola National Forest in the State of New Mexico, and for other purposes.

ACTS APPROVED—Continued

Approved December 28—Continued

H.R. 4155_____ Public Law 96–603
An act to amend the Internal Revenue Code of 1954 to simplify private foundation return and reporting requirements, and for other purposes.

H.R. 7112_____ Public Law 96–604
State and Local Fiscal Assistance Act Amendments of 1980.

H.R. 7956_____ Public Law 96–605
Miscellaneous Revenue Act of 1980.

H.R. 5737_____ Public Law 96–606
An act to amend the International Claims Settlement Act of 1949 to allow recovery by United States nationals for losses incurred in Vietnam.

S. 2363_____ Public Law 96–607
An act to provide, with respect to the national park system: for the establishment of new units; for adjustments in boundaries; for increases in appropriation authorizations for land acquisition and development; and for other purposes.

H.R. 5973_____ Public Law 96–608
An act to amend the Internal Revenue Code of 1954 to waive in certain cases the residency requirements for deductions or exclusions of individuals living abroad, to allow the tax-free rollover of certain distributions from money purchase pension plans, and for other purposes.

H.R. 5047_____ Public Law 96–609
An act to provide for the temporary suspension of certain duties, to extend certain existing suspensions of duties, and for other purposes.

S. 2729_____ Public Law 96–610
National Visitor Center Emergency Repair Act of 1980.

H.R. 8406_____ Public Law 96–611
An act to amend title XVIII of the Social Security Act to provide for medicare coverage of pneumococcal vaccine and its administration.

S. 2261_____ Public Law 96–612
An act to provide for the establishment of the Indiana Dunes National Lakeshore, and for other purposes.

H.R. 7171_____ Public Law 96–613
An act to make certain miscellaneous changes in the tax laws.

NOTE: The President completed his consideration of acts and joint resolutions passed during the second session of the 96th Congress on December 28, 1980.

Recess Appointments to Government Positions

Announcement of the Appointments. January 5, 1981

The President today announced the recess appointments of six persons. The appointments were signed on January 2.

Three of these persons had been nominated for these positions, but were not confirmed before the Senate adjourned. They are:

THOMAS M. FREDERICKS, to be an Assistant Secretary of the Interior;

REUBEN W. ASKANASE and MELBA BEALS, to be members of the Board of Directors of the Corporation for Public Broadcasting.

The other three are being appointed, for the first time, as members of the National Museum Services Board. They are:

JOHN CONNELL, of Pasadena, Calif., president and director of the Michael J. Connell Foundation, a trustee of the J. Paul Getty Museum, and is active in civic affairs and support of the arts in Los Angeles;

DOROTHY GRAHAM-WHEELER, of Winston-Salem, N.C., director of urban arts of the Arts Council, who has been active in child development and community development projects;

ALBERT T. KLYBERG, of Lincoln, R.I., director of the Rhode Island Historical Society and chair of the Rhode Island Committee for the Humanities.

Slaying of Three Persons in El Salvador

Statement by the White House Press Secretary. January 5, 1981

The Department of State spoke yesterday to our grief and dismay at the killing of two Americans and the Salvadorian with whom they worked. I want, on the President's behalf, to underscore the sense of loss and outrage we feel for what happened in El Salvador. Also on behalf of the President, I want to offer deeply felt condolences to the families of those three dedicated and brave men.

They were dedicated to the building of a just and free society in El Salvador. Their work on agrarian reform served the cause of social justice in that country as no other program has done. That work will continue. It is one of the most effective instruments to counter the objectives of both the extreme right and the extreme left.

NOTE: Press Secretary Jody Powell read the statement to reporters at 4:55 p.m. at his regular news briefing in the Briefing Room at the White House.

Michael P. Hammer, of Potomac, Md., and Mark David Pearlman, of Seattle, Wash., both with the American Institute for Free Labor Development, and José Rodolfo Viera, president of El Salvador's Institute for Agrarian Transformation, were slain in San Salvador on January 4.

Gasohol in Federal Motor Vehicles
Executive Order 12261. January 5, 1981

By the authority vested in me as President of the United States of America by Section 271 of the Energy Security Act (94 Stat. 710; Public Law 96–294; 42 U.S.C. 8871), in order to require Federal agencies which own or lease motor vehicles to use gasohol in those vehicles which are capable of operating on gasohol where it is available at reasonable prices and in reasonable quantities, it is hereby ordered as follows:

1–101. In procurement actions for unleaded gasoline motor fuel, Federal agencies shall, whenever feasible, specify that gasohol is an acceptable substitute motor fuel. In such procurements there shall be a preference for the purchase of gasohol.

1–102. Agencies may procure the components of gasohol and do their own blending.

1–103. In determining the feasibility of specifying gasohol as a substitute motor fuel in procurement actions for unleaded gasoline, agencies shall include in their considerations such factors as the availability of storage facilities for bulk purchases and the number of vehicles capable of operating on gasohol.

1–104. Agencies shall designate those vehicles which are capable of using gasohol, consistent with overall agency needs and sound vehicle management practices. Agencies shall specify the conditions governing the use of gasohol, including when gasohol shall be purchased from normal retail outlets by vehicle operators.

1–105. The use of gasohol by the Department of Defense pursuant to this Order shall be in accordance with Section 815 of the Department of Defense Authorization Act, 1980 (93 Stat. 817; Public Law 96–107; 10 U.S.C. 2388 note)

which provides for the use of gasohol to the maximum extent feasible and consistent with overall defense needs and sound vehicle management practices, as determined by the Secretary of Defense.

1–106. Vehicles used in experimental programs to test fuels other than gasohol are excepted from this Order.

1–107. The authority vested in the President by Section 271(b) of the Energy Security Act (42 U.S.C. 8871(b)) is delegated to the Secretary of Defense with respect to gasohol use by the Department of Defense, and delegated to the Administrator of General Services with respect to gasohol use by other agencies.

1–108. Federal agencies shall make available to the Department of Energy, upon request, relevant data or information they possess concerning agency gasohol usage.

1–109. For purposes of this Order "Gasohol" means a motor fuel which has an octane rating of not less than 87 $(R+M)/2$ and which consists of approximately 90 percent unleaded gasoline and approximately 10 percent anhydrous (199 proof or above) ethyl alcohol derived from biomass, as defined in Section 203(2)(A) of the Energy Security Act (94 Stat. 683; Public Law 96–294; 42 U.S.C. 8802(2)(A)).

1–110. (a) The Secretary of Defense with respect to gasohol use by the Department of Defense, and the Administrator of General Services with respect to gasohol use by other agencies, shall issue such guidelines for the implementation of this Order as they deem appropriate.

(b) Such guidelines shall provide for a determination of reasonable prices and reasonable quantities based on the local prevailing price of unleaded gasolines, the octane requirements for vehicles in the Federal fleet, local market availability of gasohol or its components, and other such factors, as may be appropriate.

JIMMY CARTER

The White House,
    January 5, 1981.

[Filed with the Office of the Federal Register, 3:39 p.m., January 6, 1981]

NOTE: The text of the Executive order was released by the White House Press Office on January 6.

White House Dinner for State and Local Officials

Remarks Following the Dinner.
January 6, 1981

There are a couple of things I've found you can't do very well with a broken collarbone. One is to do a one-step on a slick floor. [*Laughter*] And the other one is to tie a bow tie. That's been a hard thing for me.

We've been really pleased to have you here tonight. As you probably know, this is a special group for us. You're not only strong and good personal friends and political allies, but you've made a great partnership with us in, I think, reestablishing the system of federalism in our Nation that's so important to the principles that were envisioned when the Constitution was first drafted. I'm particularly grateful that so many people came tonight. You may or may not know there won't be another UDAG application before I go—[*laughter*]—except perhaps for six States and the District of Columbia. [*Laughter*] If Maryland and Georgia and a few others have some applications at the last minute, we can probably squeeze them through. [*Laughter*]

Ours is a great country, and you have proven, I think, in the last 4 years that one of the greatest difficulties that was discerned by you—that is, the deterioration of our senior cities in this country—has been reversed. You've helped me with counsel and advice and support, criticism on occasion. But in my judgment we've formed a good partnership, and I doubt that there's ever been a better relationship between the local officials of our country and the Federal Government than exists now.

And it's because of you and Gene Eidenberg and Jack Watson and others that have helped to form an urban policy that works, a good relationship with the Congress, a good understanding among the American people of the problems that are shared between local officials and the Federal Government itself. In matters concerning education, environmental quality, transportation, health, social services, there is no way to separate the responsibilities of our two levels of government. But with your urging and with your support we have always honored the first responsibilities and the preeminent prerogatives of local officials. We've tried not to encroach on your territory, but we've tried to give you support when you've needed it.

So, we've come a long way; still have a long way to go. We have a good attitude in this country, and our Nation has been blessed, in my judgment, above all others, with natural resources that God's given us, with a human attitude of brotherhood and sisterhood among a widely diverse 225 million people, most of whom, or their ancestors, who've come here looking for a better life and have found it, and who understand because of our diversity that it's better to try to understand one another and get along as best we can in the sometimes trying circumstances, rather than to fight with one another and mutually to suffer because of it.

The strength in our constitutional system, the ideals and principles and commitments, the hopes and dreams of Americans, are very well understood by you, better perhaps, better, I believe, than among any other group of people in our country. Local, county, and city officials, I think, have a better understanding of what people need and want than anyone I know. It makes it very difficult for you, and I have discerned very quickly, because of instruction by Coleman Young and many others here, Kenneth Hahn, that you need some help in Washington, and we've tried to provide it for you.

The distance that we've come together is notable, but we still have a long way to go. And I believe that if you can accurately tap the understanding and support and the commitment that the American people share with you and with me, that that progress that we have achieved and of which we are so proud can be preserved and perhaps even enhanced during the next 4 years. It's not going to be an easy time. I don't want to put an unnecessary burden or blame on the next administration. It would be difficult for me, if I were here, as President, to meet all the demands on the Federal Government and still protect the integrity of our institutions and of our financial structure, to minimize budget deficits, to meet the overwhelming demands of foreign policy and defense, the maintenance of peace, preservation of our way of life. But I think you've been overly, at least adequately, generous with me. You've understood when we couldn't meet all your desires, and I, again, feel that the reason that that occurred is because we have had a partnership.

You've understood the limitations as well as the capabilities and opportunities, and for that I'm deeply grateful. No one that I know has been more highly blessed than I have this last 4 years. It's been an extraordinary opportunity for me to serve and to learn and to have a fruitful and an enjoyable life.

The Strolling Strings, that just came in—we've heard them a lot of times, more than you have, in the last 4 years. I hope that you'll hear them more than I will the next 4 years—[*laughter*]—and that the Governors and the county officials and the city officials will continue to have a ready access to the heart of the Federal Government, both here in the White House and on Capitol Hill.

So, to close my own remarks, you are special to me, in many different ways, and because of that I particularly wanted to have for you tonight a special treat. We've had a chance to tap the tremendous artistry and talent and commitment and achievement and fame of the performers of our country. That's one of the great assets that a President and his family, Rosalynn and I, can have. And tonight we've asked someone to come here, originally from the Bronx, who knows the special opportunities of America, the achievements that we've realized, the tests that we have withstood successfully, who came to the Metropolitan Opera Company 30 years ago, as a matter of fact. She'd only been there 2 months when one of the leading sopranos could not perform that evening, and she substituted and literally made American and worldwide musical history. She sang one of the leading roles in Don Giovanni, and it electrified the performing world because of her performance.

Since then she has performed as the star in 37 operatic roles. She's made countless hundreds of very highly popular phonograph recordings, tape recordings, and she's had more operatic television performances than any other person who's ever lived. She's still young, and she's still very beautiful. And not long ago she came by here to tell me goodby and to give me a report on her trip that she just took to a new friend of ours, and that is the people in the People's Republic of China; a quarter of all the people on Earth, about a billion people, were blessed with her performance in that great new friend of ours. And tonight she's here to perform for us. And it's a great pleasure for me to introduce the person that I, as President, chose to be my seating partner tonight, Roberta Peters.

Thank you very much.

NOTE: The President spoke at 10:10 p.m. in the East Room at the White House.

United States Participation in the United Nations

Message to the Congress Transmitting a Report.   January 7, 1981

To the Congress of the United States:

I am pleased to transmit to the Congress this report of the activities of the United States Government in the United Nations and its affiliated agencies during calendar year 1979.

The international crisis created by the seizure of the American Embassy in Tehran and the taking of Americans hostage overshadowed much of the 34th General Assembly. In this atmosphere, the United States directed its efforts in the United Nations toward supporting the work of the Secretary General and the Security Council to resolve this breach of international law. The Secretary General brought the issue to the Council which unanimously called upon the Government of Iran to release the hostages. Ironically, after three years of negotiations, the Assembly adopted by consensus the Convention Against the Taking of Hostages. This Convention affirms that there is no valid

excuse for the taking of hostages and that there are no circumstances under which the seizure of hostages can be condoned.

Both the Security Council and the General Assembly focused international attention on the continued military occupation of Kampuchea by Vietnam. Of particular note during 1979 was the Security Council's termination of sanctions against Southern Rhodesia, a result of the agreement by the Lancaster House Conference.

On economic issues, UN actions ranged from highly technical meetings such as those on commodities, to continuing the work of the International Monetary Fund and to political discussions in the General Assembly on the future of international economy and development.

These discussions, attended by almost all UN members, saw a continuous, intense, and sometimes acrimonious series of exchanges between the developed and developing countries on the organization of the international economy, the nature of international economic relations, and the effects of both on economic development. This resulted in the decision by the 34th General Assembly to hold further meetings on these issues. We believe that negotiations of this kind and at this level are important and necessary to relations between developed and developing countries. However, whether the U.S. participates in these global negotiations will depend on how effectively we use but do not intrude upon the agencies of the UN and other international organizations.

The United States continues to monitor closely UN expenditures and programs and supports the Secretary General's efforts to limit budget growth.

Our participation in the United Nations and its related agencies and programs is an integral part of our foreign policy. As this report makes clear, the United Nations system of organizations is important and sometimes indispensable to the achievement of many of our central foreign policy objectives. This report should contribute to American understanding of and support for the United Nations and to the continuing active and constructive role of the United States.

JIMMY CARTER

The White House,
    January 7, 1981.

NOTE: The 399-page report is entitled "United States Participation in the UN—Report by the President to the Congress for the Year 1979."

Interagency Employee Benefit Council

Executive Order 12262.   January 7, 1981

By the authority vested in me as President by the Constitution of the United States of America, and in order to improve the administration of the Employee Retirement Income Security Act (ERISA) and to continue the improvements made by Reorganization Plan No. 4 of 1978, it is hereby ordered as follows:

1–1. *Establishment of the Council.*

1–101. There is established the Interagency Employee Benefit Council.

1–102. The Council shall be composed of the following, or their representatives:

(a) The Secretary of the Treasury.
(b) The Attorney General.
(c) The Secretary of Commerce.
(d) The Secretary of Labor.
(e) The Secretary of Health and Human Services.
(f) The Director of the Office of Management and Budget.
(g) The Administrator of the Small Business Administration.

(h) The Chairman of the Equal Employment Opportunity Commission.
(i) The Executive Director of the President's Commission on Pension Policy.

1–103. The following, or their designated representatives, are invited to participate in the activities of the Council:

(a) The Federal Trade Commission.
(b) The Securities and Exchange Commission.
(c) The National Labor Relations Board.
(d) Any other Executive agencies the Council invites.

1–104. The Secretary of Labor shall be the Chairman of the Council.

1–2. *Functions of the Council.*

1–201. The Council shall assist in interagency coordination of proposals affecting employee benefits under ERISA. It shall identify the potential economic consequences of those proposals for ERISA participants.

1–202. The Council shall develop comprehensive long-term and short-term policies applicable to the plans covered by ERISA. The Council shall identify and coordinate research into employee benefit issues affecting ERISA-covered employees, into the economic effects of private pensions, and into the effectiveness of ERISA.

1–203. The Council shall develop effective policy approaches to a comprehensive information-sharing program among ERISA agencies, including development of a common or coordinated data base, data use, and publications. The Council shall develop a program for the use of common facilities and a common information system.

1–204. The Council shall identify inconsistencies in the operation of programs under ERISA. It shall recommend to the

President ways to reduce or eliminate those inconsistencies.

1–205. Where feasible, the Council should coordinate public participation through public hearings on government-wide ERISA-related programs.

1–206. The Council shall establish and maintain a mechanism to evaluate the effectiveness of the overall ERISA program.

1–207. The Council shall submit annually to the President a summary report of significant ERISA-related achievements of the member agencies.

1–3. *Administrative Provisions.*

1–301. The Council shall meet at least once each quarter.

1–302. Each member agency with respect to matters within the jurisdiction of the agency shall cooperate with and assist the Council in performing its functions.

1–303. The Secretary of Labor shall be responsible for providing the Council with such administrative services and support as may be necessary.

1–304. The Council may establish such working groups or subcommittees as may be appropriate for the conduct of the Council's functions.

JIMMY CARTER

The White House,
    January 7, 1981.

[Filed with the Office of the Federal Register,
3:44 p.m., January 7, 1981]

Recommendations for Executive, Legislative, and Judicial Salaries

Message to the Congress Urging Approval of the Recommended Increase.   January 7, 1981

To the Congress of the United States:

If the Federal Government is to meet successfully the enormous challenges it faces in these difficult times, it must be able to attract and retain men and women of outstanding ability and experience for its highest posts.

Monetary awards are not the principal attractions offered by the public service, and complete parity with private sector salaries is neither desirable nor possible. Those who serve at the highest levels of the Federal Government expect and are willing to make some financial sacrifice to serve their country. Nevertheless, compensation levels today have fallen below the point at which they provide adequate monetary recognition of the complexity and importance of top Federal jobs.

The financial sacrifice demanded of top Federal officials is becoming far too great. Since the last quadrennial adjustment in 1977, the salaries of those officials have increased only 5.5 percent. During that same period, the CPI has risen by about 45 percent, which means that the purchasing power of these salaries has declined by about 28 percent.

I fully recognize that the salaries already being paid these officials look very large to the average taxpayer. But when we are seeking to fill an Assistant Secretary position, a Bureau Chief position, or one of the other top level policymaking positions in the Executive Branch, we want people who know the specialized field involved and who have had extensive experience and success in it. Usually, these people are already being highly paid, and there is a limit to the financial sacrifices they can afford to make.

Not only is the discrepancy between private sector executive pay large now; it is continuing to widen. Since 1977, for example, while Federal executive pay has risen only 5.5 percent, private sector executive pay has gone up about 25 percent. If this gap continues to widen, government service will be so unattractive that increasing numbers of the best qualified will refuse to serve.

These observations apply equally to the selection of judges. The Federal judiciary has traditionally drawn a substantial number of appointees from the top echelons of the legal profession. These individuals are mature, experienced, and often at the height of their career earnings. When they become judges, it is usually at a financial sacrifice. If the sacrifice we ask becomes too great, increasing numbers of those best qualified will refuse consideration for appointment. The Attorney General tells me we are already receiving many declinations from lawyers of the quality we desire. We must not allow that trend to accelerate.

In addition to the recruiting problem, there are important considerations of retention and of equity. Resignations from the Federal bench show a disturbing tendency: only seven Federal judges resigned in the 1950's, and eight in the 1960's; but 24 resigned in the 1970's. Three resigned in 1980 alone.

The Constitution wisely provided that Federal judges would be appointed for life. The founders believed, and experience has confirmed, that lifetime service enhance the integrity and independence of a judge's performance. It also strengthens public confidence that judges possess these qualities, and increases public respect for their decisions. When lifetime judges leave the bench because of inadequate salaries, the public loses more than their experience and efficiency. The public also loses the confidence in the judicial process that is central to the success of our Constitutional system.

Obviously, many judges will not leave the bench even for the much larger salaries they could earn by returning to private practice. But the devotion of these judges should not be rewarded by unfair treatment. Something must be done to encourage and reward continuous judicial service.

Turning now to career executives, you know that Executive Levels IV and V are by law the ceiling for career salaries. You know also that General Schedule salaries have risen by 31.9 percent over the period in which executive salaries rose by only 5.5 percent. As a result, more and more GS employees each year reach the executive pay ceiling.

Consequently, we now have a salary system in which up to seven levels of career executives and managers are all receiving the same pay. Career executives who are promoted to more responsible and demanding positions often receive no pay increase whatsoever to compensate them for taking on heavier responsibilities. Agencies with field organizations, which need to advance successful managers from district offices to regional offices to headquarters offices, find it increasingly difficult to persuade capable employees to move their families for "promotions" that carry no pay increase.

One result of this compression is that many experienced and valuable career executives are retiring as quickly as they become eligible for retirement. For the twelve month period ending last March, a startling 75 percent of career executives in the 55–59 age bracket who were at the executive pay ceiling and were eligible to retire, did so. The result is that talented, experienced and creative public servants are leaving when they are of maximum value to their agencies. Unless these trends are reversed, the nation cannot expect to retain a high quality senior career group.

Congress shares many of these salary problems. We all know that people do not run for office because of the salaries involved, and that many people would run for Congress even if the members drew no pay at all. But it is of vital importance to have Congressional salaries high enough to attract a broad range of people, including those who want their families to enjoy the same standard of living they would if they were carrying even moderately comparable responsibilities in other occupations.

Congressional salaries have experienced the same loss of purchasing power as those already discussed. Yet, Congressmen face even greater expense than the other groups because they must maintain two residences and have other expenses stemming from their unique responsibilities. So they, too, need pay increases.

As the law provides, a Commission on Executive, Legislative and Judicial Salaries has considered these and related salary issues. This Commission, which was composed of distinguished private citizens with no selfish interests in Federal pay scales, made the findings I have summarized above. To correct them, it has unanimously recommended salary increases averaging about 40 percent.

I have no doubt that the facts fully justify those recommendations. Nevertheless, I continue to be concerned that we balance compensation needs against Federal Government leadership in fighting inflation and in minimizing the overall costs of government. Consequently, I am recommending to you in my budget for FY 1982 that smaller increases be allowed at this time, but—just as importantly—that we commit ourselves to allowing future increases annually to prevent these salary problems from continuing to worsen.

As you know, General Schedule employees received increases in FY 1979 and FY 1980 that totaled 16.8 percent. By operation of PL 94–82, the legal salaries of top level officials also increased by these same amounts. Congress, with my concurrence, enacted appropriation language

that temporarily prohibited the *payment* of those increases to the top officials. Consequently, their payable salaries are now 16.8 percent below their legal salaries. Several judges sued over the application of that appropriation limitation to the judiciary and recently won a Supreme Court decision that means many judges will receive the 16.8 percent in question.

I believe the least we can do at this point is to give the Executive and Legislative branch officials the 16.8 percent already received by most General Schedule employees and already won by the judges. Just as important as the immediate increase, however, is adoption of the principle that we will allow whatever increase is granted General Schedule employees in October of 1981 and in subsequent years to be paid also to the top level officials, as PL 94–82 provides. Only by following this principle can we prevent the salary muddle from becoming worse every year. Experience has shown that if we wait four years to make salary adjustments in a time of rapid inflation, the needed catch-up will be so large as to be unacceptable to our citizens.

Because the case for a significant increase in the salaries of Federal judges is especially strong, I urge also that Congress give consideration to a salary scale for judges that would explicitly recognize the public importance of continuous judicial service; for example, by an annual or periodic increase for longevity in addition to the cost of living adjustments that are made from time to time.

In addition, I urge that Congress give careful consideration to the five non-salary recommendations made by the Commission, especially their proposal for a special two year study of the complex and harmful compensation problems that now exist.

The Commission concluded that the conditions I have outlined constitute ". . .

a quiet crisis, unperceived by most citizens of the nation but requiring an immediate response by the President and the Congress to safeguard the high quality of its senior officials." I agree with that conclusion and urge you to act favorably upon my recommendations. President-elect Reagan has authorized me to say that he fully supports these recommendations.

PL 95–19 provides that each House must within 60 days conduct a separate recorded vote on my recommendations for each branch of government. In addition, if you wish to accept my recommendation to make the current legal rates payable now, you should amend section 101(c) of P.L. 96–536 accordingly.

In the event that you decide you do not wish to approve increases for your own Members, I strongly urge that you allow them for officials of the Executive and Judicial branches. The gravity of the "quiet crisis" those branches face requires you to do no less.

JIMMY CARTER

The White House,
    January 7, 1981.

American Hostages in Iran
Informal Exchange With Reporters.
January 8, 1981

Q. Mr. President, is there a better chance now that the hostages may be released before you leave office? Are things looking up?

THE PRESIDENT. I don't want to raise any unwarranted expectations, Helen [Helen Thomas, United Press International]. Every time we've had a favorable response from the Iranians, later on we've been disappointed.

I sent the Deputy Secretary of State over to Algeria last night to make our own positions clear. I believe it's a proposal that would be acceptable to the American people as fair and also to the Iranians as being fair.

I hope that we can resolve it before I go out of office, but I can't predict that that will happen.

Q. Do you suspect this is your last opportunity, Mr. President, to solve this problem?

THE PRESIDENT. Well, obviously the time is getting close, but we'll continue to do our best until the last moment I'm in office. I hope we can be successful, but I can't predict that.

Q. Thank you.

THE PRESIDENT. Thank you.

NOTE: The exchange began at 9:05 a.m. on the South Lawn of the White House.

Following the remarks, the President left the White House for a trip to Plains, Ga.

Plains, Georgia
Informal Exchange With Reporters on Arrival. January 8, 1981

Q. Mr. President, will you expect to be hearing from Secretary Christopher during your stay here?

THE PRESIDENT. Yes.

Q. What are your expectations for his mission?

THE PRESIDENT. Well, Secretary Christopher always carries out his missions successfully, but what the response will be we don't know. He'll certainly do what I've assigned him to do. As a matter of fact, I've already got one report from him this morning on the plane coming back. But we don't know what the Iranian reaction is.

As I said earlier, I think the proposals that have been exchanged through the Algerians are reasonable and a foundation for resolving the differences between us, but I can't predict success. I think that would be a mistake.

Q. You haven't gotten any response yet from Iran?

THE PRESIDENT. No.

Q. Do you cling to hope?

THE PRESIDENT. I always do that.

Q. That's it. Thank you.

THE PRESIDENT. I appreciated your invitation to come to your house, although I just got it last night. Jody and Susan told me about it. I wish we—if we'd known earlier, we could have possibly——

Q. We had a small group of the old regulars.

THE PRESIDENT. I read your series, too. That's pretty accurate.

Q. Have a good day.

THE PRESIDENT. Thank you.

NOTE: The exchange began at 11:10 a.m. on a baseball field near the town.

Contribution to Tin Buffer Stock

Executive Order 12263. January 8, 1981

STRATEGIC AND CRITICAL MATERIALS TRANSACTION AUTHORITY

By the authority vested in me as President by the Constitution and the Statutes of the United States of America, including the Strategic and Critical Materials Transaction Authorization Act of 1979 (93 Stat. 1289; Public Law 96–175) (hereinafter referred to as "the Act") and Section 301 of Title 3 of the United States Code, and in order to provide for the contribution of tin to the Tin Buffer Stock established under the Fifth International Tin Agreement, the functions vested in the President by Section 5 of the Act are hereby delegated to the United States Trade Representative.

JIMMY CARTER

The White House,
January 8, 1981.

[Filed with the Office of the Federal Register, 11:42 a.m., January 8, 1981]

Natural Gas Pipeline Safety

Message to the Congress Transmitting a Report. January 8, 1981

To the Congress of the United States:

I hereby transmit to Congress the 11th Annual Report of the Natural Gas Pipeline Safety Act of 1968, covering pipeline activities for the calendar year of 1978. This report is submitted in accordance with section 14 of the Act.

Included in this report are two other elements concerning pipeline safety: the annual report on the administration of the Mineral Leasing Act of 1920, submitted in accordance with subsection 28 (w) (4) of this Act; and a report on liquid pipeline safety programs.

This report details the Department of Transportation's responsibility and progress in regulating safe pipeline transport of natural and other gases on Federal lands.

JIMMY CARTER

The White House,
January 8, 1981.

NOTE: The report is entitled "Annual Report on Pipeline Safety" (Government Printing Office).

Pipeline Safety

Message to the Congress Transmitting a Report. January 8, 1981

To the Congress of the United States:

I hereby transmit to Congress the Department of Transportation's annual report on pipeline safety. The submitted report covers pipeline safety and related activities for the calendar year of 1979. This combined report is prepared as required by section 213(c) of the Hazardous Liquid Pipeline Safety Act of 1979.

This report is the Department's First Annual Combined Report on Pipeline

Safety for 1979. The combined reports are: the 12th Annual Report of the Natural Gas Pipeline Safety Act of 1968 as amended, submitted in accordance with section 16 of the Act; and the First Annual Report of the Hazardous Liquid Pipeline Safety Act of 1979 in accordance with section 213(a) of this Act.

JIMMY CARTER

The White House,
  January 8, 1981.

NOTE: The report is entitled "Annual Report on Pipeline Safety, Calendar Year 1979" (Government Printing Office).

Nominations to Government Positions

Announcement of the Nominations.
January 8, 1981

The President today announced that he has nominated all the persons who received recess appointments during the last recess. They are:

REUBEN W. ASKANASE and MELBA BEALS, to be members of the Board of Directors of the Corporation for Public Broadcasting;

JOSEPH S. BRACEWELL, to be President of the Solar Energy and Energy Conservation Bank;

LYNN R. COLEMAN, to be Deputy Secretary of Energy;

JOHN CONNELL, DOROTHY GRAHAM-WHEELER, and ALBERT T. KLYBERG, to be members of the National Museum Services Board;

RALPH W. EMERSON, to be a member of the Foreign Claims Settlement Commission of the United States;

THOMAS W. FREDERICKS, to be an Assistant Secretary of the Interior;

LAIRD F. HARRIS and HAROLD L. THOMAS, to be Assistant Directors of the Community Services Administration;

WALTER M. HEEN, to be U.S. district judge for the District of Hawaii;

WALLACE N. HYDE, to be a Governor of the United States Postal Service;

ALICE COIG MCDONALD, to be a member of the National Council on Educational Research;

ALEX P. MERCURE, to be Under Secretary of Agriculture for Small Community and Rural Development;

JOHN C. SAWHILL, to be Chairman, and CATHERINE CLEARY, JOHN D. DEBUTTS, LANE KIRKLAND, and FRANK SAVAGE, to be members of the U.S. Synthetic Fuels Corporation;

VERNON W. THOMSON, to be a member of the Federal Election Commission;

JOHN C. TRUESDALE, to be a member of the National Labor Relations Board.

The President also announced that he has renominated four persons who were nominated in the last session of Congress, but not confirmed. They are:

THOMAS R. DONAHUE, to be a member of the Board of Directors of the Communications Satellite Corporation;

JOHN A. GRONOUSKI, to be a member of the Board for International Broadcasting;

DOROTHY SELLERS and RICARDO M. URBINA, to be associate judges of the Superior Court of the District of Columbia.

Commission on Wartime Relocation and Internment of Civilians

Appointment of Three Members.
January 8, 1981

The President today announced the appointment of three persons as members of the Commission on Wartime Relocation and Internment of Civilians. This Commission was established by Congress last year to review the facts and circumstances surrounding the internment of Asian and Aleut civilians during World War II. The three persons appointed are:

JOAN Z. BERNSTEIN, of Chevy Chase, Md., General Counsel of the Department of Health and Human Services, formerly General Counsel of the Environmental Protection Agency.

WILLIAM M. MARUTANI, of Philadelphia, Pa., judge of the Court of Common Pleas for the First Judicial District, active in the Japanese American Citizens League and a member of the American Civil Liberties Union's Advisory Committee on Minorities. As a teenager in 1942, he spent more than 6 months in internment camps in California.

ARTHUR S. FLEMMING, of Arlington, Va., Chairman of the U.S. Commission on Civil Rights and former Secretary of Health, Education, and Welfare.

John F. Kennedy Center for the Performing Arts

Appointment of Six Members of the Board of Trustees.   January 8, 1981

The President today announced the appointment of six persons as members of the Board of Trustees of the John F. Kennedy Center for the Performing Arts. They are:

RICHMOND CRINKLEY, of New York City, a producer of Broadway plays, including "The Elephant Man" and "Sweet Bird of Youth," who was formerly assistant to the Chairman of the Kennedy Center;

JUNE OPPEN DEGNAN, of San Francisco, publisher of San Francisco Review, who is active in civic affairs and the arts;

GERALD M. RAFSHOON, of Washington, D.C., president of Rafshoon Communications;

ANNETTE STRAUSS, of Dallas, Tex., vice president for public affairs and community relations of the public relations division of Bozell & Jacobs, who is very active in civic affairs and support of the arts;

HENRY STRONG, of Washington, D.C., chairman of the board and president of the Hattie M. Strong Foundation and former Vice Chairman of the Board of the Kennedy Center (reappointment);

LEW R. WASSERMAN, of Beverly Hills, Calif., chairman of the board and chief executive officer of Music Corp. of America, Inc., who was a member of the Kennedy Center Board from 1968 to 1978.

Superior Court of the District of Columbia

Nomination of Dorothy Sellers and Ricardo M. Urbina To Be Associate Judges. January 9, 1981

The President has nominated Dorothy Sellers and Ricardo M. Urbina to two vacancies on the District of Columbia Superior Court. The President originally nominated Sellers and Urbina to these positions on September 17, 1980, but the Senate failed to act on their nominations before the 96th Congress ended.

The statute governing selection of District of Columbia judges requires the President to submit nominations within 60 days after receiving recommendations from the District of Columbia Nomination Commission, but the statute is ambiguous on how this period is to be calculated. Since 55 of the 60 days had expired when the President sent up the now-expired nominations, it was necessary for the President to act within the first 5 days of the 97th Congress to ensure that there would be no legal question concerning the timeliness of the Presidential action.

Sellers has been a partner in the firm of Melrod, Redman, Gartlan since 1977. She was born May 7, 1943, in St. Louis, Mo. She received a B.A. from Stanford University in 1965 and a J.D. from George Washington Law School in 1969.

Urbina has been a professor at Howard University Law School since 1974. He was born January 31, 1946, in New York City. He received a B.A. from Georgetown University in 1967 and a J.D. from Georgetown University Law Center in 1970.

Digest of Other White House Announcements

The following listing includes the President's public schedule and other items of general interest announced by the White House Press Office and not included elsewhere in this issue.

January 5

The President met at the White House with:

—Zbigniew Brzezinski, Assistant to the President for National Security Affairs;
—Frank B. Moore, Assistant to the President for Congressional Liaison.

The President announced the recess appointment of Alice Coig McDonald as a member of the National Council on Educational Research. McDonald was nominated for this position last November, but was not confirmed before the Senate adjourned.

January 6

The President met at the White House with:

—Dr. Brzezinski;
—Mr. Moore;
—Charles T. Manatt, finance chairman of the Democratic National Committee;
—a group of black leaders.

January 7

The President met at the White House with:

—Dr. Brzezinski;
—the congressional delegation from Georgia;
—Stephen R. Aiello, Special Assistant to the President for Ethnic Affairs;
—Mr. Moore;
—the Democratic National Committee Finance Council.

The President attended a White House dinner for Democratic Governors and mayors on the State Floor.

The President transmitted to the Congress a statement by the Director of the Bureau of the Census showing the population of each State and the District of Columbia as ascertained by the 20th Decennial Census and the number of Representatives to which each State would be entitled under reapportionment.

The President transmitted to the Congress the 1979 annual report on the Administration of the Federal Railroad Safety Act of 1970.

January 8

The President met at the White House with Dr. Brzezinski.

The President transmitted to the Congress the ninth annual report on Hazardous Materials Transportation.

In the morning, the President left the White House for a visit to Plains, Ga.

NOMINATIONS SUBMITTED TO THE SENATE

The following list does not include promotions of members of the Uniformed Services, nominations to the Service Academies, or nominations of Foreign Service officers.

Submitted January 8, 1981

DOROTHY SELLERS, of the District of Columbia, to be an Associate Judge of the Superior Court of the District of Columbia for a term of 15 years, vice Edmond T. Daly, deceased.

RICARDO M. URBINA, of the District of Columbia, to be an Associate Judge of the Superior Court of the District of Columbia for a term of 15 years, vice Normalie Holloway Johnson, elevated.

JOHN A. GRONOUSKI, of Texas, to be a member of the Board for International Broadcasting for a term expiring April 28, 1983 (reappointment).

NOMINATIONS—Continued

Submitted January 8—Continued

THOMAS R. DONAHUE, of the District of Columbia, to be a member of the Board of Directors of the Communications Satellite Corporation until the date of the annual meeting of the Corporation in 1981, vice George Meany.

LYNN R. COLEMAN, of the District of Columbia, to be Deputy Secretary of Energy, vice John C. Sawhill, resigned, to which office he was appointed during the last recess of the Senate.

WALTER MEHEULA HEEN, of Hawaii, to be United States District Judge for the District of Hawaii, vice Dick Yin Wong, deceased, to which office he was appointed during the last recess of the Senate.

RALPH W. EMERSON, of the District of Columbia, to be a member of the Foreign Claims Settlement Commission of the United States for the term expiring September 30, 1981 (new position—P.L. 96–209), to which office he was appointed during the last recess of the Senate.

THOMAS W. FREDERICKS, of Colorado, to be an Assistant Secretary of the Interior, vice Forrest J. Gerard, resigned, to which office he was appointed during the last recess of the Senate.

ALEX P. MERCURE, of New Mexico, to be Under Secretary of Agriculture for Small Community and Rural Development (new position), to which office he was appointed during the last recess of the Senate.

JOSEPH S. BRACEWELL, of Texas, to be President of the Solar Energy and Energy Conservation Bank (new position), to which office he was appointed during the last recess of the Senate.

The following-named persons to be Assistant Directors of the Community Services Administration, to which offices they were appointed during the last recess of the Senate:

LAIRD F. HARRIS, of Michigan, vice Frank Jones, resigned.

HAROLD LAFAYETTE THOMAS, of the District of Columbia, vice John B. Gabusi, resigned.

The following-named persons to be members of the Board of Directors of the Corporation for Public Broadcasting for terms expiring

NOMINATIONS—Continued

Submitted January 8—Continued

March 26, 1986, to which offices they were appointed during the last recess of the Senate:

REUBEN W. ASKANASE, of Texas, vice Donald E. Santarelli, term expired.

MELBA PATTILLO BEALS, of California, vice Lucius Perry Gregg, Jr., term expired.

VERNON W. THOMSON, of Virginia, to be a member of the Federal Election Commission for the remainder of the term expiring April 30, 1983, vice Max L. Friedersdorf, resigned, to which office he was appointed during the last recess of the Senate.

ALICE COIG MCDONALD, of Kentucky, to be a member of the National Council on Educational Research for a term expiring September 30, 1982, vice John Corbally, term expired, to which office she was appointed during the last recess of the Senate.

JOHN C. TRUESDALE, of Maryland, to be a member of the National Labor Relations Board for the term of 5 years expiring August 27, 1985 (reappointment), to which office he was appointed during the last recess of the Senate.

The following-named persons to be members of the National Museum Services Board for terms expiring December 6, 1985, to which offices they were appointed during the last recess of the Senate:

JOHN CONNELL, of California, vice Gary K. Clarke, term expired.

DOROTHY GRAHAM-WHEELER, of North Carolina, vice George Horse Capture, term expired.

ALBERT T. KLYBERG, of Rhode Island, vice Charlotte Ferst, term expired.

WALLACE NATHANIEL HYDE, of North Carolina, to be a Governor of the United States Postal Service for the term expiring December 8, 1989, vice M. A. Wright, term expired, to which office he was appointed during the last recess of the Senate.

JOHN C. SAWHILL, of the District of Columbia, to be Chairman of the Board of Directors of the United States Synthetic Fuels Corporation for a term of 7 years (new position), to which office he was appointed during the last recess of the Senate.

NOMINATIONS—Continued

Submitted January 8—Continued

The following-named persons to be members of the Board of Directors of the United States Synthetic Fuels Corporation for the terms indicated, to which positions they were appointed during the last recess of the Senate:

JOHN D. DeBUTTS, of Virginia, for a term of 1 year (new position).

CATHERINE BLANCHARD CLEARY, of Wisconsin, for a term of 2 years (new position).

FRANK SAVAGE, of New York, for a term of 3 years (new position).

JOSEPH LANE KIRKLAND, of the District of Columbia, for a term of 5 years (new position).

CHECKLIST OF WHITE HOUSE PRESS RELEASES

The following listing contains releases of the White House Press Office which are not included in this issue.

Released January 7, 1981

Announcement: the President's recommendations for an increase in executive, legislative, and judicial salaries

---

ACTS APPROVED BY THE PRESIDENT

NOTE: No acts approved by the President were received by the Office of the Federal Register during the period covered by this issue.

American Hostages in Iran

Informal Exchange With Reporters.
January 12, 1981

Q. Good news from Iran today, right?

THE PRESIDENT. It looks better, but I can't predict success.

Q. Well, but are you going to be able to sign an international agreement that will satisfy them before the 20th?

THE PRESIDENT. That depends on them. We've made them a reasonable proposition.

Q. Have you heard from Warren Christopher today?

THE PRESIDENT. Yes.

NOTE: The exchange began at approximately 12:30 p.m. outside the restaurant Lion d'Or, where the President and Mrs. Carter had lunch.

National Institute of Justice Advisory Board

Appointment of Three Members.
January 12, 1981

The President today announced the appointment of three persons as members of the National Institute of Justice Advisory Board. They are:

RICHARD ARRINGTON, JR., mayor of Birmingham, Ala., former executive director of the Alabama Center for Higher Education;

ALEXANDER GREEN, of Houston, Tex., a judge of the Justice of the Peace Court and instructor of law at Thurgood Marshall School of Law;

RICHARD MORENO, of San Antonio, Tex., chief probation officer with the Bexar County Juvenile Probation Department, a member of the criminal justice planning committee of the Alamo Area Council of Governments.

President's Awards for Energy Efficiency

Remarks at the Awards Ceremony.
January 12, 1981

During the last 4 years, I've had a chance to learn a lot about the history of this country from the perspective of the White House and the 38 other people who've served there as President before I came into office. And the overwhelming sense that I have is one of the strength of our Nation—how we have been able to meet challenges from one generation to another that seem to be almost insurmountable, but to do it with success.

In the late 18th century, of course, the major challenge was the threat to our own political freedom. And the founders of this country met that challenge with exciting expressions of commitment to the worth of a human being and to the right of the people on this continent to make our own decisions. It's a great and beneficial thing for us all. As you well know, during the 19th century the major thrust was to open up new frontiers of this Nation and to do it with the excitment of exploration and achievement, but with the constant realization that mistakes made during that exciting time could very well have transformed our system of government or challenged our system of government and caused deterioration in those human freedoms that were so precious to us all. But we weathered that challenge successfully, and we laid the foundation for the early 20th century when, with the industrial revolution as an integral part of the process and the challenge of having met successfully two World Wars, our Nation arrived at its proper status, in my judgment, as a world power.

Now we face in this generation another challenge—a little more subtle, just as significant. And that is the challenge of how to preserve those things that are precious to us in a human way and at the same time to acknowledge limits on the natural resources which we have inherited and which sometimes we've not husbanded so well. It's a new thing for Americans to acknowledge limits. And in energy in particular, we've had to do it struggling against admitting that we had to conserve, that we had to save, that we couldn't any longer waste, and that we had to address this challenge along with, not superior to, the other nations on Earth.

In the last few years, we've had notable success in helping to enhance the production of additional, new, exciting energy sources in our own Nation—some not new but very precious—at the same time to eliminate some element of waste from our lives. In our homes and agriculture, in business and transportation, you have played a key role. And as President of our great Nation, even following a brief historical resumé, I'd like to express my personal thanks to you. You've proven not only that we can reduce our dependence on foreign oil supplies that rob us

financially, rob us of jobs, also endanger our own national security, but that we can do it without any deterioration in the quality of our lives.

It's not necessary for us to live a blighted life or a restricted life. In the process that you've helped to initiate, more than 150 organizations—local government, business enterprises, labor organizations, farmers—you've proven that this can be done in an exciting way, a dynamic way, a way that taps the great reserves of our country, of innovation, personal liberty, good education, natural resources, and let it be an achievement equal to, in my judgment, the exploration of our new frontiers during the last century past. So, I'm indebted to you.

In 1980 alone we reduced our oil imports by more than 20 percent, and I think in the future we'll continue that progress. And I think as different Americans see that this is a challenge worthy of a great nation and that the other nations on Earth are looking to us for leadership, as they have in the past, then there will be more of an involvement of the 226 million or so of us in this worthwhile effort. You are leaders who helped as pioneers to show the way, and as President I come over here to express my debt to you and my gratitude as well.

Some of the key executives in my own administration will, after I leave, present to you awards that will honor your organizations or your corporations or perhaps you personally or your government entity for the good work you've done for our country. You are patriots in the highest and best sense of that word, and as President I express gratification at being your partners in a noble effort and my admiration and thanks for what you've already achieved for the betterment of our Nation now and in the future.

Thank you again. God bless you all. Congratulations.

NOTE: The President spoke at 1:36 p.m. in Room 450 of the Old Executive Office Building.

Following the President's remarks, Secretary of Energy Charles W. Duncan, Jr., Deputy Secretary of Transportation William J. Beckham, Jr., Under Secretary of Housing and Urban Development Victor Marrero, and Secretary of Agriculture Bob Bergland participated in the presentation of the awards to 128 recipients.

On the same day the White House released a fact sheet on the awards program. Included in the release is a list of the recipients.

Emergency Building Temperature Restrictions

Message to the Congress Transmitting Proclamation 4813. January 13, 1981

To the Congress of the United States:

On July 10, 1979, I issued a Proclamation pursuant to the Energy Policy and Conservation Act of 1975 by which I implemented Standby Energy Conservation Contingency Plan No. 2 and imposed emergency building temperature restrictions, effective July 16, 1979. On April 15, 1980, I issued a Proclamation which continued those emergency building temperature restrictions until January 16, 1981.

I have now issued the attached Proclamation which renews the required statutory findings and continues the Plan in effect until October 16, 1981, unless sooner rescinded.

JIMMY CARTER

The White House,
   January 13, 1981.

Emergency Building Temperature Restrictions

Proclamation 4813. January 13, 1981

SECOND CONTINUATION OF EMERGENCY BUILDING TEMPERATURE RESTRICTIONS

By the President of the United States of America

A Proclamation

I find that continued implementation of the Emergency Building Temperature Restrictions, Energy Conservation Plan No. 2, is required in the national interest. This Plan was transmitted by me to the Congress on March 1, 1979, and approved by resolution of each House of Congress in the manner provided by law.

This Conservation Plan was implemented by me approximately eighteen months ago because it was clear in view of the unstable world production of crude oil that we could not rely on imports to meet our normal demand. On April 15, 1980, I continued this Plan in effect because of the decline in worldwide crude oil production compared to the previous year, the prohibition on imports of Iranian oil, and the threat to the stability of commerce in the countries of the oil-producing Persian Gulf resulting from tensions between Iran and Iraq and the Soviet Union's actions in Afghanistan.

Since then, war has broken out between Iran and Iraq, substantially interrupting crude oil production in those countries. This disruption is of significant scope and is likely to be of substantial duration. New worldwide crude oil production is now and is likely to continue to be at least two million barrels a day less than consumption through the first quarter of 1981. This shortage has resulted in increased petroleum prices, and the combined effects of the shortage and present and future price increases resulting from it may have a major adverse impact on the national economy. The war between Iran and Iraq, as well as border tensions between Syria and Jordan and the Soviet actions in Afghanistan, have also greatly increased the threat to other sources of petroleum supplies in the Middle East. Should other disruptions result, they are likely to be of an emergency nature and to further disrupt the Nation's economy.

Because of these events, the risk to the Nation from our reliance on insecure oil imports is greater than when the Plan was renewed approximately nine months ago, as well as when the Plan was implemented approximately eighteen months ago. Under applicable law, the findings that a shortage of energy supply requires implementation of the Plan must be considered anew every nine months. I therefore renew the findings and determination contained in Proclamation No. 4667 of July 10, 1979, and renewed in Proclamation No. 4750 of April 15, 1980, under sections 201(b) and 3(8) of the Energy Policy and Conservation Act (42 U.S.C. Sections 6261(b) and 6202(8)).

Now, THEREFORE, I, JIMMY CARTER, President of the United States of America, by the authority vested in me by the Constitution and laws of the United States, including section 201(b) of the Energy Policy and Conservation Act (42 U.S.C. 6261(b)), do hereby proclaim that:

1–101. The finding and determination under sections 3(8) and 201(b) of the Energy Policy and Conservation Act (42 U.S.C. 6202(8) and 6261(b)) contained in Proclamation No. 4667 of July 10, 1979, and renewed in Proclamation No. 4750 of April 15, 1980, are hereby renewed.

1–102. This Proclamation shall be transmitted to the Congress.

1–103. The provisions of the Emergency Building Temperature Restrictions, Energy Conservation Contingency Plan No. 2 (44 FR 12911 of March 8, 1979) and the regulations thereunder, or any amendments thereto, shall continue in effect until October 16, 1981, unless earlier rescinded.

1–104. In accordance with the provisions of this Plan and the regulations thereunder, the Secretary of Energy is hereby authorized to continue the administration of the program in all respects.

IN WITNESS WHEREOF, I have hereunto set my hand this thirteenth day of January, in the year of our Lord nineteen hundred and eighty-one, and of the Independence of the United States of America the two hundred and fifth.

JIMMY CARTER

[Filed with the Office of the Federal Register, 3:37 p.m., January 13, 1981]

United States-Colombia Agreement on Nuclear Energy

Message to the Congress Transmitting the Agreement. January 13, 1981

To the Congress of the United States:

I am pleased to transmit to the Congress, pursuant to Section 123(d) of the Atomic Energy Act of 1954, as amended, the text of the proposed Agreement for Cooperation Between the Government of the United States of America and the Government of the Republic of Colombia Concerning Civil Uses of Nuclear Energy and accompanying exchange of notes; my written approval, authorization and determination concerning the agreement; and the memorandum of the Director of the Arms Control and Disarmament

Agency with the Nuclear Proliferation Assessment Statement concerning the agreement. The joint memorandum submitted to me by the Secretaries of State and Energy, which includes a summary analysis of the provisions of the agreement, and the views and recommendations of the Members of the Nuclear Regulatory Commission and the Director of the Arms Control and Disarmament Agency are also enclosed.

The Nuclear Non-Proliferation Act of March 10, 1978 sets forth certain requirements for new or amended peaceful nuclear cooperation agreements with other countries. In my judgment, the proposed agreement for cooperation between the United States and Colombia, together with its accompanying exchange of notes, meets all statutory requirements.

The proposed bilateral agreement between us reflects the desire of the Government of the United States and the Government of Colombia to update the framework for peaceful nuclear cooperation between our two countries in a manner that recognizes both the shared nonproliferation objectives and the close relationship between the United States and Colombia in the peaceful application of nuclear energy. The proposed agreement will, in my view, further the non-proliferation and other foreign policy interests of the United States.

I have considered the views and recommendations of the interested agencies in reviewing the proposed agreement and have determined that its performance will promote, and will not constitute an unreasonable risk to, the common defense and security. Accordingly, I have approved the agreement and authorized its execution, and urge that the Congress give it favorable consideration.

JIMMY CARTER

The White House,
  January 13, 1981.

Refugee Resettlement Grants Program

Letter to the Speaker of the House and the President of the Senate Transmitting a Study. January 13, 1981

Sir:

In accordance with Section 412(b)(1)(B) of the Refugee Act of 1980 (Public Law 96–212), I have determined that the administration of the Reception and Placement Grants, awarded to resettlement agencies for the performance of certain initial services for refugees coming to the United States, should be retained by the Department of State.

The details of this determination are set forth in the enclosed study prepared by the U.S. Coordinator for Refugee Affairs. I concur with his comments and observations.

Respectfully,

JIMMY CARTER

NOTE: This is the text of identical letters addressed to Thomas P. O'Neill, Jr., Speaker of the House of Representatives, and Walter F. Mondale, President of the Senate.

The study is entitled "Organizational Location of Refugee Reception and Placement Grants."

United States Arms Control and Disarmament Agency

Message to the Congress Transmitting a Report. January 13, 1981

To the Congress of the United States:

In transmitting to you the 1980 Annual Report of the United States Arms Control and Disarmament Agency, I must emphasize that in 1980, although efforts to control the arms race have made some progress, they have also suffered a serious setback.

The SALT negotiations, aimed at controlling the strategic nuclear arms competition between the United States and the Soviet Union, have continued through four Administrations. The SALT II Treaty, which I signed in June 1979 with Soviet President Brezhnev, represents a significant step in the direction of such arms control. This treaty was the subject of intense national debate and of hearings by three committees of the Senate. However, the Soviet invasion of Afghanistan in December 1979 made it necessary for me to ask the Senate to delay consideration of the SALT II Treaty on the floor, although, as I informed the Congress, I intended to take up the treaty again after dealing with more urgent matters.

The subsequent Presidential campaign and election have had the effect of referring to the incoming Administration and Congress the question of what action to take with respect to the SALT II Treaty. The fact that this treaty has not been ratified raises serious issues concerning our national security and future arms control efforts.

In the period of relative calm that follows an election year, it should be possible to move quickly toward a mutually acceptable SALT II Treaty that will be ratified by the Senate. This is important to our own national security, and it is the strong wish of all our allies. In addition, while some progress has been made in other arms control negotiations—such as those seeking a Comprehensive Nuclear Test Ban Treaty, a treaty banning chemical weapons, and a treaty to achieve Mutual and Balanced Force Reductions in Europe—success in these efforts is probably dependent upon resolving the issue of SALT II. Similarly, the success of our continuing efforts to prevent the proliferation of nuclear weapons in other countries is directly related to what the major

nuclear powers do in controlling their own nuclear arsenals.

There are many serious problems in this world, but I continue to believe, as I stated in submitting the first annual arms control report of this Administration, that "The challenge of preventing war—and redirecting resources from arsenals of war to human needs—is the greatest challenge confronting mankind in this last quarter of the 20th century." We have made progress, but much remains to be done. The future depends on our success.

JIMMY CARTER

The White House,
January 13, 1981.

NOTE: The report is entitled "Twentieth Annual Report—U.S. Arms Control and Disarmament Agency" (Government Printing Office).

Highway Safety and National Traffic and Motor Vehicle Safety Acts of 1966

Message to the Congress Transmitting Two Reports. January 13, 1981

To the Congress of the United States:

The Highway Safety Act and the National Traffic and Motor Vehicle Safety Act, both enacted in 1966, initiated a cohesive national effort to reduce the deaths and injuries on the Nation's highways and require annual reports on the administration of these acts.

The report on motor vehicle safety includes the annual report required by Title I of the Motor Vehicle Information and Cost Savings Act of 1972 (bumper standards). An annual report is also required by the Energy Policy and Conservation Act of 1975 which amended the Motor Vehicle Information and Cost Savings

Act and directed the Secretary of Transportation to set, adjust and enforce motor vehicle fuel economy standards. Similar reporting requirements are contained in the Department of Energy Act of 1978 with respect to the use of advanced technology by the automobile industry. These requirements have been met in the Fourth Annual Fuel Economy Report, the highlights of which are summarized in the motor vehicle safety report.

In the Highway Safety Acts of 1973, 1976 and 1978, the Congress expressed its special interest in certain aspects of traffic safety which are addressed in the volume on highway safety.

The combination of motor vehicle and highway safety standards, enforcement, and research have reduced the fatality rate by about 39 percent. This reduction has been achieved in spite of tremendous increases in traffic volume—registered motor vehicles up 67 percent, licensed drivers up 42 percent, vehicle miles driven up 64 percent.

Even so, 51,083 people met violent deaths on the highways in 1979—up from 50,331 in 1978. Based on current trends, each person born this year can expect to be involved in a crash every 10 years. One in 60 will be killed, and one in 20 will be seriously injured.

In addition to the persistent problems of drunk driving and speeding, several influences have contributed to the upward trend in fatalities: the increasing nonobservance of the 55 mph speed limit, which in some States is only lightly enforced; the repeal, or weakening, of motorcycle helmet laws; the increasingly widespread use of vans and light trucks, which have not been subject to the majority of Federal motor vehicle safety standards; the fact that the Nation's roads are deteriorating faster than they can be maintained, especially the non-Interstate Systems, where more than 90 percent of all fatal accidents occur; and the shift to smaller, lighter cars.

While small cars made up only 38 percent of the cars on the road in 1979, small car occupants accounted for a disproportionate 55 percent of the deaths that year in two-vehicle crashes. Because of the lower weight of smaller cars, their occupants fare poorly in collisions, particularly in collisions with heavier vehicles. In a crash between a subcompact car and a full-sized model which is severe enough to cause a fatality, the occupants of the small car are eight times more likely to be killed than the occupants of the large car.

As America moves into the small car era, the consequences of ignoring the need for further safety improvements become unacceptable in both human and economic terms. Traffic safety must be given a high priority by Federal, State and municipal Governments, by the automotive industry, by private organizations, and most important of all, by the potential victims of highway accidents—the public.

JIMMY CARTER

The White House,
January 13, 1981.

NOTE: The reports are entitled "Traffic Safety '79: A Report on Activities Under the Highway Safety Act of 1966 as Amended, January 1, 1979–December 31, 1979—U.S. Department of Transportation, National Highway Traffic Safety Administration, Federal Highway Administration" and "Traffic Safety '79: A Report on Activities Under the National Traffic and Motor Vehicle Safety Act of 1966 as Amended and the Motor Vehicle Information and Cost Savings Act of 1972 as Amended and the Energy Policy and Conservation Act of 1975, January 1, 1979–December 31, 1979—U.S. Department of Transportation, National Highway Traffic Safety Administration" (Government Printing Office).

Department of Education

Message to the Congress Transmitting the First Annual Report. January 13, 1981

To the Congress of the United States:

I am pleased to transmit to the Congress the first Annual Report of the Department of Education, as required by Section 426 of Public Law 96–88, the Department of Education Organization Act.

The Report outlines the progress of the Department during Fiscal Year 1980 in the attainment of its goals, priorities, and plans. It also emphasizes this Administration's efforts to provide more responsible and effective Federal support for education.

I believe that we have made substantial progress since the Department of Education opened its doors on May 4, 1980, in providing new leadership and support for American education.

JIMMY CARTER

The White House,
   January 13, 1981.

NOTE: The report is entitled "1980 Annual Report—U.S. Department of Education" (Government Printing Office, 94 pages).

National Advisory Community Investment Board

Appointment of Two Members. January 13, 1981

The President today announced the appointment of two persons as members of the National Advisory Community Investment Board. They are:

JOHN PAUL COMERFORD, of Boston, Mass., acting president of the National Consumer Cooperative Bank;

EDWIN S. CRAWFORD, of Baltimore, Md., who is with an investment banking firm where he directs the cash management advisory service for local government.

Chadha v. Immigration and Naturalization Service

White House Statement on Justice Department Appeal of the Decision to the Supreme Court. January 13, 1981

The Department of Justice will appeal to the United States Supreme Court the recent decision of the United States Court of Appeals for the Ninth Circuit in San Francisco holding unconstitutional a legislative veto device contained in the Immigration and Nationality Act.

In the case of *Chadha* v. *INS*, decided on December 22, 1980, the Circuit Court held unconstitutional a provision authorizing one House of Congress to veto decisions by the Attorney General to stay the deportation of certain aliens. The court held that provision unconstitutional on broad separation of powers grounds and also held that the exercise of such power by one House could not be deemed as legislative in character without encroaching impermissibly on the President's veto power.

The Department of Justice argued against the constitutionality of this legislative veto device in the Ninth Circuit. The Senate and House, through their counsel, argued in support of its constitutionality. The primary reason for appealing the decision to the Supreme Court is to secure a definitive ruling from that Court on an issue which, over the last decade, has created many occasions for confrontation between the executive and legislative branches. The appeal was not filed at the request of either the House or the Senate.

In a statement on December 24, 1980, the President stated that the Ninth Circuit Court ruling sustained the position that he and other Presidents had taken in signing into law otherwise meritorious bills containing a legislative veto provision under which a resolution of one or both Houses can nullify an executive action.

NOTE: The statement by the President is printed on page 2836 of this volume.

Library of Congress Trust Fund Board

Appointment of Milton A. Wolf as a Member. January 13, 1981

The President today announced the appointment of Milton A. Wolf, of Shaker Heights, Ohio, as a member of the Library of Congress Trust Fund Board.

Wolf is president of Zehman-Wolf Construction, Inc., and is a former U.S. Ambassador to Austria.

National Advisory Council on Indian Education

Appointment of Four Members. January 13, 1981

The President today announced the appointment of four persons as members of the National Advisory Council on Indian Education. They are:

BOBBY BIGHORSE, of Oklahoma City, director of the Willard Arts Education Program, chairman of the Native American Center of Oklahoma City, and a member of the National Indian Education Association;

NADINE H. CHASE, of Bena, Minn., administrator of the Leech Lake Reservation Business Committee and chairman of the board of regents of the Community College Board of the Chippewa Tribe;

GREGORY W. FRAZIER, of Denver, Colo., chief executive of the National Urban Indian Council and a director of Indians for United Social Action;

DANNY KEVIN MARSHALL, of Puyallup, Wash., who is completing a B.S. in anthropology at Western Washington University and is active in Indian community and education affairs.

President's Council on Physical Fitness and Sports

Appointment of Milton S. Kronheim as a Member. January 13, 1981

The President today announced the appointment of Milton S. Kronheim, of the District of Columbia, to be a member of the President's Council on Physical Fitness and Sports.

Kronheim was born October 2, 1888, in Washington, D.C. He is chairman of the board of the Milton S. Kronheim & Co., Inc., of Washington and the Kronheim Co., Inc., of Baltimore. Mr. Kronheim has been very active for many years in civic and community affairs and is a sports enthusiast.

White House Dinner Honoring Labor Leaders

Toasts at the Dinner. January 13, 1981

THE PRESIDENT. This is the last night that we'll hear the Strolling Strings in the White House for a long time. I hope that you won't have to wait as long as I do to hear them again. [*Laughter*]

This is the last supper we'll have with a large number of guests, and we're particularly delighted to have this particular group. We've had a lot of Prime Ministers and Shahs and Emperors and Kings and Presidents here, Chancellors. But I believe this is the most presidents we've ever had in one night. [*Laughter*] How many presidents do we have here? Raise your hand.

And I guess all the rest of you intend to be president later on. [*Laughter*]

MR. KIRKLAND.[1] Don't encourage them. [*Laughter*]

THE PRESIDENT. Lane says don't encourage it.

It's always a delight to have our friends here with us. Later on tonight we'll have some delightful entertainment in addition to the Strolling Strings and the Marine Band. The enjoyment that we derive from these is memorable. We will never forget some of the fine experiences we've had here, and, of course, the conversations are always scintillating and very helpful as well.

I was talking a few minutes ago to Terry Herndon.[2] We talked first about Israel and how the teachers in Israel have brought about a prospective change in the government there. [*Laughter*] Terry said that a few years ago he was in Ethiopia, and the head of the teachers organization said that they were the only group in the country that might bring down Emperor Haile Selassie. They later struck. The students supported them. The parents supported the students. The Emperor fell, and the government changed. And then our attention shifted to the Reagan administration. [*Laughter*] That's as far as we got before the Strolling Strings came in. [*Laughter*]

We've got a very fine spokesman in here, and I would like to make a toast in a few minutes. But first I would like to say that I know all of you are outstanding men and women who have spoken loudly and clearly for the best interests of the working people of this Nation—Lane Kirkland and others as well, Doug Fraser[3]—but I would like to ask one particular friend of

mine who's one of the finest spokesmen for the labor movement and for the working people of this Nation that I have ever known just to say a word. Vice President Fritz Mondale.

THE VICE PRESIDENT. Thank you, Mr. President, Rosalynn.

Earlier this evening most of us were at an event at the AFL–CIO national office, where Lane Kirkland and Tom Donahue[4] conferred upon Ray Marshall one of the most moving awards that I've seen in a long, long time. I make that point because as I went around the campaign trail, I often said Ray Marshall is the best Secretary of Labor in the history of that Department. [*Applause*] I always got a good hand, as I did tonight—[*laughter*]—because he is the best Secretary of Labor in the history of the Department. And Ray and Pat have, with good grace and wisdom, stood consistently and courageously for the interests of working people in this country.

The second point I want to make is that I've been in every campaign nationally since 1948. Most of you except Ev Dubrow[5] and myself—[*laughter*]—can't remember most of them. And I was on the Truman train, and I was trained by the very best, Hubert Humphrey. And I don't recall a campaign in all those years in which I saw organized labor—the AFL–CIO, industrial unions, the building trades, the autoworkers, all the teachers—the full spectrum of working men and women more actively engaged in the election, the reelection of a President, than in 1980. And the reason, I'm convinced, is just as we've never had a better Secretary of Labor in American history serving the cause of working men and women. And if I can intervene with one interjection here,

---

[1] Lane Kirkland, president of the AFL–CIO.
[2] President, National Education Association.
[3] President, United Autoworkers of America.

[4] Secretary-treasurer, AFL–CIO.
[5] Vice president and legislative director, International Ladies' Garment Workers Union.

wherever you find independent unions you find freedom, and wherever you cannot find them you will find a dictatorial system, whether in Gdansk or El Salvador.

The reason everyone who believes in working people in this country and their rights and their justice stood for President Carter is because he's the best President of the United States.

THE PRESIDENT. I might say this is the first time I've ever called on the Vice President to join in with me in making a toast. Had I done it more frequently during the last 4 years I might have come out a little better. [*Laughter*]

I want to add my voice to that of Fritz Mondale in praising Ray Marshall. I know you've already honored him this evening, but he's an extraordinary man who has brought to the leadership in the Labor Department a true and personal knowledge of the yearnings and desires, the commitments, the frustrations, the hopes and dreams, the aspirations and the commitments of the working people of our country. He's been a good partner of mine and you, and he and Fritz Mondale and I have faced some very serious problems in this country the last 4 years. There have been very few times when we've had a basic disagreement. There have been even rarer times when we didn't consult with one another to try to face those problems with a common front. And as Fritz Mondale has said, political liberty and a free labor movement in the history of humankind are inseparable.

Our Nation has stood as a bulwark for freedom and as a beacon light for others around the world to emulate. This has been proven many times, vividly, during the last few months in Poland, when a free people there within the labor movement expressed their voices in a courageous way, overcoming years of suppression and have made remarkable progress. The sensitivity of the American labor movement to this movement toward freedom has been notable. You have given them assistance and support in a proper fashion, and our hopes and our prayers are with Mr. Walesa,[6] who left his country for the first time for the free world today, and for those who work with him. And we pray that that country will remain as it presently is at least, free of outside, direct, suppression and that breath of freedom will continue to sweep across the suppressed people of this world.

In the last few days also we recognized heroism from within your ranks directly when a fine young man who gave his life for the oppressed people in El Salvador was buried in our national cemetery here. Ray was there, the Secretary of State was there, Fritz Mondale was there. I wrote Lane Kirkland a letter expressing my admiration for Mike Hammer and wrote his family members as well.

So, your voice has not only been attuned to the special working conditions, salary scales, and voice in management of the working place of your own members, but it's reached throughout the world, indeed, in an admirable and proper fashion. And within our own Nation you always have been a strong voice for alleviating suffering, for enhancing personal freedom, and for helping those who are afflicted, sometimes poor, sometimes without an adequate voice because they don't speak good English, sometimes because they've been deprived of an education, sometimes because they've been the victims of racial or religious discrimination. And that's been an unwavering voice. And my prayer is and my expectation is the next few years that that commitment and that influence will continue.

I would like for all of you to join with me now in a toast to the free people of

---

[6] Lech Walesa, president of Solidarity, the Polish labor union.

our Nation, inspired and assisted and often led by the free labor movement of the greatest nation on Earth: To our country, to you and its people.

Thank you.

MR. KIRKLAND. May I, Mr. President?

THE PRESIDENT. Please.

MR. KIRKLAND. By your leave, Mr. President, on behalf of all of my fellow—[*inaudible*]—that you and Mrs. Carter have been kind enough to invite here tonight, I'd like to say just a few words of appreciation.

The people of the modern world demand a great deal from leadership, and they give them precious little time to meet those demands and to live up to those responsibilities. To me it seems too short a time. We've packed a great deal into it, and in that short time the accomplishments of your administration, I think, have been extraordinary and will endure and will serve the interests of ordinary people for many, many years to come.

It seemed awfully short to me, because just for a few 4 years, I've for the first time in my experience had a President who has absolutely no accent whatever. [*Laughter*] And I'm going to have to get used, I suppose, to those harsh cadences of the Middle West via Beverly Hills. And it will be painful. [*Laughter*]

Among your achievements that I think have been significant in this country's history—one of course, you've broken an old prejudice, an old taboo, that someone from the Deep South could become President of the United States. I think that fact alone will serve the country and serve the national interest and help to build a greater unity among the American people and has gone a long way toward overcoming old and longstanding divisions. But that fact in itself is minor in contrast to what you've demonstrated,

and that is that a person vigorously engaged in political life from the Southern United States is not necessarily a servant of the oligarchy, nor does he necessarily sell his people and his birthright for a fistfull of dollars, for absentee interests, but that a person from the South can, with devotion, serve the interests and advance the welfare of ordinary people, of working people, of the wretched of the Earth in a single-minded way. And that, I think, is the real message of your administration and the real service that you've done to those of us who share your southern heritage.

There has been little time. But in that time you have crammed accomplishments that we are all in the trade union movement very proud to have been a part. You have shared our struggles. You have gone to bat for us when you knew that we were right and, I guess, sometimes when you may have thought we were wrong—which is how we measure friendship. [*Laughter*] We have come to have an enormous respect, an enormous admiration, an enormous affection for yourself and for Mrs. Carter.

And, well, we in our line of work, we're not unaccustomed to taking bloody noses and coming back up fighting. It goes with the territory. And we know that it only hurts for a little while, and you can't be whipped unless you whip yourself. And the people make mistakes in a democracy. The great thing about democracy is that they'll have a chance to correct them. It's not that they're always right. If I believed they were always right, I'd have to believe that I was wrong this time, and I cannot believe that. [*Laughter*] I won't accept that.

I want to add one word to Mrs. Carter, a great lady who has graced this house and done honor to us all as few, if any, First Ladies have ever done before. And I would like to ask you all to join me in a double toast to Mrs. Carter and to the President of the United States.

THE PRESIDENT. Thank you, Lane, very much.

NOTE: The President spoke at 9:47 p.m. in the State Dining Room at the White House.

White House Dinner Honoring Labor Leaders

Remarks Introducing the After-Dinner Entertainment. January 13, 1981

About 35 years ago I went to New York for the first time and saw my first Broadway play. I spent more than half my monthly salary to get in. [*Laughter*] At the time I was a youngster at the Naval Academy in 1945, and I was making $7 a month. But it was money well spent. I never had seen anything like that before, and I was overwhelmed with the beauty of it, the emotion of it. I wept and still get emotional when I hear some of the songs from "Carousel." The performer that night was John Raitt, and, as you know, it was a superb musical achievement that has set records throughout the Nation for beauty and, in many places, for attendance as well.

Later he performed in "Carousel," "Pajama Game," more recently in "Shenandoah," both on the stage and also in motion pictures. He's a performer whose natural talent is obvious as soon as he delights the audience with the music that he provides. But I think if you go down the list of those plays and others in which he has performed, you see that they're a very good cross section of what America is. Nobody could listen to those lyrics and see the performances and remember the sentiments expressed without being filled

with a sense of patriotism, love for our country, appreciation of beauty, and the admiration of superb talent.

This is the last group that we will entertain here during this administration, and I'm very grateful that you are very close friends, all our guests this evening. And because we think so much of you and feel so close to you, we wanted to provide this special program for your entertainment.

And now John Raitt will come and delight us with selections from the plays in which he's performed, when he's delighted hundreds of thousands, even millions of Americans, with his superb talent. I know you join with me in welcoming him to the East Room of the White House to entertain some of our close friends. Thank you.

NOTE: The President spoke at 10:25 p.m. in the East Room at the White House.

National Inventors' Day, 1981

Proclamation 4814. January 14, 1981

By the President of the United States of America

A Proclamation

As the progress of science and technology is fundamental to the economic and social welfare of our society, so is the patent system essential to the advance of science and technology. This relationship is recognized in the first Article of our Constitution, which empowers the Congress "to promote the progress of science and useful arts" by securing for limited times to inventors an exclusive right to their discoveries.

Established in accordance with this constitutional mandate, our patent system dates back to the very beginning of our

Nation. Since George Washington signed the first patent act into law on April 10, 1790, the patent system has encouraged our dramatic progress from a small agrarian Nation to a great technological and industrial world leader. From the cotton gin, telephone, and electric lamp, through the transistor, modern medicines and space vehicles, the history of our creativity, ingenuity and determination is reflected in the records of our patent system.

The incentive offered by patent protection to invent and innovate has created new markets, new industries and more jobs. As a consequence, a strong and reliable patent system is a substantial element in our efforts to develop alternative energy sources, increase our productivity, improve our environment, and solve the technological challenges which will confront us in the future.

In honor of the important role played by inventors in promoting progress in the useful arts, and in recognition of the invaluable contribution of inventors to the welfare of our people, the 96th Congress, by House Joint Resolution 337, has designated February 11, 1981, as "National Inventors' Day." Because February 11 is the birthday of Thomas Alva Edison, this Nation's most prolific inventor, it is an especially appropriate day on which to honor one of our most valuable national resources, the inventive genius of our people.

Now, THEREFORE, I, JIMMY CARTER, President of the United States of America, do hereby call upon the people of the United States to honor all inventors by observing February 11, 1981, as National Inventors' Day, with appropriate ceremonies and activities.

IN WITNESS WHEREOF, I have hereunto set my hand this fourteenth day of January, in the year of our Lord nineteen hundred and eighty-one, and of the Independence of the United States of America the two hundred and fifth.

JIMMY CARTER

[Filed with the Office of the Federal Register, 4:01 p.m., January 14, 1981]

National Salute to Hospitalized Veterans' Day
Proclamation 4815.   January 14, 1981

By the President of the United States of America

A Proclamation

There are today more than 30 million living veterans of the United States Armed Forces whose military service to their Nation has significantly influenced the role of the United States in world affairs.

During Fiscal Year 1979, approximately 1.3 million of these men and women were hospitalized in the 172 Veterans Administration medical centers across the country. A similar number will be admitted for care and treatment this year and in the years to come.

In order to encourage a continuing awareness of the service and sacrifice of these Americans, I urge citizens of all ages to participate in their communities in honoring our sick and disabled hospitalized veterans. I believe it essential that we do as much as possible to express our collective appreciation to the many hospitalized men and women who have served this Nation faithfully.

Now, THEREFORE, I, JIMMY CARTER, President of the United States of America, do hereby proclaim February 14, 1981, as "National Salute to Hospitalized Veterans' Day." I invite all of our citizens to join with me in observing this day with appropriate ceremonies and activities.

IN WITNESS WHEREOF, I have hereunto set my hand this fourteenth day of January, in the year of our Lord nineteen hundred and eighty-one, and of the Independence of the United States of America the two hundred and fifth.

JIMMY CARTER

[Filed with the Office of the Federal Register, 4:02 p.m., January 14, 1981]

Earthquake in Southern Italy

Announcement of the President's Endorsement of an Assistance Program. January 14, 1981

The President has endorsed a program to match American communities with communities in southern Italy ravaged by the recent earthquake. The program, called ADOTTARE (Italian for "adopt") has been created by the National Association of Counties (NACO) and the U.S. Conference of Mayors (USCM). In a letter to Westchester County Executive Alfred Del Bello, who will serve as chairman of ADOTTARE, President Carter congratulated him and Roy Orr and Richard Hatcher, presidents of NACO and USCM respectively, for their "commendable program" and "important humanitarian effort." The President added: "This voluntary effort will be highly complementary to the Federal Government's provision of $50 million in aid which Congressman Mario Biaggi sponsored in the Congress."

Serving on the committee for this program will be John Mulroy, county executive of Onondaga County, N.Y.; William Murphy, county executive of Rensselaer County, N.Y.; Charles Worthington, county executive of Atlantic County, N.J.; Mayor Kenneth Gibson of Newark, N.J.; Mayor Kevin White of Boston, Mass.; and Mayor Louis Tullio of Erie, Pa.

The program will try to create "sister" communities for places in southern Italy which need a wide range of assistance for helping individuals and communities repair the damage from the disaster. Mr. Del Bello and his staff will act as a clearinghouse for any community in the United States wishing to join the program and be matched with a community in Italy. Communities can call Mr. Del Bello's office at (914) 682–3126 for data and advice on how to become involved in this voluntary effort.

Farewell Address to the Nation

Remarks of the President. January 14, 1981

Good evening.

In a few days I will lay down my official responsibilities in this office, to take up once more the only title in our democracy superior to that of President, the title of citizen.

Of Vice President Mondale, my Cabinet, and the hundreds of others who have served with me during the last 4 years, I wish to say now publicly what I have said in private: I thank them for the dedication and competence they've brought to the service of our country. But I owe my deepest thanks to you, to the American people, because you gave me this extraordinary opportunity to serve.

We've faced great challenges together, and we know that future problems will also be difficult. But I'm now more convinced than ever that the United States, better than any other country, can meet successfully whatever the future might bring. These last 4 years have made me more certain than ever of the inner strength of our country, the unchanging value of our principles and ideals, the stability of our political system, the ingenuity and the decency of our people.

Tonight I would like first to say a few words about this most special office, the Presidency of the United States. This is at once the most powerful office in the world and among the most severely constrained by law and custom. The President is given a broad responsibility to lead but cannot do so without the support and consent of the people, expressed formally through the Congress and informally in many ways through a whole range of public and private institutions. This is as it should be.

Within our system of government every American has a right and a duty to help shape the future course of the United States. Thoughtful criticism and close scrutiny of all government officials by the press and the public are an important part of our democratic society. Now, as in the past, only the understanding and involvement of the people through full and open debate can help to avoid serious mistakes and assure the continued dignity and safety of the Nation.

Today we are asking our political system to do things of which the Founding Fathers never dreamed. The government they designed for a few hundred thousand people now serves a nation of almost 230 million people. Their small coastal republic now spans beyond a continent, and we also now have the responsibility to help lead much of the world through difficult times to a secure and prosperous future.

Today, as people have become ever more doubtful of the ability of the Government to deal with our problems, we are increasingly drawn to single-issue groups and special interest organizations to ensure that whatever else happens, our own personal views and our own private interests are protected. This is a disturbing factor in American political life. It tends to distort our purposes, because the national interest is not always the sum of all our single or special interests. We are all Americans together, and we must not forget that the common good is our common interest and our individual responsibility.

Because of the fragmented pressures of these special interests, it's very important that the office of the President be a strong one and that its constitutional authority be preserved. The President is the only elected official charged with the primary responsibility of representing all the people. In the moments of decision, after the different and conflicting views have all been aired, it's the President who then must speak to the Nation and for the Nation.

I understand after 4 years in this office, as few others can, how formidable is the task the new President-elect is about to undertake, and to the very limits of conscience and conviction, I pledge to support him in that task. I wish him success, and Godspeed.

I know from experience that Presidents have to face major issues that are controversial, broad in scope, and which do not arouse the natural support of a political majority. For a few minutes now, I want to lay aside my role as leader of one nation, and speak to you as a fellow citizen of the world about three issues, three difficult issues: the threat of nuclear destruction, our stewardship of the physical resources of our planet, and the preeminence of the basic rights of human beings.

It's now been 35 years since the first atomic bomb fell on Hiroshima. The great majority of the world's people cannot remember a time when the nuclear shadow did not hang over the Earth. Our minds have adjusted to it, as after a time our eyes adjust to the dark. Yet the risk of a nuclear conflagration has not lessened. It has not happened yet, thank God, but that can give us little comfort, for it only has to happen once.

The danger is becoming greater. As the arsenals of the superpowers grow in size and sophistication and as other governments, perhaps even in the future dozens of governments, acquire these weapons, it may only be a matter of time before madness, desperation, greed, or miscalculation lets loose this terrible force.

In an all-out nuclear war, more destructive power than in all of World War II would be unleashed every second during the long afternoon it would take for all the missiles and bombs to fall. A World War II every second—more people killed in the first few hours than in all the wars of history put together. The survivors, if any, would live in despair amid the poisoned ruins of a civilization that had committed suicide.

National weakness, real or perceived, can tempt aggression and thus cause war. That's why the United States can never neglect its military strength. We must and we will remain strong. But with equal determination, the United States and all countries must find ways to control and to reduce the horrifying danger that is posed by the enormous world stockpiles of nuclear arms.

This has been a concern of every American President since the moment we first saw what these weapons could do. Our leaders will require our understanding and our support as they grapple with this difficult but crucial challenge. There is no disagreement on the goals or the basic approach to controlling this enormous destructive force. The answer lies

not just in the attitudes or the actions of world leaders but in the concern and the demands of all of us as we continue our struggle to preserve the peace.

Nuclear weapons are an expression of one side of our human character. But there's another side. The same rocket technology that delivers nuclear warheads has also taken us peacefully into space. From that perspective, we see our Earth as it really is—a small and fragile and beautiful blue globe, the only home we have. We see no barriers of race or religion or country. We see the essential unity of our species and our planet. And with faith and common sense, that bright vision will ultimately prevail.

Another major challenge, therefore, is to protect the quality of this world within which we live. The shadows that fall across the future are cast not only by the kinds of weapons we've built, but by the kind of world we will either nourish or neglect. There are real and growing dangers to our simple and our most precious possessions: the air we breathe, the water we drink, and the land which sustains us. The rapid depletion of irreplaceable minerals, the erosion of topsoil, the destruction of beauty, the blight of pollution, the demands of increasing billions of people, all combine to create problems which are easy to observe and predict, but difficult to resolve. If we do not act, the world of the year 2000 will be much less able to sustain life than it is now.

But there is no reason for despair. Acknowledging the physical realities of our planet does not mean a dismal future of endless sacrifice. In fact, acknowledging these realities is the first step in dealing with them. We can meet the resource problems of the world—water, food, minerals, farmlands, forests, overpopulation, pollution—if we tackle them with courage and foresight.

I've just been talking about forces of potential destruction that mankind has developed and how we might control them. It's equally important that we remember the beneficial forces that we have evolved over the ages and how to hold fast to them. One of those constructive forces is the enhancement of individual human freedoms through the strengthening of democracy and the fight against deprivation, torture, terrorism, and the persecution of people throughout the world. The struggle for human rights overrides all differences of color or nation or language. Those who hunger for freedom, who thirst for human dignity, and who suffer for the sake of justice, they are the patriots of this cause.

I believe with all my heart that America must always stand for these basic human rights at home and abroad. That is both our history and our destiny.

America did not invent human rights. In a very real sense, it's the other way around. Human rights invented America. Ours was the first nation in the history of the world to be founded explicitly on such an idea. Our social and political progress has been based on one fundamental principle: the value and importance of the individual. The fundamental force that unites us is not kinship or place of origin or religious preference. The love of liberty is the common blood that flows in our American veins.

The battle for human rights, at home and abroad, is far from over. We should never be surprised nor discouraged, because the impact of our efforts has had and will always have varied results. Rather, we should take pride that the ideals which gave birth to our Nation still inspire the hopes of oppressed people around the world. We have no cause for

self-righteousness or complacency, but we have every reason to persevere, both within our own country and beyond our borders.

If we are to serve as a beacon for human rights, we must continue to perfect here at home the rights and the values which we espouse around the world: a decent education for our children, adequate medical care for all Americans, an end to discrimination against minorities and women, a job for all those able to work, and freedom from injustice and religious intolerance.

We live in a time of transition, an uneasy era which is likely to endure for the rest of this century. It will be a period of tensions, both within nations and between nations, of competition for scarce resources, of social, political, and economic stresses and strains. During this period we may be tempted to abandon some of the time-honored principles and commitments which have been proven during the difficult times of past generations. We must never yield to this temptation. Our American values are not luxuries, but necessities—not the salt in our bread, but the bread itself. Our common vision of a free and just society is our greatest source of cohesion at home and strength abroad, greater even than the bounty of our material blessings.

Remember these words: "We hold these truths to be self-evident, that all men are created equal, that they are endowed by their Creator with certain inalienable Rights, that among these are Life, Liberty and the pursuit of Happiness."

This vision still grips the imagination of the world. But we know that democracy is always an unfinished creation. Each generation must renew its foundations. Each generation must rediscover the meaning of this hallowed vision in the light of its own modern challenges. For this generation, ours, life is nuclear survival; liberty is human rights; the pursuit of happiness is a planet whose resources are devoted to the physical and spiritual nourishment of its inhabitants.

During the next few days I will work hard to make sure that the transition from myself to the next President is a good one, that the American people are served well. And I will continue, as I have the last 14 months, to work hard and to pray for the lives and the well-being of the American hostages held in Iran. I can't predict yet what will happen, but I hope you will join me in my constant prayer for their freedom.

As I return home to the South, where I was born and raised, I look forward to the opportunity to reflect and further to assess, I hope with accuracy, the circumstances of our times. I intend to give our new President my support, and I intend to work as a citizen, as I've worked here in this office as President, for the values this Nation was founded to secure.

Again, from the bottom of my heart, I want to express to you the gratitude I feel. Thank you, fellow citizens, and farewell.

NOTE: The President spoke at 9 p.m. from the Oval Office at the White House. The address was broadcast live on radio and television.

Budget Message

Remarks at the Signing Ceremony.
January 15, 1981

THE PRESIDENT. Well, let me say first of all that this is an important annual event—the submission of the next fiscal year's budget by the President to the Congress. And before I sign these three docu-

ments—to the President-elect, to the Speaker of the House, and to the Vice President as President of the Senate—I'd like to express my deep appreciation to Jim McIntyre and to all his staff for having done a fine job in preparing this extremely complicated, but very important presentation to the Congress and to the public of the goals which I think ought to be incorporated into our Nation's decisions in the next few months.

This is a very stringent budget. In 1976, the Federal deficit amounted to about 4 percent of the Nation's gross national product. In the 1982 budget, this one, we will have reduced that percentage down less than 1 percent, a very difficult achievement in spite of the fact that we have increased the allotment of funds for basic research in this budget, have a massive program very important for reducing youth unemployment, a very large and necessary increase in the allocation of funds for strengthening our defense commitment—more than 5 percent in real growth in the 1982 budget—necessary because of the Soviet aggression in Afghanistan and other places in the world and threatened aggression in other localities.

We have pursued here in this budget the program that we initiated concerning energy, and we believe that the poor people who are suffering from increases in energy costs will be benefited by this budget. The synthetic fuels production and other actions necessary to reduce our dependence on foreign oil are adequately encompassed.

As I sign these budget documents, it's with both gratitude and anticipation. I believe that the Congress will act affirmatively on the basic premises of this document. I realize that after a chance for examination, both the Congress and the new President's administration might make some changes in this proposal. In my judgment, they'll be relatively minor in nature, because this is a sound proposal, one that I believe will stand the scrutiny of congressional deliberations and the deliberations of the other members of the future executive branch.

So, I'd like now to sign these books.

First, one for the President of the Senate.

The second one is to the Speaker of the House.

And the third one I said was to the President-elect, but I think it's to you. This is to the Director of OMB for delivery to the President-elect.

REPORTER. Any P.S., Mr. President?

THE PRESIDENT. No. P.S.'s. [*Laughter*] I'll even grant him the right to make some modifications in it if he sees fit.

Q. If he can.

THE PRESIDENT. And this has always been the case when I submit a budget. It has to go to the printers early in December or late in November. And the subsequent events in our own domestic affairs and foreign affairs requires some modification before the budget's finally passed 10 months or so later.

Jim, would you like to add a word?

MR. McINTYRE. Mr. President, I think that in the hours that we have deliberated these budget issues with you that all of us have come to realize the importance of a balanced, not in the sense of a zero sum, but in the sense of the approach to dealing with our national security and our human needs and natural resources in this country, a balanced approach to allocating our resources. And you, in my judgment, have done a superb job in sitting down and looking at these issues and balancing those difficult choices and making sound recommendations to the Congress.

Also, I'd like to thank Charlie Schultze and Bill Miller, who was not able to be with us, and my staff for all of the hard work that they put in in helping put this budget together and getting it out for you.

THE PRESIDENT. I'd like to say, Jim, I expressed my thanks earlier to your staff and to you, but this is one of the most difficult assignments that anyone in Government has, because it requires long hours, a detailed knowledge of every element of the Government bureaucracy plus the delivery of services to people. It has to be done with humaneness and with a very fine and a proper assessment of the relative priorities. I think it's a good document. I think subsequent events in the Congress and the public assessment will prove this to be true.

When will the budget be made public, and when will it be delivered to the new administration?

MR. McINTYRE. It will be made—actually, we've had our press conference this morning and copies are going to the Hill, and the embargo will be off the budget at 5 o'clock this afternoon. So, it will be public today.

THE PRESIDENT. Are your staff now basically working for the next administration?

MR. McINTYRE. Yes, they have been for several days. [*Laughter*] Some of us look around to find help, and the help is already working in other areas.

THE PRESIDENT. Well, that's good.

MR. McINTYRE. That was according to our arrangement with the Director-designate, and it's going very smoothly, Mr. President.

THE PRESIDENT. The OMB is very highly technical and highly professional, a nonpolitical staff. And I want to express again not only my thanks but my admiration to all of you.

MR. McINTYRE. Thank you, sir.

THE PRESIDENT. Thank you, Jim.

MR. McINTYRE. I appreciate it.

NOTE: The President spoke at 11:40 a.m. in the Cabinet Room at the White House.

Budget Message

*Message to the Congress Transmitting the
Fiscal Year 1982 Budget.   January 15, 1981*

To the Congress of the United States:

My administration has faced a wide
range of challenges at home and abroad,
challenges stemming from our strengths,
not our weaknesses: our strengths as a
world leader, as a developed industrial
nation, and as a heterogeneous democracy
with high goals and great ambitions.
Meeting these challenges satisfactorily
requires that we establish priorities, recognizing the limits to even our Nation's
enormous resources. We cannot do all that
we wish at the same time. But we must
provide for our security, establish the
basis for a strong economy, protect the
disadvantaged, build human and physical
capital for the future, and safeguard this
Nation's magnificent natural environment.

This budget provides for meeting these
needs, while continuing a 4-year policy of
prudence and restraint. While our budget
deficits have been higher than I would
have liked, their size has been determined
for the most part by economic conditions.
Even so, the trend has been downward. In
1976, the budget deficit equalled 4.0%
of gross national product. This was reduced to 2.3% in the budget year that

ended 3 months ago. The 1982 budget
deficit is estimated to equal only 0.9% of
gross national product.

The rate of growth in budget outlays
has been held to a minimum. In spite of
significant increases in indexed programs,
outlays for nondefense programs—after
adjusting for inflation—decreased slightly.

The 1982 budget calls for outlays of
$739 billion, an increase of 1.0% when
adjusted for inflation. Nondefense spending is projected to decline by 0.2% in real
terms. The tax reductions I proposed as
part of the economic revitalization program have been retained, but some have
been delayed or phased in over a longer
period in recognition of the continued high
inflation rate. The budget deficit—which
is now projected at $55.2 billion in 1981—
is estimated to decline to $27.5 billion in
1982.

In planning this budget, I have considered four major issues:

- What is the economic policy that will
  ensure prosperity for all while minimizing inflation?
- How much of our Nation's wealth
  should be used by the Federal
  Government?
- What are desirable spending proposals and strategies for defense, human
  resources, and investment?
- How can the management of Government be improved?

THE BUDGET TOTALS

[In billions of dollars]

	1980 actual	1981 estimate	1982 estimate	1983 estimate	1984 estimate
Outlays............................	579. 6	662. 7	739. 3	817. 3	890. 3
Receipts...........................	520. 0	607. 5	711. 8	809. 2	922. 3
Surplus or deficit (—)..........	—59. 6	—55. 2	—27. 5	—8. 0	32. 0
Budget authority....................	658. 8	726. 5	809. 8	892. 0	962. 7
Credit budget......................	131. 2	165. 4	152. 6	....	

THE ECONOMY

During the last decade we withstood a series of economic shocks unprecedented in peacetime. The most dramatic of these were the explosive increases of OPEC oil prices. But we have also faced world commodity shortages, natural disasters, agricultural shortages, and major challenges to world peace and security. Our ability to deal with these shocks has been impaired by slower productivity growth and persistent, underlying inflationary forces built up over the past 15 years.

Nevertheless, the economy has proved remarkably resilient. Real output has grown at an average annual rate of 3% since I took office, and employment has grown by 2½%. Nearly 8 million productive private sector jobs have been added to the economy. However, unacceptably high inflation remains our most difficult economic problem. This inflation requires that we hold down the growth of the budget to the maximum extent, while still meeting the demands of national security and human compassion. I have done so, as I did in my earlier budgets.

While budget restraint is essential to any appropriate economic policy, high inflation cannot be attributed solely to Government spending. The growth in budget outlays has been more the result of economic factors than the cause of them. For fiscal year 1981 alone, budget outlays must be increased by $9 billion over last year's estimate as a result of higher interest rates. Yet this increase results not only from inflation but from the monetary policies undertaken to combat it. Nearly $18 billion for 1981 reflects higher defense costs and higher automatic inflation adjustments than were anticipated a year ago.

We are now in the early stages of economic recovery following a short recession. Typically, post-recessionary periods have been marked by vigorous economic growth abetted by stimulative policies such as large tax cuts or spending programs. I am not recommending such actions, because persistent inflationary pressures dictate a restrained fiscal policy. However, I continue to recommend specific tax reductions that contribute directly to increased productivity and long-term growth.

THE SIZE AND ROLE OF GOVERNMENT

We allocate about 23% of our Nation's output through the Federal budget. (Including all levels of government, the total government share of our gross national product is about one-third.) We must come close to matching Federal outlays with tax receipts if we are to avoid excessive and inflationary Federal borrowing. This means either controlling our appetite for spending or accepting the burden of higher taxes.

The growth of budget outlays is puzzling to many Americans, but it arises from valid social and national security concerns. Other developed countries face similar pressures. We face a threat to our security, as events in Afghanistan, the Middle East, and Eastern Europe make clear. We have a steadily aging population; as a result, the biggest single increase in the Federal budget is the rising cost of retirement programs, particularly social security. We must meet other important domestic needs: to assist the disadvantaged; to provide the capital needed by our cities and our transportation systems; to protect our environment; and to revitalize American industry.

I have been concerned with the proper role of the Federal Government in designing and providing such assistance. The

Federal Government must not usurp functions that are best left to the private sector or to State and local governments. My administration has sought to make the proper assignments of responsibility, to resolve problems in the most efficient manner.

We have also recognized the need to simplify the system of Federal grants to State and local governments. Once again, I am proposing several grant consolidations in the 1982 budget, including a new proposal that would consolidate several highway programs. Previous consolidation proposals of my administration have been in the areas of youth training and employment, environment, energy conservation, airport development, and rehabilitation services. These consolidations are essential to improving our intergovernmental system. However, the Congress has so far agreed to consolidate only rehabilitation services grants. Therefore, I am proposing again the consolidations recommended earlier.

Major Budget Priorities

Spending growth can be constrained; not easily, not quickly, but it is possible. My budget priorities have been established, once again, to achieve this goal in a responsible manner.

Three years ago, in my 1979 budget message, I outlined the following principles:

• The Nation's armed forces must always stand sufficiently strong to deter aggression and to assure our security.

• An effective national energy plan is essential to reduce our increasingly critical dependence upon diminishing supplies of oil and gas, to encourage conservation of scarce energy resources, to stimulate conversion to more abundant fuels, and to reduce our large trade deficit.

• The essential human needs of our citizens must be given high priority.

• The Federal Government must lead the way in investment in the Nation's technological future.

• The Federal Government has an obligation to nurture and protect our environment—the common resource, birthright, and sustenance of the American people.

My 1982 budget is again based on these principles.

Tax policy and economic revitalization.—I continue to believe that large inflationary individual income tax cuts are neither appropriate nor possible today, however popular they might appear in the short run. My economic revitalization program stresses tax reductions on a timetable that we can afford, and that will fight inflation by encouraging capital formation and increasing industrial productivity. This program stresses:

• simplification and liberalization of depreciation allowances;

• modification of the investment tax credit to encourage investment by temporarily depressed firms and by growing new firms;

• an income tax credit to offset increases in social security taxes;

• a liberalized earned income credit to also offset social security taxes and to encourage low-income earners to work;

• a working-spouse deduction to make more equitable the way working husbands and wives are taxed; and

• more favorable tax treatment for Americans in certain areas overseas to help American exports and strengthen the dollar.

Defense.—Maintaining a strong defense has been a primary objective of this administration. In order to meet the security needs of the Nation, real spending for defense increased in 1979 and 1980 by more than the 3 percent target I set at the NATO ministerial meeting in 1977. This real growth rate in defense spending has been maintained despite the adverse effects of higher than anticipated inflation, and restrained budgets.

To meet critical remaining needs, this budget includes a $6.3 billion supplemental request for 1981, largely for military pay increases and combat readiness. Together with congressional add-ons to my earlier 1981 request, this supplemental will increase defense programs almost 8 percent in real terms over 1980. For 1982 and beyond, the budget charts a course of sustained and balanced improvements in defense programs that will require real annual increases in funding of about 5 percent per year.

The budget request reflects a careful balance between the need to meet all critical defense needs, while maintaining fiscal restraint. There will be advocates for higher defense levels, but after careful review I do not believe that higher spending would add significantly to our national security. My budget already provides for the three major defense requirements:

• *Personnel recruitment and retention.*—Our armed forces can be no better than the quality of the people who serve in them. Accordingly, I recently approved the largest pay and benefits increase in history—a $4.5 billion compensation package that provides for an average compensation increase of 16 percent. This increase in base pay, plus better housing allowances, expanded enlistment and reenlistment bonuses, and special pay enhancements for submariners and other specialists, will help attract and retain highly qualified men and women.

• *Improving combat readiness.*—Increased compensation will be a key factor in overcoming key personnel shortages, which are the major source of readiness

problems. In addition, there have been shortages in critical spare parts and, in a few cases, inadequate funds for training. The funds recommended by this budget should alleviate these problems.

• *Modernizing our forces.*—I also propose major investments to enhance substantially the capabilities of our forces. Strategic forces are being upgraded through continued procurement of Trident submarines and missiles, procurement of cruise missiles, modification of the B–52 bomber, and development of the MX missile. Army equipment, including tanks, armored vehicles, helicopters, and air defense and other missile systems, is being modernized. Fighter and attack planes are being added to Navy and Marine forces, and a continuing major shipbuilding program will add over 80 ships to our growing fleet between 1982 and 1986. The rapid deployment of our forces is being improved through the acquisition of more cargo ships and modification of airlift aircraft.

Foreign aid.—Foreign assistance remains crucial in achieving our country's international political and economic goals. From the start of my administration, I have stressed the need for substantial increases in assistance to friendly nations, many of whom are drastically harmed by constantly increasing oil prices and other external economic and security pressures. At the same time, I have insisted upon improved management of both our security and development assistance programs.

In the first 2 years of this administration, the Congress reduced my foreign aid requests but permitted some program growth. For the past 2 years, however, the Congress has failed to pass regular foreign aid appropriations. Assistance programs in 1981 are being funded under a continuing resolution that provides amounts slightly above the 1979 levels in nominal terms, and substantially below them in real terms.

I believe in the need for higher levels of aid to achieve foreign policy objectives, promote economic growth, and help needy people abroad. Foreign aid is not politically popular and represents an easy target for budget reduction. But it is not a wise one. For 1982, therefore, I am requesting a foreign assistance program level that is higher by 14% in real terms than the amount currently available for 1981. This request would reverse the recent real decline in aid and demonstrate that the United States retains its commitment to a world of politically stable and economically secure nations.

The bilateral development aid budget includes a U.S. response to the 1980 Venice Summit agreement that the major industrial countries should increase bilateral aid for food production, energy production and conservation, and family planning in the developing countries. Such an effort to increase the availability of resources on which the industrial countries depend will serve U.S. national security, and will stimulate additional actions by the private sector in the recipient countries. This U.S. effort is planned in the expectation that the other Summit countries will also increase aid in these sectors, in response to the Venice Summit agreement. We hope this initiative will lead to agreement on arrangements for increased consultation and cooperation among the major industrial countries providing increased bilateral aid to these three vital sectors.

Energy.—My administration, working with the Congress, has established fundamental new policies that will profoundly change the way the Nation produces and uses energy. They have already led to more domestic exploration and to substantial energy conservation. This energy program represents a major long-range national commitment to meeting one of our most pressing problems. It includes:

- Deregulation and decontrol of oil prices to be completed by October of this year.
- Establishment of the Synthetic Fuels Corporation, which will share with the private sector the risk in producing oil and natural gas substitutes that directly reduce U.S. oil imports.
- Support for energy research and development in technologies, such as solar and fusion energy, that the private sector would not finance.
- Development of the strategic petroleum reserve to reduce the impact of disruptions in world oil supplies.
- Energy conservation in public and nonprofit enterprises.
- Research on the environmental effects of energy production and use to assure that adverse effects on environmental quality are minimized.

Continuation of a sound energy policy is essential to the Nation's well-being in the coming decades. Such a policy must include the pricing of energy at its true cost, mechanisms to stimulate conservation, incentives for the continued development of our own domestic sources of energy, encouragement for longer-run renewable forms of energy, and equity for all our citizens as we adjust to this new reality.

Basic science and space technology.— Basic research is essential to the long-term vitality of the Nation's economy. Because the benefits of such investments cannot be fully realized by individual companies, the Federal Government plays a key role in supporting such research.

My budgets have reversed a long period of decline in Federal support for basic research. The 1982 budget continues that policy by providing for 4% real growth in support for the conduct of basic research across all Federal agencies. The budget also provides for greater efforts to foster cooperation among government, business, and universities in research.

In addition, we have recognized the growing importance of improving scientific technology in the Nation's universities as critical to the advancement of science and to the training of scientific and engineering manpower.

My administration's comprehensive space policy encourages the practical, effective use of information obtained from orbiting satellites and the coordinated use of the Space Shuttle, now nearing completion. Successful resolution of development problems is expected to lead to the first manned orbital flight of the Shuttle in 1981.

With these increases, Federal support for basic research will have increased by almost 58% over 1978.

Social programs.—This budget supports my deep commitment to programs that help our citizens develop their full potential, and to programs assisting the poor, the unemployed, the elderly, and the sick.

The most extensive such programs are *social security* and *medicare*. Parts of this system are expected to experience short-run financing problems because higher than expected unemployment has decreased payroll taxes below previous forecasts, and high inflation has increased benefit payments. Therefore, the administration continues to urge the passage of legislation that would permit the three major social security trust funds to borrow from each other. In addition, it is essential that the Congress and the American people give early consideration to medium-term financing concerns.

The reports of the Commission on Pension Policy, which I established 2 years ago, and the National Commission on Social Security should stimulate constructive debate on these issues. These Commissions will complete their final reports during the coming months.

My administration has consistently maintained a strong commitment to remedying *youth unemployment* and the problems it causes. This budget includes an increase of $1.2 billion in 1982 and an additional increase of $0.8 billion in 1983 for the youth initiative I proposed last year. This initiative emphasizes the mastery of basic arithmetic and literacy skills, as well as the link between the classroom and the workplace.

The Job Corps would be continued at this year's level, serving twice as many youth as when my administration took office. In addition, my budget provides 240,000 public service jobs for low-income, long-term unemployed persons in 1982. This program is designed for the hard-core structurally unemployed, and includes substantial training in order to place men and women in permanent jobs. At the same time, the budget continues the countercyclical public service employment program through 1982 at the 100,000 level set by the Congress for 1981. The budget also provides a slight increase for the administration's private sector jobs initiative and essentially maintains the 1980 level of summer youth employment.

I am again proposing to augment medicaid with a *child health assurance* program effective by the end of 1982. This proposal, which the House of Representatives passed last year, would extend medicaid coverage to an additional 2 million children and pregnant women.

I am also proposing a number of changes in existing programs. For example, I am again proposing that retirement benefits for government employees be adjusted for inflation once, rather than twice, a year. This change would make these adjustments comparable to those for social security and most private sector automatic adjustment practices. The Congress approved a similar administration initiative last year for the food stamp program. This proposal would save $1.1 billion in 1982.

Benefits that are adjusted by statute for inflation will comprise nearly one-third of total Federal spending in 1981. During the last year, my administration has been assessing whether these adjustments are fair and equitable. We have concluded that the Consumer Price Index has several deficiencies as a measure of the true cost of living, particularly because of the manner in which it represents housing costs. I am therefore proposing, in this budget, that future benefits be based on an alternative, more representative index. The alternative index is already calculated and published by the Bureau of Labor Statistics. This proposal is designed to improve the technique of indexing these programs, not to reduce benefits. Therefore, no cost savings are assumed in the budget.

The budget also includes legislation to make unemployment benefits more nearly uniform among the States and to coordinate benefits more precisely with unemployment rates. Although this proposal would save about $2 billion in 1982 under the unemployment rates being projected for this budget, a slightly higher rate of unemployment would trigger extended benefits nationally. In such a case, unemployment benefits would be very close to those under current law. Even with the projected change, under current economic projections $1.5 billion would be paid in 1982 for extended benefits in States where the program is triggered.

I remain committed to a national health plan that would assure basic and catas-trophic medical coverage for all Americans, as well as for prenatal and infant care. An estimated 22 million Americans lack any private or public health insurance coverage. Another 60 million people lack adequate basic coverage or protection against catastrophic medical expenses. Given the fact that adequate cost containment does not exist and the need for overall budgetary constraints, the budget does not include specific amounts for this plan. However, it is important that our Nation attempt to meet these needs and that the incentives in our health care system be restructured. A clear demonstration of success in restraining medical care costs is an essential prerequisite to the enactment of a national health plan.

My proposals to reform our welfare system should also be an enacted as soon as possible. Such a program is essential to ensuring that no American goes hungry or lacks a reasonable income, and to provide needed fiscal relief to States, counties, and cities.

IMPROVING GOVERNMENT
MANAGEMENT

This budget reinforces my commitment to use resources not only wisely, but efficiently. During my administration we have:

- installed new Offices of Inspectors General in 15 major agencies to combat waste, fraud, and abuse;

- carried out a major Government-wide reform of the civil service system;

- reorganized important areas of the Federal Government, particularly those concerned with education and energy;

- reduced permanent Federal civilian employment by 45,000;

- achieved budgetary savings directly through improved cash management; and
- reduced paperwork and established a paperwork budget.

Such efforts to streamline the way the Government conducts its business are rarely dramatic. Improved efficiency is not the product of a simple sweeping reform but, rather, of diligent, persistent attention to many aspects of Federal program management.

One important aspect of improved management has been in the budget process itself. *Zero-base budgeting* is now an integral part of the decisionmaking system, providing a more systematic basis for making decisions. We have also instituted a 3-year budget planning horizon so that the longer range consequences of short-term budget decisions are fully considered and understood.

In 1978 I made a major commitment to establish a system of controlling *Federal credit* since, in the past, the very large Federal loan guarantee programs had largely escaped the discipline of the budget process. This system is now in place.

I am gratified that the Congress has supported these efforts to improve budget control. Appropriations bills now include limits on many credit programs. The congressional budget resolutions place significantly greater emphasis on longer range budget trends and set overall credit targets.

While the credit control system provides a means of assessing and limiting Federal credit programs, I believe Federal credit programs have become unduly complex and pose an increasing threat to the effective and efficient operation of private capital markets. In particular, the Federal Financing Bank has become a major and rapidly growing source of off-budget funds for direct loans to a wide range of borrowers.

Therefore, I am recommending that a panel of outstanding financial and budget experts should be established to examine these issues. Such a panel should consider the treatment of credit activities in the budget, the adequacy of program administration, uniform rules and procedures for Federal credit programs, the role of the Federal Financing Bank, and the relationship of tax-exempt financing to overall credit and tax policies.

Conclusion

My budget recommendations reflect the major changes that have taken place in our country over recent decades. In 1950, social security and railroad retirement benefits accounted for less than 3% of budget outlays. Last year they accounted for more than one-fifth of the total. Mandatory outlays for entitlement programs, the levels of which are fixed by law, for interest on the public debt, and for payments under binding contracts account for three-fourths of total budget outlays. Because so much of the budget is committed under current law before either the President or the Congress begins the annual budget formulation process, controlling budget growth has been difficult, and the results uneven. It has been difficult because benefit payments and other legal obligations have too often been spared from annual budget scrutiny. The results have been uneven because budget restraint has fallen disproportionately on programs subject to the annual appropriations process.

My administration and the Congress began to redress this imbalance in the 1981 budget. The Congress passed, and I signed into law, a reconciliation bill that for the first time was used as a mechanism for changing a variety of entitlement and tax programs. I do not propose that we break faith with the American people by arbitrarily or unfairly reducing entitlement programs. However, these programs developed independently, and they should be made less duplicative, more consistent, and more equitable. The size of these programs, and our need for budget restraint, requires that we address these problems. I urge the Congress to build upon last year's experience and review all aspects of the budget with equal care.

The allocation of one-fifth of our Nation's resources through the Federal budget is a complex, difficult, and contentious process. Restraint on any program, small or large, is usually subject to heated debate. At a time when there is broad consensus that the size of the Federal budget is too large, we can no longer—as individuals or groups—make special pleas for exceptions to budget discipline. Too often we have taken the attitude that individual benefits or particular programs or specific tax measures are not large enough to require restraint. Too often we have taken the attitude that there must be alternative sources for reductions in programs that benefit our particular group. This attitude is in part responsible for the rapid budget growth we have experienced—and can no longer afford.

Given our Nation's needs and our economic constraints, my recommendations meet the fundamental demands of our society: a strong defense, adequate protection for the poor and the disadvantaged, support for our free enterprise economy, and investment in the Nation's future.

JIMMY CARTER

January 15, 1981.

NOTE: The President's message is printed in the report entitled "Budget of the United States Government, Fiscal Year 1982" (Government Printing Office, 638 pages).

Export of Banned or Significantly Restricted Substances
Executive Order 12264.   January 15, 1981

ON FEDERAL POLICY REGARDING THE EXPORT OF BANNED OR SIGNIFICANTLY RESTRICTED SUBSTANCES

By the authority vested in me as President by the Constitution of the United States of America, and in order to further the foreign policy interests of the United States and to provide for effective and responsible implementation of the Export Administration Act of 1979 (50 U.S.C. App. 2401 *et. seq.*) and other statutes insofar as they relate to the export of banned or significantly restricted substances, it is hereby ordered as follows:

1-1. Scope of the Order

1-101. For the purposes of this Order, the term "banned or significantly restricted substance" means:

(a) a food or class of food which

(1) is adulterated, as defined by rules or orders issued under Sec. 402(a) or (c) (21 U.S.C. 342(a) or (c)), or

(2) is in violation of emergency permit controls issued under Sec. 404 (21 U.S.C. 344)
of the Federal Food, Drug, and Cosmetic Act;

(b) a drug which is

(1) adulterated, as defined by rules or orders issued under Sec. 501(a), (b), (c), or (d) (21 U.S.C. 351(a), (b), (c), or (d)),

(2) misbranded, as defined by rules or orders issued under Sec. 502(j) (21 U.S.C. 352(j)) or

(3) a new drug or new animal drug for which an approval is not in effect under Sec. 505 (21 U.S.C. 355) or Sec. 512 (21 U.S.C. 360), respectively,

of the Federal Food, Drug, and Cosmetic Act;

(c) an antibiotic drug which has not been certified under Sec. 507 (21 U.S.C. 357) of the Federal Food, Drug, and Cosmetic Act;

(d) a drug containing insulin which has not been certified under Sec. 506 (21 U.S.C. 356) of the Federal Food, Drug, and Cosmetic Act;

(e) a device which

(1) is adulterated, as defined by rules or orders issued under Sec. 501(a) (21 U.S.C. 351(a)),

(2) is misbranded, as defined by rules or orders issued under Sec. 502(j) (21 U.S.C. 352(j)),

(3) does not conform with a performance standard issued under Sec. 514 (21 U.S.C. 360d),

(4) has not received premarket approval under Sec. 515 (21 U.S.C. 360e), or

(5) is banned under Sec. 516 (21 U.S.C. 360f)

of the Federal Food, Drug, and Cosmetic Act;

(f) a cosmetic which is adulterated, as defined by rules or orders issued under Sec. 601 (21 U.S.C. 361) of the Federal Food, Drug, and Cosmetic Act;

(g) a food additive or color additive which is deemed unsafe within the meaning of Sec. 409 (21 U.S.C. 348) or Sec. 706 (21 U.S.C. 376), respectively, of the Federal Food, Drug, and Cosmetic Act;

(h) a biological product which has been propagated or manufactured and prepared at an establishment which does not hold a license as required by Sec. 351 (42 U.S.C. 262) of the Public Health Service Act;

(i) an electronic product which does not comply with a performance standard issued under Sec. 358 (42 U.S.C. 263f) of the Public Health Service Act;

(j) a consumer product which

(1) does not comply with a consumer product safety standard adopted under Secs. 7 and 9 (15 U.S.C. 2056 and 2058) other than one relating solely to labeling,

(2) has been declared to be a banned hazardous product under Secs. 8 and 9 (15 U.S.C. 2057 and 2058),

(3) presents a substantial product hazard under Sec. 15 (15 U.S.C. 2064), or

(4) is an imminently hazardous consumer product under Sec. 12 (15 U.S.C. 2061)

of the Consumer Product Safety Act;

(k) a fabric, related material, or product which does not comply with a flammability standard (other than one relating to labeling) adopted under Sec. 4 (15 U.S.C. 1193) of the Flammable Fabrics Act;

(1) a product which is a banned hazardous substance (including a children's article) under Secs. 2 and 3 (15 U.S.C. 1261 and 1262) of the Federal Hazardous Substances Act;

(m)(1) a pesticide which, on the basis of potential risks to human health or safety or to the environment,

(A) has been denied registration for all or most significant uses under Sec. 3 (c)(6) (7 U.S.C. 136a(c)(6)),

(B) has been classified for restricted use under Sec. 3(d)(1)(C) (7 U.S.C. 136a(d)(1)(C)),

(C) has had its registration cancelled or suspended for all or most significant uses under Sec. 6 (7 U.S.C. 136d),

(D) has been proceeded against and seized under Sec. 13(b)(3) (7 U.S.C. 136k), or

(E) has not had its registration cancelled, but requires an acknowledgement statement under Sec. 17(a)(2) (7 U.S.C.

1360(a)(2)) of the Federal Insecticide, Fungicide, and Rodenticide Act, or

(2) a pesticide chemical for which a tolerance has been denied or repealed under Sec. 408 (21 U.S.C. 346(a)) of the Federal Food, Drug, and Cosmetic Act; and

(n) a chemical substance or mixture

(1) which is subject to an order or injunction issued under Sec. 5(f)(3) (15 U.S.C. 2604(f)(3)),

(2) which is subject to a requirement issued under Sec. 6(a)(1), 6(a)(2), 6(a)(5), or 6(a)(7) (15 U.S.C. 2605(a)(1), 2605(a)(2), 2605(a)(5), or 2605(a)(7)) or

(3) for which a civil action has been brought and relief granted under Sec. 7 (15 U.S.C. 2606) of the Toxic Substances Control Act.

1-102. Each agency that is responsible for the administration of a statute or statutory provision referenced in Subsection 1-101 shall compile and, within 90 days after the issuance of this Order, shall publish in the FEDERAL REGISTER a list of those substances within its jurisdiction that are banned or significantly restricted substances as defined by Subsection 1-101. Each agency shall revise the list of banned or significantly restricted substances within its jurisdiction as necessary to reflect new regulatory actions by the agency.

1-2. Regularization of Notification Procedures

1-201. Each agency that is required by statute to notify, or to be apprised of notifications to, foreign countries regarding exports of banned or significantly restricted substances to those countries shall adhere, to the extent not inconsistent with applicable law, to the following procedures:

(a) Each agency shall promptly provide to the Department of State such information regarding an export of banned or significantly restricted substances to a foreign government as is required by statute or agency regulation to be forwarded to the foreign government, either by the agency or by another party required to apprise the agency of its notification, and by the notification forms and procedures to be established by the Department of State pursuant to Subsection 1-201(b). As soon as feasible after the receipt of the required information from an agency, the Department of State shall transmit the information to the government of the foreign country to which the banned or significantly restricted substance is to be exported.

(b) the Department of State shall consult with affected agencies regarding the format and content appropriate for required notifications to foreign governments and shall establish, within 90 days after the issuance of this Order, notification forms and procedures. At a minimum, the following information shall be transmitted to foreign governments regarding banned or significantly restricted substances to be exported to them from the United States:

(1) the name of the substance to be exported;

(2) a concise summary of the agency's regulatory actions regarding that substance, including the statutory authority for such actions and the timetable for any further actions that are planned; and,

(3) a concise summary of the potential risks to human health or safety or to the environment that are the grounds for the agency's actions.

In addition, to the extent deemed appropriate by the agency with jurisdiction over the banned or significantly restricted substance to be exported, copies of additional documents may be forwarded to a foreign government, either at the same time as or subsequent to the required notification, to assist the foreign government in its assessment of the nature and extent of the risks associated with the substance.

(c) With respect to each required notification regarding an export of a banned or significantly restricted substance, each agency shall identify for the Department of State the persons or offices within that agency to be contacted in the event that the foreign government receiving the notification wishes to obtain through the Department of State additional information regarding the risks of, or regulatory actions taken with respect to, the banned or significantly restricted substance that is the subject of the notification.

(d) When it is required by statute or agency regulation that a foreign government acknowledge that it has received notification of an export of banned or significantly restricted substances, express approval of the export, or make any other type of response to notification, the notification shall advise the foreign government that its response should be directed to the Department of State for transmittal to the agency.

1–202. The procedures established by Subsection 1–201 shall not preclude an agency from contacting a foreign government directly regarding the export of banned or significantly restricted substances to that country, providing that such contacts are supplementary to, rather than substitutes for, adherence to the procedures established by Subsection 1–201.

1–203. Each United States embassy shall maintain on file, for a period of one year after transmission, copies of the notifications transmitted through the Department of State to the government of the foreign country in which the embassy is located, as well as lists of United States agency contact points sent to the Department of State in connection with those notifications.

1–3. Export Control Procedures

1–301. It is the intent of this Order to rely primarily on the notification procedures, annual report, and participation in international efforts provided for in Sections 1–2, 1–4, and 1–5, respectively, in implementing the Order, and to resort to the imposition of export controls only in a very few instances. Specifically, export controls should be limited to extremely hazardous substances, as determined by the agency primarily responsible for regulating a substance on the basis of the record compiled in connection with regulatory action taken by that agency concerning that substance—

(a) which represent a substantial threat to human health or safety or to the environment,

(b) the export of which would cause clear and significant harm to the foreign policy interests of the United States, and

(c) for which export licenses would be granted only in exceptional cases.

Export controls shall not be applied to substances specified in Sections 1–101(b) (3), 1–101(e)(4), and 1–101(m)(1)(E) of this Order. Nor shall export controls be applied to "medicine or medical supplies," which are excluded from such controls by Section 6(f) of the Export Administration Act of 1979 (50 U.S.C. App. 2405(f)). For the purposes of this Order the phrase "medicine or medical supplies" shall be construed so as to permit consideration for inclusion on the Commodity Control List of drugs and devices within the categories specified in Subsection 1–101(b–e) and representing a substantial threat to human health or safety or to the environment. Wherever practicable, export controls should be no more restrictive than the controls applicable to domestic commerce and use.

1–302. Within 90 days after the issuance of this Order, the Department of Commerce shall develop for interagency review proposed regulations to govern its consideration of applications for licenses to export banned or significantly restricted substances included on the Commodity Control List. Within 120 days after the issuance of this Order, the Department of Commerce shall publish the proposed regulations in the FEDERAL REGISTER for public comment.

1–303. In accord with its statutory role under the Export Administration Act, and consistent with the policy and standards enunciated in Subsection 1–301, the Department of State shall identify, subject to the concurrence of the Department of Commerce, candidates for inclusion on the Commodity Control List. If the Department of State and Department of Commerce are unable to agree on the inclusion on the Commodity Control List of a particural substance, the matter shall be referred to the President.

1–304. In order to assist the Department of State in the development of its advice to the Department of Commerce under subsection 1–303, there is hereby established an interagency task force, to be chaired by the Department of State. The task force shall consist of representatives of the following agencies:

(a) Department of State.

(b) Department of Commerce.

(c) Environmental Protection Agency.

(d) Food and Drug Administration, Department of Health and Human Services.

(e) Consumer Product Safety Commission.

(f) Office of the U.S. Special Trade Representative.

The Department of State, as chair of the task force, may invite representatives of non-member agencies to participate from time to time in the functions of the task force. The task force shall provide technical advice to the Department of State as to which substances should be considered candidates for inclusion on the Commodity Control List. The task force shall endeavor to reach consensus on its advice, consistent with the policy and standards enunciated in Subsection 1–301.

1–305. To the extent possible, within the limits of available information and consistent with the policy and standards enunciated in Subsection 1–301, the task force shall consider, with respect to each banned or significantly restricted substance that is proposed for inclusion on the Commodity Control List by a member of the task force:

(a) the type, extent, and severity of the potential detrimental effects of the substance;

(b) the likelihood of the effects;

(c) the duration of the effects;

(d) the ability of foreign countries to avoid or mitigate the effects;

(e) the availability of the substance from sources other than the United States;

(f) the availability of other substances or methods that would serve the same purposes as the substance; and,

(g) the importance of the beneficial uses of the substances.

1–306. Before deciding whether to grant a validated license for the export of any banned or significantly restricted substance that is included on the Commodity Control List, the Department of Commerce shall consult with the Department of State, the agency with domestic regulatory authority, and any other agency deemed relevant by the Department of

Commerce. Such consultation by the Department of Commerce is necessary within the meaning of Section 10(a)(3) of the Export Administration Act of 1979 (50 U.S.C. App. 2409(a)(3)). The Department of State shall not recommend issuing a license unless (1) it has determined that the export would not cause clear and significant harm to the foreign policy interests of the United States and (2) after appropriate consultations, it has received no objections to the export from the government of the foreign country to which the banned or significantly restricted substance is to be exported. The findings and recommendations of the Department of State shall be conveyed in writing to the Department of Commerce.

1–307. Except to the extent supplemented or further detailed by this Order, the procedures established by the Export Administration Act of 1979 (50 U.S.C. App. 2401 *et. seq.*), including required consultations with industry, shall be followed in all their particulars in the utilization of export control authority on foreign policy grounds with respect to banned or significantly restricted substances.

1–4. Annual Report on Regulatory Actions

1–401. The Regulatory Council shall compile each year a report that

(a) summarizes all final regulatory actions of the types described in Subsection 1–101 that were taken by Federal agencies by the end of the previous calendar year, including those antedating that calendar year but continuing in force, and that are of significant international interest;

(b) summarizes all proposed regulatory actions of the types described in Subsection 1–101 that were pending before agencies at the end of the previous calendar year and that are of significant international interest;

(c) indicates generally what additional information is available with respect to each of the final or proposed regulatory actions listed and how such information may be obtained; and

(d) contains such information as the Council, in consultation with affected agencies, determines is appropriate to include regarding substances the use of which in the United States is not generally banned but, on the basis of potential risks to human health or safety or to the environment, is subject to maximum exposure levels or other restrictions or conditions.

1–402. Each agency shall provide to the Regulatory Council the information necessary for the preparation of the annual report on regulatory actions. The Regulatory Council shall establish, after consultation with affected agencies and within 90 days after the issuance of this Order, a standard format and timetable for the submission of information by the agencies.

1–403. The Regulatory Council shall publish the report required by subsection 1–401 in the FEDERAL REGISTER by March 1 of each year, and the Department of State shall distribute copies of the report to foreign countries and to appropriate public and private international organizations as soon as feasible after its publication.

1–5. Participation in International Efforts

1–501. The Department of State, and other agencies and officials of the United States government in consultation with the Department of State, shall encourage and participate actively in international efforts to develop improved worldwide hazard alert systems, export notification programs, uniform hazard labeling, and other common standards and practices with respect to the export of banned or significantly restricted substances.

1–6. Evaluation

1–601. The Council on Environmental Quality, the Department of State, and the Department of Commerce, in consultation with agencies affected by this Order, shall submit to the President 18 months after the effective date of the Order and annually thereafter, a report summarizing U.S. agency activities pursuant to the Order, evaluating the effectiveness of the Order, and making any recommendations that are deemed appropriate.

1–7. Trade Secret Protection

1–701. Trade secrets or other confidential commercial or financial information that pertain to a banned or significantly restricted substance to be exported shall not be forwarded to a foreign government in the notifications or other documents prepared pursuant to this Order unless authorized or required by existing law.

JIMMY CARTER

White House,
   January 15, 1981.

[Filed with the Office of the Federal Register,
   3:24 p.m., January 15, 1981]

Export of Banned or Significantly Restricted Substances

Statement on Signing Executive Order 12264.
January 15, 1981

I have signed today an Executive order which establishes a comprehensive Federal policy on the export of hazardous products and substances that have been banned or significantly restricted for use in the United States.

The order builds upon laws that already exist and regulatory action already taken by Federal agencies. It makes our present controls over the export of banned substances more consistent and more effective. It emphasizes to other countries that the United States is a responsible trading partner and that they can trust goods bearing the label "Made in U.S.A." It establishes U.S. leadership in addressing the problems associated with the export of dangerous substances. At the same time, it protects our legitimate and important interests in international trade.

The central idea of the policy I am announcing today is full disclosure of information to our trading partners. A number of laws already require that we notify foreign countries when substances banned or significantly restricted for use at home are exported. My order improves these notifications. It will clarify for other countries the reasons why the substances in question are banned or strictly controlled in the United States and will help them judge for themselves whether they wish to allow the substances to enter and be used in their countries. We will also be publishing an annual summary of U.S. regulatory activities of international interest, which can serve as an international "hazard alert."

I am also directing the State Department and other Federal agencies to encourage greater international cooperation in controlling trade in banned substances. We will take an active part in efforts to develop common standards and practices and to improve world hazard alert systems, export notification programs, and uniform hazard labeling.

Finally, the order establishes a mechanism for imposing export controls, in a few limited circumstances, on exceptionally hazardous banned or significantly restricted substances. The order relies on existing authority under the Export Administration Act and the regulatory record that led to the banning or significant restriction of these substances. It will require export licenses for those few extremely hazardous substances that: (1) represent a substantial threat to human health or safety or to the environment; (2) the export of which would cause clear and significant harm to the foreign policy interests of the United States; and (3) for which export licenses would be granted only in exceptional cases. I intend that the strictest interpretation be applied to these standards.

The Executive order is based upon a 2½-year study by a working group composed of 22 Federal agencies. The group was chaired by Esther Peterson, my Special Assistant for Consumer Affairs, and cochaired by Robert Harris, member of the Council on Environmental Quality. In developing the policy, the working group consulted extensively with representatives of industry, labor, and citizen organizations.

The policy gives special attention to the need to foster the sale of American-made products abroad. Available evidence suggests that the volume of U.S. trade in banned substances is not large. Yet, even a very few incidents of harm to foreign citizens or the environment can seriously damage our foreign policy interests and our long-term trading interests.

As international merchants, we have an obligation not to export to unsuspecting nations products which we ourselves would not allow in our own country. This Executive order will help us meet this obligation.

Federal Consumer Programs
Executive Order 12265. January 15, 1981

PROVIDING FOR ENHANCEMENT AND COORDINATION OF FEDERAL CONSUMER PROGRAMS

By the authority vested in me as President by the Constitution of the United States of America, and in order to enlarge the membership of the Consumer Affairs Council from twelve to twenty-four, Section 1–102 of Executive Order No. 12160 of September 26, 1979, is hereby amended to read as follows:

"1–102. The Council shall consist of representatives of the following agencies and such other officers or employees of the United States as the President may designate as members:

(a) Department of Agriculture.

(b) Department of Commerce.

(c) Department of Defense.

(d) Department of Energy.

(e) Department of Health and Human Services.

(f) Department of Housing and Urban Development.

(g) Department of the Interior.

(h) Department of Justice.

(i) Department of Labor.

(j) Department of State.

(k) Department of Transportation.

(l) Department of the Treasury.

(m) ACTION Agency.

(n) Administrative Conference of the United States.

(o) Community Services Administration.

(p) Department of Education.

(q) Environmental Protection Agency.

(r) Equal Employment Opportunity Commission.

(s) Federal Emergency Management Agency.

(t) General Services Administration.

(u) Small Business Administration.

(v) Tennessee Valley Authority.

(w) Veterans Administration.

(x) Commission on Civil Rights is invited to participate.

Each agency on the Council shall be represented by the head of the agency or by a senior-level official designated by the head of the agency.".

JIMMY CARTER

The White House,
January 15, 1981.

[Filed with the Office of the Federal Register,
3:25 p.m., January 15, 1981]

Food Security Wheat Reserve

Executive Order 12266.   January 15, 1981

By the authority vested in me as President of the United States of America by Section 302(a) of the Food Security Wheat Reserve Act of 1980 (Title III of the Agricultural Act of 1980 (Public Law 96–494)), it is hereby ordered as follows:

1–101. There is hereby established a Food Security Wheat Reserve composed of a reserve stock of wheat, which shall not exceed four million metric tons.

1–102. The Secretary of Agriculture is responsible for designating, in accordance with Section 302 of the Food Security Wheat Reserve Act of 1980, the specific reserve stocks of wheat which shall comprise the Food Security Wheat Reserve.

JIMMY CARTER

The White House,
January 15, 1981.

[Filed with the Office of the Federal Register,
3:26 p.m., January 15, 1981]

Generalized System of Preferences

Executive Order 12267.   January 15, 1981

AMENDING THE GENERALIZED SYSTEM OF PREFERENCES

By the authority vested in me as President by the Constitution and statutes of the United States of America, including Title V and Section 604 of the Trade Act of 1974, as amended (19 U.S.C. 2461 *et seq.*; 19 U.S.C. 2483), and in order (1) to provide for the continuation, to the greatest extent possible, of preferential treatment under the Generalized System of Preferences (GSP) for articles which are currently eligible for such treatment from countries designated as beneficiary developing countries, notwithstanding the changes to the Tariff Schedules of the United States (TSUS) (19 U.S.C. 1202) which have resulted from the recent enactment of legislation, (2) to remove certain items from preferential treatment, (3) to make technical corrections to Executive Order No. 11888, of November 24, 1975, as amended, and (4) to make conforming modifications to the TSUS, it is hereby ordered as follows:

1–101. The Tariff Schedules of the United States are modified by amending the article description for item 652.97 by adding "and parts thereof" to the present article description therefor.

1–102. Annex II of Executive Order No. 11888 of November 24, 1975, as amended, listing articles that are eligible for benefits of the GSP when imported from any designated beneficiary country is further amended as provided in the Annex to this Order.

1–103. Annex III of Executive Order No. 11888, as amended, listing articles that are eligible for benefits of the GSP when imported from all designated beneficiary countries except those specified in General Headnote 3(c)(iii) of the TSUS, is further amended by deleting items 176.17 and 520.35 therefrom.

1–104. General Headnote 3(c)(iii) of the TSUS, listing articles that are eligible for benefits of the GSP except when imported from the beneficiary countries listed opposite those articles, is amended by deleting therefrom the following:

"176.17 _____ Philippines
520.35 _____ Thailand".

1–105. The amendments made with respect to items 470.15, 470.18, 470.25, 470.55, 708.51, 708.52, and 725.38 by Section 1–102 of this Order shall be effective as to articles that are both (1) imported on or after January 1, 1976, and (2) entered, or withdrawn from warehouse for consumption, on or after October 17, 1980, and as to which the liquidations of the entries or withdrawals have not become final and conclusive under Section 514 of the Tariff Act of 1930 (19 U.S.C. 1514).

1–106. The amendments made with respect to items 407.15, 407.16, and 408.31 by Section 1–102 of this Order shall be effective as to articles that are both (1) imported on or after January 1, 1976, and (2) entered, or withdrawn from warehouse for consumption, on or after December 2, 1980, and as to which the liquidations of the entries or withdrawals have not become final and conclusive under Section 514 of the Tariff Act of 1930 (19 U.S.C. 1514).

1–107. The amendments made by this Order, with the exception of those listed in Sections 1–105 and 1–106 shall be effective as to articles that are both (1) imported on or after January 1, 1976 and (2) entered, or withdrawn from warehouse for consumption, on or after January 16, 1981.

JIMMY CARTER

The White House,
January 15, 1981.

[Filed with the Office of the Federal Register, 3:27 p.m., January 15, 1981]

NOTE: The annex is printed in the FEDERAL REGISTER of January 17, 1981.

Hostage Relief Act of 1980
Executive Order 12268. January 15, 1981

By the authority vested in me as President by the Constitution and statutes of the United States of America, including the Hostage Relief Act of 1980 (Public Law 96–449; 94 Stat. 1967; 5 U.S.C. 5561 note) and Section 301 of Title 3 of the United States Code, and in order to provide for the implementation of that Act, it is hereby ordered as follows:

1–101. The functions vested in the President by Sections 103, 104, 105 and 301 of the Hostage Relief Act of 1980 (5 U.S.C. 5561 note) are delegated to the Secretary of State.

1–102. The Secretary of State shall consult with the heads of appropriate Executive agencies in carrying out the functions in Sections 103, 104, and 105 of the Act.

JIMMY CARTER

The White House,
January 15, 1981.

[Filed with the Office of the Federal Register, 3:28 p.m., January 15, 1981]

President's Committee on Small Business Policy

Executive Order 12269. January 15, 1981

By the authority vested in me as President by the Constitution of the United States of America, and in order to establish, in accord with the Federal Advisory Committee Act, as amended (5 U.S.C. App. I), an advisory committee on the recommendations of the White House Conference on Small Business, it is hereby ordered as follows:

1-101. There is established a President's Committee on Small Business Policy which shall be composed of seven members appointed by the President.

1-102. The Committee shall advise the President, through the Administrator of the Small Business Administration, on appropriate responses to the recommendations of the White House Conference on Small Business.

1-103. The Administrator of the Small Business Administration shall provide the Committee with such administrative services and support as may be necessary.

1-104. Notwithstanding the provisions of any other Executive Order, the functions of the President under the Federal Advisory Committee Act (5 U.S.C. App. I), except that of reporting annually to the Congress, which are applicable to the Committee, shall be performed by the Administrator of the Small Business Administration in accordance with guidelines and procedures established by the Administrator of General Services.

1-105. The Committee shall terminate on December 31, 1982, unless sooner extended.

JIMMY CARTER

The White House,
    January 15, 1981.

[Filed with the Office of the Federal Register, 3:29 p.m., January 15, 1981]

President's Council on Spinal Cord Injury

Executive Order 12270. January 15, 1981

By the authority vested in me as President by the Constitution of the United States of America, and in order to establish, in accord with the Federal Advisory Committee Act, as amended (5 U.S.C. App. I), an advisory committee on spinal cord injury, it is hereby ordered as follows:

1-101. There is established a President's Council on Spinal Cord Injury which shall be composed of twelve members appointed by the President.

1-102. The Committee shall advise the President, through the Secretary of Education, on appropriate responses to the goals of prevention, diagnosis, treatment, and reversal of spinal cord injury.

1-103. The Secretary of Education shall provide the Council with such administrative services and support as may be necessary.

1-104. Notwithstanding the provisions of any other Executive Order, the functions of the President under the Federal Advisory Committee Act (5 U.S.C. App. I), except that of reporting annually to the Congress, which are applicable to the Council, shall be performed by the Secretary of Education in accordance with guidelines and procedures established by the Administrator of General Services.

1-105. The Committee shall terminate on December 31, 1981, unless sooner extended.

JIMMY CARTER

The White House,
    January 15, 1981.

[Filed with the Office of the Federal Register, 3:30 p.m., January 15, 1981]

Continuance of Certain Federal Advisory Committees

Executive Order 12271. January 15, 1981

By the authority vested in me as President by the Constitution and statutes of the United States of America, in accordance with the provisions of the Federal Advisory Committee Act, as amended (5 U.S.C. App. I), and in order to correct typographical errors, it is hereby ordered as follows:

1–101. So much of Section 1–101(h) of Executive Order No. 12258 (relating to the President's Advisory Committee for Women) that reads "Executive Order No. 12050" is corrected to read "Executive Order No. 12135".

1–102. So much of Section 1–101(o) of Executive Order No. 12258 (relating to the Federal Advisory Council on Occupational Safety and Health) that reads "Executive Order No. 12195" is corrected to read "Exectuive Order No. 12196".

JIMMY CARTER

The White House,
  January 15, 1981.

[Filed with the Office of the Federal Register, 3:31 p.m., January 15, 1981]

American Heart Month, 1981

Proclamation 4816. January 15, 1981

By the President of the United States of America

A Proclamation

Diseases of the heart and blood vessels afflict 40 million Americans, cause 950,000 deaths annually, and cost the Nation more than $60 billion each year in lost wages and productivity and in direct costs of medical care.

Cardiovascular diseases, still our Nation's leading cause of death, have been the target of a continuing national effort since 1948. Leading this assault on illness, disability, and premature death are the American Heart Association, a private health organization supported by individual contributions, and the National Heart, Lung and Blood Institute, part of the National Institutes of Health, a Federal agency supported by tax dollars. For more than 30 years, the two organizations have worked closely together conducting and supporting research, training, education and community service directed against heart diseases. In that joint effort, they have enlisted the cooperation and resources of numerous organizations and agencies—both public and private.

Diseases of the heart and blood vessels remain the number one killer in the United States, but we have made substantial and heartening progress toward reducing the devastating toll. Deaths from coronary heart disease have declined by 25 percent during the past decade. Deaths from stroke have declined by 37 percent during the same period. These dramatic declines are a significant factor in the marked increase over the past decade in life expectancy for all Americans.

We have developed a much better understanding of the disease process and in the detection and treatment of cardiovascular disease. As a people, we have improved our overall health practices. For example, there has been a sharp drop in cigarette smoking among middle-aged men who are at the highest risk of heart attack. There has been much progress in the control of high blood pressure which is the major cause of stroke and gratifying and productive changes in our approach to diet and physical fitness.

We still have a long way to go before diseases of the heart and blood vessels are brought under control or eliminated as a major cause of suffering and premature death. In recognition of the seriousness of this menace to the Nation's health and well-being, and to encourage the consolidation and extension of our efforts against cardiovascular disease, the Congress, by joint resolution approved December 30, 1963 (77 Stat. 843; 36 U.S.C. 169b) has requested the President to issue annually a proclamation designating February as American Heart Month.

Now, THEREFORE, I, JIMMY CARTER, President of the United States of America, do hereby proclaim the month of February 1981, as American Heart Month. I invite the Governors of the States, the Commonwealth of Puerto Rico, the officials of other areas subject to the jurisdiction of the United States, and the American people, to join with me in reaffirming our commitment to the fight against cardiovascular disease.

IN WITNESS WHEREOF, I have hereunto set my hand this fifteenth day of January, in the year of our Lord nineteen hundred and eighty-one, and of the Independence of the United States of America the two hundred and fifth.

JIMMY CARTER

[Filed with the Office of the Federal Register, 10:40 a.m., January 16, 1981]

United States-Federal Republic of Germany Convention on Taxation and Fiscal Evasion

Message to the Senate Transmitting the Convention. January 15, 1981

To the Senate of the United States:

I transmit herewith for Senate advice and consent to ratification, the Convention between the United States of America and the Federal Republic of Germany for the Avoidance of Double Taxation and the Prevention of Fiscal Evasion with Respect to Taxes on Estates, Inheritances and Gifts (the Convention), signed at Bonn on December 3, 1980. For the information of the Senate, I also transmit the report of the Department of State with respect to the Convention.

The Convention is the first of its kind to be negotiated between the United States and the Federal Republic of Germany. It will apply, in the United States, to the Federal estate tax, the Federal gift tax, and the Federal tax on generation-skipping transfers, and in the Federal Republic of Germany, to the inheritance and gift tax.

In general, the Convention is similar to the estate and gift tax convention with the United Kingdom, which entered into force on November 11, 1979, and to the United States estate and gift tax convention with France, which entered into force on October 1, 1980.

The principle underlying the Convention is that the country of domicile may tax the estate and gifts of a decedent or donor on a worldwide basis, but must credit tax paid to the other State with respect to certain types of property located therein.

I recommend that the Senate give early and favorable consideration to the Convention and give advice and consent to its ratification.

JIMMY CARTER

The White House,
January 15, 1981.

Anniversary of the Birth of Martin Luther King, Jr.

Statement by the President.
January 15, 1981

Dr. Martin Luther King, Jr., was not only an eloquent spokesman for the

American civil rights movement, and for human rights everywhere. He went the difficult second mile and took the risk of living what he believed, of facing the snarling dogs and men with clubs and fire-hoses armed only with the spirit of freedom and love. Looking squarely in the eye of hatred and fear he retained his "abiding faith in America and an audacious faith in the future of mankind."

He warned us of the evils of the racism he endured each day, but also of the unseen threat of nuclear destruction, reminding us always that the God he served had something better for us if we would but listen. "Unarmed truth and unconditional love will have the final word in reality," he assured us. "Right temporarily defeated is stronger than evil triumphant."

On this 52d anniversary of his birth, when containing the dangers of nuclear weapons and securing the fundamental human rights of people throughout the world are still unmet goals, we all need his message of nonviolence, of love in action. I commend the efforts of Coretta Scott King to continue his work through the Martin Luther King, Jr. Center for Social Change.

As we honor his memory this year, may we as a nation at last take hold of the treasured birthright he sought to hand down to us—of brotherhood and freedom, peace and love for all people.

Mississippi River Commission

Nomination of Maj. Gen. William Edgar Read To Be a Member and President.
January 15, 1981

The President today announced that he will nominate Maj. Gen. William Edgar Read to be a member and President of the Mississippi River Commission.

Read is division engineer of the United States Army Engineer Divison, Lower Mississippi Valley.

Budget Rescissions and Deferrals

Message to the Congress. January 15, 1981

To the Congress of the United States:

In accordance with the Impoundment Control Act of 1974, I herewith propose 33 new rescissions of budget authority previously provided by the Congress, totalling $1,142.4 million. In addition, I am reporting 15 new deferrals totalling $1,429.9 million and revisions to three previously-reported deferrals totalling $4.4 million.

The rescission proposals affect programs of the Departments of Commerce, Education, Energy, Health and Human Services, and Housing and Urban Development as well as the Community Services Administration, the Federal Mine Safety and Health Review Commission, the Federal payment to the Postal Service Fund, and the Tennessee Valley Authority. The deferrals affect programs of the Departments of Commerce, Defense, Energy, Interior, Justice, Labor, and State, as well as the intelligence community staff, the National Consumer Cooperative Bank, the Pennsylvania Avenue Development Corporation, and the Small Business Administration.

The details of each rescission proposal and deferral are contained in the attached reports.

JIMMY CARTER

The White House,
     January 15, 1981.

NOTE: The attachments detailing the budget rescissions and deferrals are printed in the FEDERAL REGISTER of January 21, 1981.

President's Commission for a National Agenda for the Eighties

Remarks on Receiving the Commission's Final Report.   January 16, 1981

CHAIRMAN McGILL. Mr. President, I have with me your Commission on a National Agenda for the Eighties. And it is my very great honor to be able to present to you on behalf of the Commission the first copy of our final report. But I'd like to say a word or two to you first if I may, sir.

THE PRESIDENT. Please do, yes.

CHAIRMAN McGILL. The final report will be complemented by the reports of nine study panels into which we organized ourselves to carry out the broad tasks that you gave to us. Taken together, they amount to about 1,200 pages of print, about 5,000 hours of study, discussion, decisionmaking on the part of 45 commissioners and all of it accomplished in less than 14 months. The only report to have been reviewed by the entire Commission is the report that I'm giving you this morning. The panel reports were signed only by the commissioners who carried on the special work of each panel, and that would be sometimes six, sometimes nine commissioners together with appropriate staff. Accordingly, some of the recommendations of the panels appear in the final report. Others appear in altered form. And others don't appear at all. But, in general, the work proceeded in an atmosphere of harmony.

There are no simple nostrums. There are no magic formulas that will revitalize the American economy, achieve energy independence, or lubricate our political processes. We see a decade of hard decisions and rather crushing burdens for our political leaders. But the outlook of the Commission is not a grim one. We believe that we have identified a mix of policies which has a good prospect of seeing us through the eighties safely. We do not anticipate that they would be broadly acceptable to all. We don't believe they're entirely acceptable to you, sir. But we do feel that they form a basis for public debate that is likely to be an effective way to project the Commission's work into the future.

I'd like to say a few words of acknowledgement, sir. I owe a great debt to my colleagues, the commissioners. They produced an atmosphere in which we were able to address all of our differences—and they were legion—and to resolve most of them in a cordial way. We carried on our sensitive work during an election year without a single embarrassing headline, for which I think we all owe these men and women a debt, because that is the highest level of responsibility.

We owe a particular debt to the Executive Committee of the Commission, the chairpersons of the study panels. The final draft of our report is largely the work of the Executive Committee. They synthesized the nine study panel reports, structured the final report, and, I think unique among Presidential Commissions, about 50 percent of the prose is the work of the Executive Committee. We owe a very considerable debt to our professional staff who worked effectively and assiduously to get this job done on time.

And finally, sir, we owe, I think, the greatest debt of all to you. You set us free to do our work without any interference of any sort. You placed the resources of your administration fully at our disposal, and you yourself conducted yourself with dignity and honor in the midst of the greatest national difficulties. Every commissioner here knows the kinds of problems that you have confronted and what you sought to do, because our work has given us a unique perspective on the difficulties you face.

And so, we thank you, and I give you this report, sir, and ask respectfully that you discharge the Commission. Our work is done. [*Laughter*]

THE PRESIDENT. Chairman McGill has expressed my exact sentiments in the appreciation that he evoked for the work of the Commission members and for the Executive Committee. I would like to add an additional word of thanks to you as Chairman, to Hedley Donovan, who helped to evolve the idea, helped me to select the members of the Commission, and for having structured the overall concept from its very initial moments.

This is a worthwhile effort. Some of the public attention has been drawn to one or two controversial portions of the report. I'm glad that you have shared with me during the last few months an analysis of some of the kinds of issues that a President and the Government of our Nation will have to face along with the interrelationship between the private sector—of labor, management—and the other levels of government at the State and local, official level.

I don't agree with everything that I have heard about the summary of the report, and I think that's proven by the fact that some of this is a departure from the policies that I've set down. Whether or not we should proceed aggressively with the synthetic fuels program, for instance; the exact role for the PLO to play in the Mideast settlement; how to delineate between preventive health care, hospital cost containment, and a national health program—those are the kinds of questions that you have addressed. And in some instances you've come down with a little different analysis of what should be done than what I personally would prefer. In most of the report, however, as I understand it, your recommendations are compatible with what I myself would advocate, and this has strengthened my own belief that I've been correct in pursuing those ideas.

I think it's important for the American people to understand, as I tried to explain during the campaign months, that there are no simple or easy answers to very complicated problems, that they are not likely to go away, that there's no magic nostrum or magic formula for resolving these difficulties, and that the American people need not expect them. But, as I mentioned night before last in a television address, I think our Nation, above all other nations on Earth, is equipped to meet these problems successfully, not only to give our own people a better life of challenge and achievement and excitement but also to provide leadership for the rest of the world. And if we can lead toward peace or toward the husbanding of our natural resources or toward the conservation of our precious possessions or to the enhancement of liberty, to better education, to better health, to better work opportunities, to better accommodation for inevitable change in the movement of people from one part of a nation to another, then I think the rest of the world will continue to emulate what we have done ourselves. So, I believe in all those areas that the report will be very constructive, and those who shape our Nation's future I'm sure will refer to this report with interest and also with great benefit.

Finally, let me say that just the raising of these issues for public debate is an important end in itself, that the fact that the issue is addressed not just within the private circles of the Cabinet Room or the Congress, even, but through the news media and involving hundreds of thousands, perhaps millions of people will be constructive. I've always felt that the more intimately involved the vast number of Americans are in the resolution of a problem, the more sound their judgment was likely to be in the final analysis. And I'm very grateful for that as well.

I want to say in closing that you are dismissed, having done a superb job. And I'm deeply grateful to you, and so is a nation which will benefit from your work. Thank you.

NOTE: The President spoke at 9:32 a.m. at the ceremony in the Cabinet Room at the White House.

President's Commission for a National Agenda for the Eighties

Statement on Receiving the Commission's Final Report.   January 16, 1981

I want to express my personal appreciation to Dr. McGill, the Chairman, and to all the members of the Commission for a National Agenda for the Eighties. All of you have worked hard to meet the objectives and the deadlines of the Commission, and the Nation is in your debt for that. I especially want to congratulate Dr. McGill for his outstanding leadership of 44 commissioners of widely diverse talents and interests.

When I established the Commission nearly 14 months ago, I asked you to conduct a wholly independent study of the major issues for the coming decade, and you have done that. You have produced a report which contains many innovative recommendations and ideas, and they have already initiated considerable public debate.

As you know, this effort began in response to my concern that in the last decade there emerged a number of factors—such as a changing economy, increasing global interdependence, the shortage of energy supplies, and the splintering of the political system—that will affect the Nation dramatically in the 1980's. You have assessed these factors forthrightly and suggested ways in which our country might deal with these factors.

In some areas, I very much agree with your recommendations and ideas. I generally share your belief that we cannot defer the hard choices among the range of national policy and programs, that a reexamination of the roles of Federal, State, and local governments is necessary, and that the Federal Government should increasingly utilize the private sector in meeting public needs, as I have done through progress such as the targeted jobs tax credit, Title VII of the CETA programs and economic development efforts through the Urban Development Action Grant program and the Economic Development Administration. I also agree with your general statements of the goals of our society in the 1980's, in your economic, social, political and international agendas. I am particularly heartened to note that you urge us not to turn our backs on the goal of a fair and just society, and a clean environment, in our search for the indispensable economic growth. I likewise share your optimism that we can achieve economic health, and our other goals as well, if we face up to our problems. I agree with many of your specific recommendations on how we should try to achieve those goals, such as: the importance of developing long-range tax and other policies to deal with inflation, unemployment and low productivity, the great value of energy conservation, the need to continue economic deregulation and use of more flexible regulatory techniques, the need for welfare reform, the equal rights amendment, amendments to the Fair Housing Act, and campaign finance reform.

In some other areas, I strongly disagree with the views expressed in your report. For example, I disagree with the Commission's views about a synthetic fuels development program, which I view as essential to our national security and our ability to reduce our dependence on foreign oil; about a comprehensive national health insurance program, which can extend health care coverage to millions of needy Americans while controlling health care costs; and about the need for a human rights policy, which I believe is essential in the pursuit of our foreign policy.

I feel compelled to offer my views on the Commission's urban policy recommendations, since they differ in many respects from my own urban policy. The Commission correctly identified the need to make Federal grants-in-aid responsive to the needs of States and localities. They propose consolidating existing grant-in-aid programs and giving State and local officials wider discretion in the use of Federal funds. I have sought to implement these recommendations during my administration. I have also used employment tax incentives and retraining aid to encourage a mobile and productive workforce.

However, I disagree with the implication in the Commission's recommendation that the Federal Government should play a role in facilitating the population trend from the Frostbelt to the Sunbelt. We cannot abandon our older urban areas. I believe we must recognize the unique values and resources of our older urban areas in the Northeast and Midwest and their current and potential contribution to our economy and our broader national life. My urban policy has stressed incentives for the private sector

to encourage economic development in our urban and distressed rural areas, to help rebuild their tax base so they can improve their economic viability and provide additional services for their citizens. I have targeted Federal aid on areas of greatest distress. These policies are beginning to show success as the economic base of many of our urban areas have begun to stabilize and new job opportunities have been created. In my view, the Nation has been well served by this effort.

But whether I personally agree or disagree with your recommendations is not, of course, the crucial test of the Commission's success. That will be determined by others in the months and years ahead. What is most important now is that the Commission's report stimulate a public discussion of where the country should be heading in this decade. I think that test will be met, and the country will be the better for it.

Agreement on the Importation of Educational, Scientific, and Cultural Materials

Message to the Senate Transmitting a Protocol to the Agreement.
January 16, 1981

To the Senate of the United States:

With a view to receiving the advice and consent of the Senate to ratification, I transmit herewith the Protocol to the Agreement on the Importation of Educational, Scientific, and Cultural Materials, adopted at Nairobi, Kenya, on November 26, 1976, and opened for signature at the United Nations on March 1, 1977. I also transmit, for the information of the Senate, the report of the Department of State with respect to the Protocol.

The Protocol amends and expands the coverage of the Agreement on the Importation of Educational, Scientific and Cultural Materials, which was adopted at Florence in July 1950, opened for signature on November 22, 1950, and entered into force for the United States on November 2, 1966. The purpose of the original Agreement was to facilitate the international flow of educational, scientific, and cultural materials, and generally the exchange of ideas, through the extension of duty-free treatment to a range of such educational, scientific and cultural materials. The present Protocol substantially broadens the list of eligible products, including those for the advancement of the blind and other handicapped persons.

Ratification of the Protocol is expected to have important beneficial effects on United States exports of products covered by the Agreement. It will also result in important benefits for the blind and handicapped in this country. I recommend, therefore, that the Senate give early and favorable consideration to the Protocol and advise and consent to its ratification.

JIMMY CARTER

The White House,
    January 16, 1981.

Military Awards Program of the Departments of Defense and Transportation

Message to the Congress Transmitting Two Reports.   January 16, 1981

To the Congress of the United States:

Forwarded herewith in accordance with the provisions of 10 U.S.C. § 1124 are reports of the Secretary of Defense and the Secretary of Transportation on awards made during Fiscal Year 1980 to members of the Armed Forces for suggestions, inventions and scientific achievements.

Participation by military personnel in the cash awards program was authorized by the Congress in 1965. More than two million suggestion submissions since that time attest to the success which the program has had as a means of motivating military personnel to seek ways of reducing costs and improving efficiency. Of those suggestions submitted, more than 350,000 have been adopted with resultant tangible first-year benefits in excess of one billion dollars.

Of the 73,326 suggestions which were submitted by military personnel (including Coast Guard military personnel) during Fiscal Year 1980, 11,520 were adopted. Cash awards totalling $967,155 were paid for adopted suggestions during Fiscal Year 1980. These awards were based not only on tangible first-year benefits of $31,163,369 realized from adopted suggestions during the fiscal year, but also on many additional benefits and improvements of an intangible nature.

Enlisted personnel received $795,679 in awards during Fiscal Year 1980 representing 80% of the total cash awards paid during this period. Officer personnel received $194,626 during the fiscal year.

Attached are reports of the Secretary of Defense and the Secretary of Transportation containing statistical information on the military awards program and brief descriptions of some of the more noteworthy contributions made by the military personnel during Fiscal Year 1980.

JIMMY CARTER

The White House,
    January 16, 1981.

Council on Wage and Price Stability

Message to the Congress Transmitting a Report.   January 16, 1981

To the Congress of the United States:

In accordance with Section 5 of the Council on Wage and Price Stability Act, as amended, I hereby transmit to the Congress the twenty-third quarterly report of the Council on Wage and Price Stability. The report contains a description of the Council's activities during the second quarter of 1980 in monitoring both prices and wages in the private sector and various Federal Government activities that may lead to higher costs and prices without creating commensurate benefits. It discusses Council reports, analyses, and filings before Federal regulatory agencies. It also describes the Council's activities of monitoring wages and prices as part of the anti-inflation program.

The Council on Wage and Price Stability has played an important role in supplementing fiscal and monetary policies by calling public attention to wage and price developments or actions by the Government that could be of concern to American consumers.

JIMMY CARTER

The White House,
   January 16, 1981.

Presidential Medal of Freedom

Remarks at the Presentation Ceremony. January 16, 1981

One of the wonderful experiences that is enjoyed by the men who've lived in this house and served here is to meet outstanding people from around the world, and particularly from his own Nation. It's not possible to recognize in any tangible way the literally tens of thousands, even more, Americans who serve unselfishly and who serve with distinction and who garner, because of their service, the legitimate debt and thanks of their fellow citizens.

A number of years ago President Harry Truman initiated the Presidential Medal of Freedom to single out a few distinguished Americans to represent that superb service. When a few are chosen, it's done without derogation of those not chosen. It's done as an exemplification of honor in a democracy among citizens who are all equal.

I've been quite reticent, compared to some of my predecessors, about the number who have been selected. The first ceremony that I had in 1977 I honored Martin Luther King, Jr., and Jonas Salk; later, Arthur Goldberg, Margaret Meade, Ansel Adams, Rachel Carson, Lucia Chase, Hubert Humphrey, Archbishop Lakovos, Lyndon Johnson, Clarence Mitchell, Jr., Roger Tory Peterson, Admiral Hyman Rickover, Beverly Sills, Robert Penn Warren, John Wayne, Eudora Welty, and Tennessee Williams.

As you listen to those names, one of the first questions that comes to mind is why weren't they honored long ago? And I feel that way about some of those who will be honored today. Four of our honorees can't be here, and I will explain to you why as their names are called. I would like now for the military aide to come forward to present the certificates to me, and I will read the citation and perhaps say a few extra words. As I do, those who are present please come forward. Those who have representatives, come forward in their place, and I will award the medals at that time. These are done not in order of seniority or age, but according to alphabetical listing of the last names.

First, "The President of the United States of America awards this Presidential Medal of Freedom to Harold Brown."

[*At this point, the President read the citation, the text of which follows:*]

THE PRESIDENT OF THE UNITED STATES OF AMERICA AWARDS THIS PRESIDENTIAL MEDAL OF FREEDOM TO HAROLD BROWN

From the government of science to the science of government, Harold Brown has served his country first and his principles always. As an advisor to Presidents, and a president of a community of scholars, he has helped bridge the gap between the world of theory and the world of reality. Adept at translating from the language of science to the language of statecraft, he excels in translating purpose into action.

Signed, Jimmy Carter, the White House, Washington, D.C., January 16, 1981.

I have worked and served with Harold Brown for 4 years. He's a man of strength and a man of peace. He's brought level-headed judgment to one of the major departments of our country in times of testing, in times of potential war. But because of his sound judgment and the trust that others have in him, he has preserved our Nation as it should be, strong and peaceful.

It's with a great deal of honor that I present the Medal of Freedom to Harold Brown.

The next one: "The President of the United States of America awards this Presidential Medal of Freedom to Zbigniew Brzezinski."

[*The President read the citation, the text of which follows:*]

THE PRESIDENT OF THE UNITED STATES OF AMERICA AWARDS THIS PRESIDENTIAL MEDAL OF FREEDOM TO ZBIGNIEW BRZEZINSKI

Zbigniew Brzezinski served his country and the world. An author and architect of world affairs, his strategic vision of America's purpose fused principle with strength. His leadership has been instrumental in building peace and ending the estrangement of the Chinese and American people. But above all, he helped set our nation irrevocably on a course that honors America's abiding commitment to human rights.

Signed, Jimmy Carter, this date, the White House.

I doubt that anyone in my own administration has been more controversial than Dr. Brzezinski. And the reason for it is manifold, but I'd like to make two reasons. One is that he's evocative; he's a person who explores constantly better ways to do things. His Eastern European origins have given him an almost unmatched understanding of the interrelationships among the cultural entities of the Soviet Union and the satellite countries. He came here early in his life seeking freedom. He's a clear spokesman. I don't know of a single time in the last 4 years when he has ever made a public statement of any kind, privately or publicly which was not compatible with my own policies.

The other reason that he has been somewhat controversial is that he has never tried to take credit for a success, nor has he ever tried to blame me as President, or anyone else, for a failure. To me, this is a wonderful evidence of courage, because it's so easy for someone who works within the inner circles of the White House in particular and other places of leadership when something goes wrong, very quietly, very subtly to say, "I recommended one thing; the President or the Secretary of State or the Secretary of Defense did something else." Zbigniew Brzezinski has never done that. I'm deeply indebted to him, and I think that the Nation shares that debt with me.

It's with a great deal of pride and gratitude that I present the Medal of Freedom to Dr. Zbigniew Brzezinski.

I look around the room and people who know the alphabet and who work very closely with me are smiling with anticipation about the next award. "The President of the United States of America awards this Presidential Medal of Freedom to Warren Christopher."

I might say that Warren Christopher is in Algiers working as he has for the last 14 months for the freedom of the American hostages. He's listening to my voice through an open telephone line, and I'd like to read this citation.

[The President read the citation, the text of which follows:]

THE PRESIDENT OF THE UNITED STATES OF AMERICA AWARDS THIS PRESIDENTIAL MEDAL OF FREEDOM TO WARREN CHRISTOPHER

Warren Christopher has the tact of a true diplomat, the tactical skills of a great soldier, the analytical ability of a fine lawyer, and the selfless dedication of a citizen-statesman. His perseverance and loyalty, judgment and skill have won for his country new respect around the world and new regard for the State Department here at home.

Signed, Jimmy Carter, this date, White House.

Last week I was in Plains, and I was invited out to a small French restaurant between Plains and Americus by the press; it's one of the few French restaurants between Plains and Americus. *[Laughter]* And when I sat at the table eating supper, we had an informal off-the-record discussion, and the members of the press asked me, "Of all the public servants with whom you have served as President, who would you rank number one?" And I didn't hesitate a moment. I said, "Warren Christopher."

I think that those others who are being honored here today and all those that have worked with me would agree that he is indeed outstanding. I am indebted to him, and so is the Nation, far beyond what the general public knows.

And it's with a great deal of pleasure and pride and honor that I present this Medal of Freedom to his lovely wife for Warren Christopher, a distinguished American.

"The President of the United States of America awards this Presidential Medal of Freedom to Walter Cronkite." Congratulations to you.

[The President read the citation, the text of which follows:]

THE PRESIDENT OF THE UNITED STATES OF AMERICA AWARDS THIS PRESIDENTIAL MEDAL OF FREEDOM TO WALTER CRONKITE

For thousands of nights, the eyes and ears of millions of Americans have been tuned in to the eyes and ears of Walter Cronkite. He has reported and commented on the events of the last two decades with a skill and insight which stands out in the news world, in a way which has made the news of the world stand out for all of us.

There is probably not a single American who doesn't know Walter Cronkite, and of those tens of millions who know him, I don't believe there are any who distrust him. When our Nation has had great achievements, his voice has explained the significance of it, whether we have achieved peace when it was doubtful or when a man has landed on the Moon. And when our Nation has been in trouble or made mistakes and there was a danger that our public might react adversely or even panic on occasion, the calm and reassuring demeanor and voice and the inner character of Walter Cronkite has been reassuring to us all. He's a man superb on his own, but who has exemplified in the finest way the profession which he represents.

And on behalf of all Americans, I extend my congratulations and my appreciation to a distinguished American, a public servant, Walter Cronkite.

"The President of the United States of America awards this Presidential Medal of Freedom to Kirk Douglas."

[*The President read the citation, the text of which follows:*]

THE PRESIDENT OF THE UNITED STATES OF AMERICA AWARDS THIS PRESIDENTIAL MEDAL OF FREEDOM TO KIRK DOUGLAS

Acclaimed as a screen actor and director here at home, Kirk Douglas has often played a different role abroad. Acting as an ambassador of good will beyond our shores, he has travelled around the world for our State Department and the United States Information Agency. The son of Russian immigrants, he travels, too, for the opportunity to share with other peoples his love of film, and country.

I've know Kirk Douglas personally and appreciate his friendship. But more than that, I have known how dedicated he is to using his talent as an actor and a director and the esteem with which he's held by his own people in spreading the good news about this country and explaining our purposes, our ideals, our commitments, and our achievements, our hopes, and our dreams to people around the world. He's done this in a sacrificial way, almost invariably without fanfare and without claiming any personal credit or acclaim for himself.

And so, it's with a great deal of pleasure that I give him this recognition and admire his modesty and thank him for what he has meant and what he still means and will mean to the country which he loves.

"The President of the United States of America awards this Presidential Medal of Freedom to Margaret Craig McNamara."

[*The President read the citation, the text of which follows:*]

THE PRESIDENT OF THE UNITED STATES OF AMERICA AWARDS THIS PRESIDENTIAL MEDAL OF FREEDOM TO MARGARET CRAIG MCNAMARA

Margaret Craig McNamara saw a need in our society, and filled it. By creating the Reading is FUNdamental program, which has provided youngsters all over this country with millions of books, she has opened new doors in the minds of our young people and has given fresh meaning to the lives of the parents, teachers and volunteers who have joined her program.

The other night, I think in this room, I spoke to a group of people who represented local and State government in an official capacity, and I reminded them that the things that occupy our mind and to which we are dedicated are the simple things of life—things like a mother, a baby, retarded children, love for the elderly, the quality of a classroom, gentleness, love, peace, the purity of air, quietness—those kinds of things are what we try to preserve and enhance. Margaret Craig McNamara has taken this kind of commitment very long ago, when she saw two young men, I believe; talked to them quietly, found that they had never owned a book, weren't interested in reading. And she had just a simple idea of getting books and not lending them to people but letting them own their own. Since then tens of millions of books have been collected through her leadership and given to young people. It has transformed their lives.

There are hundreds of centers now all over this Nation. And she has marshaled tens of thousands of people to help in this program. She's done it quietly, because she loves others. She's dedicated a major part of her life to this effort, a simple thing of through reading, stretching the minds and the hearts of young people who wouldn't otherwise know how great God's world is and wouldn't know much about their fellow human beings. She's the kind of person who is an inspiration to all Americans who love others.

And it's with a great deal of pride that I present this Medal of Freedom to Margaret Craig McNamara.

"The President of the United States of America awards this Presidential Medal of Freedom to Karl Menninger." Dr. Menninger, as you may have anticipated, is busy enhancing the mental treatment qualities of this Nation. He's on the west coast, and honored by this award, of course, he still asked that he be excused so he could continue his work uninterrupted. A not so valuable nephew, Dr. Roy Menninger—[laughter]—has volunteered to come forward to accept the award for his uncle. And I would like to read the award now.

[*The President read the citation, the text of which follows:*

THE PRESIDENT OF THE UNITED STATES OF AMERICA AWARDS THIS PRESIDENTIAL MEDAL OF FREEDOM TO KARL MENNINGER

Karl Menninger has taught us much about ourselves and our behavior. An acute observer and social critic, he has put into action what he has put onto paper. As an author and doctor, his works range from popular, written accounts of psychiatry to studies done in his own hospital, from creating homes for parentless children to reforming the penal system. With the wisdom of his years, he truly does represent the ideas of another generation—one of the future, rather than of the past.]

All of those in this room who have been interested in improving the quality of mental health of this Nation have heard the name Karl Menninger since many years ago. He has been a pioneer, but as the closing phrase of this citation reminds us, he has never looked backward. He has always looked forward. His entire family has made the Menninger Clinic what it stands for, a powerful factor for a better life for Americans, not just in its own neighborhood but throughout the world. And with his research and with his writing, with his lecturing, with his training of other doctors, psychiatrists, psychologists, and others, he has literally transformed the mental health care attitudes of our great Nation.

To Dr. Roy Menninger, I want to express my deep thanks for accepting this award on behalf of his uncle and express

my thanks also to the entire Menninger family. It's with a great deal of pleasure that I present this award to Dr. Roy Menninger for Dr. Karl Menninger.

This is one of those, people would say, "Why wasn't it done long ago?" The President of the United States of America awards this Presidential Medal of Freedom to Edmund S. Muskie.

[*The President read the citation, the text of which follows:*]

THE PRESIDENT OF THE UNITED STATES OF AMERICA AWARDS THIS PRESIDENTIAL MEDAL OF FREEDOM TO EDMUND S. MUSKIE

As Senator and Secretary of State, candidate and citizen, Edmund S. Muskie has captured for himself a place in the public eye and the public's heart. Devoted to his nation and our ideals, he has performed heroically in a time of great challenge, with great fortitude in an era of change.

If Ed were going to rewrite this citation, he would certainly insert the word "Governor." I remember when we had the swearing-in ceremony in this room not too long ago, Ed pointed out that his love for the Governorship equaled my own, and I think those who have served in that position would agree that this is a wonderful opportunity for service before one comes to Washington to serve our whole Nation.

Ed Muskie has been a man whom I've admired ever since I've been aware of his public service and been interested myself in going into the political arena. He has performed all of his official functions admirably with a quiet sense of inner strength and demonstrated courage. He has never yielded to temptation to lower his own standards or the standards which make all public servants proud. He's a man who has transcended in all his service any particular delineation of a political party, but has stayed a loyal Democrat at the same time. He's a man admired by all and the admiration is richly deserved.

I'm particularly grateful to Ed Muskie, because he was willing to leave a sure seat in the Senate to come and serve in a very difficult position as Secretary of State in this time of transition or change. It's not an easy time. But he did it with conviction that this was the best place for him to give his tremendous talents for the further service of his fellow Americans.

He's a personal friend, as many of these honorees are, and personally and as President of our country, I'm delighted and proud to award the Medal of Freedom to Ed Muskie.

"The President of the United States of America awards this Presidential Medal of Freedom to Esther Peterson."

[The President read the citation, the text of which follows:]

THE PRESIDENT OF THE UNITED STATES OF AMERICA AWARDS THIS PRESIDENTIAL MEDAL OF FREEDOM TO ESTHER PETERSON

Once government's highest ranking woman, Esther Peterson still ranks highest among consumer advocates. She has advised Presidents and the public, and has worked for labor and business alike, always keeping the rights of all Americans to know and to be treated fairly as her highest priority. Even her staunchest foes respect her integrity and are warmed by her grace and sincere concern.

You may be surprised that in the citation the word "foes" is mentioned in relation to this lovely American, but she has made some foes. *[Laughter]* And I would guess, knowing her, that she's prouder of the foes she has made—*[laughter]*—if possible, than even some of the friends she has. She has never been afraid to address difficult issues even at the expense on occasion of personal harmony with those about whom she cares. She serves others with her entire dedicated life.

She's come to the inner circles of the White House in a major position during these last few years to work with me to make sure that the average American is not cheated, that they are told the truth, that they are treated fairly, and that when they go into the marketplace they can have some inner sense of trust in the free enterprise system which she has served so well. She's a delightful person, a person with charm, a person who makes deep friendships and deep commitments. And her deepest commitment has been to those who don't know her and who will probably never see her or maybe not even hear her voice. She serves those who are most deprived and has done that with her whole life.

I love her personally, and I congratulate her on receiving this award, the Medal of Freedom of our country.

"The President of the United States of America awards this Presidential Medal of Freedom to Gerard C. Smith." Gerry Smith.

[The President read the citation, the text of which follows:]

THE PRESIDENT OF THE UNITED STATES OF AMERICA AWARDS THIS PRESIDENTIAL MEDAL OF FREEDOM TO GERARD C. SMITH

Gerard C. Smith has represented our country in many capacities—as the first U.S. Chairman of the Trilateral Commission, as chief U.S. delegate to the Strategic Arms Limitation Talks in 1969. In helping formulate our national security policy, in promoting a better understanding of foreign relations, he has helped us all to perceive that in this nuclear age security and peace are indivisible.

In my farewell address the other night, I emphasized one subject perhaps greater than any other, and that is the control of nuclear weapons throughout the world. One way to control nuclear weapons is to have an agreement, a binding agreement, between ourselves and the Soviet Union, the other superpower, to control and to limit and hopefully to reduce, ultimately to eliminate nuclear weapons altogether. The other way is to make sure that the world understands the threat of nuclear weaponry and the threat of a nuclear war and that we can impose a policy of nonproliferation, to prevent the spread of nuclear weaponry to other nations around the world.

Gerry Smith has been involved from the very beginning of our Nation's policy of nonproliferation. He's been a teacher of leaders in this country and around the world. He's put forward our own Nation's programs and policies with distinction and commitment and tenacity. He's a great negotiator, a very successful one, and he's responsible now for the SALT treaty which is binding upon and has been for many years binding upon our Nation and the Soviet Union. Our country is indebted to Gerry Smith. And as President, I'm personally indebted to him as well.

I want to say at this time that I congratulate him; I'm honored to present the Medal of Freedom to a fine American who has served us well, Gerard C. Smith.

"The President of the United States of America awards this Presidential Medal of Freedom to Robert S. Strauss."

[The President read the citation, the text of which follows:]

The President of the United States of America Awards This Presidential Medal of Freedom to Robert S. Strauss

For Americans politics is the art of the possible. Through intelligence, ability, and the many friendships earned during his service as the leader of his party and his Nation, Robert S. Strauss has refined that art into a science. With diligence, persistence, and wit, he successfully concluded the multilateral trade negotiations at a time when many believed that they were doomed for failure. For strengthening the system of trade which links the nations of our increasingly interdependent world he has earned our gratitude and respect.

The first time I went to an international forum to meet with the leaders of other great Western nations—Japan, Canada,

Italy, Great Britain, Germany, France—I asked them about the longstanding effort to conclude a multilateral trade agreement that would enhance the quality of life, the productivity, the exchange of goods, the enhancement of peace among all the nations of the Western world. Chancellor Schmidt, President Giscard d'Estaing, at that time Prime Minister Callaghan, all told me this was a fruitless wish, that the Multilateral Trade Negotiations were dead. I decided to ask Bob Strauss to give it a try. And he succeeded.

Not only did he succeed in bringing the multiple nations together in one of the most complex negotiating efforts that I have ever seen, but he came back and convinced the Members of Congress—Democrats, Republicans, House and Senate—that the very complicated agreements that he had negotiated and which, I would guess, many of them never read, were in the best interest of our country, in the best interest of their constituents, and would do them credit on the next election day. And the Multilateral Trade Negotiation Act passed the Congress overwhelmingly. As a matter of fact, it passed so easily, that there were no violent altercations or major debates, and the event almost escaped the notice of the press, even CBS Evening News. [*Laughter*] But it was a notable achievement, and it was one that utilized the tremendous talents of this good man.

Later, Bob Strauss helped to negotiate peace between Israel and Egypt, pursuing the Camp David accords and the treaty that had been signed. And I think everyone who knows him would say that his understanding of the people of this country, his ability to get along with people of diverse views, and his ability to bring people together in an agreement that enhances the quality of life of all Americans is indeed outstanding. He's a man, as the citation says, of wit and competence and integrity.

And I'm very proud to present the Medal of Freedom to Robert Strauss.

This next one is of particular pleasure for me. "The President of the United States of America awards this Presidential Medal of Freedom to Elbert Tuttle."

[*The President read the citation, the text of which follows:*]

THE PRESIDENT OF THE UNITED STATES OF AMERICA AWARDS THIS PRESIDENTIAL MEDAL OF FREEDOM TO ELBERT TUTTLE

Elbert Tuttle is a true judicial hero. At a time when it was unpopular to do so, he carried out the mandate of Supreme Court decisions and Congressional legislation to end racial discrimination in the Deep South. With steadfast courage and a deep love and understanding of the region, he has helped to make the Constitutional principle of equal protection a reality of American life.

Those of us who have lived in the South during the time when racial discrimination was ended by the courts are perhaps the only ones here who can adequately appreciate the courage of a Federal judge like Elbert Tuttle. His decisions not only required the knowledge of the law and courage. They required a character and an earned degree of esteem from his fellow Georgians and his fellow southerners that would add additional weight to his decisions. When the people in my region would read that Judge Elbert Tuttle had ruled this way, we had a natural sense that even though some may not agree, it must be right.

I'm indebted to him personally. Both I and one of the honorees would probably never be here in the White House on this day had it not been for Elbert Tuttle and men like him. He's a man of brilliant mind. He can handle complex legal decisions easily, but he's a man of simple commitments and ideals. When he was interviewed at the time of his retire-

ment from the Federal bench on national television, the interviewer said, "Judge Tuttle, I understand that you have never drunk alcoholic beverages," and Judge Tuttle said, "That's right." And the interviewer said, "Would you mind telling our television audience why?" And Judge Tuttle said, "Because my mother told me not to." [*Laughter*] I've thought about that a lot. [*Laughter*] And a lot of people in this Nation did what was right because Judge Tuttle said, "That's what we ought to do."

I'm honored to present to him the Medal of Freedom. Federal Judge Elbert Tuttle.

Even great men like Elbert Tuttle have leaders. "The President of the United States of America awards this Presidential Medal of Freedom to Earl Warren."

[*The President read the citation, the text of which follows:*]

THE PRESIDENT OF THE UNITED STATES OF AMERICA AWARDS THIS PRESIDENTIAL MEDAL OF FREEDOM TO EARL WARREN

Earl Warren led a unanimous court that in turn led the Nation in reversing a century of judicial and social history. By affirming that separate is not equal, he and his court reaffirmed the truth of the words carved in stone at the entrance to the Supreme Court: "Equal Justice For All." As governor, presidential candidate and Chief Justice, he has truly been a citizen for all seasons.

As I stood here this afternoon, I tried to think of any man who has served in the White House as President who has benefited our Nation as much or more than Earl Warren—and I can't think of anybody. There comes a time in the evolution of society when a certain quality of understanding and integrity and leadership is a prerequisite to further progress. When hopeless, perhaps, but courageous people are being frustrated, when the times call for change, but ordinary human beings can't bring themselves to make the change because they might be criticized by their peers or those whom they would like to please, and when the trend of history must be modified or even reversed, I thank God that Earl Warren was the Chief Justice of the Supreme Court in a time like that. And with his decision, he helped to realize the aspirations and ideals expressed in the Declaration of Independence and the Constitution of our Nation.

His predecessors had not adequately done it. He departed from some long-standing decisions that they had made. I say that without criticizing them. But it took a special man to make those difficult decisions that Judge Tuttle and others followed in the administration of justice and the enhancement of equality of opportunity under the law for all the people of our Nation.

Miss Nina has come here representing her late husband, and I'm honored especially to present the Medal of Freedom to the beloved wife of one of the finest Americans who ever served in any capacity in the Government of our Nation, former Chief Justice of the Supreme Court Earl Warren.

I would like to say before I present the last medal here that Roger Baldwin, a great civil rights leader, is in the hospital in New Jersey. At 3 o'clock this afternoon, the same time as we began our ceremony here, he was presented with a Medal of Freedom by William Vanden Heuvel, Deputy Ambassador to the United Nations, on my behalf.[1]

---

[1] The text of the citation reads as follows:

THE PRESIDENT OF THE UNITED STATES OF AMERICA AWARDS THIS PRESIDENTIAL MEDAL OF FREEDOM TO ROGER NASH BALDWIN

Founder of the American Civil Liberties Union and the International League for Human

Now the President of the United States awards this next Medal of Freedom to Andrew Young.

[The President read the citation, the text of which follows:]

THE PRESIDENT OF THE UNITED STATES OF AMERICA AWARDS THIS PRESIDENTIAL MEDAL OF FREEDOM TO ANDREW YOUNG

Andrew Young brought to diplomatic service a lifetime of dedication to human rights. He helped restore trust in the United States among Third World nations, especially in Africa, demonstrating to them that American foreign policy was based on our firm belief in justice, freedom, majority rule, and opportunity for all people.

I first heard about Andrew Young when I read news reports that he was in jail along with Martin Luther King, Jr., and when I saw his photographs in the newspaper seeking, with danger to his own life, to prove that our Constitution and the rulings of Earl Warren and Judge Tuttle ought to be put into effect by human beings. He's a man of quiet demeanor, having served as a United States Congressman from my State.

When I was elected President, one of my major goals was to enhance human rights and to strengthen the ties of friendship and understanding and mutual respect between our Nation and the small, sometimes weak, new nations of the world, those whose people might be black or brown or yellow and who in the past had sometimes distrusted our country because there was a lack of understanding on our own leaders' part of them. I asked Andy Young to leave the Congress and to serve as our U.N. Ambassador. He did it reluc-

---

Rights, Roger Nash Baldwin is a leader in the field of civil rights and a legend in the field of civil liberties. He is a national resource, and an international one as well, an inspiration to those of us who have fought for human rights, a saint to those for whom he has gained them.

tantly. But when he went to the United Nations he served our Nation superbly.

Sometimes I have to admit I was surprised by some of the statements that Andy made, and I don't agree with all of them and didn't then. But if you listen closely to what he says, in the context of his statement, you see the wisdom and the continued purpose of his life expressed not just locally or domestically, but internationally.

Throughout the Asian countries, the South American countries, the African countries, and many others, Andy Young is the brightest star in the American firmament. He's the man who represents integrity and understanding, humility, purpose, and who exemplifies the quiet teachings of his Saviour, whom he represents as a preacher of the gospel. He's carried on well along with Coretta and others the heritage of Martin Luther King, Jr., and I'm deeply grateful for what Andy has meant to me personally, to me as President, and to our Nation. His beneficial service will help our Nation in many years ahead, and he's done it always with humility and with a quiet sense of calm, because he was sure that what he did was right for others. I've never known a person more unselfish than Andrew Young. And the respect that he enjoys around the world is well-deserved.

I'm honored to present the Medal of Freedom to Ambassador, former Congressman, great American, Andrew Young.

Can I ask all of the recipients of the medal to come up on the platform perhaps now for a photograph, and then we'll adjourn the meeting.

NOTE: The President spoke at 3:05 p.m. in the East Room at the White House.

The State of the Union

Annual Message to the Congress.
January 16, 1981

To the Congress of the United States:

The State of the Union is sound. Our economy is recovering from a recession. A national energy plan is in place and our dependence on foreign oil is decreasing. We have been at peace for four uninterrupted years.

But, our Nation has serious problems. Inflation and unemployment are unacceptably high. The world oil market is increasingly tight. There are trouble spots throughout the world, and 53 [1] American hostages are being held in Iran against international law and against every precept of human affairs.

However, I firmly believe that, as a result of the progress made in so many domestic and international areas over the past four years, our Nation is stronger, wealthier, more compassionate and freer than it was four years ago. I am proud of that fact. And I believe the Congress should be proud as well, for so much of what has been accomplished over the past four years has been due to the hard work, insights and cooperation of Congress. I applaud the Congress for its efforts and its achievements.

In this State of the Union Message I want to recount the achievements and progress of the last four years and to offer recommendations to the Congress for this year. While my term as President will end before the 97th Congress begins its work in earnest, I hope that my recommendations will serve as a guide for the direction this country should take so we build on the record of the past four years.

EDITORIAL NOTE: The White House announced that the number should read 52.

RECORD OF PROGRESS

When I took office, our Nation faced a number of serious domestic and international problems:

• no national energy policy existed, and our dependence on foreign oil was rapidly increasing;

• public trust in the integrity and openness of the government was low;

• the Federal government was operating inefficiently in administering essential programs and policies;

• major social problems were being ignored or poorly addressed by the Federal government;

• our defense posture was declining as a result of a defense budget which was continuously shrinking in real terms;

• the strength of the NATO Alliance needed to be bolstered;

• tensions between Israel and Egypt threatened another Middle East war; and

• America's resolve to oppose human rights violations was under serious question.

Over the past 48 months, clear progress has been made in solving the challenges we found in January of 1977:

• almost all of our comprehensive energy program have been enacted, and the Department of Energy has been established to administer the program;

• confidence in the government's integrity has been restored, and respect for the government's openness and fairness has been renewed;

• the government has been made more effective and efficient: the Civil Service system was completely reformed for the first time this century; 14 reorganization initiatives have been proposed to the Congress, approved, and implemented; two new Cabinet departments have been created to consolidate and streamline the government's handling of energy and education problems; inspectors general have been placed in each Cabinet department to combat fraud, waste and other abuses; the regulatory process has been reformed through creation of the Regulatory Council, implementation of Executive Order 12044 and its requirement for cost-impact analyses, elimination of unnecessary regulation, and passage of the Regulatory Flexibility Act; procedures have been established to assure citizen participation in government; and the airline, trucking, rail and communications industries are being deregulated;

• critical social problems, many long ignored by the Federal government, have been addressed directly; an urban policy was developed and implemented to reverse the decline in our urban areas; the Social Security System was refinanced to put it on a sound financial basis; the Humphrey-Hawkins Full Employment Act was enacted; Federal assistance for education was expanded by more than 75 percent; the minimum wage was increased to levels needed to ease the effects of inflation; affirmative action has been pursued aggressively—more blacks, Hispanics and women have been appointed to senior government positions and to judgeships than at any other time in our history; the ERA ratification deadline was extended to aid the ratification effort; and minority business procurement by the Federal government has more than doubled;

• the Nation's first sectoral policies were put in place, for the auto and steel industries, with my Administration demonstrating the value of cooperation between the government, business and labor;

• reversing previous trends, real defense spending has increased every year since 1977; the real increase in FY 1980 defense spending is well above 3 percent and I expect FY 1981 defense spending to be even higher; looking ahead, the defense program I am proposing is premised on a real increase in defense spending over the next five years of 20 percent or more;

• the NATO Alliance has proven its unity in responding to the situations in Eastern Europe and Southwest Asia and in agreeing on the issues to be addressed in the review of the Helsinki Final Act currently underway in Madrid;

• the peace process in the Middle East established at Camp David and by the Peace Treaty between Egypt and Israel is being buttressed on two fronts: steady progress in the normalization of Egyptian-Israeli relations in many fields, and the commitment of both Egypt and Israel, with United States' assistance, to see through to successful conclusion the autonomy negotiations for the West Bank and Gaza;

• the Panama Canal Treaties have been put into effect, which has helped to improve relations with Latin America;

• we have continued this Nation's strong commitment to the pursuit of human rights throughout the world, even-handedly and objectively; our commitment to a worldwide human rights policy has remained firm; and many other countries have given high priority to it;

• our resolve to oppose aggression, such as the illegal invasion of the Soviet Union into Afghanistan, has been supported by tough action.

I. Ensuring Economic Strength

ECONOMY

During the last decade our Nation has withstood a series of economic shocks unprecedented in peacetime. The most dramatic of these has been the explosive increases of OPEC oil prices. But we have also faced world commodity shortages, natural disasters, agricultural shortages and major challenges to world peace and security. Our ability to deal with these shocks has been impaired because of a decrease in the growth of productivity and the persistence of underlying inflationary forces built up over the past 15 years.

Nevertheless, the economy has proved to be remarkably resilient. Real output has grown at an average rate of 3 percent per year since I took office, and employment has grown by 10 percent. We have added about 8 million productive private sector jobs to the economy. However, unacceptably high inflation—the most difficult economic problem I have faced—persists.

This inflation—which threatens the growth, productivity, and stability of our economy—requires that we restrain the growth of the budget to the maximum extent consistent with national security and human compassion. I have done so in my earlier budgets, and in my FY '82 budget. However, while restraint is essential to any appropriate economic policy, high inflation cannot be attributed solely to government spending. The growth in budget outlays has been more the result of economic factors than the cause of them.

We are now in the early stages of economic recovery following a short recession. Typically, a post-recessionary period has been marked by vigorous economic growth aided by anti-recessionary policy measures such as large tax cuts or big, stimulation spending programs. I have declined to recommend such actions to stimulate economic activity, because the persistent inflationary pressures that beset our economy today dictate a restrained fiscal policy.

Accordingly, I am asking the Congress to postpone until January 1, 1982, the personal tax reductions I had earlier proposed to take effect on January 1 of this year.

However, my 1982 budget proposes significant tax changes to increase the sources of financing for business investment. While emphasizing the need for continued fiscal restraint, this budget takes the first major step in a long-term tax reduction program designed to increase capital formation. The failure of our Nation's capital stock to grow at a rate that keeps pace with its labor force has clearly been one cause of our productivity slowdown. Higher investment rates are also critically needed to meet our Nation's energy needs, and to replace energy-inefficient plants and equipment with new energy-saving physical plants. The level of investment that is called for will not occur in the absence of policies to encourage it.

Therefore, my budget proposes a major liberalization of tax allowances for depreciation, as well as simplified depreciation accounting, increasing the allowable rates by about 40 percent. I am also proposing improvements in the investment tax credit, making it refundable, to meet the investment needs of firms with no current earnings.

These two proposals, along with carefully-phased tax reductions for individuals, will improve both economic efficiency and tax equity. I urge the Congress to enact legislation along the lines and timetable I have proposed.

THE 1982 BUDGET

The FY 1982 budget I have sent to the Congress continues our four-year policy of prudence and restraint. While the budget deficits during my term are higher than I would have liked, their size is determined for the most part by economic conditions. And in spite of these conditions, the relative size of the deficit continues to decline. In 1976, before I took office, the budget deficit equalled 4 percent of gross national product. It had been cut to 2.3 percent in the 1980 fiscal year just ended. My 1982 budget contains a deficit estimated to be less than 1 percent of our gross national product.

The rate of growth in Federal spending has been held to a minimum. Nevertheless, outlays are still rising more rapidly than many had anticipated, the result of many powerful forces in our society:

We face a threat to our security, as events in Afghanistan, the Middle East, and Eastern Europe make clear. We have a steadily aging population and, as a result, the biggest single increase in the Federal budget is the rising cost of retirement programs, particularly social security. We face other important domestic needs: to continue responsibility for the disadvantaged; to provide the capital needed by our cities and our transportation systems; to protect our environment; to revitalize American industry; and to increase the export of American goods and services so essential to the creation of jobs and a trade surplus.

Yet the Federal Government itself may not always be the proper source of such assistance. For example, it must not usurp functions if they can be more appropriately decided upon, managed, and financed by the private sector or by State and local governments. My Administration has always sought to consider the proper focus of responsibility for the most efficient resolution of problems.

We have also recognized the need to simplify the system of grants to State and local governments. I have again proposed several grant consolidations in the 1982 budget, including a new proposal that would consolidate several highway programs.

The pressures for growth in Federal use of national resources are great. My

Administration has initiated many new approaches to cope with these pressures. We started a multi-year budget system, and we began a system for controlling Federal credit programs. Yet in spite of increasing needs to limit spending growth, we have consistently adhered to these strong budget principles:

• Our Nation's armed forces must always stand sufficiently strong to deter aggression and to assure our security.

• An effective national energy plan is essential to increase domestic production of oil and gas, to encourage conservation of our scarce energy resources, to stimulate conversion to more abundant fuels, and to reduce our trade deficit.

• The essential human needs for our citizens must be given the highest priority.

• The Federal Government must lead the way in investment in the Nation's technological future.

• The Federal Government has an obligation to nurture and protect our environment—the common resource, birthright, and sustenance of the American people.

My 1982 budget continues to support these principles. It also proposes responsible tax reductions to encourage a more productive economy, and adequate funding of our highest priority programs within an overall policy of constraint.

Fiscal restraint must be continued in the years ahead. Budgets must be tight enough to convince those who set wages and prices that the Federal Government is serious about fighting inflation but not so tight as to choke off all growth.

Careful budget policy should be supplemented by other measures designed to reduce inflation at lower cost in lost output and employment. These other steps include measures to increase investment—such as the tax proposals included in my 1982 budget—and measures

to increase competition and productivity in our economy. Voluntary incomes policies can also directly influence wages and prices in the direction of moderation and thereby bring inflation down faster and at lower cost to the economy. Through a tax-based incomes policy (TIP) we could provide tax incentives for firms and workers to moderate their wage and price increases. In the coming years, control of Federal expenditures can make possible periodic tax reductions. The Congress should therefore begin now to evaluate the potentialities of a TIP program so that when the next round of tax reductions is appropriate a TIP program will be seriously considered.

EMPLOYMENT

During the last four years we have given top priority to meeting the needs of workers and providing additional job opportunities to those who seek work. Since the end of 1976:

• almost 9 million new jobs have been added to the nation's economy

• total employment has reached 97 million. More jobs than ever before are held by women, minorities and young people. Employment over the past four years has increased by:

—17% for adult women

—11% for blacks, and

—30% for Hispanics

• employment of black teenagers increased by more than 5%, reversing the decline that occurred in the previous eight years.

Major initiatives launched by this Administration helped bring about these accomplishments and have provided a solid foundation for employment and training policy in the 1980's.

In 1977, as part of the comprehensive economic stimulus program:

• 425,000 public service jobs were created
• A $1 billion youth employment initiative funded 200,000 jobs
• the doubling of the Job Corps to 44,000 slots began and 1 million summer youth jobs were approved—a 25 percent increase.

In 1978:
• the Humphrey-Hawkins Full Employment Act became law
• the $400 million Private Sector Initiatives Program was begun
• a targeted jobs tax credit for disadvantaged youth and others with special employment barriers was enacted
• the Comprehensive Employment and Training Act was reauthorized for four years.

In 1979:
• a $6 billion welfare reform proposal was introduced with funding for 400,000 public service jobs
• welfare reform demonstration projects were launched in communities around the country
• the Vice President initiated a nationwide review of youth unemployment in this country.

In 1980:
• the findings of the Vice President's Task Force revealed the major education and employment deficits that exist for poor and minority youngsters. As a result a $2 billion youth education and jobs initiative was introduced to provide unemployed youth with the basic education and work experience they need to compete in the labor market of the 1980's.
• As part of the economic revitalization program several steps were proposed to aid workers in high unemployment communities:

—an additional 13 weeks of unemployment benefits for the long term unemployed.

—$600 million to train the disadvantaged and unemployed for new private sector jobs.
—positive adjustment demonstrations to aid workers in declining industries.
• The important Title VII Private Sector Initiatives Program was reauthorized for an additional two years.

In addition to making significant progress in helping the disadvantaged and unemployed, important gains were realized for all workers:
• an historic national accord with organized labor made it possible for the views of working men and women to be heard as the nation's economic and domestic policies were formulated.
• the Mine Safety and Health Act brought about improved working conditions for the nation's 500,000 miners.
• substantial reforms of the Occupational Safety and Health Administration were accomplished to help reduce unnecessary burdens on business and to focus on major health and safety problems.
• the minimum wage was increased over a four year period from $2.30 to $3.35 an hour.
• the Black Lung Benefit Reform Act was signed into law.
• attempts to weaken the Davis-Bacon Act were defeated.

While substantial gains have been made in the last four years, continued efforts are required to ensure that this progress is continued:
• government must continue to make labor a full partner in the policy decisions that affect the interests of working men and women
• a broad, bipartisan effort to combat youth unemployment must be sustained
• compassionate reform of the nation's welfare system should be continued with employment opportunities provided for those able to work

• workers in declining industries should be provided new skills and help in finding employment

TRADE

Over the past year, the U.S. trade picture improved as a result of solid export gains in both manufactured and agricultural products. Agricultural exports reached a new record of over $40 billion, while manufactured exports have grown by 24 percent to a record $144 billion. In these areas the United States recorded significant surpluses of $24 billion and $19 billion respectively. While our oil imports remained a major drain on our foreign exchange earnings, that drain was somewhat moderated by a 19 percent decline in the volume of oil imports.

U.S. trade negotiators made significant progress over the past year in assuring effective implementation of the agreements negotiated during the Tokyo Round of Multilateral Trade Negotiations. Agreements reached with the Japanese government, for example, will assure that the United States will be able to expand its exports to the Japanese market in such key areas as telecommunications equipment, tobacco, and lumber. Efforts by U.S. trade negotiators also helped to persuade a number of key developing countries to accept many of the non-tariff codes negotiated during the Multilateral Trade Negotiations. This will assure that these countries will increasingly assume obligations under the international trading system.

A difficult world economic environment posed a challenge for the management of trade relations. U.S. trade negotiators were called upon to manage serious sectoral problems in such areas as steel, and helped to assure that U.S. chemical exports will have continued access to the European market.

Close consultations with the private sector in the United States have enabled U.S. trade negotiators to pinpoint obstacles to U.S. trade in services, and to build a basis for future negotiations. Services have been an increasingly important source of export earnings for the United States, and the United States must assure continued and increased access to foreign markets.

The trade position of the United States has improved. But vigorous efforts are needed in a number of areas to assure continued market access for U.S. exports, particularly agricultural and high technology products, in which the United States continues to have a strong competitive edge. Continued efforts are also needed to remove many domestic disincentives, which now hamper U.S. export growth. And we must ensure that countries do not manipulate investment, or impose investment performance requirements which distort trade and cost us jobs in this country.

In short, we must continue to seek free—but fair—trade. That is the policy my Administration has pursued from the beginning, even in areas where foreign competition has clearly affected our domestic industry. In the steel industry, for instance, we have put a Trigger Price Mechanism into place to help prevent the dumping of steel. That action has strengthened the domestic steel industry. In the automobile industry, we have worked—without resort to import quotas—to strengthen the industry's ability to modernize and compete effectively.

SMALL BUSINESS

I have often said that there is nothing small about small business in America. These firms account for nearly one-half our gross national product; over half of new technology; and much more than half of the jobs created by industry.

Because this sector of the economy is the very lifeblood of our National economy, we have done much together to improve the competitive climate for smaller firms. These concerted efforts have been an integral part of my program to revitalize the economy.

They include my campaign to shrink substantially the cash and time consuming red tape burden imposed on business. They include my personally-directed policy of ambitiously increasing the Federal contracting dollars going to small firms, especially those owned by women and minorities. And they include my proposals to reinvigorate existing small businesses and assist the creation of new ones through tax reform; financing assistance; market expansion; and support of product innovation.

Many of my initiatives to facilitate the creation and growth of small businesses were made in response to the White House Conference on Small Business, which I convened. My Administration began the implementation of most of the ideas produced last year by that citizen's advisory body; others need to be addressed. I have proposed the reconvening of the Conference next year to review progress; reassess priorities; and set new goals. In the interim I hope that the incoming Administration and the new Congress will work with the committee I have established to keep these business development ideas alive and help implement Conference recommendations.

MINORITY BUSINESS

One of the most successful developments of my Administration has been the growth and strengthening of minority business. This is the first Administration to put the issue on the policy agenda as a matter of major importance. To implement the results of our early efforts in this field I submitted legislation to Congress designed to further the development of minority business.

We have reorganized the Office of Minority Business into the Minority Business Development Administration in the Department of Commerce. MBDA has already proven to be a major factor in assisting minority businesses to achieve equitable competitive positions in the marketplace.

The Federal government's procurement from minority-owned firms has nearly tripled since I took office. Federal deposits in minority-owned banks have more than doubled and minority ownership of radio and television stations has nearly doubled. The SBA administered 8(a) Pilot Program for procurement with the Army proved to be successful and I recently expanded the number of agencies involved to include NASA and the Departments of Energy and Transportation.

I firmly believe the critical path to full freedom and equality for America's minorities rests with the ability of minority communities to participate competitively in the free enterprise system. I believe the government has a fundamental responsibility to assist in the development of minority business and I hope the progress made in the last four years will continue.

II. CREATING ENERGY SECURITY

Since I took office, my highest legislative priorities have involved the reorientation and redirection of U.S. energy activities and for the first time, to establish a coordinated national energy policy. The struggle to achieve that policy has been long and difficult, but the accomplishments of the past four years make clear that our country is finally serious about the problems caused by our overdependence on foreign oil. Our progress should not be lost. We must rely on and encourage multiple forms of energy production—coal, crude oil, natural gas, solar, nuclear, synthetics—and energy conservation. The framework put in place over the last four years will enable us to do this.

NATIONAL ENERGY POLICY

As a result of actions my Administration and the Congress have taken over the past four years, our country finally has a national energy policy:

• Under my program of phased decontrol, domestic crude oil price controls will end September 30, 1981. As a result exploratory drilling activities have reached an all-time high;

• Prices for new natural gas are being decontrolled under the Natural Gas Policy Act—and natural gas production is now at an all time high; the supply shortages of several years ago have been eliminated;

• The windfall profits tax on crude oil has been enacted providing $227 billion over ten years for assistance to low-income households, increased mass transit funding, and a massive investment in the production and development of alternative energy sources;

• The Synthetic Fuels Corporation has been established to help private companies build the facilities to produce energy from synthetic fuels;

• Solar energy funding has been quadrupled, solar energy tax credits enacted, and a Solar Energy and Energy Conservation Bank has been established;

• A route has been chosen to bring natural gas from the North Slope of Alaska to the lower 48 states;

• Coal production and consumption incentives have been increased, and coal production is now at its highest level in history;

• A gasoline rationing plan has been approved by Congress for possible use in the event of a severe energy supply shortage or interruption;

• Gasohol production has been dramatically increased, with a program being put in place to produce 500 million gallons of alcohol fuel by the end of this year—an amount that could enable gasohol to meet the demand for 10 percent of all unleaded gasoline;

• New energy conservation incentives have been provided for individuals, businesses and communities and conservation has increased dramatically. The U.S. has reduced oil imports by 25 percent—or 2 million barrels per day—over the past four years.

INCREASED DEVELOPMENT OF DOMESTIC ENERGY SOURCES

Although it is essential that the Nation reduce its dependence on imported fossil fuels and complete the transition to reliance on domestic renewable sources of energy, it is also important that this transition be accomplished in an orderly, economic, and environmentally sound manner. To this end, the Administration has launched several initiatives.

Leasing of oil and natural gas on federal lands, particularly the outer continental shelf, has been accelerated at the same time as the Administration has reformed leasing procedures through the 1978 amendments to the Outer Continental Shelf Lands Act. In 1979 the Interior Department held six OCS lease sales, the greatest number ever, which resulted in federal receipts of $6.5 billion, another record. The five-year OCS Leasing schedule was completed, requiring 36 sales over the next five years.

Since 1971 no general federal coal lease sales were suspended. Over the past four years the Administration has completely revised the federal coal leasing program to bring it into compliance with the requirements of 1976 Federal Land Planning and Management Act and other statutory provisions. The program is designed to balance the competing interests that affect resource development on public lands and to ensure that adequate supplies of coal will be available to meet national needs. As a result, the first general competitive federal coal lease sale in ten years will be held this month.

In July 1980, I signed into law the Energy Security Act of 1980 which established the Synthetic Fuels Corporation. The Corporation is designed to spur the development of commercial technologies for production of synthetic fuels, such as liquid and gaseous fuels from coal and the production of oil from oil shale. The Act provides the Corporation with an initial $22 billion to accomplish these objectives. The principal purpose of the legislation is to ensure that the nation will have available in the late 1980's the option to undertake commercial development of synthetic fuels if that becomes necessary. The Energy Security Act also provides significant incentives for the development of gasohol and biomass fuels, thereby enhancing the nation's supply of alternative energy sources.

COMMITMENT TO A SUSTAINABLE ENERGY
FUTURE

The Administration's 1977 National Energy Plan marked an historic departure from the policies of previous Administrations. The plan stressed the importance of both energy *production* and *conservation*

to achieving our ultimate national goal of relying primarily on secure sources of energy. The National Energy Plan made energy conservation a cornerstone of our national energy policy.

In 1978, I initiated the Administration's Solar Domestic Policy Review. This represented the first step towards widespread introduction of renewable energy sources into the Nation's economy. As a result of the Review, I issued the 1979 Solar Message to Congress, the first such message in the Nation's history. The Message outlined the Administration's solar program and established an ambitious national goal for the year 2000 of obtaining 20 percent of this Nation's energy from solar and renewable sources. The thrust of the federal solar program is to help industry develop solar energy sources by emphasizing basic research and development of solar technologies which are not currently economic, such as photovoltaics, which generate energy directly from the sun. At the same time, through tax incentives, education, and the Solar Energy and Energy Conservation Bank, the solar program seeks to encourage state and local governments, industry, and our citizens to expand their use of solar and renewable resource technologies currently available.

As a result of these policies and programs, the energy efficiency of the American economy has improved markedly and investments in renewable energy sources have grown significantly. It now takes 3½ percent less energy to produce a constant dollar of GNP than it did in January 1977. This increase in efficiency represents a savings of over 1.3 million barrels per day of oil equivalent, about the level of total oil production now occurring in Alaska. Over the same period, Federal support for conservation and solar energy has increased by more than 3000 percent, to $3.3 billion in FY 1981, including the tax credits for solar energy and energy conservation investments—these credits are expected to amount to $1.2 billion in FY 1981 and $1.5 billion in FY 1982.

COMMITMENT TO NUCLEAR SAFETY AND SECURITY

Since January 1977, significant progress has been achieved in resolving three critical problems resulting from the use of nuclear energy: radioactive waste management, nuclear safety and weapons proliferation.

In 1977, the Administration announced its nuclear nonproliferation policy and initiated the International Fuel Cycle Evaluation. In 1978, Congress passed the Nuclear Nonproliferation Act, an historic piece of legislation.

In February 1980, the Administration transmitted its nuclear waste management policy to the Congress. This policy was a major advance over all previous efforts. The principal aspects of that policy are: acknowledging the seriousness of the problem and the numerous technical and institutional issues; adopting a technically and environmentally conservative approach to the first permanent repository; and providing the states with significant involvement in nuclear waste disposal decisions by creating the State Planning Council. While much of the plan can be and is being implemented administratively, some new authorities are needed. The Congress should give early priority to enacting provisions for away-from-reactor storage and the State Planning Council.

The accident at Three Mile Island made the nation acutely aware of the safety risks posed by nuclear power plants. In response, the President established the Kemeny Commission to review the accident and make recommendations. Virtually all of the Commission's substantive recommendations were adopted by the Administration and are now being implemented by the Nuclear Regulatory Commission. The Congress adopted the President's proposed plan for the Nuclear Regulatory Commission and the Nuclear Safety Oversight Committee was established to ensure that the Administration's decisions were implemented.

Nuclear safety will remain a vital concern in the years ahead. We must continue to press ahead for the safe, secure disposal of radioactive wastes, and prevention of nuclear proliferation.

While significant growth in foreign demand for U.S. steam coal is foreseen, congestion must be removed at major U.S. coal exporting ports such as Hampton Roads, Virginia, and Baltimore, Maryland. My Administration has worked through the Interagency Coal Task Force Study to promote cooperation and coordination of resources between shippers, railroads, vessel broker/operators and port operators, and to determine the most appropriate Federal role in expanding and modernizing coal export facilities, including dredging deeper channels at selected ports. As a result of the Task Force's efforts, administrative steps have been taken by the Corps of Engineers to reduce significantly the amount of time required for planning and economic review of port dredging proposals. The Administration has also recommended that the Congress enact legislation to give the President generic authority to recommend appropriations for channel dredging activities. Private industry will, of course, play the major role in developing the United States' coal export facilities, but the government must continue to work to facilitate transportation to foreign markets.

III. Enhancing Basic Human and Social Needs

For too long prior to my Administration, many of our Nation's basic human and social needs were being ignored or handled insensitively by the Federal government. Over the last four years, we have significantly increased funding for many of the vital programs in these areas; developed new programs where needs were unaddressed; targeted Federal support to those individuals and areas most in need of our assistance; and removed barriers that have unnecessarily kept many disadvantaged citizens from obtaining aid for their most basic needs.

Our record has produced clear progress in the effort to solve some of the country's fundamental human and social problems. My Administration and the Congress, working together, have demonstrated that government must and can meet our citizens' basic human and social needs in a responsible and compassionate way.

But there is an unfinished agenda still before the Congress. If we are to meet our obligations to help all Americans realize the dreams of sound health care, decent housing, effective social services, a good education, and a meaningful job, important legislation still must be enacted. National Health Insurance, Welfare Reform, Child Health Assessment Program, are before the Congress and I urge their passage.

Health

NATIONAL HEALTH PLAN

During my Administration, I proposed to Congress a National Health Plan which will enable the country to reach the goal of comprehensive, universal health care coverage. The legislation I submitted lays the foundation for this comprehensive plan and addresses the most serious problems of health financing and delivery. It is realistic and enactable. It does not over-promise or overspend, and, as a result, can be the solution to the thirty years of Congressional battles on national health insurance. My Plan includes the following key features:

• nearly 15 million additional poor would receive fully-subsidized comprehensive coverage;

• pre-natal and delivery services are provided for all pregnant women and coverage is provided for all acute care for infants in their first year of life;

• the elderly and disabled would have a limit of $1,250 placed on annual out-of-pocket medical expenses and would no longer face limits on hospital coverage;

• all full-time employees and their families would receive insurance against at least major medical expenses under mandated employer coverage;

• Medicare and Medicaid would be combined and expanded into an umbrella Federal program, Healthcare, for increased program efficiency, accountability and uniformity; and

• strong cost controls and health system reforms would be implemented, including greater incentives for Health Maintenance Organizations.

I urge the new Congress to compare my Plan with the alternatives—programs which either do too little to improve the health care needs of Americans most in need or programs which would impose substantial financial burdens on the American taxpayers. I hope the Congress will see the need for and the benefits of my Plan and work toward prompt enactment. We cannot afford further delay in this vital area.

HEALTH CARE COST CONTROL

Inflation in health care costs remains unacceptably high. Throughout my Administration, legislation to reduce health care cost inflation was one of my highest priorities, but was not passed by the Congress. Therefore, my FY 1982 budget proposes sharing the responsibility for health care cost control with the private sector, through voluntary hospital cost guidelines and intensified monitoring. In the longer term, the health care reimbursement system must be reformed. We must move away from inflationary cost-based reimbursement and fee-for-service, and toward a system of prospective reimbursement, under which health care providers would operate within predetermined budgets. This reimbursement reform is essential to ultimately control inflation in health care costs, and will be a significant challenge to the new Congress.

HEALTH PROMOTION AND DISEASE PREVENTION

During my Administration, the Surgeon General released *Healthy People,* a landmark report on health promotion and disease prevention. The report signals the growing consensus that the Nation's health strategy must be refocused in the 1980's to emphasize the prevention of disease. Specifically, the report lays out measurable and achieveable goals in the reduction of mortality which can be reached by 1990.

I urge the new Congress to endorse the principles of *Healthy People,* and to adopt the recommendations to achieve its goals. This will necessitate adoption of a broader concept of health care, to include such areas as environmental health, workplace health and safety, commercial product safety, traffic safety, and health education, promotion and information.

MATERNAL AND CHILD HEALTH

Ensuring a healthy start in life for children remains not only a high priority of my Administration, but also one of the most cost effective forms of health care.

When I took office, immunization levels for preventable childhood diseases had fallen to 70%. As a result of a concerted nationwide effort during my Administration, I am pleased to report that now at least 90% of children under 15, and virtually all school-age children are immunized. In addition, reported cases of measles and mumps are at their lowest levels ever.

Under the National Health Plan I have proposed, there would be no cost-sharing for prenatal and delivery services for all pregnant women and for acute care provided to infants in their first year of life. These preventive services have extremely high returns in terms of improved newborn and long-term child health.

Under the Child Health Assurance Program (CHAP) legislation which I submitted to the Congress, and which passed the House, an additional two million low-income children under 18 would become eligible for Medicaid benefits, which would include special health assessments. CHAP would also improve the continuity of care for the nearly 14 million children now eligible for Medicaid. An additional 100,000 low-income pregnant women would become eligible for prenatal care under the proposal. I strongly urge the new Congress to enact CHAP and thereby provide millions of needy children with essential health services. The legislation has had strong bipartisan support, which should continue as the details of the bill are completed.

I also urge the new Congress to provide strong support for two highly successful ongoing programs: the special supplemental food program for women, infants and children (WIC) and Family Planning. The food supplements under WIC have been shown to effectively prevent ill health and thereby reduce later medical costs. The Family Planning program has been effective at reducing unwanted pregnancies among low-income women and adolescents.

EXPANSION OF SERVICES TO THE POOR AND UNDERSERVED

During my Administration, health services to the poor and underserved have been dramatically increased. The number of National Health Service Corps (NHSC) assignees providing services in medically underserved communities has grown from 500 in 1977 to nearly 3,000 in 1981. The population served by the NHSC has more than tripled since 1977. The number of Community Health Centers providing services in high priority underserved areas has doubled during my Administration, and will serve an estimated six million people in 1981. I strongly urge the new Congress to support these highly successful programs.

MENTAL HEALTH

One of the most significant health achievements during my Administration was the recent passage of the Mental Health Systems Act, which grew out of recommendations of my Commission on Mental Health. I join many others in my gratitude to the First Lady for her tireless and effective contribution to the passage of this important legislation.

The Act is designed to inaugurate a new era of Federal and State partnership in the planning and provision of mental health services. In addition, the Act specifically provides for prevention and support services to the chronically mentally ill to prevent unnecessary institutionalization and for the development of community-based mental health services. I urge the new Congress to provide adequate support for the full and timely implementation of this Act.

HEALTH PROTECTION

With my active support, the Congress recently passed "Medigap" legislation, which provides for voluntary certification of health insurance policies supplemental to Medicare, to curb widespread abuses in this area.

In the area of toxic agent control, legislation which I submitted to the Congress recently passed. This will provide for a "super-fund" to cover hazardous waste cleanup costs.

In the area of accidental injury control, we have established automobile safety standards and increased enforcement activities with respect to the 55 MPH speed limit. By the end of the decade these actions are expected to save over 13,000 lives and 100,000 serious injuries each year.

I urge the new Congress to continue strong support for all these activities.

FOOD AND NUTRITION

Building on the comprehensive reform of the Food Stamp Program that I proposed and Congress passed in 1977, my Administration and the Congress worked together in 1979 and 1980 to enact several other important changes in the Program. These changes will further simplify administration and reduce fraud and error, will make the program more responsive to the needs of the elderly and disabled, and will increase the cap on allowable program expenditures. The Food Stamp Act will expire at the end of fiscal 1981. It is essential that the new Administration and the Congress continue this program to ensure complete eradication of the debilitating malnutrition witnessed and documented among thousands of children in the 1960's.

DRUG ABUSE PREVENTION

At the beginning of my Administration there were over a half million heroin addicts in the United States. Our continued emphasis on reducing the supply of heroin, as well as providing treatment and rehabilitation to its victims, has reduced the heroin addict population, reduced the number of heroin overdose deaths by 80%, and reduced the number of heroin related injuries by 50%. We have also seen and encouraged a national movement of parents and citizens committed to reversing the very serious and disturbing trends of adolescent drug abuse.

Drug abuse in many forms will continue to detract, however, from the quality of life of many Americans. To prevent that, I see four great challenges in the years ahead. First, we must deal aggressively with the supplies of illegal drugs at their source, through joint crop destruction programs with foreign nations and increased law enforcement and border interdiction. Second, we must look to citizens and parents across the country to help educate the increasing numbers of American youth who are experimenting with drugs to the dangers of drug abuse. Education is a key factor in reducing drug abuse. Third, we must focus our efforts on drug and alcohol abuse in the workplace for not only does this abuse contribute to low productivity but it also destroys the satisfaction and sense of purpose all Americans can gain from the work ex-

perience. Fourth, we need a change in attitude, from an attitude which condones the casual use of drugs to one that recognizes the appropriate use of drugs for medical purposes and condemns the inappropriate and harmful abuse of drugs. I hope the Congress and the new Administration will take action to meet each of these challenges.

Education

The American people have always recognized that education is one of the soundest investments they can make. The dividends are reflected in every dimension of our national life—from the strength of our economy and national security to the vitality of our music, art, and literature. Among the accomplishments that have given me the most satisfaction over the last four years are the contributions that my Administration has been able to make to the well-being of students and educators throughout the country.

This Administration has collaborated successfully with the Congress on landmark education legislation. Working with the Congressional leadership, my Administration spotlighted the importance of education by creating a new Department of Education. The Department has given education a stronger voice at the Federal level, while at the same time reserving the actual control and operation of education to states, localities, and private institutions. The Department has successfully combined nearly 150 Federal education programs into a cohesive, streamlined organization that is more responsive to the needs of educators and students. The Department has made strides to cut red tape and paperwork and thereby to make the flow of Federal dollars to school districts and institutions of higher education more efficient. It is crucial that the Department be kept intact and strengthened.

Our collaboration with the Congress has resulted in numerous other important legislative accomplishments for education. A little over two years ago, I signed into law on the same day two major bills—one benefiting elementary and secondary education and the other, postsecondary education. The Education Amendments of 1978 embodied nearly all of my Administration's proposals for improvements in the Elementary and Secondary Education Act, including important new programs to improve students' achievement in the basic skills and to aid school districts with exceptionally high concentrations of children from low-income families. The Middle Income Student Assistance Act, legislation jointly sponsored by this Administration and the Congressional leadership, expanded eligibility for need-based Basic Educational Opportunity Grants to approximately one-third of the students enrolled in postsecondary education and made many more students eligible for the first time for other types of grants, work-study, and loans.

Just three and a half months ago, my Administration and the Congress successfully concluded over two years of work on a major reauthorization bill that further expands benefits to postsecondary education. Reflected in the Education Amendments of 1980 are major Administration recommendations for improvements in the Higher Education Act—including proposals for better loan access for students; a new parent loan program; simplified application procedures for student financial aid; a strengthened Federal commitment to developing colleges, particularly the historically Black institutions; a new authorization for equipment and facilities modernization funding for the nation's major research universities; and revitalized international education programs.

Supplementing these legislative accomplishments have been important administrative actions aimed at reducing paperwork and simplifying regulations associated with Federal education programs. We also launched major initiatives to reduce the backlog of defaulted student loans and otherwise to curb fraud, abuse, and waste in education programs.

To insure that the education enterprise is ready to meet the scientific and technological changes of the future, we undertook a major study of the status of science and engineering education throughout the nation. I hope that the findings from this report will serve as a springboard for needed reforms at all levels of education.

I am proud that this Administration has been able to provide the financial means to realize many of our legislative and administrative goals. Compared to the previous administration's last budget, I have requested the largest overall increase in Federal funding for education in our nation's history. My budget requests have been particularly sensitive to the needs of special populations like minorities, women, the educationally and economically disadvantaged, the handicapped, and students with limited English-speaking ability. At the same time, I have requested significant increases for many programs designed to enhance the quality of American education, including programs relating to important areas as diverse as international education, research libraries, museums, and teacher centers.

Last year, I proposed to the Congress a major legislative initiative that would direct $2 billion into education and job training programs designed to alleviate youth unemployment through improved linkages between the schools and the work place. This legislation generated bipartisan support; but unfortunately, action on it was not completed in the final, rushed days of the 96th Congress. I urge the new Congress—as it undertakes broad efforts to strengthen the economy as well as more specific tasks like reauthorizing the Vocational Education Act—to make the needs of our nation's unemployed youth a top priority for action. Only by combining a basic skills education program together with work training and employment incentives can we make substantial progress in eliminating one of the most severe social problems in our nation—youth unemployment, particularly among minorities. I am proud of the progress already made through passage of the Youth Employment and Demonstration Project Act of 1977 and the substantial increase in our investment in youth employment programs. The new legislation would cap these efforts.

Income Security

SOCIAL SECURITY

One of the highest priorities of my Administration has been to continue the tradition of effectiveness and efficiency widely associated with the social security program, and to assure present and future beneficiaries that they will receive their benefits as expected. The earned benefits that are paid monthly to retired and disabled American workers and their families provide a significant measure of economic protection to millions of people who might otherwise face retirement or possible disability with fear. I have enacted changes to improve the benefits of many social security beneficiaries during my years as President.

The last four years have presented a special set of concerns over the financial stability of the social security system. Shortly after taking office I proposed and Congress enacted legislation to protect the stability of the old age and survivors trust fund and prevent the imminent exhaustion of the disability insurance trust fund, and to correct a flaw in the benefit formula that was threatening the long run health of the entire social security system. The actions taken by the Congress at my request helped stabilize the system. That legislation was later complemented by the Disability Insurance Amendments of 1980 which further bolstered the disability insurance program, and reduced certain inequities among beneficiaries.

My commitment to the essential retirement and disability protection provided to 35 million people each month has been demonstrated by the fact that without interruption those beneficiaries have continued to receive their social security benefits, including annual cost of living increases. Changing and unpredictable economic circumstances require that we continue to monitor the financial stability of the social security system. To correct anticipated short-term strains on the system, I proposed last year that the three funds be allowed to borrow from one another, and I urge the Congress again this year to adopt such interfund borrowing. To further strengthen the social security system and provide a greater degree of assurance to beneficiaries, given projected future economic uncertainties, additional action should be taken. Among the additional financing options available are borrowing from the general fund, financing half of the hospital insurance fund with general revenues, and increasing the payroll tax rate. The latter option is particularly unpalatable given the significant increase in the tax rate already mandated in law.

This Administration continues to oppose cuts in basic social security benefits and taxing social security benefits. The Administration continues to support annual indexing of social security benefits.

WELFARE REFORM

In 1979 I proposed a welfare reform package which offers solutions to some of the most urgent problems in our welfare system. This proposal is embodied in two bills—The Work and Training Opportunities Act and The Social Welfare Reform Amendments Act. The House passed the second of these two proposals. Within the framework of our present welfare system, my reform proposals offer achievable means to increase self-sufficiency through work rather than welfare, more adequate assistance to people unable to work, the removal of inequities in coverage under current programs, and fiscal relief needed by States and localities.

Our current welfare system is long overdue for serious reform; the system is wasteful and not fully effective. The legislation I have proposed will help eliminate inequities by establishing a national minimum benefit, and by directly relating benefit levels to the poverty threshold. It will reduce program complexity, which leads to inefficiency and waste, by simplifying and coordinating administration among different programs.

I urge the Congress to take action in this area along the lines I have recommended.

CHILD WELFARE

My Administration has worked closely with the Congress on legislation which is designed to improve greatly the child welfare services and foster care programs and to create a Federal system of adoption assistance. These improvements will be achieved with the recent enactment of H.R. 3434, the Adoption Assistance and Child Welfare Act of 1980. The well-being of children in need of homes and their permanent placement have been a primary concern of my Administration. This legislation will ensure that children are not lost in the foster care system, but instead will be returned to their families where possible or placed in permanent adoptive homes.

LOW-INCOME ENERGY ASSISTANCE

In 1979 I proposed a program to provide an annual total of $1.6 billion to low-income households which are hardest hit by rising energy bills. With the cooperation of Congress, we were able to move quickly to provide assistance to eligible households in time to meet their winter heating bills.

In response to the extreme heat conditions affecting many parts of the country during 1980, I directed the Community Services Administration to make available over $27 million to assist low-income individuals, especially the elderly, facing life threatening circumstances due to extreme heat.

Congress amended and reauthorized the low-income energy assistance program for fiscal year 1981, and provided $1.85 billion to meet anticipated increasing need. The need for a program to help low-income households with rising energy expenses will not abate in the near future. The low-income energy assistance program should be reauthorized to meet those needs.

Housing

For the past 14 months, high interest rates have had a severe impact on the nation's housing market. Yet the current pressures and uncertainties should not obscure the achievements of the past four years.

Working with the Congress, the regulatory agencies, and the financial community, my Administration has brought about an expanded and steadier flow of funds into home mortgages. Deregulation of the interest rates payable by depository institutions, the evolution of variable and renegotiated rate mortgages, development of high yielding savings certificates, and expansion of the secondary mortgage market have all increased housing's ability to attract capital and have assured that mortgage money would not be cut off when interest rates rose. These actions will diminish the cyclicality of the housing industry. Further, we have secured legislation updating the Federal Government's emergency authority to provide support for the housing industry through the Brooke-Cranston program, and creating a new Section 235 housing stimulus program. These tools will enable the Federal Government to deal quickly and effectively with serious distress in this critical industry.

We have also worked to expand homeownership opportunities for Americans. By using innovative financing mechanisms, such as the graduated payment mortgage, we have increased the access of middle income families to housing credit. By revitalizing the Section 235 program, we have enabled nearly 100,000 moderate income households to purchase new homes. By reducing paperwork and regulation in Federal programs, and by working with State and local governments to ease the regulatory burden, we have helped to hold down housing costs and produce affordable housing.

As a result of these governmentwide efforts, 5½ million more American families bought homes in the past four years than in any equivalent period in history. And more than 7 million homes have begun construction during my Administration, 1 million more than in the previous four years.

We have devoted particular effort to meeting the housing needs of low and moderate income families. In the past four years, more than 1 million subsidized units have been made available for occupancy by lower income Americans and more than 600,000 assisted units have gone into construction. In addition, we have undertaken a series of measures to revitalize and preserve the nation's 2 million units of public and assisted housing.

For Fiscal Year 1982, I am proposing to continue our commitment to lower income housing. I am requesting funds to support 260,000 units of Section 8 and public housing, maintaining these programs at the level provided by Congress in Fiscal 1981.

While we have made progress in the past four years, in the future there are reasons for concern. Home price inflation and high interest rates threaten to put homeownership out of reach for first-time homebuyers. Lower income households, the elderly and those dependent upon rental housing face rising rents, low levels of rental housing construction by historic standards, and the threat of displacement due to conversion to condominiums and other factors. Housing will face strong competition for investment capital from the industrial sector generally and the energy industries, in particular.

To address these issues, I appointed a Presidential Task Force and Advisory Group last October. While this effort will not proceed due to the election result, I hope the incoming Administration will proceed with a similar venture.

The most important action government can take to meet America's housing needs is to restore stability to the economy and bring down the rate of inflation. Inflation has driven up home prices, operating costs and interest rates. Market uncertainty about inflation has contributed to the instability in interest rates, which has been an added burden to homebuilders and homebuyers alike. By making a long-term commitment to provide a framework for greater investment, sustained economic growth, and price stability, my Administration has begun the work of creating a healthy environment for housing.

Transportation

With the passage of the Airline Deregulation Act of 1978, the Motor Carrier Act of 1980, and the Harley O. Staggers Rail Act of 1980, my Administration, working with the Congress, has initiated a new era of reduced regulation of transportation industries. Deregulation will lead to increased productivity and operating efficiencies in the industries involved, and stimulate price and service competition, to the benefit of consumers generally. I urge the new Administration to continue our efforts on behalf of deregulation legislation for the intercity passenger bus industry as well.

In the coming decade, the most significant challenge facing the nation in transportation services will be to improve a deteriorating physical infrastructure of roadways, railroads, waterways and mass transit systems, in order to conserve costly energy supplies while promoting effective transportation services.

HIGHWAYS

Our vast network of highways, which account for 90 percent of travel and 80 percent by value of freight traffic goods movement, is deteriorating. If current trends continue, a major proportion of the Interstate pavement will have deteriorated by the end of the 1980's.

Arresting the deterioration of the nation's system of highways is a high priority objective for the 1980's. We must reorient the Federal mission from major new construction projects to the stewardship of the existing Interstate Highway System. Interstate gaps should be judged on the connections they make and on their compatibility with community needs.

During this decade, highway investments will be needed to increase productivity, particularly in the elimination of bottlenecks, provide more efficient connections to ports and seek low-cost solutions to traffic demand.

My Administration has therefore recommended redefining completion of the Interstate system, consolidating over 27 categorical assistance programs into nine, and initiating a major repair and rehabilitation program for segments of the Interstate system. This effort should help maintain the condition and performance of the Nation's highways, particularly the Interstate and primary system; provide a realistic means to complete the Interstate system by 1990; ensure better program delivery through consolidation, and assist urban revitalization. In addition, the Congress must address the urgent funding problems of the highway trust fund, and the need to generate greater revenues.

MASS TRANSIT

In the past decade the nation's public transit systems' ridership increased at an annual average of 1.1% each year in the 1970's (6.9% in 1979). Continued increases in the cost of fuel are expected to make transit a growing part of the nation's transportation system.

As a result, my Administration projected a ten year, $43 billion program to increase mass transit capacity by 50 percent, and promote more energy efficient vehicle uses in the next decade. The first part of this proposal was the five year, $24.7 billion Urban Mass Transportation Administration reauthorization legislation I sent to the Congress in March, 1980. I urge the 97th Congress to quickly enact this or similar legislation in 1981.

My Administration was also the first to have proposed and signed into law a non-urban formula grant program to assist rural areas and small communities with public transportation programs to end their dependence on the automobile, promote energy conservation and efficiency, and provide transportation services to impoverished rural communities.

A principal need of the 1980's will be maintaining mobility for all segments of the population in the face of severely increasing transportation costs and uncertainty of fuel supplies. We must improve the flexibility of our transportation system and offer greater choice and diversity in transportation services. While the private automobile will continue to be the principal means of transportation for many Americans, public transportation can become an increasingly attractive alternative. We, therefore, want to explore a variety of paratransit modes, various types of buses, modern rapid transit, regional rail systems and light rail systems.

Highway planning and transit planning must be integrated and related to State, regional, district and neighborhood planning efforts now in place or emerging. Low density development and land use threaten the fiscal capacity of many communities to support needed services and infrastructure.

ELDERLY AND HANDICAPPED TRANSPORTATION

Transportation policies in the 1980's must pay increasing attention to the needs of the elderly and handicapped. By 1990, the number of people over 65 will have grown from today's 19 million to 27 million. During the same period, the number of handicapped—people who have difficulty using transit as well as autos, including the elderly—is expected to increase from 9 to 11 million, making up 4.5 percent of the population.

We must not retreat from a policy that affords a significant and growing portion of our population accessible public transportation while recognizing that the handicapped are a diverse group and will need flexible, door-to-door service where regular public transportation will not do the job.

RAILROADS

In addition, the Federal government must reassess the appropriate Federal role of support for passenger and freight rail services such as Amtrak and Conrail. Our goal through federal assistance should be to maintain and enhance adequate rail service, where it is not otherwise available to needy communities. But Federal subsidies must be closely scrutinized to be sure they are a stimulus to, and not a replacement for, private investment and initiative. Federal assistance cannot mean permanent subsidies for unprofitable operations.

WATERWAYS AND RURAL TRANSPORTATION

There is a growing need in rural and small communities for improved transportation services. Rail freight service to many communities has declined as railroads abandon unproductive branch lines. At the same time, rural roads are often inadequate to handle large, heavily-loaded trucks. The increased demand for "harvest to harbor" service has also placed an increased burden on rural transportation systems, while bottlenecks along the Mississippi River delay grain shipments to the Gulf of Mexico.

We have made some progress:

• To further develop the nation's waterways, my Administration began construction of a new 1,200 foot lock at the site of Lock and Dam 26 on the Mississippi River. When opened in 1987, the new lock will have a capacity of 86 million tons per year, an 18 percent increase over the present system. The U.S. Army Corps of Engineers has also undertaken studies to assess the feasibility of expanding the Bonneville Locks. Rehabilitation of John Day Lock was begun in 1980 and should be completed in 1982. My Administration also supports the completion of the Upper Missisippi River Master Plan to determine the feasibility of constructing a second lock at Alton, Illinois. These efforts will help alleviate delays in transporting corn, soybeans and other goods along the Mississippi River to the Gulf of Mexico.

• The Department of Transportation's new Small Community and Rural Transportation Policy will target federal assistance for passenger transportation, roads and highways, truck service, and railroad freight service to rural areas. This policy implements and expands upon the earlier White House Initiative, *Improving Transportation in Rural America,* announced in June, 1979, and the President's *Small Community and Rural Development Policy* announced in December, 1979. The Congress should seek ways to balance rail branch line abandonment with the service needs of rural and farm communities, provide financial assistance to rail branch line rehabilitation where appropriate, assist shippers to adjust to rail branch line abandonment where it takes place, and help make it possible for trucking firms to serve light density markets with dependable and efficient trucking services.

MARITIME POLICY

During my Administration I have sought to ensure that the U.S. maritime industry will not have to function at an unfair competitive disadvantage in the international market. As I indicated in my maritime policy statement to the Congress in July, 1979, the American merchant marine is vital to our Nation's welfare, and Federal actions should promote rather than harm it. In pursuit of this objective, I signed into law the Controlled Carrier Act of 1978, authorizing the Federal Maritime Commission to regulate certain rate cutting practices of some state-controlled carriers, and recently signed a bilateral maritime agreement with the People's Republic of China that will expand the access of American ships to 20 specified Chinese ports, and set aside for American-flag ships a substantial share (at least one-third) of the cargo between our countries. This agreement should officially foster expanded U.S. and Chinese shipping services linking the two countries, and will provide further momentum to the growth of Sino-American trade.

There is also a need to modernize and expand the dry bulk segment of our fleet. Our heavy dependence on foreign carriage of U.S.-bulk cargoes deprives the U.S. economy of seafaring and shipbuilding jobs, adds to the balance-of-payments deficit, deprives the Government of substantial tax revenues, and leaves the United States dependent on foreign-flag shipping for a continued supply of raw materials to support the civil economy and war production in time of war.

I therefore sent to the Congress proposed legislation to strengthen this woefully weak segment of the U.S.-flag fleet by removing certain disincentives to U.S. construction of dry bulkers and their operation under U.S. registry. Enactment of this proposed legislation would establish the basis for accelerating the rebuilding of the U.S.-flag dry bulk fleet toward a level commensurate with the position of the United States as the world's leading bulk trading country.

During the past year the Administration has stated its support for legislation that would provide specific Federal assistance for the installation of fuel-efficient engines in existing American ships, and would strengthen this country's shipbuilding mobilization base. Strengthening the fleet is important, but we must also maintain our shipbuilding base for future ship construction.

Provisions in existing laws calling for substantial or exclusive use of American-flag vessels to carry cargoes generated by the Government must be vigorously pursued.

I have therefore supported requirements that 50 percent of oil purchased for the strategic petroleum reserve be transported in U.S.-flag vessels, that the Cargo Preference Act be applied to materials furnished for the U.S. assisted construction of air bases in Israel, and to cargoes transported pursuant to the Chrysler Corporation Loan Guarantee Act. In addition, the Deep Seabed Hard Mineral Resources Act requires that at least one ore carrier per mine site be a U.S.-flag vessel.

Much has been done, and much remains to be done. The FY 1982 budget includes a $107 million authorization for Construction Differential Subsidy ("CDS") funds which, added to the unobligated CDS balance of $100 million from 1980, and the recently enacted $135 million 1981 authorization, will provide an average of $171 million in CDS funds in 1981 and 1982.

COAL EXPORT POLICY

While significant growth in foreign demand for U.S. steam coal is foreseen, congestion at major U.S. coal exporting ports such as Hampton Roads, Virginia, and Baltimore, Maryland, could delay and impede exports.

My Administration has worked through the Interagency Coal Task Force Study, which I created, to promote cooperation and coordination of resources between shippers, railroads, vessel broker/operators and port operators, and to determine the most appropriate Federal role in expanding and modernizing coal export facilities, including dredging deeper channels at selected ports.

Some progress has already been made. In addition to action taken by transshippers to reduce the number of coal classifications used whenever possible, by the Norfolk and Western Railroad to upgrade its computer capability to quickly inventory its coal cars in its yards, and by the Chessie Railroad which is reactivating Pier 15 in Newport News and has established a berth near its Curtis Bay Pier in Baltimore to decrease delays in vessel berthing, public activities will include:

• A $26.5 million plan developed by the State of Pennsylvania and Conrail to increase Conrail's coal handling capacity at Philadelphia;

• A proposal by the State of Virginia to construct a steam coal port on the Craney Island Disposal area in Portsmouth harbor;

• Plans by Mobile, Alabama, which operates the only publicly owned coal terminal in the U.S. to enlarge its capacity at McDuffie Island to 10 million tons ground storage and 100 car unit train unloading capability;

• Development at New Orleans of steam coal facilities that are expected to add over 20 million tons of annual capacity by 1983; and

• The Corps of Engineers, working with other interested Federal agencies, will determine which ports should be dredged, to what depth and on what schedule, in order to accommodate larger coal carrying vessels.

Private industry will, of course, play a major role in developing the United States' coal export facilities. The new Administration should continue to work to eliminate transportation bottlenecks that impede our access to foreign markets.

Special Needs

WOMEN

The past four years have been years of rapid advancement for women. Our focus has been two-fold: to provide American women with a full range of opportunities and to make them a part of the mainstream of every aspect of our national life and leadership.

I have appointed a record number of women to judgeships and to top government posts. Fully 22 percent of all my appointees are women, and I nominated 41 of the 46 women who sit on the Federal bench today. For the first time in our history, women occupy policymaking positions at the highest level of every Federal agency and department and have demonstrated their ability to serve our citizens well.

We have strengthened the rights of employed women by consolidating and strengthening enforcement of sex discrimination laws under the EEOC, by expanding employment rights of pregnant women through the Pregnancy Disability Bill, and by increasing federal employment opportunities for women through civil service reform, and flexi-time and part-time employment.

By executive order, I created the first national program to provide women businessowners with technical assistance, grants, loans, and improved access to federal contracts.

We have been sensitive to the needs of women who are homemakers. I established an Office of Families within HHS and sponsored the White House Conference on Families. We initiated a program targeting CETA funds to help displaced homemakers. The Social Security system was amended to eliminate the widow's penalty and a comprehensive study of discriminatory provisions and possible changes was presented to Congress. Legislation was passed to give divorced spouses of foreign service officers rights to share in pension benefits.

We created an office on domestic violence within HHS to coordinate the 12 agencies that now have domestic violence relief programs, and to distribute information on the problem and the services available to victims.

Despite a stringent budget for FY 1981, the Administration consistently supported the Women's Educational Equity Act and family planning activities, as well as other programs that affect women, such as food stamps, WIC, and social security.

We have been concerned not only about the American woman's opportunities, but ensuring equality for women around the world. In November, 1980, I sent to the Senate the Convention on the Elimination of All Forms of Discrimination Against Women. This United Nations document is the most comprehensive and detailed international agreement which seeks the advancement of women.

On women's issues, I have sought the counsel of men and women in and out of government and from all regions of our country. I established two panels—the President's Advisory Committee for Women and the Interdepartmental Task Force on Women—to advise me on these issues. The mandate for both groups expired on December 31, but they have left behind a comprehensive review of the status of women in our society today. That review provides excellent guidance for the work remaining in our battle against sex discrimination.

Even though we have made progress, much remains on the agenda for women. I remain committed to the Equal Rights Amendment and will continue to work for its passage. It is essential to the goal of bringing America's women fully into the mainstream of American life that the ERA be ratified.

The efforts begun for women in employment, business and education should be continued and strengthened. Money should be available to states to establish programs to help the victims of domestic violence. Congress should pass a national health care plan and a welfare reform program, and these measures should reflect the needs of women.

The talents of women should continue to be used to the fullest inside and outside of government, and efforts should continue to see that they have the widest range of opportunities and options.

HANDICAPPED

I hope that my Administration will be remembered in this area for leading the way toward full civil rights for handicapped Americans. When I took office, no federal agency had yet issued 504 regulations. As I leave office, this first step by every major agency and department in the federal government is almost complete. But it is only a first step. The years ahead will require steadfast dedication by the President to protect and promote these precious rights in the classroom, in the workplace, and in all public facilities so that handicapped individuals may join the American mainstream and contribute to the fullest their resources and talents to our economic and social life.

Just as we supported, in an unprecedented way, the civil rights of disabled persons in schools and in the workplace, other initiatives in health prevention—such as our immunization and nutrition programs for young children and new intense efforts to reverse spinal cord injury—must continue so that the incidence of disability continues to decline.

This year is the UN-declared International Year of Disabled Persons. We are organizing activities to celebrate and promote this important commemorative year within the government as well as in cooperation with private sector efforts in this country and around the world. The International Year will give our country the opportunity to recognize the talents and capabilities of our fellow citizens with disabilities. We can also share our rehabilitation and treatment skills with other countries and learn from them as well. I am proud that the United States leads the world in mainstreaming and treating disabled people. However, we have a long way to go before all psychological and physical barriers to disabled people are torn down and they can be full participants in our American way of life. We must pledge our full commitment to this goal during the International Year.

FAMILIES

Because of my concern for American families, my Administration convened last year the first White House Conference on Families which involved seven national hearings, over 506 state and local events, three White House Conferences, and the direct participation of more than 125,000 citizens. The Conference reaffirmed the centrality of families in our lives and nation but documented problems American families face as well. We also established the Office of Families within the Department of Health and Human Services to review government policies and programs that affect families.

I expect the departments and agencies within the executive branch of the Federal government as well as Members of Congress, corporate and business leaders, and State and local officials across the country, to study closely the recommendations of the White House Conference and implement them appropriately. As public policy is developed and implemented by the Federal government, cognizance of the work of the Conference should be taken as a pragmatic and essential step.

The Conference has done a good job of establishing an agenda for action to assure that the policies of the Federal government are more sensitive in their impact on families. I hope the Congress will review and seriously consider the Conference's recommendations.

OLDER AMERICANS

My Administration has taken great strides toward solving the difficult problems faced by older Americans. Early in my term we worked successfully with the Congress to assure adequate revenues for the Social Security Trust Funds. And last year the strength of the Social Security System was strengthened by legislation I proposed to permit borrowing among the separate trust funds. I have also signed into law legislation prohibiting employers from requiring retirement prior to age 70, and removing mandatory retirement for most Federal employees. In addition, my Administration worked very closely with Congress to amend the Older Americans Act in a way that has already improved administration of its housing, social services, food delivery, and employment programs.

This year, I will be submitting to Congress a budget which again demonstrates my commitment to programs for the elderly. It will include, as my previous budgets have, increased funding for nutrition, senior centers and home health care, and will focus added resources on the needs of older Americans.

With the 1981 White House Conference on Aging approaching, I hope the new Administration will make every effort to assure an effective and useful conference. This Conference should enable older Americans to voice their concerns and give us guidance in our continued efforts to ensure the quality of life so richly deserved by our senior citizens.

REFUGEES

We cannot hope to build a just and humane society at home if we ignore the humanitarian claims of refugees, their lives at stake, who have nowhere else to turn. Our country can be proud that hundreds of thousands of people around the world would risk everything they have—including their own lives—to come to our country.

This Administration initiated and implemented the first comprehensive reform of our refugee and immigration policies in over 25 years. We also established the first refugee coordination office in the Department of State under the leadership of a special ambassador and coordinator for refugee affairs and programs. The new legislation and the coordinator's office will bring common sense and consolidation to our Nation's previously fragmented, inconsistent, and in many ways, outdated, refugee and immigration policies.

With the unexpected arrival of thousands of Cubans and Haitians who sought refuge in our country last year, outside of our regular immigration and refugee admissions process, our country and its government were tested in being compassionate and responsive to a major human emergency. Because we had taken steps to reorganize our refugee programs, we met that test successfully. I am proud that the American people responded to this crisis with their traditional good will and hospitality. Also, we would never have been able to handle this unprecedented emergency without the efforts of the private resettlement agencies who have always been there to help refugees in crises.

Immigrants to this country always contribute more toward making our country stronger than they ever take from the system. I am confident that the newest arrivals to our country will carry on this tradition.

While we must remain committed to aiding and assisting those who come to our shores, at the same time we must uphold our immigration and refugee policies and provide adequate enforcement resources. As a result of our enforcement policy, the illegal flow from Cuba has been halted and an orderly process has been initiated to make certain that our refugee and immigration laws are honored.

This year the Select Commission on Immigration and Refugee Policy will complete its work and forward its advice and recommendations. I hope that the recommendations will be carefully considered by the new Administration and the Congress, for it is clear that we must take additional action to keep our immigration policy responsive to emergencies and ever changing times.

VETERANS

This country and its leadership has a continuing and unique obligation to the men and women who served their nation in the armed forces and help maintain or restore peace in the world.

My commitment to veterans—as evidenced by my record—is characterized by a conscientious and consistent emphasis in these general areas:

First, we have worked to honor the Vietnam veteran. During my Administration, and under the leadership of VA Administrator Max Cleland, I was proud to lead our country in an overdue acknowledgement of our Nation's gratitude to the men and women who served their country during the bitter war in Southeast Asia. Their homecoming was deferred and seemed doomed to be ignored. Our country has matured in the last four years and at long last we were able to separate the war from the warrior and honor these veterans. But with our acknowledgement of their service goes an understanding that some Vietnam veterans have unique needs and problems.

My Administration was able to launch a long sought after psychological readjustment and outreach program, unprecedented in its popularity, sensitivity and success. This program must be continued. The Administration has also grappled with the difficult questions posed by some veterans who served in Southeast Asia and were exposed to potentially harmful substances, including the herbicide known as Agent Orange. We have launched scientific inquiries that should answer many veterans' questions about their health and should provide the basis for establishing sound compensation policy. We cannot rest until their concerns are dealt with in a sensitive, expeditious and compassionate fashion.

Second, we have focused the VA health care system in the needs of the service-connected disabled veteran. We initiated and are implementing the first reform of the VA vocational rehabilitation system since its inception in 1943. Also, my Administration was the first to seek a cost-of-living increase for the recipients of VA compensation every year. My last budget also makes such a request. The Administration also launched the Disabled Veterans Outreach Program in the Department of Labor which has successfully placed disabled veterans in jobs. Services provided by the VA health care system will be further targeted to the special needs of disabled veterans during the coming year.

Third, the VA health care system—the largest in the free world—has maintained its independence and high quality during my Administration. We have made the system more efficient and have therefore treated more veterans than ever before by concentrating on out-patient care and through modern management improvements. As the median age of the American veteran population increases, we must concentrate on further changes within the VA system to keep it independent and to serve as a model to the nation and to the world as a center for research, treatment and rehabilitation.

Government Assistance

GENERAL AID TO STATE AND LOCAL
GOVERNMENTS

Since taking office, I have been strongly committed to strengthening the fiscal and economic condition of our Nation's State and local governments. I have accomplished this goal by encouraging economic development of local communities, and by supporting the General Revenue Sharing and other essential grant-in-aid programs.

GRANTS-IN-AID TO STATES AND LOCALITIES

During my Administration, total grants-in-aid to State and local governments have increased by more than 40 percent— from $68 billion in Fiscal Year 1977 to $96 billion in Fiscal Year 1981. This significant increase in aid has allowed States and localities to maintain services that are essential to their citizens without imposing onerous tax burdens. It also has allowed us to establish an unprecedented partnership between the leaders of the Federal government and State and local government elected officials.

GENERAL REVENUE SHARING

Last year Congress enacted legislation that extends the General Revenue Sharing program for three more years. This program is the cornerstone of our efforts to maintain the fiscal health of our Nation's local government. It will provide $4.6 billion in each of the next three years to cities, counties and towns. This program is essential to the continued ability of our local governments to provide essential police, fire and sanitation services.

This legislation renewing GRS will be the cornerstone of Federal-State-local government relations in the 1980's. This policy will emphasize the need for all levels of government to cooperate in order to meet the needs of the most fiscally strained cities and counties, and also will emphasize the important role that GRS can play in forging this partnership. I am grateful that Congress moved quickly to assure that our Nation's localities can begin the 1980's in sound fiscal condition.

COUNTER-CYCLICAL ASSISTANCE

Last year, I proposed that Congress enact a $1 billion counter-cyclical fiscal assistance program to protect States and localities from unexpected changes in the national economy. This program unfortunately was not enacted by the [full] Congress. I, therefore, have not included funding for counter-cyclical aid in my Fiscal Year 1982 budget. Nevertheless, I urge Congress to enact a permanent stand-by counter-cyclical program, so that States and cities can be protected during the next economic downturn.

Urban Policy

Three years ago, I proposed the Nation's first comprehensive urban policy. That policy involved more than one hundred improvements in existing Federal programs, four new Executive Orders and nineteen pieces of urban-oriented legislation. With Congress' cooperation, sixteen of these bills have now been signed into law.

ECONOMIC DEVELOPMENT

One of the principal goals of my domestic policy has been to strengthen the private sector economic base of our Nation's economically troubled urban and rural areas. With Congress' cooperation, we have substantially expanded the Federal government's economic development programs and provided new tax incentives for private investment in urban and rural communities. These programs have helped many communities to attract new private sector jobs and investments and to retain the jobs and investments that already are in place.

When I took office, the Federal government was spending less than $300 million annually on economic development programs, and only $60 million of those funds in our Nation's urban areas. Since that time, we have created the Urban Development Action Grant (UDAG) program and substantially expanded the economic development programs in the Commerce Department. My FY 1982 budget requests more than $1.5 billion for economic development grants, loans and interest subsidies and almost $1.5 billion for loan guarantees. Approximately 60 percent of these funds will be spent in our Nation's urban areas. In addition, we have extended the 10 percent investment credit to include rehabilitation of existing industrial facilities as well as new construction.

I continue to believe that the development of private sector investment and jobs is the key to revitalizing our Nation's economically depressed urban and rural areas. To ensure that the necessary economic development goes forward, the Congress must continue to provide strong support for the UDAG program and the programs for the Economic Development Administration. Those programs provide a foundation for the economic development of our Nation in the 1980's.

COMMUNITY DEVELOPMENT

The partnership among Federal, State and local governments to revitalize our Nation's communities has been a high priority of my Administration. When I took office, I proposed a substantial expansion of the Community Development Block Grant (CDBG) program and the enactment of a new $400 million Urban Development Action Grant (UDAG) program. Both of these programs have provided essential community and economic development assistance to our Nation's cities and counties.

Last year, Congress reauthorized both the CDBG and UDAG programs. The CDBG program was reauthorized for three more years with annual funding increases of $150 million, and the UDAG program was extended for three years at the current funding level of $675 million annually. My 1982 budget requests full funding for both of these programs. These actions should help our Nation's cities and counties to continue the progress they have made in the last three years.

NEIGHBORHOODS

During my Administration we have taken numerous positive steps to achieve a full partnership of neighborhood organizations and government at all levels. We have successfully fought against red lining and housing discrimination. We created innovative Self Help funding and technical resource transfer mechanisms. We have created unique methods of access for neighborhood organizations to have a participating role in Federal and State government decision-making. Neighborhood based organizations are the threshold of the American community.

The Federal government will need to develop more innovative and practical ways for neighborhood based organizations to successfully participate in the identification and solution of local and neighborhood concerns. Full partnership will only be achieved with the knowing participation of leaders of government, business, education and unions. Neither state nor Federal solutions imposed from on high will suffice. Neighborhoods are the fabric and soul of this great land. Neighborhoods define the weave that has been used to create a permanent fabric. The Federal government must take every opportunity to provide access and influence to the individuals and organizations affected at the neighborhood level.

Rural Policy

Since the beginning of my Administration, I have been committed to improving the effectiveness with which the Federal government deals with the problems and needs of a rapidly changing rural America. The rapid growth of some rural areas has placed a heavy strain on communities and their resources. There are also persistent problems of poverty and economic stagnation in other parts of rural America. Some rural areas continue to lose population, as they have for the past several decades.

In December, 1979, I announced the Small Community and Rural Development Policy. It was the culmination of several years' work and was designed to address the varying needs of our rural population. In 1980, my Administration worked with the Congress to pass the Rural Development Policy Act of 1980, which when fully implemented will allow us to meet the needs of rural people and their communities more effectively and more efficiently.

As a result of the policy and the accompanying legislation, we have:

• Created the position of Under Secretary of Agriculture for Small Community and Rural Development to provide overall leadership.

• Established a White House Working Group to assist in the implementation of the policy.

• Worked with more than 40 governors to form State rural development councils to work in partnership with the White House Working Group, and the Federal agencies, to better deliver State and Federal programs to rural areas.

• Directed the White House Working Group to annually review existing and proposed policies, programs, and budget levels to determine their adequacy in meeting rural needs and the fulfilling of the policy's objectives and principles.

This effort on the part of my Administration and the Congress has resulted in a landmark policy. For the first time, rural affairs has received the prominence it has always deserved. It is a policy that can truly help alleviate the diverse and differing problems rural America will face in the 1980's.

With the help and dedication of a great many people around the country who are concerned with rural affairs, we have constructed a mechanism for dealing effectively with rural problems. There is now a great opportunity to successfully combine Federal efforts with the efforts of rural community leaders and residents. It is my hope this spirit of cooperation and record of accomplishment will be continued in the coming years.

Consumers

In September, 1979, I signed an Executive Order designed to strengthen and coordinate Federal consumer programs and to establish procedures to improve and facilitate consumer participation in government decision-making. Forty Federal agencies have adopted programs to comply with the requirements of the Order. These programs will improve complaint handling, provide better information to consumers, enhance opportunities for public participation in government proceedings, and assure that the consumer point of view is considered in all programs, policies, and regulations.

While substantial progress has been made in assuring a consumer presence in Federal agencies, work must continue to meet fully the goals of the Executive Order. Close monitoring of agency compliance with the requirements of the Order

is necessary. Continued evaluation to assure that the programs are effective and making maximum use of available resources is also essential. As a complement to these initiatives, efforts to provide financial assistance in regulatory proceedings to citizen groups, small businesses, and others whose participation is limited by their economic circumstances must continue to be pursued.

It is essential that consumer representatives in government pay particular attention to the needs and interests of low-income consumers and minorities. The Office of Consumer Affairs' publication, *People Power: What Communities Are Doing to Counter Inflation*, catalogues some of the ways that government and the private sector can assist the less powerful in our society to help themselves. New ways should be found to help foster this new people's movement which is founded on the principle of self-reliance.

Science and Technology

Science and technology contribute immeasurably to the lives of all Americans. Our high standard of living is largely the product of the technology that surrounds us in the home or factory. Our good health is due in large part to our ever increasing scientific understanding. Our national security is assured by the application of technology. And our environment is protected by the use of science and technology. Indeed, our vision of the future is often largely defined by the bounty that we anticipate science and technology will bring.

The Federal government has a special role to play in science and technology. Although the fruits of scientific achievements surround us, it is often difficult to predict the benefits that will arise from a given scientific venture. And these benefits, even if predictable, do not usually lead to ownership rights. Accordingly, the Government has a special obligation to support science as an investment in our future.

My Administration has sought to reverse a decade-long decline in funding. Despite the need for fiscal restraint, real support of basic research has grown nearly 11% during my term in office. And, my Administration has sought to increase the support of long-term research in the variety of mission agencies. In this way, we can harness the American genius for innovation to meet the economic, energy, health, and security challenges that confront our nation.

• *International Relations and National Security.* Science and technology are becoming increasingly important elements of our national security and foreign policies. This is especially so in the current age of sophisticated defense systems and of growing dependence among all countries on modern technology for all aspects of their economic strength. For these reasons, scientific and technological considerations have been integral elements of the Administration's decision-making on such national security and foreign policy issues as the modernization of our strategic weaponry, arms control, technology transfer, the growing bilateral relationship with China, and our relations with the developing world.

Four themes have shaped U.S. policy in international scientific and technological cooperation: pursuit of new international initiatives to advance our own research and development objectives; development and strengthening of scientific exchange to bridge politically ideological, and cultural divisions between this country and other countries; formulation of programs and institutional relations to help developing countries use science and technology beneficially; and cooperation with other nations to manage technologies with local impact. At my direction, my Science and Technology Adviser has actively pursued international programs in support of these four themes. We have given special attention to scientific and technical relations with China, to new forms of scientific and technical cooperation with Japan, to cooperation with Mexico, other Latin American and Caribbean countries and several states in Black America [Africa], and to the proposed Institute for Scientific and Technological Cooperation.

In particular our cooperation with developing countries reflects the importance that each of them has placed on the relationship between economic growth and scientific and technological capability. It also reflects their view that the great strength of the U.S. in science and technology makes close relations with the U.S. technical community an especially productive means of enhancing this capability. Scientific and technological assistance is a key linkage between the U.S. and the developing world, a linkage that has been under-utilized in the past and one which we must continue to work to strengthen.

• *Space Policy.* The Administration has established a framework for a strong and evolving space program for the 1980's.

The Administration's space policy reaffirmed the separation of military space systems and the open civil space program, and at the same time, provided new guidance on technology transfer between the civil and military programs. The civil space program centers on three basic tenets: First, our space policy will reflect a balanced strategy of applications, science, and technology development. Second, activities will be pursued when they can be uniquely or more efficiently accomplished in space. Third, a premature commitment to a high challenge, space-engineering initiative of the complexity of Apollo is inappropriate. As the Shuttle development phases down, however, there will be added flexibility to consider new space applications, space science and new space exploration activities.

• Technology Development. The Shuttle dominates our technology development effort and correctly so. It represents one of the most sophisticated technological challenges ever undertaken, and as a result, has encountered technical problems. Nonetheless, the first manned orbital flight is now scheduled for March, 1981. I have been pleased to support strongly the necessary funds for the Shuttle throughout my Administration.

• Space Applications. Since 1972, the U.S. has conducted experimental civil remote sensing through Landsat satellites, thereby realizing many successful applications. Recognizing this fact, I directed the implementation of an operational civil land satellite remote sensing system, with the operational management responsibility in Commerce's National Oceanic and Atmospheric Administration. In addition, because ocean observations from space can meet common civil and military data requirements, a National Oceanic Satellite System has been proposed as a major FY 1981 new start.

• Space Science Exploration. The goals of this Administration's policy in space science have been to: (1) continue a vigorous program of planetary exploration to understand the origin and evolution of the solar system; (2) utilize the space telescope and free-flying satellites to usher in a new era of astronomy; (3) develop a better understanding of the sun and its interaction with the terrestrial environment; and (4) utilize the Shuttle and Spacelab to conduct basic research that complements earth-based life science investigations.

District of Columbia

Washington, D.C., is home to both the Federal Government and to more than half a million American citizens. I have worked to improve the relationship between the Federal establishment and the Government of the District of Columbia in order to further the goals and spirit of home rule. The City controls more of its own destiny than was the case four years ago. Yet, despite the close cooperation between my Administration and that of Mayor Barry, we have not yet seen the necessary number of states ratify the Constitutional Amendment granting full voting representation in the Congress to the citizens of this city. It is my hope that this inequity will be rectified. The country and the people who inhabit Washington deserve no less.

The Arts

The arts are a precious national resource.

Federal support for the arts has been enhanced during my Administration by expanding government funding and services to arts institutions, individual artists, scholars, and teachers through the National Endowment for the Arts. We have broadened its scope and reach to a more diverse population. We have also reactivated the Federal Council on the Arts and Humanities.

It is my hope that during the coming years the new Administration and the Congress will:

• Continue support of institutions promoting development and understanding of the arts;

• Encourage business participants in a comprehensive effort to achieve a truly mixed economy of support for the arts;

• Explore a variety of mechanisms to nurture the creative talent of our citizens and build audiences for their work;

• Support strong, active National Endowments for the Arts;

• Seek greater recognition for the rich cultural tradition of the nation's minorities;

• Provide grants for the arts in low-income neighborhoods.

The Humanities

In recently reauthorizing Federal appropriations for the National Endowment for the Humanities, the Congress has once again reaffirmed that "the encouragement and support of national progress and scholarship in the humanities . . . while primarily a matter for private and local initiative, is also an appropriate matter of concern to the Federal Government" and that "a high civilization must not limit its efforts to science and technology alone but must give full value and support to the other great branches of man's scholarly and cultural activity in order to achieve a better understanding of the past, a better analysis of the present, and a better view of the future."

I believe we are in agreement that the humanities illuminate the values underlying important personal, social, and national questions raised in our society by its multiple links to and increasing dependence on technology, and by the diverse heritage of our many regions and ethnic groups. The humanities cast light on the broad issue of the role in a society of men and women of imagination and energy—those individuals who through their own example define "the spirit of the age," and in so doing move nations.

Our Government's support for the humanities, within the framework laid down by the Congress, is a recognition of their essential nourishment of the life of the mind and vital enrichment of our national life.

I will be proposing an increase in funding this year sufficient to enable the Endowment to maintain the same level of support offered our citizens in Fiscal Year 1981.

In the allocation of this funding, special emphasis will be given to:

• Humanities education in the nation's schools, in response to the great needs that have arisen in this area;

• Scholarly research designed to increase our understanding of the cultures, traditions, and historical forces at work in other nations and in our own;

• Drawing attention to the physical disintegration of the raw material of our cultural heritage—books, manuscripts, periodicals, and other documents—and to the development of techniques to prevent the destruction and to preserve those materials; and

• The dissemination of quality programming in the humanities to increasingly large American audiences through the use of radio and television.

The dominant effort in the Endowment's expenditures will be a commitment to strengthen and promulgate scholarly excellence and achievement in work in the humanities in our schools, colleges, universities, libraries, museums and other cultural institutions, as well as in the work of individual scholars or collaborative groups engaged in advanced research in the humanities.

In making its grants the Endowment will increase its emphasis on techniques which stimulate support for the humanities from non-Federal sources, in order to reinforce our tradition of private philanthropy in this field, and to insure and expand the financial viability of our cultural institutions and life.

Insular Areas

I have been firmly committed to self-determination for Puerto Rico, the Virgin Islands, Guam, American Samoa and the Northern Mariana Islands, and have vigorously supported the realization of whatever political status aspirations are democratically chosen by their peoples. This principle was the keystone of the comprehensive territorial policy I sent the Congress last year. I am pleased that most of the legislative elements of that policy were endorsed by the 96th Congress.

The unique cultures, fragile economies, and locations of our Caribbean and Pacific Islands are distinct assets to the United States which require the sensitive application of policy. The United States Government should pursue initiatives begun by my Administration and the Congress to stimulate insular economic development; enhance treatment under Federal programs eliminating current inequities; provide vitally needed special assistance and coordinate and rationalize policies. These measures will result in greater self-sufficiency and balanced growth. In particular, I hope that the new Congress will support funding for fiscal management, comprehensive planning and other technical assistance for the territories, as well as create the commission I have proposed to review the applicability of all Federal laws to the insular areas and make recommendations for appropriate modification.

IV. Removing Governmental Waste and Inefficiency

One of my major commitments has been to restore public faith in our Federal government by cutting out waste and inefficiency. In the past four years, we have made dramatic advances toward this goal,

many of them previously considered impossible to achieve. Where government rules and operations were unnecessary, they have been eliminated, as with airline, rail, trucking and financial deregulation. Where government functions are needed, they have been streamlined, through such landmark measures as the Civil Service Reform Act of 1978. I hope that the new administration and the Congress will keep up the momentum we have established for effective and responsible change in this area of crucial public concern.

CIVIL SERVICE REFORM

In March 1978, I submitted the Civil Service Reform Act to Congress. I called it the centerpiece of my efforts to reform and reorganize the government. With bipartisan support from Congress, the bill passed, and I am pleased to say that implementation is running well ahead of the statutory schedule. Throughout the service, we are putting into place the means to assure that reward and retention are based on performance and not simply on length of time on the job. In the first real test of the Reform Act, 98 percent of the eligible top-level managers joined the Senior Executive Service, choosing to relinquish job protections for the challenge and potential reward of this new corps of top executives. Though the Act does not require several of its key elements to be in operation for another year, some Federal agencies already have established merit pay systems for GS–13–15 managers, and most agencies are well on their way to establishing new peformance standards for all their employees. All have paid out, or are now in the process of paying out, performance bonuses earned by outstanding members of the Senior Executive Service. Dismissals have increased by 10 percent, and dismissals specifically for inadequate job performance have risen

1500 percent, since the Act was adopted. Finally, we have established a fully independent Merit Systems Protection Board and Special Counsel to protect the rights of whistle-blowers and other Federal employees faced with threats to their rights.

In 1981, civil service reform faces critical challenges—all agencies must have fully functioning performance appraisal systems for all employees, and merit pay systems for compensating the government's 130,000 GS–13–15 managers. Performance bonuses for members of the Senior Executive Service will surely receive scrutiny. If this attention is balanced and constructive, it can only enhance the chances for ultimate success of our bipartisan commitment to the revolutionary and crucial pay-for-performance concept.

REGULATORY REFORM

During the past four years we have made tremendous progress in regulatory reform. We have discarded old economic regulations that prevented competition and raised consumer costs, and we have imposed strong management principles on the regulatory programs the country needs, cutting paperwork and other wasteful burdens. The challenge for the future is to continue the progress in both areas without crippling vital health and safety programs.

Our economic deregulation program has achieved major successes in five areas:

Airlines: The Airline Deregulation Act is generating healthy competition, saving billions in fares, and making the airlines more efficient. The Act provides that in 1985 the CAB itself will go out of existence.

Trucking: The trucking deregulation bill opens the industry to competition and allows truckers wide latitude on the routes they drive and the goods they haul. The bill also phases out most of the old law's immunity for setting rates. The Congressional Budget Office estimates these reforms will save as much as $8 billion per year and cut as much as half a percentage point from the inflation rate.

Railroads: Overregulation has stifled railroad management initiative, service, and competitive pricing. The new legislation gives the railroads the freedom they need to rebuild a strong, efficient railroad industry.

Financial Institutions: With the help of the Congress, over the past four years we have achieved two major pieces of financial reform legislation—legislation which has provided the basis for the most far-reaching changes in the financial services industry since the 1930's. The International Banking Act of 1978 was designed to reduce the advantages that foreign banks operating in the United States possessed in comparison to domestic banks. The Depository Institutions Deregulation and Monetary Control Act, adopted last March, provides for the phased elimination of a variety of anti-competitive barriers to financial institutions and freedom to offer services to and attract the savings of consumers, especially small savers.

Recently, I submitted to the Congress my Administration's recommendations for the phased liberalization of restrictions on geographic expansion by commercial banks. Last year the Administration and financial regulatory agencies proposed legislation to permit the interstate acquisition of failing depository institutions. In view of the difficult outlook for some depository institutions I strongly urge the Congress to take prompt favorable action on the failing bank legislation.

Telecommunications: While Congress did not pass legislation in this area, the

Federal Communications Commission has taken dramatic action to open all aspects of communications to competition and to eliminate regulations in the areas where competition made them obsolete. The public is benefitting from an explosion of competition and new services.

While these initiatives represent dramatic progress in economic deregulation, continued work is needed. I urge Congress to act on communications legislation and to consider other proposed deregulation measures, such as legislation on the bus industry. In addition, the regulatory commissions must maintain their commitment to competition as the best regulator of all.

The other part of my reform program covers the regulations that are needed to protect the health, safety, and welfare of our citizens. For these regulations, my Administration has created a management program to cut costs without sacrificing goals. Under my Executive Order 12044, we required agencies to analyze the costs of their major new rules and consider alternative approaches—such as performance standards and voluntary codes—that may make rules less costly and more flexible. We created the Regulatory Analysis Review Group in the White House to analyze the most costly proposed new rules and find ways to improve them. The Regulatory Council was established to provide the first Government-wide listing of upcoming rules and eliminate overlapping and conflicting regulations. Agencies have launched "sunset" programs to weed out outmoded old regulations. We have acted to encourage public participation in regulatory decisionmaking.

These steps have already saved billions of dollars in regulatory costs and slashed thousands of outmoded regulations. We are moving steadily toward a regulatory system that provides needed protections fairly, predictably, and at minimum cost.

I urge Congress to continue on this steady path and resist the simplistic solutions that have been proposed as alternatives. Proposals like legislative veto and increased judicial review will add another layer to the regulatory process, making it more cumbersome and inefficient. The right approach to reform is to improve the individual statutes—where they need change—and to ensure that the regulatory agencies implement those statutes sensibly.

PAPERWORK REDUCTION

The Federal Government imposes a huge paperwork burden on business, local government, and the private sector. Many of these forms are needed for vital government functions, but others are duplicative, overly complex or obsolete.

During my Administration we cut the paperwork burden by 15 percent, and we created procedures to continue this progress. The new Paperwork Reduction Act centralizes, in OMB, oversight of all agencies' information requirements and strengthens OMB's authority to eliminate needless forms. The "paperwork budget" process, which I established by executive order, applies the discipline of the budget process to the hours of reporting time imposed on the public, forcing agencies to scrutinize all their forms each year. With effective implementation, these steps should allow further, substantial paperwork cuts in the years ahead.

TIGHTENING STANDARDS FOR GOVERNMENTAL EFFICIENCY AND INTEGRITY

To develop a foundation to carry out energy policy, we consolidated scattered energy programs and launched the Synthetic Fuels Corporation; to give education the priority it deserves and at the same time reduce HHS to more manageable size, I gave education a seat at the Cabinet table, to create a stronger system for attacking waste and fraud, I reorganized audit and investigative functions by putting an Inspector General in major agencies. Since I took office, we have submitted 14 reorganization initiatives and had them all approved by Congress.

We have saved hundreds of millions of dollars through the adoption of business-like cash management principles and set strict standards for personal financial disclosure and conflict of interest avoidance by high Federal officials.

To streamline the structure of the government, we have secured approval of 14 reorganization initiatives, improving the efficiency of the most important sectors of the government, including energy, education, and civil rights enforcement. We have eliminated more than 300 advisory committees as well as other agencies, boards and commissions which were obsolete or ineffective. Independent Inspectors General have been appointed in major agencies to attack fraud and waste. More than a billion dollars of questionable transactions have been identified through their audit activities.

The adoption of business-like cash management and debt collection initiatives will save over $1 billion, by streamlining the processing of receipts, by controlling disbursements more carefully, and by reducing idle cash balances. Finally this Administration has set strict standards for personal financial disclosure and conflict of interest avoidance by high Federal officials, to elevate the level of public trust in the government.

V. PROTECTING BASIC RIGHTS AND LIBERTIES

I am extremely proud of the advances we have made in ensuring equality and protecting the basic freedoms of all Americans.

• The Equal Employment Opportunity Commission (EEOC) and the Office of Federal Contract Compliance (OFCCP) have been reorganized and strengthened and a permanent civil rights unit has been established in OMB.

• To avoid fragmented, inconsistent and duplicative enforcement of civil rights laws, three agencies have been given coordinative and standard-setting responsibilities in discrete areas: EEOC for all employment-related activities, HUD for all those relating to housing, and the Department of Justice for all other areas.

• With the enactment of the Right to Financial Privacy Act and a bill limiting police search of newsrooms, we have begun to establish a sound, comprehensive, privacy program.

Ratification of the Equal Rights Amendment must be aggressively pursued. Only one year remains in which to obtain ratification by three additional states.

The Congress must give early attention to a number of important bills which remain. These bills would:

• strengthen the laws against discrimination in housing. Until it is enacted, the 1968 Civil Rights Act's promise of equal access to housing will remain unfulfilled;

• establish a charter for the FBI and the intelligence agencies. The failure to define in law the duties and responsibilities of these agencies has made possible some of the abuses which have occurred in recent years;

• establish privacy safeguards for medical research, bank, insurance, and credit records; and provide special protection for election fund transfer systems.

EQUAL RIGHTS AMENDMENT

I remain committed as strongly as possible to the ratification of the Equal Rights Amendment.

As a result of our efforts in 1978, the Equal Rights Amendment's deadline for ratification was extended for three years. We have now one year and three States left. We cannot afford any delay in marshalling our resources and efforts to obtain the ratification of those three additional States.

Although the Congress has no official role in the ratification process at this point, you do have the ability to affect public opinion and the support of State Legislators for the Amendment. I urge Members from States which have not yet ratified the Equal Rights Amendment to use their influence to secure ratification. I will continue my own efforts to help ensure ratification of the Equal Rights Amendment.

MARTIN LUTHER KING, JR.

Dr. Martin Luther King, Jr. led this Nation's effort to provide all its citizens with civil rights and equal opportunities. His commitment to human rights, peace and non-violence stands as a monument to his humanity and courage. As one of our Nation's most outstanding leaders, it is appropriate that his birthday be commemorated as a national holiday. I hope the Congress will enact legislation this year that will achieve this goal.

FAIR HOUSING

The Fair Housing Act Amendments of 1980 passed the House of Representatives by an overwhelming bipartisan majority only to die in the Senate at the close of the 96th Congress. The leaders of both parties have pledged to make the enactment of fair housing legislation a top priority of the incoming Congress. The need is pressing and a strengthened federal enforcement effort must be the primary method of resolution.

CRIMINAL CODE

The Federal criminal laws are often archaic, frequently contradictory and imprecise, and clearly in need of revision and codification. The new Administration should continue the work which has been begun to develop a Federal criminal code which simplifies and clarifies our criminal laws, while maintaining our basic civil liberties and protections.

PRIVACY

As our public and private institutions collect more and more information and as communications and computer technologies advance, we must act to protect the personal privacy of our citizens.

In the past four years we acted on the report of the Privacy Commission and established a national privacy policy. We worked with Congress to pass legislation restricting wiretaps and law enforcement access to bank records and to reporters' files. We reduced the number of personal files held by the government and restricted the transfer of personal information among Federal agencies. We also worked with the Organization for Economic Cooperation and Development to establish international guidelines to protect the privacy of personal information that is transferred across borders.

VI. PROTECTING AND DEVELOPING OUR NATURAL RESOURCES

Two of our Nation's most precious natural resources are our environment and our vast agricultural capacity. From the beginning of my Administration, I have worked with the Congress to enhance and protect, as well as develop our natural resources. In the environmental areas, I have been especially concerned about the importance of balancing the need for resource development with preserving a clean environment, and have taken numerous actions to foster this goal. In the agricultural area, I have taken the steps needed to improve farm incomes and to increase our agricultural production to record levels. That progress must be continued in the 1980's.

Environment

Preserving the quality of our environment has been among the most important objectives of my Administration and of the Congress. As a result of these shared commitments and the dedicated efforts of many members of the Congress and my Administration, we have achieved several historic accomplishments.

PROTECTION OF ALASKA LANDS

Passage of the Alaska National Interest Lands Conservation Act was one of the most important conservation actions of this century. At stake was the fate of millions of acres of beautiful land, outstanding and unique wildlife populations, native cultures, and the opportunity to ensure that future generations of Americans would be able to enjoy the benefits of these nationally significant resources. As a result of the leadership, commitment, and persistence of my Administration and the Congressional leadership, the Alaska Lands Bill was signed into law last December.

The Act adds 97 million acres of new parks and refuges, more than doubling the size of our National Park and National Wildlife Refuge Systems. The bill triples the size of our national wilderness system, increasing its size by 56 million acres. And by adding 25 free-flowing river segments to the Wild and Scenic River System, the bill almost doubles the river mileage in that system. The Alaska Lands Act reaffirms our commitment to the environment and strikes a balance between protecting areas of great beauty and allowing development of Alaska's oil, gas. mineral, and timber resources.

PROTECTION OF NATURAL RESOURCES

In addition to the Alaska Lands Act. over the past four years we have been able to expand significantly the national wilderness and parks systems. In 1978, the Congress passed the historic Omnibus Parks Act, which made 12 additions to the National Park System. The Act also established the first two national trails since the National Trails System Act was passed in 1968. Then, in 1980, as a result of my 1979 Environmental Message, the Federal land management agencies have established almost 300 new National Recreational Trails. With the completion of the RARE II process, which eliminated the uncertainty surrounding the status of millions of acres of land, we called for over 15 million acres of new wilderness in the nation's National Forest, in 1980 the Congress established about 4.5 million acres of wilderness in the lower 48 states. In addition, the Administration recommended legislation to protect Lake Tahoe, and through and Executive Order has already established a mechanism to help ensure the Lake's protection. Finally, in 1980 the Administration established the Channel Islands Marine Sanctuary.

Administration actions over the past four years stressed the importance of providing Federal support only for water resource projects that are economically and environmentally sound. This policy should have a major and lasting influence on the federal government's role in water resource development and management. The Administration's actions to recommend to the Congress only economically and environmentally sound water resource projects for funding resulted not only in our opposing uneconomic projects but also—in 1979—in the first Administration proposal of new project starts in 4 years.

One of the most significant water policy actions of the past four years was the Administration's June 6, 1978 Water Policy Reform Message to the Congress. This Message established a new national water resources policy with the following objectives:

• to give priority emphasis to water conservation;

• to consider environmental requirements and values more fully and along with economic factors in the planning and management of water projects and programs;

• to enhance cooperation between state and federal agencies in water resources planning and management.

In addition, the Executive Office of the President established 11 policy decision criteria to evaluate the proposed federal water projects, the Water Resources Council developed and adopted a new set of Principles and Standards for water projects which is binding on all federal construction agencies, and improved regulations were developed to implement the National Historic Preservation Act and the Fish and Wildlife Coordination Act. As a result, water resource projects must be determined to be economically sound before the Administration will recommend authorization or appropriation. Over the years ahead, this policy will help to reduce wasteful federal spending by targeting federal funds to the highest priority water resource projects.

In the pursuit of this policy, however, we cannot lose sight of the vital role that sound water resource projects play in providing irrigation, power, and flood control. We must also recognize the special needs of particular regions of the country in evaluating the need for additional projects.

ADDRESSING GLOBAL RESOURCE AND
ENVIRONMENTAL PROBLEMS

The *Global 2000 Report to the President,* prepared in response to my 1977 Environment Message, is the first of its kind. Never before has our government, or any government, taken such a comprehensive, long-range look at the interrelated global issues of resources, population, and environment.

The Report's conclusions are important. They point to a rapid increase in population and human needs through the year 2000 while at the same time a decline in the earth's capacity to meet those needs— *unless* nations of the world act decisively to alter current trends.

The United States has contributed actively to a series of UN conferences on the environment, population, and resources, and is preparing for the 1981 Conference on New and Renewable Sources of Energy. Following my 1977 Environmental Message, the Administration development assistance programs have added emphasis to natural resource management and environmental protection. My 1979 Environmental Message called attention to the alarming loss of world forests, particularly in the tropics. An interagency task force on tropical forests has developed a U.S. government program to encourage conservation and wise management of tropical forests. The Administration is encouraging action by other nations and world organizations to the same purpose. The United States is a world leader in wildlife conservation and the assessment of environmental effects of government actions. The January 5, 1979, Executive Order directing U.S. government agencies to consider the effects of their major actions abroad, is another example of this leadership.

COMMITMENT TO CONTROL OF POLLU-
TION AND HAZARDOUS CHEMICALS

Over the past four years, there has been steady progress towards cleaner air and water, sustained by the commitment of Congress and the Administration to these important national objectives. In addition, the Administration has developed several new pollution compliance approaches such as alternative and innovative waste water treatment projects, the "bubble" concept, the "offset" policy, and permit consolidation, all of which are designed to reduce regulatory burdens on the private sector.

One of the most pressing problems to come to light in the past four years has been improper hazardous waste disposal. The Administration has moved on three fronts. First, we proposed the Oil Hazardous Substances and Hazardous Waste Response, Liability and Compensation Act (the "Superfund" bill) to provide comprehensive authority and $1.6 billion in funds to clean up abandoned hazardous waste disposal sites. In November 1980 the Congress passed a Superfund bill which I signed into law.

Second, the administration established a hazardous waste enforcement strike force to ensure that when available, responsible parties are required to clean up sites posing dangers to public health and to the environment. To date, 50 lawsuits have been brought by the strike force.

Third, regulations implementing subtitle C of the Resource Conservation and Recovery Act were issued. The regulations establish comprehensive controls for hazardous waste and, together with vigorous enforcement, will help to ensure that Love Canal will not be repeated.

THE FUTURE

For the future, we cannot—and we must not—forget that we are charged with the stewardship of an irreplaceable environment and natural heritage. Our children, and our children's children, are dependent upon our maintaining our commitment to preserving and enhancing the quality of our environment. It is my hope that when our descendants look back on the 1980's they will be able to affirm:

• that we kept our commitment to the restoration of environmental quality;

• that we protected the public health from the continuing dangers of toxic chemicals, from pollution, from hazardous and radioactive waste, and that we made our communities safer, healthier and better places to live;

• that we preserved America's wilderness areas and particularly its last great frontier, Alaska, for the benefit of all Americans in perpetuity;

• that we put this nation on a path to a sustainable energy future, one based increasingly on renewable resources and on energy conservation;

• that we moved to protect America's

countryside and coastland from mismanagement and irresponsibility;

• that we redirected the management
of the nation's water resources toward
water conservation, sound development
and environmental protection;

• that we faced squarely such worldwide problems as the destruction of forests, acid rain, carbon dioxide build-up
and nuclear proliferation; and

• that we protected the habitat and the
existence of our own species on this earth.

Agriculture

THE FARM ECONOMY

The farm economy is sound and its future is bright. Agriculture remains a
major bulwark of the nation's economy
and an even more important factor in the
world food system. The demand for
America's agricultural abundance, here
and abroad, continues to grow. In the
near-term, the strength of this demand is
expected to press hard against supplies,
resulting in continued price strength.

The health and vitality of current-day
agriculture represents a significant departure from the situation that existed
when I came to office four years ago. In
January 1977, the farm economy was in
serious trouble. Farm prices and farm income were falling rapidly. Grain prices
were at their lowest levels in years and
steadily falling. Livestock producers, in
their fourth straight year of record losses,
were liquidating breeding herds at an
unparalleled rate. Dairy farmers were losing money on every hundredweight of
milk they produced. Sugar prices were in
a nosedive.

Through a combination of improvements in old, established programs and
the adoption of new approaches where innovation and change were needed, my

Administration turned this situation
around. Commodity prices have steadily
risen. Farm income turned upward. U.S.
farm exports set new records each year,
increasing over 80 percent for the four
year period. Livestock producers began
rebuilding their herds. Dairy farmers began to earn a profit again.

RECENT POLICY INITIATIVES

Several major agricultural policy initiatives have been undertaken over the
past year. Some are the culmination of
policy proposals made earlier in this Administration; others are measures taken
to help farmers offset the impact of rapid
inflation in production costs. In combination, they represent a significant strengthening of our nation's food and agricultural policy. These initiatives include:

FOOD SECURITY RESERVE

The Congress authorized formation of
a 4 million ton food grain reserve for use
in international food assistance. This reserve makes it possible for the United
States to stand behind its food aid commitment to food deficit nations, even during periods of short supplies and high
prices. This corrects a serious fault in our
past food assistance policy.

COMPREHENSIVE CROP INSURANCE

The Congress also authorized a significant new crop insurance program during
1980. This measure provides farmers with
an important new program tool for sharing the economic risks that are inherent
to agriculture. When fully operational, it
will replace a hodgepodge of disaster
programs that suffered from numerous
shortcomings.

SPECIAL LOAN RATES

Another legislative measure passed late in the 2nd session of the 96th Congress authorizes the Secretary of Agriculture to provide higher loan rates to farmers who enter their grain in the farmer-owned grain reserve. This additional incentive to participate will further strengthen the reserve.

INCREASED LOAN PRICES

In July 1980, I administratively raised loan prices for wheat, feedgrains, and soybeans to help offset the effects of a serious cost-price squeeze. At the same time, the release and call prices for the grain reserve were adjusted upward.

HIGHER TARGET PRICES

The Agricultural Adjustment Act of 1980 raised the target prices for 1980-crop wheat and feed grain crops. This change corrected for shortcomings in the adjustment formula contained in the Food and Agriculture Act of 1977.

FUTURE AGENDA

The food and agricultural policies adopted by this Administration over the past four years, including those described above, will provide a firm foundation for future governmental actions in this field. Expiration of the Food and Agriculture Act of 1977 later this year will require early attention by the Congress. With relatively minor changes, most of the authorities contained in the 1977 Act should be extended in their present form. The farmer-owned grain reserve has proven to be a particularly effective means of stabilizing grain markets and should be preserved in essentially its present form.

Beyond this, it will be important for the Congress to keep a close eye on price-cost developments in the farm sector. As noted above, some of the actions I took last year were for the purpose of providing relief from the cost-price squeeze facing farmers. Should these pressures continue, further actions might be required.

My Administration has devoted particular attention to the issues of world hunger, agricultural land use, and the future structure of American agriculture. I encourage the Congress and the next Administration to review the results of these landmark enquiries and, where deemed appropriate, to act on their recommendations.

Following a careful review of the situation, I recently extended the suspension of grain sales to the Soviet Union. I am satisfied that this action has served its purpose effectively and fairly. However, as long as this suspension must remain in effect, it will be important for the next Administration and the Congress to take whatever actions are necessary to ensure that the burden does not fall unfairly on our Nation's farmers. This has been a key feature of my Administration's policy, and it should be maintained.

VII. FOREIGN POLICY

From the time I assumed office four years ago this month, I have stressed the need for this country to assert a leading role in a world undergoing the most extensive and intensive change in human history.

My policies have been directed in particular at three areas of change:

• the steady growth and increased projection abroad of Soviet military power—power that has grown faster than our own over the past two decades.

• the overwhelming dependence of Western nations, which now increasingly includes the United States, on vital oil supplies from the Middle East.

• the pressures of change in many nations of the developing world, in Iran and uncertainty about the future stability of many developing countries.

As a result of those fundamental facts, we face some of the most serious challenges in the history of this nation. The Soviet invasion of Afghanistan is a threat to global peace, to East-West relations, and to regional stability and to the flow of oil. As the unprecedented and overwhelming vote in the General Assembly demonstrated, countries across the world—and particularly the non-aligned—regard the Soviet invasion as a threat to their independence and security. Turmoil within the region adjacent to the Persian Gulf poses risks for the security and prosperity of every oil importing nation and thus for the entire global economy. The continuing holding of American hostages in Iran is both an affront to civilized people everywhere, and a serious impediment to meeting the self-evident threat to widely-shared common interests—including those of Iran.

But as we focus our most urgent efforts on pressing problems, we will continue to pursue the benefits that only change can bring. For it always has been the essence of America that we want to move on—we understand that prosperity, progress and most of all peace cannot be had by standing still. A world of nations striving to preserve their independence, and of peoples aspiring for economic development and political freedom, is not a world hostile to the ideals and interests of the United States. We face powerful adversaries, but we have strong friends and dependable allies. We have common interests with the vast majority of the world's nations and peoples.

There have been encouraging developments in recent years, as well as matters requiring continued vigilance and concern:

• Our alliances with the world's most advanced and democratic states from Western Europe through Japan are stronger than ever.

• We have helped to bring about a dramatic improvement in relations between Egypt and Israel and an historic step towards a comprehensive Arab-Israeli settlement.

• Our relations with China are growing closer, providing a major new dimension in our policy in Asia and the world.

• Across southern Africa from Rhodesia to Namibia we are helping with the peaceful transition to majority rule in a context of respect for minority as well as majority rights.

• We have worked domestically and with our allies to respond to an uncertain energy situation by conservation and diversification of energy supplies based on internationally agreed targets.

• We have unambiguously demonstrated our commitment to defend Western interests in Southwest Asia, and we have significantly increased our ability to do so.

• And over the past four years the U.S. has developed an energy program which is comprehensive and ambitious. New institutions have been established such as the Synthetic Fuels Corporation and Solar Bank. Price decontrol for oil and gas is proceeding. American consumers have risen to the challenge, and we have experienced real improvements in consumption patterns.

The central challenge for us today is to our steadfastness of purpose. We are no longer tempted by isolationism. But we must also learn to deal effectively with the contradictions of the world—the need to cooperate with potential adversaries without euphoria, without undermining our determination to compete with such adversaries and if necessary confront the threats they may pose to our security.

We face a broad range of threats and opportunities. We have and should continue to pursue a broad range of defense, diplomatic and economic capabilities and objectives.

I see six basic goals for America in the world over the 1980's:

• First, we will continue, as we have over the past four years, to build America's military strength and that of our allies and friends. Neither the Soviet Union nor any other nation will have reason to question our will to sustain the strongest and most flexible defense forces.

• Second, we will pursue an active diplomacy in the world, working—together with our friends and allies—to resolve disputes through peaceful means and to make any aggressor pay a heavy price.

• Third, we will strive to resolve pressing international economic problems—particularly energy and inflation—and continue to pursue our still larger objective of global economic growth through expanded trade and development assistance and through the preservation of an open multilateral trading system.

• Fourth, we will continue vigorously to support the process of building democratic institutions and improving human rights protection around the world. We are deeply convinced that the future lies not with dictatorship but democracy.

• Fifth, we remain deeply committed to the process of mutual and verifiable arms control, particularly to the effort to prevent the spread and further development of nuclear weapons. Our decision to defer, but not abandon our efforts to secure ratification of the SALT II Treaty reflects our firm conviction that the

United States has a profound national security interest in the constraints on Soviet nuclear forces which only that treaty can provide.

• Sixth, we must continue to look ahead in order to evaluate and respond to resource, environment and population challenges through the end of this century.

One very immediate and pressing objective that is uppermost on our minds and those of the American people is the release of our hostages in Iran.

We have no basic quarrel with the nation, the revolution or the people of Iran. The threat to them comes not from American policy but from Soviet actions in the region. We are prepared to work with the government of Iran to develop a new and mutually beneficial relationship.

But that will not be possible so long as Iran continues to hold Americans hostages, in defiance of the world community and civilized behavior. They must be released unharmed. We have thus far pursued a measured program of peaceful diplomatic and economic steps in an attempt to resolve this issue without resorting to other remedies available to us under international law. This reflects the deep respect of our nation for the rule of law and for the safety of our people being held, and our belief that a great power bears a responsibility to use its strength in a measured and judicious manner. But our patience is not unlimited and our concern for the well-being of our fellow citizens grows each day.

Enhancing National Security—American Military Strength

The maintenance of national security is my first concern, as it has been for every president before me.

We must have both the military power and the political will to deter our adversaries and to support our friends and allies.

We must pay whatever price is required to remain the strongest nation in the world. That price has increased as the military power of our major adversary has grown and its readiness to use that power been made all too evident in Afghanistan. The real increases in defense spending, therefore probably will be higher than previously projected; protecting our security may require a larger share of our national wealth in the future.

THE U.S.-SOVIET RELATIONSHIP

We are demonstrating to the Soviet Union across a broad front that it will pay a heavy price for its aggression in terms of our relationship. Throughout the last decades U.S.-Soviet relations have been a mixture of cooperation and competition. The Soviet invasion of Afghanistan and the imposition of a puppet government have highlighted in the starkest terms the darker side of their policies— going well beyond competition and the legitimate pursuit of national interest, and violating all norms of international law and practice.

This attempt to subjugate an independent, non-aligned Islamic people is a callous violation of international law and the United Nations Charter, two fundamentals of international order. Hence, it is also a dangerous threat to world peace. For the first time since the communization of Eastern Europe after World War II, the Soviets have sent combat forces into an area that was not previously under their control, into a non-aligned and sovereign state.

The destruction of the independence of the Afghanistan government and the occupation by the Soviet Union have altered the strategic situation in that part of the world in a very ominous fashion. It has significantly shortened the striking distance to the Indian Ocean and the Persian Gulf for the Soviet Union.

It has also eliminated a buffer between the Soviet Union and Pakistan and presented a new threat to Iran. These two countries are now far more vulnerable to Soviet political intimidation. If that intimidation were to prove effective, the Soviet Union could control an area of vital strategic and economic significance to the survival of Western Europe, the Far East, and ultimately the United States.

It has now been over a year since the Soviet invasion of Afghanistan dealt a major blow to U.S.-Soviet relations and the entire international system. The U.S. response has proven to be serious and far-reaching. It has been increasingly effective, imposing real and sustained costs on the USSR's economy and international image.

Meanwhile, we have encouraged and supported efforts to reach a political settlement in Afghanistan which would lead to a withdrawal of Soviet forces from that country and meet the interests of all concerned. It is Soviet intransigence that has kept those efforts from bearing fruit.

Meanwhile, an overwhelming November resolution of the United Nations General Assembly on Afghanistan has again made clear that the world has not and will not forget Afghanistan. And our response continues to make it clear that Soviet use of force in pursuit of its international objectives is incompatible with the notion of business-as-usual.

BILATERAL COMMUNICATION

U.S.-Soviet relations remain strained by the continued Soviet presence in Afghanistan, by growing Soviet military capabilities, and by the Soviets' apparent willingness to use those capabilities without respect for the most basic norms of international behavior.

But the U.S.-Soviet relationship remains the single most important element in determining whether there will be war or peace. And so, despite serious strains in our relations, we have maintained a dialogue with the Soviet Union over the past year. Through this dialogue, we have ensured against bilateral misunderstandings and miscalculations which might escalate out of control, and have managed to avoid the injection of superpower rivalries into areas of tension like the Iran-Iraq conflict.

POLAND

Now, as was the case a year ago, the prospect of Soviet use of force threatens the international order. The Soviet Union has completed preparations for a possible military intervention against Poland. Although the situation in Poland has shown signs of stabilizing recently, Soviet forces remain in a high state of readiness and they could move into Poland on short notice. We continue to believe that the Polish people should be allowed to work out their internal problems themselves, without outside interference, and we have made clear to the Soviet leadership that any intervention in Poland would have severe and prolonged consequences for East-West detente, and U.S.-Soviet relations in particular.

DEFENSE BUDGET

For many years the Soviets have steadily increased their real defense spending, expanded their strategic forces, strengthened their forces in Europe and Asia, and enhanced their capability for projecting military force around the world directly or through the use of proxies. Afghanis-

tan dramatizes the vastly increased military power of the Soviet Union.

The Soviet Union has built a war machine far beyond any reasonable requirements for their own defense and security. In contrast, our own defense spending declined in real terms every year from 1968 through 1976.

We have reversed this decline in our own effort. Every year since 1976 there has been a real increase in our defense spending—and our lead has encouraged increases by our allies. With the support of the Congress, we must and will make an even greater effort in the years ahead.

The Fiscal Year 1982 budget would increase funding authority for defense to more than $196 billion. This amount, together with a supplemental request for FY 1981 of about $6 billion, will more than meet my Administration's pledge for a sustained growth of 3 percent in real expenditures, and provides for 5 percent in program growth in FY 1982 and beyond.

The trends we mean to correct cannot be remedied overnight; we must be willing to see this program through. To ensure that we do so I am setting a growth rate for defense that we can sustain over the long haul.

The defense progam I have proposed for the next five years will require some sacrifice—but sacrifice we can well afford.

The defense program emphasizes four areas:

• It ensures that our strategic nuclear forces will be equivalent to those of the Soviet Union and that deterrence against nuclear war will be maintained;

• It upgrades our forces so that the military balance between NATO and the Warsaw Pact will continue to deter the outbreak of war—conventional or nuclear—in Europe;

• It provides us the ability to come

quickly to the aid of friends and allies around the globe;

• And it ensures that our Navy will continue to be the most powerful on the seas.

STRATEGIC FORCES

We are strengthening each of the three legs of our strategic forces. The cruise missile production which will begin next year will modernize our strategic air deterrent. B–52 capabilities will also be improved. These steps will maintain and enhance the B–52 fleet by improving its ability to deliver weapons against increasingly heavily defended targets.

We are also modernizing our strategic submarine force. Four more POSEIDON submarines backfitted with new, 4,000 mile TRIDENT I missiles began deployments in 1980. Nine TRIDENT submarines have been authorized through 1981, and we propose one more each year.

The new M–X missile program to enhance our land-based intercontinental ballistic missile force continues to make progress. Technical refinements in the basing design over the last year will result in operational benefits, lower costs, and reduced environmental impact. The M–X program continues to be an essential ingredient in our strategic posture—providing survivability, endurance, secure command and control and the capability to threaten targets the Soviets hold dear.

Our new systems will enable U.S. strategic forces to maintain equivalence in the face of the mounting Soviet challenge. We would however need an even greater investment in strategic systems to meet the likely Soviet buildup without SALT.

STRATEGIC DOCTRINE

This Administration's systematic contributions to the necessary evolution of strategic doctrine began in 1977 when I commissioned a comprehensive net assessment. From that base a number of thorough investigations of specific topics continued. I should emphasize that the need for an evolutionary doctrine is driven not by any change in our basic objective— which remains peace and freedom for all mankind. Rather, the need for change is driven by the inexorable buildup of Soviet military power and the increasing propensity of Soviet leaders to use this power in coercion and outright aggression to impose their will on others.

I have codified our evolving strategic doctrine in a number of interrelated and mutually supporting Presidential Directives. Their overarching theme is to provide a doctrinal basis—and the specific program to implement it—that tells the world that no potential adversary of the United States could ever conclude that the fruits of his aggression would be significant or worth the enormous costs of our retaliation.

The Presidential Directives include:

PD–18: An overview of our strategic objectives

PD–37: Basic space policy

PD–41: Civil Defense

PD–53: Survivability and endurance for telecommunications

PD–57: Mobilization planning

PD–58: Continuity of Government

PD–59: Countervailing Strategy for General War

These policies have been devised to deter, first and foremost, Soviet aggression. As such they confront not only Soviet military forces but also Soviet military doctrine. By definition deterrence requires that we shape Soviet assessments about the risks of war—assessments they will make using their doctrine, not ours.

But at the same time we in no way seek to emulate their doctrine. In particular, nothing in our policy contemplates that nuclear warfare could ever be a deliberate instrument for achieving our own goals of peace and freedom. Moreover, our policies are carefully devised to provide the greatest possible incentives and opportunities for future progress in arms control.

Finally, our doctrinal evolution has been undertaken with appropriate consultation with our NATO Allies and others. We are fully consistent with NATO's strategy of flexible response.

FORCES FOR NATO

We are greatly accelerating our ability to reinforce Western Europe with massive ground and air forces in a crisis. We are undertaking a major modernization program for the Army's weapons and equipment, adding armor, firepower, and tactical mobility.

We are prepositioning more heavy equipment in Europe to help us cope with attacks with little warning, and greatly strengthening our airlift and sealift capabilities.

We are also improving our tactical air forces—buying about 1700 new fighter and attack aircraft over the next five years—and increasing the number of Air Force fighter wings by over 10 percent.

We are working closely with our European allies to secure the Host Nation Support necessary to enable us to deploy more quickly a greater ratio of combat forces to the European theater at a lower cost to the United States.

SECURITY ASSISTANCE

As we move to enhance U.S. defense capabilities, we must not lose sight of the need to assist others in maintaining their own security and independence. Events since World War II, most recently in Southwest Asia, have amply demonstrated

that U.S. security cannot exist in a vacuum, and that our own prospects for peace are closely tied to those of our friends. The security assistance programs which I am proposing for the coming fiscal year thus directly promote vital U.S. foreign policy and national security aims— and are integral parts of our efforts to improve and upgrade our own military forces.

More specifically, these programs, which are part of our overall foreign aid request, promote U.S. security in two principal ways. First, they assist friendly and allied nations to develop the capability to defend themselves and maintain their own independence. An example during this past year was the timely support provided Thailand to help bolster that country's defenses against the large numbers of Soviet-backed Vietnamese troops ranged along its eastern frontier. In addition, over the years these programs have been important to the continued independence of other friends and allies such as Israel, Greece, Turkey and Korea. Second, security assistance constitutes an essential element in the broad cooperative relationships we have established with many nations which permit either U.S. bases on their territory or access by U.S. forces to their facilities. These programs have been particularly important with regard to the recently-concluded access agreements with various countries in the Persian Gulf and Indian Ocean regions and have been crucial to the protection of our interests throughout Southwest Asia.

RAPID DEPLOYMENT FORCES

We are systematically enhancing our ability to respond rapidly to non-NATO contingencies wherever required by our commitments or when our vital interests are threatened.

The rapid deployment forces we are assembling will be extraordinarily flexible: They could range in size from a few ships or air squadrons to formations as large as 100,000 men, together with their support. Our forces will be prepared for rapid deployment to any region of strategic significance.

Among the specific initiatives we are taking to help us respond to crises outside of Europe are:

• the development of a new fleet of large cargo aircraft with intercontinental range;

• the design and procurement of a force of Maritime Prepositioning Ships that will carry heavy equipment and supplies for three Marine Corps brigades;

• the procurement of fast sealift ships to move large quantities of men and material quickly from the U.S. to overseas areas of deployment;

• increasing training and exercise activities to ensure that our forces will be well prepared to deploy and operate in distant areas.

In addition, our European allies have agreed on the importance of providing support to U.S. deployments to Southwest Asia.

NAVAL FORCES

Seapower is indispensable to our global position—in peace and also in war. Our shipbuilding program will sustain a 550-ship Navy in the 1990's and we will continue to build the most capable ships afloat.

The program I have proposed will assure the ability of our Navy to operate in high threat areas, to maintain control of the seas and protect vital lines of communication—both military and economic—and to provide the strong maritime component of our rapid deployment forces. This is essential for operations in remote areas of the world, where we cannot predict far in advance the precise location of trouble, or preposition equipment on land.

MILITARY PERSONNEL

No matter how capable or advanced our weapons systems, our military security depends on the abilities, the training and the dedication of the people who serve in our armed forces. I am determined to recruit and to retain under any foreseeable circumstances an ample level of such skilled and experienced military personnel. This Administration has supported for FY 1981 the largest peacetime increase ever in military pay and allowances.

We have enhanced our readiness and combat endurance by improving the Reserve Components. All reservists are assigned to units structured to complement and provide needed depth to our active forces. Some reserve personnel have also now been equipped with new equipment.

MOBILIZATION PLANNING

We have completed our first phase of mobilization planning—the first such Presidentially-directed effort since World War II. The government-wide exercise of our mobilization plans at the end of 1980 showed, first, that planning pays off and, second, that much more needs to be done.

OUR INTELLIGENCE POSTURE

Our national interests are critically dependent on a strong and effective intelligence capability. We will maintain and strengthen the intelligence capabilities needed to assure our national security. Maintenance of and continued improvements in our multi-faceted intelligence effort are essential if we are to cope successfully with the turbulence and uncertainties of today's world.

The intelligence budget I have submitted to the Congress responds to our needs in a responsible way, providing for significant growth over the Fiscal Year 1981 budget. This growth will enable us to develop new technical means of intelligence collection while also assuring that the more traditional methods of intelligence work are also given proper stress. We must continue to integrate both modes of collection in our analyses.

Regional Policies

Every President for over three decades has recognized that America's interests are global and that we must pursue a global foreign policy.

Two world wars have made clear our stake in Western Europe and the North Atlantic area. We are also inextricably linked with the Far East—politically, economically, and militarily. In both of these, the United States has a permanent presence and security commitments which would be automatically triggered. We have become increasingly conscious of our growing interests in a third area—the Middle East and the Persian Gulf area.

We have vital stakes in other major regions of the world as well. We have long recognized that in an era of interdependence, our own security and prosperity depend upon a larger common effort with friends and allies throughout the world.

THE ATLANTIC ALLIANCE

At the outset of this Administration, I emphasized the primacy of our Atlantic relationship in this country's national security agenda. We have made important progress toward making the Atlantic Alliance still more effective in a changing security environment.

In recognition of the threat which the Soviet invasion of Afghanistan posed to Western interests in both Europe and Southwest Asia, NATO foreign and defense ministers have expressed full support for U.S. efforts to develop a capability to respond to a contingency in Southwest Asia and have approved an extensive program to help fill the gap which could be created by the diversion of U.S. forces to that region.

The U.S. has not been alone in seeking to maintain stability in the Southwest Asia area and insure access to the needed resources there. The European nations with the capability to do so are improving their own forces in the region and providing greater economic and political support to the residents of the area. In the face of the potential danger posed by the Iran-Iraq conflict, we have developed coordination among the Western forces in the area of the Persian Gulf in order to be able to safeguard passage in that essential waterway.

Concerning developments in and around Poland, the allies have achieved the highest level of cohesion and unity of purpose in making clear the effects on future East-West relations of a precipitous Soviet act there.

The alliance has continued to build on the progress of the past three years in improving its conventional forces through the Long-Term Defense Program. Though economic conditions throughout Europe today are making its achievement difficult, the yearly real increase of 3 percent in defense spending remains a goal actively sought by the alliance.

The NATO alliance also has moved forward during the past year with the implementation of its historic December 1979 decision to modernize its Theater

Nuclear Force capabilities through deployment of improved Pershing ballistic missiles and ground-launched cruise missiles in Europe. Our allies continue to cooperate actively with us in this important joint endeavor, whose purpose is to demonstrate convincingly to the Soviet Union the potential costs of a nuclear conflict in Europe. At the same time, we offered convincing evidence of our commitment to arms control in Europe by initiating preliminary consultations with the Soviet Union in Geneva on the subject of negotiated limits on long-range theater nuclear forces. Also, during 1980 we initiated and carried out a withdrawal from our nuclear weapons stockpile in Europe of 1,000 nuclear warheads. This successful drawdown in our nuclear stockpile was a further tangible demonstration of our commitment to the updating of our existing theater nuclear forces in Europe.

In the NATO area, we continued to work closely with other countries in providing resources to help Turkey regain economic health. We regretted that massive political and internal security problems led the Turkish military to take over the government on September 12. The new Turkish authorities are making some progress in resolving those problems, and they have pledged an early return to civilian government. The tradition of the Turkish military gives us cause to take that pledge seriously. We welcomed the reestablishment of Greece's links to the integrated military command structure of the Atlantic Alliance—a move which we had strongly encouraged—as a major step toward strengthening NATO's vital southern flank at a time of international crisis and tension in adjacent areas. Greek reintegration exemplifies the importance which the allies place on cooperating in the common defense and shows that the allies can make the difficult deci-

sions necessary to insure their continued security. We also welcomed the resumption of the intercommunal talks on Cyprus.

THE U.S. AND THE PACIFIC NATIONS

The United States is a Pacific nation, as much as it is an Atlantic nation. Our interests in Asia are as important to us as our interests in Europe. Our trade with Asia is as great as our trade with Europe. During the past four years we have regained a strong, dynamic and flexible posture for the United States in this vital region.

Our major alliances with Japan, Australia and New Zealand are now stronger than they ever have been, and together with the nations of western Europe, we have begun to form the basic political structure for dealing with international crises that affect us all. Japan, Australia and New Zealand have given us strong support in developing a strategy for responding to instability in the Persian Gulf.

Normalization of U.S. relations with China has facilitated China's full entry into the international community and encouraged a constructive Chinese role in the Asia-Pacific region. Our relations with China have been rapidly consolidated over the past year through the conclusion of a series of bilateral agreements. We have established a pattern of frequent and frank consultations between our two governments, exemplified by a series of high-level visits and by regular exchanges at the working level, through which we have been able to identify increasingly broad areas of common interest on which we can cooperate.

United States relations with the Association of Southeast Asian Nations

(ASEAN) have also expanded dramatically in the past four years. ASEAN is now the focus for U.S. policy in Southeast Asia, and its cohesion and strength are essential to stability in this critical area and beyond.

Soviet-supported Vietnamese aggression in Indochina has posed a major challenge to regional stability. In response, we have reiterated our security commitment to Thailand and have provided emergency security assistance for Thai forces facing a Vietnamese military threat along the Thai-Cambodian border. We have worked closely with ASEAN and the UN to press for withdrawal of Vietnamese forces from Cambodia and to encourage a political settlement in Cambodia which permits that nation to be governed by leaders of its own choice. We still look forward to the day when Cambodia peacefully can begin the process of rebuilding it social, economic and political institutions, after years of devastation and occupation. And, on humanitarian grounds and in support of our friends in the region, we have worked vigorously with international organizations to arrange relief and resettlement for the exodus of Indochinese refugees which threatened to overwhelm these nations.

We have maintained our alliance with Korea and helped assure Korea's security during a difficult period of political transition.

We have amended our military base agreement with the Philippines, ensuring stable access to these bases through 1991. The importance of our Philippine bases to the strategic flexibility of U.S. forces and our access to the Indian Ocean is self-evident.

Finally, we are in the process of concluding a long negotiation establishing Micronesia's status as a freely associated state.

We enter the 1980's with a firm strategic footing in East Asia and the Pacific, based on stable and productive U.S. relations with the majority of countries of the region. We have established a stable level of U.S. involvement in the region, appropriate to our own interests and to the interests of our friends and allies there.

THE MIDDLE EAST AND SOUTHWEST ASIA

The continuing Soviet occupation of Afghanistan and the dislocations caused by the Iraq-Iran war serve as constant reminders of the critical importance for us, and our allies, of a third strategic zone stretching across the Middle East, the Persian Gulf, and much of the Indian subcontinent. This Southwest Asian region has served as a key strategic and commercial link between East and West over the centuries. Today it produces two-thirds of the world's oil exports, providing most of the energy needs of our European allies and Japan. It has experienced almost continuous conflict between nations, internal instabilities in many countries, and regional rivalries, combined with very rapid economic and social change. And now the Soviet Union remains in occupation of one of these nations, ignoring world opinion which has called on it to get out.

We have taken several measures to meet these challenges.

MIDDLE EAST

In the Middle East, our determination to consolidate what has already been achieved in the peace process—and to buttress that accomplishment with further progress toward a comprehensive peace settlement—must remain a central goal of our foreign policy. Pursuant to their peace treaty, Egypt and Israel have made steady progress in the normalization of their relations in a variety of fields, bringing the benefits of peace directly to their people. The new relationship between Egypt and Israel stands as an example of peaceful cooperation in an increasingly fragmented and turbulent region.

Both President Sadat and Prime Minister Begin remain committed to the current negotiations to provide full autonomy to the inhabitants of the West Bank and Gaza. These negotiations have been complex and difficult, but they have already made significant progress, and it is vital that the two sides, with our assistance, see the process through to a successful conclusion. We also recognize the need to broaden the peace process to include other parties to the conflict and believe that a successful autonomy agreement is an essential first step toward this objective.

We have also taken a number of steps to strengthen our bilateral relations with both Israel and Egypt. We share important strategic interests with both of these countries.

We remain committed to Israel's security and are prepared to take concrete steps to support Israel whenever that security is threatened.

PERSIAN GULF

The Persian Gulf has been a vital crossroads for trade between Europe and Asia at many key moments in history. It has become essential in recent years for its supply of oil to the United States, our allies, and our friends. We have taken effective measures to control our own consumption of imported fuel, working in cooperation with the other key industrial nations of the world. However, there is little doubt that the healthy growth of our American and world economies will depend for many years on continued safe access to the Persian Gulf's oil production. The denial of these oil supplies would threaten not only our own but world security.

The potent new threat from an advancing Soviet Union, against the background of regional instability of which it can take advantage, requires that we reinforce our ability to defend our regional friends and to protect the flow of oil. We are continuing to build on the strong political, economic, social and humanitarian ties which bind this government and the American people to friendly governments and peoples of the Persian Gulf.

We have also embarked on a course to reinforce the trust and confidence our regional friends have in our ability to come to their assistance rapidly with American military force if needed. We have increased our naval presence in the Indian Ocean. We have created a Rapid Deployment Force which can move quickly to the Gulf—or indeed any other area of the world where outside aggression threatens. We have concluded several agreements with countries which are prepared to let us use their airports and naval facilities in an emergency. We have met requests for reasonable amounts of American weaponry from regional countries which are anxious to defend themselves. And we are discussing with a number of our area friends further ways we can help to improve their security and ours, both for the short and the longer term.

SOUTH ASIA

We seek a South Asia comprising sovereign and stable states, free of outside interference, which can strengthen their political institutions according to their own national genius and can develop their economies for the betterment of their people.

The Soviet invasion of Afghanistan has posed a new challenge to this region, and particularly to neighboring Pakistan. We are engaged in a continuing dialogue with the Pakistan government concerning its development and security requirements and the economic burden imposed by Afghan refugees who have fled to Pakistan. We are participating with other aid consortium members in debt rescheduling and will continue to cooperate through the UNHCR in providing refugee assistance. We remain committed to Pakistan's territorial integrity and independence.

Developments in the broad South/Southwest Asian region have also lent a new importance to our relations with India, the largest and strongest power in the area. We share India's interest in a more constructive relationship. Indian policies and perceptions at times differ from our own, and we have established a candid dialogue with this sister democracy which seeks to avoid the misunderstandings which have sometimes complicated our ties.

We attach major importance to strong economic assistance programs to the countries in the area, which include a majority of the poor of the non-Communist world. We believe that these programs will help achieve stability in the area, an objective we share with the countries in the region. Great progress has been achieved by these countries in increasing food production; international cooperation in harnessing the great river resources of South Asia would contribute further to this goal and help to increase energy production.

We continue to give high priority to our non-proliferation goals in the area in the context of our broad global and regional priorities. The decision to continue supply of nuclear fuel to the Indian Tarapur reactors was sensitive to this effort.

AFRICA

The United States has achieved a new level of trust and cooperation with Africa. Our efforts, together with our allies, to achieve peace in southern Africa, our increased efforts to help the poorest countries in Africa to combat poverty, and our expanded efforts to promote trade and investment have led to growing respect for the U.S. and to cooperation in areas of vital interest to the United States.

Africa is a continent of poor nations for the most part. It also contains many of the mineral resources vital for our economy. We have worked with Africa in a spirit of mutual cooperation to help the African nations solve their problems of poverty and to develop stronger ties between our private sector and African economies. Our assistance to Africa has more than doubled in the last four years. Equally important, we set in motion new mechanisms for private investment and trade.

Nigeria is the largest country in Black Africa and the second largest oil supplier to the United States. During this Administration we have greatly expanded and improved our relationship with Nigeria and other West African states whose aspirations for a constitutional democratic order we share and support. This interest was manifested both symbolically and practically by the visit of Vice President Mondale to West Africa in July (1980) and the successful visit to Washington of the President of Nigeria in October.

During Vice President Mondale's visit, a Joint Agricultural Consultative Committee was established, with the U.S. represented entirely by the private sector. This could herald a new role for the

American private sector in helping solve the world's serious food shortages. I am pleased to say that our relations with Nigeria are at an all-time high, providing the foundation for an even stronger relationship in the years ahead.

Another tenet of this Administration's approach to African problems has been encouragement and support for regional solutions to Africa's problems. We have supported initiatives by the Organization of African Unity to solve the protracted conflict in the western Sahara, Chad, and the Horn. In Chad, the world is watching with dismay as a country torn by a devastating civil war has become a fertile field for Libya's exploitation, thus demonstrating that threats to peace can come from forces within as well as without Africa.

In southern Africa the United States continues to pursue a policy of encouraging peaceful development toward majority rule. In 1980, Southern Rhodesia became independent as Zimbabwe, a multiracial nation under a system of majority rule. Zimbabwean independence last April was the culmination of a long struggle within the country and diplomatic efforts involving Great Britain, African states neighboring Zimbabwe, and the United States.

The focus of our efforts in pursuit of majority rule in southern Africa has now turned to Namibia. Negotiations are proceeding among concerned parties under the leadership of UN Secretary General Waldheim. This should lead to implementation of the UN plan for self-determination and independence for Namibia during 1981. If these negotiations are successfully concluded, sixty-five years of uncertainty over the status of the territory, including a seven-year-long war, will be ended.

Common efforts to resolve the Zimbabwean and Namibian issues have brought the United States closer both to its Western allies—Great Britain, France, the Federal Republic of Germany, and Canada—and to African states such as Tanzania, Zambia, Mozambique, Angola, and Botswana, with whom relations have at some times in the past been difficult. The success of these common undertakings demonstrates that complex problems with sometimes bitter and bloody histories can be resolved peacefully through negotiation.

In response to our active concern with issues of importance to Africans, African states have cooperated with us on issues of importance to our national interests. African states voted overwhelmingly in favor of the UN Resolution calling for release of the hostages, and for the UN Resolution condemning the Soviet invasion of Afghanistan. Two countries of Africa have signed access agreements with the U.S. allowing us use of naval and air facilities in the Indian Ocean.

Africans have become increasingly vocal on human rights. African leaders have spoken out on the issue of political prisoners, and the OAU is drafting its own Charter on Human Rights. Three countries in Africa—Nigeria, Ghana, and Uganda—have returned to civilian rule during the past year.

U.S. cooperation with Africa on all these matters represents a strong base on which we can build in future years.

Liberia is a country of long-standing ties with the U.S. and the site of considerable U.S. investment and facilities. This past April a coup replaced the government and a period of political and economic uncertainty ensued. The U.S. acted swiftly to meet this situation. We, together with African leaders, urged the release of political prisoners, and many have been released; we provided emergency economic assistance to help avoid economic collapse, and helped to involve the IMF and the banking community to bring about economic stability; and we have worked closely with the new leaders to maintain Liberia's strong ties with the West and to protect America's vital interests.

NORTH AFRICA

In early 1979, following a Libyan-inspired commando attack on a Tunisian provincial city, the U.S. responded promptly to Tunisia's urgent request for assistance, both by airlifting needed military equipment and by making clear our longstanding interest in the security and integrity of this friendly country. The U.S. remains determined to oppose other irresponsible Libyan aspirations. Despairing of a productive dialogue with the Libyan authorities, the U.S. closed down its embassy in Libya and later expelled six Libyan diplomats in Washington in order to deter an intimidation campaign against Libyan citizens in the U.S.

U.S. relations with Algeria have improved, and Algeria has played an indispensable and effective role as intermediary between Iran and the U.S. over the hostage issue.

The strengthening of our arms supply relationship with Morocco has helped to deal with attacks inside its internationally recognized frontiers and to strengthen its confidence in seeking a political settlement of the Western Sahara conflict. While not assuming a mediatory role, the U.S. encouraged all interested parties to turn their energies to a peaceful and sensible compromise resolution of the war in the Sahara and supported efforts by the Organization of African Unity toward that end. As the year drew to a close, the U.S. was encouraged by evolution in the attitudes of all sides, and is hopeful that their differences will be peacefully resolved in the year ahead so that the vast economic potential of North Africa can be developed for the well-being of the people living there.

LATIN AMERICA AND THE CARIBBEAN

The principles of our policies in this hemisphere have been clear and constant over the last four years. We support democracy and respect for human rights. We have struggled with many to help free the region of both repression and terrorism. We have respected ideological diversity and opposed outside intervention in purely internal affairs. We will act, though, in response to a request for assistance by a country threatened by external aggression. We support social and economic development within a democratic framework. We support the peaceful settlement of disputes. We strongly encourage regional cooperation and shared responsibilities within the hemisphere to all these ends, and we have eagerly and regularly sought the advice of the leaders of the region on a wide range of issues.

Last November, I spoke to the General Assembly of the Organization of American States of a cause that has been closest to my heart—human rights. It is an issue that has found its time in the hemisphere. The cause is not mine alone, but an historic movement that will endure.

At Riobamba, Ecuador, last September four Andean Pact countries, Costa Rica, and Panama broke new ground by adopting a "Code of Conduct," stating that joint action in defense of human rights does not violate the principles of nonintervention in the internal affairs of states in this hemisphere. The Organization of American States has twice condemned the coup that overturned the democratic process in Bolivia and the widespread abuse of human rights by the regime which seized power. The Inter-American Commission on Human Rights has gained world acclaim for its dispassionate reports. It completed two major country studies this year in addition to its annual report. In a resolution adopted without opposition, the OAS General Assembly in November strongly supported the work of the Commission. The American Convention on Human Rights is in force and an Inter-American Court has been created to judge human rights violations. This convention has been pending before the Senate for two years; I hope the United States this year will join the other nations of the hemisphere in ratifying a convention which embodies principles that are our tradition.

The trend in favor of democracy has continued. During this past year, Peru inaugurated a democratically elected government. Brazil continues its process of liberalization. In Central America, Hondurans voted in record numbers in their first national elections in over eight years. In the Caribbean seven elections have returned governments firmly committed to the democratic traditions of the Commonwealth.

Another major contribution to peace in the hemisphere is Latin America's own Treaty for the Prohibition of Nuclear Weapons. On behalf of the United States, I signed Protocol I of this Treaty in May of 1977 and sent it to the Senate for ratification. I urge that it be acted upon promptly by the Senate in order that it be brought into the widest possible effect in the Latin American region.

Regional cooperation for development is gaining from Central America to the Andes, and throughout the Caribbean. The Caribbean Group for Cooperation in Economic Development, which we established with 29 other nations in 1977, has helped channel $750 million in external support for growth in the Caribbean. The recent meeting of the Chiefs of State of the Eastern Caribbean set a new precedent for cooperation in that region. Mexico and Venezuela jointly and Trinidad and Tobago separately have established oil facilities that will provide substantial assistance to their oil importing neighbors. The peace treaty between El Salvador and Honduras will hopefully stimulate Central America to move forward again toward economic integration. Formation of Caribbean/Central American Action, a private sector organization, has given a major impetus to improving people-to-people bonds and strengthening the role of private enterprise in the development of democratic societies.

The Panama treaties have been in force for over a year. A new partnership has been created with Panama; it is a model for large and small nations. A longstanding issue that divided us from our neighbors has been resolved. The security of the canal has been enhanced. The canal is operating as well as ever, with traffic through it reaching record levels this year. Canal employees, American and Panamanian alike, have remained on the job and have found their living and working conditions virtually unchanged.

In 1980, relations with Mexico continued to improve due in large measure to the effectiveness of the Coordinator for Mexican Affairs and the expanded use of the U.S.-Mexico Consultative Mechanism. By holding periodic meetings of its various working groups, we have been able to prevent mutual concerns from becoming political issues. The Secretary of State visited Mexico City in November, and, along with the Mexican

Secretary of Foreign Relations, reviewed the performance of the Consultative Mechanism. The office of the Coordinator has ensured the implementation of my directive to all agencies to accord high priority to Mexican concerns. Trade with Mexico rose by almost 60 percent to nearly $30 billion, making that country our third largest trading partner.

These are all encouraging developments. Other problems remain, however.

The impact of large-scale migration is affecting many countries in the hemisphere. The most serious manifestation was the massive, illegal exodus from Cuba last summer. The Cuban government unilaterally encouraged the disorderly and even deadly migration of 125,000 of its citizens in complete disregard for international law or the immigration laws of its neighbors. Migrations of this nature clearly require concerted action, and we have asked the OAS to explore means of dealing with similar situations which may occur in the future.

We have a long-standing treaty with Colombia on Quita Sueno, Roncador, and Serrano which remains to be ratified by the Senate.

In Central America, the future of Nicaragua is unclear. Recent tensions, the restrictions on the press and political activity, an inordinate Cuban presence in the country and the tragic killing by the security forces of a businessman well known for his democratic orientation, cause us considerable concern. These are not encouraging developments. But those who seek a free society remain in the contest for their nation's destiny. They have asked us to help rebuild their country, and by our assistance, to demonstrate that the democratic nations do not intend to abandon Nicaragua to the Cubans. As long as those who intend to pursue their pluralistic goals play important roles in Nicaragua, it deserves our continuing support.

In El Salvador, we have supported the efforts of the Junta to change the fundamental basis of an inequitable system and to give a stake in a new nation to those millions of people, who for so long, lived without hope or dignity. As the government struggles against those who would restore an old tyranny or impose a new one, the United States will continue to stand behind them.

We have increased our aid to the Caribbean, an area vital to our national security, and we should continue to build close relations based on mutual respect and understanding, and common interests.

As the nations of this hemisphere prepare to move further into the 1980's, I am struck by the depth of underlying commitment that there is to our common principles: non-intervention, peaceful settlement of disputes, cooperation for development, democracy and defense of basic human rights. I leave office satisfied that the political, economic, social and organizational basis for further progress with respect to all these principles have been substantially strengthened in the past four years. I am particularly reassured by the leadership by other nations of the hemisphere in advancing these principles. The success of our common task of improving the circumstances of all peoples and nations in the hemisphere can only be assured by the sharing of responsibility. I look forward to a hemisphere that at the end of this decade has proven itself anew as a leader in the promotion of both national and human dignity.

THE INTERNATIONAL ECONOMY

A growing defense effort and a vigorous foreign policy rest upon a strong economy here in the United States. And the strength of our own economy depends upon our ability to lead and compete in the international marketplace.

ENERGY

Last year, the war between Iraq and Iran led to the loss of nearly 4 million barrels of oil to world markets, the third major oil market disruption in the past seven years. This crisis has vividly demonstrated once again both the value of lessened dependence on oil imports and the continuing instability of the Persian Gulf area.

Under the leadership of the United States, the 21 members of the International Energy Agency took collective action to ensure that the oil shortfall stemming from the Iran-Iraq war would not be aggravated by competition for scarce spot market supplies. We are also working together to see that those nations most seriously affected by the oil disruption—including our key NATO allies Turkey and Portugal—can get the oil they need. At the most recent IEA Ministerial meeting we joined the other members in pledging to take those policy measures necessary to slice our joint oil imports in the first quarter of 1981 by 2.2 million barrels.

Our international cooperation efforts in the energy field are not limited to crisis management. At the Economic Summit meetings in Tokyo and Venice, the heads of government of the seven major industrial democracies agreed to a series of tough energy conservation and production goals. We are working together with all our allies and friends in this effort.

Construction has begun on a commercial scale coal liquefaction plant in West Virginia co-financed by the United States, Japan and West Germany. An interagency task force has just reported to me on a series of measures we need to take to increase coal production and exports. This report builds on the work of the International Energy Agency's Coal Industry Advisory Board. With the assurances of a reliable United States steam coal supply at reasonable prices, many of the electric power plants to be built in the 1980's and 1990's can be coal-fired rather than oil-burning.

We are working cooperatively with other nations to increase energy security in other areas as well. Joint research and development with our allies is underway in solar energy, nuclear power, industrial conservation and other areas. In addition, we are assisting rapidly industrializing nations to carefully assess their basic energy policy choices, and our development assistance program helps the developing countries to increase indigenous energy production to meet the energy needs of their poorest citizens. We support the proposal for a new World Bank energy affiliate to these same ends, whose fulfillment will contribute to a better global balance between energy supply and demand.

INTERNATIONAL MONETARY POLICY

Despite the rapid increase in oil costs, the policy measures we have taken to improve domestic economic performance have had a continued powerful effect on our external accounts and on the strength of the dollar. A strong dollar helps in the fight against inflation.

There has also been considerable forward movement in efforts to improve the functioning of the international monetary system. The stability of the international system of payments and trade is important to the stability and good health of our own economy. We have given strong support to the innovative steps being taken by the International Monetary Fund and World Bank to help promote early adjustment to the difficult international economic problems. Recent agreement to increase quotas by fifty percent will ensure the IMF has sufficient resources to perform its central role in promoting adjustment and financing payments imbalances. The World Bank's new structural adjustment lending program will also make an important contribution to international efforts to help countries achieve a sustainable level of growth and development.

SUGAR

In 1980, Congress passed U.S. implementing legislation for the International Sugar Agreement, thus fulfilling a major commitment of this Administration. The agreement is an important element in our international commodity policy with far-reaching implications for our relations with developing countries, particularly sugar producers in Latin America. Producers and consumers alike will benefit from a more stable market for this essential commodity.

COFFEE

At year's end, Congress approved implementing legislation permitting the U.S. to carry out fully its commitments under the International Coffee Agreement. Specifically, the legislation enables us to meet our part of an understanding negotiated last fall among members of the Agreement, which defends, by use of export quotas, a price range well below coffee prices of previous years and which commits major coffee producers to eliminate cartel arrangements that manipulated future markets to raise prices. The

way is now open to a fully-functioning International Coffee Agreement which can help to stabilize this major world commodity market. The results will be positive for both consumers—who will be less likely to suffer from sharp increases in coffee prices—and producers—who can undertake future investment with assurance of greater protection against disruptive price fluctuations in their exports.

NATURAL RUBBER

In 1980, the International Natural Rubber Agreement entered into force provisionally. U.S. membership in this new body was approved overwhelmingly by the Senate last year. The natural rubber agreement is a model of its kind and should make a substantial contribution to a stable world market in this key industrial commodity. It is thus an excellent example of constructive steps to improve the operation of the world economy in ways which can benefit the developing and industrialized countries alike. In particular, the agreement has improved important U.S. relationships with the major natural rubber-producing countries of Southeast Asia.

COMMON FUND

The United States joined members of the United Nations Conference on Trade and Development, both developed and developing nations, in concluding Articles of Agreement in 1980 for a Common Fund to help international commodity agreements stabilize the prices of raw materials.

ECONOMIC COOPERATION WITH DEVELOPING NATIONS

Our relations with the developing nations are of major importance to the

United States. The fabric of our relations with these countries has strong economic and political dimensions. They constitute the most rapidly growing markets for our exports, and are important sources of fuel and raw materials. Their political views are increasingly important, as demonstrated in their overwhelming condemnation of the Soviet invasion of Afghanistan. Our ability to work together with developing nations toward goals we have in common—their political independence, the resolution of regional tensions, and our growing ties of trade for example—require us to maintain the policy of active involvement with the developing world that we have pursued over the past four years.

The actions we have taken in such areas as energy, trade, commodities, and international financial institutions are all important to the welfare of the developing countries. Another important way the United States can directly assist these countries and demonstrate our concern for their future is through our multilateral and bilateral foreign assistance program. The legislation which I will be submitting to you for FY 82 provides the authority and the funds to carry on this activity. Prompt Congressional action on this legislation is essential in order to attack such high priority global problems as food and energy, meet our treaty and base rights agreements, continue our peace efforts in the Middle East, provide economic and development support to countries in need, promote progress on North–South issues, protect Western interests, and counter Soviet influence.

Our proposed FY 1982 bilateral development aid program is directly responsive to the agreement reached at the 1980 Venice Economic Summit that the major industrial nations should increase their aid for food and energy production and for family planning. We understand that other Summit countries plan similar responses. It is also important to honor our international agreements for multilateral assistance by authorizing and appropriating funds for the International Financial Institutions. These multilateral programs enhance the efficiency of US contributions by combining them with those of many other donor countries to promote development; the proposed new World Bank affiliate to increase energy output in developing countries offers particular promise. All these types of aid benefit our long-run economic and political interests.

Progress was made on a number of economic issues in negotiations throughout the UN system. However, in spite of lengthy efforts in the United Nations, agreement has not been reached on how to launch a process of Global Negotiations in which nations might collectively work to solve such important issues as energy, food, protectionism, and population pressures. The United States continues to believe that progress can best be made when nations focus on such specific problems, rather than on procedural and institutional questions. It will continue to work to move the North-South dialogue into a more constructive phase.

FOOD—THE WAR ON HUNGER

The War on Hunger must be a continuous urgent priority. Major portions of the world's population continue to be threatened by the specter of hunger and malnutrition. During the past year, some 150 million people in 36 African countries were faced with near disaster as the result of serious drought, induced food shortages. Our government, working in concert with the UN's Food and Agricultural Organization (FAO), helped to respond to that need. But the problems of hunger cannot be solved by short-term measures. We must continue to support those activities, bilateral and multilateral, which aim at improving food production especially in developing countries and assuring global food security. These measures are necessary to the maintenance of a stable and healthy world economy.

I am pleased that negotiation of a new Food Aid Convention, which guarantees a minimum annual level of food assistance, was successfully concluded in March. The establishment of the International Emergency Wheat Reserve will enable the U.S. to meet its commitment under the new Convention to feed hungry people, even in times of short supply.

Of immediate concern is the prospect of millions of Africans threatened by famine because of drought and civil disturbances. The U.S. plea for increased food aid resulted in the organization of an international pledging conference and we are hopeful that widespread starvation will be avoided.

Good progress has been made since the Venice Economic Summit called for increased effort on this front. We and other donor countries have begun to assist poor countries develop long-term strategies to improve their food production. The World Bank will invest up to $4 billion in the next few years in improving the grain storage and food-handling capacity of countries prone to food shortages.

Good progress has been made since the Tokyo Economic Summit called for increased effort on this front. The World Bank is giving this problem top priority, as are some other donor countries. The resources of the consultative Group on International Agricultural Research will be doubled over a five-year period. The work of our own Institute of Scientific and Technological Cooperation will

further strengthen the search for relevant new agricultural technologies.

The goal of freeing the world from hunger by the year 2000 should command the full support of all countries.

The Human Dimension of Foreign Policy

HUMAN RIGHTS

The human rights policy of the United States has been an integral part of our overall foreign policy for the past several years. This policy serves the national interest of the United States in several important ways: by encouraging respect by governments for the basic rights of human beings, it promotes peaceful, constructive change, reduces the likelihood of internal pressures for violent change and for the exploitation of these by our adversaries, and thus directly serves our long-term interest in peace and stability; by matching espousal of fundamental American principles of freedom with specific foreign policy actions, we stand out in vivid contrast to our ideological adversaries; by our efforts to expand freedom elsewhere, we render our own freedom, and our own nation, more secure. Countries that respect human rights make stronger allies and better friends.

Rather than attempt to dictate what system of government or institutions other countries should have, the U.S. supports, throughout the world, the internationally recognized human rights which all members of the United Nations have pledged themselves to respect. There is more than one model that can satisfy the continuing human reach for freedom and justice:

1980 has been a year of some disappointments, but has also seen some positive developments in the ongoing struggle for fulfillment of human rights throughout the world. In the year we have seen:

• Free elections were held and democratic governments installed in Peru, Dominica, and Jamaica. Honduras held a free election for installation of a constituent assembly. An interim government was subsequently named pointing toward national presidential elections in 1981. Brazil continues on its course of political liberalization.

• The "Charter of Conduct" signed in Riobamba, Ecuador, by Ecuador, Colombia, Venezuela, Peru, Costa Rica, Panama and Spain, affirms the importance of democracy and human rights for the Andean countries.

• The Organization of American States, in its annual General Assembly, approved a resolution in support of the Inter-American Human Rights Commission's work. The resolution took note of the Commission's annual report, which described the status of human rights in Chile, El Salvador, Paraguay and Uruguay; and the special reports on Argentina and Haiti, which described human rights conditions as investigated during on-site inspections to these countries.

• The awarding of the Nobel Prize for Peace to Adolfo Perez Esquivel of Argentina for his non-violent advocacy of human rights.

• The United States was able to rejoin the International Labor Organization after an absence of two years, as that UN body reformed its procedures to return to its original purpose of strengthening employer-employee-government relations to insure human rights for the working people of the world.

The United States, of course, cannot take credit for all these various developments. But we can take satisfaction in knowing that our policies encourage and perhaps influence them.

Those who see a contradiction between our security and our humanitarian interests forget that the basis for a secure and stable society is the bond of trust between a government and its people. I profoundly believe that the future of our world is not to be found in authoritarianism: that wears the mask of order, or totalitarianism that wears the mask of justice. Instead, let us find our future in the human face of democracy, the human voice of individual liberty, the human hand of economic development.

HUMANITARIAN AID

The United States has continued to play its traditional role of safehaven for those who flee or are forced to flee their homes because of persecution or war. During 1980, the United States provided resettlement opportunities for 216,000 refugees from countries around the globe. In addition, the United States joined with other nations to provide relief to refugees in country of first asylum in Africa, the Middle East, and Asia.

The great majority of refugee admissions continued to be from Indochina. During 1980, 168,000 Indochinese were resettled in the United States. Although refugee populations persist in camps in Southeast Asia, and refugees continue to flee Vietnam, Laos and Kampuchea, the flow is not as great as in the past. One factor in reducing the flow from Vietnam has been the successful negotiation and commencement of an Orderly Departure Program which permits us to process Vietnamese for resettlement in the United States with direct departure from Ho Chi Minh Ville in an orderly fashion. The first group of 250 departed Vietnam for the United States in December, 1980.

In addition to the refugees admitted last year, the United States accepted for entry into the United States 125,000 Cubans who were expelled by Fidel Castro. Federal and state authorities, as well as private voluntary agencies, responded with unprecedented vigor to coping with the unexpected influx of Cubans.

Major relief efforts to aid refugees in countries of first asylum continued in several areas of the world. In December, 1980, thirty-two nations, meeting in New York City, agreed to contribute $65 million to the continuing famine relief program in Kampuchea. Due in great part to the generosity of the American people and the leadership exercised in the international arena by the United States, we have played the pivotal role in ameliorating massive suffering in Kampuchea.

The United States has taken the lead among a group of donor countries who are providing relief to some two million refugees in the Horn of Africa who have been displaced by fighting in Ethiopia. U.S. assistance, primarily to Somalia, consists of $35 million worth of food and $18 million in cash and kind. Here again, United States efforts can in large part be credited with keeping hundreds of thousands of people alive.

Another major international relief effort has been mounted in Pakistan. The United States is one of 25 countries plus the European Economic Community who have been helping the Government of Pakistan to cope with the problem of feeding and sheltering the more than one million refugees that have been generated by the Soviet invasion of Afghanistan.

In April, 1980, the Congress passed the Refugee Act of 1980 which brought together, for the first time, in one piece of legislation the various threads of U.S. policy towards refugees. The law laid down a new, broader definition of the term refugee, established mechanisms for arriving at a level of refugee admissions through consultation with Congress, and established the Office of the United States Coordinator for Refugees.

It cannot be ignored that the destructive and aggressive policies of the Soviet Union have added immeasurably to the suffering in these three tragic situations.

The Control of Nuclear Weapons

Together with our friends and allies, we are striving to build a world in which peoples with diverse interests can live freely and prosper. But all that humankind has achieved to date, all that we are seeking to accomplish, and human existence itself can be undone in an instant— in the catastrophe of a nuclear war.

Thus one of the central objectives of my Administration has been to control the proliferation of nuclear weapons to those nations which do not have them, and their further development by the existing nuclear powers—notably the Soviet Union and the United States.

NON-PROLIFERATION

My Administration has been committed to stemming the spread of nuclear weapons. Nuclear proliferation would raise the spectre of the use of nuclear explosives in crucial, unstable regions of the world endangering not only our security and that of our Allies, but that of the whole world. Non-proliferation is not and can not be a unilateral U.S. policy, nor should it be an issue of contention between the industrialized and developing states. The international non-proliferation effort requires the support of suppliers as well as importers of nuclear technology and materials.

We have been proceeding on a number of fronts:

• First, we have been seeking to encourage nations to accede to the Non-Proliferation Treaty. The U.S. is also actively encouraging other nations to accept full-scope safeguards on all of their nuclear activities and is asking other nuclear suppliers to adopt a full-scope safeguards requirement as a condition for future supply.

• Second, the International Nuclear Fuel Cycle Evaluation (INFCE), which was completed in 1980, demonstrated that suppliers and recipients can work together on these technically complex and sensitive issues. While differences remain, the INFCE effort provides a broader international basis for national decisions which must balance energy needs with non-proliferation concerns.

• Finally, we are working to encourage regional cooperation and restraint. Protocol I of the Treaty of Tlatelolco which will contribute to the lessening of nuclear dangers for our Latin American neighbors ought now to be ratified by the United States Senate.

LIMITATIONS ON STRATEGIC ARMS

I remain convinced that the SALT II Treaty is in our Nation's security interest and that it would add significantly to the control of nuclear weapons. I strongly support continuation of the SALT process and the negotiation of more far-reaching mutual restraints on nuclear weaponry.

CONCLUSION

We have new support in the world for our purposes of national independence and individual human dignity. We have a new will at home to do what is required to keep us the strongest nation on earth.

We must move together into this decade with the strength which comes from realization of the dangers before us and from the confidence that together we can overcome them.

JIMMY CARTER

The White House,
    January 16, 1981.

National Marine Sanctuaries

Statement on Approving Three Commerce Department Proposals. January 16, 1981

Today I have approved three proposals by the Department of Commerce to designate unique ocean areas as National Marine Sanctuaries. The three sites represent a diversity of marine ecosystems. They are: Gray's Reef, off the coast of Georgia; Looe Key, a submerged coral reef off the lower Florida Keys; and Point Reyes-Farallon Islands off the California coast.

The Gray's Reef National Marine Sanctuary encompasses an area of more than 16 square nautical miles of productive limerock reef. It is representative of a type of unusual marine habitat—a live bottom reef—found intermittently across the continental shelf in temperate and subtropical regions of our coastal waters. Ancient sedimentary rock outcrops on an otherwise flat, sandy ocean bottom form the reefs that provide habitat for an abundance and variety of marine organisms, including fish of recreational and commercial importance and threatened and endangered species. Gray's Reef is perhaps one of the most popular live bottom areas in the western Atlantic Ocean. Its nearshore location—17 miles east of Sapelo Island, Georgia—invites public use year round and offers an accessible living laboratory for marine research and education.

The Looe Key National Marine Sanctuary is an area of more than 5 square nautical miles southwest of Big Pine Key in the lower Florida Keys. This designation will protect one of the few remaining well-developed living coral reefs off the continental United States. The sanctuary area includes a spectacular "spur and groove" coral formation supporting a tremendous diversity of marine species. Because of its wide range in depth, its close proximity to land, and its broad variety of marine life, Looe Key is a popular recreational area.

Lastly, I have approved the Point Reyes-Farallon Islands National Marine Sanctuary, which encompasses a 948-square nautical mile area off the California coast. This area is extraordinary. It is characterized by irregular coastlines and submerged rocky intertidal areas and contains many biologically rich nearshore and marine habitats. It contains some of the largest seabird rookeries in the United States, providing nesting sites for at least 12 of the 16 species known to breed on the west coast. The sanctuary area also supports a large and varied marine mammal population, providing feeding, pupping, and haul-out habitat for 23 species. Whales, including several endangered species, and porpoises migrate through the sanctuary area. The sanctuary also contains highly productive communities of finfish and shellfish, kelp beds, and other marine organisms. The sanctuary will complement the Point Reyes National Seashore, the Farallon Islands National Wildlife Refuge, and State parks and refuges within the area.

In 1972 when Congress passed the law authorizing marine sanctuary designation, it recognized that while the ocean frontier is developed to meet our Nation's needs, we must balance developmental activities with prudent environmental safeguards. Sanctuary designation therefore provides for comprehensive management, but does not inhibit traditional, nonthreatening activities such as public recreational use.

In the case of the Point Reyes-Farallon Islands National Marine Sanctuary, it was particularly important to strike a balance between oil and gas development in nearby coastal waters and the protection of the sanctuary's marine resources. For this reason, oil and gas development activities within the boundary of the sanctuary will be excluded. Because of the very low oil and gas potential of the area, this provision will not affect our efforts to meet energy needs. It is supported by the Governor of California, Senator Cranston, and members of the California congressional delegation.

I should note that each sanctuary proposal is reviewed on a case-by-case basis, and decisions regarding appropriate uses, such as oil and gas development, are reviewed individually. Our decision to exclude oil and gas drilling at Point Reyes-Farallon Islands does not mean that in the future marine sanctuaries will never allow such activity. In other areas and under other conditions, it may very well be appropriate and necessary to provide energy development activities within marine sanctuaries.

My administration has worked closely with local and State governments and concerned citizens on the selection of marine sanctuaries. The designations I have approved today reflect the views of these groups. These estabilshed marine sanctuaries represent a solid foundation for our Nation's efforts to protect and manage unique marine resources. I am pleased that my administration has provided the stimulus and momentum necessary to build this program.

President's Award for Distinguished Federal Civilian Service

Announcement of Selection of Seven Persons To Receive the Award. January 16, 1981

The President today announced the selection of seven persons to receive the President's Award for Distinguished Federal Civilian Service, the highest award that can be granted to Federal civilian employees. The award was established in 1957 to recognize outstanding achievement in carrying out the Government's mission with imagination and ability. It consists of a gold medal and a citation signed by the President and is presented "with profound appreciation, highest esteem, and great personal satisfaction" to a small number of individuals each year.

The seven recipients, and the citations from their awards, are:

Morton I. Abramowitz, U.S. Ambassador to Thailand

"An outstanding diplomat, demonstrating the highest ideals of dedication and leadership, he used imagination, courage, and unmatched energy to help save thousands of Cambodian lives.

"He became the focal point of efforts to find longer-term political solutions to the dangers threatening Indochina, and his reports, analyses and recommendations provided invaluable guidance in shaping United States policies and action in Southeast Asia."

Glenn W. Burton, research leader, Forage and Turf Research Science and Education Administration, Department of Agriculture

"An internationally recognized crop breeder, his outstanding contributions to the productivity of grass lands have saved untold thousands from malnutrition or starvation.

"He proved that vegetative plantings of a pasture grass can be successful in establishing new, improved varieties, and opened a new horizon in breeding, pearl millet in India and the United States."

Alonza H. Cotton, Deputy Director, Materiel Management, Air Logistics Center, Department of the Air Force

"A recognized authority and outstanding leader in the field of logistics, he has organized and developed cost effective support systems which have had major impact on our nation's defense.

"His innovative contributions in the field of materiel management, spanning many critical periods this nation has faced, such as the Southeast Asia crisis, have assured the best support possible for United States missions throughout the world."

John T. Hughes, Deputy Director for Defense Intelligence, Defense Intelligence Agency

"A recognized authority in the field of reconnaissance intelligence and technology, he has made exceptional contributions to the security of the United States.

"His innovative accomplishments in intelligence collection management and brilliant presentations to United States and Allied leaders have had significant, positive impact on intelligence support to our military forces overseas and to the viability of NATO preparedness."

Robert T. Jones, senior staff scientist, National Aeronautics and Space Administration

"A most distinguished and honored figure in aeronautical engineering in the United States, his contributions span the entire field of aeronautical sciences, including aircraft, missile and spacecraft research.

"Of major consequence are his narrow triangular wing concept, the independence principle for three-dimensional boundary layers, and the concept of the oblique wing, boom-free supersonic airplane."

William H. Oldendorf, senior medical investigator, VA Medical Center, Brentwood, Calif., Veterans Administration

"An outstanding clinician, his work in the field of diagnostic radiology represents some of the best and most significant medical research sponsored by the Veterans Administration.

"His significant contributions to the advancement of medical practice have greatly benefited the veteran and the public. In particular, his conceptualization and demonstration of reconstruction transmission tomography is the most significant recent advancement in the non-invasive diagnosis of solid tumors."

MARY DE LA TORRE PINKARD, former Acting Director, Office of Program Standards and Evaluation, Department of Housing and Urban Development (presented posthumously)

"Recognized nationally for outstanding contributions to the Department of Housing and Urban Development's Fair Housing and Equal Opportunity Program, she participated in every major task force created to develop new programs or policy.

"She transformed legislation into operating regulations, and was the primary author of policies concerning Tenant Selection and Assignment, EEO requirements under the Model Cities Program, and the inclusion of Fair Housing and Equal Opportunity Standards in all HUD programs."

Imports of Lead Products

Proclamation 4817. January 16, 1981

PROCLAMATION TO MODIFY THE SUSPENSION IN PART OF THE TARIFF CONCESSIONS ON CERTAIN LEAD PRODUCTS

By the President of the United States of America

A Proclamation

1. On October 31, 1979, under the authority of section 101(a)(1) of the Trade Act of 1974 (the Trade Act) (19 U.S.C. 2111(a)(1)), the United States entered into a trade agreement with the United Mexican States (Mexico) containing certain tariff concessions by the United States. These tariff concessions were implemented by Proclamation No. 4707 of December 11, 1979, beginning January 1, 1980. This agreement provides that, under certain circumstances which now exist, the United States may suspend or withdraw these concessions in whole or in part.

2. An expectation, which this agreement stated to be the basis for the United States concessions therein, not having materialized, and only partially equivalent substitute concessions having been received

from Mexico, the President, by Proclamation 4792 of September 15, 1980 (45 Fed. Reg. 61589), suspended in part tariff concessions which were granted to Mexico in the October 31, 1979 agreement because adequate substitute compensatory concessions had not been provided by Mexico at that time.

3. In view of the temporary modification of the rate of duty on unwrought lead other than lead bullion by section 114 of Public Law 96–609, of December 28, 1980, and of the extent of concessions which have been received from Mexico, I determine that the suspension of the concessions under the Agreement of October 31, 1979 should be modified as set forth below.

NOW, THEREFORE, I, JIMMY CARTER, President of the United States of America, acting under the authority vested in me by the Constitution and the statutes of the United States, including sections 125 and 604 of the Trade Act (19 U.S.C. 2135 and 2483), do proclaim that:

The tariff concessions proclaimed by Proclamation No. 4707 on litharge and red lead provided for in items 473.52 and 473.56 of the Tariff Schedules of the United States (19 U.S.C. 1202), (in the case of litharge as partially suspended by Proclamation 4792) are suspended as set forth in the Annex of this proclamation.

IN WITNESS WHEREOF, I have hereunto set my hand this sixteenth day of January, in the year of our Lord nineteen hundred and eighty-one, and of the Independence of the United States of America the two hundred and fifth.

JIMMY CARTER

[Filed with the Office of the Federal Register, 10:19 a.m., January 19, 1981]

NOTE: The annex is printed in the FEDERAL REGISTER of January 21, 1981.

The proclamation was released by the White House Press Office on January 17.

Foreign Service Retirement and Disability System

Executive Order 12272. January 16, 1981

By the authority vested in me as President of the United States of America by Section 805 of the Foreign Service Act of 1946, as amended (22 U.S.C. 1065), and in order to further conform the Foreign Service Retirement and Disability System to the Civil Service Retirement and Disability System, it is hereby ordered as follows:

1–101. Section 882(c) of the Foreign Service Act of 1946, as amended (22 U.S.C. 1121(c)), shall be deemed to be amended (a) by striking out paragraph (1) thereof, and (b) by inserting in lieu thereof the provisions of Section 8340(c)(1) of Title 5 of the United States Code.

1–102. The amendment made by subsection 1–101(a) hereof shall apply with respect to annuities commencing after January 19, 1981.

JIMMY CARTER

The White House,
     January 16, 1981.

[Filed with the Office of the Federal Register,
     10:20 a.m., January 19, 1981]

NOTE: The Executive order was released by the White House Press Office on January 17.

Central Intelligence Agency Retirement and Disability System

Executive Order 12273. January 16, 1981

By the authority vested in me as President of the United States of America by Section 292 of the Central Intelligence Agency Retirement Act of 1964 for Certain Employees, as amended (50 U.S.C. 403 note), and in order to further conform the Central Intelligence Agency Retirement and Disability System to certain amendments to the Civil Service Retirement and Disability System, it is hereby ordered as follows:

1–101. Section 291(b) of the Central Intelligence Agency Retirement Act of 1964 for Certain Employees, as amended, shall be deemed to be amended (a) by striking out paragraph (1) thereof, and (b) by inserting in lieu thereof the following:

"(1) The first cost-of-living increase (if any) made to an annuity which is payable from the Central Intelligence Agency Retirement and Disability Fund to a participant who retires, or to the widow or widower of a deceased participant, shall be equal to the product (adjusted to the nearest of 1/10 of one percent) of:

a. 1/6 of the applicable percent change computed under subsection (a) of this Section, multiplied by

b. the number of full months for which the annuity was payable from the Fund before the effective date of the increase (counting any portion of a month as a full month).".

1–102. The amendment made by subsection 1–101(a) hereof shall apply with respect to annuities commencing after January 19, 1981.

JIMMY CARTER

The White House,
     January 16, 1981.

[Filed with the Office of the Federal Register,
     10:21 a.m., January 19, 1981]

NOTE: The Executive order was released by the White House Press Office on January 17.

Military Pay and Allowances

Executive Order 12274. January 16, 1981

By the authority vested in me as President and as Commander in Chief of the

Armed Forces of the United States of America by Sections 301c, 305a, and 403 of Title 37 of the United States Code, and in order to implement incentive pay for submarine duty for Navy enlisted members and officers, to implement special pay for officers serving on sea duty and increased rates of special pay for enlisted personnel serving on sea duty, and to extend the payment of basic allowances for quarters to certain members without dependents, it is hereby ordered as follows:

1-1. *Incentive Pay for Submarine Duty.*

1-101. Executive Order No. 11157, as amended, is further amended by revising Section 106 of Part I thereof to read as follows:

"Sec. 106(a). As determined by the Secretary of the Navy, a member who is entitled to basic pay, who holds or is in training leading to a submarine duty designator, who is not entitled to continuous monthly submarine duty incentive pay, and who is in and remains in the submarine service on a career basis, is also entitled to submarine duty incentive pay for the frequent and regular performance of operational submarine duty required by orders, except as provided by 37 U.S.C. 301c(c).

"(b) To the extent provided for by appropriations, a member of the Naval Reserve who is entitled to compensation under Section 206 of Title 37 of the United States Code, and who performs, under orders, duty on a submarine during underway operations, is eligible for an increase in such compensation equal to one-thirtieth of the monthly submarine duty incentive pay for the performance of that duty by a member of a corresponding grade and years of service who is entitled to basic pay when those orders specify such increased entitlement. Such member is eligible for the increase for each day served, for as long as he is quali-

fied for it, during each regular period of appropriate duty.

"(c) As determined by the Secretary of the Navy, a member who is entitled to basic pay, who holds or is in training leading to a submarine duty designator and who is in and remains in the submarine service on a career basis, is entitled to continuous monthly submarine duty incentive pay, subject to the performance of required number of years of operational submarine duty (37 U.S.C. 301c(a)(3)–(4)), except as provided by 37 U.S.C. 301c(c).

"(d) The Secretary of the Navy is hereby designated and empowered to issue additional implementing regulations with respect to entitlement of regular and reserve officers and enlisted members of the Navy to submarine duty incentive pay, or continuous monthly submarine duty incentive pay.".

1-2. *Special Pay for Career Sea Duty.*

1-201. Section 201 of Part II of Executive Order No. 11157, as amended, is further revised to read as follows:

"Sec. 201(a). The following members of a uniformed service who are entitled to receive basic pay shall be entitled to receive, additionally, career sea pay while on sea duty:

(1) enlisted members who are in pay grade E-4 or above,

(2) warrant officers,

(3) commissioned officers in pay grade O-3 or above who have over three years of sea duty, and

(4) commissioned officers in pay grades O-1 and O-2 with at least four years active service as enlisted members or as noncommissioned warrant officers and over three years of sea duty.

"(b) The period of sea duty shall include the date of reporting and the date of detachment as stated in orders. Career sea pay shall be at the rates prescribed in

Section 305a of Title 37 of the United States Code.".

1–202. Section 202 of Part II of Executive Order No. 11157, as amended, is revoked.

1–203. Part II of Executive Order No. 11157, as amended, is further revised by adding a new Section 202 as follows:

"Sec. 202. A member of a uniformed service who is entitled to career sea pay and who has served 36 consecutive months of sea duty as such period is computed under regulations of the Secretary concerned, is entitled to a monthly career sea pay premium for the thirty-seventh consecutive month and each subsequent consecutive month of sea duty service by such member when such member is entitled to career sea pay. In the regulations published by the Secretary concerned, the term 'consecutive months of sea duty' may be defined to include periods during which a member is serving in or under orders to duties, service in which qualifies the member for career sea pay, either periodically or continuously during assignment to such duties. Examples of such periods are periods of service as a member of a two crewed submarine or fleet aviation units assigned to ships, or periods for training, hospitalization, or other periods of a similar nature.".

1–204. Section 206 of Part II of Executive Order No. 11157, as amended, is further revised by deleting subsection (b).

1–3. *Basic Allowance for Quarters.*

1–301. Subsection 401 of Part IV of Executive Order No. 11157, as amended, is amended by adding new subsections (e) and (f) as follows:

"(e) The term 'deployed' shall apply to time during which the unit is at sea or in a port more than 50 miles from its home port; provided, however, time during which the unit is in a port for overhaul or extended repairs is not to be consid-

ered deployed time. Unanticipated overhauls or extended repairs which occur during a period scheduled as extended deployment in the mission assignment of the ship is time deployed unless otherwise classified by appropriate command authority.

"(f) The phrase "while the unit to which he is assigned is deployed for a period in excess of 90 days" shall apply to periods of time commencing on the 91st day the unit to which the member is assigned is deployed.".

1–302. Executive Order No. 11157, as amended, is further amended by deleting section 408 of Part IV thereof.

1–4. *Effective Date.*

1–401. The amendments made by this Order to Executive Order No. 11157, as amended, shall be effective as of January 1, 1981.

JIMMY CARTER

The White House,
    January 16, 1981.

[Filed with the Office of the Federal Register, 10:22 a.m., January 19, 1981]

NOTE: The Executive order was released by the White House Press Office on January 17.

Design Liaison Council
Executive Order 12275. January 16, 1981

By virtue of the authority vested in me as President by the Constitution of the United States of America, and in order to affirm our commitment that each Federal dollar spent on design shall be viewed as an investment in enriching the quality of American life, it is hereby ordered as follows:

1–101. To encourage good design within the Federal Government, there is hereby established an interagency Design Liaison

Council composed of the heads of the following agencies or their designees:

Department of State.

Department of the Treasury.

Department of Defense.

Department of Justice.

Department of the Interior.

Department of Agriculture.

Department of Commerce.

Department of Labor.

Department of Health and Human Services.

Department of Housing and Urban Development.

Department of Transportation.

Department of Energy.

Department of Education.

Environmental Protection Agency.

National Aeronautics and Space Administration.

Office of Personnel Management.

General Services Administration.

Veterans' Administration.

International Communication Agency.

Small Business Administration.

Federal Council on the Arts and the Humanities.

1–102. The following agencies are invited to participate in the activities of the Design Liaison Council:

Commission on Fine Arts.

Smithsonian Institution.

U.S. Postal Service.

Tennessee Valley Authority.

1–103. The representative of the Federal Council on the Arts and the Humanities shall chair the Design Liaison Council.

1–104. Representatives of other interested agencies may be invited to participate in the functions of the Design Liaison Council.

1–105. For the purposes of this Order, "design" encompasses products and processes of architecture, energy conservation, engineering, graphic design, industrial and product design, interior design, landscape architecture, urban design and city planning, and other related disciplines.

1–106. The Design Liaison Council shall encourage the exchange of information and research on design issues among federal agencies. The Council shall also recommend those changes in agency standards and procedures which will enhance the functional and visual quality of design products and processes.

JIMMY CARTER

The White House,
January 16, 1981.

[Filed with the Office of the Federal Register, 10:23 a.m., January 19, 1981]

NOTE: The Executive order was released by the White House Press Office on January 17.

Economic Report of the President

*Annual Message to the Congress.
January 17, 1981*

To the Congress of the United States:

Over the next few years our country faces several economic challenges that will test the will of our people and the capability of our government. We must find ways to bring down a stubborn inflation without choking off economic growth; we must channel a much larger share of our national output to investment and reverse a decade-long decline in productivity growth; and we must continue to reduce the Nation's dangerous vulnerability to disruptive changes in the world supply and price of oil.

In this *Economic Report* I set forth my views on how we can best meet those problems. The following *Annual Report of the Council of Economic Advisers* discusses the challenges and the policy responses in greater detail. It is useful to start by recognizing that in many respects we approach these challenges from a position of strength, with a record of significant economic progress, and the knowledge that over the past 4 years our people and our government have successfully resolved a number of difficult and potentially divisive economic issues. While it would be folly to close our minds to the stubbornness of the problems we face, it would serve the Nation equally ill to underrate our strengths and our proven ability to handle difficult issues.

STRENGTHS AND ACCOMPLISHMENTS

During the economic turmoil that characterized the decade of the 1970s, and especially during the past 4 years, the American economy succeeded in providing additional jobs for its people on a scale unsurpassed in our history. Employment grew by almost 25 percent over the decade, and by more than 11 percent in the past 4 years alone. Not only were jobs provided for a sharply rising population reaching working age, but job opportunities were opened up by the millions for new second earners, principally women. Neither Europe nor Japan came even close to the job performance of the American economy.

Along with employment, real per capita incomes grew during the past 4 years, despite the losses forced on the Nation by the huge increases in world oil prices and the effects of a slowing growth in productivity. As the year 1980 ended, per capita income, after taxes and adjusted for inflation, was some 8 percent higher than it was in 1976.

We have heard much about American industry losing its competitive edge in international markets and about the "deindustrialization" of America. In fact, during the 3 years prior to the onset of the

1980 recession—and the effects of that recession will be transient—the growth of industrial production in the United States was larger than it was in Germany, France, or the United Kingdom. The volume of American nonfarm exports rose by 35 percent between 1977 and the middle of 1980, and the share of U.S. exports among the total exports of the industrial countries rose by about 1¼ percentage points, reversing a declining trend that had been underway since the 1950s.

America's balance of payments is strong in large part because of its superior export performance. Despite a massive $40-billion annual drain of funds to pay for the oil-price increases of 1979 and 1980, our exports of goods and services now exceed our imports. Unlike the situation in most other oil-importing nations, our country's external balance is in surplus.

The dollar is also strong. After a period of weakness in its value abroad, we took decisive action 2 years ago to stabilize the dollar. Since then, in a world of sharply changing circumstances and disruptions of oil supply, the dollar has remained strong, and has risen in value compared to most major currencies.

While it is imperative that our country increase the share of its national output devoted to investment, the reason is not that investment has been weak in recent years. Between 1976 and 1980, real business investment grew almost 6 percent a year, substantially faster than GNP as a whole. Because of that rapid growth the share of business investment in GNP during the past 3 years exceeded that of any other 3-year period in the last three decades.

There are other areas where the Nation has made more progress than we sometimes realize. While we are properly concerned to limit the growth in Federal spending and voice our impatience with the waste and inefficiency that often exist in government programs, we should not forget the good that has been accomplished with these programs. Examples abound. In the early 1960s, for instance, infant mortality in the United States was scandalously high compared to other countries, and most of that high mortality was concentrated among the poor. Due in large part to programs like Medicaid, infant mortality has fallen sharply. More generally, we have dramatically improved access to medical care for the poor and the aged. Through Federal grants we have strengthened the mass transit systems of our major cities and helped our municipalities install critically needed waste treatment plants. We have helped millions of young people, who could not otherwise have afforded it, get a college education, and we have provided job training for workers who needed new skills.

Much attention is now focused on how to reduce the costs and ease the burden of Federal regulation to protect the environment, health, and safety. Concern about excessive regulatory costs is surely warranted, and my Administration has taken a number of specific steps to deal with the problem. In focusing attention on the burden of regulation, however, we should not lose sight of the substantial progress that has been made in enriching our lives, improving our health, and beautifying our country.

TACKLING DIFFICULT ISSUES

During the past 4 years the Nation has taken a series of important and in some cases painful steps to deal with its energy problems. Starting almost 2 years ago, we began to phaseout controls on domestic oil and natural gas prices. We thus moved to end the dangerous practice of holding U.S. energy prices below the world market price, a practice which tended to subsidize wasteful consumption and perpetuate our excessive dependence on oil imports.

Working with the Congress we also put in place the other principal elements of a comprehensive program to increase energy production and conserve energy use. We levied a windfall profits tax to divert the inevitable windfalls from oil decontrol to pay for the National Energy Program initiatives and to reduce the impact of decontrol on the poor.

Partly as a result of these policies we have begun to see dramatic results in both the supply and conservation of energy. There are now 70 percent more drilling rigs in operation than when my Administration took office, and the number of oil and gas wells being drilled has reached a new record. By late 1980 the United States was importing almost 30 percent less oil than it did 2 years ago and our gasoline use had dropped by more than 10 percent over the same period. While some of the reduction in energy use was due to the recession, most of it reflects real energy conservation.

What has happened in energy policy over the past 4 years augurs well for our country's future. Decontrolling domestic oil and gas was painful. It pushed up the prices each of us pay for driving and for heating our homes and added to our immediate inflation difficulties. But we showed that we were willing to take such painful steps when they were necessary in our Nation's longer-run interest. Because we are large-scale producers as well as consumers of energy, the energy problem was potentially a highly divisive issue in our country, involving the redistribution of hundreds of billions of dollars, pitting producer against consumer and one region of the Nation against another. But after prolonged and sometimes heated debate, we arrived at an appoach that took account of the legitimate concerns of all groups and at the same time furthered the national interest. Dealing with the Nation's remaining economic problems will also require painful measures and the reconciliation of a number of different interests. Our handling of the energy problem should raise our confidence that we can be successful elsewhere.

We have also had major successes in other fields. After decades of inaction, the past 4 years have seen the elimination of price-propping and competition-deadening regulations in a number of American industries. In these 4 years we witnessed more progress in economic deregulation than at any other time in the century. In the face of great skepticism and initial opposition, the executive branch, the Congress, and some of the independent regulatory agencies have deregulated or drastically reduced regulation in the airline, trucking, and railroad industries, and in banking and other financial institutions. We have also made a promising start in the communications industry. The transportation, communications, and finance industries comprise a triad that links the various strands of our economy together. Better performance in these industries should have effects far beyond their own boundaries.

The gains from deregulation will be substantial. For example, productivity and efficiency will be directly increased as transportation load factors are improved and empty backhauls reduced. One survey of studies estimates that reform in the trucking industry alone will lead to $5 billion in annual cost reductions. Even more important will be the longer-run spur to innovation and the increased flexibility that comes from opening up these industries to the fresh winds of competition.

Population trends will be working to help the country deal with some of its economic problems in the 1980s, whereas in the late 1960s and 1970s these trends required some difficult adjustments. The generation of the postwar baby boom began entering the labor market in the 1960s and the influx of new workers continued during the 1970s. The percentage of the population aged 16 to 24 rose sharply. And as birth rates slowed, women entered the labor force in ever increasing numbers. On average, the labor force became less experienced, and average productivity per worker suffered. The increased proportion of women and young people in the labor force also contributed to an increase in the average unemployment rate because the transition from school or home to job takes time and because these new workers sometimes had periods of unemployment as they explored different career possibilities.

Because of the slowdown in birth rates in the past 15 years, the 1980s will see about half as fast a growth in the labor force as in the 1970s. The proportion of experienced workers will rise, contributing to an increase in productivity, while the proportion of young people will fall, leading to a drop in unemployment.

There are a number of reasons, therefore, to confront with hope the economic challenges that face us. We have a solid record of achievement. In the fields of energy and deregulation we have already laid the foundations on which the future can build. And there are some favorable trends underway that should help raise productivity and reduce unemployment in the years ahead.

UNRESOLVED PROBLEMS

Despite much progress in recent years, we are faced with some serious problems. An inflation that was already bad became worse after the 1979 oil-price increase. Productivity growth, which had been declining sporadically for a decade, virtually ceased in the last several years. And although we have made substantial progress in adapting our economy to a world of higher oil prices, we remain dangerously vulnerable to serious supply disruptions originating abroad.

These problems are closely related to each other. Our inflation stems in part from our oil vulnerability and our slowing productivity growth. High and rising inflation, in turn, tends to cause economic reactions that depress productivity. As we make progress in one of these areas, we will also make progress in the others.

None of the problems is so intractable that we cannot overcome it. But all are so deep-seated that progress will come slowly, only with persistence, and at the cost of some sacrifice on the part of us all.

INFLATION

In the first half of the 1960s inflation averaged about 1 percent a year, so low as to be virtually unnoticeable. In the past 15 years, however, the underlying rate of inflation has risen sporadically but inexorably and it is now running at about 10 percent a year.

During those 15 years there have been three major episodes in which the rate of inflation surged upward. The first came in the late 1960s, when the Vietnam war and the Great Society programs were financed for a number of years without a tax increase. The consequent high budget deficits during a period of economic prosperity generated strong inflationary pressures

as total spending became excessive relative to the Nation's productive capacity. The second inflationary surge, which came in the early 1970s, was associated with the first massive oil-price increase, a worldwide crop shortage which drove up food prices, and an economy which again became somewhat overheated in 1972 and 1973. The third inflationary episode came in 1979 and 1980. It was principally triggered by another massive oil-price increase, but part of the rise in inflation may also have been due to overall demand in the economy pressing on available supply. Throughout the past decade, the slowing growth in productivity has pushed up the increase in business costs, adding its bit to the rise of inflation.

Late in each of the three inflationary episodes monetary and fiscal restraints were applied, and at the end of each a recession took place, with rising unemployment and idle capacity. Inflation did fall back somewhat, but at the end of each recession it had not declined to the level from which it started. And so the inflationary process has been characterized by ratchet-like behavior. A set of inflationary causes raises the rate of inflation; when the initiating factors disappear, inflation does not recede to its starting position despite the occurrence of recession; the wage-price spiral then tends to perpetuate itself at a new and higher level. Instead of an occasional 3 percentage point rise in inflation, which disappeared when the initial causes of the inflation were gone, our basic inflation rate rose first from 1 to 4 percent, then from 4 to 7 percent, and in this latest episode from 7 to 10 percent. It is this downward insensitivity of inflation in the face of economic slack that has given the last 15 years their inflationary bias.

A number of facts that are important for economic policy can be drawn from this history. *First,* excessive demand in the economy, fed by an overly large Federal budget deficit or excess growth in the money supply, was the major factor in one of the three inflationary episodes and played a subsidiary role in the other two. *Second,* twice in the last decade the tendency for government to stimulate the economy somewhat too freely during the recovery from recession probably played a role in retarding the decline of inflation or renewing its acceleration. That is why I was so insistent that a tax cut designed for quick economic stimulus not be enacted last year. *Third,* because the rate of increase in wages and prices did not decline very readily in response to the discipline of budgetary and monetary restraint, that restraint resulted only partly in reduced inflation; it also tended to retard the growth of output and employment. *Finally,* massive increases in world oil prices have twice in the past 7 years helped trigger a major inflationary episode. While we cannot eliminate our vulnerability to such shocks, a reduction in that vulnerability will improve our chances of avoiding new inflation in the future.

These realities dictate the broad tasks that economic policy must accomplish over the years ahead:

Our monetary and fiscal policies must apply steady anti-inflationary restraint to the economy. The restraint must be strong and persistent enough to convince those who set wages and prices that the government means to stand by its guns in the anti-inflation fight. But it must not be so severe or so restrictive as to prohibit even moderate economic growth and recovery, and thus collapse under its own political unreality.

We must seek means to reduce inflation at a lower cost in lost output and employment. These include measures to increase investment, the reform of regulation, and incomes policies. An increase in investment raises productivity growth which, in turn, tends to slow the rise in business costs and prices. Demand restraint will then produce more reduction of inflation and less reduction in output. Measures to lower regulatory costs and increase competition and flexibility in our economy will also directly lower inflationary pressures and let us have more economic growth without sacrificing our inflation goals. An improved set of voluntary incomes policies can directly influence wages and prices in the direction of moderation, and thereby bring inflation down faster and at lower costs.

Finally, we must build upon the foundations already laid and hasten our progress toward energy conservation and increased domestic energy supplies. We must also work to improve our capability of weathering a severe disruption in foreign oil supplies, since even a highly successful energy program will still leave our economy vulnerable to such disruptions over the coming decade.

Last August I outlined an Economic Revitalization Program that would accomplish the tasks set forth above. The specific economic policies I am recommending to the Congress in my 1982 *Budget Message* and in this *Economic Report* incorporate the elements of that revitalization program.

BUDGET AND TAX POLICIES

It is now estimated that the Federal budget for the current fiscal year 1981 will be in deficit by $55 billion, substantially more than I had hoped or planned. In part the size of that deficit reflects the loss of revenues induced by the recession from which our economy is now beginning to recover. Had the unemployment rate remained at the 6 percent level where it stood when I first submitted the 1981 budget last year, the deficit would now be less than $20 billion.

The size of the 1981 deficit also reflects three major factors which have driven up the estimates of Federal spending in the past 12 months. *First,* higher interest rates since the budget was originally submitted have added about $9 billion. *Second,* payments under many Federal programs, such as social security, are indexed to the consumer price index, which has proven in recent years to overstate significantly the actual rise in the cost of living because of the way it treats housing and mortgage interest costs. And *third,* defense spending was increased above original estimates.

As part of a program of anti-inflationary fiscal restraint I am recommending a number of steps that will help to cut the deficit in half, to $27.5 billion in the new budget for fiscal year 1982, and reduce it still further to $8 billion in 1983, despite the substantial increases in defense spending which I find it necessary to recommend for those years:

• Beyond exerting strict control over requests for new appropriations for ongoing programs, my 1982 budget sets forth a detailed list of requests to the Congress for the legislation needed to pare some $9 billion in spending in both fiscal 1982 and fiscal 1983. If enacted, these savings would help make possible a reduction in the share of GNP taken by Federal spending from 23.3 percent in 1981 to 23.0 percent in 1982 and 22.6 percent in 1983.

• The personal tax reductions which I am proposing should take effect on January 1, 1982, rather than at some earlier date in 1981.

• I am renewing my request to the Congress for a modest increase in the tax on gasoline; there is no better way to provide additional revenues for reducing the budget deficit than a measure which simultaneously reduces our imports of foreign oil.

• I still strongly support the national health insurance proposal that I earlier submitted to the Congress, but the need for budgetary restraint to control inflation requires that its introduction be delayed until more budgetary room is available and adequate cost containment is in place.

In order to avoid repetition of the recent situation in which many Federal payments rose too rapidly because they are tied to an index which does not accurately reflect changes in the cost of living, I am recommending that the Congress authorize use of a more representative index. I am informed by the Commissioner that the Bureau of Labor Statistics is now producing an index of this type and that it can quickly be made available on a timely basis.

Athough my 1982 budget emphasizes the need for fiscal restraint, and for reduction of the deficit, it also takes the first major step in a long-term program of tax reductions aimed at increasing capital formation.

The causes of the longer-term slowdown in productivity growth are many—and some of them are still unknown. But a major depressing factor has been the failure of the Nation's capital stock to increase relative to its rapidly growing labor force in the past 5 or 6 years. Unlike earlier periods, American workers have not been working with increasing amounts of capital. Improving the trend of productivity growth will require restoring the growth of capital per worker.

Higher investment will also be critically required throughout America's energy-using industries to speed up the replacement of older energy-inefficient plant and machinery with newer energy-saving capital. In addition, a large expansion of energy-producing industries—both conventional and nonconventional—will add further to investment needs.

According to estimates made by my Council of Economic Advisers, the combined tasks of restoring the earlier growth of capital per worker and meeting the Nation's energy needs call for an increase in the share of investment in GNP from its recent 10½ percent to 12½ or 13 percent during the 1980s. This would require an expansion in investment by about one-fifth above the level that might normally be expected. It will not occur without the introduction of policies to make it happen.

To begin this task, my 1982 budget incorporates the two major changes in tax laws that I outlined last August in my Economic Revitalization Program to improve incentives and provide increased sources of financing for business investment. The first and most important proposal is a major liberalization of tax allowances for depreciation. Because tax depreciation is now based on the historic cost of an asset, inflation reduces allowable tax deductions relative to the cost of replacing an asset and thus lowers the profitability of investment. Inflation also distorts the tax treatment of assets with different useful lives. I am proposing a new approach to depreciation worked out by the Department of the Treasury which substantially simplifies depreciation accounting and increases the allowable rates of depreciation by about 40 percent. This approach, unlike some other depreciation liberalization proposals that

have been introduced in the Congress, tends to avoid major distortions of economic incentives since it provides approximately equal percentage increases in allowable depreciation rates for each industry.

I also propose that the Congress expand investment incentives by improving the investment tax credit. That credit is now only partially available for short-lived assets; it should be made fully available. Even more importantly, part of the investment tax credit should be made refundable. Firms should be able to claim 30 percent of the value of the credit even if they had no tax liabilities for the year. In this way firms with substantial investment needs but with no current earnings can be supported in their efforts to rejuvenate and expand capital assets. Among these are younger and smaller firms that are just beginning to grow, and larger industries undergoing transition, such as autos and steel. The latter may temporarily be experiencing depressed profitability but still have major investment needs for retooling or for new industrial facilities.

These two proposals would reduce business tax liabilities by $9 billion in calendar year 1981, $15 billion in 1982, and by 1985 the reductions would amount to over $27 billion. We estimate that with enactment of these new incentives business investment should increase 5–10 percent above its normally expected level in 1982, with additional gains thereafter.

While providing additional incentives for business investment, we can also move on a carefully phased basis to reduce other taxes in a way that improves both economic efficiency and tax equity. The Congress should enact an income tax credit for both employers and employees that would approximately offset the scheduled rise in social security payroll taxes that occurred in January of this year. To make the benefits available to lower-income workers who have no tax liability, I also propose an increase in the earned income tax credit. But, as I pointed out earlier in this *Report,* the critical importance of reducing the budget deficit as part of the fight against inflation has led me to recommend that this reduction take effect at the beginning of 1982, by which time the growth of revenues will make such a reduction consistent with overall budgetary objectives.

At the present time one of the major inequities in our tax system is the so-called marriage penalty. Under a wide range of circumstances a husband and wife, each working, will together pay a higher tax than if they were not married. I propose that this penalty be eased by making a tax credit available to the lesser-earning spouse. The credit should be introduced in two steps, half in 1982 and the other half in 1983.

I also propose that the Congress enact several important tax reforms: income from interest and dividends should be put on an equal footing with wages and other incomes by withholding taxes at the source; the excessive issuance of several types of tax-exempt bonds should be curtailed; and the use of certain commodity futures transactions as a tax avoidance scheme should be prohibited.

The central feature of the tax policies I am proposing is their emphasis on increasing investment. By 1985, an unusually high 45 percent of the tax reductions will be directed toward spurring investment. But even this will not itself be sufficient to raise investment to the levels our country will need in the decade ahead in order to improve its productivity growth and deal with its energy problems. Careful control of Federal spending, however, will create the leeway for additional investment-oriented tax reductions in later years, within the framework of the overall budgetary restraint required to fight inflation. I do not believe that we should now commit budgetary resources to large-scale personal tax cuts which will stimulate consumption far more than investment and thereby foreclose the possibility of meeting the Nation's critical invesment requirements.

MONETARY POLICY

Monetary policy is the responsibility of the Federal Reserve System, which is independent of the Executive. I respect that independence. But there are several broad aspects of monetary policy having to do with public perceptions that do fall within the purview of the President in his role as national leader.

Sustained restraint in monetary policy is a prerequisite to lowering inflation. The Federal Reserve exercises this restraint principally by keeping a strict limit on the growth of the Nation's money supply. In October 1979 the Federal Reserve modified its earlier policies and operating procedures to increase sharply the emphasis it gives to controlling the money supply. The Federal Reserve each year sets targets for monetary growth and seeks to hold the growth of the money supply within the targets. Increasingly the public in general and the financial community in particular have come to associate the credibility of the Federal Reserve and its determination to fight inflation with its success in keeping money growth continuously within the preannounced targets. It is very important, however, that public opinion not hold the Federal Reserve to such a rigid form of monetary targeting as to deprive it of the flexibility it needs to conduct a responsible monetary policy.

Temporary fluctuations in monetary conditions can sometimes cause the money supply to overrun or underrun the targets for a short period of time without any damage to anti-inflation objectives. Furthermore, economic developments occasionally occur that may make it appropriate for the Federal Reserve to modify the targets it had originally set, or to deviate from its announced aim of lowering the targets each year. If the public interprets occasional necessary changes in the longer-run monetary target ranges or short-run deviations of actual money growth from those targets as evidence that the Federal Reserve has lessened its determination to fight inflation and as a reason to expect higher inflation in the future, the Federal Reserve is confronted with an untenable situation. If it fails to make the adjustment in the monetary targets that is called for by a major change in economic circumstances, monetary policy may produce unwanted results. But if the Federal Reserve does change the targets in the face of public misunderstanding, it risks an impairment of its credibility. The same dilemma exists with respect to allowing short-run deviations in money growth from the target ranges.

Only if the public understands the realities, and the complexities, of carrying out an anti-inflationary monetary policy can the Federal Reserve successfully apply the measured restraint necessary to wring out inflation at minimum cost in production and jobs. On the one hand, the country must face the fact that in a world with a stubborn 10 percent inflation rate, keeping a tight rein on the growth of the money supply inevitably leads to interest rates that average significantly higher than those we were accustomed to in earlier periods of lower inflation. On the other hand, the public and the financial community must not become so obsessed with the mechanics of monetary targeting that any change in targets or any short-run deviation of money growth from those targets is taken as a sign that monetary restraint has been weakened.

Without reasoned and persistent monetary restraint, inflation cannot be licked. Perhaps more than in any other area of economic policy, however, achieving success in monetary policy depends on an informed public opinion.

INCOMES POLICIES

For the past 2 years my Administration has urged business and labor to comply with a set of voluntary pay and price standards. Even though it was introduced at a very difficult time—just before the oil-price explosion of 1979—this voluntary program of wage and price restraint did moderate the pace of inflation. It significantly reduced—although it could not eliminate—the effect of the oil-price rise on the underlying inflation rate.

After 2 years of operation there is general agreement that the current pay and price standards would not continue to be effective in their present form and without additional support. For this reason we have carefully examined the possibility of strengthening a voluntary incomes policy by using the tax system to provide incentives to firms and workers to slow the rate of inflation. This approach has been labeled a tax-based incomes policy (TIP). The detailed results of our review are contained in the accompanying *Annual Report of the Council of Economic Advisers.*

Broadly, we have concluded that an approach which provided a tax reduction to workers in firms whose average pay increase did not exceed some standard, set as part of a voluntary incomes policy, would be feasible and effective in helping to lower inflation. Two major conditions apply, however. *First,* such a policy must be a supplement to, not a substitute for, fiscal and monetary restraint. Without such restraint an incomes policy will produce only fleeting reductions in inflation or none at all. *Second,* a TIP program is likely to be desirable only on a temporary basis. After several years, such a program might cease to be effective and could induce significant distortions into wage relationships throughout the economy. But as an interim device to hasten the reduction in inflation and so shorten the period of reduced output and employment growth, a TIP program could serve the Nation well.

If the growth of Federal spending is restrained, periodic tax reductions will be both feasible and necessary in the years ahead as inflation and economic growth push taxpayers into higher brackets and raise average effective tax rates. Tax-based incomes policies are novel, and most people are unfamiliar with either the opportunities they present or the difficulties they pose. It is therefore highly unlikely that a TIP program could take effect in 1981. But it would be useful for the public in general, and the Congress in particular, to begin now to evaluate the pros and cons of TIP programs so that when the time comes for the next round of Federal tax cuts a TIP program will be seriously considered.

ENERGY

I am once again proposing that the Congress increase the Federal excise tax on gasoline by 10 cents per gallon as an additional incentive to cut petroleum consumption. The need for this tax is, if anything, even greater than it was 7 months ago when the Congress over-turned my action to impose a gasoline conservation fee administratively.

We have once more seen a tightening of world oil supplies. The massive inventories built up in late 1979 and early 1980 have been drawn upon to make up for the loss of exports from Iran and Iraq. If that conflict should continue or if exports do not return to normal, the buffer which those record high inventories provided will be exhausted. Even in the last 2 months, we have seen significant escalation in prices charged by some OPEC members. National security requires us to put additional downward pressure on consumption of gasoline and other petroleum products. If we do not, OPEC may do it for us.

Paradoxically, one of the reasons given earlier for rejecting my proposed tax was that it was too small—some would have preferred a tax of 50 cents or even a dollar per gallon. Whether, over time, this Nation should move toward gasoline taxes that are comparable with those of our Western European allies is not a question that has to be answered now. In any event, to do so overnight would shock the economy excessively. At current gasoline consumption levels, a 50-cent per gallon tax would draw approximately $50 billion per year out of consumers' pockets and require excessive adjustments by consumers and industry. It is much more sensible to start with the level I have proposed.

There is other important unfinished business to attend to in energy. The Congress failed to complete work on my proposed Energy Mobilization Board, but events since August of 1979 have only made the case for the Board's creation more persuasive. It is equally important that we move ahead with the production of substitutes for petroleum. The Synthetic Fuels Corporation is established and operating. Its mission—to encourage commercial-scale production of synthetic fuels through risk-sharing with American industry—is vital.

My program of phased decontrol of domestic crude oil, along with the revamping of natural gas pricing policy contained in the Natural Gas Policy Act, is paying rich dividends. Drilling and seismic exploration have reached near-record levels. The Natural Gas Policy Act should be reviewed, however, to ensure that progress toward decontrol of new natural gas is not jeopardized by the increasing gap between oil prices and their natural gas equivalent, since world oil prices are now about twice those assumed in the act.

Our contingency planning to deal with a severe oil-supply disruption needs to be improved, since the authorities upon which many of the existing plans are based will expire at the end of September of this year. We have had underway for some time an examination of which, if any, of these authorities should be extended and what additional authorities might be required. This work should be completed as soon as possible.

Filling of the Strategic Petroleum Reserve must continue. The rate of fill should be at least the 100,000 barrels per day required by the Energy Security Act, and should, beyond that, be as high as can be accommodated without disrupting world oil markets.

INCREASING THE FLEXIBILITY OF OUR ECONOMY

Energy is not the only area where we must take additional steps to improve the ability of the economy to adjust to the changes that will be demanded of it in the years ahead. To the extent that we can reduce barriers to the flow of labor, capital, and other resources from inefficient to efficient uses, we can reduce inflationary pressures that arise from bottlenecks and economic rigidities and simultaneously speed up the pace of productivity growth.

We should not lose the momentum that has developed over the past 4 years in reducing obsolete and costly economic regulations. The Congress should complete its deliberations and pass legislation similar to that which I suggested last year to complete the task of modernizing our system of telecommunications regulation.

In the broad area of environmental, health and safety regulation, where deregulation is not an appropriate solution, we must expand on the successful beginning that has been made in providing greater flexibility and incentives for firms to meet environmental requirements in more cost-effective ways.

We must also continue our efforts to assure that the Nation's regulatory priorities are sensible. Our Nation can afford a cleaner environment, safer products, and healthier workplaces, but it does not have unlimited resources. Other national goals cry out for attention, and we cannot afford waste in attempting to achieve any of them.

During the coming years, when many of our most important industries will be facing difficult adjustment pressures, we must avoid taking shortsighted actions which block rather than promote this adjustment. Federal policies should indeed cushion the blow when sharp external shocks force an industry, its workers, and the communities within which it is located to undergo massive change in a short period of time. The programs of economic development and trade assistance which exist to meet these needs should be humanely and effectively administered. But such aid must be aimed at facilitating adjustment to change, not preventing it.

While we can and should demand that all nations abide by internationally agreed-upon rules of trade, we must avoid the temptation to use the discretion open to us to prop up weak industries.

SUMMING UP: THE NEED FOR BALANCE

In the years immediately ahead, our country will be wrestling with two central domestic issues. The first is economic in nature: How can we reduce inflation while maintaining the economic growth that keeps our people employed? The second is even broader: What is the proper role of government in our society as spender of tax revenues and regulator of industry?

I am confident we can successfully come to grips with both of these issues. We would make a costly mistake, however, if we approached these problems with the view that there is some single answer to the economic problem and a single criterion for determining the role of government. The resolution of both of these great issues demands a balancing of many approaches and many considerations. Indeed, the only helpful simple proposition is the one which states that any simple and quick answer is automatically the wrong one.

The approach I have set forth in this *Report* will successfully meet the economic challenge. But it relies on not one but a number of essential elements. To reduce inflation we must be prepared for a period of sustained budgetary and monetary restraint. But since we know that this also tends to depress the growth of output and employment, we must not conclude that the greater the restraint the better. We want a degree of restraint that takes into account society's interest in employment and production as well as its concern to lower inflation. We can im-prove our prospects significantly by introducing investment-oriented tax cuts that increase supply and productivity. But the supply response will not be so quick or so great as to constitute an answer in and of itself. And, in particular, it would be very dangerous to make budgetary policy in the belief that the supply response can be so large as to wipe out the need for fiscal prudence and budgetary restraint. We can improve our prospects still further by the use of voluntary incomes policies, strengthened when budgetary resources become available by tax incentives for wage moderation. But, again, incomes policies alone will not do the job. If we try to rely on them excessively, we will do more harm than good. Only with a balance among the various elements, and only with persistence in the realization that sure progress will come gradually, can we have both lower inflation and better growth.

Sorting out the proper role of government also requires us to strike a balance. At times Federal spending has grown too rapidly. But in recent years its growth did not result from the introduction of a host of new government programs by spendthrift politicians or a surge of profligacy by wasteful bureaucrats. It stemmed mainly from two sources: *first,* increased military spending to meet national security goals that are overwhelmingly supported by the American people; and *second,* the growth of long established and broadly accepted social security and social insurance programs that are directly or indirectly indexed against inflation or automatically responsive to an increase in unemployment.

There is some waste. There is some abuse. I have instituted a number of reforms to cut it back. I am sure my successors will continue this important effort.

But waste and abuse are not the fundamental issues. The essence of the challenge that faces us is how to balance the various benefits that government programs confer on us against their costs in terms of higher taxes, higher deficits, and sometimes higher inflation.

It is my view that we must strike the balance so as to restrict for some time the overall growth of Federal spending to less than the growth of our economy, despite the faster increase of the military component of the budget. As a consequence, in my 1982 budget I have proposed a series of program reductions. I have suggested a delay in the effective date of new programs I believe important. I have recommended improvements in the index we use to adjust Federal programs for inflation.

I think we will do a better job in striking the right balance over the years ahead if we keep two principles in mind: The first is to recognize *reality*. The choices are in fact difficult, and we should not pretend that all we have to do is find wasteful programs with zero benefits. The second is to act with *compassion*. Some government programs provide special benefits for the poor and the disadvantaged; while these programs must not be immune from review and reform, they should not bear the brunt of the reductions.

The same general viewpoint is appropriate when we approach the problem of government as regulator, especially in protecting the environment, health, and safety. When we first awoke to the fact of generations of environmental neglect, we rushed to compensate for our mistake and paid too little attention to problems of cost and effectiveness. Sometimes the laws we passed and the deadlines we set took too little account of their economic impact. For 4 years my Administration has been engaged in a major program of finding ways to make regulations more cost-effective and to strike a reasonable balance between environmental concerns and economic costs. A strong foundation has been laid. Much remains to be done. But lasting progress will not come unless we realize that there is a balance to be struck. Those who believe that virtually all regulation is bad and that the best regulation is a dead regulation will come to grips with the real problem no more successfully than the enthusiasts who believe that concern with regulatory costs is synonymous with lack of concern for the environment.

I believe that the government has indeed overregulated and that regulatory reform must continue to be a major objective of the Federal Government, as it has been during my Administration. But I also believe that true reform involves finding better ways to identify and to give proper consideration to gains as well as costs.

My reading of the distant and the nearby past gives me confidence that the American people can meet the challenges ahead. There are no simple formulas. There will be no quick victories. But an understanding of the diverse concerns we have, a pragmatic willingness to bring to bear a varied array of weapons, and persistence in the effort will bring success.

JIMMY CARTER

January 17, 1981.

NOTE: The President's message is printed in the report entitled "Economic Report of the President, Transmitted to the Congress, January 1981—Together With the Annual Report of the Council of Economic Advisers" (Government Printing Office, 357 pages).

Council on Environmental Quality

Message to the Congress Transmitting a Report. January 17, 1981

To the Congress of the United States:

I am pleased to transmit to the Congress the Eleventh Annual Report of the Council on Environmental Quality.

As the Report shows, the Nation's environmental programs are producing tangible benefits. In two dozen of our larger cities, the number of days that air quality was in violation of pollution standards declined 18 percent between 1974 and 1978. By and large, water quality in our rivers and lakes has stopped deteriorating. Levels of certain damaging pesticides in the environment have ceased to climb or have dropped, and some of the bird species in danger of extinction a few years ago are returning. The number of American homes using solar power has increased tenfold in just four years. More efficient fuel use by cars and industry has helped to produce an 18 percent decline in oil imports by mid-1980 from 1977 levels.

The signs are unmistakable that we in the United States are learning how to live in balance with nature and beginning to find sustainable ways to exist on this Nation's plentiful but finite resources. Yet there are also undeniable signs that in many other parts of the world the Earth's carrying capacity—the ability of biological systems to meet human needs—is being threatened by human activities. At the time the Declaration of Independence was signed, there were fewer than one billion people on the Earth. Now there are four and one-half billion, and there will be more than six billion by the end of this century. If present trends continue, serious food scarcities are all too probable in many poor nations of the world. The world may continue to lose substantial areas of land to desertlike conditions. In addition, some projections indicate that as much as 40 percent of the world's remaining tropical forests, and perhaps 20 percent of all the species of plants and animals on Earth, could disappear by the year 2000.

We can no longer assume as we could in the past that the Earth will heal and renew itself indefinitely. Human numbers and human works are catching up with the Earth's ability to recover. With care and careful management, our planet's resources—its water, soils, minerals, forests, fish and air—should be able to sustain us in great numbers. But to a degree unknown in past centuries, humankind is now a potent force on the face of the planet. The quality of human existence in the future will rest on careful stewardship and husbandry of the Earth's resources.

During the 1970s, the government and people of this Nation showed an extraordinary grasp of the ties between human beings and their environment and demonstrated strong leadership in creating a sustainable relationship. The 1980s are presenting new challenges. Our Nation must continue to move forward and extend the progress we have made—progress for which we are being repaid many times over.

JIMMY CARTER

The White House,
  January 17, 1981.

NOTE: The report is entitled "Environmental Quality—The Eleventh Annual Report of the Council on Environmental Quality, December 1980" (Government Printing Office, 457 pages).

American Hostages in Iran

Remarks Announcing United States-Iran Agreement for Release of the Hostages. January 19, 1981

I know you've been up all night with me and I appreciate that very much.

We have now reached an agreement with Iran which will result, I believe, in the freedom of our American hostages. The last documents have now been signed in Algiers, following the signing of the documents in Iran which will result in this agreement. We still have a few documents to sign before the money is actually transferred and the hostages are released.

The essence of the agreement is that following the release of our hostages, then we will unfreeze and transfer to the Iranians a major part of the assets which were frozen by me when the Iranians seized our Embassy compound and took our hostages. We have also reached complete agreement on the arbitration procedures between ourselves and Iran with the help of the Algerians which will resolve the claims that exist between residents of our Nation and Iran and vice-versa.

I particularly want to express my public thanks, as I have already done privately, to the Algerians, to their President, their Foreign Minister, Ben Yahia, and to the three-man negotiating teams who have done such a superb job in fair and equitable arbitration between ourselves and the officials of Iran. We don't yet know exactly how fast this procedure will go. We are prepared to move as rapidly as possible. All the preparations have been completed pending the final documents being signed.

I will have more to say to you when our American hostages are actually free. In the meantime, Jody Powell will stay in close touch with developments. Working with the Secretary of State, the Secretary of Treasury, my legal counsel, Lloyd Cutler, I'm talking frequently to Warren Christopher in Algiers. And Jody Powell will keep you informed about developments.

Thank you very much.

REPORTER. How do you feel personally, Mr. President, about having pulled this off before you leave office?

THE PRESIDENT. I'll wait until the hostages are released, and then I'll have another statement to make.

NOTE: The President spoke at 4:56 a.m. to reporters assembled in the Briefing Room at the White House.

United States-People's Republic of China Consular Convention

Message to the Senate Transmitting the Convention. January 19, 1981

To the Senate of the United States:

I am transmitting for the Senate's advice and consent to ratification the Consular Convention between the United States of America and the People's Republic of China, signed at Washington on September 17, 1980. I am also transmitting for the information of the Senate the report of the Department of State with respect to the Convention.

The signing of the Convention is a significant step in the process of improving and broadening the relationship between the United States and the People's Republic of China. Consular relations between the two countries are not now the subject of a modern formal agreement. This Convention will establish firm obligations on such important matters as free communication between a national and his consul, notification of consular officers of the arrest and detention of their nationals and permission for visits by consuls to nationals who are under detention.

I also transmit for the information of the Senate two separate exchanges of letters, signed on September 17, 1980. The first sets forth the understanding of each side that:

1) reunification of families will be promoted as quickly as possible;

2) persons who may be regarded as possessing the nationality of both countries will be permitted to travel freely;

3) persons considered to be nationals of both countries will be entitled to the consular protection of the State whose valid passport (properly visaed) they possess while visiting the other and

4) financial benefits payable by one country to persons residing in the other will be paid under mutually agreed arrangements.

The second reflects agreement that three consulates, in addition to the two already established in each country, may be established.

I welcome the opportunity through this Consular Convention to improve the relations between the two countries and their nationals. I urge the Senate to give the Convention its prompt and favorable consideration.

JIMMY CARTER

The White House,
    January 19, 1981.

The Cyprus Conflict

Letter to the Speaker of the House and the Chairman of the Senate Foreign Relations Committee. January 19, 1981

Dear Mr. Speaker: (Dear Mr. Chairman:)

In accordance with the provision of Public Law 95–384, I am submitting the following report on progress made during the past 60 days toward reaching a negotiated settlement of the Cyprus problem.

As I noted in my last report, the intercommunal talks between representatives of the Greek and Turkish Cypriot communities, which resumed in August 1980, have continued their substantive examination of the issues which divide the island. Under the chairmanship of the UN Secretary General's Special Representative on Cyprus, Ambassador Hugo Gobbi, both sides have pursued analysis and discussion of the four basic areas agreed upon for examination. Meetings were held on November 19 and 26 and December 3 and 8 before breaking for a mutually-agreed end-of-year recess. The talks resumed routinely with a meeting on January 7 and can be expected to continue in weekly sessions.

We have been encouraged by the serious, nonpolemic approach taken by the negotiators in their effort to devise mutually acceptable positions. Throughout the discussions, the negotiating atmosphere has remained businesslike and positive.

The United Nations has continued to pay close attention to Cyprus developments. In his December 1 report on Cyprus, Secretary General Waldheim reviewed developments to date, noting that "Some common ground has been indicated on certain practical questions." He suggested that while "progress so far has been slow, the discussions have been on the whole constructive . . ." and cautioned that a problem lying ahead is "the difficult issue of how and where to start the actual give-and-take which is the essence of an effective negotiating process." The Secretary General also expressed the judgment that while a complex negotiating process such as the Cyprus intercommunal talks must proceed with caution, ". . . it must also, if it is to maintain its credibility, produce concrete results."

I have noted with pleasure that the Secretary General intends to remain directly engaged in the negotiating process. He met in New York in mid-December with Cyprus Foreign Minister Rolandis and with Kenan Atakol, foreign affairs spokesman for the Turkish Cypriot community.

The United States continues fully to support the Secretary General's efforts and those of his Special Representative on Cyprus to reach mutually agreeable solutions to the Cyprus problem. This support has been conveyed on several occasions to Secretary General Waldheim and was expressed also by Secretary Muskie to Turkish Foreign Minister Turkmen and to Greek Foreign Minister Mitsotakis in separate meetings at the NATO Ministerial meeting in Brussels December 10–11, 1980.

I am also pleased to note that on December 11, 1980, the Security Council passed without dissent a resolution extending the mandate of the UN Peacekeeping Force in Cyprus (UNFICYP) to June 15, 1981. Other Security Council members continue to share our view that UNFICYP plays a vital role in maintaining the atmosphere of calm conducive to fruitful negotiation within the intercommunal talks.

The Cyprus problem remains on the international agenda. Its historical complexities suggest that only perseverance, patience and political courage of the highest order will bring about a just and lasting settlement. I remain hopeful that the good start represented by the intercom-

munal negotiations will evolve in the near future into a comprehensive solution that will benefit all the people of Cyprus.

Sincerely,

JIMMY CARTER

NOTE: This is the text of identical letters addressed to Thomas P. O'Neill, Jr., Speaker of the House of Representatives, and Charles H. Percy, chairman of the Senate Foreign Relations Committee.

Advisory Commission on Intergovernmental Relations

Appointment of Six Members. January 19, 1981

The President today announced the appointment of six persons as members of the Advisory Commission on Intergovernmental Relations. They are:

FRED E. ANDERSON, a Colorado State senator (reappointment);

BRUCE BABBITT, Governor of Arizona (reappointment);

EUGENE EIDENBERG, Assistant to the President for Intergovernmental Affairs;

DIANNE FEINSTEIN, mayor of San Francisco;

RICHARD HATCHER, mayor of Gary, Ind.;

RICHARD S. HODES, a Florida State representative and president of the National Conference of State Legislatures.

Pension Benefit Guaranty Corporation

Appointment of Thomas F. Duzak as a Member of the Advisory Committee. January 19, 1981

The President today announced the appointment of Thomas F. Duzak, of Pittsburgh, Pa., as a member of the Advisory Committee to the Pension Benefit Guaranty Corporation.

Duzak is director of the Insurance Pension and Unemployment Benefits Division of the United Steel Workers of America. He is a member of the Basic Steel Industry Task Force on Employment and Income Security and the Advisory Council on Employee Welfare and Pension Benefit Plans.

Advisory Committee for Trade Negotiations

Appointment of Edmund T. Pratt, Jr., as a Member.   January 19, 1981

The President today announced the appointment of Edmund T. Pratt, Jr., of Port Washington, N.Y., as a member of the Advisory Committee for Trade Negotiations.

Pratt is chairman and chief executive officer of Pfizer, Inc., and chairman of the New York State Council on International Business.

National Advisory Council on Adult Education

Appointment of Daniel B. Taylor as a Member. January 19, 1981

The President today announced the appointment of Daniel B. Taylor, of Charleston, W. Va., as a member of the National Advisory Council on Adult Education.

Taylor is Assistant Secretary of Education for Adult and Vocational Education. He was previously a lecturer at Harvard Graduate School of Education and State superintendent of schools for West Virginia.

National Highway Safety Advisory Committee

Appointment of Two Members. January 19, 1981

The President today announced the appointment of two persons as members of the National Highway Safety Advisory Committee. They are:

HAROLD T. "BIZZ" JOHNSON, former chairman of the House Public Works and Transportation Committee;

MARILYN BERRY THOMPSON, director of the Federal policy and director of the Washington office of New Jersey Governor Brendan Byrne.

National Advisory Committee for Juvenile Justice and Delinquency Prevention

Appointment of 12 Members. January 19, 1981

The President today announced the appointment of 12 persons as members of the National Advisory Committee for Juvenile Justice and Delinquency Prevention. They are:

C. JOSEPH ANDERSON, an attorney and former judge of the Vigo County, Ind., Circuit Court. He is a former high school teacher, deputy prosecutor, and State legislator (reappointment).

MARY ELLEN CHAMBERLIN, chairperson of the Scott County, Iowa, Juvenile Detention Planning Advisory Committee (reappointment).

AURISTELA FRIAS, a drug abuse counselor and assistant to the president of the Delancey Street Foundation (reappointment).

ROBERT D. GLASER, a student at Tulane University and a counselor at a youth crisis center in New Orleans.

BETSY HUNT, a Pennsylvania high school student and national president of National TOTS and TEENS.

CHRISTOPHER J. MAGNUS, a student of criminal justice at Michigan State University and a consultant for the Michigan Council on Crime and Delinquency.

SONIA MELARA, foster home recruitment and educational coordinator for the Santa Clara County, Calif., Department of Social Services (reappointment).

ROBERT Q. MILLAN, chairman and president of the First National Bank of Middletown, Ohio, and a member of the Ohio Council on Crime and Delinquency.

DAVID H. MOSELEY, director of the city of Seattle Division of Youth Services and chairman of the National Youth Work Alliance (reappointment).

T. GEORGE SILCOTT, president of the Urban Research Planning and Conference Center and executive director of the Wiltwyck School, a residential treatment center in New York City for emotionally disturbed children (reappointment).

MARY ANNE B. STEWART, a member of the board of trustees of the National Council on Crime and Delinquency and a board member of Family and Child Services of Washington, D.C.

BARBARA T. SYLVESTER, a member and former chairman of the South Carolina Board of Youth Services and former chairman of the State Board of Juvenile Corrections. She worked on the creation of the South Carolina Department of Mental Retardation and is chairman of the Mumford G. Fuller Developmental Center Board, a community school for retarded children. She has been designated Chairman of this Committee (reappointment).

President's Committee on the National Medal of Science

Appointment of Eight Members. January 19, 1981

The President today announced the appointment of eight persons as members of the President's Committee on the National Medal of Science. They are:

RICHARD ATKINSON, chancellor of the University of California at San Diego and former director of the National Science Foundation;

DAVID BALTIMORE, American Cancer Society professor of microbiology at Massachusetts Institute of Technology and winner of the Nobel Prize for medicine;

HERBERT BROWN, professor emeritus at Purdue University, winner of the Nobel Prize for chemistry and the National Medal of Science;

ROGER GUILLEMIN, a resident fellow at the Salk Institute and adjunct professor of medicine at the University of California at San Diego and a National Medal of Science winner;

MARY JANE OSBORN, professor of microbiology at the University of Connecticut Health Center and a member of the National Science Board;

SIDNEY TOPOL, president and chairman of the board of Science-Atlanta, Inc., an electronics firm;

STEVEN WEINBERG, professor of physics at the University of Texas and a Nobel Prize winner (reappointment);

CHIEN-SHIUNG WU, professor of physics at Columbia University and a National Medal of Science winner.

John F. Kennedy Center for the Performing Arts

Appointment of Joan Mondale as a Member of the Board of Trustees. January 19, 1981

The President has appointed Mrs. Joan Mondale to be a member of the Board of Trustees of the John F. Kennedy Center for the Performing Arts for a term expiring September 1, 1990. She will replace Mrs. Paul H. Hatch, whose term has expired.

Woodrow Wilson International Center for Scholars

Appointment of Stuart E. Eizenstat as a Member of the Board of Trustees. January 19, 1981

The President today announced the appointment of Stuart E. Eizenstat as a member of the Board of Trustees of the Woodrow Wilson International Center for Scholars.

Science and Technology
Message to the Congress Transmitting a Report. January 19, 1981

To the Congress of the United States:

I am pleased to submit to the Congress the Third Annual Science and Technology Report as required by the National Science and Technology Policy, Organization and Priorities Act of 1976.

Science and technology affect our lives in many ways, and policy decisions very often involve issues of a scientific and technical nature. Systematic assessment of scientific and technological developments is therefore a crucial element in the formation of effective public policy. My Administration has sought to make better use of science and technology in responding to challenges in many areas—energy, health, agriculture, environmental protection, national security, the quest for peace, economic productivity, and the renewal of our industrial base. The decisions, actions and programs described in this report show how developments in science and technology have interacted with recent public policies in these areas.

I hope that this report, like its predecessors and its companion, the *Five-Year Outlook* on science and technology will contribute to the informed discussion so essential to our scientific and technological capabilities and our future national strength.

JIMMY CARTER

The White House,
  January 19, 1981.

NOTE: The report is entitled "Annual Science and Technology Report to the Congress, 1980—National Science Foundation, January 1981" (Government Printing Office, 106 pages, plus appendices).

Convention on International Civil Aviation
Message to the Senate Transmitting a Protocol to the Convention. January 19, 1981

To the Senate of the United States:

I transmit herewith, for advice and consent of the Senate to ratification, a Protocol relating to an amendment to the Convention on International Civil Aviation, done at Montreal on October 6, 1980. The amendment permits a State in which an aircraft is registered to transfer its functions and duties under Articles 12, 30, 31 and 32(a) of the Convention on International Civil Aviation ("Convention") to the State of the operator leasing, chartering or interchanging that aircraft, subject to the latter State's agreement.

The Convention establishes the International Civil Aviation Organization ("ICAO") and general rules for the safe and reasonable conduct of international civil aviation. The problems which arise today from the leasing of aircraft in international operations were not envisaged in 1944 at the time the Convention was drafted. These problems involve difficulties by the States of registry in discharging their responsibilities under Articles 12 (Rules of the Air), 30 (Aircraft Radio Equipment), 31 (Certificates of Airworthiness), and 32(a) (Licenses of Personnel). Ineffective discharge of these responsibilities by States of registry tends to decrease the level of safety in flight operations. The amendment would resolve these difficulties and facilitate greater safety by allowing a State of registry and a State of the operator to agree to transfer these responsibilities to the State of the operator.

The United States expects to benefit directly from this amendment. United States nationals and companies lease by far the greatest number of civil aircraft to operators of other States. In addition, under regulations of the Department of Transportation, United States air carriers may operate and carry local traffic within the United States on aircraft registered in other States. The role of the United States as the State of the operator of leased aircraft is therefore likely to expand.

This is the first substantive amendment of the Convention. It consummates years of United States effort and furthers United States objectives to facilitate safety in international flight operations. The ICAO Assembly urged all Contracting States to ratify the amendment as soon as possible and to make any appropriate changes in their national laws. In accordance with Article 94 of the Convention, ratification by 98 Contracting States is required to bring this amendment into force. It would be desirable if the United States, originator of the amendment, were the first State to ratify it. I therefore recommend that the Senate give early and favorable consideration to the Protocol of Amendment, and advice and consent to its ratification.

JIMMY CARTER

The White House,
 January 19, 1981.

ance to Jamaica in FY 1981 to over $60 million, will be used to support the economic recovery program on the island.

The loan agreement reflects both U.S. support for the strength and vitality of the democratic process evidenced in Jamaica and elsewhere in the Caribbean over the last year and U.S. awareness of the critical economic problems facing the Caribbean countries and Jamaica in particular. The Carter administration understands the close connection between meeting the basic human needs of a people and preserving a nation's democratic institutions. We have expressed our willingness to join others in continuing to support efforts to put these countries on a sound economic footing.

Jamaican Prime Minister Edward Seaga has made clear his intentions to rebuild his country's economy, with particular emphasis on revitalizing the Jamaican private sector, and we have repeatedly expressed American support of these efforts. We have been encouraged by the efforts of his government to establish a sound economic program and the negotiations which have been held with the International Monetary Fund toward that end.

Economic Support Funds for Jamaica

White House Statement on the U.S.-Jamaican Loan Agreement.   January 19, 1981

Representatives of the United States and the Government of Jamaica today signed a loan agreement in Kingston, Jamaica, providing a total of $40 million in economic support funds to that country. The loan, which will bring U.S. assist-

President's Council on Spinal Cord Injury

Appointment of the Membership of the Council.   January 19, 1981

The President today announced the appointment of 12 persons as members of the President's Council on Spinal Cord Injury. They are:

ELMER BARTELS, commissioner of the Massachusetts Rehabilitation Commission and director emeritus of the National Spinal Cord

3025

Injury Foundation. He has also been designated Chairman of this Council.

MARIANNE J. CASHETT, director of special services at the Woodrow Wilson Rehabilitation Center in Fisherville, Va.

WILLIAM H. EDWARD, director of the military and veterans affairs program of the National Urban League.

ARTHUR I. KOBRINE, professor of neurosurgery at the George Washington University.

JUSTUS F. LEHMAN, a doctor with the department of rehabilitation medicine at the University of Washington and consultant to the Seattle Veterans Hospital.

LOUISE BOUSCAREN McKNEW, acting staff director for the U.S. Advisory Commission on Public Diplomacy.

PAUL R. MEYER, JR., president of the American Spinal Injury Association and director of the acute spinal cord injury unit at the Rehabilitation Institute of Chicago.

GILBERT S. OMENN, visiting senior fellow at the Woodrow Wilson School, Princeton University, on leave as a professor of medicine at the University of Washington.

JAMES J. PETERS, executive director of the Eastern Paralyzed Veterans Association and director of the American Paraplegic Society.

SILVIO S. VARON, professor of biology at the University of California at San Diego.

RICHARD P. VERAA, director of research for the National Spinal Cord Injury Foundation.

PATRICIA F. WALLER, incoming president of the American Association of Automotive Medicine and associate director for driver studies at the University of North Carolina Highway Safety Research Center.

United States-Iran Agreement on Release of the American Hostages

Statement of Adherence. January 19, 1981

By the authority vested in me as President by the Constitution and laws of the United States, I hereby agree and adhere, on behalf of the United States of America, to the provisions of two Declarations that are being issued today by the Government of the Democratic and Popular Republic of Algeria relating to (1) the resolution of the current crisis between the United States and Iran arising out of the detention of the fifty-two United States nationals, and (2) the settlement of claims between the United States and Iran. The two Declarations shall constitute international agreements legally binding upon the United States and Iran upon the execution of an equivalent statement of agreement and adherence by the Islamic Republic of Iran and the delivery of both statements to the Government of the Democratic and Popular Republic of Algeria.

JIMMY CARTER

The White House,
    January 19, 1981.

NOTE: The text of the statement was released by the White House Press Office on January 21.

United States-Iran Agreement on Release of the American Hostages

Statement of Adherence. January 19, 1981

By the authority vested in me as President by the Constitution and laws of the United States, I hereby agree and adhere, on behalf of the United States of America, to the provisions of the Undertakings of the Government of the United States of America and the Government of the Islamic Republic of Iran with respect to the Declaration of the Government of the Democratic and Popular Republic of Algeria. These Undertakings shall constitute an international agreement legally binding upon the United States and Iran upon the execution of an equivalent statement of agreement and adherence by the Islamic Republic of Iran and the delivery of both statements to the Government of the Democratic and Popular Republic of Algeria.

JIMMY CARTER

The White House,
    January 19, 1981.

NOTE: The text of the statement was released by the White House Press Office on January 21.

United States-Iran Agreement on Release of the American Hostages

Executive Order 12276. January 19, 1981

DIRECTION RELATING TO ESTABLISHMENT OF ESCROW ACCOUNTS

By the authority vested in me as President by the Constitution and statutes of the United States, including Section 203 of the International Emergency Economic Powers Act (50 U.S.C. 1702), Section 301 of Title 3 of the United States Code, Section 1732 of Title 22 of the United States Code, and Section 301 of the National Emergencies Act (50 U.S.C. 1631), in view of the continuing unusual and extraordinary threat to the national security, foreign policy and economy of the United States upon which I based my declarations of national emergency in Executive Order 12170, issued November 14, 1979, and in Executive Order 12211, issued April 17, 1980, in order to implement agreements with the Government of Iran, as reflected in Declarations of the Government of the Democratic and Popular Republic of Algeria dated January 19, 1981, relating to the release of U.S. diplomats and nationals being held as hostages and to the resolution of claims of United States nationals against Iran, and to begin the process of normalization of relations between the United States and Iran, it is hereby ordered that as of the effective date of this Order:

1-101. The Secretary of the Treasury is authorized to enter into, and to license, authorize, direct, and compel any appropriate official and/or the Federal Reserve Bank of New York, as fiscal agent of the United States, to enter into escrow or related agreements with a foreign central bank and with the Central Bank of Algeria under which certain money and other assets, as and when directed by the Secretary of the Treasury, shall be credited by the foreign central bank to an escrow account on its books in the name of the Central Bank of Algeria, for transfer to the Government of Iran if and when the Central Bank of Algeria receives from the Government of Algeria a certification that the 52 U.S. diplomats and nationals being held hostage in Iran have safely departed from Iran. Such agreements shall include other parties and terms as determined by the Secretary of the Treasury to be appropriate to carry out the purposes of this Order.

1-102. The Secretary of the Treasury is authorized to license, authorize, direct, and compel the Federal Reserve Bank of New York, as fiscal agent of the United States, to receive certain money and other assets in which Iran or its agencies, instrumentalities, or controlled entities have an interest and to hold or transfer such money and other assets, and any interest earned thereon, in such a manner as he deems necessary to fulfill the rights and obligations of the United States under the Declaration of the Government of the Democratic and Popular Republic of Algeria dated January 19, 1981, and the escrow and related agreements described in paragraph 1–101 of this Order. Such money and other assets may be held in interest-bearing form and where possible shall be invested with or through the entity holding the money or asset on the effective date of this Order.

1–103. Compliance with this Executive Order, any other Executive Order licensing, authorizing, directing or compelling the transfer of the assets referred to in paragraphs 1–101 and 1–102 of this Order, or any regulations, instructions, or directions issued thereunder shall to the extent thereof be a full acquittance and discharge for all purposes of the obligation of the person making the same. No person shall be held liable in any court for or with respect to anything done or omitted in good faith in connection with the administration of, or pursuant to and in reliance on, such orders, regulations, instructions, or directions.

1–104. The Attorney General shall seek to intervene in any litigation within the United States which arises out of this Order and shall, among other things, defend the legality of, and all actions taken pursuant to, each of its provisions.

1–105. The Secretary of the Treasury is delegated and authorized to exercise all functions vested in the President by the International Emergency Economic Powers Act (50 U.S.C. 1701 *et seq.*) to carry out the purposes of this Order.

1–106. This Order shall be effective immediately.

JIMMY CARTER

The White House,
    January 19, 1981.

[Filed with the Office of the Federal Register, 9:17 a.m., January 22, 1981]

NOTE: The text of the Executive order was released by the White House Press Office on January 21.

United States-Iran Agreement on Release of the American Hostages

Executive Order 12277. January 19, 1981

DIRECTION TO TRANSFER IRANIAN GOVERNMENT ASSETS

By the authority vested in me as President by the Constitution and statutes of the United States, including Section 203 of the International Emergency Economic Powers Act (50 U.S.C. 1702), Section 301 of Title 3 of the United States Code, Section 1732 of Title 22 of the United States Code, and Section 301 of the National Emergencies Act (50 U.S.C. 1631), in view of the continuing unusual and extraordinary threat to the national security, foreign policy and economy of the United States upon which I based my declarations of national emergency in Executive Order 12170, issued November 14, 1979, and in Executive Order 12211, issued April 17, 1980, in order to implement agreements with the Government of Iran, as reflected in Declarations of the Government of the Democratic and Popular Republic of Algeria dated January 19, 1981, relating to the release of U.S. diplomats and nationals being held as hostages and to the resolution of claims of United States nationals against Iran, and to begin the process of normalization of relations between the United States and Iran and in which Iran and the United States instruct and require that the assets described in this order shall be transferred as set forth below by the holders of such assets, it is hereby ordered that as of the effective date of this Order:

1–101. The Federal Reserve Bank of New York is licensed, authorized, directed, and compelled to transfer to accounts at the Bank of England, and subsequently to transfer to accounts at the Bank of England established pursuant to an escrow agreement approved by the Secretary of the Treasury, all gold bullion, and other assets (or the equivalent thereof) in its custody, of the Government of Iran, or its agencies, instrumentalities or controlled entities. Such transfers shall be executed when and in the manner directed by the Secretary of the Treasury. The Secretary of the Treasury is also authorized to license, authorize, direct, and compel the Federal Reserve Bank of New York to engage in whatever further transactions he deems appropriate and consistent with the purposes of this Order, including any transactions related to the return of such bullion and other assets pursuant to the escrow agreement.

1–102. (a) All licenses and authorizations for acquiring or exercising any right, power, or privilege, by court order, attachment, or otherwise, including the license contained in Section 535.504 of the Iranian Assets Control Regulations, with respect to the properties described in Section 1–101 of this Order are revoked and withdrawn.

(b) All rights, powers, and privileges relating to the properties described in section 1–101 of this Order and which derive from any attachment, injunction, other like proceedings or process, or other action in any litigation after November 14, 1979, at 8:10 a.m. EST, including those derived from Section 535.504 of the Iranian Assets Control Regulations, other than rights, powers, and privileges of the Government of Iran and its agencies, instrumentalities, and controlled entities, whether acquired by court order or otherwise, are nullified, and all persons claiming any such right, power, or privilege are hereafter barred from exercising the same.

(c) All persons subject to the jurisdiction of the United States are prohibited from acquiring or exercising any right, power, or privilege, whether by court order or otherwise, with respect to the properties (and any income earned thereon) referred to in Section 1–101 of this Order.

1–103. Compliance with this Order, any other Executive Order licensing, authorizing, directing, or compelling the transfer of the assets described in section 1–101 of this Order, or any regulations, instructions, or directions issued thereunder shall to the extent thereof be a full acquittance and discharge for all purposes of the obligation of the person making the same. No person shall be held liable in any court for or with respect to anything done or omitted in good faith in connection with the administration of, or pursuant to and in reliance on, such orders, regulations, instructions, or directions.

1–104. The Attorney General shall seek to intervene in any litigation within the United States which arises out of this Order and shall, among other things, defend the legality of, and all actions taken pursuant to, each of its provisions.

1–105. The Secretary of the Treasury is delegated and authorized to exercise all functions vested in the President by the International Emergency Economic Powers Act (50 U.S.C. 1701 *et seq.*) to carry out the purposes of this Order.

1–106. This Order shall be effective immediately.

JIMMY CARTER

The White House,
  January 19, 1981.

[Filed with the Office of the Federal Register, 9:18 a.m., January 22, 1981]

NOTE: The text of the Executive order was released by the White House Press Office on January 21.

United States-Iran Agreement on Release of the American Hostages

Executive Order 12278. January 19, 1981

DIRECTION TO TRANSFER IRANIAN GOVERNMENT ASSETS OVERSEAS

By the authority vested in me as President by the Constitution and statutes of the United States, including Section 203 of the International Emergency Economic Powers Act (50 U.S.C. 1702), Section 301 of Title 3 of the United States Code, Section 1732 of Title 22 of the United States Code, and Section 301 of the National Emergencies Act (50 U.S.C. 1631), in view of the continuing unusual and extraordinary threat to the national security, foreign policy and economy of the United States upon which I based my declarations of national emergency in Executive Order 12170, issued November 14, 1979 and in Executive Order 12211, issued April 17, 1980, in order to implement agreements with the Government of Iran, as reflected in Declarations of the Government of the Democratic and Popular Republic of Algeria dated January 19, 1981, relating to the release of U.S. diplomats and nationals being held as hostages and to the resolution of claims of United States nationals against Iran, and to begin the process of normalization of relations between the United States and Iran and in which Iran and the United States instruct and require that the assets described in this Order shall be transferred as set forth below by the holders of such assets, it is hereby ordered that as of the effective date of this Order:

1-101. Any branch or office of a United States bank or subsidiary thereof, which branch or office is located outside the territory of the United States and which on or after 8:10 a.m. E.S.T. on November 14, 1979 (a) has been or is in possession of funds or securities legally or beneficially owned by the Government of Iran or its agencies, instrumentalities, or controlled entities, or (b) has carried or is carrying on its books deposits standing to the credit of or beneficially owned by such Government, agencies, instrumentalities, or controlled entities, is licensed, authorized, directed, and compelled to transfer such funds, securities, and deposits, including interest from November 14, 1979, at commercially reasonable rates, to the account of the Federal Reserve Bank of New York at the Bank of England, to be held or transferred as directed by the Secretary of the Treasury. The Secretary of the Treasury shall determine when the transfers required by this section shall take place. The funds, securities and deposits described in this section shall be further transferred as provided for in the Declaration of the Government of the Democratic and Popular Republic of Algeria and its Annex.

1-102. Any banking institution subject to the jurisdiction of the United States that has executed a set-off on or after November 14, 1979, at 8:10 a.m. E.S.T. against Iranian funds, securities, or deposits referred to in section 1-101 is hereby licensed, authorized, directed, and compelled to cancel such set-off and to transfer all funds, securities, and deposits which have been subject to such set-off, including interest from November 14, 1979, at commercially reasonable rates, pursuant to the provisions of section 1-101 of this Order.

1-103. If the funds, securities, and deposits described in section 1-101 are not promptly transferred to the control of the Government of Iran, such funds, securities, and deposits shall be returned to the banking institutions holding them on the effective date of this Order and the set-offs described in section 1-102 shall be in force as if this Order had not been issued and the status of all such funds, securities, deposits and set-offs shall be *status quo ante*.

1–104. (a) All licenses and authorizations for acquiring or exercising any right, power, or privilege, by court order, attachment, or otherwise, including the license contained in Section 535.504 of the Iranian Assets Control Regulations, with respect to the properties described in Sections 1–101 and 1–102 of this Order are revoked and withdrawn.

(b) All rights, powers, and privileges relating to the properties described in Sections 1–101 and 1–102 of this Order and which derive from any attachment, injunction, other like proceedings or process, or other action in any litigation after November 14, 1979, at 8:10 a.m. E.S.T., including those derived from Section 535.-504 of the Iranian Assets Control Regulations, other than rights, powers, and privileges of the Government of Iran and its agencies, instrumentalities, and controlled entities, whether acquired by court order or otherwise, are nullified, and all persons claiming any such right, power, or privilege are hereafter barred from exercising the same.

(c) All persons subject to the jurisdiction of the United States are prohibited from acquiring or exercising any right, power, or privilege, whether by court order or otherwise, with respect to the properties (and any income earned thereon) referred to in sections 1–101 and 1–102 of this Order.

1–105. Compliance with this Order, any other Executive Order licensing, authorizing, directing, or compelling the transfer of the assets described in Sections 1–101 and 1–102 of this Order, or any regulations, instructions, or directions issued thereunder shall to the extent thereof be a full acquittance and discharge for all purposes of the obligation of the person making the same. No person shall be held liable in any court for or with respect to anything done or omitted in good faith in connection with the administration of, or pursuant to and in reliance on, such orders, regulations, instructions, or directions.

1–106. The Attorney General shall seek to intervene in any litigation within the United States which arises out of this Order and shall, among other things, defend the legality of, and all actions taken pursuant to, each of its provisions.

1–107. The Secretary of the Treasury is delegated and authorized to exercise all functions vested in the President by the International Emergency Economic Powers Act (50 U.S.C. 1701 *et seq.*) to carry out the purposes of this Order.

1–108. This Order shall be effective immediately.

JIMMY CARTER

The White House,
   January 19, 1981.

[Filed with the Office of the Federal Register,
   9:18 a.m., January 22, 1981]

NOTE: The text of the Executive order was released by the White House Press Office on January 21.

United States-Iran Agreement on Release of the American Hostages

Executive Order 12279.   January 19, 1981

DIRECTION TO TRANSFER IRANIAN GOVERNMENT ASSETS HELD BY DOMESTIC BANKS

By the authority vested in me as President by the Constitution and statutes of the United States, including Section 203 of the International Emergency Economic Powers Act (50 U.S.C. 1702), Section 301 of Title 3 of the United States Code, Section 1732 of Title 22 of the United States Code, and Section 301 of the National Emergencies Act (50 U.S.C. 1631), in view of the continuing unusual and extraordinary threat to the national security, foreign policy and economy of the United States upon which I based my declarations of national emergency in Executive Order 12170, issued November 14, 1979, and in Executive Order 12211, issued April 17, 1980, in order to implement agreements with the Government of Iran, as reflected in Declarations of the Government of the Democratic and Popular Republic of Algeria dated January 19, 1981, relating to the release of U.S. diplomats and nationals being held as hostages and to the resolution of claims of United States nationals against Iran, and to begin the process of normalization of relations between the United States and Iran and in which Iran and the United States instruct and require that the assets described in this Order shall be transferred as set forth below by the holders of such assets, it is hereby ordered that as of the effective date of this Order:

1–101. Any branch or office of a banking institution subject to the jurisdiction of the United States, which branch or office is located within the United States and is, on the effective date, either (a) in possession of funds or securities legally or beneficially owned by the Government of Iran or its agencies, instrumentalities, or controlled entities, or (b) carrying on its books deposits standing to the credit of or beneficially owned by such Government, agencies, instrumentalities, or controlled entities, is licensed, authorized, directed and compelled to transfer such funds, securities, and deposits, including interest from November 14, 1979, at commercially reasonable rates, to the Federal Reserve Bank of New York, to be held or transferred as directed by the Secretary of the Treasury.

1–102. (a) All licenses and authorizations for acquiring or exercising any right, power, or privilege, by court order, attachment, or otherwise, including the license contained in Section 535.504 of the Iranian Assets Control Regulations, with respect to the properties described in Section 1–101 of this Order are revoked and withdrawn.

(b) All rights, powers, and privileges relating to the properties described in section 1–101 of this Order and which derive from any attachment, injunction, other like proceedings or process, or other action in any litigation after November 14, 1979, at 8:10 a.m. EST, including those derived from Section 535.504 of the Iranian Assets Control Regulations, other than rights, powers, and privileges of the Government of Iran and its agencies, instrumentalities, and controlled entities, whether acquired by court order or otherwise, are nullified, and all persons claiming any such right, power, or privilege are hereafter barred from exercising the same.

(c) All persons subject to the jurisdiction of the United States are prohibited from acquiring or exercising any right, power, or privilege whether by court order or otherwise, with respect to the properties (and any income earned thereon) referred to in Section 1–101 of this Order.

1–103. Compliance with this Order, any other Executive Order licensing, authorizing, directing or compelling the transfer of the assets described in section 1–101 of this Order, or any regulations, instructions, or directions issued thereunder shall to the extent thereof be a full acquittance and discharge for all purposes of the obligation of the person making the same. No person shall be held liable in any court for or with respect to anything done or omitted in good faith in connection with the administration of, or pursuant to and in reliance on, such orders, regulations, instructions, or directions.

1–104. The Attorney General shall seek to intervene in any litigation within the United States which arises out of this Order and shall, among other things, defend the legality of, and all actions taken pursuant to, each of its provisions.

1–105. The Secretary of the Treasury is delegated and authorized to exercise all functions vested in the President by the International Emergency Economic Powers Act (50 U.S.C. 1701 *et seq.*) to carry out the purpores of this Order.

1–106. This Order shall be effective immediately.

JIMMY CARTER

The White House,
    January 19, 1981.

[Filed with the Office of the Federal Register, 9:21 a.m., January 22, 1981]

NOTE: The text of the Executive order was released by the White House Press Office on January 21.

United States-Iran Agreement on Release of the American Hostages

Executive Order 12280.   January 19, 1981

DIRECTION TO TRANSFER IRANIAN GOVERNMENT FINANCIAL ASSETS HELD BY NON-BANKING INSTITUTIONS

By the authority vested in me as President by the Constitution and statutes of the United States, including Section 203 of the International Emergency Economic Powers Act (50 U.S.C. 1702), Section 301 of Title 3 of the United States Code, Section 1732 of Title 22 of the United States Code, and Section 301 of the National Emergencies Act (50 U.S.C. 1631), in view of the continuing unusual and extraordinary threat to the national security, foreign policy and economy of the United States upon which I based my declarations of national emergency in Executive Order 12170, issued November 14, 1979, and in Executive Order 12211, issued April 17, 1980, in order to implement agreements with the Government of Iran, as reflected in Declarations of the Government of the Democratic and Popular Republic of Algeria dated January 19, 1981, relating to the release of U.S. diplomats and nationals being held as hostages and to the resolution of claims of United States nationals against Iran, and to begin the process of normalization of relations between the United States and Iran and in which Iran and the United States instruct and require that the assets described in this Order shall be transferred as set forth below by the holders of such assets, it is hereby ordered that as of the effective date of this Order:

1–101. Any person subject to the jurisdiction of the United States which is not a banking institution and is on the effective date in possession or control of funds or securities of Iran or its agencies, instrumentalities, or controlled entities is licensed, authorized, directed and compelled to transfer such funds or securities to the Federal Reserve Bank of New York to be held or transferred as directed by the Secretary of the Treasury.

1–102. (a) All licenses and authorizations for acquiring or exercising any right, power, or privilege, by court order, attachment, or otherwise, including the license contained in Section 535.504 of the Iranian Assets Control Regulations, with respect to the properties described in Section 1–101 of this Order are revoked and withdrawn.

(b) All rights, powers, and privileges relating to the properties described in section 1–101 of this Order and which derive from any attachment, injunction, other like proceedings or process, or other action in any litigation after November 14, 1979, at 8:10 a.m. EST, including those derived from Section 535.504 of the Iranian Assets Control Regulations, other than rights, powers, and privileges of the Government of Iran and its agencies, instrumentalities, and controlled entities, whether acquired by court order or otherwise, are nullified, and all persons claiming any such right, power, or privilege are hereafter barred from exercising the same.

(c) All persons subject to the jurisdiction of the United States are prohibited from acquiring or exercising any right, power, or privilege, whether by court order or otherwise, with respect to the properties (and any income earned thereon) referred to in Section 1–101 of this Order.

1–103. Compliance with this Executive Order, any other Executive Order licensing, authorizing, directing or compelling the transfer of the assets described in paragraph 1–101 of this Order, or any regulations, instructions, or directions issued thereunder shall to the extent thereof be a full acquittance and discharge for all purposes of the obligation of the person making the same. No person shall be held liable in any court for or with respect to anything done or omitted in good faith in connection with the administration of, or pursuant to and in reliance on, such orders, regulations, instructions, or directions.

1–104. The Attorney General shall seek to intervene in any litigation within the United States which arises out of this Order and shall, among other things, defend the legality of and all actions taken pursuant to, each of its provisions.

1–105. The Secretary of the Treasury is delegated and authorized to exercise all functions vested in the President by the International Emergency Economic Powers Act (50 U.S.C. 1701 *et seq.*) to carry out the purposes of this Order.

1–106. This Order shall be effective immediately.

JIMMY CARTER

The White House,
　January 19, 1981.

[Filed with the Office of the Federal Register,
　9:22 a.m., January 22, 1981]

NOTE: The text of the Executive order was released by the White House Press Office on January 21.

United States-Iran Agreement on Release of the American Hostages

Executive Order 12281.　January 19, 1981

DIRECTION TO TRANSFER CERTAIN IRANIAN GOVERNMENT ASSETS

By the authority vested in me as President by the Constitution and statutes of the United States, including Section 203 of the International Emergency Economic Powers Act (50 U.S.C. 1702), Section 301 of Title 3 of the United States Code, Section 1732 of Title 22 of the United States Code, and Section 301 of the National Emergencies Act (50 U.S.C. 1631), in view of the continuing unusual and extraordinary threat to the national security, foreign policy and economy of the United States upon which I based my declarations of national emergency in Executive Order 12170, issued November 14, 1979, and in Executive Order 12211, issued April 17, 1980, in order to implement agreements with the Government of Iran, as reflected in Declarations of the Government of the Democratic and Popular Republic of Algeria dated January 19, 1981, relating to the release of U.S. diplomats and nationals being held as hostages and to the resolution of claims of United States nationals against Iran, and to begin the process of normalization of relations between the United States and Iran and in which Iran and the United States instruct and require that the assets described in this Order shall be transferred as set forth below by the holders of such assets, it is hereby ordered that as of the effective date of this Order:

1–101. All persons subject to the jurisdiction of the United States in possession or control of properties, not including funds and securities, owned by Iran or its agencies, instrumentalities, or controlled entities are licensed, authorized, directed and compelled to transfer such properties, as directed after the effective date of this Order by the Government of Iran, acting through its authorized agent. Except where specifically stated, this license, authorization, and direction does not relieve persons subject to the jurisdiction of the United States from existing legal requirements other than those based upon the International Emergency Economic Powers Act.

1–102. (a) All licenses and authorizations for acquiring or exercising any right, power, or privilege, by court order, attachment, or otherwise, including the license contained in Section 535.504 of the Iranian Assets Control Regulations, with respect to the properties described in Section 1–101 of this Order are revoked and withdrawn.

(b) All rights, powers, and privileges relating to the properties described in section 1–101 of this Order and which derive from any attachment, injunction, other like proceedings or·process, or other action in any litigation after November 14, 1979, at 8:10 a.m. EST, including those derived from Section 535.504 of the Iranian Assets Control Regulations, other than rights, powers, and privileges of the Government of Iran and its agencies, instrumentalities, and controlled entities, whether acquired by court order or otherwise, are nullified, and all persons claiming any such right, power, or privilege are hereafter barred from exercising the same.

(c) All persons subject to the jurisdiction of the United States are prohibited from acquiring or exercising any right, power, or privilege, whether by court order or otherwise, with respect to the properties (and any income earned thereon) referred to in Section 1–101 of this Order.

1–103. Compliance with this Executive Order, any other Executive Order licensing, authorizing, directing or compelling the transfer of the assets described in paragraph 1–101 of this Order, or any regulations, instructions, or directions issued thereunder shall to the extent thereof be a full acquittance and discharge for all purposes of the obligation of the person making the same. No person shall be held liable in any court for or with respect to anything done or omitted in good faith in connection with the administration of, or pursuant to and in reliance on, such orders, regulations, instructions, or directions.

1–104. The Attorney General shall seek to intervene in any litigation within the United States which arises out of this Order and shall, among other things, defend the legality of, and all actions taken pursuant to, each of its provisions.

1–105. The Secretary of the Treasury is delegated and authorized to exercise all functions vested in the President by the International Emergency Economic Powers Act (50 U.S.C. 1701 *et seq.*) to carry out the purposes of this Order.

1–106. This Order shall be effective immediately.

JIMMY CARTER

The White House,
January 19, 1981.

[Filed with the Office of the Federal Register,
9:23 a.m., January 22, 1981]

NOTE: The text of the Executive order was released by the White House Press Office on January 21.

United States-Iran Agreement on Release of the American Hostages

Executive Order 12282. January 19, 1981

REVOCATION OF PROHIBITIONS AGAINST TRANSACTIONS INVOLVING IRAN

By the authority vested in me as President by the Constitution and statutes of the United States, including Section 203 of the International Emergency Economic Powers Act (50 U.S.C. 1702), Section 301 of Title 3 of the United States Code, Section 1732 of Title 22 of the United States Code, and Section 301 of the National Emergencies Act (50 U.S.C. 1631), in view of the continuing unusual and extraordinary threat to the national security, foreign policy and economy of the United States upon which I based my declarations of national emergency in Executive Order 12170, issued November 14, 1979, and in Executive Order 12211, issued April 17, 1980, in order to implement agreements with the Government of Iran, as reflected in Declarations of the Government of the Democratic and Popular Republic of Algeria dated January 19, 1981, relating to the release of U.S. diplomats and nationals being held as hostages and to the resolution of claims of United States nationals against Iran, and to begin the process of normalization of relations between the United States and Iran, it is hereby ordered that as of the effective date of this Order:

1–101. The prohibitions contained in Executive Order 12205 of April 7, 1980, and Executive Order 12211 of April 17, 1980, and Proclamation 4702 of November 12, 1979, are hereby revoked.

1–102. The Secretary of the Treasury is delegated and authorized to exercise all functions vested in the President by the International Emergency Economic Powers Act (50 U.S.C. 1701 *et seq.*) to carry out the purpose of this Order.

1–103. This Order shall be effective immediately.

JIMMY CARTER

The White House,
January 19, 1981.

[Filed with the Office of the Federal Register,
9:24 a.m., January 22, 1981]

NOTE: The text of the Executive order was released by the White House Press Office on January 21.

United States-Iran Agreement on Release of the American Hostages

Executive Order 12283. January 19, 1981

NON-PROSECUTION OF CLAIMS OF HOSTAGES AND FOR ACTIONS AT THE UNITED STATES EMBASSY AND ELSEWHERE

By the authority vested in me as President by the Constitution and statutes of the United States, including Section 203 of the International Emergency Economic Powers Act (50 U.S.C. 1702), Section 301 of Title 3 of the United States Code, Section 1732 of Title 22 of the United States Code, and Section 301 of the National Emergencies Act (50 U.S.C. 1631), in view of the continuing unusual and extraordinary threat to the national security, foreign policy and economy of the United States upon which I based by declarations of national emergency in Executive Order 12170, issued November 14, 1979, and in Executive Order 12211, issued April 17, 1980, in order to implement agreements with the Government of Iran, as reflected in Declarations of the Government of the Democratic and Popular Republic of Algeria dated January 19, 1981, relating to the release of U.S. diplomats and nationals being held as hostages and to the resolution of claims of United States nationals against Iran, and to begin the process of normalization of relations between the United States and Iran, it is hereby ordered that as of the effective date of this Order:

1–101. The Secretary of the Treasury shall promulgate regulations: (a) prohibiting any person subject to U.S. jurisdiction from prosecuting in any court within the United States or elsewhere any claim against the Government of Iran arising out of events occurring before the date of this Order relating to (1) the seizure of the hostages on November 4, 1979, (2) their subsequent detention, (3) injury to United States property or property of United States nationals within the United States Embassy compound in Tehran after November 3, 1979, or (4) injury to United States nationals or their property as a result of popular movements in the course of the Islamic Revolution in Iran which were not an act of the Government of Iran; (b) prohibiting any person not a U.S. national from prosecuting any such claim in any court within the United States; (c) ordering the termination of any previously instituted judicial proceedings based upon such claims; and (d) prohibiting the enforcement of any judicial order issued in the course of such proceedings.

1–102. The Attorney General of the United States is authorized and directed, immediately upon the issuance of regulations in accordance with Section 1–101, to take all appropriate measures to notify all appropriate courts of the existence of this Order and implementing regulations and the resulting termination of litigation.

1–103. The Secretary of the Treasury is delegated and authorized to exercise all functions vested in the President by the International Emergency Economic Powers Act (50 U.S.C. 1701 *et seq.*) to carry out the purpose of this Order.

1–104. This Order shall be effective immediately.

JIMMY CARTER

The White House,
    January 19, 1981.

[Filed with the Office of the Federal Register,
    9:25 a.m., January 22, 1981]

NOTE: The text of the Executive order was released by the White House Press Office on January 21.

United States-Iran Agreement on Release of the American Hostages

Executive Order 12284. January 19, 1981

RESTRICTIONS ON THE TRANSFER OF PROPERTY OF THE FORMER SHAH OF IRAN

By the authority vested in me as President by the Constitution and statutes of the United States, including Section 203 of the International Emergency Economic Powers Act (50 U.S.C. 1702), Section 301 of Title 3 of the United States Code, Section 1732 of Title 22 of the United States Code, and Section 301 of the National

Emergencies Act (50 U.S.C. 1631), in view of the continuing unusual and extraordinary threat to the national security, foreign policy and economy of the United States upon which I based my declarations of national emergency in Executive Order 12170, issued November 14, 1979, and in Executive Order 12211, issued April 17, 1980, in order to implement agreements with the Government of Iran, as reflected in Declarations of the Government of the Democratic and Popular Republic of Algeria dated January 19, 1981, relating to the release of U.S. diplomats and nationals being held as hostages and to the resolution of claims of United States nationals against Iran, and to begin the process of normalization of relations between the United States and Iran, it is hereby ordered that as of the effective date of this Order:

1–101. For the purpose of protecting the rights of litigants in courts within the United States, all property and assets located in the United States within the control of the estate of Mohammad Reza Pahlavi, the former Shah of Iran, or any close relative of the former Shah served as a defendant in litigation in such courts brought by Iran seeking the return of property alleged to belong to Iran, is hereby blocked as to each such estate or person until all such litigation against such estate or person is finally terminated.

1–102. The Secretary of the Treasury is authorized and directed (a) to promulgate regulations requiring all persons who are subject to the jurisdiction of the United States and who, as of November 3, 1979, or as of this date, have actual or constructive possession of property of the kind described in Section 1–101, or knowledge of such possession by others, to report such possession or knowledge thereof, to the Secretary of the Treasury in accordance with such regulations and (b) to make

available to the Government of Iran or its designated agents all identifying information derived from such reports to the fullest extent permitted by law. Such reports shall be required as to all individuals described in 1–101 and shall be required to be filed within 30 days after publication of a notice in the FEDERAL REGISTER.

1–103. The Secretary of the Treasury is authorized and directed (a) to require all agencies within the Executive Branch of the United States Government to deliver to the Secretary all official financial books and records which serve to identify any property of the kind described in Section 1–101 of this Order, and (b) to make available to the Government of Iran or its designated agents all identifying information derived from such books and records to the fullest extent permitted by law.

1–104. The Attorney General of the United States having advised the President of his opinion that no claim on behalf of the Government of Iran for recovery of property of the kind described in Section 1–101 of this Order should be considered legally barred either by sovereign immunity principles or by the act of state doctrine, the Attorney General is authorized and directed to prepare, and upon the request of counsel representing the Government of Iran to present to the appropriate court or courts within the United States, suggestions of interest reflecting that such is the position of the United States, and that it is also the position of the United States that Iranian decrees and judgments relating to the assets of the former Shah and the persons described in Section 1–101 should be enforced by such courts in accordance with United States law.

1–105. The Secretary of the Treasury is delegated and authorized to exercise all functions vested in the President by the International Emergency Economic

Powers Act (50 U.S.C. 1701 *et seq.*) to carry out the purposes of this Order.

1–106. This Order shall be effective immediately.

JIMMY CARTER

The White House,
   January 19, 1981.

[Filed with the Office of the Federal Register, 9:26 a.m., January 22, 1981]

NOTE: The text of the Executive order was released by the White House Press Office on January 21.

United States-Iran Agreement on Release of the American Hostages

Executive Order 12285. January 19, 1981

PRESIDENT'S COMMISSION ON HOSTAGE COMPENSATION

By the authority vested in me by the Constitution and statutes of the United States of America, and as President of the United States of America, in accordance with the Federal Advisory Committee Act, as amended (5 U.S.C. App. I), it is hereby ordered as follows:

1–1. *Establishment.*

1–101. There is established the President's Commission on Hostage Compensation, hereinafter referred to as the Commission, which shall be composed of not more than nine members who shall be appointed by the President.

1–102. The President shall designate a Chairman from among the members.

1–2. *Functions.*

1–201. The Commission shall study and analyze, and make recommendations to the President on, the question whether the United States should provide finan-cial compensation to United States nationals who have been held in captivity outside the United States, either (1) by or with the approval of a foreign government, or (2) by reason of their status as employees of the United States Government or as dependents of such employees.

1–202. The Commission shall submit a report to the President ninety days after the date of this Order. The report shall contain the Commission's recommendations as to whether legislation to deal with the foregoing compensation issue is appropriate and, if so, as to what such legislation should provide. The report shall specifically contain the Commission's recommendations concerning the compensation of United States nationals held hostage in Iran on and after November 4, 1979.

1–203. In analyzing the foregoing issues the Commission shall consider all factors which it may consider relevant, including the prior practice with respect to governmental compensation, both by the United States Government and by foreign governments, of persons held in captivity abroad.

1–204. In the performance of its functions the Commission shall specifically address the following issues:

(a) whether any legislation authorizing compensation should set forth specific legislative standards, or whether the standards by which to award compensation should be administratively developed;

(b) whether any standards developed either legislatively or administratively should be applied uniformly to civilian and military government employees, dependents of such employees, and private citizens, or whether separate criteria should be developed for these or other categories;

(c) whether an existing administrative body should determine amounts of compensation, or whether a new body should be established for this purpose; and

(d) whether compensation should be paid for injuries suffered by members of families of persons who have been held in captivity.

1–3. *Administrative Provisions.*

1–301. In performing its functions the Commission shall conduct such studies, reviews, and inquiries as may be necessary. In addition to conducting open meetings in accordance with the Federal Advisory Committee Act, the Commission shall conduct public hearings to identify critical issues and possible solutions related to compensation.

1–302. The Commission is authorized to request from any Executive agency such information that may be deemed necessary to carry out its functions under this Order. Each Executive agency shall, to the extent permitted by law, furnish such information to the Commission in the performance of its functions under this Order.

1–303. Each member of the Commission who is not otherwise employed in the Federal Government may receive, to the extent permitted by law, compensation for each day he or she is engaged in the work of the Commission at a rate not to exceed the maximum daily rate now or hereafter prescribed by law for GS–18 of the General Schedule, and may also receive transportation and travel expenses, including per diem in lieu of subsistence, as authorized by law (5 U.S.C. 5702 and 5703).

1–304. All necessary administrative staff services, support, facilities, and expenses of the Commission shall, to the extent permitted by law, be furnished by the Department of State.

1–4. *General Provisions.*

1–401. Notwithstanding the provisions of any other Executive Order, the func-

tions of the President under the Federal Advisory Committee Act, as amended (5 U.S.C. App. I), except that of reporting annually to the Congress, which are applicable to the Commission, shall be performed by the Secretary of State in accordance with guidelines and procedures established by the Administrator of General Services.

1–402. The Commission shall terminate thirty days after submitting its report.

JIMMY CARTER

The White House,
    January 19, 1981.

[Filed with the Office of the Federal Register, 9:27 a.m., January 22, 1981]

NOTE: The text of the Executive order was released by the White House Press Office on January 21.

United States-Iran Agreement on Release of the American Hostages

Message to the Congress.   January 19, 1981

To the Congress of the United States:

Pursuant to Section 204(b) of the International Emergency Economic Powers Act, 50 U.S.C. 1703, I hereby report to the Congress that I have today exercised the authority granted by this Act to take certain measures with respect to property of the Government of Iran and its controlled entities and instrumentalities.

1. On November 14, 1979, I took the step of blocking certain property and interests in property of the Government of Iran and its controlled entities and instrumentalities. This action was taken in response to a series of aggressive actions by Iran, including the attack on the United States Embassy in Tehran, the holding of U.S. citizens and diplomats as hostages,

and threats to withdraw assets from United States banks, and otherwise seek to harm the economic and political interests of the United States. Subsequently, on April 7, 1980, and April 17, 1980, I took further action restricting various kinds of transactions with Iran by persons subject to the jurisdiction of the United States.

2. Agreement has now been reached with Iran concerning the release of the hostages and the settlement of claims of U.S. nationals against Iran. Among other things this agreement involves the payment by Iran of approximately $3.67 billion to pay off principal and interest outstanding on syndicated loan agreements in which a U.S. bank is a party. This includes making all necessary payments to the foreign members of these syndicates. An additional $1.418 billion shall remain available to pay all other loans as soon as any disputes as to the amounts involved are settled and to pay additional interest to banks upon agreement or arbitration with Iran. In addition, there will be established an international tribunal to adjudicate various disputed claims by U.S. nationals against Iran; and the deposit of $1 billion by Iran from previously blocked assets as released, which will be available for payments of awards against Iran. Iran has committed itself to replenish this fund as necessary. This tribunal, among other things, will also hear certain disputes between Iranian nationals and the United States Government and contractual disputes between Iran and the United States.

In connection with this agreement, and to begin the process of normalization of relations between the two countries, I have issued and will issue, a series of Orders.

3. First, I have signed an Executive Order authorizing the Secretary of the Treasury to enter into or to direct the Federal Reserve Bank of New York to enter into escrow and depositary agreements with the Bank of England.

Under these agreements, assets in the escrow account will be returned to the control of Iran upon the safe departure of the United States hostages from Iran. I have also by this Order instructed the Federal Reserve Bank of New York, as fiscal agent of the United States, to receive other blocked Iranian assets, and, as further directed by the Secretary of the Treasury, to transfer these assets to the escrow account.

4. Second, I have signed an Executive Order directing the Federal Reserve Bank of New York to transfer to its account at the Bank of England and then to the escrow account referred to in the preceding paragraph, the assets of the Government of Iran, both transfers to take place as and when directed by the Secretary of the Treasury.

In order to assure that this transaction can be executed, and having considered the claims settlement agreement described above, I have exercised my authority to nullify, and barred the exercise of, all rights, powers or privileges acquired by anyone; I have revoked all licenses and authorizations for acquiring any rights, powers, or privileges; and I have prohibited anyone from acquiring or exercising any right, power, or privileges, all with respect to these properties of Iran. These prohibitions and nullifications apply to rights, powers, or privileges whether acquired by court order, attachment, or otherwise. I have also prohibited any attachment or other like proceeding or process affecting these properties.

5. Third, I have signed an Executive Order which directs branches and offices of United States banks located outside the United States to transfer all Iranian government funds, deposits and securities

held by them on their books on or after November 14, 1979 at 8:10 a.m. EST to the account of the Federal Reserve Bank of New York at the Bank of England in London. These assets will be transferred to the account of the Central Bank of Algeria, as escrow agent. The transfer is to include interest from the date of the blocking order at commercially reasonable rates. In addition, any banking institution that has executed a set-off subsequent to the date of the blocking order against Iranian deposits covered by this order is directed to cancel the set-off and to transfer the funds that had been subject to the set-off in the same manner as the other overseas deposits.

This Order also provides for the revocation of licenses and the nullifications and bars described in paragraph 4 of this report.

6. Fourth, I will have signed an Executive Order directing American banks located within the United States which hold Iranian deposits to transfer those deposits, including interest from the date of entry of the blocking order at commercially reasonable rates, to the Federal Reserve Bank of New York, to be held or transferred as directed by the Secretary of the Treasury. Half of these funds will be transferred to Iran and the other half (up to a maximum of $1 billion) will be placed in a security account as provided in the Declaration and the Claims Settlement Agreement that are part of the agreement we have reached with Iran. This fund will be maintained at a $500 million level until the claims program is concluded. While these transfers should take place as soon as possible, I have been advised that court actions may delay it. This Order also provides for the revocation of licenses and the nullifications and bars described in paragraph 4 of this report.

7. Fifth, I have signed an Executive Order directing the transfer to the Federal Reserve Bank of New York by non-banking institutions of funds and securities held by them for the Government of Iran, to be held or transferred as directed by the Secretary of the Treasury. This transfer will be accomplished at approximately the same time as that described in paragraph 6.

This Order also provides for the revocation of licenses and the nullifications and bars described in paragraph 4 of this report.

8. Sixth, I will sign, upon release of the hostages, an Executive Order directing any person subject to the jurisdiction of the United States who is in possession or control of properties owned by Iran, not including funds and securities, to transfer the property as directed by the Government of Iran acting through its authorized agent. The Order recites that it does not relieve persons subject to it from existing legal requirements other than those based on the International Emergency Economic Powers Act. This Order does not apply to contingent liabilities. This Order also provides for the revocation of licenses and the nullifications and bars described in paragraph 4 of this report.

9. Seventh, I will sign, upon release of the hostages, an Executive Order revoking prohibitions previously imposed against transactions involving Iran. The Executive Order revokes prohibitions contained in Executive Order No. 12205 of April 7, 1980; and Executive Order No. 12211 of April 17, 1980; and the amendments contained in Proclamation No. 4702 of November 12, 1979. The two Executive Orders limited trade and financial transactions involving Iran and travel to Iran. The proclamation restricted oil imports. In revoking these sanctions I have no intention of superseding other existing controls relating to exports including the

Arms Export Control Act and the Export Administration Act.

10. Eighth, I will sign, upon release of the hostages, an Executive Order providing for the waiver of certain claims against Iran. The Order directs that the Secretary of the Treasury shall promulgate regulations: (a) prohibiting any person subject to U.S. jurisdiction from prosecuting in any court within the United States or elsewhere any claim against the Government of Iran arising out of events occurring before the date of this Order arising out: (1) the seizure of the hostages on November 4, 1979; (2) their subsequent detention; (3) injury to the United States property or property of United States nationals within the United States Embassy compound in Tehran after November 1979; (4) or injury to United States nationals or their property as a result of popular movements in the course of the Islamic Revolution in Iran which were not an act of the Government of Iran; (b) prohibiting any person not a U.S. national from prosecuting any such claim in any court within the United States; (c) ordering the termination of any previously instituted judicial proceedings based upon such claims; and (d) prohibiting the enforcement of any judicial order issued in the course of such proceedings.

The Order also authorizes and directs the Attorney General of the United States immediately upon the issuance of such a Treasury regulation to notify all appropriate courts of the existence of the Executive Order and implementing regulations and the resulting termination of relevant litigation. At the same time, I will create a commission to make recommendations on the issue of compensation for those who have been held as hostages.

11. Finally, I will sign, upon release of the hostages, an Executive Order invoking the blocking powers of the International Emergency Economic Powers Act

to prevent the transfer of property located in the United States and controlled by the estate of Mohammed Reza Pahlavi, the former Shah of Iran, or by any close relative of the former Shah served as a defendant in litigation in United States courts brought by Iran seeking the return of property alleged to belong to Iran. This Order will remain effective as to each person until litigation concerning such person or estate is terminated. The Order also requires reports from private citizens and Federal agencies concerning this property so that information can be made available to the Government of Iran about this property.

The Order would further direct the Attorney General to assert in appropriate courts that claims of Iran for recovery of this property are not barred by principles of sovereign immunity or the act of state doctrine.

12. In addition to these actions taken pursuant to the International Economic Emergency Powers Act, other relevant statutes, and my powers under the Constitution, I will take the steps necessary to withdraw all claims now pending against Iran before the International Court of Justice. Copies of the Executive Orders are attached.

JIMMY CARTER

The White House,
    January 19, 1981.

NOTE: The text of the message was released by the White House Press Office on January 21.

Responses to Environmental Damage

Executive Order 12286.   January 19, 1981

By the authority vested in me as President of the United States of America by

Section 115 of the Comprehensive Environmental Response, Compensation, and Liability Act of 1980 (Public Law 96–510, approved December 11, 1980), it is hereby ordered as follows:

1–1. *National Contingency Plan.*

1–101. The National Oil and Hazardous Substance Pollution Contingency Plan (hereafter NCP), originally published pursuant to Section 311 of the Federal Water Pollution Control Act (Public Law 92–500, 33 U.S.C. 1321), shall be the primary vehicle for coordination of government response to releases of hazardous substances and pollutants and contaminants into the environment.

1–102. Subject to subsection 1–103 of this section, the Chairman of the Council on Environmental Quality is delegated all authority of the President under Section 105 of the Comprehensive Environmental Response, Compensation, and Liability Act of 1980, hereafter referred to as the Act. In revising the NCP the Chairman shall consult with the National Response Team (hereafter NRT) as established under the NCP, and shall coordinate all such revisions with the Director of the Federal Emergency Management Agency prior to publication for notice and comment. Each Executive agency represented on the NRT shall, as appropriate, provide technical and administrative support to the Chairman.

1–103. The Administrator of the Environmental Protection Agency is delegated all authority of the President under subsection (8)(B) of Section 105 of the Act. In exercising this authority the Administrator shall consult with the NRT.

1–2. *Determination of Remedial Action.*

The head of each Executive agency having responsibility under the NCP for determination of the appropriate remedy or remedial action is delegated all authority of the President under Section 101(24) of the Act.

1–3. *Response Activities.*

1–301. The Administrator of the Environmental Protection Agency and the Secretary of the Department in which the Coast Guard is operating are delegated, subject to the lines of jurisdiction in the NCP, all authority of the President under:

(a) Subsection (a) of Section 104 of the Act, subject to the further delegation of authority contained in section 1–303 of this Order.

(b) Subsections (c), (d), (f), and (g) of Section 104 of the Act.

(c) The first sentence of subsection (h) of Section 104 of the Act.

1–302. The Administrator of the Environmental Protection Agency is delegated, in consultation with the Executive agencies which may exercise emergency procurement powers under the NCP, all of the authority of the President under the second sentence of subsection (h) of Section 104 of the Act.

1–303. The head of each Executive agency having responsibilities for response actions under the NCP is delegated all authority of the President, to be exercised in accordance with the NCP, to undertake any necessary response actions under subsection (a) of Section 104 of the Act, and to act under subsection (b) of Section 104 of the Act, except as provided in section 1–304 below.

1–304. The Secretary of Health and Human Services, in consultation with the Administrator of the Environmental Protection Agency or the Secretary in the Department in which the Coast Guard is operating, as appropriate, is delegated all authority of the President, to be exercised in accordance with the NCP, to make the determination under subsection (b) of Section 104 of the Act relating to illness, disease and complaints thereof. The determination under subsection (i) of Section 104 as to the existence of a public health emergency shall be made by the head of the Public Health Service.

1–305. The head of each Executive agency designated in the NCP as having responsibility for determining the need for response to a release under Title I of the Act, or for enforcing the provisions of Title I of the Act, is delegated the authority to designate officers, employees and representatives under subsection (e) of Section 104 of the Act. The heads of each department and agency shall, in consultation with the Attorney General, develop guidelines or policies relating to the performance of the functions prescribed in subsection (e)(1) of Section 104. Regulations under subsection (e)(2)(C) of Section 104 respecting the manner in which data which may be entitled to protection under subsection (e)(2) of Section 104 of the Act shall be submitted and designated shall be promulgated by the Administrator of the Environmental Protection Agency in consultation with the NRT.

1–306. With respect to Department of Defense facilities, all actions taken under the delegations of this Order shall be consistent with statutes and Executive Orders protecting national security information.

1–4. *Abatement Action.*

The Administrator of the Environmental Protection Agency and the Secretary of the Department in which the Coast Guard is operating are delegated, in consultation with the Attorney General and subject to the lines of jurisdiction and procedures specified in the NCP, all authority of the President under subsection (a) of Section 106 of the Act.

1–5. *Liability.*

1–501. The Secretary of Transportation is delegated all authority of the President under subsection (c)(1)(C) of Section 107 of the Act.

1–502. The Administrator of the Environmental Protection Agency and the Secretary of the Department in which the Coast Guard is operating are delegated, subject to the lines of jurisdiction specified in the NCP and acting through the Attorney General, all authority of the President under subsection (c)(3) of Section 107 of the Act.

1–503. The head of any Executive agency designated as a trustee under the NCP, as specified in subsection (h) of Section 111 of the Act, is delegated all authority of the President under subsection (f) of Section 107 of the Act.

1–504. The Secretary of the Treasury, in consultation with the Administrator of the Environmental Protection Agency, is delegated the authority of the President under subsection (k)(4)(B) of Section 107 of the Act to establish, after a public hearing, a rule determining the feasibility of an optional system of private insurance.

1–505. The Administrator of the Environmental Protection Agency, in consultation with the Secretary of the Treasury, is delegated all authority of the President under subsection (k)(4)(D) of Section 107 of the Act and all residual authority under (k)(4)(B) of Section 107 of the Act.

1–6. *Financial Responsibility.*

1–601. The Federal Maritime Commission is delegated all authority of the President under subsection (a) of Section 108 of the Act.

1–602. The Administrator of the Environmental Protection Agency and the Secretary of Transportation are delegated all authority of the President under subsection (b) of Section 108 of the Act. The Secretary shall exercise such authority for all transportation related facilities and the Administrator shall exercise all other such authority.

1–7. *Employee Protection.*

The Secretary of Labor, in consultation with the Administrator of the Environmental Protection Agency and with the Secretary of Transportation, is delegated all authority of the President under subsection (e) of Section 110 of the Act.

1–8. *Uses of the Fund.*

1–801. This subsection of this Order refers to payment of government costs as specified in subsection (a) (4) of Section 111 of the Act. Money available in the Fund for such government costs shall be in amounts which the Director of the Office of Management and Budget shall allocate to the head of each Executive agency having responsibilities for activities specified in subsection (a) (4) of Section 111 of the Act. Each such head is delegated, with respect to the amount so allocated to his agency by the Director, all authority of the President under subsection (f) of Section 111 of the Act relating to designating Federal officials under the President's authority who may obligate money in the Fund. Any official so designated by an agency head may obligate amounts only up to the amount allocated to the agency head by the Director of the Office of Management and Budget under this subsection of this Order.

1–802. This subsection of this Order refers to payment of government response costs specified in subsection (a) (1) of Section 111 of the Act. Money available in the Fund for such government response costs shall be in a single amount which the Director of the Office of Management and Budget shall allocate to the Adminis-

trator of the Environmental Protection Agency for payment of government response costs as specified in subsection (a) (1) of Section 111 and as provided in the NCP. The Administrator of the Environmental Protection Agency is delegated, with respect to the amount so allocated by the Director, all authority of the President under subsection (f) of Section 111 of the Act relating to designating Federal officials under the President's authority who may obligate money in the Fund. Any official so designated by the Administrator may obligate amounts up to the amount allocated to the Administrator by the Director of the Office of Management and Budget under this subsection of this Order.

1–803. This subsection of this Order refers to payment of claims specified in subsections (a) (2) and (a) (3) of Section 111 of the Act. Money available in the Fund shall be allocated in amounts which the Director of the Office of Management and Budget allocates to the Administrator of the Environmental Protection Agency for payment of claims against the Fund. The Administrator of the Environmental Protection Agency is delegated, with respect to the amounts so allocated by the Director, all authority of the President under subsection (f) of Section 111 of the Act relating to designating Federal officials under the President's authority who may obligate money in the Fund for payment of claims. The claims referred to in this subsection of this Order are claims for necessary response costs as specified in subsection (a) (2) of Section 111 of the Act and for payment of claims for natural resources, other than the natural resource costs provided for under subsection (c) (1) and (c) (2) of Section 111. Any official so designated by the Administrator may obligate amounts only up to the amount allocated to the Administrator by the Director of the Office of Management and Budget under this subsection of this Order.

1–805. The Administrator of the Environmental Protection Agency, in consultation with the Attorney General, is delegated all authority of the President under the second sentence of Section 111(f) of the Act.

1–806. The head of any Executive agency designated under the NCP as trustee, as specified in subsection (h) of Section 111 of the Act, is delegated all authority of the President under subsection (b) of Section 111 of the Act.

1–807. (a) Subject to the further delegations of subsection 1–807(b) of this Order, the Administrator of the Environmental Protection Agency, in consultation with the Secretary of Transportation and with Executive agencies designated in the NCP as trustees of natural resources as specified in subsection (h) of Section 111 of the Act, is delegated all authority of the President under subsection (g) of Section 111 of the Act.

(b) The head of any Executive agency that owns or bare-boat charters and operates a public vessel is delegated the responsibility of the President under subsection (g) of Section 111 of the Act relating to appropriate notification to potential injured parties as a result of releases from such public vessel. Such notification, to the extent practicable, shall be in accordance with the regulations issued under subsection (a) of this paragraph.

1–9. *Claims Against the Fund.*

1–901. The Administrator of the Environmental Protection Agency, in consultation with the Attorney General, is delegated all authority of the President under:

a. Subsections (b)(2)(A), (B), (C), and (D) of Section 112 of the Act.

b. Subsection (b)(3) of Section 112 of the Act.

1–902. The Administrator of the Environmental Protection Agency is delegated all authority of the President under subsections (b)(4)(A), (B), (C), (E), (F), (H), and (I), and subsection (c)(3) of Section 112 of the Act. In exercising the authority of subsection (b)(4)(C) of Section 112 relating to enforcement of subpoenas in the United States District Courts, the Administrator of the Environmental Protection Agency shall act through the Attorney General.

1–903. The Administrator of the Environmental Protection Agency, in consultation with Executive agencies designated in the NCP as trustees of natural resources as specified in subsection (h) of Section 111 of the Act, is delegated all authority of the President under subsection (b)(1) of Section 112 of the Act.

1–904. The head of the Executive agency having responsibility under the NCP is delegated all authority of the President to be exercised in accordance with the NCP under subsection (b)(4) (D) of Section 112 of the Act.

1–10. *Studies.*

1–1001. The Administrator of the Environmental Protection Agency, in consultation with the NRT, is delegated all authority of the President under subsection (a)(1) of Section 301 of the Act.

1–1002. The Secretary of the Treasury is delegated all authority of the President under subsection (b) of Section 301 of the Act.

1–1003. The Secretary of the Interior, the Administrator of the National Oceanic and Atmospheric Administration, and the head of any Executive agency designated under the NCP as a trustee, as specified in subsection (h) of

Section 111 of the Act, is delegated, subject to the lines of jurisdiction specified in the NCP, all authority of the President under subsection (c) of Section 301 of the Act. Publication of all regulations under subsection (c) of Section 301 of the Act shall be coordinated with the NRT.

1–1004. The Attorney General, in consultation with the Administrator of the Environmental Protection Agency and the Council on Environmental Quality, shall conduct the study provided for in subsection (e) of Section 301 of the Act, seeking the assistance of the parties specified in that subsection.

1–11. *Litigation.*

Authority to represent the United States and the Fund, and the responsibility for the conduct and control of all litigation arising under the Act, shall be vested in the Attorney General. Nothing in this Executive Order shall be construed as delegating the President's authority to require the Attorney General to commence litigation.

1–12. *Consultation.*

1–1201. Authorities and functions delegated or assigned by this Order shall be exercised subject to consultation with the Secretaries of departments and the heads of agencies with operating or regulatory responsibilities which may be significantly affected.

1–1202. Any action which may affect the conduct of foreign relations of the United States shall be consistent with the NCP and be taken in consultation with the Secretary of State.

JIMMY CARTER

The White House,
    January 19, 1981.

[Filed with the Office of the Federal Register,
    4:36 p.m. January 28, 1981]

Digest of Other White House Announcements

The following listing includes the President's public schedule and other items of general interest announced by the White House Press Office and not included elsewhere in this issue.

January 11

The President returned to the White House from Plains, Ga.

January 12

The President met at the White House with:

—Zbigniew Brzezinski, Assistant to the President for National Security Affairs;
—Ambassador Sol M. Linowitz;
—Frank B. Moore, Assistant to the President for Congressional Liaison.

The President attended a reception in the morning for Carter/Mondale campaign staff members on the State Floor at the White House.

The President and Mrs. Carter hosted a concert and dinner for Carter/Mondale campaign fundraisers on the State Floor at the White House.

January 13

The President met at the White House with:

—Dr. Brzezinski;
—Douglas M. Costle, Administrator of the Environmental Protection Agency;
—William H. Webster, Director of the Federal Bureau of Investigation;
—Mr. Moore.

January 14

The President met at the White House with:

—Dr. Brzezinski;
—Mr. Moore.

The President and Mrs. Carter hosted a reception in the evening for administration officials on the State Floor of the White House.

January 15

The President met at the White House with:

—Dr. Brzezinski;
—Mr. Moore;
—Ambassador Ephraim Evron of Israel.

The President and Mrs. Carter hosted a reception in the afternoon for donors and lenders to the White House collection on the State Floor of the White House.

The President transmitted to Congress the second annual report on the United States Government's international activities in the field of science and technology.

January 16

The President met at the White House with:

—Dr. Brzezinski;
—Secretary of State Edmund S. Muskie, Secretary of Defense Harold Brown, Jack H. Watson, Jr., Assistant to the President, and Dr. Brzezinski;
—Mr. Moore.

The President transmitted to Congress:

—The FY 1980 annual report of the ACTION Agency;
—the 10th annual report on hazardous materials control;
—the second annual report on the status of the Weatherization Assistance Program;
—the 13th annual report of the Department of Transportation.

The President left the White House for a weekend stay at Camp David, Md.

January 18

The President returned to the White House from Camp David.

The President met at the White House during the day and evening with his advisers to discuss the situation in Iran.

January 19

The President met at the White House throughout the day and evening with his advisers to discuss developments in the United States-Iran agreement on release of the American hostages.

The White House announced that President-elect Ronald Reagan phoned the President and asked him to represent the United States when the hostages arrived in Wiesbaden, Germany, after being released in Iran. The President thanked the President-elect for his offer and reviewed the situation with him. Later in the day, when it became apparent that the hostages might not be released during the Carter Presidency, the President called the President-elect, thanked him again for the offer, and accepted his invitation to represent the United States.

January 20

The President met at the White House with Dr. Brzezinski and other administration officials to discuss continuing developments in the U.S.-Iranian agreement.

The President and Mrs. Carter welcomed President-elect and Mrs. Reagan to the White House for coffee before leaving together for the Capitol and the Inauguration.

NOMINATIONS SUBMITTED TO THE SENATE

The following list does not include promotions of members of the Uniformed Services, nominations to the Service Academies, or nominations of Foreign Service officers.

NOMINATIONS—Continued

Submitted January 15, 1981

MAJOR GENERAL WILLIAM EDGAR READ, 240–28–5658, United States Army, to be a member and President of the Mississippi River Commission, under the provisions of Section 2 of an Act of Congress, approved 28 June 1879 (21 Stat. 37) (33 U.S.C. 642).

CHECKLIST OF WHITE HOUSE PRESS RELEASES

The following listing contains releases of the White House Press Office which are not included in this issue.

Released January 12, 1981

Advance text: remarks of Zbigniew Brzezinski, Assistant to the President for National Security Affairs, to the Institut Francais des Relations Internationales in Paris, France

Fact sheet: President's Awards for Energy Efficiency (includes list of award winners)

News conference: on documents concerning Gen. Alexander M. Haig which were requested by the Senate Foreign Relations

CHECKLIST—Continued

Released January 12—Continued

Committee—by Michael H. Cardozo, Deputy Counsel to the President

Released January 14, 1981

Fact sheet: Presidential Medal of Freedom

Advance text: President's farewell address to the Nation

Released January 16, 1981

News conference: on the State of the Union message—by Stuart E. Eizenstat, Assistant to the President for Domestic Affairs and Policy

Released January 17, 1981

News conference: on the Economic Report of the President—by Charles L. Schultze, Chairman of the Council of Economic Advisers

---

ACTS APPROVED BY THE PRESIDENT

NOTE: No acts approved by the President were received by the Office of the Federal Register during the period covered by this issue.

INDEX

Letters, Messages, Telegrams

O